Civil War Naval Chronology

1861–1865

C.S.S. Arkansas rvnning through Union fleet, Mississippi River, 1862.

CIVIL WAR NAVAL CHRONOLOGY

1861–1865

Compiled by

Naval History Division
Navy Department

Washington: 1971

L. C. Card No. 71–609471

PREFACE

Concurrently with nationwide observances of the Civil War Centennial, the Naval History Division published the *Civil War Naval Chronology, 1861–1865*. It was made available between 1961 and 1965 in five paperback Parts each covering one year of the conflict. These were followed in 1966 by a Part VI containing a cumulative index, several excellent eyewitness accounts, and other significant articles of considerable interest.

The *Chronology* project was initiated, guided, and shaped by my dedicated and able predecessor, Rear Admiral E. M. Eller, USN (Ret.), during his long and highly productive tenure as Director of Naval History.

Dr. William J. Morgan, who heads our Historical Research Section, and Lieutenant Richard M. Basoco, USNR, were primarily responsible for preparation of the *Chronology* from beginning to end. Indispensable assistance and support were received from a host of individuals both within and outside of the Naval History Division. Their contributions took many forms including critical review, recommendations and strengthening of the manuscript, research, graciously allowing use of documents and illustrations, indexing, proofing. To all, appreciation was expressed in a "Summary" prefacing each Part. In this one volume edition, continuity of pagination and other considerations have dictated elimination of the summaries. We have, therefore, included herein an alphabetical listing of contributors (hopefully, with no one overlooked) so that the vital aid which made this work possible will continue to be gratefully acknowledged.

The reception accorded the *Civil War Naval Chronology* must indeed have been most gratifying to Admiral Eller and those associated with the undertaking. In presenting the Naval History Division with an Award of Distinction, the U.S. Civil War Centennial Commission characterized the *Chronology* as "a truly splendid contribution to the literature of the Civil War."

In the years following publication of the final *Chronology* part, the desirability of bringing the whole together in one bound book has been evident. This we have now done.

The volume has been prepared under the guidance of Dr. Morgan by Mr. Robert L. Scheina and Senior Chief Personnelman George K. McCuistion, USNR, a history teacher in Royal Oak, Michigan, on summer duty with the Naval History Division. It is essentially as originally published. Corrections have been made, a few illustrations changed, and, as previously noted, summaries are deleted. The comprehensive article, "The Civil War At Sea" by Admiral Eller and Commodore Dudley W. Knox, formerly an appendix to Part V, has been moved forward as an introductory essay. Likewise, the "1861–1865 Calendar" has been repositioned for more ready reference. It is hoped that these relatively few and minor adjustments will enhance the unity and usability of the volume.

Edwin B. Hooper,
Vice Admiral, USN (Ret.),
Director of Naval History.

Acknowledgements:

Allin, Larry, PN1, USNR
Anderson, Bern, Rear Admiral, USN (Ret.)
Ashbridge, Mrs. Whitney
Barthell, Edward E., Jr.
Belcher, Roy S., Captain, USN
Cooper, William B., Commander, USNR
Coward, Fred, YNC, USN
Culbert, Thomas E., YN2, USN
Cumming, Hugh S., Jr.
Daly, R. W.
Eliot, George Fielding
Eller, Ernest McNeill, Rear Admiral, USN (Ret.)
Finn, Harold B. III, Lieutenant (junior grade) USNR
Gray, J. A. C., Captain, MC, USN (Ret.)
Hayes, John D., Rear Admiral, USN (Ret.)
Heffernan, John B., Rear Admiral, USN (Ret.)
Hickey, Dermott, Commander, USN (Ret.)
Hicks, Frederick S.
Hoover, Agnes
Johns, Lionel S.
Jones, V. C.
Kirk, Nevill T.
Lanier, Monro B.
Levy, Lester S.
Long, Richard A.
Loomis, F. Kent, Rear Admiral, USN (Ret.)
Lynch, Barbara
Lyons, Patrick A., Ensign, USNR
Miller, W. M., Colonel, USMC
Proctor, Samuel
Reynolds, Lloyd L., Lieutenant (junior grade) USNR
Roberts, John C., Lieutenant (junior grade) USN
Rope, William F., Lieutenant (junior grade) USNR
Scheffenacker, Henry J.
Scheffenacker, Virginia
Skipworth, Humberson
Smith, Mrs. Carter
Smith, Ray D.
Stewart, Donald
Still, William N.
Thomas, Jesse B.
Tierney, John L., Commander, USNR
Vadnais, Henry A.
Weaver, Charles
West, Richard S., Jr.

Table of Contents

INTRODUCTORY ESSAY

THE CIVIL WAR AT SEA
by Rear Admiral Ernest McNeill Eller, U.S.N. (Ret.),
and Commodore Dudley W. Knox, U.S.N. (Ret.)

"He who rules the sea rules the world," said one of the wisest of statesmen almost 2,500 years ago. Never did these words prove truer or have more far reaching effect upon man's history than in the Civil War. In the sea lay the forces unconquerable through which, despite valor and genius of leadership, the South lost the war, the North conquered and the United States endured as a united nation for its destiny of world leadership in the nuclear space age.

This ceaseless influence of operations at sea in the Civil War has been comprehended by few Americans. Had the North prosecuted the war less vigorously and successfully at sea, or the South more effectively, the history of America and the world could have been radically changed.

George Washington said during the American Revolution: "In any operation, and under all circumstances, a decisive naval superiority is to be considered as a fundamental principle, and the basis upon which every hope of success must ultimately depend."

These same words, with slight variation, could be truly said of every major war in which the United States has become involved since those beginning days of American independence. They were strikingly true of the Civil War.

Navy Department, Washington.

The first important Northern victories in the Civil War came from the employment of sea superiority in combined operations against the Carolina coast of the Confederacy. This early sea success following Union defeat at Bull Run meant more than lift of morale in the North. It marked fateful developments in the war that forecast inevitable destruction for the South unless, as in the American Revolution, overseas nations came in to convert this into a world war with great navies joined in decisive combat.

The policy leaders in Washington settled upon the powerful forces of sea power to help crush the South—forces that in the end overthrew the bright genius of Lee. These included: (a) Blockade that starved the industrially deficient South. (b) Capture of Southern ports that facilitated the blockade and forced the South to disperse strength to counter attack from the sea. (c) Severing the South along the Mississippi and the use of the mighty highways of the western rivers to speed her destruction.

They also included, whether or not consciously realized by Northern leaders at the start, other advantages that flow from a superior Navy boldly and wisely employed.

The total benefits to the North were large indeed, for the sea's influence pervaded the Civil War and inevitably shaped the outcome like a flood tide that reaches all shores. Let us speak to the principal ones, including the three settled on as policy:

1. *The facility of movement the sea affords brought great flexibility both to strategy and to tactics.* It permitted swift adjustment to emergencies, omnipresent in war, to counter disaster and to win victory out of defeat.

For example, control of the sea and proper use of it possibly saved the Union in the first days of the war. The District of Columbia lay in the South and Confederate sympathy ran strong in the capital. President Lincoln promptly began to bring in troops. Baltimoreans rioted and cut the railroad to the North. The Capital had become an island in the Confederate sea. The railroad route through Maryland ran across overwhelmingly Southern territory. In Annapolis only one voter had cast his ballot for Lincoln in the election; most Marylanders opposed coercion if they did not favor secession.

The Federal Government's safety was precarious. In Philadelphia Captain Dupont and others placed troops on ships to steam to the Chesapeake via the Virginia Capes and took steps to move General Ben Butler and his Massachusetts volunteers from the Delaware to the head of the Chesapeake— Dupont stationed sailors with field pieces along the route across the narrow neck of land between the Delaware and Chesapeake. These low fields had seen similar operations in the American Revolution, both by the British sailing up the Bay from the south and Washington speeding south by water to win the war at Yorktown.

Butler's troops seized the railroad steamer and quickly sped to Annapolis. Since the Potomac might be closed by Virginia, the U.S. Naval Academy was the closest Federal property to Washington they could occupy. After vicissitudes solved by the troop ships coming up through the Capes, Butler landed in the Academy grounds and soon relieved Washington. With the railroad cut, the inland sea of the Chesapeake had saved the day.

Had the Bay not been used by the Federals or had the Confederates blocked its use or seized the shipping, the Capital might have fallen. With it might have gone Maryland. These events plus the important industrial facilities of Baltimore and Washington could have been decisive in swinging the delicate balance of victory to the South and thereby changing all the history of the United States.

2. *Destruction from the sea wasted and seriously weakened the South.* The South's sea coast extended for some 3,000 miles (or 8,000 if measured along the tidal line), and an equal amount along rivers and inland waterways. Every one of these thousands of miles was subject to ship attack; and before the war ended (since few points could be adequately defended), scarcely a mile but felt the devastating impact of massed naval guns suddenly appearing over the horizon. As General Robert E. Lee wrote in January 1862 from Georgia:

> Wherever his fleet can be brought no opposition to his landing can be made except
> within range of our fixed batteries. We have nothing to oppose to its heavy guns,
> which sweep over the low banks of this country with irresistible force.

Gun crew on board Union monitor exercises with boat howitzer. Note battle-scarred turret.

These incessant attacks eroded the South's resources, its strength and life. More important, they diverted from the main battlefields of decision many troops that might have swung the tide in crucial battles—what would 20,000 men taken from defense of the sea coast have meant to Lee at Gettysburg?

3. *Power afloat on the Western rivers was the spearhead for the giant drives that fatally severed the South.* The far-reaching influences of sea power have never shown more clearly in history than in these campaigns. There they combined with awful impact which steadily and inevitably cut the South to pieces along its water highways—its arteries of life or death depending on who controlled them.

We see this as early as the second day after Grant took command, September 1861, at Cairo, Illinois where the Ohio joins the Mississippi, when he based his first move on power afloat. Embarking his troops in river boats he sped up the Ohio protected by gunboats Commander John Rodgers had vigorously prepared that summer. Covering in a few hours by ship a distance it would have taken his troops days to march by land with artillery, he beat the Confederates to the draw and occupied points predominately Southern in sympathy controlling the mouths of the Tennessee and Cumberland Rivers. Thereby he not only helped save Kentucky for the Union but he paved the way for the fateful events to follow when these river highways became highways of death deep into the heart of the South.

This first operation of Grant's tells in vignette the story of the war in the West. Union armies daily gained incalculable benefits from the highly mobile heavy artillery, the concentration of power, swiftness of movement and free flow of logistics provided by the river highways.

Confederate leaders, though operating in their own homeland, suffered under the overwhelming hardship of ever being out flanked, of having large caliber guns of ships suddenly appear at vulnerable points, of witnessing secure lines collapse when Union armies penetrated them by river, of difficult logistics while more steamers poured in supplies for the Federals, of being stuck in the mud while the Union Army outmaneuvered by ship.

From Fort Henry, Fort Donelson and Island 10 in the North, and New Orleans in the South, events in the West that proved decisive in the war lay along the rivers. Victory for the North had a firm foundation in combined operations, the wise juncture of the unique powers of the sea with those of the land.

4. *Blockade that strangled the South.* Deficient in manufacturing, the Confederacy seriously needed industrial products from overseas. While never perfect, the Federal Navy's blockade severly limited imports, with increasing impact as the war advanced. Skillful blockade runners brought in much critical material and undoubtedly helped to prolong the war, but what they brought was only a fraction of what the South needed. Two examples suffice: The South almost completed several giant ironclads on the Western rivers from New Orleans to Cerro Gordo, Tennessee. These would have changed the whole course of events in that decisive area, slowing or preventing Farragut's capture of rich New Orleans and Grant's drive south behind warships to cut the Confederacy in twain. The Confederate ironclads were not completed in part because of slowness in getting armor plate, engines and shafts. All of these England could have easily provided.

Or consider small arms. In the first year of the war the South imported some 50,000 stacks of arms. In that same period the North with extensive arsenals and industrial facilities imported 700,000. The North with far lesser need imported freely from all the world; the South got the crumbs.

5. *Control of the sea helped prevent foreign intervention.* No one can define all that enters into a decision to intervene. In the American Revolution the French did, helping to contain the powerful British fleet and thus giving Washington the chance to win our freedom. We do not know how much the rapidly expanded Union Fleet and the Naval victories on the Atlantic Coast, at New Orleans and on the upper rivers entered into the decision of England and France not to intervene in support of the South. It seems clear, however, that they exerted a profound influence.

6. *In combined and amphibious operations the Federal Army gained overwhelming advantages through control of the sea.* When Army and Navy properly combined, their separate advantages were multiplied so that they bludgeoned the South into defeat from the beginning until the end of the war. Sea and land each has its unique advantages. When the two join effectively, the results are powerful and overwhelming. Afloat for example, the heaviest artillery speeds faster than cavalry. Large bodies of troops can be moved as swiftly to strategic points behind the massed concentration of naval gunfire dreadfully feared by all who have experienced it. Speeding rapidly on ships the Army can strike where the enemy is weak. This ability to appear suddenly with massed big guns and troops often gains the incalculable advantage of surprise that successful leaders in war have ever sought. Added to mobility, speed, concentration of power, and surprise, the sea provides flexibility and rapidity of maneuver of forces to attack or defend. It provides freedom of choice of operation, ease of supply and reinforcement, powerful defense for forces in straits ashore, salvation for those defeated—as for McClellan in the Peninsula Campaign.

The sea and land, indeed, so perfectly complement each other wherever water reaches, that they become like the left and right arms of a boxer. When an Army without seapower meets an enemy that enjoys superiority afloat, it is like a boxer with one hand tied behind his back trying to fight a champion.

Thus from the North's preponderance of force based at sea flowed many specific important results. Any one of several of these might have been decisive in the ultimate decision at Appomattox. For

Burning of Gosport Navy Yard, Norfolk, Virginia.

example, as we have noted, in the Spring of 1861, Washington would have probably fallen and Maryland have joined the Confederacy had the Federal Navy not controlled the Potomac and Chesapeake.

This early dependence on the sea never lessened. Not long thereafter the lead troops that occupied Alexandria in May 1861 secretly embarked in ships at the Washington Navy Yard in the night. Commander Dahlgren, confidant of Lincoln, supervised the embarkation and sailed down the Potomac through the darkness with the troops. Mobility, surprise, flexibility, concentration—these virtues of control of the sea would serve constantly to strengthen the North and destroy the South in the ensuing years.

In this same early period Commander John Rodgers went west to push the development of the gunboat fleet—wooden, tin and ironclad—that soon played a large role in the decisive operations of the west. These inland warships kept open the Ohio and upper Mississippi River thereby probably preserving Kentucky and Missouri for the Union. They solved the North's logistic problems in many operations while confounding those of the South. They both saved Grant from disaster and made possible many successful operations, for he, more than any other general in the war (and above most in any war), profoundly understood the power of the sea. Understanding it, he used it wisely in far-reaching combined operations—first in his vigorous moves south on the western rivers and later in his sledge hammer blows in Virginia. Lee, genius in war, was no less profoundly aware of influence of the sea in overall national strength for he repeatedly suffered from critical, even decisive disadvantage of lack of strength afloat.

Before Grant arrived in the East the Federal Navy's control of the sea saved McClellan and other Northern leaders from complete disaster in several operations. The story of the Civil War truly cannot be told in any of its important aspects without bringing in the influence of the sea. Many volumes could be written on its decisive effect. For the purpose of a brief survey, however, there is no finer account than that by one of the Navy's keenest minds and ablest writers, the late Commodore Dudley W. Knox. Several years ago when the Truxtun-Decatur Naval Museum opened a display on "The Navies in the Civil War", Commodore Knox prepared a summary of the operations. This noteworthy account, with minor changes, follows as he prepared it:

xv

EARLY OPERATIONS

"To a great degree the naval factor in our distressing Civil War was decisive. The Federal Navy started with the tremendous advantage of already having control of the sea, as well as of thousands of miles of ocean inlets and rivers. Diligently it exploited that control in many effective ways including worldwide protection to Federal maritime commerce, a blighting coastal blockade of huge proportions, numerous captures of coastal and river strong points, close cooperation with and support of Army operations and combat, safeguarding long military lines of communication in an age when water transport was of paramount importance, and preventing foreign intervention in the war.

"At the beginning the Confederate States had no Navy, but diligently created one from scanty means available. They were compelled to rely principally upon the conversion of merchant ships, but in time managed to construct formidable men-of-war notwithstanding poor materials and facilities, and to devise new types of ships and weapons. Their inventiveness and accomplishment under adverse circumstances were remarkable. A great windfall to the Confederacy was the early capture of the important Navy Yard at Norfolk together with the ships and huge supplies there. *Merrimack* was converted into the powerful ironclad ram *Virginia* and the large number of captured cannons permitted distribution to fortifications and ships at many distant places.

"Even before Bull Run the Confederates established control of the lower Potomac River with batteries erected on the Virginia shore, until driven away by land attack many months later to clear the river for transporting the Army to the Peninsular Campaign. Confederate naval forces also drove a Federal Squadron to sea (October 1861) from the Mississippi River's mouth, giving the South complete early command of the Father of Waters to Cairo, Illinois.

"After the disastrous defeat at Bull Run (July, 1861) the Union Army spent nine months in rehabilitation before again taking the field. During that anxious interlude the Federal Navy turned the tide by a series of victories. Confederate privateering based on Pamlico Sound, N.C., was stopped by the capture of Forts Hatteras and Clark guarding Hatteras Inlet, the main entrance to the Sound, by a naval squadron under Flag Officer Stringham (29 Aug., '61). The naval bombardment forced surrender.

"On 7 November a large expedition under Flag Officer du Pont captured the extensive anchorage of Port Royal Sound, S.C., after a sharp engagement with the defending forts by the naval squadron. It was to serve as a naval base for maintaining the blockade as well as for attacks on nearby Charleston. Soon afterwards Federal control of the coast was established southward to Florida, in support of the blockade.

"February 1862 was notable for three victories which successively electrified the North. Flag Officer Foote with a squadron of iron-clad river gunboats cooperated closely with General Grant in the capture of Forts Henry and Donelson, on the Tennessee and Cumberland Rivers. Naval bombardment of Fort Henry caused it to surrender to Foote before the Army could get into the battle. At Donelson the gunboats suffered severely but contributed substantially to Grant's victory. These two battles well proved the value of iron-clad gunboats against shore batteries, besides emphasizing the importance of combined Army-Navy operations. They also opened two great navigable rivers to Federal use.

"The large amphibious expedition of February, 1862, under Flag Officer Goldsborough and General Burnside captured Roanoke Island, lying between Albemarle and Pamlico Sounds in North Carolina. The troops landed and operated ashore under strong naval gunfire. A Confederate naval force under Flag Officer Lynch was defeated by Federal gunboats under Commander Rowan. Elizabeth City, Edenton and Newbern soon fell. Naval control of these extensive inland waters and coastline was of great value to the Federals. The control was subsequently disputed by the powerful Confederate

Alfred Waud's watercolor depicts the first major Union victory of the war at Hatteras Inlet.

Flag Officer DuPont's fleet secures Port Royal Sound as a vital base for future operations.

ironclad ram *Albemarle*. Victorious in several encounters with gunboats she was destroyed (1864) by a torpedo boat attack under Lieutenant Cushing.

"The classic first duel between armored vessels—*Monitor* vs. *Virginia* (ex-*Merrimack*)—was fought (9 March 1862) at Hampton Roads. (On the previous day *Virginia* had destroyed the *Cumberland* and *Congress* off Newport News.) The two ironclads fought intermittently for many hours without sustaining great damage. *Virginia* returned to Norfolk.

"Depending upon the Navy to protect against the menace from the *Virginia* (*Merrimack*), McClellan transported his Army by water from Northern Virginia, landed it at Fortress Monroe in April, 1862, and began his ill-fated Peninsular Campaign. Naval squadrons supported his slow advance by land on both flanks, on the York and James Rivers. Finally McClellan was forced to retreat to Malvern Hill on the James where support from gunboats contributed to saving his Army. His evacuation of the Peninsula by water was made possible and covered by the naval squadrons.

THE GREAT BLOCKADE

"The colossal blockade was at first quite thin from want of sufficient ships but it grew in effectiveness and had two profoundly important consequences. It severely restricted the import of critically-needed military supplies in a generally non-manufacturing Confederacy. It reduced to a mere trickle the export of cotton, the South's only big money producer, thus severely crippling the entire economy and ability to maintain the war.

"To blockade 3,000 miles of Confederate coastline effectively was a colossal task. Almost every available commercial steamer of any type, even ferry boats, that could mount a gun and keep the sea was purchased for this purpose, to augment regular naval vessels constantly being built. During the first year the number on blockade duty grew from a handful to nearly 200, which increased to nearly 450 at the end. Even during the first 9 months when blockaders were spread thin they captured 150 ships attempting to run through.

"While munitions and supplies came pouring into the North from Europe, the South throughout the war was almost shut off from overseas and had acute difficulty in equipping and supplying both Army and Navy—hampered by poor manufacturing facilities and limited production of suitable raw materials locally. The critical need of iron for munitions constantly exceeded production and resulted in stripping railroads, which in time seriously impaired the means of distributing even food. In 1864 rations for the Confederate Army ran so short that an officer was sent to Bermuda to purchase food. He ran the blockade outwards but the fall of Wilmington prevented sending the food in. There was universal suffering among civilians from several shortages in consumer goods, causing fantastic prices— $350 for a barrel of flour, $1 each for quinine pills, $85 a yard for woolen cloth, etc.

"The fabulous profits from successful blockade running led to the development of a special type of vessel for the purpose—a long, low- paddle-wheel steamer of about 14 knots speed. Painted a dull grey, burning nearly smokeless anthracite coal, and having telescope smoke-stacks for lowering in a danger zone, it was difficult to see even by day. The run past blockade lines was usually made on moonless nights. The protection of guns placed along the shoreline leading to a blockaded port was sought as soon as possible, and as a last resort a fugitive ship would deliberately run ashore with a view to salvaging the precious cargo afterwards.

"The integrity of the blockade was well maintained throughout the war. But it was temporarily broken twice on the Texas coast in January 1863 when Texan soldiers made surprise attacks with "Cottonclad" armed merchant steamers. At Galveston under Colonel Bayley they captured the *USS Harriet Lane* and destroyed or routed five other blockaders. At Sabine Pass under Captain W. Johnson, they captured the two blockading vessels *Morning Light* and *Velocity*.

MISSISSIPPI VALLEY STRUGGLE

"Meanwhile, Union military-naval forces had begun the tremendous task of gaining control of the lower Mississippi River, attacking from both north and south. This would split the Confederacy apart and at the same time restore the commercial outlet for Federal States in the upper valley. Grant's advance (South) up the Tennessee River, aimed at outflanking Vicksburg, met with severe resistance at Pittsburg Landing (Shiloh) where Union gunboats helped save the day. Ultimately Grant was forced to abandon this strategy in favor of a direct approach down the Mississippi.

"The chief northerly obstacle was the strong fort at Island Number Ten, near the junction of Kentucky, Tennessee and Missouri. On a dark and stormy night Federal ironclad gunboats under Flag Officer Foote bombarded the fort while one of them (*Carondelet*, Commander Walke) ran past (April, 1862). The next night *Pittsburg* followed and the two gunboats below the fort then covered the Mississippi crossing of General Pope's Army from Missouri, which then advanced by land to capture formidable Island Number Ten.

"In this affair Confederate naval resistance had been lacking because their gunboats were far away in the defense of New Orleans against Farragut's fleet, coming up from the Gulf of Mexico. Forcing

Flag Officer Farragut in U.S.S. Hartford *blasts his way through Confederate defenses to capture New Orleans.*

a passage past Forts Jackson and St. Philip, Farragut defeated the Confederate Squadron under Flag Officer Mitchell and proceeded up-river to New Orleans, which, defenseless, had no choice but to surrender (April 1862).

"Soon Farragut pressed northward against little resistance to Vicksburg, where he joined gunboats under Flag Officer Davis (Foote's successor) who had cleared the upper section of the river by defeating, off Memphis (10 May), a hastily assembled force of Confederate Rams under Captain Montgomery. This early opening of the Mississippi was but temporary. Without land forces in support the naval squadrons could not hold their gains, and had to withdraw, north and south. Confederates then hastily strengthened weak defenses along the river, so that later the Federals met stiff opposition.

"Vicksburg soon became a formidable point of unique importance. Strong batteries on high bluffs controlled the river passage. Railroads ran westward to Texas and eastward to the heart of the Confederacy forming a major transport artery to sustain the war. The Federals rightly regarded the capture of this bastion as of primary consequence. A large amphibious expedition under Sherman landed (December 1862) at Haynes Bluff just above Vicksburg, expecting a junction with Grant, marching from inland. But Grant could not get through, so both Armies withdrew northwards for a fresh joint attempt down the river.

"This new great plan which ultimately succeeded involved landing the Army on the river bank opposite Vicksburg; then marching south well past that city and crossing the river to the Vicksburg (east) side. The final phase was to strike swiftly northward across the city's eastward land communications and besiege it. Thus the Army's march would trace an enormous letter "U" with its bottom at the river crossing. All this was to be done, despite the two critical difficulties of the hazardous river crossing and keeping the Army supplied. Naval support was indispensable.

"When in January 1863, Grant's Army landed across the river from Vicksburg, supplies to that city by rail from the west were automatically cut off. But there remained a route by water down the Red River to the Mississippi below Vicksburg, that was then immune from attack by the Naval Squadron above the city, then under Porter. Farragut essayed to stop this river traffic by bringing up a squadron from New Orleans. Three of his large ships were badly damaged at Port Hudson but Farragut himself in the *Hartford* got through (March 1863). She had a long and anxious time blockading the Red River's mouth.

"Awaiting the coming of Spring, Grant attempted cutting a navigable canal across a neck of land so that supply craft could by-pass Vicksburg and reach the lower river. This failed. Meanwhile thorough investigation was made of the possibility of attacking Vicksburg from the north, on the eastern river bank. This involved extensive minor naval operations in the Yazoo River Delta. Impracticability was proved. However Haynes Bluff, on the east bank, was again occupied and a strongly held base of supplies established, which was stocked and constantly replenished down the 'Father of Waters' under naval protection. This was a key move; because the base would serve to supply the Army after it had crossed the Mississippi to the South and then moved north into a position to besiege Vicksburg on its land side. For that, no other line of supply was possible.

"In April 1863 the Union Army started marching southward along the river's west bank. Acting in concert, with a view to protecting the troop crossing, Porter ran past Vicksburg with seven ironclads during darkness of 16 April, leaving the rest of his large fleet above the city to guard Army communications. The 'run-past' was among the most spectacular events of the war. The Confederates lit large bonfires and opened a heavy bombardment, the ships replying vigorously. With loaded coal barges alongside for protection the ships made little speed, while strong eddies in the swift current swung them through large angles. Some were pivoted completely around when directly under the batteries; yet all ironclads got through without serious injury.

"On the 29th at Grand Gulf, Porter pounded Confederate shore batteries at close range for four hours, with a view to putting the Army across at that point. But the fortifications were too strong, so the Union force proceeded down-river to Bruinsburg where Grant crossed without opposition.

"At last on the Vicksburg side, the Union Army, with but scanty supplies made forced marches northward to gain contact with the well-stocked base at Haynes Bluff. This took them across Vicksburg's land communications and the long siege of that place was begun. Thereafter, until the surrender, naval forces gave vigorous combat support to the Federal Army.

"During the Vicksburg siege, the only other Confederate stronghold on the great river, Port Hudson, was taken in May by Union troops and gunboats acting jointly. Thus, when Vicksburg fell in July 1863, the Mississippi was finally open to Federal, military and commercial use throughout its length.

"The last operation of magnitude on western rivers was the ill-fated Red River Expedition in the Spring of 1864. Its origin was defensive—a precaution against the suspected designs on Texas by Napoleon III, who had landed large forces in Mexico. Admiral Porter's strong fleet of gunboats supported General Banks' Army in an up-river advance from Alexandria toward Shreveport. The defeat and hasty retreat of the Union Army forced gunboats to return down 200 miles of shallow and falling river whose banks were now strongly held by the Confederate Army. It was a hot two weeks for the Navy.

"At the refuge of Alexandria the river had so fallen that larger gunboats could not get past the 'falls.' Here the Federal Army saved the Navy. The local water level was raised sufficiently through the ingenious construction of partial dams of trees and timber cribs filled with rock, projected from each bank, under the direction of Colonel Joseph Bailey, Wisconsin Volunteers."

CONFEDERATE RAIDERS

"The greatest achievement of the Confederate Navy was to severely cripple the Federal Merchant Marine through ocean raiding operations," wrote Commodore Knox. "Although the actual damage aggregated less than 1% of the value of Union seaborne commerce during the war, the fear of much greater losses drove insurance premiums on American shipping sky-high. Thus shippers used neutral bottoms, and many American cargo carriers were sold to foreign flags. It should be noted, however, that this damage was only to shipping. Seaborne commerce, itself, under foreign flags, was highly prosperous in the North, contrasting sharply with economic ruin of the South from blockade.

"It is astonishing that a small effort accomplished so much. Of twelve ships commissioned for commerce raiding (neglecting prizes converted to similar use) only five had substantial success. The

C.S.S. Florida *running the blockade at Mobile Bay*.

Sumter got to sea from New Orleans in June, 1861, and took 18 prizes in a few months but when blockaded in Gibraltar and unable to obtain coal was sold there. Bought in England, *Florida* was equipped and commissioned as man-of-war in the Bahamas. She took 37 prizes, and her satellites 22 more, during 1½ years of raiding, coaling in neutral ports. She was finally captured in Bahia Harbor, Brazil, by the U.S. Steam Sloop *Wachusett*, a violation of neutrality which the United States later disavowed.

"The famous *Alabama*, also purchased in England, took 69 prizes in two years of raiding. Captain Semmes cleverly planned the cruise to spend only enough time in each chosen raiding area to allow for news of him to reach the United States and for hunters to arrive in pursuit. He roamed the seven seas as far as the East Indies. In January, 1863, he sank the Federal Gunboat *Hatteras* in the Gulf of Mexico, yet managed to escape retaliation. Finally reaching Cherbourg, France, for greatly needed repairs in June, 1864, he went out to meet the much more powerful USS *Kearsarge*. In the ensuing battle the gallant *Alabama* was sunk.

"Late in 1864 the former blockade runner *Tallahassee* made several cruises out of Wilmington, N. C., capturing 39 prizes.

"In October, 1864, *Shenandoah*, a fast steamer with auxiliary sail, sailed from England intending to destroy the American whaling fleet in the Bering Sea region. She went first to Australia, taking 9 prizes. Then going to the Bering Sea, she captured 39 more. The last 8 whalers were burned in a group 12 weeks after Appomattox. Several weeks later she learned of the war's end, disguised herself and reached England safely.

COASTAL OPERATIONS

"In February, 1863, Admiral du Pont received instructions from the Navy Department to take the city of Charleston, S. C. He had recently been reinforced with seven new monitors and two other ironclads of high freeboard. He maintained that a stronger force was necessary but obeying instructions attacked the outer forts on April 7th, intending to run past if practicable. It was known that the Confederates had lines of obstructions across the narrow channel at several points where heavy gunfires from the forts could concentrate.

"The first line of obstructions consisted of several rows of buoys from which a tangled mass of ropes was suspended. A ship passing through would be certain of having her propellers entangled in the ropes, and thus being held indefinitely under fire from the forts. Moreover there was also a strong probability of mines. At this line the Squadron was under rapid and accurate cross fire from 100 heavy guns and mortars in three forts for nearly two hours. Deciding against penetrating the obstructions at that time, du Pont withdrew intending to renew the attack next day, since his flagship, *New Ironsides*, had not been seriously damaged. However, upon learning that all the other ships had been badly damaged, one of them, *Keokuk*, sinking that night, he abandoned plans for attacking Charleston until stronger naval forces could be provided. He also contended that strong land forces should support the naval attack.

"Unquestionably du Pont's judgment and decisions were sound. But the Navy Department felt otherwise and superseded him in command of the squadron by Admiral Dahlgren. After receiving the support of 3,000 troops for operations on Morris Island, besides naval reinforcements, Dahlgren vigorously renewed the attacks and repeated them over a long period of time with but slight progress. The defenses were too strong. Charleston finally fell only when Sherman's Army marched across its land communications.

"Meanwhile, Confederate naval forces in Charleston had not been idle. In January, 1863, their ironclad rams *Palmetto State* and *Chicora* had raided the blockaders, capturing *Mercedita* and injuring other ships before retiring. In October the great *New Ironsides* was damaged by a torpedo from a Confederate torpedo boat *David*. A few months later the *Housatonic* was sunk by the submarine *Hunley*.

SURRENDER OF THE "TENNESSEE," BATTLE OF MOBILE BAY.

These two incidents are of especial interest as being forerunners of the vast growth of underwater warfare in the 20th Century and the first sinking of a combat ship in war by a submarine.

"At Mobile Bay (Alabama) a fort stood guard on each side of the wide entrance, and between lay a row of submerged mines—then called 'torpedoes.' Inside the extensive bay was the most powerful vessel ever to fly the Confederate flag—the ironclad ram *Tennessee* and three lightly armored small gunboats.

"On 5 August, 1864, Farragut attacked and ran through the mines with seven wooden steam frigates, each having a gunboat lashed alongside as an aid in case of severe damage to the large ship. In addition there was a division of four ironclad monitors. One of them, the *Tecumseh*, was sunk by a mine (torpedo) on the way in. Many of the mines, however, were defective from long immersion which saved other Union vessels from destruction.

"Once inside the Bay the entire Federal Squadron concentrated its main effort against the powerful ironclad *Tennessee*. She was rammed without much effect by the wooden frigates *Monongahela*, *Lackawanna* and *Hartford*, Farragut's flagship. Steady pounding with gunfire, however, principally from the large guns of the monitors, progressively took a heavy toll. With smokestack and rudder shot away, with speed drastically reduced and unable to steer, with fighting quarters filled with hot smoke, with the vessel leaking and Admiral Buchanan severely wounded, the great *Tennessee* finally had no choice but surrender.

"The last haven left for blockade runners was Wilmington, North Carolina. The peculiar configuration of its sea approaches to the Cape Fear River favored evasion by blockade runners so long as Fort Fisher stood guard. This powerful work at the tip of a narrow peninsula, had a sea face three-fourths of a mile long, and the transverse land face a quarter-mile. For its capture Admiral Porter got more than fifty large vessels, including five ironclads, mounting nearly 600 guns, with an army of 6,500 men under General Butler.

"The first attempt on 24 December, 1864, failed. It was preceded by the explosion of 150 tons of gun-powder in an old hulk at anchor 300 yards from the fort, which was not damaged. The Fleet then delivered a thunderous bombardment. Next day, while the Fleet bombarded again, the Army landed several miles away, marched close to the Fort, concluded it was too strong to be taken, reembarked and returned to Hampton Roads.

"Admiral Porter was infuriated and, upon his insistence, 8,000 troops were sent under General Terry for a second attack. It began 13 January with a landing of the troops and a heavy bombardment from the Fleet. Next day, the Fleet again bombarded the land face of the Fort. On the 15th, Fleet bombardment continued from 9 a.m. into the night. A naval landing expedition assaulting the sea face was repulsed while the Army assaulted the land face. Terry's veteran troops showed great gallantry and persistence, were given effective support from naval guns and won the victory at about 10 p.m. Soon afterwards the Fleet advanced up the river and took Wilmington. Blockade running now virtually ceased. Thus the Confederate Armies were deprived of essential supplies, even including food, and the war's end hastened.

"Grant's final campaign in Virginia received support of great value from the Federal Navy. His ability to repeatedly outflank Lee was based largely upon shifting his main base successively from Aquia Creek to Rappahannock River, York River and, finally, James River. Without naval control of Chesapeake Bay and tributaries, such main bases could not have been established or used.

"Grant's final position south of Petersburg would have been untenable without firm control of the lower James River by Union naval forces. The Confederates had for long maintained control of the river above their strong works at Drewry's Bluff. From here, to the last they operated a gunboat squadron against Federal forces. Prior to Grant's arrival, Butler's Army from Norfolk had reached City Point with strong naval support by Admiral S. P. Lee, USN, who was vigorously opposed by the Confederate Squadron under Commodore Mitchell, and later the redoubtable Admiral Raphael Semmes of high-seas fame.

"Marching from the Cold Harbor repulse, Grant crossed the James on pontoons in June, 1864. He sank obstructions in the river as an added protection against the Confederate squadron. However, the latter repeatedly bombarded the crossing and the Federal Squadron until January 1865. With the evacuation of Richmond in April, the war was virtually ended and Semmes blew up his iron-clads and abandoned the James River."

    *   *   *   *   *   *   *

The effect of control of the sea and inland waters by the North in the Civil War cannot be over-emphasized—as indeed sea power cannot be in all the United States' history. President Lincoln realized it and commented on its vast impact. After the Mississippi River had been opened in 1863 by combined military and naval operations, he wrote, "The Father of Waters goes again unvexed to the sea. . . . Nor must Uncle Sam's web feet be forgotten. At all the watery margins they have been present. Not only on the deep sea, the broad bay, the rapid river, but also up the narrow, muddy bayou, and wherever the ground was a little damp, they have been and made their tracks."

We cannot better end this brief summary of Seapower in the Civil War than by adding to the foregoing quotation the words with which last century Scharf began his incomparable *History of the Confederate States Navy*:

"It is no exaggeration of the services rendered in the late war by the navy of the United States, to say that without its aid the armies of the Union would not have been successful; that if the United States had been as destitute of a navy and of naval resources as the Southern Confederacy was, that the Union would have been dissolved; that without Farragut and Foote, Grant and Sherman would occupy in history the same plane with McDowell and Banks, Burnside and Hooker; that when the navy was not co-operating McDowell was hurled back on Washington; McClellan was driven from Richmond to seek protection under the guns of the navy on James River; that Pope was bounced from

Cedar Mountain and, ricochetting at Manassas, rested like a spent ball under the defenses of the capital; that in the West the 'tin-clad' navy conveyed the army to Fort Henry, and was its effective left wing at Donelson; that the Mississippi River from Cairo to its mouth was firmly held by the Confederates until Foote from the North and Farragut from the South broke its barriers and opened its navigation; that Vicksburg and Port Hudson successfully defied and defeated the land forces, and surrendered as much to the navy as to the army; that Sherman would never have undertaken the *march to the sea* if the navy had not provided protection on the seaboard; that Grant, in the Wilderness, diverted by Lee from his direct march on Richmond, sought the friendly help of the navy in his campaign to capture the Confederate capital; that the blockade from the Chesapeake Bay to the mouth of the Rio Grande shut the Confederacy out from the world, deprived it of supplies, weakened its military and naval strength, and compelled exhaustion, by requiring the consumption of everything grown or raised in the country; . . ."

1861

JANUARY
S	M	T	W	T	F	S
		1	2	3	4	5
6	7	8	9	10	11	12
13	14	15	16	17	18	19
20	21	22	23	24	25	26
27	28	29	30	31		

FEBRUARY
S	M	T	W	T	F	S
					1	2
3	4	5	6	7	8	9
10	11	12	13	14	15	16
17	18	19	20	21	22	23
24	25	26	27	28		

MARCH
S	M	T	W	T	F	S
					1	2
3	4	5	6	7	8	9
10	11	12	13	14	15	16
17	18	19	20	21	22	23
24	25	26	27	28	29	30
31						

APRIL
S	M	T	W	T	F	S
	1	2	3	4	5	6
7	8	9	10	11	12	13
14	15	16	17	18	19	20
21	22	23	24	25	26	27
28	29	30				

MAY
S	M	T	W	T	F	S
			1	2	3	4
5	6	7	8	9	10	11
12	13	14	15	16	17	18
19	20	21	22	23	24	25
26	27	28	29	30	31	

JUNE
S	M	T	W	T	F	S
						1
2	3	4	5	6	7	8
9	10	11	12	13	14	15
16	17	18	19	20	21	22
23	24	25	26	27	28	29
30						

JULY
S	M	T	W	T	F	S
	1	2	3	4	5	6
7	8	9	10	11	12	13
14	15	16	17	18	19	20
21	22	23	24	25	26	27
28	29	30	31			

AUGUST
S	M	T	W	T	F	S
				1	2	3
4	5	6	7	8	9	10
11	12	13	14	15	16	17
18	19	20	21	22	23	24
25	26	27	28	29	30	31

SEPTEMBER
S	M	T	W	T	F	S
1	2	3	4	5	6	7
8	9	10	11	12	13	14
15	16	17	18	19	20	21
22	23	24	25	26	27	28
29	30					

OCTOBER
S	M	T	W	T	F	S
		1	2	3	4	5
6	7	8	9	10	11	12
13	14	15	16	17	18	19
20	21	22	23	24	25	26
27	28	29	30	31		

NOVEMBER
S	M	T	W	T	F	S
					1	2
3	4	5	6	7	8	9
10	11	12	13	14	15	16
17	18	19	20	21	22	23
24	25	26	27	28	29	30

DECEMBER
S	M	T	W	T	F	S
1	2	3	4	5	6	7
8	9	10	11	12	13	14
15	16	17	18	19	20	21
22	23	24	25	26	27	28
29	30	31				

1862

JANUARY
S	M	T	W	T	F	S
			1	2	3	4
5	6	7	8	9	10	11
12	13	14	15	16	17	18
19	20	21	22	23	24	25
26	27	28	29	30	31	

FEBRUARY
S	M	T	W	T	F	S
						1
2	3	4	5	6	7	8
9	10	11	12	13	14	15
16	17	18	19	20	21	22
23	24	25	26	27	28	

MARCH
S	M	T	W	T	F	S
						1
2	3	4	5	6	7	8
9	10	11	12	13	14	15
16	17	18	19	20	21	22
23	24	25	26	27	28	29
30	31					

APRIL
S	M	T	W	T	F	S
		1	2	3	4	5
6	7	8	9	10	11	12
13	14	15	16	17	18	19
20	21	22	23	24	25	26
27	28	29	30			

MAY
S	M	T	W	T	F	S
				1	2	3
4	5	6	7	8	9	10
11	12	13	14	15	16	17
18	19	20	21	22	23	24
25	26	27	28	29	30	31

JUNE
S	M	T	W	T	F	S
1	2	3	4	5	6	7
8	9	10	11	12	13	14
15	16	17	18	19	20	21
22	23	24	25	26	27	28
29	30					

JULY
S	M	T	W	T	F	S
		1	2	3	4	5
6	7	8	9	10	11	12
13	14	15	16	17	18	19
20	21	22	23	24	25	26
27	28	29	30	31		

AUGUST
S	M	T	W	T	F	S
					1	2
3	4	5	6	7	8	9
10	11	12	13	14	15	16
17	18	19	20	21	22	23
24	25	26	27	28	29	30
31						

SEPTEMBER
S	M	T	W	T	F	S
	1	2	3	4	5	6
7	8	9	10	11	12	13
14	15	16	17	18	19	20
21	22	23	24	25	26	27
28	29	30				

OCTOBER
S	M	T	W	T	F	S
			1	2	3	4
5	6	7	8	9	10	11
12	13	14	15	16	17	18
19	20	21	22	23	24	25
26	27	28	29	30	31	

NOVEMBER
S	M	T	W	T	F	S
						1
2	3	4	5	6	7	8
9	10	11	12	13	14	15
16	17	18	19	20	21	22
23	24	25	26	27	28	29
30						

DECEMBER
S	M	T	W	T	F	S
	1	2	3	4	5	6
7	8	9	10	11	12	13
14	15	16	17	18	19	20
21	22	23	24	25	26	27
28	29	30	31			

1863

JANUARY
S	M	T	W	T	F	S
				1	2	3
4	5	6	7	8	9	10
11	12	13	14	15	16	17
18	19	20	21	22	23	24
25	26	27	28	29	30	31

FEBRUARY
S	M	T	W	T	F	S
1	2	3	4	5	6	7
8	9	10	11	12	13	14
15	16	17	18	19	20	21
22	23	24	25	26	27	28

MARCH
S	M	T	W	T	F	S
1	2	3	4	5	6	7
8	9	10	11	12	13	14
15	16	17	18	19	20	21
22	23	24	25	26	27	28
29	30	31				

APRIL
S	M	T	W	T	F	S
			1	2	3	4
5	6	7	8	9	10	11
12	13	14	15	16	17	18
19	20	21	22	23	24	25
26	27	28	29	30		

MAY
S	M	T	W	T	F	S
					1	2
3	4	5	6	7	8	9
10	11	12	13	14	15	16
17	18	19	20	21	22	23
24	25	26	27	28	29	30
31						

JUNE
S	M	T	W	T	F	S
	1	2	3	4	5	6
7	8	9	10	11	12	13
14	15	16	17	18	19	20
21	22	23	24	25	26	27
28	29	30				

JULY
S	M	T	W	T	F	S
			1	2	3	4
5	6	7	8	9	10	11
12	13	14	15	16	17	18
19	20	21	22	23	24	25
26	27	28	29	30	31	

AUGUST
S	M	T	W	T	F	S
						1
2	3	4	5	6	7	8
9	10	11	12	13	14	15
16	17	18	19	20	21	22
23	24	25	26	27	28	29
30	31					

SEPTEMBER
S	M	T	W	T	F	S
		1	2	3	4	5
6	7	8	9	10	11	12
13	14	15	16	17	18	19
20	21	22	23	24	25	26
27	28	29	30			

OCTOBER
S	M	T	W	T	F	S
				1	2	3
4	5	6	7	8	9	10
11	12	13	14	15	16	17
18	19	20	21	22	23	24
25	26	27	28	29	30	31

NOVEMBER
S	M	T	W	T	F	S
1	2	3	4	5	6	7
8	9	10	11	12	13	14
15	16	17	18	19	20	21
22	23	24	25	26	27	28
29	30					

DECEMBER
S	M	T	W	T	F	S
		1	2	3	4	5
6	7	8	9	10	11	12
13	14	15	16	17	18	19
20	21	22	23	24	25	26
27	28	29	30	31		

1865

JANUARY
S	M	T	W	T	F	S
1	2	3	4	5	6	7
8	9	10	11	12	13	14
15	16	17	18	19	20	21
22	23	24	25	26	27	28
29	30	31				

FEBRUARY
S	M	T	W	T	F	S
			1	2	3	4
5	6	7	8	9	10	11
12	13	14	15	16	17	18
19	20	21	22	23	24	25
26	27	28				

MARCH
S	M	T	W	T	F	S
			1	2	3	4
5	6	7	8	9	10	11
12	13	14	15	16	17	18
19	20	21	22	23	24	25
26	27	28	29	30	31	

APRIL
S	M	T	W	T	F	S
						1
2	3	4	5	6	7	8
9	10	11	12	13	14	15
16	17	18	19	20	21	22
23	24	25	26	27	28	29
30						

MAY
S	M	T	W	T	F	S
	1	2	3	4	5	6
7	8	9	10	11	12	13
14	15	16	17	18	19	20
21	22	23	24	25	26	27
28	29	30	31			

JUNE
S	M	T	W	T	F	S
				1	2	3
4	5	6	7	8	9	10
11	12	13	14	15	16	17
18	19	20	21	22	23	24
25	26	27	28	29	30	

JULY
S	M	T	W	T	F	S
						1
2	3	4	5	6	7	8
9	10	11	12	13	14	15
16	17	18	19	20	21	22
23	24	25	26	27	28	29
30	31					

AUGUST
S	M	T	W	T	F	S
		1	2	3	4	5
6	7	8	9	10	11	12
13	14	15	16	17	18	19
20	21	22	23	24	25	26
27	28	29	30	31		

SEPTEMBER
S	M	T	W	T	F	S
					1	2
3	4	5	6	7	8	9
10	11	12	13	14	15	16
17	18	19	20	21	22	23
24	25	26	27	28	29	30

OCTOBER
S	M	T	W	T	F	S
1	2	3	4	5	6	7
8	9	10	11	12	13	14
15	16	17	18	19	20	21
22	23	24	25	26	27	28
29	30	31				

NOVEMBER
S	M	T	W	T	F	S
			1	2	3	4
5	6	7	8	9	10	11
12	13	14	15	16	17	18
19	20	21	22	23	24	25
26	27	28	29	30		

DECEMBER
S	M	T	W	T	F	S
					1	2
3	4	5	6	7	8	9
10	11	12	13	14	15	16
17	18	19	20	21	22	23
24	25	26	27	28	29	30
31						

1864

JANUARY
S	M	T	W	T	F	S
					1	2
3	4	5	6	7	8	9
10	11	12	13	14	15	16
17	18	19	20	21	22	23
24	25	26	27	28	29	30
31						

FEBRUARY
S	M	T	W	T	F	S
	1	2	3	4	5	6
7	8	9	10	11	12	13
14	15	16	17	18	19	20
21	22	23	24	25	26	27
28	29					

MARCH
S	M	T	W	T	F	S
		1	2	3	4	5
6	7	8	9	10	11	12
13	14	15	16	17	18	19
20	21	22	23	24	25	26
27	28	29	30	31		

APRIL
S	M	T	W	T	F	S
					1	2
3	4	5	6	7	8	9
10	11	12	13	14	15	16
17	18	19	20	21	22	23
24	25	26	27	28	29	30

MAY
S	M	T	W	T	F	S
1	2	3	4	5	6	7
8	9	10	11	12	13	14
15	16	17	18	19	20	21
22	23	24	25	26	27	28
29	30	31				

JUNE
S	M	T	W	T	F	S
			1	2	3	4
5	6	7	8	9	10	11
12	13	14	15	16	17	18
19	20	21	22	23	24	25
26	27	28	29	30		

JULY
S	M	T	W	T	F	S
					1	2
3	4	5	6	7	8	9
10	11	12	13	14	15	16
17	18	19	20	21	22	23
24	25	26	27	28	29	30
31						

AUGUST
S	M	T	W	T	F	S
	1	2	3	4	5	6
7	8	9	10	11	12	13
14	15	16	17	18	19	20
21	22	23	24	25	26	27
28	29	30	31			

SEPTEMBER
S	M	T	W	T	F	S
				1	2	3
4	5	6	7	8	9	10
11	12	13	14	15	16	17
18	19	20	21	22	23	24
25	26	27	28.	29	30	

OCTOBER
S	M	T	W	T	F	S
						1
2	3	4	5	6	7	8
9	10	11	12	13	14	15
16	17	18	19	20	21	22
23	24	25	26	27	28	29
30	31					

NOVEMBER
S	M	T	W	T	F	S
		1	2	3	4	5
6	7	8	9	10	11	12
13	14	15	16	17	18	19
20	21	22	23	24	25	26
27	28	29	30			

DECEMBER
S	M	T	W	T	F	S
				1	2	3
4	5	6	7	8	9	10
11	12	13	14	15	16	17
18	19	20	21	22	23	24
25	26	27	28	29	30	31

"Sailor on Sentry" on Morris Island, Charleston harbor, was probably drawn by the contemporary artist Alfred R. Waud.

1861

I.—SOME SIGNIFICANT EVENTS OF 1861

12 April — Fort Sumter fired on by Confederate batteries—the conflict begins.

19 April — President Lincoln issued proclamation declaring blockade of Southern ports from South Carolina to Texas.

20 April — Norfolk Navy Yard partially destroyed to prevent Yard facilities from falling into Confederate hands and abandoned by Union forces.

24 May — Commander S. C. Rowan, U.S.S. *Pawnee,* demanded the surrender of Alexandria, Virginia; an amphibious expedition departed Washington Navy Yard and occupied the town.

3 August — John LaMountain made first ascent in a balloon from Union ship *Fanny* at Hampton Roads to observe Confederate batteries on Sewell's Point, Virginia.

29 August — Union forces under Flag Officer S. H. Stringham and General B. F. Butler received the unconditional surrender of Confederate-held Forts Hatteras and Clark, closing Pamlico Sound.

1 October — Confederate naval forces, including C.S.S. *Curlew, Raleigh,* and *Junaluska,* under Flag Officer W. F. Lynch, CSN, captured steamer *Fanny* (later C.S.S. *Fanny*) in Pamlico Sound with Union troops on board.

7 November— Naval forces under Flag Officer S. F. Du Pont captured Port Royal Sound.

U.S.S. *Tyler,* Commander H. Walke, and U.S.S. *Lexington*, Commander R. Stembel, supported 3000 Union troops under General Grant at the Battle of Belmont, Missouri, and engaged Confederate batteries along the Mississippi River.

8 November— U.S.S. *San Jacinto,* Captain C. Wilkes, stopped British mail steamer *Trent* in Old Bahama Channel and removed Confederate Commissioners James Mason and John Slidell.

11 November— Thaddeus Lowe made balloon observation of Confederate forces from Balloon-Boat *G. W. Parke Custis* anchored in Potomac River.

12 November— *Fingal* (later C.S.S. *Atlanta*), purchased in England, entered Savannah laden with military supplies—the first ship to run the blockade solely on Confederate government account.

21 December — Congress enacted legislation providing for the Medal of Honor.

II.—DETAILED CIVIL WAR NAVAL CHRONOLOGY

1860

NOVEMBER

1 United States Navy planned to convert seven sailing ships into steam ships of war at a cost of $3,064,000.

15 Lieutenant Thomas A. Craven, Commanding U.S. Naval Forces at Key West, notified Secretary of the Navy Isaac Toucey that due to "the present deplorable condition of affairs in the Southern States" he had moved to prevent the seizure "by any bands of lawless men" of Forts Taylor and Jefferson. Craven, in U.S.S. *Mohawk*, defended Fort Jefferson and Lieutenant Fabius Stanly, U.S.S. *Wyandotte*, held Fort Taylor. This far-sighted action on the part of Craven, who distinguished himself throughout the war, enabled the Union to retain the vital Key West posts, the importance of which, Craven noted "can not be overestimated, commanding as they do the commerce of the Gulf of Mexico."

DECEMBER

26 Following the secession of South Carolina (20 December) Major Robert Anderson, USA, removed his loyal garrison from Fort Moultrie to Fort Sumter, on an island in Charleston Harbor; this created special need for sea-borne reinforcements of troops and supplies.

27 U.S. Revenue Cutter *Aiken* was surrendered to South Carolina authorities.

1861

JANUARY

5 U.S. steamer *Star of the West*, Captain John McGowan, USRM, departed New York with an Army detachment for the relief of Fort Sumter, Charleston Harbor, South Carolina.

Secretary of the Navy Toucey ordered Fort Washington—on Maryland side of the Potomac—garrisoned "to protect public property." Forty Marines from Washington Navy Yard under Captain Algernon S. Taylor, USMC, were sent to the Fort—a vital link in the defense of the Nation's Capital by land or water.

Fort Morgan, at the entrance to Mobile Bay, Alabama, was seized and garrisoned by Alabama militia.

9 U.S. steamer *Star of the West,* Captain McGowan, was fired on by Confederate troops from Morris Island and Fort Moultrie as she attempted to enter Charleston Harbor. Cadets from the Citadel took part in this action. The relief of Fort Sumter was not effected. These were the first Confederate shots fired at a vessel flying the United States flag. *Star of the West* returned to New York.

Thirty Marines from Washington Navy Yard under First Lieutenant Andrew J. Hays, USMC, garrisoned Fort McHenry, Baltimore, until U.S. Army troops could relieve them.

10 Forts Jackson and St. Philip, Mississippi River, Louisiana, were seized by Louisiana State troops.

11 U.S. Marine Hospital two miles below New Orleans was occupied by Louisiana State troops.

12 Fort Barrancas and the Pensacola Navy Yard, Captain James Armstrong, USN, were seized by Florida and Alabama militia. Union troops escaped across the Bay to Fort Pickens on Santa Rosa Island, a position which remained in Union hands throughout the war.

14 South Carolina legislature declared any attempt to reinforce Fort Sumter would be an act of war.

16 Captain Taylor, USMC, commanding Fort Washington, wrote Colonel John Harris, Marine Corps Commandant, regarding the "defenseless and pregnable condition" of the Fort. Taylor requested rein-

Confederate battery at Morris Island fires on Star of the West, *attempting to provision Fort Sumter. These were the first shots fired by the South at a vessel flying the United States flag.*

forcements, commenting that he did "not wish to be placed in a position to detract from the high character of my corps."

18 Confederates seized U.S. lighthouse tender *Alert* at Mobile, Alabama.

20 Fort on Ship Island, Mississippi, seized by Confederates; Ship Island was a key base for operations in the Gulf of Mexico and at the mouth of the Mississippi River.

22 Guns and ammunition sold to and destined for Georgia were seized by New York authorities. This action was protested by Georgia Governor Joseph E. Brown in a letter to New York Governor Edwin Morgan. In retaliation Governor Brown seized northern ships at Savannah on 8 and 21 February 1861. Marine Guard at Brooklyn Navy Yard put under arms as a precaution against difficulty with Confederate sympathizers.

23 Commander John A. Dahlgren noted that as a precaution against an attack on the Washington Navy Yard, he had the cannon and the ammunition from the Yard magazine removed to the attic of the main building.

25 Captain Samuel F. Du Pont wrote Commander Andrew Hull Foote about the number of naval officers resigning their commissions to go to their home States in the South: "What made me most sick at heart, is the resignations from the Navy . . . I [have been] nurtured, fed and clothed by the general government for over forty years, paid whether employed or not, and for what—why to stand by the country, whether assailed by enemies from without or foes within—my oath declared 'allegiance to the United States' as well as to support the Constitution . . . I stick by the *flag* and the national government as long as we have one, whether my state does or not and she knows it."

Surrendered to Florida and Alabama militia on 12 January, the vital Pensacola Navy Yard was re-occupied by Union forces in May 1862.

28 Stephen R. Mallory, later Confederate Secretary of the Navy, hearing that U.S.S. *Brooklyn,* Captain William S. Walker, was en route to reinforce Fort Pickens, wired John Slidell that, if attempted, "resistance and a bloody conflict seems inevitable."

29 Secretaries of the Navy and War ordered that the Marines and troops on board U.S.S *Brooklyn,* Captain Walker, en route Pensacola, not be landed to reinforce Fort Pickens unless that work was taken under attack by the Confederates.

Louisiana having passed the ordinance of secession on 26 January, Secretary of the Treasury John A. Dix wired Agent William H. Jones at New Orleans ordering him not to surrender the U.S. Revenue Cutter there and to defend the American flag with force if necessary. *Robert McClelland* surrendered by Captain John G. Breshwood, USRM, to Louisiana authorities despite contrary command by Agent Jones.

30 **U.S. Revenue Schooner** *Lewis Cass,* **Captain John J. Morrison, USRM, was surrendered at Mobile to State authorities.**

31 U.S. Revenue Schooner *Washington,* Captain Robert K. Hudgins, USRM, was seized by State authorities at New Orleans, while undergoing repairs.

FEBRUARY

9 U.S.S. *Brooklyn,* Captain Walker, arrived off Pensacola. Troops were not landed at Fort Pickens in compliance with the order of 29 January, based on an interim agreement with Florida officials in which the status quo would be maintained (i.e., Forts Barrancas and McRee and Navy Yard remained in Con-

federate hands while the Union held Fort Pickens on Santa Rosa Island). *Brooklyn, Sabine, Macedonia,* and *St. Louis* remained off the harbor, but reinforcements were not put ashore at Fort Pickens until 12 April.

11 Commander Dahlgren urged Congress to approve the building of more gun-sloops and an "iron-cased" ship.

14 Confederate Congress passed a resolution authorizing "the Committee on Naval Affairs to procure the attendance at Montgomery, of all such persons versed in naval affairs as they may deem it advisable to consult with."

15 Raphael Semmes, later captain of C.S.S. *Sumter* and *Alabama,* resigned his commission in the United States Navy.

18 In his inaugural address as President of the Provisional Government of the Confederate States, Jefferson Davis said: "I . . . suggest that for the protection of our harbors and commerce on the high seas a Navy adapted to those objects will be required . . ."

20 Navy Department formally established by act of Confederate Congress.

21 Jefferson Davis appointed Stephen R. Mallory of Florida Secretary of the Confederate States Navy.

27 U.S. Congress authorized construction of seven steam sloops to augment existing naval strength. Gideon Welles, soon to be Secretary of the Navy, noted, "for steam, as well as heavy ordnance, has become an indispensable element of the most efficient naval power."

MARCH

2 U.S. Revenue Schooner *Henry Dodge,* First Lieutenant William F. Rogers, USRM, was seized at Galveston, as Texas joined the Confederacy.

4 Forty-two vessels were in commission in the United States Navy. Twelve of these ships were assigned duty with the Home Squadron, four of which were based on Northern ports. Beginning with the

Stephen R. Mallory
Secretary of the Confederate States Navy, 1861–1865

Gideon Welles
Secretary of the Navy, 1861–1869

return of *Powhatan* to New York and *Pocahontas* to Hampton Roads on 12 March and *Cumberland* to Hampton Roads on 23 March, the Department moved to recall all but three ships from foreign stations, where they were badly needed, in order to meet the greater needs of the Nation in this hour of crisis.

7   Gideon Welles of Hartford, Connecticut, took office in Washington as Secretary of the Navy.

13   It was reported by Captain J. M. Brannon, USA, commanding Fort Taylor that "everything is quiet at Key West to this date"—a tribute to the firm policing of the area by Union naval vessels. Throughout the early months of 1861 the "showing of the flag" by the Fleet maintained a peaceful equilibrium in a situation fraught with tension. The much-feared attack, expected to accompany Florida's secession (10 January), did not materialize.

17   Confederate Navy Department sent Commander Lawrence Rousseau, Commander Ebenezer Farrand, and Lieutenant Robert T. Chapman to New Orleans to negotiate for the construction of gunboats.

18   Brigadier General Braxton Bragg, CSA, issued an order forbidding passage of supplies to Fort Pickens and the U.S. squadron off Pensacola.

20   U.S. sloop *Isabella,* carrying supplies for U.S. squadron at Pensacola, was seized at Mobile.

21   Gustavus V. Fox, ex-naval officer now a civilian, reconnoitered Fort Sumter, Charleston Harbor, as directed by President Lincoln, to determine the best means of relieving the Fort. Based on his observations, Fox recommended relieving Sumter by sea: "I propose to put the troops on board of a large, comfortable sea steamer and hire two powerful light draft New York tug boats, having the necessary stores on board. These to be convoyed by the U.S.S. *Pawnee* . . . and the revenue cutter *Harriet Lane* . . . Arriving off the bar, I propose to examine by day the naval preparations and obstructions. If their vessels determine to oppose our entrance, and a feint or flag of truce would ascertain this, the armed ships must approach the bar and destroy or drive them on shore. Major Anderson would do the same upon any vessels within the range of his guns and would also prevent any naval succor being sent down from the city."

31   Secretary of the Navy Welles ordered 250 men transferred from New York to the Navy Yard at Norfolk, Virginia.

APRIL

2   President Lincoln visited the Washington Navy Yard. The President returned frequently to confer with Commander Dahlgren on the defense of the Capital and the far reaching strategy of sea power in general.

3   Confederate battery at Morris Island, Charleston, fired on American schooner *Rhoda H. Shannon.*

4   President Lincoln gave final approval to Gustavus Fox's plan to relieve Fort Sumter by sea.

5   U.S.S. *Powhatan, Pawnee, Pocahontas,* and Revenue Cutter *Harriet Lane* were ordered by Secretary of the Navy Welles to provision Fort Sumter; squadron commander was Captain Samuel Mercer in *Powhatan.*

6   Lieutenant David Dixon Porter, ordered to take command of U.S.S. *Powhatan* by President Lincoln and to reinforce Fort Pickens, Pensacola, instead of Fort Sumter, departed New York. The following day Lieutenant John L. Worden, USN, departed Washington, D.C., by rail with orders to Captain Henry A. Adams, commanding U.S.S. *Sabine* and senior officer present in the Pensacola area, to reinforce Fort Pickens.

8   Revenue Cutter *Harriet Lane,* Captain John Faunce, USRM, departed New York for relief of Fort Sumter.

9   Gustavus V. Fox sailed from New York in chartered steamer *Baltic* for the relief of Fort Sumter.

10   U.S.S. *Pawnee,* Commander Stephen C. Rowan, departed Hampton Roads for relief of Fort Sumter.

General P. G. T. Beauregard, CSA, commanding at Charleston, was instructed to demand evacuation of Fort Sumter and, if refused, to "proceed, in such manner as you may determine, to reduce it."

Secretary of the Navy Welles alerted Captain Charles S. McCauley, Commandant Norfolk Navy Yard, to condition U.S.S. *Merrimack* for a move to a Northern yard should it become necessary. At the same time Welles cautioned McCauley that, "There should be no steps taken to give needless alarm."

11 Commander James Alden was ordered to report to Captain McCauley to take command of *Merrimack*. The following day Chief Engineer Benjamin Isherwood was sent to Norfolk to put the ship's engines in working order as soon as possible.

General Beauregard's demand for evacuation of Fort Sumter refused by Major Anderson.

U.S. steamship *Coatzacoalcos* arrived in New York, returning Union troops from Texas.

12 Fort Sumter fired on by Confederate batteries—*the conflict begins.*

U.S. steamship *Baltic,* under Gustavus Fox, U.S.S. *Pawnee,* Commander Rowan, and *Harriet Lane,* Captain Faunce, USRM, arrived off Charleston to reinforce Fort Sumter. But, as Fox observed, "war had commenced" and he was unable to carry out his mission.

Under secret orders from Secretary of the Navy Welles carried by Lieutenant Worden, Fort Pickens was reinforced by landing of troops under Captain Israel Vogdes, 1st U.S. Artillery, and Marines under First Lieutenant John C. Cash, from the squadron composed of U.S.S. *Sabine,* Captain H. A. Adams, Senior Officer Present, U.S.S. *Brooklyn,* Captain W. S. Walker, U.S.S. *St. Louis,* Commander Charles H. Poor, and U.S.S. *Wyandotte,* Lieutenant J. R. Madison Mullany.

13 Fort Sumter surrendered by Major Anderson. Troops were evacuated the next day by Fox's expedition.

U.S.S. *Sabine,* Captain Adams, blockaded Pensacola Harbor.

Lieutenant Worden was seized near Montgomery, Alabama, and placed in prison, but his Pensacola mission had been accomplished.

14 Captain Du Pont wrote: "I hope those Southern gentlemen will declare war, for that will stop the shilly shallying, unite the North if it be not so already, and the line will have to be drawn by the strategic points involved, which for the defense of the Capital includes Maryland."

15 Seventeen vessels from Southern ports without U.S. clearances were seized at New York.

16 Secretary of the Navy Welles wrote Flag Officer Garrett J. Pendergrast, commanding U.S.S. *Cumberland* at Norfolk: "Until further orders the departure of the *Cumberland* to Vera Cruz will be deferred. In the meantime you will lend your assistance, and that of your command, towards putting the vessels now in the Yard in condition to be moved, placing the ordnance and ordnance stores on board for moving, and, in case of invasion, insurrection, or violence of any kind, to suppress it, repelling assualt by force, if necessary."

17 U.S.S. *Powhatan,* Lieutenant D. D. Porter, arrived off Pensacola. Under her protecting guns, 600 troops on board steamer *Atlantic* were landed at Fort Pickens to complete its reinforcement. President Lincoln had stated "I want that fort saved at all hazards." The President's wish was fulfilled, and use of the best harbor on the Gulf was denied the Confederacy for the entire war, while serving the Union indispensably in the blockade and the series of devastating assaults from the sea that divided and destroyed the South.

Jefferson Davis' proclamation invited all interested in "service in private armed vessels on the high seas" to apply for Letters of Marque and Reprisal.

Confederates placed obstacles in the channel at Norfolk, attempting to prevent the sailing of U.S. naval vessels. The subsequent passage of the obstructions by *Pawnee* and *Cumberland* proved the effort ineffective.

18 U.S.S. *Merrimack* was reported ready for sea at Norfolk by Chief Engineer Isherwood.

Secretary of the Navy Welles wrote Captain Hiram Paulding: "You are directed to proceed forthwith to Norfolk and take command of all the naval forces there afloat . . . On no account should the arms

The firing on Fort Sumter.

Troops of the New York Seventh Regiment land at the Naval Academy. Washington being cut off by rail, the New Yorkers and General Butler's Massachusetts troops were transported by steamer to Annapolis at Captain Du Pont's recommendation for the defense of the Capital.

and munitions be permitted to fall into the hands of insurrectionists, or those who would wrest them from the custody of the government; and should it finally become necessary, you will, in order to prevent that result, destroy the property."

U.S. schooner *Buchanan* (lighthouse tender), Master Thomas Cullen, was seized and taken to Richmond, Virginia.

19 President Lincoln issued proclamation declaring blockade of Southern ports from South Carolina to Texas. Of the blockade Admiral David Dixon Porter was to later write: "So efficiently was the blockade maintained and so greatly was it strengthened from time to time, that foreign statesmen, who at the beginning of the war, did not hesitate to pronounce the blockade of nearly three thousand miles of coast a moral impossibility, twelve months after its establishment were forced to admit that the proofs of its efficiency were so comprehensive and conclusive that no objections to it could be made."

Washington having been cut off by rail from the North, Captain Du Pont and others embarked troops at Philadelphia and head of the Chesapeake Bay to proceed to the relief of the Capital. Steamer *Boston* departed Philadelphia with New York Seventh Regiment on board, and ferryboat *Maryland* embarked General Benjamin F. Butler's Massachusetts Eighth Regiment at Perryville for Annapolis.

U.S. steamer *Star of the West* was seized by Confederates at Indianola, Texas.

Captain David Glasgow Farragut, though born in the South and with a southern wife, chose to remain loyal to the Union and left his home in Norfolk, Virginia, to take up residence in New York City.

20 Norfolk Navy Yard partially destroyed to prevent Yard facilities from falling into Confederate hands and abandoned by Union forces. U.S.S. *Pennsylvania, Germantown, Raritan, Columbia,* and *Dolphin* were burned to water's edge. U.S.S. *Delaware, Columbus, Plymouth,* and *Merrimack* (later C.S.S. *Virginia*)

Destruction of the Norfolk Navy Yard is only partially successful and the Confederacy gains a major facility.

Among the ships burned at the Norfolk Yard was U.S.S. Merrimack, *which the Confederates rebuilt as ironclad C.S.S.* Virginia.

were burned and sunk. Old frigate U.S.S. *United States* was abandoned. U.S.S. *Pawnee,* Commodore Paulding, and tug *Yankee,* towing U.S.S. *Cumberland,* escaped; *Pawnee* returned to Washington to augment small defenses at the Capital. This major Yard was of prime importance to the South. The Confederacy had limited industrial capacity, and possession of the Norfolk Yard provided her with guns and other ordnance materiel, and, equally as important, gave her a drydock and an industrial plant in which to manufacture crucially needed items. In large measure, guns for the batteries and fortifications erected by the Confederates on the Atlantic coast and rivers during 1861 came from the Norfolk Yard.

U.S.S. *Constitution,* Lieutenant George Rodgers, moored in Severn River off Annapolis, was towed into Chesapeake Bay by steamer *Maryland* with General Butler's troops on board. This action, preceded by resolute measures by Naval Academy staff and midshipmen, prevented Confederates from seizing historic "Old Ironsides."

U.S.S. *Anacostia,* Lieutenant Thomas S. Fillebrown, was ordered to patrol off Kettle Bottom Shoals, Virginia, to prevent the obstruction of the channel at that point; the crew was augmented by 20 Marines from the Washington Navy Yard.

Cornelius Vanderbilt offered the government the fast steamer *Vanderbilt.* Eventually the Navy acquired many private ships by charter or purchase to strengthen its blockade fleets.

U.S. coast survey schooner *Twilight,* Andrew C. Mitchell, was seized at Aransas, Texas.

21 Colonel Charles F. Smith, USA, reported to Secretary of the Navy Welles he had seized and placed under guard steamers *Baltimore, Mount Vernon, Philadelphia,* and *Powhatan* near Washington, D.C. Steamers plied between Aquia Creek and Washington; these were ordered to be outfitted at Wash-

ington Navy Yard for defense of the Capital. Aquia Creek, terminal point of railroad connection with Richmond, was the first location on the Potomac where Confederate naval officers erected batteries.

U.S.S. *Saratoga,* Commander Alfred Taylor, captured slave ship *Nightingale* with 961 slaves on board.

Secretary of the Navy Welles instructed Captain Du Pont, Commandant Philadelphia Navy Yard, to "procure five staunch steamers from ten to twelve feet draught, having particular reference to strength and speed and capable of carrying a nine-inch pivot gun . . . for coast service." Similar orders were sent to Commandants of the Navy Yards in New York and Boston.

22   Captain Franklin Buchanan, Commandant Washington Navy Yard, submitted his resignation and was relieved by Commander John A. Dahlgren; Buchanan joined the Confederate Navy and was promoted to Admiral, CSN, on 26 August 1862.   Dahlgren spurred the buildup of Union ordnance and operation of ships for the defense of Washington and Potomac River.   Of the ships (primarily chartered commercial steamers) assigned to Dahlgren's command at the Navy Yard, Secretary of the Navy Welles reported: "For several months . . . the navy, without aid, succeeded, more effectually than could have been expected, in keeping open for commercial purposes, and restricting, to a great extent, communication between the opposite shores [Potomac]."

Steamer *Boston* arrived at Annapolis with New York 7th Regiment on board, found *Maryland* aground after towing U.S.S. *Constitution* into Chesapeake Bay, and got her off, troops from both ships disembarking.   This timely arrival by water transport, recommended by Captain Du Pont at Philadelphia, was instrumental in defending Washington against possible Confederate seizure, and significant in keeping Maryland in the Union.   In the following days Butler's troops repaired the railroad and opened communications with Washington, which had been severed since the 19 April Baltimore riots.   Commander James H. Ward of U.S.S. *North Carolina* proposed to Secretary of the Navy Welles the organization of a "flying flotilla" of ships for service in Chesapeake Bay and tributaries.   The proposal was approved, ships purchased and fitted out in New York, and on 20 May 1861, U.S.S. *Freeborn,* with two small craft in tow, Commander Ward in command, arrived at Washington Navy Yard.

Secretary of the Navy Welles ordered Commander William W. Hunter to move Receiving Ship *Allegheny* at Baltimore to Fort McHenry because of strong secessionist activity in the city.

23   U.S.S. *Pawnee* reached Washington where Commodore Paulding reported to the Navy Department on the loss of the Norfolk Navy Yard.   *Pawnee's* arrival strengthened the Capital's defenses at a critical juncture.

24   U.S.S. *Cumberland,* Flag Officer Pendergrast, captured Confederate tug *Young America* and schooner *George M. Smith* with cargo of arms and ammunition in Hampton Roads.

U.S.S. *Constitution,* Lieutenant G. W. Rodgers, departed with midshipmen on board for New York and Newport, Rhode Island, under tow of U.S.S. *R. R. Cuyler* with *Harriet Lane* in company, to transfer U.S. Naval Academy.

26   U.S.S. *Commerce,* Lieutenant Peirce Crosby, captured steamer *Lancaster* at Havre de Grace, Maryland. He also pursued a steam tug "in obedience to the written orders that I had received from you [Commander Charles Steedman] to seize all tugs south of Havre de Grace," but could not catch her.

Confederate Secretary of the Navy Mallory reported: "I propose to adopt a class of vessels hitherto unknown to naval services.   The perfection of a warship would doubtless be a combination of the greatest known ocean speed with the greatest known floating battery and power of resistance . . . agents of the department have thus far purchased but two [steam vessels], which combine the requisite qualities.   These, the *Sumter* and *McRae,* are being fitted as cruisers . . . Vessels of this character and capacity cannot be found in this country, and must be constructed or purchased abroad."   Mallory discussed naval ordnance: "Rifled cannon . . . having attained a range and accuracy beyond any other form of ordnance . . . I propose to introduce them into the Navy . . . Small propeller ships, with great speed, lightly armed with these guns, must soon become as the light artillery and rifles of the deep, a most destructive element of naval warfare."

27 President Lincoln extended the blockade to ports of Virginia and North Carolina.

Secretary of the Navy Welles issued order for Union ships to seize Confederate privateers upon the high seas.

Steamer *Helmick,* loaded with powder and munitions of war for the Confederacy, was seized at Cairo, Illinois.

29 U.S.S. *United States* ordered commisioned as the first ship in the Virginia navy by Major General Robert E. Lee, Commander in Chief, Military Forces of Virginia.

30 Flag Officer Pendergrast issued notice of the blockade of Virginia and North Carolina.

MAY

1 U.S.S. *Commerce,* Lieutenant Crosby, seized steam tug *Lioness* off mouth of Patapsco River, Maryland.

2 General Winfield Scott wrote to President Lincoln suggesting a cordon capable of enveloping the seceded states and noted that "the transportation of men and all supplies by water is about a fifth of the land cost, besides the immense saving of time." On the next day Scott elaborated further to General George McClellan: "We rely greatly on the sure operation of a complete blockade of the Atlantic and Gulf ports soon to commence. In connection with such blockade, we propose a powerful movement down the Mississippi to the ocean, with a cordon of posts at proper points . . . the object being to clear out and keep open this great line of communication in connection with the strict blockade of the seaboard, so as to envelop the insurgent States and bring them to terms with less bloodshed than by any other plan." The heart of the celebrated Anaconda Plan which would strangle the Confederacy on all sides was control of the sea and inland waterways by the Union Navy; the strategy of victory was (a) strengthen the blockade, (b) split the Confederacy along the line of the Mississippi River, and (c) support land operations by amphibious assault, gunfire, and transport.

3 President Lincoln called for "the enlistment, for not less than one nor more than three years, of 18,000 seamen, in addition to the present force, for the naval service of the United States."

President Lincoln's blockade proclamation published in London newspapers.

Captain Du Pont wrote: "I am anxious for the *blockade* to get established—that will squeeze the South more than anything."

Commander Dahlgren, Commandant Washington Navy Yard, noted: "Besides the Yard, I have to hold the bridge next above, so some howitzers and a guard are there. It is from this direction that the rebels of the eastern shore may come. This Yard is of great importance, not only because of its furnishing the Navy so largely with various stores, but also as a position in the general defences of the city."

4 U.S.S. *Cumberland,* Flag Officer Pendergrast, seized schooner *Mary and Virginia* with cargo of coal, and reported the capture of schooner *Theresa C.,* running the blockade off Fort Monroe, Virginia, with cotton on board.

Steamship *Star of the West* commissioned as Receiving Ship of Confederate Navy at New Orleans.

5 U.S.S. *Valley City,* Acting Master John A. J. Brooks, captured schooner *J. O'Neil* near Pamlico River, North Carolina, after schooner was run aground by her crew.

6 Confederate Congress passed act recognizing state of war with the United States and authorized the issuing of Letters of Marque to private vessels. President Davis issued instructions to private armed vessels, in which he defined operational limits, directed "strictest regard to the rights of neutral powers," ordered privateers to proceed "With all . . . justice and humanity" toward Union vessels and crews, outlined procedure for bringing in a prize, directed that all property on board neutral ships be exempt from seizure "unless it be contraband," and defined contraband.

7   Union blockading force captured Confederate steamers *Dick Keyes* and *Lewis* near Mobile.

U.S.S. *Yankee,* Lieutenant Thomas O. Selfridge, fired on by Confederate batteries at Gloucester Point, Virginia.

8   Secretary of the Navy Welles informed Gustavus Fox: "You are appointed Chief Clerk of the Navy Department, and I shall be glad to have you enter upon the duties as soon as you conveniently can."

9   U.S.S. *Constitution,* Lieutenant G. W. Rodgers, and U.S. steamer *Baltic*, Lieutenant C. R. P. Rodgers, arrived at Newport, Rhode Island, with officers and midshipmen from the U.S. Naval Academy. The Naval Academy remained there for the duration of the war.

Confederate Secretary of the Navy Mallory, ordered Commander James D. Bulloch, CSN, to England to purchase ships, guns, and ammunition. In his instructions he said: ". . . provide as one of the conditions of payment for the delivery of the vessels under the British flag at one of our Southern ports, and, secondly, that the bonds of the Confederacy be taken in whole or in part payment. The class of vessel desired for immediate use is that which offers the greatest chances of success against the enemy's commerce . . . as side-wheel steamers can not be made general cruisers, and as from the enemy's force before our forts, our ships must be enabled to keep the sea, and to make extended cruises, propellers fast under both steam and canvas suggest themselves to us with special favor. Large ships are unnecessary for this service; our policy demands that they shall be no larger than may be sufficient to combine the requisite speed and power, a battery of one or two heavy pivot guns and two or more broadside guns, being sufficient against commerce. By getting small ships we can afford a greater number, an important consideration. The character of the coasts and harbors indicate attention to the draft of water of our vessels. Speed in a propeller and the protection of her machinery can not be obtained upon a very light draft, but they should draw as little water as may be compatible with their efficiency otherwise."

10   Blockade of Charleston initiated by U.S.S. *Niagara,* Captain William W. McKean.

Confederate Secretary of the Navy Mallory farsightedly wrote the Committee on Naval Affairs of Congress regarding proposals for new warships: "I regard the possession of an iron-armored ship as a matter of the first necessity. Such a vessel at this time could traverse the entire coast of the United States, prevent all blockades, and encounter, with a fair prospect of success, their entire Navy. If to cope with them upon the sea we follow their example and build wooden ships, we shall have to construct several at one time; for one or two ships would fall an easy prey to their comparatively numerous steam frigates. But inequality of numbers may be compensated by invulnerability; and thus not only does economy but naval success dictate the wisdom and expediency of fighting with iron against wood, without regard to first cost. Naval engagements between wooden frigates, as they are now built and armed, will prove to be the forlorn hopes of the sea, simply contests in which the question, not of victory, but of who shall go to the bottom first, is to be solved."

Secret Act of Confederate Congress, signed by President Davis, authorized "the Navy Department to send an agent abroad to purchase six steam propellers, in addition to those heretofore authorized, together with rifled cannon, small arms, and other ordnance stores and munitions of war," and appropriated a million dollars for the purpose.

11   U.S.S. *Pawnee,* Commander Rowan, ordered by Commander Dahlgren to proceed from Washington Navy Yard to Alexandria, Virginia, to protect vessels in the vicinity from attack by Confederate forces.

12   U.S.S. *Niagara,* Captain McKean, captured blockade runner *General Parkhill,* en route Liverpool to Charleston.

13   Queen Victoria proclaimed British neutrality and forbade British subjects to endeavor to break a blockade "lawfully and effectually established."

14   U.S.S. *Minnesota,* Flag Officer Silas H. Stringham, captured schooners *Mary Willis, Delaware Farmer,* and *Emily Ann* at Hampton Roads laden with tobacco for Baltimore. *Argo,* bound for Bremen from Richmond, captured on same date.

15 Secretary of the Navy Welles appointed Lieutenant Thomas M. Brasher to command U.S.S. *Bainbridge* and ordered him to proceed to Aspinwall, New Granada (Panama), to protect California steamers against "vessels sailing under pretended letters of marque issued by the insurrectionary States." California steamers transported large quantities of gold from Aspinwall to New York. Confederate ships were constantly on the alert for these vessels as the blockade tightened and the need for specie became increasingly desperate.

16 Commander John Rodgers ordered to report to the War Department to establish naval forces on the western rivers under the command of General John C. Fremont. The importance of controlling the Mississippi and its tributaries which pierced the interior in every direction was recognized immediately by the U.S. Government. This control was not only militarily strategic but was a vital factor in keeping the northwestern states in the Union. Under Rodgers, three river steamers were purchased at Cincinnati. Rodgers, overcoming no little difficulty in obtaining and training crews, getting guns and other equipment, converted the steamers to gunboats *Tyler, Lexington,* and *Conestoga.* These three gunboats, as stated by Alfred Thayer Mahan, were of inestimable service "in keeping alive the attachment to the Union where it existed."

17 U.S.S. *Minnesota,* Flag Officer Stringham, captured bark *Star* en route Richmond to Bremen.

18 Confederate schooner *Savannah,* Captain Thomas H. Baker, was commissioned by President Davis as "a private armed vessel in the service of the Confederate States on the high seas against the United States of America, their ships, vessels, goods, and effects, and those of their citizens during the pendency of the war now existing between the said Confederate States and the said United States."

Commander Dahlgren suggested a plan for the erection of batteries on commanding points along the Potomac, and "the placing of vessels of some force at two or three intervals from the kettle bottoms to the Yard [Washington] near suspected positions, with communications kept up by some fast and light steamers."

19 U.S.S. *Monticello,* Captain Henry Eagle, and U.S.S. *Thomas Freeborn,* Commander Ward, engaged Confederate battery at Sewell's Point, Virginia.

C.S.S. *Lady Davis,* Lieutenant Thomas P. Pelot, captured American ship *A. B. Thompson* off Charleston.

20 U.S.S. *Crusader,* Lieutenant T. A. Craven, captured *Neptune* near Fort Taylor, Florida.

21 U.S.S. *Constellation,* the oldest United States' warship afloat, Captain John S. Nicholas, captured slave brig *Triton* at mouth of the Congo River, Africa.

U.S.S. *Pocahontas,* Commander John P. Gillis, seized steamboat *James Guy* off Machodoc Creek, Virginia.

The Confederate government guaranteed right of patent for any invention beneficial to the war effort, reserving for the government the right to use it, and provided that, in addition to bounties otherwise provided, the government "will pay to any private armed vessel commissioned under said act 20 per centum on the value of each and every vessel of war belonging to the enemy that may be sunk or destroyed."

John A. Stevenson of New Orleans discussed with Secretary of the Navy Mallory a "plan by which the enemy's blockading navy might be driven from our coasts," and wrote President Davis, "We have no time, place, or means, to build an effective navy. Our ports are, or soon will be, all blockaded. On land we do not fear Lincoln, but what shall we do to cripple him at sea? In this emergency, and seeing that he is arming many poorly adapted vessels, I have two months past been entirely engaged in perfecting plans by which I could so alter and adapt some of our heavy and powerful tow-boats on the Mississippi as to make them comparatively safe against the heaviest guns afloat, and by preparing their bow in a peculiar manner, as my plans and model will show, render them capable of sinking by collision the heaviest vessels ever built . . ."

23 U.S.S. *Mississippi,* Flag Officer William Mervine, was compelled to put back into Boston for repairs because of sabotage damage to her condensers.

24 Commander Rowan, commanding U.S.S. *Pawnee,* demanded surrender of Alexandria, Virginia; amphibious expedition departed Washington Navy Yard, after embarking secretly at night under Commander Dahlgren's supervision, and occupied Alexandria.   Admiral D. D. Porter later noted of this event: "The first landing of Northern troops upon the Virginia shores was under cover of these improvised gunboats [U.S.S. *Thomas Freeborn, Anacostia,* and *Resolute*] . . . at Alexandria . . . Alexandria was evacuated by the Confederates upon demand of a naval officer—Commander S. C. Rowan . . . and . . . the American flag was hoisted on the Custom House and other prominent places by the officer in charge of a landing party of sailors—Lieutenant R. B. Lowry. This . . . gave indication of the feelings of the Navy, and how ready was the service to put down secession on the first opportunity offered."

Confederate States Marshal at New Orleans seized all ships from Northern states which had arrived after 6 May 1861.

25 Commander Dahlgren, Commandant Washington Navy Yard, reported capture of streamer *Thomas Colyer* by U.S.S. *Pawnee,* Commander Rowan, at Alexandria.

U.S.S. *Minnesota,* Flag Officer Stringham, seized bark *Winfred* near Hampton Roads.

26 U.S.S. *Brooklyn,* Commander Charles H. Poor, set blockade of New Orleans and mouth of Mississippi River.

U.S.S. *Powhatan,* Lieutenant D. D. Porter, set blockade at Mobile.

28 U.S.S. *Union,* Commander John R. Goldsborough, initiated blockade of Savannah.

29 Confederate privateer *J. C. Calhoun* captured American brig *Panama,* which she took to New Orleans with two earlier prizes, American schooners *Mermaid* and *John Adams.*

U.S.S. *Powhatan,* Lieutenant D. D. Porter, captured schooner *Mary Clinton* attempting to run the blockade near Southwest Pass, Mississippi River.

29–1 June Potomac Flotilla, consisting of U.S.S. *Thomas Freeborn,* Commander Ward, U.S.S. *Anacostia,* Lieutenant Napoleon Collins, and U.S.S. *Resolute,* Acting Master William Budd, engaged Confederate batteries at Aquia Creek, Virginia. Flotilla joined by U.S.S. *Pawnee,* Commander Rowan, evening of 31 May.

30 U.S.S. *Merrimack,* scuttled and burned at Norfolk Navy Yard, raised by Confederates.

U.S.S. *Quaker City,* Acting Master S. W. Mather, seized schooner *Lynchburg,* en route Richmond with cargo of coffee.

31 U.S.S. *Perry,* Lieutenant Enoch G. Parrott, captured Confederate blockade runner *Hannah M. Johnson.*

JUNE

1 U.S.S. *Union,* Commander J. R. Goldsborough, captured Confederate schooner *F. W. Johnson* with cargo of railroad iron off the coast of North Carolina.

Captain Du Pont wrote: "I do not like the tone of things in England . . . Lord Derby and Granville, etc., talk of two thousand miles of coast to be blockaded! They seem to forget so far as their rights and international interests are concerned we have only to blockade the *ports of entry*—from the Chesapeake to Galveston—any . . . venture into any other harbors or inlets of any kind is liable to capture as a smuggler. It is the intention of the Government, I presume, to connect the shore between blockaded ports by light draft cruisers to prevent the ingress of arms and contraband, and the egress of privateers—but that is our business as a war measure—an effective blockade means the covering of the ports of entry—and this will be easily done in my judgment . . ."

3 Confederate privateer *Savannah,* Captain Baker, captured American brig *Joseph* with cargo of sugar; *Savannah* was then captured by U.S.S. *Perry,* Lieutenant Parrott.

5 Revenue Cutter *Harriet Lane,* Captain Faunce, USRM, engaged Confederate battery at Pig Point, Hampton Roads.

The Potomac Flotilla attacks Confederate batteries at Aquia Creek. Early action by the Flotilla played an important role in saving Washington.

U.S.S. *Niagara,* Captain McKean, captured schooner *Aid* at Mobile.

Flag Officer Pendergrast reported the capture of bark *General Green* by U.S.S. *Quaker City,* Commander Overton Carr, at the Capes of the Chesapeake.

8 U.S.S. *Mississippi,* Flag Officer Mervine, set blockade at Key West.

U.S.S. *Resolute,* Acting Master W. Budd, having captured schooner *Somerset* at Breton's Bay, towed her close to the Virginia shore and burned her.

9 U.S.S. *Massachusetts,* Commander Melancton Smith, captured British blockade runner *Perthshire* with cargo of cotton near Pensacola.

10 U.S.S. *Union,* Commander J. R. Goldsborough, captured brig *Hallie Jackson* off Savannah with cargo of molasses.

Lieutenant John Mercer Brooke, CSN, ordered to design ironclad C.S.S. *Virginia* (ex-U.S.S. *Merrimack*).

13 U.S.S. *Mississippi,* Flag Officer Mervine, captured schooner *Forest King* at Key West.

14 American schooner *Christiana Keen,* grounded and was burned by Confederates near Upper Machodoc Creek, Virginia.

15 Major General Robert E. Lee wrote Virginia Governor John Fletcher regarding preparations for the defense of the state: "The frigate *United States* has been prepared for a school ship, provided with a deck battery of nineteen guns, 32-pounders and 9-inch Columbiads, for harbor defense. The frigate *Merrimack* has been raised and is in for the dry dock, and arrangements are made for raising the *Germantown* and *Plymouth*." Lee, showing his understanding of the serious threat posed by Union naval operations on the rivers, reported that: "Six batteries have been erected on the Elizabeth River, to guard

the approaches to Norfolk and the Navy Yard . . . to prevent ascent of the Nansemond River and the occupation of the railroad from Norfolk to Richmond, three batteries have been constructed . . . Sites for batteries on the Potomac have also been selected, and arrangements were in progress for their construction, but the entire command of that river being in the possession of the U.S. Goverment, a larger force is required for their security than could be devoted to that purpose. The batteries at Aquia Creek have only been prepared . . . On the Rappahannock River a 4-gun battery . . . has been erected."

17   U.S.S. *Massachusetts,* Commander M. Smith, captured schooner *Achilles* near Ship Island, Mississippi.

18   U.S.S. *Union,* Commander J. R. Goldsborough, captured Confederate blockade runner *Amelia* at Charleston with cargo of contraband from Liverpool.

Major General Robert E. Lee wrote Lieutenant Robert Randolph Carter, CSN, commander of C.S.S. *Teaser*: "It is desired that the C.S. steam tender *Teaser* shall unite with the batteries at Jamestown Island in defense of James River, and be employed in obtaining intelligence of the movements of hostile vessels and the landing of troops either side of the river . . . It is suggested that you establish a system of signals as a means of communication with the troops, and take every precaution not to jeopardize the safety of your boat by proceeding too far beyond the protection of the guns of the batteries . . ."

19   U.S.S. *Massachusetts,* Commander M. Smith, captured blockade running brig *Nahum Stetson* off Pass à l'Outre, Louisiana.

23   Confederate Navy began reconstruction of ex-U.S.S. *Merrimack* as ironclad C.S.S. *Virginia* at Norfolk.

U.S.S. *Massachusetts,* Commander M. Smith, captured Mexican schooner *Brilliant,* with cargo of flour, and Confederate schooners *Trois Freres, Olive Branch, Fanny,* and *Basile* in the Gulf of Mexico.

24   U.S.S. *Pawnee,* Commander Rowan, and U.S.S. *Thomas Freeborn,* Commander Ward, shelled Confederate batteries at Mathias Point, Virginia.

25   Secretary of the Navy Welles received a report that "the rebels in New Orleans are constructing an infernal submarine vessel to destroy the *Brooklyn,* or any vessel blockading the mouth of the Mississippi . . . a projectile with a sharp iron or steel pointed prow to perforate the bottom of the vessel and then explode." It was also reported that "a formidable floating battery [is] being built at Mobile, to be mounted with large guns of immense size and range to drive away or capture the ships, by engaging them at long range."

26   U.S.S. *Minnesota,* Flag Officer Stringham, captured bark *Sally Magee* off Hampton Roads.

27   Blockade Strategy Board met under the chairmanship of Captain Du Pont and included as members Commander Charles H. Davis, USN, Major John G. Barnard, USA Corps of Engineers, and Professor Alexander D. Bache, Superintendent U.S. Coast Survey, to consider and report on the major problems of the blockade and to plan amphibious operations to seize vital bases on the Southern coast. Recommendations made by the Blockade Strategy Board, an early example of a "Joint Staff," had a profound effect on the course of the conflict and pointed the way to the successful naval actions at Hatteras Inlet, Port Royal, and New Orleans. The broad policies the Board early set forth were essentially followed to their culmination at Appomattox.

U.S.S. *Resolute,* Acting Master W. Budd, burned a Confederate supply depot on Virginia shore of the Potomac River.

U.S.S. *Thomas Freeborn,* Commander Ward, U.S.S. *Reliance,* Acting Lieutenant Jared P. K. Mygatt, with two boats under Lieutenant James C. Chaplin, from U.S.S. *Pawnee,* Commander Rowan, attacked Confederate forces at Mathias Point, Virginia. Commander Ward was killed in the action. Naval actions at Mathias Point, Aquia Creek, and elsewhere caused Admiral D. D. Porter to observe of these early operations on the Potomac and Chesapeake: ". . . the country was too busy watching the black clouds gathering in the South and West to note the ordinary events that were taking place on the Potomac, yet they formed the small links in the chain, which in the end, shackled the arms of the great rebellion."

28 Confederate privateer *Jefferson Davis,* formerly slaver *Echo,* Captain Louis M. Coxetter, sailed from Charleston, later made numerous captures of Union ships along the coast, and caused much consternation on the Eastern seaboard.

Captain Du Pont, Chairman of the Blockade Strategy Board, wrote: "The order we received . . . set forth . . . the selection of two ports, one in South Carolina, another in the confines of Georgia and Florida, for coal depots . . . it seems impossible to supply the blockading fleet with coal without these depots."

28–29 Side-wheel steamer *St. Nicholas,* making scheduled run between Baltimore and Georgetown, D.C., was captured by Confederates who had boarded her posing as passengers at the steamer's various stopping points on the Potomac River. Confederates were led by Captain George N. Hollins, CSN, who took command of *St. Nicholas,* and Colonel Richard Thomas, CSA, who boarded disguised as a woman. *St. Nicholas* then began search for U.S.S. *Pawnee,* but, not finding her, put out into the Chesapeake Bay, where she seized schooners *Margaret* and *Mary Pierce* and brig *Monticello* the following day, 29 June.

30 C.S.S. *Sumter,* Commander Semmes, ran the blockade at the mouth of Mississippi River and escaped to sea through Pass à l' Outre, eluding U.S.S. *Brooklyn,* whereupon the crew "gave three hearty cheers for the flag of the Confederate States, thus . . . thrown to the breeze on the high seas by a ship of war," launching Semmes' famous career as a commerce raider.

U.S.S. *Reliance,* Lieutenant Mygatt, seized and destroyed sloop *Passenger* in the Potomac River.

JULY

1 U.S.S. *Minnesota,* Flag Officer Stringham, captured schooner *Sally Mears* at Hampton Roads.

Confederate privateer *Petrel* evaded blockaders and put to sea from Charleston.

2 U.S.S. *South Carolina,* Commander James Alden, initiated blockade of Galveston.

3 C.S.S. *Sumter,* Commander Semmes, captured and burned American ship *Golden Rocket* near Isle of Pines, off the coast of Cuba.

4 U.S.S. *South Carolina,* Commander Alden, captured blockade running schooners *Shark, Venus, Ann Ryan, McCanfield, Louisa,* and *Dart* off Galveston.

5 U.S.S. *South Carolina,* Commander Alden, captured blockade running schooners *Falcon* and *Coralia* off Galveston.

U.S.S. *Dana,* Acting Master's Mate Robert B. Ely, captured sloop *Teaser* in Nanjemoy Creek, Maryland.

6 U.S.S. *South Carolina,* Commander Alden, captured blockade running schooner *George G. Baker* off Galveston.

Confederate privateer *Jefferson Davis* captured American brig *John Welsh* and schooner *Enchantress* east of Cape Hatteras.

C.S.S. *Sumter,* Commander Semmes, arrived at Cienfuegos, Cuba, with seven U.S. vessels taken as prizes—*Cuba, Machias, Ben Dunning, Albert Adams, Naiad, West Wind, Lewis Kilham.* Semmes appointed a Cuban agent for custody of the prizes, expressing to the Governor there that he had entered that port "with the expectation that Spain will extend to cruisers of the Confederate States the same friendly reception that in similar circumstances she would extend to the cruisers of the enemy . . ."

7 U.S.S. *South Carolina,* Commander Alden, captured schooner *Sam Houston* off Galveston.

Confederate privateer *Jefferson Davis* captured American schooner *S. J. Waring* about 150 miles off Sandy Hook, New Jersey.

U.S.S. *Pocahontas,* Comander Benjamin M. Dove, fired on and damaged C.S.S. *George Page* in Aquia Creek, Virginia.

Two floating torpedoes (mines) in the Potomac River were picked up by U.S.S. *Resolute,* Acting Master W. Budd—the earliest known use of torpedoes by the Confederates. During the course of the war a variety of ingenious torpedoes destroyed or damaged some 40 Union ships, forecasting the vast growth to come in this aspect of underwater naval warfare.

9 U.S.S. *South Carolina,* Commander Alden, seized and destroyed schooner *Tom Hicks* with cargo of lumber off Galveston.

Confederate privateer *Jefferson Davis* captured American brig *Mary E. Thompson* of Bangor en route Antigua, and schooner *Mary Goodell* of New York en route Buenos Aires.

10 U.S.S. *Minnesota,* Flag Officer Stringham, captured Confederate brig *Amy Warwick* in Hampton Roads.

12 U.S.S. *South Carolina,* Commander Alden, captured Confederate schooner *General T. J. Chambers* off Galveston with cargo of lumber.

13 U.S.S. *Massachusetts,* Commander M. Smith, seized schooner *Hiland* near Ship Island, Mississippi.

14 U.S.S. *Daylight,* Commander Samuel Lockwood, initiated blockade of Wilmington, North Carolina.

15 Captain Du Pont wrote: "The Department are [sic] worried about the privateers increasing so. Lieutenant Semmes has sent . . . [vessels] into Cuba, but the Captain General ordered them to be immediately restored to their commanders." Du Pont also noted that the privateer *Jefferson Davis,* "which has ventured so far north," was also causing concern. Confederate privateers struck out boldly against Northern commerce and generated distress among shipping interests. However, as the naval blockade tightened and ports and coastal havens were seized by amphibious assault and other naval actions, operations of Confederate raiders became increasingly difficult and restricted.

16 Blockade Strategy Board reported to Secretary of the Navy Welles on the necessity of halting Confederate commerce: ". . . it is an important object in the present war that this trade, home and foreign, should be interrupted . . . The most obvious method of accomplishing this object is by putting down material obstructions; and the most convenient form of obstruction, for transportation and use, is that of old vessels laden with ballast . . . sunk in the appropriate places." This was the first suggestion for the "stone fleet". Elimination of water-borne trade by the Union Navy blockade (more effective than the "stone fleet" obstructions at harbor entrances), meant the economic ruination of the Confederacy.

U.S.S. *St. Lawrence,* Captain Hugh Y. Purviance, captured British blockade runner *Herald,* bound from Beaufort, North Carolina, to Liverpool.

William Tilghman, a Negro, overwhelmed Confederate prize crew on board schooner *S. J. Waring* and took possession of the vessel, carrying her into New York on 22 July.

18 Confederate schooner *Favorite* was captured by U.S.S. *Yankee,* Commander T. T. Craven, on Yeocomico River; *Favorite* was sunk later at Piney Point on the Potomac River.

Commander Ridgely, U.S. Receiving Ship *Allegheny,* reported his ship had received a battery of guns from the Washington Navy Yard and was standing by in the harbor for the protection of Annapolis.

Confederate Secretary of the Navy Mallory reported: "The frigate *Merrimack* [later C.S.S. *Virginia*] has been raised and docked at an expense of $6,000, and the necessary repairs to hull and machinery to place her in her former condition is estimated by experts at $450,000. The vessel would then be in the river, and by the blockade of the enemy's fleets and batteries rendered comparatively useless. It has therefore been determined to shield her completely with 3-inch iron [4-inch armor was used], placed at such angles as to render her ball-proof, to complete her at the earliest moment, to arm her with the heaviest ordnance, and to send her at once against the enemy's fleet. It is believed that thus prepared she will be able to contend successfully against the heaviest of the enemy's ships and to drive them from Hampton Roads and the ports of Virginia. The cost of this work is estimated by the constructor and engineer in charge at $172,523, and as time is of the first consequence in this enterprise I have not hesitated to commence the work and to ask Congress for the necessary appropriation."

19   Captain-General of Cuba released all vessels brought into Cuban ports as prizes by C.S.S. *Sumter.*

20   U.S.S. *Mount Vernon,* Commander Oliver S. Glisson, seized sloop *Wild Pigeon* on the Rappahannock River.

   U.S.S. *Albatross,* Commander George A. Prentiss, recaptured *Enchantress* off Hatteras Inlet (see 6 July 1861).

21   U.S.S. *Albatross,* Commander Prentiss, engaged C.S.S. *Beaufort,* Lieutenant R. C. Duvall, in Oregon Inlet, North Carolina. *Albatross,* heavier gunned, forced *Beaufort* to withdraw.

   Confederate privateer *Jefferson Davis* captured American bark *Alvarado* in Atlantic (25°04′ N, 50°00′ W).

   U.S. Marines commanded by Major Reynolds took part in the First Battle of Bull Run: 9 Marines killed, 19 wounded, 16 missing in action. Commander Dahlgren wrote of the loss of two naval howitzers in the battle. The Confederates also had a naval battery at Manassas.

24   Congress approved bill authorizing the appointment of an Assistant Secretary of the Navy.

   Act "to provide for the temporary increase of the Navy" passed by Congress; gave President authority to take vessels into the Navy and appoint officers for them, to any extent deemed necessary; this confirmed action that had been taken by President Lincoln since April.

25   John LaMountain began balloon reconnaissance ascensions at Fort Monroe, Virginia.

   C.S.S. *Sumter,* Commander Semmes, captured schooner *Abby Bradford* in the Caribbean Sea and, denied the right to enter Venezuela with Confederate prizes, dispatched her to a Southern port.

   Confederate privateer *Mariner,* Captain W. B. Berry, captured American schooner *Nathaniel Chase* off Ocracoke Inlet, North Carolina.

   Confederate privateer *Gordon* captured American brig *William McGilvery* off Cape Hatteras with cargo of molasses.

   Confederate privateer *Dixie* captured American schooner *Mary Alice* off the east coast of Florida.

   U.S.S. *Resolute,* Acting Master W. Budd, brought two schooners and one sloop as prizes into Washington, D.C.

27   C.S.S. *Sumter,* Commander Semmes, captured American bark *Joseph Maxwell* off Venezuela.

28   U.S.S. *Union,* Commander J. R. Goldsborough, destroyed former American brig *B. T. Martin* north of Cape Hatteras, where she had been run aground by Confederates. *B. T. Martin* had been captured previously by Confederate privateer *York.*

   Confederate privateer *Gordon* captured American schooner *Protector* off Cape Hatteras.

   U.S.S. *St. Lawrence,* Captain Purviance, sank Confederate privateer *Petrel* off Charleston.

29   U.S.S. *Yankee,* Commander T. T. Craven, and U.S.S. *Reliance,* Lieutenant Mygatt, engaged Confederate battery at Marlborough Point, Virginia.

   Four U.S. steamers engaged Confederate battery at Aquia Creek, Virginia, for three hours.

31   Confederate privateer *Dixie* captured American bark *Glenn* and took her to Beaufort, North Carolina.

AUGUST

1   President Lincoln appointed Gustavus V. Fox Assistant Secretary of the Navy. Fox, the energetic ex-naval officer who had led the unsuccessful Fort Sumter expedition in April, became Secretary Welles' right hand man in the Department. His large acquaintance among naval officers and forthright, "unofficial" style made him a useful troubleshooter. By the informal correspondence which he elicited from the chief naval commanders, the Navy Department was able to keep in intimate touch with problems in the several squadrons.

St. Lawrence *destroys privateer* Petrel. *Though small in numbers at the outset of the war, Union ships vigorously demonstrated the reality of the blockade proclaimed by President Lincoln.*

3   John LaMountain made first ascent in a balloon from Union ship *Fanny* at Hampton Roads to observe Confederate batteries on Sewell's Point, Virginia—a small beginning for the potent aircraft carrier in the tridimensional Navy of the Twentieth Century.

Congress authorized Secretary of the Navy Welles to "appoint a board of three skillful naval officers to investigate the plans and specifications that may be submitted for the construction or completing of iron or steel-clad steamships or steam batteries . . . there is hereby appropriated . . . the sum of one million five hundred thousand dollars." Commodore Joseph Smith, Captain Hiram Paulding, Commander Charles H. Davis appointed to the Ironclad Board on 8 August.

U.S.S. *Wabash,* Captain Mercer, recaptured American schooner *Mary Alice,* which had been taken by Confederate ship *Dixie,* and captured brig *Sarah Starr,* a blockade runner, off Charleston.

U.S.S. *South Carolina,* Commander Alden, engaged Confederate batteries at Galveston.

4   Cutter from U.S.S. *Thomas Freeborn,* Lieutenant Eastman, captured schooner *Pocahontas,* loaded with wood, and sloop *Mary Grey* in Pohick Creek, Virginia.

5   U.S.S. *Jamestown,* Commander Charles Green, burned Confederate prize bark *Alvarado* near Fernandina, Florida.

Confederate privateer *Jefferson Davis* captured large American brig *Santa Clara* off Puerto Rico.

7   War Department contracted with J. B. Eads of St. Louis for construction of seven shallow-draft iron-clad river gunboats. The Eads gunboats—*Cairo, Carondelet, Cincinnati, Louisville, Mound City, Pitts-burg,* and *St. Louis*—were the core of the Union force on the western waters. Built with the aid of Naval Constructor Samuel M. Pook, USN, they were the key to Grant's great series of campaigns that, beginning in February 1862, ultimately split the South and had a decisive influence on the war.

U.S.S. *Massachusetts,* Commander M. Smith, captured blockade running sloop *Charles Henry* near Ship Island, Mississippi.

8   U.S.S. *Santee,* Captain Eagle, captured schooner *C. P. Knapp* in the Gulf of Mexico.

9   Confederate privateer *York* captured schooner *George G. Baker.* U.S.S. *Union,* Commander J. R. Golds-borough, recaptured *George G. Baker. York* was set afire off Cape Hatteras by her crew to prevent capture by *Union.*

11 Blockade runner *Louisa,* pursued by U.S.S. *Penguin,* Commander John L. Livingston, struck shoal near Cape Fear, North Carolina, and sank.

12 Gunboats U.S.S. *Tyler, Lexington,* and *Conestoga,* procured and fitted out by Commander J. Rodgers, arrived at Cairo, Illinois, to protect the strategic position at the junction of the Ohio and Mississippi Rivers, and to scout the rivers for Confederate batteries and troop movements.

13 Commander Bulloch, CSN, writing from London to Confederate Secretary of the Navy Mallory, said: "After careful examination of the shipping lists of England, and inspecting many vessels, I failed to find a single wooden steamer fit for war purposes, except one paddle steamer, too large and costly and drawing too much water for our coast. Wood as a material for ships has almost entirely gone out of use in the British merchant service, and their iron ships, though fast, well built, and staunch enough for voyages of traffic, are too thin in the plates and light in the deck frames and stanchions to carry guns of much weight. I therefore made arrangements to contract with two eminent builders for a gun vessel each . . ."

U.S.S. *Powhatan,* Lieutenant D. D. Porter, recaptured schooner *Abby Bradford* off the mouth of the Mississippi River.

15 U.S.S. *Tyler* and *Conestoga,* Lieutenant S. L. Phelps, scouted the Mississippi for Confederate fortifications and movements as far south as New Madrid, Missouri, while U.S.S. *Lexington,* Lieutenant Roger N. Stembel, operating with the Army, made a similar reconnaissance of the river north to Cape Girardeau, Missouri.

U.S.S. *Resolute,* Acting Master W. Budd, while on a reconnaissance mission, engaged Confederate troops at Mathias Point, Virginia.

16 President Lincoln declared the inhabitants of the Confederate States to be in a state of insurrection and forbade all commercial intercourse with them.

17 Lieutenant Reigart B. Lowry wrote Assistant Secretary of the Navy Fox regarding the progress for sinking a stone fleet to block the inlets to the North Carolina sounds: "We have nineteen schooners properly loaded with stone, and all our preparations are complete to divide them in two divisions and place them in tow of this steamer [*Adelaide*] and of the *Governor Peabody.* I think all arrangements are complete, as far as being prepared to 'sink and obstruct' . . . the obstructing party could place their vessels in position, secure them as we propose, by binding chains, spars on end in the sand to settle by action of the tide, anchors down, and finally sink them in such a way as to *block* the channel so effectually that there could be no navigation through them for several months to come, at least till by the aid of our *new* gunboats the outside blockade could be effectual."

18 Confederate privateer *Jefferson Davis,* Captain Coxetter, wrecked on the bar trying to enter St. Augustine, Florida, ending a most successful cruise. Charleston *Mercury* (26 August 1861) said: "The name of the privateer *Jefferson Davis* has become a word of terror to the Yankees. The number of her prizes and the amount of merchandise which she captured have no parallel since the days of the *Saucy Jack* [1812 privateer]."

19–21 Assistant Secretary of the Navy Fox ordered 200 Marines to report to Commander Dahlgren at the Washington Navy Yard for duty on board ships of the Potomac Flotilla for the purpose of scouring the Maryland countryside—especially Port Tobacco—for locations suspected of being Confederate depots for provisions and arms to be used for invading Maryland.

21 U.S.S. *Vandalia,* Commander Samuel Phillips Lee, captured Confederate blockade runner *Henry Middleton* off Charleston with a cargo of spirits, turpentine, and rosin.

22 Commander J. Rodgers reported that six hundred Confederate troops occupying Commerce, Missouri, withdrew at the approach of the Union gunboats. This action prevented the erection of Confederate batteries at a location which would have effectively impeded navigation.

 U.S.S. *Lexington,* Commander Stembel, seized steamer *W. B. Terry* at Paducah, Kentucky, for trading with Confederates.

 Steamer *Samuel Orr* was seized by Confederates at Paducah, Kentucky, and taken up the Tennessee River.

23 U.S.S. *Release* and *Yankee* engaged Confederate batteries at the mouth of Potomac Creek, Virginia.

24 President Davis appointed James M. Mason, Special Commissioner to the United Kingdom, and John Slidell, Special Commissioner to France.

26 Squadron under Flag Officer Stringham, U.S.S. *Minnesota, Wabash, Monticello, Pawnee,* Revenue Cutter *Harriet Lane,* U.S. tug *Fanny* and two transports carrying about 900 troops under Major General Butler, departed Hampton Roads (later joined by U.S.S. *Susquehanna* and *Cumberland*) for Hatteras Inlet, N.C., for first combined amphibious operation of the war. Hatteras Inlet was the main channel into Pamlico Sound and the most convenient entrance for blockade runners bringing supplies to the Confederate Army in Virginia. The Navy early recognized the strategic importance of the inlet and invited the Army to cooperate in its capture. The operation was designed to check Confederate privateering and to begin the relentless assault from the sea that would divert a large portion of Confederate manpower from the main armies.

 Captain A. H. Foote ordered to relieve Commander J. Rodgers in command of the Army's gunboat flotilla on the western rivers.

 U.S. tug *Fanny,* Lieutenant Crosby, reported the capture of blockade running sloop *Mary Emma* at the headwaters of Manokin River, Maryland.

 U.S.S. *Daylight,* Commander Lockwood, re-captured brig *Monticello* in Rappahannock River.

27 Flag Officer Stringham's Squadron anchored off Hatteras Inlet and prepared to land the troops and take Forts Hatteras and Clark under attack.

28 Flag Officer Stringham's Squadron commenced bombardment of Forts Hatteras and Clark; Marines and troops were landed from surf boats above the Forts under cover of naval gunfire. The ship's heavy cannonade forced the Confederates to evacuate Fort Clark. Commodore Samuel Barron, CSN, with two small vessels joined the defenders that evening.

 Commander Dahlgren, Commandant of Washington Navy Yard, sent 400 seamen on steamboat *Philadelphia* to Alexandria, to report to Brigadier General William B. Franklin for the defense of Fort Ellsworth. This timely naval reinforcement strengthened the Fort's defenses and consequently that of the Nation's Capital.

 U.S.S. *Yankee,* Commander T. T. Craven, captured schooner *Remittance* near Piney Point, Virginia.

29 Hatteras Inlet was secured as Forts Hatteras and Clark surrendered unconditionally to Flag Officer Stringham and General Butler. The Union triumph sealed off commerce raiding and blockade running from Pamlico Sound. Hatteras Inlet became a coal and supply depot for the blockading ships. Of this most successful joint operation Admiral D. D. Porter later wrote: "This was our first naval victory, indeed our first victory of any kind, and should not be forgotten. The Union cause was then

Flag Officer Stringham's Fleet bombards Forts Hatteras and Clark. This joint action in cooperation with Army troops under General Butler produced the first real Union victory of the war.

in a depressed condition, owing to the reverses it had experienced. The moral effect of this affair was very great, as it gave us a foothold on Southern soil and possession of the Sounds of North Carolina if we chose to occupy them. It was a death-blow to blockade running in that vicinity, and ultimately proved one of the most important events of the war."

U.S.S. *R. R. Cuyler,* Captain Francis B. Ellison, seized and burned Confederate ship *Finland,* which was prepared to receive cargo of cotton and run the blockade, off Apalachicola, Florida.

30 Confederate tug *Harmony* attacked U.S.S. *Savannah,* Captain Joseph B. Hull, at Newport News, inflicting damage before withdrawing.

31 C.S.S. *Teaser* shelled Newport News.

U.S.S. *George Peabody,* Lieutenant Lowry, captured brig *Henry C. Brooks* in Hatteras Inlet.

U.S.S. *Jamestown,* Commander Green, captured British blockade running schooner *Aigburth* off Florida coast.

SEPTEMBER

1 President Lincoln received news late at night from Secretary of the Navy Welles of Flag Officer Stringham's victory at Hatteras Inlet, in the initial Army-Navy expedition of the war. Coming shortly after the defeat at Bull Run, it electrified the North and greatly raised morale.

U.S.S. *Dana,* Acting Master's Mate Ely, captured blockade running schooner *T. J. Evans* off Clay Island, Maryland, with a cargo including blankets, surgical instruments, and ordnance supplies.

4 Captain Du Pont wrote: "The first fruits of the labors of . . . [the Blockade Strategy Board] came out on the North Carolina coast [Hatteras Inlet] . . . we will secure the whole of those inland sounds and passages and hold all that coast by a flotilla . . . the great morale effect and encouragement to the country are of incalculable service just now."

Off Hatteras Inlet
United States Flag ship
Minnesota
August 30. 1861

No 133

Honl
Gideon Welles
Secretary of Navy

Sir

I have the honor to
inform you that we have been
eminently Successful in our
Expidition. All that could be
wished by the most hopeful has
been accomplished

This Morning, we are
taking on Board the Minnesota
Officers and Men Six hundred and
fifteen Captured with the Forts
at Hatteras Inlet which Surren
dered Yesterday after Bombardment
from the Fleet of parts of two days

I shall forward a full account
immediately on my arrival at New
York whither I have concluded to land
them as requested in Your Commu
nication in reference to Prisoners Com
ing into possession of the Navy. after land
ing them I shall return to Hampton Roads

Respectfully yr Mo St
S. H. Stringham
Flg Offir
Atlantic Blockadig Squadron

Flag Officer Stringham notifies Secretary Welles of the Union victory at Hatteras Inlet.

C.S.S. *Yankee* (also known as C.S.S. *Jackson*) and Confederate batteries at Hickman, Kentucky, fired on U.S.S. *Tyler,* Commander J. Rodgers, and *Lexington,* Commander Stembel, while the gunboats were reconnoitering Mississippi River south from Cairo.

U.S.S. *Jamestown,* Commander Green, captured Confederate schooner *Colonel Long,* removed her cargo, and scuttled her off the coast of Georgia.

5 Captain A. H. Foote reported at St. Louis, Missouri, to relieve Commander J. Rodgers in command of naval operations on the western rivers.

6 Gunboats U.S.S. *Tyler,* Commander J. Rodgers, and U.S.S. *Lexington,* Commander Stembel, spearheaded operations by which General Grant, in his first move after taking command at Cairo, seized strategic Paducah and Smithland, Kentucky, at the mouths of the Tennessee and Cumberland Rivers. Captain Foote, newly designated naval commander in the west, participated in the operation. This initial use of strength afloat by Grant, aimed at countering a Confederate move into the State, helped preserve Kentucky for the Union, and foreshadowed the General's great reliance on naval mobility and support throughout the campaigns which divided the Confederacy and placed the entire Mississippi under Union control.

U.S. consul in London reported purchase by Confederates of steamers *Bermuda, Adelaide,* and *Victoria.*

9 U.S.S. *Cambridge,* Commander William A. Parker, captured schooner *Louisa Agnes* off Nova Scotia.

10 U.S.S. *Conestoga,* Lieutenant S. L. Phelps, and U.S.S. *Lexington,* Commander Stembel, covering a troop advance, silenced the guns of a Confederate battery and damaged gunboat C.S.S. *Yankee* at Lucas Bend, Missouri.

U.S.S. *Pawnee,* Commander Rowan, captured schooner *Susan Jane* in Hatteras Inlet. Other blockade runners, unaware that the Union Navy now controlled the inlet, were also taken as prizes.

U.S.S. *Cambridge,* Commander W. A. Parker, captured British blockade running schooner *Revere* off Beaufort, North Carolina, with cargo of salt and herring.

11 U.S.S. *South Carolina,* Commander Alden, captured *Soledad Cos* with a cargo of coffee off Galveston.

13 U.S.S. *Susquehanna,* Captain John S. Chauncey, captured blockade running British schooner *Argonaut,* with cargo of fish, bound from Nova Scotia to Key West.

C.S.S. *Patrick Henry,* Commander John R. Tucker, exchanged fire with U.S.S. *Savannah,* Captain Hull, and U.S.S. *Louisiana,* Lieutenant Alexander Murray, off Newport News; shot on both sides fell short.

14 In the early morning darkness sailors and Marines from U.S.S. *Colorado,* rowing in to Pensacola Harbor, boarded and burned Confederate privateering schooner *Judah,* and spiked guns at Pensacola Navy Yard.

U.S.S. *Albatross,* Commander Prentiss, captured schooner *Alabama* near the mouth of the Potomac River.

16 Ironclad Board reported to Secretary of the Navy Welles: "For river and harbor service we consider iron-clad vessels of light draught, or floating batteries thus shielded, as very important . . . Armored ships or batteries may be employed advantageously to pass fortifications on land for ulterior objects of attack, to run a blockade, or to reduce temporary batteries on the shores of rivers and the approaches to our harbors." The Board recommended construction of three ironclads (*Monitor, Galena,* and *New Ironsides*). These ships, and those that followed, revolutionized naval warfare.

U.S.S. *Conestoga,* Lieutenant S. L. Phelps, captured Confederate steamers *V. R. Stephenson* and *Gazelle* on Cumberland River, Kentucky.

16-17 Landing party from U.S.S. *Pawnee,* Commander Rowan, destroyed guns and fortifications on Beacon Island, closing Ocracoke Inlet, North Carolina. Admiral D. D. Porter later wrote: "The closing of these inlets [Hatteras and Ocracoke] to the Sounds of North Carolina sent the blockade runners elsewhere to find entrance to Southern markets, but as channel after channel was closed the smugglers' chance diminished . . .''

17 Confederates evacuated Ship Island, Mississippi; landing party from U.S.S. *Massachusetts* took possession. Ship Island eventually became the staging area for General Butler's troops in the amphibious operations below New Orleans.

18 U.S.S. *Rescue,* Master Edward L. Haines, captured Confederate schooner *Harford* with cargo of wheat and tobacco on the Potomac River.

Flag Officer Du Pont was appointed Commander South Atlantic Blockading Squadron. Du Pont wrote : "My appointment as a flag officer will be dated today . . . Things have taken an active turn, and this day is an epoch in naval history—seniority and rotation have seen their last day. Selection with as much regard to seniority as the good of the service will admit, is now the order of the day."

Secretary of the Navy Welles wrote Flag Officer Louis M. Goldsborough, appointed to command North Atlantic Blockading Squadron: "It is essentially necessary that the Navy should at this time put forth all its strength and demonstrate to the country and to foreign powers its usefulness and capability in protecting and supporting the Government and the Union. There must be no commercial intercourse with the ports that are in insurrection, and our Navy must, by its power, energy, and activity, enforce the views of the President and the Government on this subject. Privateers to depredate on our commerce and rob our countrymen pursuing their peaceful avocations must not be permitted . . ."

19 U.S.S. *Gemsbok,* Acting Master Edward Cavendy, captured blockade running schooner *Harmony,* en route Nova Scotia to Ocracoke, North Carolina.

21 Boat under Midshipman Edward A. Walker from U.S.S. *Seminole,* Commander Gillis, captured sloop *Maryland* on the Potomac River.

22 U.S.S. *Gemsbok,* Acting Master Cavendy, captured schooner *Mary E. Pindar* off Federal Point, North Carolina, attempting to run the blockade with cargo of lime.

Flag Officer McKean assumed command of the Gulf Blockading Squadron.

23 U.S.S. *Lexington,* Commander Stembel, proceeded to Owensboro, Kentucky, "for the purpose of keeping the Ohio River open" and in order to protect Union interests in the area. Such expeditions deep into territory with Confederate sympathies were fundamental in containing Southern advances in the border states.

U.S.S. *Cambridge,* Commander W. A. Parker, captured British schooner *Julia* bound for Beaufort, North Carolina.

Flag Officer L. M. Goldsborough assumed command of North Atlantic Blockading Squadron including operations in the Chesapeake.

24 U.S.S. *Dart,* Acting Master William M. Wheeler, captured Confederate schooner *Cecelia* off Louisiana, thereafter fitted out as Union cruiser by U.S.S. *Huntsville,* Commander Cicero Price.

25 C.S.S. *Sumter,* Commander Semmes, captured American ship *Joseph Park* off northeast coast of South America; three days later burned her at sea.

U.S.S. *Jacob Bell,* Lieutenant Edward P. McCrea, and U.S.S. *Seminole,* Lieutenant Charles S. Norton, engaged Confederate battery at Freestone Point, Virginia.

Secretary of the Navy Welles instructed Flag Officer Du Pont, commanding South Atlantic Blockading Squadron: "The Department finds it necessary to adopt a regulation with respect to the large and increasing number of persons of color, commonly known as 'contrabands,' now subsisted at the navy yards and on board ships-of-war. These can neither be expelled from the service, to which they have resorted, nor can they be maintained unemployed, and it is not proper that they should be compelled to render necessary and regular services without compensation. You are therefore authorized, when their services can be made useful, to enlist them for the naval service, under the same forms and regulations as apply to other enlistments. They will be allowed, however, no higher rating than 'boys,' at a compensation of ten dollars per month and one ration per day."

28 U.S.S. *Susquehanna,* Captain Chauncey, captured Confederate schooner *San Juan,* bound for Elizabeth City, North Carolina, with cargo of salt, sugar, and gin.

29 U.S.S. *Susquehanna,* Captain Chauncey, captured schooner *Baltimore* off Hatteras Inlet.

30 U.S.S. *Dart,* Acting Master Wheeler, captured schooner *Zavalla* off Vermillion Bay, Louisiana.

U.S.S. *Niagara,* Captain John Pope, captured pilot boat *Frolic* at South West Pass of the Mississippi River.

Cecelia, prize and tender to U.S.S. *Huntsville,* Commander Price, captured blockade running schooner *Ranchero* west of Vermillion Bay.

OCTOBER

1 Confederate naval forces, including C.S.S. *Curlew, Raleigh,* and *Junaluska,* under flag Officer William F. Lynch, CSN, captured steamer *Fanny* (later C.S.S. *Fanny*) in Pamlico Sound with Union troops on board. Colonel Claiborne Snead, CSA, reported: "The victory was important in more respects than one. It was our first naval success in North Carolina and the first capture made by our arms of an armed war-vessel of the enemy, and dispelled the gloom of recent disasters. The property captured [two rifled guns and large amount of army stores] was considerable, much needed, and highly esteemed . . ."

Secretary Welles, in a letter to Secretary Seward, opposed issuing letters of marque because it would be "a recognition of the assumption of the insurgents that they are a distinct and independent nationality."

3 Captain Eagle, commanding U.S.S. *Santee,* reported return of U.S.S. *Sam Houston* to Galveston with schooner *Reindeer,* captured off San Luis Pass, Texas. The schooner, deemed worthless, was sunk.

4 U.S.S. *South Carolina,* Commander Alden, captured Confederate schooners *Ezilda* and *Joseph H. Toone* off South West Pass of the Mississippi River with four to five thousand stand of arms.

5 Two boats from U.S.S. *Louisiana,* Lieutenant A. Murray, destroyed Confederate schooner being fitted out as a privateer at Chincoteague Inlet, Virginia.

U.S.S. *Monticello,* Lieutenant Daniel L. Braine, drove off Confederate troops and steamers attacking Union soldiers in the vicinity of Hatteras Inlet.

6 U.S.S. *Flag,* Commander Louis C. Sartori, captured Confederate blockade running schooner *Alert* near Charleston.

7 U.S.S. *Tyler,* Commander Walke, and U.S.S. *Lexington,* Commander Stembel, exchanged fire with Confederate batteries at Iron Bluffs, near Columbus, Kentucky.

U.S.S. *Louisiana,* Lieutenant A. Murray, captured schooner *S. T. Garrison,* with cargo of wood, near Wallops Island, Virginia.

9 Confederate steamer *Ivy,* Lieutenant Joseph Fry, attacked U.S. blockading vessels at Head of Passes, Mississippi River; no damage caused but long range of *Ivy's* guns concerned naval officers.

10 U.S.S. *Daylight,* Commander Lockwood, silenced Confederate battery attacking American ship *John Clark* anchored in Lynnhaven Bay, Virginia.

Confederate troops at Tampa Bay captured American sloop *William Batty.*

11 Lieutenant Abram D. Harrell of U.S.S. *Union,* with 3 boat crews, cut out and burned Confederate schooner in Dumfries Creek on the Potomac River.

12 Confederate metal-sheathed ram *Manassas*, Commodore Hollins, CSN, in company with armed steamer *Ivy* and *James L. Day*, attacked U.S.S. *Richmond, Vincennes, Water Witch, Nightingale*, and *Preble* near Head of Passes, Mississippi River. In this offensive and spirited action by the small Confederate force, *Manassas* rammed *Richmond*, forced her and *Vincennes* aground under heavy fire before withdrawing. Acting Master Edward F. Devens of *Vincennes* observed: "From the appearance of the *Richmond*'s side in the vicinity of the hole, I should say that the ram had claws or hooks attached to her . . . for the purpose of tearing out the plank from the ship's side. It is a most destructive invention . . . [*Manassas*] resembles in shape, a cigar cut lengthwise, and very low in the water. She must be covered with railroad iron as all the shells which struck her glanced off, some directly at right angles. You could hear the shot strike quite plainly. They did not appear to trouble her much as she ran up the river at a very fast rate."

Confederate ship *Theodora* ran the blockade at Charleston with Mason and Slidell, Commissioners to England and France respectively, on board.

Confederate privateer *Sallie* captured American brig *Granada* in the Atlantic (33° N, 71° W).

U.S.S. *Dale*, Commander Edward M. Yard, captured schooner *Specie* east of Jacksonville, bound for Havana with large cargo of rice.

Secretary of the Navy Welles wrote Flag Officer Du Pont: "In examining the various points upon the coast, it has been ascertained that Bull's Bay, St. Helena, Port Royal, and Fernandina, are each and all accessible and desirable points for the purposes indicated [Fleet coaling and supply stations], and the Government has decided to take possession of at least two of them." Coaling and supply depots seized by the Navy on the Southern coast allowed blockaders to remain on station for longer periods without returning to Northern navy yards.

Warning given that Confederates had lined James River with powerful submarine batteries (mines).

13 U.S.S. *Keystone State*, Commander Gustavus H. Scott, captured Confederate steamer *Salvor* near the Tortugas Islands with cargo of coffee, cigars, and munitions.

14 In the presence of Lieutenant A. Murray of U.S.S. *Louisiana*, citizens of Chincoteague Island, Virginia, took the oath of allegiance to the United States and presented a petition in which they stated their "abhorrence of the secession heresy."

15 U.S.S. *Roanoke, Flag, Monticello*, and *Vandalia* captured and burned blockade runner *Thomas Watson* on Stono Reef, off Charleston.

16 U.S.S. *South Carolina*, Commander Alden, captured schooner *Edward Barnard* with cargo of turpentine on board at South West Pass, Mississippi River.

17 Flag Officer Du Pont wrote: "There is no question that Port Royal is the most important point to strike, and the most desirable to have first and hold . . . Port Royal alone admits the large ships— and gives us such a naval position on the sea coast as our Army is holding across the Potomac." Subsequently, the strategic importance of Port Royal to the Union Navy and the blockade substantiated this judgment.

Confederate privateer *Sallie*, Master Henry S. Lebby, captured American brig *Betsey Ames* opposite the Bahama Banks with cargo including machinery.

18 U.S.S. *Gemsbok*, Acting Master Cavendy, captured brig *Ariel* off Wilmington with cargo of salt.

19 U.S.S. *Massachusetts*, Commander M. Smith, engaged C.S.S. *Florida*, Lieutenant Charles W. Hays, in Mississippi Sound. Though the battle was inconclusive, Captain Levin M. Powell of U.S.S. *Potomac* noted one result that could be bothersome to Union naval forces: "The caliber and long range of the rifled cannon [of *Florida*] . . . established the ability of these fast steam gunboats to keep out of the range of all broadside guns, and enables them to disregard the armament or magnitude of all ships thus armed, or indeed any number of them, when sheltered by shoal water."

21 Charles P. Leavitt, Second Virginia Regiment, wrote the Confederate Secretary of War: "I have invented an instrument of war which for a better name I have called a submarine gunboat . . . My plan is simple. A vessel is built of boiler iron of about fifty tons burden . . . but made of an oval form with the propeller behind. This is for the purpose of having as little draft of water as possible for the purpose of passing over sand-bars without being observed by the enemy. The engines are of the latest and best style so as to use as little steam as possible in proportion to the power received. The boilers are so constructed as to generate steam without a supply of air. The air for respiration is kept in a fit condition for breathing by the gradual addition of oxygen, while the carbonic acid is absorbed by a shower of lime water . . . I propose to tow out my gun-boat to sea and when within range of the enemy's guns it sinks below the water's surface so as to leave no trace on the surface of its approach, a self-acting apparatus keeping it at any depth required. When within a few rods of the enemy it leaps to surface and the two vessels come in contact before the enemy can fire a gun. Placed in the bow of the gun-boat is a small mortar containing a self-exploding shell. As it strikes the engines are reversed, the gun-boat sinks below the surface and goes noiselessly on its way toward another ship. After a few ships are sunk the enemy can scarcely have the temerity to remain in our waters . . . I have written you on this subject in order to obtain an opportunity to draft out my invention, which with the means at command in Richmond can be done in a week . . . " Although Leavitt's scheme was not adopted, it was an interesting indication of early thinking about submarines in the South. Ultimately the Confederacy built *H. L. Hunley,* first submarine to be used successfully in combat.

22 Captain T. T. Craven, commanding Potomac River Flotilla, reported the Potomac River was commanded by Confederate batteries at all important points below Alexandria.

23 Officers and men of privateer *Savannah* went on trial in New York, charged with "piracy."

25 John Ericcson began construction of single-turret, two-gun ironclad U.S.S. *Monitor* at Greenpoint, New York.

Flag Officer Du Pont wrote Assistant Secretary of the Navy Fox of the continuing importance of amphibious training: "Landing a brigade today to exercise Ferry boats and Surf boats—reaping immense advantages from the experiment by seeing the defects."

U.S.S. *Rhode Island,* Lieutenant Stephen D. Trenchard, captured schooner *Aristides* off Charlotte Harbor, Florida.

26 U.S.S. *Conestoga,* Lieutenant S. L. Phelps, transported Union troops to Eddyville, Kentucky, for attack on Confederate cavalry at Saratoga.

C.S.S. *Nashville,* Lieutenant Pegram, ran the blockade out of Charleston.

27 U.S.S. *Santee,* Captain Eagle, captured brig *Delta* off Galveston.

C.S.S. *Sumter,* Commander Semmes, captured and burned American schooner *Trowbridge* in the Atlantic after removing a five months' supply of provisions.

27–28 Boat expedition from U.S.S. *Louisiana* led by Lieutenant Alfred Hopkins surprised and burned three Confederate vessels at Chincoteague Inlet, Virginia.

29 Large Union expedition to Port Royal, South Carolina, sailed from Fort Monroe, under command of Flag Officer Du Pont in U.S.S. *Wabash.* Comprising 77 vessels, it was the largest U.S. Fleet ever assembled to that date. Army forces numbered about 16,000 men, commanded by Brigadier General Thomas W. Sherman. Port Royal Sound, about equi-distant from Savannah and Charleston, was of recognized importance, and one of the first locations fortified by the Confederates against the entrance of Union ships.

30 Confederate privateer *Sallie* captured American brig *B. K. Eaton.*
Confederate forces sank stone-filled barges to obstruct Cumberland River near Fort Donelson, Tennessee, against the advance of Union gunboats.

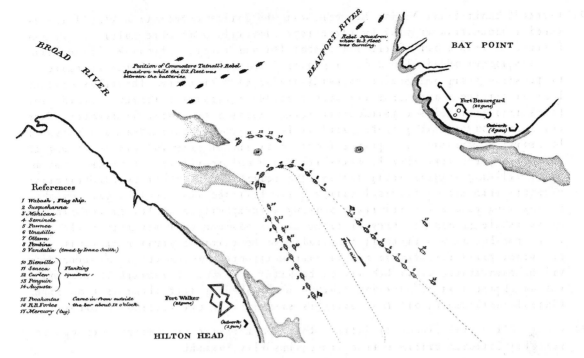

The plan of attack at Port Royal demonstrated the detailed planning of Flag Officer Du Pont which helped decide the issue.

NOVEMBER

1 Violent storm struck the Port Royal Sound Expedition off the Carolina coast, widely scattering naval vessels, transports, and supply ships and jeopardizing the success of this major undertaking. However, the damage to the Fleet was less than could have been expected. All ships had been furnished with secret instructions to be opened at sea only in case of separation from the Fleet.

2 U.S.S. *Sabine,* Captain Cadwalader Ringgold, rescued Major John G. Reynolds and a battalion of U.S. Marines under his command from U.S. transport *Governor,* unit of the Port Royal Sound Expedition, sinking off Georgetown, South Carolina.

British steamer *Bermuda* ran the blockade at Charleston with 2000 bales of cotton.

4 Coast Survey Ship *Vixen* entered Port Royal Sound to sound channel escorted by U.S.S. *Ottawa* and *Seneca.* Confederate naval squadron under Commodore Tattnall took Union ships under fire.

5 U.S.S. *Ottawa, Pembina, Seneca,* and *Pawnee* engaged and dispersed small Confederate squadron in Port Royal Sound, fired on Fort Beauregard and Fort Walker.

6 U.S.S. *Rescue,* Lieutenant William Gwin, captured and burned schooner *Ada* hard aground in Corrotoman Creek, Virginia.

Captain Purviance, commander of U.S.S. *St. Lawrence,* reported capture of British schooner *Fanny Lee,* running the blockade at Darien, Georgia, with cargo of rice and tobacco.

7 Naval forces under Flag Officer Du Pont captured Port Royal Sound. While Du Pont's ships steamed in boldly, the naval gunners poured a withering fire into the defending Forts Walker and Beauregard with extreme accuracy. The Confederate defenders abandoned the Forts, and the small Confederate naval squadron under Commodore Tattnall could offer only harassing resistance but did rescue troops

Flag Ship Wabash
Off Hilton Head — Port Royal Harbor
1861 — November 8th

Sir,

I have the honor to inform you that yesterday I attacked the Enemies Batteries on Bay Point and Hilton Head — Forts Beauregard and Walker — and succeeded in silencing them after an engagement of four hours duration and driving away the Squadron of Rebel Steamers under Commodore Tattnall. The reconnoissance of yesterday made us acquainted with the superiority of Fort Walker and to that I directed my special efforts, engaging it at a distance of first eight and afterwards six hundred yards — But the plan of attack brought the Squadron sufficiently near Fort Beauregard to receive its fire, and the ships were frequently fighting the Batteries on both sides at the same time.

The action was begun on my part at twenty six minutes after nine and at half past two the American Ensign was hoisted on the flag staff of Fort Walker, & this morning, at sunrise, on that of Fort Beauregard —

The defeat of the Enemy terminated in utter route and confusion; their quarters and encampments were abandoned without an attempt to carry away either public or private property

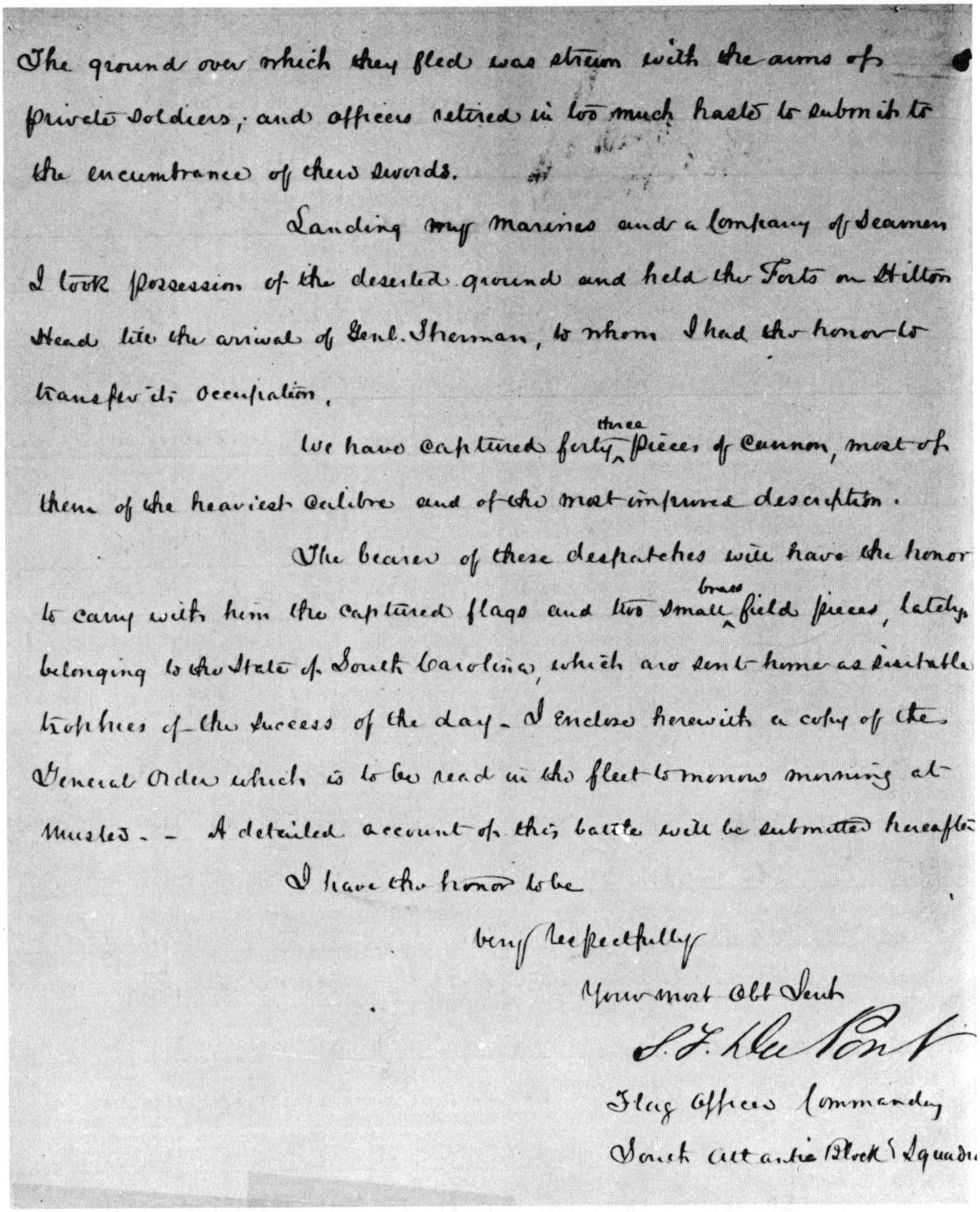

The ground over which they fled was strewn with the arms of private soldiers; and officers retired in too much haste to submit to the encumbrance of their swords.

Landing my Marines and a Company of Seamen I took possession of the deserted ground and held the Forts on Hilton Head till the arrival of Genl. Sherman, to whom I had the honor to transfer its occupation.

We have captured forty _three_ pieces of cannon, most of them of the heaviest calibre and of the most improved description.

The bearer of these despatches will have the honor to carry with him the captured flags and two small _brass_ field pieces, lately belonging to the State of South Carolina, which are sent home as suitable trophies of the success of the day — I enclose herewith a copy of the General Order which is to be read in the fleet to morrow morning at Muster. — A detailed account of this battle will be submitted hereafter

I have the honor to be

very respectfully
Your most obt Sevt
S. F. Du Pont
Flag Officer Commandg
South Atlantic Block Squadr

Flag Officer Du Pont reports his victory at Port Royal Sound to Secretary of the Navy Welles.

Du Pont's squadron—the largest ever assembled by the Navy up to that time poured a withering fire with extreme accuracy into Forts Walker and Beauregard compelling the Confederates to withdraw.

by ferrying them to the mainland from Hilton Head. Marines and sailors were landed to occupy the Forts until turned over to Army troops under General T. W. Sherman. Careful planning and skillful execution had given Du Pont a great victory and the Union Navy an important base of operations. The Confederates were compelled to withdraw coastal defenses inland out of reach of naval gunfire. Du Pont wrote: "It is not my temper to rejoice over fallen foes, but this must be a gloomy night in Charleston."

U.S.S. *Tyler,* Commander Walke, and U.S.S. *Lexington,* Commander Stembel, supported 3000 Union troops under General Grant at the Battle of Belmont, Missouri, and engaged Confederate batteries along the Mississippi River. The arrival of Confederate reinforcements compelled Grant to withdraw under pressure. Grape, canister, and shell from the gunboats scattered the Confederates, enabling Union troops to re-embark on their transports. Grant, with characteristic restraint, reported that the gunboats' service was "most efficient," having "protected our transports throughout."

8   U.S.S. *San Jacinto,* Captain Wilkes, stopped British mail steamer *Trent* in Old Bahama Channel and removed Confederate Commissioners Mason and Slidell. The action sparked a serious international incident.

Boat expedition under Lieutenant·James E. Jouett from U.S.S. *Santee* surprised and captured Confederate crew of schooner *Royal Yacht,* and burned the vessel at Galveston.

U.S.S. *Rescue,* Lieutenant Gwin, shelled Confederate battery at Urbana Creek, Virginia, and captured large schooner.

9   Gunboats of Flag Officer Du Pont's force took possession of Beaufort, South Carolina, and, by blocking the mouth of Broad River, cut off this communication link between Charleston and Savannah.

Major General Robert E. Lee wrote Confederate Secretary of War Judah P. Benjamin regarding the effects of the Union Navy's victory at Port Royal: "The enemy having complete possession of the water and inland navigation, commands all the islands on the coast and threatens both Savannah and Charleston, and can come in his boats, within 4 miles of this place [Lee's headquarters, Coosawhatchie, South Carolina]. His sloops of war and large steamers can come up Broad River to Mackay's Point, the mouth of the Pocotaligo, and his gunboats can ascend some distance up the Coosawhatchie and Tulifinny. We have no guns that can resist their batteries, and have no resources but to prepare to meet them in the field."

11 Thaddeus Lowe made balloon observation of Confederate forces from Balloon-Boat *G. W. Parke Custis* anchored in Potomac River. *G. W. Parke Custis* was procured for $150, and readied for the service at the Washington Navy Yard. Lowe reported: "I left the navy-yard early Sunday morning, the 10th

Commd's office
Navy Yard Washington
Augt 12th 1861

Sir,

In reply to your letter of
the 9th inst, I have to state, that
the boat "G. W. Custis" is
122 feet long
14½ " beam
5½ " depth of hold
She is propelled by oars or poles or
towed by Steamer. She will carry
about 75 ton in 2½ feet Water; in
deep Water her Capacity is 120 tons.
Her age is between 7 & 8 years, planking built de only 11 months old.

The Master of the yard say
She will require some bracing and
Caulking to make a Coal barge of
her, that she is worth the money
asked for her $150 —

I have the honor to be
Very respectfully
Yr ob St
J. Dahlgren
Comdr

Como Jos Smith
&c &c &c

Description of Balloon-Boat G. W. Parke Custis by Commander John A. Dahlgren.

Thaddeus Lowe conducts aerial observation of Confederate positions from Balloon-Boat G. W. Parke Custis. *This and John LaMountain's earlier ascension from* Fanny *paved the way for the Navy's present effective use of the air as an element of sea power.*

I–36

instant . . . towed out by the steamer *Coeur de Lion,* having on board competent assistant aeronauts, together with my new gas generating apparatus, which, though used for the first time, worked admirably. We located at the mouth of Mattawoman Creek, about three miles from the opposite or Virginia shore. Yesterday [11 November] proceeded to make observations accompanied in my ascensions by General Sickles and others. We had a fine view of the enemy's camp-fires during the evening, and saw the rebels constructing new batteries at Freestone Point."

12 *Fingal* (later C.S.S. *Atlanta*), purchased in England, entered Savannah laden with military supplies—the first ship to run the blockade solely on Confederate government account.

   U.S.S. *W. G. Anderson,* Acting Lieutenant William C. Rogers, captured Confederate privateer *Beauregard* near Abaco.

13 U.S.S. *Water Witch,* Lieutenant Aaron K. Hughes, captured blockade running British brigantine *Cornucopia* off Mobile.

14 U.S. cutter *Mary,* Captain Pease, seized Confederate privateer *Neva* at San Francisco, California.

15 Confederate Commissioners Mason and Slidell disembarked from U.S.S. *San Jacinto,* Captain Wilkes, at Fort Monroe.

   U.S.S. *Dale,* Commander Yard, captured British schooner *Mabel* east of Jacksonville.

16 Confederate Secretary of the Navy Mallory advertised for plans and bids for building four seagoing ironclads capable of carrying four heavy guns each.

17 U.S.S *Connecticut,* Commander Maxwell Woodhull, captured British schooner *Adeline,* loaded with military stores and supplies off Cape Canaveral, Florida.

18 U.S.S. *Monticello,* Lieutenant Braine, engaged Confederate battery near New Inlet, North Carolina.

   U.S.S. *Conestoga,* Lieutenant S. L. Phelps, on expedition up Cumberland River, dispersed Confederate forces and silenced battery at Canton, Kentucky.

19 C.S.S. *Nashville,* Lieutenant Pegram, captured and burned American clipper ship *Harvey Birch,* bound from Le Havre to New York.

21 U.S.S. *New London,* Lieutenant Abner Read, with U.S.S. *R. R. Cuyler* and crew members of U.S.S. *Massachusetts,* captured Confederate schooner *Olive* with cargo of lumber in Mississippi Sound; same force took steamer *Anna,* with naval stores, the following day.

22 Two days of combined gunfire commenced from U.S.S. *Niagara,* Flag Officer McKean, U.S.S. *Richmond,* Captain Francis B. Ellison, and Fort Pickens against Confederate defenses at Fort McRee, the Pensacola Navy Yard, and the town of Warrington, terminating the following day with damage to Confederate positions and to U.S.S. *Richmond.*

   U.S. Marine Corps authorized to enlist an additional 500 privates and proportionate number of noncommissioned officers.

23 C.S.S. *Sumter,* Commander Semmes, evaded U.S.S. *Iroquois* at Martinique and steamed on course for Europe.

   Confederate gunboat *Tuscarora* accidentally destroyed by fire near Helena, Arkansas.

24 Landing party from U.S.S. *Flag,* Commander J. Rodgers, U.S.S. *Augusta, Pocahontas, Seneca,* and *Savannah,* took possession of the Tybee Island, Savannah Harbor. "This abandonment of Tybee Island," Du Pont reported, "is due to the terror inspired by the bombardment of Forts Walker and Beauregard, and is a direct fruit of the victory of the 7th [capture of Port Royal Sound]."

25 First armor plate for shipment to C.S.S. *Virginia* (ex-U.S.S. *Merrimack*) accepted by Confederate Secretary of the Navy Mallory.

U.S.S. *Penguin,* Acting Lieutenant Thomas A. Budd, captured blockade running schooner *Albion* near North Edisto, South Carolina, with cargo of arms, munitions, and provisions.

C.S.S. *Sumter,* Commander Semmes, captured American brig *Montmorenci* off Leeward Islands.

26 C.S.S. *Savannah,* Commodore Tattnall, and three steamers sortied against Union fleet in Cockspur Roads, Savannah; unsuccessful in effort to draw blockading vessels within range of Fort Pulaski's guns.

Flag Officer Du Pont observed the blockade's increasing pressure on the South's economy: "The flag is hoisted on the lighthouse and martello tower at Tybee . . . Shoes are $8 a pair in Charleston. Salt $7 a bushel, no coffee—women going into the interior—[Captain James L.] Lardner has closed the port so effectively that they can no longer get fish even."

C.S.S. *Sumter,* Commander Semmes, captured and burned American schooner *Arcade* north of Leeward Islands.

27 U.S.S. *Vincennes,* Lieutenant Samuel Marcy, boarded and seized blockade running British bark *Empress,* aground at the mouth of the Mississippi River, with large cargo of coffee.

28 U.S.S. *New London,* Lieutenant A. Read, captured Confederate blockade runner *Lewis,* with cargo of sugar and molasses, and schooner *A. J. View,* with cargo of turpentine and tar, off Ship Island, Mississippi.

29 Lieutenant Worden, later commanding officer of U.S.S. *Monitor,* arrived in Washington after seven months as a prisoner in the South.

30 U.S.S. *Wanderer,* Lieutenant James H. Spotts, captured blockade running British schooner *Telegraph* near Indian Key, Florida.

U.S.S. *Savannah,* Commander John S. Missroon, with other ships in company, seized Confederate schooner *E. J. Waterman,* after the vessel grounded at Tybee Island with cargo of coffee on board.

DECEMBER

1 U.S.S. *New London,* Lieutenant A. Read, captured sloop *Advocate* in Mississippi Sound.

U.S.S. *Seminole,* Commander Gillis, seized sloop *Lida,* from Havana, off St. Simon's Sound, Georgia, with cargo of coffee, lead, and sugar.

2 In his first annual report, Secretary of the Navy Welles reported to President Lincoln that: "Since the institution of the blockade one hundred and fifty-three vessels have been captured . . . most of which were attempting to violate the blockade . . . When the vessels now building and purchased are . . . ready for service, the condition of the navy will be . . . a total of 264 vessels, 2,557 guns, and 218,016 tons. The aggregate number of seamen in the service . . . is now not less than 22,000 . . . The amount appropriated at the last regular session of Congress for the naval service for the current year was $13,168,675.86. To this was added at the special session in July last $30,446,875.91—making for the fiscal year ending June 30, 1862, an aggregate of $43,615,551.77. This sum will not be sufficient . . ."

C.S.S. *Patrick Henry,* Commander Tucker, attacked four Union steamers above Newport News; *Patrick Henry* damaged in the two hour action.

Lieutenant Robert D. Minor, CSN, reported a laboratory had been organized at New Orleans "for the supply of ordnance stores for the vessels fitting out at this station."

3 C.S.S. *Sumter,* Commander Semmes, captured and burned at sea American ship *Vigilant,* bound from New York to the West Indies.

U.S.S. *Santiago de Cuba,* Commander Ridgely, captured British blockade running schooner *Victoria.*

4 Confederate steamers *Florida* and *Pamlico* attacked U.S.S. *Montgomery,* Commander Thompson D. Shaw, off Horn Island Pass, Mississippi Sound.

5   Flag Officer Du Pont, regarding expedition to Wassaw Sound, Georgia, and plans for the use of the "stone fleet," wrote: "*Ottawa, Pembina,* and *Seneca* penetrated into Wassaw . . . the 'stone fleet' are all at Savannah, and I hardly know what to do with them—for with Wassaw that city is more effectively closed than a bottle with wire over the cork . . . I am sending to [Captain James L.] Lardner to know if he can plant them on the Charleston bar . . . One good thing they [the 'stone fleet's' appearance at Savannah] did, I have not a doubt they were taken for men-of-war, and led to giving up the Wassaw defenses . . ."

6   U.S.S. *Augusta,* Commander Parrott, captured British blockade runner *Cheshire* off South Carolina.

8   C.S.S. *Sumter,* Commander Semmes, captured and burned American bark *Eben Dodge* in the mid-Atlantic (30°57' N, 51°49' W), equipped for whaling voyage in Pacific.

    U.S.S. *Rhode Island,* Lieutenant Trenchard, seized British blockade runner *Phantom* with cargo of sugar off Cape Lookout, North Carolina.

9   U.S.S. *New London,* Lieutenant A. Read, captured schooner *Delight* and sloops *Express* and *Osceola* off Cat Island Passage, Mississippi.

    U.S.S. *Harriet Lane,* Lieutenant Robert H. Wyman, and other vessels of the Potomac Flotilla engaged Confederate forces at Freestone Point, Virginia.

10 U.S.S. *Isaac Smith,* Lieutenant James W. A. Nicholson, on expedition up Ashepoo River, South Carolina, landed on Otter Island and took possession of abandoned Confederate fort; Nicholson turned over command of the fort to the Army.

11 U.S.S. *Bienville,* Commander Steedman, captured schooner *Sarah and Caroline* off St. John's River, Florida.

    U.S.S. *South Carolina,* Commander Alden, captured Confederate sloop *Florida* off lighthouse at Timbalier, Louisiana.

12 U.S.S. *Alabama,* Commander Edward Lanier, captured British ship *Admiral* off Savannah, attempting to run the blockade.

    U.S.S. *Isaac Smith,* Lieutenant J. W. A. Nicholson, on a reconnaissance in the Ashepoo River, South Carolina, with Marine detachment embarked, scattered Confederate troops by gunfire and landed Marines to destroy their quarters.

15 U.S.S. *Stars and Stripes,* Lieutenant Reed Werden, captured blockade running schooner *Charity* off Cape Hatteras.

    U.S.S. *Jamestown,* Commander Green, captured Confederate sloop *Havelock* near Cape Fear, North Carolina.

17 Flag Officer Foote, Commanding U.S. Naval Forces, Western Waters, issued General Order regarding observance of Sunday on board ships of his flotilla: "It is the wish . . . that on Sunday the public worship of Almighty God may be observed . . . and that the respective commanders will either themselves, or cause other persons to pronounce prayers publicly on Sunday . . ." Foote added: "Discipline to be permanent must be based on moral grounds, and officers must in themselves, show a good example in morals, order, and patriotism to secure these qualities in the men." Since 1775 Navy Regulations have required that religious services be held on board ships of the Navy in peace and war.

    Seven "stone fleet" vessels sunk at entrance of Savannah Harbor.

19 Confederate forces demolished lighthouse on Morris Island, Charleston.

20 "Stone fleet" sunk at Charleston by Captain C. H. Davis. Steamer *Gordon* ran the blockade off Wilmington.

21 U.S. Congress authorized Medal of Honor, the Nation's highest award.

24 U.S.S. *Gem of the Sea,* Lieutenant Irvin B. Baxter, captured and destroyed British blockade runner *Prince of Wales* off Georgetown, South Carolina.

Confederate Secretary of the Navy Mallory wrote Major General Leonidas Polk, commanding troops at Columbus, Kentucky, requesting furlough of troops to assist in construction of ironclad gunboats at Memphis. Mallory commented: "One of them at Columbus would have enabled you to complete the annihilation of the enemy."

25 U.S.S. *Fernandina,* Acting Lieutenant George W. Browne, captured schooner *William H. Northrup* off Cape Fear, North Carolina.

26 Confederate Fleet, including C.S.S. *Savannah,* Commodore Tattnall, *Resolute, Sampson, Ida,* and *Barton,* attacked Union blockading ships at mouth of Savannah River. Before returning to his anchorage under the guns of Fort Pulaski, Tattnall forced the blockaders to move seaward temporarily.

U.S.S. *Rhode Island,* Lieutenant Trenchard, captured Confederate schooner *Venus* southeast of Sabine Pass, off the Louisiana coast.

27 Flag Officer Du Pont wrote regarding the *"Trent* Affair": "I hope now that our politicians will begin to learn, that something is necessary to be 'a great universal Yankee Nation etc.' than politics and party. We should have armies and navies and have those appurtenances which enable a nation to defend itself and not be compelled to submit to humiliation [releasing Mason and Slidell] . . . Thirty ships like the *Wabash* would have spared us this without firing a gun, with an ironclad frigate or two."

28 U.S.S. *New London,* Lieutenant A. Read, captured Confederate schooner *Gipsey* with cargo of cotton in Mississippi Sound.

29 C.S.S. *Sea Bird,* Flag Officer Lynch, evaded Union gunfire and captured large schooner near Hampton Roads carrying fresh water to Fort Monroe.

30 U.S.S. *Santee,* Captain Eagle, captured schooner *Garonne* off Galveston.

Flag Officer Foote wrote Assistant Secretary of the Navy Fox of the pay scale he was using: "In the case of Masters, and Pilots, I have been obliged, in order to secure the services of efficient Men, to pay 1st Masters $150. per month, 2nd Masters $125. 3rd Masters $100. and 4th Masters $80. per month, while Pilots are paid $175. per month. These prices are much less than the incumbents received in ordinary times, while they have before been provided with table furniture and stores, bedding &c., which I have not allowed them."

31 Biloxi, Mississippi, surrendered to a landing party of seamen and Marines covered by U.S.S. *Water Witch, New London,* and *Henry Lewis;* a small Confederate battery was destroyed, two guns and schooner *Captain Spedden* captured.

Flag Officer Foote wrote Assistant Secretary of the Navy Fox about the delay in fitting out mortar boats: "I did say and still consider the mortar boats very defective. They are built of solid timber and when armed and manned will be awash with the deck . . . all will leak more or less. Still I would have them fitted out, with all their defects." Foote made excellent use of the mortar boats later at Island No. 10.

U.S.S. *Augusta,* Commander Parrott, captured Confederate schooner *Island Belle* attempting to run the blockade near Bull's Bay, South Carolina.

Two boats, under Acting Masters A. Allen and H. L. Sturges, from U.S.S. *Mount Vernon,* destroyed lightship off Wilmington which had been fitted out as a gunboat by Confederates.

31–2 January Naval squadron under Commander C. R. P. Rodgers, including gunboats *Ottawa, Pembina,* and *Seneca* and four armed boats carrying howitzers, joined General Stevens' troops in successful amphibious attack on Confederate positions at Port Royal Ferry and on Coosaw River. Gunboat fire covered the troop advance, and guns and naval gunners were landed as artillery support. Army signal officers acted as gunfire observers and coordinators on board the ships. The action disrupted Confederate plans to erect batteries and build troop strength in the area intending to close Coosaw River and isolate Federal troops on Port Royal Island. General Stevens wrote: "I would do great injustice to my own feelings did I fail to express my satisfaction and delight with the recent cooperation of the command of Captain Rodgers in our celebration of New Year's Day. Whether regard be had to his beautiful working of the gunboats in the narrow channel of Port Royal, the thorough concert of action established through the signal officers, or the masterly handling of the guns against the enemy, nothing remained to be desired. Such a cooperation . . . augurs everything. propitious for the welfare of our cause in this quarter of the country."

1862

I.—SOME SIGNIFICANT EVENTS OF 1862

9 January— Flag Officer D. G. Farragut was appointed to command the Western Gulf Blockading Squadron—the beginning of the New Orleans campaign.

16 January— Seven armored river gunboats were commissioned, thus providing the naval force for the overwhelming combined operations in the west.

6 February— Naval forces under Flag Officer A. H. Foote captured strategic Fort Henry on the Tennessee River. This breached the Confederate line and opened the flood gates for the flow of Union power deep into the South.

7-8 February— Joint amphibious expedition under Flag Officer L. M. Goldsborough and Brigadier General A. E. Burnside captured Roanoke Island—the key to Albemarle Sound.

14 February— Gunboats under Flag Officer A. H. Foote attacked Fort Donelson on the Cumberland River in conjunction with troops under Brigadier General U. S. Grant. The fort capitulated on 16 February.

3 March— Forces under Flag Officer S. F. Du Pont took Fernandina, Florida, and the surrounding area in joint operations against the South Atlantic coast.

8 March— Ironclad ram C.S.S. *Virginia*, Captain F. Buchanan, destroyed wooden blockading ships U.S.S. *Cumberland* and *Congress* in Hampton Roads.

9 March— U.S.S. *Monitor*, Lieutenant J. L. Worden, engaged C.S.S. *Virginia*, Lieutenant C. ap R. Jones, in the historic first battle of ironclads.

14 March— Joint amphibious assault under Commander S. C. Rowan and Brigadier General A. E. Burnside captured New Bern, North Carolina—"an immense depot of army fixtures and manufactures, of shot and shell. . . ."

17 March— C.S.S. *Nashville*, Lieutenant R. B. Pegram, ran the blockade out of Beaufort, North Carolina—a "Bull Run of the Navy."

4 April— U.S.S. *Carondelet*, Commander H. Walke, dashed past Confederate batteries on Island No. 10 to support Major General J. Pope's assault on the island.

7 April— Island No. 10, vital to the Confederate defense of the upper Mississippi, surrendered to the naval forces of Flag Officer A. H. Foote.

24 April— Flag Officer D. G. Farragut's fleet ran past Forts Jackson and St. Philip, destroyed the defending Confederate flotilla below New Orleans, and, next day, compelled the surrender of the South's largest and wealthiest city.

10 May— Confederates destroyed the Norfolk and Pensacola Navy Yards in actions caused by the forced Southern withdrawal from her coasts.

11 May— C.S.S. *Virginia* was blown up by her crew off Craney Island to prevent her capture by advancing Union forces.

15 May— The James River Flotilla under Commander J. Rodgers advanced unsupported to within eight miles of Richmond before being turned back at Drewry's Bluff by batteries manned in part by Confederate Navy and Marine personnel.

6	June—	Gunboats under Captain C. H. Davis and rams under Colonel C. R. Ellet, Jr., destroyed the upper Mississippi portion of the Confederate River Defense Fleet under Captain J. E. Montgomery at the Battle of Memphis. The Tennessee city surrendered.
28	June—	Flag Officer D. G. Farragut's fleet successfully passed the heavy Vicksburg batteries; three days later, 1 July, his forces were joined by those of Flag Officer C. H. Davis: the fresh and salt-water fleets met for the first time.
1–2	July—	Flag Officer L. M. Goldsborough's fleet covered the withdrawal of Major General G. B. McClellan's army after the battle of Malvern Hill.
15	July—	C.S.S. *Arkansas*, Lieutenant I. N. Brown, engaged and ran through the Union fleet above Vicksburg, partially disabling U.S.S. *Carondelet* and *Tyler*.
16	July—	David Glasgow Farragut promoted to Rear Admiral, the first officer to hold that rank in the history of the U.S. Navy.
24	August—	Commander R. Semmes assumed command of celebrated raider C.S.S. *Alabama*.
26	August—	Franklin Buchanan promoted to Admiral, ranking officer in the Confederate Navy.
25	September—	U.S.S. *Kensington* and *Rachel Seaman* and mortar schooner *Henry Janes* bombarded Sabine City, Texas, and forced Confederate troops to withdraw from the city.
1	October—	The Western Gunboat Fleet was transferred from the War Department to the Navy.
31	October—	During October the Confederate Torpedo Bureau was established under Lieutenant H. Davidson, continuing work pioneered by Commander M. F. Maury.
3	November—	C.S.S. *Cotton* and shore batteries engaged Union squadron at Berwick Bay, Louisiana. The squadron suffered considerable damage before the gallant Confederate gunboat expended all its ammunition and was compelled to withdraw.
12	December—	U.S.S. *Cairo*, Lieutenant Commander T. O. Selfridge, was sunk in the Yazoo River, the first ship to be destroyed by a Confederate torpedo.
31	December—	U.S.S. *Monitor*, Commander J. P. Bankhead, foundered and was lost at sea off Cape Hatteras.

II.—DETAILED CIVIL WAR NAVAL CHRONOLOGY

1862

JANUARY

1 U.S.S. *Yankee*, Lieutenant Eastman, and U.S.S. *Anacostia*, Lieutenant Oscar C. Badger, exchanged fire with Confederate batteries at Cockpit Point, Potomac River; *Yankee* was damaged slightly. Attacks by ships of the Potomac Flotilla were instrumental in forcing the withdrawal of strong Confederate emplacements along the river. Batteries at Cockpit and Shipping Point were abandoned by 9 March 1862.

Flag Officer Foote reported to Secretary of the Navy Welles that he was sending U.S.S. *Lexington*, Lieutenant Shirk, to join U.S.S. *Conestoga*, Lieutenant S. L. Phelps, which had been rendering valuable service in her river cruising ground, protecting "Union people" on the borders of the Ohio River and its tributaries; indeed, the control of the rivers advanced Union frontiers deep into territory sympathetic to the South. Foote added: "I am using all possible dispatch in getting all the gunboats ready for service. There is great demand for them in different places in the western rivers."

Confederate Commissioners Mason and Slidell left Boston for England, via Provincetown, Massachusetts, where they boarded H.M.S. *Rinaldo*.

2 Flag Officer L. M. Goldsborough ordered U.S.S. *Louisiana*, *Lockwood*, *I. N. Seymour*, *Shawsheen*, and *Whitehall* (forced to return to Newport News because of engine trouble) to Hatteras Inlet, "using a sound discretion in time of departing." Goldsborough wrote Secretary of the Navy Welles the next day: "When they arrive there, twelve of this squadron will have been assembled in that quarter. With the rest we are driving on as fast as possible." Since early December

Andrew Hull Foote
Flag Officer, USN

Gustavus V. Fox
Assistant Secretary of the Navy

II–3

extensive preparations for the joint attack on Roanoke Island—the key to Albemarle Sound—had been underway in a move not only to seal off the North Carolina coast, but also to back up General McClellan's Peninsular Campaign by threatening Confederate communications.

Flag Officer Foote wrote Secretary of the Navy Welles: "I hope to be able to send 60 men on board of each gunboat within the week. We are waiting for the 1,000 men to fill up our complement . . . The carpenters and engineers are behindhand in their work." Eads' completion of the gunboats had been much delayed beyond his contract time. This placed a great strain upon the wooden gunboats, whose daily service in the rivers was demonstrated by General Grant's typical communication with Foote: "Will you please direct a gunboat to drop down the river . . . to protect a steamer I am sending down to bring up produce for some loyal citizens of Kentucky?"

Steamer *Ella Warley* evaded U.S.S. *Mohican*, Commander Godon, in a heavy fog and ran the blockade into Charleston.

5 Flag Officer L. M. Goldsborough, replying to a telegram from Brigadier General Ambrose E. Burnside, the Army commander for the Roanoke Island expedition, wrote that "the sooner you start your first brigade [for Hatteras Inlet] the better, and so, too, with all vessels you have which are to be towed or which require choice weather in order to arrive safely." President Lincoln was reported as "anxious to hear of the departure of the expedition."

6 One of Flag Officer Foote's primary problems was the manning of the new ironclad gunboats, which were becoming available behind contract date at St. Louis and Mound City. The Navy Department sent a draft of 500 seamen; the rest had to be recruited or detailed from the Army. That the Army was reluctant to give up its best men for service afloat was demonstrated by Grant's letter to Major General Halleck, in which he wrote that he had a number of offenders in the guardhouse and suggested, "In view of the difficulties of getting men for the gunboat service, that these men be transferred to that service . . ."

7 Lieutenant S. L. Phelps, U.S.S. *Conestoga*, on an expedition up the Tennessee and Cumberland Rivers gained valuable intelligence about Confederate activity at Forts Henry and Donelson. "The rebels," he reported to Flag Officer Foote, "are industriously perfecting their means of defense both at Dover and Fort Henry. At Fort Donelson (near Dover) they have placed obstructions in the river, 1½ miles below their battery, on the left bank and in the bend where the battery comes in sight . . . The fire of gunboats here [at Fort Donelson] would be at a bad angle . . . The forts are placed, especially on the Cumberland, where no great range can be had, and they can only be attacked in one narrow and fixed line . . . It is too late now to move against the works on either river, except with a well-appointed and powerful naval force." As early as mid-December 1861, Phelps had reconnoitered the Cumberland and warned of the immense difficulties involved in a naval assault on Fort Donelson, the strategically located Confederate stronghold. "None of the works can be seen," he observed, "till approached to within easy range." The difficult assault on Fort Donelson five weeks later gave truth to Phelps' careful observation. Meanwhile, Flag Officer Foote reconnoitered down the Mississippi with U.S.S. *Tyler*, *Lexington*, and *Essex*, the latter one of the first two ironclads ready. Pursuing a Confederate gunboat, Foote proceeded within range of the batteries at Columbus and found "one of the submarine batteries." But learning that the river was generally clear of these, he was able to report that "my object was fully attained."

General McClellan's orders to Brigadier General Burnside illustrated the Army's reliance on strength afloat: ". . . you will," he wrote, "after uniting with Flag-Officer Goldsborough at Fort Monroe, proceed under his convoy to Hatteras Inlet . . . [the] first point of attack will be Roanoke Island and its dependencies. It is presumed that the Navy can reduce the batteries . . . and cover the landing of your troops . . ." McClellan also detailed the Army's follow-up operations in conjunction with the gunboats at Fort Macon, New Bern, and Beaufort.

8   General Robert E. Lee, confounded by the strength and mobility of the Union Navy, observed. "Wherever his fleet can be brought no opposition to his landing can be made except within range of our fixed batteries. We have nothing to oppose to its heavy guns, which sweep over the low banks of this country with irresistable force. The farther he can be withdrawn from his floating batteries the weaker he will become, and lines of defense, covering objects of attack, have been selected with this view."

9   Orders from the Navy Department appointed Flag Officer Farragut to command Western Gulf Blockading Squadron, flagship U.S.S. *Hartford*, then at Philadelphia. The bounds of the command extended from West Florida to the Rio Grande, but a far larger purpose than even the important function of blockade lay behind Farragut's appointment. Late in 1861 the administration had made a decision that would have fateful results on the war. The full list of senior officers in the Navy was reviewed for a commander for an enterprise of first importance—the capture of New Orleans, the South's "richest and most populous city," and the beginning of the drive of sea-based power up the Father of Waters to meet General Grant, who would soon move south behind the spearhead of the armored gunboats. On 21 December 1861, in Washington, Farragut had written his wife: "Keep your lips closed, and burn my letters; for perfect silence is to be observed— the first injunction of the Secretary. I am to have a flag in the Gulf and the rest depends upon myself. Keep calm and silent. I shall sail in three weeks." Meanwhile, the tight blockade was causing grave concern in New Orleans. The *Commercial Bulletin* reported: "The situation of this port makes it a matter of vast moment to the whole Confederate State that it should be opened to the commerce of the world within the least possible period . . . We believe the blockading vessels of the enemy might have been driven away and kept away months ago, if the requisite energy had been put forth . . . The blockade has remained and the great port of New Orleans has been hermetically sealed . . ."

10   Concern continued to grow in the Union fleet as to what preparations should be taken to meet the unfinished ex-*Merrimack*. As early as 12 October 1861, Flag Officer L. M. Goldsborough had written Secretary of the Navy Welles: ". . . I am now quite satisfied that . . . she will, in all probability, prove to be exceedingly formidable . . . Nothing, I think, but very close work can possibly be of service in accomplishing the destruction of the *Merrimack*, and even of that a great deal may be necessary." Goldsborough ordered tugs *Dragon* and *Zouave* to remain constantly in company with U.S.S. *Congress* and *Cumberland*, "so as to tow them into an advantageous position in case of an attack from the *Merrimack* or any other quarter." However, at this date—two months before the historic engagements in Hampton Roads—Union naval commanders were seeking a defense against the powerful Confederate ironclad. Commander William Smith, captain of the ill-fated *Congress*, had said earlier, "I have not yet devised any plan to defend us against the *Merrimack*, unless," he added, "it be with hard knocks."

Flag Officer Foote's gunboats convoyed General Grant's troops as diversionary moves were begun a short distance down the Mississippi and later up the Tennessee to prevent a Confederate build-up of strength at Fort Henry.

Brigadier General John C. Pemberton, CSA, reported on the effectiveness of the Union gunboats at Port Royal Ferry and on the Coosaw River (see last entry, 31 December–1 January 1861): "Although the enemy did not land in force at Page's Point or Cunningham's Bluff, it was entirely practicable for him to have done so under cover of his gunboats. . . .At no time during his occupation of the river bank did he leave their [the gunboats'] protection, and, finally, when withdrawing to the island, did so under a fire from his vessels almost as heavy as that under which he had landed . . . by far the larger proportion of the [Confederate] casualties being from the shells of the fleet."

Naval vessels under Flag Officer Goldsborough and Army transports ready at Hampton Roads for the amphibious expedition against Roanoke Island which sealed off Albemarle Sound.

11 U.S.S. *Essex*, Commander W. D. Porter, and U.S.S. *St. Louis*, Lieutenant Leonard Paulding, engaged Confederate gunboats in a running fight in the Mississippi River, near Lucas Bend, Missouri. The Confederates withdrew under the protecting batteries at Columbus.

Responding to inquiries from the Navy Department on the mortar boats, Flag Officer Foote wrote: "I am aware that an officer of great resources can overcome almost insuperable difficulties." Foote had the enormous problem of being thrown into a region without naval bases or the usual resources of the seacoast. In his own words, the western rivers area was "this wilderness of naval wants".*

Having sent similar orders the previous day to U.S.S. *Henry Brinker*, Flag Officer L. M. Goldsborough ordered U.S.S. *Delaware, Philadelphia, Hunchback, Morse, Southfield, Commodore Barney, Commodore Perry*, and schooner *Howard* to Hatteras Inlet as the build up of forces in the area for the assault on Roanoke Island continued.

12 Union amphibious expedition to Roanoke Island, North Carolina, departed Fort Monroe under Flag Officer L. M. Goldsborough and General Burnside. Seizure of Hatteras Inlet by the Navy the previous August allowed Federal control of Pamlico Sound, but heavily fortified Roanoke

---

* Foote's long report revealed some of these. In this part of the *Chronology*, a larger portion of the problems he met in outfitting and manning his ships is detailed than those of commanders in other areas. They had the same type of difficulties, however, for there is never enough of anything, except trouble, in the transition from a peace to war economy.

Island dominated the narrow connection between Pamlico and Albemarle Sounds, the latter of which Confederates used for active blockade running. Capture of strategic Roanoke Island, which one Confederate general termed "that post which I regard as the very key of the rear defenses of Norfolk and the navy yard," would give the Union control of Albemarle Sound and the waters penetrating deeply into North Carolina, over which passed important railroad bridges south of Norfolk.

U.S.S. *Pensacola*, Captain Henry W. Morris, successfully ran down the Potomac past the Confederate batteries at Cockpit and Shipping Points. *Pensacola* reached Hampton Roads on 13 January, demonstrating that the restriction of travel on the river, imposed by the Confederate batteries, was being steadily lessened.

13 Lieutenant Worden ordered to command U.S.S. *Monitor*. Three days later Worden wrote Secretary of the Navy Welles from New York: ". . . I have this day reported for duty for the command of the U.S. Steamer building by Captain Ericsson." Within two months, *Monitor*, Worden, and Ericsson were to have their names written indelibly in the annals of naval warfare.

Flag Officer Foote ordered three gunboats up the Cumberland and two up the Tennessee River on demonstrations.

15 Flag Officer Foote advised Lieutenant Paulding of U.S.S. *St. Louis*, "I must enjoin you to save your ammunition. No gun must be fired without your order . . . You will be particular in noting the range of the first shot, its heighth and distance. I was surprised yesterday, at Columbus, to see three or four of your shells bursting at such an elevation . . . I am aware of your difficulties in a new and undisciplined crew and officers, but make these criticisms rather as indicative of correcting things in the future. Save your ammunition and let the first gun show you how to aim for the second." Foote was constantly beset with the problem of having too much to do with too little material, even to the point of being unable to train adequately his crews in gunnery. That he met these difficulties successfully, however, was demonstrated in the Union's steady sweep down the western rivers.

Major General Mansfield Lovell, CSA, at the request of Confederate Secretary of War Benjamin, with the assistance of Lieutenant Thomas B. Huger, CSN, took over 14 steamers at New Orleans to be armed and used to bolster defenses in the area. The plan which came from the War Department was to outfit the steamships with iron rams to attack the Union river gunboats. Secretary of War Benjamin wrote: "Each Captain will ship his own crew, fit up his own vessel, and get ready within the shortest possible delay. It is not proposed to rely on cannons, which these men are not skilled in using, nor on firearms. The men will be armed with cutlasses. On each boat, however, there will be one heavy gun, to be used in case the stern of any of the [Union] gunboats should be exposed to fire, for they are entirely unprotected behind, and if attempting to escape by flight would be very vulnerable by shot from a pursuing vessel."

16 Gunfire and boat crews, including Marines, from U.S.S. *Hatteras*, Commander Emmons, destroyed a Confederate battery, seven small vessels loaded with cotton and turpentine ready to run the blockade, a railroad depot and wharf, and the telegraph office at Cedar Keys, Florida. A small detachment of Confederate troops was taken prisoner. Such unceasing attack from the sea on any point of her long coastline and inland waterways cost the South sorely in losses, economic disruption, and dispersion of strength in defense.

Flag Officer Foote reported: "The seven gunboats built by contract were put in commission today." The Eads gunboats augmented Foote's wooden force and would turn the tide in the Union's effort to split the Confederacy.

U.S.S. *Albatross*, Commander Prentiss, destroyed British blockade runner *York* near Bogue Inlet, North Carolina, where *York* had been run aground.

17 U.S.S. *Conestoga*, Lieutenant S. L. Phelps, and U.S.S. *Lexington*, Lieutenant Shirk, reconnoitered the Tennessee River below Fort Henry, attempting to determine the location of a reported "masked battery" at the foot of Panther Creek Island. Having become convinced that the battery had been removed, Phelps fired "a few shells" at the fort, but the range was too great for his guns to reach. ". . . our batteries," reported General Albert S. Johnston, CSA, "though ready, did not reply." As early as October 1861, the Navy had initiated a careful examination of the Confederate works in the area in preparation for the projected Army-Navy assault on Fort Henry. Lieutenant Phelps reported the results of a 5 October reconnaissance: "I examined the fort [Henry] carefully at a distance of from 2 to 2½ miles . . . The fortification is quite an extensive work and armed with heavy guns, mounted en barbette, and garrisoned by a considerable force. It is situated about 1½ miles above the head of Panther Creek Island . . . There is no channel upon one side of the island, and a narrow and somewhat crooked one upon the other, which continues so till within a mile of the fort, where the water becomes of a good depth from bank to bank, some 600 yards." Detailed knowledge and careful preparations in large measure provided for the ultimate success of the February offensive operations against both Forts Henry and Donelson with the objective of driving the Confederates out of Kentucky where they held a line across the southern part of the state.

General Robert E. Lee's orders to Brigadier General James H. Trapier, commanding in Florida, illustrated the growing impact of the Union blockade: "Arrangements have been made for running into Mosquito Inlet, on the east coast of Florida, arms and ammunition, by means of small fast steamers. The department considers it necessary that at least two moderate sized guns be placed at New Smyrna, to protect the landing in the event of our steamers being chased by the enemy's gunboats. . . . The cargoes of the steamers are so valuable and vitally important, that no precaution should be omitted."

U.S.S. *Connecticut*, Commander Woodhull, captured blockade running British schooner *Emma* off the Florida Keys.

18 U.S.S. *Midnight*, Lieutenant James Trathen, and U.S.S. *Rachel Seaman*, Acting Master Quincy A. Hooper, shelled Velasco, Texas. Lieutenant Trathen reported that "One object had been gained in this instance, making the enemy expend his ammunition." Colonel Joseph Bates, commanding at Velasco, wrote: "While the enemy remain on their vessels, with their long-range guns, &c., they can annoy and harass us, but when they come on land we will whip them certain."

C.S.S. *Sumter*, Commander Semmes, captured and burned bark *Neapolitan*, with cargo of fruit and sulphur, in the Straits of Gibraltar and captured and bonded bark *Investigator* with cargo of iron. U.S.S. *Kearsarge* was ordered to Cadiz, Spain, in an effort to track her down.

19 U.S.S. *Itasca*, Lieutenant Charles H. B. Caldwell, captured schooner *Lizzie Weston* off Florida en route Jamaica with cargo of cotton.

20 Secretary of the Navy Welles ordered the Gulf Blockading Squadron divided into two squadrons upon the arrival of Farragut at Key West: Eastern Gulf Blockading Squadron, Flag Officer McKean, and Western Gulf Blockading Squadron, Flag Officer Farragut. Farragut's area of responsibility began on the Florida coast at the mouth of the Choctawhatchee River and extended over the Gulf to the west; McKean's jurisdiction covered the Florida Gulf and east coasts as far as Cape Canaveral and also included Cuba and the Bahamas.

Boarding party from U.S.S. *R. R. Cuyler*, Lieutenant F. Winslow, assisted by U.S.S. *Huntsville* and two cutters from U.S.S. *Potomac*, captured blockade running schooner *J. W. Wilder*, grounded about 15 miles east of Mobile.

Flag Officer L. M. Goldsborough, having arrived at Hatteras Inlet on 13 January, ordered Commander Rowan to be certain that all officers in the squadron had been instructed in the use of the

C.S.S. Sumter *under Commander Raphael Semmes captures Union merchantman as the South strikes back against Northern commerce.*

Bormann fuze in the 9-inch schrapnel shells, which were to be used in the attack on Roanoke Island. Careful planning and training were essential elements of victory at Roanoke Island as elsewhere.

20–21 C.S.S. *Sea Bird*, Flag Officer Lynch, with C.S.S. *Raleigh* in company, reconnoitered Hatteras Inlet and "there saw a large fleet of steamers and transports." Lynch pointed out in a letter to Confederate Secretary of the Navy Mallory the importance of the area which Roanoke Island controlled: "Here is the great thoroughfare from Albemarle Sound and its tributaries, and if the enemy obtain lodgments or succeed in passing here he will cut off a very rich country from Norfolk market."

21 Lieutenant S. L. Phelps, on the basis of his own reconnaissance missions and intelligence reports reaching him, re-emphasized the advisability of using mortar boats at Fort Donelson, noting that "the position of Fort Donelson is favorable for the greatest effect of bombshells, both in and about it. Effective mortar boats must prove the most destructive adversaries earth forts can have to contend with." However, Flag Officer Foote, urged into early action by the Army commanders, was unable to use mortar boats to "soften up" the Confederate works at Donelson.

U.S.S. *Ethan Allen*, Acting Lieutenant William B. Eaton, captured schooner *Olive Branch* bound from Cedar Keys, Florida, to Nassau with cargo of turpentine.

22 U.S.S. *Lexington*, Lieutenant Shirk, with Brigadier General Charles F. Smith on board, conducted one of the frequent gunboat reconnaissances up the Tennessee River, and fired a few long-range shots at Fort Henry. The rising waters were making operations feasible as the new armored gunboats were becoming available. Shirk reported: "The river is so full at present (and is still rising) that whenever there is water there is a channel."

Lieutenant Worden reported the steady progress toward completion of U.S.S. *Monitor*. Awaiting the 11-inch guns which would make up the ironclad's battery, Worden noted that "It will take four or five days to sight them after they arrive."

Obstructions in Charleston Harbor—Union forces sank "stone fleets" to strengthen the blockade . . .

II–10

23 Flag Officer L. M. Goldsborough wrote from Hatteras Inlet that the 17 naval vessels present (two others reported later) for the Roanoke Island expedition were over the bar inside Pamlico Sound. Bad weather and the shallow, tortuous channel, which Goldsborough termed "this perplexing gut," delayed entry of the naval vessels into the Sound, and presented extreme difficulties when attempting to get the heavily-laden troop transports over the bar.

Flag Officer Foote sent another insistent plea for men to Secretary of the Navy Welles, this time cutting his needs to the bone: "Can we have 600 men? Army officers object to their men shipping. Boats, except the *Benton*, are in commission waiting for men." Twelve days later, Assistant Secretary of the Navy Fox wired Foote: "The Secretary of War today gave directions to detail from several Massachusetts regiments those soldiers who have been seamen up to the number of 600. These will be sent to you without arms or officers in detachments of 100, commencing next Monday."

Schooner *Samuel Rotan*, tender to U.S.S. *Colorado*, Captain Bailey, captured steamer *Calhoun* in East Bay, Mississippi River, with cargo of powder, coffee, and chemicals.

24 U.S.S. *Mercedita*, Commander Stellwagen, and other ships of the Gulf Blockading Squadron chased aground schooner *Julia* and an unidentified bark attempting to run the blockade at the mouth of the Mississippi River; both were laden with cotton and were burned to prevent capture.
A Union lightboat off Cape Henry went aground and was captured by Confederates.

25 Flag Officer French Forrest, CSN, commanding the Navy Yard at Norfolk, wrote Major General Huger: "I have just learned that one of the enemy's vessels has been driven ashore with several

and Confederates planted torpedoes as a lethal menace to the blockading ships.

hundred gallons of oil on board . . . We are without oil for the *Merrimack*, and the importance of supplying this deficiency is too obvious for me to urge anthing more in its support." As was true throughout the economy of the blockaded Confederacy, lack of critical supplies delayed the construction of the ironclad ram.

Secretary of the Navy Welles wrote Flag Officer Du Pont, commanding the South Atlantic Blockading Squadron: "The importance of a rigorous blockade at every point under your command can not be too strongly impressed or felt. By cutting off all communication we not only distress and cripple the States in insurrection, but by an effective blockade we destroy any excuse or pretext on the part of foreign governments to aid and relieve those who are waging war upon the Government."

U.S.S. *Arthur*, Acting Lieutenant John W. Kittredge, captured schooner *J. J. McNeil* off Pass Cavallo, Texas.

26 The second "stone fleet" sunk in Charleston harbor at Maffitt's Channel. The first "stone fleet" had been sunk in the Main Channel on 20 December 1861.

26–29 Union squadron commanded by Captain Davis, comprising U.S.S. *Ottawa*, *Seneca*, and other vessels, with 2400 troops under Brigadier General Horatio G. Wright conducted a strategic reconnaissance of Wassaw Sound, Georgia. Telegraph lines between Fort Pulaski and Savannah were severed. Five Confederate gunboats under Commodore Tattnall were engaged while attempting to carry stores to Fort Pulaski. Though the exchange of fire was sharp, three of Tattnall's steamers made good their passage to the fort, the other two being unable to get through. In his report of the reconnaissance operation, Captain Davis noted: "As a demonstration the appearance of the naval and military forces in Wilmington and Wassaw Sound has had complete success. Savannah was thrown into a state of great alarm, and all the energies of the place have been exerted to the utmost to increase its military defenses, for which purpose troops have been withdrawn from other places." On the Confederate side, General Robert E. Lee commented: "If the enemy succeeds in removing the obstacles [in Wall's Cut and Wilmington Narrows] there is nothing to prevent their reaching the Savannah River, and we have nothing afloat that can contend against them."

Constantly probing and attacking along the South Atlantic coast, part of Flag Officer Du Pont's squadron enters Wassaw Sound to reconnoiter above Fort Pulaski.

BUREAU OF ORDNANCE AND HYDROGRAPHY,
NAVY DEPARTMENT,
Washington City, January 27, 1862.

MY DEAR FOOTE: I have yours of the 22d and rely upon it that your services, almost superhuman as they are and have been, are not only appreciated by me, but by all your friends around us, from the President down; and let me add that the mistake of Hitchcock's naval career has been his declension of your command; and now, although he is trying hard to get a ship, he will never get one.

With reference to the mortar rafts, Uncle Abe, as you already know, has gone into that business with a will, making his first demonstration, *entre nous*, by pitching General Ripley out of his Ordnance Bureau. I have told him how the work can be done expeditiously, and take my word for it, my friend, that the wires have not ceased vibrating since, nor will they until the thing is done.

Yesterday a. m. came your second telegram, which I immediately sent to the White House, and in the evening I was with him for two hours, and Meigs will be instructed to-day to carry out your views about either buying or chartering a steamer and also with reference to the suggestions you make for the *Benton*.

I have carefully studied the plans of the mortar rafts, and quite agree with you that they will be shaken to pieces by the mortars. However, the way to decide as to their strength would be to mount a mortar on one of the staunchest and fire twenty or thirty rounds, and the result will be conclusive one way or the other.

I send you a paper showing the manner the mortars are arranged on board Porter's vessels, where they work beautifully, and as your log boats will be fitted similarly the sketch may prove of interest.

With reference to the men you require, Fox told me they had been ordered, but since there has been some unexpected hitch, which shall be cleared up the moment I see the President to-night.

Be certain that I shall do all I can for you, come fair weather or foul, and I make no doubt, nor ever have, but that the whole thing will redound to your reputation and honor.

*   *   *   *   *   *   *

Yours, faithfully,

H. A. WISE.

Lieutenant Wise writes Flag Officer Foote of President Lincoln's deep personal interest in the naval operations on the western waters. (Extracted from Official Records of the Union and Confederate Navies in the War of the Rebellion, Series I, Volume 22.)

28 Flag Officer Foote wrote Major General Halleck: "General Grant and myself are of the opinion that Fort Henry, on the Tennessee River, can be carried with four gunboats and troops and be permanently occupied." Halleck replied the next day that he was waiting only for a report on the condition of the road from Smithland to the fort, and would then give the order for the attack. Seeking to push forward, Foote hurried an answer the same day, noting: "Lieutenant Phelps has been with me [at Cairo] for a day or two, and in consultation with General Grant we have come to the conclusion that, as the Tennessee will soon fall, the movement up that river is desirable early next week (Monday), or, in fact, as soon as possible." Flag Officer Foote and General Grant worked closely and cooperated fully with each other throughout the planning and preparations for the attack. Though inclement weather was to prevent Grant and his troops from taking part in the action at Fort Henry, the understandings and mutual respect formed here were to serve the Union cause brilliantly in other joint operations on the western waters as well as in General Grant's later campaigns in the east.

"On the 28th . . ." Flag Officer L. M. Goldsborough reported to Secretary of the Navy Welles, "all the vessels composing the naval branch of our combined expedition, intended by my arrangements to participate in the reduction of Roanoke Island and operate elsewhere in its vicinity, were over the bulkhead at Hatteras Inlet and in readiness for service, but . . . it was not until the 5th [of February] . . . that those composing the army branch of it were similarly situated." Goldsborough, however, used the time lapse to good advantage: "During our detention at the inlet," he wrote, "we resorted to every means in our power to get accurate information of the enemy's position and preparation . . ."

Captain John Marston wrote Secretary of the Navy Welles that "as long as the *Merrimack* is held as a rod over us, I would by no means recommend that she [U.S.S. *Congress*] should leave this place." Marston wrote in reply to a letter from the Secretary four days earlier in which he had suggested that *Congress* should go to Boston. Varying rumors as to the readiness of *Virginia* (ex-*Merrimack*) kept Union blockading forces in Hampton Roads in a constant state of vigilance.

Boat crews under Acting Master William L. Martine from U.S.S. *De Soto* boarded and captured blockade runner *Major Barbour* at Isle Derniere, Louisiana, with cargo including gunpowder, niter, sulphur, percussion caps, and lead.

29 U.S. Storeship *Supply*, Commander George M. Colvocoresses, captured schooner *Stephen Hart* south of Sarasota, Florida, with cargo of arms and munitions.

30 U.S.S. *Monitor*, the Union's first sea-going ironclad vessel, launched at Greenpoint, New York. Assistant Secretary of the Navy Fox wired John Ericsson, referring to *Monitor's* launching: "I congratulate you and trust she will be a success. Hurry her for sea, as the *Merrimack* is nearly ready at Norfolk, and we wish to send her here."

Major General Halleck ordered the combined operation up the Tennessee, warned General Grant that the roads were quagmires, and directed that the movement of troops, munitions, and supplies be convoyed by gunboats.

U.S.S. *Conestoga*, Lieutenant S. L. Phelps, and U.S.S. *Lexington*, Lieutenant Shirk, reconnoitered the Tennessee River, making final preparations for the attack on Fort Henry. Phelps, who performed yeoman service on the western waters, reported: "In the right channel, and near the foot of the island, are numerous buoys, evidently marking the location of some kind of explosive machine or obstruction; these I think we can rake out with our boats."

U.S.S. *Kingfisher*, Acting Lieutenant Joseph P. Couthouy, captured blockade runner *Teresita*, bound from Havana to Matamoras.

Confederate Commissioners Mason and Slidell arrived at Southampton, England.

31 Lieutenant Henry A. Wise wrote Flag Officer Foote regarding a conversation with President Lincoln on the western operations. The Commander in Chief was interested in the mortars because he wanted Foote to have enough gunpower "to rain the rebels out." Wise stated: "He is an evidently practical man, understands precisely what he wants, and is not turned aside by anyone when he has his work before him. He knows and appreciates your past and present arduous services, and is firmly resolved to afford you every aid in the work in hand. The additional smooth howitzers you asked for were ordered two days ago." Meanwhile, Foote telegraphed the Bureau of Ordnance, requesting powder and primers. He added: "I am apprehensive that the Army will not permit the men, as the colonels and captains do not readily give their assent. I am shipping men by 'runners at Chicago and elsewhere.' I can move with four armed [armored] and three other gunboats at any moment, and am only waiting for men (with the exception of the *Benton*) to be ready with all the gunboats." The Army could not be blamed, as Foote well understood, for reluctance to weaken its units. They, too, had been given jobs to do and had to present trained, effective units in the hour of need.

A British memorandum reaching the Confederacy, regarding the effectiveness of the Union blockade and sinking of the stone fleet in Charleston harbor, presented the views of various European nations: "About 10 days ago the English foreign office submitted the two following questions to the maritime powers of Europe: First. Is the sinking of the stone fleet. . .an outrage on civilization? Second. Is the blockade effective . . . Is it now binding? France . . . pronounces the destruction of the harbor . . . 'vindictive vandalism' . . . the blockade to be 'ineffective and illegal' . . . Prussia winds up by declaring the sinking of the stone fleet to be a crime and outrage on civilization . . . Sardinia agrees with France, but . . . in even stronger terms . . . Austria declares 'blockade altogether illegal' . . . Spain declares blockade . . . 'altogether ineffective' . . ." On the other hand, Secretary of the Navy Welles strongly maintained that the effectiveness of the blockade did "destroy any pretext on the part of foreign governments to aid the Confederacy."

FEBRUARY

1 Flag Officer Foote telegraphed Washington from Cairo: "I leave early to-morrow with four armored gunboats on an expedition cooperating with the Army. Senior officer will telegraph you during my absence. Nothing new about the mortars. Twenty-nine men shipped from regiments yesterday and three to-day."

U.S.S. *Portsmouth*, Commander Swartwout, captured blockade running steamer *Labuan* at the mouth of the Rio Grande River with cargo of cotton.

U.S.S. *Montgomery*, Lieutenant Jouett, captured schooner *Isabel* in the Gulf of Mexico.

2 U.S.S. *Hartford*, Flag Officer Farragut, departed Hampton Roads for Ship Island, Mississippi, where Farragut took command of the Western Gulf Blockading Squadron preparatory to the assault on New Orleans.

In his battle plan and orders to gunboats, Flag Officer Foote emphasized the need for coolness and precision of fire: "Let it be also distinctly impressed upon the mind of every man firing a gun that, while the first shot may be either of too much elevation or too little, there is no excuse for a second wild fire, as the first will indicate the inaccuracy of the aim of the gun, which must be elevated or depressed, or trained, as circumstances require. Let it be reiterated that random firing is not only a mere waste of ammunition, but, what is far worse, it encourages the enemy when he sees shot and shell falling harmlessly about and beyond him . . . The Commander in Chief has every confidence in the spirit and valor of officers and men under his command, and his only solicitude arises lest the firing should be too rapid for precision, and that coolness and order, so essential to complete success, should not be observed, and hence he has in this general

CAIRO, *January 28, 1862.*

General Grant and myself are of the opinion that Fort Henry, on the Tennessee River, can be carried with four ironclad gunboats and troops, and be permanently occupied. Have we your authority to move for that purpose when ready?

A. H. FOOTE,
Flag-Officer.

Major-General HALLECK.

NOTE.—I made the proposition to move on Fort Henry first to General Grant.

ST. LOUIS, [*January*] *29, 1862.*

I am waiting for General Smith's report on road from Smithland to Fort Henry. As soon as that is received will give order. Meantime, have everything ready.

H. W. HALLECK,
Major-General.

Commodore FOOTE,
Cairo.

CAIRO, *January 29, 1862.*

GENERAL: I have just received your telegram in relation to Fort Henry and will be ready with four ironclad boats early on Saturday. Lieutenant Commanding Phelps has been with me for a day or two, and in consultation with General Grant we have come to the conclusion that, as the Tennessee will soon fall, the movement up that river is desirable early next week (Monday), or, in fact, as soon as possible.

Four mortars and beds are en route from Pittsburg and more will soon be forwarded.

I send Lieutenant Prichett with orders to report to you, agreeable to your suggestion to General Grant.

I have the honor to be, your obedient servant,

A. H. FOOTE,
Flag-Officer.

Major-General HALLECK,
Commanding Army of the West, St. Louis, Mo.

P. S.—The roads are said to be good from Paducah to Fort Henry, even at this season.

A. H. FOOTE.

Flag Officer Foote and General Grant urge the combined attack on Fort Henry. (Extracts from Official Records of the Union and Confederate Navies in the War of the Rebellion, Series I, Volume 22.)

order expressed his views, which must be observed by all under his command." He directed Lieutenant S. L. Phelps, upon the surrender of Fort Henry, to proceed with "*Conestoga, Tyler,* and *Lexington* up the river to where the railroad bridge crosses, and, if the army shall not already have got possession, he will destroy so much of the track as will entirely prevent its use by the rebels. He will then proceed as far up the river as the stage of water will admit and capture the enemy's gunboats and other vessels which might prove available to the enemy."

3 Having left his headquarters at Cairo on 2 February en route Fort Henry, Flag Officer Foote ordered U.S.S. *Essex* and *St. Louis* to proceed from Paducah to Pine Bluff, 65 miles up the Tennessee, "for the purpose of protecting the landing of the troops on their arrival at that point." The Army commanders had recognized for some time that the mobility and fire power of the gunboats were vital in support of land forces operating along the rivers. Brigadier General C. F. Smith had well expressed this earlier: "The *Conestoga,* gunboat, admirably commanded by Lieutenant Phelps of the Navy, is my only security in this quarter. He is constantly moving his vessel up and down the Tennessee and Cumberland." The same day, Foote wrote Secretary of the Navy Welles that he would have had more ships to take against the fort but for want of men. "The volunteers from the Army to go in the gunboats exceed the number of men required, but the derangement of companies and regiments" had permitted few to transfer afloat. Major General Halleck wired Foote from St. Louis: "General Grant is authorized to furnish men for temporary gunboat duty by detail. Men will be sent from here as soon as collected. Arrange with General Grant for temporary crews, so that there may be no delay." The following day, Commander Kilty, left in charge of naval matters at Cairo by Foote, advised Halleck that permanent details were needed, not temporary ones. Grant advised Halleck: "Will be off up the Tennessee at 6 o'clock. Command, 23 regiments in all." Grant's troops embarked in transports at Cairo and Paducah; Foote's gunboats took the lead. Behind this spearhead and battering ram, the dismemberment of the South began.

C.S.S. *Nashville,* Lieutenant Robert B. Pegram, departed Southampton, England. H.M.S. *Shannon* stood by to enforce the Admiralty ruling that U.S.S. *Tuscarora* could not leave the port for twenty-four hours after the sailing of *Nashville.*

4 Brigadier General Lloyd Tilghman, gallant defender of Fort Henry, informed General John B. Floyd: "Gunboats and transports in Tennessee River. Enemy landing in force 5 miles below Fort Henry." After initiating the debarkation of troops below Fort Henry, Flag Officer Foote, in U.S.S. *Cincinnati* with General Grant on board, took the four ironclad gunboats that he had been able to man up the Tennessee for reconnoitering, and exchanged shots with the Confederate gunners. Torpedoes, planted in the river but torn loose by the flooding waters, floated by. Foote had some fished out for inspection. He and Grant went aft to watch the disassembling of one. According to a reminiscence, suddenly there was a strange hiss. The deck was rapidly cleared. Grant beat Foote to the top of the ladder. When Foote asked the General about his hurry, Grant replied that "the Army did not believe in letting the Navy get ahead of it."

5 U.S.S. *Keystone State,* Commander William E. Le Roy, captured British blockade runner *Mars* with cargo of salt off Fernandina, Florida.

6 Naval forces under Flag Officer Foote, comprising the partially ironclad gunboats U.S.S. *Essex, Carondelet, Cincinnati, St. Louis* and wooden gunboats U.S.S. *Tyler, Conestoga,* and *Lexington,* captured strategic Fort Henry on the Tennessee River. Originally planned as a joint expedition under Flag Officer Foote and General Grant, heavy rains the two days before the attack delayed the troop movements, and the gunboats attacked alone. Accurate fire from the gunboats pounded the fort and forced Brigadier General Tilghman, CSA, with all but four of his defending guns useless, to strike his flag and surrender to Foote. U.S.S. *Essex,* Commander W. D. Porter, was disabled during the engagement. In continuing operations the three days following the capitulation of Fort Henry, U.S.S. *Tyler, Conestoga,* and *Lexington,* under Lieutenant S. L. Phelps, swept

the Tennessee for Confederate transports, seized the unfinished steamer *Eastport*, and destroyed a railroad bridge spanning the river. Leaving *Carondelet* on station as guardship, Foote proceeded the evening of the 6th with the three other ironclads, all damaged, to Cairo to direct preparation for the assault on Fort Donelson. He saw the vast possibilities in breaching the Confederate defenses at the center. From far up in Kentucky, south and west to the Mississippi at Columbus, all hung in the balance. Fort Donelson would open the second door for the flood of Union power to sweep into the South. With the center broken, collapse would follow. The significant possibilities opening for the Union and the disaster awaiting the South had resulted in considerable part not only from Foote's indomitable drive to get the ships ready and to make them effective but also from his bold leadership in action. He indeed deserved Secretary of the Navy Welles' congratulations: "The labor you have performed and the services you have rendered in creating the armed flotilla of gunboats on the Western waters, and in bringing together for effective operation the force which has already earned such renown, can never be overestimated. The Department has observed with no ordinary solicitude the armament that has so suddenly been called into existence, and which, under your well-directed management, has been so gloriously effective." Though the Confederate gunners had fought their weapons well, General Albert S. Johnston, CSA, noted the results of the action: "The capture of that Fort [Henry] by the enemy gives them the control of the navigation of the Tennessee River, and their gunboats are now ascending the river to Florence . . . Should Fort Donelson be taken it will open the route to the enemy to Nashville, giving them the means of breaking the bridges and destroying the ferry-boats on the river as far as navigable."

U.S.S. *Sciota*, Lieutenant Edward Donaldson, captured sloop *Margaret* off Isle au Breton, attempting to run the blockade with cargo of cotton.

C.S.S. *Louisiana* launched at Jefferson City, Louisiana. Delay followed delay in completing the machinery for this large ironclad which would have been a powerful addition to the defense of New Orleans.

7   U.S.S. *Conestoga*, Lieutenant S. L. Phelps, forced Confederates on the Tennessee River to abandon and burn steamers *Samuel Orr*, *Appleton Belle*, and *Lynn Boyd* to prevent their falling into Union hands. *Samuel Orr* was loaded with torpedoes, "which," Phelps observed, "very soon exploded; the second one was freighted with powder, cannon, shot, grape, balls, etc. Fearing an explosion from the fired boats (there were two together), I had stopped at a distance of 1,000 yards; but even there our skylights were broken by the concussion; the light upper deck was raised bodily, doors were forced open, and locks and fastenings everywhere broken. The whole river for half a mile around about was completely beaten up by the falling fragments and the shower of shot, grape, balls, etc."

Brigadier General John A. McClernand, wrote Flag Officer Foote that he was giving the name Fort Foote to the captured Fort Henry. He congratulated the Flag Officer: "As an acknowledgment of the consummate skill with which you brought your gunboats into action yesterday, and of the address and bravery displayed by yourself and your command, I have taken the liberty of giving the late Fort Henry the new and more appropriate name of Fort Foote. Please pardon the liberty I have taken without first securing your concurrence, as I am hardly disposed to do, considering the liberty which you took in capturing the fort yesterday without my cooperation." Meanwhile, Tennessee Governor Isham G. Harris advised Confederate Secretary of War Benjamin from Nashville: "Fort Henry fell yesterday. Memphis and Clarksville Railroad bridge over Tennessee destroyed . . . A large increase of force to defend this [state] from Cumberland Gap to Columbus is an absolute and imperative necessity. If not successfully defended, the injury is irreparable."

U.S.S. *Bohio*, Acting Master William D. Gregory, captured schooner *Eugenie Smith*, en route from Havana to Matamoras.

General Grant's troops having been delayed by heavy rains, Flag Officer Foote's gunboats attack Fort Henry on the Tennessee River alone and compel its surrender—the beginning of the Union's steady sweep down the western waters.

7-8 Joint amphibious expedition under Flag Officer L. M. Goldsborough and Brigadier General Burnside captured Roanoke Island. The Union force departed its anchorage at Hatteras Inlet on 5 February, but was delayed one day en route by foul weather. Naval bombardment of Confederate defenses—especially Fort Bartow at Pork Point—began the morning of 7 February, continuing until dark when the action was broken off. Confederate Flag Officer Lynch, commanding Southern naval forces at Roanoke Island, paid tribute to the accuracy of the Union naval fire when he reported: "The soldiers in the battery [Pork Point] sustained their position under a terrific fire . . . At times the entire battery would be enveloped in the sand and dust thrown up by shot and shell . . . The earthwork . . . was very much cut up . . ." Late in the afternoon, under cover of naval gunfire, General Burnside's troops were landed at Ashby's Point. By 9:00 a.m., 8 February, the attack was resumed, and by 4:00 p.m. the obstructions which had been sunk by the Confederates were cleared sufficiently to permit passage of the Union fleet into Albermarle Sound. At this time the American flag was raised over Pork Point. C.S.S. *Curlew*, disabled during the attack, was destroyed to prevent her capture, and the remainder of the small gunboat fleet under Flag Officer Lynch, able to offer only token, long-range resistance to the Union squadron, withdrew up Pasquotank River (see 10 February). The joint amphibious victory at Roanoke Island, and follow-up operations in the Sounds, cut off Norfolk from its main supply lines, secured the North Carolina coast, and was, as Admiral D. D. Porter later noted, "a great loss to the enemy and one he deeply mourned." The evacuation of Norfolk three months later, caused in part by the loss of Roanoke Island, was a far greater loss. The abandonment of the great industrial navy yard and the destruction of C.S.S. *Virginia* were serious reverses that had far-reaching effect upon the Confederacy's ability to resist at sea.

8 A Confederate gunner captured at Fort Henry made the following statement attesting to the extreme effectiveness of U.S.S. *Carondelet*'s gunfire during the attack: "The center boat, or the boat with the red stripes around the top of her smokestacks, was the boat which caused the greatest execution. It was one of her guns which threw a ball against the muzzle of one of our guns, disabling it for the remainder of the contest. The *Carondelet* (as I subsequently found her name to be) at each shot committed more damage than any other boat. She was the object of our hatred, and many a gun from the fort was leveled at her alone. To her I give more credit than any other boat in capturing one of our strongest places." The success of Flag Officer Foote's armored gunboats spread panic and exaggerated their capabilities in Confederate as well as Union minds. General Johnston wrote in a letter to the Confederate War Department: "The slight resistance at Fort Henry indicates that the best open earthworks are not reliable to meet successfully a vigorous attack of ironclad gunboats." He concluded that Fort Donelson would also fall. This would open the way to Nashville. "The occurence of the misfortune of losing the fort will cut off the communication of the force here under General Hardee from the south bank of the Cumberland. To avoid the disastrous consequences of such an event, I ordered General Hardee yesterday to make, as promptly as it could be done, preparations to fall back to Nashville and cross the river. The movements of the enemy on my right flank would have made a retrograde in that direction to confront the enemy indispensable in a short time. But the probability of having the ferriage of this army corps across the Cumberland intercepted by the gunboats of the enemy admits of no delay in making the movement. Generals Beauregard and Hardee are, equally with myself, impressed with the necessity of withdrawing our force from this line at once."

Captain Buchanan ordered C.S.S. *Patrick Henry*, Commander Tucker, and C.S.S. *Jamestown*, Lieutenant Joseph N. Barney, to be kept in a constant state of readiness "to cooperate with the *Merrimack* when that ship is ready for service."

U.S.S. *Conestoga*, Lieutenant S. L. Phelps, seized steamers *Sallie Wood* and *Muscle* at Chickasaw, Alabama. The Confederates destroyed three other vessels to prevent their capture, bringing the total losses resulting from the fall of Fort Henry to nine.

10 Following the capture of Roanoke Island, a naval flotilla, including embarked Marines, under Commander Rowan in U.S.S. *Delaware*, pursuing Flag Officer Lynch's retiring Confederate naval force up the Pasquotank River, engaged the gunboats and batteries at Elizabeth City, North Carolina. C.S.S. *Ellis* was captured and C.S.S. *Seabird* was sunk; C.S.S. *Black Warrior*, *Fanny*, and *Forrest* were set on fire to avoid capture; the fort and batteries at Cobb's Point were destroyed. Of Commander Rowan's success, Admiral Daniel Ammen later wrote: "Nothing more brilliant in naval 'dash' occured during the entire Civil War than appears in this attack." One example of "dash" was called to Flag Officer L. M. Goldsborough's attention by Commander Rowan. "I would respectfully call your attention to one incident of the engagement which reflects much credit upon a quarter gunner of the *Valley City* and for which Congress has provided rewards in the shape of medals. A shot passed through her magazine and exploded in a locker beyond containing fireworks. The commander, Lieutenant Commander Chaplain, went there to aid in suppressing the fire, where he found John Davis, quarter gunner, seated with commendable coolness on an open barrel of powder as the only means to keep the fire out." For demonstrating such courage, "while at the same time passing powder to provide the division on the upper deck while under fierce enemy fire," Davis was awarded the Congressional Medal of Honor by General Order 11, 3 April 1863.

Flag Officer Foote, amidst repairing battle damages and working feverishly to get other gunboats ready, received repeated requests from Major General Halleck to "send gunboats up the Cumberland. Two will answer if he can send no more. They must precede the transports. I am straining every nerve to send troops to take Dover and Clarksville. Troops are on their way. All we want is gunboats to precede the transports."

Secretary of the Navy Welles forwarded to Commander D. D. Porter the names of 22 sailing vessels and 7 steamers which would comprise the Mortar Flotilla. This potent force, to which would be added U.S.S. *Owasco*," as soon as she can be got ready," conducted an intensive bombardment of Forts Jackson and St. Philip, preparatory to Flag Officer Farragut's drive past these heavy works to New Orleans.

General Robert E. Lee wrote Confederate Secretary of War Benjamin: "From the reports of General Mercer as to the inability of the batteries of Saint Simon's and Jekyl Islands to withstand the attack of the enemy's fleet, the isolated condition of those islands, and the impossibility of reenforcing him with guns or men, I have given him authority, should he retain that opinion upon a calm review of the whole subject, to act according to his discretion; and, if deemed advisable by him, to withdraw to the mainland, and take there a defensible position for the protection of the country . . ."

Captain Buchanan reported that *Merrimack* had not yet received her crew, "not withstanding all my efforts to procure them from the Army." Shortage of trained seamen restricted the Confederacy's efforts to build naval strength.

Flag Officer Lynch's outgunned Confederate fleet is destroyed by Commander Rowan's naval forces at Elizabeth City, North Carolina, in followup operations after the Union success at Roanoke Island.

11 Flag Officer Foote, foreseeing the realities of the situation into which he was being pulled by the tide of events, wrote Secretary of the Navy Welles: "I leave [Cairo] again to-night with the *Louisville*, *Pittsburg*, and *St. Louis* for the Cumberland River, to cooperate with the army in the attack on Fort Donelson . . . I shall do all in my power to render the gunboats effective in the fight, although they are not properly manned . . . If we could wait ten days, and I had men, I would go with eight mortar boats and six armored boats and conquer." Despite the serious difficulties they faced, Foote and his gunboat fleet made what General Grant was to term admiringly "a gallant attack."

13-15 U.S.S. *Pembina*, Lieutenant John P. Bankhead, discovered a battery of "tin-can" torpedoes (mines) while engaged in sounding Savannah River above the mouth of Wright's River. The mines, only visible at low tide, were connected by wires and moored individually to the bottom. The following day, Bankhead returned and effected the removal of one of the "infernal machines" for purposes of examination. On the 15th, Bankhead "deemed it more prudent to endeavor to sink the remaining ones than to attempt to remove them," and sank the mines by rifle fire. Torpedoes were planted in large numbers in the harbors and rivers of the Confederacy, constituting a major hazard which Union commanders had to consider and reckon with in planning operations.

14 Gunboats U.S.S. *St. Louis*, *Carondelet*, *Louisville*, *Pittsburg*, *Tyler*, and *Conestoga* under Flag Officer Foote joined with General Grant in attacking Fort Donelson on the Cumberland River. Donelson, on high ground, could subject the gunboats to a plunging fire and was a more difficult objective than Fort Henry. Foote did not consider the gunboats properly prepared for the assault on Donelson so soon after the heavy action at Fort Henry; nevertheless, at the "urgent request" of both Grant and General Halleck to reduce the fortifications, Foote moved against the Confederate works. Bitter fire at close range opened on both sides. *St. Louis*, the flagship, was hit fifty-nine times and lost steering control, as did *Louisville*. Both disabled vessels drifted down stream; the gunboat attack was broken off. Flag Officer Foote sustained injuries which forced him to give up command three months later. Fort Donelson surrendered to Grant on 16 February. Major General Lewis Wallace, speaking of the renewed gunboat support on 15 February, summed up the substantial role of the gunboats in the victory: "I recollect yet the positive pleasure the sounds [naval gunfire] gave me . . . the obstinacy and courage of the Commodore . . ." Was the attack "of assistance to us"? "I don't think there is room to question it. It distracted the enemy's attention, and I fully believe it was the gunboats . . . that operated to prevent a general movement of the rebels up the river or across it, the night before the surrender." Coming quickly after the fall of Fort Henry, the capture of Fort Donelson by a combined operation had a heavy impact on both sides. News of the fall of Fort Donelson created great excitement in New Orleans where the press placed much blame on Secretary of the Navy Mallory because "we are so wretchedly helpless on the water." With their positions in Kentucky now untenable, the Confederates had to withdraw, assuring that state to the Union. On the Mississippi, Confederate forces fell back on Island No. 10. Nashville could not be held, and the Union armies were poised to sweep down into the heart of the South.

Armed boat from U.S.S. *Restless*, Acting Lieutenant Edward Conroy, captured and destroyed sloop *Edisto* and schooners *Wandoo*, *Elizabeth*, and *Theodore Stoney* off Bull's Bay, South Carolina; all ships carried heavy cargoes of rice for Charleston.

Confederate ships sank obstructions in Cape Fear River near Fort Caswell, North Carolina, in an effort to block the channel.

U.S.S. *Galena*, experimental seagoing ironclad, launched at Mystic, Connecticut.

15 Four Confederate gunboats under Commodore Tattnall attacked Union batteries at Venus Point, on Savannah River, Georgia, but were forced back to Savannah. Tattnall was attempting to effect the passage of steamer *Ida* from Fort Pulaski to Savannah.

Flag Officer Foote's squadron engages Fort Henry, Tennessee River. Though the gunboats were severely damaged by plunging fire from the fort, they contributed materially to the victory that compelled a Confederate withdrawal along a broad front.

16 Gunboats of Flag Officer Foote's force destroyed the "Tennessee Iron Works" above Dover on the Cumberland River. General McClellan wired Flag Officer Foote from Washington: "Sorry you are wounded. How seriously? Your conduct magnificent. With what force do you return? I send nearly 600 sailors for you to-morrow."

17 Ironclad C.S.S. *Virginia* (ex-U.S.S. *Merrimack*) commissioned, Captain Franklin Buchanan commanding.

Flag Officer Foote informed Secretary of the Navy Welles: "I leave immediately with a view of proceeding to Clarksville with eight mortar boats and two ironclad boats, with the *Conestoga*, wooden boat, as the river is rapidly falling. The other ironclad boats are badly cut up and require extensive repairs. I have sent one of the boats already since my return and ordered a second to follow me, which, with eight mortars, hope to carry Clarksville."

18 U.S.S. *Ethan Allen*, Acting Lieutenant Eaton, entered Clearwater harbor, Florida, and captured schooner *Spitfire* and sloops *Atlanta* and *Caroline*.

19 Confederates evacuated Clarksville, Tennessee. Colonel W. H. Allen, CSA, reported to General Floyd: "Gunboats are coming; they are just below point; can see steamer here. Will try and see how many troops they have before I leave. Lieutenant Brady set bridge on fire, but it is burning very slowly and will probably go out before it falls." Asking in a postscript that any

orders for him be sent "promptly," Allen noted that "I will have to go in a hurry when I go." Union forces under Flag Officer Foote occupied Fort Defiance and took possession of the town. Foote urged an immediate move on Nashville and notified Army headquarters in Cairo: "The Cumberland is in a good stage of water and General Grant and I believe we can take Nashville."

Trial run of two-gun ironclad U.S.S. *Monitor* in New York harbor. Chief Engineer Alban C. Stimers, USN, reported on the various difficulties that were presented during the trial run of *Monitor* and concluded that her speed would be approximately 6 knots, "though Captain Ericsson feels confident of 8."

U.S.S. *Delaware*, Commander Rowan, and U.S.S. *Commodore Perry*, Lieutenant Flusser, on a reconnaissance of the Chowan River, engaged Confederate troops at Winton, North Carolina. The following day Rowan's force covered the landing of Union troops who entered the town, destroying military stores and Confederate troop quarters before re-embarking.

U.S.S. *Brooklyn*, Captain T. T. Craven, and U.S.S. *South Carolina*, Lieutenant Hopkins, captured steamer *Magnolia* in the Gulf of Mexico with large cargo of cotton.

General Robert E. Lee, harassed by the Confederate inability to cope with the guns of the Union fleet, wrote Brigadier General Trapier regarding the defenses of Florida: "In looking at the whole defense of Florida, it becomes important to ascertain what points can probably be held and what points had better be relinquished. The force that the enemy can bring against any position where he can concentrate his floating batteries renders it prudent and proper to withdraw from the islands to the main-land and be prepared to contest his advance into the interior. Where an island offers the best point of defense, and is so connected with the main that its communications cannot be cut off, it may be retained. Otherwise it should be abandoned."

20 Flag Officer Farragut arrived at Ship Island to begin what Secretary of the Navy Welles termed the "most important operation of the war"—the assault on New Orleans. In his instruction of 10 February to the Flag Officer, Welles observed: "If successful, you open the way to the sea for the great West, never again to be closed. The rebellion will be riven in the center, and the flag to which you have been so faithful will recover its supremacy in every State." For some weeks prior to Farragut's arrival, Union forces had been gathering at the Ship Island staging area. As early as 30 December, General Bragg, CSA, had written from Mobile: "The enemy's vessels, some twenty, are below, landing supplies and large bodies of troops on Ship Island." With an inadequate naval force, however, the Confederates were unable to contest the steady build-up of Northern strength.

Major General John E. Wool at Fort Monroe, on hearing a report that Newport News was to be attacked by *Virginia*, wrote Secretary of War Edwin M. Stanton: "We want a larger naval force than we have at present." Meanwhile, the same day, Secretary of the Navy Welles was writing Lieutenant Worden: "Proceed with the U.S.S. *Monitor*, under your command, to Hampton Roads, Virginia . . ."

Brigadier General George W. Cullum, General Halleck's Chief of Staff at Cairo, relayed an urgent message from General McClellan regarding the gunboats to Lieutenant S. L. Phelps: "General McClellan gives most emphatic order to have gun and mortar boats here ready by Monday morning. Must move on Columbus with at least four serviceable gunboats and mortar boats. Only two gunboats at all serviceable here, and but one mortar boat, three being ashore."

Flag Officer L. M. Goldsborough wrote Assistant Secretary of the Navy Fox: "At Washington, and also at Newberne [North Carolina] the obstructions in the river are very formidable, and admirably placed. They consist of a double row of piles thoroughly well driven by steam, and sunken vessels. The rows are at right angles to the shore and parallel with each other. One stretches all the way from the right bank nearly over to the left, and the other all the way from the left bank nearly over to the right, and there is a battery of considerable force on either bank between them; so that attacking vessels must first go bows on to one, and then after passing it, be raked aft by one and forward by the other at the same time." The Confederates sought to reduce the Union Navy's effectiveness by well-placed obstructions, making passage of shore batteries difficult and costly.

Armed boat expedition from U.S.S. *New London*, Lieutenant A. Read, captured 12 small sloops and schooners at Cat Island, Mississippi, suspected of being used as pilot vessels by blockade runners.

U.S.S. *Portsmouth*, Commander Swartwout, captured sloop *Pioneer* off Boca Chica, Texas, with cargo of tobacco.

21 Flag Officer Farragut formally relieved Flag Officer McKean as Commander, Western Gulf Blockading Squadron. As his other ships arrived, he assembled them at the Southeast Pass and sent those whose draft permitted over the bar to conduct the blockade "in the river." Secretary of the Navy Welles had sent Farragut supplementary confidential instructions, spelling out what had been discussed in conference: "When the *Hartford* is in all respects ready for sea, you will proceed to the Gulf of Mexico with all possible dispatch . . . There will be attached to your squadron a fleet of bomb-vessels and armed steamers, enough to manage them," under Commander D. D. Porter. Key West, preserved for the Union by the energy and foresight of naval commanders, would play the key role it has played throughout the United States' history as a naval base, rendezvous and training center for operations east, west, and south. He instructed Farragut to "proceed up the Mississippi River and reduce the defenses which guard the approaches to New Orleans, when you will appear off that city and take possession of it under the guns of your squadron, and hoist the American flag therein, keeping possession until troops can be sent to you . . . There are other operations of minor importance which will commend themselves to your judgement and skill, but which must not be allowed to interfere with the great object in view—the certain capture of the city of New Orleans."

22 Union naval vessels entered Savannah River through Wall's Cut, isolating Fort Pulaski.

U.S.S. Hartford—*Farragut's flagship at New Orleans and Mobile Bay.*

Flag Officer Farragut ordered Coast Survey team to sound the Mississippi passes and to mark out the safest channel.

23 Flag Officer Du Pont wrote Senator James W. Grimes from Iowa, a member of the Committee on Naval Affairs of his departure for continued operations on the South Atlantic Coast: "I am off tomorrow with a large division of my squadron to complete my work on the lower coast, and if God is with us, in some three weeks I hope to hold everything by and inside or outside blockade from Cape Canaveral to Georgetown, S.C." The Confederacy would withdraw inland as a result of Du Pont's efforts.

Flag Officer Foote, with Brigadier General Cullum, reconnoitered the Mississippi River down to Columbus, the anchor of the powerful Confederate defenses. He reported proceeding "with four ironclad boats, two mortar boats and three transports containing 1,000 men." Lieutenant Gwin, in U.S.S. *Tyler*, conducted a reconnaissance of the Tennessee River to Eastport, Mississippi. At Clifton, Tennessee, Gwin seized 1,100 sacks and barrels of flour and some 6,000 bushels of wheat.

24 Captain Buchanan, CSN, ordered to command James River, Virginia, naval defenses, and to fly his flag on board C.S.S. *Virginia*; the squadron consisted of C.S.S. *Virginia*, and the small gunboats C.S.S. *Patrick Henry*, *Jamestown*, *Teaser*, *Raleigh*, and *Beaufort*. In his orders to Buchanan, Secretary of the Navy Mallory added: "The *Virginia* is a novelty in naval construction, is untried, and her powers unknown; and hence the department will not give specific orders as to her attack upon the enemy. Her powers as a ram are regarded as very formidable, and it is hoped you will be able to test them. Like the bayonet charge of infantry, this mode of attack, while the most destructive, will commend iself to you in the present scarcity of ammunition. It is one also that may be rendered destructive at night against the enemy at anchor. Even without guns the ship would, it is believed, be formidable as a ram. Could you pass Old Point and make a dashing cruise in the Potomac as far as Washington, its effect upon the public mind would be important to our cause. The condition of our country, and the painful reverses we have just suffered, demand our utmost exertions; and convinced as I am that the opportunity and the means for striking a decisive blow for our navy are now, for the first time, presented, I congratulate you upon it, and know that your judgment and gallantry will meet all just expectations. Action, prompt and successful just now, would be of serious importance to our cause."

U.S.S. *Harriet Lane*, Lieutenant Jonathan M. Wainwright, captured schooner *Joanna Ward* off the coast of Florida. Wainwright was the grandfather of the General of the same name who was compelled to surrender Bataan in World War II.

25 U.S.S. *Monitor* commissioned in New York, Lieutenant John L. Worden commanding. Captain Dahlgren described *Monitor* as "a mere speck, like a hat on the surface."

U.S.S. *Cairo*, Lieutenant Nathaniel Bryant, arrived at Nashville, convoying seven steam transports with troops under Brigadier General William Nelson, one of two ex-naval officers assigned to duty with the Army. Troops were landed and occupied the Tennessee capital, an important base on the Cumberland River, without opposition. Meanwhile, the demand for the gunboats mounted steadily. From President Lincoln to widely seperated field commanders, everyone recognized their importance. General McClellan wired Major General Halleck: "I learn from telegraph of Commodore Foote to the Navy Department that you have ordered that no gunboats go above Nashville. I think it may greatly facilitate Buell's operations to send a couple at least of the lighter ones to Nashville. Captain Maynadier, Tenth Infantry, will be ordered to Commodore Foote, at his request, as his ordnance officer for mortar boats." With the fall of Forts Henry and Donelson the Confederates retreated precipitously, abandoning strong positions, valuable ordnance, and supplies. Moreover, at Nashville and elsewhere on the river they lost badly needed manufacturing facilities. Flag Officer Foote quoted a Nashville paper as stating: "We had nothing to fear from a land attack, but the gunboats are the devil."

U.S.S. *Kingfisher*, Acting Lieutenant Couthouy, captured blockade runner *Lion* in the Gulf of Mexico after a three day chase.

U.S.S. *Mohican*, Commander Godon, and U.S.S. *Bienville*, Commander Steedman, captured blockade running British schooner *Arrow* off Fernandina, Florida.

U.S.S. *R. B. Forbes*, Acting Lieutenant William Flye, grounded in a gale near Nag's Head, North Carolina, and was ordered destroyed by her commanding officer to prevent her falling to the Confederates. She had been ordered to the mortar flotilla below New Orleans.

26 C.S.S. *Nashville*, Lieutenant Pegram, captured and burned schooner *Robert Gilfillan*, bound from Philadelphia to Haiti with cargo of provisions.

U.S.S. *Bienville*, Commander Steedman, captured schooner *Alert* off St. John's, Florida.

New Orleans "Committee of Safety" reported to President Davis regarding the "most deplorable condition" of the finances of the Navy Department there, stating that it was preventing the enlistment of men and that the "outstanding indebtedness . . . can not be less than $600,000 or $800,000" owing to foundries and machine shops, draymen, and other suppliers, and that for months "a sign has been hanging over the paymaster's office of that department, 'No funds.' " The Committee stated that "unless the proper remedy is at once applied, workmen can no longer be had."

27 Delayed one day by a lack of ammunition for her guns, U.S.S. *Monitor*, Lieutenant Worden, departed the New York Navy Yard for sea, but was compelled to turn back to the Yard because of steering failure. The same day at Norfolk, Flag Officer Forrest, CSN, commanding the Navy Yard, reported that want of gun powder, too, was delaying the readiness of *Virginia* to begin operations against the Union blockading ships.

28 C.S.S. *Nashville*, Lieutenant Pegram, ran the blockade into Beaufort, North Carolina.

MARCH

1 U.S.S. *Tyler*, Lieutenant Gwin, and U.S.S. *Lexington*, Lieutenant Shirk, engaged Confederate forces preparing to strongly fortify Shiloh (Pittsburg Landing), Tennessee. Under cover of the gunboats' cannon, a landing party of sailors and Army sharpshooters was put ashore from armed boats to determine Confederate strength in the area. Flag Officer Foote commended Gwin for his successful "amphibious" attack where several sailors met their death along with their Army comrades. At the same time he added: "But I must give a general order that no commander will land men to make an attack on shore. Our gunboats are to be used as forts, and as they have no more men than are necessary to man the guns, and as the Army must do the shore work, and as the enemy want nothing better than to entice our men on shore and overpower them with superior numbers, the commanders must not operate on shore, but confine themselves to their vessels."

Flag Officer Foote again requested funds to keep the captured *Eastport*. He telegraphed: "I have applied to the Secretary of the Navy to have the rebel gunboat, *Eastport*, lately captured in the Tennessee River, fitted up as a gunboat, with her machinery in and lumber. She can be fitted out for about $20,000, and in three weeks. We want such a fast and powerful boat. Do telegraph about her, as we now have carpenters and cargo ahead on her and she is just what we want. I should run about in her and save time and do good service. Our other ironclad boats are too slow. The *Eastport* was a steamer on the river, and she, being a good boat, would please the West. No reply yet from the Secretary and time is precious." Had the Confederates been able to complete this fine ship, over 100 feet longer than the armored gunboats, before the rise of the rivers enabled the Federal forces to move with such devastating effect, she could well have disrupted the whole series of Union victories and postponed the collapse of Confederate defenses.

U.S.S. *Mount Vernon*, Commander Glisson, captured blockade running British schooner *British Queen* off Wilmington with cargo including salt and coffee.

3   Flag Officer Du Pont, commanding joint amphibious expedition to Fernandina, Florida, reported to Secretary of the Navy Welles that he was "in full posssesion of Cumberland Island and Sound, of Fernandina and Amelia Island, and the river and town of St. Mary's." Confederate defenders were in the process of withdrawing heavy guns inland from the area and offered only token resistance to Du Pont's force. Fort Clinch on Amelia Island, occupied by an armed boat crew from U.S.S. *Ottawa*, had been seized by Confederates at the beginning of the war and was the first fort to be retaken by the Union. Commander Drayton on board *Ottawa* took a moving train under fire near Fernandina, while launches under Commander C. R. P. Rodgers captured steamer *Darlington* with a cargo of military stores. Du Pont had only the highest praise for his association with Brigadier General Wright, commanding the brigade of troops on the expedition: "Our plans of action have been matured by mutual consultation, and have been carried into execution by mutual help." The Fernandina operation placed the entire Georgia coast actually in the possession or under the control of the Union Navy. DuPont wrote Senator Grimes three days later that: "The victory was bloodless, but most complete in results." DuPont also noted that: "The most curious feature of the operations was the chase of a train of cars by a gunboat for one mile and a half—two soldiers were killed, the passengers rushed out in the woods. . . ." The expedition was a prime example of sea-land mobility and of what General Robert E. Lee meant when he said: "Against ordinary numbers we are pretty strong, but against the hosts our enemies seem able to bring everywhere, there is no calculating."

4   Union forces covered by Flag Officer Foote's gunboat flotilla, now driving down the Mississippi, occupied strongly fortified Columbus, Kentucky, which the Confederates had been compelled to evacuate. Foote reported that the reconnaissance by U.S.S. *Cincinnati* and *Louisville* two days earlier had hastened the evacuation, the "rebels leaving quite a number of guns and carriages, ammunition, and large quantity of shot and shell, a considerable number of anchors, and the remnant of chain lately stretched across the river, with a large number of torpedoes." The powerful fort, thought by many to be impregnable, had fallen without a struggle. Brigadier General Cullum wrote: "Columbus, the Gibraltar of the West, is ours and Kentucky is free, thanks to the brilliant strategy of the campaign, by which the enemy's center was pierced at Forts Henry and Donelson, his wings isolated from each other and turned, compelling thus the evacuation of his strongholds at Bowling Green first and now Columbus."

Confederate Secretary of the Navy Mallory summarized his Navy's needs to President Davis: ". . . fifty light-draft and powerful steam propellers, plated with 5-inch hard iron, armed and equipped for service in our own waters, four iron or steel-clad single deck, ten gun frigates of about 2,000 tons, and ten clipper propellers with superior marine engines, both classes of ships designed for deep-sea cruising, 3,000 tons of first-class boiler-plate iron, and 1,000 tons of rod, bolt, and bar iron are means which this Department could immediately employ. We could use with equal advantage 3,000 instructed seamen, and 4,000 ordinary seamen and landsmen, and 2,000 first rate mechanics."

Commander Daniel B. Ridgely, U.S.S. *Santiago de Cuba*, reported the capture of sloop *O.K.* off Cedar Keys, Florida, in February. Proceeding to St. Mark's, Florida, *O.K.* foundered in heavy seas.

5   Flag Officer Foote observed that the gunboats could not immediately attack the Confederate defenses at Island No. 10, down the river from Columbus. "The gunboats have been so much cut up in the late engagements at Forts Henry and Donelson in the pilot houses, hulls, and disabled machinery, that I could not induce the pilots to go in them again in a fight until they are repaired. I regret this, as we ought to move in the quickest possible time, but I have declined doing it, being utterly unprepared, although General Halleck says go, and not wait for repairs; but that can not be done without creating a stampede amongst the pilots and most of the newly made

officers, to say nothing of the disasters which must follow if the rebels fight as they have done of late." Two days later he added other information: "The *Benton* is underway and barely stems the strong current of the Ohio, which is 5 knots per hour in this rise of water, but hope, by putting her between two ironclad steamers to-morrow, she will stem the current and work comparatively well . . . I hope on Wednesday [12 March] to take down seven ironclad gunboats and ten mortar boats to attack Island No. 10 and New Madrid. As the current in the Mississippi is in some places 7 knots per hour, the ironclad boats can hardly return here, therefore we must go well prepared, which detains us longer than even you would imagine necessary from your navy-yard and smooth-water standpoint . . . We are doing our best, but our difficulties and trials are legion."

Flag Officer Farragut issued a general order to the fleet in which he stressed gunnery and damage control training. "I expect every vessel's crew to be well exercised at their guns . . . They must be equally well trained for stopping shot holes and extinguishing fire. Hot and cold shot will no doubt be freely dealt us, and there must be stout hearts and quick hands to extinguish the one and stop the holes of the other."

U.S.S. *Water Witch*, Lieutenant Hughes, captured schooner *William Mallory* off St. Andrew's Bay, Florida.

6 Lieutenant Worden reported U.S.S. *Monitor* had passed over the bar in New York harbor with U.S.S. *Currituck* and *Sachem* in company. "In order to reach Hampton Roads as speedily as possible," Worden wrote Secretary of the Navy Welles, "whilst the fine weather lasts, I have been taken in tow by the tug [*Seth Low*]."

Commander Semmes, C.S.S. *Sumter*, wrote J. M. Mason, Confederate Commissioner in London, " . . . it is quite manifest that there is a combination of all the neutral nations against us in this war and that in consequence we shall be able to accomplish little or nothing outside of our own waters. The fact is, we have got to fight this war out by ourselves, unaided, and that, too, in our own terms . . ." The foreign intervention so much hoped for by the Confederacy was in large measure forestalled by the impressive series of Union naval successes and the effectiveness of the blockade.

U.S.S. *Pursuit*, Acting Lieutenant David Cate, captured schooner *Anna Belle* off Apalachicola, Florida.

8 Ironclad C.S.S. *Virginia*, Captain Buchanan, destroyed wooden blockading ships U.S.S. *Cumberland* and U.S.S. *Congress* in Hampton Roads. *Virginia*, without trials or under way-training, headed directly for the Union squadron. She opened the engagement when less than a mile distant from *Cumberland* and the firing became general from blockaders and shore batteries. *Virginia* rammed *Cumberland* below the waterline and she sank rapidly, "gallantly fighting her guns," Buchanan reported in tribute to a brave foe, "as long as they were above water." Buchanan next turned *Virginia's* fury on *Congress*, hard aground, and set her ablaze with hot shot and incendiary shell. The day was *Virginia's* but it was not without loss. Part of her ram was wrenched off and left imbedded in the side of stricken *Cumberland*, and Buchanan received a wound in the thigh which necessitated his turning over command to Lieutenant Catesby ap R. Jones. Secretary of the Navy Mallory wrote to President Davis of the action: "The conduct of the Officers and men of the squadron . . . reflects unfading honor upon themselves and upon the Navy. The report will be read with deep interest, and its details will not fail to rouse the ardor and nerve the arms of our gallant seamen. It will be remembered that the *Virginia* was a novelty in naval architecture, wholly unlike any ship that ever floated; that her heaviest guns were equal novelties in ordnance; that her motive power and obedience to her helm were untried, and her officers and crew strangers, comparatively, to the ship and to each other; and yet, under all these disadvantages, the dashing courage and consummate professional ability of Flag Officer Buchanan and his associates achieved the most remarkable victory which naval annals record."

C.S.S. Virginia, *Captain Buchanan, rams and sinks wooden blockading ship U.S.S.* Cumberland.

U.S.S. *Monitor*, Lieutenant Worden, arrived in Hampton Roads at night. The stage was set for the dramatic battle with C.S.S. *Virginia* the following day. "Upon the untried endurances of the new *Monitor* and her timely arrival," observed Captain Dahlgren, "did depend the tide of events . . ."

Flag Officer Foote's doctor reported on the busy commander's injury received at Fort Donelson where, as always, he was in the forefront: "Very little, if any, improvement has taken place in consequence of neglect of the main [requirements] of a cure, viz, absolute rest and horizontal position of the whole extremity."

U.S.S. *Bohio*, Acting Master W. D. Gregory, captured schooner *Henry Travers* off Southwest Pass, mouth of the Mississippi River.

9 Engagement lasting four hours took place between U.S.S. *Monitor*, Lieutenant Worden, and C.S.S. *Virginia*, Lieutenant Jones, mostly at close range in Hampton Roads. Although neither side could claim clear victory, this historic first combat between ironclads ushered in a new era of war at sea. The blockade continued intact, but *Virginia* remained as a powerful defender of the Norfolk area and a barrier to the use of the rivers for the movement of Union forces. Severe

damage inflicted on wooden-hulled U.S.S. *Minnesota* by *Virginia* during an interlude in the fight with *Monitor* underscored the plight of a wooden ship confronted by an ironclad. The broad impact of the *Monitor-Virginia* battle on naval thinking was summarized by Captain Levin M. Powell of U.S.S. *Potomac* writing later from Vera Cruz: "The news of the fight between the *Monitor* and the *Merrimac[k]* has created the most profound sensation amongst the professional men in the allied fleet here. They recognize the fact, as much by silence as words, that the face of naval warfare looks the other way now—and the superb frigates and ships of the line . . . supposed capable a month ago, to destroy anything afloat in half an hour . . . are very much diminished in their proportions, and the confidence once reposed in them fully shaken in the presence of these astounding facts." And as Captain Dahlgren phrased it: "Now comes the reign of iron—and cased sloops are to take the place of wooden ships."

Naval force under Commander Godon, consisting of U.S.S. *Mohican*, *Pocahontas*, and *Potomska*, took possession of St. Simon's and Jekyl Islands and landed at Brunswick, Georgia. All locations were found to be abandoned in keeping with the general Confederate withdrawal from the seacoast and coastal islands.

U.S.S. *Pinola*, Lieutenant Crosby, arrived at Ship Island, Mississippi, with prize schooner *Cora*, captured in the Gulf of Mexico.

Landing party from U.S.S. *Anacostia* and *Yankee* of the Potomac Flotilla, Lieutenant Wyman, destroyed abandoned Confederate batteries at Cockpit Point and Evansport, Virginia, and found C.S.S. *Page* blown up.

C.S.S. Virginia *and U.S.S.* Monitor *engage in the historic first action between ironclads which changed the course of naval warfare, Hampton Roads, 9 March 1862.*

10 Amidst the Herculean labors of lightening and dragging heavy ships through the mud of the "19 ft. bar" that turned out to be 15 feet, and organizing the squadron, Flag Officer Farragut reported: "I am up to my eyes in business. The *Brooklyn* is on the bar, and I am getting her off. I have just had Bell up at the head of the passes. My blockading shall be done inside as much as possible. I keep the gunboats up there all the time . . . Success is the only thing listened to in this war, and I know that I must sink or swim by that rule. Two of my best friends have done me a great injury by telling the Department that the *Colorado* can be gotten over the bar into the river, and so I was compelled to try it, and take precious time to do it. If I had been left to myself, I would have been in before this."

Tug U.S.S. *Whitehall*, Acting Master William J. Baulsir, was accidentally destroyed by fire off Fort Monroe.

11 Landing party from U.S.S. *Wabash*, Commander C. R. P. Rodgers, occupied St. Augustine, Florida, which had been evacuated by Confederate troops in the face of the naval threat.

Two Confederate gunboats under construction at the head of Pensacola Bay were burned by Confederate military authorities to prevent their falling into Northern hands in the event of the anticipated move against Pensacola by Union naval forces.

12 Landing party under Lieutenant Thomas H. Stevens of U.S.S. *Ottawa* occupied Jacksonville, Florida, without opposition.

U.S.S. *Gem of the Sea*, Lieutenant Baxter, captured British blockade runner *Fair Play* off Georgetown, South Carolina.

Gunboats U.S.S. *Tyler*, Lieutenant Gwin, and U.S.S. *Lexington*, Lieutenant Shirk, engaged a Confederate battery at Chickasaw, Alabama, while reconnoitering the Tennessee River.

13 Major General John P. McCown, CSA, ordered the evacuation of Confederate troops from New Madrid, Missouri, under cover of Flag Officer Hollins' gunboat squadron consisting of C.S.S. *Livingston*, *Polk*, and *Pontchartrain*.

Flag Officer Foote advised Major General Halleck of the problems presented the partly armored ironclads by an attack downstream, much different difficulties than those encountered going up rivers in Tennessee: "Your instructions to attack Island No. 10 are received, and I shall move for that purpose to-morrow morning. I have made the following telegram to the Navy Department, which you will perceive will lead me to be cautious, and not bring the boats within short range of the enemy's batteries. Generally, in all our attacks down the river, I will bear in mind the effect on this place and the other rivers, which a serious disaster to the gunboats would involve. General Strong is telegraphing Paducah for transports, as there are none at Cairo. The ironclad boats can not be held when anchored by stern in this current on account of the recess between the fantails forming the stern yawing them about, and as the sterns of the boats are not plated, and have but two 32-pounders astern, you will see our difficulty of fighting downstream effectually. Neither is there power enough in any of them to back upstream. We must, therefore, tie up to shore the best way we can and help the mortar boats. I have long since expressed to General Meigs my apprehensions about these boats' defects. Don't have any gunboats for rivers built with wheels amidships. The driftwood would choke the wheel, even if it had a powerful engine. I felt it my duty to state these difficulties, which could not be obviated, when I came here, as the vessels were modeled and partly built."

Commander D. D. Porter reported the arrival of the mortar flotilla at Ship Island, and five days later took them over the bar and into the Mississippi in preparation for the prolonged bombardment of Forts Jackson and St. Philip.

Union gunboats steam up the Neuse River at night, supporting and transporting Army troops in the capture of New Bern, North Carolina.

14 Joint amphibious attack under Commander Rowan and Brigadier General Burnside captured
     Confederate batteries on the Neuse River and occupied New Bern, North Carolina, described by
     Rowan as "an immense depot of army fixtures and manufactures, of shot and shell . . ." Com-
     mander Rowan, with 13 war vessels and transports carrying 12,000 troops, departed his anchorage
     at Hatteras Inlet on 12 March, arriving in sight of New Bern that evening. Landing the troops,
     including Marines, the following day under the protecting guns of his vessels, Rowan continued
     close support of the Army advance throughout the day. The American flag was raised over
     Forts Dixie, Ellis, Thompson, and Lane on 14 March, the "formidable" obstructions in the
     river—including torpedoes—were passed by the gunboats, and troops were transported across
     Trent River to occupy the city. In addition to convoy, close gunfire support, and transport
     operations, the Navy captured two steamers, stores, munitions, and cotton, and supplied a how-
     itzer battery ashore under Lieutenant Roderick S. McCook, USN. Wherever water reached,
     combined operations struck heavy blows that were costly to the Confederacy.

C.W.R. 40

U. S. Iron Clad Steamer "Monitor"
Hampton Roads, March 12, 1862

Sir:

Lieutenant, Commanding John L. Worden
having been disabled in the action of the 9th Inst
between this vessel and the Rebel Iron Clad Frigate
Merrimac, I submit to you the following report.

We arrived at Hampton Roads at 9. P. M.
on the 8th Inst, and immediately received orders from
Captain Marston to proceed to Newport News
and protect the Minnesota from the attack of the
Merrimac. Acting Master Howard came on board
and volunteered to act as Pilot. We left Hampton Roads
at 10 P. M. and reached the Minnesota at 11.30 P. M.
The Minnesota being aground, Capt Worden sent
me on board of her to enquire if we could render her
any assistance, and to state to Capt Van Brunt
that we should do all in our power to protect
her from the attack of the Merrimac.
I then returned to this vessel and, at 1. A. M. on the
9th Inst anchored near the Minnesota. At 4. A. M.
supposing the Minnesota to be afloat and coming
down upon us got underweigh and stood out of the
channel. Finding that we were mistaken, Anchored at
5.30 A. M. At 8 A.M. perceived the Merrimac
underweigh and standing towards the Minnesota
hove up the anchor and went to Quarters,

At 8.45 A.M. we opened fire upon the Merrimac and continued the action untill 11.30 A.M. then Capt Worden was injured in the eyes by the explosion of a shell from the Merrimac upon the outside of the eye hole in the Pilot House. exactly opposite his eye. Capt Worden then sent for me and told me to take charge of the vessel. We continued the action untill 12.15. P.M. when the Merrimac retreated to Sewalls Point.

and we went to the Minnesota and remained by her untill she was afloat

I am Sir, very Respectfully
Your Obedient Servant
S. D. Greene
Lieut. Ex. Officer

Hon Gideon Welles
Secretary of the Navy
Washington D.C.

Lieutenant Samuel Dana Greene of U.S.S. Monitor *reports to Secretary Welles on the historic engagement with C.S.S.* Virginia.

Catesby ap R. Jones
Lieutenant, CSN

John L. Worden
Lieutenant, USN

Flag Officer Foote departed Cairo with seven gunboats (U.S.S. *Louisville* was soon forced to return for repairs) and ten mortar boats to undertake the bombardment of Island No. 10, which stood astride the sweep of Union forces down the Mississippi. Foote wired Major General Halleck: ". . . I consider it unsafe to move without troops to occupy No. 10 if we [naval forces] capture it . . . should we pass No. 10 after its capture, the rebels on the Tennessee side would return and man their batteries and thus shut up the river in our rear . . ."

15 Flag Officer Foote's flotilla moved from Hickman, Kentucky, down river to a position above Island No. 10. Foote reported, "The rain and dense fog prevented our getting the vessels in position [to commence the bombardment] . . ."

Union mortar boats bombarded Confederate river fortifications with telling effect.

16 Union gunboats and mortar boats under Flag Officer Foote commenced bombardment of strongly fortified and strategically located Island No. 10 in the Mississippi River. After the loss of Forts Henry and Donelson, and as General Grant continued to wisely use the mobile force afloat at his disposal, the Confederates fell back on Island No. 10, concentrated artillery and troops, and prepared for an all-out defense of this bastion which dominated the river. Meanwhile, Lieutenant Gwin reported the operations of the wooden gunboats on the Tennessee River into Mississippi and Alabama where they kept constantly active: "I reported to General Grant at Fort Foote on the 7th instant and remained at Danville Bridge, 25 miles above, awaiting the fleet of transports until Monday morning, by direction of General Grant, when, General Smith arriving with a large portion of his command, forty transports, I convoyed them to Savannah, arriving there without molestation on the 11th. The same evening, with General Smith and staff on board, made a reconnaissance of the river as high as Pittsburg. The rebels had not renewed their attempts to fortify at that point, owing to the vigilant watch that had been kept on them in my absence by Lieutenant Commanding Shirk."

U.S.S. *Owasco*, Lieutenant John Guest, captured schooners *Eugenia* and *President* in the Gulf of Mexico with cargoes of cotton.

17 First elements of the Army of the Potomac under General McClellan departed Alexandria, Virginia, for movement by water to Fort Monroe and the Navy-supported Peninsular Campaign aimed at capturing Richmond. His strategy was based on the mobility, flexibility, and massed gunfire support afforded by the Union Navy's control of the Chesapeake; indeed, he was to be saved from annihilation by heavy naval guns.

U.S.S. *Benton*, with Flag Officer Foote on board, was lashed between U.S.S. *Cincinnati* and *St. Louis* to attack Island No. 10 and Confederate batteries on the Tennessee shore at a range of 2,000 yards. "The upper fort," Foote reported, "was badly cut up by the *Benton* and the other boats with her. We dismounted one of their guns . . ." In the attack, Confederate gunners scored hits on *Benton* and damaged the engine of *Cincinnati*. A rifled gun burst on board *St. Louis* and killed or wounded a number of officers and men.

C.S.S. *Nashville*, Lieutenant Pegram, ran the blockade out of Beaufort, North Carolina, through the gunfire of U.S.S. *Cambridge*, Commander W. A. Parker, and U.S.S. *Gemsbok*, Lieutenant Cavendy. News of the escape of *Nashville* caused concern to run high in Washington. Assistant Secretary of the Navy Fox wrote Flag Officer L. M. Goldsborough: "It is a terrible blow to our naval prestige . . . you can have *no* idea of the feeling here. It is a Bull Run of the Navy."

C.S.S. Nashville—*the escape of this commerce raider through the blockade off Beaufort, N.C., caused considerable concern in Washington.*

18 U.S.S. *Florida, James Adger, Sumpter, Flambeau,* and *Onward* captured British blockade runner *Emily St. Pierre* off Charleston. The master and steward, left on board, overpowered prize master Josiah Stone off Cape Hatteras, recaptured the vessel, and sailed to Liverpool, England.

19 Flag Officer Foote's forces attacking Island No. 10 continued to meet with strong resistance from Confederate batteries. "This place, Island No. 10," Foote observed, "is harder to conquer than Columbus, as the island shores are lined with forts, each fort commanding the one above it. We are gradually approaching . . . The mortar shells have done fine execution . . ."

Flag Officer Farragut described the noose of seapower: "I sent over to Biloxi yesterday, and robbed the post-office of a few papers. They speak volumes of discontent. It is no use—the cord is pulling tighter, and I hope I shall be able to tie it. God alone decides the contest; but we must put our shoulders to the wheel."

20 Confederate President Davis wrote regarding the defense of the James River approach to Richmond: "The position of Drewry's Bluff, seven or eight miles below Richmond . . . was chosen to obstruct the river against such vessels as the *Monitor.* The work is being rapidly completed. Either Fort Powhatan or Kennon's Marsh, if found to be the proper positions, will be fortified and obstructed as at Drewry's Bluff, to prevent the ascent of the river by ironclad vessels. Blockading the channel where sufficiently narrow by strong lines of obstructions, filling it with submersive batteries [torpedoes], and flanking the obstructions by well-protected batteries of the heaviest guns, seem to offer the best and speediest chances of protection with the means at our disposal against ironclad floating batteries." The Confederate Navy contributed in large part to these successful defenses that for three years resisted penetration. Naval crews proved especially effective in setting up and manning the big guns, many of which had come from the captured Navy Yard at Norfolk.

21 Major General Halleck wrote Flag Officer Foote, commenting on the Navy's operations against the Confederate batteries guarding Island No. 10: "While I am certain that you have done everything that could be done successfully to reduce these works, I am very glad that you have not unnecessarily exposed your gunboats. If they had been disabled, it would have been a most serious loss to us in the future operations of the campaign . . . Nothing is lost by a little delay there." Foote's gunboat and mortar boat flotilla continued to bombard the works with telling effect.

22 C.S.S. *Florida,* Acting Master John Low, sailing as British steamer *Oreto,* cleared Liverpool, England, for Nassau. The first ship built in England for the Confederacy, *Florida*'s four 7-inch rifled guns were sent separately to Nassau in steamer *Bahama.* Commander Bulloch, CSN, wrote Lieutenant John N. Maffitt, CSN: "Another ship will be ready in about two months . . . Two small ships can do but little in the way of materially turning the tide of war, but we can do something to illustrate the spirit and energy of our people . . ."

General Lovell wrote Secretary of War Benjamin that he had six steamers of the River Defense Fleet to protect New Orleans. Lovell added: "The people of New Orleans thought it strange that all the vessels of the Navy should be sent up the river and were disposed to find fault with sending in addition fourteen steamers leaving this city without a single vessel for protection against the enemy . . ." Confederate officials in Richmond were convinced than the greatest threat to New Orleans would come from upriver rather than from Flag Officer Farragut's force below Forts Jackson and St. Philip.

Boat crew from U.S.S. *Penguin,* Acting Lieutenant T. A. Budd, and U.S.S. *Henry Andrew,* Acting Master Mather, was attacked while reconnoitering Mosquito Inlet, Florida. Budd, Mather, and three others were killed.

Flag Officer Foote's gunboats and mortars attack Island No. 10.

24 Lieutenant Gwin, U.S.S. *Tyler*, reported the typically ceaseless activity of the gunboats: ". . . since my last report, dated March 21, I have been actively employed cruising up and down the river. The *Lexington* arrived this morning. The *Tyler*, accompanied by the *Lexington*, proceeded up the river to a point 2 miles below Eastport, Mississippi, where we discovered the rebels were planting a new battery at an elevation above water of 60 (degrees), consisting of two guns, one apparently in position. We threw several shell into it, but failed to elicit a reply. The battery just below Eastport, consisting of two guns, then opened upon us. Their shot fell short. I stood up just outside of their range and threw three or four 20 [second] shell at that battery, none of which exploded, owing to the very defective fuze (army). The rebels did not respond. I have made no regular attack on their lately constructed batteries, as they are of no importance to us, our base of operations being so much below them. I have deemed it my duty, however, to annoy them, where I could with little or no risk to our gunboats . . . The *Lexington*, Lieutenant Commanding Shirk, will cruise down the river from this point. The *Tyler* will cruise above."

U.S.S. *Pensacola*, towing a chartered schooner into which she had discharged guns and stores at Ship Island, arrived at the mouth of the Mississippi. She grounded and failed on four attempts to cross the bar even though water conditions were favorable and small steamships were towing her through the mud—on one occasion parting a hawser that killed two men and injured others.

25 C.S.S. *Pamlico*, Lieutenant William G. Dozier, and C.S.S. *Oregon*, Acting Master Abraham L. Myers, engaged U.S.S. *New London*, Lieutenant Read, at Pass Christian, Mississippi. The rifled gun on board *Pamlico* jammed during the nearly two hour engagement, and the Confederate vessels broke off the action, neither side having been damaged in the test of the strength of Flag Officer Farragut's gathering forces. Transports with General Butler and troops arrived at Ship Island which, until Pensacola was retaken, became the principal base for operations west of Key West. Flag Officer Farragut wrote: "I am now packed and ready for my departure to the mouth of the Mississippi River . . . I spent last evening very pleasantly with General Butler. He does not appear to have any very difficult plan of operations, but simply to follow in my wake and hold what I can take. God grant that may be all that we attempt . . . victory. If I die in the attempt, it will only be what every officer has to expect. He who dies in doing his duty to his country, and at peace with his God, has played out the drama of life to the best advantage."

Confederate Secretary of the Navy Mallory ordered Flag Officer Tattnall to relieve the injured Flag Officer Buchanan and "take command of the naval defenses on the waters of Virginia and hoist your flag on board the *Virginia*."

Reports of Confederate ironclads on the river disturbed Union commanders far and wide. Major General Halleck wired Flag Officer Foote: "It is stated by men just arrived from New Orleans that the rebels are constructing one or more ironclad river boats to send against your flotilla. Moreover, it is said that they are to be cased with railroad iron like the *Merrimack*. If this is so I think a single boat might destroy your entire flotilla, pass our batteries and sweep the Western rivers. Could any of your gunboats be clad in the same way so as to resist the apprehended danger? If not, how long would it require to build a new one for that purpose? I have telegraphed to the Secretary of War for authority to have any suitable boat altered or prepared; or if there be none suitable, to build a new one. As no time is to be lost, if any one of the gunboats now in service will bear this change it should be taken in preference to building a new one. I shall await your answer. Could not the *Essex* be so altered?" Flag Officer Foote sent Lieutenant Joseph P. Sanford, his ordnance officer, to confer with the General on the subject and replied: "There is no vessel now in the flotilla that can be armored as you suggest. This [*Benton*] is the only one which could bear the additional weight of iron required and she already is so deep and wanting in steam power that it would make her utterly useless with the additional weight of iron. I suggest that a strong boat be fitted up in St. Louis and armored—in fact, two vessels—in the shortest possible manner, with a view of protecting the river at Cairo, or Columbus would do better, if it was fortified with heavy guns sweeping the river below. These boats will require at least a month to be fitted up. As to the place, etc., Lieutenant Sanford will consult with you. Commander Porter of the *Essex*, is also in St. Louis, who is fitting out the *Essex*, and who will remain there for the present. He will attend to the new boats and get them ready in the shortest possible time."

Gunboat U.S.S. *Cairo*, Lieutenant Bryant, seized guns and equipment abandoned by Confederate troops evacuating Fort Zollicoffer, six miles below Nashville.

Gunboat U.S.S. *Cayuga*, Lieutenant Harrison, captured schooner *Jessie J. Cox*, en route from Mobile to Havana with cargo of cotton and turpentine.

26 Flag Officer Foote, off Island No. 10, dispatched a warning to Commander Alexander M. Pennock, his fleet captain at Cairo: "You will inform the commanders of the gunboats *Cairo*, *Tyler*, and *Lexington* not to be caught up the river with too little water to return to Cairo. They, of course, before leaving, will consult the generals with whom they are cooperating. As it is reported on the authority of different persons from New Orleans that the rebels have thirteen gunboats finished and ready to move up the Mississippi, besides the four or five below New Madrid, and the *Manassas*, or ram, at Memphis, the boats now up the rivers and at Columbus or Hickman, should be ready to protect Cairo or Columbus in case disaster overtakes us in our flotilla." Union commanders

in the west and elsewhere recognized how much the margin of Union superiority and the power to thrust deep into the Confederacy depended upon the gunboats, and care was exercised not to lose the effectiveness of this mobile force. Meanwhile, greatly concerned about threats of Confederate naval ironclads, Secretary of War Stanton wired the President of the Board of Trade at Pittsburg: "This Department desires the immediate aid of your association in the following particulars: 1st. That you would appoint three of its active members most familiar with steamboat and engine building who would act in concert with this Department and under its direction, and from patriotic motives devote some time and attention for thirty days in purchasing and preparing such means of defense on the Western waters against ironclad boats as the engineers of this Department may devise . . . My object is to bring the energetic, patriotic spirit and enlightened, practical judgment of your city to aid the Government in a matter of great moment, where hours must count and dollars not be squandered."

Two armed boats from U.S.S. *Delaware*, Lieutenant Stephen P. Quackenbush, captured schooners *Albemarle* and *Lion* at the head of Pantego Creek, North Carolina.

Fort Pitt Iron Works, Pittsburgh, Pennsylvania—the North's industrial capacity and access to raw materials were tremendous advantages.

27 Secretary of War Stanton instructed Engineer Charles Ellet, Jr., "You will please proceed immediately to Pittsburg, Cincinnati, and New Albany and take measures to provide steam rams for defense against ironclad vessels on the Western waters." The next day he wired Ellet at Pittsburg: "General [James K.] Moorhead has gone to Pittsburg to aid you and put you in communication with the committee there. The rebels have a ram at Memphis. Lose no time." Later Stanton described the Ellet rams to General Halleck: "They are the most powerful steamboats, with upper cabins removed, and bows filled in with heavy timber. It is not proposed to wait for putting on iron. This is the mode in which the *Merrimack* will be met. Can you not have something of the kind speedily prepared at St. Louis also?"

Armed boat expedition from U.S.S. *Restless*, Acting Lieutenant Conroy, captured schooner *Julia Worden* off South Carolina, with cargo of rice for Charleston, and burned sloop *Mary Louisa* and schooner *George Washington*.

Flag Officer Du Pont reported to Secretary of the Navy Welles that Confederate batteries on Skiddaway and Green Islands, Georgia, had been withdrawn and placed nearer Savannah, giving Union forces complete control of Wassaw and Ossabaw Sounds and the mouths of the Vernon and Wilmington Rivers, important approaches to the city.

28 Commander Henry H. Bell reported a reconnaissance in U.S.S. *Kennebec* of the Mississippi River and Forts Jackson and St. Philip. He noted that the "two guns from St. Philip reached as far down the river as any from Jackson" and called attention to the obstruction, "consisting of a raft of logs and eight hulks moored abreast," across the river below St. Philip. Scouting missions of this nature enabled Flag Officer Farragut to make the careful and precise plans which ultimately led to the successful passage of the forts and the capture of New Orleans.

Lieutenant Stevens reported his return to Jacksonville with a launch and cutter from U.S.S. *Wabash* and steamers U.S.S. *Darlington* and *Ellen* after raising yacht *America* which had been found sunk by the Confederates earlier in the month far up St. John's River, Florida. Stevens reported that it was "generally believed she was bought by the rebels for the purpose of carrying Slidell and Mason to England."

29 U.S.S. *R. R. Cuyler*, Lieutenant F. Winslow, captured blockade running schooner *Grace E. Baker* off the coast of Cuba.

Boat under command of Acting Master's Mate Henry Eason from U.S.S. *Restless*, captured schooner *Lydia and Mary* with large cargo of rice for Charleston, and destroyed an unnamed schooner in Santee River, South Carolina.

30 Flag Officer Foote ordered Commander Henry Walke, U.S.S. *Carondelet:* "You will avail yourself of the first fog or rainy night and drift your steamer down past the batteries, on the Tennessee shore, and Island No. 10 . . . for the purpose of covering General Pope's army while he crosses that point to the opposite, or to the Tennessee side of the river, that he may move his army up to Island No. 10 and attack the rebels in the rear while we attack them in front." Five days later Walke made his heroic dash past Island No. 10 to join the Army at New Madrid.

APRIL

1 Combined Army-Navy boat expedition under Master John V. Johnston, USN, of gunboat U.S.S. *St. Louis* and Colonel George W. Roberts landed and spiked the guns of Fort No. 1 on the Tennessee shore above Island No. 10, Mississippi River (night of 1–2 April). Colonel Roberts reported: "To the naval officers in command of the boats great praise is due for the admirable manner in which our approach was conducted."

C.S.S. *Gaines*, Commander Hunter, recaptured Confederate schooner *Isabel* off Mobile. *Isabel* had been under tow of U.S.S. *Cayuga*, Lieutenant Harrison, but was cast off in a heavy gale in the Gulf of Mexico.

2 General McClellan and his staff arrived at Fort Monroe on board steamer *Commodore*. In the Peninsular Campaign to capture Richmond, the General intended to take full advantage of Union command of the seas for logistic support and offensive operations. He wrote: "Effective naval cooperation will shorten this operation by weeks." He proposed to outflank Confederate defenders by water movements up the James and York Rivers supported by the Navy. The ominous presence of C.S.S. *Virginia* at the mouth of the James River dictated that Flag Officer L. M. Goldsborough keep his main naval strength at Hampton Roads alerted against future attacks by the Confederate ironclad. Union gunboats frequently bombarded Yorktown, under siege by McClellan's army, until the city was evacuated on 3 May.

U.S.S. *Mount Vernon*, Commander Glisson, with U.S.S. *Fernandina* and *Cambridge*, destroyed schooner *Kate* attempting to run the blockade near Wilmington.

3 Armed boats from U.S.S. *Mercedita*, Commander Stellwagen, and U.S.S. *Sagamore*, Lieutenant Andrew J. Drake, captured Apalachicola, Florida, without resistance and took pilot boats *Cygnet* and *Mary Olivia*, schooners *New Island*, *Floyd*, and *Rose*, and sloop *Octavia*.

DEAR SIR: I wish to give you my views as briefly as possible.

It is said that the enemy have eleven gunboats below Island No. 10, and, as I understand, they are supposed to have others fitted up as rams ascending the Mississippi, one of which has reached Memphis.

I propose to strengthen the hulls of some of the swift, strong towboats, which I am told can only be obtained here, and fit them up as speedily as possible, to be used as extempore rams.

To go down to Island No. 10, or any other stronghold of the rebels, and at a proper time during the contest, when the rebel gunboats seem to be in a favorable position, run down before the batteries and drive our rams at full headway into the rebel boats, doing what I can by preliminary preparations to save the men if our own boats should be sunk.

These boats, the river men here say, will all make 18 or 20 miles an hour down the Mississippi. It will be very difficult to hit them at that speed, and I will try to protect the engines and boilers against any ordinary shot.

It is not impossible that I can so strengthen our own hulls as to sink any Mississippi boat we can hit fairly, and yet save our own.

I seek good boats, and do not intend to make alterations which will injure them materially for future use, if they are not lost in the service.

If successful in sinking the rebel gunboats at Island No. 10, I would proceed down the river and lay our boats up under General Pope's guns.

I shall need a few strong and swift towboats of a smaller class, and these would then be used as pickets to watch the approach of the rams or other hostile boats below New Madrid.

I may need, also, one or two larger old boats to shelter our rams in running under the enemy's batteries. This is about my plan to meet the present condition of things, though the conditions may change materially before I am ready.

To carry out this plan, we ought to have at least as many boats as there are boats to be run down. Indeed, we ought to provide more. No boat can stop to strike twice, and some may not hit their adversaries fairly, or may get the worst of it.

The men must take service with a full knowledge of the dangerous nature of the duty, the enemy's fire being the least of the dangers. I would like to be authorized to assure them that their names will be reported to the Secretary of War, who will recommend them if they do well to the President and Congress. I think this will be valued more than specific rewards.

Very respectfully, your obedient servant,

CHARLES ELLET, Jr.

Hon. E. M. STANTON,
Secretary of War.

Charles Ellet Jr. gives Secretary of War Stanton his views regarding construction and use of a ram fleet. (Extract from Official Records of the Union and Confederate Navies in the War of the Rebellion, Series I, Volume 22.)

Flag Officer Du Pont and Brigadier General Henry W. Benham planned to cut off Fort Pulaski from Savannah in joint operations along the Georgia coast. Du Pont immediately ordered U.S.S. *Mohican*, Commander Godon, to reconnoiter the Wilmington River to determine the best means of obstructing it as part of the projected attack.

U.S.S. *Susquehanna*, Captain Lardner, captured British blockade runner *Coquette* off Charleston.

U.S.S. Carondelet, *Commander Walke, dashes past Confederate batteries on Island No. 10 to support the Union Army at New Madrid.*

Three armed boats from U.S.S. *Isaac Smith*, Lieutenant J. W. A. Nicholson, captured British blockade runner *British Empire* with cargo of provisions, dry goods, and medicines in Matanzas Inlet, Florida.

4 U.S.S. *Carondelet*, Commander Walke, shrouded by a heavy storm at night, successfully ran past Island No. 10, Mississippi River, and reached Major General John Pope's army at New Madrid. For his heroic dash through flaming Confederate batteries, Walke strengthened *Carondelet* with cord-wood piled around the boilers, extra deck planking, and anchor chain for added armor protection. "The passage of the *Carondelet*," wrote A. T. Mahan, "was not only one of the most daring and dramatic events of the war; it was also the death blow to the Confederate defense of this position." With the support of the gunboats, the Union troops could now safely plan to cross the river and take the Confederate defenses from the rear.

U.S.S. *Pursuit*, Acting Lieutenant Cate, captured sloop *LaFayette* at St. Joseph's Bay, Florida, with cargo of cotton.

C.S.S. *Carondelet*, Lieutenant Washington Gwathmey, with C.S.S. *Pamlico* and *Oregon*, engaged gunboats U.S.S. *J. P. Jackson*, *New London*, and *Hatteras*, and troops on board steamer *Lewis*, but could not prevent the landing of 1,200 men at Pass Christian, Mississippi, and the destruction of the Confederate camp there. *J. P. Jackson*, Acting Lieutenant Selim E. Woodworth, captured steamer *P. C. Wallis* near New Orleans with cargo of turpentine, pitch, rosin, and oil.

5 Brigadier General Benham informed Flag Officer Du Pont of a reported Confederate build-up of strength at Wilmington Island, "possibly for an effort to relieve or reinforce the garrison of Fort Pulaski." The General added that he was "most earnestly wishing" for further naval strength in the area. As reports of expected Confederate action at Fort Pulaski continued to reach Du Pont, he made every effort to render maximum support to the Army.

Flag Officer Farragut on board U.S.S. *Iroquois* made a personal reconnaissance in the area of Forts Jackson and St. Philip. The forts opened fire, but Farragut, observing from a mast, remained as "calm and placid as an onlooker at a mimic battle."

Launch from U.S.S. *Montgomery*, Lieutenant Charles Hunter, captured and destroyed schooner *Columbia* near San Luis Pass, Texas, loaded with cotton.

6 U.S.S. *Tyler*, Lieutenant Gwin, and U.S.S. *Lexington*, Lieutenant Shirk, protected the advanced river flank of General Grant's army at the Battle of Shiloh (Pittsburg Landing) and slowed the initially successful attack of the Confederates. Major General Polk, CSA, reported that the Confederate forces "were within from 150 to 400 yards of the enemy's position, and nothing seemed wanting to complete the most brilliant victory of the war but to press forward and make a vigorous assault on the demoralized remnant of his forces. At this juncture his gunboats dropped down the river, near the landing where his troops were collected, and opened a tremendous cannonade of shot and shell over the bank, in the direction from where our forces were approaching." Fire from the two wooden gunboats helped maintain Union positions until reinforcements arrived, and the next day contributed to forcing the Confederate retreat. "In this repulse," wrote Grant, "much is due to the presence of the gunboats." General Beauregard, CSA, attributed the Confederate loss the following day in large part to the presence of the gunboats. "During the night [of the 6th] the rain fell in torrents, adding to the discomforts and harassed condition of the men. The enemy, moreover, had broken their rest by a discharge at measured intervals of heavy shells thrown from the gunboats; therefore, on the following morning the troops under my command were not in condition to cope with an equal force of fresh troops, armed and equipped like our adversary, in the immediate possession of his depots and sheltered by such an auxiliary as the enemy's gunboats." One of the Army divisions at Shiloh was commanded by Major General Nelson, a former naval officer assigned to the Army, "who," Lieutenant Gwin observed,

"greatly distinguished himself." Gwin went on to report of the battle, "I think this has been a crushing blow to the rebellion."

U.S.S. *Carondelet*, Commander Walke, made a reconnaissance down the Mississippi River from New Madrid to Tiptonville, exchanging shots with shore batteries and landing to spike Confederate guns in preparation for covering the river crossing by Major General Pope's troops.

U.S.S. *Pursuit*, Acting Lieutenant Cate, captured steamer *Florida* loading cotton at North Bay, head of Bear Creek, Florida.

7 U.S.S. *Pittsburg*, Lieutenant Egbert Thompson, ran past the batteries at Island No. 10 and joined U.S.S. *Carondelet* in covering the crossing of Major General Pope's army to the Tennessee side of the Mississippi River to move against Island No. 10. The General's words to Flag Officer Foote attested to the importance he attached to naval support: ". . . the lives of thousands of men and the success of our operations hang upon your decision. With the two boats all is safe . . ."

Island No. 10, described by Brigadier General William W. Mackall, CSA, commanding the island, as "the key of the Mississippi," surrendered to the naval forces of Flag Officer Foote. Besides the heavy cannon and munitions captured, four steamers were taken and gunboat C.S.S. *Grampus* was sunk before the surrender. Capture of Island No. 10 opened the river to Union gunboats and transports south to Fort Pillow. Congress tendered Flag Officer Foote a vote of thanks "for his eminent services and gallantry at Fort Henry, Fort Donelson, and Island No. 10, while in command of the naval forces of the United States." Mobile naval strength had sealed the fate of the Confederacy on the upper Mississippi River, and was knifing into the heart of the South.

After surrender of Island No. 10, U.S.S. *Mound City*, Commander Augustus H. Kilty, seized Confederate ship *Red Rover*, which had been damaged by mortar fire. Temporarily repaired, *Red Rover* was moved to Cairo where she was converted to the Navy's first hospital ship. She joined the river fleet under Commander Pennock, on 10 June and shortly received her first patients. *Red Rover* was officially transferred to the Navy on 1 October 1862 and commissioned 26 December.

U.S.S. Red Rover, *the Navy's first hospital ship, well served the sick and wounded on the western waters.*

Sisters of the Holy Cross volunteered and served on board as nurses—pioneers of the U.S. Navy Nurse Corps—treating the sick and wounded. From Civil War *Red Rover* to the present, fine medical facilities afloat have promoted the efficiency and staying power of the combatant fleets.

U.S.S. *Pensacola*, Captain Morris, and U.S.S. *Mississippi*, Commander M. Smith, were successfully brought over the bar at the Passes and into the Mississippi River after several previous attempts to do so had met with failure. These were the two heaviest vessels ever to enter the river and figured prominently in the attack on New Orleans. "Now," Flag Officer Farragut wrote, "we are all right."

Commander Semmes' log of C.S.S. *Sumter* recorded: "Received a telegram from Mr. Mason [J. M. Mason, Confederate Commissioner in London] ordering me to lay the *Sumter* up and to permit the officers and such of the crew as prefer it to return to the Confederate States." This action in large measure was caused by a serious breakdown of *Sumter's* boilers at Gibraltar.

8 General Robert E. Lee wrote Confederate Secretary of the Navy Mallory: ". . . it is my opinion that they [General McClellan's army] are endeavoring to change their base of operations from James to York River. This change has no doubt been occasioned by their fear of the effect of the *Virginia* upon their shipping in the James. General Magruder informs me that their gunboats and transports have appeared off Shipping Point, on the Poquosin, near the mouth of the York, where they intend, apparently, to establish a landing for stores, preparatory to moving against our lines at Yorktown."

9 U.S.S. *Ottawa*, Lieutenant Stevens, U.S.S. *Pembina*, and *Ellen* escorted transports *Cosmopolitan* and *Belvedere* out of Jacksonville, as Union forces evacuated the area.

Flag Officer Hollins telegraphed Confederate Secretary of the Navy Mallory from Fort Pillow for authority to bring his force to the support of New Orleans. Mallory, convinced that the serious threat to New Orleans would come from Flag Officer Foote's force in the upper river rather than from Farragut's fleet below, denied Hollin's request.

10 Gunboat U.S.S. *Kanawha*, Lieutenant John C. Febiger, captured blockade running schooners *Southern Independence*, *Victoria*, *Charlotte*, and *Cuba* off Mobile.

U.S.S. *Whitehead*, Acting Master Charles A. French, captured schooners *Comet*, *J. J. Crittenden*, and sloop *America* in Newbegun Creek, North Carolina.

U.S.S. *Keystone State*, Commander LeRoy, chased blockade runner *Liverpool*, which ran aground outside North Inlet, South Carolina, and was destroyed by her crew.

11 C.S.S. *Virginia*, Flag Officer Tattnall, rounded Sewell's Point to make her second appearance in Hampton Roads. Under *Virginia's* protection, C.S.S. *Jamestown*, Lieutenant Barney, and C.S.S. *Raleigh*, Lieutenant Commander Joseph W. Alexander, captured three Union transports. Because of major strategic considerations on both sides, no second *Monitor-Virginia* duel ensued. *Monitor's* mission was to contain *Virginia* in support of General McClellan's campaign on the Peninsula, and *Virginia* safeguarded the important Norfolk area and the mouth of the James River.

Fort Pulaski, Georgia, surrendered after enduring an intensive two day bombardment by Union artillery. Commander C. R. P. Rodgers and a detachment of sailors from U.S.S. *Wabash* manned Battery Sigel the second day of the engagement and "kept up a steady and well-directed fire until the fort hauled down its flag, at 2 p.m." The Navy gunners' participation in the action was at the invitation of Major General David Hunter, commander of the Army forces, and demonstrated once again the closeness of cooperation achieved by the two services.

Flag Officer Farragut expressed his views on the outcome of the anticipated assault on New Orleans: "God dispenses His will according to his judgment, and not according to our wishes or

April 12th . 1862 .

Sir:

The "Merrimac" and consorts all made their appearance yesterday morning, and remained between Sewell's Point and Newport News, out of gunshot from Fort Monroe and the Rip Raps, until late in the afternoon, when they returned to their anchorage under Craney Island. Among the hundreds of sailing vessels congregated here, several had anchored, contrary to my advice repeatedly and formally urged upon the proper authorities on shore, in an exposed position, well over towards Newport News, and three of them were captured by the enemy's vessels. Except this, nothing further

of

Flag Officer Goldsborough reports the second appearance of C.S.S. Virginia *in Hampton Roads to Secretary Welles.*

of any importance occurred.

"Had the "Merrimac" engaged the "Monitor", which she might have done, I was quite prepared, with several vessels, to avail myself of a favorable moment and run her down. This experiment however must not be made too rashly, or until the right opportunity presents itself, as, to fail in it, would be to enable the "Merrimac" to place herself before Yorktown &c.—

I am very respectfully
yr ob't servant,
L. M Goldsborough.
Flag officer,
Com'dg N. Atl. Block. Sq.

Hon Gideon Welles
Secretary of the Navy
Washington D. C.

expectations. The defeat of our army at Corinth, which I saw in the rebel papers, will give us a much harder fight; men are easily elated or depressed by victory. But as to being prepared for defeat, I certainly am not. Any man who is prepared for defeat would be half defeated before he commenced. I hope for success; shall do all in my power to secure it, and trust to God for the rest. I trust in Him as a merciful being; but really in war it seems as if we hardly ought to expect mercy, when men are destroying one another upon questions of which He alone is the judge. Motive seems to constitute right and wrong."

Commander T. A. Craven, U.S.S. *Tuscarora*, reported that C.S.S. *Sumter*, Commander Semmes, had been abandoned at Gibraltar. *Tuscarora* had closely blockaded *Sumter* in port. The Confederate Congress expressed thanks "to Captain Raphael Semmes and the officers and crew of the steamer *Sumter*, under his command, for gallant and meritorious services rendered by them in seriously injuring the enemy's commerce upon the high seas, thereby setting an example reflecting honor upon our infant Navy which can not be too highly appreciated by Congress and the people of the Confederate States." In her spectacular though abbreviated career, *Sumter* captured 18 vessels and dealt Union shipping a heavy blow. "Well," Semmes remarked, "we have done the country some service, having cost the United States at least $1,000,000 in one way or another."

Secretary of the Navy Welles wrote President Lincoln: "It is of the greatest importance that the exportation of anthracite coal from ports of the United States to any and all foreign ports should be absolutely prohibited. The rebels obtain the coal for their steamers from Nassau and Havana, and the fact that it burns without smoke enables them to approach blockaded ports with greater security, as all other coals throw out so much smoke as to render their presence visible a great distance at sea."

13   U.S.S. *Tyler*, Lieutenant Gwin, and U.S.S. *Lexington*, Lieutenant Shirk, convoyed Army troops from Shiloh (Pittsburg Landing) to Chickasaw, Alabama. The expedition destroyed a bridge at Bear Creek, Alabama, used by the Memphis and Charleston Railroad.

Coast Survey party under Ferdinand H. Gerdes, began surveying the Mississippi River below Forts Jackson and St. Philip. Harassed by fire from the forts and riflemen on the river banks, Gerdes' party worked for five days to provide Flag Officer Farragut with a reliable map of the river, forts, water batteries, and the obstruction across the river.

Lieutenant Eaton of U.S.S. *Beauregard* demanded the surrender of the Confederate garrison at Fort Brooke, Tampa Bay, Florida. His demands were refused and Eaton shelled the fort before withdrawing.

14   Union mortar boats of Flag Officer Foote's force commenced regular bombardment of Fort Pillow, Tennessee—the next Army-Navy objective on the drive down the Mississippi.

Potomac Flotilla ascended the Rappahannock River and destroyed Confederate batteries and captured three vessels.

15   U.S.S. *Keystone State*, Commander LeRoy, captured blockade runner *Success* off Georgetown, South Carolina.

16   Flag Officer Farragut, after careful planning and extensive preparations, moved his fleet up the Mississippi to a position below Forts Jackson and St. Philip, guarding the approaches to New Orleans and mounting over 100 guns. High water in the river had flooded the forts. Confederate garrisons worked night and day to control the water and strengthen the forts against the impending assault. A chain obstruction supported by hulks spanned the river. Above the forts a Confederate flotilla, Flag Officer John K. Mitchell, included the potentially powerful but uncompleted ironclad *Louisiana*. Most of the others were small, makeshift gunboats. There were also a number of fire rafts readied to be set adrift to flow with the current into the midst of the Union fleet. Against these combined defenses Farragut, flying his flag in U.S.S. *Hartford*,

brought seventeen ships carrying 154 guns and a squadron of 20 mortar boats under Commander D. D. Porter.

18 Confederate Congress, hoping to stem the constant sweeping of the seas and inland waters by the Union fleets, passed an act authorizing contracts for the purchase of not more than six ironclads to be paid for in cotton.

Union mortar boats, Commander D. D. Porter, began a five day bombardment of Fort Jackson. Moored some 3,000 yards from Fort Jackson, they concentrated their heavy shells, up to 285 pounds, for six days and nights on this nearest fort from which they were hidden by intervening woods. The garrison heroically endured the fire and stuck to their guns.

19 Mortar schooner U.S.S. *Maria J. Carlton*, Acting Master Charles E. Jack, bombarding Fort Jackson, was sunk by Confederate fire. Commander Bell observed that the Confederate guns were being worked "beautifully and with effect."

U.S.S. *Huron*, Lieutenant John Downes, captured schooner *Glide* loaded with cotton, rice, and flour off Charleston.

20 U.S.S. *Itasca*, Lieutenant Caldwell, and U.S.S. *Pinola*, Lieutenant Crosby, under direction of Commander Bell, breached the obstructions below Forts Jackson and St. Philip under heavy fire, opening the way for Flag Officer Farragut's fleet. Brigadier General Johnson K. Duncan, CSA, commanding the forts, complained that the River Defense Fleet had sent no fire rafts down "to light up the river or distract the attention of the enemy at night" and had stationed no ship below to warn of the approach of *Itasca* and *Pinola*. This lack of coordination proved most costly to the Confederacy.

Lieutenant Wyman, commanding Potomac Flotilla, reported the capture of *Eureka, Monterey, Lookout, Sarah Ann, Sydney Jones, Reindeer, Falcon, Sea Flower*, and *Roundout* at the mouth of the Rappahannock River.

21 Flag Officer Farragut explained the delay in the attack on New Orleans: "We have been bombarding the forts for three or four days, but the current is running so strong that we cannot stem it sufficiently to do anything with our ships, so that I am now waiting a change of wind, which brings a slacker tide, and we shall be enabled to run up. . . . Captain Bell went last night to cut the chain across the river. I never felt such anxiety in my life as I did until his return. One of his vessels got on shore, and I was fearful she would be captured. They kept up a tremendous fire on him; but Porter diverted their fire with a heavy cannonade. They let the chain go, but the man sent to explode the petard did not succeed; his wires broke. Bell would have burned the hulks, but the illumination would have given the enemy a chance to destroy his gunboat, which got aground. However, the chain was divided, and it gives us space enough to go through."

U.S.S. *Tyler*, Lieutenant Gwin, captured steamer *Alfred Robb* on the Tennessee River.

22 Two boats from U.S.S. *Arthur*, Acting Lieutenant Kittredge, captured a schooner and two sloops at Aransas Pass, Texas, but were forced to abandon the prizes and their own boats when attacked by Confederate vessels and troops.

23 Brigadier General Duncan, the commander of Fort Jackson, wrote General Lovell in New Orleans: "Heavy and continued bombardment all night, and still progressing. No further casualties, except two men slightly wounded. God is certainly protecting us. We are still cheerful, and have an abiding faith in our ultimate success. We are making repairs as best we can. Our barbette guns are still in working order. Most of them have been disabled at times. The health of the troops continues good. Twenty-five thousand [actually about five thousand] XIII-inch shells have been fired by the enemy, thousands of which fell in the fort. They must soon exhaust themselves; if not, we can stand it as long as they can."

U.S. Flag Ship "Hartford"
Mississippi River
April 20th 1862

General Order

The Flag Officer after having heard all the opinions expressed by the different Commanders. is of the opinion that whatever is to be done. will have to be done quickly. or we will be again reduced to a Blockading Squadron. without the means of carrying on the Bombardment, As we have nearly expended all the Shells & Fuzes, and material for making Cartridges, He has always entertained the same opinions which are expressed by Com'dr Porter, that is, that there are three modes of attack, and the question is, which, is the one to be adopted? His own opinion is, that a Combination of two should be made, viz— The Forts should be run, and when a force is once above the Forts to protect the troops, they should landed at Quarantine. from the Gulf side, by bringing them through the Bayou, and then our forces should move up the River. mutually aiding each other, as it can be done to advantage. When, in the opinion of the Flag Officer. the propitious time has arrived. the signal will be made to weigh, and advance to the Conflict. If, in his opinion, at the time of arriving at the respective positions of the different Divisions of the Fleet, we have the advantage of
the Enemy

he will make the signal for "close action" No 8 and abide by the result longer. to be conquered, Drop anchor or keep underweigh, as in their opinion is best Unless the signal above mentioned is made. It will be understood that the first order of sailing will be formed after leaving Fort "St. Philip," and we will proceed up the River, in accordance with the original opinion expressed.

The program of the orders of sailing accompanies this General Order, and the Commanders will hold themselves in readiness for the service as indicated.

Very Respectfully
Your Obt Servt

Flag Officer Western
Gulf Block'g Squadron

Flag Officer Farragut's operational order for running the forts below New Orleans.

C.S.S. Manassas—*powerful armored ram destroyed defending New Orleans against Farragut's force.*

23-24 Expedition commanded by Lieutenant Flusser, including U.S.S. *Lockwood*, *Whitehead*, and *Putnam*, blocked the mouth of Albemarle and Chesapeake Canal, near Elizabeth City, North Carolina, sinking a schooner and other obstructions inside the canal.

24 Flag Officer Farragut's fleet ran past Forts Jackson and St. Philip and engaged the defending Confederate flotilla. At 2:00 a.m., U.S.S. *Hartford* had shown Farragut's signal for the fleet to get underway in three divisions to steam through the breach in the obstructions which had been opened by U.S.S. *Pinola* and *Itasca*. A withering fire from the forts was answered by roaring broadsides from the ships. *Hartford*, grounded in the swift current near Fort St. Philip, was set afire by a Confederate fireraft. Farragut's leadership and the disciplined training of the crew saved the flagship. U.S.S. *Varuna* was rammed by two Confederate ships and sunk. In the ensuing melee, C.S.S. *Warrior*, *Stonewall Jackson*, *General Lovell*, and *Breckinridge*, tender *Phoenix*, steamers *Star* and *Belle Algerine*, and Louisiana gunboat *General Quitman* were destroyed. The armored ram C.S.S. *Manassas* was driven ashore by U.S.S. *Mississippi* and sunk. Steam tenders C.S.S. *Landis* and *W. Burton* surrendered; *Resolute* and *Governor Moore* were destroyed to prevent capture. "The destruction of the Navy at New Orleans," wrote Confederate Secretary of the Navy Mallory, "was a sad, sad blow . . ." When the Union Navy passed the forts and disposed of the Confederate forces afloat, the fate of New Orleans was decided. Farragut had achieved a brilliant victory, one which gave true meaning to the Flag Officer's own words: "The great man in our country must not only plan but execute."

C.S.S. *Nashville* made a successful run into Wilmington with 60,000 stand of arms and 40 tons of powder.

25 Flag Officer Farragut's fleet, having silenced Confederate batteries at Chalmette en route, anchored before New Orleans. High water in the river allowed the ships' guns to dominate the city over the levee top. Captain Bailey went ashore to demand the surrender. The Common Council of New Orleans resolved that: ". . . having been advised by the military authorities that the

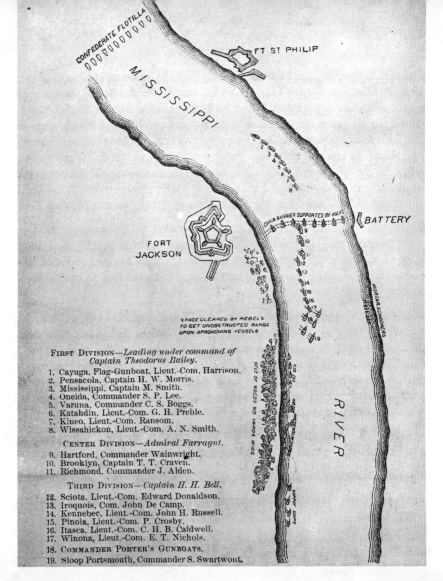

CONFEDERATE FLOTILLA

MISSISSIPPI

FT ST PHILIP

FORT JACKSON

CHAIN BARRIER SUPPORTED BY HULKS

BATTERY

MORTAR SCHOONERS WESTERN

RIVER

SPACE CLEARED BY REBELS
TO GET UNOBSTRUCTED RANGE
UPON APPROACHING VESSELS

First Division—*Leading under command of Captain Theodorus Bailey.*

1. Cayuga, Flag-Gunboat, Lieut.-Com. Harrison.
2. Pensacola, Captain H. W. Morris.
3. Mississippi, Captain M. Smith.
4. Oneida, Commander S. P. Lee.
5. Varuna, Commander C. S. Boggs.
6. Katahdin, Lient.-Com. G. H. Preble.
7. Kineo, Lieut.-Com. Ransom.
8. Wissahickon, Lieut.-Com. A. N. Smith.

Center Division—*Admiral Farragut.*

9. Hartford, Commander Wainwright.
10. Brooklyn, Captain T. T. Craven.
11. Richmond, Commander J. Alden.

Third Division—*Captain H. H. Bell.*

12. Sciota, Lieut.-Com. Edward Donaldson.
13. Iroquois, Com. John De Camp.
14. Kennebec, Lieut.-Com. John H. Russell.
15. Pinola, Lieut.-Com. P. Crosby.
16. Itasca, Lieut.-Com. C. H. B. Caldwell.
17. Winona, Lieut.-Com. E. T. Nichols.
18. Commander Porter's Gunboats.
19. Sloop Portsmouth, Commander S. Swartwout.

Planning, leadership, and bold action combine to forge Farragut's complete victory at New Orleans, which placed the South's largest and wealthiest city in Union hands.

city is indefensible, [we] declare that no resistance will be made to the forces of the United States." Loss of New Orleans, the largest and wealthiest seaport in the South, was a critical blow to the Confederacy. With the rapid capitulation of Forts Jackson and St. Philip, the delta of the Mississippi was open to the water-borne movement of Union forces which were free to steam up river to join those coming south in the great pincer which would sever the Confederacy. "Thus," reported Secretary of the Navy Welles, "the great southern depot of the trade of the immense central valley of the Union was once more opened to commercial intercourse and the emporium of that wealthy region was restored to national authority; the mouth of the Mississippi was under our control and an outlet for the great West to the ocean was secured."

C.S.S. *Mississippi*, launched on 19 April and described by Confederate naval officers as "the strongest . . . most formidable war vessel that had ever been built," was destroyed by fire at New Orleans to prevent her capture by the Union fleet. Had the Tredegar Iron Works, Richmond, completed her shaft on time, *Mississippi* might have been readied to throw her weight into the defense of New Orleans.

Commander Charles H. McBlair, CSN, notified the Confederate Navy Department that as a result of the passage of the forts below New Orleans by Flag Officer Farragut's fleet that he intended to take the unfinished ram C.S.S. *Arkansas*, building at Memphis, up the Yazoo River to be completed. McBlair also reported that arrangements had been made to destroy the *Tennessee* on the stocks to prevent her capture if Memphis fell. In June *Arkansas* was moved down the Yazoo to Liverpool Landing where a raft across the river and shore batteries protected the ram from the Federal gunboats while work went forward on her.

U.S.S. *Maratanza*, Commander George H. Scott, began shelling Gloucester and Yorktown, Virginia, in support of General McClellan's Peninsular Campaign.

U.S.S. *Katahdin*, Lieutenant George Preble, captured schooner *John Gilpin* below New Orleans.

U.S.S. *Santiago de Cuba*, Commander Ridgely, captured blockade runner *Ella Warley* at sea 120 miles off Port Royal.

26 Flag Officer Farragut, from flagship U.S.S. *Hartford*, issued a general order after his victory at New Orleans: "Eleven o'clock this morning is the hour appointed for all the officers and crews of the fleet to return thanks to Almighty God for His great goodness and mercy in permitting us to pass through the events of the last two days with so little loss of life and blood. At that hour the church pennant will be hoisted on every vessel of the fleet, and their crews assembled will, in humiliation and prayer, make their acknowledgments therefor to the great dispenser of all human events."

Fort Macon, North Carolina, surrendered to combined land-sea forces under Commander Lockwood and Brigadier General John G. Parke. U.S.S. *Daylight*, *State of Georgia*, *Chippewa*, and *Gemsbok* heavily bombarded the fort; blockade runners *Alliance* and *Gondar* were captured after the fort's surrender.

U.S.S. *Onward*, Acting Lieutenant J. Frederick Nickels, forced schooner *Chase* aground on Raccoon Keys near Cape Romain, South Carolina, and subsequently destroyed her.

U.S.S. *Flambeau*, Lieutenant John H. Upshur, captured blockade runner *Active* near Stono Inlet, South Carolina.

U.S.S. *Santiago de Cuba*, Commander Ridgely, captured schooner *Mersey* off Charleston.

U.S.S. *Uncas*, Acting Master Lemuel G. Crane, captured schooner *Belle* off Charleston.

27 Fort Livingston, Bastian Bay, Louisiana, surrendered to the Navy. Boat crew from U.S.S. *Kittatinny* raised the United States flag over the fort.

U.S.S. *Mercedita*, Commander Stellwagen, captured steamer *Bermuda* northeast of Abaco with large cargo of arms shipped from Liverpool.

U.S.S. *Wamsutta*, Lieutenant Alexander A. Semmes, and U.S.S. *Potomska*, Acting Lieutenant Pendleton G. Watmough, exchanged fire with dismounted Confederate cavalry concealed in woods on Woodville Island, Riceboro River, Georgia.

28 Forts Jackson and St. Philip, isolated since being passed by Flag Officer Farragut's fleet and the fall of New Orleans, surrendered to the Navy; the terms of capitulation were signed on board U.S.S. *Harriet Lane*, Commander D. D. Porter's flagship. C.S.S. *Louisiana*, *Defiance*, and *McRae* were destroyed to prevent their capture.

Steamer *Oreto* (C.S.S. *Florida*) arrived at Nassau, British West Indies.

29 Expedition under Lieutenant Alexander C. Rhind in U.S.S. *E. B. Hale* landed and destroyed Confederate battery at Grimball's, Dawho River, South Carolina, and exchanged fire with field pieces near Slann's Bluff.

Gunboat U.S.S. *Kanawha*, Lieutenant Febiger, captured blockade running British sloop *Annie* between Ship Island and Mobile, bound for Havana with cargo of cotton.

30 U.S.S. *Santiago de Cuba*, Commander Ridgely, captured schooner *Maria* off Port Royal.

MAY

1 U.S.S. *Hatteras*, Commander Emmons, captured schooner *Magnolia* near Berwick Bay, Louisiana, with cargo of cotton.

U.S.S. *Jamestown*, Commander Green, captured British blockade runner *Intended* off the coast of North Carolina with cargo of salt, coffee, and medicines.

U.S.S. *Huron*, Lieutenant Downes, captured schooner *Albert* off Charleston.

Schooner *Sarah* ran aground at Bull's Bay, South Carolina, and was destroyed by her own crew to prevent capture by U.S.S. *Onward*, Acting Lieutenant Nickels.

U.S.S. *Marblehead*, Lieutenant Somerville Nicholson, shelled the Confederate positions at Yorktown.

2 U.S.S. *Restless*, Acting Lieutenant Conroy, captured British blockade runner *Flash* off the coast of South Carolina.

3 U.S.S. *R. R. Cuyler*, Lieutenant F. Winslow, captured schooner *Jane* off Tampa Bay, Florida, with cargo including pig lead.

4 U.S.S. *Corwin*, Lieutenant Thomas S. Phelps, captured schooner *Director* and launch marked "U.S. brig *Dolphin*" in York River near Gloucester Point; guard boat *General Scott* and sloop *Champion*, both loaded with Confederate Army stores, were burned to prevent capture.

Boat crew from U.S.S. *Wachusett*, Commander W. Smith, raised United States flag at Gloucester Point, Virginia, after General McClellan's troops occupied Yorktown; two Confederate schooners were captured.

U.S.S. *Calhoun*, Lieutenant Joseph E. DeHaven, captured sloop *Charles Henry* off St. Joseph, Louisiana, and raised the United States flag over Fort Pike, which had been evacuated.

Lieutenant English, commanding U.S.S. *Somerset*, reported the capture of steamer *Circassian* between Havana and Matanzas.

Union forces at Ragged Island burned schooner *Beauregard*, laden with coal for C.S.S. *Virginia*.

U. S. Flag Ship Hartford
Off the city of New Orleans
April 26th 1862

General Order

Of all the duties of a Commanding Officer
none is so gratifying as that of making praise
to those under his command

The Flag Officer announces to the Fleet, that
the conduct of both Officers & Men, during
the trying events of the mornings of the 24th
and 25th instants, met his highest admiration
their steading courage, and intrepidity, could
not have been surpassed, and I apprehend
have rarely been equaled, and however much
we may deplore the loss of our Brave Shipmates
who so gloriously fell in the discharge of
their duty, we cannot but derive pleasure from
the knowledge that our chances were equal,
and that their families and friends will derive
the benefit from the glorious part they bore in
the conflict —.

D. G. Farragut
Flag Officer
W. Gulf Blockade Squadron

Flag Officer Farragut gives full praise to the conduct of his officers and men . . .

U. S. Flag Ship "Hartford"
Off the City of New Orleans
April 26th 1862.

General Order.

Eleven O'clock this morning is the hour appointed for all the Officers and Crews of the Fleet to return thanks to Almighty God for His great Goodness and Mercy in permitting us to pass through the Events of the last two days with so little loss of life and Blood

At that hour the Church Pennant will be hoisted by every Vessel of the Fleet, and their Crews assembled will in humiliation and prayer make their acknowledgements therefor to the Great Dispenser of All human Events.

D. G. Farragut
Flag Officer, Western
Gulf Blockading Squadron.

and thanks for the decisive victory won by his squadron at New Orleans.

No. 15.

U. S. Flag Ship "Hartford"
At anchor off the City of New Orleans.
April 29th 1862.

Sir:

I am happy to announce to you
that our Flag waves over both Forts,
Jackson and St. Phillip, and at New
Orleans over the Custom House. I am
taking every means to secure the occupation by General Butler of all the Forts along
the Coast. Berwick's Bay and Fort Pike
have been abandoned, in fact there is
a general Stampede, and I shall endeavor
to follow it up. (As soon as I see Genl Butler
safely in possession of this place I will
sail for Mobile with the Fleet.)
I am bringing up the Troops now as
fast as possible. We have destroyed all the
Forts above the City, 4 in number, which
are understood to be all the impediments
between this and Memphis.
I am.
Very Respectfully
Your Obedient Servant.

D. G. Farragut
Flag Officer Western
Gulf Blockading Squadron

Flag Officer Farragut reports the capture of New Orleans and Forts Jackson and St. Philip.

5 President Lincoln, with Secretaries Stanton and Chase on board, proceeded to Hampton Roads on steamer *Miami* to personally direct the stalled Peninsular Campaign. The following day, Lincoln informed Flag Officer L. M. Goldsborough: "I shall be found either at General Wool's [Fort Monroe] or on board the *Miami*." The President directed gunboat operations in the James River and the bombardment of Sewell's Point by the blockading squadron in the five days he acted as Commander-in-Chief in the field.

U.S.S. *Calhoun*, Lieutenant DeHaven, captured schooner *Rover* with cargo of brick in Lake Pontchartrain, Louisiana.

Boat from U.S.S. *Corwin*, Lieutenant T. S. Phelps, captured sloop *Water Witch*, abandoned the previous day by Confederates above Gloucester Point, Virginia.

6 U.S.S. *Calhoun*, Lieutenant DeHaven, captured steamer *Whiteman* in Lake Pontchartrain.

U.S.S. *Ottawa*, Lieutenant J. Blakeley Creighton, captured schooner *General C. C. Pinckney* off Charleston.

6–7 U.S.S. *Wachusett*, Commander W. Smith, U.S.S. *Chocura*, and *Sebago* escorted Army transports up the York River, supported the landing at West Point, Virginia, and countered a Confederate attack with accurate gunfire. U.S.S. *Currituck*, Acting Master William F. Shankland, sent on a reconnaissance of the Pamunkey River by Smith on the 6th, captured *American Coaster* and *Planter* the next day. Shankland reported that some twenty schooners had been sunk and two gunboats burned by the Confederates above West Point.

8 U.S.S. *Monitor, Dacotah, Naugatuck, Seminole*, and *Susquehanna*—"by direction of the President"— shelled Confederate batteries at Sewell's Point, Virginia, as Flag Officer L. M. Goldsborough reported, "mainly with the view of ascertaining the practicability of landing a body of troops thereabouts" to move on Norfolk. Whatever rumors President Lincoln had received about Confederates abandoning Norfolk were now confirmed; a tug deserted from Norfolk and brought news that the evacuation was well underway and that C.S.S. *Virginia*, with her accompanying small gunboats, planned to proceed up the James or York River. It was planned that when *Virginia* came out, as she had on the 7th, the Union fleet would retire with U.S.S. *Monitor* in the rear hoping to draw the powerful but under-engined warship into deep water where she might be rammed by high speed steamers. The bombardment uncovered reduced but considerable strength at Sewell's Point. *Virginia* came out but not far enough to be rammed. Two days later President Lincoln wrote Flag Officer Goldsborough: "I send you this copy of your report of yesterday for the purpose of saying to you in writing that you are quite right in supposing the movement made by you and therein reported was made in accordance with my wishes verbally expressed to you in advance. I avail myself of the occasion to thank you for your courtesy and all your conduct, so far as known to me, during my brief visit here." President Lincoln, acting as Commander-in-Chief in the field at Hampton Roads, also directed Flag Officer Goldsborough: "If you have tolerable confidence that you can successfully contend with the *Merrimack* without the help of the *Galena* and two accompanying gunboats, send the *Galena* and two gunboats up the James River at once" to support General McClellan. This wise use of power afloat by the President silenced two shore batteries and forced gunboats C.S.S. *Jamestown* and *Patrick Henry* to return up the James River.

Landing party from U.S.S. *Iroquois*, Commander James S. Palmer, seized arsenal and took possession of Baton Rouge, Louisiana.

9 Captain Davis assumed temporary command of the Western Flotilla, relieving Flag Officer Foote who was failing from the wound suffered at Fort Donelson. Foote had made a series of major contributions toward reopening the "Father of Waters." In the words of Admiral Mahan: "Over the birth and early efforts of that little fleet he had presided; upon his shoulders had fallen

the burden of anxiety and unremitting labor which the early days of the war, when all had to be created, everywhere entailed. He was repaid, for under him its early glories were achieved and its reputation established.''

President Lincoln himself, after talking to pilots and studying charts, reconnoitered to the eastward of Sewell's Point and found a suitably unfortified landing site near Willoughby Point. The troops embarked in transports that night. The next morning they landed near the site selected by the President. The latter, still afloat, from his ''command ship'' *Miami* ordered U.S.S. *Monitor* to reconnoiter Sewell's Point to learn if the batteries were still manned. When he found the works abandoned, President Lincoln ordered Major General Wool's troops to march on Norfolk, where they arrived late on the afternoon of the 10th.

10 Norfolk Navy Yard set afire before being evacuated by Confederate forces in a general withdrawal up the peninsula to defend Richmond. Union troops under Major General Wool crossed Hampton Roads from Fort Monroe, landed at Ocean View, and captured Norfolk.

Pensacola reoccupied by Union Army and Navy forces. Military installations in the area, including the Navy Yard, Forts Barrancas and McRee, C.S.S. *Fulton*, and an ironclad building on the Escambia River, were destroyed by the Confederates the preceding day before withdrawing. Commander D. D. Porter reported to Secretary of the Navy Welles: ''The rebels had done their work completely. The yard is a ruin.'' Abandonment of the important Pensacola coastal area had been in preparation by the Confederates for months after Flag Officer Foote's stunning successes on the upper Mississippi made redeployment of guns and troops necessary. Flag Officer Farragut's momentous victory at New Orleans precipitated the final evacuation. Colonel Thomas M. Jones, CSA, commanding at Pensacola, reported: ''On receiving information that the enemy's gunboats had succeeded in passing the forts below New Orleans with their powerful batteries and splendid equipments, I came to the conclusion that, with my limited means of defense, reduced, as I have been by the withdrawal of nearly all my heavy guns and ammunition, I could not hold them in check or make even a respectable show of resistance.''

Confederate River Defense Fleet—C.S.S. *General Bragg*, *General Sumter*, *General Sterling Price*, *General Earl Van Dorn*, *General M. Jeff Thompson*, *General Lovell*, *General Beauregard*, and *Little Rebel*—made a spirited attack on Union gunboats and mortar flotilla at Plum Point Bend, Tennessee. The Confederate fleet, Captain James E. Montgomery, attacked Mortar Boat No. 16, stationed just above Fort Pillow and engaged in bombarding the works. U.S.S. *Cincinnati*, Commander Stembel, coming to the mortar boat's defense, was rammed by *Bragg* and sank on a bar in eleven feet of water. *Van Dorn* rammed U.S.S. *Mound City*, Commander Kilty, forcing her to run aground to avoid sinking. The draft of the Confederate vessels would not permit them to press the attack into the shoal water in which the Union squadron steamed, and, having sustained various but minor injuries, Montgomery withdrew under the guns of Fort Pillow. *Cincinnati* and *Mound City* were quickly repaired and returned to service.

U.S.S. *Unadilla*, Lieutenant Collins, captured schooner *Mary Teresa* attempting to run the blockade at Charleston.

Ironclad steamer U.S.S. *New Ironsides* launched at Philadelphia.

11 C.S.S. *Virginia* blown up by her crew off Craney Island to avoid capture. The fall of Norfolk to Union forces denied *Virginia* her base, and when it was discovered that she drew too much water to be brought up the James River, Flag Officer Tattnall ordered the celebrated ironclad's destruction. ''Thus perished the *Virginia*,'' Tattnall wrote, ''and with her many highflown hopes of naval supremacy and success.'' For the Union, the end of *Virginia* not only removed the formidable threat to the large base at Fort Monroe, but gave Flag Officer Goldsborough's fleet free passage up the James River as far as Drewry's Bluff, a factor which was to save the Peninsular Campaign from probable disaster.

Flag Officer Tattnall ordered the celebrated ironclad C.S.S. Virginia *abandoned and destroyed off Craney Island to prevent her capture.*

Josiah Tattnall Flag Officer, CSN

U.S.S. *Bainbridge*, Commander Thomas M. Brasher, captured schooner *Newcastle* at sea with cargo of turpentine and cotton.

U.S.S. *Kittatinny*, Acting Master Charles W. Lamson, captured blockade running British schooner *Julia* off Southwest Pass, Mississippi River, with cargo of cotton.

U.S.S. *Hatteras*, Commander Emmons, captured steamer *Governor A. Mouton* off Berwick **Bay,** Louisiana.

12 U.S.S. *Maratanza*, Lieutenant Stevens, and other gunboats made a reconnaissance of Pamunkey River in support of an Army advance to the new supply base at White House, Virginia, within twenty-two miles of Richmond.

Officers and crew of C.S.S. *Virginia* were ordered to report to Commander Farrand to establish a battery below Drewry's Bluff on the left bank of the river to prevent the ascent of Union gunboats. The battery was to be organized and commanded by Lieutenant Catesby ap R. Jones.

13 Confederate steamer *Planter*, with her captain ashore in Charleston, was taken out of the harbor by an entirely Negro crew under Robert Smalls and turned over to U.S.S. *Onward*, Acting Lieutenant Nickels, of the blockading Union squadron. "At 4 in the morning," Flag Officer Du Pont reported, ". . . she left her wharf close to the Government office and headquarters, with palmetto and Confederate flag flying, passed the successive forts, saluting as usual by blowing her steam whistle. After getting beyond the range of the last gun she quickly hauled down the rebel flags and hoisted a white one . . . The steamer is quite a valuable acquisition to the squadron . . ." Du Pont added in a letter to Senator Grimes: "You should have heard his [Small's] modest reply when I asked him what was said of the carry away of General Ripley's barge sometime ago. He said they made a great fuss but perhaps they would make more 'to do' when they heard of the steamer having been brought out."

U.S.S. *Iroquois*, Commander Palmer, and U.S.S. *Oneida*, Commander S. P. Lee, occupied Natchez, Mississippi, as Flag Officer Farragut's fleet moved steadily toward Vicksburg.

U.S.S. *Bohio*, Acting Master W. D. Gregory, captured schooner *Deer Island* in Mississippi Sound with cargo of flour and rice.

Boat crew from U.S.S. *Calhoun*, Lieutenant DeHaven, captured Confederate gunboat *Corypheus*, moored in Bayou Bonfouca, Louisiana.

Guns of U.S.S. Galena.

John Rodgers
Commander, USN

14 U.S.S. *Calhoun*, Lieutenant DeHaven, captured schooner *Venice* in Lake Pontchartrain with cargo of cotton.

15 James River Flotilla, including U.S.S. *Monitor, Galena, Aroostook, Port Royal,* and *Naugatuck,* under Commander J. Rodgers encountered obstructions sunk across the river and at close range hotly engaged sharpshooters and strong Confederate batteries, manned in part by sailors and Marines, at Drewry's Bluff, Virginia. For his part in the ensuing action, Corporal John B. Mackie, a member of *Galena's* Marine Guard, was cited for gallantry in a letter to Secretary of the Navy Welles; in Department of the Navy General Order 17, issued on 10 July 1863, Mackie was awarded the first Medal of Honor authorized a member of the Marine Corps. In the bombardment, *Galena* was heavily damaged but, unsupported, Rodgers penetrated the James River to within eight miles of Richmond before falling back. Rodgers stated at this time that troops were needed to take Drewry's Bluff in the rear. Had this been done, Richmond might well have fallen.

U.S.S. *Sea Foam*, Acting Master Henry E. Williams, and U.S.S. *Matthew Vassar*, Acting Master Hugh H. Savage, captured sloops *Sarah* and *New Eagle* off Ship Island, Mississippi, with cargo of cotton.

16 Union naval squadron under Commander S. P. Lee in U.S.S. *Oneida*, advancing up the Mississippi River toward Vicksburg, shelled Grand Gulf, Mississippi.

17 Joint expedition including U.S.S. *Sebago*, Lieutenant Murray, and U.S.S. *Currituck*, Acting Master Shankland, with troops embarked on transport *Seth Low*, at the request of General McClellan ascended the Pamunkey River to twenty-five miles above White House. Confederates burned

Commander Rodgers' squadron, including U.S.S. Monitor, *engages Confederate positions on the James River during the Peninsular Campaign to capture Richmond.*

seventeen vessels, some loaded with coal and commissary stores. The river was so narrow at this point that the Union gunboats were compelled to return stern foremost for several miles. General McClellan reported that the "expedition was admirably managed, and all concerned deserve great credit."

U.S.S. *Hatteras*, Commander Emmons, captured sloop *Poody* off Vermilion Bay, Louisiana.

18 Commander S. P. Lee submitted a demand from Flag Officer Farragut and General Butler for the surrender of Vicksburg; Confederate authorities refused and a year-long land and water assault on the stronghold began. As Flag Officer Du Pont observed: "The object is to have Vicksburg and the entire possession of the river in all its length and shores."

U.S.S. *Hunchback*, Acting Lieutenant Colhoun, and U.S.S. *Shawsheen*, Acting Master Thomas J. Woodward, captured schooner *G. H. Smoot* in Potecasi Creek, North Carolina.

20 Union gunboats occupied the Stono River above Cole's Island, South Carolina, and shelled Confederate positions there. Flag Officer Du Pont reported to Secretary of the Navy Welles: "The *Unadilla*, *Pembina*, and *Ottawa*, under Commander Marchand . . . succeeded in entering Stono and proceeded up the river above the old Fort opposite Legareville. On their approach the barracks were fired and deserted by the enemy . . . This important base of operations, the Stono, has thus been secured for further operations by the army against Charleston. . ."

U.S.S. *Whitehead*, Acting Master French, captured schooner *Eugenia* in Bennet's Creek, North Carolina.

21 Boat expedition from U.S.S. *Hunchback*, Acting Lieutenant Colhoun, and U.S.S. *Whitehead*, Acting Master French, captured schooner *Winter Shrub* in Keel's Creek, North Carolina, with cargo of fish.

22 U.S.S. *Mount Vernon*, Commander Glisson, captured steamer *Constitution* attempting to run the blockade at Wilmington.

U.S.S. *Whitehead*, Acting Master French, captured sloop *Ella D* off Keel's Creek, North Carolina, with cargo of salt.

24 U.S.S. *Bienville*, Commander Mullany, captured British blockade runner *Stettin* off Charleston.

U.S.S. *Amanda*, Acting Lieutenant Nathaniel Goodwin, and U.S.S. *Bainbridge*, Commander Brasher, captured steamer *Swan* west of Tortugas with cargo of cotton and rosin.

25 Confederate gunboat under command of Captain F. N. Bonneau, guarding the bridge between James and Dixon Islands, Charleston harbor, exchanged fire with Union gunboats. Captain Bonneau claimed several hits on the gunboats.

26 Lieutenant Isaac N. Brown, CSN, ordered to take command of C.S.S. *Arkansas* and "finish the vessel without regard to expenditure of men or money." Captain Lynch after inspecting the unfinished ram reported to Secretary of the Navy Mallory that: "the *Arkansas* is very inferior to the *Merrimac[k]* in every particular. The iron with which she is covered is worn and indifferent, taken from a railroad track, and is poorly secured to the vessel; boiler iron on stern and counter; her smoke-stack is sheet iron." Nevertheless, with great energy to overcome shortages and difficulties of every nature, Lieutenant Brown completed *Arkansas*, reinforced her bulwarks with cotton bales, and mounted a formidable armament of 10 guns. Lieutenant George W. Gift, CSN, who served in the ship later recorded that "within five weeks from the day we arrived at Yazoo City, we had a man-of-war (such as she was) from almost nothing—the credit for all of which belongs to Isaac Newton Brown, the commander of the vessel." A number of Army artillerists volunteered to act as gunners on board the ram.

Reconnaissance Balloon Boat on the James River.

U.S.S. *Brooklyn*, Captain T. T. Craven, and gunboats U.S.S. *Kineo*, Lieutenant George M. Ransom, and U.S.S. *Katahdin*, Lieutenant Preble, shelled Grand Gulf, Mississippi.

U.S.S. *Huron*, Lieutenant Downes, captured British blockade runner *Cambria* off Charleston.

U.S.S. *Pursuit*, Acting Lieutenant Cate, captured schooner *Andromeda* near the coast of Cuba with cargo of cotton.

27   U.S.S. *Bienville*, Commander Mullany, seized blockade running British steamer *Patras* off Bull's Island, South Carolina, from Havana with cargo of powder and arms.

U.S.S. *Santiago de Cuba*, Commander Ridgely, captured schooner *Lucy C. Holmes* off Charleston with cargo of cotton.

28   U.S.S. *State of Georgia*, Commander Armstrong, and U.S.S. *Victoria*, Acting Master Joshua D. Warren, captured steamer *Nassau* near Fort Caswell, North Carolina.

Assistant Secretary of the Navy Fox wrote Senator Grimes: "I beg of you for the enduring good of the service, which you have so much at heart, to add a proviso [to the naval bill] abolishing the spirit ration and forbidding any distilled liquors being placed on board any vessel belonging to, or chartered by the U. States, excepting of course, that in the Medical Department. All insubordination, all misery, every deviltry on board ships can be traced to *rum*. Give the sailor double the value or more, and he will be content." Congressional Act approved 14 July 1862 abolished the spirit ration in the Navy.

29   U.S.S. *Keystone State*, Commander LeRoy, captured British blockade runner *Elizabeth* off Charleston.

U.S.S. *Bienville*, Commander Mullany, captured blockade runners *Providence*, with cargo of salt and cigars, *Rebecca*, with cargo of salt, and *La Criolla*, with cargo of provisions, off Charleston.

31   Commander Rowan, commanding U.S.S. *Philadelphia*, reported the capture of schooner W. F. *Harris* in Core Sound, North Carolina.

U.S.S. *Keystone State*, Commander LeRoy, captured blockade running British schooner *Cora* off Charleston.

JUNE

2   Boat from U.S.S. *New London*, Lieutenant A. Read, captured yachts *Comet* and *Algerine* near New Basin, Louisiana.

Eleven men in two boats under Acting Master Samuel Curtis from U.S.S. *Kingfisher*, while on an expedition up Aucilla River, Florida, to obtain fresh water, were surprised by Confederate attackers; two were killed and nine were captured.

2–3   U.S.S. *Unadilla*, Lieutenant Collins, U.S.S. *Pembina*, *E. B. Hale*, *Ellen*, and *Henry Andrew* provided close gun-fire support for Army landings and operations on James Island, South Carolina.

3   U.S.S. *Gem of the Sea*, Lieutenant Baxter, captured blockade runner *Mary Stewart* at the entrance of South Santee River, South Carolina.

U.S.S. *Montgomery*, Lieutenant C. Hunter, captured blockade running British schooner *Will-O'-The-Wisp* transferring powder and percussion caps to a lighter near the mouth of the Rio Grande River.

4   Confederates evacuated Fort Pillow, Tennessee, on the Mississippi River during the night of 4–5 June after sustaining prolonged bombardment by Union gunboats and mortars. On 5 June the Union fleet under Captain Davis and transports moved down the river to within two miles of Memphis.

5   Tug assigned to U.S.S. *Benton*, Captain Davis, captured steamer *Sovereign* near Island No. 37 in the Mississippi River.

Confederate steamer *Havana* set afire in Deadman's Bay, Florida, to prevent her capture by U.S.S. *Ezilda*, tender to U.S.S. *Somerset*, Lieutenant English.

6   U.S.S. *Benton*, *Louisville*, *Carondelet*, *St. Louis*, and *Cairo* under Captain Davis, and rams *Queen of the West* and *Monarch* under Colonel Charles Ellet, Jr., engaged Confederate River Defense Fleet, C.S.S. *Earl Van Dorn*, *General Beauregard*, *General M. Jeff Thompson*, *Colonel Lovell*, *General Bragg*, *General Sumter*, *General Sterling Price*, and *Little Rebel* under Captain Montgomery in the Battle of Memphis. In the ensuing close action *Queen of the West* was rammed and Colonel Ellet mortally wounded. The Confederate River Defense Fleet was destroyed; all ships, excepting *Van Dorn*, were either captured, sunk, or grounded on the river bank to avoid sinking. Memphis surrendered to Captain Davis, and the pressure of relentless naval power had placed another important segment of the Mississippi firmly under Union control.

U.S.S. *Pembina*, Lieutenant Bankhead, seized schooner *Rowena* in Stono River, South Carolina.

7   Lieutenant Wyman, commander of Potomac Flotilla, reported U.S.S. *Anacostia* had captured sloop *Monitor* in Piankatank River, Virginia.

7–10   U.S.S. *Wissahickon*, Commander John DeCamp, and U.S.S. *Itasca*, Lieutenant Caldwell, shelled Confederate batteries at Grand Gulf, Mississippi; they were joined 10 June by gunboats U.S.S. *Iroquois* and *Katahdin*.

8   U.S.S. *Penobscot*, Lieutenant John M. B. Clitz, burned schooner *Sereta*, grounded and deserted off Shallotte Inlet, North Carolina.

9   Secretary of the Navy Welles wrote Senator John P. Hale, Chairman of the Senate Naval Committee, and expressed his belief that the only security against any foreign war was having a Navy second to none: "The fact that a radical change has commenced in the construction and armament of ships, which change in effect dispenses with the navies that have hitherto existed, is obvious, and it is a question for Congress to decide whether the Government will promptly take the initiatory step to place our country in the front rank of maritime powers . . . Other nations, whose

Close action at the Battle of Memphis.   The city surrendered to Captain Charles Henry Davis, USN.

wooden ships-of-war far exceed our own in number, cannot afford to lay them aside, but are compelled to plate them with iron at very heavy cost.   They are not unaware of the disadvantage of this proceeding, but it is a present necessity.   It must be borne in mind, however, that those governments which are striving for naval supremacy are sparing no expense to strengthen themselves by building iron vessels, and already their dock-yards are undergoing the necessary preparation for this change in naval architecture . . ."

On a joint expedition up the Roanoke River to Hamilton, North Carolina, U.S.S *Commodore Perry*, Lieutenant Flusser, accompanied by U.S.S. *Shawsheen* and *Ceres* with troops embarked, came under small arms fire for two hours from Confederates along the banks.   Troops were landed at Hamilton without opposition where steamer *Wilson* was captured.

11   U.S.S. *Susquehanna*, Commander Robert B. Hitchcock, captured blockade runner *Princeton* in the Gulf of Mexico.

U.S.S. *Bainbridge*, Commander Brasher, captured schooner *Baigorry* with cargo of cotton in the Gulf of Mexico.

14   U.S.S. *William G. Anderson*, Acting Master N. D'Oyley, captured schooner *Montebello*, moored in Jordan River, Mississippi.

U.S. tug *Spitfire* captured steamer *Clara Dolsen* in White River, Arkansas.

15   U.S.S *Corwin*, Lieutenant T. S. Phelps, captured schooner *Starlight* on Potopotank Creek, Virginia.

U.S.S. *Tahoma*, Lieutenant John C. Howell, and U.S.S. *Somerset*, Lieutenant English, crossed the bar of St. Marks River, Florida, and shelled the Confederate fort near the lighthouse for forty minutes.   The artillery company stationed there withdrew, and the sailors landed destroyed the battery, and burned the buildings used as barracks.

16   C.S.S. *Maurepas* and steamers *Eliza G.* and *Mary Patterson* were sunk in White River, Arkansas, to obstruct the advance of Union gunboats.

U.S.S. *Somerset*, Lieutenant English, captured blockade running schooner *Curlew* off Cedar Keys, Florida.

17 Joint expedition, made at the request of Major General Halleck to open Army communications on the White River, under Commander Kilty in U.S.S. *Mound City*, with U.S.S. *St. Louis*, *Lexington*, and *Conestoga*, and a regiment of troops, engaged Confederate batteries at St. Charles, Arkansas. *Mound City* took a direct hit at close range, exploding her steam drum and causing heavy casualties. Covered by the gunboats, the troops landed and successfully stormed the earthworks. This action gave control of the White River to the Union fleet.

U.S.S. Mound City *is hit and explodes during action on the White River, Arkansas.*

Captain Blake, Superintendent of the U.S. Naval Academy, wrote Assistant Secretary of the Navy Fox regarding the curriculum of the Academy: "To make the Academy a school for engineers would require considerable changes in the Academic Course. Descriptive geometry, which was struck out of it sometime since, should be restored, for it is needed in the study and comprehension of machines. There should also be an extension of the course of Analytical Geometry and Calculus, by means of which many of the formulas relating to steam, and the steam engine, are derived, and the course of drawing, which now embraces mechanical drawing to some degree, should be extended. We should also have more chemistry." Through the years the Naval Academy curriculum has been reviewed and revised to meet the demands of new technology and new dimensions in sea power.

Charles H. Davis appointed Flag Officer and Commander of U.S. Naval Forces on the Mississippi, relieving Flag Officer Foote. Davis had been in actual command since the departure of Foote on 9 May. Secretary of the Navy Welles congratulated Foote for the "series of successful actions which have contributed so largely to the suppression of the rebellion throughout the Southwest."

19 U.S. sloop *Florida*, tender to U.S.S. *Morning Light*, Acting Lieutenant Henry T. Moore, captured sloop *Ventura* off Grant's Pass, Mobile Bay, with cargo of rice and flour.

Admiral Buchanan, CSN, wrote to Lieutenant Catesby ap R. Jones about the destruction of C.S.S. *Virginia*: "I have great confidence in my old friend Commodore T[attnall] and cannot believe that he acted withou⸱ reflection, or was governed by any other motives than those his judgment told him was right . . . . There is one thing very certain: The destruction of the *Virginia* saved Richmond, for if you all had not been at the bluff [Drewry's] Richmond would have been shelled and perhaps taken."

Commander Maury, CSN, reported to Secretary of the Navy Mallory on his mining operations near Chaffin's Bluff in the James River. Electric torpedoes (mines) made of boiler plate encased in water-tight wooden casks were planted with the assistance of C.S.S. *Teaser*, Lieutenant Davidson. Maury noted that one of the galvanic batteries had been loaned for this service by the University of Virginia.

20 Commander Semmes wrote Confederate Secretary of the Navy Mallory: "It will doubtless be a matter of delicacy and management to get the *Alabama* safely out of British waters without suspicion, as Mr. [Charles F.] Adams, the Northern envoy, and his numerous satellites are exceedingly vigilant in their espionage. We can not, of course, think of arming her in a British port. This must be done at some concerted rendezvous, to which her battery and most of her crew must be sent in a merchant vessel . . . I think well of your suggestion of the East Indies as a cruising ground, and hope to be in the track of the enemy's commerce in those seas as early as October or November next, when I shall doubtless be able to make other rich 'burnt offerings' upon the altar of our country's liberties . . .''

Lieutenant Hunter Davidson, commanding C.S.S. *Teaser*, the first mine-layer, ordered to relieve Commander Matthew F. Maury "in the charge of devising, placing, and superintending submarine batteries in the James River, and you will exercise your discretion as to the ways and means of placing obstacles of this and of any other character to oppose the enemy's passage of the river."

U.S.S. *Madgie*, Acting Master Frank B. Meriam, took 3,000 bushels of rice from a vessel at Barrett's Island, near Darien, South Carolina, and captured schooner *Southern Belle* above that city.

U.S.S. *Beauregard*, Acting Master David Stearns, seized blockade running British schooner *Lucy* off Deadman's Point Bay, Florida.

U.S.S. *Keystone State*, Commander LeRoy, captured blockade running British schooner *Sarah* with cargo of cotton off Charleston.

Two boats under command of Acting Master Theodore B. DuBois of U.S.S. *Albatross* captured steam tug *Treaty* and schooner *Louisa* near Georgetown, South Carolina.

21 Joint expedition under Lieutenant Rhind, U.S.S. *Crusader*, with U.S.S. *Planter* in company, ascended to Simmons Bluff, Wadmelaw River, South Carolina. Lieutenant Rhind landed with troops and destroyed a Confederate encampment.

U.S.S. *Bohio*, Acting Master W. D. Gregory, captured sloop *L. Rebecca* bound from Biloxi to Mobile.

26 General McClellan notified Flag Officer L. M. Goldsborough that the urgency for safely bringing the provision transports from the Pamunkey to the James River was "a matter of vital importance and may involve the existence of the Army." A Confederate offensive had cut McClellan's line of communications with his main base at White House on the Pamunkey River.

U.S.S. *Kensington*, Acting Master Frederick Crocker, with mortar schooners *Horace Beals* and *Sarah Bruen*, proceeding towards Vicksburg, silenced a Confederate battery near Cole's Creek, Mississippi River.

U. S. Flag Ship Hartford
Below Vicksburgh. June 25. 1862.

General Order.

The Mortar Boats and GunBoats of the Mortar Fleet having been placed by Comdr Porter according to his judgment, to the best advantage to act upon the Batteries on the heights, & the Fort below the hospital, at 4 A. M tomorrow they will open fire upon the same and on the city of Vicksburg

At the display of the signal for the ships and GunBoats to weigh, they will form in a double line of sailing, the Richmond (1) leading the ships. Hartford (2) next. and Brooklyn (3) third. The GunBoats will form another line so as to fire between the ships. in the following order, Iroquois (1) & Oneida (2) ahead, but on the port bow of the Richmond so as to fire into the Forts at the upper end of the town without interfering with the fire of the Richmond; next in order the Wissahickon and Sciota, in a line with the Iroquois and Oneida but on the port bow of the Flag Ship so as to fire between the Richmond and Flag Ship; next the Winona & Pinola on port bow of the Brooklyn.

The Hartford will as often as occasion offers fire her bow guns on the Forts at the upper end of the town but the broadside batteries of all the ships

Flag Officer Farragut's carefully prepared plan for bringing his fleet past the Vicksburg batteries.

ships will be particularly directed to the guns in the Forts below and on the heights   The fire use of shrapnel is considered the best projectile, but great care must be taken in the cutting of fuses, so as always to be sure that they burst short of their distination.   When close enough give them grape.

The enclosed diagram will show the position of the respective vessels in the order of attack.

When the vessels reach the bend in the river the Wissahikon, Sciota, Winona, and Pinola will continue on and pass up but should the action be continued by the enemy the ships and Iroquois and Oneida will stop their engines and drop down the river again keeping up their fire until directed otherwise

D. G. Farragut,

Flag Officer
Comdg West Gulf Squad

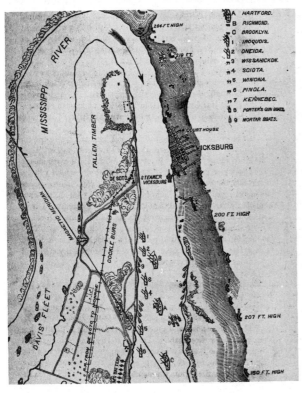

U.S.S. *Mount Vernon*, Commander Glisson, with U.S.S. *Mystic* and *Victoria* chased blockade runner *Emily* standing in for Wilmington. *Emily* grounded and a boat crew commanded by Acting Master W. N. Griswold from *Mount Vernon* boarded and destroyed her while under heavy fire from Fort Caswell.

27 U.S.S. *Bohio*, Acting Master W. D. Gregory, captured sloop *Wave*, bound from Mobile to Mississippi City with cargo of flour.

U.S.S. *Bienville*, Commander Mullany, captured schooner *Morning Star* off Wilmington.

U.S.S. *Cambridge*, Commander W. A. Parker, chased blockade runner *Modern Greece* ashore off Wilmington, where she was subsequently destroyed with cargo of gunpowder, rifled cannon, and other arms.

28 Flag Officer Farragut's fleet, supported by mortar boats under Commander D. D. Porter, successfully passed Vicksburg while exchanging a heavy fire with Confederate batteries. Farragut was acting under orders from President Lincoln to "clear the river."

Flag Officer Davis wrote Secretary of the Navy Welles: "Our recent experience in the navigation of White River has made it apparent that in order to acquire control of the tributaries of the Mississippi, and to maintain that control during the dry season, it will be necessary to fit up immediately some boats of small draft for this special purpose. These boats will be sufficiently protected about the machinery and pilot houses against musketry. They will be selected for their light draft and their capacity to receive a suitable armament of howitzers, fieldpieces, or other light guns, and to accommodate the requisite number of men; and, finally, for their susceptibility of protection."

U.S.S. *Braziliera* captured schooner *Chance* with cargo of salt off Wassaw Sound, Georgia.

28-29 U.S.S. *Marblehead*, Lieutenant S. Nicholson, and U.S.S. *Chocura*, Lieutenant Thomas H. Patterson, in the Pamunkey River, supported Army withdrawal from White House, Virginia, with gunfire and transport. Other Union gunboats escorted transports and moved up the James and Chickahominy Rivers in close support of General McClellan's army.

29 U.S.S. *Susquehanna*, Commander Hitchcock, in company with U.S.S. *Kanawha*, Lieutenant Commander J. C. Febiger, captured blockade running British steamer *Ann* near Mobile with cargo of arms and ammunition.

29-30 Confederate troops fired on U.S.S. *Lexington*, Lieutenant Shirk, on White River between St. Charles and Clarendon, Arkansas.

30 Major General McClellan, compelled to withdraw down the James and dependent upon the Navy for gunfire support and transportation, reported: "I returned from Malvern to Haxall's, and . . . went on board of Captain Rogers' gunboat U.S.S. *Galena* to confer with him in reference to the condition of our supply vessels and the state of things on the river. It was his opinion that it would be necessary for the army to fall back to a position below City Point, as the channel there was so near the southern shore that it would not be possible to bring up the transports should the enemy occupy it. Harrison's Landing was, in his opinion, the nearest suitable point. . . . Concurring in his opinion, I selected Harrison's Bar as the new position of the army." McClellan noted one of many instances of invaluable naval support as the Confederates pressed to cut off the Union movement to the river: "The rear of the supply trains and the reserve artillery of the army reached Malvern Hill about 4 p.m. At about this time the enemy began to appear in General Fitz John Porter's front, and at 5 o'clock advanced in large force against his flank, posting artillery under cover of a skirt of timber, with a view to engage our force on Malvern Hill. . . . The gunboats rendered most efficient aid at this time, and helped drive back the enemy." Naval gunfire support was controlled through a system of liaison in which "fall-of-

shot'' information was sent by Army signal personnel ashore to Army signal personnel afloat in the gunboats by the Myer's system of signalling.

U.S.S. *Quaker City*, Commander Frailey, captured brig *Model* with cargo of coal in the Gulf of Mexico.

Flag Officer Du Pont ordered U.S.S. *South Carolina*, Commander Almy, to join U.S.S. *Wyandotte* in blockading Mosquito Inlet near New Smyrna, Florida. The inlet had become increasingly important to the Confederates as an unloading point for blockade runners bringing arms from Nassau.

JULY

1 The Western Flotilla of Flag Officer Davis joined the fleet of Flag Officer Farragut above Vicksburg. Farragut wrote: ''The iron-clads are curious looking things to us salt-water gentlemen; but no doubt they are better calculated for this river than our ships. . . . They look like great turtles. Davis came on board . . . . We have made the circuit (since we met at Port Royal) around half the United States and met on the Mississippi.'' The meeting of the fresh-water and salt-water squadrons had considerable psychological value throughout the North, but it did not imply control over the river so long as the Gibraltar-like fortress of Vicksburg remained unsubdued. In a military sense this temporary joining of the squadrons pointed up the necessity for the arduous, year-long amphibious campaign which was necessary to capture Vicksburg.

President Lincoln recommended to the Congress that Flag Officer Foote be given a vote of thanks for his efforts on the western waters. The President knew well the import of the defeats dealt the Confederacy by the gunboats on the upper Mississippi. He recognized that Foote's forces had cleared the Tennessee and Cumberland Rivers, and had succeeded in splitting the Confederacy as far as Vicksburg on the Father of Waters.

U.S.S. *De Soto*, Captain W. M. Walker, captured British schooner *William* attempting to run the blockade at Sabine Pass, Texas.

1-2 Flag Officer L. M. Goldsborough's fleet covered the withdrawal of General McClellan's army after a furious battle with Confederate forces under General Robert E. Lee at Malvern Hill. Dependent on the Navy for his movement to Harrison's Landing, chosen by McClellan at Commodore J. Rodgers recommendation because it was so situated that gunboats could protect both flanks of his army, the General acknowledged the decisive role played by the Navy in enabling his troops to withdraw with a minimum loss: ''Commodore Rodgers . . . placed his gunboats so as to protect our flanks and to command the approaches from Richmond . . . During the whole battle Commodore Rodgers added greatly to the discomfiture of the enemy by throwing shell among his reserve and advancing columns.'' The Washington *National Intelligencer* of 7 July described the gunboats' part in the action at Malvern Hill: ''About five o'clock in the afternoon the gunboats *Galena*, *Aroostook*, and *Jacob Bell* opened from Turkey Island Bend, in the James River, with shot and shell from their immense guns. The previous roar of field artillery seemed as faint as the rattle of musketry in comparison with these monsters of ordnance that literally shook the water and strained the air. . . . They fired about three times a minute, frequently a broadside at a time, and the immense hull of the *Galena* careened as she delivered her complement of iron and flame. The fire went on . . . making music to the ears of our tired men. . . . [Confederate] ranks seemed slow to close up when the naval thunder had torn them apart. . . .'' During the engagement at White Oak Swamp, too, the *Intelligencer* reported, the gunboats ''are entitled to the most unbounded credit. They came into action just at the right time, and did first rate service.'' The Navy continued to safeguard the supply line until the Army of the Potomac was evacuated to northern Virginia in August, bringing to a close the unsuccessful Peninsular Campaign.

At Malvern Hill, gunfire support by the James River Flotilla prevented the probable annihilation of General McClellan's troops . . .

and protected the troop's flanks during and after the withdrawal to Harrison's landing.

2 U.S.S. *Western World*, Acting Master Samuel B. Gregory, captured blockade running British schooner *Volante* in Winyah Bay, South Carolina, with cargo of salt and fish.

3 U.S.S. *Quaker City*, Commander Frailey, captured blockade running British brig *Lilla* off Hole-in-the-Wall, Virginia.

   U.S.S. *Hatteras*, Commander Emmons, captured schooner *Sarah* bound for Sabine Pass, Texas, with cargo of sugar and molasses.

4 U.S.S. *Maratanza*, Lieutenant Stevens, engaged C.S.S. *Teaser*, Lieutenant Davidson, at Haxall's on the James River. *Teaser* was abandoned and captured after a shell from *Maratanza* exploded

Capture of C.S.S. Teaser *in James River.* Teaser, *commanded by Lieutenant Hunter Davidson, was equipped for mine laying and balloon reconnaissance.*

her boiler. In addition to placing mines in the river, Davidson had gone down the river with a balloon on board for the purpose of making an aerial reconnaissance of General McClellan's positions at City Point and Harrison's Landing. By this time both Union and Confederate forces were utilizing the balloon for gathering intelligence; *Teaser* had been the Southern counterpart of U.S.S. *G. W. Parke Custis*, from whose deck aerial observations had been made the preceding year. The balloon, as well as a quantity of insulated wire and mine equipment, were found on board *Teaser*. Six shells with "peculiar fuzes" were also taken and sent to Captain Dahlgren at the Washington Navy Yard for examination.

Commander J. Rodgers reported to Flag Officer L. M. Goldsborough on the stationing of the gunboats supporting the Army's position at Harrison's Landing: "It is now too late, I hope, for the enemy to attack the army here with any chance of success. The troops are in good spirits and everyone seems confident." Major General McClellan advised President Lincoln that "Captain Rodgers is doing all in his power in the kindest and most efficient manner." General Robert E. Lee came to the same conclusion in a letter to Confederate President Davis: "The enemy is strongly posted in the neck formed by Herring creek and James River . . . The enemy's batteries occupy the ridge along which the Charles City road runs, north to the creek, and his gunboats lying below the mouth of the creek sweep the ground in front of his batteries—Above his encampments which lie on the river, his gunboats also extend; where the ground is more favorable to be

U. S. S Galena off Harrison Bar
July 4th 1862

Sir

Every thing is quiet and goes on finely — I send a sketch of the position of the Gun boats — The army is in high spirits — They are entrenching their front and by noon will be thoroughly ready for all comers —

" I feel anxious about the navigation — I fear that the enemy may occupy the bluffs which command the Channel below us; this would be inconvenient at the least —

" The enemy are at Haxhalls above City point — they sent up a balloon this morning — but it remained up only a few moments — The Monitor and Maratanza will make a reconnoisance this evening in that direction —

" If Capts McKinstry and Jenkins are in charge of the river below this, I can bring more vessels here to guard our flanks —

" At present there are eight — only two up the river — four down and the Galena and Port Royal, as a reserve, to throw these force where needed — The Stepping Stones I shall use to carry orders. —

" This is the present arrangement of the vessels — or was this morning — The Monitor and Maratanza have gone above City point on a reconnoisance —

At west end of base opposite Jordans Pt	At East end of base opposite Windmill Pt	Reserve to move to either end of base
Maratanza	Aroostook	Galena
Yankee	Monitor	Port Royal
2	Southfield	Stepping Stones tug
	Currituck	2
	4	

Total 8
Aug 4

Commander John Rodgers reports to Flag Officer Goldsborough on the naval support of the Army's position at Harrison's Landing, Virginia.

Guarding Navigation below

Mohaska   At Jamestown Island   Up Chickahominy
Com Barney   Jacob Bell   Delaware
Dragon – tug   Satellite
Sebago   2
Morse
   5

I have not seen the Dacotah nor the Wachusetts — These powerful vessels will, if they remain below, allow the Mohaska and Morse to move up here —

     It it now too late I hope for the enemy to attack the army here with any chance of success — The troops are in good spirits and every one seems confident —

                            I have the honor to be
                            Very Respectfully
                            Your Obt Servant

To Flag Officer
     L. M. Goldsborough   John Rodgers
     Comd N. A. Block Squadron   Commander

Sketch of position of
gun boats on James River

searched by their cannon. As far as I can now see there is no way to attack him to advantage; nor do I wish to expose the men to the destructive missiles of his gunboats . . . I fear he is too secure under cover of his boats to be driven from his position . . ."

U.S.S. *Rhode Island*, Commander Trenchard, captured blockade running British schooner *R. O. Bryan* off the coast of Texas.

5 Act to reorganize the U.S. Navy Department increased the number of Bureaus to eight: Yards and Docks, Equipment and Recruiting, Navigation, Ordnance, Construction and Repair, Steam Engineering, Provisions and Clothing, Medicine and Surgery. This act, and other far-reaching measures were guided through Congress by Senator Grimes of Iowa, who had an outstanding appreciation of sea power.

U.S.S. *Hatteras*, Commander Emmons, captured sloop *Elizabeth* off the Louisiana coast.

6 Commodore Wilkes ordered to command James River Flotilla as a division of the North Atlantic Blockading Squadron, Flag Officer L. M. Goldsborough. Secretary of the Navy Welles' instructions to Wilkes stated: "You will immediately place yourself in communication with Major General McClellan, Commanding the Army of the Potomac, near Harrison's Landing . . . It will be your special duty to keep open the navigation of James River and afford protection to all vessels transporting troops or supplies, and generally to cooperate with the army in all military movements."

7 Commander J. Rodgers reported to Flag Officer L. M. Goldsborough on the convoying of Army transports on James River: "There is to be a convoy of gunboats each day from Harrison's Bar to near the mouth of the Chickahominy, going and returning each day. As there was no better reason for the time than the arrival and departure of the mail from Old Point, it was agreed that at 9 a.m. all the transportation down should sail, convoyed by gunboats—I had selected four for it. And at 3 p.m. all the army transportation to this point should come up, convoyed by the same force." Convoy and cover of supply ships by the gunboats were indispensable to General McClellan's army.

U.S.S. *Tahoma*, Lieutenant John C. Howell, captured schooner *Uncle Mose* off Yucatan Bank, Mexico, with cargo of cotton.

U.S.S. *Quaker City*, Commander Frailey, in company with U.S.S. *Huntsville*, captured blockade running British steamer *Adela* off the Bahama Islands.

Boats from U.S.S. *Flag*, Commander James H. Strong, and U.S.S. *Restless*, Acting Lieutenant Conroy, captured British blockade runner *Emilie* in Bull's Bay, South Carolina.

President Lincoln and military party departed Washington on board U.S.S. *Ariel* to visit General McClellan with the Army of the Potomac at Harrison's Landing, Virginia.

9 General Robert E. Lee wrote President Davis, advising him of the Confederate troops' inability to move against the Union forces on the James River because of the presence of the Navy gunboats: "After a thorough reconnaissance of the position taken up by the enemy on James River, I found him strongly posted and effectually flanked by his Gunboats. . . . I caused field batteries to play on his forces, and on his transports, from points on the river below. But they were too light to accomplish much, and were always attacked with superior force by the Gunboats. . . ."

U.S.S. *Commodore Perry*, Lieutenant Flusser, U.S.S. *Shawsheen*, Acting Master Woodward, and U.S.S. *Ceres*, Acting Master John MacDiarmid, embarked on an expedition up Roanoke River and landed a field piece and force of soldiers and sailors at Hamilton, North Carolina, where steamer *Wilson* was captured.

U.S.S. *Arthur*, Acting Lieutenant Kittredge, captured schooner *Reindeer* with cargo of cotton near Aransas Pass, Texas.

10 Flag Officer Du Pont, learning of the action at Malvern Hill, wrote: "The *Mississippi*, [Army] transport passed us this morning. We boarded her and got papers to the 5th. The captain of the transport told the boarding officer that McClellan's army would have been annihilated but for the gunboats." Continual Confederate concern about the gunboats was noted by a British Army observer, Colonel Garnet J. Wolseley, who wrote that he "noted with some interest the superstitious dread of gunboats which possessed the Southern soldiers. These vessels of war, even when they have been comparatively harmless had several times been the means of saving northern armies."

U.S.S. *Arthur*, Acting Lieutenant Kittredge, captured sloop *Belle Italia* at Aransas Pass, and schooner *Monte Christo* was burned by Confederates at Lamar, Texas, to prevent her falling into Union hands.

11 President Lincoln, demonstrating his appreciation of the role sea power had played thus far in the Civil War, recommended to the Congress that votes of thanks be given to Captains Lardner, Davis, and Stringham, and to Commanders Dahlgren, D. D. Porter, and Rowan.

Congress passed an act for the relief of relatives of the officers and men who died on board U.S.S. *Cumberland* and *Congress* when C.S.S. *Virginia* destroyed those vessels and threatened to break the blockade of Norfolk four months before.

12 U.S.S. *Mercedita*, Commander Stellwagen, captured blockade running schooners *Victoria* and *Ida* off Hole-in-the-Wall, Abaco, Bahamas, the former laden with cotton, the latter with general cargo, including cloth, shoes, needles and salt.

13 Commodore Wilkes reported operations of the James River Flotilla to Secretary of the Navy Welles: "The Army transports are daily convoyed up and down by the gunboats, besides having others stationed off the principal salient points where the rebels have come down to fire at our vessels passing. They almost daily make some attempts to annoy these unarmed boats, but seldom venture to do anything. I believe it is in my power to keep the river open effectually. . . . I found . . . a necessity of active and prompt measures to bring the flotilla into operation, as the duties on the river require, and the effective protection of the two flanks of the army. . . . I would ask the Assistant Secretary's attention to the subject of torpedoes, and also barbed rockets that will enter wood and be the means of firing any bridges or other works of wood. If we had some Congreve rockets, they would prove effective in driving the sharpshooters out of the woods."

14 Congress passed an act stating that: ". . . the spirit ration in the Navy of the United States shall forever cease, and . . . no distilled spiritous liquors shall be admitted on board vessels of war, except as medical stores . . . there shall be allowed and paid to each person in the Navy now entitled to the ration, five cents per day in commutation and lieu thereof, which shall be in addition to their present pay." Assistant Secretary of the Navy Fox and officers generally held that it was in the Navy's best interest to abolish the spirit ration.

15 U.S.S. *Carondelet*, Commander Walke, U.S.S. *Tyler*, Lieutenant Gwin, and ram *Queen of the West*, carrying Army sharp shooters on reconnaissance of the Yazoo River, engaged Confederate ironclad ram *Arkansas*, Lieutenant Isaac N. Brown. In a severe fight as Union ships withdrew, *Arkansas* partially disabled *Carondelet* and *Tyler*. Entering the Mississippi, *Arkansas* ran through fire from the Union fleet to refuge under the Vicksburg batteries in a heavily damaged condition and with many casualties. Farragut's fleet pursued *Arkansas*, but, as the Flag Officer reported, "it was so dark by the time we reached the town that nothing could be seen except the flashes of the guns." In the heavy cannonade as Farragut's ships continued down river below Vicksburg, U.S.S. *Winona*, Lieutenant Edward T. Nichols, and U.S.S. *Sumter*, Lieutenant Henry Erben, were substantially damaged. The daring sortie of *Arkansas* emphatically underscored the need to reduce Vicksburg. Major General Earl Van Dorn, CSA, said that Lieutenant Brown had "immortalized his single vessel, himself, and the heroes under his command, by an achievement

U.S.S. Monitor's *turret in July 1862 still shows the scars from her history making engagement with C.S.S.* Virginia *in Hampton Roads* . . .

the most brilliant ever recorded in naval annals." Secretary Mallory added: "Naval history records few deeds of greater heroism or higher professional ability than this achievement of the *Arkansas*." Lieutenant Brown was promoted to Commander, and the Confederate Congress later expressed thanks to Brown and his men "for their signal exhibition of skill and gallantry . . . in the brilliant and successful engagement of the sloop of war *Arkansas* with the enemy's fleet."

16 David Glasgow Farragut, in recognition of his victory at New Orleans, promoted to Rear Admiral, the first officer to hold that rank in the history of the U.S. Navy.

The measure passed by Congress which created the rank of Rear Admiral also revamped the existing rank structure to include Commodore and Lieutenant Commander and established the number of Rear Admirals at 9; Commodores, 18; Captains, 36; Commanders, 72; and the remainder through Ensign at 144 each. The act provided that "The three senior rear admirals [Farragut, L. M. Goldsborough, and Du Pont] shall wear a square blue flag at the mainmast head; the next three at the foremast head, and all others at the mizzen." Rear Admirals were to rank with Major Generals in the Army.

and part of her crew relaxes topside after enduring temperatures in excess of 100° below decks.

C.S.S. Arkansas, *Lieutenant Isaac N. Brown, heroically runs through the combined Union fleets to refuge at Vicksburg.*

Congress approved a bill transferring "the western gunboat fleet constructed by the War Department for operations on the western waters" to the Navy Department. Actual enactment of the measure took place on 1 October 1862.

Commander Woodhull, U.S.S. *Cimarron*, reported from Harrison's Landing: "I have placed my vessel, as directed, on the extreme right flank of the army; so also the other gunboats under my charge, as will give us full command of the open country beyond the line."

U.S.S. *Huntsville*, Acting Lieutenant William C. Rogers, seized blockade running British schooner *Agnes* off Abaco with cargo of cotton and rosin.

17 Congress passed an act which established that "every officer, seaman, or marine, disabled in the line of duty, shall be intitled to receive for life, or during his disability, a pension from the United States, according to the nature and degree of his disability, not exceeding in any case his monthly pay."

17-18 Twenty Marines from U.S.S. *Potomac* participated in an expedition up Pascagoula River, Mississippi. Under First Lieutenant George W. Collier, the Marines, whose force was augmented by an equal number of sailors, acted with U.S.S. *New London* and *Grey Cloud* to capture or destroy a steamer and two schooners rumored to be loading with cotton, and to destroy telegraphic communications between Pascagoula and Mobile. The expedition succeeded in disrupting communications, but, pursuing the Confederate vessels upstream, it was engaged by cavalry and infantry troops and forced to turn back to care for the wounded.

Rear Admiral David Glasgow Farragut, first officer to hold the rank in the U.S. Navy.

Captain Franklin Buchanan was promoted to Admiral, CSN, for his gallant actions while commanding C.S.S. Virginia.

18 Secretary of the Navy Welles notified Flag Officers commanding squadrons of a bill authorizing the President to appoint annually three midshipmen to the Naval Academy from the enlisted boys of the Navy. "They must be of good moral character, able to read and write well, writing from dictation and spelling with correctness, and to perform with accuracy the various operations of the primary rules of arithmetic, viz, numeration, and the addition, subtraction, multiplication, and division of whole numbers." Each Flag Officer was requested to nominate one candidate from his command "not over 18 years of age."

19 Naval court martial meeting in Richmond acquitted Flag Officer Tattnall with honor for ordering the destruction of C.S.S. *Virginia* on 11 May after the evacuation of Norfolk. The court found that "the only alternative . . . was to abandon and burn the ship then and there, which in the judgment of the court, was deliberately and wisely done. . . ."

21 U.S. steamers *Clara Dolsen* and *Rob Roy* and tug *Restless* under Commander Alexander M. Pennock, with troops embarked, arrived from Cairo to protect Evansville, Indiana, at the request of Governor Morton. Troops were landed and retook Henderson, Kentucky, from Confederate guerrillas, several boats were burned, and the Ohio was patrolled against attack from the Kentucky side of the river. Major General John Love wrote to Commander Pennock expressing the "gratitude with which the citizens of Indiana and of this locality will regard the prompt cooperation of yourself and your officers in this emergency, which threatened their security." The mobility which naval control of the river gave to Union forces neutralized repeated Confederate attempts to re-establish positions in the border states.

Confederate artillery at Argyle Landing, Mississippi River, destroyed naval transport U.S.S. *Sallie Woods*.

U.S.S. *Huntsville*, Acting Lieutenant W. C. Rogers, captured steamer *Reliance* in Bahama Channel.

22 U.S.S. *Essex*, Commander W. D. Porter, and ram *Queen of the West*, Lieutenant Colonel Ellet, attacked C.S.S. *Arkansas*, Commander I. N. Brown, at anchor with a disabled engine at Vicksburg.

Although many of his officers and crew were ashore sick and wounded after the action of 15 July, Commander Brown fought his ship gallantly. After attempting to ram, the *Essex* became closely engaged in cannon fire with *Arkansas*. Breaking off the engagement, *Essex* steamed through a hail of shell past the shore batteries and joined Rear Admiral Farragut's fleet which had remained below Vicksburg after passing the city on 15 July. *Queen of the West* rammed *Arkansas* but with little effect. She rejoined Flag Officer Davis' fleet in a shattered condition. The day after repelling the attack by *Essex* and *Queen of the West*, Commander Brown defiantly steamed *Arkansas* up and down the river under the Vicksburg batteries. A member of *Arkansas*'s crew, Dabney M. Scales, described the action in a vivid letter to his father: "At 4 o'clock on the morning of the 22nd, I was awakened by the call to quarters. Hurrying to our stations, with not even a full complement of men for 3 guns; our soldiers having left just the night before; we discovered the enemy coming right down upon us. . . . We did not have men enough to heave the anchor up and get underway, before the enemy got to us, even if we had had steam ready. So we had to lay in to the bank, and couldn't meet him on anything like equal terms. . . . The *Essex* came first, firing on us with her three bow guns. We replied with our two bow guns as long as they could be brought to bear, which was not a very long time, as our vessel being stationary, the enemy soon came too much on our broadside for these guns, and their crews had to be shifted to the broadside guns. In the meantime, the *Essex* ranged up alongside us, and at the distance of 20 feet poured in a broads. which crashed against our sides like—nothing that I ever heard before. . . . We were so close that our men were burnt by the powder of the enemy's guns. . . . All this time the Ram [*Queen of the West*] was not idle, but came close down on the heels of his consort. . . . We welcomed him as warmly as we could with our scanty crew. Just before he got to us, we managed by the helm and with the aid of the starboard propellor, to turn our bow outstream a little, which prevented him from getting a fair lick at us. As it was, he glanced round our side and ran aground just astern of us." Meanwhile, the Confederate Secretary of War in a general order praised *Arkansas*'s feats of the week before: "Lieutenant Brown, and the officers and crew of the Confederate steamer *Arkansas*, by their heroic attack upon the Federal fleet before Vicksburg equaled the highest recorded examples of courage and skill. They proved that the Navy, when it regains its proper element, will be one of the chief bulwarks of national defense and that it is entitled to a high place in the confidence and affection of the country."

President Davis telegraphed Governor John J. Pettus of Mississippi: "Captain Brown of the *Arkansas*, requires boatmen, and reports himself doomed to inactivity by the inability to get them. We have a large class of river boatmen and some ordinary seamen on our Gulf Coast who must now be unemployed. Can you help Captain Brown to get an adequate crew?"

23 Assistant Secretary of the Navy Fox wrote Major General John G. Barnard: "Part of the mortar fleet are ordered to James River and should be there by the 1st proximo. There is no army to cooperate at Vicksburg where we have been lying two months, and the keeping open James River up to McClellan's position is the first duty of the Navy, so we ordered twelve of the vessels there. If a fort is erected below you on the right bank of the James (and I see no obstacle) or if offensive or defensive operations are undertaken I think the mortar will not come amiss. . . . The iron boats are progressing . . . We have forty underweigh, and are putting others in hand as fast as contracts for engines shall be made. The machinery for manufacturing marine engines is limited." The Union Navy's rapid transformation from wood to iron doomed the Confederacy's effort with ironclads and rams to break the noose of Federal seapower.

24 Rear Admiral Farragut's fleet departed its station below Vicksburg, as the falling water level of the river and sickness among his ships' crews necessitated withdrawal to Baton Rouge and New Orleans. Farragut's return to the lower Mississippi made abundantly clear the strategic significance of Vicksburg for, although the Navy held the vast majority of the river, Confederate control of Vicksburg enabled the South to continue to get some supplies for her armies in the

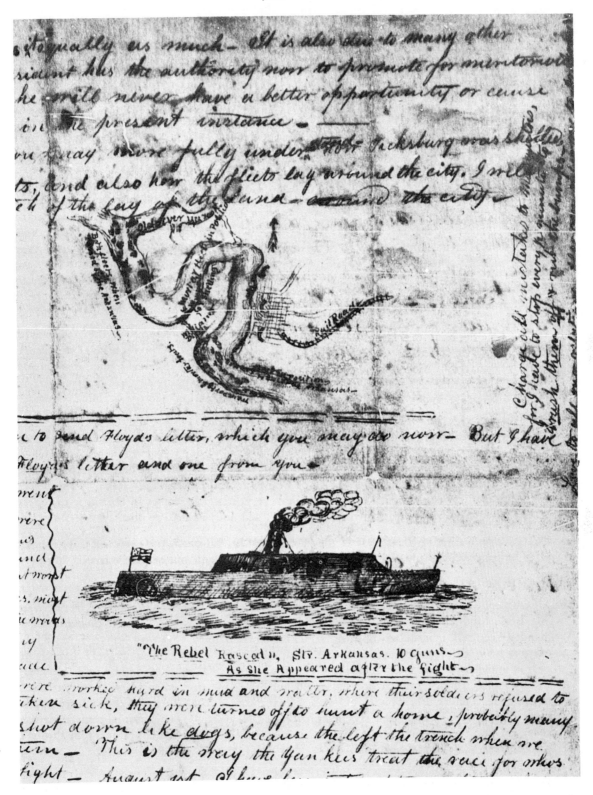

In a letter to his father, Midshipman Dabney Scales included these interesting sketches of the Union forces in the Mississippi River near Vicksburg and his ship C.S.S. Arkansas.

East from Texas, Arkansas, and Louisiana.   To prevent as much of this as possible, Rear Admiral Davis and Major General Samuel R. Curtis provided for combined Army-Navy expeditions along the banks of the Mississippi from Helena, Arkansas, to Vicksburg. Though supplies continued to move across the river, this action prevented the Confederates from maintaining and reinforcing batteries at strategic points, an important factor in the following year's operations.

U.S.S. *Quaker City*, Commander Frailey, captured blockade runner *Orion* at Campeche Bank, south of Key West, Florida.

U.S.S. *Octorara*, Commander D. D. Porter, captured British blockade runner *Tubal Cain* east of Savannah.

25 Steamer *Cuba* ran the blockade into Mobile.

26 Confederates boarded and burned schooner *Louisa Reed* in the James River.

27 U.S.S. *Yankee*, Lieutenant Commander William Gibson, and U.S.S. *Satellite*, Acting Master Amos Foster, captured schooner *J. W. Sturges* in Chippoak Creek, Virginia.

28 U.S.S. *Hatteras*, Commander Emmons, captured Confederate brig *Josephine* off Ship Shoal, Louisiana, en route to Havana with cargo of cotton.

Bark *Agrippina*, Captain Alexander McQueen, was ordered to rendezvous in the Azores with steamer *Enrica* (afterwards C.S.S. *Alabama*) which was to depart Liverpool pursuant to arrangements made by Commander Bulloch in London, for the purpose of transferring guns, ammunition, coal, and other cargo to *Alabama*. Under the command of Captain Raphael Semmes, the renowned Confederate cruiser *Alabama* ravaged the seas, dealing serious damage to Union commerce.

29 U.S.S. *Mount Vernon*, Commander Glisson, and U.S.S. *Mystic*, Lieutenant Commander Arnold, captured blockade running British brig *Napier* near Wilmington.

Writing of Union reverses in the East, which he ascribed to the deception of Northern commanders by false reports of the size of Confederate armies, Rear Admiral Farragut stated: "The officers say I don't believe anything. I certainly believe very little that comes in the shape of reports . . . I mean to be whipped or to whip my enemy, and not be scared to death."

31 U.S.S. *Magnolia*, Acting Lieutenant W. Budd, captured British steamer *Memphis* off Cape Romain with large cargo of cotton and rosin. She had run the blockade out of Charleston on 26 July.

JULY–AUGUST

31–1 Confederate batteries at Coggins' Point took Union forces under fire on the James River between Harrison's Landing and Shirley, Virginia, sinking two Army transports. U.S.S. *Cimarron*, Commander Woodhull, immediately opened counter fire on the battery. Praising Gunner's Mate John Merrett who, although extremely ill and awaiting transfer to a hospital, bravely manned his station in the main magazine, Commander Woodhull wrote: "Merrett is an old man-of-warsman; his discipline, courage, and patriotism would not brook inaction when his ship was in actual battle. His conduct, I humbly think, was a great example to all lovers of the country and its cause . . . it is the act of a fine specimen of the old Navy tar." This mutual respect between the naval officer and the long service enlisted man enabled the Navy to maintain its tone throughout the Civil War despite expansion.

AUGUST

1 U.S.S. *Thomas Freeborn*, Acting Master James L. Plunkett, captured schooner *Mail* in Coan River, Virginia, with cargo including salt.

U.S.S. *Penobscot*, Lieutenant Clitz, captured sloop *Lizzie* off New Inlet, North Carolina, with cargo including salt.

2 William H. Aspinwall, a Union merchant and long time booster of ironclads, wrote Assistant Secretary of the Navy Fox suggesting an innovation in weaponry to which can be traced the modern torpedo: "I have been thinking for some time about the probability that a properly shaped cylindrical shot fired 6 or 8 feet under water will be the next improvement on iron clad vessels. At short range great effect could be attained below the iron plating. . . . I have the plan for firing a gun projecting 6 or 8 or 10 feet below the water line of a vessel, which I think would work well, if it is found that shot can be relied on to do the intended injury—under water."

C.S.S. *Florida*, Lieutenant Maffitt, about to take to sea from Nassau, was released by the Admiralty Court after having been seized by H.M.S *Greyhound*.

3 U.S.S. *Santiago de Cuba*, Commander Ridgely, seized blockade runner *Columbia* north of Abaco with cargo of arms.

4 U.S.S. *Unadilla*, Lieutenant Collins, captured British steamer *Lodona* attempting to run the blockade at Hell Gate, Georgia.

U.S.S. *Huron*, Lieutenant Downes, seized schooner *Aquilla* near Charleston with cargo of turpentine.

5 Assistant Secretary of the Navy Fox observed that: "The Richmond Engineer [*Enquirer*] said that the first federal [army] officer meeting a navy officer at James River after McClellan's 'strategic move' [withdrawing from Malvern Hill to Harrison's Landing] threw his arms around his neck and said 'Oh my dear Sir, we ought to have a gunboat in every family!'"

6 C.S.S. *Arkansas*, Lieutenant Henry Stevens temporarily in command, having become unmanageable due to engine failure while advancing to support a Confederate attack on Baton Rouge, was engaged by U.S.S. *Essex*, Commander W. D. Porter. Lieutenant Stevens recognized his helpless condition, shotted his guns, and ordered *Arkansas* destroyed to prevent her capture. He reported: "It was beautiful to see her, when abandoned by Commander and crew, and dedicated to sacrifice, fighting the battle on her own hook." Without naval support and under fire from U.S.S. *Sumter*, *Cayuga*, *Kineo*, and *Katahdin*, the Confederate thrust was repelled. When the wounded and ill Commander Brown had departed *Arkansas* on a brief leave, he had realized that critical repairs were necessary and that his ship was not ready for combat. He ordered Stevens not to move her until his return. Nevertheless, General Van Dorn, to ensure the success of his expedition, ordered *Arkansas* into the fatal Baton Rouge action. Had *Arkansas* been fit for battle, the Confederates might have taken Baton Rouge and reopened the important Red River supply line then under Union blockade.

7 President Lincoln, with Secretaries Seward and Stanton, visited Captain Dahlgren at the Washington Navy Yard for a two hour demonstration of the "Rafael" repeating cannon. Later Dahlgren took the party on board a steamer to cool off and rest.

C.S.S. *Florida* departed Nassau and began her renowned career under Lieutenant Maffitt.

8 Confederate Secretary of the Navy Mallory wrote Commander Bulloch in London: "I am pleased to learn that the credit of my department stands well in England, and sensible of the great importance of maintaining it. I am endeavoring to place funds to your credit, which the scarcity and very high rate of exchange render difficult. We have just paid 200 and 210 per cent for 80,072.3.9, which amount is now in the hands of John Fraser & Co. of Charleston, with orders to place the same to your credit in England." The tightening blockade constantly constricted the Southern economy.

10   Rear Admiral Farragut reported to Secretary of the Navy Welles that he had partially destroyed Donaldsonville, Louisiana, in reprisal for the firing by guerrilla forces on steamers "passing up and down the river." Farragut wrote that he had "sent a message to the inhabitants that if they did not discontinue this practice, I would destroy their town. The last time I passed up to Baton Rouge to the support of the army, I . . . heard them firing upon the vessels coming up, first upon the *Sallie Robinson* and next upon the *Brooklyn*. In the latter case they made a mistake, and it was so quickly returned that they ran away. The next night they fired again upon the *St. Charles*. I therefore ordered them to send their women and children out of the town, as I certainly intended to destroy it on my way down the river, and I fullfilled my promise to a certain extent. I burned down the hotels and wharf buildings, also the dwelling houses and other buildings of a Mr. Phillippe Landry, who is said to be a captain of guerrillas." Though Farragut had no taste for devastating private property, he felt justified in doing so if private citizens endangered the lives of his men.

    U.S.S. *Resolute*, Acting Master James C. Tole, captured schooner *S.S. Jones* near the Virginia coast.

11   Rear Admiral Farragut, having received his promotion, "hoisted my flag at the main." His general order to the fleet on this date ascribed the promotion to "the gallantry of the officers and men of the fleet . . . [and] your Admiral feels assured that you will never disappoint these high expectations. A new field is now opening before you. To your ordinary duties is added the contest with the elements. Let it be your pride to show the world that danger has no greater terror for you in one form than in another; that you are as ready to meet the enemy in the one shape as in the other, and that you, with your wooden vessels, have never been alarmed by fire rafts, torpedoes, chain booms, ironclad rams, ironclad gunboats, or forts. The same Great Power preserves you in the presence of all."

12   U.S.S. *Arthur*, Acting Lieutenant Kittredge, captured armed schooner *Breaker* at Aransas Pass, Texas. Confederate schooner *Elma* and sloop *Hannah* were burned at Corpus Christi to prevent their capture by *Arthur*.

13   Rear Admiral Du Pont wrote Assistant Secretary of the Navy Fox on the subject of Confederate rams and ironclads at Savannah and Charleston: "The Savannah one, not at all the *Fingal*, is more of a floating battery, doubtless with 10 inch guns (8 of them) but she has a list, leaks, and has not power to go against stream. She may be used to cover vessels running the blockade by putting herself between them and the *Forts* if entering Savannah River. . . . The Charleston vessels are not yet ready and I *hope* are progressing slowly, one is simply an ironclad, size of *Pembina*— the other more of a ram." Because of the power which C.S.S. *Virginia* had promised and demonstrated, the Confederacy made every effort to ready other ironclads to strike against the blockading forces. However, lack of critical material and industrial facilities prevented the South from mounting a truly serious threat. On the Savannah River, ironclad rams *Georgia* and *Atlanta* were launched, but both were too slow and drew too much water to be fully effective. *Atlanta* showed herself to Du Pont's squadron on 31 July, when she steamed down the river toward Fort Pulaski and returned to Savannah. Some six months later, Master H. Beverly Littlepage, CSN, wrote Lieutenant Catesby ap R. Jones of her: "We are still at anchor in the river between Fort Jackson and the first obstructions, only a few hundred yards from the *Georgia*. I understand it is the intention of the commodore [Tattnall] that the *Atlanta* shall be moored as near the stern of the *Georgia* as she can get so that by springing her either of her broadsides may be made to bear on the obstructions in the event of the anticipated attack. I think I can safely affirm that the *Atlanta* will never go outside of the obstructions again or, at least for some time. . . . There is no

ventilation below at all, and I think it will be impossible for us to live on her in the summer. . . . I would venture to say that if a person were blindfolded and carried below and then turned loose he would imagine himself in a swamp, for the water is trickling in all the time and everything is so damp." C.S.S. *Georgia*, for want of adequate engines, was used as a floating battery. The ironclads concerning Du Pont at Charleston were C.S.S. *Palmetto State*, a ram, and gunboat C.S.S. *Chicora*. *Palmetto State*'s keel had been laid in January under Flag Officer Duncan N. Ingraham. Two months later *Chicora*'s keel was laid—in the rear of the Charleston post office—under the direction of James M. Eason, who built two additional ironclads at Charleston, C.S.S. *Charleston* (whose keel was laid in December 1862) and C.S.S. *Columbia*, which was not completed before the fall of Charleston. Lieutenant James H. Rochelle, who commanded *Palmetto State* late in the war, described the vessels: "The iron-clads were . . . slow vessels with imperfect engines, which required frequent repairing. . . . Their armor was four inches thick, and they were all of the type of the *Virginia*. . . . Each of the iron-clads carried a torpedo fitted to the end of a spar some 15 or 20 feet long, projecting from the bow on a line with the keel, and so arranged that it could be carried either triced up clear of the water or submerged five or six feet below the surface. . . . Every night one or more of the iron-clads anchored in the channel near Sumter for the purpose of resisting a night attack on Sumter or a dash into the harbor by the Federal vessels." Of *Columbia* Rochelle wrote: "She had a thickness of six inches of iron on her casemate, and was otherwise superior to the other iron-clads. Unfortunately, the *Columbia* was bilged in consequence of the ignorance, carelessness or treachery of her pilot, and rendered no service whatever." For all their defects, the Charleston vessels, particularly *Palmetto State* and *Chicora*, did in a measure, as naval constructor John L. Porter forecast in a 20 June 1862 letter to Eason, "afford great protection to the harbor of Charleston when completed."

U.S.S. *Kensington*, Acting Master Crocker, seized schooner *Troy* off Sabine Pass, Texas, with cargo of cotton.

14 U.S.S. *Pocahontas*, Lieutenant George B. Balch, and steam tug *Treaty*, Acting Lieutenant Baxter, on an expedition up the Black River from Georgetown, South Carolina, exchanged fire with Confederate troops at close range along both banks of the river for a distance of 20 miles in an unsuccessful attempt to capture steamer *Nina*.

15 Commodore Wilkes, commanding James River Flotilla, ordered U.S.S. *Galena*, Commander J. Rodgers, U.S.S. *Port Royal*, and U.S.S. *Satellite* to cover the withdrawal of the left wing of General McClellan's army from Harrison's Landing over the Chickahominy. Rodgers was directed to "communicate with General Pleasonton and inform him that you are to cover his cavalry force until such time as the services of the gunboats may no longer be useful to him."

Confederate steamer *A. B.* (or *A. Bee*), aground at the entrance of the Nueces River near Corpus Christi, was burned to avoid capture by U.S.S. *Arthur*, Acting Lieutenant Kittredge.

16 Naval forces under Lieutenant Commander S. L. Phelps, including U.S.S. *Mound City*, *Benton*, and *General Bragg*, and rams *Monarch*, *Samson*, *Lioness*, and *Switzerland*, under Colonel Ellet, convoyed and covered Army troops under Colonel Charles R. Woods in a joint expedition up the Mississippi from Helena as far as the Yazoo River. The force was landed at various points en route, capturing steamer *Fairplay* above Vicksburg, with large cargo of arms, and dispersing Confederate troop encampments. The joint expedition also destroyed a newly erected Confederate battery about 20 miles up the Yazoo River.

Confederate Secretary of the Navy Mallory wrote of the desperate need of iron for the South's ships: "The want of iron is severely felt throughout the Confederacy, and the means of increasing its production demand, in my judgment, the prompt consideration of Congress. The Government has outstanding contracts amounting to millions of dollars, but the iron is not forthcoming to meet the increasing public wants. Scrap iron of all classes is being industriously collected by

Ellet's Rams strengthened the Union offensive down the western rivers.

agents of the Government, and we are now rolling railroad iron into plates for covering ships. . . ." Chronic lack of iron drastically restricted Confederate ship construction, and eventually weighed heavily in the final decision. As Commander Maury had written: "Our necessities cry out for a Navy in war; and when peace comes, it will profit us but little to be affluent and free, if we are continually liable to be pillaged by all . . . the breadth of our plantations and the value of our staples will be of small advantage if the others may have the mastery in our own waters." Weakness in naval power made the Confederate supply problems insurmountable.

16–18 Union naval force, comprising U.S.S. *Sachem, Reindeer, Belle Italia,* and yacht *Corypheus,* under command of Acting Lieutenant Kittredge, bombarded Corpus Christi. On 18 August a landing party of sailors from *Belle Italia,* supported by ships' gunfire, attempted to seize a Confederate battery but was driven back by a cavalry force. Lieutenant Kittredge was captured while ashore on 14 September. Confederate General H. P. Bee characterized Kittredge as "an honorable enemy" and a "bold and energetic leader." Lacking troop strength to occupy and hold Corpus Christi, Sabine City or Galveston, Rear Admiral Farragut's ships nonetheless effectively controlled the Texas coast and pinned down Confederate forces which were vitally needed elsewhere.

17 Joint landing party from U.S.S. *Ellis,* Master Benjamin H. Porter, and Army boats destroyed Confederate salt works, battery, and barracks near Swansboro, North Carolina. This constant attack from the sea destroyed the South's resources and drained her strength.

18 Secretary of the Navy Welles wrote Commodore Wilkes: "Our naval operations in James River have, from the time you were placed in command of the flotilla, depended almost entirely on army movements; and notwithstanding the army has left your vicinity, your future action and the orders you may receive will, for a time at least, and in a great degree, be controlled by developments elsewhere."

Secretary of the Navy Welles, regarding the right of search, instructed squadron and cruiser commanders: "Some recent occurrences in the capture of vessels, and matters pertaining to the blockade, render it necessary that there should be a recapitulation of the instructions heretofore . . . given . . . It is essential, in the remarkable contest now waging, that we should exercise great forbearance, with great firmness, and manifest to the world that it is the intention of our Government, while asserting and maintaining our own rights, to respect and scrupulously regard the right of others . . . You are specially informed that the fact that a suspicious vessel has been indicated to you . . . does not in any way authorize you to depart from the practice of the rules of visitation, search, and capture prescribed by the law of nations."

19 Captain John A. Winslow of U.S.S. *St. Louis* reported the burning by Confederates of Union steamer *Swallow*, aground below Memphis.

21 Rear Admiral Farragut commented on the intervention of foreign powers in the Civil War: "I don't believe it, and, if it does come, you will find the United States not so easy a nut to crack as they imagine. We have no dread of 'rams' or 'he-goats,' and, if our Editors had less, the country would be better off. Now they scare everybody to death."

U.S.S. *Bienville*, Commander Mullany, captured British blockade runner *Eliza*, bound from Nassau to Shallotte Inlet, North Carolina.

22 Secretary of the Navy Welles ordered Rear Admiral L. M. Goldsborough, commanding North Atlantic Blockading Squadron, to "assist the army, as far as you may be able, in embarking the troops at Fortress Monroe and Newport News, as desired by Major General Halleck." The withdrawal northward of the Army of the Potomac by water transport brought to a close the Peninsular Campaign.

Rear Admiral Farragut instructed Lieutenant Commander Philip C. Johnson, commanding U.S.S. *Tennessee*, that "you will stop at Pilot Town [Louisiana] and bring Lieutenant McClain Tilton and the Marine guard, together with all the stores you can [to the Pensacola Navy Yard]." Earlier in the year the Marines had garrisoned the town.

U.S.S. *Keystone State*, Commander Le Roy, captured British schooner *Fanny* with cargo of salt, near St. Simon's Sound, Georgia.

23 U.S.S. *Adirondack*, Captain Guert Gansevoort, ran on a reef outside Man of War Cay, Little Bahamas, and was abandoned after efforts to save her failed.

U.S.S. *Bienville*, Commander Mullany, seized British blockade runner *Louisa* off Cape Romain, South Carolina.

U.S.S. *James S. Chambers*, Acting Master D. Frank Mosman, seized schooner *Corelia* off the coast of Cuba.

23-24 Boat crew from U.S.S. *Essex*, Captain W. D. Porter, was fired upon by Confederate guerrillas at Bayou Sara, Louisiana. *Essex* shelled the town.

24 Raphael Semmes took command of C.S.S. *Alabama* at sea off the island of Terceira, Azores. Of *Alabama*, Semmes said, "She was indeed a beautiful thing to look upon." As Semmes finished reading his orders promoting him to Captain and appointing him to command *Alabama*, the Confederate ensign replaced the English colors at the mast head, a gun was fired, and "The air was rent by a deafening cheer from officers and men. The band, at the same time, playing Dixie." Thus, the celebrated raider was christened to begin her storied two year career.

U.S.S. *Isaac N. Seymour*, Acting Master Francis S. Wells, ran aground and sank in Neuse River, North Carolina.

U.S.S. *Henry Andrew*, Lieutenant Arthur S. Gardner, wrecked after grounding during a heavy gale 15 miles south of Cape Henry, Virginia.

U.S.S. *Stars and Stripes*, Lieutenant McCook, captured British ship *Mary Elizabeth*, attempting to run the blockade into Wilmington with cargo of salt and fruit.

U.S. yacht *Corypheus*, tender to U.S.S. *Arthur*, Acting Lieutenant Kittredge, captured schooner *Water Witch* off Aransas Bay, Texas.

Confederate blockade runner makes port under fire from blockading ships.

25 Typical log entry (this of U.S.S. *Benton*) describing the relentless naval operations on the western waters: "At 7 [a.m.] sent a boat ashore, which destroyed seven skiffs and one batteau. At 11:40 came to at Bolivar Landing [Mississippi]. At 11:45 General Woods landing troops; opened fire upon the enemy. We opened fire with our bow and starboard guns in protecting the landing of the troops . . . fired a number of shots in direction of the rebel force."

26 Captain Franklin Buchanan promoted to Admiral in the Confederate Navy "for gallant and meritorious conduct in attacking the enemy's fleet in Hampton Roads and destroying the frigate *Congress*, sloop of war *Cumberland* . . . whilst in command of the squadron in the waters of Virginia on the 8th of March, 1862."

Confederate steamer *Yorktown*, running the blockade from Mobile to Havana, sprung a leak and foundered at sea off Ship Island with cargo of cotton.

27 U.S.S. *South Carolina*, Commander John J. Almy, destroyed abandoned schooner *Patriot*, aground near Mosquito Inlet, Florida.

U.S.S. *Santiago de Cuba*, Commander Ridgely, captured blockade runner *Lavinia* north of Abaco with cargo of turpentine.

29 U.S.S. *Pittsburg*, Lieutenant Thompson, escorted steamers *White Cloud* and *Iatan* with Army troops embarked to Eunice, Arkansas. The gunboat shelled and dispersed Confederate forces from a camp above Carson's Landing on the Mississippi shore. Landing the troops under cover of *Pittsburg*'s guns for reconnaissance missions en route, Lieutenant Thompson at Eunice seized a large wharf boat, fitted out as a floating hotel. This type of persistent patrolling of the Mississippi and tributaries by the Union Navy in support of Army operations was instrumental in preventing the Confederates from establishing firm positions.

The James River Flotilla having carried out its mission in support of General McClellan's army, the Navy Department ordered Commodore Wilkes to turn the ships over to Rear Admiral L. M. Goldsborough and to proceed to Washington to assume command of the Potomac Flotilla.

30 U.S.S. *Passaic* launched at Greenpoint, New York. A newspaper reporter observed: "A fleet of monsters has been created, volcanoes in a nutshell, breathing under water, fighting under shelter, steered with mirrors, driven by vapor, running anywhere, retreating from nothing. These floating carriages bear immense ordnance, perfected by new processes, and easily worked by new and simple devices. . . ."

U.S.S. *R. R. Cuyler*, Acting Master Simeon N. Freeman, captured schooner *Anne Sophia* at sea east of Jacksonville.

31 U.S. transport *W. B. Terry*, Master Leonard G. Klinck, carrying cargo of coal for Union gunboats, ran aground at Duck River Shoals, Tennessee River, and was captured by Confederate troops.

U.S.S. *William G. Anderson*, Acting Master D'Oyley, seized schooner *Lily* off Louisiana with cargo of gun powder.

SEPTEMBER

1 C.S.S. *Florida*, Lieutenant Maffitt, put into Havana after suffering a yellow fever epidemic on board which was fatal to several crew members.

Rear Admiral S. P. Lee relieved Rear Admiral L. M. Goldsborough as Commander, North Atlantic Blockading Squadron.

2 U.S.S. *Restless*, Acting Lieutenant Conroy, captured sloop *John Thompson* off South Carolina with cargo of turpentine.

3 U.S.S. *Essex*, Commodore W. D. Porter, in pursuit of C.S.S. *Webb*, had a landing party fired on at Natchez, Mississippi, from which Union forces had withdrawn on 25 July. *Essex* bombarded the town for an hour, after which the mayor "unconditionally surrendered" the city to Porter.

4 First session of the Naval Investigating Committee of the Confederate Congress was held in Richmond to examine Secretary Mallory's administration of naval affairs and the causes of the Southern disaster at New Orleans. The final report of the committee was favorable to Mallory.

C.S.S. *Florida*, Lieutenant Maffitt, ran the blockade into Mobile Bay. Many of the crew were suffering from yellow fever and Maffitt determined to make the bold dash into Mobile. Running past the broadside of U.S.S. *Oneida*, Commander Preble, *Florida* also evaded U.S.S. *Winona* and *Rachel Seaman* before coming to anchor under the guns of Fort Morgan in a much damaged condition. This *Florida* incident brought forth orders for stricter enforcement of the blockade.

U.S.S. *William G. Anderson*, Acting Master D'Oyley, captured schooner *Theresa* in the Gulf of Mexico with cargo including salt.

U.S.S. *Shepherd Knapp*, Acting Lieutenant Henry S. Eytinge, captured bark *Fannie Laurie* off South Edisto River, South Carolina.

C.S.S. Florida—*successful commerce raider built in England for the Confederacy.*

5 Rear Admiral Du Pont wrote Secretary of the Navy Welles, again expressing concern about reports of Confederate ironclads building at Charleston: "The iron-clads or rams built at Charleston have been described to me, by intelligent persons who have seen them, as well protected by their armor, but as not formidable for offensive operations against our vessels, in consequence of their deficiency in steam power, it having been intended to place in them engines taken from old steamers belonging to South Carolina. If it be true that English steam engines have been provided for them, as reported to me by the Department, it becomes my duty to urge upon it the necessity of sending some iron-clad vessels of our own, to render our position off Charleston tenable. Vessels even imperfectly covered with armor emerging from the protection of forts, and always provided with a place of refuge, would be comparatively secure, while they might do great harm to wooden ships, especially of the light class which forms the chief material of this squadron. If by any possibility the blockading force off Charleston could be destroyed, or compelled to retire, it would produce a moral impression to our disadvantage even more disastrous than the actual loss itself. If it be possible to send the *Ironsides* to take up a position off that [Charleston] harbor, the efforts of the enemy would be completely frustrated."

C.S.S. *Alabama*, Captain Semmes, seized and burned ship *Ocmulgee* near the Azores, the first of many Union whalers and merchant vessels to fall prey to the feared commerce raider.

6 U.S.S. *Louisiana*, Acting Lieutenant Richard T. Renshaw, joined with Union troops in repelling the Confederate attack on Washington, North Carolina. Major General John G. Foster reported that *Louisiana* "rendered most efficient aid, throwing her shells with great precision, and clearing the streets, through which her guns had range." U.S. Army gunboat *Picket* was destroyed by an accidental magazine explosion during engagement.

7 C.S.S. *Alabama*, Captain Semmes, captured and burned schooner *Starlight* near the Azores.

U.S.S. *Essex*, Commodore W. D. Porter, steamed down the Mississippi to New Orleans past Confederate batteries at Port Hudson, Louisiana. *Essex* was struck with heavy shot 14 times. Porter noted that the Port Hudson batteries "would seriously interrupt the free navigation of the Lower Mississippi."

8   Commodore Wilkes ordered to command a "Flying Squadron"—including U.S.S. *Wachusett*, *Dacotah, Cimarron, Sonoma, Tioga, Octorara*, and *Santiago de Cuba*. The squadron was originated specifically to seek out and capture commerce raiders C.S.S. *Alabama* and *Florida*. Though the squadron seized several vessels engaged in blockade running, the two noted raiders eluded Wilkes' force.

    A landing party from U.S.S. *Kingfisher* destroyed salt works at St. Joseph's Bay, Florida, that could produce some 200 bushels a day. Three days later, similar works at St. Andrew's Bay were destroyed by a landing party from U.S.S. *Sagamore*.

    C.S.S. *Alabama*, Captain Semmes, captured and burned whaling ship *Ocean Rover* near the Azores.

9   C.S.S. *Alabama*, Captain Semmes, captured and burned whaling ships *Alert* and *Weather Gauge* near the Azores.

11   U.S.S. *Patroon*, Acting Master William D. Urann, and U.S.S. *Uncas*, Acting Master Crane, engaged Confederate batteries at St. John's Bluff, Florida. *Uncas* suffered damage, but temporarily forced the abandonment of the batteries.

12   Rear Admiral Du Pont wrote Senator Grimes of Iowa expressing his "warm appreciation of your tremendous labors in behalf of the Navy during the last session. I believe this to be emphatically the opinion of the whole service." Grimes had strongly backed the bill creating the rank of Rear Admiral in the Navy. In reply the Senator stated: "I am in no wise deserving of the kind compliments you lavish upon me. . . . you know that up to my time [in Congress] it was supposed that all information in relation to your branch of the public service was confined to a select 'guild' about the Atlantic cities, no one from the interior having presumed to know anything about it. If I have been of any real service it has been in breaking down and eradicating that idea, in assisting to nationalize the Navy—in making the frontiersman as well as the longshoreman feel that he was interested in it and partook of its glory."

13   C.S.S. *Alabama*, Captain Semmes, seized and burned whaling ship *Altamaha* near the Azores.

14   C.S.S. *Alabama*, Captain Semmes, seized and burned whaling ship *Benjamin Tucker* near the Azores.

15   Lieutenant Commander Samuel Magaw, commander of U.S.S. *Thomas Freeborn*, reported the seizure and burning of schooner *Arctic* in Great Wicomico River, Maryland.

16   Confederate Congress passed a resolution expressing thanks to Commander Ebenezer Farrand, CSN, senior officer in command of the combined naval and military forces at Drewry's Bluff on 15 May, "for the great and signal victory achieved over the naval forces of the United States in the engagement . . . at Drewry's Bluff;" Farrand was praised for his "gallantry, courage, and endurance in that protracted fight . . ." which Confederate statesmen knew could have been so disastrous to their cause.

    C.S.S. *Alabama*, Captain Semmes, captured and burned whaling ship *Courser* near the Azores.

17   Rear Admiral S. P. Lee, concerned by frequent reports as to the building by the Confederates of "*Merrimack II*," again wrote Assistant Secretary of the Navy Fox asking that an ironclad be sent to Norfolk to support his forces there. "I feel the necessity," he wrote, "of having a fast steamer convenient as to size & draft, with bow & stern strengthened, and iron plated suitable for ramming, carrying effective guns in broadside, & fitted so as to work two heavy rifled guns at each end—bow & stern—capable of throwing such projectiles as will most readily penetrate iron plating." On 22 September Fox, sympathetic to Lee's needs, answered: "The *Ironsides* will probably be with you on Wednesday [24 September]. . . . With the *Ironsides* you will feel no anxiety. She is fast, and has a terrible battery, and is a match for the whole Southern navy. If the *Merrimac*[k] #2 comes down I trust they will follow her up and destroy her."

U.S.S. *W. G. Anderson*, Acting Master D'Oyley, seized schooner *Reindeer* in the Gulf of Mexico (27N, 93W) with cargo of cotton.

C.S.S. *Alabama*, Captain Semmes, captured and burned whaling ship *Virginia* near the Azores.

18 C.S.S. *Alabama*, Captain Semmes, captured and burned whaling ship *Elisha Dunbar* near the Azores. "The whaling season at the Azores being at an end," Semmes later wrote, ". . . I resolved to change my cruising-ground, and stretch over to the Banks of New Foundland . . ."

19 Ram *Queen of the West*, Medical Cadet Charles R. Ellet, escorting two troop transports, had a sharp engagement with Confederate infantry and artillery above Bolivar, Mississippi.

20 Answering a letter in which Assistant Secretary of the Navy Fox had written, "We must have Charleston. . . .", Rear Admiral Du Pont replied: "Do not go it half cocked about Charleston—it is a bigger job than Port Royal . . . *failure* now at Charleston is ten times the failure elsewhere. . . ." The same day, Du Pont wrote Senator Grimes in Iowa: "The thorn in *my* flesh is *Charleston*, they have been allowed seventeen months to prepare its defenses—and in no part of the wretched Confederacy has there been more industry, energy, and intelligent zeal, and science displayed—It is a *cul de sac* and resembles more a porcupine's hide turned outside in than anything else, with no outlet—you go into a bag—no running the forts as at New Orleans. We have to do what never has been done, take *regular* forts by gunboats—this *must be done*, but it is no ordinary work . . . One thing only oppresses us, that just in proportion to the extent of the honor and glory of the success, and the prestige gained at home and abroad—so will be the deep mortification and moral injury if we fail at this wicked seat of the rebellion—hence we want quiet calm preparation of plans." Du Pont's estimate of the stubbornness of the Confederate defenses at Charleston, as well as his appreciation of the probable effect on the North of a Union failure in his particular quarter proved correct. Throughout the fall of 1862 the ironclads were being built which Du Pont would command against the symbol of the Confederacy.

21 U.S.S. *Albatross*, Commander Henry French, captured schooner *Two Sisters* off the Rio Grande River.

22 Writing during a storm ("I suppose the true equinoctial gale"), Rear Admiral Farragut noted that "these are the times that try the commander of a squadron. I could not sleep last night, thinking of the blockaders. It is rough work lying off a port month in and month out . . . I have 6 vessels off Mobile, so that one can always come in for coal. They are all the time breaking down and coming in for repairs."

U.S.S. *Wyandank*, Acting Master John McGowan, Jr., captured schooner *Southerner* on Coan River, Virginia.

23 U.S.S. *Alabama*, Lieutenant Commander William T. Truxtun, captured blockade running British schooner *Nelly* off Ossabaw Sound, Georgia, with cargo including drugs and salt.

25 U.S.S. *Kensington*, Acting Master Crocker, U.S.S. *Rachel Seaman*, Acting Master Hooper, and mortar schooner *Henry Janes*, Acting Master Lewis Pennington, bombarded Confederate batteries at Sabine Pass, Texas. The action was broken off when the defending troops evacuated the fort, having spiked the guns. Though Sabine City surrendered to Acting Master Crocker the next day and a force under Acting Master Hooper severed communications between Sabine Pass and Taylor's Bayou by burning the railroad bridge and seized the mails on 27 September, the expedition sent by Rear Admiral Farragut could not occupy the area because there were no troops available for that purpose. As Rear Admiral Farragut noted some three months later, "It takes too much force to hold the places for me to take any more, or my outside fleet will be too much reduced to keep up the blockade and keep the river open"—the two primary missions of the squadron.

Crewmen of U.S.S. Pensacola *man the yards in a salute to President Lincoln.*

Nevertheless, the attacks were a constant drain on the Confederates and imposed widespread dispersion of strength to protect against them anytime ships hove over the horizon.

U.S.S. *Florida*, Lieutenant Commander Robert W. Scott, captured British schooner *Agnes*, attempting to run the blockade at St. Andrew's Sound, Georgia.

26 U.S.S. *State of Georgia*, Commander Armstrong, and U.S.S. *Mystic*, Lieutenant Commander Arnold, chased a blockade running schooner (name unknown) ashore at New Inlet, North Carolina, and destroyed her.

Rear Admiral Du Pont sought to extend his policy of "mobile support" logistics by requesting an afloat fuel storage in the form of a coal hulk capable of holding a thousand tons and fitted out with hoisting equipment. Coal schooners from the North unloaded into this hulk and men-of-war coaled from it as needed while on station. This practice antedated the modern use of fleet oilers in furthering the fleet's efficiency and effectiveness. Storeships, receiving ships, and machinery repair hulks were already being employed at this time at Port Royal.

27 U.S.S. *Kittatinny*, Acting Master Lamson, captured schooner *Emma* off the coast of Texas with cargo of cotton.

28 U.S.S. *State of Georgia*, Commander Armstrong, and U.S.S. *Mystic*, Lieutenant Commander Arnold, captured blockade running British steamer *Sunbeam* near New Inlet, North Carolina.

30 Assistant Secretary of the Navy Fox wrote Commodore Blake, Superintendent of the Naval Academy at Newport, regarding training at the Academy: "The seamanship is of the utmost importance, in my opinion, notwithstanding steam, and iron clads. I share the old Jack Tar

feeling that a sailor can do anything, and that a man is not good for much, who is not a thorough seaman. D. D. Porter was particularly struck at seeing your boys scrubbing copper: he was always afraid they were getting too scientific, too conceited, but his experience at Newport seems to have un-deceived him."

OCTOBER

1 The Western Gunboat Fleet, brought into being by Commander J. Rodgers and Flag Officer Foote, under jurisdiction of the War Department for operations on the western waters, was transferred to the Navy Department and renamed the Mississippi Squadron. David Dixon Porter was appointed Acting Rear Admiral and ordered to relieve Rear Admiral Davis, who had commanded naval forces on the western waters since 17 June. Noting that the naming of Porter, then a Commander, would be open to criticism, Secretary of the Navy Welles observed: "His selection will be unsatisfactory to many, but his field of operations is peculiar, and a young and active officer is required for the duty to which he is assigned." However, Rear Admiral Foote, 55 years old when he took command, bold and indefatigable, had achieved miracles. No fleet commanders in the west achieved as much as he and Farragut, who was even five years older. Audacity and drive are born of the soul, and do not die ever in some great leaders.

2 Commodore Harwood reported the capture of sloop *Thomas Reilly* by U.S.S. *Thomas Freeborn*, Lieutenant Commander Magaw.

3 Responding to a request for assistance in an anticipated assault on gathering Confederate forces at Franklin, Virginia, a naval expedition under Lieutenant Commander Flusser, comprising U.S.S. *Commodore Perry*, *Hunchback*, and *Whitehead*, engaged Confederate troops on the Blackwater River for six hours. The river having been obstructed, the gunboats could not reach Franklin and returned down stream as Confederate troops were felling trees in the river behind the gunboats in an attempt to "blockade the river in our rear." Enclosing the reports of the gunboat captains, Commander Davenport, Senior Officer in the Sounds of North Carolina, wrote Rear Admiral S. P. Lee: "While I can not praise too highly the gallantry and heroism displayed by officers and men on the occasion, I think it extremely hazardous for our gunboats unprotected as the men are by bulwarks or any other defenses, to go on expeditions up these narrow and tortuous channels."

A joint expedition under Commander Steedman and Brigadier General John M. Brannon engaged and captured a Confederate battery at St. John's Bluff and occupied Jacksonville, Florida, which had been almost entirely evacuated by Southern troops. The Union forces had arrived at the mouth of the river on 1 October and, in operations through 12 October, the gunboats convoyed and supported the Army troops, forcing a general withdrawal by the Confederates. Calling Steedman's action "most hearty and energetic," General Brannon reported: "The entire naval force under his command exhibited a zeal and perseverance in every instance, whether in aiding my forces to effect a landing, the ascent of St. John's River (230 miles), or the assistance to one of my transports unfortunately injured in crossing the bar, that is deserving of all praise." Captain Godon, temporarily commanding the South Atlantic Blockading Squadron, noted at operation's end: "We retain possession of St. John's River as far as Jacksonville." Amphibious assaults continued to force Confederate defenses away from the coastal areas.

C.S.S. *Alabama*, Captain Semmes, captured ship *Brilliant*, bound from New York to Liverpool, near 40° N, 50° W. Semmes later commented that ". . . her destruction must have disappointed a good many holders of bills of exchange drawn against her cargo . . . for the ship alone and the freight-moneys which they lost by her destruction [came] to the amount of $93,000. The cargo was probably even more valuable than the ship."

Naval forces under Commander William B. Renshaw in U.S.S. *Westfield*, including U.S.S. *Harriet Lane*, *Owasco*, *Clifton*, and mortar schooner *Henry Janes*, bombarded and captured the defenses of the harbor and city of Galveston. Six days later, Galveston formally surrendered to Commander Renshaw. Rear Admiral Farragut reported to Secretary of the Navy Welles: "I am happy to inform you that Galveston, Corpus Christi, and Sabine City and the adjacent waters are now in our possession. . . . All we want, as I have told the Department in my last dispatches, is a few soldiers to hold the places, and we will soon have the whole coast." The failure to have a sizeable effective Marine Corps to send ashore in conjunction with fleet operations reduced considerably the effectiveness of the Navy and may have lengthened the war.

4   U.S.S. *Somerset*, Lieutenant Commander English, attacked Confederate salt works at Depot Key, Florida. The landing party from *Somerset* was augmented by a strong force from U.S.S. *Tahoma*, Commander John C. Howell, and the salt works were destroyed. Salt at this time was among the most critical "stretegic materials" in the Confederacy. This action at Depot Key was one of innumerable such landing and raiding operations all along the far-flung Confederate coastline which, often lacking dramatic appeal, nonetheless exacted ceaseless activity and untiring effort, and were instrumental in bringing the Confederacy to defeat.

Raiding party from U.S.S. *Thomas Freeborn*, Lieutenant Commander Magaw, entered Dumfries, Virginia, and destroyed the telegraph office and wires of the line from Occoquan to Richmond via Fredericksburg.

6   U.S.S. *Rachel Seaman*, Acting Master Crocker, captured British schooner *Dart* attempting to run the blockade at Sabine Pass.

C.S.S. Alabama—*celebrated commerce raider begins her career in 1862 under Captain Raphael Semmes.*

7 William Gladstone, British Chancellor of the Exchequer, remarked at a banquet in Newcastle, England, that "there is no doubt that Jefferson Davis and other leaders of the South have made an army; they are making it appears a navy; and they have made, what is more than either—they have made a nation." Upon reading of Gladstone's statement, Assistant Secretary of the Navy Fox observed: "It is a most interesting piece of history. . . ."

C.S.S. *Alabama*, Captain Semmes, captured and burned bark *Wave Crest* and brig *Dunkirk* southeast of Nova Scotia.

Lieutenant Commander Edward P. Williams in Army transport *Darlington*, with sailors and troops embarked, captured steamer *Governor Milton* in St. John's River, Florida. In continuing Union operations in the river, Williams had seized the vessel—termed by Commander Steedman "one of their best boats"—which had been used in transporting guns and munitions to St. John's Bluff.

8 Steamer *Blanche*, anchored off Havana, was set afire to prevent seizure by U.S.S. *Montgomery*, Commander C. Hunter.

C.S.S. *Alabama*, Captain Semmes, captured and released on bond packet *Tonawanda* southeast of Nova Scotia.

11 U.S.S. *Monticello*, Lieutenant Commander Braine, captured blockade running British schooner *Revere* off Frying Pan Shoals, North Carolina.

C.S.S. *Alabama*, Captain Semmes, captured and burned *Manchester* southeast of Nova Scotia bound from New York to Liverpool. "The *Manchester*," Semmes wrote, "brought us a batch of late New York papers. . . . I learned from them where all the enemy's gun boats were, and what they were doing. . . . Perhaps this was the only war in which the newspapers ever explained, before-hand, all the movements of armies and fleets, to the enemy."

U.S.S. *Maratanza*, Commander Scott, was damaged by Confederate battery at Cape Fear River, North Carolina, and was forced to retire seaward.

12 Commander Matthew Fontaine Maury, on board blockade runner *Herald*, departed Charleston for England to attempt to purchase vessels for the Confederacy. Midshipman James M. Morgan, who accompanied Maury, recorded an interesting incident that demonstrated that the "Pathfinder of the Seas" had lost none of his famed abilities. The captain of *Herald*, according to Morgan, was new to deep water sail, lost his way, and "told Commander Maury that something terrible must have happened, as he had sailed his ship directly over the spot where the Bermuda Islands ought to be." Maury advised him to slow down till evening when he could shoot the stars. At that time, having obtained a fix, Maury gave the captain a course and speed that would raise the light at Port Hamilton about 2 o'clock in the morning. Maury and his son turned in; the rest anxiously stayed up to watch: "four bells struck and no light was in sight. Five minutes more passed and still not a sign of it; then grumbling commenced and the passengers generally agreed with the man who expressed the opinion that there was too much D . . . d science on board . . . at 10 minutes past 2 the masthead lookout called 'Light Ho!' " Lacking funds and under close scrutiny by Union officials who immediately protested through diplomatic channels any attempts to outfit vessels for the Confederacy, Maury, like other Confederate agents, met with only limited success. Nonetheless, he did purchase and arrange for the outfitting of C.S.S. *Georgia* the following spring. Maury was adamant in his opinion that the South had to pursue a policy that would bring about the existence of an effective Navy. Earlier he had written under the pseudonym of Ben Bow: "We cannot, either with cotton or with all the agricultural staples of the Confederacy put together, adopt any course which will make cotton and trade stand us as a nation in the stead of a navy."

Raphael Semmes
Captain, CSN

Matthew Fontaine Maury
Commander, CSN

U.S.S. *Restless*, Acting Lieutenant Conroy, captured blockade running schooner *Elmira Cornelius* off the South Carolina coast.

13 U.S.S. *America*, Acting Master Jonathan Baker, seized schooner *David Crockett* attempting to run the blockade out of Charleston with cargo of turpentine and rosin.

14 U.S.S. *Memphis*, Acting Lieutenant Watmough, captured blockade running British steamer *Ouachita* at sea off Cape Romain, South Carolina.

15 C.S.S. *Alabama*, Captain Semmes, captured and burned bark *Lamplighter* southeast of Nova Scotia.

Boat crew under command of Master's Mate Edwin Janvrin of U.S.S. *Rachel Seaman*, and boat crew under command of Second Assistant Engineer Timothy W. O'Connor of U.S.S. *Kensington*, destroyed Confederate railroad bridge by fire at Taylor's Bayou, Texas, preventing the transportation of heavy artillery to Sabine Pass, and burned schooners *Stonewall* and *Lone Star* and barracks. The constant drain on the South of these unceasing attacks along her sea perimeter and up the rivers is portrayed almost daily in similar accounts. Some were quite unusual even for versatile sailors. In a river expedition during the month Lieutenant Commander Ransom "captured 1,500 head of cattle en route for the enemy, and succeeded by great perseverance in getting them down to New Orleans."

Boat crews from U.S.S. *Fort Henry*, Acting Lieutenant Edward Y. McCauley, reconnoitering Apalachicola River, Florida, captured sloop *G. L. Brockenborough* with cargo of cotton.

20 Steamer *Minho* ran aground after running the blockade out of Charleston. Rear Admiral Du Pont reported that ". . . it appears that . . . she will perhaps become a wreck, as there is much water in the hold, and part of the cargo [is] floating about in the vessel. So much of the cargo, it is stated ["by the Charleston papers"], as may be destroyed by water will be nearly a total loss."

21 U.S.S. *Louisville*, Lieutenant Commander Meade, escorted steamer *Meteor*, whose embarked Army troops were landed at Bledsoe's Landing and Hamblin's Landing, Arkansas. The towns were

burned in reprisal for attacks by Confederate guerrillas on mail steamer *Gladiator* early in the morning, 19 October. "The people along the river bank," Meade reported to Rear Admiral D. D. Porter, "were duly informed that every outrage by the guerrillas upon packets would be similarly dealt with."

22 A naval battery consisting of three 12 pounder boat howitzers from U.S.S. *Wabash* took part in and furnished artillery support for Union infantry troops at the battle of Pocotaligo, South Carolina. One of the gun crew, who was seriously injured, was ordinary seaman Oscar W. Farenholt, the first enlisted man in the Navy to reach flag rank. The battery from *Wabash* took part as artillery in amphibious operations all along the South Atlantic coast.

U.S.S. *Penobscot*, Commander Clitz, captured blockade running British brig *Robert Bruce* off Cape Fear, North Carolina.

Lieutenant William B. Cushing reported that U.S.S. *Ellis* captured and destroyed blockade runner *Adelaide* at New Topsail Inlet, North Carolina, with cargo of turpentine, cotton, and tobacco.

23 C.S.S. *Alabama*, Captain Semmes, captured and burned American bark *Lafayette* south of Halifax, Nova Scotia.

24 Sailors on horseback—a landing party from U.S.S. *Baron De Kalb*, Captain Winslow, debarked at Hopefield, Arkansas, to engage a small Confederate scouting party. Mounting horses which were procured, as Captain Winslow reported, "by impressement," the *Baron De Kalb* sailors engaged in a 9 mile running fight which ended with the capture of the Confederate party.

25 Rear Admiral Du Pont again wrote Secretary of the Navy Welles of the reported building of ironclads by the Confederacy in its attempt to break the blockade. Du Pont remarked: "The idea seemed to be to open the Savannah river, then come to Port Royal, and thence off Charleston, and raise the blockade. . . . I submit that the *Ironsides* and *Passaic* should be dispatched at an early day."

26 C.S.S. *Alabama*, Captain Semmes, captured and burned schooner *Crenshaw* south of Halifax, Nova Scotia.

27 Boat crews from U.S.S. *Flag*, Lieutenant Commander Charles C. Carpenter, captured British steamer *Anglia* at Bull's Bay, South Carolina.

Rear Admiral S. P. Lee wrote Assistant Secretary of the Navy Fox regarding the difficulty of blockading the coast of North Carolina: "Our supremacy in the Sounds of N[orth] C[arolina] can . . . only be maintained by iron clads adapted to the navigation there. . . . The defense of the Sounds is a very important matter. . . ."

28 Party led by Lieutenant John Taylor Wood, CSN, boarded, captured, and fired ship *Alleghanian* at anchor in Chesapeake Bay off the mouth of the Rappahannock River with cargo of guano from Baltimore for London.

C.S.S. *Alabama*, Captain Semmes, captured and burned bark *Lauraetta* south of Halifax, Nova Scotia.

U.S.S. *Montgomery*, Commander C. Hunter, captured blockade running steamer *Caroline* near Pensacola.

U.S.S. *Sagamore*, Lieutenant Commander George A. Bigelow, captured blockade running British schooner *Trier* off Indian River Inlet, Florida.

29 Landing party from U.S.S. *Ellis*, Lieutenant Cushing, destroyed large Confederate salt works at New Topsail Inlet, North Carolina. Cushing reported that "it could have furnished all Wilmington with salt."

U.S.S. *Dan* exchanged fire with Confederate troops near Sabine Pass; *Dan* shelled the town and on 30 October a party was landed under protection of the ship's guns to burn a mill and several buildings.

C.S.S. *Alabama*, Captain Semmes, seized brigantine *Baron de Castine* south of Nova Scotia. "The vessel being old and of little value," Semmes reported, "I released her on a ransom bond and converted her into a cartel, sending some forty-five prisoners on board of her—the crews of the three last ships burned."

30 Assistant Secretary of the Navy Fox wrote Edward G. Flynn regarding that man's expressed desire to attempt capture or destruction of commerce raider *290* (C.S.S. *Alabama*): "The [Navy] Department has published that it will give $500,000 for the capture and delivery to it of that vessel, or $300,000 if she is destroyed; the latter however is to be contingent upon the approval of Congress." The concern over *Alabama*'s highly successful commerce raiding was attested to when Fox wrote Rear Admiral Farragut: "The raid of '290' [*Alabama*] has forced us to send out a dozen vessels in pursuit."

U.S.S. *Connecticut*, Lieutenant Commander Milton Haxtun, captured blockade running British schooner *Hermosa* off the mouth of the Sabine River.

U.S.S. *Daylight*, Acting Master Warren, captured schooner *Racer* between Stump Inlet and New Topsail Inlet, North Carolina, with cargo of salt.

Rear Admiral Du Pont issued a general order which provided that, on capture of foreign vessels attempting to run the blockade, "the flag of the country to which they belong must be worn until their cases are adjudicated. The American flag will be carried at the fore to indicate that they are, for the time, under charge of United States officers."

31 During October the Confederate Congress formalized a Torpedo Bureau in Richmond under Brigadier General Gabriel J. Rains and a Naval Submarine Battery Service under Lieutenant Hunter Davidson. The purpose was to organize and improve methods of torpedo (mine) warfare, in which Commander Mathew Fontaine Maury had pioneered. The Confederacy, of necessity, developed a variety of underwater torpedoes, for it had a long coastline with many navigable rivers to protect and slight naval strength with which to oppose the formidable Union fleet. That the efforts, while failing to lift the ceaseless pressure of the Northern naval forces, were nonetheless a serious threat was attested to at war's end by Secretary of the Navy Welles, who observed that the torpedoes were "always formidable in harbors and internal waters, and . . . have been more destructive to our naval vessels than all other means combined."

U.S.S. *Reliance*, Acting Master Andrew J. Frank, captured sloop *Pointer* at Alexandria, Virginia. Although cleared through the Alexandria Custom House as being without cargo, *Pointer* was found to be carrying groceries, dry goods, and whiskey.

U.S.S. *Restless*, Acting Lieutenant Conroy, captured sloop *Susan McPherson* off the coast of South Carolina.

Landing party from U.S.S. *Mahaska*, Commander Foxhall A. Parker, destroyed Confederate gun positions on Wormley's Creek and at West Point, Virginia. The attack was continued on 1 November.

31 OCTOBER–7 NOVEMBER

Naval expedition under Commander Davenport, comprising U.S.S. *Hetzel*, *Commodore Perry*, *Hunchback*, *Valley City*, and Army gunboat *Vidette*, opened fire on an encampment at Plymouth, North Carolina, forcing the Confederate troops there to withdraw. Davenport was subsequently ordered to meet General John G. Foster at Williamston on 3 November to support an Army assault on Hamilton, North Carolina. "It was agreed upon," Commander Davenport reported,

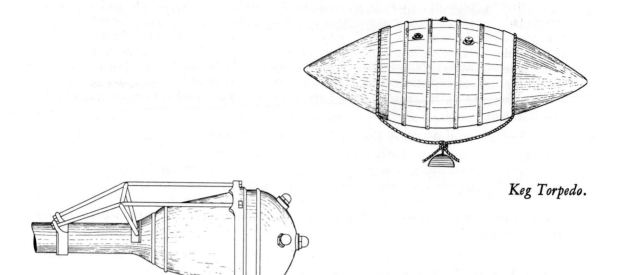

Keg Torpedo.

Spar Torpedo.

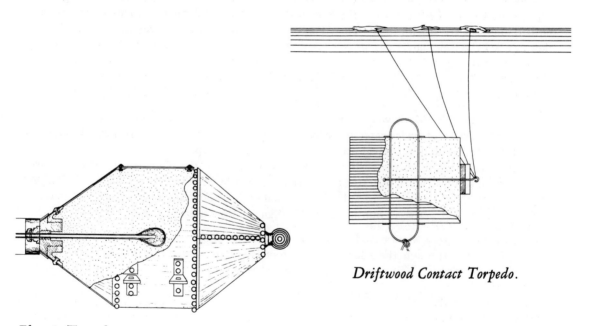

Driftwood Contact Torpedo.

Electric Torpedo.

Examples of Confederate Torpedoes.

(Extracted from J. Thomas Scharf's History of the Confederate States Navy)

". . . that we would begin our advance on Hamilton that night. . . . At 11 a.m. [4 November], having failed as yet in receiving any signal from the army, I made general signal 'to get underway' and proceeded up the river . . ." The force also included U.S.S. *Seymour*, which had arrived that morning. Hamilton was evacuated by the Confederates and Union troops took possession of the town. Davenport's gunboats "proceeded a few miles farther up the river to divert the attention of the enemy, while the army continued its march to Tarboro"; *Seymour* was sent down river the next day (5 November) to destroy the works at Rainbow Bluff. On 7 November the Union troops, failing to reach Tarboro, returned to Hamilton, and 300 sick and wounded soldiers were placed on board the gunboats to be transported to Williamston.

NOVEMBER

1 U.S.S. *Louisville*, Lieutenant Commander Meade, captured steamer *Evansville* in the Mississippi River above Island No. 36.

U.S.S. *Thomas Freeborn*, Lieutenant Commander Magaw, captured three unnamed boats at Maryland Point, on the Potomac River; the boats were attempting to run goods across from Maryland to Virginia.

2 Rear Admiral D. D. Porter wrote Assistant Secretary of the Navy Fox seeking authority over the Ellet rams: "I am extremely anxious to get possession of Ellet's Rams; they are the class of vessels I particularly want at this moment. The old 'Pook Turtles' are fit only for fighting—they cannot get along against the current without a tow. . . . Do settle the Ram business, and let me know by telegraph. The Commander will have to be instructed, or he will not give them up. I have notified him that I will not permit any naval organization on this River besides the Mississippi Squadron. . . ." Fox agreed with Porter and pressed the matter with the President. On 7 November the Assistant Secretary convinced President Lincoln that the Ellet rams belonged under control of the Navy. In a White House conference with Secretary of the Navy Welles, Secretary of War Stanton, and General Halleck, Lincoln transferred all war vessels on the Mississippi to the Navy. The action provided for greater efficiency of operations on the western waters.

C.S.S. *Alabama*, Captain Semmes, captured and burned whaling ship *Levi Starbuck* near Bermuda.

3 C.S.S. *Cotton*, Lieutenant Edward W. Fuller, and shore batteries engaged U.S.S. *Calhoun*, *Kinsman*, *Estrella*, and *Diana* in Berwick Bay, Louisiana. In this close and spirited action against heavy odds, Captain Fuller caused considerable damage to the Union squadron until exhaustion of cartridges forced *Cotton* to retire. Captain Fuller reported that the legs of the men's pants were cut off for use as improvised cartridge bags to fire parting shots as he withdrew.

Commander Henry K. Thatcher wrote Assistant Secretary of the Navy Fox about the Mediterranean cruise of historic U.S.S. *Constellation* and his request for additional ships on this station: "I feel a considerable degree of national pride in wishing our force here to be increased . . . for the prevailing opinion here, evidently is, that our country is not sufficiently strong to admit of withdrawing another vessel from the blockade. But the paramount object is that of the efficient protection of our commerce and citizens who are engaged in commercial pursuits and to be prepared, should any rebel cruisers venture into the Mediterranean."

U.S.S. *Penobscot*, Commander Clitz, destroyed blockade running British ship *Pathfinder* after forcing her aground off Shallotte Inlet, North Carolina.

4 The blockade continued to clench the Confederacy in an ever-tightening grip. Rear Admiral S. P. Lee, commanding the North Atlantic Blockading Squadron, advised Assistant Secretary of the Navy Fox: "There is no doubt that a large trade was carried on with Wilmington through

Shallotte Inlet 25 miles below, & New Topsail Inlet 15 miles above Wilmington. I have shut both doors."

U.S.S. *Jacob Bell*, Acting Ensign George E. McConnell, captured and burned schooner *Robert Wilbur* in Nomini Creek, off the Potomac River.

U.S.S. *Hale*, Captain Alfred T. Snell, captured pilot boat *Wave* and an unnamed schooner in Nassau Sound, Florida.

U.S.S. *Daylight*, Acting Master Warren, and U.S.S. *Mount Vernon*, Acting Lieutenant Trathen, forced blockade running British bark *Sophia* aground and destroyed her near Masonboro Inlet, North Carolina.

U.S.S. *Coeur de Lion*, Acting Master Charles H. Brown, with U.S.S. *Teaser* and schooner *S. H. Poole*, evacuated Union families and their property from Gwynn's Island, Virginia.

5 U.S.S. *Louisiana*, Acting Lieutenant R. T. Renshaw, captured schooner *Alice L. Webb* at Rose Bay, North Carolina.

6 U.S.S. *Teaser*, Ensign Sheridan, captured sloop *Grapeshot* in Chesapeake Bay.

7 U.S.S. *Potomska*, Acting Lieutenant W. Budd, escorted Army transport *Darlington* up Sapelo River, Georgia. *Potomska* being unable to proceed far up river because of her draft, Budd transferred to the Army vessel, which was engaged by Confederates at Spaulding's. *Darlington*, undamaged, continued up the Sapelo to Fairhope, where a landing party destroyed salt works "and other things that might be of use to the enemy." Taken under attack once again upon returning past Spaulding's, *Darlington* put forces ashore and destroyed public property and captured arms. "We were greatly aided here by the *Potomska*," reported Lieutenant Colonel Oliver T. Beard, "which, from a bend below, shelled the woods. Under the guns of the *Potomska* we landed . . . I am greatly indebted to Lieutenant Budd for the success of this day."

U.S.S. *Kinsman*, Acting Master George Wiggin, and steamer *Seger* burned steamers *Osprey* and *J. P. Smith* in Bayou Cheval, Louisiana.

8 C.S.S. *Alabama*, Captain Semmes, captured and burned ship *T. B. Wales* southeast of Bermuda.

U.S.S. *Resolute*, Acting Master Tole, captured sloop *Capitola* at Glymont, Maryland. *Capitola* was carrying cargo and passengers across to Virginia in violation of the blockade.

9 Greenville, North Carolina, surrendered to joint Army-Navy landing force under Second Assistant Engineer J. L. Lay of U.S.S. *Louisiana*.

10 Commander Maury, enroute to Liverpool, England, wrote his wife from Halifax, Nova Scotia, that he had arrived after a "boisterous passage of 5½ days from Bermuda" in which he and his 12-year old son suffered from sea sickness. "The steamer in which we came was quite equal in dirt and all uncomfortableness to that between Calais and Dover. . . . This is a place of 25 or 30,000 inhabitants. They are strongly 'secesh' here. The Confederate flag has been flying from the top of the hotel all day, in honor, I am told 'of our arrival'." Hand organs ground out Dixie all day under the window; Maury, world famous as "Pathfinder of the Seas," having run the blockade, was proceeding to England on a mission for the Confederacy.

11 U.S.S. *Kensington*, Acting Master Crocker, captured schooner *Course* off the Florida coast.

12 U.S.S. *Kensington*, Acting Master Crocker, captured British blockade runner *Maria* off the Florida coast.

Crew exercising a Dahlgren gun on board Union gunboat.

14 Rear Admiral Farragut had sailed from the Mississippi River in August to base at Pensacola where his crews recuperated and repaired the ships preparatory to attacking Mobile. However, reports of growing Confederate fortifications on the river and other developments drew him back to the scene of his fame. On this date from on board U.S.S. *Hartford* at New Orleans he wrote Secretary of the Navy Welles: "I am once more in the Mississippi River. I deemed that my presence here would be well, as the French admiral is here with two vessels at the city and a frigate at the bar; there is also an English corvette off the city, and we sailors understand each other better in many cases than landsmen. General Butler also informed me that he was operating very largely for his forces on the Opelousas, which was an additional reason for my entering the river. I enclose herewith Lieutenant-Commander Buchanan's report. He is commanding the naval forces cooperating with the army in Opelousas, and has already had two fights with the enemy's steamers and land forces. These little vessels require a sheet of boiler iron around them as a protection against musketry, when they would be able to run up the whole length of the river and catch all the boats in the branches. I called on General Butler for the purpose of ascertaining when he could give me a small force to attack Fort Gaines, and to notify him that when the Department wished it I would attack the forts and go through Mobile Bay without his assistance, but it would embarrass me very much not to have my communication open with the outside, and that with 1,000 men to menace Gaines in the rear I felt certain they would soon abandon both forts, once we got inside. He promised to assist in the operation as soon as General Weitzel returned from Opelousas, although he urges me to attack Port Hudson first, as he wishes to break up the rendezvous before we go outside. It will take at least 5,000 men to take Port Hudson. I am ready for anything, but desire troops to hold what we get. The general has really not half troops enough; he requires at least 20,000 more men to hold the places and do good service in this river and occupy Galveston, whither he proposes to send a regiment."

15 President Lincoln, with Secretaries Seward and Chase, drove to the Washington Navy Yard to view the trial of the Hyde rocket. Captain Dahlgren joined the group for the experiment. Though a defective rocket accidentally exploded, the President escaped injury.

16 U.S.S. *T. A. Ward*, Acting Master William L. Babcock, captured sloop *G. W. Green* and an unnamed seine boat at St. Jerome's Creek, Maryland, attempting to cross to the Virginia shore with contraband.

17 U.S.S. *Kanawha*, Lieutenant Commander Febiger, and U.S.S. *Kennebec*, Lieutenant Commander John H. Russell, chased a schooner ashore near Mobile where she was set afire and destroyed by her crew. Union ships prevented Confederate coast guard from boarding the vessel to extinguish the flames. Of the effectiveness of the blockade in the Gulf, Rear Admiral Farragut noted: "Blockading is hard service, and difficult to carry on with perfect success . . . I don't know how many [blockade runners] escape, but we certainly make a good many prizes."

U.S.S. *Cambridge*, Commander W. A. Parker, forced blockade running British schooner *J. W. Pindar* aground at Masonboro Inlet, North Carolina, and sent boat crew to destroy the vessel. The boat swamped and the crew was captured after firing the schooner.

Assistant Secretary of the Navy Fox wrote Major General Butler at New Orleans: "I think [General] McClernand will be down your way near the last of December and if you and Farragut can open the Mississippi as far as Red River and block that leaky place, we shall be able with our Mississippi squadron to keep that big river open to commerce and New Orleans will rise from its lethargy."

18 C.S.S. *Alabama*, Captain Semmes, arrived at Martinique and was blockaded by U.S.S. *San Jacinto*, Commander William Ronckendorff. In foul weather the evening of 19 November, *Alabama* evaded *San Jacinto* and escaped.

U.S.S. *Monticello*, Lieutenant Commander Braine, chased blockade running British schooners *Ariel* and *Ann Maria* ashore and destroyed them near Shallotte Inlet with cargoes of salt, flour, sugar, and lard.

19 U.S.S. *Wissahickon*, Lieutenant Commander John L. Davis, and U.S.S. *Dawn*, Acting Lieutenant John S. Barnes, engaged Fort McAllister on Ogeechee River, Georgia. *Wissahickon* was hit and temporarily disabled in the exchange of fire. Persistent and vigilant actions of this nature by the Union Navy pinned down Confederate manpower that could have been used in land actions elsewhere. *Wissahickon* and *Dawn* at this time had the mission of blockading C.S.S. *Nashville* in Ossabaw Sound, Georgia, and preventing her from becoming another commerce raider like C.S.S. *Alabama*.

20 U.S.S. *Seneca*, Lieutenant Commander Gibson, captured schooner *Annie Dees* running the blockade out of Charleston with cargo of turpentine and rosin.

U.S.S. *Montgomery*, Commander C. Hunter, captured sloop *William E. Chester* near Pensacola Bay.

Confederates at Matagorda Bay, Texas, captured boat crew from U.S. mortar schooner *Henry Janes*, Acting Master Pennington. The men were ashore to procure fresh beef for the mortar schooner.

22–24 Joint Army-Navy expedition to vicinity of Mathews Court House, Virginia, under Lieutenant Farquhar and Acting Master's Mate Nathan W. Black of U.S.S. *Mahaska* destroyed numerous salt works together with hundreds of bushels of salt, burned three schooners and numerous small boats, and captured 24 large canoes.

23 Landing party from U.S.S. *Ellis*, Lieutenant Cushing, captured arms, mail, and two schooners at Jacksonville, North Carolina. While under attack from Confederate artillery, *Ellis* grounded on 24 November. After every effort to float the ship failed, Lieutenant Cushing ordered her set afire

on 25 November to avoid capture. Cushing reported: "I fired the *Ellis* in five places and having seen that the battle flag was still flying, trained the gun on the enemy so that the vessel might fight herself after we had left her."

24 Boat from U.S.S. *Reliance*, Acting Master William P. Dockray, captured longboat *New Moon*, suspected of running the blockade on the Potomac River, off Alexandria.

U.S.S. *Monticello*, Lieutenant Commander Braine, destroyed two Confederate salt works near Little River Inlet, North Carolina.

U.S.S. *Sagamore*, Lieutenant Commander English, captured two British blockade runners, schooner *Agnes* and sloop *Ellen*, in Indian River, Florida.

25 U.S.S. *Kittatinny*, Acting Master Lamson, captured British blockade runner *Matilda*, bound from Havana to Matamoras.

26 U.S.S. *Kittatinny*, Acting Master Lamson, captured schooner *Diana*, bound from Campeche to Matamoras.

27 Rear Admiral Farragut wrote from his flagship at New Orleans: "I am still doing nothing, but waiting for the tide of events and doing all I can to hold what I have, & blockade Mobile. So soon as the river rises, we will have Porter down from above, who now commands the upper squadron, and then I shall probably go outside . . . We shall spoil unless we have a fight occasionally."

29 In late November Captain H. A. Adams was ordered to special duty at Philadelphia as coordinator of coal supply. All coal used in the U.S. Navy at that time was anthracite and came from the eastern district of Pennsylvania, being forwarded to Philadelphia either by rail or barge down the Schuylkill River. There it was loaded into coal schooners and sent to the various blockading squadrons. Before Captain Adams was ordered to this duty, squadron commanders had considerable difficulty in keeping their ships supplied with coal and often had to borrow from the Army. To illustrate the amount of coal required by the squadrons, Rear Admiral Du Pont notified the Navy Department in mid-December that the consumption of coal in his South Atlantic Blockading Squadron alone was approximately 950 tons a week.

U.S.S. *Mount Vernon*, Acting Lieutenant Trathen, captured blockade runner *Levi Rowe* off New Inlet, North Carolina, with cargo of rice.

30 C.S.S. *Alabama*, Captain Semmes, captured and burned bark *Parker Cook* off the Leeward Islands.

DECEMBER

1 In his second annual report, Secretary of the Navy Welles informed President Lincoln: "We have at this time afloat or progressing to rapid completion a naval force consisting of 427 vessels . . . armed in the aggregate with 1,577 guns, and of the capacity of 240,028 tons . . . The number of persons employed on board our naval vessels, including receiving ships and recruits, is about 28,000; and there are not less than 12,000 mechanics and laborers employed at the different navy yards and naval stations."

Lieutenant Maffitt, commanding C.S.S. *Florida*, wrote: "As the *Alabama* and *Florida* are the only two cruisers we have just now, it would be a perfect absurdity to tilt against their more than three hundred, for the Federals would gladly sacrifice fifty armed ships to extinguish the two Confederates."

Rear Admiral Du Pont again remarked on the Charleston defenses and his growing forces with which to attack them in a letter to Senator Grimes: "The rebel defenses of Charleston are still progressing—The English officers who have been in and the blockade runners whom we capture, smile at the idea of its being taken, and say it is stronger than Sebastabol—but they said the same of New Orleans. . . . I am very glad to learn that John Rodgers and Worden [commander of U.S.S. *Monitor* during the engagement with C.S.S. *Virginia*] were with Drayton on his last trial of the *Passaic*, for the more we learn of the new tools we have to use the better—two rams are completed at Charleston to add to the harbor defenses—but for the strong force I have off here [Port Royal], I think they would have attempted to raid across the bar.''

U.S.S. *Sagamore*, Lieutenant Commander English, captured blockade running British schooner *By George* off Indian River, Florida, with cargo including coffee and salt.

U.S.S. *Tioga*, Commander Clary, captured schooner *Nonsuch* at Bahama Banks.

2 Confederate steamer *Queen of the Bay*, Captain H. Willke, CSA, sounding Corpus Christi Pass, was chased by boats under Acting Ensign Alfred H. Reynolds and Master's Mate George C. Dolliver from U.S.S. *Sachem*. Captain Willke ran *Queen of the Bay* aground on Padre Island, deployed his men, and took Union boats under fire. Reynolds, seriously wounded, was compelled to land on nearby Mustang Island and abandon his boats to the Confederates before retreating overland 30 miles to rejoin *Sachem* at Aransas Bay, Texas.

3 U.S.S. *Cambridge*, Commander W. A. Parker, captured schooner *J. C. Roker* off the coast of North Carolina with cargo of salt.

U.S.S. *Daylight*, Acting Master Warren, captured British blockade runner *Brilliant* attempting to run cargo of salt into Wilmington.

U.S.S. *Cambridge*, Commander W. A. Parker, captured schooner *Emma Tuttle* off Cape Fear.

4 U.S.S. *Anacostia*, *Coeur de Lion*, *Currituck*, and *Jacob Bell*, under Acting Master Shankland, engaged by Confederate batteries at Port Royal, Virginia. In the exchange of fire which lasted over an hour, *Jacob Bell* was damaged.

Rear Admiral Farragut stated: "My people are carrying on the war in various parts of the coast, & it takes all my energies to keep them supplied with provisions and coal. I have a great many irons in the fire and have to look sharp to keep some of them from burning . . . We have either taken or destroyed all the steamers that run from Havanna & Nassau to this coast, except the *Cuba* and *Alice* . . . I have all the coast except Mobile Bay, and am ready to take that the moment I can get troops.''

5 Boats from U.S.S. *Mahaska*, Commander F. A. Parker, and U.S.S. *General Putnam*, under Lieutenant Elliot C. V. Blake of *Mahaska*, captured and destroyed "several fine boats," a schooner and two sloops in branches of Severn River, Maryland, and brought back schooners *Seven Brothers* and *Galena*. Although the captain of *Galena* claimed to be a Union man, Commander Parker reported his belief that the captain was endeavoring "to carry water on both shoulders.''

C.S.S. *Alabama*, Captain Semmes, captured and released on bond schooner *Union* off Haiti.

Lieutenant Commander John G. Walker, U.S.S. *Baron De Kalb*, reported capture of steamer *Lottie* 30 miles above Memphis.

6 U.S.S. *Diana*, Acting Master Ezra Goodwin, captured steamers *Southern Methodist* and *Naniope* near Vicksburg laden with molasses and sugar.

7 C.S.S. *Alabama*, Captain Semmes, captured California steamer *Ariel* off the coast of Cuba with 700 passengers on board, including 150 Marines and Commander Louis C. Sartori, USN.

8 President Lincoln sent a recommendation of thanks to the Congress on behalf of Commander Worden for his part as commanding officer of U.S.S. *Monitor* during her Hampton Roads engagement with C.S.S. *Virginia*.

U.S.S. *Daylight*, Acting Master Warren, seized sloop *Coquette* off New Topsail Inlet, North Carolina, with cargo of whiskey, potatoes, apples, and onions.

9   Rear Admiral Bailey, on assuming command of the Eastern Gulf Blockading Squadron, stated: "The outward pressure of our Navy, in barring the enemy's ports, crippling the power, and exhausting the resources of the States in rebellion; in depriving them of a market for their peculiar productions, and of the facilities for importing many vital requisites for the use of their Army and peoples, is slowly, surely, and unostentatiously reducing the rebellion to such straits as must result in their unconditional submission, even though our gallant Army does not achieve another victory."

10 U.S.S. *Currituck*, Acting Master Thomas J. Linnekin, engaged Confederate battery on Brandywine Hill, Virginia.

U.S.S. *Sagamore*, Lieutenant Commander English, captured British schooner *Alicia* attempting to run the blockade out of Indian River, Florida, with cargo of cotton.

U.S.S. *Southfield*, Lieutenant Charles F. W. Behm, was disabled by a shot through the steam chest off Plymouth, North Carolina, while rendering close fire support to troops under attack by Confederate forces.

11 Assistant Secretary of the Navy Fox wrote Rear Admiral D. D. Porter of the readying of ironclads for the fleet and observed: "We shall soon be ready to try the Iron Clads against the few southern Forts yet in the hands of the Rebels."

12 U.S.S. *Cairo*, Lieutenant Commander Thomas O. Selfridge, on an expedition up the Yazoo River to destroy torpedoes, was sunk by one of the "infernal machines" and Selfridge reported: "The *Cairo* sunk in about twelve minutes after the explosion, going totally out of sight, except the top of her chimneys, in 6 fathoms of water." *Cairo* was the first of some 40 Union vessels to be torpedoed during the war.   The torpedo which destroyed *Cairo* was a large demijohn fired with a friction primer by a trigger line from torpedo pits on the river bank.   Rear Admiral D. D. Porter later observed: "It was an accident liable to occur to any gallant officer whose zeal carries him to the post of danger and who is loath to let others do what he thinks he ought to do himself." Despite the loss of *Cairo*, Porter wrote: "I gave Captain Walke orders to hold Yazoo River at all hazards . . . We may lose three or four vessels, but will succeed in carrying out the plan for the capture of Vicksburg."

12–16 Naval force under Commander Murray including U.S.S. *Delaware, Shawsheen, Lockwood,* and *Seymour* with armed transports in the Neuse River supported an Army expedition to destroy railroad bridges and track near Goldsboro, North Carolina; low water prevented the gunboats from advancing more than about 15 miles up the river.

15 Assistant Secretary of the Navy Fox wrote Rear Admiral S. P. Lee, proposing an assault on Wilmington: "Though the popular clamor centers upon Charleston I consider Wilmington a more important point in a military and political point of view and I do not conceal from myself that it is more difficult of access on account of the shallowness of the bars, and more easily defended inside by obstructions, yet it must be attacked and we have more force than we shall possess again since the Iron Clads must go South so soon as four are ready."   Nonetheless, Wilmington, guarded by the guns of Fort Fisher, remained a bastion of Confederate strength and one of the few havens for blockade runners until nearly the end of the war.

16 General Banks arrived at New Orleans with additional troops to supersede General Butler and prepare for increased operations on the river.

18 Assistant Secretary of the Navy Fox wrote: "I believe there is no work shop in the country capable of making steam machinery or iron plates and hulls that is not in full blast with Naval

U.S.S. Cairo *is torpedoed and sinks in the* Yazoo River. Cairo *was the first Union ship sunk by Confederate torpedoes.*

orders. Before another year we shall be prepared to defend ourselves with reasonable hopes of success against a foreign enemy, and in two years we can take the offensive with vessels that will be superior to any England is now building." Because of this extensive building program, by war's end the U.S. Navy was the most powerful force afloat in the world.

19 Rear Admiral Farragut advised Secretary of the Navy Welles that he had recommended "the occupation of Baton Rouge" to General Banks on his arrival. "He . . . ordered his transports to proceed directly to that city." Commander James Alden in *Richmond* with 2 gunboats covered the landing. "Baton Rouge is only 12–15 miles from Port Hudson. I am ready to attack the latter place and support General Banks the moment he desires to move against it." The powerful combined operations that were destroying the Confederacy at its heart gathered strength for the crushing attacks of 1863.

20 Rear Admiral D. D. Porter in his flagship U.S.S. *Black Hawk* joined General William T. Sherman at Helena, Arkansas, and prepared for the joint assault on Vicksburg. The fleet under Admiral Porter's command for the Vicksburg campaign was the largest ever placed under one officer up to that time, equal in number to all the vessels composing the U.S. Navy at the outbreak of war.

Medal of Honor awarded to Boatswain's Mate Thomas Gehegan for personal valor while serving on board U.S.S. Pinola *with Flag Officer Farragut's fleet at New Orleans, April 24 and 25, 1962. A total of 327 Civil War sailors and Marines were awarded the Medal of Honor.*

22 U.S.S. *Huntsville*, Acting Lieutenant W. C. Rogers, seized schooner *Courier* off Tortugas with cargo including salt, coffee, sugar, and dry goods.

Captain Dahlgren, confidant of and advisor to the President, went to the White House at the request of President Lincoln to observe the testing of a new type of gunpowder.

24 U.S.S. *New Era*, Acting Master Frank W. Flanner, arrived off Columbus, Kentucky, to support the Army, which was threatened with imminent attack by a large Confederate force. *New Era* .had been dispatched to Columbus at the urgent request of General J. M. Tuttle, and brought a much-needed Army howitzer, ammunition, and a Master's Mate to take charge of one of the batteries. Confederate occupation of Columbus would have seriously disrupted the flow of supplies to the fleet and Army poised below for the Vicksburg assault.

U.S.S. *Charlotte*, Acting Master Bruner, captured steamer *Bloomer* in Choctawhatchee River, Florida.

27 Rear Admiral D. D. Porter received a request from Brigadier General Willis A. Gorman for assistance in the forthcoming campaign in Arkansas. Though his fleet was "fully employed," Porter nevertheless ordered U.S.S. *Conestoga* to begin the requested patrolling action "between the White and Arkansas rivers as occasion may require. But," he added in his instructions to Lieutenant Commander Selfridge, "Arkansas is the main point to look after. We will occupy it soon with troops." Meanwhile, that day Porter's squadron was involved in a heated engagement with Confederate batteries on the Yazoo. U.S.S. *Benton*, Lieutenant Commander Gwin, continuing to carry on the removal of torpedoes after *Cairo's* destruction a fortnight before, with U.S.S. *Cincinnati*, *Baron de Kalb*, *Louisville*, *Lexington*, *Marmora*, and ram *Queen of the West* in company, returned the fire of the battery's eight heavy guns at Drumgould's Bluff. As Porter observed, "The old war horse, *Benton*, has been much cut up, and the gallant, noble Gwin, I fear, mortally wounded." Nonetheless, Porter was able to report that the Yazoo was cleared of torpedoes to within one-half mile of the battery and to remark "we gave the enemy enough to occupy them to-day, and drew off a large portion of their force." Cooperating fully with the Army during the preparations for renewed engagements along the Mississippi, the Navy constantly harassed Confederate forces at Drumgould's Bluff, as well as those at Haynes' Bluff and elsewhere, as the squadron's mobile fire power kept Confederate troops off balance and dispersed.

U.S.S. *Magnolia*, Acting Master Charles Potter, captured British schooner *Carmita* northwest of Marquesas Keys, Florida, attempting to run the blockade.

U.S.S. *Roebuck*, Master John Sherrill, captured British schooner *Kate* attempting to run into St. Mark's River, Florida, with cargo of salt, coffee, copper, and liquor.

28 U.S.S. *Anacostia*, Acting Master Nelson Provost, seized schooner *Exchange* in the Rappahannock River.

28–30 Rear Admiral D. D. Porter's gunboats supported General Sherman's attempt to capture Confederate-held Chickasaw Bluffs, a vantage point upstream from Vicksburg. "Throughout these operations," Porter wrote, "the Navy did everything that could be done to ensure the success of General Sherman's movement." Though the Navy supplied shore bombardment from the squadron and created diversionary movements, the Union troops, hindered by heavy rains and faced by the timely arrival of Confederate reinforcements, were forced to withdraw.

29 U.S.S. *Magnolia*, Acting Master Potter, seized blockade running British sloop *Flying Fish* off Tortugas.

31 U.S.S. *Monitor*, Commander Bankhead, foundered and was lost off Cape Hatteras en route from Hampton Roads to Beaufort, North Carolina. During the short career of the first Union seagoing ironclad, she had fought C.S.S. *Virginia* in the historic engagement that ushered in a new era in warfare, had supported General McClellan's Peninsular Campaign, and had effected for all time momentous changes in naval tactics and ship construction.

The Confederate embargo, the capture of New Orleans, and the Union Navy's blockade combined to curtail greatly the export of the South's major product, cotton. Meanwhile, the North's control of the seas, threatened only by a few Confederate commerce raiders, granted the Union access to the world markets for the importation of war materials and exportation of produce such as wheat, which was a major factor in deterring European powers from recognizing the Confederacy.

U.S.S. Monitor *is lost at sea*.

Men wanted

FOR

THE NAVY!

All able bodied men and boys

Will be enlisted into the **NAVAL SERVICE**

upon application at the Naval Rendezvous.

Come forward and serve your Country

WITHOUT CONSCRIPTION!

Roanoke Island, Dec. 8th, 1863.

1863

I.—SOME SIGNIFICANT EVENTS OF 1863

1 January— C.S.S. *Bayou City* and *Neptune* engaged the Union fleet at Galveston, forcing the North's withdrawal from that foothold on the Texas coast. U.S.S. *Harriet Lane* was captured and U.S.S. *Westfield* was destroyed.

9–11 January— Gunboats under Rear Admiral D. D. Porter, with troops embarked, compelled the surrender of Fort Hindman (Arkansas Post) on the Arkansas River.

11 January— C.S.S. *Alabama*, Captain R. Semmes, engaged and sank U.S.S. *Hatteras*, Lieutenant Commander H. C. Blake, off Galveston.

14 January— Joint Army-Navy forces attacked Confederate positions at Bayou Teche, Louisiana, compelling a Southern withdrawal and the subsequent destruction of gunboat C.S.S. *Cotton*.

21 January— C.S.S. *Josiah Bell* and *Uncle Ben* captured U.S.S. *Morning Light* and *Velocity*, temporarily lifting the blockade of Sabine Pass, Texas.

30 January— U.S.S. *Commodore Perry* and Army troops severed Confederate supply lines to Richmond via the Perquimans River, North Carolina.

31 January— C.S.S. *Palmetto State* and *Chicora* attacked the blockading fleet off Charleston; U.S.S. *Mercedita* and *Keystone State* were heavily damaged and struck their flags.

14 February— U.S.S. *Queen of the West* grounded in the Black River and was abandoned under heavy fire.

24 February— C.S.S. *William H. Webb* and *Queen of the West* engaged and sank ram U.S.S. *Indianola* below Warrenton, Mississippi.

28 February— U.S.S. *Montauk*, *Wissahickon*, *Seneca*, and *Dawn* shelled and destroyed blockade runner *Rattlesnake* (formerly C.S.S. *Nashville*) under the guns of Fort McAllister, Georgia. For more than a month Union ironclads had been bombarding the fort guarding the approaches to Savannah.

11 March— Ships of the Yazoo Pass Expedition, begun in February with the objective of cutting off Vicksburg in the rear, engaged Fort Pemberton, Mississippi. The expedition ultimately had to retire without achieving its purpose.

14 March— Rear Admiral D. G. Farragut passed the heavy batteries at Port Hudson with U.S.S. *Hartford* and *Albatross* to establish an effective blockade of the vital Red River supply lines.

31 March— Confederate troops opened a sustained attack on Union forces at Washington, North Carolina, but Northern warships, moving swiftly to the support of the soldiers, halted the assault.

7 April— Rear Admiral S. F. Du Pont's ironclad squadron engaged strong Confederate forts in Charleston harbor in an attempt to penetrate the defenses and capture the city. The ironclads were heavily damaged and the attack was broken off; U.S.S. *Keokuk* sank the next day.

16–17 April—	Gunboats under Rear Admiral D. D. Porter escorting Army transports successfully passed the Vicksburg batteries preparatory to attacking Grand Gulf.
3 May—	Rear Admiral Porter's force and troops under Major General U. S. Grant forced the evacuation of Grand Gulf. Porter reported: "The Navy holds the door to Vicksburg."
17 June—	C.S.S. *Atlanta*, with two wooden steamers in company, engaged U.S.S. *Weehawken* and *Nahant* in Wassaw Sound, Georgia. The heavy Confederate warship grounded and was compelled to surrender.
4 July—	Vicksburg surrendered after a lengthy bombardment and siege by Union naval and land forces. President Lincoln wrote: "The Father of Waters again goes unvexed to the sea."
9 July—	Port Hudson, Louisiana, surrendered after prolonged attack by Northern sea and land forces. The Union had won the war in the West.
10 July—	Rear Admiral J. A. Dahlgren's ironclads renewed the bombardment of Charleston defenses, opening on Fort Wagner, Morris Island.
13 July	Yazoo City, Mississippi, was captured by a joint Army-Navy expedition.
1 August—	Rear Admiral D. D. Porter relieved Rear Admiral D. G. Farragut of command of the lower half of the Mississippi and assumed command of the River from New Orleans to the headwaters.
5 August—	U.S.S. *Commodore Barney* was severely damaged by Confederate electric torpedo in the James River above Dutch Gap, Virginia.
29 August—	Confederate submarine *H. L. Hunley*, Lieutenant J. A. Payne, CSN, sank for the first time in Charleston harbor after making practice dives preparatory to attacking the blockading fleet.
6 September—	Morris Island, Charleston harbor, was evacuated by Confederate forces after nearly 2 months of intensive bombardment from afloat and ashore.
8 September—	C.S.S. *Uncle Ben* and shore batteries turned back a Union expedition to take Sabine Pass, Texas. U.S.S. *Clifton* and *Sachem* were disabled and surrendered.
5 October—	C.S.S. *David*, Lieutenant W. T. Glassell, exploded a spar torpedo against U.S.S. *New Ironsides* in an attempt to destroy the heavy blockader off Charleston. *New Ironsides* was damaged but not destroyed.
15 October—	Submarine *H. L. Hunley* sank for the second time in Charleston harbor. The part owner for whom she was named and a crew of seven perished in the accident, but she was again recovered and a third crew volunteered to man her.
31 October—	During October instruction began for 52 midshipmen at the Confederate States Naval Academy on board C.S.S. *Patrick Henry* in the James River.
2–4 November—	Naval forces convoyed and supported Army troops at Brazos Santiago, Texas, where the Union secured a valuable position on the Mexican border. As a result of this operation, Brownsville, Texas, was also evacuated.
7 December—	Steamer *Chesapeake* en route Portland, Maine, was seized off Cape Cod by Confederates disguised as passengers and carried to Nova Scotia.

II.—DETAILED CIVIL WAR NAVAL CHRONOLOGY

1863

JANUARY

1 Confederate warships under Major Leon Smith, CSA, defeated Union blockading forces at Galveston in a fierce surprise attack combined with an assault ashore by Confederate troops that resulted in the capture of the Northern Army company stationed there. Smith's flotilla included the improvised cotton-clad gunboats C.S.S. *Bayou City* and *Neptune*, with Army sharpshooting boarding parties embarked, and tenders *John F. Carr* and *Lucy Gwin*. The Union squadron under Commander William B. Renshaw, U.S.S. *Harriet Lane, Owasco, Corypheus, Sachem, Clifton,* and *Westfield*, was caught off guard. Despite the surprise, *Harriet Lane*, Commander Jonathan M. Wainwright, put up a gallant fight. She rammed *Bayou City*, but without much damage. In turn she was rammed by *Neptune*, which was so damaged by the resulting impact and a shot from *Harriet Lane* taken at the waterline that she sank in 8 feet of water. *Bayou City*, meanwhile, turned and rammed *Harriet Lane* so heavily that the two ships could not be separated. The troops from the cotton-clad clambered over the bulwarks to board *Harriet Lane*. Commander Wainwright was killed in the wild hand-to-hand combat and his ship was captured.

    In the meantime, *Westfield*, Commander Renshaw, had run aground in Bolivar Channel prior to the action, could not be gotten off, and was destroyed to prevent her capture. Renshaw and a boat crew were killed when *Westfield* blew up prematurely. The small ships comprising

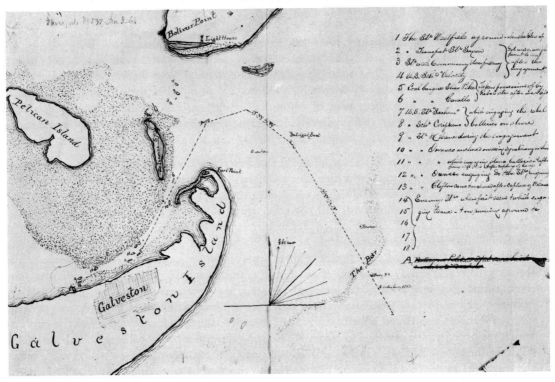

This contemporary chart was drawn to show the position of Union ships at Galveston when taken under attack by a small Confederate squadron on 1 January.

U.S.S. Westfield, *Commander Renshaw, was destroyed by her crew to prevent capture at Galveston after she had grounded.*

the remainder of the blockading force ran through heavy Confederate fire from ashore and stood out to sea. Surprise and boldness in execution, as often in the long history of warfare, had won another victory. The tribute paid by Major General John Bankhead Magruder, CSA, was well deserved: "The alacrity with which officers and men, all of them totally unacquainted with this novel kind of service, some of whom had never seen a ship before, volunteered for an enterprise so extraordinarily and apparently desperate in its character, and the bold and dashing manner in which the plan was executed, are certainly deserving of the highest praise."

The extensive use of Confederate torpedoes in the western waters required similar ingenuity on the part of Union forces to cope with them. Colonel Charles R. Ellet proposed a plan to clear the Yazoo of torpedoes, to enable the gunboats to operate more freely. He wrote: "My plan was to attach to the bow of a swift and powerful steamboat [*Lioness* was chosen] a strong framework, consisting of two heavy spars, 65 feet in length, firmly secured by transverse and diagonal braces and extending 50 feet forward of the steamer's bow. A crosspiece, 35 feet in length, was to be bolted to the forward extremities of these spars. Through each end of this crosspiece and through the center a heavy iron rod, 1½ inches in diameter and 10 feet long, descended into the river, terminating in a hook. An intermediate hook was attached to each bar 3 feet from the bottom. The three bars were strengthened by a light piece of timber halfway down, through which they were passed and bolted. . . . The torpedoes are sunk in the water, but the cords by which they are fired are attached to buoys floating on the surface. My belief was that the curved hooks of the rake would catch these cords, and, driven by the powerful boat, would either explode the torpedoes or tear them to pieces and break the ropes, thus rendering them harmless to succeeding vessels." In fundamental principle, the method compares with the sweeping of mines in World War II and Korea.

3 U.S.S. *Currituck*, Acting Master Thomas J. Linnekin, captured sloop *Potter* between the mouths of the Potomac and Rappahannock Rivers.

Confederate commerce raiding schooner *Retribution*, Master Thomas B. Power, chased merchant ships *Gilmore Meredith* and *Westward* back into the harbor at Havana.

4 A joint Army-Navy expedition under Rear Admiral David D. Porter and Major General W. T. Sherman got underway up the White River, Arkansas, aiming at the capture of Fort Hindman at Arkansas Post. Hindman, described by Porter as a "tough little nut," mounted 11 guns. With a small coal supply available, Porter had the gunboats towed upriver by Army transports to conserve his fuel as much as possible. The gunboats included U.S.S. *Baron de Kalb, Louisville, Cincinnati, Signal, Marmora, Lexington, New Era, Romeo, Rattler, Glide*, and flagship *Black Hawk*. This date Porter also ordered ram *Monarch* to join him at the mouth of the Arkansas River.

Rear Admiral Samuel F. Du Pont wrote Charles Henry Davis regarding the Confederate defenses of Charleston: "The work on the defenses of Charleston has never ceased since the fall of Sumter, some 20 long months under successive generals; and the man who commenced it [General Beauregard] is now giving the closing touches and I believe he has exhausted his science and applied every conceivable means. He is fully confident that he can successfully defend the harbor, and the British officers who go in, and the blockade runners whom we catch smile at the idea of its being taken, representing it stronger than Sebastopol. A deserter from Morris Island confirms the above feeling of confidence, and says they expect to sink every gunboat as fast as they approach."

Referring to the proposed Union attack on Charleston, Du Pont said: "I have always been of the opinion that it should be a joint operation, carefully devised—and I trust that I am not

Gunboats under Rear Admiral Porter bombard Fort Hindman (Arkansas Post) and force its surrender. The victory was especially important at this time because it offset Northern loses in other areas.

insensible to the honor of a *naval* capture—Though I am infinitely more alive to the absolute *necessity* of *success* than any special glory to our arm of service, or of personal distinction to myself. We cannot afford a failure in this crisis, political as well as military through which we are now passing—the more so, that desirable as the taking of Charleston is, the contest will still go on, until the rebel armies are broken and dispersed."

Major General Ulysses S. Grant wired Commander Alexander M. Pennock at Cairo, asking for gunboat support as Confederate troops began renewed attempts to regain positions in Tennessee: "Some light-draft gunboats now in Tennessee would be of great value. Forrest has got to the east bank, but there are strong signs of his recrossing in the vicinity of Savannah [Tennessee]. Can any be sent?" Though hampered by low water on the rivers, Pennock had foreseen the possible Southern action; he replied: "Have already ordered all available boats to ascend [the] Tennessee with the rise."

This date, Pennock received word from Army headquarters at Evansville, Indiana, that 14 steamers had departed for Nashville with essential supplies and would need convoy service from Smithland, Kentucky. The fleet captain at Cairo wired back: "Two gunboats have been waiting since yesterday at Smithland. Commanding naval officer will make such arrangements as he deems proper on arrival of the fleet at Smithland." Control over the inland waterways by the Union Navy assured the Army of continuous logistic and convoy support. As on the railroads, troops and supplies moved freely on the rivers. In addition, the powerful armament of the gunboats swept aside opposition.

U.S.S. *Quaker City*, Commander James M. Frailey, captured sloop *Mercury* off Charleston with important Confederate dispatches on board. Rear Admiral Du Pont described "the most important of all" as a letter bearing on the ironclads building in England which urged "the absolute importance of hastening them forward as the only thing that offers succor and relief . . . We want succor or we must die."

5 Boat crews from U.S.S. *Sagamore*, Lieutenant Commander Earl English, seized blockade running British sloop *Avenger* in Jupiter Inlet, Florida, with cargo of coffee, gin, salt, and baled goods.

6 Confederate troops captured and burned steamboat *Jacob Musselman* near Memphis. The commander of the Confederate company, Captain James H. McGehee, was acting under orders to reconnoiter the area, "burning cotton in that country and annoying the enemy on the Mississippi River" wherever possible. Attacks such as this emphasized the Union's reliance on naval control of the waterways to transport and convoy troops and supplies in areas already dominated by the North. Had this force afloat been weaker, the Confederacy might well have re-established vital positions in the west and elsewhere.

Assistant Adjutant General John A. Rawlins, writing from Holly Springs, Mississippi, informed Colonel William W. Lowe, commanding at Fort Henry, of a reported large number of "flat boats and other craft for crossing the Tennessee. You will therefore please request the gunboats, which are reported to be up the river, to use every means for their destruction, that the enemy may be prevented from crossing into West Tennessee and Kentucky. They should proceed up the river as far as the water will permit." The gunboats had constant work to do on the upper waters as well as near Vicksburg.

U.S.S. *Pocahontas*, Lieutenant Commander William M. Gamble, captured blockade runner *Antona* off Cape San Blas, Florida.

7 Confederate Secretary of the Navy Stephen R. Mallory wrote Commander James D. Bulloch in Liverpool regarding urgently needed ships to be built in England: ". . . Push these ships ahead as rapidly as possible. Our difficulty lies in providing you with funds, but you may rely upon receiving cotton certificates sooner or later. You speak of having under consideration plans of

armored ships of about 2300 tons and to draw 14 feet, and of certain parties who are willing to build without cash advances, and to deliver the ships armed and equipped, beyond British juris- diction. Close with this proposition at once by all means, and give any reasonable bonus after agreeing upon the times of such delivery, for earlier delivery, together with a bonus for extra speed. . . . I am convinced that every ship may and should be used as a ram when opportunities are presented. . . . Our river high-pressure boats, carrying their boilers on deck, frequently run against a sand bar or a snag, going at great speed, and bring all up standing, without deranging their boilers or engines in the least. The contact of the *Virginia* with the *Cumberland* was not felt on board the former, and the moving vessel that runs squarely into a stationary one rarely receives injury.''

7–9 Joint Army-Navy expedition up the Pamunkey River destroyed boats, barges and stores at West Point and White House, Virginia. U.S.S. *Mahaska* and *Commodore Morris*, under Commander Foxhall A. Parker, supported the Army movement and convoyed transport *May Queen*. Rear Admiral Samuel P. Lee reported: "A more extensive enterprise was projected, but want of water at the obstructions prevented its full success; as a reconnaissance it is valuable." Major General Erasmus D. Keyes felt that "the success of the land part of the expedition was largely indebted to Captain Parker's admirable management of his vessels. On this and many other occasions I have noticed the zeal and good judgment of that naval officer."

8 General Grant wired Commander Pennock in Cairo: "Can I have gunboats at Memphis to convoy reinforcements to Vicksburg? I will want them by the eleventh." The fleet captain, facing problems that had beset the gunboats since the squadron's inception, replied: "Will send one light-draft gunboat, bullet-proof, one-fourth manned. I can do no more. Can't you place under the command of her captain soldiers enough to work her guns?" The next day, 9 January, Grant and Pennock again exchanged telegrams relative to the Army's need for gunboats. "There is no gunboat in Tennessee River above Fort Henry," the General wired Cairo. "There is 10 feet water and rising." Pennock reported: "Two [gunboats] have orders to ascend Tennessee with rise."

U.S.S. *Sagamore*, Lieutenant Commander English, seized blockade running British sloop *Julia* off Jupiter Inlet with cargo of salt.

U.S.S. *Tahoma*, Lieutenant Commander Alexander A. Semmes, captured blockade runner *Silas Henry*, aground in Tampa Bay with cargo of cotton.

9 Boat crews from U.S.S. *Ethan Allen*, Acting Master Isaac A. Pennell, destroyed "a very large salt manufactory" south of St. Joseph's, Florida. Pennell noted that the works were "capable of making 75 bushels of salt per day" and reported that it was "the fourth salt manufactory I have destroyed since I have been on this station."

9–11 U.S.S. *Baron De Kalb*, *Louisville*, *Cincinnati*, *Lexington*, *Rattler*, and *Black Hawk*, under Rear Admiral Porter in tug *Ivy*, engaged and, with the troops of Major General W. T. Sherman, forced the surrender of Fort Hindman at Arkansas Post. Ascending the Arkansas River, Porter's squadron covered the landing of the troops and shelled Confederates from their rifle pits, enabling McClernand's troops on 9 January to take command of the woods below the fort and approach unseen. Though the Army was not in a position to press the attack on 10 January, the squadron moved to within 60 yards of the staunchly defended fort to soften the works for the next day's assault. A blistering engagement ensued, the fort's 11 guns pouring a withering fire into the gunboats. U.S.S. *Rattler*, Lieutenant Commander Watson Smith, attempted to run past the fort to provide enfilade support, but was caught on a snag placed in the river by the Confederates, received a heavy raking fire, and was forced to return downstream.

Porter's gunboats renewed the engagement the next morning, 11 January, when the Army launched its assault, and "after a well directed fire of about two and one-half hours every gun in the fort was dismounted or disabled and the fort knocked all to pieces. . . ." Ram *Monarch* and U.S.S. *Rattler* and *Glide,* under Lieutenant Commander W. Smith, knifed upriver to cut off any attempted escape. Brigadier General Thomas J. Churchill, CSA, surrendered the fort—including some 36 defending Confederate naval officers and men—after a gallant resistance to the fearful pounding from the gunboats. Porter wrote Secretary of the Navy Welles: "No fort ever received a worse battering, and the highest compliment I can pay those engaged is to repeat what the rebels said: 'You can't expect men to stand up against the fire of those gunboats.' "

After the loss of Fort Hindman, Confederates evacuated other positions on the White and St. Charles Rivers before falling waters forced the gunboats to retire downstream. Porter wrote: "The fight at Fort Hindman was one of the prettiest little affairs of the war, not so little either, for a very important post fell into our hands with 6,500 prisoners, and the destruction of a powerful ram at Little Rock [C.S.S. *Pontchartrain*], which could have caused the Federal Navy in the West a great deal of trouble, was ensured. . . . Certain it is, the success at Arkansas Post had a most exhilarating effect on the troops, and they were a different set of men when they arrived at Milliken's Bend than they were when they left the Yazoo River." A memorandum in the Secretary's office added: "The importance of this victory can not be estimated. It happened at a moment when the Union arms were unsuccessful on three or four battlefields. . . ."

10   Under orders from Farragut to "reestablish the blockade as soon as you can" at Galveston, Commodore Henry H. Bell in U.S.S. *Brooklyn,* with other ships in company, bombarded the port. Because of the danger of grounding, Bell decided not to attempt to force an entrance. "It is with a bitter and lasting sense of grief I give it up," he wrote, "as the blockade of the port with *Harriet Lane* is a difficult task for so small a fleet as is in the Gulf. There will be censure, inconsiderate censure, but I can't help it. I can't overcome the difficulty of shoal water and a crooked, narrow channel without pilots, or small draft vessels to assist such [ships] as ground."

U.S.S. *Octorara,* Commander Napoleon Collins, captured blockade running British schooner *Rising Dawn* in North West Providence Channel with large cargo of salt.

C.S.S. *Retribution,* Master Power, captured brig *J. P. Ellicott,* bound from Boston to Cienfuegos. Next day, she was retaken by her own crew from the Confederate prize crew and sailed to St. Thomas Island where she was turned over to U.S.S. *Alabama,* Commander Edward T. Nichols.

11   C.S.S. *Alabama,* Captain Raphael Semmes, sank U.S.S. *Hatteras,* Lieutenant Commander Homer C. Blake, after a heated and close night engagement some thirty miles off Galveston. "My men," reported Semmes, "handled their pieces with great spirit and commendable coolness, and the action was sharp and exciting while it lasted; which, however, was not very long, for in just *thirteen minutes* after firing the first gun, the enemy hoisted a light, and fired an off-gun, as a signal that he had been beaten. We at once withheld our fire, and such a cheer went up from the brazen throats of my fellows, as must have astonished even a Texan, if he had heard it." *Hatteras* was severely punished, whereas damage to *Alabama* was so slight "that there was not a shot-hole which it was necessary to plug, to enable us to continue our cruise; nor was there a rope to be spliced." *Hatteras* went down in 9½ fathoms, *Alabama* saving all hands. Other Union ships in the Galveston area steamed out in vain in chase of the raider. Semmes observed: "There was now as hurried a saddling of steeds for the pursuit as there had been in the chase of the young Lochinvar, and with as little effect, for by the time the steeds were given the spur, the *Alabama* was distant a hundred miles or more."

Confederate troops captured steamboat *Grampus No. 2* near Memphis laden with large cargo of coal, and later burned her at Mound City, Arkansas.

U.S.S. *Matthew Vassar,* Acting Master Hugh H. Savage, captured schooner *Florida* off Little River Inlet, South Carolina, with cargo of salt.

13   Joint Army-Navy expedition from Memphis on board U.S.S. *General Bragg,* Lieutenant Joshua Bishop, destroyed buildings at Mound City, Arkansas, in reprisal for Confederate attacks on

river steamers. Bishop reported: "Ascertained that there was quite a force of guerrillas in the neighborhood, who intended destroying steamers; that their rendezvous was at Mound City, Marion, and Hopefield. . . . At 9 a.m. left Bradley's Landing and proceeded to Mound City, firing shells at intervals into the woods, as it was supposed there were guerrillas thereabouts. At 10 landed at Mound City and disembarked the troops. The infantry made prisoners of several citizens, who had been harboring guerrillas. . . ."

U.S.S. *Currituck*, Acting Master Linnekin, captured schooner *Hampton* at Dividing Creek, Virginia. The day before, Linnekin destroyed the salt works at Dividing Creek, works that had been "extensively engaged" in supplying Richmond with the important item.

14 Joint Army-Navy forces, including U.S.S. *Kinsman*, *Estrella*, *Calhoun*, and *Diana*, under Lieutenant Commander Thomas McK. Buchanan, attacked Confederate defenses in Bayou Teche, below Franklin, Louisiana. Vigorous prosecution of the action by the naval vessels forced withdrawal of the Southern defenders and permitted removal of the formidable obstructions sunk in an effort to halt the ships. Gunboat C.S.S. *Cotton*, Lieutenant Edward W. Fuller, engaged the attacking force, but was compelled to withdraw, subsequently being set afire and destroyed by her crew to prevent capture. During the engagement, a torpedo exploded under U.S.S. *Kinsman*, Acting Lieutenant George Wiggin, unshipping her rudder. Lieutenant Commander Buchanan was killed by shore fire.

Joint expedition under Lieutenant Commander John G. Walker and Brigadier General Willis A. Gorman, including gunboats U.S.S. *Baron De Kalb* and *Cincinnati* with two Army transports in tow, arrived at St. Charles, Arkansas, on the White River in a move to follow up the advantage gained by the Fort Hindman victory. The commanders discovered that the Confederates had

C.S.S. Alabama *sinks U.S.S.* Hatteras *off Galveston. The Union redoubled its efforts to capture the "ghost ship of the Confederacy."*

abandoned their position and withdrawn up river on board *Blue Wing*. While *Cincinnati* remained at St. Charles, *Baron De Kalb* proceeded up the White River in pursuit.

U.S.S. *Columbia*, Lieutenant Joseph P. Couthouy, ran aground on the coast of North Carolina. High winds and heavy seas aborted initial attempts to get her off, and by the 17th, when the weather moderated, *Columbia* was in Confederate hands. She was destroyed by fire and Couthouy and some 11 other crew members were taken prisoner.

15 President Lincoln conferred with Captain John A. Dahlgren at the Washington Navy Yard regarding gunpowder development in one of his frequent trips to the yard to observe tests and weapon progress.

U.S.S. *Octorara*, Commander Collins, seized blockade running British sloop *Brave* in North West Providence Channel, Bahamas, with cargo of salt and sponge.

16 C.S.S. *Florida*, Lieutenant John N. Maffitt, ran the blockade out of Mobile in the early morning after having remained in that port for some 4 months in order to complete repairs to her equipment. Confusion in the blockading fleet enabled *Florida* to escape, for the Confederate commerce raider passed within 300 yards of U.S.S. *R. R. Cuyler*, Commander George F. Emmons. Upon her arrival at Havana on 20 January to debark prisoners from her first prize, U.S. Consul-General Robert W. Shufeldt described the raider: "The *Florida* is a bark-rigged propeller, quite fast under steam and canvas; has two smoke-stacks fore and aft of each other, close together; has a battery of four 42's or 68's of a side, and two large pivot guns. Her crew consists of 135 men . . . is a wooden vessel of about 1,500 tons." Farragut was concerned by *Florida*'s escape: "This squadron, as Sam Barron used to say, 'is eating its dirt now'—*Galveston* skedaddled, the *Hatteras* sunk by

Under Lieutenant John Maffitt C.S.S. Florida *runs the blockade out of Mobile to resume her career on the high seas.*

the *Alabama*, and now the *Oreto* [*Florida*] out. . . .   The Admiral's son, Loyall Farragut, completed the letter: "Father's eyes have given out; so I will finish this letter. He has been very much worried at these things, but still tries to bear it like a philosopher. He knows he has done all in his power to avert it, with the vessels at his disposal. If the Government had only let him take Mobile when he wished to, the *Oreto* would never have run out."

Captain Semmes, with a keen interest in the advancement of scientific knowledge, recorded the following observation from on board C.S.S. *Alabama*: ". . . the old theory of Dr. Franklin and others, was, that the Gulf Stream, which flows out of the Gulf of Mexico, between the north coast of Cuba, and the Florida Reefs and Keys, flows *into* the Gulf, through the channel between the west end of Cuba, and the coast of Yucatan, in which the *Alabama* now was. But the effectual disproof of this theory is, that we know positively, from the strength of the current, and its volume, or cross section, in the two passages, that more than twice the quantity of water flows out of the Gulf of Mexico, than flows into it through this passage. Upon Dr. Franklin's theory, the Gulf of Mexico in a very short time would become dry ground. Nor can the Mississippi River, which is the only stream worth noticing, in this connection, that flows into the Gulf of Mexico, come to his relief, as we have seen that that river only empties into the Gulf of Mexico, about *one three thousandth* part as much water, as the Gulf Stream takes out. We must resort, of necessity, to an under-current from the north, passing into the Gulf of Mexico, under the Gulf Stream, rising to the surface when heated, and thus swelling the volume of the outflowing water."

U.S.S. *Baron De Kalb*, Lieutenant Commander J. G. Walker, arrived at Devall's Bluff, Arkansas, on the White River. A landing party went ashore and "took possession of all the public property," including guns and munitions. Walker reported: "Upon the arrival of General Gorman's troops I drew off my men and turned everything over to the army." Next day, *Baron De Kalb* continued the pursuit of Confederate steamer *Blue Wing*, which was reported to have departed Devall's Bluff just before the Union gunboat arrived.

17 U.S.S. *Baron De Kalb*, Lieutenant Commander Walker, with U.S.S. *Forest Rose* and *Romeo* and an Army transport in company, proceeded up White River to Des Arc, Arkansas. "At that place," Walker reported, "I found 39 rebel soldiers in the hospital, whom I paroled. I also found and brought away 171 rounds of fixed ammunition, 72 cartridges, and 47 shot for 12-pounder rifled gun. I took possession of the post-office. . . . The troops reached Des Arc about an hour after me, and searched the town for arms and public property." Having cleared out Confederate strong points, the squadron withdrew downstream.

18 Following the operations on the White River, Rear Admiral Porter once more turned his attentions to the Southern citadel at Vicksburg. In a general order to gunboats on the Yazoo River, he directed: "All the gunboats on their way up will return down river and give convoy to the transports as far as Milliken's Bend, where they will cover them."

Porter wrote Secretary Welles concerning the unsuccessful Vicksburg operation of December 1862, then added: "The operations to come will be of a different character; it will be a tedious siege, the first step, in my opinion, toward a successful attack on Vicksburg, which has been made very strong by land and water. I have always thought the late attempt was premature, but sometimes these dashes succeed . . . The operations of the navy in the Yazoo are worthy to be ranked amongst the brightest events of the war. The officers in charge of getting up the torpedoes and clearing 8 miles of river distinguished themselves by their patient endurance and cool courage under a galling fire of musketry from well-protected and unseen riflemen, and the crews of the boats exhibited a courage and coolness seldom equaled. The navy will scarcely ever get credit for these events; they are not brilliant enough to satisfy our impatient people at the North, who know little of the difficulties . . . or how much officers and men are exposing themselves. . . . The Department may rest assured that the navy here is never idle. The army depends on us to take entire charge of them on the water. . . . We expect to disembark the troops opposite

Vicksburg in four or five days. In the meantime, I want to gather up the fleet, which are operating at different points with the army. My opinion is that Vicksburg is the main point. When that falls all subordinate posts will fall with it." The buildup was begun.

U.S.S. *Wachusett*, Rear Admiral Charles Wilkes, and U.S.S. *Sonoma*, Commander Thomas H. Stevens, seized steamer *Virginia* off Mugeres Island, Mexico. *Virginia* was sent to Key West for adjudication.

U.S.S. *Zouave*, Pilot John A. Phillips, captured sloop *J. C. McCabe* in the James River.

Confederate steamer *Tropic* accidentally caught fire and burned attempting to run the blockade at Charleston with cargo of cotton and turpentine.

19 C.S.S. *Florida*, Lieutenant Maffitt, captured and burned brig *Estelle* bound from Santa Cruz to Boston with cargo of sugar, molasses, and honey. The master of *Estelle* wrote: "Generosity and courtesy on the part of enemies should not pass unheeded by, as the rigors of a sad and un-natural war may be somewhat mitigated by politeness and manly forbearance. I would add that Captain Maffitt returned our personal effects, but retained the chronometer and charts."

Secretary Welles wired Commander Pennock in Cairo, asking that he give all possible assistance to the Army: "General Rosecrans desires a naval force to protect the transports in the Cumberland. Can you not send some vessels for the purpose?" Next day, 20 January, Rosecrans telegraphed Pennock, pressing the issue: "It is very desirable that a couple of good gunboats should go up the Cumberland and destroy means of crossing as high up as Somerset. How soon can it be done?" After receiving two more such messages on 22 January, Pennock advised the harried General on the 24th: "The *Silver Lake* leaves for Cumberland River to-day. Has short crew. The *Lexington*, with heavy guns, will also leave to-morrow evening. No more boats to send; with these there will be five in that river. . . . Will do all I can to assist you." Rosecrans responded that he was "greatly obliged" and would "furnish more crews if possible." This joint cooperation kept the upper rivers open to the Union and prevented the Confederates from mounting an effective counteroffensive. Secretary Welles advised Porter of President Lincoln's personal interest in the Vicksburg operation: "The President is exceedingly anxious that a canal from which practical and useful results would follow should be cut through the peninsula opposite Vicksburg. If a canal were cut at a higher point up the river than the first one, as you some time since suggested, so as to catch the current before it has made the curve, and also avoid the bluffs below the city, it would probably be a success. The Department desires that this plan may be tried whenever you may deem it expedient and can have the cooperation of the army." This was one of several plans to get the Army transports downstream past Vicksburg so that the Union troops could encircle the stronghold from the rear. The batteries were thought to be too powerful for a successful run past them with the big and cumbersome transports. When the "ditch" was begun, as Porter later wrote, "it was hoped that when the river rose it would cut its way through, but that wished for event did not come to pass until after the fall of Vicksburg. The enemy mounted heavy guns opposite the mouth of the canal and prevented any work upon it."

An intercepted letter from Nassau indicated the blockade's effectiveness: "There are men here who are making immense fortunes by shipping goods to Dixie. . . . Salt, for example, is one of the most paying things to send in. Here in Nassau it is only worth 60 cents a bushel, but in Charleston brings at auction from $80 to $100 in Confederate money, but as Confederate money is no good out of the Confederacy they send back cotton or turpentine, which, if it reaches here, is worth proportionally as much here as the salt is there. . . . It is a speculation by which one makes either 600 to 800 per cent or loses all."

20 C.S.S. *Florida*, Lieutenant Maffitt, entered Havana. A correspondent for the New York *Herald* noted that: "Captain Maffitt is no ordinary character. He is vigorous, energetic, bold, quick

Lieutenant John N. Maffitt, CSN, destroyed Union commerce.

Rear Admiral Charles Wilkes, USN, scoured the seas unsuccessfully for him.

and dashing, and the sooner he is caught and hung the better it will be for the interest of our commercial community. He is decidedly popular here, and you can scarcely imagine the anxiety evinced to get a glance at him. . . . Nobody, unless informed, would have imagined the small, black-eyed, poetic-looking gentleman, with his romantic appearance, to be a second Semmes, probably in time to be a more celebrated and more dangerous pirate.''

21 C.S.S. *Josiah Bell* and *Uncle Ben*, under Major Oscar M. Watkins, CSA, attacked and captured the small blockaders U.S.S. *Morning Light*, Acting Master John Dillingham, and *Velocity*, Acting Master Nathan W. Hammond, at Sabine Pass. The two Confederate cottonclads came down into the Pass the preceding evening, and in the morning stood out to meet the Union blockaders. Watkins reported: ''When within 1,000 yards of the enemy Captain [Matthew] Nolan's sharpshooters [on *Josiah Bell*] opened a terrific fire, which swept their decks [on *Morning Light*] and soon caused their commanding officer to strike his flag. . . . In the meantime the *Ben* bore down gallantly on the schooner [*Velocity*], receiving her fire and the broadside from the sloop of war at short range . . . The schooner was surrendered unconditionally, and, putting Captain [Charles] Fowler in charge of the sloop, we started for Sabine Pass.'' Two days later the Confederates burned *Morning Light* because she could not be brought over the bar at Sabine Pass. As Watkins later observed: ''The captured vessels would be worse than useless in battle, for I could not spare seamen enough to maneuver them, nor were there among my excellent artillerists any who were skillful in the use of guns mounted on ship carriages.''

The ceaseless, if not always dramatic, operations of the Potomac Flotilla, Commodore Andrew A. Harwood, were continually evidenced by the maintenance of the blockade in the Potomac and Rappahannock Rivers area, where Confederates repeatedly attempted to smuggle goods from shore to shore. Union barges *J.C. Davis* and *Liberty* broke loose from their anchorage at Cornfield Harbor, Maryland, and drifted to Coan River, Virginia, where they were boarded this date and captured. Upon hearing of the incident, Acting Master Benjamin C. Dean, U.S.S. *Dan Smith*, ordered a cutter into Coan River ''to rescue the crews and recapture or destroy the boats.'' This was accomplished under Acting Ensign Francis L. Harris—an unnoticed act that typified the constant pressure that kept the South always on the defensive.

Unofficial.

Navy Department
January 23 1863.

Dear Sir:

Your undaunted experiment with the "Weehawken" has filled us with admiration after several sleepless nights, for the gale of Tuesday night was a hurricane. You were very rash with the Delaware under your lee, but Blair says daring men are always protected. When the Monitor went down the "I told you so" people were to be met everywhere: Now have disposed of them. I congratulate you. Your brave act has been of more use to us than a victory. Send us an official report of the most minute character

Assistant Secretary of the Navy Gustavus Fox expressed the admiration of many for the gallantry of Captain John Rodgers in riding out a violent storm at sea. Rodgers, in an act typifying his indomitable spirit, chose to test the characteristics of his monitor, Weehawken, *under the most severe conditions.*

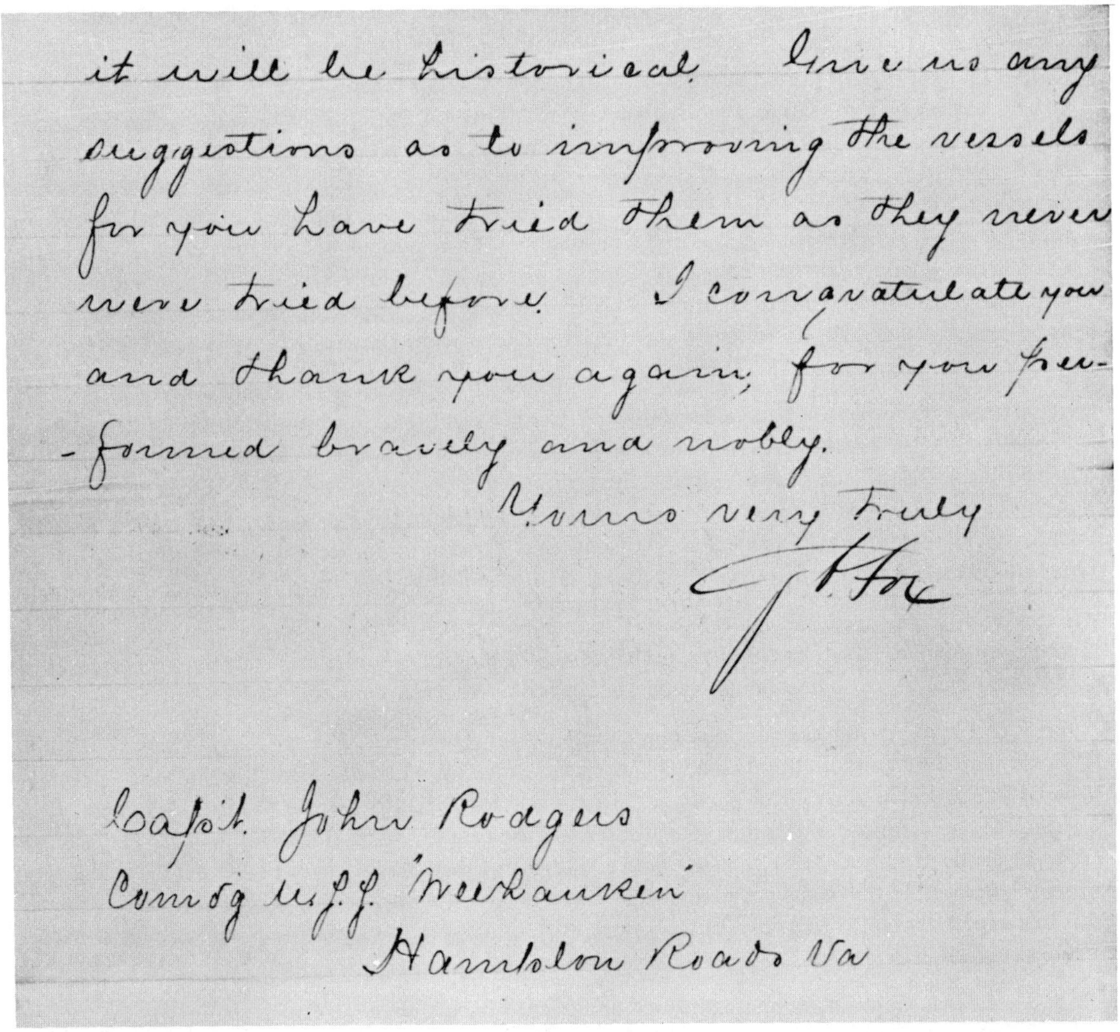

it will be historical. Give me any suggestions as to improving the vessels for you have tried them as they never were tried before. I congratulate you and thank you again; for you performed bravely and nobly.

Yours very truly

J. Fox

Capt. John Rodgers
Com'dg U.S.S. "Weehawken"
Hampton Roads Va

U.S.S. *Ottawa*, Lieutenant Commander William D. Whiting, captured schooner *Etiwan* off Charleston with cargo of cotton.

U.S.S. *Chocura*, Lieutenant Commander William T. Truxtun, seized blockade running British schooner *Pride* at sea east of Cape Romain, South Carolina, with cargo of salt.

U.S.S. *Daylight*, Acting Master Joshua D. Warren, forced a blockade running schooner (name unknown) aground off New Topsail Inlet, North Carolina, and destroyed her.

22 U.S.S. *Commodore Morris*, Lieutenant Commander James H. Gillis, keeping a constant vigil for contraband goods being carried on the river, seized oyster sloop *John C. Calhoun*, schooner *Harriet*, and sloop *Music* near Chuckatuck Creek, Virginia.

The chronic shortage of iron, as well as other critical materials, plagued the Confederacy thoughout the conflict. The Secretary of War appointed a committee to determine what railroad tracks could best be "dispensed with" in order to provide iron "for the completion of public vessels."

C.S.S. *Florida*, Lieutenant Maffitt, captured and burned brigs *Windward* and *Corris Ann* near Cuba.

23 U.S.S. *Cambridge*, Commander William A. Parker, captured schooner *Time* off Cape Fear, North Carolina, with cargo of salt, matches, and shoes.

24 Rear Admiral Porter reported his arrival at the mouth of the Yazoo River to Secretary Welles and noted the progress at Vicksburg: "The army is landing on the neck of land opposite Vicksburg. What they expect to do I don't know, but presume it is a temporary arrangement. I am covering their landing and guarding the Yazoo River. The front of Vicksburg is heavily fortified, and unless we can get troops in the rear of the city I see no chance of taking it at present, though we cut off all their supplies from Texas and Louisiana." Observing that his gunboats had trapped 11 Confederate steamers up the Yazoo obtaining provisions for Port Hudson, Porter wrote: "This will render the reduction of that place [Port Hudson] an easier task than it otherwise would have been, as there are no steamers on the river except two that will be kept at Vicksburg."

With reference to the projected attack on Charleston, Rear Admiral Du Pont wrote Welles: "The Department is aware that I have never shrunk from assuming any responsibilities which circumstances called for nor desired to place any failure of mine on others. But the interests involved in the success or failure of this undertaking strikes me as so momentous to the nation at home and abroad at this particular period that I am confident it will require no urging from me to induce the Department to put at my disposal every means in its power to insure success especially by sending additional ironclads, if possible, to those mentioned in your dispatch."

Secretary Mallory wrote President Davis rejecting a request that an Army officer be named to command *Harriet Lane*, captured at Galveston on 1 January, "over the heads of nine-tenths of the naval officers . . . even could it be done legally, which it cannot."

25 U.S.S. *Currituck*, Acting Master Linnekin, captured sloop *Queen of the Fleet* at Tapp's Creek, Virginia. On 30 January Commodore Harwood, commanding the Potomac Flotilla, advised Secretary Wells of the recent activity of *Currituck*. "I enclose for the information of the Department," he reported, "a certificate of capture of a sloop and nine canoes, with thirteen prisoners and a quantity of contraband goods, by the *Currituck*. I have this day placed them in the hands of the civil authorities. All the captures have been made between the mouths of the Potomac and the Piankatank rivers. . . . These canoes were full of freight, which has been brought to the [Washington Navy] yard."

26 C.S.S. *Alabama*, Captain Semmes, captured and burned bark *Golden Rule* off Haiti in the Caribbean Sea. Semmes noted in his log: "This vessel had on board masts, spars, and a complete set of

Rear Admiral Du Pont prepares for the attack on Charleston by testing his monitors at Fort McAllister, Savannah, Georgia. Repeated engagements showed that the ironclads possessed great defensive endurance but suffered offensively from a slowness of fire.

rigging for the U.S. brig *Bainbridge*, lately obliged to cut away her masts in a gale at Aspinwall [Panama].'' He later added: "I had tied up for a while longer, one of the enemy's gun-brigs, for want of an outfit. It must have been some months before the *Bainbridge* put to sea.''

27 Ironclad U.S.S. *Montauk*, Commander John L. Worden, and U.S.S. *Seneca, Wissahickon, Dawn*, and mortar schooner *C. P. Williams* engaged Confederate batteries at Fort McAllister, Georgia, on the Ogeechee River. Worden was acting under orders from Rear Admiral Du Pont to test the new ironclads; though McAllister was an important objective itself, Du Pont was primarily readying his forces for the spring assault on Charleston—for the success of which the Department relied greatly on the monitor class vessels. Worden, unable to proceed within close range of the fort because of formidable sunken obstructions which "from appearances" were "protected by torpedoes," engaged for four hours before withdrawing. Worden reported that the Confederate fire was "very fine, striking us quite a number of times, doing us no damage.''

Du Pont wrote to Benjamin Gerhard: "The monitor was struck some thirteen or fourteen times, which would have sunk a gunboat easily, but did no injury whatever to the *Montauk*— speaking well for the impenetrability of those vessels—though the distance was greater than what could constitute a fair test. But the slow firing, the inaccuracy of aim, for you can't see to aim properly from the turret . . . give no corresponding powers of aggression. . . . I asked myself this morning while quietly dressing, if one ironclad cannot take eight guns—how are five to take 147 guns in Charleston harbor.''

C.S.S. *Alabama*, Captain Semmes, captured and burned brig *Chastelaine* off Alta Vela in the Caribbean Sea. *Chastelaine* was en route to Cienfuegos, Cuba, to take on sugar and rum for delivery in Boston.

U.S.S. *Hope*, Master John E. Rockwell, seized blockade running British schooner *Emma Tuttle* off Charleston.

28 Secretary Welles noted that the official report of the 1 January Confederate attack at Galveston had not yet come in, but added: "Farragut has prompt, energetic, excellent qualities, but no fondness for written details or self-laudation; does but one thing at a time, but does that strong and well; is better fitted to lead an expedition through danger and difficulty than to command an extensive blockade; is a good officer in a great emergency, will more willingly take great risks in order to obtain great results than any officer in high position in either Navy or Army, and unlike most of them, prefers that others should tell the story of his well-doing rather than relate it himself.''

U.S.S. *Sagamore*, Lieutenant Commander English, captured and destroyed blockade running British sloop *Elizabeth* at the mouth of Jupiter Inlet, Florida.

29 U.S.S. *Lexington*, Lieutenant Commander Samuel L. Phelps, and other gunboats on the Cumberland and Tennessee Rivers continued to convoy Army transports and maintain supply lines. During one expedition between Cairo and Nashville, Phelps reported: "Meeting with a transport that had been fired upon by artillery 20 miles above Clarksville, I at once went to that point and, landing, burned a storehouse used by the rebels as a resort and cover. On leaving there to descend to Clarksville, where I had passed a fleet of thirty-one steamers with numerous barges in tow, convoyed by three light-draft gunboats under Lieutenant Commander [LeRoy] Fitch, *Lexington* was fired upon by the enemy, who had two Parrott guns, and struck three times, but the rebels were quickly dislodged and dispersed. I then returned to Clarksville and, agreeable to the arrangement already made by Lieutenant Commander Fitch, left that place at midnight with the whole fleet of boats, and reached Nashville the following night [30 January] without so much as a musket shot having been fired upon a single vessel of the fleet. Doubtless the lesson of the previous day had effected this result.''

Rear Admiral Du Pont continued to experiment with the ironclads in hopes of improving their efficiency. The smokestack of U.S.S. *New Ironsides*, Captain Thomas Turner, was cut to within 4 feet of the deck to leave the line of sight ahead entirely clear, rather than partially obstructed. The problems created were greater than those solved. Turner reported that ". . . the alteration can not be made without seriously impairing the efficiency of this ship in action . . . I am inclined to believe that under any circumstances, enduring for several hours with the smokestack down, the whole ship would be so filled with gas as to create much suffering and partially to disable the crew, and that it might hazard the chances of a successful expedition." Du Pont ordered the smokestack restored. "So," he wrote, "we will have to go it blind. . . . If we don't run ashore going in, it will be because God is with us."

U.S.S. *Brooklyn*, Commodore H. H. Bell, with gunboats U.S.S. *Sciota*, *Owasco*, and *Katahdin*, tested Confederate batteries under construction at Galveston. He learned that two of the fort's guns were capable of firing past the squadron—more than 2½ miles.

U.S.S. *Unadilla*, Lieutenant Commander Stephen P. Quackenbush, seized British blockade runner *Princess Royal* attempting to run into Charleston with cargo of arms, ammunition, and two steam engines for ironclads. "The P[rincess] R[oyal]," Du Pont wrote, "we have had on our list, traced her through consular reports from the Thames to Halifax, etc. She has a valuable cargo. . . ."

30 U.S.S. *Isaac Smith*, Acting Lieutenant Francis S. Conover, conducted an expedition up the Stono River, South Carolina. Above Legareville, on her return, she was caught in a heavy cross fire, forced aground, and captured by the Confederates. U.S.S. *Commodore McDonough*, Lieutenant Commander George Bacon, attempted without success to prevent the capture.

U.S.S. *Commodore Perry*, Lieutenant Commander Charles W. Flusser, on a joint expedition with Army troops, landed at Hertford, North Carolina, and destroyed two bridges over the Perquimans River. As a result of the successful mission, Flusser reported: "There are now no bridges remaining on the Perquimans, so that the goods sent from Norfolk to the enemy on the south side of the Chowan (by whom they are conveyed to Richmond) have to be passed over a ford, and the roads leading from that ford can be guarded by the troops at Winfield." Three days later (2 February), *Commodore Perry* anchored at the mouth of the Yeopim River; two boats were sent into the river and succeeded in capturing three Confederate small boats. Two of the captures contained cargoes including salt. The constant harassment and interruption of supply lines through the Union Navy's control of the waterways hurt the Confederacy sorely.

Grant informed Porter of a plan to cut a canal through Lake Providence, Louisiana, to effect the passage of troops to the rear of Vicksburg. "By enquiry," he wrote, "I learn that Lake Providence, which connects with Red River through Tensas Bayou, Washita [Ouachita] and Black rivers, is a wide and navigable way through. As some advantage may be gained by opening this, I have ordered a brigade of troops to be detailed for the purpose, and to be embarked as soon as possible. I would respectfully request that one of your light-draft gunboats accompany this expedition." Porter immediately ordered U.S.S. *Linden*, Acting Master Thomas E. Smith, to cooperate with General Grant. The Admiral later noted of this operation: "Several transports were taken in, but there were miles of forest to work through and trees to be cut down. The swift current drove the steamers against the trees and injured them so much that this plan had to be abandoned."

31 Under Flag Officer Duncan N. Ingraham, rams C.S.S. *Chicora*, Commander John R. Tucker, and C.S.S. *Palmetto State*, Lieutenant John Rutledge, attacked the Union blockading fleet off Charleston early in the morning in a fog. *Palmetto State* rammed U.S.S. *Mercedita*, Captain Stellwagen, and fired into her, forcing the gunboat to strike her colors in a "sinking and perfectly defenseless condition." *Chicora* engaged U.S.S. *Keystone State*, Commander William E. LeRoy, severely crippling her before U.S.S. *Memphis*, Captain Pendleton G. Watmough, took her in tow "in a

Ironclads C.S.S. Chicora *and* Palmetto State *constituted two of the South's best means of defending Charleston harbor if the Union ships could pass the forts and obstructions . . . .*

They struck at the blockading fleet offensively on 31 January, forcing its temporary withdrawal outside the bar. The blockade, however, remained unbroken.

sinking condition." Commander LeRoy reported: "Our steam chimneys being destroyed, our motive power was lost and our situation became critical. There were 2 feet of water in the ship and leaking badly, water rising rapidly, the forehold on fire. . . . I regret to report our casualties as very large, some 20 killed and 20 wounded." U.S.S. *Quaker City* was damaged by a shell "which," Commander Frailey reported, "entered this vessel amidships about 7 feet above the water line, cutting away a portion of the guard beam and a guard brace, and thence on its course through the ship's side, exploding in the engine room, carrying away there the starboard entablature brace, air-pump dome, and air-pump guide rod, and making sad havoc with the bulkheads." U.S.S. *Augusta,* Commander Enoch G. Parrott, took a shot "in the port side, passing a little above our boiler." U.S.S. *Housatonic,* Captain William R. Taylor, engaged the two rams before they withdrew toward Charleston harbor. General P. G. T. Beauregard, who claimed in vain that the blockade had been broken, wrote Flag Officer Ingraham: "Permit me to congratulate you and the gallant officers and men under your command for your brilliant achievement of last night, which will be classed hereafter with those of the *Merrimack* and *Arkansas*."

Major General Horatio G. Wright wrote Commander Pennock in Cairo and noted "the importance to the army service of keeping the line of the Cumberland River between its mouth and Nashville constantly open to the use of our steam transports," and requested that he "assign to that portion of the river an ironclad gunboat, plated with sufficiently heavy iron to resist field artillery, to assist in the above object." Recognizing the Army's dependence on the gunboats, Pennock and the gunboat commanders had complied with the request before it was made. *Lexington* had been added to the naval forces in the River, and, the same date that Wright was making his request of Pennock, Lieutenant Commander Fitch was advising from Smithland, Kentucky, that: "The *Robb* joined me yesterday at this place. Nothing very serious up Tennessee River. Have sent the *Robb* and *St. Clair* to Paducah to bring up our coal barge. . . . Have another large convoy to take to Nashville and one to bring down. No danger of either being blockaded by the rebels."

C.S.S. *Retribution*, Master Power, captured schooner *Hanover*, in West Indian waters.

FEBRUARY

1 Ironclad U.S.S. *Montauk*, Commander Worden, with U.S.S. *Seneca*, *Wissahickon*, *Dawn*, and mortar schooner *C. P. Williams*, again tested the defenses of Fort McAllister—described by Rear Admiral Du Pont as "rather a thorn in my flesh." On the 28th of January, Worden had learned, through "a contraband," the position of the obstructions and torpedoes which had effectively blocked his way in the assault of 27 January. "This information," Worden reported," with the aid of the contraband, whom I took on board, enabled me to take up a position nearer the fort in the next attack. . . ."

Ammunition supplies replenished, *Montauk* moved to within 600 yards of McAllister in the early morning; the gunboats took a position one and three-quarters miles below the fort. Worden opened fire at 7:45 a.m., and reported at "7:53 a.m. our turret was hit for the first time during this action at which time the enemy were working their guns with rapidity and precision." The Confederate fire was concentrated on the ironclad, which took some 48 hits in the 4-hour engagement.

Colonel Robert H. Anderson, commanding Fort McAllister, paid tribute to the accuracy of the naval gunfire: "The enemy fired steadily and with remarkable precision. Their fire was terrible. Their mortar fire was unusually fine, a large number of their shells bursting directly over the battery. The ironclad's fire was principally directed at the VIII-inch columbiad, and . . . the parapet in front of this gun was so badly breached as to leave the gun entirely exposed."

General Beauregard added: "For hours the most formidable vessel of her class hurled missiles of the heaviest caliber ever used in modern warfare at the weak parapet of the battery, which was almost demolished; but, standing at their guns, as became men fighting for homes, for honor, and for independence, the garrison replied with such effect as to cripple and beat back their adversary, clad though in impenetrable armor and armed with XV and XI inch guns, supported by mortar boats whose practice was of uncommon precision."

Rear Admiral Porter wrote Secretary Welles: "I have the honor to report that, hearing that there was a lot of cotton at Point Chicot, on the Mississippi, belonging to the so-called Confederate Government, and that the agents were moving it back into the country or about to burn it, I sent up the ram *Monarch*, Colonel Ellet, and the *Juliet*, Acting Lieutenant [Edward] Shaw, and seized 250 bales, which I now have and am using to protect the boilers of those vessels that are vulnerable. There are now altogether 300 bales in the squadron, which I recommend should be sold when no longer needed and the proceeds placed in the Treasury. All cotton on the river belongs to the rebel Government, and on that they depended to carry on the war. I recommend that it be all seized and sold for the benefit of the Government. There is authority enough on record to justify me in taking cotton under certain circumstances, but not enough to take it in all cases. Eight thousand bales will pay the expenses of the squadron per year, and I think there will be no difficulty in obtaining that amount when Colonel Ellet gets his brigade ready and we can penetrate some 6 or 8 miles into the interior, where it is all stowed away.''

Captain Percival Drayton reconnoitered the Wilmington River, Georgia, with U.S.S. *Passaic* and *Marblehead*. He reported to Du Pont: ''. . . I went . . . within sight of Wassaw or Thunderbolt, and two and a quarter miles distant when I was stopped by shallow water. . . . The Batteries were very extensive, and large bodies of troops drawn up on the shore. I was not fired on although quite within range; a battery which is about a mile nearer than ones I saw, was covered by the wood and I was not high enough to open it. I saw two small steamers but nothing that looked like the *Fingal*.'' Du Pont's ships were constantly active, enabling the Union forces to prevent the Confederates from launching a decisive counteroffensive along the South Atlantic coast.

U.S.S. *Two Sisters*, Acting Master William A. Arthur, seized sloop *Richards* from Havana off Boca Grande, Mexico.

U.S.S. *Tahoma*, Lieutenant Commander A. A. Semmes, and U.S.S. *Hendrick Hudson*, Lieutenant David Cate, captured blockade running British schooner *Margaret* off St. Petersburg.

2 Ram U.S.S. *Queen of the West*, Colonel C. R. Ellet, attacked Confederate steamer *City of Vicksburg*, which lay under the batteries of that citadel. Ellet had hoped to get underway to make the attack before daybreak, but the necessity of readjusting the wheel put the engagement off until it was fully light and ''any advantage which would have resulted from the darkness was lost to us.'' The Confederates opened a heavy fire on *Queen of the West* as she approached the city, but succeeded in hitting her only three times before she reached the steamer. Ellet reported: ''Her position was such that if we had run obliquely into her as we came down the bow of the *Queen* would inevitably have glanced. We were compelled to partially round to in order to strike. The consequence was that at the very moment of collision the current, very strong and rapid at this point, caught the stern of my boat, and, acting on her bow as a pivot, swung her around so rapidly that nearly all her momentum was lost.''

Having anticipated this eventuality, Ellet had ordered the starboard gun shotted with incendiary shell, which now set *City of Vicksburg* aflame, though this was rapidly extinguished by the Confederates. *City of Vicksburg* fired into *Queen of the West*, which had bulwarks of cotton built up around her sides and one shell set the ram afire near the starboard wheel; meanwhile, the discharge of her own gun set *Queen* in flames in the bow. ''The flames spread rapidly and the dense smoke rolling into the engine room suffocated the engineers. I saw that if I attempted to run into the *City of Vicksburg* again that my boat would certainly be burned. . . . After much exertion, we finally put the fire out by cutting the burning bales loose.'' *Queen of the West* then steamed downstream under orders to destroy all Confederate vessels encountered.

Unable to ascend the Big Black River because of the narrowness of the stream, Ellet continued down the Mississippi. On 3 February, below the mouth of the Red River, he met Confederate steamer *A. W. Baker* coming up river. *Baker*, ''not liking the *Queen*'s looks,'' ran ashore but was captured. She had just delivered her cargo to Port Hudson and was returning for another. Ellet had placed a guard on board when another steamer, *Moro*, was seen coming down stream. ''A shot across her bows,'' Ellet reported, ''brought her to . . . laden with 110,000 pounds of pork, nearly 500 hogs, and a large quantity of salt, destined for the rebel army at Port Hudson.''

Running short of coal, Ellet turned back upriver, destroying 25,000 pounds of meal awaiting transportation to Port Hudson. Stopping at the mouth of the Red River to release the civilians captured on *Baker* and *Moro*, he also seized steamer *Berwick Bay*. She, too, carried a large cargo

U.S.S. Queen of the West, *steaming past Vicksburg to blockade the mouth of the Red River below, engages* City of Vicksburg *in a fierce battle under the guns of the Mississippi citadel.*

for Port Hudson: 200 barrels of molasses, 10 hogsheads of sugar, 30,000 pounds of flour, and 40 bales of cotton. Ellet ordered his prizes destroyed and returned to his position below Vicksburg. Some $200,000 worth of property had been destroyed by *Queen of the West.*

Of the intrepid Ellet, Porter remarked: "I can not speak too highly of this gallant and daring officer. The only trouble I have is to hold him in and keep him out of danger. He will undertake anything I wish him to without asking questions, and these are the kind of men I like to command." This was one of a series of important operations that seriously disrupted Confederate supply channels and built up to the eventual fall of Vicksburg in mid-summer.

C.S.S. *Alabama* experienced a fire on board which was rapidly extinguished but which prompted Captain Semmes to write: "The fire-bell in the night is sufficiently alarming to the landsman, but the cry of fire at sea imports a matter of life and death—especially in a ship of war, whose boats are always insufficient to carry off her crew, and whose magazine and shell-rooms are filled with powder, and the loaded missiles of death."

U.S.S. *Mount Vernon*, Lieutenant James Trathen, drove blockade running schooner *Industry* aground off New Topsail Inlet, North Carolina, and burned her.

3 The long, tortuous Army-Navy operation against Fort Pemberton at Greenwood, Mississippi, was begun with the opening of the levee at Yazoo Pass to gain access to the Yazoo River above Haynes' Bluff and reach Vicksburg from the rear. The next day Acting Master G. W. Brown, of U.S.S. *Forest Rose*, which was standing by to enter the opening, reported that "the water is gushing through at a terrible rate. . . . After cutting two ditches through and ready for the water, we placed a can of powder (50 pounds) under the dam, which I touched off by means of three mortar fuzes joined together. It blew up immense quantities of earth, opening a passage for the water, and loosened the bottom so that the water washed it out very fast. We then sunk three more shafts, one in the entrance of the other ditch, and the other two on each side of the mound between the two ditches, and set them off simultaneously, completely shattering the

mound and opening a passage through the ditch. . . . [creating] a channel 70 or 75 yards wide. It is thought that it will be at least four or five days before we can enter." The plan of attack called for gunboats and Army transports to go through the Pass into Moon Lake, down the Coldwater and Tallahatchie Rivers to the Yazoo, take Pemberton, effect the capture of Yazoo City, and proceed down to assault Vicksburg on its less strongly defended rear flanks.

U.S.S. *Lexington, Fairplay, St. Clair, Brilliant, Robb,* and *Silver Lake,* under Lieutenant Commander Fitch, supported Army troops at Fort Donelson and repulsed a Confederate attack at that point. Proceeding up the Cumberland River on convoy duty from Smithfield, Kentucky, Fitch's squadron met steamer *Wild Cat* coming down river some 24 miles below Dover, Tennessee, bearing a message from Colonel Abner C. Harding, commanding at Donelson, which reported that he was being assaulted in force by Confederate troops. Fitch pushed his squadron "on up with all possible speed" and arrived in the evening to find the defending troops "out of ammunition and entirely surrounded by the rebels in overwhelming numbers, but still holding them in check." Not expecting the presence of the gunboats, the Confederates had taken a position which enabled the mobile force afloat to rake them effectively with a telling fire from the guns. "The rebels were so much taken by surprise," Fitch reported, "that they did not even fire a shot, but immediately commenced retreating. So well directed was our fire on them that they could not even carry off a caisson that they had captured from our forces, but were compelled to abandon it, after two fruitless attempts to destroy it by fire." Fitch then stationed his vessels to prevent the return of the Southern forces.

C.S.S. *Alabama,* Captain Semmes, captured and burned at sea schooner *Palmetto,* bound from New York to San Juan, Puerto Rico, with cargo of provisions. Of the chase of *Palmetto,* Semmes said: "It was beautiful to see how the *Alabama* performed her task, working up into the wind's eye, and overhauling her enemy, with the ease of a trained courser coming up with a saddle-nag."

U.S.S. *Sonoma,* Commander Stevens, captured blockade running British bark *Springbok* off the Bahamas.

3–8 U.S.S. *Tyler,* Lieutenant Commander James M. Prichett, patrolled the Yazoo River and confiscated 113 bales of cotton. This was in keeping with Porter's plan to seize all Confederate cotton for the dual purpose of preventing its being shipped out through the blockade and to protect the vessels of his Mississippi Squadron. Porter advised Secretary Welles: "Three hundred more bales are in my possession, captured from rebel parties, but I am using it at present for protecting the boilers of the different boats. When no longer needed, I will forward it to Cairo."

4 Rear Admiral Du Pont wrote Major General David Hunter: "Among the defects in matters of detail on the ironclads is the absence of all means of making the navy signals. . . . It has been suggested to me, however, that the army code, which we have on various occasions found so useful, might be employed at times on these vessels from the side not engaged or exposed at the moment. In order to effect this, I propose, if agreeable to you, that several of the young officers of the squadron should be instructed in the code, and will be greatly obliged if you will issue the necessary orders, with such restrictions as may be required." Du Pont added, "I learn the code now forms part of the instruction at the Naval Academy." Hunter replied in the usual spirit of cooperation: "It will afford me sincere pleasure to comply with your request in regard to the army signal code, orders having been already issued to the chief signal officer of this Department to furnish all requisite facilities and instruction to such of your officers as you may assign to this service."

U.S.S. *New Era,* temporarily under Acting Ensign William C. Hanford, captured steamer *W. A. Knapp* with cargo of cloth at Island No. 10.

6 Rear Admiral Porter ordered Lieutenant Commander W. Smith to command the expedition through Yazoo Pass aimed at the capture of Yazoo City as part of the planned move on Vicksburg: "You will proceed with the *Rattler* and *Romeo* to Delta, near Helena, where you will find the *Forest Rose* engaged in trying to enter the Yazoo Pass. You will order the *Signal*, now at White River, to accompany you; and if the *Cricket* comes down while you are at Delta, detain her also, or the *Linden*. . . . Do not engage batteries with the light vessels. The *Chillicothe* will do the fighting." To this force was later added U.S.S. *Baron De Kalb* and *Marmora* and towboat *S. Bayard* in lieu of *Cricket* and *Linden*. "If this duty is performed as I expect it to be," Porter wrote, "we will strike a terrible blow at the enemy, who do not anticipate an attack from such a quarter."

Lieutenant Commander Thomas O. Selfridge, U.S.S. *Conestoga*, reported intelligence gathered from a reconnaissance mission—one of many which the Navy conducted to facilitate precise planning and preparation for future operations. "From the information gathered by Lieutenant [Cyrenius] Dominy, of the *Signal*, I should judge the rebels have no heavy guns in the river up to Little Rock. A passenger told him that after the capture of the post [Arkansas Post] the gunboats were daily expected, but the idea was now generally given up. The [Confederate] ram *Pontchartrain* has not had steam up for some time. Some men are still at work upon her. She requires a good deal of pumping to keep her free. She has as yet no guns. She has no officers of consequence. . . . She is represented as being casemated with 20 inches of wood and railroad iron to abaft her wheels. [Thomas C.] Hindman is represented with 16,000 troops at Little Rock, [James] McCullough with 6,000 at Pine Bluff fortifying, [John S.] Marmaduke with 3,000 cavalry at Dardanelle. These numbers are greatly overestimated as effective troops, as Little Rock is represented as full of sick soldiers." Selfridge also proposed an immediate attack on Little Rock and the destruction of the ram. Though his plan was not followed, both his aims were achieved during the year; Little Rock was occupied on 10 September and *Pontchartrain* was destroyed by the Confederates to prevent her capture. The Union's ability to move on the river highways in Arkansas, as elsewhere, pinned down Confederate strength and caused constant loss.

Ships of the Mississippi Squadron, photographed here off Mound City, Illinois, restlessly patrolled the western rivers, protecting Army transports and positions and preventing the Confederacy from gaining offensive footholds.

7   Rear Admiral Porter reported to Secretary Welles: "Vicksburg was by nature the strongest place on the river, but art has made it impregnable against floating batteries—not that the number of guns is formidable, but the rebels have placed them out of our reach, and can shift them from place to place in case we should happen to annoy them (the most we can do) in their earthworks. . . . The people in Vicksburg are the only ones who have as yet hit upon the method of defending themselves against our gunboats, viz, not erecting water batteries, and placing the guns some distance back from the water, where they can throw a plunging shot, which none of our ironclads could stand. I mention these facts to show the Department that there is no possible hope of any success against Vicksburg by a gunboat attack or without an investment in the rear of the city by a large army. We can, perhaps, destroy the city and public buildings, but that would bring us no nearer the desired point (the opening of the Mississippi) than we are now. . . ." The fall of Vicksburg came only after a long combined land and water siege and attack as Porter indicated.

U.S.S. *Forest Rose*, Acting Master G. W. Brown, succeeded in entering Yazoo Pass and proceeded into Moon Lake as far as the mouth of the Old Pass. Brown learned that Confederates were obstructing Coldwater River by felling trees across it. He reported another difficulty to Porter: "We cannot enter the pass with this boat until the trees are trimmed and some of the overhanging trees cut down." The density of the woods would slow the vessels greatly and damage the smokestacks and upper works severely.

In a letter to Secretary Mallory, a daring plan for a raiding expedition on the Great Lakes was proposed by Lieutenant William H. Murdaugh, CSN. Four naval officers would make their way to Canada and purchase a small steamer, man her with Canadians, and reveal the object of the cruise only when underway. The crew was to be armed with revolvers and cutlasses. The steamer was to carry torpedoes, explosives, and incendiary materials.

At Erie, Pennsylvania, Murdaugh planned to carry U.S.S. *Michigan* by boarding, and then advance on Lake Ontario through the Welland Canal to destroy locks and shipping. The scheme was to pass through Lake Huron into Lake Michigan, "and make for the great city of Chicago. At Chicago burn the shipping and destroy the locks of the Illinois and Michigan Canal, connecting Lake Michigan and the Mississippi River. Then turn northward, and, touching at Milwaukee and other places, pass again into Lake Huron, go through the Sault St. Marie, and destroy the lock of the Canal of that name. Then the vessel could be run into Georgian Bay, at the bottom of which is a railway connecting with the main Canadian lines, and be run ashore and destroyed." The bold venture was approved by the Navy Department, but, as Lieutenant Murdaugh wrote, President Davis believed that "it would raise such a storm about the violation of the neutrality laws that England would be forced to stop the building of some ironclads and take rigid action against us everywhere. So the thing fell through and with it my great chance."

Commander Ebenezer Farrand, CSN, reported to Governor John G. Shorter of Alabama the successful launching of ironclads C.S.S. *Tuscaloosa* and *Huntsville* at Selma, "amid enthusiastic cheering." Both warships were taken to Mobile.

U.S.S. *Glide*, Acting Ensign Charles B. Dahlgren, was destroyed accidentally by fire at Cairo, Illinois.

8   U.S.S. *Commodore McDonough*, Lieutenant Commander Bacon, and an Army transport reconnoitered the Stono and Folly Rivers, South Carolina, at the request of Major General John G. Foster and "discovered that the enemy had not taken advantage of our absence to erect any new batteries."

9   Illustrative of the continuing, vital importance of the inland rivers was the report of Lieutenant Commander Fitch, commanding U.S.S. *Fairplay*, from Smithfield, Kentucky: "I have the honor to report my return from Nashville, having landed in safety at that place with some 45 steamers. This makes 73 steamers and 16 barges we have convoyed safely to Nashville since the river has been navigable for our boats."

III-25

Rear Admiral Du Pont wrote Secretary Welles of the difficulties in obtaining logistical support for his blockading squadron—a major problem for all naval commanders: "Our requisitions for general stores, I have reason to believe, are immediately attended to by the bureaus in the Department . . . but there seem to be unaccountable obstacles to our receiving them. . . . We have been out of oil for machinery. Coal is not more essential . . . We were purchasing from transports or wherever it could be found, two or three barrels at a time. Finally the *Union* came with some, but it was stored under her cargo and the captain wished to defer its delivery until his return from the Gulf, which, however, I would not allow. The vessel was to have brought important parts of the ration, such as sugar, coffee, flour, butter, beans and dried fruit with clothing but she did not. The articles named are exhausted on the store ships of this squadron. My commanding officers complain that their wants are not supplied, and I have been so tried by the increasing demands for articles which I could not supply that I can defer no longer addressing the Department on the subject."

U.S.S. *Coeur de Lion*, Acting Master Charles H. Brown, captured blockade running schooner *Emily Murray* off Machodoc Creek, Virginia, with cargo of lumber, sugar, and whiskey.

10 Confederate troops disabled ram *Dick Fulton* at Cypress Bend, Arkansas, by gunfire.

11 Rear Admiral Porter was continually concerned with supply problems. He wrote Commander Pennock at Cairo: "As circumstances occur I have to change the quantity of coal required here and find it impossible to hit upon any particular quantity. It is likely that we shall want a large amount, and I want a stack of 160,000 bushels sent to the Yazoo River, besides the monthly allowance already required, viz, 70,000 bushels here, 40,000 at White River and 20,000 at Memphis." Stressing the need to have logistic support rapidly available for his mobile forces, Porter added: "You will also have the *Abraham* filled up with three months' provisions and stores for the squadron, or as much as she can carry, and keep her ready at all times with her machinery in order and in condition to move at a moment's notice to such point as I may designate. Circumstances may occur when it will be necessary to move the wharf boat, and you will arrange for the most expeditious plan to do so. . . . You will see from what I have written the importance of carrying out my order to the letter, for much depends on my being in such a position with the squadron that I can not be hampered, and can be in a condition to move where I please."

12 As on the East Coast and on the western waters at and above Vicksburg, great demands were placed on Farragut's fleet in the lower Mississippi and along the Gulf coast. Farragut observed: "Everyone is calling on me to send them vessels, which reminds me of the remark of the musician, 'It is very easy to say blow! blow! but where the devil is the wind to come from?' "

Starting to visit his blockading units at Ship Island, Mobile, and Pensacola, Farragut was called back to New Orleans by conditions at Vicksburg. He wrote Secretary Welles: ". . . I have the same appeal made to me from all quarters, viz, for more force. The ships are all out of coal, and the enemy threatens to attack us. The *Susquehanna* has kept on the blockade, to my astonishment. I had hoped that the *Colorado* would have been here to relieve her before this. My force in this river is reduced to the fixed force of the *Pensacola* and *Portsmouth* and the *Hartford, Richmond, Essex,* and three gunboats, viz, *Kineo, Albatross,* and *Winona.* This is a very small force to give protection to the river commerce and be ready to pass or attack the batteries on the river. Commodore H. H. Bell does not think it prudent to leave Galveston without a ship, and Commodore [Robert B.] Hitchcock does not think it proper to leave Mobile without a ship, as the enemy have doubtless a much stronger force inside than we have outside. Still, they would not come out except on a very calm day. The moment that I can withdraw a ship from the river I will do so, as the gunboats will be all-sufficient when Port Hudson and Vicksburg are taken and the other high points on the river occupied to prevent the enemy from fortifying them."

U.S.S. *Queen of the West,* Colonel C. R. Ellet, steamed up Red River and ascended Atchafalaya River where a landing party destroyed twelve Confederate Army wagons. That night, *Queen of the West* was fired on near Simmesport, Louisiana. Next day, Ellet returned to the scene of the attack and destroyed all the buildings on three adjoining plantations in reprisal. The vessel had previously run below Vicksburg to disrupt Confederate trade in the Red River area.

Lincoln conferred with Assistant Secretary Fox on the projected naval assault on Charleston. Two days later, the President discussed ammunition for the ironclads to be used against that port with Captain Dahlgren. Lincoln was reported to be "restless about Charleston."

C.S.S. *Florida*, Lieutenant Maffitt, captured ship *Jacob Bell* in West Indian waters, bound from Foo-Chow, China, to New York with cargo of tea, firecrackers, matting, and camphor valued at more than $2,000,000. *Jacob Bell* was burned on the following day.

U.S.S. *Conestoga*, Lieutenant Commander Selfridge, seized steamers *Rose Hambleton* and *Evansville* off White River, Arkansas.

13 U.S.S. *Indianola*, Lieutenant Commander George Brown, ran past the batteries at Vicksburg to join U.S.S. *Queen of the West* in blockading the Red River. Rear Admiral Porter's instructions to Brown added: "Go to Jeff Davis' plantation load up with all the cotton you can find and the best single male Negroes." Towing two barges filled with coal, *Indianola* steamed slowly past the upper batteries undetected. Abreast the point, *Indianola* was sighted and a heavy fire opened upon her without effect.

Lieutenant Commander W. Smith, commanding the light draft expedition into Yazoo Pass, arrived at Helena, Arkansas. Porter ordered U.S.S. *Baron De Kalb*, Lieutenant Commander J. G. Walker, to join the forces. Unable to enter the pass with his vessels, Smith observed: "A heavy army force is clearing this, which in places, at turns, may not admit of our vessels

C.S.S. Florida *destroys clipper ship* Jacob Bell *on 12 February. The merchant vessel's cargo was valued at more than $2,000,000.*

U.S.S. Indianola *runs past Vicksburg to join* Queen of the West *in blockading the mouth of the Red River. Though Confederate batteries opened a blistering cannonade,* Indianola *escaped unscathed.*

getting through. Our force takes the trees from the stream while the rebels on the other end cut them from both sides to fall across. The army is expected to be through with this pass in one week."

Commander A. Ludlow Case, U.S.S. *Iroquois*, reported the steady strengthening of Confederate positions in the Wilmington area. Noting that they were "working like beavers," Case wrote: "From their apparent great energy I am induced to believe that in the event of our capture of Charleston this is to be the point for the blockade runners. . . . They now have four casemated batteries west of Fort Fisher completed and a fifth nearly so, each mounting two or three guns, built of heavy framework, and covered deeply with sand and sodded. . . . The defenses are much more formidable and much more judiciously arranged, on account of detached batteries, than those at the South Bar, Fort Caswell, etc. . . . If a vessel now gets inside of the blockaders she can soon run under cover of the batteries and anchor until the tide serves for crossing the bar. A few months ago this would have been impossible, the defenses at that time being such as to make an immediate crossing of the bar absolutely necessary." Wilmington did, in fact, become the primary port for blockade runners in the last half of the Civil War for precisely this reason.

Commander James H. North, CSN, wrote from Glasgow to Secretary Mallory: "I can see no prospect of recognition from this country [Great Britain]. . . . If they will let us get our ships out when they are ready, we shall feel ourselves most fortunate. It is now almost impossible to make the slightest move or do the smallest thing, that the Lincoln spies do not know of it.',

U.S.S. *New Era*, Acting Ensign Hanford, captured steamer *White Cloud*, carrying Confederate mail, and steamer *Rowena*, carrying drugs, on the Mississippi River near Island No. 10.

14 U.S.S. *Queen of the West*, Colonel C. R. Ellet, patrolling the Red River, seized steamer *Era No. 5* with a cargo of corn-some 15 miles above the mouth of Black River. Ellet continued up river to investigate reports of the presence of three Confederate vessels at Gordon's Landing. *Queen of the West* was taken under heavy fire by shore batteries. Attempting to back down river, the pilot ran her aground, directly under the Confederate guns. "The position," Ellet wrote, "at once became a very hot one; 60 yards below we would have been in no danger. As it was, the enemy's shot struck us nearly every time." *Queen of the West*'s chief engineer reported that the escape pipe had been shot away; the steam pipe was severed. Ellet ordered the ship abandoned. A formidable vessel was now in Confederate hands.

Though efforts steadily increased to maintain the tight blockade of the Southern coast, daring Confederates—stirred by patriotism and the lure of profit—continued to elude the Union warships. Captain Sands, U.S.S. *Dacotah*, off Cape Fear River, North Carolina, reported a typical example: "I had a picket boat from this vessel inside the bar, and one from the *Monticello* was anchored on the bar in 13-feet of water. The latter saw nothing of the blockade runner [*Giraffe*], but my picket boat, in charge of Acting Master W[illiam] Earle, saw her pass between him and the shore, and came near being run over by her soon after discovering her. The boat was anchored in 12-feet of water on the western side of the channel, with the fort [Fort Fisher] bearing N.N.E., and the steamer passed between her and the beach, evidently having tracked the beach along, where, under cover of the dark land, she could not be seen a quarter of a mile off in the obscurity of the hour before daylight. . . . The *Chocura* was stationed at the Western Bar, the *Monticello* farther west, near the shore, and the *Dacotah* guarding the approaches to the bar. Yet neither vessel, with all their accustomed watchfulness, saw anything of the blockade runner, and it is with much chagrin that I am obliged thus to report a rebel success."

U.S.S. *Forest Rose*, Acting Master G. W. Brown, captured stern-wheel steamer *Chippewa Valley* with cargo of cotton at Island No. 63.

Commander Clary, U.S.S. *Tioga*, reported the capture of blockade running British schooner *Avon* with cargo including liquor near the Bahamas.

15 Rear Admiral Porter ordered Acting Lieutenant Robert Getty, U.S.S. *Marmora:* "Proceed to Delta, the old Yazoo Pass, and report to Lieutenant Commander Watson Smith as part of his expedition. . . . If you meet any vessel taking in cotton below White River, seize vessel, cotton, and all, and leave her at White River. . . ." By this time, as Brigadier General Gorman remarked, secrecy was "out of the question," and it had become necessary to prepare for a more extended expedition than had been originally anticipated.

U.S.S. *Sonoma*, Commander Stevens, captured brig *Atlantic*, bound from Havana to Matamoras.

16 President Lincoln, greatly interested in the naval assault on Charleston, reviewed plans for the attack with Assistant Secretary of the Navy Fox.

17 Rear Admiral Porter wrote Secretary Welles: "I have reason to believe that the enemy's troops at Port Hudson are in a strait for want of provisions, and if pushed by General [Nathan P.] Banks' troops that fort will fall into our hands. It is situated in a swampy, muddy region 60 miles from any railroad, and the rains, which have exceeded anything I ever saw in my life, have ren-

Patrolling the Black River, U.S.S. Queen of the West *grounded under heavy Confederate shore fire. Abandoned, she falls into Southern hands. A formidable ship, the ram greatly enhanced the South's strength on the Mississippi. However . . .*

just two months later, 14 April, C.S.S. Queen of the West *was engaged by Union gunboats and destroyed, ending that threat to Northern domination of the river.*

dered hauling by wagon impossible. Our vessels above them cut off all hope of supply or aid of any kind from Red River and they must, in a short time, make a retreat. . . ." Porter's estimate was overly optimistic. Loss of *Queen of the West* and other events to follow would re-open the Red River supply line so that Port Hudson sustained its position into the summer of 1863.

Confederate troops captured and burned U.S. tug *Hercules* opposite Memphis. The Confederates attempted to seize seven coal barges at the same place, but were unable to "run them off," according to Captain McGehee, commanding the Southern force, "owing to the terrific fire from the gunboats which were lying at the Memphis wharf."

18 U.S.S. *Victoria*, Acting Lieutenant Edward Hooker, captured brig *Minna* near Shallotte Inlet, North Carolina, with cargo of salt and drugs.

Cutter from U.S.S. *Somerset*, Lieutenant Commander Alexander F. Crosman, captured blockade runner *Hortense*, bound from Havana to Mobile.

19 The Confederate Navy Department made a decision to mount an expedition to attempt to destroy the Union monitors at Charleston. Secretary Mallory sent the following orders to Lieutenant William A. Webb, CSN, for a strike against the Northern forces: "Should it be deemed advisable to attack the enemy's fleet by boarding, the following suggestions are recommended for your consideration: . . . First—Row-boats and barges, of which Charleston can furnish a large number. Second—Small steamers, two or three to attack each vessel. Third—the hull of a single-decked vessel without spars, divided into several watertight compartments by cross bulk-heads, and with decks and hatches tight, may have a deckload of compressed cotton so placed on either side, and forward and aft, so as to leave a space fore and aft in the centre. A light scaffold to extend from the upper tier of cotton ten or fifteen feet over the side, and leading to the enemy's turret when alongside the iron-clad, and over which it can be boarded, at the same time that boarding would be done from forward and aft. This could be made permanent or to lower at will. The boarding force to be divided into parties of tens and twenties, each under a leader. One of these parties to be prepared with iron wedges, to wedge between the turret and the deck; a second party to cover the pilot house with wet blankets; a third party of twenty to throw powder down the smoke-stack or to cover it; another party of twenty provided with turpentine or camphine in glass vessels to smash over the turret, and with an inextinguishable liquid fire to follow it; another party of twenty to watch every opening in the turret or deck, provided with sulphuretted cartridges, etc., to smoke the enemy out. Light ladders, weighing a few pounds only, could be provided to reach the top of the turret."

Rear Admiral Du Pont wrote of the blockade: "No vessel has ever attempted to run the blockade except by stealth at night—which fully established internationally the effectiveness of the block-ade—but it is not sufficient for our purpose, to keep out arms and keep in cotton—unfortunately our people have considered a total exclusion possible and the government at one time seemed to think so. A cordon of ships covering the arc from Bulls Bay to Stono, some twenty-one miles moored together head and stern—would do it easy—but that we have not the means to accom-plish. I have forty ships of all classes, sometimes more—never reaching fifty—a considerable number are incapable of keeping at sea or at outside anchorage—the wear and tear and ceaseless breaking of American machinery compared with English or even French now, keep a portion of the above always in here [Port Royal] repairing. If I had not induced the Department to estab-lish a floating machine shop, which I had seen the French have in China, the blockade would have been a total failure. . . . Steam however is the new element in the history of blockades, which no one at first understands, as both sides have it—but it is all in favor of the runner—he chooses his time, makes his bound and rushes through, his only danger a chance shot—while the watcher has banked fires, has chains to slip, has guns to point and requires certainly fifteen minutes to get full way on his ship. It is wonderful how many we catch, how many are wrecked, there is another on the beach now with the sea breaking over her. . . ."

C.S.S. *Retribution*. Acting Master Power, captured brig *Emily Fisher* in West Indian waters.

20 U.S.S. *Crusader*, Acting Master Thomas I. Andrews, captured schooner *General Taylor* in Mobjack Bay, Virginia.

21 Lieutenant Commander W. Smith reported the readiness of his expedition to enter Yazoo Pass: "Our party, consisting of the *Chillicothe, Baron De Kalb, Marmora, Romeo, Forest Rose, S. Bayard* (side-wheel towboat), and three barges of coal, containing 12,000, 10,000 and 5,000 bushels, are all snug at the entrance of Yazoo Pass, ready to go through the moment the stream is clear and the working boats get out of the way. A small army transport is to go through with us, with the excess of men over the 500, which the light-drafts will carry. . . . I expect the *Signal* from Memphis to-night. I am to receive the troops to-morrow." The difficulty in removing both Confederate-placed and natural obstructions had slowed the proposed movement to a crawl.

C.S.S. *Alabama*, Captain Semmes, captured and burned at sea ship *Golden Eagle* and bark *Olive Jane*. Of the former, Semmes wrote:"I had overhauled her near the.termination of a long voyage. She had sailed from San Francisco, in ballast, for Howland's Island, in the Pacific; a guano island of which some adventurous Yankees had taken possession. There she had taken in a cargo of guano, for Cork. . . . This ship [*Golden Eagle*] had buffeted the gales of the frozen latitudes of Cape Horn, threaded her pathway among its ice-bergs, been parched with the heats of the tropic, and drenched with the rains of the equator, to fall into the hands of her enemy, only a few hundred miles from her port. But such is the fortune of war. It seemed a pity, too, to destroy so large a cargo of a fertilizer, that would else have made fields stagger under a wealth of grain. But those fields would have been the fields of the enemy; or if it did not fertilize his fields, its sale would pour a stream of gold into his coffers; and it was my business upon the high seas, to cut off, or dry up this stream of gold. . . . how fond the Yankees had become of the qualifying adjective, 'golden,' as a prefix to the names of their ships. I had burned the *Golden Rocket*, the *Golden Rule*, and the *Golden Eagle*."

U.S.S. *Thomas Freeborn*, Lieutenant Commander Samuel Magaw, and U.S.S. *Dragon*, Acting Master George E. Hill, engaged a Confederate battery below Fort Lowry, Virginia, while reconnoitering the Rappahannock River. *Freeborn* was struck and one Confederate gun was silenced.

23 Boat crews from Coast Survey schooners *Caswell*, William H. Dennis, and *Arago*, William S. Edwards, boarded and seized blockade running schooner *Glide*, aground near Little Tybee Island, Georgia, with cargo of cotton. Possession of the prize was relinquished to U.S.S. *Marblehead*, Lieutenant Commander Robert W. Scott, upon her arrival at the scene.

U.S.S. *Dacotah*, Captain Sands, and U.S.S. *Monticello*, Lieutenant Commander Daniel Braine, closed Fort Caswell, North Carolina, to engage a large steamer attempting to run the blockade. The fort opened on the Union ships and an exchange of fire ensued; the steamer was out of range of the Union warships.

U.S.S. *Potomska*, Acting Lieutenant William Budd, captured blockade running British schooner *Belle* in Sapelo Sound, Georgia, with cargo of coffee and salt.

U.S.S. *Kinsman*, Acting Lieutenant Wiggen, transporting a detachment of troops, struck a snag and sank in Berwick Bay, Louisiana. Six men were reported missing.

24 C.S.S. *William H. Webb* and *Queen of the West*, with C.S.S. *Beatty* in company, engaged U.S.S. *Indianola*, Lieutenant Commander G. Brown, below Warrenton, Mississippi. The Confederate squadron, under Major Joseph L. Brent, CSA, had reached Grand Gulf just 4 hours behind the

Northern vessel which was returning upstream to communicate with Rear Admiral Porter above Vicksburg.

Knowing his speed was considerably greater than that of *Indianola*, Brent determined to attempt overtaking the ironclad and attacking her that night. Shortly before 10 p.m., the Confederate vessels were seen from *Indianola* and Brown "immediately cleared for action...." *Queen of the West* opened the action, attempting to ram the *Indianola;* she knifed into the coal barge lashed to the ship's port side and cut it in two but did little damage to *Indianola*. *Webb* dashed up and rammed *Indianola* at full speed. The impact swung *Indianola* around; *Queen of the West* again struck only a glancing blow. *Queen of the West* maneuvered into a position to ram, this time astern, and succeeded in shattering the framework of the starboard wheelhouse and loosening iron plating. At this time *Webb* completed circling upstream in order to gain momentum and rammed *Indianola*, crushing the starboard wheel, disabling the starboard rudder, and starting a number of leaks.

Being in what Brown termed "an almost powerless condition," *Indianola* was allowed to fill with water to assure her sinking, run on to the west bank of the river and surrendered to Lieutenant Colonel Frederick B. Brand of C.S.S. *Beatty*, which had been "hovering round to enter the fight when an opportunity offered." Loss of *Indianola* was keenly felt. Secretary Welles wrote Porter: "The disastrous loss of the *Indianola* may, if she has not been disabled, involve the most serious results to the fleet below." Porter expressed the view: "The importance of this move to our army here can not be estimated. We had already broken the communications of the enemy in Texas with Vicksburg and Port Hudson. We had cut off all supplies and means of transportation, having destroyed some of their best boats. In a week more the water would have surrounded Port Hudson, and there being no means of getting away, they would have been

Confederates attempt to destroy Indianola *as Union ruse with a dummy gunboat succeeds.*

obliged to evacuate in time. We hoped in a short time to force this thing by getting one or two more gunboats below, and troops enough to land close to Port Hudson. That place evacuated, General Banks could have ascended the river. . . . There is no use to conceal the fact, but this has, in my opinion, been the most humiliating affair that has occurred during this rebellion. . . . My only hope is that she has blown up." This ended Porter's move to blockade the Red River by detached vessels while he kept the body of the fleet above Vicksburg. The South also held *Queen of the West* and had bright prospects for raising *Indianola* and placing her in a serviceable condition.

A deserter from Confederate receiving ship *Selma* gave the following information about submarine experiments and operations being conducted by Horace L. Hunley, James R. McClintock, B. A. Whitney, and others, at Mobile, where the work was transferred following the fall of New Orleans to Rear Admiral Farragut: "On or about the 14th an infernal machine, consisting of a submarine boat propelled by a screw which is turned by hand, capable of holding five persons, and having a torpedo which was to be attached to the bottom of the vessel, left Fort Morgan at 8 p.m. in charge of a Frenchman who invented it. The invention was to come up at Sand Island, get the bearing and distance of the nearest vessel." He added that this failed but that other attempts would be made. This submarine went down in rough weather off Fort Morgan, but no lives were lost. Hunley and his colleagues built another in the machine shop of Park and Lyons, Mobile; this was to be the celebrated *H. L. Hunley*, the first submarine to sink an enemy vessel in combat.

Cutters from U.S.S. *Mahaska*, Lieutenant Elliot C. V. Blake, captured and destroyed sloop *Mary Jane* and barge *Ben Bolt* in Back Creek, York River, Virginia.

U.S.S. *State of Georgia*, Commander James F. Armstrong, seized blockade running British schooner *Annie* at sea off Cape Romain, South Carolina, with cargo of salt and drugs.

Rear Admiral Theodorus Bailey, commanding the East Gulf Blockading Squadron, reported the capture of schooner *Stonewall* by U.S.S. *Tahoma*, Lieutenant Commander A. A. Semmes, near Key West.

24–25 U.S.S. *Conemaugh*, Lieutenant Commander Thomas H. Eastman, chased blockade running British steamer *Queen of the Wave* aground near the mouth of the North Santee River, South Carolina. Unable to get *Queen of the Wave* off the bar, he destroyed her on 7 March.

25 The light draft gunboat expedition entered Yazoo Pass after a lengthy delay while Army troops cleared away obstructions in the river. Reporting to Rear Admiral Porter the next day, Lieutenant Commander W. Smith briefly noted some of the difficulties encountered: "If we get through this with our casemates still up and wheels serviceable, it will be as much as can reasonably be expected. There is about room for one of your tugs handled skillfully. Our speed is necessarily less than the current, as backing is our only and constant resort against dangers and to pass the numerous turns. This gives every vagrant log a chance to foul our wheels, and as many do foul them; delays are frequent. Our damages so far, though not serious, are felt."

Confederates worked feverishly to raise ex-U.S.S. *Indianola*. C.S.S. *Queen of the West* was sent up river to Vicksburg to obtain a pump and other materials, but soon was seen returning below Warrenton. She brought news of a large Union "gunboat" passing the Vicksburg batteries and approaching the small Confederate squadron. According to Colonel Wirt Adams, CSA, "All the vessels at once got underway in a panic, and proceeded down the river, abandoning without a word the working party and fieldpieces on the wreck." He continued: "The Federal vessel did not approach nearer than 2½ miles, and appeared very apprehensive of attack."

After making further fruitless efforts to free *Indianola* of water, the next evening the working party fired the heavy XI-inch Dahlgren guns into each other and burned her to the water line. The Union ruse had worked. The "gunboat" was a barge, camouflaged to give the appearance of a formidable vessel of war, that Rear Admiral Porter had floated down river. A Confederate paper reported bitterly: "The Yankee barge sent down the river last week was reported to be an ironclad gunboat. The authorities, thinking that this monster would retake the *Indianola*, immediately issued an order to blow her up. . . . It would really seem we had no use for gunboats on the Mississippi, as a coal barge is magnified into a monster, and our authorities immediately order a boat—that would have been worth a small army to us—to be blown up."

U.S.S. *Vanderbilt*, Acting Lieutenant Charles H. Baldwin, seized blockade running British steamer *Peterhoff* off St. Thomas. An international dispute arose as to the disposition of the mails carried on board the steamer, and eventually Lincoln ruled that they should be returned to the British. Though *Peterhoff* was initially condemned as a lawful prize, some 4 years later this decision was reversed.

27 C.S.S. *Alabama*, Captain Semmes, captured and released on bond ship *Washington* in the mid-Atlantic. Semmes noted: "She was obstinate, and compelled me to wet the people on her poop, by the spray of a shot, before she would acknowledge that she was beaten."

28 U.S.S. *Montauk*, Commander Worden, supported by U.S.S. *Wissahickon*, *Seneca*, and *Dawn*, shelled and destroyed blockade runner *Rattlesnake*, formerly C.S.S. *Nashville*, lying under the guns of Fort McAllister in the Ogeechee River. For some 8 months *Rattlesnake* had been lying at the fort, awaiting an opportunity to run the blockade. The day before (27 February), Worden had noticed *Rattlesnake*'s renewed movements above McAllister; subsequent reconnaissance indicated that the vessel had grounded. "Believing that I could, by approaching close to the battery," Worden reported, "reach and destroy her with my battery, I moved up at daylight this morning. . . ." The Union squadron found *Rattlesnake* still aground, and, under heavy fire from the

U.S.S. Montauk *destroys blockade runner* Rattlesnake *(formerly C.S.S. Nashville) near Fort McAllister, Georgia. Though unable to run out,* Rattlesnake *had long commanded Northern attention and was termed by Commander John Worden a "troublesome pest."*

fort, began bombarding her. The gunboats contributed enfilading fire from long range. Within 20 minutes *Rattlesnake* was aflame. *Montauk* dropped down river about 8:30 and struck a torpedo. The explosion—described by her Second Assistant Engineer, Thomas A. Stephans, as "violent, sudden"—fractured the iron hull and caused sufficient damage to warrant running *Montauk* onto a mud bottom to effect repairs. About 9:30, *Rattlesnake*'s magazine ignited and the vessel blew up "with terrific violence, shattering her smoking ruins." Thus occurred the "final disposition," as Worden wrote, "of a vessel which has so long been in the minds of the public as a troublesome pest."

The Navy portion of the expedition through Yazoo Pass reached the Coldwater River and spent the next 2 days (through 2 March) waiting for the Army transports to join up. The time was utilized in making repairs on damaged smokestacks and wheels, in readying the rams *Fulton* and *Lioness* which, along with gunboat U.S.S. *Petrel*, had joined on the 28th, and in collecting bales of cotton for protecting the bulwarks of the vessels.

U.S.S. *Wyandank*, Acting Master Andrew J. Frank, captured schooners *Vista* and *A. W. Thompson* at Piney Point, Virginia.

U.S.S. *New Era*, Acting Ensign Hanford, seized steamer *Curlew* at Island No. 10 in the Mississippi River.

MARCH

2 Rear Admiral Farragut wrote Secretary Welles from New Orleans: "I have recently seen persons from Mobile, and they all concur in the statement that provisions are very high, and very scarce even at those high figures. Flour, $100 per barrel; bacon and meat of every kind, $1 per pound; meal, $20 per sack." Farragut, chafing under the relative inactivity of "doing nothing but blockading," also advised the Secretary of his planned operations, writing that he would attack Galveston as soon as there were sufficient troops. "At present," he added, "I am all ready to make an attack on or run the batteries at Port Hudson, so as to form a junction with the army and navy above Vicksburg. . . . The army of General Banks will attack by land or make a reconnaissance in force at the same time that we run the batteries. . . . My first object will be destroy the boats and cut off the supplies from the Red River. We expect to move in less than a week. I shall take the four ships, *Hartford*, *Mississippi*, *Richmond*, and *Monongahela*, and three gunboats and the *Brooklyn*, if she arrives in time."

Amidst the ever-present difficulties of command on the western waters, Rear Admiral Porter found time to be concerned with the well being of private citizens. He instructed Lieutenant Commander Selfridge, U.S.S. *Conestoga*: "Mrs. Twiddy, at Wilson and Mitchell's Landing, Bolivar, has 130 bales of cotton which she is desirous of sending to Cairo. This cotton must be seized the same as all other cotton and turned over to the civil authorities at Cairo, and, after it has been sold, Mrs. Twiddy can, by proving her loyalty to the Government, receive the value for it. She has also permission to go up to Cairo herself and take all her effects. If it is necessary, a gunboat will protect her self and property. When she is ready to go she will hoist a white flag, but you had better run down there occasionally and see how she is getting on. You will make a full report to me of all the particulars of this case. . . ." Three weeks later, U.S.S. *Bragg* took Mrs. Twiddy, her cotton, and her personal effects to Cairo.

C.S.S. *Alabama*, Captain Semmes, captured and burned at sea ship *John A. Parks*, after transferring on board *Alabama* provisions and stores. Semmes remarked that this capture threw *Alabama*'s carpenter into "ecstacies" since the cargo included white pine lumber; ". . . if I had not put some restraint on my zealous officer of the adze and chisel, I believe he would have converted the *Alabama* into a lumberman."

Both navies suffered from a lack of trained seamen. Youth, however, made valiant efforts to meet the needs of the services and, like the Union "powder monkey" above, made valuable contributions.

III–37

Surgeon Ninian Pinkney, USN, informed Porter that he had succeeded, "after a most fatiguing time," in obtaining the Commercial Hotel in Memphis for use by the Navy as a hospital. "It is," he reported, "admirably located and well adapted for hospital purposes." Such facilities, together with hospital ship *Red Rover*, greatly increased the Navy's capability to care for the sick and injured in the fleet.

3   Ironclads U.S.S. *Passaic*, *Nahant*, and *Patapsco*, with three mortar boats and gunboats U.S.S. *Seneca*, *Dawn*, and *Wissahickon*, under Captain Drayton, again engaged Fort McAllister at Savannah for 6 hours. Rear Admiral Du Pont held that the series of engagements was vital "before entering upon more important operations . . ."—the assault on Charleston. Du Pont wanted to subject the ironclads to the stresses and strains of battle, as well as give the crews additional gunnery practice.

Lieutenant Commander W. Smith's Yazoo Pass expedition moved down the Coldwater River. "We are advancing but slowly," he reported. "This stream is not so much wider or clearer than the pass as to make much difference in either speed or the amount of damage inflicted on these vessels. Our hull has suffered as much to-day as on any day yet. We can only advance with the current; faster than that brings us foul. Our speed is not more than 1½ miles per hour, if that. Wheels and stacks have escaped through care, but with over 200 feet above water, and less than 3 in it, without steerageway, light winds play with us, bringing the sides and trees in rough contact. I imagine that the character of this navigation is different from what was expected. We will get through in fighting condition, but so much delayed that all the advantages of a surprise to the rebels will have been lost."

Commenting on the loss of *Indianola* the preceding month, Assistant Secretary Fox wrote Du Pont: "These disasters must come, they are sure to follow a long course of uninterrupted success and we will look at them at the Department with a determination that they shall not lead us to doubt either ultimate victory or the brave officers and men who will surely win it."

Rear Admiral Porter wrote Fox from above Vicksburg: "There is delightful concert here between the Army and Navy. Grant and Sherman are on board almost every day. . . . we agree in everything, and they are disposed to do everything for us they can, they are both able men, and I hope sincerely for the sake of the Union that nothing may occur to make a change here."

Boat crew under Acting Master's Mate George Drain from U.S.S. *Matthew Vassar* destroyed a large boat at Little River Inlet, North Carolina. Proceeding up the western branch of the river to destroy salt works, the boat grounded and the crew was captured by Confederate troops.

4   U.S.S. *James S. Chambers*, Acting Master Luther Nickerson, seized blockade running Spanish sloop *Relampago* and schooner *Ida*. The schooner, beached at Sanibel Island, Florida, when she could not escape, was destroyed by the crew of *James S. Chambers*.

5   The Yazoo Pass expedition neared the junction of the Coldwater and Tallahatchie Rivers. Lieutenant Commander W. Smith reported: "The river is clearer, and we make better speed. If we reach the Tallahatchie this evening, which our advance may do, our total distance from Delta will be but 50 miles, not 6 miles per day. . . . I hope to make better speed from this time through." The next evening found Smith's forces some 12 miles down the Tallahatchie, where he was compelled to leave U.S.S. *Petrel* because of damage to her wheel; *Petrel* was reported once again "in line" on the 10th after rapid repairs.

Captain Sands, U.S.S. *Dacotah*, reported the appearance at New Inlet, on the Cape Fear River, of a Confederate ironclad. "I would feel somewhat more at ease," he wrote Rear Admiral S. P. Lee, "if we had an ironclad at each of these main inlets to Cape Fear River, to fend off an attack upon the wooden vessels by this Confederate ram, although, without such aid, we will do our best to prevent its success. But without some such assistance the blockade may be at any time broken by even this single yet formidable (because ironclad) ram." Sands later reported that the ram had had to return inside the Cape Fear River "because she could not stand the sea."

U.S.S. *Lockwood* returned to New Bern, North Carolina, from an expedition up the Pungo River where a bridge was destroyed, "which the enemy had built to facilitate the removal of the products from that section into the interior," and some arms, stores, and a small schooner were captured.

U.S.S. *Aroostook*, Lieutenant Commander Samuel R. Franklin, chased blockade running sloop *Josephine*, forced her aground near Fort Morgan, Mobile Bay, and, with U.S.S. *Pocahontas*, Lieutenant Commander Gamble, destroyed her by gunfire.

6   Major General Hunter wrote Rear Admiral Du Pont, requesting naval support for "an important mission in the southerly part of this department [the Union Army's Department of the South]. . . ." On the 10th, U.S.S. *Norwich* and *Uncas* convoyed the troop transports up the St. John's River where the soldiers were landed and again occupied Jacksonville, Florida. Commander James M. Duncan reported: "In the afternoon of that day some skirmishing took place outside of the town, upon which I threw several shell in the supposed direction of the enemy, which very soon dispersed them. During the next day," he added cryptically, "another skirmish took place with the like result."

C.S.S. *Florida*, Lieutenant Maffitt, captured and fired ship *Star of Peace* bound from Calcutta to Boston with cargo of saltpeter and hides.

7   The capture of blockade runners caused Rear Admiral S. P. Lee, commanding the North Atlantic Blockading Squadron, a shortage of officers. "Owing to the increase of blockade runners off the coast of North Carolina, and frequent captures made of them, I would request that six officers capable of taking charge of prizes may be ordered to this squadron. The vessels blockading off Cape Fear are greatly in want of them, owing to the number they have heretofore sent away in prizes, which leaves our vessels very deficient in officers."

8   U.S.S. *Sagamore*, Lieutenant Commander English, captured sloop *Enterprise* bound from Mosquito Inlet, Florida, to Nassau with cargo of cotton.

9   Commander Pennock, Fleet Captain of the Mississippi Squadron, informed Lieutenant Commander Fitch, U.S.S. *Lexington*, of reports of proposed Confederate action along the Tennessee: "You will have to keep a good watch soon on the Tennessee River. The enemy's plan is to fall back on Tennessee with all the forces they can raise, and deal Rosecrans a crushing blow. Now we must keep all the vessels you can spare up the Tennessee as high as they can go. The chance is the enemy will cross over somewhere as high up as Decatur [Alabama]. At all events get all the information you can, and be ready to meet them. . . . I do not think the rebels will attempt to cross into Tennessee if we have two boats at Decatur, another at Waterloo. Both these points command important railroads. . . . The time has come when we must begin to drive the rebels off the banks of the Tennessee."

Though the low water in the river did not allow the gunboats to go up the Tennessee as far as Decatur, by the 14th Rear Admiral Porter informed Secretary Welles: "The entire Mississippi banks have been alive with guerrillas, and we have successfully guarded every point and driven them [back]; and my object is to keep them away. As fast as the vessels are bought and fitted they are now sent to the Cumberland and Tennessee. We are doing all we can for General Rosecrans, and will, as heretofore done, keep him supplied. The only trouble is want of men. We can get the vessels faster than we can get crews."

U.S.S. *Bienville*, Commander J. R. Madison Mullany, captured schooner *Lightning* south of Port Royal with cargo of coffee and salt.

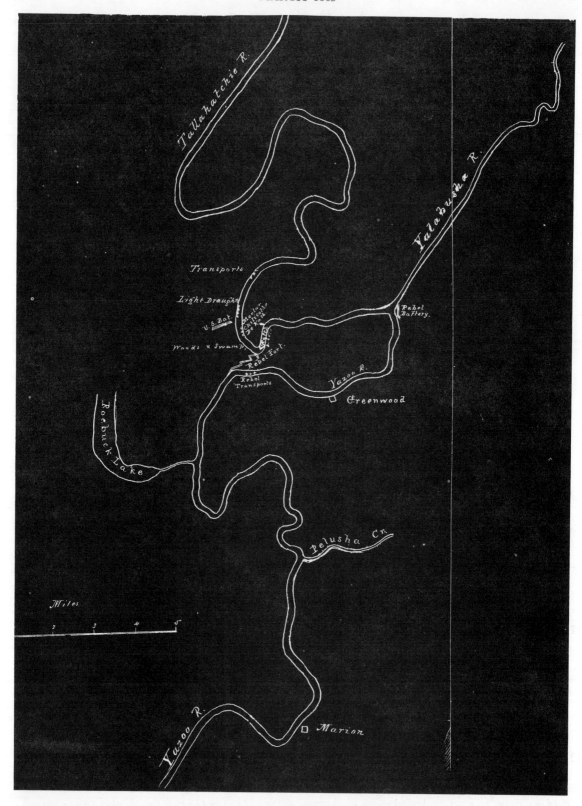

Contemporary map of the area in which the Yazoo Pass expedition operated under Lieutenant Commander Watson Smith. The effort to invest Vicksburg from the rear was turned back at Fort Pemberton.

III–40

U.S.S. *Quaker City*, Commander Frailey, seized British blockade runner *Douro* bound from Wilmington to Nassau with cargo of cotton, turpentine, and tobacco.

10 U.S.S. *Chillicothe*, Lieutenant Commander James P. Foster, destroyed a large bridge, a sawmill, and a flat-bottomed boat on the Tallahatchie River above Fort Pemberton, Mississippi. Earlier that afternoon Confederate steamer *Thirty-fifth Parallel* was destroyed to prevent her capture by the Union forces. According to Commander I. N. Brown, CSN, former commander of C.S.S. *Arkansas* who had been on board the steamer, *Thirty-fifth Parallel*, "from the extreme narrowness of the stream, ran into the woods and disabled herself, so that, to save falling into the hands of the enemy, I ordered her burned, which was done as the enemy came in sight."

U.S.S. *Gem of the Sea*, Acting Lieutenant Irvin B. Baxter, captured and destroyed sloop *Petee* attempting to run the blockade at Indian River Inlet, Florida, with cargo of salt.

11 The Yazoo Pass expedition's first attack on Fort Pemberton, Mississippi, on the Tallahatchie River commenced. Pemberton was a cotton and earthwork mounting a heavy Whitworth rifle, four other cannon, and several field pieces. U.S.S. *Chillicothe*, Lieutenant Commander J. P. Foster, was damaged by two shots from the fort, which was engaged at a range of 800 yards. Late in the afternoon, *Chillicothe* renewed the engagement, followed by U.S.S. *Baron De'Kalb*, Lieutenant Commander J. G. Walker. Under heavy fire, the vessels were compelled to withdraw once again. *Chillicothe* had one gun crew "rendered perfectly useless, 3 men being killed outright, 1 mortally wounded, and 10 others seriously wounded, while the other 5 of the gun's crew had their eyes filled with powder. This occurred in this way: One of the enemy's largest shell penetrated the port slide (3 inches thick) and struck the tulip of the *Chillicothe*'s port gun, and, exploding, ignited her shell just after it was in the muzzle of her port gun, and it not being home exploded at or about the muzzle, carrying away the two forward port slides, weighing 3,200 pounds, and a portion of the turret's backing, and tearing the bolts out of a large space of the armor, besides setting the cotton on fire that had been placed forward of the turret after the reconnaissance of the morning." Finding it difficult to bring more than one vessel's guns to bear on the fort, in front of which C.S.S. *St. Philip* (formerly steamer *Star of the West*) had been sunk as an obstruction, Lieutenant Commander W. Smith had a 30 pound Parrott gun moved on shore from U.S.S. *Rattler* "to annoy the rebel's best gun at about 600 yards. . . ." The following day was spent in repairing *Chillicothe* and readying an additional Parrott gun ashore.

Assistant Secretary Fox wrote Rear Admiral Du Pont, stressing the importance of the impending attack on Charleston: "The French Minister told the Chairman of Foreign Relations in the Senate that he was officially advised by his Consul at Charleston that 30 steamers had entered that port since January 1st and that trade was greater between Charleston and foreign ports than it had ever been before since the City was in existence."

12 Rear Admiral Farragut, in his flagship U.S.S. *Hartford*, arrived at Baton Rouge to make the final preparations for the passage of Port Hudson. Three days earlier he had ordered U.S.S. *Richmond*, Captain James Alden, to proceed to Baton Rouge and await him. He stationed U.S.S. *Essex*, *Genesee*, and *Albatross*, as well as the mortar boats, at the head of Profit Island and issued instructions warning against possible boarding by Confederates.

U.S.S. *Kittatinny*, Acting Master Charles W. Lamson, captured *D. Sargent* bound from Galveston to Honduras with cargo of cotton.

13 U.S.S. *Chillicothe*, Lieutenant Commander J. P. Foster, and U.S.S. *Baron De Kalb*, Lieutenant Commander J. G. Walker, and a mortar schooner, reengaged the Confederate works at Fort Pemberton as the Yazoo Pass expedition attempted to move down the Tallahatchie River to Greenwood, Mississippi. In action described by Walker as "severe," *Chillicothe* sustained 38 hits in an exchange of fire lasting about an hour and a half. Her ammunition exhausted, *Chillicothe* retired; *De Kalb*

135

General Order

For passing "Port Hudson."

The Ships will each take a Gunboat on
the Port Side and secure her as well aft
as possible, so as to leave the Port Battery
clear for the enemy's Battery on the Port side
of the River going up, after we round
the point opposite Port Hudson —

Each Ship will keep a very little on the
Starboard Quarter of her next ahead, so as
to give free range to her chase guns, without risk of damage from premature
explosion of Shrapnel or Shells —

The Captains will bear in mind that the
object is to run the batteries at the least
possible damage to our Ships, and thereby
secure an efficient force above for the
purpose of rendering such assistance as
may be required of us by the Army at
Vicksburg or if not required there, to our
Army at Baton Rouge —

If they succeed in getting past the Batteries,
The Gunboats will proceed up to the
mouth of the Red River, and keep up the
police of the River between that River and
Port Hudson, capturing anything they can.
Should any vessel be disabled so that she
is unable to pass Port Hudson, she will use
the Gunboat to the best advantage, if
the Captain thinks he can get by, try it —
if he thinks not, let the Gunboat drop
her down below the range of the Batteries —
If both are disabled, then club down
with a light anchor or use the sails, as

as in his judgment may seem best —but I expect all to go by, who are able, and I think the best protection against the enemy's fire, is a well directed fire from our own Guns, Shell and Shrapnel at a distance, and Grape when within 4 or 500 Yards —

D. G. Farragut
Rear Admiral

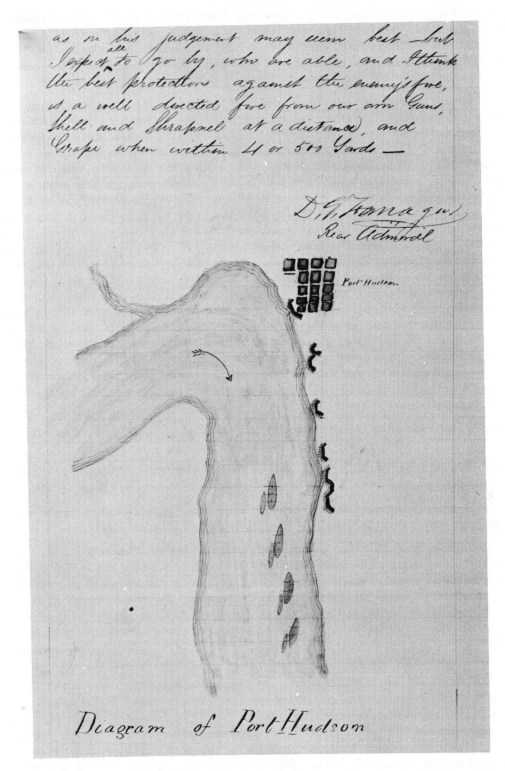

Diagram of Port Hudson

Rear Admiral Farragut's General Order for the passage of Port Hudson. "The best protection against the enemy's fire, is a well directed fire from our own guns."

continued to engage the fort some 3 more hours before withdrawing. Lieutenant Colonel James H. Wilson, USA, remarked: "The rebel position is a strong one by virtue of the difficulties of approach. . . ." The gunboats were unable to bring their full fire power to bear on the works, and the Army was unable to render effective assistance. Thus, though the fort was damaged by the attack, the follow up operations could not be pressed to force withdrawal.

Rear Admiral Du Pont wrote Professor Alexander D. Bache of the Coast Survey with reference to the projected Charleston attack and the ironclads: "We are steadily preparing for the great experiment, to see whether 20 guns, counting one broadside of the *Ironsides*, can silence or overcome some hundreds. I am not without hope, but would have more, were it not for obstructions—unfortunately the Army can give us no assistance. I did a very wise thing, though I think not many persons in my place would have done it—in trying the ironclads, four of them at least, against a live target in the shape of Fort McAllister. The experience has been invaluable, for they were wholly unfit to go into action—some things are not encouraging as they might be, but it is a great thing to know your tools, forewarned, etc. Then Dahlgren writes the life of his fifteen inch [gun] is 300 [firings]! This is about the worst thing yet—for I look for such pounding as done to the *Montauk*, today, by the torpedo—it is bad and hard to mend—but we can, we think, close the leak from the inside for the present. Our papers instructed the rebels at what spot to aim at and they did *exactly* but I have sent for more iron—all this, entre nous—I thought you would like a few words on the subject. One word more—nothing is more difficult for me to explain than the indisposition on the part of the inventors, who are often men of genius to wish to exclude from all knowledge or participation, the very people who are to use and give effect to their instruments and inventions. I saw an amendment to a Senate bill to exclude the submitting of some plans for iron ships to Navy officers! Now if Mr. [John] Ericsson could have had such men as Drayton and John Rodgers at his elbow from the beginning, these vessels would have been much better to handle. . . ."

C.S.S. *Florida*, Lieutenant Maffitt, captured and burned ship *Aldebaran*, from New York, near 29° N., 51° W., with cargo of provisions and clocks.

U.S.S. *Huntsville*, Acting Lieutenant William C. Rogers, seized blockade running British schooner *Surprise* off Charlotte Harbor, Florida, bound for Havana with cargo of cotton.

U.S.S. *Octorara*, Commander Collins, seized blockade running British schooner *Florence Nightingale* with cargo of cotton in the North East Providence Channel, Bahama Islands.

13-14 Confederate troops launched a surprise night attack against Fort Anderson on the Neuse River, North Carolina. Union gunboats U.S.S. *Hunchback*, *Hetzel*, *Ceres*, and *Shawsheen*, supported by a revenue cutter and an armed schooner, forced the Confederates to break off their heavy assault and withdraw. Colonel Jonathan S. Belknap, USA, wrote Commander Henry K. Davenport: "Your well-directed fire drove the enemy from the field; covered the landing of the Eighty-fifth New York, sent to the relief of the garrison, and the repulse of the rebel army was complete. Allow me, commodore, in the name of the officers and men of my command, to express my admiration of the promptitude and skill displayed by your command on that occasion. The Army is proud of the Navy."

14 Rear Admiral Farragut with his squadron of seven ships attacked the strong Confederate works at Port Hudson, attempting to effect passage. With typical thoroughness, the Admiral had inspected his squadron the day before "to see that all arrangements had been made for battle," and consulted with Major General Banks. His general order for the passage had previously been written and distributed to each commanding officer. Just before the attack, Farragut held a conference with the commanders on board the flagship and then received word from General Banks that he was in position and ready to begin an attack ashore in support of the passage. The mortars had begun to fire. Shortly after 10 p.m., the fleet was underway, the heavier ships, *Hartford*, *Rich-*

mond, and *Monongahela* to the inboard or fort side of the smaller *Albatross*, *Genesee*, and *Kineo*. *Mississippi* brought up the rear.

Moving up the river "in good style," *Hartford*, with *Albatross* lashed alongside, weathered the hail of shot from the batteries. Major General Franklin Gardner, commanding at Port Hudson, noted: "She returned our fire boldly." Passing the lower batteries, the current nearly swung the flagship around and grounded her, "but," Farragut reported, "backing the *Albatross*, and going ahead strong on this ship, we at length headed her up the river." Though able to bring only two guns to bear on the upper batteries, Farragut successfully passed those works.

Following the flagship closely, *Richmond* took a hit in her steam plant, disabling her. "The turning point [in the river] was gained," Commander Alden reported, "but I soon found, even with the aid of the *Genesee*, which vessel was lashed alongside, that we could make no headway against the strong current of the river, and suffering much from a galling cross fire of the enemy's batteries, I was compelled though most reluctantly, to turn back, and by the aid of the *Genesee* soon anchored out of the range of their guns." Next in line, *Monongahela* ran hard aground under Port Hudson's lower batteries where she remained for nearly half an hour, taking severe punishment. At least eight shots passed entirely through the ship. The bridge was shot from underneath Captain James P. McKinstry, injuring him and killing three others. With *Kineo's* aid, *Monongahela* was floated and attempted to resume her course upriver. "We were nearly by the principal battery," Lieutenant Nathaniel W. Thomas, the executive officer wrote, "when the crank pin of the forward engine was reported heated, and the engine stopped, the chief engineer reporting that he was unable to go ahead." The ship became unmanageable and drifted downstream, where she anchored out of range of the Confederate guns.

Meanwhile, on board U.S.S. *Mississippi*, Captain Melancton Smith saw *Richmond* coming downstream but, because of the heavy smoke of the pitched battle, was unable to sight *Monongahela*. Thinking she had steamed ahead to close the gap caused by *Richmond's* leaving the line ahead formation, he ordered his ship "go ahead fast" to close the supposed gap. In doing so, *Mississippi* ran aground and despite every effort could not be brought off. After being fired in four places, she was abandoned. At 3 a.m., *Mississippi* was seen floating in flames slowly down river; 2½ hours later, she blew up, "producing an awful concussion which was felt for miles around." Lieutenant George Dewey, destined to become hero of Manila Bay in 1898, was First Lieutenant of *Mississippi*. Thus ended one of the war's fiercest engagements; only *Hartford* and *Albatross* had run the gantlet.

Rear Admiral Porter, "having made arrangements with General Grant by which the army could cooperate with us" as the Yazoo Pass expedition faltered, launched the difficult and hazardous Steele's Bayou, Mississippi, expedition aimed at gaining entrance to the Yazoo River for the purpose of taking Vicksburg from the rear. The expedition—comprising U.S.S. *Louisville*, *Cincinnati*, *Carondelet*, *Pittsburg*, *Mound City*, four mortars and four tugs—made its way to Black Bayou, "a place about 4 miles long leading into Deer Creek." At that point further progress was impeded by the dense forest. Porter set his men to clearing the way by pulling up the trees or pushing them over with the ironclads. "It was terrible work," he reported to Welles, "but in twenty-four hours we succeeded in getting through these 4 miles and found ourselves in Deer Creek, where we were told there would be no more difficulties."

Boat crews under Acting Master Andrews, commanding U.S.S. *Crusader*, on an expedition to Milford Haven, Virginia, destroyed a blockade running schooner without cargo.

15 Armed boats from U.S.S. *Cyane*, Lieutenant Commander Paul Shirley, boarded and seized schooner *J. M. Chapman*, preparing to get underway from San Francisco. *J. M. Chapman* was suspected of having been outfitted as a Confederate commerce raider. She was found to have a crew of 4, and below decks 17 more men were concealed together with a cargo of guns, ammunition, and other military stores. Shirley reported that he discharged the cargo and confined the prisoners on Alcatraz.

Whether viewed from the batteries (top) or the fleet, the attempt by Rear Admiral Farragut to pass Port Hudson resulted in a violent action. Only the Admiral's flagship, U.S.S. Hartford, *and a gunboat successfully negotiated the passage. U.S.S.* Mississippi *was destroyed in the engagement.*

C.S.S. *Alabama*, Captain Semmes, captured and released on bond ship *Punjaub*, from Calcutta for London, northeast of Brazil.

16 U.S.S. *Chillicothe*, Lieutenant Commander J. P. Foster, resumed the attack on Fort Pemberton, Mississippi. In a brief engagement, the gunboat was struck eight times which rendered her guns unworkable and forced her to retire. Foster reported, "The *Chillicothe*'s loss on the 11th, 13th, and today is 22 killed, wounded, and drowned." Next day, the Yazoo Pass expedition fell back, and no further major effort was mounted against the Confederate position. The Army was unable to land because the country was flooded. Brigadier General Isaac F. Quinby shortly ordered the troops withdrawn and on 10 April the Confederate defenders could report "Yazoo Pass expedition abandoned."

Rear Admiral Porter later analyzed the results of the undertaking: Although some cotton was taken, "the result was a failure in the main object. The enemy burned two large steamers [*Parallel* and *Magnolia*] loaded with cotton. . . . built two formidable forts, Pemberton and Greenwood on the Tallahatchie and Yallabusha [sic], and blocked the way effectually. General Pemberton showed a great deal of ability in his defense of Vicksburg, all through, and won the respect of his opponents by his zeal and fidelity to his cause, to say nothing of his spirit of endurance. But in nothing did he show more energy than in watching the Federal tactics, and guarding against all attempts made to turn his flanks, especially by way of the streams which would have commanded the approaches to Vicksburg if held by the enemy. Pemberton took care that these passes should never be left unguarded in the future."

Reporting to Secretary Welles on the passage of Port Hudson, Rear Admiral Farragut wrote: "Concerning the *Hartford*, I cannot speak too highly of her captain, officers, and crew. All did their duty as far as came under my observation, and more courage and zeal I have never seen displayed. The officers set a good example to their men, and their greatest difficulty was to make them understand why they could not fire when the smoke was so dense that the pilot could not navigate. . . . To the good firing of the ships we owe most of our safety, for, according to my theory, the best way to save yourself is to injure your adversary. . . ." Welles replied: "The Department congratulates you and the officers and men of the *Hartford* upon the gallant passage of the Port Hudson batteries. . . . Although the remainder of your fleet were not successful in following their leader, the Department can find no fault with them. All appear to have behaved gallantly, and to have done everything in their power to secure success. Their failure can only be charged to the difficulties in the navigation of the rapid current of the Mississippi, and matters over which they had no control."

General Grant ordered troops under Major General W. T. Sherman to cooperate with Porter's gunboats as the expedition attempted to force its way from Steele's Bayou into the Yazoo River. "The ironclads," Sherman noted, "push their way along unharmed, but the trees and overhanging limbs tear the wooden boats all to pieces." The troops rendered great assistance to the ships in helping to clear Black Bayou and entangled obstructions.

U.S.S. *Octorara*, Commander Collins, seized sloop *Rosalie* and schooner *Five Brothers* with cargo of cotton at sea east of Florida.

18 U.S.S. *Wissahickon*, Lieutenant Commander John L. Davis, seized and destroyed steamer *Georgiana* attempting to run the blockade into Charleston with a valuable cargo including rifled guns. *Georgiana* was said to be pierced for 14 guns and earlier consular reports indicated that "she is an armed vessel intended for a cruise against our merchantmen." Described as a swift vessel, she was termed "another confederate to the pirate *Alabama*." Upon hearing of her fate, Secretary Welles wrote Rear Admiral Du Pont: "I am exceedingly gratified with the confirmation of the destruction of the *Georgiana*. It would have been better would she have been captured but the fact that she is disposed of is a relief. We had serious apprehensions in regard to her. In disposing

of both her and the *Nashville* you have rendered great service to our commerce, for had they got abroad they would have made sad havoc with our shipping. We shall have an account to settle with John Bull one of these days for this war which is being carried on against us by British capital and by Englishmen under the Confederate flag.''

19 Rear Admiral Farragut in U.S.S. *Hartford*, with U.S.S. *Albatross* in company, engaged Confederate batteries at Grand Gulf as the ships steamed up the Mississippi toward Vicksburg. After successfully passing the heavy Confederate works at Port Hudson, Farragut had proceeded to the mouth of the Red River on the 16th. Next day, he steamed up to Natchez, tearing down a portion of the telegraph lines to Port Hudson. He anchored for the night of the 18th below Grand Gulf and ran the batteries early the next morning, suffering eight casualties in the engagement. He came to anchor just below Warrenton, Mississippi, where, on the 20th, he communicated with Grant and Porter and sought replenishment of his coal supply.

Rear Admiral Porter reported that the Steele's Bayou expedition had reached within 1½ miles of Rolling Fork, Mississippi. ''Had the way been as good as represented to me, I should have been in Yazoo City by this time; but we have been delayed by obstructions which I did not mind much, and the little willows, which grow so thick that we stuck fast hundreds of times.'' In a later summary report to Secretary Welles, Porter noted: ''We had succeeded in getting well into the heart of the country before we were discovered. No one would believe that anything in the shape of a vessel could get through Black Bayou, or anywhere on the route.'' As the gunboats continued to struggle against unfriendly natural hazards, Confederates felled trees to further obstruct the channel and sharpshooters took the ships under fire. To prevent additional obstructions being placed at Rolling Fork, Porter sent ashore 2 boat howitzers and 300 men under Lieutenant John M. Murphy, commanding U.S.S. *Carondelet*. However, with Confederate troop strength in the area growing and receiving reports of obstructions being placed ahead and trees being felled in his rear, Porter was shortly compelled to break off the attempt to reach the Yazoo in order to avoid complete entrapment.

Rear Admiral Du Pont wrote Assistant Secretary Fox: ''We are hard at work on the ironclads. They require so much, and the injury of the *Montauk* is very great. I crawled on 'all fours' to see for myself. . . . The *Patapsco*'s pumps are not yet in order. I had dispatched the *Weehawken* to Edisto this morning to establish our base of operations, but an equinoctial gale sent her back. I may send her to Savannah River in lieu. . . . I am anxiously awaiting the arrival of the *Keokuk*. Her less draft than the others is very important. I think these monitors [*Keokuk* was a citadel ironclad, not a monitor] are wonderful conceptions, but, oh, the errors of details, which would have been corrected if these men of genius could be induced to pay attention to the people who are to use their tools and inventions.''

U.S.S. *Octorara*, Commander Collins, seized blockade running British schooner *John Williams* near the Bahamas.

20 From below Warrenton, Rear Admiral Farragut sent the following message to General Grant and a similar one to Rear Admiral Porter: ''Having learned that the enemy had the Red River trade open to Vicksburg and Port Hudson and that two of the gunboats of the upper fleet [*Queen of the West* and *Indianola*] had been captured, I determined to pass up and, if possible, recapture the boats and stop the Red River trade, and this I can do most effectively if I can obtain from Rear Admiral Porter or yourself coal for my vessels. . . . I shall be most happy to avail myself of the earliest moment to have a consultation with yourself and Rear Admiral Porter as to the assistance I can render you at this place; and, if none, then I will return to the mouth of the Red River and carry out my original designs.'' Porter replied: ''I would not attempt to run the batteries at Vicksburg if I were you; it won't pay, and you can be of no service up here at this moment. Your services at Red River will be a godsend; it is worth to us the loss of the [U.S.S.] *Mississippi* at

this moment and it is the severest blow that could be struck at the South. They obtain all their supplies and ammunition in that way." Grant floated a coal barge down the river to Farragut, who steamed above Warrenton to meet the vital cargo.

U.S.S. *Ethan Allen*, Acting Master Pennell, seized blockade running British schooner *Gypsy* off St. Joseph's Bay, Florida, with cargo including merchants' tools.

21 U.S.S. *Victoria*, Acting Lieutenant Hooker, and U.S. schooner *William Bacon*, captured blockade running British steamer *Nicolai I* in "thick and rainy" weather off Cape Fear. The steamer was carrying a cargo of dry goods, arms, and ammunition, and had been turned back 2 days earlier in an attempt to run into Charleston.

22 Though troops sent by General W. T. Sherman had reached the gunboats of the Steele's Bayou expedition at Rolling Fork the day before, it was Rear Admiral Porter's decision that their numbers were not sufficient to insure success. The soldiers had met the gunboats without provisions of their own and without any field artillery. "Under the circumstances," Porter wrote, "I could not afford to risk a single vessel, and therefore abandoned the expedition." Unable to turn around in the narrow waters, the gunboats unshipped their rudders and drifted backwards. Coming to a bend in the river, "where the enemy supposed they had blockaded us completely, having cut a number of trees all together . . .," the gunboats and Union troops fought their way through as the withdrawal continued. Sherman arrived with additional troops, but Porter noted: "We might now have retraced our steps, but we were all worn-out. The officers and men had for six days and nights been constantly at work, or sleeping at the guns. We had lost our coal barge, and the provision vessel could not get through, being too high for such purposes. Taking everything into consideration, I thought it best to undertake nothing further without being better prepared, and we finally, on the 24th, arrived at Hill's plantation, the place we started from on the 16th."

Thus ended what Porter accurately described as "a most novel expedition. Never did those people expect to see ironclads floating where the keel of a flat boat never passed." Though it did not achieve its primary goal, the daring expedition was not a failure. By destroying all bridges encountered, it had "cut off for the present all the means of transporting provisions to Vicksburg." In addition, a vast quantity of corn was destroyed and many horses, mules, and cattle were taken. An estimated 20,000 bales of cotton were destroyed and enough was taken "to pay for the building of a good gunboat." Porter recognized, too, the "moral effect of penetrating into a country deemed inaccessible. There will be no more planting in these regions for a long time to come. The able-bodied negroes left with our army, carrying with them all the stores left by their masters. . . ." Despite these positive results, the Admiral succinctly summed up a deeper meaning of the abandonment of the Steele's Bayou expedition: "With the end of this expedition ends all my hopes of getting Vicksburg in this direction. Had we been successful we could have made a sure thing of it. . . ." By land and water, the long siege and the bitter fighting for Vicksburg would now continue.

Rear Admiral Farragut advised General Grant that the Confederates were building "a very formidable casemated work" at Warrenton. "I fired at it yesterday, but I think did it little or no injury. I see they are at work on it again and shall interrupt them to-day with an occasional shot or shell to prevent their annoying me on my way down, but if you think proper to make a little expedition over that way to destroy it, my two vessels will be at your service as long as I am here." Grant replied: "As you kindly offered me the cooperation of your vessels and the use of them to transport troops to Warrenton, should I want them to send an expedition to destroy their batteries, I have determined to take advantage of the offer. . . . I send no special instruction for this expedition further than to destroy effectually the batteries at Warrenton and to return to their camp here. They will be glad to receive any suggestions or directions from you." Farragut, writing Captain Henry Walke, expressed the view that the blockade of the Red River

With deep sorrow I call you to-
-gether to announce the death of
our late executive officer, Lt. Com-
-mander A. B. Cummings at New
Orleans. It has pleased God
to take from among us our gallant
friend in the fullness of his en-
-ergies & usefulness. You all well
know the importance of his ser-
-vices in this ship; his conscientious
devotion to duty; his justice & even
temper in maintaining discipline;
his ability in preparing for emer-
-gencies & his coolness in meeting
them. All these qualities he brought
to his country in the hour of need
and he has sealed his devotion
with his life. The fatal cannon
shot struck him where he stood
on the "bridge" cheering the men
at the guns and directing their
fire. He was thrown down upon
the deck but his presence of mind
still remained — he said: "Quick!
boys, pick me up." "put a tourni-
-quet on my leg"; "Send my letters
to my wife"; "Tell them I fell
in doing my duty."
When below he said to the

Commander James Alden gave this memorable address to the officers and men of U.S.S. Richmond upon the death of his executive officer, Lieutenant Commander Andrew B. Cummings, from a wound suffered at Port Hudson on 14 March. Alden said: "We cannot do our duty better, but let us at least try to do it as well."

Surgeons. "If there are others more hurt attend to them first"
"Nolan, are you here too"? He enquired about "Howard" & his thoughts were directly of others & of success in the fight. When told that the noise he heard was from the escape of steam & that the ship could no longer stem the current he exclaimed: "I would rather lose the other leg than go back" Can nothing be done? there is a South wind! where are the sails?

Friends; The high object of our country in this war is "that peace "& happiness; truth & justice, relig-"ion & piety may be established "among us for all generations".

For this sacred cause has fallen the Christian gentleman whose death we now lament; for this cause have fallen all the brave men whose blood has stained these decks — We cannot do our duty better, but let us at least try to do it as well.

(Signed)

James Alden
Com. & Senior Officer pres.

III–51

could be better effected with the aid of one of the Ellet rams, which were above Vicksburg. To Grant he noted that a ram would be more suitable for landing the troops at Warrenton than either U.S.S. *Hartford* or *Albatross*.

U.S.S. *Tioga*, Commander Clary, captured blockade running British steamer *Granite City* at sea off Eleuthera Island and British schooner *Brothers* off Abaco. Both carried assorted cargoes including medicines and liquor.

23   Concerned with the fate of his ships that had failed to pass the Port Hudson batteries, Rear Admiral Farragut wrote his wife from U.S.S. *Hartford* below Vicksburg: "I passed the batteries of Port Hudson with my chicken (U.S.S. *Albatross*) under my wing. We came through in safety. . . . Would to God I only knew that our friends on the other ships were as well as we are! We are all in the same hands, and He disposes of us as He thinks best. . . . You know my creed: I never send others in advance when there is a doubt; and, being one on whom the country has bestowed its greatest honors, I thought I ought to take the risks which belong to them. So I took the lead. . . ."

Lieutenant Webb, CSN, issued instructions to Lieutenant William G. Dozier regarding the defense of Charleston harbor in the event of an attack by the Union ironclads. Should the ironclads steam past the batteries in the harbor, elaborate plans were made to sink them by torpedoes.

C.S.S. *Alabama*, Captain Semmes, captured ship *Morning Star* and burned whaling schooner *Kingfisher* off the Brazilian coast near the equator.

U.S.S. *Arizona*, Acting Lieutenant Daniel P. Upton, took blockade running sloop *Aurelia* off Mosquito Inlet, Florida, with cargo of cotton.

24   Brigadier General Alfred W. Ellet informed Captain Walke that he intended to send rams *Lancaster* and *Switzerland* past the Vicksburg batteries to support Farragut at Warrenton and in blockading the Red River. "You will not," the General informed Colonel C. R. Ellet, commanding

U.S.S. Lafayette, *once Admiral Porter's flagship off Grand Gulf, Mississippi.*

the ram fleet, "in the event that either boat is disabled, attempt, under fire of the batteries, to help her off with the other boat, but will run on down, it being of primary importance that one boat at least should get safely by."

U.S.S. *Mount Vernon*, Acting Lieutenant Trathen, seized British schooner *Mary Jane* attempting to run the blockade near New Inlet, North Carolina, with cargo of soap, salt, flour, and coffee.

25 Before daybreak, rams *Switzerland* and *Lancaster* got underway to run past Vicksburg to join Rear Admiral Farragut below with U.S.S. *Hartford* and *Albatross*. Colonel C. R. Ellet reported: "The wind was extremely unfavorable, and notwithstanding the caution with which the boats put out into the middle of the stream, the puff of their escape pipes could be heard with fatal distinctness below. The flashing of the enemy's signal lights from battery to battery as we neared the city showed me that concealment was useless." Under full steam, the rams rounded the bend into a concentrated fire from the Confederate works. On board *Switzerland*, Colonel Ellet noted: "Shot after shot struck my boat, tearing everything to pieces before them." *Lancaster*, under Lieutenant Colonel John A. Ellet, followed, steaming steadily down river, "but," the senior Ellet reported, "I could see the splinters fly from her at every discharge." Directly in front of the main Vicksburg batteries, a shell plunged into *Switzerland*'s boiler, stopping the engines. The pilots, who "stood their posts like men," kept the ram in the river and she floated down, still under a hail of shot, to safety. The *Lancaster*, meanwhile, received a fatal shot which pierced her steam drum "and enveloped the entire vessel in a terrible cloud of steam. . . . About this time," reported her commanding officer, "a heavy plunging shot struck her in the frailest part of her stern, passing longitudinally through her and piercing the hull in the center near the bow, causing an enormous leak in the vessel." She sank almost immediately. The planned joint attack on Warrenton was called off because of the extensive repairs required by the *Switzerland*.

Farragut wrote Rear Admiral Porter about the difficulties of maintaining the blockade of the Red River with so few ships: "My isolated position requires that I should be more careful of my ships than I would be if I had my fleet with me. I can not get to a machine shop, or obtain the most ordinary repairs without fighting my way to them." Coal and provisions were set adrift on barges above Vicksburg and floated to Farragut below.

C.S.S. *Alabama*, Captain Semmes, captured ships *Charles Hill* and *Nora* near the equator off the coast of Brazil. Semmes described the capture: "It was time now for the *Alabama* to move. Her main yard was swung to the full, sailors might have been seen running up aloft, like so many squirrels, who thought they saw 'nuts' ahead, and pretty soon, upon a given signal the top-gallant sails and royals might have been seen fluttering in the breeze, for a moment, and then extending themselves to their respective yard-arms. A whistle or two from the boatswain and his mates, and the trysail sheets are drawn aft and the *Alabama* has on those seven-league boots . . . . A stride or two, and the thing is done. First, the *Charles Hill*, of Boston, shortens sail, and runs up the 'old flag,' and then the *Nora*, of the same pious city, follows her example. They were both laden with salt, and both from Liverpool."

U.S.S. *Kanawha*, Lieutenant Commander William K. Mayo, took schooner *Clara* attempting to run the blockade at Mobile.

U.S.S. *State of Georgia*, Commander Armstrong, and U.S.S. *Mount Vernon*, Acting Lieutenant Trathen, captured blockade running schooner *Rising Dawn* off New Inlet, North Carolina, with large cargo of salt.

U.S.S. *Fort Henry*, Acting Lieutenant Edward Y. McCauley, captured blockade running sloop *Ranger*, from Havana, off Cedar Keys, Florida.

U.S.S. *Wachusett*, Lieutenant Commander Charles E. Fleming, seized British blockade runner *Dolphin* between Puerto Rico and St. Thomas Island.

26   Assistant Secretary Fox notified Rear Admiral Du Pont: "We have sent you down the semi-submarine boat 'Alligator' that may be useful in making reconnaissances." *Alligator*, designed by the French inventor Brutus de Villeroy and built for the government in Philadelphia, was 46 feet long, 4½ feet in breadth, and carried a crew of 17 men. She was designed to be propelled by folding oars, but these were replaced at the Washington Navy Yard by a hand operated screw propellor.

27   U.S.S. *Hartford* engaged and passed below the Confederate batteries being erected at Warrenton. Two days later U.S.S. *Albatross* joined Rear Admiral Farragut, having waited above the batteries to obtain further coal and provisions which had been floated down on barges from the fleet above Vicksburg.

  U.S.S. *Pawnee*, Commander Balch, supported an Army landing on Cole's Island, South Carolina; Balch joined the Army command ashore for a reconnaissance of the island.

  U.S.S. *Hendrick Hudson*, Lieutenant Cate, seized British schooner *Pacifique* at St. Mark's, Florida.

28   U.S.S. *Diana*, Acting Master Thomas L. Peterson, reconnoitering the Atchafalaya River, Louisiana, with troops embarked, was attacked by Confederate sharpshooters and fieldpieces. In action that lasted almost 3 hours, casualties were heavy, *Diana*'s "tiller ropes were shot away, the engines disabled, and she finally drifted ashore when it was impossible to fight or defend her longer, and she ultimately surrendered to the enemy."

  C.S.S. *Florida*, Lieutenant Maffitt, captured bark *Lapwing*, bound from Boston to Batavia with cargo of coal. Maffitt transferred a howitzer and ammunition to the captured bark and renamed her *Oreto* for use as a tender under Lieutenant S. N. Averett.

  U.S.S. *Stettin*, Acting Master Edward F. Devens, seized blockade running British steamer *Aries* off Bull's Bay with cargo of liquor.

29   General Grant wrote Rear Admiral Porter requesting gunboat assistance in an anticipated move below Vicksburg. "It looks to me, admiral," Grant wrote, "as a matter of vast importance that one or two vessels should be put below Vicksburg, both to cut off the enemy's intercourse with the west bank of the river entirely and to insure a landing on the east bank for our forces if wanted . . . . Without the aid of gunboats it will hardly be worthwhile to send troops to New Carthage or to open the passage from here there; preparatory surveys for doing this are now being made." Porter replied the same day: "I am ready to cooperate with you in the matter of landing troops on the other side. . . . If it is your intention to occupy Grand Gulf in force it will be necessary to have vessels there to protect the troops or quiet the fortifications now there. If I do send vessels below it will be the best vessels I have, and there will be nothing left to attack Haynes' Bluff, in case it should be deemed necessary to try it. . . . Before making a gunboat move I should like to get the vessels back from the Yazoo Pass Expedition."

  Commander Duncan, U.S.S. *Norwich*, reported to Rear Admiral Du Pont the evacuation of Jacksonville, Florida, by Union troops after destroying the greater part of the city.

  U.S.S. *South Carolina*, Commander John J. Almy, captured schooner *Nellie* off Port Royal.

30   C.S.S. *Florida*, Lieutenant Maffitt, seized bark *M. J. Colcord*, loaded with provisions, from New York and bound for Cape Town, South Africa. The provisions were taken on board *Florida*, the crew was put on board Danish brig *Christian*, and the prize was destroyed. Maffitt wrote: "Living like lords on Yankee plunder."

  U.S.S. *Monticello*, Lieutenant Commander Braine, captured blockade running British schooner *Sue* off Little River, North Carolina.

31 Confederate troops opened a sustained attack and siege of the Union position at Washington, North Carolina. The assaulting forces erected numerous batteries along the Pamlico River in an effort to check the Union Navy. Nonetheless, the senior naval officer, Commander Davenport, moved quickly to aid the beleaguered Union soldiers. He dispatched all but two gunboats guarding New Bern to Washington and left only one at Plymouth. Before the attack was broken up on 16 April, the warships' heavy gunfire support swung the balance in stopping the Confederates. In addition, small boats transported desperately needed ammunition to the troops and ultimately it was the waterborne supplies reaching the garrison that induced the Confederates to withdraw. "We were compelled to give up the siege of Washington," Major General A. P. Hill wrote, "as the Yankee supply boats ran the blockade. Two more days would have starved the garrison out." Once again the flexibility of Union naval units had preserved a vital position for the North.

Ram *Switzerland*, Colonel C. R. Ellet, repairs completed, steamed below Warrenton and joined U.S.S. *Hartford* and *Albatross* under Rear Admiral Farragut. The three ships ran past the batteries at Grand Gulf that night, anchored, and next day continued downriver to the mouth of the Red River, destroying Confederate supply skiffs and flatboats en route.

Commander John Guest wrote Rear Admiral S. P. Lee regarding a method for the removal of the ever-dangerous Confederate torpedoes by "raft and grapnel." He believed: "It is perfectly feasible and is decidedly the best means wherever there is a tideaway. A hulk could do as well [to which Admiral Lee objected, 'No! they can be sunk, but rafts can't.'] in some cases with four or five grapnel hung over the side & spars rigged out forward & aft to give a greater *spread* to the grapnels. . . . After clearing the channel of torpedoes the hulk might be allowed to drift so as to point out obstructions, or with powder in her and a wire might be used to blow out obstructions."

U.S.S. *Memphis*, Lieutenant Commander Watmough, captured British schooner *Antelope* attempting to run the blockade into Charleston with cargo of salt.

U.S.S. *Two Sisters*, Acting Master Arthur, took schooner *Agnes* off Tortugas with cargo of cotton.

31–1 April   Lieutenant Commander Gillis, in U.S.S. *Commodore Morris*, with soldiers embarked proceeded up the Ware River, Virginia, to investigate reports of a large quantity of grain being stored in the area. Thousands of bushels were found at Patterson Smith's plantation. While engaged in seizing the grain the next day, 1 April, the landing party of soldiers and sailors were attacked by Confederate cavalry. Gillis reported: "The men were immediately formed . . . and a few well directed shots caused a wavering in their ranks, and a cheer and a charge on the part of both sailors and soldiers turned an attack into a retreat. . . ." Gillis deemed it necessary to destroy the remainder of the grain, "making altogether some 22,000 bushels of grain that the rebels have thus been deprived of." The constant loss of essential food stuffs sorely hurt the South.

APRIL

1 Preparations for the naval assault on Charleston moved into their final week. Rear Admiral Du Pont sent ironclads U.S.S. *Passaic*, *Montauk*, *Patapsco*, and *Keokuk* to the North Edisto River and gunboat *Sebago* to Calibogue Sound. To Commander John C. Beaumont, commanding *Sebago*, the Admiral wrote that his objective was "to cover the approaches to the west end of Hilton Head Island and prevent any descent upon it from boats with troops, etc., and to give notice by signal to the picket stations on shore, you will use your own discretion as to your position." Du Pont assigned Captain Charles Steedman to protect the Army at Hilton Head Island while he himself led the offensive against Charleston. Next day, 2 April, Du Pont left Port Royal for the North Edisto, flying his pennant in U.S.S. *James Adger*.

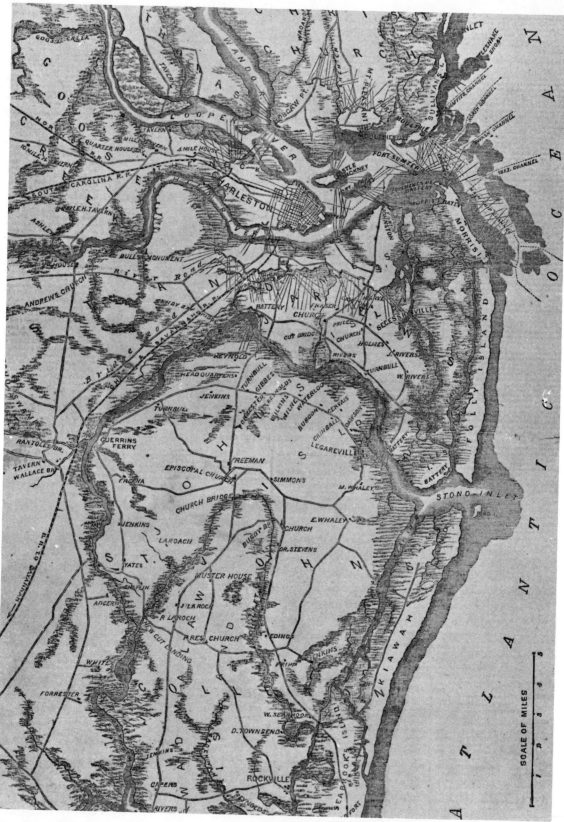

The Charleston area: the scene of massive operations throughout 1863.

III–56

U.S.S. *Tuscumbia*, with Rear Admiral Porter and Generals Grant and W. T. Sherman on board, reconnoitered the Yazoo River to determine the practicability of landing a force at Haynes' Bluff. Grant believed that an attack "would be attended with immense sacrifice of life, if not with defeat." This closed the last hope of turning Vicksburg's fortifications by the right, and gave added weight to the Grand Gulf operation below Vicksburg about which Grant and Porter had just exchanged letters. On 2 April, Secretary Welles wrote Porter a letter strongly urging the occupation of the Mississippi between Vicksburg and Port Hudson, which would be "the severest blow that can be struck upon the enemy, [and] is worth all the risk encountered by Rear-Admiral Farragut."

2   Assistant Secretary Fox wrote Rear Admiral Farragut that President Lincoln, with characteristic understanding of how to use naval strength, was "rather disgusted with the flanking expeditions [at Yazoo Pass and Steele's Bayou], and predicted their failure from the first. . . . he always observed that cutting the Rebels in two by our force in the river was of greater importance. . . . Grant . . . has kept our Navy trailing through swamps to protect his soldiers when a force between Vicksburg and Port Hudson, the same length of time, would have been of greater injury to the enemy."

Lincoln informed Secretary Welles that Farragut had to be strengthened. Welles accordingly wrote Rear Admiral Du Pont to send all but two of his ironclads to New Orleans after the Charleston attack.

2-9   An armed boat expedition of sailors and Marines under Acting Lieutenant McCauley, U.S.S. *Fort Henry*, reconnoitered the Bayport, Florida, area. The boats stood in for Bayport on the evening of the 2nd, arriving off the city the next morning. The first launch, exhibiting the "sluggish" qualities that were to be trying throughout the reconnaissance, slowed the expedition's progress through the intricate channel. "This waste of time," McCauley reported, "gave the rebels leisure to make all preparations for our reception." Two Confederate sloops and two small schooners ran into a bayou and grounded seeking to avoid destruction. Sloop *Helen*, carrying corn, was captured south of the harbor and destroyed. The Union boat crews engaged and forced the evacuation of a defending battery, and the Confederates burned a schooner with cargo of cotton. McCauley reported: "Having gained my object in her destruction and the clearing of the battery, the disabling of two of my guns, the unwieldiness of the first launch, which made it difficult to bring her gun to bear; the uncertainty of aim in the sea that was running, and consequent waste of ammunition, and the warnings of Mr. Ashley, the pilot, that if the ebb tide found us there we should be left aground, made me give up my design of trying to set the vessels in the bayou on fire by shelling." The boats withdrew out of range of a rifled gun which the Confederates brought up. In the next week the expedition examined the Chassahowitzka, Crystal, Homosassa, Withlacoochee, Waccassassa, and Suwannee Rivers, as small boats carried the message of seapower where deeper draft vessels could not pass.

3   Expedition under Lieutenant Commander Fitch, including U.S.S. *Lexington, Brilliant, Robb, Silver Lake,* and *Springfield*, destroyed Palmyra, Tennessee, in retaliation for Confederate guerrillas firing on a Union convoy (2 April), crippling U.S.S. *St. Clair* and damaging Army transports *Eclipse* and *Luminary*.

U.S.S. *New London*, Lieutenant Commander Abner Read, and U.S.S. *Cayuga*, Lieutenant Commander David A. McDermut, captured blockade running British schooner *Tampico* off Sabine Pass with cargo of cotton.

4   Rear Admiral Du Pont issued his order of battle and plan of attack on Charleston: ". . . The Squadron will pass up the main ship channel without returning the fire of the batteries on Morris Island, unless signal should be made to commence action. The ships will open fire on Fort Sumter when within easy range, and will take up a position to the northward and westward of that

fortification, engaging its left or northeast face at a distance of from 600 to 800 yards firing low and aiming at the center embrasure. The commanding officers will instruct their officers and men to carefully avoid wasting shot and will enjoin upon them the necessity of precision rather than rapidity of fire. Each ship will be prepared to render every assistance possible to vessels that may require it. The special code of signals prepared for the ironclad vessels will be used in action. After the reduction of Fort Sumter it is probable that the next point of attack will be the batteries on Morris Island. The order of battle will be the line ahead. . . . A squadron of reserve, of which Captain J. F. Green will be the senior officer, will be formed outside the bar and near the entrance buoy, consisting of the following vessels, *Canandaigua, Housatonic, Huron, Unadilla, Wissahickon,* and will be held in readiness to support the ironclads when they attack the batteries on Morris Island.''

President Lincoln wrote regarding harbor defense: "I have a single idea of my own about harbor defences. It is a steam-ram, built so as to sacrifice nearly all capacity for carrying to those of speed and strength. . . . her business would be to guard a particular harbour, as a Bull-dog guards his master's door.''

C.S.S. *Alabama*, Captain Semmes, captured ship *Louisa Hatch* off the coast of Brazil with large cargo of coal. Semmes took the prize with him so that he would still have a means of obtaining a supply of coal if he failed to rendezvous as planned with the bark *Agrippina* at Fernando de Noronha Island. Semmes' foresight again paid off, for the bark did not arrive at the island. After coaling and provisioning from *Louisa Hatch*, Semmes burned her on 17 April.

5   With ironclads and enough steamers to take them in tow if knocked out of action, Rear Admiral Du Pont departed North Edisto for Charleston, arriving off the Confederate stronghold that afternoon. As a last step before the assault, preparations were made to buoy the Stono bar to fix a safe channel. U.S.S. *Patapsco*, Commander Ammen, and U.S.S. *Catskill*, Commander George Rodgers, remained inside the bar to protect the buoys.

6   Commander Balch, U.S.S. *Pawnee*, reported that the Stono Bar had been buoyed, preparatory to the assault on Charleston. Rear Admiral Du Pont crossed the bar, his flag in U.S.S. *New Ironsides*, Captain Turner. Intending to attack Charleston that day, the Admiral took the other ironclads in with him: U.S.S. *Passaic*, Captain Drayton; *Weehawken*, Captain J. Rodgers; *Montauk*, Captain Worden; *Patapsco*, Commander Ammen; *Catskill*, Commander G. Rodgers; *Nantucket*, Commander Donald McD. Fairfax; *Nahant*, Commander John Downes; and *Keokuk*, Commander Alexander C. Rhind. After reaching an anchorage inside the bar, Du Pont reported, ". . . the weather became so hazy, preventing our seeing the ranges, that the pilots declined to go farther.''

Captain William F. Lynch, CSN, wrote Senator George Davis of North Carolina from Wilmington regarding the status of ships building in the waters of that state: "One ironclad, the *North Carolina*, building here, is very nearly ready for her crew. . . . The other, the *Raleigh*, is now ready for her iron shield, and can in eight weeks be prepared for service, as far as the material is concerned. At Whitehall, upon the Neuse, we have a gunboat [*Neuse*] in nearly the same state of forwardness as the *Raleigh;* at Tarboro we have one with the frame up, the keel of one [*Albemarle*] is laid near Scotland Neck. . . .''

Assistant Secretary Fox wrote Commodore Rowan about a method of countering Confederate torpedoes at Mobile: "It strikes me that a small grapnel might be thrown several hundred yards ahead and hauled in so as to break the connections of their torpedoes. A small charge of powder, a wooden sabot, a grapnel and chain fast to a line, fired from a XV-inch gun, are all the elements. I advise you to prepare these arrangements, for you certainly will find torpedoes near Fort Morgan.''

U.S.S. *Huntsville*, Acting Lieutenant W. C. Rogers, captured sloop *Minnie* off Charlotte Harbor, Florida, with cargo of cotton.

7 Rear Admiral Du Pont, with nine ironclads, engaged the strong Confederate forts in Charleston harbor. The Richmond *Whig*, unaware of the outcome of the battle, editorialized on 8 April: "At last the hour of trial has come for Charleston."

Du Pont made signal to get underway at noon, "this," the Admiral reported, "being the earliest hour at which, owing to the state of the tide, the pilots would consent to move." U.S.S. *Weehawken*, in the van pushing a raft to clear torpedoes from the path of the line ahead column, fouled the torpedo grapnels attached to the raft, delaying the movement for an hour, and continued to impede the column's progress throughout so that it was nearly 3 o'clock before the ships came within range of Forts Moultrie and Sumter in the harbor.

Weehawken opened on Fort Sumter shortly after 3, followed by the other monitors. The Confederates had not only heavily obstructed the channels to Charleston, but they had also marked them with range indicators for their gunners in the forts, "which," Ammen later observed, "greatly increased the accuracy of the fire from the forts as the vessels passed."

As *Weehawken* became hotly engaged, a torpedo exploded near her; "it lifted the vessel a little," the indomitable Captain John Rodgers reported, "but I am unable to preceive that it has done us any damage." Of greater concern to the commander of the lead ship were the obstructions extending from Fort Moultrie to Fort Sumter. "The appearance was so formidable," Rodgers wrote, "that, upon deliberate judgment, I thought it not right to entangle the vessel in obstructions which I did not think we could have passed through, and in which we should have been caught." He swung his ship's bow to seaward to prevent being swept against the obstructions by the strong flood tide which made the ironclads virtually unmanageable at times during the engagement. *Weehawken* steamed a few hundred feet southward to give the ships in the rear opportunity to turn in her wake. Engaged for 40 minutes, the lead ironclad was hit 53 times and was taking water through a shot hole which had been made in the deck.

Next in line, *Passaic* had her XI-inch gun disabled for several hours and the turret was temporarily unable to turn. All the plates forming the upper edge of the turret were broken and the pilot house badly dented while she was receiving some 35 hits from the forts. *Montauk*, maneuvering with difficulty, was struck some 14 times with little effect as she, like *Passaic*, turned in *Weehawken's* wake away from the obstructions. *Patapsco*, endeavoring to turn short of *Montauk's* wake, lost headway and failed to obey the helm. She became a sitting target for the guns of Forts Sumter and Moultrie and took 47 hits. Backing, she was brought under control and turned seaward. The flagship, *New Ironsides*, had become unmanageable in the heavy current, and *Catskill* passed her, approaching to within some 600 yards of Sumter where the pointblank fire of her guns blasted a barbette gun from its mount. Caught in the forts' crossfire like the others, *Catskill* received 20 shots, one of which broke the deck plates and deck planking forward, causing her to take water. Meanwhile, *New Ironsides* narrowly escaped destruction as she lay directly over a Confederate electric torpedo containing 2,000 pounds of powder near Fort Wagner. Every effort to fire the torpedo failed, and it was later discovered that a connecting wire had been cut by a wagon passing over it.

Nantucket followed *Catskill* past the flagship and was badly battered by 51 hits, one jamming her turret. *Nahant* took 36 hits: 3 disabled the turret; the impact of another broke off a segment of interior iron weighing nearly 80 pounds which wreaked havoc with the steering gear. Nuts from iron bolts sheered off, fatally wounding the helmsman and injuring the pilot.

Keokuk was compelled to run ahead of the crippled *Nahant* to avoid getting foul of her in the narrow channel and strong tide. This brought the last ironclad less than 600 yards from Fort Sumter, where she remained for half an hour. Colonel Alfred Rhett, CSA, wrote: "She received our undivided attention. . . ." *Keokuk* was riddled by 90 hits, one-fifth of which pierced her at or below the waterline. She was withdrawn from the action and anchored overnight outside of range of the forts, where the crew was able to keep her afloat only because of the calm seas. Next day, 8 April, a breeze came up, *Keokuk* took on more water, and, rapidly filling, sank.

Under Rear Admiral Du Pont ships of the South Atlantic Blockading Squadron assault the strong Confederate harbor defenses on 7 April in an effort to capture Charleston. The fleet was forced to retire, however, after the monitors sustained heavy damage.

With darkness approaching and his ironclads severely battered, Du Pont broke off the action. He reported to Secretary Welles: "When I withdrew the ironclad vessels from action on the evening of the 7th, I did so because I deemed it too late in the day to attempt to force a passage through the obstructions which we had encountered, and I fully intended to resume offensive operations the next day; but when I received the reports of the commanders of the ironclads as to the injuries those vessels had sustained and their performance in action I was fully convinced that a renewal of the attack could not result in the capture of Charleston, but would, in all probability, end in the destruction of a portion of the ironclad fleet and might leave several of them sunk within reach of the enemy (which opinion I afterwards learned was fully shared in by all their commanders). I therefore determined not to renew the attack."

The Confederates had beaten back a serious threat and gained a stunning victory; Du Pont was thankful that the result was "a *failure* instead of a *disaster*." He wrote General Hunter: "I am now satisfied that that place cannot be taken by a purely naval attack, and I am admonished by the condition of these vessels that a persistence in our efforts would end in disaster and might cause us to leave some of our ironclads in the hands of the enemy, which would render it difficult for us to hold those parts of the coast which are now in our possession." Hunter replied: "No country can ever fail that has men capable of facing what your ironclads had yesterday to endure." Admiral Porter later wrote: "It was certainly the hardest task undertaken by the Navy during the war."

Rear Admiral Porter informed Welles that Army troops had been sent up "to take possession of the country through which we lately took the gunboats. When that is secured we can reach the Yazoo as we please, provided the water keeps up. I am preparing to pass the batteries of Vicksburg with most of the fleet. General Grant is marching his army below, and we are going to endeavor to turn Vicksburg and get to Jackson by a very practicable route. . . . The enemy, owing to our late raids on them, have much reduced their force at Vicksburg. They are cut off from all supplies from below; so is Port Hudson." The long joint operation against the Southern stronghold was moving into its final stages.

In a recent artist's conception, U.S.S. Keokuk, a citadel ironclad, is shown sinking off Charleston on 8 April. She had been riddled by nearly 100 shot during the engagement the day before.

U.S.S. *Barataria*, Acting Ensign James F. Perkins, on a reconnaissance mission with troops embarked, struck a snag in Lake Maurepas, Louisiana, and was destroyed by her crew to prevent capture.

8 Mr. Edward C. Gabaudan, secretary to Farragut, arrived on board U.S.S. *Richmond* with a dispatch from the river above after safely floating in a small boat past the Port Hudson batteries. Loyall Farragut, the Admiral's son, vividly described Gabaudan's memorable exploit: "A small dug-out was covered with twigs, ingeniously arranged to resemble the floating trees which were a common sight on the Mississippi. At nightfall Mr. Gabaudan lay down in the bottom of his little craft under the brush, with his revolver and a small paddle by his side, and silently drifted out into the current, followed by the prayers of his shipmates. He reached the *Richmond* in safety, with but one adventure, which came near being his last. His frail bark was swept in so close to the shore that he could distinctly hear the sentinels talking. The size of his craft attracted attention, and a boat put out to make an examination. Gabaudan felt that his time had come; but with a finger on the trigger of his revolver, he determined to fight for his liberty, and quietly awaited discovery. Fortunately for him, the rebels were not in a pulling humor that night, and seemed satisfied with a cursory glance. His mind was greatly relieved when they pronounced him to be 'only a log,' and returned to the shore. About ten o'clock p.m. a rocket was seen to dart up into the air some miles below, a signal of the success of the perilous undertaking."

U.S.S. *Gem of the Sea*, Acting Lieutenant Baxter, seized blockade running British schooner *Maggie Fulton* off Indian River Inlet, Florida. "I am confident," Baxter reported to Rear Admiral Bailey, "that no vessels have run in or out of either Jupiter or Indian River inlets since the 6th of March, 1863, as our boats are in the river whenever the bar will permit them to cross."

9 John A. Quinterro, Confederate Commissioner in Monterrey, Mexico, wrote Secretary of War Benjamin: "Narciso Monturio [of Barcelona, Spain] . . . has invented a vessel for submarine navigation. She is called 'Ictineo' (fishlike vessel). As a man-of-war she can prevent not only the bombardment of the ports, but also the landing of the enemy. If . . . the necessary number of vessels [are] built, no Federal squadron would dare to approach our coasts. . . . The 'Ictineos' have guns which fire under water and also rams and torpedoes. They can navigate in a depth of about twenty-five fathoms. . . . The inventor creates an artificial atmosphere . . . and carries with him the elements of existence." The Confederates were continuously alert for any development that might contest the stranglehold of the North's overwhelming naval superiority.

10 President Jefferson Davis said: "We began this struggle without a single gun afloat, while the resources of our enemy enabled them to gather fleets which, according to their official list published in August last, consisted of 427 vessels, measuring 340,036 tons, and carrying 3,268 guns. Yet we have captured, sunk, or destroyed a number of these vessels, including two large frigates and one sloop of war, while four of their captured steam boats are now in our possession, adding to the strength of our little Navy, which is rapidly gaining in numbers and efficiency."

An expedition led by Lieutenant Commander Selfridge of U.S.S. *Conestoga* cut across Beulah Bend, Mississippi, and destroyed guerrilla stations that had harassed Union shipping on the river.

Boat crew under Lieutenant Benjamin F. Day from U.S.S. *New London*, while reconnoitering Confederate strength in the Sabine City area, captured a small sloop and four prisoners, including Captain Charles Fowler, who had commanded C.S.S. *Josiah Bell* when U.S.S. *Morning Light* and *Velocity* were captured in January 1863.

Landing party under Acting Master John C. Dutch, U.S.S. *Kingfisher*, captured Confederate pickets on Edisto Island, South Carolina.

11 General Beauregard, believing that a renewal of the naval attack on Charleston was imminent, wrote Lieutenant Webb, CSN, regarding an offensive measure to remove this threat: "Upon further reflection, after the discussion of yesterday with Captain Tucker and yourself, I think it would be preferable to attack each of the enemy's seven iron-clads (six monitors and one ironsides), now inside the bar, with at least two of your spar-torpedo row-boats, instead of the number (six in all) already agreed upon. I believe it will be as easy to surprise at the same time the whole of those iron-clads as a part of them. . . . about dark on the first calm night (the sooner the better) I would rendezvous all my boats at the mouth of the creek in the rear of Cummings Point, Morris Island. There I would await the proper hour of the night, which should not be too late, in order to take advantage of the present condition of the moon. . . . Having arrived at the point of the beach designated [opposite the fleet] I would form line of attack, putting my torpedoes in position, and would give orders that my boats should attack by twos any monitor or ironsides they should encounter on their way out, answering to the enemy's hail 'Boats on secret expedition' or merely 'Contrabands'. . . . I feel convinced that with nerve and proper precaution on the part of your boats' crews, and with the protection of a kind Providence, not one of the enemy's monsters, so much boasted of by them, would live to see the next morning's sun." The next day, however, the Union ironclads withdrew outside the bar, foiling the proposed torpedo attack.

Threatened by a "large force" of Confederates, Army commanders at Suffolk, Virginia, requested gunboat support from Rear Admiral S. P. Lee, who speedily replied that there were already three small naval vessels "up the Nansemond or at its mouth." Next day, 12 April, he sent U.S.S. *Commodore Barney*, Lieutenant William B. Cushing, "to assist in repelling the enemy, who are surrounding Suffolk."

Meanwhile, Southerners threatened Union positions on the York River as well, and Yorktown was felt to be in danger. Another appeal for naval support was sent to Lee, who ordered U.S.S. *Commodore Morris* to aid U.S.S. *Crusader* in that area. Whether in the North Carolina Sounds or the Virginia rivers, the demand for the services of the gunboats of the North Atlantic Squadron was great. As Admiral Porter later wrote: "After all, most of these gun-boats were merely improvised for the occasion, and the Army transports, armed with field pieces, would have answered the same purpose. But the soldiers were not used to managing steamers up the narrow streams or handling guns behind the frail bulwarks of wooden gunboats. Only sailors could do that kind of work, and the Army were only too glad to have them do it."

Secretary Welles instructed Rear Admiral Du Pont to "retain a strong force off Charleston, even should you find it impossible to carry the place." Though the large-scale attack 4 days before had failed, it was believed that the presence of the fleet at Charleston would keep the Confederates "in apprehension of a renewed attack, in order that they may be occupied and not come North or go West to the aid of the rebels with whom our forces will soon be in conflict. . . ." The Union's ability to strike with vigor at a variety of points under seapower's flexibility continued to keep Confederate strength dispersed.

12 Rear Admiral Porter advised Secretary Welles of developments in the proposed move below Vicksburg: "I have been endeavoring since I came here to get the batteries of these vessels changed, and have succeeded at last in getting three 11-inch guns placed in the bow of each one. This makes them much more effective. . . . [Major General Grant] proposes to embark his army at Carthage, seize Grand Gulf under fire of the gunboats, and make it the base of his operations. . . . The squadron will pass the [Vicksburg] batteries and engage them while the transports go by in the smoke, passing down, of course, at night. . . . In this operation I act in obedience to the orders of the Department to cooperate with the army, and shall do my best to make them successful." Though preoccupied with the plans to get below Vicksburg, Porter did not neglect other areas of need on the western waters. He ordered eight gunboats to the mouths of the Arkansas and White Rivers to meet any contingency at that point, and reported, "Every point on the Missis-

Flag Ship New Ironsides

Inside Charleston Bar

April 8. 1863

Sir,

I yesterday moved up with Eight Iron clads and this ship and attacked Fort Sumpter, intending to pass it and commence action on its North West face in accordance with my order of battle.

The heavy fire we received from it and Fort Moultrie, and the nature of the obstructions compelled the attack from the outside — It was fierce and obstinate and the gallantry of the Officers & men of the vessels engaged was conspicuous.

Owing to the condition of the tide and an unavoidable accident I had been compelled to delay action until late in the afternoon, and towards evening finding no impression made upon the Fort I made the signal to withdraw the ships, intending to renew the attack this morning.

But the Commanders of the Monitors came on board and reported verbally the injuries to their vessels, when without hesitation or consultation, for I never hold councils of war, I determined not to renew the attack, for in my judgment it would have converted a failure into a disaster, and I will only add that Charleston cannot be taken by a purely naval attack, and tho army could give me no Co-operation — Had I succeeded in entering the harbor I should have had twelve hundred men and thirty two guns, but five of the 8 Iron clads were wholly a partially disabled after a brief engagement.

I have alluded above only to Forts Sumpter and Moultrie but the vessels were also exposed to the fire of the batteries on Cummings Point, Mt Pleasant, The Redan and Fort Beauregard.

Very Respectfully
Your Obed. Servt.

S. F. Du Pont

Extracts from Rear Admiral Du Pont's report to Secretary Welles on his 7 April Charleston assault.

sippi is guarded or patrolled where there is likelihood of a guerilla. The river from Cairo to Vicksburg is as quiet as in time of peace." Porter also sent a sizable force into the Tennessee and Cumberland Rivers. "There are now (or soon will be) 23 vessels in the Tennessee River (including the Marine Brigade), 14 of which carry in all 97 guns, many of them of heavy caliber. The Cumberland River will be reinforced in like manner, as I can spare the light-drafts from below."

Porter wrote Welles about the shortage of men in his Mississippi Squadron: "I have been filling up deficiencies from the army. General Grant has supplied me with 800 soldiers, who are now very efficient. About 600 contrabands are employed in the place of discharged men, and we man the guns with them, the men sent from the North are light built (mostly boys). We are much in need of more experienced men for petty officers. . . ."

Blockade running steamer *Stonewall Jackson*, attempting to get into Charleston, dashed past U.S.S. *Flag* and *Huron*. The blockaders poured a hail of shell after her, several of which holed her hull. Her commander finding escape impossible, *Stonewall Jackson* was run aground and destroyed with her cargo, including Army artillery and some 40,000 Army shoes.

The crew of a launch under Acting Master George C. Andrews, CSN, which had left Mobile on 6 April, captured steamboat *Fox* in the coal yard at à Pass l'Outre, Mississippi. Andrews succeeded in running *Fox* into Mobile through the blockaders' fire on 15 April.

13 U.S.S. *Annie*, Acting Ensign James S. Williams, captured schooner *Mattie* off the Florida Gulf coast.

14 As two days of heavy fighting near Suffolk, Virginia, closed, Lieutenant Cushing informed Rear Admiral S. P. Lee that U.S.S. *Mount Washington* had been temporarily disabled and grounded under heavy fire but had been brought off by U.S.S. *Stepping Stones*. Cushing's own ship, U.S.S. *Commodore Barney*, had been raked heavily by a Confederate shore battery, but he wrote: "I can assure you that the *Barney* and her crew are still in good fighting trim, and we will beat the enemy or sink at our post." The gunboats repeatedly drove Confederate gunners from their rifle pits, only to see them return when the ships' fire slackened. The gunboats were a decisive factor in the Confederates' inability to move across the river to surround the Union troops.

U.S.S. *Estrella*, Lieutenant Commander Augustus P. Cooke; U.S.S. *Arizona*, Acting Lieutenant Upton; and U.S.S. *Calhoun*, Acting Master Meltiah Jordan, supporting operations ashore by General Banks' troops, engaged and destroyed ram C.S.S. *Queen of the West*, Lieutenant E. W. Fuller, in Grand Lake, Louisiana. C.S.S. *Diana* and *Hart* were destroyed on 18 April to prevent their capture. General Banks reported: "Great credit is due to the energy and efficiency shown by the officers of the Navy in this operation."

U.S.S. *Sonoma*, Commander Stevens, captured schooner *Clyde* in the Gulf of Mexico with cargo of cotton and rosin.

U.S.S. *Huntsville*, Acting Lieutenant W. C. Rogers, took blockade running British schooner *Ascension* off the Florida Gulf coast.

Commander Charles F. M. Spotswood wrote Commander Mitchell concerning service on ironclad C.S.S. *Georgia* on the Savannah station: ". . . *anything* that floats at sea will suit me. . . . for being shut up in an Iron Box (for she is not a vessel) is horrible, and with no steam power to move her, in fact she is made fast here to a pile pier. . . . She is not a fit command for a Sargent of Marines. . . ."

C.S.S. *Missouri* was launched at Shreveport, Louisiana. Though the steamer mounted six guns, she never saw action and remained above the obstructions in the Red River until war's end.

15 C.S.S. *Alabama*, Captain Semmes, captured whalers *Kate Cory* and *Lafayette* off the island of Fernando de Noronha, Brazil. Semmes burned *Lafayette* this date and *Kate Cory* two days later.

U.S.S. *Monticello*, Lieutenant Commander Braine, captured schooner *Odd Fellow* near Little River, North Carolina, with cargo of turpentine and rosin.

U.S.S. *William G. Anderson*, Acting Lieutenant Frederic S. Hill, took schooner *Royal Yacht* in the Gulf of Mexico with cargo of cotton.

16 U.S.S. *Hendrick Hudson*, Acting Lieutenant Cate, captured blockade running British schooner *Teresa* off the coast of Florida.

U.S.S. *Vanderbilt*, Lieutenant Baldwin, seized British blockade runner *Gertrude* off the Bahama Islands.

16–17 Gunboats under Rear Admiral Porter engaged and ran past the Confederate batteries at Vicksburg shepherding Army transports to New Carthage below the Southern citadel. The force included U.S.S. *Benton, Lafayette, Louisville, Pittsburg, Mound City, Carondelet,* and *Tuscumbia*; U.S.S. *General Sterling Price* was lashed to the starboard side of *Lafayette* for the passage, as was tug *Ivy* to *Benton*. Each ship, except *Benton*, also towed a coal barge containing 10,000 bushels of coal. *Lafayette*, Captain Walke, hampered by the ship lashed to her side, received nine "effective" shots through her casemate and had her coal barge sunk. Transport *Henry Clay* was sunk, with no loss of life, during the passage and another, *Forest Queen*, was temporarily disabled but was successfully aided by *Tuscumbia*, Lieutenant Commander James W. Shirk. Under fire for 2½ hours, beginning shortly after 11 p.m. on the 16th, the squadron suffered what Porter termed only "very light" loss. He reported that all ships were ready for service within half an hour after the passage. "Altogether," he remarked, "we were very fortunate; the vessels had some narrow escapes, but were saved in most instances by the precautions taken to protect them. They were covered with heavy logs and bales of wet hay, which were found to be an excellent defense." A memorandum in the Secretary of the Navy's office recorded: "The passage of the fleet by Vicksburg was a damper to the spirits of all rebel sympathizers along the Mississippi for everyone was so impressed with the absurdity of our gunboats getting safely past their batteries without being knocked to pieces that they would not admit to themselves that it would be undertaken until they saw the gunboats moving down the river all safe and sound. Vicksburg was despaired of from that moment." The successful steaming of the squadron past the heavy batteries contributed to the early seizure of Grand Gulf, the eventual fall of Vicksburg itself, and ultimately the total control of the entire Mississippi.

17 U.S.S. *Wanderer*, Acting Master Eleazer S. Turner, took schooner *Annie B* southwest of Egmont Key, Florida, bound for Havana with cargo of cotton.

C.S.S. *Florida*, Lieutenant Maffitt, captured and destroyed ship *Commonwealth* off the coast of Brazil, bound from New York to San Francisco.

18 Boat expedition to reconnoiter Sabine City under command of Lieutenant Commander Read, U.S.S. *New London*, and Lieutenant Commander McDermut, U.S.S. *Cayuga*, was surprised at the lighthouse and driven off by Confederate troops.

U.S.S. *Susquehanna*, Commodore Hitchcock, captured schooner *Alabama* off the Florida Gulf coast with cargo including wine, coffee, nails, and dry goods.

U.S.S. *Stettin*, Acting Master James R. Beers, seized steamer *St. Johns* off Cape Romain, South Carolina.

U.S.S. *Gem of the Sea*, Acting Lieutenant Baxter, captured and destroyed blockade running British schooner *Inez* off Indian River Inlet, Florida.

19 U.S.S. *Housatonic*, Captain William Taylor, took sloop *Neptune*, attempting to run the blockade out of Charleston with cargo of cotton and turpentine.

U.S.S. *Powhatan*, Captain Steedman, captured schooner *Major E. Willis* near Charleston with cargo of cotton.

20 A joint Army-Navy attack succeeded in capturing a strong Confederate position at Hill's Point on the Nansemond River, Virginia, taking 5 howitzers and some 160 prisoners, as well as denying the South the use of an effective position from which to shell the flotilla guarding the Union Army position near Suffolk. Brigadier General George W. Getty wrote Rear Admiral S. P. Lee: "I beg to express my most sincere thanks to Captain Lamson, USN, his officers and crews for the gallantry, energy and ability displayed by them in the operations . . . resulting in the capture of one of the enemy's batteries on the west side of the Nansemond, and a number of prisoners." Later that night, 20 April, the Confederates evacuated their battery at Reed's Ferry, and Lieutenant Cushing reported: "All is now clear at this point [the western branch of the Nansemond], and if the army fortify, we can hold the position against any force, the gunboats protecting both flanks." Though there were intermittent skirmishes for almost 2 weeks following this action, the back of the planned Confederate offensive was broken. As Cushing wrote on 21 April: "I think that active work is nearly over in this quarter." Both Cushing and Lamson were cited by Secretary Welles for their gallantry and meritorious services.

U.S.S. *General Sterling Price*, Commander Selim E. Woodworth, and U.S.S. *Tuscumbia*, Lieutenant Commander Shirk, reconnoitered down the Mississippi River from New Carthage to the Confederate stronghold at Grand Gulf in preparation for the Union assault. Rear Admiral Porter reported to Major General Grant: "The rebels are at work fortifying. Three guns mounted on a bluff 100 feet high, pointing upriver. Two deep excavations are made in the side of the hill (fresh earth); it can not be seen whether guns are mounted on them or not." Porter urged Grant to move as quickly as possible: "My opinion is that they will move heaven and earth to stop us if we don't go ahead. I could go down and settle the batteries, but if disabled would not be in condition to cover the landing when it takes place, and I think it should be done together. If the troops just leave all their tents behind and take only provisions, we can be in Grand Gulf in four days. I don't want to make a failure, and am sure that a combined attack will succeed beautifully."

U.S.S. *Estrella*, Lieutenant Commander Cooke, with U.S.S. *Clifton*, *Arizona*, and *Calhoun*, engaged and received the surrender of Fort Burton, Butte à la Rose, Louisiana. Third Assistant Engineer George W. Baird noted in his diary: "The fight was short, sharp and decisive. It was done after the style of Daddy Farragut: we rush in. . . . We rushed right up to it and the four black vessels all firing made a savage appearance."

Porter reported the results of an examination of the hulk of U.S.S. *Indianola*, captured by the Confederates and subsequently sunk below Vicksburg: "Her hull and machinery seem to be uninjured; the woodwork on deck has all been burned. The casemate for the 11-inch guns has been blown to pieces; the iron plates lying around the deck. I have had it taken to strengthen the gunboats now here. The 11-inch gun carriages are still in the wreck, much shattered. The 9-inch gun carriages were burned when the rebels heard a gunboat (the imitation monitor) was coming down. One 11-inch and one 9-inch gun were removed and a few shells." Recommending that an attempt be made to raise *Indianola*, Porter added: "It would be a great comfort to have the *Indianola* afloat once more and still on the Navy list."

U.S.S. *Octorara*, Commander Collins, captured British blockade runner *W. Y. Leitch* east of Florida with cargo of salt.

U.S.S. *Lodona*, Commander Edmund R. Colhoun, seized British schooner *Minnie* attempting to run the blockade at Bull's Bay, South Carolina, with cargo of salt.

The naval station at Mound City, Illinois, was one of the major facilities on the western waters.

A landing party under Lieutenant Commander George U. Morris, U.S.S. *Port Royal*, captured cotton awaiting transportation at Apalachicola, Florida. Three prisoners and a quantity of canister, shot, and chain were also taken.

C.S.S. *Oreto*, Lieutenant Samuel W. Averett, captured at sea and bonded ship *Kate Dyer* bound for Antwerp, Belgium.

21 Secretary Mallory wrote Commander Bullock: "The recent repulse of the enemy before Charleston will show the world that we have not been idle with regard to ordnance and that the enemy's ironclads suffered severely. At a recent experimental trial of the triple-banded Brooke navy gun, a wrought iron bolt was driven through 8 inches of iron and 18 inches of wood. The distance was 260 yards, 16 pounds of powder, with a bolt of 140 pounds."

Rear Admiral Dahlgren noted in his private journal: "I had a conversation with the Secretary about Charleston. He is not satisfied and thinks Du Pont gave up too soon. I reminded him that Du Pont was a judicious and brave officer, and that the Captains of the iron-clads who were chosen officers concurred with Du Pont."

Rear Admiral Porter, in U.S.S. *Lafayette*, personally reconnoitered the Confederate works at Grand Gulf. He found a "strong fort" under construction and shelled the workers out. Confederate steamer *Charm* attempted to land supplies for the fort but was driven back up the Big Black River. By the 24th, Porter had stationed his gunboats so that they commanded the upper battery at Grand Gulf and closed off the mouth of the Big Black, "through which ammunition and supplies are brought down, and by which the rebels have hitherto obtained supplies from

Red River." Porter continued to call for quick action. "Dispatch," he urged Major General McClernand, "is all important at this moment."

Confederate guns at Vicksburg opened fire on Union Army steamers attempting a night passage of the batteries. *Tigress* was sunk and *Empire City* was totally disabled; *Moderator* was badly damaged, but *J. W. Cheeseman*, *Anglo-Saxon*, and *Horizon* passed safely.

Farragut on board U.S.S. *Hartford* wrote to Rear Admiral Bailey about his passage of Port Hudson: "My disaster in passing Port Hudson was a misfortune incidental to battle, but the damage, with the exception of the loss of the *Mississippi* was nothing: the smoke was so thick that the pilots could not see. I worked through by the compass as I did by Jackson and had my pilot in the mizzentop. . . . I have now been absent from my command six weeks and know nothing of what is going on below. . . . they say no news is good news, and I hear of no disasters, and therefore hope for the best."

U.S.S. *Octorara*, Commander Collins, seized blockade running British schooner *Handy* east of Florida with cargo of salt.

U.S.S. *Rachel Seaman*, Acting Lieutenant Quincy A. Hooper, captured schooner *Nymph* attempting to run the blockade off Pass Cavallo, Texas, with cargo including coffee, rice, shoes, and medicine.

22   U.S.S. *Mount Vernon*, Acting Lieutenant Trathen, captured schooner *St. George* off New Inlet, North Carolina, with cargo including salt and rum.

Rear Admiral Farragut gave his thoughts on changes in the Navy uniform in a letter to Assistant Secretary Fox: "Pray do not let those officers at Washington be changing our uniform every week or two. . . . I wish that uniform [for Rear Admiral] had been simply a broad stripe of lace on

Extracts from Rear Admiral Farragut's letter to Assistant Secretary Fox recommending changes in the official uniform.

the cuff—say an inch and a quarter wide—with a narrow stripe of a quarter of an inch above it, and a little rosette with a silver star in the centre. The star is the designation of the Admiral and therefore should be visible . . . but this adding stripes until they reach a man's elbow, appears to me to be a great error . . . you must count the stripes to ascertain the officer's rank, which at any distance is almost impossible. . . ." The practical uniform, Farragut believed, should be "well suited to the necessities of the service—easy to procure—not expensive—easily preserved—and the grades distinctly marked." It is essentially the one in use today.

23 Steamers *Merrimac, Charleston,* and *Margaret and Jessie* successfully ran the blockade into Wilmington. Brigadier General William H. C. Whiting, CSA, reported: "The *Merrimac* brings me three splendid Blakely guns, 8-inch rifled 13-pounders."

C.S.S. *Florida,* Lieutenant Maffitt, captured and burned at sea bark *Henrietta* bound for Rio de Janeiro with cargo including flour.

U.S.S. *Tioga,* Commander Clary, seized blockade running British sloop *Justina* bound from Indian River, Florida, to Nassau with cargo of cotton.

U.S.S. *Pembina,* Lieutenant Commander Jonathan Young, captured sloop *Elias Beckwith* near Mobile.

24 The extent to which the South was forced to dispersion of troops and weapons was graphically illustrated in an exchange of messages between General Beauregard at Charleston and Secretary of War J. A. Seddon. This date, Beauregard wrote requesting Whitworth guns, "one to place on Morris Island, to cover at long range the bar and enable us to get guns off the *Keokuk,* also to keep the enemy from replacing buoys and surveying [the] bar; the other to place on Sullivan's Island to cover vessels running the blockade [which] frequently run ashore." Next day, Seddon replied: "I regret to be unable to spare the guns even for the object mentioned. The claims of Wilmington and the Mississippi are now paramount."

U.S.S. *De Soto,* Captain William M. Walker, captured blockade running schooners *General Prim* and *Rapid,* bound from Mobile to Havana, and sloops *Jane Adelie* and *Bright* with cargoes of cotton in the Gulf of Mexico.

C.S.S. *Alabama,* Captain Semmes, captured and burned whaler *Nye* off the coast of Brazil with cargo of sperm and whale oil. Semmes later wrote: "The fates seemed to have a grudge against these New England fishermen, and would persist in throwing them in my way, although I was not on a whaling-ground. This was the sixteenth I had captured—a greater number than had been captured from the English by Commodore David Porter, in his famous cruise in the Pacific, in the frigate *Essex,* during the war of 1812."

C.S.S. *Florida,* Lieutenant Maffitt, captured and destroyed ship *Oneida,* bound from Shanghai to New York with cargo of tea.

U.S.S. *Western World,* Acting Master Samuel B. Gregory, and U.S.S. *Samuel Rotan* took schooners *Martha Ann* and *A. Carson* off Horn Harbor, Virginia.

U.S.S. *Pembina,* Lieutenant Commander Young, captured schooner *Joe Flanner,* bound from Havana to Mobile.

25 C.S.S. *Georgia,* Lieutenant W. L. Maury, captured ship *Dictator* with cargo of coal off the Cape Verde Islands. Maury burned the prize the next day.

26 U.S.S. *Lexington,* Lieutenant Commander Fitch, joined the ram fleet under Brigadier General Alfred W. Ellet to engage and disperse Confederate cavalry concentrated at the mouth of Duck River, Tennessee.

C.S.S. *Alabama*, Captain Semmes, captured and burned ship *Dorcas Prince* at sea, east of Natal, Brazil, with cargo of coal.

U.S.S. *De Soto*, Captain W. M. Walker, seized British schooner *Clarita* in the Gulf of Mexico, bound from Havana to Matamoras.

U.S.S. *Sagamore*, Lieutenant Commander English, captured schooner *New Year* of Tortugas, Florida, with cargo of turpentine and cotton.

27 Rear Admiral Porter issued a general order concerning the attack on Grand Gulf: "It is reported that there are four positions where guns are placed, in which case it is desirable that all four places should be engaged at the same time. The *Louisville, Carondelet, Mound City,* and *Pittsburg* will proceed in advance, going down slowly, firing their bow guns at the guns in the first battery on the bluff, passing 100 yards from it, and 150 yards apart from each. As they pass the battery on the bluff they will fire grape, canister, and shrapnel, cut at one-half second, and percussion shell from rifled guns." Porter gave specific orders for the subsequent actions of the gunboats, and instructed: "The *Lafayette* will drop down . . . stern foremost, until within 600 yards, firing her rifled guns with percussion shells at the upper battery. The *Tuscumbia* will round to outside the *Benton*, not firing over her while so doing; after rounding to, she will keep astern and inside of the *Benton*, using her bow guns while the *Benton* fires her broadside guns. The *Tuscumbia* and *Benton* will also fire their stern guns at the forts below them whenever they will bear, using shell together."

Under Acting Master Louis A. Brown, boat crews from U.S.S. *Monticello* and *Matthew Vassar* boarded and destroyed British blockade runner *Golden Liner* in Murrell's Inlet, South Carolina. The ship contained a cargo of flour, brandy, sugar, and coffee.

U.S.S. *Preble*, Acting Master William F. Shankland, was accidentally destroyed by fire while at anchor off Pensacola.

28 U.S. tug *Lily*, Acting Master R. H. Timmonds, attempting to cross the bow of U.S.S. *Choctaw*, Lieutenant Commander Francis M. Ramsay, at anchor in the Yazoo River, was swept by the current into *Choctaw*'s ram and sunk.

29 Gunboats under Rear Admiral Porter engaged the heavy Confederate works at Grand Gulf, "which," the Admiral acknowledged, "were very formidable." In the 5½-hour battle, the gunboats silenced the lower batteries but could succeed in stopping the fire from the upper forts only "for a short time." Army transports passed safely below the batteries at night. Grand Gulf had been strongly fortified since Rear Admiral Farragut passed the batteries the preceeding summer, "to prevent his coming up again," and four batteries were placed a quarter of a mile apart, completely commanding the Mississippi River.

Though U.S.S. *Benton, Tuscumbia,* and *Pittsburg* were "pretty much cut up" in the engagement, the expedition was successful and the net result was summed up by Porter: "We are now in a position to make a landing where the general [Grant] pleases."

A Confederate soldier wrote on 30 April from Grand Gulf remarking on the state of affairs after the gunboat attack: "We came here two weeks ago and have had hot times ever since. Enemy from their gunboats have shelled us every day. Yesterday our batteries gave them a fight. The firing beat Oak Hill, Elkhorn, Corinth, Hutchin's Bridge, or anything I ever heard. I believe, too, they gave us rather the worst of it. We did not sink a single boat, while they silenced one of our batteries, dismounted 4 pieces, killed Colonel [William] Wade, commanding artillery, and one of his staff, and some 5 or 6 men."

29 April–1 May Union Army and Navy expedition feigned an attack on Confederate batteries at Haynes' Bluff on the Yazoo River. The force consisted of U.S.S. *Tyler, Choctaw, DeKalb, Signal, Romeo, Linden, Petrel, Black Hawk,* and 3 mortar boats under Lieutenant Commander Breese and

Rear Admiral David D. Porter
Mississippi Squadron

Gunboats under Rear Admiral Porter bombard Grand Gulf.

Firing for more than five hours, the ships contributed to the eventual evacuation of the heavily fortified works early in May. (Bottom picture is from a painting which was in the possession of Admiral Porter at one time.)

10 large transports carrying troops under command of Major General W. T. Sherman. The feint was made to prevent Confederates from reinforcing Grand Gulf. On the 29th the expedition proceeded as far as Chickasaw Bayou. As the force departed on the morning of the 30th, *Petrel*, remained at Old River on station; the remaining vessels moved up the Yazoo with *Choctaw* and *DeKalb* opening fire on the main works at Drumgould's Bluff and *Tyler* and *Black Hawk* opening on the fieldworks and batteries. Though instructed not to conduct an actual assault, the feint was so vigorously prosecuted that *Choctaw*, Lieutenant Commander Ramsay, was struck 53 times by Confederate guns. The soldiers were landed and "marched up toward Haynes' Bluff on the only roadway, the levee, making quite a display, and threatening one also." Naval gunfire supported the soldiers throughout the demonstration, which lasted through 1 May. The evening of the 1st, the expedition returned to the mouth of the Yazoo. Porter reported to Secretary Welles: "The plan succeeded admirably, though the vessels were more exposed than the occasion called for; still as they met with no casualties, with the exception of the hulls, it mattered but little."

U.S.S. *Juniata*, Commander John M. B. Clitz, captured schooner *Harvest* at sea north of the Bahamas with cargo of cotton.

30 April–1 May   Major General Grant ferried his troops across the Mississippi River at Bruinsburg to commence the work of isolating Vicksburg from reinforcements.

MAY

1   As requested by Secretary Mallory, the Confederate Congress enacted legislation "To create a Provisional Navy of the Confederate States." The object of the act, as explained by Captain Semmes, was ". . . without interfering with the rank of the officers in the Regular Navy, to cull out from the navy-list, younger and more active men, and put them in the Provisional Navy, with increased rank. The Regular Navy became, thus, a kind of retired list, and the Secretary of the Navy was enabled to accomplish his object of bringing forward younger officers for active service, without wounding the feelings of the older officers, by promoting their juniors over their heads, on the same list." At this time the Confederate Congress also provided that: ". . . all persons serving in the land forces of the Confederate States who shall desire to be transferred to the naval service, and whose transfer as seamen or ordinary seamen shall be applied for by the Secretary of the Navy, shall be transferred from the land to the naval service. . . ." The Confederate Navy suffered from an acute shortage of seamen. Mallory complained that the law was not complied with, and that hundreds of men had applied for naval duty but were not transferred.

Boat expedition from U.S.S. *Western World*, Acting Master S. B. Gregory, and U.S.S. *Crusader*, Acting Master Andrews, destroyed two Confederate schooners aground at Milford Haven, Virginia.

U.S.S. *Kanawha*, Lieutenant Commander Mayo, captured schooner *Dart*, bound from Havana to Mobile.

2   Captain John Rodgers wrote Secretary Welles relative to the April attack on Charleston: "The punishment which the monitors are able to stand is wonderful—but it cannot be denied that their gun gear is more liable to accident than was foreseen. Battles are won by two qualities, ability to endure, and ability to injure. The first we possess in an unrivalled degree—the latter one more sparingly. No vessels have ever been under such a fire as that of Charleston before, since the guns are new inventions only perfected since the Crimean War. When a man is in a tight place, he is to do the best he can—that best is often not a pleasant choice. Still if it is the best he can do, it is a great want of wisdom not to do the best he can. Experiment before the most formidable modern artillery has demonstrated that the monitors are more liable to lose their power of shooting than was foreseen—but it does not appear that these deficiencies are irremediable even in the present monitors. . . . the vessels were fast getting hors de combat. No one can say what would have been the result of a renewal of the fight—but if after a renewal we had been driven out, and left a single monitor to fall into the enemy's hands then the whole character of

the war would have changed—the wooden blockade would have been at an end—as far at least as Charleston is concerned, as far indeed as she could get along the coast. Seeing the damage we received and not knowing the injury we were doing, the Admiral did not choose to risk the chances of a combat à l'outrance which if it went against us would entail such momentous consequences. It was not fair game. In losing a couple of monitors to them we should receive far more injury than the taking of Charleston would advance our cause."

Two boat crews from U.S.S. *Roebuck*, Acting Master John Sherrill, seized blockade running British schooner *Emma Amelia* off St. Joseph's Bay, Florida, with cargo including flour and wine.

U.S.S. *Perry*, Acting Master William D. Urann, captured blockade running schooner *Alma*, bound from Bermuda to Beaufort, South Carolina, with cargo of salt and liquor.

U.S.S. *Sacramento*, Captain Charles S. Boggs, seized blockade running British schooner *Wanderer* off Murrell's Inlet, North Carolina, with cargo of salt and herring.

2–9 Union gunboats under Lieutenant Commander Selfridge, protecting steamers from guerrilla activity in the Greenville, Mississippi, vicinity, responded quickly when such action required it. On 2 May steamer *Era* was fired upon 3 miles above Greenville. U.S.S. *Cricket*, Acting Lieutenant Amos R. Langthorne, engaged the Confederate battery and then convoyed steamer *Champion* downstream the following day. In *Cricket*'s absence, steamer *Minnesota* was destroyed by Southern guerrilla troops. U.S.S. *Conestoga* drove the force away and remained in the area until the evening of the 7th, when, after coaling U.S.S. *Cricket* and *Rattler*, she returned to the mouth of the White River. Next day, Selfridge ordered U.S.S. *General Bragg* to "destroy the property in the vicinity of the recent firing upon the gunboat *Cricket* and transport *Minnesota*." On the 9th this order was carried out and "houses etc. . . . affording a protection to the enemy" were destroyed, after which the Union ships returned to their normal stations.

3 Having paved the way for a final assault on Grand Gulf with the attack of 29 April (see entry that date), Rear Admiral Porter once again moved his gunboats against the strong Confederate batteries. The Southerners, however, finding their position totally untenable, Grant having taken his army into the country back of Grand Gulf, had evacuated. The great land-sea pincer could now close on Vicksburg. As Porter remarked to Secretary Welles: ". . . it is with great pleasure that I report that the Navy holds the door to Vicksburg." In a general order the Admiral praised those under his command: "I take this occasion to thank the officers and men engaged in the attack on the forts at Grand Gulf for the unflinching gallantry displayed in that affair. Never has there been so long and steady a fight against forts so well placed and ably commanded. . . . We have met losses which we can not but deplore; still, we should not regret the death of those who died so nobly at their guns. Officers and men, let us always be ready to make the sacrifice when duty requires it."

Porter departed Grand Gulf with his gunboat squadron and rendezvoused that evening with the Farragut fleet at the mouth of the Red River. After obtaining supplies, he proceeded up the River the next day with U.S.S. *Benton*, *Lafayette*, *Pittsburg*, *Sterling Price*, ram *Switzerland*, and tug *Ivy*. U.S.S. *Estrella* and *Arizona* joined en route. The evening of 5 May, the ships arrived at Fort De Russy, Louisiana, "a powerful casemated work" which the Confederates had recently evacuated in the face of the naval threat. Porter pushed past a heavy obstruction in the river and proceeded to Alexandria, Louisiana, which he took possession of formally on the morning of the 7th, "without encountering any resistance." Subsequently turning the town over to Army troops, and unable to continue upriver because of the low water, Porter's force returned to Fort De Russy and partially destroyed it. Porter also sent U.S.S. *Sterling Price*, *Pittsburg*, *Arizona*, and ram *Switzerland* up the Black River on a reconnaissance. At Harrisonburg these ships encountered heavy batteries, which they engaged with little effect because of the position of the guns "on

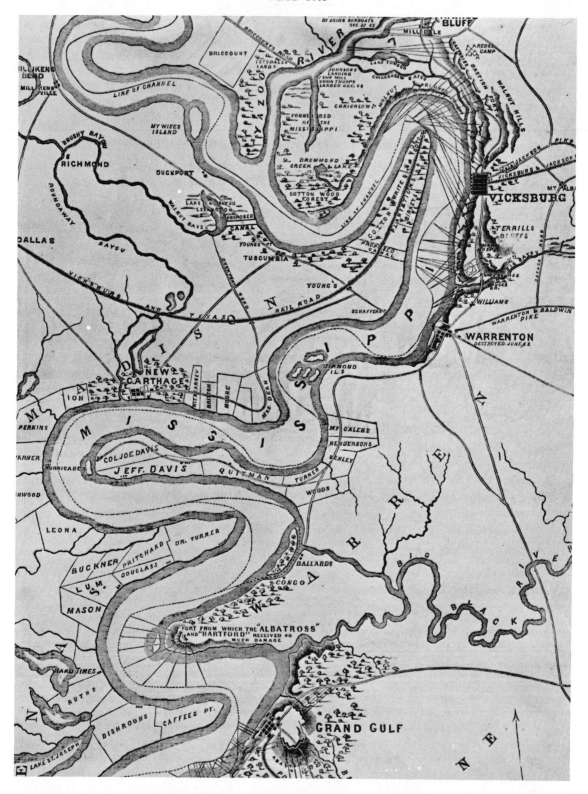

The Mississippi River from the mouth of the Yazoo to Grand Gulf. Until Vicksburg fell in early July 1863, this section of the Father of Waters was the scene of concentrated action.

high hills." Leaving the larger portion of his force at the Red River, Porter returned to Grand Gulf on the 13th.

Confederate troops under Captain Edward E. Hobby, CSA, captured a launch and drove off two other boats from U.S.S. *William G. Anderson*, Acting Lieutenant Hill, at St. Joseph's Island, Texas. The Union boats were salvaging cotton from a sloop which had been run ashore on 30 April.

3 C.S.S. *Alabama*, Captain Semmes, captured and burned bark *Union Jack* and ship *Sea Lark* off Brazil.

4 A part of Rear Admiral Porter's squadron having arrived off the Red River the previous evening, Rear Admiral Farragut sent a dispatch to Secretary Welles: "Feeling now that my instructions of October 2, 1862, have been carried out by my maintenance of the blockade of Red River until the arrival of Admiral Porter . . . I shall return to New Orleans as soon as practicable, leaving the *Hartford* and *Albatross* at the mouth of Red River to await the result of the combined attack upon Alexandria, but with orders to Commodore Palmer to avail himself of the first good opportunity to run down past Port Hudson." As the Admiral left *Hartford*, the crew manned the rigging and filled the air with cheers in tribute to him.

U.S.S. *Albatross*, Lieutenant Commander John E. Hart, on a reconnaissance up the Red River, engaged armed iron steamers *Grand Duke* and *Mary T* and Confederate cavalry near Fort De Russy. The Union gunboat sustained considerable damage and was compelled to withdraw.

U.S.S. *Chocura*, Lieutenant Commander Truxtun, with U.S.S. *Maratanza* in company, seized sloop *Express* off Charleston with cargo of salt.

U.S.S. *Kennebec*, Lieutenant Commander John H. Russell, captured schooner *Juniper*, bound from Havana to Mobile.

5 Major General John A. Dix wrote Rear Admiral S. P. Lee, requesting naval assistance and support during an expedition on the York River: "I need two gunboats to cover the landing of the troops." Lee assigned U.S.S. *Commodore Morris*, *Morse*, and *Mystic* to this duty and directed Lieutenant Commander Gillis to ". . . give the army all the assistance in your power." Two days later the Union vessels convoyed the Army transports as far as West Point and supported the landing. Guarding the troops until the soldiers' line of entrenchments was secure, Gillis detailed *Morse* and *Mystic* to remain on station to "repel any attack that may be made, as their guns command the peninsula completely."

U.S.S. *Tahoma*, Lieutenant Commander A. A. Semmes, captured schooner *Crazy Jane* in the Gulf of Mexico northwest of Charlotte Harbor, Florida, with cargo of cotton and turpentine.

6 Commander North, CSN, wrote Secretary Mallory from Scotland regarding ships being built in England: "For the first time I begin to fear that our vessels stand in much danger of being seized by this Government. I have written to our minister in France to know if this ship can be put under the French flag; this will involve some expense, but shall not consider a few thousand pounds . . . if we can only succeed in getting out . . . aiding to raise the blockade and making captures of some of their vessels, which may prove valuable additions to our little navy."

Rear Admiral Dahlgren noted in his private journal: "Captain Drayton came in about suppertime from New York, where he had brought the *Passaic* from Port Royal. He says it would be madness to go into Charleston again, and all the Captains who were in the action so agree fully. He thinks Dupont intended to renew the attack, but when the Captains of the iron-clads assembled in his ship, and made their reports, he gave it up."

C.S.S. *Florida*, Lieutenant Maffitt, captured brig *Clarence* off the coast of Brazil. *Clarence* was converted into a Confederate cruiser under Lieutenant Charles Read who wrote: "I propose to take the brig which we have just captured, and with a crew of twenty men to proceed to Hampton Roads and cut out a gunboat or steamer of the enemy." Maffitt concurred with the daring plan and ordered *Clarence* to raid Union shipping at either Hampton Roads or Baltimore.

U.S.S. *R. R. Cuyler*, Lieutenant Commander James E. Jouett, captured steamer *Eugenie* bound from Havana to Mobile.

U.S.S. *Dragon*, Acting Master G. E. Hill, seized schooner *Samuel First* attempting to run the blockade above Potomac Creek, Virginia.

7　The Charleston *Mercury* reported: "The guns of this famous ironclad [U.S.S. *Keokuk*] now lie on the South Commercial wharf. They consist of two long XI-inch columbiads, and will be mounted for our defense, valuable acquisitions, no less than handsome trophies of the battle of Charleston Harbor. . . . The turret had to be unbolted, or unscrewed, and taken off before the guns could be slung for removal. This was an unpleasant job of some difficulty, the labor being performed under water, when the sea was smooth, and in the night time only. Those engaged in the undertaking, going in the small boat of the fort, were sometimes protected from the enemy by the presence of our gunboats; at other times not. One gun was raised last week, being removed by the old lightboat. General Ripley himself, night before last, went down to superintend the removal of the second gun. Enterprise, even with scant means, can accomplish much."

8　Secretary Welles received Rear Admiral Porter's dispatch regarding the fall of Grand Gulf and informed President Lincoln. "The news," wrote Welles, "was highly gratifying to the President, who had not heard of it until I met him at the Cabinet-meeting."

Union Mortar Flotilla under Commander Charles H. B. Caldwell, supported by U.S.S. *Richmond*, Captain Alden, opened the bombardment of the Confederate works at Port Hudson, Louisiana.

U.S.S. *Canandaigua*, Captain Joseph F. Green, seized blockade running steamer *Cherokee* off Charleston with cargo of cotton.

U.S.S. *Flag*, Commander James H. Strong, captured schooner *Amelia* attempting to run the blockade out of Charleston late at night with cargo of cotton. While under tow, *Amelia* developed a serious leak in a storm on the 15th and had to be abandoned.

U.S.S. *Primrose*, Master William T. Street, captured schooner *Sarah Lavinia* at Corrotoman Creek, Virginia.

9　Captain Case, commanding U.S.S. *Iroquois*, reported that the Confederates were mounting guns on the northern faces of Fort Fisher at Wilmington. "They appear," he wrote Rear Admiral S. P. Lee, "to be large caliber." This defensive strengthening of the Southern position was in keeping with the view voiced by Lieutenant John Taylor Wood, CSN, in a 14 February 1863, letter to President Davis concerning the defenses of Wilmington: "The batteries covering the water approaches, as far as I am able to judge, are well placed and admirably constructed. But the great want, the absolute necessity of the place if it is to be held against naval attack, is heavy guns, larger caliber." So well did the Confederates do their job that Fort Fisher successfully dominated Cape Fear until the massive amphibious operation in January 1865.

U.S.S. *Aroostook*, Lieutenant Commander Franklin, seized schooner *Sea Lion* bound from Mobile to Havana with cargo of cotton.

10　U.S.S. *Mound City*, Lieutenant Commander Bryon Wilson, reconnoitering near Warrenton, Mississippi took a recently constructed battery under fire and "in a short time it was all in a blaze." Rear Admiral Porter observed: "Thus ended a fort in the space of an hour which had taken the rebels five months to build, working mostly day and night." This form of constant hammering by the gunboats at every point along the western waters sapped Confederate strength and resources.

Boat crews from U.S.S. *Owasco*, Lieutenant Commander John Madigan, Jr., and U.S.S. *Katahdin*, Lieutenant Commander Philip C. Johnson, burned blockade runner *Hanover* off Galveston.

12 Writing of the significance of Farragut's operations in the Mississippi below Vicksburg, Commodore H. H. Bell said: "I am one of those who attaches more importance to the admiral's brilliant move up the river than to anything that has been done by navy or army since capture of New Orleans. It was the finishing stroke to that great blow, and I am glad the admiral did it single handed, unassisted from other quarters. The want of provisions soon became sensibly felt from Vicksburg to Richmond. . . . It was better than any battle, for it is of wider influence and more generally felt than any battle. Man cannot hold together without food. . . . It was gallantly done, and I think the admiral has fairly wedded his name to the Mississippi through all ages to come."

Having begun an expedition up the Tennessee River on 5 May to destroy "every kind of boat that could serve the rebels to cross the river," gunboats under Lieutenant Commander S. L. Phelps supported an Army assault on Confederate troops at Linden, Tennessee. "Along the river," Phelps reported, "I heard of detachments of rebel cavalry at various points. . . . At Linden . . . there was a rebel force of this kind posted. I arranged with Colonel [William K. M.] Breckenridge to cross his small force and cover different points with the gunboats, places to which he could retreat if need be, while he should attempt to surprise Linden." Taking the Union cavalry on board the gunboats, Phelps transported them across the river "with little noise," thereby enabling the surprise attack to be completely successful. In many effective ways mobile naval support of Army movements extended the effective use of seapower deep into the arteries of the Confederacy.

U.S.S. *Conemaugh*, Commander Reed Werden, and U.S.S. *Monticello*, Lieutenant Commander Braine, stood in close to shore at Murrell's Inlet, South Carolina, and bombarded five schooners aground there. Werden reported: "It affords me pleasure to state that so accurate was our firing that in less than an hour we had fired about 100 bales of cotton on the beach near the schooners, set one schooner on fire, and more or less injured all the others in spars and hull."

13 The persistent Army-Navy siege and assault on Vicksburg compelled Confederate strategists to withdraw much needed troops from the eastern front in an effort to bring relief to their beleagured forces in the west. General Beauregard and others warned repeatedly of the possible disasters such loss of strength in the Charleston area and elsewhere might bring. This date, Confederate Secretary of War James A. Seddon wrote to those objecting to the transfer of troops from Charleston to Vicksburg: ". . . I beg you to reflect on the vital importance of the Mississippi to our cause, to South Carolina, and to Charleston itself. Scarce any point in the Confederacy can be deemed more essential, for the 'cause of each is the cause of all,' and the sundering of the Confederacy [along the line of the Mississippi] would be felt as almost a mortal blow to the most remote parts."

General Banks wrote Rear Admiral Farragut that the withdrawal of U.S.S. *Hartford* and other ships down river from above Port Hudson "would lose to us all that has been gained in the campaigns for the passage of the fleet to this day, as it would reopen to Port Hudson the now closed avenue of supplies." Farragut responded on 15 May and directed that Commodore James S. Palmer remain above "so long as he can contribute to the fall of Port Hudson."

Boat expedition from U.S.S. *Kingfisher*, Acting Master John C. Dutch, departed St. Helena Sound for Edisto, South Carolina, where previous reconnaissance missions had revealed a large quantity of corn was stored. The expedition returned five days later with 800 bushels. "My object," Dutch reported, "in doing this was, first, to prevent its falling into rebel hands, and, second, to supply the people in this vicinity."

Transports carrying troops and supplies on the western waters, such as those on the Tennessee River in the two photographs above, were convoyed and protected by the Navy's river gunboats.

U.S.S. *Huntsville*, Acting Lieutenant W. C. Rogers, captured schooner *A. J. Hodge* at sea off the east Florida coast.

U.S.S. *Daffodil*, Acting Master E. M. Baldwin, seized blockade running British schooner *Wonder* off Port Royal.

C.S.S. *Florida*, Lieutenant Maffitt, captured ship *Crown Point* off the coast of Brazil. After removing stores, Maffitt burned the prize.

U.S.S. *De Soto*, Captain Walker, seized schooner *Sea Bird* from Havana, off Pensacola Bay.

14 Boat crew from U.S.S. *Currituck*, Acting Master Linnekin, captured schooner *Ladies' Delight* near Urbanna, Virginia.

15 Writing Benjamin F. Isherwood, Chief of the Bureau of Steam Engineering, regarding the U.S. naval floating machine shop at Port Royal, Rear Admiral Du Pont said: "This establishment is a most essential and important accession to the efficiency of this squadron, turning out an amount of work highly creditable to all concerned with it and particularly to Chief Engineer McCleery whose attention is ceaseless to the wants of the steamers now by long service so frequently requiring repairs. In this connection I would call the attention of the Bureau to the necessity of sending out a small store vessel in which the materials required for work at the machine shop, now constantly increasing since the arrival of the ironclads, could be stored, and that some person be carefully selected to take charge thereof. The machine shop, as the Bureau is aware is in two old hulks, one of which is taken up entirely as a workshop and for quarters; and the other is in too decayed a condition to be suitable for the purpose of stowage."

U.S.S. *Canandaigua*, Captain J. F. Green, captured blockade running sloop *Secesh* off Charleston with cargo of cotton.

U.S.S. *Kanawha*, Lieutenant Commander Mayo, seized blockade running British brig *Comet* 20 miles east of Fort Morgan, Mobile Bay.

Some 35 Confederates seized mail steamers *Arrow* and *Emily* at Currituck bridge and forced the crews to pilot them to Franklin, Virginia.

16 Commander Bulloch wrote Secretary Mallory from London: ". . . I had understood, and Mr. Slidell was under the impression, that French builders, being anxious to establish business connections with the South and to compete with England for the custom of the Confederate States after the war, would be willing to deal with us largely upon credit . . . I found that French builders, like the English, wanted money, and were not willing to lay down the ships unless I could give security in the shape of cotton certificates. . . ." Chronic currency shortage constantly blocked Confederate ambitions abroad.

U.S.S. *Two Sisters*, Acting Master's Mate John Boyle, captured schooner *Oliver S. Breese* off the Anclote Keys, Florida, bound from Havana to Bayport, Florida.

Store ship U.S.S. *Courier*, Acting Master Walter K. Cressy, captured blockade running sloops *Angelina* and *Emeline* off the South Carolina coast, bound from Charleston to Nassau with cargoes of cotton.

U.S.S. *Powhatan*, Captain Steedman, captured sloop *C. Routereau* off Charleston with small cargo of cotton and turpentine.

17 Confederate blockade runner *Cuba* was burned by her crew in the Gulf of Mexico to prevent capture by U.S.S. *De Soto*, Captain W. M. Walker. Rear Admiral Bailey reported: "Her cargo cost $400,000 in specie at Havana, and was worth at Mobile a million and a quarter."

U.S.S. *Courier*, Acting Master Cressy, captured schooner *Maria Bishop* at sea off Cape Romain, South Carolina, with cargo of cotton.

Flag Officer Silas H. Stringham, in U.S.S. *Minnesota*, reported the capture of schooner *Almira Ann* near the Chickahominy River, Virginia, with cargo of timber.

U.S.S. *Kanawha*, Lieutenant Commander Mayo, captured schooner *Hunter* bound from Mobile to Havana with cargo of cotton.

18 Gunboats under Rear Admiral Porter joined with troops under Generals Grant and W. T. Sherman in assaulting Confederate works to the rear of Vicksburg. Porter had departed for the operation on the Yazoo River on the 15th. He reported to Secretary Welles: "Leaving two of the ironclads at Red River, one at Grand Gulf, one at Carthage, three at Warrenton, and two in the Yazoo, left me a small force to cooperate with; still, I disposed of them to the best advantage." Observing that Grant's troops had cut off Confederates at Snyder's Bluff, Porter ordered U.S.S. *Baron De Kalb*, *Choctaw*, *Linden*, *Romeo*, *Petrel*, and *Forest Rose* up the Yazoo to assist the Army. Upon the Union occupation of Snyder's Bluff, Porter quickly sent up provisions for the troops, and U.S.S. *De Kalb*, Lieutenant Commander J. G. Walker, pushed on to Haynes' Bluff—which the Southerners were evacuating. Porter noted that "guns, forts, tents, and equipage of all kinds fell into our hands." Quickly taking advantage of the opportunities presented by the fall of the heavy works, the Admiral moved the gunboats into position and began to shell the hill batteries at Vicksburg. On the 19th six mortars began to fire "night and day as rapidly as they could."

Union mortar boats played important parts throughout the war in the west.

U.S.S. *Linden*, Acting Lieutenant T. E. Smith, escorted five Army transports down the Mississippi. The lead transport, *Crescent City*, was fired into by a Confederate masked battery at Island No. 82, wounding some soldiers. *Linden* immediately opened fire, and drove the artillerists from their battery. Under the ships' guns, troops were landed and the buildings in the area were destroyed in retaliation.

U.S.S. *Kanawha*, Lieutenant Commander Mayo, took schooner *Ripple* bound from Mobile to Havana with cargo of cotton.

U.S.S. *Shepherd Knapp*, Acting Lieutenant Henry Eytinge, ran aground on a reef at Cape Haitien, West Indies, could not get off, and was stripped of all usable stores, provisions, and instruments before being abandoned.

Boat crew under Acting Master's Mate N. Mayo Dyer from U.S.S. *R. R. Cuyler* boarded, captured, and burned schooner *Isabel* near Fort Morgan, Mobile Bay.

U.S.S. *Octorara*, Commander Collins, captured British blockade runner *Eagle* near the Bahamas. Collins reported that the chase had failed "to heave to till we had disabled her machinery. . . ."

18-21 Confederate troops planted torpedoes in Skull Creek, South Carolina, "with a view of destroying the enemy's vessels, which are constantly passing through this thoroughfare."

19 As Union Army troops advanced on Vicksburg, Generals Grant and Sherman sought continuous naval support for their movements. Grant wrote Rear Admiral Porter: "If you can run down and throw shell in just back of the city it will aid us and demoralize an already badly beaten enemy." Sherman requested similar assistance: "My right [flank] is on the Mississippi. We have possession of the bluff down a mile or more below the mouth of the Bayou. Can't you send immediately a couple of gunboats down? They can easily see and distinguish our men, and can silence a water battery that is the extremity of their flank on the river and enfilade the left flank of their works." U.S.S. *Benton*, Lieutenant Commander James A. Greer, was ordered into action at once by Porter: "The moment you see the forts on the hills opening on our troops advancing toward the town, move up and open at long range with shell on such forts as may be firing. . . . The object is to disconcert the enemy, and by firing shell at your longest range, you can do so. Do not come in range of the guns above the city, as there are no forts there that can trouble our army. Fire on the forts on the hill, and try and drop your shell in them."

Lieutenant Commander Reigart B. Lowry wrote Secretary Welles urging that naval officers and seamen not employed at sea be used to man forts and seacoast defenses: "The most successful defenses made against us . . . at various points of the Mississippi and the seacoast have been made by ex-naval officers and seamen; in the last defense of Port Hudson the guns were worked by seamen and naval men, so at Vicksburg, at Galveston, and Charleston. The defenses of Sebastopol were entirely defended by Russian seamen for many months, while from the fort guarding that port they beat back the combined fleets of England and France."

U.S.S. *Huntsville*, Acting Lieutenant W. C. Rogers, seized blockade running Spanish steamer *Union* in the Gulf of Mexico west of St. Petersburg.

Mortar schooner U.S.S. *Sophronia*, Acting Ensign William R. Rude, seized schooner *Mignonette* at Piney Point, Virginia, attempting to smuggle whiskey.

U.S.S. *De Soto*, Captain W. M. Walker, captured schooner *Mississippian* in the Gulf of Mexico, bound from Mobile to Havana with cargo of cotton and turpentine.

20 Rear Admiral Farragut reported to Secretary Welles: "We are again about to attack Port Hudson. General Banks supported by the *Hartford*, *Albatross* and some of the small gunboats, will attack from above, landing probably at Bayou Sara, while General Augur will march up from Baton

Rouge and will attack the place from below. . . . my vessels are pretty well used up, but they must work as long as they can."

Writing of the reports he had made to the Navy Department after the Charleston attack, Rear Admiral Du Pont noted: "I did not call a failure, a reconnaissance. I told them, to renew the attack would be to convert failure into disaster. I told them moreover that Charleston could not be taken by a purely naval attack—*nor can it be* in the ordinary professional acceptation of the term—not that there is not power enough in the country to do it—but there is nothing to justify its application or to reward its success—commensurate with the sacrifice etc. When Admiral Sir Charles Napier informed the Admiralty that to attack Cronstadt would be the destruction of the British fleet—or when the combined fleets withdrew from the attack of the forts at Sebastopol, it was not intended to convey, there was not wealth and life enough in Britain and France to accomplish it. Blood and treasure may do almost anything in war. Suvorov bridged marshes with human bodies, by forcing his advance guard into them, until the remainder of his army found a foot-hold on their fallen comrades."

Boat crew under Acting Master's Mate Charles W. Fisher of U.S.S. *Louisiana* captured schooner *R. T. Renshaw* in the Tar River, above Washington, North Carolina.

21 General Grant wrote Rear Admiral Porter, informing him of an anticipated Army attack on Vicksburg and requesting the assistance of the gunboats: "I expect to assault the city at 10 a.m. tomorrow. I would request, and earnestly request it, that you send up the gunboats below the city and shell the rebel entrenchments until that hour and for thirty minutes after. If the mortars could all be sent down to near this point on the Louisiana shore, and throw shells during the night, it would materially aid me. I would like at least to have the enemy kept annoyed during the night." Porter responded and "kept six mortars playing rapidly on the works and town all night; sent the *Benton*, *Mound City*, and *Carondelet* up to shell the water batteries, and other places where troops might be resting during the night." Early the morning of 22 May, *Mound City*, Lieutenant Commander Wilson, engaged the hill batteries. An hour later she was joined by U.S.S. *Benton*, *Tuscumbia*, and *Carondelet*. The combined fire temporarily silenced the Confederate work. Leaving *Tuscumbia* to prevent further action by the hill batteries, Porter proceeded with the other three gunboats against the water batteries. These guns opened on the Union ships "furiously," but Porter forced his way to within a quarter of a mile of them. By this time the gunboats had been engaged for an hour longer than Grant had requested, and, with no Army assault apparently forthcoming, the Admiral directed his ships to drop back out of range. The gunboats were hit "a number of times" but suffered little severe damage; they were, however, nearly out of ammunition when the attack was broken off. The Admiral later learned that the troops ashore had attacked Vicksburg, an unsuccessful assault that had been obscured from the squadron's view by the smoke and noise of its own guns and the Confederate batteries. Praising Grant's effort, Porter remarked: "The army had terrible work before them, and are fighting as well as soldiers ever fought before, but the works are stronger than any of us dreamed of." Brigadier General John McArthur in turn praised the work of the gunboats. He wrote Porter: "I received your communication regarding the silencing of the two batteries below Vicksburg, and in reply would say that I witnessed with intense satisfaction the firing on that day, being the finest I have yet seen."

Under Lieutenant Commander J. G. Walker, U.S.S. *Baron De Kalb*, *Choctaw*, *Forest Rose*, *Linden*, and *Petrel* pushed up the Yazoo River from Haynes' Bluff to Yazoo City, Mississippi. As the gunboats approached the city, Commander Isaac N. Brown, CSN, who had commanded the heroic ram C.S.S. *Arkansas* the preceding summer, was forced to destroy three "powerful steamers, rams" and a "fine navy yard, with machine shops of all kinds, sawmills, blacksmith shops, etc. . . ." to prevent their capture. Porter noted that "what he had begun our forces finished," as the city was evacuated by the Southerners. The Confederate steamers destroyed were *Mobile*, *Republic*, and "a monster, 310 feet long and 70 feet beam." Had the latter been completed, "she would have given us much trouble." Porter's prediction to Secretary Welles at the end of the expedition, though overly optimistic in terms of the time that would be required, was nonetheless a clear summary of the effect of the gunboats' sweep up the Yazoo: "It is a mere question of a few hours, and then, with the exception of Port Hudson (which will follow Vicksburg), the Mississippi will be open its entire length."

Rear Admiral Farragut wrote Captain John R. Goldsborough, commanding the blockading force off Mobile: "I am much gratified to find that you are adding to the successes of the day by the number of captures recently made. . . . I know that your service is one of great anxiety, and irksome, with but little compensation save the pleasure of knowing that you are doing your duty toward your country. I know your officers would be glad to be with me in the river, and gladly would I bring them here to my assistance were it not indispensable to have them on the blockade. I feel as if I was about to make the last blow at them [the Confederates] I shall for some time to come. The fall of Port Hudson will place Admiral Porter in command of the river, and I shall join my fleet outside, and trust I shall call on my officers outside for their exertions in the reductions of the last two places—Mobile and Galveston."

U.S.S. *Union*, Acting Lieutenant Edward Conroy, seized blockade running British schooner *Linnet* in the Gulf of Mexico, west of Charlotte Harbor, Florida.

U.S.S. *Currituck*, Acting Master Linnekin, U.S.S. *Anacostia*, Acting Master Nelson Provost, and U.S.S. *Satellite*, Acting Master John F. D. Robinson, captured schooner *Emily* at the mouth of the Rappahannock River.

22   Small boats from U.S.S. *Fort Henry*, Lieutenant Commander McCauley, captured sloop *Isabella* in Waccassassa Bay, Florida.

Union Army steamer *Allison* destroyed schooner *Sea Bird* after seizing her cargo of coal near New Bern, North Carolina.

24   Confederates fired on the commissary and quartermaster boat of the Marine Brigade under Brigadier General A. W. Ellet above Austin, Mississippi, on the evening of 23 May. Before dawn, this date, Ellet's forces went ashore, engaged Confederate cavalry some 8 miles outside of Austin, and, after a 2-hour engagement, compelled the Southerners to withdraw. Finding evidence of smuggling and in reprisal for the firing of the previous evening, Ellet ordered the town burned. "As the fire progressed," Ellet reported, "the discharge of firearms was rapid and frequent in the burning buildings, showing that fire is more penetrating in its search [for hidden weapons] than my men had been; two heavy explosions of powder also occurred during the conflagration."

A boat expedition under Acting Master Edgar Van Slyck from U.S.S. *Port Royal*, Lieutenant Commander Morris, captured sloop *Fashion* above Apalachicola, Florida, with cargo of cotton. Van Slyck also burned the facility at Devil's Elbow where the sloop had been previously repaired and destroyed a barge near *Fashion*.

24-30   Lieutenant Commander J. G. Walker ascended the Yazoo River with U.S.S. *Baron De Kalb*, *Forest Rose*, *Linden*, *Signal*, and *Petrel* to capture transports and to break up Confederate movements. Fifteen miles below Fort Pemberton, Walker found and burned four steamers which were sunk on a bar blocking the river. Fire was exchanged with Confederate sharp shooters as the Union gunboats returned downriver. A landing party destroyed a large sawmill, and at Yazoo City "brought away a large quantity of bar, round, and flat iron from the navy yard." Walker next penetrated the Sunflower River for about 150 miles, destroying shipping and grain before returning to the mouth of the Yazoo River. Admiral Porter reported to Secretary Welles: "Steamers to the amount of $700,000 were destroyed by the late expedition—9 in all."

25 C.S.S. *Alabama*, Captain Semmes, captured and burned ship *Gildersleeve* and bonded *Justina* off Bahia, Brazil.

26 General Banks wrote Rear Admiral Farragut of the status of the assault on Port Hudson, adding: "Please let the mortars destroy the enemy's rest at night." The Admiral answered: "I shall continue to harass the enemy occasionally day and night. He was pretty well exercised last night both by the *Hartford* and the mortars. . . . We have several mortar boats up half a mile nearer, and the ships will be ready to open the moment you give us notice. . . . We will aid you all we can."

Commander Davenport reported the assistance rendered the Army in the occupation of Wilkinson's Point, North Carolina. U.S.S. *Ceres*, *Shawsheen*, and *Brinker* reconnoitered the area along the Neuse River, capturing and destroying a number of small schooners and boats. The gunboats then covered the landing of the troops and remained on station until the Army was solidly entrenched in its position.

27 U.S.S. *Cincinnati*, Lieutenant Bache, ". . . in accordance with Generals Grant's and Sherman's urgent request," moved to enfilade some rifle pits which had barred the Army's progress before Vicksburg. Though Porter took great precautions for the ship's safety by packing her with logs and hay, a shot entered *Cincinnati*'s magazine, "and she commenced filling rapidly." Bache reported: "Before and after this time the enemy fired with great accuracy, hitting us almost every time. We were especially annoyed by plunging shots from the hills, an 8-inch rifle and a 10-inch smoothbore doing us much damage. The shots went entirely through our protection— hay, wood, and iron." *Cincinnati*, suffering 25 killed or wounded and 15 probable drownings, went down with her colors nailed to the mast. General Sherman wrote: "The style in which the *Cincinnati* engaged the battery elicited universal praise." And Secretary Welles expressed "the Department's appreciation of your brave conduct."

Confederate defenders turned back a major assault on Port Hudson, inflicting severe losses on the Union Army. General Banks' troops fell back into siege position and appealed to Rear Admiral Farragut to continue the mortar and ship bombardment night and day, and requested naval officers and Marines to man a heavy naval battery ashore. A week later, Farragut reported the situation to Welles: "General Banks still has Port Hudson closely invested and is now putting up a battery of four IX-inch guns and four 24 pounders. The first will be superintended by Lieutenant [Commander] Terry, of the *Richmond*, and worked by four of her gun crews and to be used as a breaching battery. We continue to shell the enemy every night from three to five hours, and at times during the day when they open fire on our troops. . . . I have the *Hartford* and two or three gunboats above Port Hudson; the *Richmond*, *Genesee*, *Essex*, and this vessel [*Monongahela*], together with the mortar boats below, ready to aid the army in any way in our power."

C.S.S. *Chattahoochee*, Lieutenant John J. Guthrie, was accidentally sunk with what one Southern newspaper termed "terrible loss of life" by an explosion in her boilers. Occurring while the gunboat was at anchor in the Chattahoochee River, Georgia, the accident cost the lives of some 18 men and injured others. She was later raised but never put to sea and was ultimately destroyed at war's end by the Confederates.

From Grand Gulf Lieutenant Commander Elias K. Owen, U.S.S. *Louisville*, reported to Rear Admiral Porter that, in accord with his order of the 23d, the destruction of the abandoned Rock Hill Point Battery had begun. He also informed the Admiral that at "the earnest request of Colonel [William] Hall, late commanding this post, I went up Big Black some three miles and destroyed a raft the enemy had placed across the river, chained at both ends. . . ."

U.S.S. *Coeur de Lion*, Acting Master William G. Morris, burned schooners *Charity*, *Gazelle*, and *Flight* in the Yeocomico River, Virginia.

U.S.S. *Brooklyn*, Commodore H. H. Bell, captured sloop *Blazer* with cargo of cotton at Pass Cavallo, Texas.

28 Rear Admiral Porter instructed his gunboat squadron that "it will be the duty of the commander of every vessel to fire on people working on the enemy's batteries, to have officers on shore examining the heights, and not to have it said that the enemy put up batteries in sight of them and they did nothing to prevent it." The heavy firepower of the Union vessels—massed, mobile artillery—seriously hindered Confederate defenses and was a decisive factor in battle.

U.S.S. *Brooklyn*, Commodore H. H. Bell, captured sloop *Kate* at Point Isabel, Texas, with cargo of cotton.

29 Major General Grant sent two communiques to Rear Admiral Porter, requesting naval assistance for Army operations near Vicksburg. In the first he informed the Admiral that a force under Major General Frank P. Blair, Jr., was attempting "to clear out the enemy between the [Big] Black and Yazoo rivers, and, if possible, destroy the Mississippi Central Railroad Bridge" over the former. Grant pointed out that there was "great danger" of the Confederates cutting this expedition off in the rear and asked that Porter send "one or two gunboats to navigate the Yazoo as high up as Yazoo City," so that Blair would be assured an escape route if necessary.

In the second letter, Grant asked Porter: "Will you have the goodness to order the Marine Brigade to Haynes' Bluff, with directions to disembark and remain in occupation until I can relieve them by other troops? I have also to request that you put at the disposal of Major S. C. Lyford, chief of ordnance, two siege guns, ammunition, and implements complete, to be placed to the rear of Vicksburg. After they are in battery, and ready for use, I should be pleased to have them

General Grant, who had a splendid understanding of sea power and used it to the best advantage, and Rear Admiral Porter confer to plan the joint strategy in the siege of Vicksburg.

manned by crews from your fleet." Porter immediately replied that the brigade would leave early the next morning but that he had only one suitable large gun for use ashore and that one he was fitting on a mortar boat for close support "to throw shell into the [rifle] pits in front of Sherman." There were, however, six 8-inch guns on board U.S.S. *Manitou*, he told Grant, and he would have them landed as soon as that ship returned from Yazoo City.

Also on this date, Lieutenant Commander Greer, U.S.S. *Benton*, reported firing on Confederates building rifle pits on the crest and side of a hill near the battery that commanded the canal. He drove them away after firing for an hour. This action was renewed during the next 2 days for brief intervals and Greer, on 31 May, reported to Porter: "They return to their work as soon as the boats drop down."

C.S.S. *Alabama*, Captain Semmes, captured and burned *Jabez Snow* in the South Atlantic, bound from Cardiff to Montevideo, Uruguay, with cargo of coal.

U.S.S. *Cimarron*, Commander Andrew J. Drake, took blockade runner *Evening Star* off Wassaw Sound, Georgia, with cargo of cotton.

30   U.S.S. *Forest Rose*, Acting Lieutenant G. W. Brown, and U.S.S. *Linden*, Acting Lieutenant T. E. Smith, reconnoitered Quiver River, Mississippi. A boat expedition from the two ships captured and burned *Dew Drop* and *Emma Bett*.

U.S.S. *Rhode Island*, Commander Stephen D. Trenchard, gave chase to blockade runner *Margaret and Jessie* off Eleuthera Island. Taking a shot in the boiler, the fleeing steamer was run ashore to keep from sinking with a large cargo of cotton.

Boat expedition under Lieutenant Commander Chester Hatfield captured schooner *Star* and sloop *Victoria* at Brazos Santiago, Texas; the latter was burned as she grounded in the attempt to bring her out into the Gulf.

Blockade runner *A. D. Vance* sailed from Great Britain to Wilmington; this was the first of 11 successful runs through the blockade for the vessel.

31   U.S.S. *Carondelet*, Lieutenant Murphy, patrolling the Mississippi River below Vicksburg, proceeded to Perkins Landing, Louisiana, where Army troops were found cut off from the Union headquarters. Murphy "shelled the woods . . . and thus prevented the enemy from advancing and throwing an enfilading fire on the troops ashore," while awaiting the arrival of a transport which could rescue the soldiers. As *Forest Queen* arrived and the Union troops began to board her, a large force of Confederates pressed an attack. *Carondelet*'s guns laid down a heavy fire, saving the troops and forcing the Southerners eventually to break off the assault. *Carondelet* remained at Perkins' Landing after *Forest Queen* departed, saved those stores and material which it was possible to take on board, and destroyed the rest to prevent its capture by Confederates.

Rear Admiral Porter, accompanied by some of the fleet officers, went ashore, mounted horses and rode to Major General W. T. Sherman's headquarters before Vicksburg. Sherman reported that the Admiral, referring to the loss of U.S.S. *Cincinnati* on 27 May, was "willing to lose all the boats if he could do any good." Porter also volunteered to place a battery ashore. To that end, Lieutenant Commander Selfridge visited Sherman on the first of June and reported that he was prepared to land two 8-inch howitzers and to man and work them if the Army would haul the guns in to position and build a parapet for them. On 5 June Selfridge told Porter that one gun was in position and "I shall have the other gun mounted to-night. . . ." Frequent joint efforts of this nature hastened the end of Vicksburg.

U.S.S. *Pawnee*, Commander Balch, and U.S.S. *E. B. Hale*, Acting Lieutenant Edgar Brodhead, supported an Army reconnaissance to James Island, South Carolina, and covered the troop landing. Balch reported: "The landing was successfully accomplished and the reconnaissance made, our forces meeting with no opposition, and they were embarked at 9 a.m. and returned to their camps without a casualty of any kind." Colonel Charles H. Simonton, CSA, commanding at James Island, warned: "This expedition of the enemy removes all [their] fear of our supposed batteries on the Stono, and no doubt we will have visits from them often."

U.S.S. *Sunflower*, Acting Master Edward Van Sice, seized schooner *Echo* off the Marquesas Keys with cargo of cotton.

JUNE

1 U.S. Consul Seth C. Hawley at Nassau wrote Assistant Secretary of State Frederick W. Seward, commenting on the continued attempts to run the blockade despite the danger of capture or destruction. Naming 28 ships that had run or attempted to run the blockade since 10 March, Hawley observed that 13 had not been successful. "This proportion of loss seems too large to allow the business to be profitable, but this view is deceptive. The number of successful and unsuccessful voyages must be compared to make a sound conclusion. . . . To arrive at the probable profits of the business, I made an estimate in the case of the *Ella and Annie*. She came into the business in April, has made two successful voyages and is now absent on the third venture.

"One voyage outward cargo, say	$100,000
One voyage expense, etc	$ 15,000
	$115,000
She returns with 1,300 bales of cotton, weighing an average of 400 pounds per bale, equal to 45 cents per pound, or	$234,000
From which deduct the cost	$115,000
Leaves profit	$119,000

"Assume that she makes the average four voyages and is lost on the fifth with her cargo, the account would stand thus: Four voyages, profit at $119,000 each, is $476,000; deduct cost of steamer, $100,000, and cargo, $100,000, equal $200,000, leaves as profit on four voyages, $276,000. This estimate of profits is far less; it is not half as great as the figures made by those engaged in the business." Thus patriotism and the great profit realized from a successful run through the blockade combined to induce adventurous Southerners to risk the perils posed by the Union fleet.

In seeking to stop the activities of Confederate blockade runners, vigorous naval officers were not always confined to the water. On hearing that four men engaged in blockade running were ashore near Lawson's Bay on the Rappahannock River, Acting Master Street of U.S.S. *Primrose* took a landing party 4 miles inland and surrounded the house the men had been reported to be in. "On searching the house," Street wrote, "we found four men secreted under the bedding. . . . We also obtained $10,635 in notes and bonds belonging to the prisoners. . . ."

The Confederate Navy Department assumed complete control of the Selma, Alabama, Iron Works. Under the command of Commander Catesby ap R. Jones, the iron works became a naval ordnance works where naval guns were cast. Between June 1863 and April 1864, nearly 200 guns were cast there, most of them 6.4-inch and 7-inch Brooke rifles.

2 C.S.S. *Alabama*, Captain Semmes, after a chase of 8 hours in the South Atlantic, captured and burned bark *Amazonian*, bound from New York to Montevideo with cargo including commercial mail.

U.S.S. *Anacostia*, Acting Master Provost, and U.S.S. *Primrose*, Acting Master Street, took sloop *Flying Cloud* at Tapp's Creek, Virginia.

3 Rear Admiral Porter, writing from his flagship, U.S.S. *Black Hawk*, informed General Grant that he had sent six 8-inch guns up the Yazoo River, "to be placed where required," and two 9-inch guns to Warrenton as well. The Admiral also wrote to Lieutenant Commander Greer, U.S.S. *Benton*, urging a continual fire from the gunboats into the Vicksburg positions. "The town," he noted, "will soon fall now, and we can afford to expend a little more ammunition."

U.S.S. *Stars and Stripes*, Acting Master Charles L. Willcomb, captured sloop *Florida* at St. Marks Bay, Florida, with cargo of cotton and tar.

3-4 Ram U.S.S. *Switzerland*, Lieutenant Colonel J. Ellet, reconnoitered the Atchafalaya River as far as Simmesport, Louisiana, upon hearing reports that Confederate General Kirby Smith might be advancing to engage the Union position above Port Hudson. Half a mile above Simmesport, heavy rifle fire was opened on the ram. "Strongly posted behind the levee and heavy earthworks, within 100 yards of the channel of the river," Ellet reported, "they poured a perfect storm of Minie balls upon us as we passed in front of the town. The fire of the artillery was also very severe." After a vigorous exchange in which *Switzerland* sustained seven hits, the ram withdrew. Next day, U.S.S. *Lafayette* and *Pittsburg* "proceeded to Simmesport and shelled the rebels away from their breastworks, fired their camp and the houses which had been occupied as their quarters." The gunboats then returned to their positions at the mouth of the Red River.

4 U.S.S. *Commodore McDonough*, Lieutenant Commander Bacon, with steamer *Island City*, transport *Cossack*, and Army gunboat *Mayflower* in company, transported and supported an Army action at Bluffton, South Carolina. The troops disembarked without incident under the protection of the gunboat, and proceeded to Bluffton where they met strong Confederate resistance. With naval gunfire support, the town was destroyed and the troops were enabled to reembark with the mission successfully completed.

4-5 Joint Army-Navy expedition including U.S.S. *Commodore Morris*, Lieutenant Commander Gillis; U.S.S. *Commodore Jones*, Lieutenant Commander John G. Mitchell; Army gunboat *Smith Briggs*, and transport *Winnissimet* with 400 troops embarked, ascended the Mattapony River for the purpose of destroying a foundry above Walkerton, Virginia, where Confederate ordnance was being manufactured. The troops were landed at Walkerton and marched to the Ayletts area where the machinery, a flour mill, and a large quantity of grain were destroyed. Reembarking the troops and captured livestock, the force fell down river as the gunboats "dropped shells into many deserted houses and completely scoured the banks, and sweeping all the points on the river." Rear Admiral S. P. Lee reported that: "The vigilant dispositions of Lieutenant Commander Gillis kept the river below clear, and the rebels, attempting demonstrations at several points on the banks, were dispersed by the gunboats." Brigadier General Henry A. Wise, CSA, called the joint expedition a "daring and destructive raid." Constant destruction along the coasts and up the rivers seriously hampered the already industrially deficient South.

5 C.S.S. *Alabama*, Captain Semmes, captured ship *Talisman* in the mid-Atlantic en route Shanghai. Semmes wrote in his log: "Received on board from this ship during the day some beef and pork and bread, etc., and a couple of brass 12-pounders, mounted on ship carriages. There were four of these pieces on board, and a quantity of powder and shot, two steam boilers, etc., for fitting up a steam gunboat. . . . at nightfall set fire to the ship, a beautiful craft of 1,100 tons."

U.S.S. *Wissahickon*, Lieutenant Commander Davis, attacked and sank a steamer (name unknown) attempting to run the blockade out of Charleston.

6 Rear Admiral Lee reported to Secretary Welles regarding the urgent need of additional vessels on the blockade: "The two entrances to Cape Fear River make the blockade of Wilmington very difficult. The vessels on one side cannot support those on the other, and each side, particularly the New Inlet side, requires a large blockading force. Two vessels like the *New Ironsides* are

required to protect this blockade against the enemy's ironclads. . . . swift and suitably armed schooners are needed to capture the blockade runners. The fact that these last now go together adds to the difficulty of capturing them, and requires additional strength for this purpose. The blockade requires more and better vessels and must eventually fail without them." The North's industrial strength and free access to the world's markets, assured by control of the seas, made the necessary naval buildup possible. The exact opposite was true of the Confederacy. Secretary Mallory, writing Commander Bulloch in Liverpool on 8 June, lamented: "We need ironclads, ironclads, ironclads. . . ."

C.S.S. *Clarence* (prize of C.S.S. *Florida*), Lieutenant Read, launched a brief but highly successful cruise against Union commerce by capturing and burning bark *Whistling Wind* with cargo of coal in the Atlantic east of Cape Romain, South Carolina. Read reported: "She was insured by the U.S. Government for the sum of $14,000."

C.S.S. *Florida*, Lieutenant Maffitt, captured and burned ship *Southern Cross*, bound from Mexico to New York with cargo of wood.

U.S.S. *Tahoma*, Lieutenant Commander A. A. Semmes, seized schooner *Statesman*, aground at Gadsen's Point, Florida, with cargo of cotton.

Steamer *Lady Walton* surrendered to U.S.S. *Tyler*, Lieutenant Commander Prichett, at the mouth of White River, Arkansas.

7 U.S.S. *Choctaw*, Lieutenant Commander Ramsay, and U.S.S. *Lexington*, Lieutenant Commander Bache, defended Union troops at Milliken's Bend, Mississippi, from the assault by a superior number of Confederate soldiers. The Union troops withdrew to the river bank where the guns of the ships could be brought into action. "There," Rear Admiral Porter noted, "the gunboats opened on the rebels with shell, grape, and canister. . . ." and compelled the Confederates to fall back. Confederate Major General John G. Walker wrote: ". . . it must be remembered that the enemy behind a Mississippi levee, protected on the flanks by gunboats, is as securely posted as it is possible to be outside a regular fortification."

C.S.S. *Clarence*, Lieutenant Read, seized schooner *Alfred H. Partridge* bound from New York to Matamoras with cargo of arms and clothing. "I took the captain's bond for the sum of $5,000 for the delivery of the cargo to loyal citizens of the Confederate states," Read wrote.

8 Crew from a Confederate launch commanded by Master James Duke, CSN, boarded and captured steam tug *Boston* at Pass a l'Outre, Mississippi River, and put to sea, then capturing and burning Union barks *Lenox* and *Texana*. Duke carried *Boston* safely into Mobile on 11 June. This bold action caused Rear Admiral Farragut considerable concern. Recalling a similar event on 12 April, he wrote the blockade commander off Mobile: "She is the second vessel that has been captured off the mouth of the Mississippi and carried through our blockading squadron into Mobile. I cannot understand how the blockade is run with such ease when you have so strong a numerical force."

C.S.S. *Georgia*, Lieutenant W. L. Maury, captured ship *George Griswold* with cargo of coal off Rio de Janeiro. Maury released the prize on bond.

9 Union mortar boats continued to bombard Vicksburg. From dawn until nearly noon, they poured 175 shells into the city as the Confederate position, cut off from supplies and relief, grew steadily more desperate. Heavy rains curtailed the mortar activity the next day, only some 75 shells being fired, but on the 11th the attack was stepped up once again and Ordnance Gunner Eugene Mack reported that 193 mortar shells fell on the river stronghold. Rear Admiral Porter wrote Secretary Welles: "The mortars keep constantly playing on the city and works, and the gunboats throw in their shell whenever they see any work going on at the batteries, or new bat-

Lieutenant Charles Read, CSN, led a daring raid on Northern commerce.

Flag Officer Duncan Ingraham, CSN, strengthened Charleston naval defenses.

teries being put up. Not a soul is to be seen moving in the city, the soldiers lying in their trenches or pits, and the inhabitants being stowed in caves or holes dug out in the cliffs. If the city is not relieved by a much superior force from the outside, Vicksburg must fall without anything more being done to it. I only wonder it has held out so long. . . ."

C.S.S. *Clarence*, Lieutenant Read, captured and burned brig *Mary Alvina*, bound from Boston to New Orleans with cargo of commissary stores. Read, upon interrogating prisoners, concluded that it would not be possible to carry out his intention to harass Union shipping in Hampton Roads. "No vessels," he wrote, "were allowed to go into Hampton Roads unless they had supplies for the U.S. Government, and then they were closely watched. . . . I determined to cruise along the coast and try to intercept a transport for Fortress Monroe and with her endeavor to carry out the orders of Commander Maffitt [see 6 May 1863], and in the meantime do all possible injury to the enemy's commerce."

10 Major General Banks, besieging Port Hudson, signalled Rear Admiral Farragut: "Please send to Springfield Landing 500 blank cartridges, 50 schrapnel, 500 shell, and 50 solid shot for the IX-inch navy guns. Please let me know when they will be there." The return signal read: "The ammunition that you asked for will be at Springfield Landing at 5 p.m."

Rear Admiral Du Pont ordered U.S.S. *Weehawken*, Captain J. Rodgers, and U.S.S. *Nahant*, Commander Downes, to Wassaw Sound, Georgia, where it was reported that the powerful ram C.S.S. *Atlanta*, Commander Webb, was preparing to attack the wooden blockader U.S.S. *Cimarron*. A week later Du Pont's wise foresight would save the day for the Union blockade there.

Confederate officer prisoners of war being transported to Fort Delaware on board steamer *Maple Leaf* overpowered the guard, took possession of the steamer, and landed below Cape Henry, Virginia.

11 Rear Admiral Farragut wrote Major General Banks regarding the continuous bombardment of Port Hudson: "You must remember that we have been bombarding this place five weeks, and we are now upon our last 500 shells, so that it will not be in my power to bombard more than three

or four hours each night, at intervals of five minutes. . . . I was under the impression that our shelling only served two purposes—to break their rest and silence their guns, when they opened in our sight; the last he has ceased to do, and they have now become indifferent to the former. After the people have been harassed to a certain extent they become indifferent to danger, I think, but we will do all in our power to aid you."

Steamer *Havelock* ran past U.S.S. *Memphis*, *Stettin*, and *Ottawa* at Charleston but was so severely battered by the blockaders' fire that she was found at daybreak aground on Folly Island and ablaze. Captain Turner, U.S.S. *New Ironsides*, reported that she was "a total wreck."

U.S.S. *Florida*, Commander Bankhead, captured blockade running steamer *Calypso* attempting to dash into Wilmington with cargo including drugs, provisions, and plating for ironclads.

Boat crew from U.S.S. *Coeur De Lion*, Acting Master W. G. Morris, seized and burned schooners *Odd Fellow* and *Sarah Margaret* in Coan River, Virginia.

12 C.S.S. *Clarence*, Lieutenant Read, captured bark *Tacony* off Cape Hatteras and shortly thereafter took schooner *M. A. Shindler* from Port Royal to Philadelphia in ballast. Read determined to transfer his command to *Tacony*, she "being a better sailor than the *Clarence*," and was in the process of transferring the howitzer when another schooner, *Kate Stewart*, from Key West to Philadelphia, was sighted. "Passing near the *Clarence*," Read reported, "a wooden gun was pointed at her and she was commanded to heave to, which she did immediately. . . . As we were now rather short of provisions and had over fifty prisoners, I determined to bond the schooner *Kate Stewart* and make a cartel of her." Read then destroyed both *Clarence* and *M. A. Shindler* and stood in chase of another brig, *Arabella*, which he soon overhauled. She had a neutral cargo, and Read "bonded her for $30,000, payable thirty days after peace." Thus the career of C.S.S. *Clarence* was at an end. In a week's time she had made six prizes, three of which had been destroyed, two bonded, and her successor, C.S.S. *Tacony*, sailed against Union shipping under the same daring skipper and his crew.

13 C.S.S. *Georgia*, Lieutenant W. L. Maury, captured bark *Good Hope* (22°15′ S.–37°1′ W.) bound from Boston to Cape of Good Hope; the prize was burned at sea on 14 June after provisions and stores were removed.

U.S.S. *Juniata*, Commander Clitz, captured blockade running schooner *Fashion* off the coast of Cuba with cargo of salt and soda.

U.S.S. *Sunflower*, Acting Master Van Sice, captured schooner *Pushmataha* off Tortugas.

13–15 Confederate guerrillas fired into U.S.S. *Marmora*, Acting Lieutenant Getty, near Eunice, Arkansas, and on the morning of the 14th, took transport *Nebraska* under fire. In retaliation, Getty sent a landing party ashore and destroyed the town, "including the railroad depot, with locomotive and car inside, also the large warehouse. . . ." The next day, 15 June, landing parties from *Marmora* and U.S.S. *Prairie Bird*, Acting Lieutenant Edward E. Brennand, destroyed the town of Gaines Landing in retaliation for a guerrilla attempt to burn the Union coal barge there and for firing on *Marmora*.

14 President Lincoln authorized the Secretary of the Treasury to "cooperate by the revenue cutters under your direction with the Navy in arresting rebel depredations on American commerce and transportation and in capturing rebels engaged therein." The directive was largely the result of Lieutenant Read's continued raid on Union commerce near Northern shores.

Rear Admiral Porter wired Secretary Welles: "The situation of affairs here has altered very little. We are still closing on the enemy. General Grant's position is a safe one, though he should have all the troops that can possibly be sent to him. We have mounted six heavy navy guns in the rear of Vicksburg and can give the army as many as they want. I think the town can't hold out

Under Commander William Webb, ram C.S.S. Atlanta *constituted a grave threat to Union blockading forces off Wassaw Sound, Georgia.*

longer than the 22d of June. The gunboats and mortars keep up a continual fire.'' The intrepid defenders of Vicksburg held out against the crushing water and land siege for 2 weeks beyond Admiral Porter's estimate.

C.S.S. *Florida*, Lieutenant Maffitt, captured ship *Red Gauntlet* in West Indian waters.

C.S.S. *Georgia*, Lieutenant W. L. Maury, captured at sea and bonded bark *J. W. Seaver* with cargo of machinery for Russia.

U.S.S. *Lackawanna*, Captain John B. Marchand, captured blockade running steamer *Neptune*, bound from Havana to Mobile.

15   C.S.S. *Atlanta*, Commander Webb, got underway in the early evening and passed over the lower obstructions in the Wilmington River, preparatory to an anticipated attack on the Union forces in Wassaw Sound, Georgia. Webb dropped anchor at 8 p.m. and spent the remainder of the night coaling. The next evening, "about dark," the daring Confederate later reported, "I proceeded down the river to a point of land which would place me in 5 or 6 miles of the monitors, at the same time concealing the ship from their view, ready to move on them at early dawn the next morning.''

C.S.S. *Tacony*, Lieutenant Read, captured and burned brig *Umpire* with cargo of sugar and molasses off the Virginia coast (37°40′ N., 70°31′ W.). Read's exploits created much concern and a large force was sent to search for him. Secretary Welles noted in his diary: "None of our vessels have succeeded in capturing the Rebel pirate *Tacony* which has committed great ravages along the coast.''

U.S.S. *Juliet*, Acting Lieutenant Shaw, seized steamer *Fred Nolte* on the White River, Arkansas.

U.S.S. *Lackawanna*, Captain Marchand, captured steamer *Planter* with cargo of cotton in the Gulf of Mexico.

16   Acting Master John C. Bunner, U.S.S. *New Era*, obtained a report that Confederate troops "meditated an attack on either Columbus, Hickman, Island 10, or New Madrid. . . .'' Bunner at once proceeded above Island No. 10, found and destroyed nine boats and flats. He reported:

"I do not think the enemy can procure transportation enough to attack the island with any hope of success, but am careful that none at all shall remain at his service in this vicinity."

U.S.S. *Circassian*, Acting Lieutenant William B. Eaton, captured blockade running sloop *John Wesley* off St. Marks, Florida, bound for Havana with cargo of cotton.

C.S.S. *Florida*, Commander Maffitt, captured ship *B. F. Hoxie* in West Indian waters. After removing silver bars valued at $105,000, Maffitt burned the prize.

17 C.S.S. *Atlanta*, Commander Webb, with wooden steamers *Isondiga* and *Resolute*, engaged U.S.S. *Weehawken*, Captain J. Rodgers, and U.S.S. *Nahant*, Commander Downes, in Wassaw Sound. A percussion torpedo was fitted to the ram's bow, "which," Webb wrote, "I knew would do its work to my entire satisfaction, should I but be able to touch the *Weehawken*. . . ." *Atlanta* grounded coming into the channel, was gotten off, but repeatedly failed to obey her helm. *Weehawken* poured five shots from her heavy guns into the Confederate ram, and *Nahant* moved into attacking position. With two of his gun crews out of action, with two of three pilots severely injured, and with his ship helpless and hard aground, Webb was compelled to surrender. His two wooden escorts had returned upriver without engaging.

Captain Rodgers reported: "The *Atlanta* was found to have mounted two 6-inch and two 7-inch rifles, the 6-inch broadside, the 7-inch working on a pivot either as broadside or bow and stern guns. There is a large supply of ammunition for these guns and other stores, said to be of great value by some of the officers of the vessel. There were on board at the time of capture, as per muster roll, 21 officers and 124 men, including 28 marines."

In a message of congratulations to Captain Rodgers, Secretary Welles wrote: "Every contest in which the ironclads have been engaged against ironclads has been instructive, and affords food for reflection. The lessons to be drawn are momentous. . . . Your early connection with the Mississippi Flotilla and your participation in the projection and construction of the first ironclads on the Western waters, your heroic conduct in the attack on Drewry's Bluff, the high moral courage that led you to put to sea in the *Weehawken* upon the approach of a violent storm in order to test the seagoing qualities of these new craft at a time when a safe anchorage was close under your lee, the brave and daring manner in which you, with your associates, pressed the ironclads under the concentrated fire of the batteries in Charleston harbor and there tested and proved the endurance and resisting power of these vessels, and your crowning successful achieve-

U.S.S. Weehawken *engages C.S.S.* Atlanta *in Wassaw Sound, Georgia. Failing to obey her helm properly, the Confederate ram was virtually helpless under the monitor's guns and was compelled to surrender.*

ment in the capture of the *Fingal*, alias *Atlanta*, are all proofs of a skill and courage and devotion to the country and the cause of the Union, regardless of self, that can not be permitted to pass unrewarded. . . . For these heroic and serviceable acts I have presented your name to the President, requesting him to recommend that Congress give you a vote of thanks in order that you may be advanced to the grade of commodore in the American Navy."

Boat expedition under Acting Master Sylvanus Nickerson from U.S.S. *Itasca* captured blockade runner *Miriam* at Brazos Santiago, Texas, with cargo of cotton.

18 Rear Admiral Farragut in U.S.S. *Monongahela* steamed down river from Port Hudson to Plaquemine, Louisiana, where a raid by a company of Confederate cavalry had burned two Army transports. It was feared that the Confederate intent was to capture Donaldsonville, Louisiana, cutting off the flow of supplies between New Orleans and General Banks before Port Hudson. U.S.S. *Winona*, Lieutenant Commander Aaron W. Weaver, shelled the Confederate cavalrymen from the town. The Admiral reported: "The moral effect of our force gathering about them so quickly was very good both against the enemy and in favor of the soldiers and ourselves." Farragut concentrated three or four gunboats at Donaldsonville, and General Banks wrote several days later: "The result at Donaldsonville was very gratifying, and I feel greatly indebted to the officers of the Navy for the assistance they gave, and the distinguished part they played in this most creditable affair."

U.S.S. *General Sterling Price*, Commander Woodworth, and U.S.S. *Mound City*, Lieutenant Wilson, returned to their positions below Vicksburg after a 3-day reconnaisance down the Mississippi River as far as Cole's Creek. During the expedition, some 60 to 70 barges, skiffs, and boats were destroyed which could have been used to transport Confederate troops. Meanwhile, U.S.S. *Benton*, Lieutenant Commander Greer, supplied Major General Francis J. Herron with two 32-pounders, complete with ammunition and equipment and a crew to man them. Of this battery, General Herron later wrote: "The battery, under the command of Acting Master J. Frank Reed, of the *Benton*, did excellent service, and I can not speak too highly of the bravery and energy of this young officer. Indeed, during the whole of my operations, I received valuable assistance and a hearty cooperation from the Navy."

U.S.S. *Tahoma*, Lieutenant Commander A. A. Semmes, captured British blockade runner *Harriet* near Anclote Keys, Florida; *Tahoma* chased British blockade runner *Mary Jane* ashore and destroyed her at Clearwater.

U.S.S. *James S. Chambers*, Acting Master L. Nickerson, captured schooner *Rebekah* off Tampa Bay.

19 Secretary Mallory wrote to Commander Bulloch in Liverpool: "I have heretofore requested you to purchase upon the best terms you can make a very fast steamer suitable for blockade running between Nassau, Bermuda, Charleston, and Wilmington. A capacity for stowing from 600 to 1,000 bales of cotton upon not over 10 feet draft would be desirable. With such a vessel I can place exchange for our use in England every month."

A naval battery mounted to fire across the river at Cerro Gordo, Tennessee, manned by crew from U.S.S. *Robb*, Acting Ensign Hanford, was hotly engaged by Confederate troops. Hanford reported: "They [the Confederates] charged four abreast (dismounted) and came to within 20 yards of the cannon's mouth, while canister was being fired into them like rain."

Mortar schooner U.S.S. *Para*, Acting Master Edward G. Furber, captured blockade running schooner *Emma* off Mosquito Inlet, Florida.

20 A heavy combined Army-Navy bombardment of Vicksburg, lasting 6 hours, hammered Confederate positions. Supporting the Army, Porter pressed mortars, gunboats, and scows into action from 4 a.m. until 10. The naval force met with no opposition, and the Admiral noted: "The only demonstration made by the rebels from the water front was a brisk fire of heavy guns

from the upper batteries on two 12-pounder rifled howitzers that were planted on the Louisiana side by General Ellet's Marine Brigade, which has [sic] much annoyed the enemy for two or three days, and prevented them from getting water." After this extensive bombardment, reports reached Porter that the Southerners were readying boats with which to make a riverborne evacuation of the city. Emphasizing the need for continued vigilance, the Admiral informed his gunboat commanders: "If the rebels start down in their skiffs, the current will drift them to about abreast of the houses where the mortars are laid up, and they will land there. In that case the vessels must push up amidst them, run over them, fire grape and canister and destroy all they can, looking out that they are not boarded."

C.S.S. *Alabama*, Captain Semmes, captured bark *Conrad* from Buenos Aires for New York with cargo of wool. Semmes commissioned her as a cruiser under the name C.S.S. *Tuscaloosa* and wrote: "Never perhaps was a ship of war fitted out so promptly before. The *Conrad* was a commissioned ship, with armament, crew, and provisions on board, flying her pennant, and with sailing orders signed, sealed, and delivered, before sunset on the day of her capture."

C.S.S. *Tacony*, Lieutenant Read, captured ship *Isaac Webb*, bound from Liverpool to New York. The prize had some 750 passengers on board and, being unable "to dispose of the passengers, I bonded her for $40.000." The same day, *Tacony* captured and burned fishing schooner *Micawber* at sea off the New England coast.

U.S.S. *Primrose*, Acting Master Street, captured sloop *Richard Vaux* off Blakistone Island, Potomac River.

21 C.S.S. *Tacony*, Lieutenant Read, captured and burned ship *Byzantium*, with cargo of coal, and bark *Goodspeed*, in ballast, off the coast of New England.

U.S.S. *Owasco*, Lieutenant Commander Madigan, and U.S.S. *Cayuga*, Lieutenant Commander William H. Dana, took sloop *Active* attempting to run blockade out of Sabine Pass, Texas, with cargo of cotton.

U.S.S. *Santiago De Cuba*, Commander Robert H. Wyman, seized blockade running British steamer *Victory* off Palmetto Point, Eleuthera Island, after a long chase; *Victory* was from Wilmington and carried a cargo of cotton, tobacco, and turpentine.

U.S.S. *Florida*, Commander Bankhead, captured schooner *Hattie* off Frying Pan Shoals, North Carolina, with cargo of cotton and naval stores.

22 C.S.S. *Tacony*, Lieutenant Read, captured fishing schooners *Florence*, *Marengo*, *E. Ann*, *R. Choate*, and *Ripple* off the New England coast. Read reported: "The *Florence* being an old vessel I bonded her and placed seventy-five prisoners on her. The other schooners were burned."

U.S.S. *Shawsheen*, Acting Master Henry A. Phelon, while on a reconnaissance in Bay River, North Carolina, captured schooner *Henry Clay* up Spring Creek. An armed boat went up Dimbargon Creek and captured a small schooner carrying turpentine before *Shawsheen* returned to New Bern.

U.S.S. *Itasca*, Lieutenant Commander Robert F. R. Lewis, seized British blockade runner *Sea Drift* near Matagorda Island, Texas, with cargo including gunpowder, lead, and drugs.

23 C.S.S. *Tacony*, Lieutenant Read, captured and burned fishing schooners *Ada* and *Wanderer* off the New England coast.

U.S.S. *Pursuit*, Lieutenant William P. Randall, took sloop *Kate* in Indian River, Florida.

U.S.S. *Flambeau*, Lieutenant Commander John H. Upshur, seized British schooner *Bettie Cratzer*, off Murrell's Inlet, South Carolina, bound from New York to Havana and suspected of being a blockade runner.

C.S.S. Tacony *destroys fishing schooners and merchant vessels.* Under Lieutenant Charles Read, *Tacony* raised havoc with Union shipping from Norfolk to New England.

23–30   Under Commander Pierce Crosby, gunboats *Commodore Barney*, *Commodore Morris*, *Western World*, and *Morse*, with Army gunboats *Smith Briggs* and *Jesup*, escorted and covered an Army landing at White House on the Pamunkey River, Virginia.   Arriving on the 26th, Crosby reported that he "found all quiet on the river," but stationed the gunboats at White House and *Jesup* at West Point, with instructions for two of his ships to "run [daily] from White House to West Point to protect the army transports and examine the banks of the river to discover signs of the enemy should they be near. . . ."   A naval landing party at White House destroyed rails and a turn-table inside an earthwork on which the Confederates intended to place a railroad car mounting a heavy gun.

24   Rear Admiral Dahlgren was detached from duty at the Washington Navy Yard and as Chief of the Bureau of Ordnance and ordered to relieve Rear Admiral Du Pont at Port Royal in command of the South Atlantic Blockading Squadron.   Originally, the Navy Department ordered Rear Admiral Foote to the Blockading Squadron, but the hero of the western waters suffered a relapse from his long illness occasioned by the wound sustained at Fort Donelson and was unable to accept the command.

Brigadier General A. W. Ellet, commanding the Marine Brigade, reported to Rear Admiral Porter on his observations of the continued naval bombardment of Vicksburg: "Your mortars are doing good work this morning.   Every shell is thrown into the city, or bursts immediately over it."

C.S.S. *Tacony*, Lieutenant Read, captured ship *Shatemuc*, from Liverpool to Boston with a large number of emigrants on board.   Read bonded her for $150,000.   *Tacony* later captured fishing

Officers and men on board U.S.S. Commodore Barney. *The gunboat was one of many actively patrolling the rivers of Virginia in support of Army operations.*

schooner *Archer.* "As there were now a number of the enemy's gunboats in search of the *Tacony,*" Read wrote, "and our howitzer ammunition being all expended, I concluded to destroy the *Tacony,* and with the schooner *Archer* to proceed along the coast with the view of burning the shipping in some exposed harbor, or of cutting out a steamer." Therefore, the next morning Read, applied the torch to the *Tacony* and stood in for the New England coast with *Archer.*

U.S.S. *Sumpter,* Acting Lieutenant Peter Hays, collided with transport steamer *General Meigs* in heavy mist near Hampton Roads and sank.

25 Rear Admiral Du Pont, unaware that Dahlgren had been ordered to relieve him in command of the South Atlantic Blockading Squadron, wrote in these terms of Rear Admiral Foote:". . . I infer he is very ill, and could hardly be fit to come for some time to this situation even if he recovers. I trust God he will, for I think he can ill be spared. I always thought he represented the best traits of the New England character with its best shade of puritanism—a sort of Northern Stonewall Jackson, without quite his intellect and judgment, but equal pluck and devotion."

C.S.S. *Georgia,* Lieutenant W. L. Maury, captured ship *Constitution* bound from Philadelphia to Shanghai with cargo of coal.

Boats from U.S.S. *Crusader,* Acting Master Roland F. Coffin, on a reconnaissance of Pepper Creek, near New Point Comfort, Virginia, to determine if an armed boat was being outfitted for "preying on the commerce of Chesapeake Bay" was fired on by a Confederate party. In retaliation Master Coffin burned several houses in the area, one belonging to "a noted rebel and blockade runner named Kerwan."

Blockade runner Ruby *was run ashore at Folly Island, South Carolina, to avoid capture. Confederates subsequently dismantled the steamer. Her machinery is shown in the photograph above.*

Lieutenant Commander English, U.S.S. *Sagamore*, reported the capture of blockade running British schooner *Frolic* off Crystal River, Florida, with cargo of cotton and turpentine, bound for Havana.

U.S.S. *Santiago De Cuba*, Commander Wyman, took steamer *Britannia* off Palmetto Point, Eleuthera Island, with cargo of cotton.

26 Rear Admiral Andrew Hull Foote died in New York City of the wound received while brilliantly leading the naval forces on the Western rivers. The next day the Navy Department announced: "A gallant and distinguished naval officer is lost to the country. The hero of Fort Henry and Fort Donelson, the daring and inimitable spirit that created and led to successive victories the Mississippi Flotilla, the heroic Christian sailor, who in the China Seas and on the coast of Africa, as well as the great interior rivers of our country, sustained with unfaltering fidelity and devotion the honor of our flag and the causes of the Union—Rear-Admiral Andrew Hull Foote—is no more. . . . Appreciating his virtues and his services, a grateful country had rendered him while living its willing honors, and will mourn his death."

Ships, rifled cannon, mortar boats, and Army guns laid down a heavy bombardment barrage which was answered bravely by the Confederate gunners at Port Hudson. Captain Alden in U.S.S. *Richmond* reported to Rear Admiral Farragut: "The *Genessee's* firing was as fine as usual. The *Essex* stood up manfully and did her work handsomely. She was the only vessel hit, and, strange to say, although the enemy's fire was for the most part of the engagement—which lasted some four hours—concentrated upon her, was struck only three times, but one of those was near proving fatal to her. The shot passed through her starboard smokepipe, down through the deck, through the coal bunker, grazing the starboard boiler, down through the machinery and steam pipes, over the galley, and through the wheelhouse into the water. . . . They all seem to be very much pleased with the operation of the naval battery on shore. . . . It had done, as you know, splendid service under the command of our gallant executive officer, Lieutenant Commander [Edward] Terry, before you were called away, and is still, I am happy to say, earning new laurels."

Rear Admiral Porter wrote Secretary Welles of the operations at Vicksburg: "I was in hopes ere this to have announced the fall of Vicksburg, but the rebels hold out persistently, and will no doubt do so while there is a thing left to eat. In the meantime, they are hoping for relief from General Johnston—a vain hope, for even if he succeeded in getting the better of General Sherman . . . his forces would be so cut up that he could take no advantage of any victory that he might gain. General Sherman has only to fall back to our entrenchments at Vicksburg, and he could defy twice his own force. The rebels have been making every effort to bring relief to Vicksburg through Louisiana, but without avail. With the few men we have at Young's Point and the gunboats, we keep them in check. . . . They have lined the river bank and are annoying the transports a little, but the gunboats are so vigilant and give them so little rest that they have done no damage worth mentioning. I have lined the river from Cairo to Vicksburg with a good force. . . . I am having the *Cincinnati*'s guns removed, and Colonel Woods, of the army, is erecting a battery on shore with them. I have now ten heavy naval guns landed from the gunboats, in the rear of Vicksburg, some of them manned by sailors. They have kept up a heavy fire for some days, doing great execution."

26–27 C.S.S. *Archer*, Lieutenant Read, made the Portland, Maine, light. Read picked up two fishermen, "who," he reported, "taking us for a pleasure party, willingly consented to pilot us into Portland." From the fishermen Read learned that revenue cutter *Caleb Cushing* and a passenger steamer, *Chesapeake*, "a staunch, swift propeller," were at Portland and would remain there over night. Steamer *Forest City* was also in Portland and two gunboats were building there. At once Read made a daring plan: he would enter the harbor and at night "quietly seize the cutter and steamer."

Lieutenant Read, CSN, destroys U.S. revenue cutter Caleb Cushing *shortly after capturing her in the harbor at Portland, Maine.*

U.S. Ship "Constellation,"
Leghorn, Italy, June 29, '63.

Sir:

I have the honor to inform the Department that I have learned from many private sources, which I have every reason to believe reliable, that a very fast steamer, said to be called "The Southerner", has been built in England destined for a Confederate cruiser against the U.S. commerce in the Mediterranean; and from the fact that a rebel Commander, T. Jefferson Page, late of the U.S. Navy, is now at Florence, and believed to be awaiting the arrival of this steamer, with the intention of assuming the command, I have reason to believe these reports to be true. It is said, and generally believed here, that this vessel will arrive in a Mediterranean port with regular papers and cargo; but in all respects fitted in such a manner that she can at once be converted into a privateer. I have therefore believed it to be my duty to lay these facts before the Department, trusting that a

Under Commodore H. K. Thatcher, U.S.S. Constellation, the Nation's oldest warship afloat, spent most of her Civil War days cruising in the Mediterranean Sea supporting Union interests in that area of the world.

well armed U.S. Steamer may be speedily
sent into the Mediterranean with a view
to aiding in preventing the destruction of
our extensive commerce in this sea.

At this season of prevailing calms the
Constellation, though an efficient vessel of her
class, could not successfully pursue a steamer.

I have the honor to be,
Sir,
Very respectfully,
Your ob't Servant,
Henry K. Thatcher
Commodore.

At sunset he boldly sailed in, anchoring "in full view of the shipping." Read discussed the plan with his crew and admitted there were difficulties in the scheme. Engineer Eugene H. Brown was doubtful that he could get the engines of the steamer started without the assistance of another engineer, and Read pointed out that "as the nights were very short it was evident that if we failed to get the steamer underway, after waiting to get up steam, we could not get clear of the forts before we were discovered." Read decided to concentrate on capturing the revenue cutter. At 1:30 in the morning, 27 June, Read's crew boarded and took *Caleb Cushing*, "without noise or resistance." Luck and time were running out on Read's courageous band, however, for, with a light breeze and the tide running in, the cutter was still under the fort's guns at daybreak. By midmorning, when *Caleb Cushing* was but 20 miles off the harbor, Read saw "two large steamers and three tugs . . . coming out of Portland." He cleared for action and fired on the leading steamer, *Forest City*, as soon as she was in range. After firing five shells from the pivot gun, Read "was mortified to find that all the projectiles for that gun were expended." About to be caught in a crossfire from the steamers and in a defenseless position, Read ordered the cutter destroyed and the men into the lifeboats. "At 11:30 I surrendered myself and crew to the steamer *Forest City* [First Lieutenant James H. Merryman, USRS]." Read had yet another moment of success: at noon *Caleb Cushing* blew up.

So ended an exploit of gallant dash and daring by Read and his small crew. From the date of their first capture to the destruction of the revenue cutter off Portland, the doughty Confederate seamen had taken 22 prizes.

27 C.S.S. *Florida*, Lieutenant Maffitt, seized and bonded whaling schooner *V. H. Hill* en route to Bermuda.

Commander A. G. Clary, U.S.S. *Tioga*, reported the capture of blockade running British schooner *Julia* off the Bahamas with cargo of cotton.

28 Rear Admiral Dahlgren noted in his private journal: "The French Admiral called yesterday. He said he thought there were torpedoes near Sumter, and that fifteen monitors might take it if they fired faster. He said we fired once in eleven or twelve minutes for each turret."

C.S.S. *Georgia*, Lieutenant W. L. Maury, captured ship *City of Bath* off Brazil.

Armed boats from U.S.S. *Fort Henry*, Lieutenant Commander McCauley, captured schooner *Anna Maria* in Steinhatchee River, Florida, with cargo of cotton.

28–30 As the advance of General Robert E. Lee's armies into Maryland (culminating in the Battle of Gettysburg) threatened Washington, Baltimore, and Annapolis, the U.S. Navy Department ordered Rear Admiral S. P. Lee to send ships immediately for the defense of the Capital and other cities. This was a move reminiscent of the opening days of the war when naval protection was vital to the holding of the area surrounding the seat of government.

29 Lieutenant Commander Shirk reported the interception of a letter from Confederate General Martin L. Smith at Vicksburg to his wife. "He says," Shirk wrote, "everything looks like taking a trip North. All seem to think that Saturday or Sunday will tell the fall of Vicksburg." The Confederates were being realistic rather than pessimistic, for, though they had long and bravely resisted against tremendous odds with supply lines severed, the fall of the fortress on the Mississippi was at hand.

30 Captain Semmes of C.S.S. *Alabama* wrote in his journal: "It is two years to-day since we ran the blockade of the Mississippi in the *Sumter*. . . . Two years of almost constant excitement and

anxiety, the usual excitement of battling with the sea and the weather and avoiding dangerous shoals and coasts, added to the excitement of the chase, the capture, the escape from the enemy, and the battle. And then there has been the government of my officers and crew, not always a pleasant task, for I have had some senseless and unruly spirits to deal with; and last, though not least, the bother and vexation of being hurried out of port when I have gone into one by scrupulous and timid officials, to say nothing of offensive espionage. All these things have produced a constant tension of the nervous system, and the wear and tear of body in these two years would, no doubt, be quite obvious to my friends at home, could they see me on this 30th day of June, 1863.''

Captain Josiah Tattnall wrote Commander William W. Hunter: "The ironclad steamer *Savannah* being completed in all respects and ready for service with the exception of her officers in which she is deficient, I have the pleasure to transfer her to your command.''

U.S.S. *Ossipee*, Captain Gillis, captured schooner *Helena* off Mobile.

JULY

1 Major General Rosecrans asked Captain Pennock in Cairo for gunboat assistance in operations on the Tennessee River. The Confederates repeatedly attempted to establish bases along this waterway, but the Union Navy had several gunboats stationed on the Tennessee and Cumberland Rivers to frustrate such moves. These unheralded but nonetheless eventful actions by the forces afloat, as Admiral Mahan later wrote, showed ''the unending and essential work performed by the navy in keeping the communications open, aiding isolated garrisons, and checking the growth of the guerilla war.''

Commander Caldwell, upon being detached from command of U.S.S. *Essex* and the mortar flotilla at Port Hudson, reported to Rear Admiral Farragut: "From the 23 of May to the 26 of June there followed a constant succession of bombardments and artillery fights between the *Essex* and mortar vessels on one side and the rebel batteries on the other. We have fired from this vessel 738 shells and from the mortar vessels an aggregate of 2,800 XIII-inch shells.'' The continued bombardment of the strong Southern works was instrumental in forcing its surrender after the fall of Vicksburg.

James M. Tindel wrote Confederate Secretary of State Judah P. Benjamin from Mobile, proposing the capture of Pacific Mail Steamers, Union ships carrying on an active trade along the west coast. The expedition, Tindel wrote, would proceed first to Matamoras. ''There the expedition would be divided, one portion to proceed overland to San Francisco to make an attempt to capture one of the steamers plying between that port and the Isthmus, the other to sail as a neutral from some port near Aspinwall [Panama], to make a similar attempt on the steamer sailing from that port. . . .'' The Confederates recognized that the success of such a mission would cause considerable excitement and greatly disrupt shipping in the area, but the Union moved to strengthen its Pacific Squadron in the last 6 months of the year and Confederate plans bore no fruit.

J. B. Jones, a clerk in the Confederate War Department, noted in his diary that President Davis had ''decided that the obstructions below the city [Richmond] shall not be opened for the steam iron-clad *Richmond* to go out until another iron-clad be in readiness to accompany her.''

2 General Grant, before Vicksburg, wrote Rear Admiral Porter that ''the firing from the mortar boats this morning has been exceedingly well directed on my front. One shell fell into the large fort, and several along the line of the rifle pits. Please have them continue firing in the same direction and elevation.'' U.S.S. *General Sterling Price*, *Benton*, and *Mound City* had shelled the heavy battery, which had earned the sobriquet ''Whistling Dick'' because of its power and effectiveness.

C.S.S. *Alabama*, Captain Semmes, captured ship *Anna F. Schmidt* in the South Atlantic with cargo of clothes, medicines, clocks, sewing machines, and ''the latest invention for killing bed-bugs.''

Semmes put the torch to the prize. "We then wheeled about and took the fork of the road again, for the Cape of Good Hope."

U.S.S. *Samuel Rotan*, Acting Lieutenant William W. Kennison, seized schooner *Champion* off the Piankatank River, Virginia.

U.S.S. *Cayuga*, Lieutenant Commander Dana, captured blockade running sloop *Blue Bell* in Mermentau River, Louisiana, with cargo of sugar and molasses.

U.S.S. *Covington*, Acting Lieutenant George P. Lord, captured steamer *Eureka* near Commerce, Mississippi, with cargo of whiskey.

U.S.S. *Juniata*, Commander Clitz, seized blockade running British schooner *Don Jose* at sea with cargo of salt, cotton, and rum.

3 Major General Grant and Lieutenant General Pemberton, CSA, the gallant and tireless commander of the Vicksburg defenses, arranged an armistice to negotiate the terms of capitulation of the citadel. Only with the cessation of hostilities did the activity of the fleet under Rear Admiral Porter come to a halt off Vicksburg.

Boats from U.S.S. *Fort Henry*, Lieutenant Commander McCauley, captured sloop *Emma* north of Sea Horse Key, Florida, with cargo of tar and Confederate mail.

4 Vicksburg, long under assault and siege by water and land, capitulated to General Grant. W. T. Sherman congratulated Rear Admiral Porter for the decisive role played by the Navy in effecting the surrender: "No event in life could have given me more personal pride or pleasure than to have met you to-day on the wharf at Vicksburg—a Fourth of July so eloquent in events as to need no words or stimulants to elevate its importance. . . . In so magnificent a result I stop not to count who did it; it is done, and the day of our nation's birth is consecrated and baptized anew in a victory won by the United Navy and Army of our country." Observing that he must continue to push on to finish the operations in the west by seizing Port Hudson, Sherman added: "It does seem to me that Port Hudson, without facilities for supplies or interior communication, must soon follow the fate of Vicksburg and to leave the river free, and to you the task of preventing any more Vicksburgs or Port Hudsons on the banks of the great inland sea. Though farther apart, the Navy and Army will still act in concert, and I assure you I shall never reach the banks of the river or see a gunboat but I will think of Admiral Porter, Captain Breese, and the many elegant and accomplished gentlemen it has been my good fortune to meet on armed or unarmed decks of the Mississippi squadron."

Major General Herron spoke as warmly in a letter to Porter: "While congratulating you on the success of the Army and Navy in reducing this Sebastopol of Rebeldom, I must, at the same time, thank you for the aid my division has had from yourself and your ships. The guns received from the *Benton*, under charge of Acting Master Reed, a gallant and efficient officer, have formed the most effective battery I had, and I am glad to say that the officer in charge has well sustained the reputation of your squadron. For the efforts you have made to cooperate with me in my position on the left, I am under many obligations."

Porter noted the statistical contributions of the Squadron in compelling the fall of Vicksburg. Writing Secretary Welles that 13 naval guns had been used ashore, many with officers and men from the fleet to work them, he added: "There has been a large expenditure of ammunition during the siege; the mortars have fired 7,000 mortar shells, and the gunboats 4,500; 4,500 have been fired from the naval guns on shore, and we have supplied over 6,000 to the different army corps." General Grant wrote: "The navy, under Porter, was all it could be during the entire campaign. Without its assistance the campaign could not have been successfully made with twice the number of men engaged." Reflecting on the fall of Vicksburg, Porter wrote: "What bearing this will have on the rebellion remains yet to be seen, but the magnitude of the success must go

Rear Admiral Porter wires Secretary Welles to inform him of the surrender of Vicksburg, 4 July 1863.

far toward crushing out this revolution and establishing once more the commerce of the States bordering on this river.   History has seldom had an opportunity of recording so desperate a defense on one side, with so much courage, ability, perseverance, and endurance on the other. . . . Without a watchful care over the Mississippi, the operations of the army would have been much interfered with, and I can say honestly that officers never did their duty better than those who have patrolled the river from Cairo to Vicksburg. . . . The capture of Vicksburg leaves us a large army and naval forces free to act all along the river. . . . The effect of this blow will be felt far up the tributaries of the Mississippi.''

Navy Department,
July 13, 1863.

Sir:

Your despatch of the 4th instant announcing the surrender of Vicksburg on the anniversary of the great historic day in our national annals, has been received. The fall of that place insures a severance of the rebel territory and must give to the country the speedy, uninterrupted navigation of the rivers which water and furnish the ocean outlet to the great central valley of the Union. For the past year the key to the Mississippi has been Vicksburg, and so satisfied of this was the rebel chief who pioneered the rebellion and first gave the order to open the fires of civil strife, that he staked his cause upon its retention. By the Herculean efforts of the Army under the admirable leadership of General Grant, and the persistent and powerful cooperation of the Navy commanded by yourself, this great result under the providence of Almighty God has been achieved. A slave empire divided by this river into equal parts with liberty in possession of its banks and freedom upon its waters, cannot exist. The work of rescuing and setting free this noble artery, whose unrestricted vital current is essential to our nationality commenced with such ability by the veteran Farragut and the lamented Foote and continued by Davis, is near its consummation. You have only to proceed onward and meet that veteran chief whose first act may to dash through the gates by which the rebels assumed to bar the entrance to the Mississippi, whose free communication to and above New Orleans he has ever since proudly maintained.

Secretary Welles congratulates Rear Admiral Porter and his command for the "great result" at Vicksburg. With the fall of this bastion, and the rapid surrender of Port Hudson, the war in the west was won.

When the Squadrons of the Upper and lower Mississippi shall combine, and the noble river be again free to a united people, the nation will feel its integrity restored—and the names of the heroic champions who signalized themselves in this invaluable service will be cherished and honored. Present and future millions on the shores of those magnificent rivers which patriotism and valor shall have emancipated, will remember with unceasing gratitude the naval heroes who so well performed their part in these eventful times.

To yourself, your officers and the brave and gallant sailors who have been so fertile in resources—so persistent and enduring through many months of trial and hardship, and so daring under all circumstances, I tender in the name of the President the thanks and congratulation of the whole country on the fall of Vicksburg.

Very respectfully, &c

Gideon Welles
Secy of the Navy

Rear Admiral
    David D. Porter,
Commdg Mississippi Squadron,
    Vicksburg, Miss.

A moment's pause after the surrender of Vicksburg.

III–109

Indeed, the effect was felt throughout the North and South, for, as Porter had noted, Port Hudson could not long hold out, and the war in the west was won. The great produce of the Midwest could flow freely down the Mississippi to New Orleans, and the South was severed.

Raphael Semmes later wrote: "This [the surrender of Vicksburg] was a terrible blow to us. It not only lost us an army, but cut the Confederacy in two, by giving the enemy the command of the Mississippi River. . . . Vicksburg and Gettysburg mark an era in the war. . . . We need no better evidence of the shock which had been given to public confidence in the South, by those two disasters, than the simple fact, that our currency depreciated almost immediately a thousand per cent!"

President Lincoln could write: "The Father of Waters again goes unvexed to the sea. . . . Nor must Uncle Sam's web feet be forgotten. At all the watery margins they have been present. Not only on the deep sea, the broad bay, the rapid river, but also up the narrow, muddy bayou, and wherever the ground was a little damp, they have been and made their tracks."

U.S.S. *Tyler*, Lieutenant Commander Prichett, repulsed an attack on Helena, Arkansas, by a large body of Confederate troops. The Southerners had penetrated the outposts of the outnumbered Union Army, under Major General Benjamin M. Prentiss, when *Tyler* steamed into action and, in Porter's words, "saved the day. . . ." *Tyler*'s heavy fire halted the Confederate attack and compelled a withdrawal. The Southern losses were heavy; Lieutenant Commander S. L. Phelps, commanding the Second Division of the Mississippi Squadron, reported that "our forces have buried 380 of his killed, and many places have been found where he had himself buried his dead. His wounded number 1,100 and the prisoners are also 1,100. . . ."

Mahan, later analyzing the contributions of *Tyler*'s action at Helena, wrote that ". . . to her powerful battery and the judgment with which it was used must be mainly attributed the success of the day; for though the garrison fought with great gallantry and tenacity, they were outnumbered two to one."

Prentiss advised Porter of Prichett's "valuable assistance" during the battle: "I assure you, sir, that he not only acquitted himself with honor and distinction during the engagement proper, but with a zeal and patience as rare as they are commendable, when informed of an attack on this place lost no time and spared no labor to make himself thoroughly acquainted with the topography of the surrounding country. And I attribute not a little of our success in the late battle to his full knowledge of the situation and his skill in adapting the means within his command to the end to be obtained." The Union's force afloat, lead by capable and tireless commanders, repeatedly shattered Confederate hopes for taking the offensive.

5 Rear Admiral S. P. Lee, commanding the North Atlantic Blockading Squadron, wrote Assistant Secretary Fox regarding measures for a successful blockade: "The blockade requires smart, active vessels to move about close inside, large vessels with heavy batteries, if ironclads cannot be got to protect the blockade and well armed swift steamers to cruise in pairs outside." Captain Raphael Semmes later paid tribute to the effectiveness of this cordon thrown up by the Union fleet around the lengthy Confederate coast: "We were being hardpressed too, for material, for the enemy was maintaining a rigid blockade of our ports."

6 Rear Admiral John A. Dahlgren relieved Rear Admiral Du Pont as Commander, South Atlantic Blockading Squadron, at Port Royal. Since April, when Du Pont's ironclads had proved unequal to the task of beating down Fort Sumter, Du Pont had wanted to explain to the country the reason for their failure, i.e., the weaknesses of the monitors in their cast-iron and wrought-iron parts. To have published this would have cleared the Admiral, but it also would have lowered the Union Navy's most widely publicized weapon in public opinion. Du Pont and Secretary Welles fell out over this difference, and Du Pont's retirement from active duty resulted. Dahlgren did not fare any better in his later attempts to take Charleston than did his predecessor.

Rear Admiral John A. Dahlgren took command of the South Atlantic Blockading Squadron early in July 1863. Flanked in this photograph by members of his staff on board U.S.S. Pawnee, *he moved swiftly to reopen the Union assault on Charleston harbor.*

U.S.S. *De Soto*, Captain W. M. Walker, captured blockade runner *Lady Maria* off Clearwater, Florida, with cargo of cotton.

C.S.S. *Alabama*, Captain Semmes, captured and burned ship *Express* off the coast of Brazil. She was carrying a cargo of guano.

7 Confederate forces under General John H. Morgan captured steamers *John T. McCombs* and *Alice Dean* at Brandenburg, Kentucky. The famous "Morgan's Raiders" moved up the Ohio, causing great concern in the area. The Union Navy blunted the Southern thrust.

U.S.S. *Monongahela*, Commander Read, and U.S.S. *New London*, Lieutenant Commander George H. Perkins, engaged Confederate field batteries behind the levee about 12 miles below Donaldsonville, Louisiana. Read, characterized by Farragut as "one of the most gallant and enterprising officers in my squadron," was mortally wounded in the action.

C.S.S. *Florida*, Commander Maffitt, captured ship *Sunrise*, bound from New York to Liverpool. Maffitt released her on $60,000 bond.

8 Lieutenant Commander Fitch, U.S.S. *Moose*, received word at Cincinnati that General Morgan, CSA, was assaulting Union positions and moving up the banks of the Ohio River. He had also captured steamers *John T. McCombs* and *Alice Dean* (see 7 July). Fitch immediately notified the ships under his command stationed along the river, and got underway himself with U.S.S. *Victory* in company. Next day the ships converged on Brandenburg, Kentucky, only to find that Morgan's troops, 6,000 strong, had just beaten them to the river and crossed into Indiana. "Not knowing which direction Morgan had taken," Fitch reported, "I sent the *Fairfield* and *Silver Lake* to patrol from Leavenworth, [Indiana] up to Brandenburg during the night, and the *Victory* and *Springfield* to patrol from Louisville down [to Brandenburg]." By thus deploying his forces, Fitch was

able to cover the river for some 40 miles. The morning of 10 July Fitch learned the Confederates were moving northward and, joined by U.S.S. *Reindeer* and *Naumkeag*, ascended the Ohio, "keeping as near Morgan's right flank as I possibly could." The chase, continuing until 19 July, was conducted by U.S.S. *Moose, Reindeer, Victory, Springfield, Naumkeag*, and steamer *Alleghany Belle*. U.S.S. *Fairplay* and *Silver Lake* remained to patrol between Louisville and Cannelton, Indiana.

Under command of Acting Ensigns Henry Eason and James J. Russell, two cutters from U.S.S. *Restless* and *Rosalie* captured schooner *Ann* and one sloop (unnamed) in Horse Creek, Florida, with cargoes of cotton.

C.S.S. *Florida*, Commander Maffitt, captured and burned brig *W. B. Nash* and whaling schooner *Rienzi* off New York. The latter carried a cargo of oil.

9   Port Hudson, Louisiana, surrendered after a prolonged attack by Union naval and land forces. The journal of U.S.S. *Richmond* recorded: "This morning at daylight our troops took possession of the rebel stronghold. . . . At 10 a.m. the *Hartford* and *Albatross* came down from above the batteries and anchored ahead of us. General Banks raised the stars and stripes over the citadel and fired a salute of thirty-five guns." A week later Rear Admiral Farragut wrote from New Orleans: "We have done our part of the work assigned to us, and all has worked well. My last dash past Port Hudson was the best thing I ever did, except taking New Orleans. It assisted materially in the fall of Vicksburg and Port Hudson." The long drive to wrest control of the entire Mississippi River, beginning in the north at Fort Henry and in the south at New Orleans early in 1862, was over.

Farragut, off Donaldsonville, Louisiana, wrote Rear Admiral Porter: "The Department, I presume, anticipated the fall of Vicksburg and Port Hudson by the time their dispatch would reach me, in which they tell me that 'I will now be able to turn over the Mississippi River to you and give my more particular attention to the blockade on the different points on the coast.' . . . There are here, as above, some 10,000 Texans, who have 15 or 20 pieces of light artillery, and have cut embrasures in the levee and annoy our vessels very much." Farragut requested Porter to send down one or two ironclads which "would then be able to keep open the communications perfectly between Port Hudson and New Orleans."

Commander Bulloch wrote Secretary Mallory from Paris regarding the ironclads being built in Europe for the South. Noting that it had not been difficult to sign crews for commerce raiders C.S.S. *Alabama* and *Florida* because they held out to the men, "not only the captivating excitement of adventure but the positive expectation of prize money," he revealed that it was a much greater problem to man the ironclads. "Their grim aspect and formidable equipment," he wrote, "clearly show that they are solely intended for the real danger and shock of battle. . . ."
    Recognizing that Wilmington was the key port through which blockade runners were finding passage, Bulloch recommended that the warships be sent to that port "as speedily as possible . . . [to] entirely destroy the blockading vessels." Once this was accomplished, the ships could turn their attentions elsewhere for "a decisive blow in any direction, north or south." Bulloch suggested that they could steam up the coast, striking at Washington, Philadelphia, and Portsmouth, New Hampshire. The high hopes placed on these ironclads were to no avail, however, for they were seized by the British prior to their completion and never reached Confederate waters.

Boat crew from U.S.S. *Tahoma*, Lieutenant Commander A. A. Semmes, captured an unnamed flatboat with cargo of sugar and molasses near Manatee River, Florida.

10   Under Rear Admiral Dahlgren, ironclads U.S.S. *Catskill*, Commander G. W. Rodgers; *Montauk*, Commander Fairfax; *Nahant*, Commander Downes; and *Weehawken*, Commander Colhoun, bombarded Confederate defenses on Morris Island, Charleston harbor, supporting and covering a landing by Army troops under Brigadier General Quincy A. Gillmore. Close in support of

the landing was rendered by small boats, under Lieutenant Commander Francis M. Bunce, armed with howitzers, from the blockading ships in Light House Inlet. The early morning assault followed the plan outlined by General Gillmore a week earlier in a letter to Rear Admiral Du Pont: "I cannot safely move without assistance from the Navy. We must have that island or Sullivan's Island as preliminary to any combined military and naval attack on the interior defenses of Charleston harbor. . . . I consider a naval force abreast of Morris Island as indispensable to cover our advance upon the Island and restrain the enemy's gunboats and ironclads."

The ironclads were abreast of Fort Wagner by midmorning and bombarded the works until evening, but could not dislodge the determined and brave defenders.

The Confederates poured a withering fire into Dahlgren's ships. "The enemy," the Admiral reported, "seemed to have made a mark of the *Catskill*." She was hit some 60 times, many of which were "very severe." Despite the battering she received, Rodgers had *Catskill* ready to renew the attack the following day. Dahlgren added: "The *Nahant* was hit six times, the *Montauk* twice, and the *Weehawken* escaped untouched." Colonel Robert F. Graham, CSA, reported that during the attack, as the Confederates were forced to withdraw within Fort Wagner, "the iron monitors followed us along the channel, pouring into us a fire of shell and grape," and that casualties were heavy. The prolonged, continuing bombardment of the Southern works at Charleston had begun.

Commodore Montgomery, commandant of the Boston Navy Yard, ordered U.S.S. *Shenandoah*, Captain Daniel B. Ridgely, and U.S.S. *Ethan Allen*, Acting Master Pennell, to search for C.S.S. *Florida*, Commander Maffitt. Two days before, the commerce raider had destroyed two ships near New York, and now was reported to be "bound for the Provincetown mackeral fleet." The recent exploits of Lieutenant Read in C.S.S. *Clarence*, *Tacony*, and *Archer* had created great concern as to the safety of even New England waters.

The activity of *Florida* reinforced these fears, which had already been expressed to Lincoln in a resolution urging "the importance and necessity of placing along the coast a sufficient naval and military force to protect the commerce of the country from piratical depradations of the rebels. . . ." On 7 July the President had requested Secretary Welles to "do the best in regard to it which you can. . . ."

Rear Admiral Dahlgren leads his monitor fleet against the defenses at Charleston.

Assistant Secretary Fox wrote Rear Admiral Farragut, congratulating him upon "the final opening of the Mississippi" through the Union victories at Vicksburg and Port Hudson. "You smashed in the door [at New Orleans] in an unsurpassed movement and the success above became a certainty. . . . Your last move past Port Hudson has hastened the downfall of the Rebs."

U.S.S. *New London*, Lieutenant Commander G. H. Perkins, en route from Donaldsonville to New Orleans, was taken under fire and disabled by Confederate artillery at White Hall Point. Perkins went to Donaldsonville to obtain troops to prevent the ship's capture. While Farragut commended Perkins' handling of the ship, he informed him that "the principle was wrong—a commander should never leave his vessel under such circumstances."

Commander Bulloch informed Secretary Mallory that he was going to sell the bark *Agrippina*, which had been purchased initially to take stores and armament to C.S.S. *Alabama* at Terceira (see 28 July 1862). During the year she had made three voyages but had lost contact with Captain Semmes, the unresting commerce raider, and it would be too costly to maintain her as a tender.

11   General Grant, acting on reports that the Confederates were building their strength at Yazoo City, wrote Rear Admiral Porter: "Will it not be well to send up a fleet of gunboats and some troops and nip in the bud any attempt to concentrate a force there?" Porter agreed to escort troops up the river next day.

Charles Francis Adams, U.S. Ambassador to Great Britain, protested the building of ironclads and the outfitting of blockade runners by citizens of Great Britain to Foreign Secretary Earl John Russell. Such acts, Adams noted, "procrastinate the struggle" and increase the "burden of war." The Ambassador's diplomatic protests served the Union cause well and helped to frustrate Confederate efforts to obtain additional support in Britain.

U.S.S. *Yankee*, Acting Ensign James W. Turner, captured schooner *Cassandra* at Jones Point on the Rappahannock River with cargo of whiskey and soda.

Rear Admiral Hiram Paulding, Commandant of the New York Navy Yard, stationed gunboats around Manhattan to assist in maintaining order during the Draft Riots.

12   General Beauregard, commanding the Confederate defenses at Charleston, wrote Captain Tucker, commander of the forces afloat at that city, regarding grave danger which the Union ironclads presented not only to the defenses of Fort Wagner but to the complete defense of Charleston. "It has therefore," he noted, "become an urgent necessity to destroy, if possible, part or all of these ironclads. . . ." He suggested an attack by a gunboat and a "torpedo ram." Within the week, he was again pressing the need to make "some effort . . . to sink either the *Ironsides* or one of the monitors. . . . The stake is manifestly a great one, worthy of no small risk. . . . One monitor destroyed now will have greater moral and material effect, I believe, than two sunk at a later stage in our defense." This was a forecast of the daring and colorful attempts to be made by the Charleston defenders in the *David* attack on *New Ironsides* and the heroic assault by *H. L. Hunley*, the first submarine successfully used in action.

U.S.S. *Penobscot*, Lieutenant Commander Joseph E. De Haven, chased blockade runner *Kate* ashore at Smith's Island, North Carolina. Some 3 weeks later (31 July), *Kate* was floated by the Confederates and towed under the protecting batteries at New Inlet, but was abandoned on the approach of Union ships.

13   A combined expedition up the Yazoo River captured Yazoo City, Mississippi. U.S.S. *Baron de Kalb*, *Kenwood*, *Signal*, *New National*, and *Black Hawk*, under Lieutenant Commander J. G. Walker, convoyed some 5,000 troops under Major General Herron in the operation. Arriving below Yazoo City in midafternoon, *Baron de Kalb*, leading the force, struck a torpedo and sank within 15

minutes. "Many of the crew were bruised by the concussion, which was severe, but no lives were lost," Rear Admiral Porter reported. As the troops landed, the Confederates evacuated the city.

Commander I. N. Brown, commander of the heavy artillery and ships at Yazoo City, ordered shipping in the area destroyed to prevent its falling into Union hands. Subsequently, a correspondent for the Atlanta *Appeal* wrote: "Though the Yankees gained nothing, our loss is very heavy in boats and material of a character much needed. Commander Brown scuttled and burned the *Magenta*, *Mary Keene*, *Magnolia*, *Pargoud*, *John Walsh*, *R. J. Lockland*, *Scotland*, *Golden Age*, *Arcadia*, *Ferd Kennett*, *E. J. Gay*, *Peytona*, *Prince of Wales*, *Natchez* and *Parallel* in the Yazoo River, and *Dewdrop*, *Emma Bett*, *Sharp* and *Meares* in the Sunflower. We have only left, of all the splendid fleet which sought refuge in the Yazoo River, the *Hope*, *Hartford City*, *Ben McCulloch* and *Cotton Plant*, which are up the Tallahatchie and Yalobusha. . . . This closes the history of another strongly defended river." In addition, the Union force captured steamer *St. Mary*. The spectacular Union victories in the West did not eliminate the need for continued attention by the forces afloat on the rivers. "While a rebel flag floats anywhere," Porter observed, "gunboats must follow it up."

U.S.S. *Forest Rose*, Acting Lieutenant G. W. Brown, with U.S.S. *Petrel* in company, captured steamer *Elmira* on the Tensas River, Louisiana. Meanwhile, another phase of the expedition under Lieutenant Commander Selfridge, U.S.S. *Rattler* and *Manitou*, captured steamer *Louisville* in the Little Red River. She was described as "one of the finest of the Mississippi packets." Selfridge reported to Porter: "The result of the expedition is the capture of the steamers *Louisville* and *Elmira*, 2 small steamers burned, 15,000 rounds smoothbore ammunition, 1,000 rounds Enfield [rifle shells], ditto. . . ." He also destroyed a large sawmill "with some 30,000 feet of lumber," and a quantity of rum, sugar and salt.

U.S.S. *Katahdin*, Lieutenant Commander P. C. Johnson, seized British blockade runner *Excelsior* off San Luis Pass, Texas. "With the exception of 2 bales of cotton," Johnson reported, "she had no cargo."

A landing party from U.S.S. *Jacob Bell*, Acting Master Gerhard C. Schulze, went ashore near Union Wharf on the Rappahannock River, and seized contraband goods consisting of blockade running flatboats and cargo of alcohol, whisky, salt, and soda. Lacking transport for the captured goods, Schulze destroyed them.

14 Naval forces under Rear Admiral S. P. Lee, including U.S.S. *Sangamon*, *Lehigh*, *Mahaska*, *Morse*, **Commodore Barney**, **Commodore Jones**, **Shokokon**, and **Seymour**, captured Fort **Powhatan** on the James River, Virginia. Acting on orders from Secretary Welles to threaten Richmond and assist military movements in the vicinity, Lee reported: "We destroyed two magazines . . . and twenty platforms for gun carriages to-day." The last Confederate defense below Chaffin's and Drewry's Bluff had fallen.

J. B. Jones, clerk in the Confederate War Department, recorded in his diary that General Beauregard had written from Charleston "for a certain person here skilled in the management of torpedoes—but Secretary Mallory says the enemy's gun-boats are in the James River and he cannot be sent away. I hope," he added, "both cities [Charleston and Richmond] may not fall!" A lack of technicians in adequate numbers was one of many hindrances to the Confederate efforts.

U.S.S. *R. R. Cuyler*, Lieutenant Commander Jouett, captured steamer *Kate Dale* off Tortugas with cargo of cotton.

U.S.S. *Jasmine*, Acting Master Alfred L. B. Zerega, captured sloop *Relampago* near the Florida Keys bound from Havana with cargo including copper boiler tubing.

15 Rear Admiral Farragut wrote Rear Admiral Porter: "I feel that the time has now arrived contemplated by the honorable Secretary of the Navy, when I should turn over the Mississippi to you down to New Orleans, and then pay my attention to the blockade of the Gulf. . . ." Farragut noted that he would take a brief leave, offered by Secretary Welles, "prior to the work he expects of me in the fall. I suppose some work to be done by the vessels yet to be sent to me, Galveston and Mobile perhaps, and that will finish my work. . . ." On 1 August Porter wrote Welles that he had "assumed the charge of the Mississippi. . . ."

Boat crews from U.S.S. *Stars and Stripes* and *Somerset*, under Lieutenant Commander Crosman, landed at Marsh's Island, Florida, and destroyed some 60 bushels of salt and 50 salt boilers.

U.S.S. *Yankee*, Acting Ensign Turner, captured schooner *Nanjemoy* in the Coan River, Virginia.

U.S.S. *Santiago de Cuba*, Commander Wyman, captured steamer *Lizzie* east of the Florida coast.

16 Batteries at Grimball's Landing on the Stono River, South Carolina, opened a heavy fire on U.S.S. *Pawnee*, Commander Balch, and U.S.S. *Marblehead*, Lieutenant Commander Scott, while Confederate troops assaulted a Union position on James Island under command of Brigadier General Alfred H. Terry. Though *Pawnee*, struck some 40 times by the accurate shorefire, and *Marblehead* were compelled to drop downriver, they nonetheless provided important support for the Union troops and were instrumental in forcing the Confederates to break off the attack. Brigadier General Terry reported that the ships "opened a most effective fire upon my left. The enemy, unable to endure the concentric fire to which they were exposed, fell back and retreated. . . . I desire to express my obligations to Captain Balch, U.S. Navy, commanding the naval forces in the river, for the very great assistance he rendered to me. . . ."

C.S.S. Stonewall, *built for the Confederacy in France under a contract awarded in mid-July 1863, caused much international controversy but took no active part in the war. She was photographed (above) at Ferrol, Spain, in March 1865.*

Porter wrote Farragut from Vicksburg: "The plan of the enemy is, to have flying batteries all along the river, and annoy us in that way. They have already planted one twenty-five miles below here, one at Rodney, and are going to put another at Ellis's Cliffs. We shall be kept busy chasing them up." Nonetheless, on this date the merchant steamer *Imperial* arrived at New Orleans. She had left St. Louis on 8 July and her arrival at the Mississippi's port city without incident illustrated that the great river truly "again goes unvexed to the sea."

Commander Bulloch awarded a contract to Lucien Arman, a naval constructor at Bordeaux, France, for the construction of "two steam rams, hulls of wood and iron, 300 horsepower, two propellers, with two armored turrets. . . ." The general plans had been drawn up by Commander M. F. Maury and approved by Secretary Mallory. The Confederate agent also specified that the ships would have to have a speed of "not less than 12 knots" in a calm sea. Only one of the rams, later commissioned C.S.S. *Stonewall*, ever reached Confederate hands. She arrived in Havana late in the war and was eventually surrendered to the Union. Without the material and industrial capacity to fill their naval needs at home, the South turned with increasing frequency to Europe in hopes of building a Navy capable of breaking the North's stranglehold.

Expedition from U.S.S. *Port Royal*, Lieutenant Commander G. U. Morris, captured cotton ready to be run through the blockade at Apalachicola, Florida.

C.S.S. *Georgia*, Lieutenant W. L. Maury, captured ship *Prince of Wales*, of Bath, Maine, in the mid-South Atlantic (24°14' S., 28°1' W.); Maury released her on bond.

17 Rear Admiral Dahlgren, preparing to renew the attack on Fort Wagner, wrote Secretary Welles about the critical shortage of men in his squadron. Men were being required to bombard by day and blockade by night. The Admiral asked for 500 Marines: ". . . there will be occasion for them." On 28 July Welles informed Dahlgren that U.S.S. *Aries* had departed Boston with 200 men and upon her return from Charleston would bring 200 more sailors from New York to him. He added, "A battalion of marines, about 400 in number, will leave New York on the steamer *Arago* on Friday next."

U.S. ram *Monarch*, with troops embarked, participated in the reoccupation of Hickman, Kentucky, which had been taken by Confederate cavalry 2 days earlier. Brigadier General Alexander Asboth had high praise for the ram and her mobility: "It would be in the best interests of the service to place the ram *Monarch* on the Mississippi between Island No. 10 and Columbus, where she could operate with my land forces appearing at any point threatened or attacked on this part of the river, so much exposed to rebel raids. Without the cooperation of a ram or gunboat it will be difficult for my very limited force to act with efficiency and the desired degree of success. . . ."

18 The combined attack on Fort Wagner, Charleston harbor, was renewed. Rear Admiral Dahlgren's force consisted of U.S.S. *Montauk*, *New Ironsides*, *Catskill*, *Nantucket*, *Weehawken*, and *Patapsco*. The gunboats U.S.S. *Paul Jones*, *Ottawa*, *Seneca*, *Chippewa*, and *Wissahickon* provided long-range support with effect. The heavy fire from the ironclads commenced shortly after noon, the range closing as the tide permitted to 300 yards. The naval bombardment at this distance silenced the fort "so that for this day not a shot was fired afterwards at the vessels. . . ." At sunset Gillmore ordered his troops to attack the fort. "To this moment," Dahlgren reported, "an incessant and accurate fire had been maintained by the vessels, but now it was impossible [in the dim light] to distinguish whether it took effect on friend or foe, and of necessity was suspended." Deprived of naval gunfire support, the Union assault ashore was repulsed with heavy losses.

A delegation from Portsmouth, New Hampshire, bearing a letter from the Governor, was received by Secretary Welles. The group was seeking additional defenses for the city. "Letters from numerous places on the New England coast are received to the same effect," Welles wrote in his diary. "Each of them wants a monitor, or cruiser, or both." The Secretary pointed out that the shore defenses came under the War Department rather than the Navy, and that the local municipality should bear some of the responsibility for its own defense. The successful raid along the New England coast by Lieutenant Read in C.S.S. *Tacony* the preceding month and persistent rumors of other Confederate cruisers in the area since his capture had alarmed the northern seaboard.

U.S.S. *De Soto*, Captain W. M. Walker; U.S.S. *Ossipee*, Captain Gillis; and U.S.S. *Kennebec*, Lieutenant Commander Russell, seized steamers *James Battle* and *William Bagley* in the Gulf of Mexico. The cargo of the former was cotton and rosin, and she was described by Rear Admiral Bailey as "the finest packet on the Alabama River and was altered to suit her for a blockade runner, at a large expense." *William Bagley*, too, carried a cargo of cotton from Mobile.

Boat crews from U.S.S. *Vincennes*, Lieutenant Commander Henry A. Adams, Jr., and U.S.S. *Clifton*, Acting Lieutenant Frederick Crocker, captured barge *H. McGuin* in Bay St. Louis, Mississippi.

U.S.S. *Jacob Bell*, Acting Master Schulze, with U.S.S. *Resolute* and *Racer* in company, drove off Confederate troops firing on ship *George Peabody*, aground at Mathias Point, Virginia.

19 After seeking to intercept the troops of General Morgan for some 10 days and 500 miles, the gunboat squadron under Lieutenant Commander Fitch engaged the Confederate raiders as they attempted to effect a crossing of the Ohio River at Buffington Island. U.S.S. *Moose* and steamer *Alleghany Belle* repeatedly frustrated the Southerners' attempts to cross. Pressed from the rear by Union troops and subjected to heavy fire from the gunboats, Morgan's soldiers made a scattered retreat into the hills, leaving their artillery on the beach. This audacious Southern thrust into the North was broken up. Some 3,000 Confederates were taken prisoner. Major General Ambrose E. Burnside heralded the "efficient services" of Fitch in achieving the "brilliant success" of the engagement. "Too much praise," he wrote Rear Admiral Porter, "cannot be awarded the naval department at this place for the promptness and energy manifested in this movement." And Brigadier General Jacob D. Cox noted: "The activity and energy with which the squadron was used to prevent the enemy recrossing the Ohio, and to assist in his capture, was worthy of the highest praise."

Feeling that "Morris Island must be held at all cost," Brigadier General Thomas Jordan, General Beauregard's chief of staff, asked for reinforcements from Fort Sumter. Brigadier General Roswell S. Ripley replied that he had reinforcements but doubted that they could be transported to Morris Island. "The *Sumter* is here with [Colonel] Graham's regiment, but it is broad daylight, and she can not land within 2,000 yards of the *Ironsides* and monitors."

Major General W. T. Sherman wrote Rear Admiral Porter of the Army's capture of Jackson, Mississippi. No longer could the Confederates utilize it as a base for organizing attacks on Mississippi River steamer traffic. The operation was not as complete a success as either Sherman or Porter had hoped. "Having numerous bridges across the Pearl River," the General wrote, ". . . and a railroad in full operation to the rear, he [General Joseph E. Johnston, CSA] succeeded in carrying off most of his material and men. Had the Pearl River been a Mississippi, with a patrol of gunboats, I might have accomplished your wish in bagging the whole. . . ." Sherman added in an aside that during a supper held for the general officers at the governor's mansion in Jackson, "'Army and Navy Forever' was sung with a full and hearty chorus."

U.S.S. *Canandaigua*, Captain Green, sighted sidewheel steamer *Raccoon* attempting to run the blockade into Charleston and headed her off. The blockade runner, going aground near Moultrie House, was destroyed next day by her crew to prevent capture.

20 U.S.S. *Shawsheen*, Acting Master Phelon, captured schooners *Sally*, *Helen Jane*, *Elizabeth*, *Dolphin*, and *James Brice* near Cedar Island, Neuse River, North Carolina.

21 Rear Admiral Dahlgren wrote Secretary Welles of the continuing operations against Fort Wagner: "I have already silenced Fort Wagner and driven its garrison to shelter [on the 18th], and can repeat the same, but this is the full extent to which artillery can go; the rest can only be accomplished by troops. General Gillmore tells me he can furnish but a single column for attack, and it is, of course, impossible for me to supply the deficiency, when the crews of the vessels are already much reduced in number and working beyond their strength to fulfill the various duties of blockade, cannonading, and boat patrols by night. Time is all important," he added, "for the enemy will not fail to use it in guarding weak points. He is already putting up fresh works."

Boats from U.S.S. *Owasco*, Lieutenant Commander Madigan, and U.S.S. *Cayuga*, Lieutenant Commander Dana, captured and destroyed schooner *Revenge* at Sabine Pass.

22 In a move to bolster Union Army strength ashore, Rear Admiral Dahlgren ordered Commander F. A. Parker to take charge of a four-gun naval battery to be placed on Morris Island "for the work against Fort Sumter." General Gillmore, expressing appreciation to Dahlgren for the battery, noted that he would cooperate fully with Commander Parker: "His guns and men will, of course, remain under his immediate control."

According to figures compiled by the New York Chamber of Commerce on the effectiveness of Confederate raiders, "150 vessels, including two steamers, representing a tonnage of upward of 60,000 tons and a value of over $12,000,000 have been captured by the rebel privateers *Alabama*, *Florida*, *Georgia*, and the vessels seized and armed by them. . . . The result is, that either American ships lie idle at our own and foreign ports, unable to procure freights, and thus practically excluded from the carrying trade, or are transferred to foreign flags."

23 Brigadier General Ripley proposed the use of a fire ship against U.S.S. *New Ironsides* and other Union ships at Charleston. The fire ship, he suggested, would be loaded with explosives. "Should this explode close to the *Ironsides*, or other vessel, the effect must be to destroy her; and if two or three are in juxtaposition, the two or three may be got rid of." He pointed out that some 20 Union ships were generally stationed in a narrow waterway. Though Ripley thought the chances of success were "fair," General Beauregard asked the advice of the Confederate naval leaders, Commodore Ingraham and Captain Tucker, and, when Ingraham reported his estimate of the odds for success at "five in one hundred" and Tucker's at "thirty in one hundred," he determined not to carry out the plan. Late in 1864 the Union acted on a similar proposal by General Butler at Wilmington. Over 200 tons of powder were exploded on a ship to cover an Army assault on Fort Fisher. The experiment was unsuccessful.

24 Rear Admiral Dahlgren's ironclads and gunboats, including U.S.S. *New Ironsides*, *Weehawken*, *Patapsco*, *Montauk*, *Catskill*, *Nantucket*, *Paul Jones*, *Ottawa*, *Seneca*, and *Dai Ching*, bombarded Fort Wagner in support of Army operations ashore. Dahlgren reported the effort a success, noting that the ship's fire "silenced the guns of Wagner and drove its garrison to shelter. This enabled our army to progress with the works which they had advanced during the night and to arm them." The Admiral added in his diary that "General Gillmore telegraphed that his operation had succeeded, and thanked me for the very efficient fire of the vessels." The next day, learning from Gillmore that a Confederate offensive was planned for the 26th, Dahlgren quickly brought his forces afloat into action once again. Issuing detailed instructions to prevent an attack, Dahlgren added: "The enemy must not obtain the advantage he seeks, nor attempt it with impunity."

Because of the French occupation of Mexico City some 6 weeks before and the apparently hostile attitude of Emperor Napoleon III toward the United States, General Banks at New Orleans was ordered to prepare an expedition to Texas. For some time Secretary Welles had advocated a similar move in order to halt the extensive blockade running via Matamoras and the legally neutral Rio Grande River. "The use of the Rio Grande to evade the blockade," he recorded in his diary, "and the establishment of regular lines of steamers to Matamoras did not disturb some of our people, but certain movements and recent givings-out of the French have alarmed Seward, who says Louis Napoleon is making an effort to get Texas; he therefore urges the immediate occupation of Galveston and also some other point." The expedition could take two routes: striking by amphibious assault along the Texas coast, or via the Red River into the interior. In either case, a joint Army-Navy assault would be necessary. The expedition, after a beginning marked by delays and frustrations, got underway early in 1864.

Dahlgren again wrote Welles about "how much I am pushed in order (first) to conduct operations on Morris Island, (second) to maintain the blockade, (third) to cover the points which have been exposed by the withdrawal of troops concentrated here. . . ." In addition, Dahlgren's duties required his forces to be active at Wassaw Sound where a Confederate ram was being built and at Port Royal where the Southerners had long hoped to recapture the vital Union supply station, as well as along the entire southeastern Atlantic coast. Squadron commanders were always faced with demands greater than they had ships and men to meet.

Rear Admiral Porter directed that all ships in his Mississippi Squadron be provided with an apparatus to destroy torpedoes while on expeditions up narrow rivers. Since a torpedo exploding with 100 pounds of powder would not injure a ship 10 feet away, Porter proposed "that each vessel be provided with a rake projecting 20 or 30 feet beyond the bow. . . . The rake will be provided with iron teeth (spikes will do) to catch the torpedo or break the wires." The serious threat of the Confederate torpedoes, even in waters dominated by the Union, could never be ignored by naval commanders and dictated persistent caution.

Confederate torpedoes in rivers both east and west were a major hazard for Union naval commanders. U.S.S. Saugus, in Trent's Reach, James River, (above) demonstrates the use of torpedo nets—one means of trying to offset the Southern threat.

Secretary Mallory wrote President Davis asking that men be transferred from the Army to man ships at Mobile, Savannah, Charleston, and Wilmington. "The vessels at these points," he wrote, "have not the men to fight their own guns and men to spare for any enterprises against the enemy." The Navy had no conscription and suffered from a critical want of seamen.

U.S.S. *Iroquois*, Captain Case, captured blockade runner *Merrimac* off the coast of North Carolina with cargo of cotton, turpentine, and tobacco.

U.S.S. *Arago*, Commander Henry A. Gadsden, captured steamer *Emma* off Wilmington with cargo of cotton, rosin, and turpentine.

27 C.S.S. *Florida*, Commander Maffitt, sailed from Bermuda after having coaled and refitted. Three weeks later, Maffitt put into harbor at Brest, France, for extensive repairs, which would consume 6 months and take from the seas one of the most successful of the Confederate commerce raiders. During this period, Maffitt, in poor health, asked to be relieved of his command.

General Beauregard asked Captain Tucker, commanding Confederate naval forces at Charleston, to "place your two ships, the ironclads, in a position immediately contiguous to Cumming's Point. . . ." Beauregard noted that the addition of the ironclads would "materially strengthen our means of defense" and the Confederate hold on Morris Island. Tucker subsequently replied: "Flag Officer Ingraham, commanding station, Charleston, has informed me officially that he has but 80 tons of coal to meet all demands, including the ironclads, and has admonished me of the necessity of economy in consumption." However, a fresh supply of coal arrived in August in time to enable the ironclads to help evacuate Fort Wagner. Critical shortages of coal hampered Southern efforts afloat and even that which was obtained was "soft" rather than "hard" coal. It burned with a heavy smoke and was much less efficient than anthracite coal.

U.S.S. *Clifton*, Lieutenant Crocker, with U.S.S. *Estrella*, *Hollyhock*, and *Sachem* in company on a reconnaissance of the Atchafalaya River to the mouth of Bayou Teche, Louisiana, engaged Confederate batteries.

28 Under the command of Lieutenant Commander English, U.S.S. *Beauregard* and *Oleander* and boats from U.S.S. *Sagamore* and *Para* attacked New Smyrna, Florida. After shelling the town, the Union force "captured one sloop loaded with cotton, one schooner not laden; caused them to destroy several vessels, some of which were loaded with cotton and about ready to sail. They burned large quantities of it on shore. . . . Landed a strong force, destroyed all the buildings that had been occupied by troops." The Union Navy's capability to strike swiftly and effectively at any point on the South's sea perimeter kept the Confederacy off balance.

Commander John C. Carter, commanding U.S.S. *Michigan* on a cruise visiting principal cities on Lake Erie to recruit men for the Navy, reported that his call at Detroit was particularly opportune. "I found the people suffering under serious apprehensions of a riot in consequence of excitement in reference to the draft. . . . The presence of the ship perhaps did something toward overawing the refractory, and certainly did much to allay the apprehensions of the excited, doubting people. All fears in reference to the riot had subsided before I left." During August, *Michigan* was called on for similar service at Buffalo, New York.

29 Rear Admiral Farragut recalled Commodore H. H. Bell from blockade duty on the Texas coast to assume command of the West Gulf Blockading Squadron during his absence. Bell hoisted his broad pennant on board U.S.S. *Pensacola*.

U.S.S. *Rosalie*, Acting Master Peter F. Coffin, seized blockade running British schooner *Georgie* in the Caloosahatchee River, near Fort Myers, Florida. The schooner had been abandoned and carried no cargo.

U.S.S. *Niphon*, Acting Master Joseph B. Breck, seized British blockade runner *Banshee* at New Inlet, North Carolina.

U.S.S. *Shawsheen*, Acting Master Phelon, captured schooner *Telegraph* in Rose Bay, North Carolina. She had been abandoned after a chase of some 16 miles.

30   Rear Admiral Dahlgren advised Secretary Welles that "the position of affairs" at Morris Island had not "materially changed" in the last 5 days.   He reported that the Army's advanced batteries, 600 yards from Fort Wagner, were in operation and that "Every day two or three of the ironclads join in and sweep the ground between Wagner and Cumming's Point, or else fire directly into Wagner. . . . It is to be remembered," he added, "that Wagner is the key to Sumter, wherefore the enemy will spare no effort for the defense, and will protect any result to the last."   Dahlgren also observed that one of the "many little things" which would be of assistance to him would be "the electric light which Professor Way exhibited here, and which Professor Henry (Smithsonian Institution) knows of; it would either illuminate at night, if needed, or would serve to signal. . . ."   As a man of science as well as an operational commander, the Admiral was quick to seek the advantages offered by new developments.   The calcium light was brought down and enormously assisted in the capture of Fort Wagner by slowing down and halting Confederate repairs to the fort which previously were made under cover of night.

31   C.S.S. *Tuscaloosa*, Lieutenant John Low, captured ship *Santee*, bound from Akyab to Falmouth with cargo of rice.   *Santee* was released on bond.

AUGUST

1   Prior to departing for the North on board U.S.S. *Hartford*, Rear Admiral Farragut wrote Rear Admiral Porter from New Orleans: "I congratulate you upon your arrival at this city and rejoice that we have been able to meet here to make the transfer of the charge of the Mississippi River from New Orleans to the headwaters, and at the same time to receive the announcement from you that the entire Mississippi to St. Louis is free from the annoyances of the rebels, and that I can carry with me the glad tidings that it is open to commerce. . . . I hope that it will not be closed or interrupted again, but that peace and tranquility will soon follow these glorious events."

Confederate steamer *Chesterfield*, landing troops and ammunition at Cumming's Point, Morris Island, Charleston harbor, was taken under fire by a Union gunboat.   She was forced to seek safety at Fort Sumter before she completed the landing of her stores.   Brigadier General Ripley noted that the Union was "for the first time, attempting to interrupt our communication with Morris Island."   Urging that some measures be taken to protect the Confederate transports, Ripley observed that if such actions continued, "our transportation, which is already of the weakest kind, will soon be cut up, and when that is gone our first requisite for carrying out the defense of Charleston is taken from us."   General Beauregard asked Flag Officer Tucker on 2 August to provide "at least one of the ironclad rams . . . to drive away such vessels as disturbed and interrupted our means of transportation last night."

U.S.S. *Yankee*, Acting Ensign Turner, captured sloop *Clara Ann* near Coan River, Virginia, with cargo including whiskey.

2   The day after assuming command of the entire Mississippi River, Rear Admiral Porter wrote Secretary Welles: "The wharves of New Orleans have a most desolate appearance, and the city looks less thriving than it did when I was last here, a year since.   It is to be hoped that facilities will be afforded for the transportation of produce from above.   Almost everything is wanted, and provisions are very high. . . . I think we have arrived at a stage . . . when trade and commerce should be encouraged.   With trade, prosperity will again commence to enter this once flourishing city, and a better state of feeling be brought about."

U.S.S. Commodore Barney *avoids destruction by an electric torpedo in the James River only because the circuit is closed too quickly by an over-eager Confederate.*

4 Four boat crews under Lieutenants Alexander F. Warley and John Payne from C.S.S. *Chicora* and *Palmetto State* and a Confederate Army detachment captured a Union picket station and an unfinished battery at Vincent's Creek, Morris Island. The sharp engagement took place at night, after Confederates discovered that the Union men, under Acting Master John Haynes, USN, had been observing Southern movements at Cumming's Point and signaling General Gillmore's batteries so that effective artillery fire could be thrown on transports moving to the relief of Fort Wagner.

5 U.S.S. *Commodore Barney*, Acting Lieutenant Samuel Huse, was severely damaged when a 1,000-pound electric torpedo was exploded near her above Dutch Gap, Virginia. The explosion, reported Captain Guert Gansevoort, senior officer present, produced "a lively concussion" and washed the decks "with the agitated water." "Some 20 men," he added, "were either swept or jumped overboard, two of whom are missing and may have been drowned." Had the anxious Confederate torpedoman waited another moment to close the electrical circuit, *Commodore Barney* surely would have been destroyed. The incident took place during a joint Army-Navy reconnaissance of the James River which had begun the previous day. "This explosion . . .," wrote Lieutenant Hunter Davidson, CSN, in charge of the Submarine Battery Service, "effectively arrested their progress up the river. . . ." On 6 August U.S.S. *Sangamon, Cohasset*, and *Commodore Barney* were taken under fire by Confederate shore artillery and *Commodore Barney* was again disabled, this time by a shot through the boilers. Returning downstream, the expedition was subjected to a heavy shorefire, *Commodore Barney* receiving more than 30 hits.

C.S.S. *Juno*, Lieutenant Philip Porcher, captured a launch, commanded by Acting Master Edward Haines, from U.S.S. *Wabash* in Charleston harbor. The launch was a part of the night patrol on guard duty; Haines, hearing the report that a Confederate steamer was coming out into the harbor, went to investigate. "Soon after getting underway," he reported, "I made out a steamer standing down the channel close to Morris Island." He opened on her with the launch's howitzer. *Juno*, reconnoitering the harbor with a 65-pound torpedo attached to her bow in the event that she should meet a Union ship, was otherwise unarmed, for she had been trimmed down to become a blockade runner, and her only means of defense was to run the launch down. Engineer James H. Tomb, CSN, reported: "We immediately headed for her, striking her about amidships; but not having much headway on the *Juno*, the launch swung around to port, just forward of the wheel. . . ." Haines' men then tried to carry *Juno* by boarding despite heavy musket fire but were overwhelmed by superior numbers.

Rear Admiral Porter praised the work of the Coast Survey men assigned to him in a letter to A. D. Bache, Superintendent of the Coast Survey. The charts prepared by the Survey were of great value to the Navy in its efforts on the western waters, for they "have added a good deal to the geographical knowledge already procured." Because of the charts, Porter added, "gunboats have steamed through where the keel of a canoe never passed, and have succeeded in reaching points in the enemy's country where the imagination of man never dreamed that he would be molested by an enemy in such a shape. You will see by the charts that what was once considered a mere ditch, capable of passing a canoe, is really a navigable stream for steamers. . . . I have found them [officers of the Coast Survey] always prompt and ready to execute my orders, never for a moment taking into consideration the dangers and difficulties surrounding them."

A detachment of Marines arrived at Charleston harbor to augment Union forces. Rear Admiral Dahlgren quickly cut the number of Marines on board the ships of his squadron to a minimum and sent the resulting total of some 500 Marines, under Major Jacob Zeilin, ashore on Morris Island. Dahlgren ordered that the Marines be ready "to move on instant notice; rapidity of movement is one of the greatest elements of military power."

C.S.S. *Alabama*, Captain Semmes, captured bark *Sea Bride* off Table Bay, Cape of Good Hope, with cargo of provisions. The capture took place within view of cheering crowds ashore. A local newspaperman wrote: "They did cheer, and cheer with a will, too. It was not, perhaps, taking the view of either side, Federal or Confederate, but in admiration of the skill, pluck and daring of the *Alabama*, her Captain, and her crew, who afford a general theme of admiration for the world all over." Semmes subsequently sold the bark to an English merchant.

6   U.S.S. *Fort Henry*, Lieutenant Commander McCauley, captured sloop *Southern Star* at St. Martin's Reef, Florida, with cargo of turpentine.

C.S.S. *Florida*, Commander Maffitt, captured and released on bond *Francis B. Cutting* in the mid-North Atlantic.

U.S.S. *Antona*, Acting Master Lyman Wells, seized blockade running British schooner *Betsey* off Corpus Christi.

U.S.S. *Paw Paw*, Acting Master Augustus F. Thompson, struck a snag in the Mississippi River and sank within 15 minutes near Hardin's Point, Arkansas.

7   With Charleston under heavy attack by combined Union forces, General Beauregard asked that the "transportation of Whitney's submarine boat from Mobile here" be expedited. "It is," he added, "much needed." Beauregard was referring to the submarine constructed at Mobile on plans furnished by Horace L. Hunley, James R. McClintock, and Baxter Watson. She was the *H. L. Hunley*, a true submersible fashioned from a cylindrical iron steam boiler, which comprised her main center section, and tapered bow and stern sections. Designed for a crew of nine—one to

In August 1863, C.S.S. Alabama *was off Cape Town, South Africa.   Lieutenants Richard F. Armstrong and Arthur Sinclair, Jr. are shown on deck near a 32-pounder.*

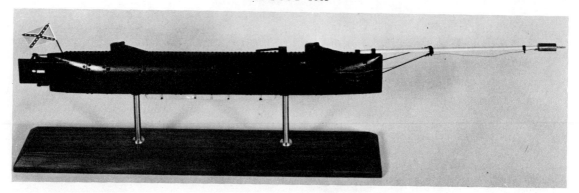

The career of Confederate submarine H. L. Hunley *was marked by deeds of great courage by the men who manned her before she became the first such ship to be successfully used in combat. This photograph is of a model built by the noted model maker Floyd D. Houston for the Truxtun-Decatur Naval Museum, Washington, D.C.*

steer her and eight to turn her hand-cranked propeller—*H. L. Hunley*, according to McClintock, was 40 feet in length, 3½ feet in breadth at her widest point, and 4 feet in depth. Her speed was about 4 knots. In the next 6 months the little craft would become famous and her gallant crews would launch a new era in war at sea.

Secretary Mallory sent Lieutenant Maffitt his appointment as a commander in the Confederate States Navy, effective 29 April 1863. He congratulated the intrepid captain of C.S.S. *Florida* "and the officers and men under your command upon the brilliant success of your cruise, and I take occasion to express the entire confidence of the Department that all that the skill, courage, and coolness of a seaman can accomplish with the means at your command will be achieved." The value of Maffitt's exploits in *Florida*, as well as those of Confederate captains in other commerce raiders, was far greater than even the large number of merchant ships that were captured and destroyed, for their operations required the Union to use many ships and men and expend huge sums of money in attempts to run them down that could otherwise have been diverted to the war effort in coastal waters and the rivers.

U.S.S. *Mound City*, Lieutenant Commander Wilson, fired on and dispersed Confederate cavalry making a raid on an encampment at Lake Providence, Louisiana.

8 U.S.S. *Sagamore*, Lieutenant Commander English, seized British sloop *Clara Louisa* off Indian River, Florida. Later the same day he captured British schooners *Southern Rights* and *Shot* and Confederate schooner *Ann* off Gilbert's Bar.

10 Rear Admiral Farragut arrived at New York. In a message of welcome Secretary Welles said: "I congratulate you on your safe return from labors, duties, and responsibilities unsurpassed and unequaled in magnitude, importance, and value to the country by those of any naval officers. I will not enumerate the many signal achievements you have accomplished from that most splendid one which threw open the gates of the Mississippi and restored the Crescent City again to the Union to the recent capture of Port Hudson, the last formidable obstruction to the free navigation of the river of the great central valley." Three days later, a group of leading New York citizens sent a letter of tribute to the Admiral: "The whole country, but especially this commercial metropolis, owes you a large debt of gratitude for the skill and dauntless bravery with which, during a long life of public duty, you have illustrated and maintained the maritime rights of the nation, and also for the signal ability, judgment, and courtesy with which, in concert with other branches of the loyal national forces, you have sustained the authority of the government, and recovered and defended national territory."

U.S.S. *Princess Royal*, Commander Melancthon B. Woolsey, seized brig *Atlantic* off the mouth of the Rio Grande River with cargo of cotton. Sent to New Orleans for adjudication, she was recaptured by her master and crew and taken to Havana.

U.S.S. *Cayuga*, Lieutenant Commander Dana, captured blockade running schooner *J. T. Davis* off the mouth of the Rio Grande River with cargo of cotton.

11   Rear Admiral Dahlgren, seeking to clear the way for his ironclads through the heavy Confederate obstructions in Charleston harbor, suggested that "a vessel constructed of corrugated iron" and "fashioned like a boat, but closed perfectly on the top, so that it could be submerged very quickly" could be a means of delivering a large amount of powder directly upon the obstructions. Such a weapon, Dahlgren wrote Secretary Welles, "would dislocate any nice arrangements." Dahlgren later described to Welles the nature of the formidable harbor defenses at Charleston against which the Admiral pitted his ironclads. There was a "continuous line of works" extending from Fort Moultrie on the right to Fort Johnson on the left. Fort Ripley, supported by C.S.S. *Chicora, Charleston,* and *Palmetto State,* and Castle Pinckney were to the right beyond Moultrie. A line of piles had been driven into the harbor in front of Fort Ripley. Rope obstructions were stretched between Forts Sumter and Moultrie, and anchored torpedoes were placed in the harbor as well.

12   Rear Admiral Charles H. Bell, commanding the Pacific Squadron, ordered U.S.S. *Narragansett,* Commander Stanly, to cruise regularly between San Francisco and Acapulco, Mexico, for the protection of Pacific mail steamers. In addition, he warned Stanly to keep two-thirds of his officers on board the ship at all times, and to maintain a regular sea watch whenever in a port with Confederate sympathies to avoid being boarded and taken.

U.S.S. *Princess Royal*, Commander Woolsey, seized British schooner *Flying Scud* at Brazos, Texas. She was reported to have run the blockade and landed 65,000 pounds of powder, 7 tons of horseshoes, and thousands of dollars worth of medical supplies.

13–14   A naval force under Lieutenant Bache reconnoitered the White River above Clarendon, Arkansas, "to gain information as to the whereabouts of [Confederate General Sterling] Price's Army, to destroy the telegraph at Des Arc and capture the operator, and catch the steamboats *Kaskaskia* and *Thos. Sugg.*" The force, including U.S.S. *Lexington,* Lieutenant Bache; U.S.S. *Cricket,* Acting Lieutenant Langthorne; and U.S.S. *Marmora,* Acting Lieutenant R. Getty, with Army troops embarked, burned a large warehouse at Des Arc, destroyed the telegraph lines for a half a mile, and "obtained some information that we wanted. . . ." Next day, the gunboats proceeded upriver, *Lexington* and *Marmora* advancing to Augusta, and *Cricket* searching the Little Red River for the Confederate steamers. At Augusta, Bache learned that " the Southern army were [sic] concentrating at Brownsville, intending to make their line of defense on Bayou Meto. Price was there and Kirby Smith in Little Rock. Marmaduke had recrossed the White some days before, and was then crossing the Little Red."

    Returning downstream, Bache left *Marmora* to guard the mouth of the Little Red River and ascended the tributary himself, meeting *Cricket.* Langthorne had captured steamers *Kaskaskia* and *Thomas Sugg* with cargoes of cotton, horses, and arms at Searcy and had also destroyed General Marmaduke's pontoon bridge across the river, thereby slowing his movements. Reporting on the successful expedition, Bache noted: "The capture of the two boats, the only means of transportation the rebels had on this river, is a great service to us." Though operations of this nature passed almost unnoticed by the public, it was precisely the Navy's ability to thrust incessantly into the vitals of the Confederacy that helped to keep the South on the defensive.

14   Timely intelligence reports played an important role in alerting the Union blockaders. This date, Rear Admiral Bailey advised Lieutenant Commander McCauley, U.S.S. *Fort Henry:* "I have information that the steamers *Alabama* and *Nita* sailed from Havana on the 12th, with a view of

Crew members on board U.S.S. Pawnee. *The starboard battery and quarterdeck are shown.*

running the blockade, probably at Mobile, but possibly between Tampa Bay and St. Marks [Florida]; also that the steamers *Montgomery* (formerly *Habanero*), the *Isabel*, the *Fannie*, the *Warrior*, and the *Little Lily* were nearly ready for sail, with like intent. . . . the *Isabel*, which sailed on the 7th, has undoubtedly gone either to Bayport, the Waccasassa, or the Suwanee River. You will therefore keep a sharp lookout for any of these vessels. . . .'' Four of the seven ships were captured by the blockading forces within a month.

U.S.S. *Bermuda*, Acting Master J. W. Smith, seized British blockade runners *Carmita*, with cargo of cotton, and *Artist*, with cargo including liquor and medicine, off the Texas coast.

15 Submarine *H. L. Hunley* had arrived in Charleston on two covered railroad flat cars. Brigadier General Jordan advised Mr. B. A. Whitney that a reward of $100,000 dollars would be paid by John Fraser and Company for the destruction of U.S.S. *New Ironsides*. He added that "a similar sum for destruction of the wooden frigate *Wabash*, and the sum of fifty thousand dollars for every Monitor sunk" was also being offered. The next day, Jordan ordered that "every assistance" be rendered in equipping the submarine with torpedoes. Jordan noted that General Beauregard regarded *H. L. Hunley* as the most formidable engine of war for the defense of Charleston now at his disposition & accordingly is anxious to have it ready for service. . . .''

16 U.S.S. *Pawnee*, Commander Balch, escaped undamaged when a floating Confederate torpedo exploded under her stern, destroying a launch, shortly after midnight at Stono Inlet, South Carolina. Four hours later, another torpedo exploded within 30 yards of the ship. In all, four devices exploded close by, and two others were picked up by mortar schooner *C. P. Williams*. In addition, a boat capable of holding 10 torpedoes was captured by *Pawnee*. Commander Balch

informed Rear Admiral Dahlgren that the torpedoes were "ingenious and exceedingly simple" and suggested that "they may be one of the means" which the Confederates would use to destroy Northern ships stationed in the Stono River. The threat posed by the torpedoes floating down rivers caused grave concern among Northern naval commanders, and Dahlgren came to grips with it at once. Within 10 days, Lieutenant Commander Bacon, U.S.S. *Commodore McDonough*, reported from Lighthouse Inlet that a net had been stretched across the Inlet "for the purpose of stopping torpedoes. . . ."

Rear Admiral Porter wrote Assistant Secretary Fox regarding an attack on Mobile: "I think the only way to be successful is a perfect combination of Army and Navy—it is useless for either branch of service to attempt anything on a grand scale without the aid of the other." Though joint operations were planned for some time, it was Rear Admiral Farragut who, a year later, was to steam into Mobile Bay, achieve a great naval victory and close the last Gulf port open to the Confederacy.

U.S.S. *Rhode Island*, Commander Trenchard, seized blockade running British steamer *Cronstadt* north of Man of War Cay, Abaco, with cargo of turpentine, cotton, and tobacco.

U.S.S. *De Soto*, Captain W. M. Walker, captured steamer *Alice Vivian* in the Gulf of Mexico with cargo of cotton.

U.S.S. *Gertrude*, Acting Master Cressy, captured steamer *Warrior* bound from Havana to Mobile with cargo of coffee, cigars, and dry goods.

17 Naval forces under Rear Admiral Dahlgren, including ironclads U.S.S. *Weehawken, Catskill, Nahant, Montauk, Passaic, Patapsco, New Ironsides*, and gunboats *Canandaigua, Mahaska, Cimarron, Ottawa, Wissahickon, Dai Ching, Seneca*, and *Lodona*, renewed the joint attack on Confederate works in Charleston harbor in conjunction with troops of Brigadier General Gillmore. The naval battery ashore on Mossie Island under Commander F. A. Parker contributed some 300 rounds to the bombardment, "the greater portion of which," Parker reported, "struck the face of Sumter or its parapet." U.S.S. *Passaic* and *Patapsco* also concentrated on Fort Sumter, though the Navy's chief fire mission, as it would be for the next 5 days of the engagement, was to heavily engage Confederate batteries and sharpshooters at Fort Wagner in support of Gillmore's advance.

In the face of the Union threat, Flag Officer Tucker, flying his flag in C.S.S. *Chicora*, ordered Lieutenant Dozier to have the torpedo steamers under his command "ready for action without the least delay" in the event that the ironclads passed Fort Sumter. During the day's fierce exchange of fire, Dahlgren's Chief of Staff, Captain G. W. Rodgers, U.S.S. *Catskill*, was killed by a shot from Fort Wagner. "It is but natural that I should feel deeply the loss thus sustained, for the close and confidential relation which the duties of fleet captain necessarily occasion impressed me deeply with the worth of Captain Rodgers. Brave, intelligent, and highly capable, [he was] devoted to his duty and to the flag under which he passed his life. The country," added the Admiral in his report to Secretary Welles, "can not afford to lose such men."

U.S.S. *De Soto*, Captain W. M. Walker, captured steamer *Nita*, from Havana, in Apalachicola Bay, Florida, with cargo of provisions and medicines. Walker observed: "The fact that steamers are employed at great cost with all the attendant risk, in transporting provisions from Havana to Mobile is the most conclusive evidence I have yet had of the scarcity of supplies in the Gulf States."

U.S.S. *Satellite*, Acting Master Robinson, seized schooner *Three Brothers* in Great Wicomico River, Maryland.

U.S.S. *Crocus*, Acting Ensign J. LeGrand Winton, ran aground at night and was wrecked at Bodie's Island, North Carolina.

Confederate torpedoes presented Northern naval commanders with a difficult problem. They constituted a threat in every harbor, inlet, and river to which the South had access. These torpedo drawings accompanied the report of Commander Balch after U.S.S. Pawnee *had a narrow escape from destruction on August 16, 1863.*

18 U.S.S. *Niphon*, Acting Master Breck, chased steamer *Hebe* north of Fort Fisher, Wilmington. She was carrying a cargo of drugs, clothing, coffee, and provisions when she was run aground and abandoned. Because of a strong gale, Breck determined to destroy her rather than attempt to get her off. Three boat crews sent to the steamer for that purpose were captured by the Confederates when the boats were either stove in or swamped by the heavy seas. U.S.S. *Shokokon*, Lieutenant Cushing, assisted in the destruction of *Hebe* by commencing "a heavy fire, that soon riddled her." Rear Admiral Lee reported in summation: "She was as thoroughly burned as the water in her would allow."

C.S.S. *Oconee*, Lieutenant Oscar F. Johnston, foundered in heavy seas near St. Catherine's Sound, Georgia, after running the blockade out of Savannah the night before. She was carrying a cargo of cotton "on navy account," Secretary Mallory reported. All hands were saved, but 2 days later a boat containing 4 officers and 11 men was captured by U.S.S. *Madgie*, Acting Master Woodbury H. Polleys. Polleys noted that "it was probably her [*Oconee's*] intention to obtain plate iron on her return trip, in order to ironclad the new rams now building at Savannah."

19 Boat expedition from U.S.S. *Norwich* and *Hale*, under Acting Master Charles F. Mitchell, destroyed a Confederate signal station near Jacksonville. "The capture of this signal station," Acting Master Frank B. Meriam, commander of *Norwich*, reported, ". . . will either break up this end of the line or it will detain here to protect it the troops, five small companies (about 200 men) of infantry, two full companies of cavalry, and one company of artillery, that I learn are about being forwarded to Richmond." Throughout the war the Navy's ability to strike repeatedly at a variety of places pinned down Confederate manpower that was vitally needed on the main fronts.

U.S.S. *Restless*, Acting Master William R. Browne, captured schooner *Ernti* with cargo of cotton southwest of the Florida Keys.

21 Confederate torpedo boat *Torch*, Pilot James Carlin, formerly a blockade runner, made a gallant night attempt to sink U.S.S. *New Ironsides*, Captain Stephen C. Rowan, in the channel near Morris Island. The small steamer, which was constructed from the hulk of an unfinished gunboat at Charleston, sailed low in the water, was painted gray and burned anthracite coal to avoid detection. She took on much water and her engines were of dubious quality when she made her run on the heavy Union blockader. When but 40 yards away from *New Ironsides*, Carlin ordered the engines cut and pointed her at his prey. The boat failed to respond properly to her helm, and, as *New Ironsides* swung about her anchor slowly with the tide, the torpedo failed to make contact with the ship's hull. While alongside the Union ship, Carlin could not start the engines for some minutes, but the daring Confederate kept up a cool conversation with the officer of the deck on *New Ironsides*, who finally became alarmed but was unable to depress any of the guns sufficiently to fire into the little craft. At this moment, the torpedo boat's engines started, and Carlin quickly made his way back to Charleston, two shots from *New Ironsides* falling 20 feet to either side of his torpedo boat. General Beauregard, seeking to lift the blockade and the continuing bombardment of his forces at Forts Wagner and Sumter, wrote Carlin: "I feel convinced that another trial under more favorable circumstances will surely meet with success, notwithstanding the known defects of the vessel."

C.S.S. *Florida*, Commander Maffitt, captured and burned ship *Anglo Saxon* with cargo of coal near Brest, France.

21-22 Following 4 days of intensive bombardment of Forts Wagner, Sumter, and Gregg from afloat and ashore, naval forces under Rear Admiral Dahlgren moved to press a close attack on heavily damaged Fort Sumter late at night. U.S.S. *Passaic*, Lieutenant Commander Edward Simpson, in advance of the other ironclads, grounded near the fort shortly after midnight. "It took so much time to get her off," the Admiral wired Brigadier General Gillmore, "that when I was

A Confederate craft photographed after the Civil War in Charleston harbor—a torpedo boat?

informed of the fact that I would have had but little time to make the attack before daylight . . . [the assault] was unavoidably postponed. . . ." Dahlgren wrote Secretary Welles of the difficulties attendant upon an all-out naval offensive because of the multitude of duties his ships had to perform. He noted that one ironclad had to be stationed at Savannah and that another was repairing at Port Royal. The remaining five had to work closely in support of Army operations ashore, "for the trenches can not be advanced nor even the guns kept in play, unless the ironclads keep down Wagner, and yet in doing so the power of the ironclads is abated proportionally." This same date, Brigadier General Johnson Hagood, CSA, commanding Fort Wagner, testified to the effectiveness of the Union Navy's gunfire support: "The fire from the fleet, enfilading the land face and proving destructive, compelled us to cease firing. As soon as the vessels withdrew the sharpshooters resumed their work."

22 Boat crew from U.S.S. *Shokokon*, Lieutenant Cushing, destroyed schooner *Alexander Cooper* in New Topsail Inlet, North Carolina. "This was," Rear Admiral Lee wrote, "a handsome affair, showing skill and gallantry." Ten days before, Cushing had sighted the blockade runner while he was on a reconnaissance of the Inlet. "This schooner," he said, "I determined to destroy, and as it was so well guarded I concluded to use strategy." The evening of the 22nd, he sent two boats' crews ashore under command of Acting Ensign Joseph S. Cony. The men landed, shouldered a dingy, and carried it across a neck of land to the inlet. Thus the assault took place from behind the Confederate works with marked success. In addition to burning *Alexander Cooper*, Cony destroyed extensive salt works in the vicinity and took three prisoners back to *Shokokon*.

U.S.S. *Cayuga*, Lieutenant Commander Dana, captured schooner *Wave* with cargo of cotton southeast of Corpus Christi.

23 Confederate boat expedition under Lieutenant Wood, CSN, captured U.S.S. *Reliance*, Acting Ensign Henry Walter, and U.S.S. *Satellite*, Acting Master Robinson, off Windmill Point, on the Rappahannock River. Wood had departed Richmond 11 days before with some 80 Confederates and

4 boats placed on wheels. These were launched on the 16th, 25 miles from the mouth of the Piankatank River and rowed into the bay. Concealing themselves by day and venturing forth by night, the Confederates sought for a week to find Union ships in an exposed position. Shortly after 1 o'clock in the morning, 23 August, *Reliance* and *Satellite* were found at anchor "so close to each other," Wood reported, "that it was necessary to board both at the same time." The two ships were quickly captured and taken up the Rappahannock to Urbanna. A "daring and brilliantly executed" plan, the capture of the two steamers shocked the North. Only a limited supply of coal on board the prizes and poor weather prevented Wood from following up his initial advantage more extensively. (See 25 August.)

As operations against the Charleston defenses continued, ironclads under Rear Admiral Dahlgren, including U.S.S. *Weehawken, Montauk, Nahant, Passaic,* and *Patapsco,* opened on Fort Sumter shortly after 3 a.m. Confederate batteries at Fort Moultrie replied, and three of the monitors turned their attention to that quarter as fog set in, obscuring the view of both sides. "Finding Sumter pretty well used up," Dahlgren wrote, "I concluded to haul off [at daybreak], for the men had been at work two days and two nights and were exhausted." Much of the firing had been within a range of 1,000 yards. Later that morning U.S.S. *New Ironsides,* Captain Rowan, steamed abreast of and engaged Fort Wagner for an hour. In the exchange *New Ironsides* lost a dinghy which was cut away by a shot from a Confederate X-inch gun.

24 General Dabney H. Maury, CSA, reported: "The submarine boat sent to Charleston found that there was not enough water under the *Ironsides* for her to pass below her keel; therefore they have decided to affix a spike to the bow of the boat, to drive the spike into the *Ironsides,* then to back out, and by a string to explode the torpedo which was to be attached to the spike." *H. L. Hunley* had originally been provided with a floating copper cylinder torpedo with flaring triggers which she could tow some 200 feet astern. The submarine would dive beneath the target ship, surface on the other side, and continue on course until the torpedo struck the ship and exploded. When the method proved unworkable, a spar torpedo containing 90 pounds of powder was affixed to the bow. A volunteer crew commanded by Lieutenant Payne, CSN, of C.S.S. *Chicora* took charge of *H. L. Hunley* in the next few days.

25 The recently captured U.S.S. *Satellite,* now commanded by Lieutenant Wood, CSN, seized schooners *Golden Rod,* with cargo of coal, *Coquette,* and *Two Brothers* with cargoes of anchor and chain, at the mouth of the Rappahannock River; the schooners were taken up river by their captors. "The *Golden Rod,*" Wood wrote, "drawing too much water to go up, was stripped and burned. The other two were towed up to Port Royal. . . ." There they, too, were stripped of useful parts and destroyed together with ex-U.S.S. *Reliance* and *Satellite* which Wood had taken by boarding just two days earlier.

Reviewing the effect of the joint operations at Charleston, Secretary Welles noted in his diary: "The rebel accounts of things at Charleston speak of Sumter in ruins, its walls fallen in, and a threatened assault on the city. I do not expect immediate possession of the place, for it will be defended with desperation, pride, courage, nullification chivalry, which is something Quixotic, with the Lady Dulcineas to stimulate the Secession heroes; but matters are encouraging. Thus far, the Navy has been the cooperating force, aiding and protecting the army on Morris Island."

U.S.S. *William G. Anderson,* Acting Lieutenant F. S. Hill, captured schooner *Mack Canfield* off the mouth of the Rio Grande River with cargo of cotton.

26 Secretary Welles ordered U.S.S. *Fort Jackson,* Captain Alden, to cruise the track taken by blockade runners steaming between Bermuda and Wilmington. Information had reached Welles that two large Whitworth guns, weighing 22 tons each, had been carried to Bermuda by the blockade runner *Gibraltar,* formerly C.S.S. *Sumter,* and he was hoping to intercept the guns at sea before the ship carrying them could even make an attempt to run the blockade.

Welles requested that Rear Admiral Dahlgren submit weekly reports and sketches of damage inflicted on the ironclads by Confederate guns at Charleston harbor. "These reports and sketches," he wrote, "are important to the Bureau and others concerned, to enable them to understand correctly and provide promptly for repairing the damages; and frequently measures for improving the ironclads are suggested by them."

Boat crew from U.S.S. *Beauregard*, Acting Master Francis Burgess, seized schooner *Phoebe* off Jupiter Inlet, Florida.

27 U.S.S. *Sunflower*, Acting Master Van Sice, captured schooner *General Worth* in the straits of Florida.

U.S.S. *William G. Anderson*, Acting Lieutenant F. S. Hill, captured schooner *America* off the coast of Texas with cargo of cotton.

U.S.S. *Preble*, Acting Master William F. Shankland, was destroyed by accidental fire at Pensacola.

28 C.S.S. *Alabama*, Captain Semmes, and C.S.S. *Tuscaloosa*, Lieutenant Low, joined briefly in the Bay of Angra Pequena on the African coast. Semmes ordered *Tuscaloosa* to proceed on a cruise to the coast of Brazil.

Lieutenant George W. Gift, CSN, wrote that he had just visited C.S.S. *Tennessee* and *Nashville* which were building above Mobile. Of *Nashville*, he reported: "She is of immense proportions and will be able to whip any Yankee craft afloat—when she is finished. . . ." In an earlier letter he had written of her: "She is tremendous! Her officers' quarters are completed. The wardroom, in which I am most interested, is six staterooms and a pantry long, and about as broad between the rooms as the whole *Chattahoochee*. Her engines are tremendous, and it requires all her width, fifty feet, to place her boilers. She is to have side wheels. The *Tennessee* is insignificant alongside her. She . . . will mount fourteen guns. . . ."

29 Confederate submarine *H. L. Hunley*, Lieutenant Payne, sank in Charleston harbor for the first time. After making several practice dives in the harbor, the submarine was moored by lines fastened to steamer *Etiwan* at the dock at Fort Johnson. When the steamer moved away from the dock unexpectedly, *H. L. Hunley* was drawn onto her side. She filled with water and rapidly sank, carrying with her five gallant seamen. Payne and two others escaped. *H. L. Hunley* was subsequently raised and refitted, as, undaunted by the "unfortunate accident," another crew volunteered to man her.

Secretary Mallory wrote Commander North in Glasgow, Scotland, urging the rapid completion of the ships being built for the Confederacy. "The terrible ordeal through which our country is passing and the knowledge that our ships in England, would, if present here, afford us incalculable relief, intensifies my deep regret at their noncompletion. . . ." Mallory wrote Commander Bulloch this day on the same subject. Remarking on his "regret and disappointment" that the ships building in England were unfinished, the Secretary added: "Their presence at this time upon our coast would be of incalculable value, relieving, as they would be able to do, the blockade of Charleston and Wilmington. . . ." From the beginning of the war, the Confederacy had sought full recognition from the European powers. After Vicksburg and Gettysburg, the South found assistance from Europe increasingly difficult to obtain.

Commodore H. H. Bell ordered Lieutenant Commander Cooke to "proceed in the *Estrella* up the river to Donaldsonville or as far as Morganza, and report your presence to Commander Robert Townsend, of the U.S. ironclad *Essex*, for assisting in patrolling the river as far as Morganza against the operations of guerillas." The need for gunboats to patrol the Mississippi to guard transports and merchantmen against surprise raids never ended.

30 A detachment of the Marine Brigade, assigned to Rear Admiral Porter's Mississippi Squadron, captured three Confederate paymasters at Bolivar, Mississippi. The paymasters, escorted by 35 troops who were also taken prisoner, were carrying $2,200,000 in Confederate currency to pay their soldiers at Little Rock. "This," Porter commented, "will not improve the dissatisfaction now existing in Price's army, and the next news we hear will be that General Steele has possession of Little Rock."

Captain Samuel Barron, CSN, was ordered to England, "by the first suitable conveyance from Wilmington or Charleston." Secretary Mallory hoped that the ships being constructed there under the direction of Commander Bulloch would be completed by the time that Barron arrived, and that he could proceed to sea at once. Such was not to be, however, and 18 months later Barron resigned his Navy commission while he was still overseas.

C.S.S. *Georgia*, Lieutenant W. L. Maury, captured and bonded ship *John Watts* with cargo of teakwood in the mid-South Atlantic (34°3′S., 18°6′E.).

Confederate transport steamer *Sumter* was sunk by batteries on Sullivan's Island, Charleston harbor, when Southern artillerists on the island mistook her for a Union monitor in the fog and heavy weather.

31 U.S.S. *Gem of the Sea*, Acting Lieutenant Baxter, captured sloop *Richard* in Peace Creek, Florida, with cargo of cotton.

SEPTEMBER

1 Rear Admiral Lee issued the following instructions to the officers of his North Atlantic Blockading Squadron: "Blockaders must not waste fuel by unnecessary moving about in the daytime. . . . The blockaders must not lie huddled together by day or night, and especially in thick weather; there must be specified day anchorages and night positions. . . . Vessels should weigh anchor before sunset and be in their night positions by dark, as when the draft of vessels or stage of the tide permits, escapes are made out at or near to evening twilight, without showing black smoke, and inward in the morning at daylight. The distance to be kept from the bar, the batteries, and the beach must be regulated by the state of the weather and atmosphere and the light. When vessels anchor at night, they must be underway one hour before dawn of day, so as not to expose their position, and to be ready to chase. . . ."

Major General Whiting, CSA, issued regulations for blockade runners at the port of Wilmington. The specific instructions were intended to prevent Union spies from having ready access to the best remaining haven for blockade runners.

Commander Catesby ap R. Jones, commanding the Confederate naval gun foundry and ordnance works at Selma, Alabama, ordered a small quantity of munitions to Admiral Franklin Buchanan for the defense of Mobile. Munitions were in increasingly short supply, and the bulk of those available were being ordered to Charleston.

1–2 Dahlgren, flying his flag in U.S.S. *Weehawken*, took the ironclads against Fort Sumter late at night following an intensive, day-long bombardment by Army artillery. Moving to within 500 yards of the Fort, the ships cannonaded it for 5 hours, "demolishing," as Brigadier General Ripley, CSA, reported, "nearly the whole of the eastern scarp. . . ." Confederates returned a heavy fire from Fort Moultrie, scoring over 70 hits on the ironclads. One shot struck *Weehawken*'s turret, driving a piece of iron into the leg of Captain Oscar C. Badger, severely wounding him. Noting that he was the third Flag Captain he had lost in 2 months, Dahlgren wrote: "I shall feel greatly the loss of Captain Badger's services at this time." The Admiral broke off the attack as the flood tide set in, "which," Dahlgren said, had he remained, "would have exposed the monitors unnecessarily."

2–3   Boat expedition under Acting Ensign William H. Winslow and Acting Master's Mate Charles A. Edgcomb from U.S.S. *Gem of the Sea*, Acting Lieutenant Baxter, reconnoitered Peace Creek, Florida. The expedition was set in motion by Baxter because of "reliable information that there was a band of guerrillas, or regulators, as they style themselves, organizing in the vicinity of Peace Creek, with the intention of coming down this harbor [Charlotte Harbor] for the purpose of capturing the refugees on the islands in this vicinity and also the sloop *Rosalie*. . . ." The Union force destroyed buildings used as a depot for blockade runners and a rendezvous for guerrillas as well as four small boats.   Baxter reported: "I think this expedition will have a tendency to break up the blockade running and stop the regulators from coming down here to molest the refugees in this vicinity."

4   Commodore H. H. Bell, commanding the West Gulf Blockading Squadron in the absence of Farragut, notified Welles of a joint amphibious expedition to be mounted at New Orleans aimed at the capture of Sabine Pass, Texas. ". . . Major General Banks," he wrote, "having organized a force of 4,000 men under Major General [William B.] Franklin to effect a landing at Sabine Pass for military occupation, and requested the cooperation of the navy, which I most gladly acceded to, I assigned the command of the naval force to Acting Volunteer Lieutenant Frederick Crocker, commanding U.S.S. *Clifton*, accompanied by the steamer *Sachem*, Acting Volunteer Lieutenant Amos Johnson; U.S.S. *Arizona*, Acting Master Howard Tibbits; and U.S.S. *Granite City*, Acting Master C. W. Lamson.   These being the only available vessels of sufficiently light draft at my disposal for that service. . . . It was concerted that the squadron of four gunboats . . . shall make the attack alone, assisted by about 180 sharpshooters from the army; and having driven the enemy from his defenses, and destroyed or driven off the rams the transports are then to advance and land their troops."   All possible secrecy was to be observed in carrying out the joint operation, which was planned as the first step in preventing any possible moves by the French troops in Mexico to cross the Rio Grande River.   Sabine Pass in Union hands could serve as a base for operations into the interior of Texas.

Major General Jeremy F. Gilmer wrote Secretary Mallory, seeking assistance in holding Morris Island "to the last extremity."   He requested "the service of as many sailors as you can possibly give us from Richmond, Wilmington, Savannah, and other points—not less that [sic] 200—to be employed as oarsmen to convey troops and *materiel* to and from that island."   For some time Confederate sailors had been performing this vital mission, for, as the siege and intensive bombardment progressed, it had become necessary to relieve the embattled soldiers at Fort Wagner every 3 days.   As Union batteries found the range of Cumming's Point, where the Southern transport steamers were landing troops and supplies, most of these movements then had to be carried on by rowboats crossing Vincent's Creek.   This was hazardous, for armed small boats from the blockading ships closely patrolled the area throughout the night.   Nonetheless, Confederate sailors worked tirelessly to support the Army garrison on Morris Island until Fort Wagner was finally evacuated.

Small boats manned by Union sailors under Lieutenant Francis J. Higginson transported troops in an attempted night assault on Fort Gregg at Cumming's Point, Morris Island.   "The object," Brigadier General Gillmore reported, "was to spike the guns and blow up the magazine."   At the mouth of Vincent's Creek a boat carrying a wounded Confederate soldier was captured, but the shots fired alerted the defenders at Fort Gregg and the secret attack was called off.   A similar attempt the next night found the Southerners ready and no further attempts were made. Gillmore reported that Lieutenant Higginson "has rendered good service.   Major [Oliver S.] Sanford . . . speaks highly of his presence of mind and personal bravery, as well as his efficiency as a commander.   I give this testimonial unasked because it is deserved."

6 Having been under constant bombardment from land and sea for nearly 60 days, Confederate forces secretly evacuated Morris Island by boat at night. Two days before, Colonel Lawrence M. Keitt, commanding Fort Wagner, had reported the ''rapid and fatal'' effects of the shore bombardment combined with the accurate firing from U.S.S. *New Ironsides*, Captain Rowan. One hundred of his 900 defenders had been killed in the bombardment of 5 September. ''Is it desirable to sacrifice the garrison?'' he asked. ''To continue to hold it [Fort Wagner] is [to] do so.'' The next day, 6 September, General Beauregard wrote that Forts Wagner and Gregg had undergone a ''terrible bombardment'' for some 36 hours. Describing Wagner as ''much damaged; repairs impossible,'' the commander of the Charleston defenses added: ''Casualties [the last 2 days] over 150; garrison much exhausted: nearly all guns disabled. Communications with city extremely difficult and dangerous; Sumter being silenced. Evacuation of Morris Island becomes indispensable to save garrison. . . .'' That night Confederate transports assembled between Fort Johnson, on James Island, and Fort Sumter under protection of ironclad C.S.S. *Charleston*, and barges manned by seamen from C.S.S. *Chicora* and *Palmetto State* effected the evacuation. Not until the last group of Confederate soldiers was being evacuated did the Union commanders become aware of what was taking place. ''Then,'' Brigadier General Ripley reported, ''his guard boats discovered the movement of our boats engaged in the embarkation, and, creeping up upon the rear, succeeded in cutting off and capturing three barges containing Lieutenant Hasker [CSN] and boat's crew of the *Chicora*, and soldiers of the Army.'' The Richmond *Sentinel* of 7 September summarized: ''The enemy now holds Cumming's Point, in full view of the city.''

Landing party from U.S.S. *Argosy*, Acting Ensign John C. Morong, seized Confederate ordnance supplies and 1,200 pounds of tobacco at Bruinsburg, Mississippi.

6–7 Army transports and naval warships of the joint amphibious expedition arrived at Sabine Pass and anchored off the bar. Union plans called for the seizure of Sabine Pass as a base for strategic operations against western Louisiana and eastern and central Texas. Through a series of mishaps, as Major General Franklin reported, ''the attack, which was intended to be a surprise, became an open one, the enemy having had two nights' warning that a fleet was off the harbor, and during Monday [7 September] a full view of most of the vessels comprising it. . . .''

7–8 Following the evacuation of Morris Island, Rear Admiral Dahlgren demanded the surrender of Fort Sumter on the 7th; the fort had been so hammered by sea and shore bombardment that one observer noted that its appearance ''from seaward was rather that of a steep, sandy island than that of a fort.'' ''I replied,'' General Beauregard wrote, ''to take it if he could.'' Preparatory to renewing the assault, Dahlgren ordered U.S.S. *Weehawken*, Commander Colhoun, between Cumming's Point, Morris Island, and Fort Sumter. *Weehawken* grounded in the narrow channel and could not be gotten off until the next day. That evening U.S.S. *New Ironsides*, *Nahant*, *Lehigh*, *Montauk*, and *Patapsco* reconnoitered the obstructions at Fort Sumter and heavily engaged Fort Moultrie. ''I drew off,'' Dahlgren recorded in his diary, ''to give attention to *Weehawken*.'' Beginning the morning of 8 September the grounded ironclad was subjected to heavy fire from Fort Moultrie and Sullivan's and James Islands. *Weehawken* gallantly replied from her helpless position as other Union ironclads closed to assist. ''Well done *Weehawken*,'' Dahlgren wired Colhoun, praising his effective counter-fire; ''don't give up the ship.'' U.S.S. *New Ironsides*, Captain Rowan, positioned herself between *Weehawken* and the Fort Moultrie batteries, drawing off Confederate fire. Struck over 50 times, *New Ironsides* finally withdrew ''for want of ammunition''; *Weehawken* was finally floated with the aid of tugs.

8 The joint Army-Navy attack on Sabine Pass opened as U.S.S. *Clifton*, Acting Lieutenant Crocker, crossed the bar and unsuccessfully attempted to draw the fire of the fort and cotton-clad steamer C.S.S. *Uncle Ben*. *Clifton* was followed across the bar by U.S.S. *Sachem*, *Arizona*, *Granite City*, and Army transports. *Sachem* and *Arizona* advanced up the Louisiana (right) channel and *Clifton* and *Granite City* moved up the Texas (left) channel; they opened on the Confederate batteries preparatory to landing the troops. The Confederate gunners withheld fire until the gunboats

were within close range and then countered with a devastating cannonade. A shot through the boiler totally disabled *Sachem;* another shot away the wheel rope of *Clifton* and she grounded under the Confederate guns. Crocker fought his ship until, with 10 men killed and nine others wounded, he deemed it his duty "to stop the slaughter by showing the white flag, which was done, and we fell into the hands of the enemy." *Sachem,* after flooding her magazine, also surrendered and was taken under tow by C.S.S. *Uncle Ben.*

With the loss of *Clifton*'s and *Sachem*'s firepower, the two remaining gunboats and troop transports recrossed the bar and departed for New Orleans. The Sabine Pass expedition had, in the words of Commodore H. H. Bell, "totally failed." Nevertheless, Major General Banks reported: "In all respects the cooperation of the naval authorities has been hearty and efficient. Fully comprehending the purposes of the Government, they entered upon the expedition with great spirit. Commodore Bell gave all the assistance in his power, and Captain Crocker, of the *Clifton,* now a prisoner, deserves especial mention for his conspicuous gallantry." In a vote of thanks to the small defending garrison for the victory which prevented "the invasion of Texas," the Confederate Congress called the action "one of the most brilliant and heroic achievements in the history of this war."

8–9 Rear Admiral Dahlgren mounted a boat attack on Fort Sumter late at night. Commander Stevens led the assault comprising more than thirty boats and some 400 sailors and Marines. The Confederates, apprised in advance of the Union's intentions because they had recovered a key

The heavy guns defending Charleston harbor, such as these on Johnson Island (with Fort Sumter in the background), roared out against Union ships. . . .

But the two views of Fort Sumter's walls shown in these photographs testify to the severe pounding the defenders received in return.

to the Northern signal code from the wreck of U.S.S. *Keokuk*, waited until the boats were nearly ashore before opening a heavy fire and using hand grenades. C.S.S. *Chicora* contributed a sweeping, enfilading fire. Dahlgren noted that "Moultrie fired like the devil, the shells breaking around us and screaming in chorus." The attack was repulsed, and more than 100 men were captured. For the next several weeks, a period of relative quiet at Charleston prevailed.

10 As Little Rock, Arkansas, was falling to Major General Frederick Steele, U.S.S. *Hastings*, Lieutenant Commander S. L. Phelps, arrived at Devall's Bluff on the White River to support the land action. Though the river was falling rapidly, Phelps advised the General: "I shall be glad to be of service to you in every way possible." Phelps added that he would have gone over to Little Rock to congratulate Steele if he "could have obtained conveyance . . . Horseback riding," he wrote dryly, "for such a distance is rather too much for the uninitiated." A week later Phelps reported to Rear Admiral Porter: "I have been up this river 150 miles, where we found a bar over which we could not pass. Numerous bodies of men cut off from General Price's army [after the fall of Little Rock to Steele] were fleeing across White River to the eastward. We captured 3 rebel soldiers, 2 cavalry horses and equipments, and brought down a number of escaped conscripts, who have come to enlist in our army." This type of naval operation far into the Confederate interior continued to facilitate shore operations.

11 U.S.S. *Seminole*, Commander Henry Rolando, seized blockade running British steamer *William Peel* off the Rio Grande River with large cargo of cotton.

12 U.S.S. *Eugenie*, Acting Master's Mate F. H. Dyer, captured steamer *Alabama* off Chandeleur Islands, Louisiana.

Blockade running steamer *Fox* was destroyed by her own crew to prevent capture at Pascagoula, Mississippi, by U.S.S. *Genesee*, Commander William H. Macomb.

13 U.S.S. *Cimarron*, Commander Hughes, seized British blockade runner *Jupiter* in Wassaw Sound, Georgia. The steamer was aground when captured and her crew had attempted to scuttle her.

Some 20 crew members from U.S.S. *Rattler*, Acting Master Walter E. H. Fentress, were captured by Confederate cavalry while attending church services at Rodney, Mississippi.

U.S.S. *De Soto*, Captain W. M. Walker, captured steamer *Montgomery* in the Gulf of Mexico south of Pensacola.

16 U.S.S. *San Jacinto*, Lieutenant Commander Ralph Chandler, captured blockade running steamer *Lizzie Davis* off the west coast of Florida. She had been bound from Havana to Mobile with cargo including lead.

U.S.S. *Coeur De Lion*, Acting Master W. G. Morris, seized schooner *Robert Knowles* in the Potomac River for violating the blockade.

17 Reports of Confederate vessels building in the rivers of North Carolina were a source of grave concern to the Union authorities. Secretary Welles wrote Secretary of War Stanton suggesting an attack to insure the destruction of an ironclad—which would be C.S.S. *Albemarle* and a floating battery, reported nearing completion up the Roanoke River. Should they succeed in getting down the river, Welles cautioned, "our possession of the sounds would be jeoparded [sic]."

U.S.S. *Adolph Hugel*, Acting Master Frank, seized sloop *Music* off Alexandria, Virginia, for a violation of the blockade.

19 Small boat expedition under command of Acting Masters John Y. Beall and Edward McGuire, CSN, captured schooner *Alliance* with cargo of sutlers' stores in Chesapeake Bay. The daring raid was continued 2 days later when schooner *J. J. Houseman* was seized. On the night of the 22nd, the force took two more schooners, *Samuel Pearsall* and *Alexandria*. All but *Alliance* were cast adrift at Wachapreague Inlet. Beall attempted to run the blockade in *Alliance* but she grounded

at Milford Haven and was burned on the morning of 23 September, after U.S.S. *Thomas Freeborn*, Acting Master Arthur, opened fire on her. Beall escaped and returned to Richmond. A joint Army-Navy effort was mounted to stop these raids, but Beall and his men destroyed several lighthouses on Maryland's Eastern Shore prior to being captured on 15 November 1863.

Horace L. Hunley wrote General Beauregard requesting that command of the submarine bearing his name be turned over to him. "I propose," Hunley said, "if you will place the boat in my hands to furnish a crew (in whole or in part) from Mobile who are well acquainted with its management & make the attempt to destroy a vessel of the enemy as early as practicable." Three days later, Brigadier General Jordan, Beauregard's Chief of Staff, directed that the submarine be "cleaned and turned over to him with the understanding that said Boat shall be ready for service in two weeks." Under Hunley's direction, a crew was brought to Charleston from Mobile, the *H. L. Hunley* was readied, and a number of practice dives carried out preparatory to making an actual attack.

Coal schooner *Manhasset* was driven ashore in a gale at Sabine Pass. The wreck was subsequently seized by Confederate troops.

20   The general report submitted this date by Lieutenant Commander J. P. Foster, commanding the second district of the Mississippi Squadron, to Rear Admiral Porter illustrated the restrictive effect gunboat patrols had on Confederate operations along the Mississippi. Foster had taken command of the Donaldsonville, Louisiana to the mouth of the Red River section of the Mississippi in mid-August. From Bayou Sara he wrote: "Since taking command of the *Lafayette* I have made a tour of my district and find everything quiet below Bayou Sara and very little excitement between this place and Red River, no vessels having been fired into since the rebels were shelled by the *Champion* [30 August]. The disposition of this ship, *Neosho*, and *Signal*, I think, has had a beneficial influence upon the rebels, insomuch as they have not shown themselves upon the river banks since I have been down here."

22   Acting Master David Nichols and a crew of 19 Confederate seamen captured Army tug *Leviathan* before dawn at South West Pass, Mississippi River, but were taken prisoner later that morning when U.S.S. *De Soto*, Captain W. M. Walker, recaptured the prize in the Gulf of Mexico some 40 miles off shore. Nichols and his men had departed Mobile 2 or 3 days before in the small cutter *Teaser*. Reaching South West Pass, they pulled the cutter into the marshes and made their way on foot to the coal wharf where *Leviathan* lay. They seized the tug, described by Captain Walker as "a new and very fast screw steamer, amply supplied with coal and provisions for a cruise," and put to sea at once. Shortly thereafter, Commodore Bell ordered Navy ships in pursuit. At midmorning, U.S.S. *De Soto* fired three shots at the tug and brought her to.

Flag Officer Tucker assigned Lieutenant William T. Glassell, CSN, to command C.S.S. *David*, "with a view of destroying as many of the enemy's vessels as possible. . . ." Glassell, who had arrived in Charleston on 8 September from Wilmington on "special service," would take the torpedo boat against U.S.S. *New Ironsides* 2 weeks later.

Expedition under Acting Master George W. Ewer from U.S.S. *Seneca* destroyed the Hudson Place Salt Works near Darien, Georgia. Ewer reported that the works, producing some 10 or 15 bushels of salt a day, were now "completely useless."

U.S.S. *Connecticut*, Commander Almy, seized blockade running British steamer *Juno* off Wilmington with cargo of cotton and tobacco.

25   Epidemic sickness was one of the persistent hazards of extended blockade duty in warm climate. This date, to illustrate, Commodore H. H. Bell reported to Secretary Welles from New Orleans: "I regret to inform the Department that a pernicious fever has appeared on board the United States steamers repairing at this port from which some deaths have ensued. Some of the cases

THE CONSCRIPT BILL!
HOW TO AVOID IT!!
U. S. NAVY.
1,000 MEN WANTED, FOR 12 MONTHS!

Seamen's Pay, - - - - - - - - $18.00 per month.
Ordinary Seamen's Pay, ... 14.00 " "
Landsmen's Pay, ... 12.00 " "
$1.50 extra per month to all, Grog Money.

$50,000,000 PRIZES!

Already captured, a large share of which is awarded to Ships Crews.   The laws for the distributing of Prize money carefully protects the rights of all the captors.

PETTY OFFICERS,—PROMOTION.—Seamen have a chance for promotion to the offices of Master at Arms, Boatswain's Mates, Quarter Gunners, Captain of Tops, Forecastle, Holds, After-Guard, &c.
Landsmen may be advanced to Armorers, Armorers' Mates, Carpenter's Mates, Sailmakers' Mates, Painters, Coopers, &c.
PAY OF PETTY OFFICERS,—From $20.00 to $45.00 per month.
CHANCES FOR WARRANTS, BOUNTIES AND MEDALS OF HONOR.—All those who distinguish themselves in battle or by extraordinary heroism, may be promoted to forward Warrant Officers or Acting Masters' Mates,—and upon their promotion receive a guaranty of $100, with a medal of honor from their country.
All who wish may leave HALF PAY with their families, to commence from date of enlistment.
Minors must have a written consent, sworn to before a Justice of the Peace.

For further information apply to U. S. NAVAL RENDEZVOUS,
E. Y. BUTLER, U. S. N. Recruiting Officer,
No. 14 FRONT STREET, SALEM, MASS.

FROM WRIGHT & POTTER'S BOSTON PRINTING ESTABLISHMENT, No. 4 SPRING LANE, CORNER OF DEVONSHIRE STREET.

have been well-defined yellow fever, and others are recognized here by the names of pernicious and congestive fever."

U.S.S. *Tioga*, Commander Clary, captured steamer *Herald* near the Bahamas with cargo of cotton, turpentine, and pitch.

27 U.S.S. *Clyde*, Acting Master A. A. Owens, seized schooner *Amaranth* near the Florida Keys with cargo including cigars and sugar.

28 Secretary Welles noted in his diary that the chances of European intervention in the war on behalf of the Confederacy were dimming. He wrote: "The last arrivals indicate a better tone and temper in England, and I think in France also. From the articles in their papers . . . I think our monitors and heavy ordnance have had a peaceful tendency, a tranquillizing effect. The guns of the *Weehawken* have knocked the breath out of the British statesmen as well as the crew of the *Atlanta* [see 17 June 1863]."

29 U.S.S. *Lafayette*, Lieutenant Commander J. P. Foster, and U.S.S. *Kenwood*, Acting Master John Swaney, arrived at Morganza, Louisiana, on Bayou Fordoche to support troops under Major General Napoleon J. T. Dana. More than 400 Union troops had been captured in an engagement with Confederates under Brigadier General Thomas Green. Foster noted, "the arrival of the gunboats was hailed . . . with perfect delight." Next day, the presence of the ships, he added, "no doubt . . . deterred [the Confederates] from attacking General Dana in his position at Morganza as they had about four brigades to do it with, while our forces did not amount to more than 1,500." Foster ordered gunboats to cover the Army and prevent a renewal of the action.

U.S.S. *St. Louis*, Commander George H. Preble, returned to Lisbon, Portugal, after an unsuccessful cruise of almost a hundred days in search of Confederate commerce raiders. Preble reported significantly to Secretary Welles that although the *St. Louis* had "repeatedly crossed and recrossed the sea routes (to and from) between the United States and the Mediterranean and Europe, we have in all this cruise met with but one American merchant vessel at sea. This fact, on a sea poetically supposed to be whitened by our commerce, illustrates the difficulties attendant upon a search after the two or three rebel cruisers afloat." In addition, the scarcity of American flag merchant sail testified to the effectiveness of the few Southern raiders.

30 U.S.S. *Rosalie*, Acting Master Peter F. Coffin, seized British schooner *Director* attempting to run the blockade at Sanibel River, Florida, with cargo of salt and rum.

OCTOBER

2 U.S.S. *Bermuda*, Acting Master J. W. Smith, seized blockade running British schooner *Florrie* near Matagorda, Texas, with cargo including medicine, wine, and saddles.

5 C.S.S. *David*, Lieutenant Glassell, exploded a torpedo against U.S.S. *New Ironsides*, Captain Rowan, in Charleston harbor but did not destroy the heavy warship. Mounting a torpedo containing some 60 pounds of powder on a 10-foot spar fixed to her bow, the 50-foot *David* stood out from Charleston early in the evening. Riding low in the water, the torpedo boat made her way down the main ship channel and was close aboard her quarry before being sighted and hailed. Almost at once a volley of small arms fire was centered on her as she steamed at full speed at *New Ironsides*, plunging the torpedo against the Union ship's starboard quarter and "shaking the vessel and throwing up an immense column of water. . . ." As the water fell, it put out the fires in *David*'s boilers and nearly swamped her; the torpedo boat came to rest alongside *New Ironsides*. Believing the torpedo boat doomed, Lieutenant Glassell and Seaman James Sullivan abandoned ship and were subsequently picked up by the blockading fleet. However, Engineer Tomb at length succeeded in relighting *David*'s fires and, with pilot Walker Cannon, who had remained on board because he could not swim, took her back to Charleston. Though *David* did not succeed in sinking

Confederate David *rams a spar torpedo into the hull of U.S.S.* New Ironsides *in Charleston harbor. The huge blockader sustained considerable damage but was not destroyed.*

New Ironsides, the explosion was a "severe blow" which eventually forced the Union ship to leave the blockade for repairs. "It seems to me," Rear Admiral Dahlgren wrote, noting the tactical implications of the attack, "that nothing could have been more successful as a first effort, and it will place the torpedo among certain offensive means." Writing of the attack's "unsurpassed daring," Secretary Mallory noted: "The annals of naval warfare record few enterprises which exhibit more strikingly than this of Lieutenant Glassell the highest qualities of a sea officer."

The near success of *David's* torpedo attack on *New Ironsides* prompted Dahlgren to emphasize further the need for developing defensive measures against them. "How far the enemy may seem encouraged," he wrote Welles, "I do not know, but I think it will be well to be prepared against a considerable issue of these small craft. It is certainly the best form of the torpedo which has come to my notice, and a large quantity of powder may as well be exploded as 60 pounds . . . The vessels themselves should be protected by outriggers, and the harbor itself well strewn with a similar class of craft. . . . The subject merits serious attention, for it will receive a greater development." He added to Assistant Secretary Fox: "By all means let us have a quantity of these torpedoes, and thus turn them against the enemy. We," Dahlgren said, paying tribute to the industrial strength that weighed so heavily in the Union's favor, "can make them faster than they can."

British blockade runner *Concordia* was destroyed by her crew at Calcasieu Pass, Louisiana, to prevent her capture by boats from U.S.S. *Granite City*, Acting Master Lamson.

6 U.S.S. *Beauregard*, Acting Master Burgess, captured sloop *Last Trial* at Key West with cargo of salt.

U.S.S. *Virginia*, Lieutenant C. H. Brown, seized British blockade runner *Jenny* off the coast of Texas with cargo of cotton.

7 An expedition under Acting Chief Engineer Thomas Doughty from U.S.S. *Osage* captured and burned steamers *Robert Fulton* and *Argus* in the Red River. Acting Lieutenant Couthouy, commanding *Osage*, had ordered the operation upon learning that a Confederate steamer was tied up to the river bank. The naval force travelled overland from the Mississippi to the Red "after great labor in getting through entanglements of the bushes and other undergrowth. . . ." Doughty succeeded in capturing *Argus* shortly before *Robert Fulton* was sighted steaming downriver. He ordered her to come to. "She did so," he reported, "and I found myself in possession of 9 prisoners and two steamboats." Doughty burned *Argus* immediately and then destroyed *Robert Fulton* when he was unable to get her over the bar at the mouth of the Red River. "This is a great loss to the rebels at this moment," Rear Admiral Porter wrote, "as it cuts off their means of operating across that part of Atchafalaya where they lately came over to attack Morganza. This capture will deter others from coming down the Red River."

Boat crew from U.S.S. *Cayuga*, Lieutenant Commander Dana, boarded and destroyed blockade runner *Pushmataha* which had been chased ashore and abandoned off Calcasieu River, Louisiana. *Pushmataha* carried a cargo of a ram, claret, and gunpowder, and had been set on fire by her crew. "One of a number of kegs of powder had been opened," reported Dana, "and a match, which was inserted in the hole, was on fire; this was taken out and, with the keg, thrown overboard by Thomas Morton, ordinary seaman"—an unsung act of heroism. Dana chased ashore another schooner carrying gunpowder which was blown up before she could be boarded.

9 Secretary Welles commended Rear Admiral Dahlgren on the work of the South Atlantic Blockading Squadron off Charleston the preceding month and cited Brigadier General Gillmore's "brilliant operations" on Morris Island. Noting that, though the first step in the capture of Charleston was taken, the remainder would be full of risk, he added: "While there is intense feeling pervading the country in regard to the fate of Charleston . . . the public impatience must not be permitted to hasten your own movements into immature and inconsiderate action against your own deliberate convictions nor impel you to hazards that may jeopardize the best interest of the country without adequate results. . . ."

C.S.S. *Georgia*, Lieutenant W. L. Maury, captured and burned ship *Bold Hunter* off the coast of French West Africa. She had been bound for Calcutta with cargo of coal.

10 Secretary Welles transmitted to Rear Admiral Porter a War Department request for gunboat assistance for the operations of Major General W. T. Sherman on the Tennessee River. Porter replied that the shallowness of the water prevented his immediate action but promised: "The gunboats will be ready to go up the moment a rise takes place. . . ." Ten days later, General Grant urged: "The sooner a gunboat can be got to him [Sherman] the better." Porter answered that gunboats were on their way up the Tennessee and Cumberland Rivers. "My intention," he wrote, "is to send every gunboat I can spare up the Tennessee. I have also sent below for light-drafts to come up. Am sorry to say the river is at a stand." By the 24th two gunboats were at Eastport to join Sherman's operations.

U.S.S. *Samuel Rotan*, Acting Lieutenant Kennison seized a large yawl off Horn Harbor, Virginia, with cargo including salt.

11 U.S.S. *Nansemond*, Lieutenant Roswell H. Lamson, chased ashore and destroyed at night steamer *Douro* near New Inlet, North Carolina. She had a cargo of cotton, tobacco, turpentine, and rosin. *Douro* had been captured previously on 9 March 1863 by U.S.S. *Quaker City*, but after being condemned she was sold and turned up again as a blockade runner. Noting this, Commander Almy, senior officer at New Inlet, wrote: "She now lies a perfect wreck . . . and past ever being bought

Confederate David torpedo boats.

General P. G. T. Beauregard commanded the defenses of Charleston. He encouraged use of the torpedo boats and used the small Confederate forces afloat well.

and sold again." Rear Admiral S. P. Lee informed Assistant Secretary Fox: "The *Nansemond* has done well off Wilmington. She discovered followed & destroyed the *Douro at night*, the first instance of the kind, I believe."

U.S.S. *Union*, Acting Lieutenant Conroy, seized steamer *Spaulding* at sea east of St. Andrew's Sound, Georgia. She had run the blockade out of Charleston the previous month with cargo of cotton and was attempting to return from Nassau, "which," Conroy wrote, "we have spoiled. . . ."

U.S.S. *Madgie*, Acting Master Polleys, in tow of U.S.S. *Fahkee*, Acting Ensign Francis R. Webb, sank in rough seas off Frying Pan Shoals, North Carolina.

12 U.S.S. *Kanawha*, Lieutenant Commander Mayo, and U.S.S. *Eugenie*, Lieutenant Henry W. Miller, attempted to destroy a steamer aground under the guns of Fort Morgan in Mobile Bay and were taken under fire by the fort. *Kanawha* was damaged during the engagement.

13 U.S.S. *Victoria*, Acting Lieutenant John MacDiarmid, seized a sloop (no name reported) west of Little River, North Carolina, with cargo of salt and soap.

Guard boat from U.S.S. *Braziliera*, Acting Master William T. Gillespie, captured schooner *Mary* near St. Simon's, Georgia.

13-14 U.S.S. *Queen City*, Acting Lieutenant G. W. Brown, with troops embarked, departed Helena, Arkansas, for Friar's Point, Mississippi, where the soldiers landed and surrounded the town. The morning of the 14th, the warehouses were searched and more than 200 bales of cotton and several prisoners were seized.

15 Confederate submarine *H. L. Hunley*, under the command of the part owner for whom she was named, sank in Charleston harbor while making practice dives under Confederate receiving ship *Indian Chief*. A report of the "unfortunate accident" stated: "The boat left the wharf at 9:25 a.m. and disappeared at 9:35. As soon as she sunk, air bubbles were seen to rise to the surface of the water, and from this fact it is supposed the hole in the top of the boat by which the men entered was not properly closed. It was impossible at the time to make any effort to rescue the unfortunate men, as the water was some 9 fathoms deep." Thus the imaginative and daring Horace L. Hunley and his gallant seven man crew perished. The submarine had claimed the lives of its second crew. When the submarine was raised for a second time, a third crew volunteered to man her. Her new captain was Lieutenant George Dixon, CSA. Under Dixon and Lieutenant William A. Alexander, *H. L. Hunley* was reconditioned, but, as a safety precaution, General Beauregard directed that she not dive again. She was fitted with a spar torpedo. Time and again in the next 4 months the submarine ventured into the harbor at night from her base on Sullivan's Island, but until mid-February 1864 her attempts to sink a blockader were to no avail. The fact that the Unions ships frequently remained on station some 6 or 7 miles away and put out picket boats at night; the condition of tide, wind, and sea; and the physical exhaustion of the submarine crew who sometimes found themselves in grave danger of being swept out to sea in the underpowered craft were restricting factors with which Lieutenant Dixon and *H. L. Hunley* had to cope.

U.S.S. *Honduras*, Acting Master Abraham N. Gould, seized British steamer *Mail* near St. Petersburg, Florida. She had been bound from Bayport to Havana with cargo of cotton and turpentine. The capture was made after a 3-hour chase in which U.S.S. *Two Sisters*, *Sea Bird*, and *Fox* also participated.

U.S.S. *Commodore*, Acting Master John R. Hamilton, and U.S.S. *Corypheus*, Acting Master Francis H. Grove, destroyed a Confederate tannery at Bay St. Louis, Mississippi. Grove wrote that they had "completely destroyed the buildings, vats, and mill for grinding bark; also a large amount of hides stored there, said to be worth $20,000."

16   Mr. Jules David wrote from Victoria, Vancouver Island, "as president of a Southern association existing in this and the adjoining colony of British Columbia," requesting Confederate Secretary of State Benjamin to assist him in obtaining for his organization "a letter of marque to be used on the Pacific." Mr. David added that much could be done on that coast "to harass and injure our enemies," and stated that the group he represented had "a first-class steamer of 400 tons, strongly built, and of an average speed of 14 miles." Southern sympathizers like Mr. David hoped to strike a blow for the Confederacy by raiding Union commerce.

Commodore H. H. Bell reported that U.S.S. *Tennessee*, Acting Lieutenant Wiggin, had seized blockade running British schooner *Friendship* off Rio Brazos, Texas, with cargo of munitions from Havana, and caused schooner *Jane* to be destroyed by her own crew to prevent capture.

16–17   Upon learning that blockade runners *Scottish Chief* and *Kate Dale* were being loaded with cotton and nearly ready to sail from Hillsboro River, Florida, Rear Admiral Bailey sent U.S.S. *Tahoma*, Lieutenant Commander A. A. Semmes, and U.S.S. *Adela*, Acting Lieutenant Louis N. Stodder, to seize them. "It was planned between myself and Captain Semmes," Bailey reported, "that he should, with the *Tahoma*, assisted by the *Adela*, divert attention from the real object of the expedition by shelling the fort and town [Tampa], and that under cover of night men should be landed at a point on old Tampa Bay, distant from the fort to proceed overland to the point on the Hillsboro River where the blockade runners lay, there to destroy them." This plan was put into effect and some 100 men from the two ships marched 14 miles overland. At daylight, 17 October, as the landing party boarded the blockade runners, two crew members made good their escape and alerted the garrison. Nevertheless, the Union sailors destroyed *Scottish Chief* and *Kate Dale*. A running battle ensued as they attempted to get back to their ships. Bailey reported 5 members of the landing party killed, 10 wounded, and 5 taken prisoner. Lieutenant Commander Semmes noted: "I regret sincerely our loss, yet I feel a great degree of satisfaction in having impressed the rebels with the idea that blockade-running vessels are not safe, even up the Hillsboro River."

17   Boat crews from U.S.S. *T. A. Ward*, Acting Master William L. Babcock, destroyed schooner *Rover* at Murrell's Inlet, South Carolina. The schooner was laden with cotton and ready to run the blockade. Three days later, a landing party from *T. A. Ward* went ashore under command of Acting Ensign Myron W. Tillson to reconnoiter the area and obtain water. They were surprised by Confederate cavalry and 10 of the men were captured.

Lieutenant Commander William Gibson, U.S.S. *Seneca*, reported to Rear Admiral Dahlgren that the blockaded steamer *Herald* had escaped the previous night from Darien, Georgia and recommended that the ships of the blockading squadron there be "properly armed." Gibson noted: "One gunboat in this sound can not guard all the estuaries and creeks formed by the flowing of the Altamaha to the sea, especially since the port of Charleston has been effectually closed and the enemy seeks other channels of unlawful commerce."

18   Rear Admiral Dahlgren, writing Secretary Welles that the role of the Navy in the capture of Morris Island was "neither known nor appreciated by the public at large," noted that in the 2-month bombardment of the Confederates the ironclads of his squadron had fired more than 8,000 shot and shells and received nearly 900 hits. The Admiral added: "By the presence and action of the vessels the right flank of our army and its supplies were entirely covered; provisions, arms, cannon, ammunition . . . were landed as freely as if an enemy were not in sight, while by the same means the enemy was restricted to the least space and action. Indeed, it was only by night, and in the line from Sumter, that food, powder, or relief could be introduced, and that very sparingly. The works of the enemy were also flanked by our guns so that he was confined to his works and his fire quelled whenever it became too serious. . . ."

The sunken Confederate submarine, *H. L. Hunley*, was found in 9 fathoms of water by a diver in Charleston harbor. Efforts were begun at once to recover the little craft, deemed vital to the defenses of Charleston.

20   Commander Bulloch advised Secretary Mallory from Liverpool that the ironclads known as *294* and *295*, being built in England, had been seized by the British Government. Bulloch felt the action stemmed from the fact that "a large number of Confederate naval officers have during the past three months arrived in England. The *Florida* came off the Irish coast some six weeks since, and proceeding to Brest, there discharged the greater portion of her crew, who were sent to Liverpool. These circumstances were eagerly seized upon by the United States representative here, and they have so worked upon Lord Russell as to make him believe that the presence of these officers and men has direct reference to the destination of the rams. . . ."

U.S.S. *Annie*, Acting Ensign Williams, seized blockade running British schooner *Martha Jane* off Bayport, Florida, bound to Havana with cargo of some 26,600 pounds of sea island cotton.

21   U.S.S. *Nansemond*, Lieutenant R. H. Lamson, chased blockade running steamer *Venus* ashore near Cape Fear River, North Carolina. Four shots from the blockader caused the steamer to take on water. Lamson attempted to get *Venus* off in the morning but found it "impossible to move her, [and] I ordered her to be set on fire." A notebook found on board *Venus* recorded that 75 ships had been engaged in blockade running thus far in 1863, of which 32 had been captured or destroyed.

U.S.S. *Currituck*, Acting Lieutenant Hooker, and U.S.S. *Fuchsia*, Acting Master Street, captured steamer *Three Brothers* in the Rappahannock River, Virginia.

U.S.S. *J. P. Jackson*, Lieutenant Lewis W. Pennington, captured schooner *Syrena* near Deer Island, Mississippi.

22   Union steamer *Mist* was boarded and burned at Ship Island, Mississippi, by Confederate guerrillas when she attempted to take on a cargo of cotton without the protection of a Union gunboat. A week later Rear Admiral Porter wisely wrote Major General W. T. Sherman: "Steamers should not be allowed to land anywhere but at a military port, or a place guarded by a gunboat. . . ."

23   U.S.S. *Norfolk Packet*, Acting Ensign George W. Wood, captured schooner *Ocean Bird* off St. Augustine Inlet, Florida.

24   U.S.S. *Hastings*, Lieutenant Commander S. L. Phelps, and U.S.S. *Key West*, Acting Master Edward M. King, arrived at Eastport, Mississippi, to support Army operations along the Tennessee River. Low water had delayed the movement earlier in the month and would prevent full operations for some time, but Major General W. T. Sherman was "gratified" with the gunboats' arrival. The joint operations extended into mid-December as the Union moved to solidify its position in the South's interior. Sherman wrote Rear Admiral Porter of Phelps' arrival: "Of course we will get along together elegantly. All I have he can command, and I know the same feeling pervades every sailor's and soldier's heart. We are as one."

U.S.S. *Calypso*, Acting Master Frederick D. Stuart, captured blockade running British schooner *Herald* off Frying Pan Shoals, North Carolina, with cargo of salt and soda.

U.S.S. *Conestoga*, Acting Master Gilbert Morton, seized steamer *Lillie Martin* and tug *Sweden*, suspected of trading with the Confederates, near Napoleon, Mississippi.

25   U.S.S. *Kittatinny*, Acting Master Isaac D. Seyburn, captured schooner *Reserve*, off Pass Cavallo, Texas.

26 Union ironclads began an intensive two week bombardment of Fort Sumter. At month's end, General Beauregard wrote of the ''terrible bombardment'' and noted that the land batteries and ships had hammered the fort with nearly 1,000 shots in 12 hours. Within a week of the bombardment's opening, Commander Stevens, U.S.S. *Patapsco*, called the effect of the firing ''hardly describable, throwing bricks and mortar, gun carriages and timber in every direction and high into the air.'' But, as Rear Admiral Dahlgren noted: ''There is an immense endurance in such a mass of masonry, and the ruins may serve as shelter to many men.'' The embattled defenders heroically held on.

27 Colonel L. Smith, CSA, commanding the Marine Department of Texas, reported the status of the small gunboats in the area. C.S.S. *Clifton*, *Sachem*, and *Jacob A. Bell* were at Sabine Pass; C.S.S. *Bayou City*, *Diana*, and *Harriet Lane* were at Galveston Bay; C.S.S. *Mary Hill* was at Velasco, and C.S.S. *John F. Carr* was at Saluria. *Bayou City* and *Harriet Lane* were without guns and the remainder mounted a total of 15 cannon.

Union expedition to capture Brazos Santiago, and the mouth of the Rio Grande River departed New Orleans convoyed by U.S.S. *Monongahela*, Commander Strong; U.S.S. *Owasco*, Lieutenant Commander Edmund W. Henry; and U.S.S. *Virginia*, Acting Lieutenant C. H. Brown. This was the beginning of another Union move not only to wrest Texas from Confederate control but to preclude the possibility of a movement into the State by French troops in Mexico.

U.S.S. *Granite City*, Acting Master C. W. Lamson, captured schooner *Anita* off Pass Cavallo, Texas, with cargo of cotton.

28 C.S.S. *Georgia*, Lieutenant W. L. Maury, anchored at Cherbourg, France, concluding a 7-month cruise against Union commerce. During this period the raider destroyed a number of prizes and bonded the remainder for a total of $200,000. A short time later, Flag Officer Samuel Barron, CSN, advised Secretary Mallory that the ship had been laid up: ''The *Georgia*, Commander W. L. Maury, arrived in Cherbourg a few days ago almost broken down; she has lost her speed, not now

Under Lieutenant William L. Maury, C.S.S. Georgia *cruised the high seas in search of Union commerce. After a successful seven month voyage, she put into Cherbourg, France, for repairs.*

going under a full head of steam over 6 knots an hour, and is good for nothing as a cruiser under sail."

29   With a sizable naval force already supporting Army operations along the Tennessee River, Rear Admiral Porter ordered the officers of his Mississippi Squadron "to give all the aid and assistance in their power" to Major General W. T. Sherman. Next day Porter advised Secretary Welles: "The *Lexington*, *Hastings*, *Key West*, *Cricket*, *Robb*, *Romeo*, and *Peosta* are detached for duty in the Tennessee River; and the *Paw Paw*, *Tawah*, *Tyler*, and one or two others will soon join them, which will give a good force for that river."

30   U.S.S. *Vanderbilt*, Commander Baldwin, captured bark *Saxon*, suspected of having rendezvoused with and taken cargo from C.S.S. *Tuscaloosa* at Angra Pequena, Africa.

    U.S.S. *Annie*, Acting Ensign Williams, seized blockade running British schooner *Meteor* off Bayport, Florida.

31   During October instruction began for 52 midshipmen at the Confederate States Naval Academy. Lieutenant W. H. Parker, CSN, was Superintendent of the "floating academy" housed on board C.S.S. *Patrick Henry* at Drewry's Bluff on the James River.

    The initial move to establish a Naval Academy was taken in December 1861 when the Confederate Congress passed a bill calling for "some form of education" for midshipmen. Further legislation in the spring of 1862 provided for the appointment of 106 acting midshipmen to the Naval Academy. In May 1862, the *Patrick Henry* was designated as the Academy ship, and alterations were undertaken to ready her for this role.

    In general the curriculum, studies, and discipline at the new school were patterned after that of the United States Naval Academy. The training was truly realistic as the midshipmen were regularly called upon to take part in actual combat. When they left the Academy, they were seasoned veterans. Commander John M. Brooke, CSN, wrote to Secretary Mallory about the midshipmen as follows: "Though but from 14 to 18 years of age, they eagerly seek every opportunity presented for engaging in hazardous enterprises; and those who are sent upon them uniformly exhibit good discipline, conduct, and courage."

    Mallory reported to President Davis: "The officers connected with the school are able and zealous, and the satisfactory progress already made by the several classes gives assurance that the Navy may look to this school for well-instructed and skillful officers." The Naval Academy continued to serve the Confederate cause well until war's end.

NOVEMBER

2–3   The report of Lieutenant Commander Greenleaf Cilley, U.S.S. *Catskill*, indicated extensive Confederate preparations to meet any Union attempt to breach the obstructions between Forts Sumter and Moultrie as the furious Northern bombardment of Fort Sumter continued. "Two boats under sail were seen moving from Sumter toward Sullivan's Island," Cilley wrote. "About 11 p.m. a balloon with two lights attached rose from Sumter and floated toward Fort Johnson. . . . At midnight a steamer left Sumter and moved toward Fort Johnson. At sunrise . . . observed the three rams [C.S.S. *Charleston*, *Chicora*, and *Palmetto State*] and the side-wheel steamer anchored in line of battle ahead from Johnson toward Charleston, and each with its torpedo topped up forward of the bows."

3–4   Naval forces under Commander Strong, including U.S.S. *Monongahela*, *Owasco*, and *Virginia*, convoyed and supported troops commanded by General Banks at Brazos Santiago, Texas. The landing began on the 2nd and continued the next day without opposition. On the 4th Brownsville, Texas, was evacuated, and the Union foothold on the Mexican border was secured. Major General Dana wrote Commander Strong thanking him for the "many services you have rendered this expedition, particularly for the gallant service rendered by Captain Henry and the crew of the *Owasco* in saving the steam transport *Zephyr* from wreck during the late storm [encountered

C.S.S. Patrick Henry *served the South in the James River as school ship of the Confederate States Naval Academy when instruction began for 52 midshipmen in October 1863.*

enroute on 30 October] and towing her to the rendezvous, and to you and your crew for assisting the steam transport *Bagley* in distress; also especially for the signal gallantry of your brave tars in landing our soldiers through the dangerous surf yesterday at the mouth of the Rio Grande." The naval force also quickly effected the capture of several blockade runners in the vicinity.

3 Rear Admiral Dahlgren closely examined Fort Sumter from his flagship during the evening and "could plainly observe the further effects of the firing; still," he added, "this mass of ruin is capable of harboring a number of the enemy, who may retain their hold until expelled by the bayonet. . . ."

U.S.S. *Kenwood*, Acting Master Swaney, captured steamer *Black Hawk* off Port Hudson, Louisiana, with cargo of cotton.

4 U.S.S. *Virginia*, Acting Lieutenant C. H. Brown, seized blockade running British schooner *Matamoras* at the mouth of the Rio Grande River with cargo including shoes, axes, and spades for the Confederate Army.

5 Ships of the South Atlantic Blockading Squadron continued to cannonade Fort Sumter in concert with Army batteries ashore on Morris Island. Rear Admiral Dahlgren described the results of the combined bombardment: "The only original feature left is the northeast face, the rest is a pile of rubbish."

U.S.S. *Virginia*, Acting Lieutenant C. H. Brown, seized blockade running British bark *Science*, and, in company with U.S.S. *Owasco*, Lieutenant Commander Henry, captured blockade running British brigs *Volante* and *Dashing Wave* at the mouth of the Rio Grande River.

Rear Admiral Porter wrote Major General Banks in response to the General's long expressed request for gunboats near and below New Orleans. The Admiral advised him that a dozen gunboats were being fitted out, and added: "This will give you 22 gunboats in your department, with those now there, and I may be able to do more after we drive the rebels back from the Tennessee River." Banks wrote in mid-December that this assistance would "render it impossible for the enemy to annoy us, as they have heretofore done, by using against us the wonderful network of navigable waters west of the Mississippi River.''

Blockade runner *Margaret and Jessie* was captured at sea east of Myrtle Beach, South Carolina, after a prolonged chase by Army transport *Fulton* and U.S.S. *Nansemond*, Lieutenant R. H. Lamson. The chase had been started the preceding evening by U.S.S. *Howquah*, Acting Lieutenant Mac-Diarmid, which kept the steamer in sight throughout the night. U.S.S. *Keystone State*, Commander Edward Donaldson, joined the chase in the morning and was at hand when the capture was effected, putting an end to the career of a ship that had run the blockade some 15 times.

U.S.S. *Beauregard*, Acting Master Burgess, seized blockade running British schooner *Volante* off Cape Canaveral, Florida, with cargo including salt and dry goods.

6 Faced with the problem of passing through the maze of complicated Confederate obstructions near Fort Sumter if the capture of Charleston was to be effected from the sea, the North experimented with another innovation by John Ericsson, celebrated builder of U.S.S. *Monitor*. This date, U.S.S. *Patapsco*, Commander Stevens, tested Ericsson's anti-obstruction torpedo. The device, which was a cast-iron shell some 23 feet long and 10 inches in diameter containing 600 pounds of powder, was suspended from a raft which was attached to the ironclad's bow and held in position by two long booms. The demonstration was favorable, for the shock of the explosion was "hardly perceptible" on board *Patapsco* and, though a "really fearful" column of water was thrown 40 or 50 feet into the air, little of the water fell on the ironclad's deck. Even in the calm water in which the test was conducted, however, the raft seriously interfered with the ship's maneuverability. Rear Admiral Dahlgren noted significantly that "perfectly smooth water" was "a miracle here. . . ." Stevens expressed the view that the torpedo was useful only against fixed objects but that for operations against ironclads "the arrangement and attachment are too complicated" and that "something in the way of a torpedo which can be managed with facility" was needed.

C.S.S. *Alabama*, Captain Semmes, captured and destroyed bark *Amanda* in the East Indies with cargo of hemp and sugar.

7 Merchant steamer *Allen Collier*, with cargo of cotton, was burned by Confederate guerrillas at Whitworth's Landing, Mississippi, after she left the protection of U.S.S. *Eastport*, Acting Ensign Sylvester Pool. The uneasy quiet on the river required constant gunboat cover.

Cutter from U.S.S. *Sagamore*, Lieutenant Commander Charles E. Fleming, captured blockade running British schooner *Paul* off Bayport, Florida.

8 U.S.S. *James Adger*, Commander Thomas H. Patterson, and U.S.S. *Niphon*, Acting Master Breck, captured steamer *Cornubia* north of New Inlet, North Carolina.

9 U.S.S. *James Adger*, Commander Patterson, captured blockade runner *Robert E. Lee* off Cape Lookout Shoals, North Carolina. The steamer had left Bermuda 2 days before with cargo including shoes, blankets, rifles, saltpeter, and lead. She had been one of the most famous and successful blockade runners. Her former captain, Lieutenant John Wilkinson, CSN, later wrote: "She had run the blockade twenty-one times while under my command, and had carried abroad between six thousand and seven thousand bales of cotton, worth at that time about two millions of dollars in gold, and had carried into the Confederacy equally valuable cargoes.''

Intelligence data on the Confederate naval capability in Georgia waters reached Union Army and Navy commanders. C.S.S. *Savannah*, Commander Robert F. Pinkney, had two 7-inch and two 6-inch Brooke rifled guns and a torpedo mounted on her bow as armament. She carried two other torpedoes in her hold. Her sides were plated with 4 inches of rolled iron and her speed was about seven knots "in smooth water." C.S.S. *Isondiga*, a wooden steamer, was reported to have old boilers and "unreliable" machinery. The frames for two more rams were said to be on the stocks at Savannah, but no iron could be obtained to complete them. C.S.S. *Resolute*, thought by the Union commanders to be awaiting an opportunity to run the blockade, had been converted to a tender, and all the cotton at Savannah was being transferred to Wilmington for shipment through the blockade. C.S.S. *Georgia*, a floating battery commanded by Lieutenant Washington Gwathmey, CSN, was at anchor near Fort Jackson and was reported to be "a failure." Such information as this enabled Union commanders to revise their thinking and adjust their tactics to the new conditions in order to maintain the blockade and move against the coast with increasing effectiveness.

Rear Admiral Porter wrote Secretary Welles suggesting that the Coast Survey make careful maps of the area adjacent to the Mississippi River "where navigation is made up of innumerable lakes and bayous not known to any but the most experienced pilots." The existence of these waterways, he added, "would certainly never be known by examining modern charts." A fortnight later, the Secretary recommended to Secretary of the Treasury Salmon P. Chase that surveys similar to those completed by the Coast Survey for Rear Admiral S. P. Lee along the North Carolina coast be made in accordance with Porter's request. Welles noted that the operations of the Mississippi Squadron and the transport fleet would be "greatly facilitated" and volunteered naval assistance for such an effort.

Admiral Buchanan ordered Acting Midshipman Edward A. Swain to report to Fort Morgan to take "command of the C.S.S. *Gunnison* and proceed off the harbor of Mobile and destroy, if possible, the U.S.S. *Colorado* or any other vessel of the blockading squadron. . . ." *Gunnison* was a torpedo boat.

U.S.S. *Niphon*, Acting Master Breck, captured blockade runner *Ella and Annie* off Masonboro Inlet, North Carolina, with cargo of arms and provisions. In an effort to escape, *Ella and Annie* rammed *Niphon*, but, when the two ships swung broadside, the runner was taken by boarding.

The repeated thrusts of the Union fleet at Charleston were blunted by stout Confederate defenses. Some of the ordnance used against the fleet are pictured above, including "floating" and "keg" torpedoes and a variety of shot and shell.

10 As an intensive two-week Union bombardment of Fort Sumter drew to a close, General Beauregard noted: "Bombardment of Sumter continues gradually to decrease. . . . Total number of shots [received] since 26th, when attack recommenced, is 9,306."

Major General James B. McPherson reported to Lieutenant Commander E. K. Owen, U.S.S. *Louisville*, that he anticipated an attack by Confederate troops near Goodrich's Landing, Louisiana. "I have to request," the General wrote, "that you will send one or two gunboats to Goodrich's Landing to assist General [John P.] Hawkins if necessary." For more than two months McPherson relied on naval support in the face of Southern movements in the area.

U.S.S. *Howquah*, Acting Lieutenant MacDiarmid, captured blockade running steamer *Ella* off Wilmington.

C.S.S. *Alabama*, Captain Semmes, captured and burned clipper ship *Winged Racer* in the Straits of Sunda off Java, with cargo of sugar, hides, and jute. "She had, besides," wrote Semmes, "a large supply of Manila tobacco, and my sailors' pipes were beginning to want replenishing."

11 C.S.S. *Alabama*, Captain Semmes, captured and destroyed clipper ship *Contest* after a long chase off Gaspar Strait with cargo of Japanese goods for New York.

14 U.S.S. *Bermuda*, Acting Lieutenant J. W. Smith, recaptured schooner *Mary Campbell* after she had been seized earlier the same day by Confederates under command of Master Duke, CSN, whose daring exploits five months before (see 8 June 1863) had resulted in the capture of a Union ship near New Orleans. *Bermuda* also took an unnamed lugger which the Confederates had used to capture *Mary Campbell*. The captures took place off Pensacola after the ships had come out of the Perdido River under Duke's command. Lieutenant Smith reported that ". . . the notorious James Duke . . . also captured the *Norman*, with which vessel he, with 10 of his crew, had made for the land upon my heaving in sight, and I have reason to believe that he beached and burned her. . . ."

The relentless pressure exerted on the Confederacy by the Union Navy was becoming increasingly apparent. Paymaster John deBree, CSN, reported to Secretary Mallory: "Restricted as our resources are by the blockade and by the reduced number of producers in the country, it has . . . been the main object to feed and clothe the Navy without a strict regard to those technicalities that obtain in times of peace and plenty." DeBree noted that the Confederate Navy had to purchase its cloth largely from blockade runners and "necessarily had to pay high prices. . . . Still, the closing of the Mississippi River losing us the benefit of a full supply of shoes, blankets and cloth, . . . rendered the necessity so urgent that we were obliged to adopt this method of clothing our half naked and fast increasing Navy. . . ." The paymaster reported that the lack of shoes was "our great difficulty" and that shoes were being made out of canvas rather than leather. "For leather shoes we will have to await the arrival of shipments from abroad; and in this, more than any other particular, we feel the inconvenience caused by the loss of our goods . . . by the closing of the Mississippi River." The Confederacy's ability to continue the war was becoming ever more dependent on supplies run through the blockade, and the blockade was tightening.

General Beauregard commented on the limitations of the Confederate ships at Charleston: "Our gunboats are defective in six respects: First. They have no speed, going only from 3 to 5 miles an hour in smooth water and no current. Second. They are of too great draft to navigate our inland waters. Third. They are unseaworthy by their shape and construction. . . . Even in the harbor thay are at times considered unsafe in a storm. Fourth. They are incapable of resisting the enemy's XV-inch shots at close quarters. . . . Fifth. They can not fight at long range. . . . Sixth. They are very costly, warm, uncomfortable, and badly ventilated; consequently sickly."

Nonetheless, the General was forced to rely heavily on them in his plans for the defense of Charleston from sea attack. Lacking the industrial capacity, funds and material to construct in strength the desperately needed ships of war, the Confederacy nevertheless accomplished much with inadequate ships.

U.S.S. *Dai Ching*, Lieutenant Commander James C. Chaplin, captured schooner *George Chisholm* off the Santee River, South Carolina, with cargo of salt.

15 U.S.S. *Lodona*, Acting Lieutenant Brodhead, seized blockade running British schooner *Arctic* southwest of Frying Pan Shoals, North Carolina, with cargo of salt.

15–16 Fort Moultrie opened a heavy, evening bombardment on Union Army positions at Cumming's Point, Morris Island. Brigadier General Gillmore immediately turned to Rear Admiral Dahlgren for assistance. "Will you have some of your vessels move up, so as to prevent an attack by boats on the sea face of the point," he wired late at night. The Admiral answered "at once" and ordered the tugs on patrol duty to keep "a good lookout." U.S.S. *Lehigh*, Commander Andrew Bryson, grounded while covering Cumming's Point and was taken under heavy fire the next morning before U.S.S. *Nahant*, Lieutenant Commander John J. Cornwell, got her off. Landsmen Frank S. Gile and William Williams, gunner's mate George W. Leland, coxswain Thomas Irving, and seaman Horatio N. Young from *Lehigh* were subsequently awarded the Medal of Honor for heroism while carrying a line from their ship to *Nahant*, thus enabling *Lehigh* to work free from her desperate position.

16 The effect of the Union's western successes was severely felt by the Confederate effort in the east. Commander John K. Mitchell wrote Secretary Mallory that there was a critical shortage of fuels for manufacturing purposes and naval use. "The occupation of Chattanooga by the enemy in August has effectually cut off the supply from the mines in that region, upon which the public works in Georgia and South Carolina and the naval vessels in the waters of those States were dependent. Meager supplies have been sent to Charleston from this place [Richmond] and from the Egypt mines in North Carolina. . . ." He reported that there was a sufficient amount of coal in the Richmond area to supply the Confederate ships operating in Virginia waters and rivers, and he felt that wood was being successfully substituted for coal at Charleston and Savannah. Mitchell paid tribute to the thoroughness of the Union blockade when he wrote of the economic plight of the Confederate States: "The prices of almost all articles of prime necessity have advanced from five to ten times above those ruling at the breaking out of the war, and, for many articles, a much greater advance has been reached, so that now the pay of the higher grades of officers, even those with small families, is insufficient for the pay of their board only; how much greater, then, must be the difficulty of living in the case of the lower grades of officers, and, the families of enlisted persons. This difficulty, when the private sources of credit and the limited means of most of the officers become exhausted, must soon, unless relief be extended to them by the Government, reach the point of destitution, or of charitable dependence, a point, in fact, already reached in many instances."

16–17 U.S.S. *Monongahela*, Commander Strong, escorted Army transports and covered the landing of more than a thousand troops on Mustang Island, Aransas Pass, Texas. *Monongahela*'s sailors manned a battery of two howitzers ashore, and the ship shelled Confederate works until the outnumbered defenders surrendered. General Banks wrote in high praise of the "great assistance" rendered by *Monongahela* during this successful operation.

17 U.S.S. *Mystic*, Acting Master William Wright, assigned to the North Atlantic Blockading Squadron, seized schooner *Emma D.* off Yorktown, Virginia. The same day, Assistant Secretary Fox wrote Rear Admiral S. P. Lee praising the effectiveness of the squadron: "I congratulate you upon the captures off Wilmington. Nine steamers have been lost to the rebels in a short time, all due to the 'fine spirit' of our people engaged in the blockade. It is a severe duty and well

maintained and Jeff Davis pays us a higher compliment than our own people when he declares that there is but one port in 3500 miles (recollect that the whole Atlantic front of Europe is but 2900 miles) through which they can get in supplies."

18 Merchant schooner *Joseph L. Garrity*, 2 days out of Matamoras bound for New York, was seized by five Southern sympathizers under Thomas E. Hogg, later a Master in the Confederate Navy. They had boarded the ship as passengers. Hogg landed *Joseph L. Garrity's* crew "without injury to life or limb" on the coast of Yucatan on 26 November, and sailed her to British Honduras where he entered her as blockade runner *Eureka* and sold her cargo of cotton. Three of the crew were eventually captured in Liverpool, England, and charged with piracy, but on 1 June 1864, Confederate Commissioner James Mason informed Secretary of State Benjamin that they had been acquitted of the charge. In the meantime, *Garrity* was turned over to the custody of the U.S. commercial agent at Belize, British Honduras, and ultimately returned to her owners.

Acting Master C. W. Lamson, U.S.S. *Granite City*, reported the capture of schooner *Amelia Ann* and Spanish bark *Teresita*, with cargo of cotton, both attempting to run the blockade at Aransas Pass, Texas.

Captain Thomas A. Faries, CSA, commanding a battery near Hog Point, Louisiana, mounted to interdict the movement of the Union shipping on the Mississippi River, reported an engagement with U.S.S. *Choctaw*, *Franklin*, and *Carondelet*. "The *Choctaw*, left her position above, and, passing down, delivered a very heavy fire from her bow, side, and stern guns, enfilading for a short time the four rifle guns in the redoubt."

20 Rear Admiral Farragut, eager to return to sea duty in the Gulf, informed Secretary Welles from New York that U.S.S. *Hartford* and *Brooklyn* "will not be ready for sea in less than three weeks, from the best information I can obtain. I particularly regret it, because I see that General Banks is in the field and my services may be required." The Admiral noted that he had received a letter from Commodore Bell, commanding in his absence, which indicated that there were not enough ships to serve on the Texas coast and maintain the blockade elsewhere as well. Farragut noted that some turreted ironclads were building at St. Louis and suggested: "They draw about 6 feet of water and will be the very vessels to operate in the shallow waters of Texas, if the Department would order them down there." Three days later, the Secretary asked Rear Admiral Porter to "consider the subject and inform the Department as early as practicable to what extent Farragut's wishes can be complied with." Porter replied on the 27th that he could supply Farragut with eight light drafts "in the course of a month" and that "six weeks from to-day I could have ten vessels sent to Admiral Farragut, if I can get the officers and men. . . ."

21 U.S.S. *Grand Gulf*, Commander George M. Ransom, and Army transport *Fulton* seized blockade running British steamer *Banshee* south of Salter Path, North Carolina.

22 U.S.S. *Aroostook*, Lieutenant Chester Hatfield, captured schooner *Eureka* off Galveston. She had been bound to Havana with cargo of cotton.

U.S.S. *Jacob Bell*, Acting Master Schulze, transported and supported a troop landing at St. George's Island, Maryland, where some 30 Confederates, some of whom were blockade runners, were captured.

23 The threat of Confederate torpedoes in the rivers and coastal areas became an increasing menace as the war progressed. The necessity of taking proper precautions against this innovation in naval warfare slowed Northern operations and tied up ships on picket duty that might otherwise have been utilized more positively. This date, Secretary Welles wrote Captain Gansevoort, U.S.S. *Roanoke*, at Newport News: "Since the discovery of the torpedo on James River, near Newport News, the Department has felt some uneasiness with regard to the position of your vessel, as it is evidently the design of the rebels to drift such machines of destruction upon her. . . .

Lacking sufficient naval power to contest Union forces afloat, the Confederacy sought to make progress up its rivers as difficult as possible by sinking obstructions such as these hulks in the James River.

Vigilance is demanded.'' Upon receipt of this instruction, Gansevoort replied 2 days later: ''The *Roanoke* lies in the deepest water here, and until very lately, when the necessary force has been temporarily reduced by casualties to machinery, a picket boat has been kept underway during all night just above this anchorage to prevent such missiles from approaching the ship. This precaution has been renewed now that the *Poppy* has been added to this disposable force, and in addition I have caused . . . a gunboat to be anchored above us to keep a sharp lookout for torpedoes.''

24   Rear Admiral Lee wrote Secretary Welles regarding a conversation with General Benjamin F. Butler while reconnoitering the Sounds of North Carolina: ''I gave him my views respecting the best method of attacking Wilmington, viz, either to march from New Berne and seize the best and nearest fortified inlet on the north of Fort Fisher, thence to cross and blockade the Cape Fear River, or to land below Fort Caswell (the key to the position) and blockade the river from the right bank between Smithville and Brunswick.'' Four days later, Commander W. A. Parker supported the Admiral's views after making his own observations. Recommending a joint Army-Navy assault to capture Fort Fisher, he wrote: ''I am of the opinion that 25,000 men and two or three ironclads should be sent to capture this place, if so large a force can be conveniently furnished for this purpose. . . . The ironclads . . . should be employed to divert the attention of the garrison at Fort Fisher during the landing of our troops at Masonboro Inlet, and to prevent the force there from being used to oppose the debarkation. . . . Fort Fisher would probably fall after a short resistance, as I have been informed that the heavy guns all point to seaward, and there is but slight provision made to resist an attack from the interior.'' Union efforts in the east were concentrated on the capture of Charleston at this time, however, and a thrust at Wilmington was postponed. The city continued as a prime haven for blockade runners until early 1865.

Under cover of U.S.S. *Pawnee*, Commander Balch, and U.S.S. *Marblehead*, Lieutenant Commander Richard W. Meade, Jr., Army troops commenced sinking piles as obstructions in the Stono River above Legareville, South Carolina. The troops, protected by *Marblehead*, had landed the day before. The naval force remained on station at the request of Brigadier General Schimmelfennig to preclude a possible Confederate attack.

25 The valiant but overpowered Confederate Navy faced many problems in the struggle for survival. One of them was the inability to obtain enough ordnance. Commander Brooke reported to Secretary Mallory this date that ordnance workshops had been established at Charlotte, Richmond, Atlanta, and Selma, Alabama. While great efforts were made to meet Southern needs, Brooke wrote: "The deficiency of heavy ordnance has been severely felt during this war. The timely addition of a sufficient number of heavy guns would render our ports invulnerable to the attacks of the enemy's fleets, whether ironclads or not. . . ."

U.S.S. *Fort Hindman*, Acting Lieutenant John Pearce, captured steamer *Volunteer* off Natchez Island, Mississippi.

26 U.S.S. *James Adger*, Commander Patterson, seized British blockade runner *Ella* off Masonboro Inlet, North Carolina, with cargo of salt.

U.S.S. *Antona*, Acting Master Zerega, captured schooner *Mary Ann* southeast of Corpus Christi with cargo of cotton.

27 U.S.S. *Two Sisters*, Acting Master Charles H. Rockwell, seized blockade running schooner *Maria Alberta* near Bayport, Florida.

28 U.S.S. *Chippewa*, Lieutenant Commander Thomas C. Harris, convoyed Army transport *Monohassett* and *Mayflower* up Skull Creek, South Carolina, on a reconnaissance mission. Though Confederate troops had established defensive positions from which to resist attacks, *Chippewa*'s effective fire prevented them from halting the movement. "The object of the expedition was fully accomplished," Harris reported, "and the reconnaissance was complete."

29 U.S.S. *Kanawha*, Lieutenant Commander Mayo, captured schooner *Albert* (or *Wenona*) attempting to run the blockade out of Mobile, with cargo of cotton, rosin, turpentine, and tobacco.

At the request of Major General Banks, a gun crew from U.S.S. *Monongahela*, Commander Strong, went ashore to man howitzers in support of an Army attack on Pass Cavallo, Texas.

30 Secretary Mallory emphasized the necessity for the proper training of naval officers in his annual report on the Confederate States Navy. It was, he wrote, "a subject of the greatest importance." He observed: "The naval powers of the earth are bestowing peculiar care upon the education of their officers, now more than ever demanded by the changes in all the elements of naval warfare. Appointed from civil life and possessing generally but little knowledge of the duties of an officer and rarely even the vocabulary of their profession they have heretofore been sent to vessels or batteries where it is impossible for them to obtain a knowledge of its most important branches, which can be best, if not only, acquired by methodical study." Mallory noted that there were 693 officers and 2,250 enlisted men in the Confederate Navy. He reported that while Union victories at Little Rock and on the Yazoo River had terminated the Department's attempts to construct ships in that area, construction was "making good progress at Richmond, Wilmington, Charleston, Savannah, Mobile, on the Roanoke, Peedee, Chattahoochee, and Alabama Rivers. . . ." Two major problems Mallory enumerated troubled the Confederacy throughout the conflict. the lack of skilled labor to build ships and the inability to obtain adequate iron to protect them. In the industrial North, neither was a difficulty—a factor which helped decide the course of the war.

Confederate naval officers and men played vital roles in Southern shore defenses throughout the war. This date, Secretary Mallory praised the naval command at Drewry's Bluff which guarded the James River approach to Richmond. The battery, he reported, "composed of seamen and marines, is in a high state of efficiency and the river obstructions are believed to be sufficient, in connection with the shore and submarine batteries, to prevent the passage of the enemy's ships. An active force is employed on submarine batteries and torpedoes."

DECEMBER

2 Rear Admiral Porter reported: "In the operations lately carried on up the Tennessee and Cumberland rivers, the gunboats have been extremely active and have achieved with perfect success all that was desired or required of them. . . . With the help of our barges, General Sherman's troops were all ferried over in an incredibly short time by the gunboats, and he was enabled to bring his formidable corps into action in the late battle of Chattanooga, which has resulted so gloriously for our arms." The Mississippi Squadron continued to patrol the rivers relentlessly, restricting Confederate movements and countering attempts to erect batteries along the banks.

Commodore H. H. Bell, pro tem commander of the West Gulf Blockading Squadron, reported to Secretary Welles the estimated Confederate naval strength at Mobile Bay. C.S.S. *Gaines* and *Morgan* mounted ten guns; C.S.S. *Selma* mounted four, as did the nearly completed ironclad C.S.S. *Nashville*. All were sidewheelers. Ironclad rams C.S.S. *Baltic*, *Huntsville*, and *Tennessee* all mounted four guns each. The latter, Admiral Buchanan's flag ship, was said to be "strong and fast." C.S.S. *Gunnison* was fitted as a torpedo boat carrying 150 pounds of powder and another screw steamer was reported being fitted out, though a fire had destroyed her upper works. In addition to two floating batteries mounting 3 guns each and 10 transport steamers at Mobile Bay, the report noted: "At Selma there is a large vessel building, to be launched in January. There are three large rams building on the Tombigbee River, to be launched during the winter." Rear Admiral Farragut would face four of these ships in Mobile Bay the following year. Lack of machinery, iron, and skilled mechanics prevented the rest from being little more than the phantoms which rumor frequently includes in estimates of enemy strength.

Boat expedition from U.S.S. *Restless*, Acting Master William R. Browne, reconnoitered Lake Ocala, Florida. Finding salt works in the area, the Union forces destroyed them. "They were in the practice of turning out 130 bushels of salt daily." Rear Admiral Bailey reported. "Besides destroying these boilers, a large quantity of salt was thrown into the lake, 2 large flatboats, and 6 ox carts were demolished, and 17 prisoners were taken. . . ." These destructive raids, destroying machinery, supplies, armament, and equipment, had a telling and lasting effect on the South, already short of all.

3 Rear Admiral Dahlgren issued the following orders to emphasize vigorous enforcement of the blockade and vigilance against Confederate torpedo boats: "Picket duty is to be performed by four monitors, two for each night, one of which is to be well advanced up the harbor, in a position suitable for preventing the entrance or departure of any vessel attempting to pass in or out of Charleston Harbor, and for observing Sumter and Moultrie, or movements in and about them, taking care at the same time not to get aground, and also to change the position when the weather appears to render it unsafe. The second monitor is to keep within proper supporting distance of the first, so as to render aid if needed." The Admiral added: "The general object of the monitors, tugs, and boats on picket is to enforce the blockade rigorously, and to watch and check the movements of the enemy by water whenever it can be done, particularly to detect and destroy the torpedo boats and the picket boats of the rebels."

U.S.S. *New London*, Lieutenant Commander Weld N. Allen, captured blockade running schooner *del Nile* near Padre Pass Island, Texas, with cargo including coffee, sugar, and percussion caps.

5 Boat crew under Acting Ensign William B. Arrants from U.S.S. *Perry* was captured while reconnoitering Murrell's Inlet, South Carolina, to determine if a ship being outfitted there as a blockade runner could be destroyed. Noting that a boat crew from *T. A. Ward* had been captured in the same area 2 months before, Rear Admiral Dahlgren wrote: "These blunders are very annoying, and yet I do not like to discourage enterprise and dash on the part of our officers and men. Better to suffer from the excess than the deficiencies of these qualities."

6 U.S.S. *Weehawken*, Commander Duncan, sank while tied up to a buoy inside the bar at Charleston harbor. *Weehawken* had recently taken on an extra load of heavy ammunition which reduced the freeboard forward considerably. In the strong ebb tide, water washed down an open hawse pipe and a hatch. The pumps were unable to handle the rush of water and *Weehawken* quickly foundered, drowning some two dozen officers and men.

U.S.S. *Violet*, Acting Ensign Thomas Stothard, and U.S.S. *Aries*, Acting Lieutenant Devens, sighted blockade running British steamer *Ceres* aground and burning at the mouth of the Cape Fear River, North Carolina. During the night, *Ceres* floated free and, the flames having been extinguished, was seized by *Violet*.

7 In his third annual report to the President, Secretary Welles wrote: "A blockade commencing at Alexandria, in Virginia, and terminating at the Rio Grande, has been effectively maintained. The extent of this blockade . . . covers a distance of three thousand five hundred and forty-nine

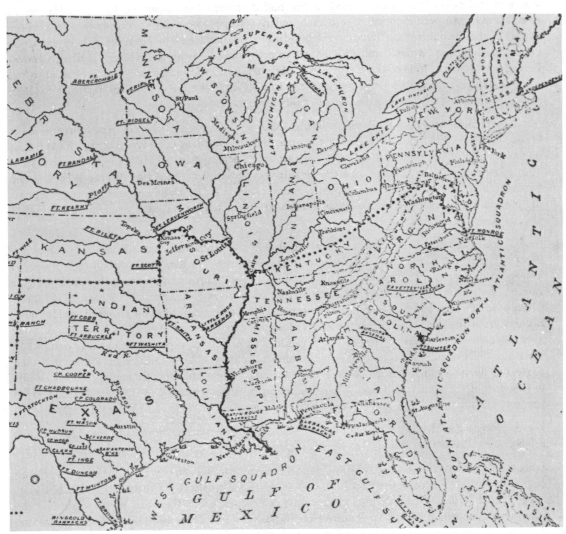

As 1863 ended, the war in the west had been won by the Union and the South was split along the Mississippi River; the North pressed in from all sides along the coasts; and only Mobile and Wilmington were major ports open to Confederate blockade runners.

statute miles, with one hundred and eighty-nine harbor or pier openings or indentations, and much of the coast presents a double shore to be guarded . . . a naval force of more than one hundred vessels has been employed in patrolling the rivers, cutting off rebel supplies, and co-operating with the armies . . . The distance thus traversed and patrolled by the gunboats on the Mississippi and its tributaries is 3,615 miles, and the sounds, bayous, rivers and inlets of the States upon the Atlantic and the Gulf, covering an extent of about 2,000 miles, have also been . . . watched with unceasing vigilance." Welles reported a naval strength of 34,000 seamen and 588 ships displacing 467,967 tons, mounting 4,443 guns. More than 1,000 ships had been captured by alert blockaders, as the results of weakness at sea were driven home to the beleaguered South. The North's mighty force afloat had severed the Confederacy along the Mississippi and pierced ever deeper into her interior; amphibious assaults from the sea had driven her still further from her coasts; and the vise of the blockade clamped down more tightly on an already withering economy and military capability.

Steamer *Chesapeake* of the New York and Portland Line, en route to Portland, Maine, was seized off Cape Cod by a group of 17 Confederate sympathizers led by John C. Braine. The bizarre undertaking had been planned at St. John, New Brunswick, by Captain John Parker (whose real name seems to have been Vernon G. Locke), former commander of the Confederate privateer *Retribution*. Parker ordered Braine and his men to New York where they purchased side arms

After boldly seizing steamer Chesapeake *on 7 December by posing as passengers, Confederates sail into the Bay of Fundy to put prisoners ashore.*

and boarded *Chesapeake* as passengers. At the appropriate moment they threw aside their disguises, and, after a brief exchange of gunfire in which the second engineer was killed, took possession of the steamer. They intended to make for Wilmington after coaling in Nova Scotia. Captain Parker came on board in the Bay of Fundy and took charge.

News of the capture elicited a quick response in the Navy Department. Ships from Philadelphia northward were ordered out in pursuit. On 17 December U.S.S. *Ella and Annie*, Acting Lieutenant J. Frederick Nickels, recaptured *Chesapeake* in Sambro Harbor, Nova Scotia. She was taken to Halifax where the Vice Admiralty Court ultimately restored the steamer to her original American owners. Most of the Confederates escaped and John Braine would again cause the Union much concern before the war ended.

Assistant Secretary Fox transmitted a list of ships reported to be running the blockade and urged Rear Admiral Lee to prosecute the blockade even more vigorously. "While the captures are numerous, it is not the less evident that there are many that escape capture." Some ships would successfully run the blockade until the end of the war.

8   Acting Master W. T. Gillespie, U.S.S. *Braziliera*, reported that blockade running British schooner *Antoinette* ran aground on Cumberland Island, Georgia, and was a total wreck. "I have saved her anchors, chains, and sails, which will be of service to me," he wrote Rear Admiral Dahlgren: "nothing else, either of cargo or outfit, of any value, remaining."

The disabled merchant steamer *Henry Von Phul* was shelled by a Confederate shore battery near Morganza, Louisiana. U.S.S. *Neosho*, Acting Ensign Edwin F. Brooks, and U.S.S. *Signal*, Acting Ensign William P. Lee, steamed up to defend the ship and silenced the battery. Union merchantmen were largely free from such attacks when convoyed by a warship.

9   In his annual message to the Congress, President Lincoln noted that the blockade was increasing in efficiency, but "illicit trade is not entirely suppressed" and that the production of war vessels had created new forms of naval power.

U.S.S. *Circassian*, Acting Lieutenant Eaton, seized blockade running British steamer *Minna* at sea east of Cape Romain, South Carolina. The steamer was carrying cargo including iron, hardware, and powder. In addition, Eaton reported, "she has also as cargo a propellor and shaft and other parts of a marine engine, perhaps intended for some rebel ironclad."

U.S.S. *Kennebec*, Lieutenant Commander William P. J. McCann, captured schooner *Marshall Smith* off Mobile. She was attempting to run to Havana with cotton and turpentine.

10   U.S.S. *Bloomer*, Acting Ensign Edwin Crissey, and her tender, *Caroline*, reported to Acting Master W. R. Browne, U.S.S. *Restless*, to participate in an attack on the extensive salt works at St. Andrew's Bay, Florida. Next day, *Restless* bombarded the town of St. Andrew's, which had been used as a supply station for the salt works and as quarters for some 275 Confederate troops. "Selecting the largest group of houses," Browne reported, "we succeeded in firing it, our third shell bursting in one of the houses at the southeast end. The wind being E.S.E. communicated the flames quickly to the others, consisting of 32 houses and shanties, which were speedily reduced to ashes. . . ." Meanwhile *Bloomer* and *Caroline* destroyed the salt works lining the shores of the Bay. Remarking on the size of the main works, which produced some 400 bushels of salt daily, Browne wrote: "It was in fact a complete village, covering a space of three-fourths of a square mile, employing many hands and 16 ox and mule teams constantly to haul salt to Eufaula Sound, and from thence conveyed to Montgomery, at which place it is selling at fabulous prices—$40 and $45 per bushel. At this place, [St. Andrew's Bay] were 27 buildings, and 22 large steam boilers, and 300 kettles averaging 200 gallons each, which cost the Government $5 per gallon, all of which were totally destroyed, besides 2,000 bushels of salt, and storehouses filled with corn meal, bacon, sirup, and other provisions, enough to supply these employed for

three months. . . ." The Union expedition also destroyed an unnamed schooner with cargo of 100 bales of cotton up Bear Creek.

Confederate troops burned schooner *Josephine Truxillo* and barge *Stephany* on Bayou Lacomb, Louisiana. Next day they burned schooner *Sarah Bladen* and barge *Helana* on Bayou Bonfouca.

11 Confederate troops fired on U.S.S. *Indianola* in the Mississippi in an attempt to destroy her, but the effective counterfire of U.S.S. *Carondelet*, Acting Master James C. Gipson, drove them off. The Union Navy was exerting great effort to get *Indianola* off the bar on which she had sunk in February, and on 23 November Gipson had written Rear Admiral Porter: "I will do all that lies in my power to protect her from destruction."

Major General D. H. Maury, CSA, wrote of reports that had reached him of a Union naval attack on Mobile "at an early day." Maury prophetically stated that "I expect the fleet to succeed in running past the outer forts," but he added, "I shall do all I can to prevent it, and to hold the forts as long as possible."

14 General Beauregard ordered Lieutenant Dixon, CSA, to proceed with submarine *H. L. Hunley* to the mouth of Charleston harbor and "sink and destroy any vessel of the enemy with which he can come in conflict." The General directed that "such assistance . . . as may be practicable" be rendered to Lieutenant Dixon.

15 Captain Semmes, after cruising for some time in Far Eastern waters, determined to change his area of operations. Leaving the island of Condore in C.S.S. *Alabama*, he wrote: "The homeward trade of the enemy is now quite small, reduced, probably, to twenty or thirty ships per year, and these may easily evade us by taking the different passages to the Indian Ocean. . . . there is no cruising or chasing to be done here, successfully, or with safety to oneself without plenty of coal, and we can only rely upon coaling once in three months. . . . So I will try my luck around the Cape of Good Hope once more, thence to the coast of Brazil, and thence perhaps to Barbados for coal, and thence—? If the war be not ended, my ship will need to go into dock to have much of her copper replaced, now nearly destroyed by such constant cruising, and to have her boilers

Throughout 1863 the Union tried to float Indianola, *sunk and surrendered in February. Above, sailors are hard at work on her where the falling waters of the Mississippi left her high and dry.*

overhauled and repaired, and this can only be properly done in Europe." The cruise of the most famous Confederate commerce raider went into its final 6 months.

Captain Barron advised Secretary Mallory from Paris of the great difficulty encountered in purchasing or seeking to repair Confederate ships in European ports. The "difficulties and expense and some delay," he said, were due to "the spies" of U.S. Ambassador Charles Francis Adams in London. Barron reported that they "are to be found following the footsteps of any Confederate agent in spite of all the precautions we can adopt. . . ." The shrewd U.S. diplomat moved time and again to frustrate Southern efforts in Europe.

Admiral Buchanan wrote Commander C. ap R. Jones regarding C.S.S. *Tennessee*: "The *Tennessee* will carry a battery of two 7-inch Brooke guns and four broadsides, 6.4 or 9 inch. . . . There is a great scarcity of officers and I know not where I will get them. I have sent the names of 400 men who wish to be transferred from the Army to the Navy, and have received only about twenty." Jones replied, "Strange that the Army disregard the law requiring the transfer of men."

16   In acknowledging resolutions of congratulations and appreciation passed by the Chamber of Commerce of New York for "one of the most celebrated victories of any time"—the capture of New Orleans—Rear Admiral Farragut wrote: "That we did our duty to the best of our ability, I believe; that a kind Providence smiled upon us and enabled us to overcome obstacles before which the stoutest of our hearts would have otherwise quailed, I am certain."

Thomas Savage, U.S. Consul-General at Havana, reported to Commodore H. H. Bell regarding blockade runners in that port: "A schooner under rebel colors, called *Roebuck*, 41 tons, with cotton arrived from Mobile yesterday. She left that port, I believe, on the 8th. She is the only vessel that has reached this port from Mobile for a very long time. . . . The famous steamer *Alice*, which ran the blockade at Mobile successfully so many times, is now on the dry dock here fitting out for another adventure."

U.S.S. *Huron*, Lieutenant Commander Stevens, captured blockade runner *Chatham* off Doboy Sound, Georgia, with cargo of cotton, tobacco, and rosin.

U.S.S. *Ariel*, Acting Master William H. Harrison, captured sloop *Magnolia* off the west coast of Florida. She was inbound from Havana with cargo of spirits and medicines.

17   Lieutenant Commander Fitch, U.S.S. *Moose*, reported that he had sent landing parties ashore at Seven Mile Island and Palmyra, Tennessee, where they had destroyed distilleries used by Confederate guerrilla troops.

U.S.S. *Roebuck*, Acting Master Sherrill, seized blockade-running British schooner *Ringdove* off Indian River, Florida, with cargo including salt, coffee, tea, and whiskey.

19   Expedition under Acting Master W. R. Browne, comprising U.S.S. *Restless*, *Bloomer*, and *Caroline*, proceeded up St. Andrew's Bay, Florida, to continue the destruction of salt works. A landing party went ashore under *Bloomer*'s guns and destroyed those works not already demolished by the Southerners when reports of the naval party were received. Browne was able to report that he had "cleared the three arms of this extensive bay of salt works . . . Within the past ten days," he added, "290 salt works, 33 covered wagons, 12 flatboats, 2 sloops (5 ton each) 6 ox carts, 4,000 bushels of salt, 268 buildings at the different salt works, 529 iron kettles averaging 150 gallons each, 105 iron boilers for boiling brine [were destroyed], and it is believed that the enemy destroyed as many more to prevent us from doing so."

20   Steamer *Antonica* ran aground on Frying Pan Shoals, North Carolina, attempting to run the blockade Boat crews from U.S.S. *Governor Buckingham*, Acting Lieutenant William G. Saltonstall, captured her crew but were unable to get the steamer off. Rear Admiral S. P. Lee noted:

"She will be a total loss. . . ." *Antonica* had formerly run the blockade a number of times under British registry and name of *Herald*, "carrying from 1,000 to 1,200 bales of cotton at a time."

U.S.S. *Connecticut*, Commander Almy, seized British blockade running schooner *Sallie* with cargo of salt off Frying Pan Shoals, North Carolina.

U.S.S. *Fox*, Acting Master George Ashbury, captured steamer *Powerful* at the mouth of Suwannee River, Florida. The steamer had been abandoned by her crew on the approach of the Union ship, and, unable to stop a serious leak, Ashbury ordered the blockade runner destroyed.

21 Rear Admiral Dahlgren wrote Secretary Welles that, after 10 days of "wretched" weather at Charleston, a quantity of obstructions had been washed down from the upper harbor by the "wind, rain, and a heavy sea." The Admiral added: "The quantity was very considerable, and besides those made of rope, which were well known to us, there were others of heavy timber, banded together and connected by railroad iron, with very stout links at each end. . . . This is another instance of the secrecy with which the rebels create defenses; for although some of the deserters have occupied positions more or less confidential, not one of them has even hinted at obstructions of this kind, while, on the other hand, the correspondents of our own papers keep the rebels pretty well posted in our affairs. . . ."

Admiral Buchanan wrote Commander C. ap R. Jones at the Confederate Naval Gun Foundry and Ordnance Works, Selma, Alabama: "Have you received any orders from Brooke about the guns for the *Tennessee*? She is all ready for officers, men, and guns, and has been so reported to the Department many weeks since, but none have I received."

22 Captain Semmes of C.S.S. *Alabama* noted the effect of Confederate commerce raiding on Northern shipping in the Far East: "The enemy's East India and China trade is nearly broken up. Their ships find it impossible to get freights, there being in this port [Singapore] some nineteen sail, almost all of which are laid up for want of employment. . . . the more widely our blows are struck, provided they are struck rapidly, the greater will be the consternation and consequent damage of the enemy."

23 Rear Admiral Farragut advised Secretary Welles from the New York Navy Yard that U.S.S. *Hartford*, which had served so long and well as his flagship in the Gulf, was again ready for sea save for an unfilled complement. The Admiral, anxious to return to action, suggested that the sailors might be obtained in Boston and other ports.
Rear Admiral Dahlgren ordered retaliatory steps taken against the Confederates operating in the Murrell's Inlet area where two Union boat crews had recently been captured (see 17 October and 5 December). "I desire . . .," he wrote Captain Green, U.S.S. *Canandaigua*, "to administer some corrective to the small parties of rebels who infest that vicinity, and shall detail for that purpose the steamers *Nipsic, Sanford, Geranium,* and *Daffodil*, also the sailing bark *Allen* and the schooner *Mangham*, 100 marines for landing, and four howitzers, two for the boats, two on field carriages, with such boats as may be needed." The force left its anchorage at Morris Island on 29 December.

24 Commander C. ap R. Jones wrote Admiral Buchanan that guns for C.S.S. *Tennessee* would be sent from the Selma Gun Foundry "as soon as they are ready." Jones added: "We had an accident that might have been very serious. An explosion took place while attempting to cast the bottom section of a gun pit. The foundry took fire, but was promptly extinguished. Fortunately but two of the molds were burned. I had a narrow escape, my hat, coat, and pants were burned. Quite a loss in these times, with our depreciated currency and fixed salaries. As a large casting is never made without my being present, I consider my life in greater danger here than if I were in command of the *Tennessee*, though I should expect hot work in her occasionally. What chance have I for her?"

U.S.S. *Fox*, Acting Master Ashbury, seized blockade running British schooner *Edward* off the mouth of the Suwannee River, Florida, after a two hour chase during which the schooner attempted to run down the smaller Union ship. She was carrying a cargo of lead and salt from Havana.

C.S.S. *Alabama*, Captain Semmes, captured and burned bark *Texan Star* in the Strait of Malacca with cargo of rice.

U.S.S. *Sunflower*, Acting Master Van Sice, captured blockade runner *Hancock* near the lighthouse at Tampa Bay with cargo including salt and borax.

U.S.S. *Antona*, Acting Master Zerega, seized blockade running schooner *Exchange* off Velasco, Texas, with cargo including coffee, nails, shoes, acids, wire, and cotton goods.

25   Confederate batteries on John's Island opened an early morning attack on U.S.S. *Marblehead*, Lieutenant Commander Meade, near Legareville, South Carolina, in the Stono River. *Marblehead* sustained some 20 hits as U.S.S. *Pawnee*, Commander Balch, contributed enfilading support, and mortar schooner *C. P. Williams*, Acting Master Simeon N. Freeman, added her firepower to the bombardment. After more than an hour, the Confederates broke off the engagement and withdrew. Meade later seized two VIII-inch sea coast howitzers.

U.S.S. *Daylight*, Acting Lieutenant Francis S. Wells, and U.S.S. *Howquah*, Acting Lieutenant MacDiarmid, transported troops from Beaufort, North Carolina, to Bear Inlet, where the soldiers and sailors were landed without incident under the *Daylight's* protecting guns. Wells reported: "Four extensive salt works in full operation were found at different points along the coast and near the inlet, which were all thoroughly destroyed. . . ."

26   C.S.S. *Alabama*, Captain Semmes, captured and burned ships *Sonora* and *Highlander*, both in ballast, at anchor at the western entrance of the Straits of Malacca. "They were monster ships," Semmes wrote, "both of them, being eleven or twelve hundred tons burden." One of the masters told the commerce raider: "Well, Captain Semmes, I have been expecting every day for the last three years to fall in with you, and here I am at last. . . . The fact is, I have had constant visions of the *Alabama*, by night and by day; she has been chasing me in my sleep, and riding me like a night-mare, and now that it is all over, I feel quite relieved."

As the year drew to a close, it became evident that the much-hoped-for European aid, if not actual intervention, on behalf of the Confederacy would not be forthcoming. This was expressed by Henry Hotze, Confederate Commercial Agent in London, in a letter this date to Secretary of State Benjamin: ". . . it is absolutely hopeless to expect to receive any really serviceable vessels of war from the ports of either England or France, and . . . our expenditure should therefore be confined to more practicable objects and our naval staff be employed in eluding, since we can not break, the blockade."

26–31   U.S.S. *Reindeer*, Acting Lieutenant Henry A. Glassford, with Army steamer *Silver Lake No. 2* in company, reconnoitered the Cumberland River at the request of General Grant. The force moved from Nashville to Carthage without incident but was taken under fire five times on the 29th. The Confederates' positions, Glassford reported, "availed them nothing, however, against the guns of this vessel and those of the *Silver Lake No. 2*; they were completely shelled out of them . . ." The gunboats continued as far as Creelsboro, Kentucky, before "the river gave unmistakable signs of a fall." The ships subsequently returned to Nashville.

29   Under Captain Green, U.S.S. *Nipsic*, *Sanford*, *Geranium*, *Daffodil*, and *Ethan Allen* departed Morris Island for Murrell's Inlet to destroy a schooner readying to run the blockade and disperse Confederate troops that had been harassing Union gunboats. The force arrived at an anchorage some 15 miles from Murrell's Inlet the following day, rendezvousing with U.S.S. *George Mangham*.

Charles H. Bell
Rear Admiral, USN

Theodorus Bailey
Rear Admiral, USN

Preparations for landing commenced immediately, but debarkation was delayed by heavy seas. With surprise lost, part of the purpose of the landing was frustrated. However, on 1 January, U.S.S. *Nipsic*, Commander James H. Spotts, landed sailors and Marines at Murrell's Inlet and succeeded in destroying the blockade runner with cargo of turpentine. The ships then returned to Charleston.

Boat crews from U.S.S. *Stars and Stripes*, Acting Master Willcomb, destroyed blockade running schooner *Caroline Gertrude*, aground on a bar at the mouth of Ocklockonee River, Florida. Attempting to salvage the schooner's cargo of cotton, the Union sailors were taken under heavy fire by Confederate cavalry ashore and returned to their ship after setting the blockade runner ablaze.

30   Expedition under command of Acting Ensign Norman McLeod from U.S.S. *Pursuit*, destroyed two salt works at the head of St. Joseph's Bay, Florida.

31   U.S.S. *Kennebec*, Lieutenant Commander McCann, captured blockade runner *Grey Jacket*, bound from Mobile to Havana, with cargo of cotton, rosin, and turpentine.

U.S.S. *Sciota*, Lieutenant Commander Perkins, and U.S.S. *Granite City*, Acting Master Lamson, with troops embarked, made a reconnaissance from Pass Cavallo, Texas, and landed the soldiers on the Gulf shore of Matagorda Peninsula in action continuing through 1 January. While *Granite City* covered the troops ashore from attacks by Confederate cavalry, *Sciota* reconnoitered the mouth of the Brazos River. Returning to the landing area, *Sciota* anchored close to the beach and shelled Confederate positions. *Granite City* fell down to Pass Cavallo to call up U.S.S. *Monogahela*, *Penobscot*, and *Estrella* to assist. Confederate gunboat *John F. Carr* closed and fired on the Union troops, "making some very good hits," but was driven ashore by a severe gale and destroyed by fire. The Union troops were withdrawn on board ship. Reporting on the operation, Lieutenant Colonel Frank S. Hasseltine wrote: "Captain Perkins, of the *Sciota*, excited my admiration by the daring manner in which he exposed his ship through the night in the surf till it broke all about him, that he might, close to us, lend the moral force of his XI-inch guns and howitzers, and by his gallantry in bringing us off during the gale. To Captain Lamson, of the *Granite City*, great credit is due for his exertion to retard and drive back the enemy. By the loss he inflicted upon them it is clear but for the heavy sea he would have freed us from any exertion."

Though the war's decisive areas of combat were east of the Mississippi, the attention of the Navy Department continued to be nationwide. Secretary Welles advised Rear Admiral C. H. Bell, commanding the Pacific Squadron, that it would be wise to keep at least one ship constantly on duty in San Francisco in order to give "greater security to that important city. . . ." Welles promised to send Bell two additional steamers to augment his squadron.

Secretary Welles noted in his diary: "The year closes more satisfactorily than it commenced. . . . The War has been waged with success, although there have been in some instances errors and misfortunes. But the heart of the nation is sounder and its hopes brighter."

1864

I.—SOME SIGNIFICANT EVENTS OF 1864

2 February	Confederate boat expedition led by Commander J. T. Wood captured and destroyed U.S.S. *Underwriter* in the Neuse River, North Carolina.
17 February	Confederate submarine *H. L. Hunley* sank Union blockader *Housatonic* off Charleston—the first submarine to sink a ship in combat.
12 March	Ships of Rear Admiral D. D. Porter's Mississippi Squadron moved up the Red River to commence the unsuccessful Army-Navy campaign to gain a foothold in the Texas interior.
19 April	C.S.S. *Albemarle*, Commander J. W. Cooke, sank U.S.S. *Southfield* and forced the remainder of the Union squadron at Plymouth, North Carolina, to withdraw. Having gained control of the waterways in the area, the Confederates were able to capture Plymouth on 20 April.
5 May	U.S.S. *Sassacus*, *Wyalusing*, and *Mattabesett* engaged C.S.S. *Albemarle* off the mouth of the Roanoke River as the Union sought in vain to regain control near Plymouth.
6 May	Confederate torpedo destroyed U.S.S. *Commodore Jones* in the James River, Virginia, one of several losses the Union suffered from torpedoes during the year.
13 May	The last of Rear Admiral Porter's squadron, after being trapped by low water, dashed through the hurriedly constructed Red River dams to safety below the Alexandria rapids.
19 June	U.S.S. *Kearsarge*, Commander J. A. Winslow, sank C.S.S. *Alabama*, Captain R. Semmes, off Cherbourg, France, ending the career of the South's most famous commerce raider.
5 August	Rear Admiral D. G. Farragut's fleet steamed by Forts Morgan and Gaines, through the deadly torpedo field blocking the channel, and into Mobile Bay. In the fierce engagement with the forts and Admiral F. Buchanan's small squadron, Farragut won a victory worthy of his great name.
6 August	C.S.S. *Tallahassee*, Commander J. T. Wood, put to sea from Wilmington, launching a brief but highly successful cruise against Northern shipping.
23 August	Fort Morgan, the last of the three forts at Mobile Bay to remain in Confederate hands, capitulated.
7 October	U.S.S. *Wachusett*, Lieutenant N. Collins, captured C.S.S. *Florida*, Lieutenant C. M. Morris, at Bahia, Brazil. Thus, in the same year were the cruises of the dread raiders *Alabama* and *Florida* ended.
19 October	C.S.S. *Shenandoah*, Lieutenant J. I. Waddell, commissioned off the Madeira Islands.
27 October	Torpedo launch commanded by Lieutenant W. B. Cushing destroyed ram C.S.S. *Albemarle* in the Roanoke River, assuring the North of renewed control of the waters around Plymouth, North Carolina.
4 November	Confederate raiders captured small gunboats U.S.S. *Key West*, *Tawah*, and *Elfin* near Johnsonville on the Tennessee River.
13 December	Rear Admiral Farragut arrived in New York City, for a period of rest after his arduous duty in the Gulf of Mexico and was acclaimed as a conquering hero. Ten days later he was promoted to the newly established rank of Vice Admiral.
21 December	Flag Officer W. W. Hunter destroyed the last of the Confederate Savannah Squadron to prevent its capture by the advancing forces of General W. T. Sherman.
24–25 December	A joint Army-Navy operation under Rear Admiral Porter and Major General B. F. Butler unsuccessfully attempted to take the Confederate stronghold of Fort Fisher, Wilmington, by amphibious assault.

II.—DETAILED CIVIL WAR NAVAL CHRONOLOGY
1864

JANUARY

1   As the New Year opened, the Union once more focused its attention on Wilmington. Since 1862 the Navy had pressed for a combined assault on this major east coast port, ideally located for blockade running less than 600 miles from Nassau and only some 675 from Bermuda. Despite the efforts of the fleet, the runners had continued to ply their trade successfully. In the fall of 1863, a British observer reported that thirteen steamers ran into Wilmington between 10 and 29 September and that fourteen ships put to sea between 2 and 19 September. In fact, James Randall, an employee of a Wilmington shipping firm, reported that 397 ships visited Wilmington during the first two and a half to three years of the war. On 2 January, Secretary of the Navy Gideon Welles again proposed an attack on the fortifications protecting Wilmington, "the only port by which any supplies whatever reach the rebels. . . ." He suggested to Secretary of War Edwin M. Stanton that a joint operation be undertaken to seize Fort Caswell: "The result of such operation is to enable the vessels to lie inside, as is the case at Charleston, thus closing the port effectually." However, Major General Henry W. Halleck advised Stanton that campaigns to which the Army was committed in Louisiana and Texas would not permit the men for the suggested assault to be spared. Thus, although the Navy increasingly felt the need to close Wilmington, the port remained a haven for blockade runners for another year.

  U.S.S. *Huron*, Lieutenant Commander Francis H. Baker, sank blockade running British schooner *Sylvanus* in Doboy Sound, Georgia, with cargo of salt, liquor, and cordage.

2   Major General Stephen A. Hurlbut, Army commander at Memphis, wired Secretary Welles: "The *Tennessee* at Mobile will be ready for sea in twenty days. She is a dangerous craft. Buchanan thinks more so than the *Merrimack* . . . ."

  Commander Robert Townsend reported the seizure of steamer *Ben Franklin* in the lower Mississippi River "for flagrant violation of the Treasury Regulations."

3   U.S.S. *Fahkee*, with Rear Admiral Samuel P. Lee embarked, sighted steamer *Bendigo* aground at Lockwood's Folly Inlet, South Carolina. Three boat crews were sent to investigate; after it was discovered that the blockade runner had been partially burned to prevent capture and that there was seven feet of water in the hold, Lee ordered *Bendigo* destroyed by gunfire from U.S.S. *Fort Jackson*, *Iron Age*, *Montgomery*, *Daylight*, and *Fahkee*.

4   Estimating the situation west of the Mississippi, Lieutenant General E. Kirby Smith, CSA, wrote to Major General Richard Taylor, CSA: "I still think Red and Washita [Ouachita] Rivers, especially the former, are the true lines of operation for an invading column, and that we may expect an attempt to be made by the enemy in force before the rivers fall. . . ." Within eight weeks Rear Admiral David D. Porter was leading such a joint expedition aimed at the penetration of Texas, which would not only further weaken Confederate logistic support from the West, but also would counter the threat of Texas posed by the French ascendancy in Mexico.

  U.S.S. *Tioga*, Lieutenant Commander Edward Y. McCauley, seized an unnamed schooner near the Bahamas, bound from Nassau to Havana with cargo including salt, coffee, arms, shoes, and liquors.

5   Commander George B. Balch reported to Rear Admiral John A. Dahlgren, commanding the South Atlantic Blockading Squadron, that prices continue to rocket in blockaded Charleston: " . . . boots sell at $250 a pair."

7 Following reports from an informant, Rear Admiral Dahlgren ordered all ships of the Charleston blockading force to take stringent precautions against attack by Southern torpedo boats, and noted: "There is also one of another kind, which is nearly submerged and can be entirely so. It is intended to go under the bottoms of vessels and there to operate." Regarding the submarine *H. L. Hunley*, he warned: "It is also advisable not to anchor in the deepest part of the channel, for by not leaving much space between the bottom of the vessel and the bottom of the channel it will be impossible for the diving torpedo to operate except on the sides, and there will be less difficulty in raising a vessel if sunk."

Major General Benjamin F. Butler's plan to send Army steamer *Brewster*, Ensign Arnold Harris, Jr., into Wilmington harbor under the guise of a blockade runner "for the purpose of making an attempt upon the shipping and blockade runners in the harbor" was abandoned upon learning of the Confederates' protective precautions. Brigadier General Charles K. Graham reported to Rear Admiral Lee that while it might be possible to run past Forts Caswell and Fisher under the proposed ruse, it would be frustrated by the chain that stretched across the channel at Fort Lee;

Gun crew on Union ship loads a boat howitzer mounted on a field carriage.

all blockade runners were required to come to at that point until permission for their further advance was received from Wilmington. Under these circumstances, Graham concluded, "it would be madness to make the attempt."

U.S.S. *Montgomery*, Lieutenant Edward H. Faucon, and U.S.S. *Aries*, Lieutenant Edward F. Devens, chased blockade runner *Dare*. The steamer, finding escape impossible, was beached at North Inlet, South Carolina, and was abandoned by her crew. Boat crews from both *Montgomery* and *Aries* boarded but, failing to refloat the prize, set her afire.

U.S.S. *San Jacinto*, Lieutenant Commander Ralph Chandler, captured schooner *Roebuck* at sea, bound from Havana for Mobile.

8 Captain Raphael Semmes, C.S.S. *Alabama*, noted in his journal that he had identified himself to an English bark as U.S.S. *Dacotah* in search of the raider *Alabama*. The bark's master replied: "It won't do; the *Alabama* is a bigger ship than you, and they say she is iron plated besides." Had Semmes' ship been armored in fact, the outcome of his battle with U.S.S. *Kearsarge* six months later might have been different.

U.S.S. *Kennebec*, Lieutenant Commander William P. McCann, chased blockade runner *John Scott* off Mobile for some eight hours and captured her with cargo of cotton and turpentine. *John Scott*'s pilot, William Norval, well known for his professional skill and for aiding the blockade runners, was sent by Commodore Henry K. Thatcher to New Orleans, where he was imprisoned.

9 Reflecting the increased Union concern over Confederate torpedoes, President Abraham Lincoln granted an interview to one Captain Lavender, a New England mariner, to discuss a device for discovering and removing underwater obstructions. Though many ideas for rendering Confederate torpedoes ineffective were advanced, none solved the problem, and torpedoes sank an increasing number of Union ships.

Mr. James O. Putnam, U.S. Consul at L'Havre, France, notified Captain John Winslow of U.S.S. *Kearsarge* "that it was the purpose of the commanders of the *Georgia*, the *Florida*, and *Rappahannock*, to rendezvous at some convenient and opportune point, for the purpose of attacking the *Kearsarge* after she has left Brest." This attack never took place; six months later it was *Kearsarge* which met another Confederate raider, *Alabama*, off Cherbourg.

Rear Admiral Charles H. Bell, commanding the Pacific Squadron, advised Secretary Welles of the report that a Confederate privateer was outfitting at Victoria, Vancouver Island: "I would also respectfully suggest the expediency of having at all times a small steamer, under the direction of the [Mare Island] navy yard, ready to be despatched at a few hours' notice whenever a similar occasion arises. The want of a vessel so prepared may be of incalculable injury to the mercantile interests of our western coast."

10 While helping to salvage the hulk of grounded and partially burned blockade runner *Bendigo* near Lockwood's Folly Inlet, South Carolina, U.S.S. *Iron Age*, Lieutenant Commander Edward E. Stone, herself grounded. Efforts to get her off were futile, and, as Confederates positioned a battery within range, the ship was ordered destroyed to prevent her capture. Reporting on the loss of the small screw steamer and on blockade duty in general, Rear Admiral Lee noted: "This service is one of great hardship and exposure; it has been conducted with slight loss to us, and much loss to the rebels and their allies, who have lost twenty-two vessels in six months, while our loss has only been two vessels on the Wilmington blockade during the war."

Boat crews from U.S.S. *Roebuck*, Acting Master John Sherrill, captured blockade-running Confederate sloop *Maria Louise* with cargo of cotton off Jupiter Inlet, Florida.

11 Flag Officer Samuel Barron, senior Confederate naval officer in France, reported to Secretary of the Navy Stephen Mallory, that he had placed Lieutenant Charles M. Morris in command of

C.S.S. *Florida*, relieving Commander Joseph N. Barney whose ill health prevented active service afloat. *Florida* had completed her repairs and on a trial run "made 13 knots under steam." C.S.S. *Rappahannock* was "repairing slowly but surely;" she would be armed with the battery from C.S.S. *Georgia*, no longer fit for duty as a cruiser. He concluded: "You are doubtless, sir, aware that three Confederate 'men-of-war' are now enjoying the hospitality and natural courtesies of this Empire—a strange contrast with the determined hostility, I may almost say, of Earl Russell . . . . Louis Napoleon is not Lord John Russell!"

U.S.S. *Minnesota, Daylight, Aries,* and *Governor Buckingham* intercepted blockade-runner *Ranger*, Lieutenant George W. Gift, CSN, and forced her aground at the Western Bar of Lockwood's Folly Inlet, South Carolina. Since Southern sharpshooters precluded salvage, *Ranger*, carrying a cargo for the Confederate government, was destroyed by Union forces. *Aries*, Acting Lieutenant Edward F. Devens, also investigated a fire observed between Tubb's and Little River Inlets and found the "fine-looking double propeller blockade runner" *Vesta* beached and in flames. *Vesta* had been sighted and chased the night before by U.S.S. *Keystone State, Quaker City,* and *Tuscarora*.

U.S.S. *Honeysuckle*, Acting Ensign Cyrus Sears, captured blockade running British schooner *Fly* near Jupiter Inlet, Florida.

Boat crews from U.S.S. *Roebuck*, Acting Master Sherrill, captured blockade running British schooner *Susan* at Jupiter Inlet with cargo including salt.

12 Under cover of U.S.S. *Yankee, Currituck, Anacostia, Tulip,* and *Jacob Bell*, commanded by Acting Lieutenant Edward Hooker, Union cavalry and infantry under General Gilman Marston landed on the peninsula between the Potomac and Rappahannock Rivers, capturing "a small body of the enemy and a large number of cavalry horses." The small gunboats supported the Army operations on the 13th and 14th, and covered the reembarkation of the soldiers on the 15th.

13 Captain Thornton A. Jenkins, senior officer present off Mobile, wrote Commodore Henry H. Bell, temporary commander of the West Gulf Blockading Squadron: "I must be permitted to say that, in my judgment, our present weakness at this point, and the incalculable benefits to accrue in the event of success, are a most tempting invitation to the enemy to attack us and endeavor to raise the blockade by capturing or destroying our vessels and to open the way to other successes." Rear Admiral Farragut, who had arrived in Key West, Florida, on 12 January, was soon to resume command of the West Gulf Squadron.

Rear Admiral Dahlgren urged Secretary Welles to employ torpedo boats in Charleston harbor similar to the Confederate "David". "Nothing better could be devised for the security of our own vessels or for the examination of the enemy's position," he wrote. "The length of these torpedo boats might be about 40 feet, and 5 to 6 feet in diameter, with a high-pressure engine that will drive them 5 knots. It is not necessary to expend much finish on them."

Boat crew from U.S.S. *Two Sisters*, Acting master Thomas Chatfield, captured schooner *William* off Suwannee River, Florida, with cargo of salt, bagging, and rope.

14 C.S.S. *Alabama*, Captain Semmes, captured and burned ship *Emma Jane* off the coast of Malabar, southwest India.

Small boats from U.S.S. *Roebuck*, Acting Master Sherrill, chased blockade running British sloop *Young Racer* and forced her aground north of Jupiter Inlet, Florida, with cargo of salt. The sloop was destroyed by her crew.

Having failed in efforts to pull the grounded U.S.S. *Iron Age* off the beach at Lockwood's Folly Inlet, the Federal blockaders applied the torch and blew her up. "As an offset to the loss . . .," reported Lieutenant Commander Stone, "I would place the capture or destruction of 22 blockade runners within the last six months by this squadron [the North Atlantic Blockading Squadron]."

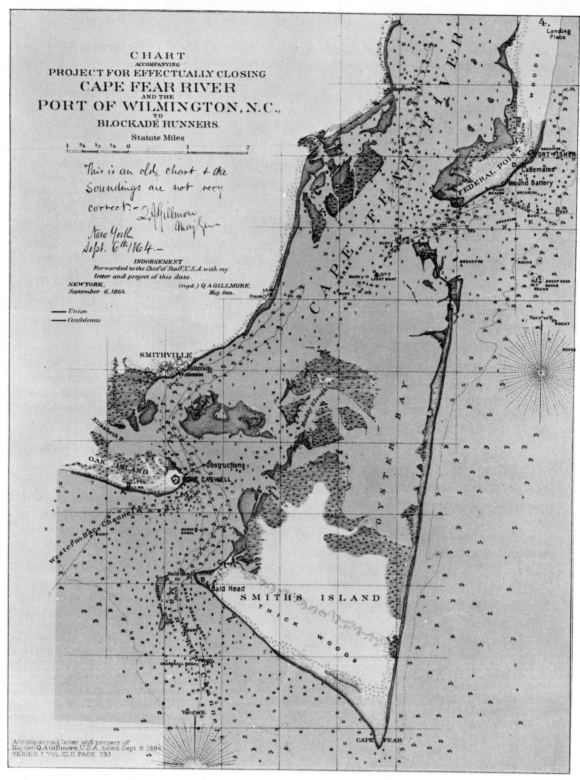

Chart of the Cape Fear River approaches to Wilmington.

U.S.S. *Union*, Acting Lieutenant Edward Conroy, captured blockade running steamer *Mayflower* near Tampa Bay, Florida, with cargo of cotton.

15 Regarding Southern Red River defenses, Major General Taylor, CSA, wrote to Brigadier General William R. Boggs: "At all events, we should be prepared as far as possible, and I trust the remaining 9-inch gun and the carriages for the two 32-Dahlgrens will soon reach me. For the 9-inch and 32-pound rifle now in position at Fort De Russy, there were sent down only 50 rounds of shot and shell; more should be sent at once. The *Missouri*, I suppose, will come down on the first rise."

Secretary Mallory ordered Commander James W. Cooke to command C.S.S. *Albemarle* at Halifax, North Carolina, and to complete her. Under Cooke's guidance she was rapidly readied for service and played a major role in Albemarle Sound from April until her destruction in October.

Commodore H. H. Bell wrote confidentially to Commander Robert Townsend, U.S.S. *Essex*, off Donaldsonville, Louisiana: "The rams and ironclads on Red River and in Mobile Bay are to force the blockade at both points and meet here [New Orleans], whilst the army is to do its part. Being aware of these plans, we should be prepared to defeat them. The reports in circulation about their ironclads and rams being failures may be true in some degree; but we should remember that they prevailed about the redoubtable *Merrimack* before her advent." Of the ironclads, however, only C.S.S. *Tennessee* could be regarded as formidable.

U.S.S. *Beauregard*, Acting Master Francis Burgess, captured blockade running British schooner *Minnie* south of Mosquito Inlet, Florida, with cargo including salt and liquor.

16 Secretary Mallory wrote Captain John K. Mitchell of the Confederate James River Squadron urging that action be taken against the Union squadron downriver at the earliest opportunity. ". . . I think that there is a passage through the obstructions at Trents' Reach. I deem the opportunity a favorable one for striking a blow at the enemy if we are able to do so. In a short time many of his vessels will have returned to the River from Wilmington and he will again perfect his obstructions. If we can block the River at or below City Point, Grant might be compelled to evacuate his position. . . ." The clamor for action increased as the months passed. On 15 May Lieutenant Robert D. Minor, First Lieutenant and ordnance officer for the Squadron, wrote his wife: "There is an insane desire among the public to get the iron clads down the river, and I am afraid that some of our higher public authorities are yeilding to this pressure of public opinion—but *I for one am not* and in the squadron we know too much of the interest at stake to act against our judgement even if those high in authority wish to hurry us into an action unprepared and against vastly superior forces. . . ."

The Richmond *Enquirer* reported that 26 ships on blockading station off Wilmington "guard all the avenues of approach with the most sleepless vigilance. The consequences are that the chances of running the blockade have been greatly lessened, and it is apprehended by some that the day is not far distant when it will be an impossibility for a vessel to get into that port without incurring a hazard almost equivilant to positive loss. Having secured nearly every seaport on our coast, the Yankees are enabled to keep a large force off Wilmington."

Henry Hotze, commercial agent of the Confederate States, wrote from London to Secretary of State Judah P. Benjamin suggesting complete government operation of blockade running: "The experiments thus far made by the Ordnance, Niter, and other Bureaus, as also the Navy Department, demonstrates that the Government can run the blockade with equal if not greater chances than private enterprise. But the public loses the chief advantages of the system, first, by the competition of private exportation; secondly, by the complicated and jarring machinery which only serves to grind out large profits in the shape of commissions, etc.; thirdly, by confounding the distinctive functions of different administrative departments. If blockade running was constituted an arm of the national defense, each would perform only its appropriate work, which

War Department
Washington City,

January 18th 1864.

The
 Secretary of The Navy
  Washington, D.C.
   Sir.

The Secretary of War instructs me to submit to you, the accompanying letter of the 17th November last, received at this Department, from Head Quarters, Department of the Gulf, communicating the contents of a letter, dated at Richmond, Va which was found in a captured rebel mail, in which some particulars are given of the locating of torpedoes in certain named rivers; and enclosing a communication obtained from the same mail, and also dated at Richmond, giving a description and covering a diagram of a proposed submarine torpedo vessel, suggested to be used on the coast of Texas.

I have the honor to be,
Your obedient Servant
Edw. R. S. Canby
Brig Genl: A. A. G.

Letter from Brigadier General Canby to Secretary Welles enclosing captured plans for a Confederate "submarine torpedo vessel, suggested to be used on the coast of Texas."

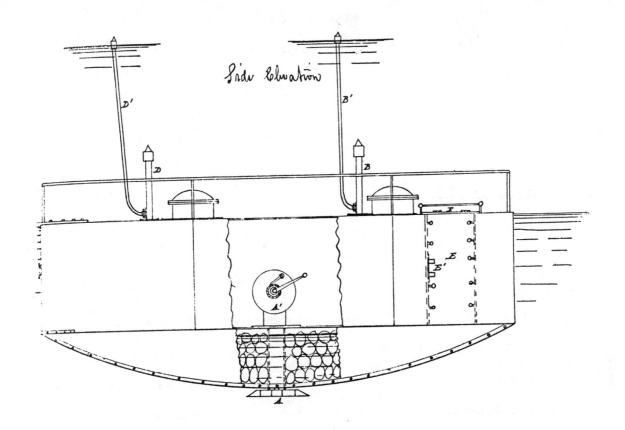

Side Elevation

Plan view.

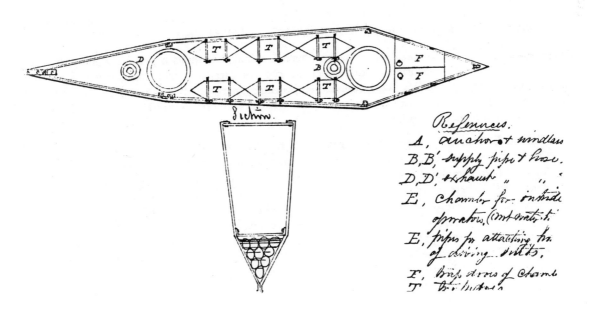

Section

IV-9

therefore would be well done. The Treasury would procure without competition the raw material and regulate the disposition of the proceeds; the Navy, abandoning the hope of breaking the blockade and throwing all its available energies into eluding it, would purchase, build, and man the vessels for this purpose. . . ." As the war progressed, more and more blockade runners commanded by naval officers did operate under the Confederate government.

Boat crews from U.S.S. *Fernandina*, Acting Master Edward Moses, captured sloop *Annie Thompson* in St. Catherine's Sound, Georgia, with cargo of cotton, tobacco, and turpentine.

U.S.S. *Gertrude*, Acting Master Henry C. Wade, captured blockade running schooner *Ellen* off Mobile with an assorted cargo.

17 Rear Admiral Farragut, eager to attack at Mobile but needing ironclads to cope with Confederate ram *Tennessee*, wrote Rear Admiral Porter: "I am therefore anxious to know if your monitors, at least two of them, are not completed and ready for service; and if so, can you spare them to assist us? If I had them, I should not hesitate to become the assailant instead of awaiting the attack. I must have ironclads enough to lie in the bay to hold the gunboats and rams in check in the shoal water."

18 Rear Admiral Farragut arrived off Mobile Bay to inspect Union ships and the Confederate defenses. He had sailed from New York in his renowned flagship *Hartford* after an absence of five months, and was to officially resume command of the West Gulf Blockading Squadron on January 22 at New Orleans. Farragut was concerned about the reported strength of the Confederate ram *Tennessee*, then in Mobile Bay, and determined to destroy her and silence the forts, closing Mobile to the blockade runners. To this end, he immediately began to build up his forces and make plans for the battle.

Secretary Welles directed Captain Henry Walke, U.S.S. *Sacramento*, to search for "the piratical vessels now afloat and preying upon our commerce," adding: "You will bear in mind that the principal object of your pursuit is the *Alabama*." *Alabama* had by this date taken more than 60 prizes, and the effect of all raiders on Union merchantmen was evident in the gradual disappearance of the U.S. flag from the ocean commerce lanes. Boat crews from U.S.S. *Roebuck*, Acting Master Sherrill, captured sloop *Caroline* off Jupiter Inlet, Florida, with cargo of salt, gin, soda, and dry goods.

U.S.S. *Stars and Stripes*, Acting Master Charles L. Willcomb, captured blockade running steamer *Laura* off Ocklockonee River, Florida, with cargo including cigars.

19 Boats from U.S.S. *Roebuck*, Acting Master Sherrill, seized British schooner *Eliza* and sloop *Mary* inside Jupiter Inlet, Florida. Both blockade runners carried cargoes of cotton. Three days later *Mary*, en route to Key West, commenced leaking, ran aground, and was wrecked. The prize crew and most of the cotton were saved. In ten days, Sherrill's vigilance and initiative had enabled him to take six prizes.

Thomas E. Courtenay, engaged in secret service for the Confederacy, informed Colonel Henry E. Clark, that manufacture of "coal torpedoes" was nearing completion, and stated: "The castings have all been completed some time and the coal is so perfect that the most critical eye could not detect it." These devices, really powder filled cast iron bombs, shaped and painted to resemble pieces of coal, were to be deposited in Federal naval coal depots, from where they would eventually reach and explode ships' boilers. During the next few months Rear Admiral Porter, commanding the Mississippi Squadron, became greatly concerned over Confederate agents assigned to distribute the coal torpedoes, and wrote Secretary Welles that he had "given orders to commanders of vessels not to be very particular about the treatment of any of these desperadoes if caught—only summary punishment will be effective."

21 U.S.S. *Sciota*, Lieutenant Commander George H. Perkins, in company with U.S.S. *Granite City*, Acting Master Charles W. Lamson, joined several hundred troops in a reconnaisance of the Texas coast. *Sciota* and *Granite City* covered the troops at Smith's Landing, Texas, and the subsequent foray down the Matagorda Peninsula. From the war's outset this type of close naval support and cooperation with the army had been a potent factor in Union success in all theaters of the conflict.

22 Rear Admiral Dahlgren wrote Assistant Secretary of the Navy Gustavus V. Fox regarding Charleston: ". . . do not suppose that I am idle because no battles are fought; on the contrary, the blockade by four monitors of such a place as this, and the determined intentions of the rebels to operate with torpedoes, keep all eyes open."

Acting Ensign James J. Russell, U.S.S. *Restless*, accompanied by two sailors, captured blockade running schooner *William A. Kain* in St. Andrew's Bay, Florida. Russell and his men had intended originally to reconnoiter only, but after discovering and capturing the Captain and several of the crewmembers of the blockade runner in the woods near the vessel, he determined to take her himself. Compelling his prisoners to row him out to *Kain*, Russell captured the remaining crew members and managed to sail *Kain* from Watson's Bayou out into the bay and under the protection of *Restless*'s guns.

23 Rear Admiral Dahlgren in a letter to President Lincoln wrote: "The city of Charleston is converted into a camp, and 20,000 or 25,000 of their best troops are kept in abeyance in the vicinity, to guard against all possible contingencies, so that 2,000 of our men in the fortifications of Morris and Folly Islands, assisted by a few ironclads, are rendering invaluable service. . . . No man in the country will be more happy than myself to plant the flag of the Union where you most desire to see it." The Union's ability to attack any part of the South's long coastline from the sea diverted important numbers of Confederate soldiers from the main armies.

26 William L. Dayton, U.S. Minister to France, noted in a dispatch to Secretary of State Seward: "I must regret that, of the great number of our ships of war, enough could not have been spared to look after the small rebel cruisers now in French ports. It is a matter of great surprise in Europe, that, with our apparent naval force, we permit such miserable craft to chase our commerce from the ocean; it affects seriously our prestige."

28 Captain Henry S. Stellwagen, commanding U.S.S. *Constellation*, reported from Naples "It is my pleasant duty to inform you of the continued [friendly] demonstrations of ruling powers and people of the Kingdom of Italy toward our country and its officers." When the problems of blockading the hazardous Atlantic and Gulf coasts and running down Confederate commerce raiders compelled the Navy Department to employ its steamers in these tasks, sailing warships were sent out to replace them on the foreign stations. These slow but relatively powerful vessels, the historic *Constellation* in the Mediterranean, *St. Louis* west of Gibraltar on the converging trade routes, *Jamestown* in the East Indies, became available to escort merchant ships and, more important, to deter the approach of raiders. Though they received few opportunities to carry out their military missions, these veterans of the Old Navy rendered most effective service protecting American interests and maintaining national prestige abroad.

U.S. Army steamer *Western Metropolis* seized blockade running British steamer *Rosita* off Key West with cargo including liquor and cigars. Acting Lieutenant Lewis W. Pennington, USN, and Acting Master Daniel S. Murphy, USN, on board as passengers, assisted in the capture.

U.S.S. *Beauregard*, Acting Master Burgess, seized blockade running British sloop *Racer* north of Cape Canaveral, Florida, with cargo of cotton.

29 Commander Thomas H. Stevens, U.S.S. *Patapsco*, reported to Rear Admiral Dahlgren on an extended reconnaissance of the Wilmington River, Georgia, during which Confederate sharpshooters

were engaged. Stevens concluded: "From what I can see and learn, an original expedition against Savannah at this time by a combined movement of the land and sea forces would be probably successful." Though the Navy kept the city under close blockade and engaged the area's defenses, troops for the combined operation did not become available until late in the year.

Lieutenant Commander James C. Chaplin, U.S.S. *Dai Ching*, reported to Dahlgren information obtained from the master of blockade runner *George Chisholm* [see 14 November 1863 for capture]: ". . . vessels running out from Nassau, freighted with contraband goods for Southern ports . . . always skirt along on soundings and take the open sea through the North East Providence Channel by Egg and Royal Islands, steering from thence about N.N.W. course toward Wilmington or ports adjacent on the Carolina coast, while those bound to Mobile run down on the east side of Cuba through Crooked Island Passage, sweeping outside in a considerable circle to avoid the United States cruisers in the vicinity. The vessels bound to the coast of the Carolinas take their point of departure from a newly erected light-house in the neighborhood of Man of War Cay. They are provided with the best of instruments and charts, and, if the master is ignorant of the channels and inlets of our coast, a good pilot. They are also in possession of the necessary funds (in specie) to bribe, if possible, captors for their release. Such an offer was made to myself . . . of some £800. The master of a sailing vessel, before leaving port, receives $1,000 (in coin), and, if successful, $5,000 on his return; those commanding steamers $5,000 on leaving and $15,000 in a successful return to the same port."

31 In planning the strategy for the joint Army-Navy Red River Campaign, Major General William T. Sherman wrote to Major General Nathaniel P. Banks: "The expedition on Shreveport should be made rapidly, by simultaneous movements from Little Rock on Shreveport, from Opelousas on Alexandria, and a combined force of gun-boats and transports directly up Red River. Admiral Porter will be able to have a splendid fleet by March 1." The Army relied on Porter's gunboats both to spearhead attack with its powerful guns and to keep open the all-important supply line.

An expedition comprising some 40 sailors and 350 soldiers with a 12-pound howitzer, under command of Lieutenant Commander Charles W. Flusser, marched inland from the Roanoke River, North Carolina, "held the town of Windsor several hours, and marched back 8 miles to our boats without a single shot from the enemy."

FEBRUARY

1 Army expedition supported by minor naval forces (including converted ferry boat U.S.S. *Commodore Morris*, Lieutenant Commander James H. Gillis, and launches from U.S.S. *Minnesota*) was repulsed by Confederate sharpshooters near Smithfield, Virginia, with the loss of Army gunboat *Smith Briggs*. The troops, whose original object had been the capture of a Confederate camp and a quantity of tobacco on Pagan Creek, re-embarked on the transports and withdrew downstream.

U.S.S. *Sassacus*, Lieutenant Commander Francis A. Roe, captured blockade runner *Wild Dayrell* aground at Stump Inlet, North Carolina. Roe attempted to get the steamer off for two days but, unable to do so, burned her.

Boat expedition from U.S.S. *Braziliera*, Acting Master William T. Gillespie, captured sloop *Buffalo* with cargo of cotton near Brunswick, Georgia.

2 Early in the morning, a Confederate boat expedition planned and boldly led by Commander John Taylor Wood, CSN, captured and destroyed 4-gun sidewheel steamer U.S.S. *Underwriter*, Acting Master Jacob Westervelt, anchored in the Neuse River near New Bern, North Carolina. The boats had been shipped by rail from Petersburg, Virginia, to Kinston, North Carolina, and from there started down the Neuse. Wood, grandson of President Taylor and nephew of Jefferson Davis, silently approached *Underwriter* about 2:30 a.m. and was within 100 yards of the gunboat before the boats were sighted. *Underwriter's* guns could not be brought to bear in time,

John Taylor Wood
Commander, CSN

Lloyd J. Beall
Colonel, CSMC

and the Confederates quickly boarded and took her in hand-to-hand combat, during which Wester-velt was killed. Unable to move *Underwriter* because she did not have steam up, Wood destroyed her while under the fire of nearby Union batteries. He later wrote Colonel Lloyd J. Beall, Commandant of the Confederate Marine Corps, commending the Marines who had taken part in the expedition: "Though their duties were more arduous than those of the others, they were always prompt and ready for the performance of all they were called upon to do. As a body they would be a credit to any organization, and I will be glad to be associated with them on duty at any time." Lieutenant George W. Gift, CSN, who took part in what Secretary Mallory termed "this brilliant exploit," remarked: "I am all admiration for Wood. He is modesty personified, conceives boldly and executes with skill and courage."

Major General W. T. Sherman, who had recently arrived at Vicksburg on board U.S.S. *Juliet*, Acting Master J. Stoughton Watson, preparatory to commencing his expedition to Meridian, Mississippi, expressed his appreciation for the assistance Watson had given him. "I am very obliged to you personally and officially for the perfect manner [in which] you have contributed to my wants. You have enabled me to assemble and put in motion troops along the Mississippi, and have contributed to the personal comfort of myself and staff." In order to further assist Sherman's move, stern-wheel gunboats *Marmora*, *Romeo*, *Exchange* and tinclad *Petrel* supported a diversionary expedition up the Yazoo River. Sherman had written Lieutenant Commander Elias K. Owen, commanding the gunboats: "I desire to confuse the enemy as to our plans [to march across Mississippi and attack Meridian], and know that the appearance of a force up the Yazoo as far as possible will tend to that result." Moreover, such a showing of the flag would impress the people with the force available to Union commanders should it be necessary to use it.

U.S. Tug *Geranium*, Acting Ensign David Lee, captured eight members of the Confederate Torpedo Corps off Fort Moultrie, in Charleston Harbor, while they were attempting to remove stores from a grounded blockade runner.

2–4 Blockade runner *Presto* was discovered aground under the batteries of Fort Moultrie. Monitors U.S.S. *Lehigh*, Commander Andrew Bryson, *Nahant*, Lieutenant Commander John J. Cornwell, and *Passaic*, Lieutenant Commander Edward Simpson, fired on the steamer for three days, finally satisfying themselves on 4 February that she was destroyed.

2–22 Major General Quincy A. Gillmore advised Rear Admiral Dahlgren of his intention " . . . to throw a force into Florida on the west bank of St. John's River." He requested the support of two or three naval gunboats for the operation. Dahlgren promply detailed small screw steamers U.S.S. *Ottawa* and *Norwich* to convoy the Army troops to Jacksonville, and ordered screw steamer U.S.S. *Dai Ching*, and sidewheelers *Mahaska* and *Water Witch* up the St. John's. The Admiral himself went to Florida to take a personal hand in directing his forces to " . . . keep open the communications by the river and give any assistance to the troops which operations may need. . . . " With the gunboats deployed according to Dahlgren's instructions, the soldiers, under Brigadier General Truman Seymour, landed at Jacksonville, moved inland, captured fieldpieces and took a large quantity of cotton. As Dahlgren prepared to return to Charleston on 10 February, General Gillmore wrote: "Please accept my thanks for the prompt cooperation afforded me." A strong Confederate counterattack commenced on 20 February and compelled the Union troops to fall back on Jacksonville where the gunboats stood by to defend the city; naval howitzers were put ashore in battery, manned by seamen. Commander Balch, senior naval officer present, reported: "I had abundant reasons to believe that to the naval force must our troops be indebted for protection against a greatly superior force flushed with victory." Seymour expressed his appreciation for Balch's quick action " . . . at a moment when it appeared probable that the vigorous assistance of the force under your command would be necessary."

Officers and men attend divine services on board U.S.S. Passaic *off Charleston.*

3 U.S.S. *Petrel*, *Marmora*, *Exchange*, and *Romeo*, under Lieutenant Commander Owen, silenced Confederate batteries at Liverpool, Mississippi, on the Yazoo River, as naval forces began an expedition to prevent Southerners from harassing Major General W. T. Sherman's expedition to Meridian, Mississippi. In the next two weeks, Owen's light-draft gunboats pushed up the Yazoo River as far as Greenwood, Mississippi, engaging Confederate troops en route. Confederates destroyed steamer *Sharp* to prevent her capture before the Union naval force turned back. "This move," Rear Admiral Porter later reported to Secretary Welles, "has had the effect of driving the guerrillas away from the Mississippi River, as they are fearful it is intended to cut them off."

U.S.S. *Midnight*, Acting Master Walter H. Garfield, captured blockade running schooner *Defy* off Doboy Light, Georgia, with cargo of salt.

4 A boat under command of Acting Master's Mate Henry B. Colby from U.S.S. *Beauregard* captured *Lydia* at Jupiter Narrows, Florida, with small cargo of cotton and turpentine.

4–5 U.S.S. *Sassacus*, Lieutenant Commander Roe, chased steamer *Nutfield* aground off New River Inlet, North Carolina. When it proved impossible to get her off, her cargo of Enfield rifles and quinine was salvaged and she was destroyed.

5 J. L. McPhail, Maryland's Provost Marshal General, wrote Commander Foxhall A. Parker of the Potomac Flotilla, informing him that a known Southern sympathizer was the agent for schooner *Ann Hamilton*'s owners. McPhail recommended that she be taken, but it later developed that U.S. Revenue Steamer *Hercules* had already seized *Ann Hamilton* off Point Lookout, Maryland, on 4 February. A search of the schooner confirmed McPhail's suspicions: quantities of salt and lye and more than $15,000 in Confederate money were found on board. Parker ordered her to Washington for adjudication.

Captain John R. Tucker reported that the boiler of C.S.S. *Chicora* had given out and that henceforth she could be used only as a floating battery in the defenses of Charleston harbor.

U.S.S. *De Soto*, Captain Gustavus H. Scott, seized blockade running British steamer *Cumberland* in the Gulf of Mexico south of Santa Rosa Island with cargo of arms, gunpowder, and dry goods.

6 Special Commissioner of the Confederate States A. Dudley Mann wrote Secretary of State Benjamin from London: "The iron hull is superseding the wooden hull just as steam is superseding canvas. The rich and exhaustless ore fields and coal mines of the 'Island Giant', her numerous workshops and shipyards, the abundance and constant augmentation of her seamen, will probably in less than a score of years produce for her a mercantile navy three times as large as that of all the world besides. The old American Union was her only rival in bottom carrying. That rival has disappeared." Mann here referred to the fact that the U.S. merchant vessels were increasingly sailing under foreign registry because of Southern commerce raiders.

U.S.S. *Cambridge*, Commander William F. Spicer, found blockade running steamer *Dee* aground and in flames near Masonboro, North Carolina. She had grounded the preceding night and was set afire to prevent capture. Spicer completed the destruction of the blockade runner with her cargo of lead, bacon, and spirits.

7 Confederate steamer *St. Mary's*, trapped in McGirt's Creek, above Jacksonville, Florida, by U.S.S. *Norwich*, Acting Master Frank B. Meriam, was sunk and her cargo of cotton destroyed to prevent its falling into Union hands.

8 Commander Catesby ap R. Jones, commanding the Confederate Naval Gun Factory at Selma, Alabama, wrote Admiral Franklin Buchanan at Mobile of the fighting qualities of the Union monitors: "The revolving turret enables the monitor class to bring their guns to bear without reference to the movements or turning of the vessel. You who fought the *Virginia* know well how to appreciate that great advantage. You doubtless recollect how often I reported to you

that we could not bring one of her ten guns to bear. In fighting that class, it is very important to prevent the turret from revolving, which I think may be done either with the VII-inch or 6.4-inch rifles or 64 pounder, provided their projectiles strike the turret at or near its base where it joins the deck. . . . If the turret is prevented from revolving, the vessel is then less efficient than one with the same guns having the ordinary ports, as the monitors' ports are so small that the guns can not be trained except by the helm."

9   Acting Master Gerhard C. Schulze "received six refugees" on board U.S.S. *Jacob Bell* off Blakistone Island, Virginia. One of the men, Joseph Lenty, an Englishman, had worked in Richmond for four years and brought the North further news of recent refinement by Confederates of their ingenious torpedoes. ". . . they are now making a shell which looks exactly like a piece of coal, pieces of which were taken from a coal pile as patterns to imitate. I have made these shells myself. I believe these shells have power enough to burst any boiler. After they were thrown, in a coal pile I could not tell the difference between them and coal myself." The "coal torpedo" was reported to have been placed in production late in January 1864 and was suspected of having been the agent of several unexplained explosions and fires during the remainder of the war (see 27 November 1864). A general order issued by Rear Admiral Porter on the subject testified to the genuine alarm with which Union commanders viewed the new weapon: "The enemy have adopted new inventions to destroy human life and vessels in the shape of torpedoes, and an article resembling coal, which is to be placed in our coal piles for the purpose of blowing the vessels up, or injuring them. Officers will have to be careful in overlooking coal barges. Guards will be placed over them at all times, and anyone found attempting to place any of these things amongst the coal will be shot on the spot."

Life on board Confederate commerce raiders was taxing and little relieved by relaxation. This date C.S.S. *Alabama* made one of her few "port calls", putting into the island of Johanna between Africa and Madagascar for provisions. Captain Semmes later wrote: "I gave my sailors a run on shore, but this sort of 'liberty' was awful hard work for Jack. There was no such thing as a glass of grog to be found in the whole town, and as for a fiddle, and Sal for a partner—all of which would have been a matter of course in civilized countries—there were no such luxuries to be thought of. They found it a difficult matter to get through with the day, and were all down at the beach long before sunset—the hour appointed for their coming off—waiting for the approach of the welcome boat. I told Kell to let them go on shore as often as they pleased, but no one made a second application."

Commander T. H. Stevens, U.S.S. *Patapsco*, reported that one of his cutters commanded by Acting Ensign Walter C. Odiorne captured blockade running schooner *Swift* off Cabbage Island, Georgia, with cargo of fish.

10   C.S.S. *Florida*, Lieutenant Charles M. Morris, escaped to sea from Brest, France, having been laid up for repairs since the preceding August. "The *Florida*," reported Captain Winslow of *Kearsarge*, "took advantage of a thick, rainy night and left at 2 o'clock, proceeding through the southern passage." Morris' sailing instructions, received from Flag Officer Samuel Barron, contained the terse reminder: ". . . you are to do the enemy's property the greatest injury in the shortest time." Winslow was finding, as the British found during the Napoleonic Wars, that Brest was a very difficult port to blockade.

U.S.S. *Florida*, Commander Peirce Crosby, forced blockade runner *Fanny and Jenny* aground near Masonboro Inlet, North Carolina. Immediately thereafter, Crosby sighted blockade runner *Emily* aground nearby. Unable to get either steamer afloat and under fire from a Confederate Whitworth battery, Crosby burned them. *Fanny and Jenny* carried an assorted cargo including a quantity of coal; *Emily* carried a cargo of salt. On *Fanny and Jenny* was also found a solid gold jewel-studded sword inscribed: "To General Robert E. Lee, from his British sympathizers."

Seven-inch banded Brooke gun. Brooke was Chief of the Office of Ordnance and Hydrography in Richmond, 1863–1864.

John M. Brooke Commander, CSN

Crosby reported that information given him by the captured crew members of *Fanny and Jenny* indicated that ten blockade runners had sailed from Nassau for Wilmington "... during this dark of the moon. Three have been destroyed, and one put back, broken down, leaving six others to be heard from."

11 U.S.S. *Queen*, Acting Master Robert Tarr, captured schooner *Louisa* off the mouth of the Brazos River, Texas, with cargo of powder and Enfield rifles.

12 Commander John M. Brooke, in charge of the Confederate Navy's Office of Ordnance and Hydrography wrote Flag Officer Barron in France for "material for cartridge bags, which is now much needed." Brooke asked Barron to purchase some 22,000 yards of material and ship it to Nassau. From there blockade runners would attempt to run it through the blockade, in 1000 yard lots to avoid losing it all in the event of capture. It was becoming increasingly difficult for the South to procure basic war materials, a problem which was compounded by the lack of good railroads for internal transportation and control of most of her rivers by the Federal fleet.

13 Rear Admiral Farragut reported to Assistant Secretary of Navy Fox that information given him indicated "that those publications about vessels running into Mobile are false [and] that no vessel has gotten in during the last six weeks and then only one, that the *Isabel* has been in there 4 months ... that there are but 3 steamers, the *Denbigh*, and *Isabel* and *Austin*; the 2 last are loaded ready to run out and the *Denbigh* was so disabled by the Fleet when she attempted to run out the other night that she had to be towed up to the City [Mobile]—and her cotton is at the Fort."

14 Lieutenant Commander Charles A. Babcock reported on a reconnaissance mission conducted the preceding day by U.S.S. *Morse* on the York River and Potopotank Creek, Virginia. A sloop, with a cargo of corn and small schooner *Margaret Ann* were seized and taken to Yorktown. Babcock also swept the river from Moody's Wharf to Purtan Island Point to verify reports that Confederate torpedoes had been planted there. None were found in that area, but Babcock wrote: "I do not believe there are any torpedoes below Goff's Point, but across from Goff's Point to Terrapin Point and in the forks of the river at West Point I believe, from information received, that there are certainly torpedoes placed there."

The blockading forces off Mobile raise the Stars and Stripes: "Our flag is there!"

15   U.S.S. *Forest Rose*, Acting Lieutenant John V. Johnston, came to the relief of Union soldiers who were being hard-pressed by attacking Confederate troops at Waterproof, Louisiana.   The 260-ton gunboat compelled the Southerners to retire under a heavy bombardment.   The commander of

the Northerners ashore wrote Johnston: "I hope you will not consider it [mere] flattering when I say I never before saw more accurate artillery firing than you did in these engagements, invariably putting your shells in the right place ordered. My officers and men now feel perfectly secure against a large force, so long as we have the assistance of Captain Johnston and his most excellent drilled crew. . . ."

Rear Admiral C. H. Bell of the Pacific Squadron ordered Commander William E. Hopkins, U.S.S. *Saginaw*, to cruise in Mexican waters and warned: "It is believed that on that part of the coast of Mexico which you will visit during your present cruise there are many persons calling themselves citizens of the United States who are watching an opportunity to seize upon any vessel suitable to make depredations on our commerce. You must, therefore, be extremely careful, particularly when at anchor, that no boats approach without being ready to repel any attempt which may be made to take you by surprise. A sufficient watch on deck at night, with arms at hand, and the men drilled to rush on deck without waiting to dress, is absolutely indispensable in a low-deck vessel like the *Saginaw*."

The Confederate Congress tendered its thanks to Commander John Taylor Wood, his officers, and men "for the daring and brilliantly executed plans which resulted in the capture of the United States transport schooner *Elmore*, on the Potomac River; of the ship *Allegheny* [see *Alleghanian*, 28 October 1862] . . . and the United States transport schooners *Golden Rod*, *Coquette*, and *Two Brothers*, on the Chesapeake [see 25 August 1863]; and, more recently, in the capture from under the guns of the enemy's works of the United States gunboat *Underwriter*, on the Neuse River, near New Berne, North Carolina [see 2 February 1864], with the officers and crews of the several vessels brought off as prisoners."

Flag Officer Barron reported from Paris to Secretary Mallory: "From all the information I can get there seems to be scarcely a single Yankee vessel engaged in regular trade between any two places. But should our efforts to keep cruisers afloat abate or prove less successful doubtless their enterprise will again be brought into lively activity to relieve their present more than half-starved commerce."

U.S.S. *Virginia*, Acting Lieutenant Charles H. Brown, seized blockade running British schooner *Mary Douglas* off San Luis Pass, Texas, with cargo of bananas, coffee, and linen.

Rear Admiral Farragut's fleet off Mobile bombards Fort Powell.

16   Union naval forces, composed of double-ender U.S.S. *Octorara*, Lieutenant Commander William W. Low, converted ferryboat U.S.S. *J. P. Jackson*, Acting Lieutenant Miner B. Crowell, and six mortar schooners, began bombarding Confederate works at Fort Powell as Rear Admiral Farragut commenced the long, arduous campaign that six months later would result in the closing of Mobile Bay. The bombardment of Fort Powell by gunboats was a continuing operation, though the mortar boats were eventually withdrawn.

Rear Admiral Dahlgren, alert to the potential offered by torpedoes, ordered 100 of them made by Benjamin Maillefert, an engineering specialist. Late the preceding November, Maillefert had proposed using torpedoes to clear the obstructions in the channel between Fort Sumter and Charleston: "Each of these charges will be provided with a clockwork arrangement, which shall determine the exact time of firing; they are to contain 110 to 125 pounds of gunpowder each. . . ." This date Dahlgren, satisfied with the tests during the intervening period, wrote: "Having witnessed the action of your time torpedoes, I think they may be serviceable in operating against the rebels at Charleston and elsewhere." By war's end both North and South were using torpedoes, forecasting the great roles this underwater ordnance would play in the 20th century.

U.S.S. *Montgomery*, Acting Lieutenant Faucon, seized blockade running British steamer *Pet* off Lockwood's Folly Inlet, South Carolina.

Lieutenant Minor, CSN, reported on the condition of C.S.S. *Neuse*, then building at Kinston, North Carolina: ". . . Lieutenant Comdg. [William] Sharp has a force of one hundred and seventy-two men employed upon her. . . . As you are aware the Steamer has two layers of iron on the forward end of her shield, but none on either broadside, or on the after part. The carpenters are now calking the longitudinal pieces on the hull, and if the iron can be delivered more rapidly, or in small quantities with some degree of regularity, the work would progress in a much more

Line engraving by Conrad Wise Chapman of Confederate submarine H. L. Hunley which sank U.S.S. Housatonic *off Charleston.*

satisfactory manner. The boiler was today lowered into the vessel and when in place, the main deck will be laid in . . . . The river I am told is unprecedently low for the season of the year . . . I am satisfied not more than five feet can be now carried down the channel. . . . And as the Steamer when ready for service will draw between six or seven feet, it is very apparent that to be useful, she must be equipped in time to take advantage of the first rise. . . .''

16–23   U.S.S. *Para*, Acting Master Edward G. Furber, escorted troops up the St. Mary's River to Woodstock Mills, Florida, to obtain lumber. The 200-ton schooner engaged Confederates along the river banks and covered the transports while a large quantity of lumber was taken on board. On 21 February, *Para* captured small steamer *Hard Times*.

17   Confederate submarine *H. L. Hunley*, Lieutenant George E. Dixon, CSA, destroyed U.S.S. *Housatonic*, Captain Charles W. Pickering, off Charleston, and became the first submarine to sink an enemy ship in combat. After *Hunley* sank the preceding fall for the second time (see 15 October 1863), she was raised, a new volunteer crew trained, and for months under the cover of darkness moved out into the harbor where she awaited favorable conditions and a target. This night, the small cylindrical-shaped craft with a spar torpedo mounted on the bow found the heavy steam sloop of war *Housatonic* anchored outside the bar. Just before 9 o'clock in the evening, Acting Master John K. Crosby, *Housatonic*'s officer of the deck, sighted an object in the water about 100 yards off but making directly for the ship. ''It had the appearance of a plank moving in the water.'' Nevertheless *Housatonic* slipped her cable and began backing full; all hands were called to quarters. It was too late. Within two minutes of her first sighting, *H. L. Hunley* rammed her torpedo into *Housatonic*'s starboard side, forward of the mizzenmast. The big warship was shattered by the ensuing explosion and ''sank immediately.''

     The Charleston *Daily Courier* reported on 29 February: ''The explosion made no noise, and the affair was not known among the fleet until daybreak, when the crew were discovered and released from their uneasy positions in the rigging. They had remained there all night. Two officers and three men were reported missing and were supposed to be drowned. The loss of the *Housatonic* caused great consternation in the fleet. All the wooden vessels are ordered to keep up steam and to go out to sea every night, not being allowed to anchor inside. The picket boats have been doubled and the force in each boat increased.''

     Dixon and his daring associates perished with *H. L. Hunley* in the attack. The exact cause of her loss was never determined, but as Confederate Engineer James H. Tomb later observed: ''She was very slow in turning, but would sink at a moment's notice and at times without it.'' The submarine, Tomb added, ''was a veritable coffin to this brave officer and his men.'' But in giving their lives the gallant crew of *H. L. Hunley* wrote a fateful page in history—for their deed foretold the huge contributions submarines would make in later years in other wars.

17–19   Boat expedition under the command of Acting Ensign J. G. Koehler, U.S.S. *Tahoma*, destroyed a large Confederate salt works and a supply of salt near St. Marks, Florida.

18   Commander James D. Bulloch wrote Secretary Mallory from Liverpool of his disappointment over the inability of the Confederacy to obtain ironclads in Europe and suggested, as Henry Hotze had a month before (see 16 January 1864), that the Navy Department ''. . . take the blockade-running business into its own hands. . . .'' Bulloch added: ''The beams and decks of these steamers could be made of sufficient strength to bear heavy deck loads without exciting suspicion, and then if registered in the name of private individuals and sailed purely as commercial ships they could trade without interruption or violation of neutrality between our coasts and the Bermudas, Bahamas, and West Indies. When three or more of the vessels happened to be in harbor at the same time a few hours would suffice to mount a couple of heavy guns on each, and at early dawn a successful raid might be made upon the unsuspecting blockaders. . . . After a raid or cruise the vessels could be divested of every appliance of war, and resuming their private ownership and commercial names, could bring off cargoes of cotton to pay the cost of the cruise.

... Such operations are not impracticable, and if vigorously carried on without notice and at irregular periods, would greatly increase the difficulty of blockading our harbors, and would render hazardous the transportation of troops along the line of our coasts and through the Gulf of Mexico.'' Bulloch's proposal to disguise raiders as merchantmen became a reality in the 20th century as a practice followed by European belligerents.

> U.S.S. Sloop "Canandaigua"
> Off Charleston S.C.
> February 18th 1864
>
> Sir.
>
> I have respectfully to report that a boat belonging to the "Housatonic" reached this ship last night at about 9.20 giving me information that that vessel had been sunk at 8.45 P.M. by a Rebel Torpedo Craft.
>
> I immediately slipped our Cable and started for her anchorage, and on arriving near it at 9.35 descovered her sunk with her hammock nettings under water, despatched all boats and rescued from the wreck twenty one (21) officers and one hundred and Twenty nine men.

Extract from a report by Lieutenant Francis J. Higginson, on board U.S.S. Canandaigua, *regarding the destruction of blockader* Housatonic *by submarine* H. L. Hunley.

President Lincoln ended the blockade of Brownsville, Texas, and opened the port for trade.

20 Rear Admiral Dahlgren, greatly concerned by the loss of U.S.S. *Housatonic*, wrote in his diary: "The loss of the *Housatonic* troubles me very much. . . . Torpedoes have been laughed at; but this disaster ends that." The day before, he had written Secretary Welles urging that the Union develop and use torpedo boats to combat similar Confederate efforts. Under the impression that the submarine *H. L. Hunley* had been another "David" torpedo boat, the Admiral suggested "a large reward of prize money for the capture or destruction of a 'David'. I should say not less than $20,000 or $30,000 for each. They are worth more than that to us."

Rear Admiral Lee wrote Assistant Secretary of the Navy Fox about the blockade off Wilmington. He reported that "the number of blockade runners captured or destroyed since July 12, [is] 26, and since the blockade was strengthened last fall the number is 23 steamers lost to the trade. . . . I don't believe that many prizes will be made hereafter; the runners now take to the beach too readily when they see a blockader by day or night. . . . I think the additions to the runners are less than the numbers destroyed, etc. . . . The blockade off Wilmington is the blockade of two widely separated entrances each requiring as much force as Charleston did if not more. Experience teaches that a mere inner line will not answer for blockading in this steam era. Now the blockaders are from 1 to 2 miles, and more, apart. . . . Wilmington and its entrances and adjacent inlets require more attention than all the rest of the coast. The depots at Bermuda and Nassau are tributary to it." The Admiral also continued to urge an attack on Wilmington: "I long to cooperate with an army capable of investing Richmond or Wilmington, *a la* Vicksburg."

21 Lieutenant Commander Francis M. Ramsay off the mouth of the Red River reported that the water in the river was too low for three Confederate gunboats at Shreveport to get over the falls. This boded ill for the success of the Federals' Red River expedition soon to be undertaken.

22 Secretary Mallory wrote Flag Officer Barron, CSN, in Paris: "If you could raise the blockade of Wilmington, an important service would thereby be rendered, a service which would enable neutrals to carry a great deal of cotton from that port. . . . A dash at the New England ports and commerce might be made very destructive and would be a heavy blow in the right direction. A few days' cruising on the banks might inflict severe injury on the fisheries. The interception of the California steamers also offers good service. . . . Unless you determine to strike a blow which necessarily requires a combination of your force, it would be judicious to send the ships in opposite directions to distract the enemy in pursuit. It would be well, too, to give instructions looking to the occasional disguise and change of name of each vessel for the same purpose. Their advent upon the high seas will raise a howl throughout New England, and I trust it may be well founded. The destruction of a few ships off New York and Boston, Bath and Portland would raise insurance upon their coasting trade a hundred per cent above its present rates." Mallory well recalled the profound effect Lieutenant Charles W. Read's cruise in June 1863 had had on New England mercantile interests.

Tinclad U.S.S. *Whitehead*, Acting Master William N. Welles, ordered on an expedition up the Roanoke River by Lieutenant Commander Flusser, destroyed a corn mill used by Confederate troops near Rainbow Bluff, North Carolina. Torpedoes were reported to be planted in the river above that point, which Flusser observed "would argue rather fear of our advance than an intention on their part to attack." Flusser made this remark in the wake of repeatedly expressed concern over a rumored massive Confederate attack on Union positions in the sounds of North Carolina.

U.S.S. *Virginia*, Acting Lieutenant C. H. Brown, captured blockade running British schooner *Henry Colthirst*, off San Luis Pass, Texas, with cargo of gunpowder, hardware, and provisions.

U.S.S. *Linden*, Acting Master Thomas M. Farrell, attempting to aid transport *Ad. Hines*, hit a snag in the Arkansas River and sank.

23 Rear Admiral C. H. Bell wrote Secretary Welles from U.S.S. *Lancaster* at Acapulco, Mexico: "Such is the present state of affairs at Acapulco that it is believed by both native and foreign populations that the presence of man-of-war alone prevented an attempt to sack and destroy the town by the Indians in the interior, encouraged by the governor, General Alvarez. . . ." Far from the main theaters of the Civil War, a U.S. naval vessel was carrying out the traditional mission of protecting American interests and keeping the peace.

24 U.S.S. *Nita*, Acting Lieutenant Robert B. Smith, chased blockade runner *Nan-Nan* ashore in the East Pass of Suwannee River, Florida. The steamer's crew fired her to prevent her falling into Union hands, but part of *Nan-Nan*'s cargo of cotton, thrown overboard during the chase, was recovered.

25 U.S.S. *Roebuck*, Acting Master Sherrill, seized blockade running British sloop *Two Brothers* in Indian River, Florida, with cargo including salt, liquor, and nails.

26 While on night picket duty at Charleston harbor, a boat commanded by Acting Master's Mate William H. Kitching, Jr., from U.S.S. *Nipsic*, was captured by a Confederate cutter from C.S.S. *Palmetto State*. The Union boat encountered her captors in a thick fog and was unable to withdraw rapidly enough against the flood tide to escape. Kitching and his five crew members were taken prisoner and confined initially on board C.S.S. *Charleston* near Fort Sumter.

26–27 Boat expedition under the command of Acting Master E. C. Weeks, U.S.S. *Tahoma*, destroyed a large salt works belonging to the Confederate government on Goose Creek, near St. Marks, Florida. As Rear Admiral Bailey noted in his report to Secretary Welles: ". . . the works to be destroyed were under the protection of a rebel cavalry company, whose pickets the expedition succeeded in eluding."

27 U.S.S. *Roebuck*, Acting Master Sherrill, seized blockade running British sloop *Nina* with cargo of liquors and coffee, and schooner *Rebel* with cargo of salt, liquor, and cotton, at Indian River Inlet, Florida.

Lieutenant David Porter McCorkle, CSN, wrote Commander C. ap R. Jones relaying information he had received from Lieutenant Augustus McLaughlin of the Columbus, Georgia, naval station: "The *Muscogee* draws too much water; she has to be altered. It will be a long time before the *Muscogee* will be ready. . . ." On 16 March the editor of the Columbus *Enquirer* bitterly invited the public to "take a stroll below the wharf to see how much money has been wasted on a slanting 'dicular looking craft." *Muscogee*, he said, looked like an ark, and "nothing short of a flood will float it."

28 Lieutenant Minor, CSN, reporting on the progress being made on the ram C.S.S. *Albemarle*, told Secretary Mallory: ". . . with the exception of some little connecting work to be completed [the ironclad] may be considered as ready. Steam will probably be raised on Friday next. The iron is all on the hull . . . the carpenters are now bolting the first layers of plate on the shield, and as long as iron is available the work will progress. The Rudder is in place. Shell room and magazine prepared. Officer quarters arranged and berth deck ready for either hammocks if allowed the ship or bunks if the canvas cannot be obtained. . . . The ship is now afloat and when ready for service will I think draw between 7 to 8 feet. . . . The guns, carriages, and equipment have not yet arrived, but are expected on the 4th of March. . . ." *Albemarle* was launched less than two months later, on 17 April.

U.S.S. *Penobscot*, Lieutenant Commander Andrew E. K. Benham, seized British schooner *Lilly* attempting to run the blockade at Velasco, Texas, with cargo of powder.

29 The U.S. consular agent at Calais, France, sent Captain Winslow, U.S.S. *Kearsarge*, a detailed description of C.S.S. *Rappahannock*, Lieutenant William P. A. Campbell, under the impression

C.S.S. Rappahannock *lies at a pier at Calais, France.*

that she would soon attempt to begin a cruise on the high seas. *Rappahannock* had been purchased for the Confederacy in England by Commander Matthew Fontaine Maury the previous year and in November had been brought to Calais to continue necessary repairs. Late in January, Flag Officer Barron had instructed Campbell to rendezvous with C.S.S. *Georgia*, Lieutenant William E. Evans, as soon as possible in order to transfer the latter's guns to *Rappahannock*. Though *Georgia* subsequently made her way to the appointed place of rendezvous off Morocco, *Rappahannock* never left Calais, detained by want of crew members and the French Government. She did, however, serve the Confederacy as a depot for men and supplies intended for other ships.

Two boats from U.S.S. *Monticello* led by Lieutenant William B. Cushing landed at Confederate-held Smithville, North Carolina, at night to attempt the capture of General Louis Hebert. The daring Cushing found his way with three of his men to the General's quarters in the middle of town and within fifty yards of the Confederate barracks. Cushing was disappointed to find that Hebert had gone to Wilmington earlier that day and instead reported to Rear Admiral Lee: ''I send Captain Kelly, C.S. Army, to you, deeply regretting that the general was not in when I called.''

U.S.S. *Penobscot*, Lieutenant Commander Benham, captured blockade running schooners *Stingray* and *John Douglas* with cargoes of cotton off Velasco, Texas.

U.S.S. *Virginia*, Acting Lieutenant C. H. Brown, captured Confederate schooner *Camilla* with cargo of cotton off the coast at Galveston, Texas. The sloop *Catherine Holt* was also captured with cargo of cotton, but she went aground off San Luis Pass and was burned.

29–5 March Prior to the launching of the Red River campaign, Rear Admiral Porter ordered a naval reconnaissance expedition under Lieutenant Commander Ramsay to ascend the Black and Ouachita Rivers, Louisiana. The force included paddle wheel monitor U.S.S. *Osage* and gunboats *Ouachita*, *Lexington*, *Fort Hindman*, *Conestoga*, and *Cricket*. Ramsay moved up the Black River and met with no resistance until late in the afternoon, 1 March, when Confederate sharpshooters took his ships under fire below Trinity. The gunboats countered with a hail of grape, canister, and shrapnel and steamed above the city before anchoring for the night. Next day Ramsay's vessels entered the Ouachita River and *Osage*, Acting Master Thomas Wright, suffered a casualty which disabled her turret. Below Harrisonburg, Louisiana, which the naval force shelled on 2 March, Confederate troops again opened fire on the naval force, centering their attention on *Fort Hindman*, which took 27 hits. One of them disabled *Fort Hindman*'s starboard engine and Ramsay dropped her back, transferring to *Ouachita*. She took 3 hits but suffered no serious damage, and the gunboats silenced the Southern fire ashore. Ramsay proceeded as far as Catahoula Shoals and Bayou Louis without further incident. "I found plenty of water to enable me to proceed to Monroe," Ramsay reported, "but the water was falling so fast I deemed it best to return." The gunboats returned to the mouth of the Red River on 5 March after spending the 3rd and 4th landing at various places and capturing field pieces and cotton, briefly engaging Confederate troops once more.

MARCH

1 Commander George H. Preble, U.S.S. *St. Louis*, reported that C.S.S. *Florida*, Lieutenant Morris, succeeded in getting to sea from Funchal, Madeira, where she had sailed after leaving Brest. Preble lamented: "Nelson said the want of frigates in his squadron would be found impressed on his heart. I am sure the want of steam will be found engraven on mine. Had the *St. Louis* been a steamer, I would have anchored alongside of her, and, unrestricted by the twenty-four hour rule, my old foe could not have escaped me." *St. Louis* gave chase but could not come up with *Florida*. Had the crews of these sailing vessels been used to man newly built steamers, the pursuit of the Confederate cruisers might have been more successful.

U.S.S. *Connecticut*, Commander Almy, took blockade running Bristish steamer *Scotia* with cargo of cotton at sea off Cape Fear, North Carolina.

U.S.S. *Roebuck*, Acting Master Sherrill, seized blockade running British steamer *Lauretta* off Indian River Inlet, Florida, with cargo of salt.

1–2 At the request of Brigadier General Henry W. Wessells, Lieutenant Commander Flusser took double-ender U.S.S. *Southfield* and tinclad *Whitehead* up the Chowan River, North Carolina, to aid Army steamer *Bombshell* which had been cut off by Confederates above Petty Shore. Flusser had received reports earlier of Confederate torpedoes being planted at that point and concluded that he "dared not attempt, with boats of such great draft . . . to run by." The gunboats were engaged by shore artillery as night fell, and, unable to fire effectively or navigate safely in the darkness, Flusser dropped down stream about a mile to await morning before continuing operations. On 2 March *Southfield* and *Whitehead* kept up a constant bombardment of the Confederate position to enable *Bombshell* to dash by, which the Army steamer finally did later in the day. It was subsequently learned that the shore batteries had been withdrawn shortly after the gunboats had opened on them in the morning.

2 Rear Admiral Porter, in anticipation of the proposed campaign into Louisiana and Texas, arrived off the mouth of the Red River to coordinate the movements of his Mississippi Squadron with those of the Army. Previous attempts to gain control of Texas by coastal assault had not succeeded (see 8 September 1863), and a joint expedition up the Red River to Shreveport was decided upon. From there the Army would attempt to occupy Texas. Ten thousand men from Major General W. T. Sherman's army at Vicksburg would rendezvous with Major General N. P. Banks' army and Porter's gunboats at Alexandria by 17 March. The naval forces would provide vital convoy and gunfire support up the river to Shreveport, where Major General Frederick Steele was to join them from Little Rock. This date, however, Porter wrote Secretary Welles, advising him of an unforeseen development that cast dark shadows on the entire expedition: "I came down here anticipating a move on the part of the army up toward Shreveport, but as the river is lower

than it has been known for years, I much fear that the combined movement can not come off, without interfering with plans formed by General Grant." Porter was referring to the fact that the troops Sherman had detailed for the Red River campaign were committed to Grant after 10 April for his spring campaign. To wait for a rise in the river, Porter feared, would mean failure to meet that deadline; however, to ascend the river at its present stage would also jeopardize the large scale movement. Porter nevertheless pushed swiftly ahead to ready his squadron for the operation.

Rear Admiral Farragut wrote his son Loyall about his recent sighting of the Confederate ram *Tennessee*, commenting that "she is very long, and I thought moved very slowly." Nevertheless, this heavily armored and well-fought ship was to prove a formidable opponent for the Admiral's squadron in Mobile Bay.

3   U.S.S. *Dan Smith*, Acting Master Benjamin C. Dean, seized blockade running British schooner *Sophia* stranded in Altamaha Sound, Georgia, with an assorted cargo. *Sophia* was subsequently lost at sea in a heavy gale which disabled her and forced her abandonment on 8 May 1864 by Acting Ensign Paul Armandt and the prize crew.

4   British authorities instructed the Governor of the Cape of Good Hope, Sir Philip E. Wodehouse, to restore C.S.S. *Tuscaloosa* to Confederate authorities. *Tuscaloosa* had been captured under the name *Conrad* by Captain Semmes in C.S.S. *Alabama* on 20 June 1863 and sent on a cruise under Lieutenant John Low, CSN. On 26 December *Tuscaloosa* had put into Simon's Bay, Cape of Good Hope, after searching for Union merchantmen off the coast of Brazil. The next day the Governor had the bark seized for violating neutrality laws because she had never been properly adjudicated in a prize court. Low promptly protested on the grounds that he had previously entered Simon's Bay in August, at which time his ship took on supplies and effected repairs "with the full knowledge and sanction of the authorities." No protest had been made by the Governor at that time. Unsuccessfully seeking for more than three weeks the release of his ship, Low paid off his crew and with Acting Midshipman William H. Sinclair made his way to Liverpool, where he arrived late in February. The reversal of Governor Wodehouse's action was accounted for by the "peculiar circumstances of the case. The *Tuscaloosa* was allowed to enter the port of Cape Town, and to depart, the instructions of the 4th of November not having arrived at the Cape before her departure. The captain of the *Alabama* was thus entitled to assume that . . . [Low] might equally bring . . . [*Tuscaloosa*] a second time into the same harbor. . . ." The decision, however, came too late for the Confederates. *Tuscaloosa* was never reclaimed by the South and was eventually turned over to the Union. Semmes later said of the incident: "Besides embalming the beautiful name '*Tuscaloosa*' in history this prize-ship settled the law point I had been so long contesting with Mr. Seward and Mr. Adams, to wit: that 'one nation cannot inquire into the antecedents of the ships of war of another nation;' and consequently that when the *Alabama* escaped from British waters and was commissioned, neither the United States nor Great Britain could object to her *status* as a ship of war."

Captain Semmes wrote in his journal: "My ship is weary, too, as well as her commander, and will need a general overhauling by the time I can get her into dock. If my poor service shall be deemed of any importance in harrassing and weakening the enemy, and thus contributing to the independence of my beloved South, I shall be amply rewarded." It was her need for upkeep and repairs that three and a half months later brought her under the guns of U.S.S. *Kearsarge* off Cherbourg, France.

U.S.S. *Pequot*, Lieutenant Commander Stephen P. Quackenbush, seized blockade running British steamer *Don* at sea east of Fort Fisher, North Carolina, with cargo including Army shoes, blankets, and clothing. Captain Cory, master of the steamer, reported that he had made nine attempts to run into Wilmington during his career but had succeeded only four times.

President of the Confederate States of America,

TO ALL unto these Presents shall come, Send Greeting:-

Know Ye, That we have granted, and by these Presents do grant, License and Authority to *Raphael Semmes* , Commander of the *Steam Barque* called the *Alabama* of the Burden of Tons *1200* or thereabout, and mounting *ten* Guns to fit out and set forth the said *barque* in a warlike Manner, and by and with the said *barque* and the crew thereof, by Force of Arms, to attack, subdue, scuttle, and take all ships belonging to the United States of America or any vessel carrying Soldiers, Arms, Gunpowder, Ammunition, Provisions, or any other goods of a military nature to any of the Army of the United States or Ships of War employed against the Confederate States of America in a hostile manner. And to take by force if necessary any vessel, barge, or floating transporter belonging to said United States or persons loyal to the same, including Tackle, Apparel, Ladings, Cargoes, and Furniture on the High Seas or between high and low water mark, Rivers and inlets accepted. (the Ships and Vessels belonging to Inhabitants of Bermuda, the Bahama Islands, and Great Britain and other persons with Intent to settle or serve the cause of the Confederate States of America you shall suffer to pass unmolested, the Commanders thereof permitting a peaceable Search and after giving satisfactory account of Ladings and Destination) And that said Ships or Vessels apprehended as aforesaid, and the Prize taken, to carry to a Port or Harbor within the Domains of any Neutral State willing to admit the same or any port of the Confederate States, in Order that the Courts therein instituted to hear such claims may Judge in such cases at the Port or in the State where the same shall be impounded. The sufficient securities, bonds and sureties having been given by the owners that they nor any person in command of this vessel shall not exceed or transfer the Powers and Authorities contained in this commission. And We will and require all Officers whatsoever in the Service of the Confederate States to give assistance to the said *Captain* in the Premises. This Commission shall remain active and in Force until this Government of the United Confederate States of America shall issue Orders to the contrary.

By order of the President of the Confederate States of America

Port of:.............

Given under my hand this *22nd* of *June* *1863* at *Richmond*

Jefferson Davis
President

---

5 Commander John Taylor Wood, CSN, led an early morning raid on the Union-held telegraph station at Cherrystone Point, Virginia. After crossing Chesapeake Bay at night with some 15 men in open barges, Wood landed and seized the station. Small Union Army steamers *Aeolus* and *Titan*, unaware that the station was in enemy hands, put into shore and each was captured by the daring Southerners. Wood then destroyed the telegraph station and surrounding warehouses, and disabled and bonded *Aeolus* before boarding *Titan* and steaming up the Piankatank River as far as possible. A joint Army-Navy expedition to recapture her was quickly organized, but Wood evaded U.S.S. *Currituck* and *Tulip* in the still early morning haze. A force of five gunboats under Commander F. A. Parker followed the Confederates up the river on the 7th, where *Titan* was found destroyed by Wood, "together with a number of large boats prepared for a raid."

Acting Master Thomas McElroy, commanding U.S.S. *Petrel*, reported a Confederate attack on Yazoo City. Heavy gunfire support by *Petrel* and U.S.S. *Marmora*, Acting Master Thomas Gibson, helped drive the Confederate troops off. In addition, McElroy wrote, "I am proud to say that the Navy was well represented [ashore] by 3 sailors, who . . . stood by their guns through the whole action, fighting hand to hand to save the gun and the reputation of the Navy. The sailors are highly spoken of by the army officers. . . ."

6 A Confederate "David" torpedo boat commanded by First Assistant Engineer Tomb, CSN, attacked U.S.S. *Memphis*, Acting Master Robert O. Patterson, in the North Edisto River near Charleston. The "David" was sighted some 50 yards to port and a heavy volley of musket fire directed at her, but Tomb held his small craft on course. The spar torpedo containing 95 pounds of powder was thrust squarely against *Memphis*' port quarter, about eight feet below the waterline, but failed to explode. Tomb turned away and renewed the attack on the starboard quarter. Again the torpedo struck home, but this time only a glancing blow because *Memphis* was now underway. The two vessels collided, damaging the "David", and Tomb withdrew under heavy fire. The faulty torpedo had prevented the brave Tomb from adding an 800-ton iron steamer to a growing list of victims.

U.S.S. *Morse*, Lieutenant Commander Babcock, ascended the York River, Virginia, at the Army's request to assist a Union cavalry detachment under the command of Colonel Ulric Dahlgren, son of the Navy's famous Admiral. From Purtan Island Point *Morse*, a converted ferryboat, was slowed by the necessity of sweeping the river in front of the ship for torpedoes. Anchoring for the night off Terrapin Point, the gunboat continued upriver next morning and fired signal guns to attract the attention of the cavalry. Off Brick House Farm a boat carrying five cavalrymen put out to *Morse*. They reported that the Union force had been cut off and captured by a greatly superior Confederate unit of cavalry and infantry. Young Dahlgren, who had lost a leg at Gettysburg, was killed in the engagement. His grief-stricken father wrote in his diary, "How busy is death—oh, how busy indeed!"

Major General W. T. Sherman appointed Brigadier General Andrew J. Smith to command the forces of his Army in the Red River expedition. He directed Smith: ". . . proceed to the mouth of the Red River and confer with Admiral Porter; confer with him and in all the expedition rely on him implicitly, as he is the approved friend of the Army of the Tennessee, and has been associated with us from the beginning. . . ." Long months of arduous duty together in the west had forged a close bond between Sherman and Porter.

U.S.S. *Grand Gulf*, Commander George M. Ransom, captured blockade running British steamer *Mary Ann* which had run out of Wilmington with cargo of cotton and tobacco.

U.S.S. *Peterhoff*, Acting Lieutenant Thomas Pickering, was run into by U.S.S. *Monticello* and sunk off New Inlet, North Carolina. The following day, U.S.S. *Mount Vernon* destroyed *Peterhoff* to prevent possible salvage by the Confederates.

8 U.S.S. *Conestoga*, Lieutenant Commander Thomas O. Selfridge, was rammed by U.S.S. *General Price*, Lieutenant J. E. Richardson, about ten miles below Grand Gulf, Mississippi, and sank in four minutes with the loss of two crew members. The collision resulted from a confusion in whistle signals on board *General Price*. Lieutenant Commander Selfridge, who achieved a conspicuously successful record in the war, had singularly bad luck in having his ships sunk under him. He commented later in his memoirs: "Thus for the third time in the war, I had my ship suddenly sunk under me. It is a strange coincidence that the names of these three ships all begin with the letter 'C', and that two of these disasters occurred on the 8th day of March; the other on the 12th of December." Selfridge had been on board U.S.S. *Cumberland* during her engagement with C.S.S. *Virginia* in Hampton Roads on 8 March 1862, and had commanded U.S.S. *Cairo* when she was struck by a torpedo and sank instantly in the Yazoo River on 12 December 1862. Admiral Porter, upon hearing the young officer's report on the sinking of *Conestoga*, replied: "Well, Selfridge, you do not seem to have much luck with the top of the alphabet. I think that for your next ship I will try the bottom." Thus Lieutenant Commander Selfridge took command of the paddle wheel monitor U.S.S. *Osage*, and, after she grounded in the Red River, was sent as captain of the new gunboat U.S.S. *Vindicator*—further down the alphabet.

U.S.S. *Virginia*, Acting Lieutenant C. H. Brown, captured blockade running sloop *Randall* off San Luis Pass, Texas.

9 Rear Admiral Porter directed Lieutenant Commander James A. Greer, U.S.S. *Benton*, to advise him as soon as General Sherman's troops were sighted coming downriver on transports. The Admiral wanted to move quickly upon the arrival of the troops in order to meet Major General Banks at Alexandria on 17 March. Porter had gathered his gunboats at the mouth of the Red River for the move. They included ironclads U.S.S. *Essex*, *Benton*, *Choctaw*, *Chillicothe*, *Ozark*, *Louisville*, *Carondelet*, *Eastport*, *Pittsburg*, *Mound City*, *Osage*, and *Neosho*; large wooden steamers *Lafayette* and *Ouachita*; and small paddle-wheelers *Lexington*, *Fort Hindman*, *Cricket*, and *Gazelle*.

Confederate Secretary of War James A. Seddon authorized Thomas E. Courtenay to employ "a band of men, not exceeding twenty-five in number, for secret service against the enemy. . . . For the destruction of property of the enemy or injury done, a percentage shall be paid in 4 per cent bonds, in no case to exceed 50 per cent of the loss to the enemy, and to be awarded by such officer or officers as shall be charged with such duty. . . . The waters and railroads of the Confederate States used by the enemy are properly the subjects and arenas of operations. . . ." Courtenay had aided in the development of the coal torpedo (see 19 January 1864).

U.S.S. *Shokokon*, *Morse*, and *General Putnam*, under Lieutenant Commander Babcock, convoyed an Army expedition up the York and Mattapony Rivers. After disembarking troops from the transports, Babcock remained at Sheppard's Landing throughout the 10th as requested by Brigadier General Isaac J. Wistar. Then the naval force withdrew downriver, arriving at Yorktown on the 12th. While enroute on the 11th, Babcock met a naval force under Acting Lieutenant Edward Hooker of the Potomac Flotilla and arranged for him to "keep a vigilant lookout for our forces, and also prevent any rebels from crossing from the mouth of the Piankatank River to Mosquito Point on the Rappahannock." As Rear Admiral Lee wrote: ". . . the naval part of the expedition was well arranged and executed."

U.S.S. *Yankee*, Acting Lieutenant Hooker, reconnoitered the Rappahannock River to within a mile of Urbanna, Virginia. "We learned," he reported to Commander F. A. Parker, "that there is now no force of any importance at or near Urbanna, although the presence of troops a short time ago was confirmed." Two days later, "Major General Butler having requested me to 'watch the Rappahannock from 10 miles below Urbanna to its mouth,' " Parker directed Hooker to "lend such assistance . . . as you can. . . ." Continuing operations in the river by the Union Navy tended to deny to the Confederates use of the inland waters for even marginal logistic support of their operations. This decisive function of seapower was just as valid on the inland waters as on the high sea.

10 Confederate steamer *Helen*, commanded by Lieutenant Philip Porcher, CSN, was lost at sea in a gale while running a cargo of cotton from Charleston to Nassau. Secretary Mallory wrote that Porcher "was one of the most efficient officers of the service, and his loss is deeply deplored."

U.S.S. *Virginia*, Acting Lieutenant C. H. Brown, captured schooner *Sylphide* off San Luis Pass, Texas, with cargo including percussion caps.

11 U.S.S. *Aroostook*, Lieutenant Commander Chester Hatfield, captured blockade-running British schooner *Mary P. Burton* in the Gulf of Mexico south of Velasco, Texas, with cargo of iron and shot.

Boats under Acting Ensign Henry B. Colby, from U.S.S. *Beauregard*, and Acting Master George Delap, from U.S.S. *Norfolk Packet*, seized British schooner *Linda* at Mosquito Inlet, Florida, with cargo including salt, liquor, and coffee.

U.S.S. *San Jacinto*, Commander James F. Armstrong, captured schooner *Lealtad*, which had run the blockade at Mobile with cargo of cotton and turpentine.

Schooner *Julia Baker* was boarded by Confederate guerrilla forces near Newport News, Virginia. After taking $2,500 in cash and capturing the master and five men, the boarders burned the schooner.

U.S.S. *Beauregard*, Acting Master Francis Burgess, captured blockade running British sloop *Hannah* off Mosquito Inlet, Florida, with cargo of cotton cloth.

12 Rear Admiral Porter's gunboats moved up the Red River, Louisiana, to open the two month operation aimed at obtaining a lodgement across the border in Texas. U.S.S. *Eastport*, Lieutenant Commander Samuel L. Phelps, pushed ahead to remove the obstructions in the river below Fort De Russy, followed by ironclads U.S.S. *Choctaw*, *Essex*, *Ozark*, *Osage*, and *Neosho* and wooden steamers *Lafayette*, *Fort Hindman*, and *Cricket*. Porter took ironclads U.S.S. *Benton*, *Chillicothe*,

Rear Admiral Porter's squadron assembles for the long but ill-fated Red River campaign.

Louisville, Pittsburg, and *Mound City* and wooden paddlewheelers *Ouachita, Lexington,* and *Gazelle* into the Atchafalaya River to cover the Army landing at Simmesport. A landing party from *Benton,* Lieutenant Commander Greer, drove back Confederate pickets prior to the arrival of the transports. Next morning, 13 March, the soldiers disembarked and pursued the Confederates falling back on Fort De Russy. Meanwhile, *Eastport* and the gunboats which had continued up the Red River reached the obstructions which the Southerners had taken five months to build. "They supposed it impassable," Porter observed, "but our energetic sailors with hard work opened a passage in a few hours." *Eastport* and *Neosho* passed through and commenced bombarding Fort De Russy as the Union troops began their assault on the works; by the 14th it was in Union hands. Porter wrote: "The surrender of the forts at Point De Russy is of much more importance than I at first supposed. The rebels had depended on that point to stop any advance of army or navy into rebeldom. Large quantities of ammunition, best engineers, and best troops were sent there. . . ."

U.S.S. *Columbine,* Acting Ensign Francis W. Sanborn, supporting an Army movement up the St. John's River, Florida, captured Confederate river steamer *General Sumter.* Acting Master John C. Champion, commanding a launch from U.S.S. *Pawnee* which was in company with tug *Columbine,* took command of the prize, and the two vessels pushed on up the St. John's, reaching Lake Monroe on the 14th. That afternoon the naval force captured steamer *Hattie* at Deep Creek. The expedition continued for the next few days, destroying a Southern sugar refinery and proceeding to Palatka, where the Army was taking up a fortified position.

U.S.S. *Aroostook,* Lieutenant Commander Hatfield, captured schooner *Marion* near Velasco, Texas, with cargo of salt and iron. *Marion* sank in a gale off Galveston on the 14th.

U.S.S. *Massachusetts,* Acting Lieutenant William H. West, captured sloop *Persis* in Wassaw Sound, Georgia, with cargo of cotton.

15 After ordering ironclads U.S.S. *Benton* and *Essex* to remain at Fort De Russy in support of the Army detachment engaged in destroying the works, Rear Admiral Porter convoyed the main body of troops up the Red River toward Alexandria, Louisiana. Porter dispatched U.S.S. *Eastport, Lexington,* and *Ouachita* ahead to try to overtake the Confederate vessels seeking to escape above the Alexandria rapids. The Confederate ships were too far ahead, however, and the Union gunboats arrived at the rapids half an hour behind them. Confederate steamer *Countess* grounded in her hasty attempt to get upstream and was destroyed by her crew to prevent capture.

U.S.S. *Nyanza,* Acting Lieutenant Samuel B. Washburn, captured schooner *J. W. Wilder* in the Atchafalaya River, Louisiana.

16 Lieutenant Commander Flusser reported to Rear Admiral Lee on information reaching him regarding the Confederates' progress in completing C.S.S. *Albemarle* on the Roanoke River, North Carolina. The ram was reported to have two layers of iron and to be ready to proceed to Williamston on 1 April. Two days later Flusser again wrote Lee, informing him that he had just heard the rumor that *Albemarle* was to have 7 inches of plating. "I think," he observed, "the reporters are putting on the iron rather heavy. I am inclined to believe her armor is not more than stated in one of my former letters—3 inches." *Albemarle* actually carried two layers of 2-inch armor. By 24 March Flusser reported that intelligence, "which would seem reliable," indicated that the ironclad ram was at Hamilton and that the torpedoes placed by the Confederates in the Roanoke River below Williamston were being removed to permit her passage downstream.

Nine Union vessels had arrived at Alexandria, Louisiana, by morning and a landing party under Lieutenant Commander Selfridge, U.S.S. *Osage,* occupied the town prior to the arrival of Rear Admiral Porter and the troops. At Alexandria, Porter's gunboats and the soldiers awaited the arrival of Major General Banks' Army, which was delayed by heavy rains.

C.S.S. Albemarle *dominated the waters near Plymouth, North Carolina, from her first appearance in April until her destruction in October 1864.*

James W. Cooke
Commander, CSN

Rear Admiral James L. Lardner, commander of the West Indies Squadron, ordered U.S.S. *Neptune*, Commander Joseph P. Sanford, and U.S.S. *Galatea*, Commander John Guest, to convoy California steamers operating in the Caribbean. This was a measure designed to protect the merchant ships, which often carried quantities of vital Union gold, from the highly regarded Confederate cruisers.

18 Lieutenant General E. Kirby Smith, CSA, ordered steamer *New Falls City* taken to Scopern's Cut-off, below Shreveport on the Red River, where she was to be sunk if the Union movement threatened that far upriver. Next day the General directed that thirty topedoes be placed below Grand Ecore to obstruct the Red River. An officer from C.S.S. *Missouri* was detailed for this duty. General Smith's foresight would shortly pay dividends, for the hulk of *New Falls City* did block the way of the Union gunboats and U.S.S. *Eastport* was to be severely damaged by a torpedo.

20 Arriving off Capetown, South Africa, Captain Semmes, C.S.S. *Alabama*, noted that there were no Union cruisers in the vicinity, though he was well aware that many had been dispatched from Northern ports to capture him. He recalled later: "That huge old coal-box, the *Vanderbilt*, having thought it useless to pursue us farther, had turned back, and was now probably doing a more profitable business, by picking up blockade-runners on the American coast. This operation *paid*—the Captain might grow rich upon it. Chasing the *Alabama* did not."

U.S.S. *Honeysuckle*, Acting Ensign Sears, captured blockade running sloop *Florida* in the Gulf of Mexico west of Florida, with cargo of powder, shot, nails, and coffee.

U.S.S. *Tioga*, Lieutenant Commander Edward Y. McCauley, captured blockade running sloop *Swallow*, bound from the Combahee River, South Carolina, to Nassau, laden with cotton, rosin, and tobacco.

Lieutenant Charles C. Simms, C.S.S. *Baltic*, wrote Commander C. ap R. Jones that naval constructor John L. Porter "has made a very unfavorable report on the condition of the ship [*Baltic*] and recommended that the iron be taken from her and put upon one of the new boats that were built. . . . Between you and I [sic] the *Baltic* is rotten as punk and is about as fit to go into action as a mud scow." By July *Baltic* had been dismantled and her armor transferred to C.S.S. *Nashville*.

21 Confederate forces at Sabine Pass, Texas, destroyed steamer *Clifton* (ex-U.S.S. *Clifton*, see 8 September 1863) to prevent her capture by blockading Union naval forces. The 900-ton *Clifton* had been attempting to run out of the Texas port when she grounded and could not be floated.

U.S.S. *Hendrick Hudson*, Lieutenant Commander Charles J. McDougal, rammed blockade runner *Wild Pigeon*, bound from Havana to the Florida coast; she struck *Wild Pigeon* amidships and the schooner sank immediately.

Confederate Secretary Mallory wrote Commander Bulloch in Europe disagreeing with Bulloch's conclusion that the Confederacy needed no additional cruisers since ". . . there is no longer any American commerce for them to prey upon." Mallory countered "We have, it is true, inflicted a heavy blow and great discouragement upon the Federal foreign commerce, but the coasting trade and fisheries, embracing the California trade, has suffered but little from our cruisers, and it can and must be struck."

24 A closely coordinated Army-Navy expedition departed Beaufort, North Carolina, on board side-wheel steamer U.S.S. *Britannia*. Some 200 soldiers were commanded by Colonel James Jourdan, while about 50 sailors from U.S.S. *Keystone State*, *Florida*, and *Cambridge* were in charge of Commander Benjamin M. Dove. The aim of the expedition was the capture or destruction of two schooners used in blockade running at Swansboro, North Carolina, and the capture of a Confederate army group on the south end of Bogue Island Banks. Arriving off Bogue Inlet late at night, the expedition encountered high winds and heavy seas which prevented landing on the beach. Early on the morning of the 25th, a second attempt was made under similarly difficult conditions, but a party got through to Bear Creek where one of the schooners was burned. Bad weather persisted throughout the day and the expedition eventually returned to Beaufort on the 26th with its mission only partially completed.

Rear Admiral Porter reported that his forces had seized more than 2,000 bales of cotton, as well as quantities of molasses and wool, since entering the Red River.

U.S.S. *Stonewall*, Master Henry B. Carter, captured sloop *Josephine* in Sarasota Sound, Florida, with cargo of cotton.

25 U.S.S. *Peosta*, Acting Lieutenant Thomas E. Smith, and U.S.S. *Paw Paw*, Acting Lieutenant A. Frank O'Neil, engaged Confederate troops who had launched a heavy assault on Northern positions at Paducah, Kentucky. Under the wooden gunboats' fire the Southerners were halted and finally forced to withdraw. The value of the force afloat was recognized by Brigadier General Mason Brayman, who later wrote of the action: "I wish to state during my short period of service here the Navy has borne a conspicuous part in all operations. The *Peosta*, Captain Smith, and *Paw Paw*, Captain O'Neil, joined Colonel Hicks at Paducah, and with gallantry equal to his own shelled the rebels out of the buildings from which their sharpshooters annoyed our troops. A large number took shelter in heavy warehouses near the river and maintained a furious fire upon the gunboats, inflicting some injury, but they were promptly dislodged and the buildings destroyed. Fleet Captain Pennock, of the Mississippi Squadron, representing Admiral Porter in his absence, and Lieutenant Commander Shirk, of the Seventh Division, who had charge above Cairo and on the Tennessee, were prompt, vigilant, and courageous and cooperated in everything. That the river line was kept open, considering the inadequate force at my control, I regard as due in a great degree to the cooperation of the Navy."

Close cooperation and support between land and sea forces continued to mark Northern efforts in the Civil War. On 21 March, Major General Quincy A. Gillmore wrote Commodore Stephen C. Rowan that, though the Army had five steam transports operating in the vicinity of Port Royal on picket duty and as transports, he had "no officer possessing sufficient experience to properly outfit and command such vessels. My steamboat masters are citizens, and know nothing of artillery. My artillery officers are not sailors, and are not acquainted with naval gunnery." The General thus requested that an officer from the blockading squadron be assigned to assist

Cartoon depicting the Confederacy as a scorpion surrounded by Union strength afloat and ashore. "When' cornered,' and no avenue of escape appearing," read the original caption in part, "it usually stings itself to death—striking its poisonous sting into its own head, which is the softest and consequently most vulnerable part of its body."

the Army in this regard. "It would," Gillmore wrote, "be of advantage to this army. . . ." This date, Rowan, temporarily commanding the naval forces in the absence of Rear Admiral Dahlgren, ordered Acting Ensign William C. Hanford to assist the General as requested.

Secretary Welles called President Lincoln's attention to the scarcity of seamen in ships afloat and suggested the transfer of 12,000 men from the Army to the Navy. The transfer was later effected as a result of a bill sponsored by Senator Grimes of Iowa.

Lieutenant Commander Babcock, U.S.S. *Morse*, submitted a report to Rear Admiral Lee on all the Confederate material seized by his ship between 1 and 12 February on the York River. He wrote that the articles included a small schooner, a sloop, corn, wheat, oats, salt, tobacco, plows, a cultivator, plow points, plow shares, and molding boards. Seemingly inconsequential in themselves, these articles lost were multiplied manyfold by the ceaseless efforts of the Navy in river and coastal waters; it was their steady attrition which was so sorely felt by Confederate fighting men and civilians alike.

A boat expedition under Acting Master Edward H. Sheffield from U.S.S. *Winona*, Lieutenant Commander A. W. Weaver, after making extensive reconnaissance of the area, captured blockade runner *Little Ada* loading cotton at McClellansville in the South Santee River, South Carolina. As Union sailors sought to bring the prize out, Confederate artillery opened on the vessel with devastating accuracy. The attack by Sheffield, carried on deep in Confederate-held territory, had begun in darkness, but as it was now fully light, the riddled prize had to be quickly abandoned to prevent capture of the boarding party.

Major General Banks arrived at Alexandria—a week later than originally planned. The main force of the Red River expedition was now assembled.

28   The versatility of Union gunboat crews was continually tested. Crewmen from U.S.S. *Benton*, Lieutenant Commander Greer, had gone ashore the 27th near Fort De Russy and taken some 13 bales of cotton from an abandoned plantation. They returned this date, Greer reported, and "got 18 bales from the same place, which they baled themselves, using up an old awning for the purpose."

Secretary Welles ordered Commander John C. Carter to have U.S.S. *Michigan* "prepared for active service as soon as the ice will permit." *Michigan*, an iron side-wheel steamer, was at Erie, Pennsylvania, and it was rumored that the Confederates were planning a naval raid from Canada against a city on the Great Lakes.

U.S.S. *Kingfisher*, Acting Master John C. Dutch, ran aground and was totally wrecked in St. Helena Sound, South Carolina.

29   The low level of the Red River continued to hinder Rear Admiral Porter's efforts to get his gunboats above the rapids at Alexandria for the assault on Shreveport. He reported: "After a great deal of labor and two and a half days' hard work, we succeeded in getting the *Eastport* over the rocks on the falls, hauling her over by main force. . . ." All the Army transports maneuvered safely above the rapids, but hospital ship *Woodford* was battered against the rocks and sank. Porter added: "I shall only be able to take up a part of the force I brought with me, and leave the river guarded all the way through."

C.S.S. *Florida*, Lieutenant Morris, at 150°11′ N, 34°25′ W, captured ship *Avon* with a 1,600 ton cargo of guano. After removing the crew, Morris used the prize for gunnery practice and finally destroyed her by burning.

29–30   A boat expedition under the command of Acting Master James M. Williams, U.S.S. *Commodore Barney*, with a detachment of sailors under the command of Acting Master Charles B. Wilder, U.S.S. *Minnesota*, ascended Chuckatuck Creek late at night seeking to capture a party of Confederate troops reported to be in that vicinity. After landing at Cherry Grove, Virginia, shortly before dawn, the sailors silently surrounded the Confederate headquarters and took 20 prisoners. Rear Admiral Lee reported to Secretary Welles that ". . . it gives me pleasure to commend the energy and zeal displayed by these officers in planning and carrying out to a successful termination an expedition of no little difficulty."

30   Captain John B. Marchand, commanding the Third Division of the Western Gulf Blockading Squadron, reported to Fleet Captain Percival Drayton on the difficulty of trying to maintain a tight blockade through the passes and inlets around Galveston: "This place has great advantages for blockade running, as, in addition to the regular channels, the shores, both to the northward and southward, are represented to be bold. I have been credibly informed that good large schooners have hugged the shore so close as to be dragged along for miles by lines from the land by soldiers and sailors into Galveston."

31   A boat crew under the command of Acting Master's Mate Francisco Silva, returned to U.S.S. *Sagamore* after destroying two blockade running schooners near Cedar Keys, Florida. Three boats had initiated the search for a blockade runner sighted on the 28th, but two had turned back after an unsuccessful search of nearly six hours, as night was falling and the weather threatening. Silva, however, continued to search for the next two days ". . . with heavy rain squalls and an ugly sea running." Despite the adverse conditions, Silva succeeded in destroying schooner *Etta*

and a second schooner whose name could not be ascertained. Blockade duty was seldom highly dramatic or widely publicized, but the resolute determination of the forces afloat to choke off Confederate commerce took a prohibitive toll of Southern shipping and kept the Confederacy in a constant state of need.

APRIL

1 Army transport *Maple Leaf*, returning from carrying troops to Palatka, Florida, was destroyed by a Confederate torpedo in the St. John's River. She was one of several victims in this river which on 30 March the Southerners had mined with twelve floating torpedoes, each containing 70 pounds of powder. On 16 April Army transport *General Hunter* was similarly destroyed at almost the same place near Mandarin Point. Confederate torpedoes continued to play an increasing role in the defense of rivers and harbors. As Major General Patton Anderson, CSA, noted, the torpedoes "taught him [the Northerner] to be cautious in the navigation of our waters."

Secretary Welles wrote Rear Admiral C. H. Bell expressing concern that Confederate raiders would strike at the California trade. Intelligence had been received suggesting as a destination "for the *Florida* and *Georgia* the straits of Le Maire, between the island of Tierra del Fuego and Staten Island, through which . . . nine out of every ten California-bound ships pass, in plain sight from either shore. . . . the protection of the land in these straits is such that the rebel steamers could lie almost obscured and in comparatively smooth water . . . while escape [by] merchantmen would be impossible."

During the last year of the war on the Mississippi bands of Confederate guerrillas kept up their efforts to surprise and destroy Union gunboats isolated on patrol duty. This date the Secretary of War forwarded to Secretary Welles a captured letter written by Confederate Navy Secretary Mallory about the plans of guerrillas. Welles relayed the information next day to Rear Admiral Porter.

3 As Major General Banks began his preliminary deployments for the Red River campaign, iron-clads U.S.S. *Eastport, Mound City, Osage, Ozark, Neosho, Chillicothe, Pittsburg,* and *Louisville* and steamers *Fort Hindman, Lexington,* and *Cricket* convoyed Major General A. J. Smith's corps from Alexandria to Grand Ecore, Louisiana. The troops disembarked (with the exception of a division under Brigadier General T. Kilby Smith) and marched to join Banks at Natchitoches for the overland assault on Shreveport, to be supported by ships of the Mississippi Squadron.

4 U.S.S. *Sciota*, Lieutenant Commander Perkins, captured schooner *Mary Sorly* attempting to run the blockade at Galveston with cargo of cotton. She had previously been U.S. Revenue Cutter *Dodge*, seized by the Confederates at Galveston at the war's outbreak.

5 The naval force in the St. John's River, Florida, under Commander Balch continued to patrol the river and convoy Army operations as it had for a month. On 4 April Union troops evacuated Palatka in accord with a general troop movement northward, but U.S.S. *Ottawa*, Lieutenant Commander Breese, which had protected the soldiers there, remained in the river, moving to Picolata "where some two regiments are stationed." U.S.S. *Pawnee*, Commander Balch, remained on duty at Jacksonville, while double-ender U.S.S. *Mahaska*, Lieutenant Commander Robert F. Lewis, and wooden screw steamers U.S.S. *Unadilla*, Lieutenant Commander James Stillwell, and U.S.S. *Norwich*, Acting Master Frank B. Meriam, continued to convoy troops on the river. This date, Brigadier General John P. Hatch summed up the vital contributions made by the Navy in controlling the inland waterways: ". . . I consider it very important, I may say necessary, that the naval force should be retained here as a patrol of the river, to aid us in the event of an attack, and to cover the landing of troops at other points. . . . The length of the river now occupied (100 miles) requires for its thorough patrol a naval force of the size of the present squadron."

Late in March, Union forces at Plymouth, North Carolina, had sunk hulks, some with percussion torpedoes attached, to obstruct the Roanoke River and provide additional defense against "the ironclad up this river." Lieutenant Commander Flusser, reporting another of the rumors which were circulating freely regarding the Confederate ironclad ram *Albemarle*, wrote Rear Admiral Lee that the large ship was said to be of such light draft "that she may pass over our obstructions in the river without touching them." The draft of *Albemarle*, approximately nine feet, had been reported by Flusser on 27 March as being "6 to 8 feet"—according to a carpenter who had worked on her.

6   Secretary Mallory wrote Flag Officer Barron in Paris regarding the possible operations of ships being fitted out in France: "If the vessels about to get to sea can be united with the two you sent off [C.S.S. *Florida* and *Georgia*], they might strike a blow at the enemy off Wilmington, during the summer, and then separate to meet for a blow at another point. I commend the light infantry system to your judgment. An invited clash at a point north heretofore indicated to you, then a separation for a reunion and dash at a second point, and a second separation for a third one, etc., with the intervals sufficient to draw the enemy's attention to distant chasing, would produce very important results." While Mallory's reasoning was sound in proposing such a hit-and-run cruise, it was not to happen. C.S.S. *Florida* would be captured before year's end; *Georgia* would soon be sold; and *Rappahannock*, like the ironclads contracted for in France, would never take to the high seas under the Confederate flag.

U.S.S. *Estrella*, Lieutenant Commander Augustus P. Cooke, captured mail schooner *Julia A. Hodges* in Matagorda Bay, Texas.

7   Rear Admiral Porter detailed Lieutenant Commander Phelps to remain in command of the heavier gunboats at Grand Ecore while he personally continued to advance up the Red River toward Shreveport with ironclads U.S.S. *Osage*, *Neosho*, and *Chillicothe* and wooden steamers *Fort Hindman*, *Lexington* and *Cricket*. The Admiral hoped to bring up the remaining gunboats if the water level began to rise.

U.S.S. *Beauregard*, Acting Master Edward C. Healy, seized blockade running British schooner *Spunky* near Cape Canaveral, Florida, with an assorted cargo.

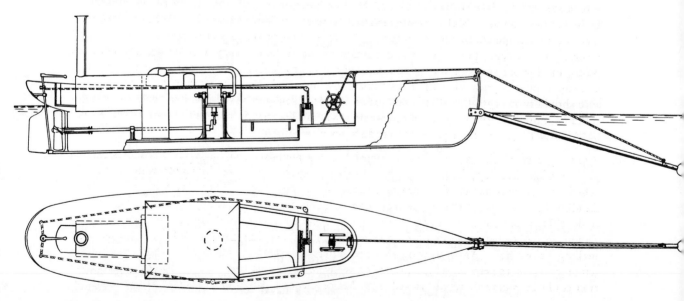

Drawings of Confederate torpedo boat Squib *which attacked U.S.S.* Minnesota *off Newport News, Virginia.*

9   Confederate torpedo boat *Squib*, Lieutenant Hunter Davidson, successfully exploded a spar torpedo against large steam frigate U.S.S. *Minnesota*, Lieutenant Commander John H. Upshur, off Newport News, Virginia. *Squib* was described by Acting Master John A. Curtis, second in command of the torpedo boat, as being constructed of wood, "about thirty-five feet long, five feet wide, drew three feet of water, two feet freeboard; designed by Hunter Davidson. . . . The boiler and engine were encased with iron; forward of the boiler was the cockpit, where the crew stood and from where we steered her." The attack, described by a Northern naval officer observer as "a deed as daring as it was vicious", took place about two o'clock in the morning. The officer of the deck saw a small boat 150 to 200 yards off, just forward of the port beam. To his hail, the Confederates replied "*Roanoke*." Acting Ensign James Birtwistle ordered her to stay clear. Davidson answered "aye, aye!" Although Birtwistle could discern no visible means of propulsion, the small Confederate boat continued to close *Minnesota* rapidly. *Minnesota* attempted to open fire, but, the distance between the two being so slight, her gun could not be brought to bear. *Squib* rammed her powder charge of more than 50 pounds into the blockader's port quarter. The log of *Minnesota* recorded: ". . . a tremendous explosion followed." Curtis wrote that he closed his eyes at the moment of impact, "opening them in about a second, I think, I never beheld such a sight before, nor since. The air was filled with port shutters and water from the explosion, and the heavy ship was rolling to starboard, and the officer of the deck giving orders to save yourselves and cried out 'Torpedo, torpedo!'"

Little damage resulted, though "the shock was quite severe." Nevertheless, as Secretary Mallory later said of the attack: "The cool daring, professional skill, and judgement exhibited by Lieutenant Davidson in this hazardous enterprise merit high commendation and confer honor upon a service of which he is a member." As the blockader reeled under the blow, the fate of the seven Southerners was gravely imperiled, for *Squib* was sucked under the port quarter. As *Minnesota* rolled back to port, however, Curtis reported, "the pressure of the water shoved us off." But so close aboard her adversary did she remain that Curtis leaped on the torpedo boat's forward deck and pushed against *Minnesota* to get the small craft clear. *Squib* escaped under heavy musket fire. Union tug *Poppy* did not have steam up and could not pursue the torpedo boat, which withdrew safely up the James River. Davidson, a pioneer in torpedo warfare, was promoted to Commander for his "gallant and meritorious conduct."

The concern caused by the attack on *Minnesota*, coming as it did shortly after the Confederate submarine *H. L. Hunley* had sunk U.S.S. *Housatonic*, was widespread. William Winthrop, United States Consul at Malta, wrote assistant Secretary of State Frederick W. Seward concerning precautions recommended for the future. "In these days of steam and torpedoes, you may rest assured that outlying picket boats and a steam tug at all hours ready to move are not sufficient protection for our ships of war, where a squadron is at anchor. They require something more, and this should be in having their own boats rowing round all night, so that in a measure every ship should protect itself. If this precaution be not taken, any vessel in a dark and foggy night could be blown out of the water, even while a watchful sentry on board might still have his cry of 'All's well' yet on his lips as the fiendish act was accomplished."

10 Steaming toward Shreveport, Rear Admiral Porter's gunboats and the Army transports arrived at Springfield Landing, Louisiana, where further progress was halted by Confederate ingenuity, which Porter later described to Major General W. T. Sherman: "When I arrived at Springfield Landing I found a sight that made me laugh. It was the smartest thing I ever knew the rebels to do. They had gotten that huge steamer, *New Falls City*, across Red River, 1 mile above Loggy Bayou, 15 feet of her on shore on each side, the boat broken down in the middle, and a sand bar making below her. An invitation in large letters to attend a ball in Shreveport was kindly left stuck up by the rebels, which invitation we were never able to accept." Before this obstruction could be removed, word arrived from Major General Banks of his defeat at the Battle of

Sabine Cross-Roads near Grand Ecore and retreat toward Pleasant Hill. The transports and troops of Brigadier General T. K. Smith were ordered to return to the major force and join Banks. The high tide of the Union's Red River campaign had been reached. From this point, with falling water level and increased Confederate shore fire, the gunboats would face a desperate battle to avoid being trapped above the Alexandria rapids.

11 U.S.S. *Nita*, Lieutenant Robert B. Smith, captured blockade runner *Three Brothers* at the mouth of the Homosassa River, Florida, with an assorted cargo.

Confederate troops attack Rear Admiral Porter's squadron from the banks of the Red River.

U.S.S. Osage *helped to repulse Confederates firing on the gunboats from the high banks of the Red River.*

Thomas O. Selfridge, Jr.
Lieutenant Commander, USN

U.S.S. *Virginia*, Acting Lieutenant C. H. Brown, captured blockade runner *Juanita* off San Luis Pass, Texas. However, on 13 April she went aground, was recaptured, and the prize crew, under Acting Ensign N.A. Blume, was taken prisoner.

12   As Rear Admiral Porter's gunboats and Brigadier General T. K. Smith's transports retraced their course down the Red River from Springfield Landing, Louisiana, Confederate guns took them under heavy fire from the high bluffs overlooking the river. At Blair's Landing, dismounted cavalry supported by artillery, engaged the Union fleet. The 450-ton wooden side-wheeler U.S.S. *Lexington*, Lieutenant Bache, silenced the shore battery but the Confederate cavalry poured a hail of musket fire into the rest of the squadron. Lieutenant Commander Selfridge reported: "I waited till they got into easy shelling range, and opened upon them a heavy fire of shrapnel and canister. The rebels fought with unusual pertinacity for over an hour, delivering the heaviest and most concentrated fire of musketry that I have ever witnessed." What Porter described as "this curious affair, . . . a fight between infantry and gunboats", was finally decided by the gunboats' fire, which inflicted heavy losses on the Confederates, including the death of their commander, General Thomas Green. This engagement featured the use of a unique instrument, developed by Chief Engineer Thomas Doughty of U.S.S. *Osage* and later described by Selfridge as "a method of sighting the turret from the outside, by means of what would now be called a periscope. . . ." The high banks of the Red River posed a great difficulty for the ships' gunners in aiming their cannon from water level. Doughty's ingenious apparatus helped to solve that problem. Selfridge wrote that: "On first sounding to general quarters, . . . [I] went inside the turret to direct its fire, but the restricted vision from the peep holes rendered it impossible to see what was going on in the threatened quarter, whenever the turret was trained in the loading position. In this extremity I thought of the periscope, and hastily took up station there, well protected by the turret, yet able to survey the whole scene and to direct an accurate fire." Thus was the periscope, a familiar sight on gun turrets and on submarines of this century, brought into Civil War use on the Western waters.

Confederate cavalry and infantry commanded by Major General Nathan B. Forrest, CSA, commenced an attack on Fort Pillow, Tennessee. The small 160-ton gunboat U.S.S. *New Era*, Acting Master James Marshall, steamed in to support the Union soldiers. Her few guns drove the Confederates from their first position before the fort, but by mid-afternoon Forrest's Army mounted an overwhelming assault on the fort and carried it, though still under the fire of *New Era*. Acting Master Marshall received refugees from the fort on board *New Era*, but after the captured artillery was turned on his vessel, he was forced to withdraw upstream out of range.

Returning to the fort on 14 April, Marshall found it evacuated and with the added gunfire support of the lately arrived steamers *Platte Valley*, Captain Riley, Master, and *Silver Cloud*, Acting

Master William Ferguson, scattered the Confederates as they withdrew. The raid on Fort Pillow was one of many attacks made by Forrest during March and April, causing considerable concern among Union commanders and taxing the resources of the Mississippi Squadron. Forrest's favorite operating ground was between the Tennessee and Mississippi Rivers, where Union gunboats could not oppose his raids.

Major General Hurlbut wrote Secretary Welles regarding the preparation by Confederates of a submerged torpedo boat reported to be intended for use in Mobile Bay: "The craft, as described to me, is a propeller about 30 feet long, with engine of great power for her size, and boiler so constructed as to raise steam with great rapidity. She shows above the surface only a small smoke outlet and pilot house, both of which can be lowered and covered. The plan is to drop down within a short distance of the ship, put out the fires, cover the smoke pipe and pilot house, and sink the craft to a proper depth; then work the propeller by hand, drop beneath the ship, ascertaining her position by a magnet suspended in the propeller, rise against her bottom, fasten the torpedo by screws, drop their boat away, pass off a sufficient distance, rise to the surface, light their fires, and work off." While there is no evidence that the vessel described by Hurlbut ever was taken to Mobile, another submersible torpedo boat, *Saint Patrick*, was constructed by Captain Halligan at Selma, Alabama. Halligan's submarine was taken to Mobile in late 1864 and unsuccessfully attacked U.S.S. *Octorara* in early 1865.

U.S.S. *Estrella*, Lieutenant Commander Cooke, supported Army steamers *Zephyr* and *Warrior* on a reconnaissance expedition in Matagorda Bay, Texas. As the ships approached Matagorda Reef, two Confederate vessels were sighted and fired upon, but escaped. Acting Master Gaius P. Pomeroy took charge of the two Army transports and skillfully sailed them into the upper bay where the soldiers were landed. After completing the reconnaissance and capturing two small schooners, the expedition returned to Pass Cavallo. Brigadier General Fitz Henry Warren, commander of the troops on the foray, praised Pomeroy: "He took general charge of two steam transports, and by his attention, industry, and good seamanship impressed me most favorably as to his qualities for command and a higher position . . . in the great work in which we are all engaged."

Boats from U.S.S. *South Carolina*, Acting Lieutenant William W. Kennison, and U.S.S. *T. A. Ward*, Acting Master William L. Babcock, seized blockade running British steamer *Alliance*, which had run aground on Daufuskie Island, South Carolina, with cargo including glass, liquor, and soap.

13   John S. Begbie, an agent of the Albion Trading Company of London, with which the Confederacy dealt, wrote Confederate States Commissioner John Slidell in Paris regarding Southern regulations on pilots, and said that he was informed: "1. Pilots are liable to the conscription. 2. If losing their ship are forced to enlist. 3. If demanding or receiving more than the Government regulation pilotage they are, if found out, deprived of their license and obliged to serve." In protesting against these regulations, he went on: "If it is desirable and in the interest of the Confederate Government that steamers should run in with stores and out with cotton, paying the Government debts and influencing greatly their credit, surely pilots are much more usefully employed to the State as pilots than as fighting men. The very few of them there are could never be felt as a loss to the army, while one dozen of them taken out of their number is sensibly felt and greatly aggravates the difficulty of steamers getting in, which is surely difficult enough already. If a pilot loses his ship, do not let him be deprived of his license unless he is grievously to blame; but if so, at once into the ranks with him, not otherwise; the best of pilots may lose his ship."

U.S.S. *Rachel Seaman*, Acting Master Charles Potter, seized blockade running British schooner *Maria Alfred* near the Mermentau River, Louisiana, with an assorted cargo.

U.S.S. *Nyanza*, Acting Lieutenant Washburn, captured schooner *Mandoline* in Atchafalaya Bay, Louisiana, with cargo of cotton.

13-14 A joint Army–Navy expedition advanced up the Nansemond River, Virginia, to capture Confederate troops in the area and destroy Confederate torpedo boat *Squib* which was thought to have been in that vicinity after her 9 April thrust at U.S.S. *Minnesota*. The naval force deployed by Rear Admiral Lee included converted ferryboats U.S.S. *Stepping Stones*, *Commodore Morris*, *Commodore Perry*, *Commodore Barney*, *Shokokon*, and two launches from *Minnesota*. A handful of prisoners was taken and information was obtained indicating that *Squib* had departed Smithfield for Richmond on the 10th. Acting Lieutenant Charles B. Wilder, who commanded *Minnesota*'s two launches, was killed in an engagement with snipers near Smithfield. Of Wilder, Lieutenant Commander Upshur, *Minnesota*'s commanding officer, wrote: ". . . true to the reputation he had won among his shipmates for promptness and gallantry, he fell while in the act of firing a shot at the enemy."

14 Small paddle-wheel steamers of the Mississippi Squadron continued to engage Confederate raiders in Western Kentucky along the Mississippi and Ohio rivers. At Paducah, Lieutenant Commander James W. Shirk, U.S.S. *Peosta*, with *Key West*, Acting Lieutenant Edward M. King, *Fairplay*, Acting Master George J. Groves and *Victory*, Acting Master Frederick Read, took up defensive positions on the river to meet an anticipated Confederate blow. On 12 April, Shirk had reported: "The rebels are in force around us. The colonel and the gunboats are waiting for an attack." This date, Confederate troops entered Paducah, were taken under fire by the Union ships and withdrew. Meanwhile, on 13 April, Confederates appeared before Columbus, Kentucky, which was protected by U.S.S. *Moose*, Lieutenant Commander LeRoy Fitch, U.S.S. *Hastings*, Acting Master John S. Watson, and U.S.S. *Fairy*, Acting Master Henry S. Wetmore. Here too the Southerners were held at bay by the presence of the light gunboats. These small warships, mostly converted river steamers, played a major role in frustrating the Confederate thrust. Secretary Welles, concerned about Confederate activities in the area, wrote in his diary: " . . . respecting Rebel movements in western Kentucky—at Paducah, Columbus, Fort Pillow, etc. Strange that an army of 6000 Rebels should be moving unmolested within our lines. But for the gunboats, they would repossess themselves of the defenses . . ."

Rear Admiral Porter's position in the Red River became increasingly critical as the water level stubbornly refused to rise, threatening to strand the gunboats. Porter wrote Welles: "I found the fleet at Grand Ecore somewhat in an unpleasant situation, two of them being above the bar, and not likely to get away again this season unless there is a rise of a foot. . . . If nature does not change her laws, there will no doubt be a rise of water, but there was one year—1846—when there was no rise in Red River, and it may happen again. The rebels are cutting off the supply by diverting different sources of water into other channels, all of which would have been stopped had our Army arrived as far as Shreveport. . . . Had we not heard of the retreat of the Army, I should still have gone on to the end."

Porter expressed his appreciation of the services rendered by the river pilots, whose duties were both hazardous and arduous: "There is a class of men who have during this war shown a good deal of bravery and patriotism and who have seldom met with any notice from those whose duty it is to report such matters. I speak of the pilots on the Western Waters. Without any hope of future reward through fame, or in a pecuniary way, they enter into the business of piloting the transports through dangers that would make a faint-hearted man quail. Occupying the most exposed position. . . . managing their vessels while under fire. . . . I beg leave to pay this small tribute to their bravery and zeal, and must say as a class I never knew a braver set of men."

15 U.S.S. *Eastport*, Lieutenant Commander Phelps, struck a Confederate torpedo in the Red River some eight miles below Grand Ecore. The shock of the explosion almost threw the leadsman forward overboard and Phelps, who was in his cabin aft, reported "a peculiar trembling sensation." He immediately ran *Eastport* into shoal water where she grounded. For six days Phelps, assisted by other gunboats in the river, attempted to bail and pump out the water. At last, 21 April, he was able to get underway with carpenters working day and night to close the leak. In the next five days *Eastport* could move only 60 miles downstream while grounding some eight times. The last time, unable to float her, Rear Admiral Porter ordered Phelps to transfer his men to U.S.S. *Fort Hindman* and destroy *Eastport*. On 26 April Phelps, the last man to leave her decks, detonated more than 3,000 pounds of powder and shattered the gunboat. He wrote: "The act has been the most painful one experienced by me in my official career." The ironclad was completely destroyed, "as perfect a wreck as ever was made by powder," Porter noted. "She remains a troublesome obstruction to block up the channel for some time to come." *Eastport* had been captured from the Confederates while still building in the Tennessee River following the seizure of Fort Henry more than two years before (see 6 February 1862).

U.S.S. *Virginia*, Acting Lieutenant C. H. Brown, forced sloop *Rosina* aground and destroyed her at San Luis Pass, Texas.

16 Secretary Mallory wrote Commander Bulloch in England to have 12 small marine engines and boilers built for torpedo boats (40 to 50 feet in length, 5 to 6 feet beam, and drawing 3 feet of water). Twenty-five miles of "good" insulated wire and the "best" gun cotton to be used for torpedoes were also ordered. Unable to produce elements essential for pursuing the torpedo warfare that had been found so effective, the South looked hopefully to Europe for the materials.

17 Confederate troops launched a sustained attack on Plymouth, North Carolina. Union gunboats moved to support their troops ashore and were promptly taken under fire by the Southern batteries. Next day, the fighting at Plymouth intensified as the Confederates pressed the assault. Union Army steamer *Bombshell*, commanded temporarily by Acting Ensign Thomas B. Stokes, was sunk during the engagement, but by 9 o'clock in the evening the Southern advance had been halted. Lieutenant Commander Flusser reported: "The *Southfield* and *Miami* took part and the general says our firing was admirable." The Southern attack required naval support in order to achieve success, and Flusser added meaningfully: "The ram [*Albemarle*] will be down to-night or to-morrow."

U.S.S. *Owasco*, Lieutenant Commander Edmund W. Henry, seized blockade running British schooner *Lilly* at Velasco, Texas.

18 The following dispatch from Brigadier General John McArthur to Acting Master McElroy, U.S.S. *Petrel*, exemplified naval support of Army operations and the dependence placed on it. "An expedition under command of Colonel Scofield starts from Haynes' Bluff for Yazoo City tomorrow. . . . marching by land. You will please to move up and cooperate with them, calculating to reach Yazoo City on Thursday night; afterwards patrolling the river sufficiently to keep open communications between that point and this place."

Boats from U.S.S. *Beauregard*, Acting Master Edward C. Healy, seized blockade running British schooner *Oramoneta* in Matanzas Inlet, Florida, with cargo of salt and percussion caps.

Landing party from U.S.S. *Commodore Read*, Commander F. A. Parker, destroyed a Confederate base together with a quantity of equipment and supplies at Circus Point on the Rappahannock River, Virginia.

U.S.S. *Fox*, Acting Master Charles T. Chase, captured and burned schooner *Good Hope* at the mouth of the Homosassa River, Florida, with cargo of salt and dry goods.

19 C.S.S. *Albemarle*, Commander Cooke, attacked Union warships off Plymouth, North Carolina, at 3:30 in the morning. The heralded and long-awaited ram had departed Hamilton on the evening of the 17th. While en route, "a portion of the machinery broke down" and "the rudderhead broke off," but repairs were promptly made; and, despite the navigational hazards of the crooked Roanoke River, Cooke anchored above Plymouth at 10 p.m. on the 18th. Failing to

C.S.S. Albemarle, *having sunk U.S.S.* Southfield, *steams to engage the gunboat* Miami *in the action that returned control of the waters in the vicinity of Plymouth, North Carolina, to the South.*

rendezvous with Confederate troops as planned, Cooke dispatched a boat to determine the position of the Union gunboats and shore batteries. Shortly after midnight, 19 April, the party returned and reported that *Albemarle* could pass over the Union obstructions because of the high stage of the water. Cooke weighed anchor and stood down to engage. Meanwhile, anticipating an attack by the ram, Lieutenant Commander Flusser lashed wooden double-enders U.S.S. *Miami* and *Southfield* together for mutual protection and concentration of firepower. As *Albemarle* appeared, he gallantly headed the two light wooden ships directly at the Southern ram, firing as they approached. *Albemarle* struck *Southfield*, Acting Lieutenant Charles A. French, a devastating blow with her ram. It was reported that she "tore a hole clear through to the boiler" and Cooke stated that his ship plunged ten feet into the side of the wooden gunboat. Though backing immediately after the impact, *Albemarle* could not at once wrench herself free from the sinking *Southfield* and thus could not reply effectively to the fire poured into her by *Miami*. At last her prow was freed as *Southfield* sank, and Cooke forced Flusser's ship to withdraw under a heavy cannonade. Small steamer U.S.S. *Ceres* and 105-ton tinclad *Whitehead* moved downriver also. The shot of the Union ships had been ineffective against the heavily plated, sloping sides of the ram.

Early in the engagement, Lieutenant Commander Flusser had been killed. Brigadier General Wessells, commanding Union troops at Plymouth, noted: "In the death of this accomplished sailor the Navy has lost one of its brightest ornaments, and he will be long remembered by those who knew and loved him. . . ." Major General John J. Peck, commanding the District of North Carolina, called him a "noble sailor and gallant patriot"; and Rear Admiral Lee wrote: "His patriotic and distinguished services had won for him the respect and esteem of the Navy and the country. He was generous, good, and gallant, and his untimely death is a real and great loss to the public service."

Albemarle now controlled the water approaches to Plymouth and rendered invaluable support to Confederate army moves ashore giving the South a taste of the priceless advantage Union armies enjoyed in all theaters throughout the war. On 20 April Plymouth fell to the Southern attack. General Peck gave testimony to one profound meaning of seapower when he wrote: ". . . but for the powerful assistance of the rebel ironclad ram and the floating iron sharpshooter battery the *Cotton Plant*, Plymouth would still have been in our hands." For the success of *Albemarle*, the Confederate Congress tendered Commander Cooke a vote of thanks, and Secretary Mallory wrote: "The signal success of this brilliant naval engagement is due to the admirable skill and courage displayed by Commander Cooke, his officers and men, in handling and fighting his ship against a greatly superior force of men and guns." Great hopes were placed in *Albemarle* as they had been in *Virginia (Merrimack)* two years earlier.

A "David" torpedo boat commanded by Engineer Tomb, CSN, attempted to sink U.S.S. *Wabash*, Captain John De Camp, off Charleston. The "David", the same one that had been used in the attack on U.S.S. *Memphis* on 6 March, was sighted while still 150 yards distant from the blockader. Alertly the large steam frigate slipped her cable and rapidly got under way, pouring a hail of musket fire at the approaching "David". When only 40 yards off, Tomb was turned back by heavy swells that threatened to swamp the boat.

U.S.S. *Virginia*, Acting Lieutenant C. H. Brown, took blockade running Mexican schooner *Alma* off the coast of Texas with assorted cargo.

21 Rear Admiral Lee emphasized the urgent need to destroy C.S.S. *Albemarle*. If the ram could not be disposed of by ship's gunfire, the Admiral suggested that an attempt be made with torpedoes. However, Lee wrote Commander Henry K. Davenport, senior officer in the North Carolina sounds: "I propose that two of our vessels should attack the ram, one on each side at close quarters, and drive her roof in. That railroad iron will not stand the concussion of our heavy guns. . . . Our vessels must maneuver to avoid being rammed, and once close alongside, there will be no danger of firing into each other. . . . I think the ram must be weak, and must fail if attacked on the side." Lieutenant Commander William T. Truxtun, U.S.S. *Tacony*, wrote Davenport on the same day: "The ironclad, from all accounts, is very much like the first *Merrimack*, with a very long and very sharp submerged prow. . . . The loss of so good a vessel as the *Southfield* and so valuable a life as that of the brave Flusser should show the impossibility of contending successfully with a heavy and powerful ironclad with nothing but one or two very vulnerable wooden vessels."

U.S.S. *Petrel*, Acting Master McElroy, U.S.S. *Prairie Bird*, Acting Ensign John W. Chambers, and transport *Freestone* steamed up the Yazoo River to operate with Union troops attacking Yazoo City. Coming abreast the city, *Petrel* was fired upon by a Confederate battery and sharpshooters. The river was too narrow to come about, so *Petrel* steamed past the batteries to avoid the direct line of fire. The 170-ton *Prairie Bird*, however dropped downriver out of range of the batteries. McElroy made preparation to join her, but on April 22nd, was again taken under attack by rifle and artillery fire and disabled. McElroy attempted to destroy *Petrel* to prevent her being taken as a prize, but was captured before he could successfully put his small wooden gunboat to the torch. Reporting the capture, Confederate General Wirt Adams wrote: "I removed her fine armament of eight 24-pounder guns and the most valuable stores and had her burned to the water's edge."

Boat crews from U.S.S. *Howquah*, *Fort Jackson*, and *Niphon*, commanded by Acting Lieutenant Joseph B. Breck, destroyed Confederate salt works on Masonboro Sound, North Carolina. The sailors landed under cover of darkness at 9 p.m. without being detected and rapidly demolished the works while taking some 160 prisoners. Breck then returned to the ships, which were standing by to cover the operation with gunfire if necessary. Major General W. H. C. Whiting, CSA, noted that the incident demonstrated the necessity of maintaining a guard to protect "these points", and that henceforth there would be no salt works constructed at Masonboro Inlet. The Union Navy conducted a regular campaign against Southern salt works as the need for salt was critical in the Confederacy.

Boat crews from U.S.S. *Ethan Allan*, Acting Master Isaac A. Pennell, landed at Cane Patch, near Murrell's Inlet, South Carolina, and destroyed a salt work which Pennell, who led the expedition himself, described as "much more extensive than I expected . . ." After mixing most of the 2,000 bushels of salt into the sand of the beach, the Union sailors fired the four salt works as well as some 30 buildings in the surrounding area. The next day, off Wither's Swash, Pennell sent Acting Master William H. Winslow and Acting Ensign James H. Bunting ashore with two boat crews to destroy a smaller salt work.

Rear Admiral Dahlgren wrote Secretary Welles suggesting that since "the demands of the public service elsewhere will prevent the detail of more ironclads for service at Charleston, which will necessarily postpone any serious attack on the interior defenses of the harbor," the combined Army and Navy forces should focus their attention and efforts on occupying Long Island and attacking Sullivan's Island. The demands elsewhere to which Dahlgren referred were the preparations for the assault on Mobile Bay by Rear Admiral Farragut.

Boat expedition commanded by Acting Master John K. Crosby from U.S.S. *Cimarron* destroyed a rice mill and 5,000 bushels of rice stored at Winyah Bay, South Carolina. The blockaded South could ill afford to lose such food stuffs.

U.S.S. *Eureka*, Acting Ensign Isaac Hallock, nearing the shore below Urbanna, Virginia, to capture two small boats, was taken under heavy fire by concealed Southern soldiers. The 85-foot, 50-ton steamer, though surprised by the attack, replied immediately and forced the Confederates to withdraw. Commander F. A. Parker, commanding the Potomac Flotilla, remarked: "It was quite a gallant affair and reflects a great deal of credit upon both the officers and men of the *Eureka*. . . ."

U.S.S. *Owasco*, Lieutenant Commander Henry, seized blockade running British schooner *Laura* with cargo of guns in the Gulf of Mexico off Velasco, Texas.

Boat expedition under Acting Ensign Christopher Carven, U.S.S. *Sagamore*, took over 100 bales of cotton and destroyed 300 additional bales near Clay Landing, on the Suwannee River, Florida.

22 C.S.S. *Neuse*, Lieutenant Benjamin P. Loyall, got underway at Kinston, North Carolina, and began steaming downriver to operate on the State's inland waters. She grounded just below Kinston, however, and could not be gotten off. General Montgomery D. Corse reported: "I fear she will be materially injured if not floated soon. The water has fallen 7 feet in the last four days, and is still falling." The Confederates could not float the ram and nearly a year later she was burned to prevent her capture.

23 C.S.S. *Alabama*, Captain Semmes, captured and destroyed ship *Rockingham* with cargo of guano at sea west of the Cape Verde Islands. Semmes said of the capture: "It was the old spectacle of the panting, breathless fawn, and the inexorable stag-hound. A gun brought his colors to the peak, and his main-yard to the mast. . . . We transferred to the *Alabama* such stores and provisions as we could make room for, and the weather being fine, we made a target of the prize, firing some shot and shell into her with good effect and at five p.m. we burned her and filled away on our course." Ominously, during this gunnery practice, many of *Alabama*'s shells failed to explode.

25 Major General W. T. Sherman, in Nashville preparing for his campaign against Atlanta, requested gunboat assistance from Fleet Captain Pennock in Cairo to protect his lines of supply and communication. "I wish," he wrote, "you would notify Captain Shirk that we will, in May, be

actively engaged beyond the Tennessee [River] and I have no doubt the enemy will work up along the Mobile and Ohio Railroad and try and cross the Tennessee to attack my lines of communication. What we want is the earliest possible notice of such movement sent to Nashville and also keep my headquarters here advised where a gunboat could be found with which to throw men across to the west bank of the Tennessee when necessary. For some time [Major General James B.] McPherson's command will be running up the Tennessee as far as Clifton [Tennessee] which is the shortest line of march to Pulaski and Decatur. Please facilitate this movement all you can.'' Five days later Sherman reiterated his request to Pennock. Knowing that the Mississippi Squadron, like squadrons in the Gulf and on the East Coast, suffered from a shortage of men, the General offered to man and equip any gunboats sent to aid him if Rear Admiral Porter could provide the officers. Sherman added: ''I want the [Tennessee] River above Mussel Shoals patrolled as soon as possible, as it will set free one garrison.'' Pennock advised Porter: ''I shall use all the means in my power to forward this movement and to meet at the same time the constantly occurring emergencies which we shall have as long as rebels remain in western Kentucky and Tennessee.''

26 At the request of Brigadier General William Birney, U.S.S. *Ottawa*, Lieutenant Commander S. Livingston Breese, and a launch from U.S.S. *Pawnee* under Acting Master John C. Champion convoyed transports *Harriet A. Weed* and *Mary Benton* up the St. John's River, Florida, The move was prompted by reports of Confederates operating near Union-held Fort Gates and threatening St. Augustine. Several small craft were destroyed by the joint expedition and one small sloop was captured before the Union force withdrew on the 28th.

U.S.S. *Union*, Acting Lieutenant Edward Conroy, captured schooner *O.K.* attempting to run the blockade between Tampa Bay and Charlotte Harbor.

26–27 Attempting to reach Alexandria, Union gunboats under Rear Admiral Porter fought a running engagement with Confederate troops and artillery along the Red River. Wooden gunboats U.S.S. *Fort Hindman*, Acting Lieutenant John Pearce, U.S.S. *Cricket*, Acting Master Henry Gorringe, U.S.S. *Juliet*, Acting Master J. S. Watson, and two pump steamers were attacked by a large force while making final preparations to blow up U.S.S. *Eastport* (see 15 April). The Confederates charged *Cricket* in an attempt to carry her by boarding, but were driven back by a heavy volley of grape and canister from the gunboats. Later in the day, near the mouth of the Cane River at Deloach's Bluff, Louisiana, Southern troops, this time with artillery as well as muskets, again struck Porter's ships, wreaking havoc. *Cricket*, the Admiral's flagship, was hit repeatedly by the batteries, but finally succeeded in rounding a bend in the river downstream and out of range. Pump Steamer *Champion No. 3* took a direct hit in her boiler, drifted out of control, and was captured. *Juliet*'s engine was disabled by Confederate shot, but *Champion No. 5*, though badly hit, succeeded in towing her upstream out of range. *Fort Hindman* covered the withdrawal of the disabled vessels, and the night of April 26 was spent in making urgent repairs. Confederate Major General Richard Taylor, commanding forces along the river, described his plans as follows: ''My dispositions for the day are to . . . keep up a constant fight with the gunboats, following them with sharpshooters and killing every man who exposes himself.'' On 27 April the ships made a second attempt to pass the batteries. *Fort Hindman* took a shot which partially disabled her steering, and she drifted past the Confederate guns. *Champion No. 5* was so damaged that she grounded, was abandoned, and burned. *Juliet* succeeded in getting through, but was severely damaged. Ironclad U.S.S. *Neosho*, Acting Lieutenant Samuel Howard, attempting to assist the embattled gunboats, arrived after the riddled ships had passed the batteries, having endured what Porter later described as ''the heaviest fire I ever witnessed.'' By day's end on the 27th, Porter had reassembled his squadron at Alexandria and began to plan means to pass the Red River rapids.

27 President Jefferson Davis appointed Jacob Thompson representative of the Confederate States in Canada ''to carry out such instructions as . . . received . . . verbally'' from the President.

It was from Canada that Thompson sponsored plans to liberate prisoners of war held on Johnson's Island in Lake Erie, assisted an expedition to burn steamboats on the inland rivers, coordinated the return of escaped Confederate prisoners through Canada via Halifax to Bermuda, and sought to maintain liaison with the organization known as "Sons of Liberty" in the North which was opposed to continuance of the war.

C.S.S. *Alabama*, Captain Semmes, captured and burned bark *Tycoon* at sea east of Salvador, Brazil, with cargo of merchandise, including some valuable clothing. Semmes described the capture: "We now hailed, and ordered him to heave to, whilst we should send aboard of him, hoisting our colors at the same time. . . . The whole thing was done so quietly, that one would have thought it was two friends meeting."

28 Rear Admiral Porter, stranded above the rapids at Alexandria, advised Secretary Welles of the precarious position in which his gunboats found themselves due to the falling water level of the Red River and the withdrawal forced upon Major General Banks: ". . . I find myself blockaded by a fall of 3 feet of water, 3 feet 4 inches being the amount now on the falls; 7 feet being required to get over; no amount of lightening will accomplish the object. . . . In the meantime, the enemy are splitting up into parties of 2,000 and bringing in the artillery . . . to blockade points below here. . . ." Porter faced the distinct possibility of having to destroy his squadron to prevent its falling into Confederate hands. ". . . you may judge of my feelings," he wrote Welles, "at having to perform so painful a duty." Only by the most ingenious planning and the strenuous efforts of thousands of soldiers and sailors was such a disaster avoided. The Admiral summed up the results of "this fatal campaign" which "has upset everything" to date: "It has delayed 10,000 troops of General Sherman, on which he depended to open the State of Mississippi; it has drawn General Steele from Arkansas and already given the rebels a foothold in that country; it has forced me to withdraw many light-clad vessels from points on the Mississippi to protect this army. . . ."

Commander John K. Mitchell, CSN, in charge of the Office of Orders and Detail, wrote: "A deficiency of lieutenants and younger officers continues, owing to the impossibility of obtaining persons suitably qualified. The total number of officers of all grades, commissioned, warranted, and appointed, now in the service amounts to 753, all of whom, except 26, are on duty. The

Rear Admiral Porter's squadron photographed in the Red River at Alexandria, Louisiana.

total number of enlisted persons now employed in the Navy within the Confederacy is 3,960, and abroad about 500, making a total of 4,460."

29 Major General Taylor, CSA, seeking to take full advantage of the vulnerable position of Rear Admiral Porter's gunboats above the Alexandria rapids sought "to convert one of the captured transports into a fire ship to burn the fleet now crowded above the upper falls." This date, however, Union Army and Navy commanders accepted a daring plan proposed by Lieutenant Colonel Joseph Bailey to raise the water level of the Red River and enable the vessels to pass the treacherous rapids. Bailey's proposal was to construct a large dam of logs and debris across the river to back up water level to a minimum depth of seven feet. The dams would be broken and the ships would ride the crest of the rushing waters to safety. Work on the dam commenced early the next day. Porter later wrote: "This proposition looked like madness, and the best engineers ridiculed it, but Colonel Bailey was so sanguine of success that I requested General Banks to have it done . . . two or three regiments of Maine men were set to work felling trees . . . every man seemed to be working with a vigor seldom seen equalled. . . . These falls are about a mile in length, filled with rugged rocks, over which at the present stage of water it seemed to be impossible to make a channel."

An expedition up the Rappahannock River including boats from U.S.S. *Yankee*, Acting Lieutenant Edward Hooker, and U.S.S. *Fuchsia*, assisted by U.S.S. *Freeborn* and *Tulip*, engaged Confederate cavalry and destroyed a camp under construction at Carter's Creek, Virginia.

U.S.S. *Honeysuckle*, Acting Ensign Cyrus Sears, captured blockade running schooner *Miriam*, west of Key West, Florida, with assorted cargo. Sears had boarded *Miriam* on 28 April, thought her papers in order, and released her. Keeping her under surveillance however, he found that she was not on her predicted course and boarded her again. This time upon inspection of the ship's cargo he discovered mail for the Confederate States and seized the vessel.

30 Secretary Mallory reported on existing Confederate naval strength on the East Coast. In the James River, under Flag Officer French Forrest, eight ships mounting 17 guns were in commission, including school ship *Patrick Henry;* under Commander Robert F. Pinkney on the inland waters of North Carolina there were two commissioned ships mounting 4 guns; and on the Cape Fear River, under Flag Officer William F. Lynch, there were three ships and a floating battery in commission mounting a total of 12 guns.

Reporting to President Davis regarding the operations of the Confederate Navy Department, Secretary Mallory said: "Special attention is called to the necessity of providing for the education and training of officers for the navy, and to the measures adopted by the department upon the subject. Naval education and training lie at the foundation of naval success; and the power that neglects this essential element of strength will, when the battle is fought, find that its ships, however formidable, are but built for a more thoroughly trained and educated enemy. . . . While a liberal education at the ordinary institutions of learning prepares men for useful service not only in the Army, but in most branches of public affairs, special education and training, and such as these institutions cannot afford, are essential to form a naval officer. In recognition of the necessity of this special training, every naval power of the earth has established naval colleges and schools and practice ships, and the radical and recent changes in the chief elements of naval warfare have directed to these establishments marked attention."

Confederate blockade runners *Harriet Lane*, *Alice* (also called *Matagorda*), and *Isabel*, escaped through the Union squadron blockading Galveston under cover of darkness and rain squalls. U.S.S. *Katahdin*, Lieutenant Commander J. Irwin, sighted a large steamer passing rapidly inshore near the Southwest Channel at about 9:15 p.m. Since *Harriet Lane* had been reported as too large to use this channel, Irwin thought the vessel to be another blockade runner and did not fire a gun or send up the agreed-upon signal lest he divert the other blockaders from the Main

Channel. *Harriet Lane* passed within 100 yards of *Katahdin*, but was not seen clearly because of the heavy rain. Irwin gave chase, hoping to cross the path of the steamer to seaward, and in the early morning sighted four ships fleeing from him. Though the Union vessel initially gained on the blockade runners, eventually they pulled away. *Katahdin* fired all of her Parrott shell at the closest of the steamers without effect. Irwin continued the chase until daylight on 2 May before turning back to rejoin the fleet off Galveston. All of the blockade runners were laden with cotton—*Alice* threw over some 300 bales to increase her speed during the chase. *Harriet Lane* had been closely watched in Galveston Harbor by the blockaders, and her escape caused indignation in official Washington.

U.S.S. *Conemaugh*, Lieutenant Commander James C. P. De Krafft, captured schooner *Judson* 18 miles east of Mobile with cargo of cotton.

U.S.S. *Vicksburg*, Lieutenant Commander Daniel L. Braine, seized blockade running British schooner *Indian* at sea east of Charleston. She carried a cargo of only one hogshead of palm oil.

MAY

1 Wooden side-wheelers U.S.S. *Morse*, Lieutenant Commander Babcock, and U.S.S. *General Putnam*, Acting Master Hugh H. Savage, convoyed 2,500 Army troops up the York River to West Point, Virginia, where the soldiers were landed under the ships' guns and occupied the town. Another side-wheel steamer, U.S.S. *Shawsheen*, Acting Master Henry A. Phelon, joined the naval forces later in the day and operated with *General Putnam* in the Pamunkey River "for covering our troops and resisting any attack which might be made by the enemy." *Morse* patrolled the Mattapony River where, Babcock reported, "my guns would sweep the whole plain before the entrenchments." Army movements, as Rear Admiral Lee had observed of an earlier plan by Major General Benjamin F. Butler, required "a powerful cooperating naval force to cover his landing, protect his position, and keep open his communications."

U.S.S. *Fox*, Acting Master Charles T. Chase, captured sloop *Oscar* outbound from St. Marks, Florida, with cargo of cotton.

2-9 Colonel Bailey and his regiments of Maine and New York soldiers succeeded, after eight days of gruelling work, in nearly completing the dam across the Red River at Alexandria, and hopes rose that Rear Admiral Porter would be able to save the Mississippi Squadron, marooned above the rapids. On 9 May, two of the stone-filled barges which had been sunk as parts of the dam gave way under the increasing pressure of the backed-up water. The barges, however, swung into position to form a chute over the rapids, and Porter quickly ordered his lighter draft vessels to attempt a passage through the gap. As the water was falling, ironclads *Osage* and *Neosho* and wooden steamers *Fort Hindman* and *Lexington* careened over the rapids with little damage. As Porter later recalled about this thrilling moment: "Thirty thousand voices rose in one deafening cheer, and universal joy seemed to pervade the face of every man present." But all of Porter's vessels were not yet safe, as the larger ships of the squadron remained above the falls. "The accident to the dam," the Admiral related, "instead of disheartening Colonel Bailey, only induced him to renew his exertions, after he had seen the success of getting four vessels through." Bailey and his men, despite the fact that eight days of the heaviest labor had been swept away, turned immediately to work on a new dam.

3 U.S.S. *Chocura*, Lieutenant Commander Bancroft Gherardi, captured blockade running British schooner *Agnes* off the mouth of the Brazos River, Texas, with cargo of cotton. Later that same day, *Chocura* overhauled and captured Prussian schooner *Frederick the Second*, also laden with cotton, which had run the blockade with *Agnes*.

U.S.S. *Virginia*, Acting Lieutenant C. H. Brown, captured schooner *Experiment* off the Texas coast and destroyed her after removing the cotton cargo.

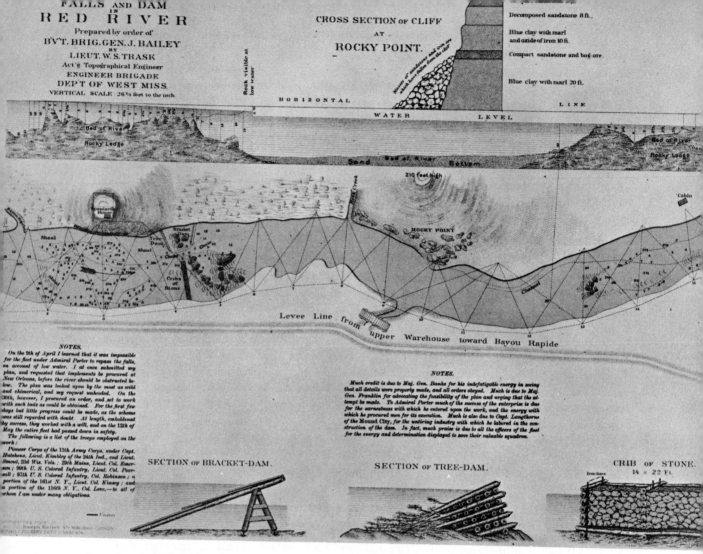

FALLS AND DAM IN RED RIVER

Prepared by order of
BV'T. BRIG. GEN. J. BAILEY
BY
LIEUT. W. S. TRASK
Act'g Topographical Engineer
ENGINEER BRIGADE
DEP'T OF WEST MISS.
VERTICAL SCALE 26⅔ feet to the inch.

CROSS SECTION OF CLIFF
AT
ROCKY POINT.

Decomposed sandstone 8 ft.

Blue clay with marl
and oxide of iron 10 ft.

Compact sandstone and bog ore.

Blue clay with marl 20 ft.

HORIZONTAL   WATER   LEVEL   LINE

SECTION OF BRACKET-DAM.   SECTION OF TREE-DAM.   CRIB OF STONE.
14 × 22 Ft.

NOTES.

NOTES.

Drawing of the Red River from Bayou Rigolets to Alexandria, Louisiana, showing the position and construction of the dams built by Colonel Bailey to save Rear Admiral Porter's squadron which was trapped upstream by low water.

4   Flag Officer Barron in Paris wrote Secretary Mallory: "I have the honor to inform you that the *Georgia*, after having received in the port of Bordeaux all necessary aid and courtesy, has arrived in Liverpool, where I have turned her over to Commander J. D. Bulloch, agent for the Navy Department in Europe, to be disposed of for the benefit of the Government. . . . the plans which I had formed for equipping the *Rappahannock* for service as a man-of-war have been a second time frustrated by the unexplained and unjustifiable action of the French authorities in detaining the *Rappahannock* in the port of Calais. Had she been permitted to sail on the day appointed by her commander her concerted meeting with the *Georgia* would have taken place in a fine, out-of-the-way harbor on the coast of Morocco, in and about which place the *Georgia* had six days of uninterrupted good weather and secure from the notice of all Europeans." As the tide of war turned relentlessly against the Confederacy, foreign governments became increasingly reluctant to involve themselves in the conflict by allowing raiders to outfit in their harbors, and Union diplomatic moves to choke off this source of Southern sea power intensified.

4-7   Steamers U.S.S. *Sunflower*, Acting Master Edward Van Sice, and *Honduras*, Acting Master John H. Platt, and sailing bark *J. L. Davis*, Acting Master William Fales, supported the capture of Tampa, Florida, in a combined operation. The Union ships carried the soldiers to Tampa and provided a naval landing party which joined in the assault. Van Sice reported of the engagement: "At 7 A.M. the place was taken possession of, capturing some 40 prisoners, the naval force cap-

ALEXANDRIA

Actual photographs (above and below) show the dams constructed in the Red River which enabled the Union gunboats to pass over the falls above Alexandria, Louisiana.

turing about one-half, which were turned over to the Army, and a few minutes after 7 the Stars and Stripes were hoisted in the town by the Navy." The warships also captured blockade running sloop *Neptune* on 6 May with cargo of cotton. Brigadier General Daniel Woodbury later wrote to Rear Admiral Bailey, Commander of the East Gulf Blockading Squadron: "I wish to acknowledge the important service you have rendered to the army department by placing the gunboat *Honduras* in my charge, and by your special and general instructions to the commanding Officers of your squadron to assist and cooperate in any military operations."

5 C.S.S. *Albemarle*, Commander Cooke, with *Bombshell*, Lieutenant Albert G. Hudgins, and *Cotton Plant* in company, steamed into Albemarle Sound and engaged Union naval forces in fierce action off the mouth of the Roanoke River. *Bombshell* was captured early in the action after coming under severe fire from U.S.S. *Sassacus*, and *Cotton Plant* withdrew up the Roanoke. *Albemarle* resolutely continued the action. *Sassacus*, Lieutenant Commander Roe, gallantly rammed the heavy ironclad but with little effect. *Sassacus* received a direct hit in her starboard boiler, killing several sailors and forcing her out of action. Side-wheelers U.S.S. *Mattabesett*, Captain M. Smith, and U.S.S. *Wyalusing*, Lieutenant Commander Walter W. Queen, continued to engage the Southern ram until darkness halted the action after nearly three hours of intensive fighting. As Assistant Surgeon Samuel P. Boyer, on board *Mattabesett*, wrote: "Shot and shell came fast like hail." *Albemarle* withdrew up the Roanoke River and small side-wheelers U.S.S. *Commodore Hull* and *Ceres* steamed to the river's mouth on picket duty to guard against her reentry into the sound. The ironclad had returned to her river haven, but she had given new evidence that she was a mighty force to be reckoned with. Captain Smith reported: "The ram is certainly very formidable. He is fast for that class of vessel, making from 6 to 7 knots, turns quickly, and is armed with heavy guns. . . ." And Lieutenant Commander Roe noted: ". . . I am forced to think that the *Albemarle* is more formidable than the *Merrimack* or *Atlanta*, for our solid 100-pounder rifle shot flew into splinters upon her iron plates." *Albemarle*'s commander was more

Union ships engage C.S.S. Albemarle *in Albemarle Sound. U.S.S.* Sassacus *was disabled in the action. Ships shown include (from left to right):* Commodore Hull, Wyalusing, Sassacus, Albemarle, *and* Mattabesett.

Enlisting Articles
C. S. Naval Submarine battery Service.

We the undersigned, for, and in consideration of the Sums set opposite our names, do individually agree,

Article 1st.

To enter the C. S. Naval Submarine battery Service. —

Article 2nd

To do our duty in said Service loyally and faithfully, —

Article 3rd.

To obey all lawful orders of those set over us in authority.

Article 4th.

Under no circumstances now, or hereafter, to make known to any one not employed on this Service, anything regarding the methods used, for arranging, or exploding its Submarine batteries, excepting only, by permission of the Hon. Secty of the Navy, or the Commdg Officer of said Service.

This agreement to remain to inforce whilst its Articles are adhered to, or until the expiration of thirty days, from the day on which we may give the Commdg Officer of this Service, written notice of our desire to be discharged. — the Certificate of Employment to be returned before the discharge is delivered. — To all of which we hereunto Subscribe ourselves.

The Enlisting Articles for the Confederate Navy's Submarine Battery (Torpedo) Service.

critical of her performance. Three days later he wrote Secretary Mallory that the ram "draws too much water to navigate the sounds well, and has not sufficient bouyancy. In consequence she is very slow and not easily managed. Her decks are so near the water as to render it an easy task for the enemy's vessels to run on her, and any great weight soon submerges the deck." For the next five months Union efforts in the area focused on *Albemarle*'s destruction.

While Rear Admiral Porter's fleet awaited the opportunity to pass over the Red River rapids, the ships below Alexandria were incessantly attacked by Confederate forces. This date, wooden steamers U.S.S. *Covington*, Acting Lieutenant George P. Lord, U.S.S. *Signal*, Acting Lieutenant Edward Morgan, and transport *Warner* were lost in a fierce engagement on the Red River near Dunn's Bayou, Louisiana. On 4 May, *Covington* and *Warner* had been briefly attacked by infantry, and the next morning the Confederates reappeared with two pieces of artillery and a large company of riflemen. *Warner*, in the lead, soon went out of control, blocked the river at a bend near Pierce's Landing, and despite the efforts of Lord and Morgan was forced to surrender. *Signal* also became disabled and although *Covington* attempted to tow her upstream, she went adrift out of control and came to anchor. The gunboats continued the hot engagement, but Lord finally burned and abandoned *Covington* after his ammunition was exhausted and many of the crew were killed. After continuing to sustain the Confederate cannonade alone, the crippled *Signal* was finally compelled to strike the colors. The Southerners then sank *Signal* as a channel obstruction.

Chief Engineer Henry A. Ramsay of the newly established Confederate Navy Yard, Charlotte, North Carolina, advised Commander Brooke, Chief of the Naval Bureau of Ordnance, that because of difficulties in recruiting skilled workers and a shortage of mechanics he was unable to operate some of the equipment for arming Southern ironclads; nor could he repair the locomotives assigned to that station by Secretary Mallory. He added: "I understand from you that the iron-clad *Virginia* [No. II] at Richmond is now in readiness for action except her gun carriages and wrought-iron projectiles, which are being made at these works. If we had a full force of mechanics this work would have been finished in one-half the time. . . ." Two days later, Lieutenant David P. McCorkle wrote Brooke in a similar vein from the Naval Ordnance Works at Atlanta, Georgia. This chronic shortage of skilled workers combined with the material shortages occasioned by the blockade could not be surmounted by the Confederacy.

6 U.S.S. *Commodore Jones*, Acting Lieutenant Thomas Wade, was destroyed by a huge 2,000-pound electric torpedo in the James River while dragging for torpedoes with U.S.S. *Mackinaw* and *Commodore Morris*. From the Norfolk Naval Hospital, Wade later reported that the torpedo "exploded directly under the ship with terrible effect, causing her destruction instantly, absolutely blowing the vessel to splinters." Other observers said that the hull of the converted ferryboat was lifted completely out of the water by the force of the explosion which claimed some 40 lives. A landing party of sailors and Marines went ashore immediately and captured two torpedomen and the galvanic batteries which had detonated the mine. One of the Confederates, Jeffries Johnson, refused to divulge information regarding the location of torpedoes under interrogation, but he "signified his willingness to tell all" when he was placed in the bow of the forward ship on river duty, and Johnson became the war's "unique minesweeper."

Early in the evening, C.S.S. *Raleigh*, Flag Officer Lynch, steamed over the bar at New Inlet, North Carolina, and engaged U.S.S. *Britannia* and *Nansemond*, forcing them to withdraw temporarily and enabling a blockade runner to escape. Captain Sands, senior officer present, commented: "The principal object [of *Raleigh*'s attack], it seems to me . . . is for her to aid the outgoing and incoming of the runners by driving off the vessels stationed on and near the bar. . . ." Early the next morning, *Raleigh* renewed the engagement, exchanging fire with wooden steamers U.S.S. *Howquah* and *Nansemond*. Two other steamers, U.S.S. *Mount Vernon* and *Kansas*, also opened on the ram, and at 6 a.m. Lynch broke off the action. Attempting to cross the bar at the mouth of Cape Fear

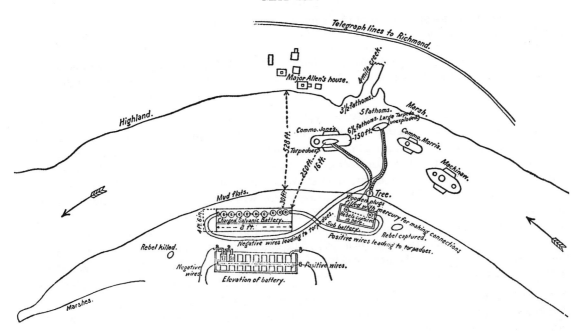

This sketch of the Confederate galvanic batteries which destroyed U.S.S. Commodore Jones *was drawn by Jefferson Young, a First Assistant Engineer of U.S.S.* Mackinaw.

River, *Raleigh* grounded and was severely damaged. Lynch order her destroyed; his action was sanctioned by a subsequent court of inquiry. Thus, the Confederacy lost another formidable ram, one upon which Southern Army commanders had been depending to defend the inner bars from Union attack.

U.S.S. *Granite City*, Acting Master C. W. Lamson, and U.S.S. *Wave*, Acting Lieutenant Benjamin A. Loring, were captured by Confederate troops in Calcasieu River, Louisiana. Steamer *Granite City* and tinclad *Wave* had been dispatched to Calcasieu Pass to receive refugees on 28 April and both ships carried out this duty until the morning of the captures, landing a small army detachment on shore as pickets. The Southerners, with artillery and about 350 sharpshooters from the Sabine Pass garrison, overwhelmed the Union landing party, and took the ships under fire on the morning of 6 May. After an hour's engagement, *Granite City* surrendered; upon receiving shot in her boiler and steam drum, *Wave* shortly followed suit. On the 10th U.S.S. *New London*, Acting Master Lyman Wells, unaware that the Confederates had surprised and taken the Union vessels, arrived off Calcasieu. Wells sent one boat to *Granite City*, which did not return. On the morning of the 11th, he sent another boat, under the command of Acting Ensign Henry Jackson, toward *Granite City* under flag of truce. Seeing a Confederate flag flying from her, Jackson tried to shoot it down and was killed by a Southern sharpshooter. Upon receiving Acting Master Wells' report, Rear Admiral Farragut immediately planned to recapture the vessels but, having insufficient ships of light draft available, was forced to postpone his efforts.

U.S.S. *Dawn*, Acting Lieutenant John W. Simmons, transported soldiers to capture a signal station at Wilson's Wharf, Virginia. After landing the troops two miles above the station, Simmons proceeded to Sandy Point to cover the attack. When the soldiers were momentarily halted, a boat crew from *Dawn* spearheaded the successful assault.

U.S.S. *Grand Gulf*, Commander George M. Ransom, captured blockade running British steamer *Young Republic* at sea east of Savannah with cargo of cotton and tobacco. Two weeks later, Rear Admiral Lee congratulated Ransom on the seizure and wrote: "Every capture made by the blockaders deprives the enemy of so much of the 'sinews of war,' and is equal to the taking of a supply train from the rebel Army."

U.S.S. *Eutaw*, *Osceola*, *Pequot*, *Shokokon*, and *General Putnam*, side-wheelers of Rear Admiral Lee's North Atlantic Blockading Squadron, supported the landing of troops at Bermuda Hundred, Virginia.

7   U.S.S. *Shawsheen*, Acting Ensign Charles Ringot, was disabled, captured and destroyed by Confederates in James River. *Shawsheen*, a 180-ton side-wheel steamer, had been ordered to drag the river for torpedoes above Chaffin's Bluff, and had anchored near shore shortly before noon so that the crew could eat, when Confederate infantry and artillery surprised the gunboat. A shot through the boiler forced many sailors overboard to avoid being scalded. Lieutenant Colonel W. M. Elliott, CSA, reported that *Shawsheen* was completely disabled and "though reluctantly, she nevertheless hauled down her colors and displayed the white flag in token of surrender. A boat was dispatched to enforce the delivery of the prisoners on board, the enemy's boats being made available to bring them off. The officer was also instructed to fire the vessel, which was effectively done, the fire quickly reaching the magazine, exploding it, consigning all to the wind and waves."

The Confederacy, hampered by limited armaments and foundries, sought to make optimum use of every piece of captured Union ordnance. This date, Major General Camille J. Polignac, CSA, pointed out the significance of the Southern capture of U.S.S. *Signal* and *Covington* and their two Parrott guns (see 6 May): "It is very important and desirable that these fruits of our victories over the enemy's gunboats shall be saved to us, as well as lost to them."

9   Rear Admiral Farragut again wrote Secretary Welles requesting ironclads for the reduction of Mobile Bay: "I am in hourly expectation of being attacked by almost an equal number of vessels, ironclads against wooden vessels, and a most unequal contest it will be, as the *Tennessee* is represented as impervious to all their experiments at Mobile so that our only hope is to run her down,

C.S.S. Tennessee, *Admiral Buchanan's gallant flagship, was the primary object of Union interest as the opposing forces readied themselves for the battle for control of Mobile Bay.*

which we shall certainly do all in our power to accomplish; but should we be unsuccessful the panic in this part of the country will be beyond all control. They will imagine that New Orleans and Pensacola must fall." At this time Admiral Buchanan was trying to float *Tennessee* over the Mobile bar using watertight caissons or "camels". Until that could be effected, there would be no engagement with Farragut's fleet.

U.S.S. *Connecticut*, Commander Almy, seized blockade running British steamer *Minnie* with cargo of cotton, tobacco, turpentine, and $10,000 in gold. The steamer was a well-known successful blockade runner. On 16 April 1864, John T. Bourne, Confederate commercial agent at St. Georges, Bermuda, had advised B. W. Hart Company, of London: "Steamer *Minnie*, Captain [Thomas S.] Gilpin, has made a splendid trip bringing 700 & odd bales of cotton & good lot of Tobacco paying for herself & the *Emily*."

10 U.S. Army transport *Harriet A. Weed*, supporting troop movements in the St. John's River, was destroyed by a torpedo. Sinking in less than a minute, the steamer became the third victim of stepped-up Confederate torpedo activity in the St. John's River in less than six weeks. While reconnoitering the river near *Harriet A. Weed*'s hulk, U.S.S. *Vixen* recovered a torpedo of the type that destroyed the transport. The keg torpedo was, reported Charles O. Boutelle of the Coast Survey, "simple and effectual. . . ."

U.S.S. *Mound City*, Acting Lieutenant Amos R. Langthorne, and U.S.S. *Carondelet*, Lieutenant Commander John G. Mitchell, grounded near where work was proceeding on the wing dams across the Red River rapids above Alexandria. Next day, as the Red River slowly continued to rise behind the two wing dams, ironclads *Mound City*, *Carondelet*, and U.S.S. *Pittsburg*, Acting Lieutenant William R. Hoel, were finally hauled across the upper falls above the obstructions by throngs of straining soldiers. As the troops looked on in tense anticipation, the gunboats, all hatches battened down, successfully lurched through the gap between the dams to safety. Rear Admiral Porter later reported to Secretary Welles: "The passage of these vessels was a beautiful sight, only to be realized when seen." U.S.S. *Ozark*, *Louisville*, and *Chillicothe*, ironclads which had crossed the upper falls, were preparing to follow the next day.

U.S.S. *Connecticut*, Commander Almy, captured blockade running British steamer *Greyhound*, Lieutenant George H. Bier, CSN, with cargo of cotton, tobacco, and turpentine on the Government account.

12 Rear Admiral Lee, prompted by the recent loss of U.S.S. *Commodore Jones* and *Shawsheen*, ordered Lieutenant Roswell H. Lamson to command a special "torpedo and picket division" in the James River. The force would comprise side-wheelers U.S.S. *Stepping Stones*, *Delaware*, and *Tritonia*. In addition to patrolling and reconnoitering the river banks and dragging the river itself for torpedoes, Lee directed Lamson: "By night keep picket vessels and boats ahead and underway with alarm signals to prevent surprise from rebel river craft, rams, torpedo 'Davids,' and fire rafts."

Flag Officer Barron in Paris wrote Secretary Mallory: "To-day I have heard indirectly and confidentially that the *Alabama* may be expected in a European port on any day. Ship and captain both requiring to be docked. Captain Semmes' health has begun to fail, and he feels that rest is needful to him. If he asks for a relief, I shall order Commander T. J. Page to take his place in command, and shall not hesitate to relieve the other officers if they ask for respite from sea duty after their long, arduous, and valuable service on the sea. There are numbers of fine young officers here who are panting for active duty on their proper element, and will cheerfully relieve their brother officers who have so handsomely availed themselves of the opportunities afforded them of rendering such distinguished service to their country and illustrating the naval profession."

Boat expedition under Acting Lieutenant William Budd, U.S.S. *Somerset*, transported a detachment of troops to Apalachicola, Florida, to disperse a Confederate force thought to be in the vicinity.

After disembarking the troops, Budd and his launches discovered a body of Confederate sailors embarking on a boat expedition, and after a brief exchange succeeded in driving them into the town and capturing their boats and supplies. The Confederates, led by Lieutenant Gift, CSN, had planned to capture U.S.S. *Adela*.

U.S.S. *Beauregard*, Acting Master Edward C. Healy, seized blockade running sloop *Resolute* off Indian River, Florida.

13 Climaxing two weeks of unceasing effort to save the gunboats and bring to a close the unsuccessful Red River campaign, U.S.S. *Louisville, Chillicothe,* and *Ozark*, the last ships of Rear Admiral Porter's stranded fleet, succeeded in passing over the rapids above Alexandria, Louisiana. By mid-afternoon the gunboats steamed down the river, convoying Army transports; thus ended one of the most dramatic exploits of the war, as Lieutenant Colonel Bailey's ingenuity and the inexhaust-ible energy of the men working on the obstructions raised the level of the river enough to save the Mississippi Squadron. Porter later wrote to Secretary Welles: "The water had fallen so low that I had no hope or expectation of getting the vessels out this season, and as the army had made arrangements to evacuate the country I saw nothing before me but the destruction of the best part of the Mississippi squadron. . . ." He rightly praised the work of Colonel Bailey: "Words are inadequate to express the admiration I feel for the abilities of Lieutenant Colonel Bailey. This is without a doubt the best engineering feat ever performed . . . he has saved to the Union a valuable fleet, worth nearly $2,000,000. . . . ." Bailey's services received prompt recognition, for in June he was promoted and he later received the formal thanks of Congress.

Small sidewheel steamer U.S.S. *Ceres*, Acting Master Henry H. Foster, with Army steamer *Rockland* and 100 embarked soldiers in company, conducted a raiding expedition on the Alligator River, North Carolina, captured Confederate schooner *Ann S. Davenport* and disabled a mill supplying ground corn for the Southern armies.

15 As ships of Rear Admiral Porter's gunboat fleet neared the mouth of the Red River, they met continued resistance from Confederate shore batteries and riflemen. U.S.S. *St. Clair*, a 200-ton stern-wheeler under Acting Lieutenant Thomas B. Gregory, engaged a battery near Eunice's Bluff, Louisiana. Gregory exchanged fire with the artillerists until the transports he was con-voying were out of danger, then continued downriver.

U.S.S. *Kansas*, Lieutenant Commander Pendleton G. Watmough, captured blockade running British steamer *Tristram Shandy* at sea east of Fort Fisher with cargo of cotton, tobacco, and turpentine.

Gunboats of the Red River Squadron careen over the hastily-built dams above Alexandria, Louisiana, to safety below the rapids.

16 Ships of the Mississippi Squadron were constantly occupied with safeguarding river transportation from Southern attack. Side-wheeler U.S.S. *General Price*, Acting Lieutenant Richardson, engaged a Confederate battery which had taken transport steamer *Mississippi* under fire near Ratliff's Landing, Mississippi. U.S.S. *Lafayette*, Lieutenant Commander J. P. Foster, and U.S.S. *General Bragg*, Acting Lieutenant Cyrenius Dominy, converged upon the battery and the three heavy steamers forced the Confederate gunners back from the river, enabling the transport to proceed.

Having crossed the rapids of the Red River at Alexandria, Rear Admiral Porter next had to traverse the many bars in the River near its mouth. The Admiral found that the water was higher there than had been anticipated and reported to Secretary Welles: "Providentially we had a rise from the backwater of the Mississippi, that river being very high at that time, the backwater extending to Alexandria, 150 miles distant, enabling us to pass all the bars and obstructions with safety." After battling low water, rapids, and the harassing forces of General Taylor for two months along the Red River, Porter and his gunboats again entered the Mississippi.

A landing party from U.S.S. *Stockdale*, Acting Lieutenant Thomas Edwards, was fired upon by Confederate cavalry at the mouth of the Tchefuncta River in Lake Pontchartrain, Louisiana. Edwards succeeded in forcing the Confederates to withdraw, but not until two of his officers had been captured and one killed.

18 After encountering many difficulties and setbacks Admiral Buchanan succeeded in floating the formidable Confederate ram *Tennessee* over Dog River Bar and out into Mobile Bay. With Rear Admiral Farragut's fleet forming outside the bay, the stage was now being set for one of the most dramatic and decisive naval battles of the War.

C.S.S. *Florida*, Lieutenant Morris, captured and burned schooner *George Latimer* of Baltimore at 34°55′ N, 55°13′ W, with cargo of flour, lard, bread, and kerosene.

19 U.S.S. *General Price*, Acting Lieutenant Richardson, engaged a Confederate battery on the banks of the Mississippi River at Tunica Bend, Louisiana. The Southerners, who had been attempting to destroy transport steamer *Superior*, were forced to evacuate their river position. Richardson put ashore a landing party which burned a group of buildings used by the Confederates as a headquarters from which attacks against river shipping were launched.

21 Gunfire from ironclad steamer U.S.S. *Atlanta*, Acting Lieutenant Thomas J. Woodward, and U.S.S. *Dawn*, Acting Lieutenant John W. Simmons, dispersed Confederate cavalry attacking Fort Powhatan on the James River, Virginia. *Dawn*, a wooden steamer, remained above the fort during the night to prevent another attack.

22 During the long period of watchful waiting and preparation off Mobile, Rear Admiral Farragut wrote his son Loyall: "I am lying off here, looking at Buchanan and awaiting his coming out. He has a force of four ironclads and three wooden vessels. I have eight or nine wooden vessels. We'll try to amuse him if he comes. . . . I have a fine set of vessels here just now, and am anxious for my friend Buchanan to come out."

U.S.S. *Kineo*, Lieutenant Commander John Waters, seized blockade-running British schooner *Sting Ray* off Velasco, Texas. However, the prize crew put on board the schooner was overwhelmed by the original crew. The schooner was grounded on the Texas coast, where the Union sailors were turned over to the custody of Confederate troops.

U.S.S. *Crusader*, Lieutenant Peter Hays, captured schooner *Isaac L. Adkins* at the mouth of the Severn River, Maryland, with cargo of corn and oats.

23 U.S.S. *Columbine*, Acting Ensign Sanborn, was captured after a heated engagement with Confederate batteries and riflemen at Horse Landing, near Palatka, Florida. *Columbine*, a 130-ton side-wheeler operating in support of Union Army forces and with soldiers embarked, lost steering control and ran onto a mud bank, where she was riddled by the accurate Confederate fire. With some 20 men killed and wounded, Sanborn surrendered "to prevent the further useless expenditure of human life." Shortly after taking the prize, the Southerners destroyed her to avoid recapture by U.S.S. *Ottawa*, Lieutenant Commander Breese. *Ottawa*, cooperating with the Army in the same operation, had also been fired upon the night before and suffered damage but no casualties before compelling the Confederate battery at Brown's Landing to withdraw. Rear Admiral Dahlgren wrote: "The loss of the *Columbine* will be felt most inconveniently; her draft was only 5 or 6 feet, and having only two such steamers, the services of which are needed elsewhere, can not replace her."

24 President Lincoln, ever ready to recognize the contributions of the officers and men in service afloat, recommended the promotion of Lieutenant Commander Francis A. Roe and First Assistant Engineer James M. Hobby for their distinguished conduct in the fierce battle between U.S.S. *Sassacus* and C.S.S. *Albemarle* in Albemarle Sound, North Carolina, on 5 May.

Confederate soldiers captured and burned steamer *Lebanon* near Ford's Landing, Arkansas. Six days later, Union transport *Clara Eames* and her cargo of cotton were taken and burned near Gaines Landing, Arkansas, after she was disabled by artillery fire. Confederates continually ranged along the banks of the western rivers engaging Union shipping in hit-and-run raids. The actions were a constant reminder of the continuing need for naval gunboat support and vigilance on these all important waterways.

Accurate gunfire from wooden steamer U.S.S. *Dawn*, Acting Lieutenant Simmons, compelled Confederate troops to break off an attack on the Union Army position at Wilson's Wharf on the James River. Other ships quickly moved to support the troops. Rear Admiral Lee later reported that General E. A. Wild, commanding the Army defenses, praised the Navy's work: "He stated to me that the gunboats were of great assistance to him in repelling their attack."

25 Boat crew from U.S.S. *Mattabesett*, Captain M. Smith, made an unsuccessful attempt to destroy C.S.S. *Albemarle* in the Roanoke River near Plymouth, North Carolina. After ascending the Middle River with two 100-pound torpedoes, Charles Baldwin, coal heaver, and John W. Lloyd, coxswain, swam across the Roanoke carrying a towline with which they hauled the torpedoes to the Plymouth shore. Baldwin planned to swim down to the ram and position a torpedo on either side of her bow. Across the river, Alexander Crawford, fireman, would then explode the weapons. However, Baldwin was discovered by a sentry when within a few yards of *Albemarle* and the daring mission had to be abandoned. John Lloyd cut the guidelines and swam back across the river to join John Laverty, fireman, who was guarding the far shore. They made their way to the dinghy in which they had rowed upriver and, with Benjamin Lloyd, coal heaver, who had acted as boatkeeper, made their way back to the *Mattabesett*. On 29 May Baldwin and Crawford, exhausted, returned to the ship. Captain Smith reported: "I can not too highly commend this party for their courage, zeal, and unwearied exertion in carrying out a project that had for some time been under consideration. The plan of executing it was their own, except in some minor details. . . ." As Smith recommended, each of the five sailors was awarded the Medal of Honor for their heroic efforts.

A joint Army-Navy expedition advanced up the Ashepoo and South Edisto Rivers, South Carolina, with the object of cutting the Charleston and Savannah Railroad. Union naval forces, under Lieutenant Commander Edward E. Stone, included converted ferryboat U.S.S. *Commodore McDonough*, and wooden steamers *E. B. Hale*, *Dai Ching*, and *Vixen* and a detachment of Marines. The Navy pushed up the South Edisto, while Army transports moved up the Ashepoo convoyed by *Dai Ching*. Stone landed the Marines and howitzers and on the morning of the 26th opened fire on Willstown, South Carolina. The naval commander, unable to make contact with General Birney to coordinate a further assault, withdrew next morning. Transport *Boston* ran aground in the Ashepoo and was destroyed to prevent her capture.

26 The unsuccessful Red River campaign having drawn to a close, General Banks' army on 20 May crossed the Atchafalaya River near Simmesport, Louisiana, protected by Rear Admiral Porter's fleet. Porter, whose health was beginning to fail after many months of arduous duty on the western waters, arrived at his headquarters at Cairo, Illinois, this date, and reported to Secretary Welles on the end of the expedition: "I have the honor to report my arrival at this place, four days from Red River. The army had all crossed the Atchafalaya, and General Smith's division had embarked; the gunboats covered the army until all were over. . . . The river is quiet between this [Ohio River] and Red River. . . ."

Rear Admiral Farragut wrote Rear Admiral Bailey, then at Key West, about the torpedo preparations made by Confederate Admiral Buchanan in Mobile Bay: "I can see his boats very industriously laying down torpedoes, so I judge that he is quite as much afraid of our going in as we are of his coming out; but I have come to the conclusion to fight the devil with fire, and therefore shall attach a torpedo to the bow of each ship, and see how it will work on the rebels—if they can stand blowing up any better than we can."

Commander Carter, U.S.S. *Michigan*, reported to Secretary Welles from Buffalo, New York, of the cruise of his iron side-wheeler on Lake Erie "relative to supposed armed vessel intended to raid on the lake cities . . .", but he could "find no foundation for the rumors relative thereto . . . matters quiet at present. . . ."

Illustrative of the global demands placed on the Union Navy was the request of Robert H. Pruyn, U.S. Minister to Japan, that Captain Cicero Price bring U.S.S. *Jamestown* without delay to the port of Kanagawa, which the Japanese threatened to close to foreign commerce.

28 After a six-hour chase, U.S.S. *Admiral*, Lieutenant William B. Eaton, captured blockade running steamer *Isabel*, south of Galveston, Texas, with a cargo of powder and arms. Eaton commented in his report that "She was ably handled, and her commander evinced the most desperate courage, not surrendering until two broadsides at close quarters had been poured into him, and our Marines pouring in such an incessant fire of musketry that not a man could remain on deck, and not until then did the captain of her show a light as a signal of submission." *Isabel*, a highly successful blockade runner which was reported to have made more than 20 trips through the blockade at Mobile and Galveston, was severely damaged, and despite Eaton's efforts to save her, sank at Quarantine Station on the Mississippi River on 2 June.

U.S.S. *Ariel*, Acting Master James J. Russell, captured sloop *General Finegan* north of Chassahowitzka Bay, Florida. The blockade runner's crew attempted to set her afire, but *Ariel* saved the cargo of cotton and turpentine and then destroyed *General Finegan* as unseaworthy.

29 U.S.S. *Cowslip*, Acting Ensign Richard Canfield, captured sloop *Last Push* off the coast of Mississippi with cargo of corn.

30 Mounting evidence pointed to a Confederate naval assault on Union forces in the James River below Richmond. This date, John Loomis, a deserter from C.S.S. *Hampton*, reported that three ironclads and six wooden gunboats, all armed with torpedoes, had passed the obstructions at Drewry's Bluff and were below Fort Darling, awaiting an opportunity to attack. The ironclads were C.S.S. *Virginia II*, Flag Officer John K. Mitchell, C.S.S. *Richmond*, Lieutenant William H. Parker, and C.S.S. *Fredericksburg*, Commander Thomas R. Rootes. Two days later, Archy Jenkins, a Negro from Richmond, confirmed this statement and added: "They are putting two barges and a sloop lashed together, filled with shavings and pitch and with torpedoes, which they intend

No 207 : Hartford.

Flag-Ship : Western Gulf Blockading Squadron,

Off Mobile Bar-

May- 25- 1864.

Sir:

My mail from New Orleans this morning

I ran in shore yesterday, and took a good look at the Iron Clad Tennessee. She flies the Blue Flag of Admiral Buchanan. She has four Ports of a side, out of which she fights, I understand from the refugees, four 7 in. Brook's Rifles. and 2 (?) Columbiads, She has a torpedo fixture on the bow.

Their Four Iron Clads and Three wooden Gun Boats make quite a formidable appearance. I see by the Rebel papers, Buchanan is advertised to raise the Blockade so soon as he is ready.. As I have before informed the Department, if I had the military force to place on the Isthmus and on Dauphin Island, say Three Thousand men, and one or two Iron Clads, I would not hesitate to

IV-64

run in and attack him,—but, if I was to run in, and in so doing get my vessels crippled, it would be in his power to retire to the shoal water with his Iron Clads, (In fact all their vessels draw much less water than ours) and thus destroy us without our being able to get at him. But if he takes the offensive and comes out of Port, I hope to be able to contend with him. The Department has not

Torpedoes are not so agreeable when used both sides,—therefore I have reluctantly brought myself to it. I have always deemed it unworthy of a chivalrous nation,—but it does not do to give your Enemy such a decided superiority over you.

Very Respectfully
Yr. Obdt. Servt.—
D. G. Farragut
Rear Admiral

Extracts from Rear Admiral Farragut's letter to Secretary Welles regarding C.S.S. Tennessee and prospects for the attack on Mobile Bay.

The Confederate James River Squadron, stationed above the obstructions near Fort Darling, defend the river approach to Richmond.

to set on fire, and when it reaches the fleet it will blow up and destroy the fleet. . . . They all say they know 'they can whip you all; they are certain of it.' They believe in their torpedoes in preference to everything." "In view of the novel attack contemplated," Rear Admiral Lee wrote Secretary Welles, ". . . one or more ironclads could be added to my force here, considering the importance of this river to the armies of Generals Grant and Butler."

U.S.S. *Keystone State*, Commander Crosby, and U.S.S. *Massachusetts*, Acting Lieutenant William H. West, captured blockade running British steamer *Caledonia* at sea south of Cape Fear after a three hour chase in which the steamer's cargo of bacon, leather, and medical supplies was thrown overboard.

31 U.S.S. *Commodore Perry*, Acting Lieutenant Amos P. Foster, engaged Confederate artillery on the James River, Virginia, in a two hour exchange during which the converted ferryboat was damaged by six hits.

Secretary Welles ordered U.S.S. *Constellation*, Captain Stellwagen, detached from duty in the Mediterranean to report to Rear Admiral Farragut in the Western Gulf Blockading Squadron.

JUNE

1 Rear Admiral Dahlgren wrote in his diary off Charleston: "Of the seven monitors left, two are here out of order, and the *Passaic* no better. The Rebels have four; wonder if they will come out and try their luck."

U.S.S. *Exchange*, a 210-ton wooden paddle-wheeler under Acting Master James C. Gipson, engaged two Confederate batteries on the Mississippi River near Columbia, Arkansas, sustaining serious damage. Gipson, who was wounded during the heated encounter, described the action: "They waited until I had passed by the lower battery, when they opened a destructive crossfire. As I had just rounded a point of a sand bar, I could not back down, consequently there was no other alternative but run by the upper battery if possible. . . . I opened my port broadside guns, replying to theirs; but unfortunately the port engine was struck and disabled, causing her to work very slow, keeping us under fire about forty-five minutes. I had barely got out of range of their guns when the engine stopped entirely. . . . I immediately let go the anchor . . . expecting every moment they would move their battery above us and open again; but we succeeded in getting out, although pretty badly damaged."

2 Union gunboats convoying transports on the western rivers continued to be harassed by hostile field artillery along the banks. Lieutenant Commander Owen, U.S.S. *Louisville*, after sustaining

severe damage in an exchange at Columbia, Arkansas, wrote to Rear Admiral Porter: "The strength of the enemy in the neighborhood is undoubtedly great, and nothing but a military expedition can clear the banks. We can convoy boats every day with the usual loss of men and injury to boats, as the river is now, but it is falling rapidly, and vessels are of necessity being driven close under the enemy's guns." Next day, at Memphis, Lieutenant Commander John G. Mitchell, U.S.S. *Carondelet*, also observed: "Not a steamer arrives here from Cairo but what has been fired upon by gangs numbering from 12 to 100 men." The warships were encountering difficulties similar to those Rear Admiral Farragut had faced on the Texas coast in the fall of 1862: the ships could dominate the waterways and coasts, but troops were needed to prevent the buildup of Confederate artillery and troublesome guerilla activity.

U.S.S. *Wamsutta*, Acting Master Charles W. Lee, chased blockade running British steamer *Rose* aground at Pawley's Island, South Carolina, with small cargo including liquor and destroyed her.

U.S.S. *Victoria*, Acting Master Alfred Everson, chased blockade running steamer *Georgiana McCaw* aground near Wilmington and destroyed her with large cargo of provisions.

Landing party from U.S.S. *Cowslip*, Acting Ensign Canfield, captured five sloops and one steam boiler, destroyed six large boats, four salt works, and three flat boats during a raid up Biloxi Bay, Mississippi.

3 A Confederate boat expedition of some 130 officers and men under the command of Lieutenant Thomas P. Pelot, CSN, surprised and captured U.S.S. *Water Witch*, Lieutenant Commander Austin Pendergrast, in an early morning raid off Ossabaw Island, Georgia. In pitch darkness at 2 o'clock in the morning, Pelot silently guided his party to the anchored blockaders' and was within 50 yards of her when discovered. Before the Union sailors could man their stations, the Confederates had boarded *Water Witch* and a wild hand-to-hand melee ensued. "The fight," Rear Admiral Dahlgren recorded in his diary after learning of the incident, "was hard, but brief." Though the Southerners overwhelmed the defenders, Pelot and five others were killed and 17 were wounded in taking the prize. Lieutenant Joseph Price, who assumed command of the expedition when Pelot fell, said of his comrade: "In his death the country has lost a brave and gallant officer, and society one of her highest ornaments." *Water Witch*, a 380-ton sidewheeler, was taken into the Vernon River and moored above the obstructions guarding Savannah. Secretary Mallory wrote: "The plan and gallant execution of the enterprise reflect great credit upon all who were associated with it, and upon the service which they adorn. The fall of Lieutenant Pelot and his gallant associates in the moment of victory, and the suffering of his companions wounded, sadden the feelings of patriotic pleasure with which this brilliant achievement is everywhere received." The valor with which Southern sailors fought on against great and ever-increasing odds helped keep Confederate hopes alive throughout the last dark year of the war.

Commander Bulloch wrote Secretary Mallory, enumerating some of the difficulties he experienced as Confederate Naval Agent abroad: "At no time since the completion of the *Alabama* has there been anything like money enough in hand, or within my control to pay for the ships actually under contract, and if no political complications had to delay the completion of these ships and they had been ready for delivery at the dates specified in the contracts, I should not have been able to pay for them. . . . If these were ordinary times and the agent of your department could treat openly and in person with the European governments, we could doubtless obtain very good ships from several of the Continental navies, but acting through intermediaries who care for nothing beyond their commissions, we can not get anything but the cast-off vessels of other services, which either possess some radical defect of design rendering them unfit for cruisers, or are so delapidated as to be worthless."

U. S. Str. "Mendota"
James River June 3rd 1864

My dear Admiral.

I promised before leaving
New York, to write and let you know what
was going on in this part of the world. I
should be much pleased to do so, but,
strange as it may seem, though we are
only about four miles from Head Quarters,
our latest, and indeed almost only news
from there, we receive through an occasion-
-al stray New York paper, and I cannot
say that I receive the newspaper accounts
with that full measure of confidence I
should like to. Our "Specials", do tell.

now in command. Scarcely a night or
day passes that an assault is not made
on our lines, but so far they have all been
repulsed. Our iron clads and some of the
Gun boats, with Admiral Lee, are at the right
flank, and generally have something to say
in these attacks. The sight at night is
beautiful. The sky is illuminated by the
flashing guns and bursting shells, and
the noise is equal to a small thunder
storm. The most of our vessels are engaged
in guarding prominent points along the
river to keep open the navigation. My

IV–68

repeated stoppages moreover. To crown
all with my own personal grievances,
my cabin is about as uncomfortable
as it will can be. It leaks all over, deck,
skylight, combings and stairway. I am
sorry I did not bring an umbrella with
me. I make the best I can of all these
ills, and intend to do my best to worry
through the campaign, satisfied to bear
all present ills and many more to
end this business successfully and
gloriously. Hoping that yourself
and family are enjoying good health
and with my kind remembrances to

Extracts from a letter from Commander Edward T. Nichols to Rear Admiral Hiram Paulding. Nichols describes operations and conditions on the James River.

Men of U.S.S. Mendota, *the ship from which Nichols wrote Paulding. The gun shown on deck is a 100-pounder Parrott.*

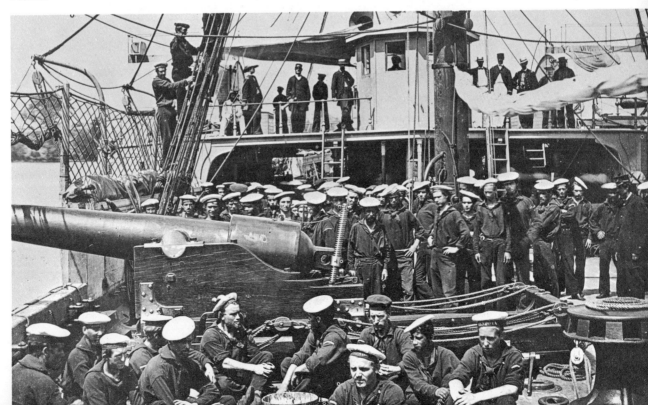

In response to the increasing number of Confederate hit-and-run attacks upon river shipping on the western waters, Major General Canby wrote to Rear Admiral Porter offering the cooperation of land forces: "I have ordered reserves of troops and of water transportation to be held in readiness at different points on the Mississippi, for the purpose of operating against any rebel force that may attempt to interrupt the navigation of the river. If you will direct naval commanders to give early notice of any movements of this kind to the commanders of the military districts, a sufficient military force can be sent at once to cooperate with the gunboats in destroying or driving off the rebels."

U.S.S. *Coeur de Lion*, Acting Master William G. Morris, seized schooner *Malinda* in the Potomac River for violating the blockade.

4   The success of C.S.S. *Tacony* against shipping off the New England coast the previous year (see 20–27 June 1863) prompted a committee in Gloucester, Massachusetts, to address a request to Secretary Welles: "In behalf of the citizens and businessmen of this town interested in the fishing business, to ask your attention to the necessity of some protection for our fishing fleet the coming season. . . . it is necessary that a steamer, properly armed, should be detailed for the special service of cruising in the Gulf of St. Lawrence until the close of the fishing season." Welles ordered U.S.S. *Ticonderoga*, Captain Charles Steedman, on this duty.

U.S.S. *Fort Jackson*, Captain Sands, captured blockade running steamer *Thistle* at sea east of Charleston. Her cargo, except for a cotton press, was thrown overboard during the six hour chase.

5   U.S.S. *Keystone State*, Commander Crosby, seized blockade running British steamer *Siren* off Beaufort harbor, North Carolina, with cargo including hoop iron and liquor.

6   Lieutenant Commander Owen, U.S.S. *Louisville*, covered the embarkation of 8,000 Union troops under General A. J. Smith on transports near Sunnyside, Arkansas, on the Mississippi River. Under Owen's charge, the transports had landed the Federal force on 4 June, and the soldiers had engaged Confederate units near Bayou Macon, Louisiana, forcing the Southerners into the interior. Owen noted in his report to Rear Admiral Porter: "The object that brought the enemy here in the first place doubtless still remains, and I may expect him any time after the departure of General Smith. Unless Marmaduke's forces, with his artillery, are driven away or destroyed, they will very much annoy navigation between Cypress Bend and Sunnyside."

U.S.S. *Metacomet*, Lieutenant Commander Jouett, captured blockade running steamer *Donegal* off Mobile with large cargo of munitions.

7   Confederate transport steamer *Etiwan* grounded off Fort Johnson and was sunk by Union batteries on Morris Island, Charleston harbor.

Suspecting that Confederates were using cotton to erect breastworks on the banks of the Suwannee River, Florida, boat expedition commanded by Acting Ensign Louis R. Chester, composed of men from U.S.S. *Clyde* and *Sagamore*, proceeded upriver and captured over 100 bales of cotton in the vicinity of Clay Landing.

8   Lieutenant Commander Ramsay, U.S.S. *Chillicothe*, led an expedition up the Atchafalaya River, Louisiana, accompanied by U.S.S. *Neosho*, Acting Lieutenant Howard, and U.S.S. *Fort Hindman*, Acting Lieutenant Pearce, to silence a Confederate battery above Simmesport. The Union gunboats, after a short engagement, forced the Southerners to abandon their position and a landing party captured the guns.

9   Illustrative of the vast difference in capabilities of the two navies were the reactions North and South during the aftermath of the capture of U.S.S. *Water Witch* on 6 June. The Northern fleet was concerned that she might escape to sea and attack Union coastal positions. "We must try to block the *Water Witch*," Rear Admiral Dahlgren wrote, anticipating an offensive effort such as

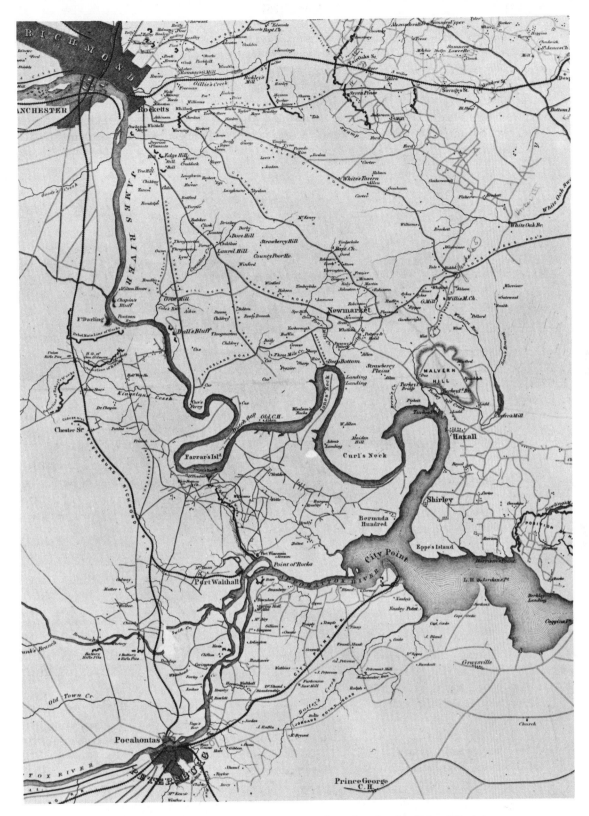

Map showing the James River area from Richmond to Coggins Point, Virginia.

IV–71

he would make in similar circumstances. The South, however, hoping to conserve this unexpected gain in strength by the capture, had no intention of risking the gunboat in such an adventure. Rather, every effort was made to bring her to Savannah as additional defense for the city. Flag Officer William W. Hunter, CSN, this date ordered Lieutenant William W. Carnes, CSN, commanding *Water Witch:* "Keep powder enough to blow her up—say 100 pounds—in the event the enemy may be enabled to recapture her." The North, with free access to the sea and with an abundance of material and great facilities available, could remain on the offensive; the South, in desperate need of ships and supplies, was committed to the defensive.

Secretary Welles decided "to retire the Marine officers who are past the legal age, and to bring in Zeilin as Commandant of the Corps." Retirement of over-age naval and marine officers was one of the difficult administrative problems of the war.

The stringent material limitations with which the Confederate Navy had to operate greatly restricted its capabilities and prevented its taking offensive action. Menaced by the advance of Major General Butler's troops along the James River below Drewry's Bluff and by the Union squadron at Trent's Reach, Flag Officer Mitchell, commanding the Confederate James River Squadron, sought to attack "without delay . . . the enemy in Trent's Reach." This date, the leading officers of his squadron advised against such an assault "under existing circumstances." They wrote Mitchell that the Union squadron was "a force equal to, if not superior to our own", that it was better supported ashore, that the Southern ships were not manueverable enough for efficient use in the narrow confines of the Reach, and that obstructions would additionally hamper their movements. Thus, they were opposed to risking the "whole force" of Southern naval strength in an attack and suggested instead the more defensive but potentially less costly alternative of sending fire rafts and floating torpedoes downriver against the Union squadron.

U.S.S. *Proteus,* Commander Robert W. Shufeldt, captured blockade running British schooner *R.S. Hood* at sea north of Little Bahama Bank.

U.S.S. *New Berne,* Acting Lieutenant Thomas A. Harris, chased blockade running steamer *Pevensey* aground near Beaufort, North Carolina, with cargo including arms, lead, bacon, and clothing. She blew up shortly thereafter.

U.S.S. *Rosalie,* Acting Master Peter F. Coffin, captured steamer *Emma* at Marco Pass, Florida, with cargo of blacksmith's coal.

10 U.S.S *Elk,* Acting Lieutenant Nicholas Kirby, captured blockade running sloop *Yankee Doodle* at the middle entrance of the Pearl River, Mississippi Sound, with cargo of cotton.

U.S.S. *Union,* Acting Lieutenant Edward Conroy, took sloop *Caroline* attempting to run the blockade at Jupiter Inlet, Florida.

11 C.S.S. *Alabama,* Captain Semmes, badly in need of repairs, arrived at Cherbourg, France. Lieutenant Arthur Sinclair, CSN, an officer on board the Confederate raider, later recorded his impressions upon entering this, her last port: "We have cruised from the day of commission, August 24, 1862, to June 11, 1864, and during this time have visited two-thirds of the globe, experiencing all vicissitudes of climate and hardships attending constant cruising. We have had from first to last two hundred and thirteen officers and men on our payroll, and have lost *not one* by disease, and but one by accidental death." The Confederate Commissioner in France, John Slidell, assured Semmes that he anticipated no difficulty in obtaining French permission for *Alabama* to use the docking facilities. William L. Dayton, U.S. Minister to France, immediately protested the use of the French port by a vessel with a character "so obnoxious and so notorious". Intelligence of the material condition and strength of *Alabama* was relayed by the American Vice-Consul at Cherbourg to Captain Winslow of U.S.S. *Kearsarge* at Flushing.

Two officers, Acting Master James R. Wheeler and Paymaster J. Adams Smith, on board U.S.S. Kearsarge.

Captain Raphael Semmes on board C.S.S. Alabama.

12 U.S.S. *Flag*, Commander James C. Williamson, captured blockade running sloop *Cyclops* shortly after she ran out of Charleston with cargo of cotton.

U.S.S. *Lavender*, Acting Master John H. Gleason, struck a shoal off North Carolina in a severe squall. The 175-ton wooden steamer was destroyed and nine crewmen lost before the survivors were rescued on 15 June by Army steamer *John Farron*.

13 U.S.S. *Kearsarge*, Captain Winslow, sailed from Dover, England, to blockade C.S.S. *Alabama* at Cherbourg.

14 U.S.S. *Kearsarge*, Captain Winslow, arrived off Cherbourg, France. The ship log recorded: "Found the rebel privateer *Alabama* lying at anchor in the roads." *Kearsarge* took up the blockade in international waters off the harbor entrance. Captain Semmes stated: ". . . My intention is to fight the *Kearsarge* as soon as I can make the necessary arrangements. I hope they will not detain me more than until tomorrow evening, or after the morrow morning at furthest. I beg she will not depart before I am ready to go out." With the famous Confederate raider at bay, *Kearsarge* had no intention of departing—the stage was set for the famous duel. As a poet on board *Alabama* wrote:

> "We're homeward, we're homeward bound,
> And soon shall stand on English ground.
> But ere that English land we see,
> We first must fight the *Kearsargee*."

U.S.S. *Courier*, Acting Master Samuel C. Gray, ran aground and was wrecked on Abaco Island, Bahamas; the sailing ship's crew and stores were saved.

15 Confederate artillery opened fire in the early morning hours on wooden side-wheeler U.S.S. *General Bragg*, Acting Lieutenant Dominy, lying off Como Landing, Louisiana. The return fire from *General Bragg* forced the Southerners to move to Ratliff's Landing where they fired on small paddle-wheel steamer U.S.S. *Naiad*, Acting Master Henry T. Keene. U.S.S. *Winnebago*, a double-turreted river monitor, alerted by the sound of gunfire, soon hove into sight, and the combined firepower of the three ships temporarily silenced the field battery. Next day, *General Bragg* was again taken under fire by Confederate guns on the river bank and another spirited engagement ensued, during which a shot disabled the ship's engine.

Confederate transport *J. R. Williams*, carrying supplies up the Arkansas River, Oklahoma, from Fort Smith to Fort Gibson, was taken under fire by Union artillery. The steamer was run aground and abandoned by her crew, and Federal forces subsequently destroyed her.

Lieutenant Bache, commanding U.S.S. *Lexington*, and a boat crew from U.S.S. *Tyler*, captured three steamers off Beulah Landing, Mississippi. Reports had reached Bache that steamers *Mattie*, *M. Walt*, and *Hill*, were "in communication with rebel soldiers, openly receiving them on the boats, and trading with them. . . ."

16 Captain Semmes, C.S.S. *Alabama*, wrote Flag Officer Barron in Paris: "The position of *Alabama* here has been somewhat changed since I wrote you. The enemy's steamer, the *Kearsarge*, having appeared off this port, and being but very little heavier, if any in her armament than myself, I have deemed it my duty to go out and engage her. I have therefore withdrawn for the present my application to go into dock, and am engaged in coaling ship." Semmes noted in his journal: "The enemy's ship still standing off and on the harbor."

16 Commander Catesby ap R. Jones, commandant of the Confederate Naval Gun Foundry and Ordnance Works at Selma, Alabama, wrote Major General Dabney H. Maury at Mobile that the submersible torpedo boat *Saint Patrick*, built by John P. Halligan, would be launched "in a few days." He added: "It combines a number of ingenious contrivances, which, if experiments show

that they will answer the purposes expected, will render the boat very formidable. It is to be propelled by steam (the engine is very compact), though under water by hand. There are also arrangements for raising and descending at will, for attaching the torpedo to the bottom of vessels, etc. Its first field of operation will be off Mobile Bay, and I hope you may soon have evidence of its success." Although the South hoped to take *Saint Patrick* against the blockading forces off Mobile as the submarine *H. L. Hunley* had operated earlier in the year off Charleston, delay followed delay in getting her to sea and it was not until January 1865 that she went into action.

A minor joint expedition under Acting Lieutenant George W. Graves, commander of U.S.S. *Lockwood*, departed New Bern, North Carolina. Graves with a detachment of sailors from U.S.S. *Louisiana* and a dozen soldiers, embarked on Army transport *Ella May*. Small sidewheeler U.S.S. *Ceres* was in company. Near the mouth of Pamlico River schooners *Iowa*, *Mary Emma*, and *Jenny Lind* were captured and two others destroyed. With U.S.S. *Valley City* joining the expedition, Graves scoured the Pungo River area for five more days before returning to New Bern, where he arrived early on 23 June.

16–17 U.S.S. *Commodore Perry*, Acting Lieutenant A. P. Foster, shelled Fort Clifton, Virginia, at the request of Major General Butler. Bombardment by the ship's heavy guns was almost a daily part of continuing naval support of Army operations along the James River.

17 C.S.S. *Florida*, Lieutenant Morris, at 30° N, 62°40' W, captured and burned brig *W. C. Clarke* bound from Machias, Maine, to Matanzas with cargo of lumber.

19 "The day being Sunday and the weather fine, a large concourse of people—many having come all the way from Paris—collected on the heights above the town [Cherbourg], in the upper stories of such of the houses as commanded a view of the sea, and on the walls and fortifications of the harbor. Several French luggers employed as pilot-boats went out, and also an English steam-yacht, called the *Deerhound*. Everything being in readiness between nine and ten o'clock, we got underway, and proceeded to sea, through the western entrance of the harbor; the *Couronne* [French ironclad] following us. As we emerged from behind the mole, we discovered the *Kearsarge* at a distance of between six and seven miles from the land. She had been apprised or our intention of coming out that morning, and was awaiting us." Thus Captain Raphael Semmes drew the scene as the historic *Kearsarge-Alabama* battle unfolded.

Alabama mounted 8 guns to *Kearsarge*'s 7. Yet, Captain Winslow of *Kearsarge* enjoyed a superiority in weight of broadside including two heavy XI-inch Dahlgren guns while Semmes had but one heavy gun, an VIII-inch. Perhaps his greatest advantage was superior ammunition, since *Alabama*'s had deteriorated during her long cruise. Furthermore, Winslow had protected the sides of his ship and the vulnerable machinery by hanging heavy chains over the sides from topside to below the waterline. *Kearsarge*'s complement numbered 163; *Alabama*'s, 149.

The antagonists closed to about one and a half miles, when Semmes opened the action with a starboard broadside. Within minutes the firing became fierce from both ships as they fought starboard to starboard on a circular course. Lieutenant Sinclair, CSN, wrote: "Semmes would have chosen to bring about yard-arm quarters, fouling, and boarding, relying upon the superior physique of his crew to overbalance the superiority of numbers; but this was frustrated." Shot and shell from the heavier guns of *Kearsarge* crashed into *Alabama*'s hull, while the Union sloop of war, her sides protected by the chain armor, suffered only minor damage. One shell from *Alabama* lodged in the *Kearsarge*'s sternpost but failed to explode. "If it had exploded," wrote John M. McKenzie, who was only 16 years old at the time of the battle, "the *Kearsarge* would have gone to the bottom instead of the *Alabama*. But our ammunition was old and had lost its strength." Southern casualties were heavy as both sides fought valiantly. "After the lapse of about one hour and ten minutes," Semmes reported, "our ship was ascertained to be in a sinking condition, the enemy's shells having exploded in our side, and between decks, opening large apertures through which the water rushed with great rapidity. For some few minutes I had

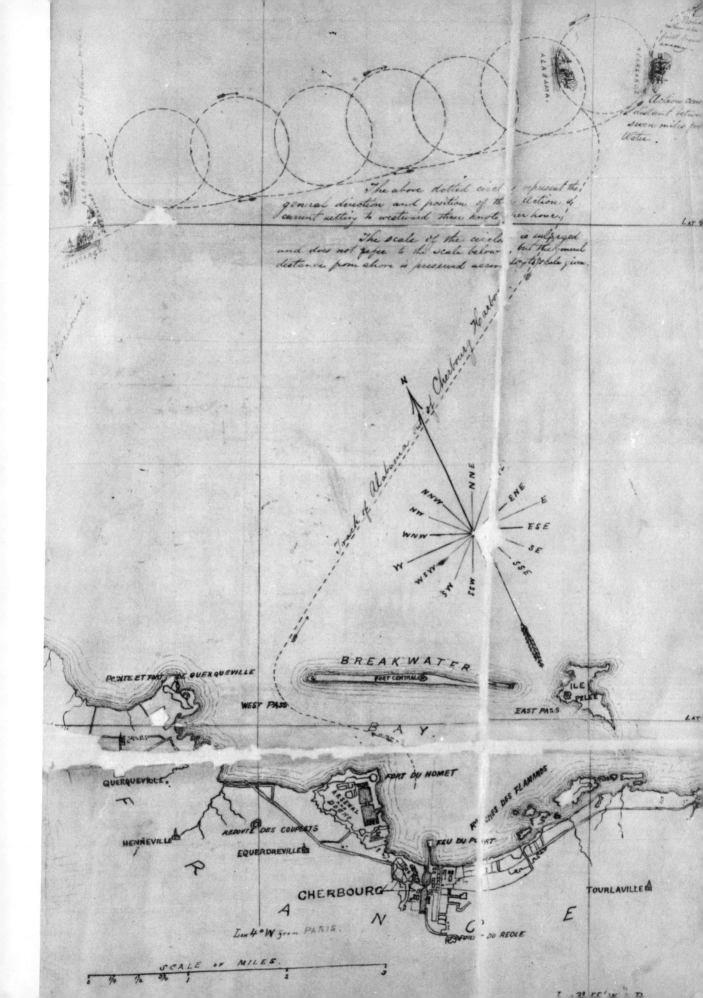

The above dotted circles represent the
general direction and position of the Action &
current setting to westward three knots per hour.

The scale of the circles is enlarged
and does not refer to the scale below, but their actual
distance from shore is preserved according to scale given.

Track of Alabama out of Cherbourg Harbor

N

NNW
NW
WNW
W
WSW
SW
SSW
SSE
SE
ESE
E
ENE
NNE

BREAKWATER
FORT CENTRAL

POINTE ET FORT DE QUERQUEVILLE

WEST PASS

ILE
PELEE

EAST PASS

BAY

QUERQUEVILLE

FORT DU HOMET

ARSENAL

ROCHES DES FLAMANDS

REDOUTE DES COUPERTS

HENNEVILLE

EQUERDREVILLE

FEU DU PORT

R

CHERBOURG

A

N

C

E

TOURLAVILLE

Lon 4° W from PARIS.

FORT DU REOLE

SCALE OF MILES.

(Left) Reproduction of the original chart submitted by Captain Winslow showing the tracks of U.S.S. Kearsarge and C.S.S. Alabama during their engagement. (Above) Two views of the spirited, broadside-to-broadside battle which resulted in the destruction of the South's most storied commerce raider.

hopes of being able to reach the French coast, for which purpose I gave the ship all steam, and set such of the fore and aft sails as were available. The ship filled so rapidly, however, that before we had made much progress, the fires were extinguished in the furnaces, and we were evidently on the point of sinking. I now hauled down my colors to prevent the further destruction of life, and dispatched a boat to inform the enemy of our condition."

Alabama settled stern first and her bow raised high in the air as the waters of the English Channel closed over her. Boats from *Kearsarge* and French boats rescued the survivors. The English yacht *Deerhound*, owned by Mr. John Lancaster, picked up Captain Semmes with 13 of his officers and 27 crew members and carried them to Southampton.

The spectacular career of the Confederacy's most famous raider was closed. Before her last battle Semmes reminded his men: "You have destroyed, and driven for protection under neutral flags, one-half of the enemy's commerce, which, at the beginning of the war, covered every sea." *Alabama* had captured and burned at sea 55 Union merchantmen valued at over four and one-half million dollars, and had bonded 10 others to the value of 562 thousand dollars. Another prize, *Conrad*, was commissioned C.S.S. *Tuscaloosa*, and herself struck at Northern shipping. Flag Officer Barron lamented: "It is true that we have lost our ship; the ubiquitous gallant *Alabama* is no more, but we have lost no honor."

For Winslow and *Kearsarge* the victory was well deserved and rewarding. Throughout the North news of *Alabama*'s end was greeted with jubilation and relief. Secretary Welles wrote the Captain: "I congratulate you for your good fortune in meeting the *Alabama*, which had so long avoided the fastest ships of the service . . . for the ability displayed in the contest you have the thanks of the Department. . . . The battle was so brief, the victory so decisive, and the comparative results so striking that the country will be reminded of the brilliant actions of our infant Navy, which have been repeated and illustrated in this engagement . . . Our countrymen have reason to be satisfied that in this, as in every naval action of this unhappy war, neither the ships, the guns, nor the crews have deteriorated, but that they maintain the ability and continue the renown which have ever adorned our naval annals." Winslow received a vote of thanks from Congress, and was promoted to Commodore with his commission dated 19 June 1864, his victory day.

20   Side-wheelers U.S.S. *Morse*, Lieutenant Commander Babcock, and U.S.S. *Cactus*, Acting Master Newell Graham, dislodged Confederate batteries which had opened fire on Army supply wagon trains near White House, Virginia. Rear Admiral Lee reported: "Deserters afterwards reported that a force estimated at 10,000 of Wade Hampton's and Fitzhugh Lee's cavalry intended attacking our trains, but were deterred from the attempt by the fire of the gunboats." For three weeks Babcock had supported the Army at White House. The Admiral noted: "I should not fail to call attention to the hearty, efficient, and successful service which Lieutenant Commander Babcock has rendered to the Army in opening and protecting its communications and in repelling the assaults of the enemy." Next day, U.S.S. *Shokokon*, Acting Master William B. Sheldon, similarly dispersed an attack on Union transport *Eliza Hancox* at Cumberland Point, Virginia.

Secretary Mallory wrote Flag Officer Barron in Paris: "I am surprised at the expression of your opinion that a battery for a certain vessel can not be purchased in England, because her laws permit the exportation of guns and ordnance stores daily, and no system of espionage, it would seem, could prevent their shipment for one port and their being landed at another, or placed at another on board the ship awaiting them. Could they not be shipped for any port in the United States, in the Mediterranean, China, Brazil, or Austria, and carried to a given rendezvous? They will involve the charter of a steamer, or other vessel, and be thereby expensive; but such expense is not to be compared for a moment with the risks of her attempting, unarmed, to reach the Confederacy, watched as she is." The procedure suggested by Mallory had been used successfully by the Confederacy before, notably in the case of C.S.S. *Alabama*.

Officers of U.S.S. Kearsarge.   Captain John A. Winslow is third from left.

Photo of the shot from C.S.S. Alabama which was embedded in Kearsarge's sternpost but failed to explode. This section was presented to President Lincoln and is now on display at the Naval Historical Display Center in Washington, D.C.   (The wire mesh seen in the photograph supports the structure of the sternpost.)

U.S.S. "Benton"
Off Natchez June 20" 1864.

Sir,

Enclosed I have the honor to forward a copy of the key to cypher code used by the Rebel General Kirby Smith's command. It was brought in by a Major who deserted and gave himself up.

General Canby has a copy and I will send one to Captains Ramsay and Foster.

Very Respectfully
Your Obd: Servt:
Jos A. Greer
Lieut: Comdr

Comdg "Benton" and 5" Dist: Miss River

Rear Admiral
David D Porter,
Comdg Miss: Squadron.

i m p r s o w o f i a a t i r u a l y
1 2 3 4 5 6 7 8 9 10 11 12 13 14 15 16 17 18 19 20

a b c d e f g h i j k l m n o p
13 21 12 22 4 10 23 24 1 25 26 14 2 8 7 3
18 17 16

q r s t u v w x y z
27 5 6 11 28 29 30 31 20 32
15

I, me, mine   o   which 7'   but φ   am, is, are c-)

you, your, yours 1'   what 8'   to III   was, were ÷

we, us, our, ours 2'   there 9'   for V̆   be. ⊙

he, him, his 3'   the ✚   from ⌿   will ﬃ

they, them, theirs 4'   a ✛   at ∪   changes ☒

who, whom, whose 5'   and ⊕   on-x had =

that 6'   not ✦   it ∧   with ↯

Millions ∪   thousands ⨍   hundreds ℗

Some letters occuring more than once in the Key word
have more than one number, either of which may be
used; it is best to use them alternately.
The characters may be used, or the words spelled —
where the word occurs often it is better to do both.
double letters, as ll— ac— ss— &c are written 14. 12. 3.
numerals as 32— 21— 1. 2. 3. are written 32. 20. 1. 2. 3.
if exceeding the largest number used in the alphabet the
number is written without any dot, simply thus 40. 80.
90. 60. Millions, thousands and hundreds are indicated by placing the number before the characters
When deemed expedient for greater security, each letter
may be numbered by the number of its fifth letter.
thus a would take the number or numbers of e.
and e the numbers of i. and i. the number of a.
x the number of v. &c— when this is done. it must be
indicated by placing (5̽) immediately before the
word in which the change begins.— and when

the original order is resumed it will be indicated
by displacing (1) immediately before the word x
x (#)

20–24 Iron screw steamer U.S.S. *Calypso*, Acting Master Frederick D. Stuart, and wooden side wheeler U.S.S. *Nansemond*, Acting Ensign James H. Porter, transported and supported an Army expedition in the vicinity of New River, North Carolina. The object was to cut the Wilmington and Weldon Railroad, but Confederates had learned of the attempt and, taking up defensive positions in strength, compelled the Union troops to withdraw under cover of the ships' guns.

21 Rear Admiral Farragut viewed the forthcoming operation at Mobile Bay both as an event of tactical and strategic importance and as an encounter which would pit the new against the old in naval warfare. Reflecting on the relative strengths of his own and Admiral Buchanan's fleet at Mobile, he wrote: "This question has to be settled, iron *versus* wood; and there never was a better chance to settle the question of the sea-going qualities of iron-clad ships."

A joint Confederate Army-Navy long-range bombardment opened on the Union squadron in the James River at Trent's and Varina Reaches. The Confederate ships, commanded by Flag Officer Mitchell in the ironclad flagship *Virginia II*, included: ironclad ram C.S.S. *Fredericksburg*, Commander Rootes; 166-ton gunboats *Hampton*, Lieutenant John S. Maury, *Nansemond*, Lieutenant Charles W. Hayes, and *Drewry*, Lieutenant William H. Hall; small steamer *Roanoke*, Lieutenant Mortimer M. Beton, and 85-ton tug *Beaufort*, Lieutenant Joseph Gardner. Ironclad ram C.S.S. *Richmond*, Lieutenant W. H. Parker, initially intended to join in the bombardment, suffered a casualty getting underway and had to be towed upriver to a position near the obstructions below Richmond. An engine failure in *Virginia II* could not be repaired until afternoon, when it was too late to move farther downstream to engage at more effective range. The Union gunboats and monitors concentrated their fire on the Army shore batteries during the exchange; neither fleet suffered serious damage.

22 U.S.S. *Lexington*, Acting Ensign Henry Booby, withstood a surprise Confederate strike on White River Station, Arkansas, and forced the attacking Confederate troops to withdraw.

23 U.S.S. *Tecumseh*, Commander Tunis A. M. Craven, was ordered to proceed to sea "as soon as practicable" by Rear Admiral Lee. The monitor, departing the James River where she had been on duty since April, was to deploy under secret orders that were not to be opened until "you discharge your pilot." Unknowingly, *Tecumseh* was beginning her last operation.

23–24 Lieutenant Cushing, with Acting Ensign J. E. Jones, Acting Master's Mate Howorth and fifteen men, all from U.S.S. *Monticello*, reconnoitered up Cape Fear River to within 3 miles of Wilmington, North Carolina. They rowed past the batteries guarding the western bar on the night of the 23rd, and despite three narrow escapes pulled safely ashore below Wilmington as day dawned on the 24th. The expedition had begun as an attempt to gain information about C.S.S. *Raleigh*, which Cushing was unaware had been wrecked after the engagement on 6 May. He learned that the ram had been "indeed, destroyed, and nothing now remains of her above water."

Cushing also gained much other valuable information. C.S.S. *Yadkin*, 300-ton flagship of Flag Officer Lynch, "mounted only two guns, did not seem to have many men." Ironclad sloop C.S.S. *North Carolina* was at anchor off Wilmington; she "would not stand long against a monitor." His report continued: "Nine steamers passed in all, three of them being fine, large blockade runners." The scouting detachment captured a fishing party and a mail courier, gaining valuable intelligence on river obstructions and fortifications. That night, the expedition returned to the blockading fleet, after being detected and hotly pursued in the harbor. Only Cushing's ingenuity enabled the Union sailors to throw the Confederates off the track and cross the bar to safety. As late as the 28th, Confederates were still searching the harbor area for the daring raiders.

Cushing, who received a letter of commendation for his action from Secretary Welles, called special attention to his officers, Jones and Howorth ("whom I select because of their uniform enterprise and bravery"), and singled out David Warren, coxwain, William Wright, yeoman, and John Sullivan, seaman, who were awarded the Medal of Honor for their part in the expedition. Rear Admiral Porter later wrote: "There was not a more daring adventure than this in the whole course of the war. There were ninety-nine chances in a hundred that Cushing and his party would be killed or captured, but throughout all his daring scheme there seemed to be a method, and, though criticised as rash and ill-judged, Cushing returned unscathed from his frequent expeditions, with much important information. In this instance it was a great source of satisfaction to the blockading vessels to learn that the 'Raleigh' was destroyed, and that the other iron-clad ram was not considered fit to cross the bar."

24 U.S.S. *Queen City*, Acting Master Michael Hickey, lying at anchor off Clarendon, Arkansas, on the White River, was attacked and destroyed in the early morning hours by two regiments of Confederate cavalry supported by artillery. The 210-ton wooden paddle-wheeler, taken by surprise, was disabled immediately, and Hickey surrendered her. Lieutenant Bache, U.S.S. *Tyler*, attempted to retake the ship, but when within a few miles of the location "heard two successive reports, which proved subsequently to have been the unfortunate *Queen City* blowing up. [Confederate General] Shelby, hearing us coming, had destroyed her." Bache proceeded with wooden steamers *Tyler*, U.S.S. *Fawn*, Acting Master John R. Grace, and U.S.S. *Naumkeag*, Acting Master John Rogers, to Clarendon, where he engaged the Confederate battery hotly for forty-five minutes. *Naumkeag* succeeded in recapturing one howitzer and several crewmen from *Queen City* as the Confederates fell back from the riverbank.

26 U.S.S. *Norfolk Packet*, Acting Ensign George W. Wood, captured sloop *Sarah Mary* off Mosquito Inlet, Florida, with cargo of cotton.

27 U.S.S. *Proteus*, Commander Robert W. Shufeldt, seized British blockade running steamer *Jupiter* northwest of Man-of-War Cay, Bahamas. Her cargo had been thrown overboard.

U.S.S. *Nipsic*, Lieutenant Commander Alexander F. Crosman, captured sloop *Julia* off Sapelo Sound, Georgia, with cargo of salt.

29-30 Converted ferryboat U.S.S. *Hunchback*, Lieutenant Joseph P. Fyffe, supported by single turretted monitor U.S.S. *Saugus*, Commander Colhoun, bombarded Confederate batteries at Deep Bottom on the James River and caused their eventual removal. Rear Admiral Lee reported: "The importance of holding our position at Deep Bottom is obvious. Without doing so our communications are cut there, and our wooden vessels can not remain above that point, and the monitors would be alone and exposed to the enemy's light torpedo craft from above and out of Four Mile Creek. The enemy could then plant torpedoes there to prevent the monitors passing by for supplies."

30 Immediately upon returning to command of the West Gulf Blockading Squadron, Rear Admiral Farragut moved to obtain monitors for the inevitable engagement with C.S.S. *Tennessee* in Mobile Bay. Earlier in June Secretary Welles had written to Rear Admiral Porter of the matter: "It is of the greatest importance that some of the new ironclads building on the Mississippi should be sent without fail to Rear Admiral Farragut. Are not some of them ready? If not, can you not hurry them forward?" Porter responded that light-draft monitors U.S.S. *Winnebago* and *Chickasaw* were completed, and this date issued orders for the two vessels, which were to play an important part in the Battle of Mobile Bay, to report to Farragut at New Orleans.

Acting Ensign Edward H. Watkeys, commanding a launch from U.S.S. *Roebuck*, captured sloop *Last Resort* off Indian River Inlet, Florida, with cargo of cotton.

U.S.S. *Glasgow*, Acting Master N. Mayo Dyer, forced blockade running steamer *Ivanhoe* to run aground near Fort Morgan at Mobile Bay. Because the steamer was protected by the fort's guns, Rear Admiral Farragut attempted at first to destroy her by long-range fire from U.S.S. *Metacomet* and *Monongahela*. When this proved unsuccessful, Farragut authorized his Flag Lieutenant,

Union guard boats on picket duty off Mobile kept a look out for blockade runners, sometimes helped to destroy them, and often gained intelligence as to Confederate operations.

J. Crittenden Watson, to lead a boat expedition to burn *Ivanhoe*. Under the cover of darkness and the ready guns on board U.S.S. *Metacomet* and *Kennebec*, Watson led four boats directly to the grounded steamer and fired her in two places shortly after midnight 6 July. Farragut wrote: "The admiral commanding has much pleasure in announcing to the fleet, what was anxiously looked for last night by hundreds, the destruction of the blockade runner ashore under the rebel batteries by an expedition of boats. . . . the entire conduct of the expedition was marked by a promptness and energy which shows what may be expected of such officers and men on similar occasions."

JULY

1   Secretary Mallory wrote President Davis that due to a shortage of mechanics the ordnance works at Selma, Alabama, could not "make more than one gun in a week, whereas with a proper number of mechanics it could manufacture with carriages and equipments complete, three in a week, and in a few months one every day. . . ." Shortage of skilled craftsmen was a handicap the South could never overcome. The manpower and material shortages at Selma specifically crippled the progress of the ironclad squadron Admiral Buchanan was desperately trying to develop in Mobile Bay. Only ram *Tennessee* was ready when the critical moment arrived on 5 August.

C.S.S. *Florida*, Lieutenant Morris, captured and burned bark *Harriet Stevens* at sea southwest of Bermuda with cargo of lumber, cement, and gum opium; Morris sent the opium in a blockade runner for hospital use.

U.S.S. *Merrimac*, Acting Lieutenant W. Budd, captured blockade running sloop *Henrietta* at sea west of Tampa, Florida, with cargo of cotton.

2   U.S.S. *Keystone State*, Commander Crosby, captured blockade running British steamer *Rouen* at sea off Wilmington. The steamer had thrown her cargo of cotton overboard during the four hour chase, and was not brought to until *Keystone* had fired 22 shots at her, "all of them falling quite near and some directly over her."

2-9 Single-turreted monitors U.S.S. *Lehigh*, Lieutenant Commander A. A. Semmes, U.S.S. *Montauk*, Lieutenant Commander A. W. Johnson, and other ships of the South Atlantic Blockading Squadron supported Army troops in a demonstration up the Stono River, South Carolina. Hearing that Confederate forces were about to move against the blockaders off Charleston, Rear Admiral Dahlgren and Major General Foster planned a diversionary expedition up the Stono River, intending to cut the important Charleston-Savannah railroad. Union monitors and gunboats shelled Confederate works on both sides of the river with telling effect in support of movements ashore. Brigadier General Schimmelfennig, troop commander, reported to Dahlgren on 6 July: "I take pleasure in informing you of the excellent practice by your gunboats and monitors on Stono River yesterday. They drove the enemy out of his rifle pits and prevented him from erecting an earthwork which he had commenced. As I shall probably have to occupy that line again before long, this fire of your monitors will undoubtedly save many lives on our side, for which I desire to express to them my thanks." Dahlgren's vessels later effectively covered the Army withdrawal from Stono River.

4 U.S.S. *Hastings*, Acting Lieutenant J. S. Watson, engaged Confederate sharpshooters on the White River above St. Charles, Arkansas. Lieutenant Commander Phelps, embarked in the 300-ton, 8-gun *Hastings*, commented in his report to Rear Admiral Porter: "I had been at a loss to know how we should celebrate the Fourth, being underway and having so much of a convoy in charge, but this attack occurring about noon furnished the opportunity of at once punishing the enemy and celebrating the day by firing cannon." It had been a year before, on 4 July 1863, that Union forces had commemorated Independence Day with decisive victories at Gettysburg and Vicksburg, the latter pivoting on the Union Navy. With control of the Western waters assured, the North was certain of victory.

U.S.S. *Magnolia*, Acting Lieutenant William S. Cheesman, captured three boats at sea several hundred miles east of Florida with small cargo of cotton and turpentine. The intrepid Southern boatsmen had been at sea for some 40 days attempting to reach Nassau. The attempt to run the blockade in small boats, powered by sail and oars, was an extreme measure even for the South's struggling economy.

6 Illustrating the great paucity of Confederate naval power and the strategic importance of C.S.S *Albemarle* to the defense of North Carolina, Brigadier General Lawrence S. Baker, CSA, wrote to Commander Maffitt, captain of the ironclad, cautioning him against risking his vessel: "I beg leave to remind you of the importance to the Confederacy of the country opened to us by the taking of Plymouth, to suggest that its recapture now engages the serious attention of the U.S. Government, and that the loss of the gunboat which you command would be irreparable and productive of ruin to the interests of the government, particularly in this State and district, and indeed would be a heavy blow to the whole country. . . . I have no doubt that in event of an attack by you the most desperate efforts will be made to destroy your boat, and thus open the approach to Plymouth and Washington [North Carolina]." While criticism was leveled at the Confederate Navy Department for not bringing *Albemarle* into action, her presence at Plymouth constituted a powerful threat to Union control of the North Carolina sounds, demanded a vigilant patrol by many Northern ships, and prevented recapture of the area by Union troops. Few ships better illustrate the important relationship between a nation's land and sea-based power.

Captain Cicero Price, U.S.S. *Jamestown*, wrote Secretary Welles from Yokohama, Japan, regarding the celebration of Independence Day in that far-off port: "The Fourth was very handsomely celebrated here, all the foreign ships of war participating by dressing their ships, as well as saluting. It was very marked on the part of the British." With the tide of war ashore as well as afloat having swung irrevocably in favor of the Union, British intervention on behalf of the South could no longer be considered a possibility.

7–12 Small schooners U.S.S. *Ariel*, Acting Master Russell, *Sea Bird*, Acting Ensign Ezra L. Robbins, and *Stonewall*, Acting Master Henry B. Carter, and 29-ton sloop *Rosalie*, Acting Master Coffin, transported Union troops on a raid on Brookville, Florida. After disembarking the soldiers, *Ariel* and *Sea Bird* proceeded to Bayport, Florida, where a landing party captured a quantity of cotton and burned the customs house. The Union troops joined the two schooners at Bayport on 11 July, and the force returned to Anclote Keys the next day.

8 U.S.S. *Fort Jackson*, Captain Sands, captured blockade running British steamer *Boston* at sea off the South Carolina coast with cargo of copperas, salt, and soap.

U.S.S. *Kanawha*, Lieutenant Commander Bushrod B. Taylor, forced blockade running steamer *Matagorda* aground near Galveston. *Kanawha*, joined by U.S.S. *Penguin* and *Aroostook*, opened fire and destroyed the steamer, which carried cargo including cotton.

C.S.S. *Florida*, Lieutenant Morris, captured whaling bark *Golconda* at sea southwest of Bermuda with 1,800 barrels of whale oil. "After taking what supplies of oil we required," Morris reported, "I burned her."

U.S.S. *Sonoma*, Lieutenant Commander Edmund O. Matthews, captured steamer *Ida* off the Stono River, South Carolina, with cargo of cotton.

U.S.S. *Azalea*, Acting Master Frederick W. Strong, and U.S.S. *Sweet Brier*, Acting Ensign J. D. Dexter, captured blockade running schooner *Pocahontas* off Charleston with cargo of cotton. Weak at sea, the South could not protect by convoy the daring merchantmen that sought to run the blockade.

9 In a confidential letter to Secretary Welles, Rear Admiral Lee disclosed the plans then being considered for an expedition to destroy the Confederate ram, C.S.S. *Albemarle*: "I concur in Captain Smith's opinion that it would be inexpedient to fight the ram with our long double-enders in that narrow river [the Roanoke]. I proposed to Lieutenant Cushing a torpedo attack, either by means of the india-rubber boat heretofore applied for, which could be transported across the swamp opposite Plymouth, or a light-draft, rifle-proof, swift steam barge, fitted with a torpedo." Cushing, who had already proved his audacity and ability on earlier expeditions into the Cape Fear River (see 29 February and 23–24 June 1864) immediately began plans for the new adventure, destined to be one of the most dramatic and dangerous of the war. He wrote Lee: "Deeming the capture or destruction of the rebel ram *Albemarle* feasible, I beg leave to state that I am acquainted with the waters held by her, and am willing to undertake the task." The Admiral saw in Cushing an officer with the spirit and skill to accomplish this difficult mission, and noted in closing his letter to Welles: "He is entirely willing to make an attempt to destroy the ram, and I have great confidence in his gallantry."

Major John Tyler, CSA, Assistant Adjutant General, wrote Major General Sterling Price regarding a proposed attack on Point Lookout, Maryland, to release Confederate prisoners: "The plan is that he [Lieutenant General Jubal Early] shall seize Baltimore and hold it with his infantry while his cavalry proceeds to Point Lookout to liberate our prisoners there concentrated to the extent of nearly 30,000. In the meantime Captain [John Taylor] Wood, of the Navy, proceeds from Wilmington with 5 gunboats and 20,000 stand of arms for the same point by water. If successful in thus liberating and arming our imprisoned soldiers, Washington will be assaulted and no doubt carried. This I regard as decidedly the most brilliant idea of the war." Rumors of this daring plan reached Lieutenant Stuyvesant, U.S.S. *Minnesota*, on 18 July and he warned the Navy Department and Rear Admiral Lee that Wood was reported to have left Richmond with 800 volunteers on the 7th and 8th. While the projected expedition caused considerable excitement among the Union authorities, President Davis had already, on 10 July, advised against the attempt. Wood reported that he was ready to run the blockade out of Wilmington on 9 July, but the Confederate

President replied: "The object and destination of the expedition have somehow become so generally known that I fear your operations will meet unexpected obstacles." The idea was abandoned, but illustrated the bold and daring measures considered by the South during the last year of the war.

C.S.S. *Florida*, Lieutenant Morris, captured and burned bark *Greenland*, with cargo of coal, and schooner *Margaret Y. Davis*, in ballast, at sea off Cape Henry, Virginia.

U.S.S. *Gettysburg*, Acting Master William M. Gloin, captured blockade running steamer *Little Ada* at sea off Cape Romain with cargo of pig lead and potash after a lengthy chase.

10 C.S.S. *Florida*, Lieutenant Morris, captured and burned bark *General Berry* with cargo of hay and straw. The action took place only 35 miles from Maryland's eastern shore as Morris continued his dashing raid on Union coastal shipping. Shortly thereafter, Morris gave chase to bark *Zelinda*, which he captured in ballast. He reported: "Put an officer and prize crew on board of her, with orders to follow us, went in chase of a schooner to the eastward. Found her to be the *Howard* . . . with a cargo of fruit belonging to English merchants. Bonded the schooner for $6,000, and put all of the prisoners (sixty-two in all) on board. . . ." Morris then removed *Zelinda*'s provisions and burned her. *Florida* made yet another capture that day, the mail steamer *Electric Spark;* her passengers were transferred to a passing British ship, *Lane*. Seeking to create the impression that he had made a tender of *Electric Spark*, Morris scuttled her during the night rather than putting her to the torch. This prize had yielded a quantity of cash in addition to other important articles, including mail. Morris, recognizing that Union ships would by this time be in hot pursuit of him, turned *Florida* on an easterly course into the broad Atlantic, whose vastness provided refuge for commerce raiders.

Reflecting the widespread concern caused by the recent captures made by C.S.S. *Florida*, Lieutenant Morris, off the coast of Virginia and Maryland, Rear Admiral Lee dispatched screw steamers U.S.S. *Mount Vernon*, Lieutenant Commander Henry A. Adams, Jr., and U.S.S. *Monticello*, Lieutenant Cushing, to "cruise together, and on finding the *Florida* will make a joint attack on her and capture her." The career of *Florida*, one of the most successful raiders, was nearing an end, but the honor of capturing her was to go neither to Adams nor Cushing. Many ships went out after her, but few got even a glimpse of the wily cruiser. This date Lee also ordered out U.S.S. *Ino*, Acting Lieutenant French, with another approach in mind: "Disguise the *Ino*, her battery, officers, and crew, and play the merchantman in appearance so as to entice her [C.S.S. *Florida*] alongside, when you, being prepared, will open upon her suddenly and effectually."

U.S.S. *Monongahela*, Commander Strong, U.S.S. *Lackawanna*, Captain Marchand, U.S.S. *Galena*, Lieutenant Commander Clark H. Wells, U.S.S. *Sebago*, Lieutenant Commander William E. Fitzhugh, opened fire on steamer *Virgin*, described as "a very large" blockade runner, aground near Fort Morgan, at Mobile Bay, Alabama. Under cover of Fort Morgan's cannon, a river steamer attempted to tow *Virgin* off, but was forced to withdraw by the accurate shelling from the blockaders. The next day, however, the Confederates towed *Virgin* into Mobile Bay.

U.S.S. *Roebuck*, Acting Master William L. Martine, captured blockade running British schooner *Terrapin*, at Jupiter Inlet, Florida, with cargo of cotton and turpentine.

11 Landing party from U.S.S. *James L. Davis*, Acting Master Griswold, destroyed Confederate salt works near Tampa, Florida. The works were capable of producing some 150 bushels of salt per day. On 16 July a similar raid near Tampa was carried out in which a salt work consisting of four boilers was destroyed.

12 U.S.S. *Whitehead*, Acting Ensign George W. Barrett, and U.S.S. *Ceres*, Acting Master Foster, in company with transport steamer *Ella May*, conducted a joint expedition up the Scuppernong River to Columbia, North Carolina. *Whitehead*, a small tinclad, and *Ceres*, a 140-ton

Rear Admiral Farragut and Captain Drayton on board flagship U.S.S. Hartford.

paddle-wheeler, landed troops near Columbia, and the soldiers succeeded in destroying a bridge and a quantity of grain.

U.S.S. *Penobscot*, Lieutenant Commander Benham, captured blockade running schooner *James Williams* off Galveston with cargo including medicines, coffee, and liquor.

13 Colonel Albert J. Myer, USA, forwarded intelligence regarding the naval defenses of Mobile Bay to Rear Admiral Farragut. Myer reported: "A line of piles driven under water extends from the shoal water near Fort Gaines, across Pelican Pass Channel, and to the edge of the main ship channel. One informant describes this obstruction as five rows of piles driven closely together. The other informant does not know how many are the piles or how closely driven. . . . From the western edge of the main ship channel, where the fixed obstructions terminate, a torpedo line extends eastward across that channel to a point differently estimated as at 400 yards and as at nearly one-half mile from Fort Morgan." A "torpedo party" of seven men was reported to be in charge of the underwater weapons. These torpedoes almost turned back the Admiral's assault on Mobile Bay less than a month later.

Flag Officer Barron wrote Secretary Mallory from Paris: "In the course of this week . . . I hope to have the pleasure of reporting the *Rappahannock* at sea . . . She is strictly watched by Federal cruisers in the channel: *Kearsarge* at Dover, *Niagara* at or off Cherbourg, and *Sacramento* off Ushant. This disposition of the enemy's ships increases the risks and affords decided chances of capture; but if we be permitted to leave port with the number of officers and men on board I shall assuredly encounter all the chances and risks, knowing your anxiety and the great importance of keeping a sufficient number of vessels afloat to keep up the rates of maritime insurance in the United States, and a wholesome dread of our active and enterprising little Navy amongst their commercial marine." Despite Barron's strong efforts, however, *Rappahannock* remained in port until the war ended.

13-14 In order to protect the rear of Union Army emplacements around Annapolis, Maryland, against Confederate raiders Lieutenant Commander Braine, U.S.S. *Vicksburg*, detailed a boat expedition under the command of Acting Ensign Francis G. Osborn to destroy all means of crossing South River.

14 Acting Master George R. Durand, U.S.S. *Paul Jones*, was captured while making an attempt in Ossabaw Sound, Georgia, to destroy C.S.S. *Water Witch;* a former Union ship which had been taken in June, 1864. Durand concealing himself and his men by day and moving by night, made his way toward the prize steamer only to be discovered and captured by a Confederate patrol.

Screw steamer U.S.S. *Pequot*, Lieutenant Commander Quackenbush, and converted ferryboat U.S.S. *Commodore Morris*, Acting Master Robert G. Lee, engaged Confederate batteries in the vicinity of Malvern Hill, James River, Virginia, for four hours, sustaining no serious damage. Two days later the batteries opened on U.S.S. *Mendota*, Commander Nichols, *Pequot*, and *Commodore Morris*. *Mendota*, a double-ender, sustained minor damage and several casualties. Presence of the battery below Four Mile Creek temporarily closed the navigation of the James River.

18 Rear Admiral Farragut wrote of his plans for the attack on Mobile Bay: "I propose to go in according to programme—fourteen vessels, two and two, as at Port Hudson; low steam; flood tide in the morning with a light southwest wind; ironclads on the eastern side, to attack the *Tennessee*, and gunboats to attack rebel gunboats as soon as past the forts." It was characteristic of the Admiral's farsighted attention to detail to have battle plans drawn up and his fleet ready for action when the most favorable moment to move forward arrived.

Governor Samuel Corry of Maine wrote Secretary Welles regarding the exploits of C.S.S. *Florida*. Gravely concerned by the captures the cruiser had made recently, he asked that one or two gunboats constantly patrol the coast, and stated: "We are at war with a brave, energetic adversary, fruitful in resources, ready to strike at any exposed point, and which, with one or two piratical cruisers, besides destroying a great amount of tonnage, has driven a large share of our commerce under the protection of the flags of other nations."

Secretary Mallory wrote Commander Bulloch in Liverpool, England, that ". . . we can operate effectually against the enemy's blockading fleets with torpedo boats . . . As these boats select their own time for operating and may thus secure a smooth sea, and as they must operate at night, and avoid being seen, it is important that they should be as low in the water as may be consistent with their safety. They are expected to carry from five to seven men, coal for twenty-four hours, and four torpedoes with their shifting poles, and to go at least 10 miles an hour with all on board . . . The torpedo is usually made of copper or iron boiler plate, contains from 40 to 100 pounds of powder and is prepared with three sensitive tubes which explode on impact . . . The torpedo boats are miniature swift steamers, and they must be strongly built and as light as may be consistent with strength . . . I suppose these boats might be built and sent to us without interference by the authorities; but if not they might be built in sections and thus sent over. We are so destitute of mechanics, however, that they should be sent us complete as possible . . ."

21 U.S.S. *Prairie Bird*, Acting Master Thomas Burns, seized steamer *Union* on the Mississippi River for violation of revenue laws and giving "aid and comfort to the enemy".

22 Lieutenant Charles S. Cotton and Acting Ensign John L. Hall led a landing party from U.S.S. *Oneida* on a daring expedition that resulted in the capture of a Confederate cavalry patrol near Fort Morgan, Mobile Bay. The sailors rowed in from *Oneida* under cover of darkness, and lay in wait for a nightly Southern patrol which had been under observation for some time. Surprise was complete, and Hall marched a detachment four miles further inland to destroy the patrol's camp site. Lieutenant Cotton reported: "The results of the expedition were—captured, 1 lieutenant and 4 privates of the Seventh Alabama Cavalry, arms and ammunition; 5 horses, with their equipments complete, and all the camp equipage and stores."

23 Army transport *B. M. Runyan*, with some 500 military and civilian passengers on board, sank in the Mississippi River near Skipwith's Landing, Mississippi, after hitting a snag. U.S.S. *Prairie Bird*, Acting Master Thomas Burns, rescued 350 survivors and salvaged part of the cargo. Rescue and humanitarian operations have been a continuing naval mission throughout our history.

24 Confederate guerrillas captured and burned steamer *Kingston*, which had run aground the preceding day between Smith's Point and Windmill Point on the Virginia shore of Chesapeake Bay.

25 As Union naval forces in Albemarle Sound kept a close watch on the powerful ram C.S.S. *Albemarle*, Acting Master's Mate John Woodman with three companions made the first of his three daring reconnaissance expeditions up the Roanoke River to Plymouth, North Carolina. Reported Woodman: "The town appeared very quiet; very few persons were moving about; I could hear the blacksmiths and carpenters at work in the town near the river." The ram, he added, was "lying at the wharf near the steam sawmill." The danger posed by the Confederate ship was to be a prime object of Northern concern for several more months, and prevented the Union forces from aggressive operations in the Plymouth area.

Boats from U.S.S. *Hartford*, *Monongahela*, and *Sebago*, commanded by Rear Admiral Farragut's flag lieutenant, J. C. Watson, reconnoitered the Mobile Bay area in an attempt to discover the type and number of water mines laid by Confederates off Fort Morgan. Watson and his men located and cut loose many of the torpedoes; they were aided by the fact that a number were inoperative. This hazardous work was indispensable to the success of the Navy's coming operations against Mobile. Several similar night operations were conducted.

U.S.S. *Undine*, Acting Master John L. Bryant, struck a snag and sank in the Tennessee River near Clifton, Tennessee. Bryant immediately set to work raising his small gunboat, while at the same time placing her guns ashore to help defend the city, which was threatened by Confederate troops. On 31 July, after the arrival of pump steamer *Little Champion*, and under constant danger of attack, Bryant succeeded in raising *Undine* and returning her to action.

26-27 Pickets from U.S.S. *Shokokon*, Acting Master Sheldon, were attacked ashore by Confederate sharpshooters at Turkey Bend, in the James River. *Shokokon*, a 710-ton double-ender mounting

Union monitor in background patrols the James River. Because of monitors and gunboats the North dominated the waters below Drewry's Bluff.

5 guns, supported the embattled landing party with gunfire, and succeeded in preventing its capture. Next day, *Shokokon* engaged a Confederate battery at the same point on the River.

27 Rear Admiral Lee sent tugs *Belle*, *Martin*, and *Hoyt*, fitted as torpedo boats, to Commander Macomb, commanding Union naval forces off New Bern, North Carolina. The tugs, which were to be used against reported Confederate ironclads in that vicinity, carried spar torpedoes, described by Lee as follows: "This form of torpedo is intended to explode on impact, and to be placed on a pole or rod projecting not less than 15 feet, and if possible 20 feet, beyond the vessel using it. It contains 150 pounds of powder." Initially the Union violently rejected torpedo warfare introduced by the South, but as the war progressed the North also utilized it to advantage.

Colonel Lewis B. Parsons, USA, Assistant Quartermaster and Chief of Western River Transportation, wrote to Lieutenant Commander Phelps, Navy commander on the White River, about the unavailability of sufficient gunboats to convoy the vital supply ships on the river: "I am now in receipt of letters from three different officers, urgently enquiring if something can be done to prevent the detention of boats for convoys, in consequence of which, it is extremely difficult to send stores and supplies from Helena, Memphis, and other points. . . . I have no doubt everything is being done in your power and consistent with your means, but considering the importance of the subject and the expenditure, is it not advisable to increase the means, so that convoys, *if necessary, may be sent as boats arrive?* If this can not be done, would it not do if two or three gunboats be stationed at different and dangerous points and boats be permitted to proceed without convoys?" The Navy's efforts to keep open the essential river supply routes in the West were beset with many problems, including a scarcity of ships for convoy against constant harassment by Confederate guerrillas.

Rear Admiral Bailey wrote Secretary Welles from Key West describing the severe epidemic of yellow fever among the officers and men of his squadron: "My worst fears have been more than realized, and for more than two months the disease has held its course without abatement and is now as virulent as at any time. . . . The mortality on the island I am told has reached as high as 12 to 15 in a day. . . . The squadron is much crippled. . . ."

27–30 Boat crew commanded by Lieutenant J. C. Watson made daylight reconnaissances of the Mobile Bay channel. Watson and his men, towed into the bay by the small tug *Cowslip*, sounded the outer channel and marked the outside limits of the Confederate torpedo fields with buoys for the coming attack on the defenses of the bay.

28 Large side-wheel double-enders U.S.S. *Mendota*, Commander Nichols, and U.S.S. *Agawam*, temporarily commanded by Lieutenant George Dewey, shelled Confederate positions across Four Mile Creek, on the James River, in support of Union moves to clear the area and restore full Northern use of the river at that point.

28–29 Tinclad U.S.S. *Whitehead*, Acting Ensign Barrett, joined with Army steamers *Thomas Colyer* and *Massasoit* in an expedition up the Chowan River, North Carolina, to confiscate contraband. Steamer *Arrow* was captured at Gatesville with cargo of cotton and tobacco.

30 Landing party from U.S.S. *Potomska*, Acting Lieutenant Robert P. Swann, destroyed two large Confederate salt works near the Back River, Georgia. Returning to *Potomska*, Swann and his men were taken under fire by Confederates and a sharp battle ensued. "Our arms," Swann reported, "the Spencer rifles, saved us all from destruction, as the rapidity with which we fired caused the enemy to lie low, and their firing was after the first volley very wild. . . . We fought them three-quarters of an hour, some of the time up to our knees in mud, trying to land and capture them, and some of the time in the water with the boats for a breastwork." Finally able to regain the *Potomska*, Swann's party received a commendation from Rear Admiral Dahlgren for the bravery and skill they had demonstrated on the expedition.

In strongly refuting a recommendation that ram C.S.S. *Albemarle* be kept as a threat in being at Plymouth and not venture out to offer battle, Secretary Mallory wrote: ". . . she was not designed as a floating battery merely, and while her loss must not be lightly hazarded, the question of when to attack the enemy must be left to the judgment of the naval officer in command, deciding in view of the relation she bears to the defenses of North Carolina."

AUGUST

1–4 Landing party under Commander George M. Colvocoresses, composed of 115 officers and men, raided a meeting of civilians forming a coastal guard at McIntosh Court House, Georgia. Colvocoresses marched his men overland after coming ashore during the night of 2 August, destroyed a bridge to prevent being cut off by Confederate cavalry, and captured some 26 prisoners and 22 horses before making his way safely back to U.S.S. *Saratoga*. Rear Admiral Dahlgren, amused at the circumstances of the expedition and pleased with its results, reported to the men of his squadron: "Captain Colvocoresses having been favored with a sight of the notice in a Savannah paper, and feeling considerable interest in the object of the meeting, concluded that he would attend it also, which he did, with a number of United States citizens serving at the time on board the U.S.S. *Saratoga* as officers, seamen, and marines. . . . When the appointed time arrived, Mr. Miller [Boatswain Philip J. Miller] set fire to the bridge [outside the town] and at the signal the main body rushed out and joined the meeting. . . . Captain Colvocoresses then read to the meeting from the newspaper the order of Colonel Gaulden [CSA] for their assembling, and, regretting that the Colonel had failed to attend, he invited the meeting to accompany him, which they did, and arrived safely on board the *Saratoga*, where they meet daily under the United States flag." The Admiral later reported to Secretary Welles of the prisoners: ". . . it is hoped that under the old flag the deliberations may be of a more beneficial tendency, as the parties are now relieved of their proposed responsibility as a coast guard."

Colonel Gaulden, not to be outdone, published an explanatory letter in the Savannah *Republican* adding a challenge to the observant naval Captain: "As the Captain seems to be a reader of your paper, I take this opportunity to make my compliments to him and to say that when he calls to see me again I shall be at home, and will try and give him a more respectful reception."

2 After months of attempting to ready C.S.S. *Rappahannock* and negotiating her clearance from French authorities in Calais, Flag Officer Barron reluctantly concluded that she could not be taken to sea under the Confederate flag. This date, he received a letter from Lieutenant Charles M. Fauntleroy, commanding *Rappahannock*, informing him that while the French would now permit her put to sea, her crew could not exceed 35 men. Barron at once replied: "I agree with you in the 'absolute impossibility of navigating the ship' with so small a complement as thirty-five, including yourself and officers. You will therefore proceed to pay off and discharge your officers and crew, keeping sufficient officers and men to look after the public property, and lay up the ship until we determine upon what course we shall pursue in regard to her." Private agents acting for the Confederacy had purchased *Rappahannock* from the British in November, 1863, at Sheerness, where she was refitting. Concerned that the British, suspecting that she was to be used as a cruiser, would detain her, the Confederates ran *Rappahannock* out of port on 24 November. Her officers joined in the channel, and intended to rendezvous with C.S.S. *Georgia* off the French coast, where she would take on armament. However, in passing out of the Thames estuary her bearings burned out and she was taken across the channel to Calais for repairs. Though the South had entertained high hopes for her as a commerce raider, she was destined never to put to sea under the "Stars and Bars". Fauntleroy, disillusioned with the command which cost the South so much in time and effort, termed her "The Confederate White Elephant".

3 Rear Admiral Farragut's Fleet Captain, Percival Drayton, wrote the senior officer at Pensacola, Captain Thornton A. Jenkins, urging that the monitor *Tecumseh* be hurried to Mobile for Farragut's attack. "If you can get the *Tecumseh* out to-morrow, do so; otherwise I am pretty certain that the admiral won't wait for her. Indeed, I think a very little persuasion would have taken him in to-day, and less to-morrow. The army are to land at once, and the admiral does not want to be thought remiss." Farragut himself wrote Jenkins, adding in a tone indicative of his indomitable spirit: "I can lose no more days. I must go in day after to-morrow morning at daylight or a little after. It is a bad time, but when you do not take fortune at her offer you must take her as you can find her."

Lieutenant J. C. Watson and his boat crew made a final night expedition into the waters of Mobile Bay under the guns of Fort Morgan. Although they were constantly in danger of being discovered by the lights of the Fort, the bold sailors worked all night to deactivate and sink Confederate torpedoes in the channel preparatory to Farragut's dash into Mobile Bay.

U.S.S. *Miami*, Acting Lieutenant George W. Graves, engaged Confederate batteries at Wilcox's Landing, Virginia. Proceeding toward heavy firing, Graves had discovered batteries at Wilcox's Landing firing on Union transports. He immediately opened a brisk cannonade, and after an hour the Confederates withdrew. Next day, *Miami*, accompanied by U.S.S. *Osceola*, Commander

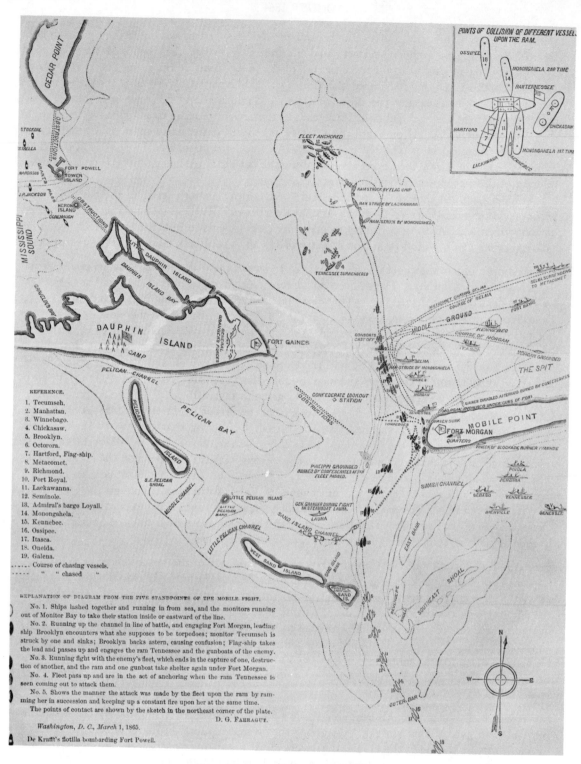

Diagram of the battle of Mobile Bay.

IV–94

Clitz, drove off batteries which were firing on another group of transports near Harrison's Landing, on the James River. Throughout the embattled South, Union gunboats kept communications and supply lines open despite the dogged determination of the Confederates to sever them.

5 Rear Admiral Farragut took his squadron of 18 ships, including four monitors, against the heavy Confederate defenses of Mobile Bay. Soon after 6 a.m., the Union ships crossed the bar and moved into the bay. The monitors *Tecumseh*, *Manhattan*, *Winnebago*, and *Chickasaw* formed a column to starboard of the wooden ships in order to take most of the fire from Fort Morgan, which they had to pass at close range. The seven smaller wooden ships were lashed to the port side of the larger wooden screw steamers, as in the passage of Port Hudson, Mississippi River.

Shortly before 7 o'clock, *Tecumseh*, Commander T. A. M. Craven, opened fire on Fort Morgan. The action quickly became general. The Confederate squadron under Admiral Buchanan, including the heavy ram *Tennessee* (6 guns) and the smaller ships *Gaines* (6 guns), *Selma* (4 guns), and *Morgan* (6 guns), moved out to engage the attackers. Craven headed *Tecumseh* straight at *Tennessee*, bent on engaging her at once. Suddenly, a terrific explosion rocked the Union monitor. She careened violently and went down in seconds, the victim of one of the much-feared torpedoes laid by the Confederates for harbor defense. Amidst the confusion below decks as men struggled to escape the sinking ship, Craven and the pilot, John Collins, arrived at the foot of the ladder leading to the main deck. The captain stepped back. "After you, pilot," he said. Collins was saved, but there was no afterwards for the heroic Craven. He and some 90 officers and men of *Tecumseh*'s crew of 114 went down with the ship. Captain Alden called them "intrepid pioneers of that death-strewed path."

Alden, in *Brooklyn*, was to *Tecumseh*'s port when the disaster occurred; the heavy steamer stopped and began backing to clear "a row of suspicious-looking buoys" directly under *Brooklyn*'s bow. The entire line of wooden vessels was drifting into confusion immediately under the guns of Fort Morgan. Farragut, lashed in the rigging to observe the action over the smoke billowing from the guns, acted promptly and resolutely, characteristic of a great leader who in war must constantly meet emergencies fraught with danger. The only course was the boldest—through the torpedo field. "Damn the torpedoes," he ordered; "full speed ahead" (Flag Lieutenant John C. Watson later recalled that Farragut's exact words were: "Damn the torpedoes! Full speed ahead, Drayton! Hard astarboard; ring four bells! Eight bells! Sixteen bells!") His flagship *Hartford* swept past *Brooklyn* into the rows of torpedoes; the fleet followed. The torpedoes were heard bumping against the hulls but none exploded. The Union force steamed into the bay.

Hardly past one hazard, Farragut was immediately faced with another: Buchanan attempted to ram *Hartford* with *Tennessee*. The Union ship slipped by her slower, clumsier antagonist, returning her fire but also being raked by the fire of gunboat C.S.S. *Selma*, Lieutenant Peter U. Murphey. Wooden double-ender U.S.S. *Metacomet*, Lieutenant Commander Jouett, engaged *Selma* and, though sustaining considerable damage, compelled her to strike her colors shortly after 9 a.m. Meanwhile, *Tennessee* also attempted in vain to ram *Brooklyn*. C.S.S. *Gaines*, Lieutenant John W. Bennett, advanced to engage the Union ships as they entered the bay, but she suffered a steering casualty early in the action. ". . . subjected to a very heavy concentrated fire from the *Hartford*, *Richmond*, and others at short range . . .", Bennett soon found his command in a sinking condition. He ran her aground near Fort Morgan and salvaged most of the ammunition and small arms before she settled in two fathoms. C.S.S. *Morgan*, Commander George W. Harrison, briefly engaged *Metacomet* to assist *Selma* prior to her surrender, but as the action took place at high speed, *Morgan* could not maintain her position and faced the possibility of being cut off and captured by two Union ships. Harrison determined to take her under Fort Morgan's guns and later he saved her by boldly running the gauntlet of Federal ships to Mobile.

Meanwhile, 300-ton side-wheeler U.S.S. *Philippi*, Acting Master James T. Seaver, "wishing to be of assistance to the fleet in case any vessels were disabled," grounded near Fort Morgan attempting to get into the bay. The fort's heavy guns quickly found the range and riddled

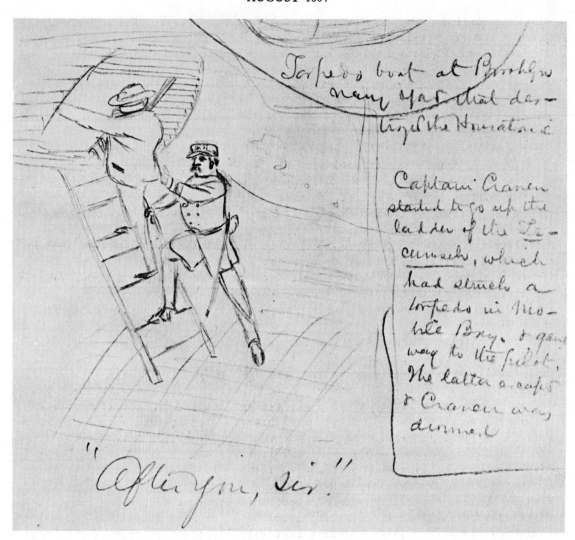

Torpedo boat at Brooklyn navy Yard that des-
troyd the Housatonic

Captain Craven
started to go up the
ladder of the Te-
cumseh, which
had struck a
torpedo in Mo-
bile Bay. & gave
way to the pilot,
The latter escaped
& Craven was
drowned

"After you, sir."

This rough contemporary sketch from the Civil War collection of the Library of Congress depicts and describes the gallant act of Captain T. A. M. Craven in giving his life to save that of his pilot after Tecumseh *struck a Confederate torpedo at Mobile Bay. (The words appearing at top right of the illustration refer to a sketch drawn on the same page by the artist but not included here. The artist apparently but mistakenly thought he was drawing* H. L. Hunley, *the submarine that destroyed* Housatonic.)

Philippi with shot and shell, forcing Seaver and his crew to abandon ship. A boat crew from C.S.S. *Morgan* completed her destruction by setting her afire. The Union fleet, having steamed up into the bay, anchored briefly. Buchanan heroically carried the fight to his powerful opponents alone. Farragut reported: "I was not long in comprehending his intention to be the destruction of the flagship. The monitors and such of the wooden vessels as I thought best adapted for the purpose were immediately ordered to attack the ram, not only with their guns, but bows on at full speed, and then began one of the fiercest naval combats on record."

For more than an hour the titanic battle raged. Steam sloop of war *Monongahela* struck *Tennessee* a heavy blow but succeeded only in damaging herself. *Lackawanna* rammed into the Confederate ship at full speed but, said Farragut, "the only perceptible effect on the ram was to give her a heavy list." A shot from *Manhattan*'s 15-inch gun, however, made a greater impression on those on board *Tennessee*. Lieutenant Wharton, CSN, reported: "The *Monongahela* was hardly clear of us when a hideous-looking monster came creeping up on our Port side, whose slowly revolving turret revealed the cavernous depths of a mammoth gun. 'Stand clear of the Port side!' I shouted. A moment after a thundrous report shook us all, while a blast of dense, sulpherous smoke covered our port-holes, and 440 pounds of iron, impelled by sixty pounds of powder, admitted daylight through our side, where, before it struck us, there had been over two feet of solid wood, covered with five inches of solid iron. This was the only 15-inch shot that hit us fair. It did not come through; the inside netting caught the splinters, and there were no casualties from it. I was glad to find myself alive after that shot.''

Hartford struck a glancing blow and poured a broadside into *Tennessee* from a distance of ten feet. *Chickasaw* pounded the ram with heavy shot; steam sloops *Lackawanna* and *Hartford* had collided, but had regained position and, with *Ossipee* and *Monongahela*, were preparing to run down Buchanan's ship. The intrepid Confederate Admiral had been seriously wounded and relinquished command to Commander James D. Johnston. The rain of shells knocked out the ironclad's steering. Unable to maneuver and taking on water, *Tennessee* struggled on against her overwhelmingly superior foes despite the terrible cannonade that pounded her mercilessly. Ultimately, Buchannan and Johnston concurred that *Tennessee* must surrender to prevent loss of life to no fruitful end. At 10 o'clock a white flag was hoisted. Farragut acknowledged the tenacity and ability with which the Confederate seamen had fought: "During this contest with the rebel gunboats and *Tennessee* . . . we lost many more men than from the fire of the batteries of Fort Morgan.''

Secretary Welles warmly congratulated the Admiral on his stunning triumph: "In the success which has attended your operations you have illustrated the efficiency and irresistible power of a naval force led by a bold and vigorous mind, and insufficiency of any batteries to prevent the passage of a fleet thus led and commanded. You have, first on the Mississippi and recently in the bay of Mobile, demonstrated what had been previously doubted, the ability of naval vessels, properly manned and commanded, to set at defiance the best constructed and most heavily armed fortifications. In these successive victories you have encountered great risks, but the results have vindicated the wisdom of your policy and the daring valor of our officers and seamen.''

Costly as the victory was to the Union and stubbornly as Mobile Bay was defended by the Confederates, the result of the struggle was the closing of the last major Gulf port to the South. With the bay itself controlled by Farragut's fleet, it was inevitable that the land fortifications which had been bypassed would be compelled to surrender. That afternoon, *Chickasaw*, Lieutenant Commander George H. Perkins, stood down and engaged Fort Powell at a distance of less than 400 yards. The Confederate work could not meet such an assault from its rear, and during the night it was evacuated and blown up. Forts Gaines and Morgan would fall soon as well, and henceforth Northern naval efforts could be concentrated in the East, though vigilance and ' mopping up'' operations would continue elsewhere until war's end. Of the stunning victory at Mobile, the distinguished naval historian Commodore Dudley W. Knox wrote: "Success there had been mainly due to the genius of Farragut, who had shown all the attributes of a great leader. He had been skillful and thorough in planning, cautious in awaiting adequate military and naval reinforcements, bold in attack, quick in perceptions and decisions during the greatest emergencies of battle, superbly courageous in setting an example, ever ready to take personal risks, as well as to assume those demanded by his heavy responsibility, and resolute beyond measure until the victory was won.''

6 Powerful C.S.S. *Albemarle*, Captain J. W. Cooke, steamed from Plymouth, N.C., to the mouth of the Roanoke River, causing great concern among the Union blockading ships before returning to Plymouth. Commander Harrell, U.S.S. *Chicopee*, reported: ". . . the ram made its appearance this morning at a few minutes before 4 a.m. It advanced as far as the mouth of the river and halted. . . . From the number of people in sight on the beach, no doubt it was expected that an engagement would ensue. . . . The ram is now lying in the river blowing off steam. I do not

think, however that she will advance. Should she do so, however, I will endeavor to draw her down toward the fleet. I shall now pay my respects to those gentlemen on the beach in the shape of a few shells."

C.S.S. *Tallahassee*, Commander Wood, ran out of Wilmington harbor, and after eluding several blockaders off the bar, embarked on one of the most destructive commerce raiding cruises of the war. "This extemporaneous man-of-war," Jefferson Davis later wrote, ". . . soon lit up the New England coast with her captures. . . ." In the next two weeks Wood, whom Davis called "an officer of extraordinary ability and enterprise," took or destroyed more than 30 ships.

7 Colonel Charles D. Anderson, CSA, commanding Fort Gaines at Mobile Bay, proposed the surrender of his command to Rear Admiral Farragut. U.S.S. *Chickasaw*, Lieutenant Commander Perkins, had bombarded the fort the day before, and Anderson wrote: "Feeling my inability to maintain my present position longer than you may see fit to open upon me with your fleet, and feeling also the uselessness of entailing upon ourselves further destruction of life, I have the honor to propose the surrender of Fort Gaines, its garrison, stores, etc." Before 10 a.m., 8 August, the Stars and Stripes were flying over the works.

8 Sailors in the Civil War were often called upon to perform duties far removed from ordinary shipboard routine. This date, Rear Admiral Dahlgren wrote to the commanders of ships in the South Atlantic Blockading Squadron on the subject of naval infantry: "It has frequently happened that the peculiar nature of the duties in this command has required the service of bodies of men to be landed from vessels to act for a short time as infantry, assisted by light fieldpieces. In order to meet similar exigencies commanders of vessels will take pains to select from their crews such men as may seem to have a turn for this kind of duty and have them drilled with small arms until they have attained the necessary proficiency. . . . The light-infantry drill will be best adapted to this service, and to the habits of the seamen."

U.S.S. *Violet*, Acting Ensign Thomas Stothard, ran aground off the western bar at Cape Fear River, North Carolina, and was destroyed. Stothard and his men labored to keep *Violet* afloat for five hours, but seeing that the water was gaining, fired her magazine and abandoned the small wooden steamer.

| . Fathoms | Courses | WIND. | | TEMPERATURE. | | | REMARKS on this 5th day of *August* 1864 |
| | | Direction. | Force. | Weather. | Air. | Water. | Barometer. |

At 9.15 a.m. This Ship hauled down the Confederate colors, having been badly disabled in the Engagement this morning, and surrendered to Rear Admiral "D. G. Farragut" of the U.S. Navy. A. V. L. "Pierre Giraud" of the U.S.S. "Ossipee" was the first to board her and take charge. Received the surrender in Rear Admiral "Farraguts" name. At 10.30 a.m. Hoisted the American Colors on this vessel.

Actg Vol Lieut "Pierre Giraud" in charge. Actg "Master "Charles W. Adams" reported for duty on board. Also "George Billings Actg Masters mate. Received the following men from U.S.S. "Ossipee" Vz:
"Henry Wolf" (Sea) "Wm Butler" (Lds) "Wm Goodman" (Lds) "James McGrath (Lds) "John McClellah (Lds) Edward Wall (Boy) "Miles Burke" (Boy). The prisoners of this vessel were then distributed on board of different Vessels of this Squadron,

ter coming to anchor near the "Flag Ship "Hartford". At 1.30 P.M. "Fort Powell" blew up.

(Left) C.S.S. Tennessee *carries the bold but futile fight to Rear Admiral Farragut's squadron in Mobile Bay.* (Above) Tennessee's *log showing the first entries after her capture by the Union.* (Inset) Commander James D. Johnston, CSN, Tennessee's *last Confederate captain, took command when Admiral Buchanan was injured.*

IV–99

9 Though the Union fleet under Rear Admiral Farragut controlled Mobile Bay and Forts Powell and Gaines were in Northern hands, Brigadier General Richard L. Page, formerly a U.S. naval officer and until recently a Commander in the Confederate Navy, gallantly refused to surrender Fort Morgan to the overwhelming forces opposing him. Federal naval forces took station in the Bay while troops began the land investment of Fort Morgan. After a brief bombardment, Farragut and Union Army commander Major General Gordon Granger advised Page: "To prevent the unnecessary sacrifice of human life which must follow the opening of our batteries, we demand the unconditional surrender of Fort Morgan and its dependencies." Undaunted, the Confederate officer replied: "I am prepared to sacrifice life, and will only surrender when I have no means of defense." He was fighting his fort as he would have his ship.

Ram *Tennessee*, whose big guns had so valiantly sought to defend Confederate possession of Mobile Bay on 5 August, now in Union hands, bombarded Fort Morgan. Her log recorded: "At 10 a.m. having no steam up on this vessel, the U.S. gunboat *Port Royal* took us in tow down towards the Fort Morgan. Anchored between the Middle Ground and the fort and opened our battery upon the fort." At 10 p.m. *Winnebago* towed *Tennessee* back up to her anchorage.

Part of the destruction that accompanied the explosion of a clockwork torpedo planted on board a Union transport at City Point, Virginia, by members of the Confederate Torpedo Corps.

Whilst I believe we will never require the Armoured vessels to meet those of the enemy I think it would be imprudent to withdraw them. At least two such vessels, in my judgment, should be kept in the upper James. They stand a constant threat to the enemy and prevent him taking the offensive. There is no disguising the fact that if the enemy should take the offensive, on the water, altho' we probably would destroy his whole James River Navy, such damage would be done our shipping and stores, all accumulated on the water near where the conflict would begin, that our victory would be dearly bought.

I have the honor to be &c

Very Respectfully

U. S. Grant

Lieutenant General Grant writes Rear Admiral Lee stressing the need for maintaining adequate forces afloat in the James River.

Reflecting Union concern regarding the great strength of C.S.S. *Albemarle*, Rear Admiral Lee wrote to Commander Macomb, commanding off Albemarle Sound, of the measures to employ in the event of another engagement with her: "The Department is of the opinion that too light charges of powder were used in the engagement of May 5 with the *Albemarle*, and that the IX-inch with 13 pounds and the 100-pounder rifle with 10 pounds of powder can effect nothing, and that even using XI-inch guns the vessels should touch the ram while engaging her and the XI-inch guns be fired with 30 pounds of powder and solid shot."

Two resourceful members of the Confederate Torpedo Corps, John Maxwell and R. K. Dillard, planted a clockwork torpedo containing twelve pounds of powder on a Union transport at City Point, Virginia, causing a huge explosion which rocked the entire area. Maxwell and Dillard succeeded in getting through Union lines to the wharf area, where Maxwell convinced the trusting wharf sentry that he had been ordered by the captain of the ammunition barge to deliver a box on board. The box was accepted and the two Confederates hastily started back for Richmond. When the torpedo exploded an hour later, it set in motion a devastating chain reaction which spread the holocaust from the barges to storage buildings on shore and even to General Grant's headquarters. Grant hurried off a message to General Halleck in Washington: "Five minutes ago an ordnance boat exploded, carrying lumber, grape, canister, and all kinds of shot over this point. Every part of the yard used as my headquarters is filled with splinters and fragments of shell."

Lieutenant General Grant wrote to Rear Admiral Lee, in response to a question as to the usefulness of the Union ironclads on the James River: ". . . I think it would be imprudent to withdraw them. At least two such vessels, in my judgment, should be kept in the upper James. They stand a constant threat to the enemy and prevent him taking the offensive." From experience Grant well understood the vital part sea power played in the struggle between North and South, whether on the ocean, the Western rivers, or the restricted waters of the James. The General was a master at employing the unique advantages of strength based afloat in combined operations to overwhelm opposition.

Blockade running steamer *Prince Albert* went aground off Fort Moultrie at Charleston and was destroyed by U.S.S. *Catskill*, Commander Napoleon B. Harrison, and the Morris Island batteries.

10 Rear Admiral Farragut continued steady day and night bombardment, battering down the walls of Fort Morgan resolutely defended by his former shipmate, General Page.

Writing from Paris, Flag Officer Barron, reported to Secretary Mallory that all Confederate midshipmen except the *Alabama*'s had been examined for promotion. Though its ships were few in numbers, the Confederacy continued an active and systematic training program for young naval officers. In his annual report to President Davis, Secretary Mallory stressed the value of training to the naval service: "Naval education and training lie at the foundation of naval success; and the power that neglects this essential element of strength will, when the battle is fought, find that its ships, however formidable, are but built for a more thoroughly trained and educated enemy. . . . While a liberal education at the ordinary institutions of learning prepares men for useful service not only in the Army, but in most branches of public affairs, special education and training, and such as these institutions cannot afford, are essential to form a naval officer." The Confederate Naval Academy, on board C.S.S. *Patrick Henry* in the James River, translated this active interest in proper naval training into concrete instruction, and provided trained officers to the Southern cause until her loss when Richmond fell in 1865.

Secretary Mallory wrote Commander Bulloch in Liverpool of the continuing importance of commerce raiding to the Confederacy: "It seems certain that we can not obtain such ships as we specially want; but we must not therefore desist in our attempts and must do the best we can under the circumstances which surround us. The enemy's distant whaling grounds have not been visited by us. His commerce constitutes one of his reliable sources of national wealth no less than one of his best schools for seamen, and we must strike it, if possible." The Secretary's desires were to be carried out with even greater success than he had anticipated by C.S.S. *Shenandoah*.

One of the additional difficulties of naval operations in the lowlands surrounding the James River, Virginia, was the high incidence of sickness. This date, Flag Officer Mitchell, commanding the Confederate James River Squadron, wired Major General George E. Pickett: "Our crews are so much reduced in number from sickness that we shall have to discontinue our picket guard at Osborne's on James River to enable us to man our batteries, in order that we may act against the enemy. About one-third of the men are sick." Later in the month, a board of surgeons inspected the ships of the squadron with a view toward reducing the prevalence of malaria and other disabling diseases. The conclusions reached in the subsequent report illustrated the hazard of duty on board river gunboats: "We consider the causes of the great amount of sickness on board said vessels to be, first, and chiefly, that exposure to malaria, the necessary consequence of a residence upon the waters of James River; as secondary causes to this, but in our opinion highly conducive to the hurtful influence, we would enumerate the heated atmosphere of the ironclads, especially when at quarters for and during action, the want of proper exercise on shore, and of a deficient supply of vegetables and fruits for the ships' companies. . . ." Difficult living conditions and sickness were common, especially in the summer, for both navies in the James River as well as elsewhere throughout the tidewaters of the South.

10-11   Small steamers U.S.S. *Romeo*, Acting Master Thomas Baldwin, and U.S.S. *Prairie Bird*, Acting Master Thomas Burns, and transport steamer *Empress* engaged battery at Gaines Landing, Arkansas, on the Mississippi River which the Confederates had secretly wheeled into place. On 10 August, *Empress* had been attacked by the batteries, enduring a withering fire which disabled her and killed Captain John Molloy. *Romeo* closed, fired upon the Confederate guns, and towed *Empress* to safety. Next day, however, the Southerner's artillery again opened heavily on *Prairie Bird* which was passing the same point near Gaines Landing. Hearing the firing from upstream, *Romeo* came down and joined in the brisk engagement; the Confederates ultimately broke off the action and withdrew. All three ships were severely damaged in the two-day exchange, *Empress* alone taking some sixty-three hits.

Cruising within 80 miles of Sandy Hook, New Jersey, C.S.S. *Tallahassee*, Commander Wood, took seven prizes, including schooners *Sarah A. Boyce* and *Carrol*, brigs *Richards* and *Carrie Estelle*, cargo of logs, pilot boats *James Funk* (No. 22) and *William Bell* (No. 24), and bark *Bay State*, cargo of

C.S.S. Tallahassee *raided Union commerce during a brief but highly successful cruise under Commander John Taylor Wood.*

wood. All were scuttled or burned except *Carrol*, which was bonded for $10,000 and sent to New York with the passengers and crews of the other ships. Rear Admiral Hiram Paulding, Commandant of the New York Navy Yard, immediately wired Secretary Welles: "Pirate off Sandy Hook, capturing and burning." By evening, Paulding had three ships in pursuit of *Tallahassee*. Welles, hoping to head off the Southern raider and prevent another cruise similar to the June 1863 raid of Lieutenant Charles Read in C.S.S. *Tacony*, telegraphed naval commanders at Hampton Roads, Philadelphia, and Boston, ordering a large-scale search for Wood.

12 C.S.S. *Tallahassee*, Commander Wood, seized six more prizes while continuing her devastating cruise off the New York coast. Wood burned ships *Atlantic*, *Adriatic*, and *Spokane*, cargo of lumber; attempted to scuttle brig *Billow*, cargo of lumber, and released bark *Suliote* and schooner *Robert E. Packer*, cargo of lumber, on bond. *Billow* did not sink and was retaken by U.S.S. *Grand Gulf*, Commander Ransom, two days later.

Ram *Tennessee* got up steam for the first time since her capture by Rear Admiral Farragut on 5 August. She had been fitted with a new stack on the 11th and this date tried it out by steaming around the bay. On the 13th *Tennessee* steamed down and opened on Fort Morgan.

13 Reports of C.S.S. *Tallahassee*'s destructive success created much alarm in northern seaports. This date, John D. Jones, president of the Board of Underwriters, wired Secretary Welles from New York: "Confederate steamer *Tallahassee* is reported cruising within 60 miles of this port. She has already captured six vessels. Will you please have the necessary measures taken, if not already done, to secure her capture?" Half an hour after receipt of this message, Welles replied: "Three vessels left New York Navy Yard yesterday afternoon; more leave to-day. Vessels left Hampton Roads last night; more leave to-day. Several vessels leave Boston to-day and to-morrow. Every vessel available has been ordered to search for pirate." In addition this date, Captain C. K. Stribling, Commandant of the Philadelphia Navy Yard, despatched three ships "in pursuit of the pirate." However, *Tallahassee*, Commander Wood, continued her "depredations", burning schooner *Lammot Du Pont*, cargo of coal, and bark *Glenavon*.

U.S.S. *Agawam*, Commander Rhind, engaged three different Confederate batteries near Four Mile Creek on the James River. The 975-ton double-ender was fired upon early in the afternoon, countered immediately and maintained a heavy fire for over four hours when, "finding our ammunition running short, having expended 228 charges, we weighed anchor and dropped down." Next day *Agawam* again engaged the batteries, in support of Union troops advancing along the river.

Ships of the Confederate James River Squadron, including C.S.S. *Virginia II*, Commander R. B. Pegram, C.S.S. *Richmond*, Lieutenant J. S. Maury, C.S.S. *Fredericksburg*, Commander Rootes, C.S.S. *Hampton*, Lieutenant John W. Murdaugh, C.S.S. *Nansemond*, Lieutenant Charles W. Hays, C.S.S. *Drewry*, Lieutenant William W. Hall, shelled Union Army positions near Dutch Gap, Virginia. At the request of the Confederate Army, Flag Officer Mitchell kept up the fire, intended to support Confederate troop movements in the area, for over 12 hours. The Union entrenchments, however, were largely beyond the range of his guns and hidden by hills. Union gunboats took position below the James River barricade; but their guns could not reach the ships of Mitchell's squadron. The Confederate fire was, however, returned briskly by Union shore emplacements. Mitchell ordered his ships to return to their anchorages at nightfall.

14 As all-out Union efforts to capture C.S.S. *Tallahassee*, Commander Wood, increased, the cruiser seized and scuttled ship *James Littlefield* with cargo of coal. Rear Admiral Paulding noted in New York: "Our vessels must fall in with her. They strip everybody of everything valuable."

15 Rumors concerning C.S.S. *Albemarle* continued to reach Union naval forces in Albemarle Sound. Colonel David W. Wardrop, Union Army commander in the area, wrote to Commander Macomb:

"I have received information from parties heretofore reliable that the enemy have been fitting up some of their boats with torpedoes, and are intending to attack the fleet in conjunction with the ram on Tuesday next. It is also confidently reported that a second ram will be done in a fortnight. They are very busy up the Roanoke River, but it is very difficult to learn what is being done. . . ."

Rear Admiral Farragut's fleet sustained its pounding of Fort Morgan with shot from its heavy guns. Typical of the action that took place in Mobile Bay from the time the ships dominated its waters on 5 August until General Page, the determined defender of Fort Morgan, finally capitulated was a log entry of U.S.S. *Manhattan*, Commander Nicholson: "At 7 [p.m.] opened fire on Fort Morgan. At 8 Fort Morgan opened fire on this ship and fired two shot. From 8 to midnight: Continuing to fire on Fort Morgan; Morgan fired one shot at this ship. At 10:20 ceased firing having fired 7 XV-inch shell. Fort fired on our encampment on shore from 9 till end of watch."

C.S.S. *Tallahassee*, Commander Wood, captured and scuttled schooners *Mary A. Howes*, *Howard*, *Floral Wreath*, *Restless*, *Etta Caroline*, and bonded schooner *Sarah B. Harris* off New England.

U.S.S. *Niagara*, Commodore Thomas T. Craven, captured steamer *Georgia* off the coast of Portugal. *Georgia* was formerly C.S.S. *Georgia*, which had been sold to British merchants in June of 1864. American Ambassador to England Charles Francis Adams recommended that she be taken when she put to sea under private ownership because of her previously belligerent status. *Georgia* was later condemned by a prize court in Boston.

16 Ships of the James River Division, North Atlantic Blockading Squadron, transported and supported Union troops in an advance from Dutch Gap, Virginia. Captain M. Smith described the supporting deployment: "The *Mount Washington* was detained to transport the troops from Dutch Gap to Aiken's [Landing], and to lie off that point and use her 32 pounder, holding herself ready to reembark troops if necessary. Just above her the *Delaware*, a little farther above the *Mackinaw*, and at the bend of Dutch Gap the *Canonicus* were stationed to cover the advance by shelling the enemy's line, the *Canonicus* also devoting attention to Signal Hill Battery." Throughout the long months of virtually stalemated operations in the James River area, naval forces operated intimately with the Army, facilitating the small advances that were made and checking reverses with the big guns that could swiftly be brought to bear on points of decision near the river.

C.S.S. *Tallahassee*, Commander Wood, captured and burned off New England bark *P. C. Alexander*, and schooners *Leopard*, *Pearl*, *Sarah Louise*, and *Magnolia*.

Boat expedition by Commander Colvocoresses, U.S.S. *Saratoga*, consisting of men from that ship and *T. A. Ward*, Acting Master Babcock, captured some 100 prisoners and a quantity of arms on a daring raid into McIntosh County, Georgia. Commander Colvocoresses also destroyed a salt works and a strategic bridge across the South Newport River on the main road to Savannah.

17 General Robert E. Lee, attempting to consolidate his position on the James River below Richmond, turned to the ships of Flag Officer Mitchell's squadron for gunfire support. "The enemy is on Signal Hill, fortifying," he telegraphed. "Please try and drive him off. Our picket line is reestablished with the exception of Signal Hill." Ironclads C.S.S. *Virginia II*, Lieutenant Johnston, and C.S.S. *Richmond*, Lieutenant J. S. Maury, promptly steamed to a position above Signal Hill where they took the Union position under fire. Shortly thereafter scouts reported that Union forces had fallen back and that Lee's troops now commanded the hill.

Running short of coal, Commander Wood headed C.S.S. *Tallahassee* for Halifax, Nova Scotia, where he hoped to refuel in order to continue his devastating attack on Federal commerce. Enroute, *Tallahassee* destroyed schooners *North America* and *Josiah Achorn* and released brig *Neva* on bond.

18 Attesting to the effectiveness of the patrol maintained on the Mississippi River by Union gun-boats, Lieutenant General Richard Taylor, CSA, wrote General E. Kirby Smith, CSA, regarding the impossibility of crossing the river with large bodies of troops: "I have dispatched the War Department to the effect that I consider the crossing of any considerable body of troops impossible. Accurate observations have been made of the enemy's gunboats between Red River and Vicksburg, and from the strictness of the guard maintained no success can be anticipated." The original Northern strategy of splitting the Confederacy along the Mississippi River under the efforts of Rodgers, Foote, Farragut, and Porter continued in widening influence to war's end.

C.S.S. *Tallahassee*, Commander Wood, put into Halifax to replenish coal supply. U.S. Consul Mortimer M. Jackson wired Secretary Welles: "*Tallahassee* has just come into port. Will protest against her being coaled here." Welles, in turn, at once wired U.S.S. *Pontoosuc*, Lieutenant Commander George A. Stevens, which had put into Eastport, Maine, the preceding day, to steam to the Nova Scotia capital "without delay". Consul Jackson protested the sale of coal for the cruiser to Lieutenant Governor Richard G. MacDonnell, but was informed: ". . . his excellency does not consider it his duty to detain the *Tallahassee*, or any man-of-war of a belligerent state, on the chance of evidence being hereafter found of her having violated international law, and in the absence of proof to that effect he can not withhold from her commander the privilege of obtaining as much coal as may be necessary to carry him to a port of the Confederate States. . . ." MacDonnell, however, also asked Admiral Sir James Hope to advise him as to the amount of coal that would be required for *Tallahassee* to steam from Halifax to Wilmington. Next day, the Lieutenant Governor advised Wood, who had put into port with 40 tons of coal, that he could depart Halifax with no more than 100 tons of coal on board. However, the Confederate cruiser, which put to sea on the night of the 19th, sailed with somewhat more than that quantity. As Wood later reported: "I am under many obligations to our agent, Mr. Wier, for transacting our business, and through his management about 120 tons of coal were put aboard, instead of half this quantity."

20 U.S.S. *Pontoosuc*, Lieutenant Commander Stevens, entered Halifax. Stevens learned that *Tallahassee* had sailed late the night before and that he had failed to intercept her by only seven hours. *Pontoosuc* departed immediately in pursuit. Based on information reported by Consul Jackson, Stevens steamed north into the Gulf of St. Lawrence, while Wood, feeling that he did not have sufficient fuel to actively pursue his raids, had set a course for Wilmington. This date, *Tallahassee* captured brig *Roan* and burned her. She was the last prize taken on this brief but most effective cruise.

22–24 Boat expedition from U.S.S. *Potomska*, Acting Lieutenant Swann, captured prisoners and some small arms and destroyed over 2,000 barrels of rosin and turpentine on the Satilla and White

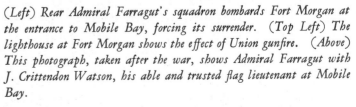

(Left) Rear Admiral Farragut's squadron bombards Fort Morgan at the entrance to Mobile Bay, forcing its surrender. (Top Left) The lighthouse at Fort Morgan shows the effect of Union gunfire. (Above) This photograph, taken after the war, shows Admiral Farragut with J. Crittendon Watson, his able and trusted flag lieutenant at Mobile Bay.

Rivers, Georgia. Wherever water reached, Confederate supplies were fair game for alert Union sailors.

23   Having doggedly withstood naval bombardment for more than two weeks, and invested by Union soldiers ashore, Brigadier General Page surrendered Fort Morgan, the last Confederate bastion at Mobile Bay. "My guns and powder had all been destroyed, my means of defense gone, the citadel, nearly the entire quartermaster stores, and a portion of the commissariat burned by the enemy's shells," he reported. "It was evident the fort could hold out but a few hours longer under a renewed bombardment. The only question was: Hold it for this time, gain the eclat, and sustain the loss of life from the falling of the walls, or save life and capitulate?"

Acting Master's Mate Woodman made his second dangerous reconnaissance up the Roanoke River, North Carolina, to gather intelligence on C.S.S. *Albemarle* and the defenses of Plymouth. Woodman reported: "At 10 a.m. I arrived on the Roanoke River, opposite Plymouth. The ram *Albemarle* was lying alongside of the wharf at Plymouth, protected with timbers, extending completely around her. . . ." Woodman, who would make yet another reconnaissance mission, gained much vital information upon which Lieutenant Cushing planned the expedition which ended *Albemarle*'s career.

23–25   Boat expedition under Commander Colvocoresses, U.S.S. *Saratoga*, composed of men from *Saratoga*, U.S.S. *T. A. Ward*, Acting Master Babcock, and U.S.S. *Braziliera*, Acting Master Gillespie, engaged Confederate pickets along Turtle River, Georgia. The expedition aimed at the capture of an encampment at Bethel, Georgia, but the Confederates there were alerted by the firing downstream and escaped. On 15 September the daring and resourceful Colvocoresses was commended by Secretary Welles for his three successful forays into Southern territory.

24   U.S.S. *Keystone State*, Commander Crosby, and U.S.S. *Gettysburg*, Lieutenant R. H. Lamson, captured blockade running steamer *Lilian*, off Wilmington with cargo of cotton. Both Union ships fired on *Lilian*; when she finally hove to she was in a sinking condition. Crosby managed to repair the damage and sent her to Beaufort. She was subsequently purchased by the Navy and assigned to the squadron under the same name.

U.S.S. *Narcissus*, Acting Ensign William G. Jones, captured schooner *Oregon* in Biloxi Bay, Mississippi Sound.

25   C.S.S. *Tallahassee*, Commander Wood, successfully ran the blockade into Wilmington, after being chased and fired at by several blockading vessels. Rear Admiral Lee issued orders urging "upmost vigilance" to prevent her re-entry onto the high seas. In his cruise, cut short by lack of coal, Wood took some 31 prizes, all but eight of which were destroyed.

Stirred by the heavy toll of Union shipping taken by C.S.S. *Tallahassee*, the Navy Department redoubled efforts to track down remaining raiders. Secretary Welles dispatched warships in search of *Tallahassee* and instructed: "Telegraph your arrival at each port you may enter to the Navy Department, but your departure therefrom need not be delayed in waiting for an answer, unless you consider an answer necessary. . . . Report the length of time under sail, under steam, and under both sail and steam, respectively; also all vessels spoken or boarded, and other incidents of interest or importance during the cruise."

27   In failing health and with the assault on the city of Mobile delayed indefinitely awaiting adequate troops, Rear Admiral Farragut wrote Secretary Welles requesting to be relieved of his duties: "It is evident that the army has no men to spare for this place beyond those sufficient to keep up an alarm, and thereby make a diversion in favor of General Sherman. . . . Now, I dislike to make of show of attack unless I can do something more than make a menace, but so long as I am able I am willing to do the bidding of the Department to the best of my abilities. I fear, however, my health is giving way. I have now been down in this Gulf and the Caribbean Sea

nearly five years out of six, with the exception of the short time at home last fall, and the last six months have been a severe drag on me, and I want rest, if it is to be had." Two months later the great leader set course to the North for a well earned leave.

U.S.S. *Niphon*, Acting Lieutenant Joseph B. Breck, and U.S.S. *Monticello*, Acting Master Henry A. Phelon, conducted an expedition up Masonboro Inlet, North Carolina, to silence a Confederate battery which was reported to have been erected in the vicinity. The two screw steamers shelled the shoreline and a number of buildings at Masonboro; landing parties went ashore and captured a quantity of rifles, ammunition, foodstuffs.

29 While removing Confederate obstructions from the channel leading into Mobile Bay, five sailors were killed and nine others injured when a torpedo exploded. Farragut regretted the unfortunate loss, but resolutely pressed on with the work: "As it is absolutely necessary to free the channel of these torpedoes, I shall continue to remove them, but as every precaution will be used, I do not apprehend any further accident." Like the loss of *Tecumseh*, this event demonstrated that although some torpedoes had been made inactive by long immersion, many were very much alive when Farragut made the instant decision, "Damn the torpedoes . . . ."

30 Small stern-wheeler U.S.S. *Fawn*, Acting Master Grace, convoyed Union infantry and artillery embarked in transport *Kate Hart*, on an expedition up the White River from Devall's Bluff, Arkansas. The troops were to join with General West's cavalry, then searching for General Shelby's force of Confederate raiders. *Fawn* and the transport returned to Devall's Bluff on 2 September, and commenced a second foray with larger forces embarked in transports *Nevada*, *Commercial*, and *Celeste* that afternoon. Next day, above Peach Orchard Bluffs, Confederate batteries opened on the convoy, but were dislodged from their riverbank position by *Fawn*'s gunfire. Unable to proceed water-borne because of the low level of the river, scouts and cavalry were sent ahead to communicate with General West, and returned, escorted by *Fawn*, to Devall's Bluff on 6 September. Shelby's forces continued to elude the Union troops and harass shipping on the White River.

31 Blockade running British steamer *Mary Bowers* ran aground between Rattlesnake Shoals and Long Island, South Carolina, and was a total loss. She was bound for Charleston where, it was reported, she was to load a cargo of cotton for Halifax.

SEPTEMBER

2 Small, 8-gun paddle-wheeler U.S.S. *Naiad*, Acting Master Keene, engaged Confederate battery near Rowe's Landing, Louisiana, and, after a brisk exchange, silenced it.

3 President Lincoln ordered a 100-gun salute at the Washington Navy Yard at noon on Monday, the 5th of September, and upon receipt of the order, at each arsenal and navy yard in the United States "for the recent brilliant achievements of the fleet and land forces of the United States in the harbor of Mobile and in the reduction of Fort Powell, Fort Gaines, and Fort Morgan. . . ." The President also proclaimed that on the following Sunday thanksgiving should be given for Rear Admiral Farragut's victory at Mobile and for the capture of Atlanta by General Sherman. These events, said Lincoln, "call for devout acknowledgment to the Supreme Being in whose hands are the destinies of nations."

5 Unaware as yet of Rear Admiral Farragut's letter of the week before (see 27 August) regarding his failing health, Secretary Welles wrote the Admiral asking him to take command of the North Atlantic Blockading Squadron and prepare to attack Wilmington, the last major port open to the Confederates. Welles regarded its capture as "more important, practically, than the capture of Richmond." It was natural that, not knowing of Farragut's personal wishes, he should turn to his most successful and indomitable officer for the accomplishment of this last vital task. "You are selected," wrote Welles, "to command the naval force, and you will endeavor to be at Port Royal by the latter part of September, where further orders will await you." It was not until

mid-month that the Secretary received Farragut's letter of 27 August.   On 22 September the hero of Mobile Bay wrote Welles upon receipt of his instructions to proceed to Port Royal and reiterated his request to go North on leave.   Welles, meanwhile, had taken steps to select a new squadron commander in lieu of Farragut, and the same day, 22 September, he wrote Rear Admiral Porter: "Rear Admiral D. G. Farragut was assigned to the command of the North Atlantic Squadron on the 5th instant, but the necessity of rest on the part of that distinguished officer renders it necessary that he should come immediately North.   You will, therefore, on receipt of this order consider yourself detached from the command of the Mississippi Squadron . . . and relieve Acting Rear Admiral Lee in command of the North Atlantic Blockading Squadron."   Thus, because of Admiral Farragut's poor health, Porter was given the opportunity to prepare and lead the massive assault against the South's most important remaining seaport.

U.S.S. *Keystone State*, Commander Crosby, and U.S.S. *Quaker City*, Lieutenant Silas Casey, captured blockade running British steamer *Elsie* off Wilmington with cargo of cotton.   *Elsie* had been chased the previous night upon standing out of Wilmington, but the blockading vessels had lost her in the darkness.   This date, however, *Keystone State* sighted her, and with *Quaker City*, opened fire.   *Elsie* almost escaped, but a shell exploding in her forward hold forced her to heave to.

6   U.S.S. *Proteus*, Commander Shufeldt, captured blockade running British schooner *Ann Louisa* in the Gulf of Mexico.

8   U.S.S. *Tritonia, Rodolph, Stockdale,* and an Army transport commenced a two-day expedition under Acting Lieutenant George Wiggin to destroy large salt works at Salt House Point near Mobile Bay.   Only *Rodolph* and *Stockdale* crossed the bar and entered Bon Secours River.   Arriving at the Point at mid-morning, Wiggin sent two boat crews ashore and demolition of the salt works began immediately.   So extensive were the works that destruction was not completed until late afternoon the next day.   Wiggin reported: "I found some of the works well built and very strong, particularly one known as the Memphis Works, said to have cost $60,000. . . .   Another work, which was very strong and well built, said to have cost $50,000."   Rear Admiral Farragut, who had ordered the attack, observed: "There were 55 furnaces, in which were manufactured nearly 2,000 bushels of salt per day, and their destruction must necessarily inconvenience the rebels."

9   Acting under orders from Rear Admiral Farragut, 500-ton screw steamer U.S.S. *Kanawha*, Lieutenant Commander Taylor, reinstituted the blockade of Brownsville, Texas.   The blockade had been lifted in mid-February by Presidential proclamation (see 18 February 1864), but on 15 August Secretary of State Seward had informed Secretary Welles that it should be re-enforced once more because of the withdrawal of Union troops stationed in the area.   Three days later, Welles directed Farragut to resume the blockade "as early as practicable".   On 3 September the Admiral reported to Welles that, "I am now increasing the blockading force off the coast of Texas, the recent operations here now enabling me to spare vessels for that purpose."   Farragut relayed the Department's message to his senior subordinate on the Texas coast, Commander Melancthon B. Woolsey, who on 8 September replied: "The *Kanawha* sailed hence last night with orders to blockade the Brazos Santiago (one of the points of approach to Brownsville).   She also bore orders to the *Aroostook* to blockade the Rio Grande . . . the blockade of those places will be resumed from to-morrow morning (9th)."   At this point in the war Union strength at sea was such that specific ports like Brownsville could be reclosed as necessary, while at the same time the iron ring of the entire coastal blockade tightened.

As the conflict drew into its final stage, Southern authorities turned increasingly to blockade runners manned and financed by the Navy.   These allowed the Confederacy to employ some of its excellent officers at sea and insured that entire cargoes brought in would be of direct benefit to the government.   This date, Commander Maffitt, one of the Confederacy's most successful and experienced captains, was detached from command of C.S.S. *Albemarle* and ordered to Wilmington to command the new blockade runner *Owl*.

10 An expedition from U.S.S. *Wyalusing*, Lieutenant Commander Earl English, landed at Elizabeth City on the Pasquotank River, North Carolina, and seized several of the leading citizens for inter-rogation regarding the burning of mail steamer *Fawn* on the Albemarle and Chesapeake Canal the night before.   The naval landing party encountered little resistance at Elizabeth City, and suc-ceeded in capturing 29 prisoners.   English learned that the *Fawn* expedition had been led by members of C.S.S. *Albemarle*'s crew.

U.S.S. *Santiago de Cuba*, Captain Glisson, captured blockade running steamer *A. D. Vance* at sea northeast of Wilmington with cargo of cotton.

U.S.S. *Magnolia*, Acting Lieutenant Cheesman, seized steamer *Matagorda* at sea off Cape San Antonio, Cuba, with cargo of cotton.

11 Acting Lieutenant Wiggin led an expedition up Fish River at Mobile Bay to seize an engine used by Confederates in a sawmill and to assist Union soldiers in obtaining lumber.   Tinclad U.S.S. *Rodolph*, Acting Lieutenant George D. Upham, and wooden side-wheeler U.S.S. *Stockdale*, Acting Master Spiro V. Bennis, with Wiggin embarked, convoyed Army transport *Planter* to Smith's mill, where they took the engine, 60,000 feet of lumber, and some livestock.   Loading the lumber on board a barge in tow of *Planter* took almost until nightfall, and in the dusk of the return down-stream, Confederate riflemen took the ships under fire and felled trees ahead of them.   The gun-boats returned the fire rapidly and *Rodolph* broke through the obstructions, enabling the remaining ships to pass downriver.

U.S.S. *Augusta Dinsmore*, Acting Lieutenant Miner B. Crowell, captured schooner *John* off Velasco, Texas, with cargo of cotton.

A vital part of the follow-up operations at Mobile Bay included the hazardous duty of dragging for torpedoes to clear the area for navigation.   Despite the efforts of the squadron, a number of ships were lost to torpedoes in the vicinity of Mobile.

13 Rear Admiral Farragut's sailors continued to clear the main ship channel at Mobile Bay of torpedos such as the one that had sunk U.S.S. *Tecumseh* on 5 August. He reported to Secretary Welles that 22 torpedos had been raised. He added: "This part of the channel is now believed to be clear, for, though beyond doubt many more were originally anchored here, report says they have sunk over one hundred to the bottom." Despite the Admiral's efforts, Union ships would be destroyed in the vicinity of Mobile Bay by torpedoes in the months to come.

15 Though the Union forces dominated Mobile Bay, the South still possessed a number of ships at Mobile itself. Farragut informed Welles that C.S.S. *Nashville*, an ironclad which, he said, had been waiting for her plating for at least 12 months, was now ready for service. Farragut described her as mounting "six of their heaviest rifles and has heavier backing and greater speed than the *Tennessee*." Referring to the battle of Mobile Bay the month before, the Admiral added: "If she had gotten out fully equipped, the rebels would have made a stronger fight on the 5th day of August. . . ." The Mobile defenses also counted on the casemated ironclads *Tuscaloosa* and *Huntsville*, "covered with 4 inches of iron, but, I understand, very unmanageable", and three gunboats. "I have them guarded," Farragut wrote, "by the two ironclads, the *Winnebago* and *Chickasaw*, and four of our gunboats."

16 Commander Bulloch wrote Secretary Mallory from Liverpool: "The loss of the *Alabama* occurred just at a time when the financial condition of the Navy Department began to improve and . . . I took immediate steps to look up a successor. I have now the satisfaction to inform you of the purchase of a fine composite ship, built for the Bombay trade, and just returned from her first voyage. She is 1,160 tons builder's measurement, classed A-1 . . . frames, beams, etc., of iron, but planked from keel to gunwhale with East Indian teak. . . . My broker has had her carefully examined by one of Lloyd's inspectors, who pronounced her a capital ship in every respect. . . . The log of the ship shows her to be a fast sailor under canvas, for with screw up she has made 330 miles in 24 hours by observation." Bulloch was describing the steamer *Sea King*, a ship which would shortly become renowned as the raider C.S.S. *Shenandoah*. He also informed Mallory that contracts had been let for the torpedo boats which the Secretary had ordered two months before (see 18 July).

Boat expedition from U.S.S. *Ariel*, Acting Master Russell, captured over 4,000 pounds of cotton in the vicinity of Tampa Bay, Florida.

19 Confederates under Acting Master John Yates Beall captured and burned steamers *Philo Parsons* and *Island Queen* on Lake Erie. Captain Charles H. Cole, CSA, a Confederate secret agent in the Lake Erie region, conceived the plan and received the assistance of Jacob Thompson, Southern agent in Canada, and the daring Beall. The plan was for Cole to aid in the capture of iron sidewheeler U.S.S. *Michigan*, which was then guarding the Confederate prisoners at Johnson's Island, near Sandusky, Ohio, by befriending her officers and attempting to bribe them. Beall was to approach with a captured steamer from the mouth of Sandusky Bay and board *Michigan*, after which the prisoners would be released and the whole force would embark on a guerrilla expedition along the lake. Beall and his 19 men came on board *Philo Parsons* as passengers but soon seized the steamer and took her to Middle Bass Island, on the way from Detroit to Sandusky. While there, Beall was approached by an unsuspecting steamer, *Island Queen*, which he quickly captured and burned. He then landed the passengers and cargoes of the two ships and proceeded with his improvised man-of-war to Sandusky. Meanwhile, Commander J. C. Carter of *Michigan* had discovered Cole's duplicity and had him arrested, along with his assistant in the plot. As Beall and his men approached Sandusky, the prearranged signals were not made. Confronted with uncertain circumstances and overwhelming odds, Beall and his men reluctantly but wisely abandoned their part in the plan and took *Philo Parsons* to Sandwich, Canada, where she was stripped and burned. The Confederates then dispersed.

James D. Bulloch
Commander, CSN

John Y. Beall
Master, CSN

Secretary Mallory, in a telegram to Commander Maffitt, gave his orders regarding the new Confederate-owned blockade runners: "It is of the first importance that our steamers should not fall into the enemy's hands. Apart from the specific loss sustained by the country in the capture of blockade runners, these vessels, lightly armed, now constitute the fleetest and most efficient part of his blockading force off Wilmington. . . . As commanding officer of the *Owl* you will please devise and adopt thorough and efficient means for saving all hands and destroying the vessel and cargo whenever these measures may become necessary to prevent capture."

A boat expedition commanded by Acting Ensign Semon in U.S.S. *Niphon*, landed at Masonboro Inlet, North Carolina, to gain intelligence on the defenses of Wilmington and the strength of its garrison. In planning for the forthcoming assault on the defenses of Wilmington, Semon also learned that raider C.S.S. *Tallahassee* was at Wilmington, along with several blockade runners.

22 Upon learning that Farragut's health prevented him from accepting command of the forthcoming operations against Wilmington, Secretary Welles paid eloquent tribute to the Admiral and his accomplishments: "In accordance with the view of the Department and the universal wish of the country, the orders of the 5th instant [see 5 September 1864] were given to you; but a life so precious must not be thrown away by failing to heed the monitions which the greatest powers of physical endurance receive as a warning to rest. The country will again call upon you, perhaps, to put the finishing blow to the rebellion." The distinguished Admiral's service in the Civil War was over, but not before he had achieved a permanent place among the great naval heroes of all time. From New Orleans to Port Hudson to Mobile Bay, David Glasgow Farragut, first Admiral in the U.S. Navy, had shown the leadership, courage, intelligence, and devotion to duty which have ever since been shining examples for all who are privileged to serve the Nation at sea.

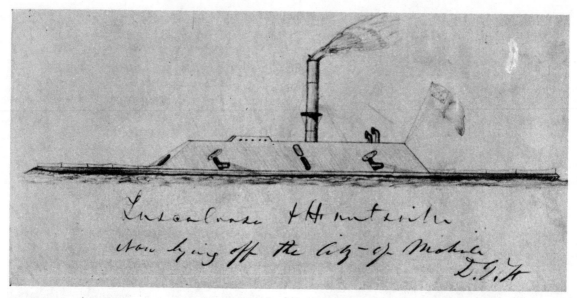

Rear Admiral Farragut's squadron controlled Mobile Bay, but the Confederates had a naval force at the city itself. Above is a rough sketch of C.S.S. Tuscaloosa *and* Huntsville, *with Farragut's notation.*

23 Small side-wheeler U.S.S. *Antelope*, Acting Master John Ross, struck a snag and sank in the Mississippi River below New Orleans.

24 Under command of Acting Master William T. Street, wooden steamer U.S.S. *Fuchsia*, and side-wheelers *Thomas Freeborn* and *Mercury* proceeded to Milford Haven, Virginia, near which Confederates were believed to be preparing a number of boats to attack the blockading force at the mouth of the Piankatank River. Leaving *Fuchsia* and *Thomas Freeborn* at Milford Haven, Street took armed boats in tow of *Mercury* and proceeded up Stutt's Creek. Some three miles upstream a force of 40 sailors was landed, under Acting Master William A. Arthur and Acting Ensign Philip Sheridan. Four Confederate boats were destroyed, five were captured, and a fishery demolished. Though the Rappahannock River area was dominated by the Northern forces, Union ships had to be continually on the alert to prevent audacious Southern raids.

General Robert E. Lee wrote Secretary of War Seddon of another dilemma posed by the South's weakness at sea: "Since the fitting out of the privateer *Tallahassee* and her cruise from the port of Wilmington, the enemy's fleet of blockaders off that coast has been very much increased, and the dangers of running the blockade rendered much greater. The question arises whether it is of more importance to us to obtain supplies through that port or to prey upon the enemy's commerce by privateers sent from thence. . . . It might be well therefore, if practicable, to divert the enemy's attention from Wilmington Harbor and keep it open as long as possible as a port of entry. While it is open the energies . . . should be exerted . . . to get in two or three years' supplies so as to remove all apprehension on this score."

25 U.S.S. *Howquah*, Acting Lieutenant John W. Balch, U.S.S. *Niphon*, Acting Master Edmund Kemble, and U.S.S. *Governor Buckingham*, Acting Lieutenant John MacDiarmid, chased ashore and destroyed blockade running steamer *Lynx* off Wilmington with cargo of cotton. The three Union screw steamers were fired upon by *Lynx* and by shore batteries; Balch reported: ". . . one 30-pounder percussion shell struck the main rail on the starboard bow, cutting it through, also striking the forward end of the 30-pounder pivot carriage, cutting the breech in two and disabling the carriage, glancing over, striking the main rail on the port side, and falling on the deck (I have

the shot now on board).   Fortunately this shell did not explode." *Lynx* sustained several close-range broadsides and was run ashore in flames, where she continued to burn throughout the night until consumed.

26 Major General Whiting, C.S.A., Army commander in Wilmington, wrote to Governor Vance of North Carolina requesting that C.S.S. *Tallahassee* and *Chickamauga* be retained in Wilmington for the defense of that port: "The Confederate steamers *Tallahassee* and *Chickamauga* are now nearly ready for sea, and will leave this port for the purpose of operating against the enemy's commerce. Should they leave on this service the few vessels they might destroy would be of little advantage to our cause, while it would excite the enemy to increase the number of the blockading squadron to such an extent as to render it almost impossible for vessels running the blockade to escape them."   Notwithstanding these objections and those of General Lee two days before, the raiders were sent to sea.

As Union forces on the James River pressed their attempt to bypass the obstructions at Trent's Reach by digging a canal at Dutch Gap, senior Confederate Army officers became increasingly concerned as to their ability to hold the defensive position before Richmond.   Major General George E. Pickett wrote from Chesterfield: "If they wish to complete the canal, they will be compelled to occupy this bank of the river; any attempt to do this ought to be prevented by the gunboats." General Robert E. Lee, ever aware of the meaning of seapower, concurred and added: "The navy can readily prevent the enemy from crossing the river at the point indicated by General Pickett, if an understanding be come to by which they shall move promptly to the spot upon being notified of the existence of danger."   Flag Officer Mitchell, commander of the Confederate James River Squadron, reported four days later: "I have offered repeatedly to the commanding generals on both sides of the James River to cooperate with them, and shall always be happy to answer any call for this purpose, and feel thankful for any information which will enable the squadron to move promptly when its services can be useful."

C.S.S. *Florida*, Lieutenant Morris, captured bark *Mondamin* off the northeastern coast of South America.

27 Acting Ensign Semon made his second reconnaissance expedition to Masonboro Inlet and Wilmington.   Semon again gained important information concerning Confederate blockade runners, the defensive dispositions of forces in the area, and made arrangements to procure pilots for the operation against Wilmington.   He learned for the first time that C.S.S. *North Carolina*, one of the ironclads built for the defense of Wilmington, had sunk at her pier at Smithville, her bottom eaten out by worms.   *North Carolina* drew too much water to pass over the bars at the mouth of the Cape Fear River, and had spent virtually her entire career at Smithville.   Concerned about the state of Wilmington's defenses, Major General Whiting wrote Secretary Mallory on 6 October: "It is men and guns that are wanted as well as the ships, not only to man the naval batteries now being substituted for the *North Carolina* and the *Raleigh* [beached on 7 May 1864], which were to defend the inner bars, but to guard or picket the entrance and river, a duty devolving upon the Navy, and for which there are neither forts nor vessels here."   An additional ironclad was laid down but was never finished because of lack of armor.

U.S.S. *Arkansas*, Acting Lieutenant David Cate, captured schooner *Watchful* in the Gulf of Mexico south of Barataria Bay, Louisiana.   *Watchful* carried a cargo of lumber and arms.

28 Rear Admiral Porter, on his detachment from command of the Mississippi Squadron, wrote a farewell to his officers and men, in which he reflected on the far-reaching accomplishments of naval power on the western waters: "When I first assumed command of this squadron the Mississippi was in possession of the rebels from Memphis to New Orleans, a distance of 800 miles, and over 1,000 miles of tributaries were closed against us, embracing a territory larger than some of the kingdoms of Europe.   Our commerce is now successfully, if not quietly, transported on the broad Mississippi from one end to the other, and the same may almost be said with regard to its tribu-

taries.'' Porter, who was to be relieved by Rear Admiral S. P. Lee, soon proceeded to Hampton Roads, assumed command of the North Atlantic Blockading Squadron, and turned his attention to the reduction of Wilmington.

29 Steamer *Roanoke*, bound for New York from Havana, was captured by Confederates under Acting Master John C. Braine, CSN, just off the Cuban coast. Braine's actions caused the Richmond government concern and embarrassment, since his expedition was organized and carried out from the neutral port of Havana. The resourceful and audacious Braine had outlined his idea to Secretary Mallory earlier in the year, and the Secretary had given his approval, with the stipulation that neutral rights were to be strictly observed. With that understanding, Braine was commissioned a temporary Acting Master. Instead of boarding the vessel as a passenger in New York, however, he chose to capture her on the Havana end of the voyage. With a small group of Confederates, he was able to overwhelm the ship's officers and take over the ship, steering her for Bermuda. After attempting to smuggle supplies and coal from that island, unsuccessfully, he determined that the fine steamer could not be brought through the blockade to the Confederacy and she was burned off Bermuda. Braine was held by the British but subsequently released, and was to be heard from again.

29–30 U.S.S. *Niphon*, Acting Master Kemble, forced blockade running British steamer *Night Hawk* aground off Fort Fisher and burned her. Late on 29 September, *Niphon* fired upon *Night Hawk* as she attempted to run into New Inlet, and observed her go aground. A boat crew led by Acting Ensign Semon boarded the steamer, and under the fire of Fort Fisher set her ablaze and brought off the crew as prisoners. Ensign Semon's conduct on this occasion became the subject of a diplomatic note from the British Ambassador, the latter alleging cruel treatment of the officers of *Night Hawk* and a premature burning of the ship. Semon was subsequently cleared of all implications of misconduct by a court of inquiry.

29–1 October Ships of the Confederate James River Squadron, Flag Officer Mitchell, supported Southern troops in attacks against Fort Harrison, Chaffin's Farm, James River, Virginia. Though the Confederates failed to retake Fort Harrison, with the aid of heavy fire from Mitchell's ships, they prevented Union soldiers from capturing Chaffin's Bluff.

OCTOBER

1 U.S.S. *Niphon*, Acting Master Kemble, ran British blockade runner *Condor* aground off New Inlet, North Carolina. *Niphon* was prevented from destroying the steamer by intense fire from Fort Fisher. Among the passengers on board *Condor* was one of the most famous Confederate agents of the war, Mrs. Rose O'Neal Greenhow. Mrs. Greenhow, fearful of being captured on the grounded runner with her important dispatches, set out in a boat for shore, but the craft overturned in the heavy surf. The crew managed to get ashore, but the woman, weighted down by $2,000 in British gold in a pouch around her neck, drowned.

Major General John G. Walker, CSA, reported to the Confederate States War Department that 10 sailors and marines under Captain W. F. Brown, CSMC, and Lieutenant Marcus J. Beebee, CSN, had disguised themselves as passengers on board steamer *Ike Davis* and had captured her off Brazos, Texas. After overpowering the crew and imprisoning them below, the Confederates took *Ike Davis* into Matagorda Bay, Texas.

3 Captain Semmes, commander of the famous raider C.S.S. *Alabama*, embarked from England in steamer *Tasmanian* for Havana, from where he hoped to return to the Confederacy and report to President Davis for further assignment. The gallant Captain later recalled: "I considered my career upon the high seas closed by the loss of my ship, and had so informed Commodore Barron, who was our Chief of Bureau in Paris." While his most celebrated deeds were behind him, Semmes was to play an able part in the final naval efforts of the Confederacy.

HARPER'S WEEKLY.
A JOURNAL OF CIVILIZATION.

VOL. VIII.—No. 413.]   NEW YORK, SATURDAY, NOVEMBER 26, 1864.   [SINGLE COPIES TEN CENTS. $4.00 PER YEAR IN ADVANCE.

Entered according to Act of Congress, in the Year 1864, by Harper & Brothers, in the Clerk's Office of the District Court for the Southern District of New York.

CAPTAIN NAPOLEON COLLINS.—PHOTOGRAPHED BY BRADY.—[SEE PAGE 757.]

CAPTAIN C. M. MORRIS.—[SEE PAGE 757.]

THE CAPTURED REBEL PRIVATEER "FLORIDA" AND THE UNITED STATES STEAMER "WACHUSETT."—[SEE PAGE 757.]

Harper's Weekly *tells of the capture of the vaunted commerce raider C.S.S.* Florida.

4   C.S.S. *Florida*, Lieutenant Morris, arrived in Bahia, Brazil, for provisions and coal. Within three days *Florida*'s brilliant career as commerce raider would be closed.

Confederates destroyed the lighthouse at the entrance from Albemarle to Croatan Sound, North Carolina. Commander William H. Macomb, U.S.S. *Shamrock*, reported: "It was blownup and afterwards set on fire so as to make the destruction complete."

5   U.S.S. *Mobile*, Acting Lieutenant Pierre Giraud, seized blockade running British schooner *Annie Virdon* south of Velasco, Texas, with cargo of cotton.

5–6   Boat expedition commanded by Acting Ensign Henry Eason, U.S.S. *Restless*, destroyed large salt works on St. Andrew's Bay, Florida, along with 150 buildings used to house the compound and its employees. Salt works, providing as they did both a foodstuff and an invaluable preservative, were a constant target for fast-hitting Union boat expeditions aimed at drying up the source of intended supplies for Southern armies.

6   Acting Master Charles W. Lee, U.S.S. *Wamsutta*, reported that blockade running steamer *Constance* had run aground and sunk near Long Island in Charleston harbor while trying to enter the port. Lee wrote: ". . . as she is completely submerged in about 3 fathoms water I could ascertain nothing about her except that she is a Clyde-built vessel, of the class of the *Mary Bowers*, and was evidently bound in."

7   U.S.S. *Wachusett*, Commander Napoleon Collins, captured C.S.S. *Florida*, Lieutenant Morris, in Bahia harbor, Brazil, and towed her out to sea. Collins, who had been scouring the sea lanes for the Confederate raider for many months, saw her enter Bahia on 4 October and anchored close by the next morning. Collins offered to meet Morris outside the harbor in a ship duel, but the Confederate captain wisely declined. The Brazilian authorities, recognizing the explosiveness of the situation, exacted promises from both Lieutenant Morris and the U.S. Consul, Thomas Wilson, that no attacks would be made in Brazilian waters. Collins was not to allow elusive *Florida* to escape, however, and plans were laid to attack her shortly after midnight on the 7th. At 3 a.m. he slipped his cable, steamed past the Brazilian gunboat anchored between his ship and *Florida*, and rammed the famous raider on her starboard quarter. After a brief exchange of cannon fire, Lieutenant Porter, commanding *Florida* in Morris's absence, surrendered the ship. By this time the harbor was alive, and as *Wachusett* towed her long-sought prize to sea, the coastal fort opened fire on her.

Collins' actions, though cheered in the North where *Florida* was a household name because of her continued "depredations", were in violation of international law, and prompt disavowal of them was made by Secretary of State Seward. *Florida* was taken to Hampton Roads, arriving there on 12 November. She was ordered returned to the Brazilian Government, but before she could be made ready for sea she mysteriously sank. Commander Collins was courtmartialed and ordered to be dismissed from the naval service. At the trial, the dauntless captain admitted his actions had violated international law, offering in his defense only the following statement: "I respectfully request that it may be entered on the records of the court as my defense that the capture of the *Florida* was for the public good."

Secretary Welles concurred, especially in view of the vast damage done by C.S.S. *Florida* to Union commerce, and, restored Collins to his command. The furor over the capture, however, did not die down. At length, to further satisfy Brazil, a 21-gun salute as an "amende honorable" was fired by U.S.S. *Nipsic* in Bahia harbor, 23 July 1866.

U.S.S. *Aster*, Acting Master Samuel Hall, chased blockade runner *Annie* ashore at New Inlet, North Carolina, under the guns of Fort Fisher, but the 285-ton wooden steamer ran aground herself and was destroyed to prevent capture. U.S.S. *Niphon*, Acting Master Kemble, rescued Hall and his men and, under a hail of fire from Confederate batteries, towed out U.S.S. *Berberry*, which had become disabled trying to pull *Aster* off the shoal.

The torpedo was, I believe, the invention of Engineer Lay of the navy and introduced by Chief Engineer Wood. It has many defects and I would not again attempt its use. Everything being complete we started to the Southard taking the boats through the canals to Chesapeake Bay, and losing one in going down to Norfolk. This was a great misfortune and I have never understood how so stupid a thing occurred. I forget the name of the volunteer Ensign to whose care it was entrusted, but am pleased to know that he was taken prisoner. I trust that his bed was not of down, or his food that of princes while in rebel hands.

(Top) *The torpedo launch used by Lieutenant Cushing to destroy ram C.S.S.* Albemarle. (Bottom) *Extract from Cushing's post-war journal regarding the loss of one of his two launches while en route from New York to Norfolk.*

8 Steamer *Sea King* sailed from London under merchant captain G. H. Corbett to rendezvous with S.S. *Laurel* at Madeira. *Sea King* carried a number of Confederate officers including Lieutenant William C. Whittle; *Laurel* put to sea later the same day carrying Lieutenant James I. Waddell, who, when the rendezvous was effected, would take command of *Sea King* and commission her as C.S.S. *Shenandoah*. *Laurel* also carried the armaments and supplies that would sustain *Shenandoah* on her long voyage as a Confederate raider. Commander Bulloch later reported *Shenandoah*'s

"safe departure" and "that the entire expedition is far away at sea, beyond the reach of interference of any United States authority in Europe. . . ."

Steam Picket Boat No. 2, Acting Ensign Andrew Stockholm, was captured by Confederate troops in Wicomico Bay, Virginia. The boat was one of two purchased by Lieutenant Cushing in New York for the expedition against C.S.S. *Albemarle*, and was en route in company with Picket Boat No. 1 to Fortress Monroe. Mechanical troubles forced No. 2 ashore for repairs, and while these were in progress, No. 1 continuing ahead, Stockholm and his men were attacked by a body of guerrillas. He reported: "I immediately returned their fire, and fought them until I had expended my last cartridge; previous to which I had slipped my cable, and in trying to get out of the enemy's reach, grounded on a sand bar." Stockholm succeeded in burning the boat and destroying his supplies before he and his men were captured. Lieutenant Cushing was highly indignant at what he considered the unnecessary loss of one of his boats, and later wrote of it: "This was a great misfortune and I have never understood how so stupid a thing could have happened. I forget the name of the volunteer ensign to whose care it was intrusted, but am pleased to know that he was taken prisoner. I trust that his bed was not of down or his food that of princes while in rebel hands."

Flag Officer Mitchell wrote Secretary Mallory regarding the enlistment of Union deserters for duty with the James River Squadron: "I beg that no more deserters from the enemy be sent to the squadron in future, for they are apt not only to desert themselves, but induce others to do so who might otherwise continue loyal. The fidelity of no man can be relied upon who has ever proved a traitor to any flag he has engaged to serve under. They form a dangerous element on board a ship." The difficulty of procuring qualified and competent officers and men to man the ships of the James River Squadron was to continue to the end of the war.

9 A Confederate battery near Freeman's wharf, Mobile Bay, opened fire on side-wheeler U.S.S. *Sebago*, Lieutenant Commander Fitzhugh, which was guarding the approaches to Mobile. "There was no evidence of earthworks when these guns were fired," Fitzhugh reported; "they were so masked as to make them difficult to be seen." *Sebago* returned the Confederate fire for an hour, sustaining five casualties.

10 U.S.S. *Key West*, Acting Lieutenant King, U.S.S. *Undine*, Acting Master Bryant, in company with transports *City of Pekin*, *Kenton*, and *Aurora*, were surprised by Confederate shore batteries off Eastport, Mississippi, on the Tennessee River, and after a severe engagement, were forced to retire downriver. The combined operation to take Eastport was designed to secure the river at that point against the crossing of General Forrest's cavalry and provide an outpost against the threatened advance of Confederate General Hood from the East. Departing Clifton, Tennessee, on 9 October with the gunboats in the van, the force steamed up the river and cautiously approached Eastport. Finding no evidence of the Southerners, the Federal troops began to land. Suddenly, masked batteries on both sides of the river opened a severe crossfire, immediately disabling transports *Aurora* and *Kenton* and causing widespread confusion among the troops. *Key West* and *Undine*, both steamers of about 200 tons, engaged the batteries hotly. Seeing the two disabled transports drifting downstream out of control, Lieutenant King ordered *Undine* to follow them, while he stayed at Eastport to cover *City of Pekin* as troops re-embarked and to escort her downstream in retreat.

U.S.S. *Montgomery*, Lieutenant Faucon, captured blockade running British steamer *Bat* near Wilmington with cargo of coal and machinery.

12 Rear Admiral David Dixon Porter assumed command of the North Atlantic Blockading Squadron, relieving Acting Rear Admiral Lee. In one of his early general orders, Porter said: "It will be almost useless to enjoin on all officers the importance of their being vigilant at all times. We have

an active enemy to deal with, and every officer and man must be on the alert . . . ." Porter's efforts would soon turn to the most effective means of enforcing the blockade—the capture of Wilmington, the main port of entry.

Rear Admiral Cornelius K. Stribling relieved Captain Greene as commander of the East Gulf Blockading Squadron. Captain Greene had assumed temporary command upon the departure of Rear Admiral Bailey in August 1864.

U.S.S. *Chocura*, Lieutenant Commander Richard W. Meade, Jr., captured blockade running British schooner *Louisa* off Aransas Pass, Texas, with cargo including iron and tools.

13   Rear Admiral Farragut, a leader with keen understanding of men as well as great skill and courage, wrote to his son, Loyall, from Mobile Bay regarding the young man's studies: ". . . remember also that one of the requisite studies for an officer is *man*. Where your analytical geometry will serve you once, a knowledge of men will serve you daily. As a commander, to get the right men in the right place is one of the questions of success or defeat."

13–15   Boat expedition from U.S.S. *Braziliera*, Acting Master Gillespie, and U.S.S. *Mary Sanford*, Acting Master Zaccheus Kempton, freed a number of slaves from a plantation on White Oak Creek, Georgia, and engaged a company of Confederate cavalry at Yellow Bluff. The Union gunboats succeeded in driving off the Southerners.

15   Acting Master's Mate Woodman completed his third daring and successful reconnaissance of the Confederate position at Plymouth, North Carolina, reporting C.S.S. *Albemarle* moored to the wharf as before, and the apparent abandonment of efforts to raise the captured steamer *Southfield*.

18   Major General Thomas, commanding Union forces in Tennessee, wired Major General Sherman concerning his plans for opposing General Hood's thrust into Tennessee: "I have arranged with Lieutenant [Commander] Greer, commanding gunboat fleet on lower Tennessee, to patrol the river as far up as Eastport [Mississippi]. Lieutenant Glassford, commanding between Bridgeport and Decatur [Alabama] patrols that portion on the river daily, and cooperates with me very cordially." As Hood approached Tuscumbia and his rendezvous with General Forrest's cavalry, Union commanders became increasingly concerned with measures to keep the Confederates from crossing the Tennessee River in Alabama, and relied heavily on the gunboats of the Mississippi Squadron for this duty as well as for intelligence. During the climactic campaign between the forces of Thomas and those of Hood, the close cooperation and support of naval forces played a key role.

19   *Sea King*, the sleek, fast ship Commander Bulloch had obtained for the Confederate cause in England, rendezvoused with tender *Laurel* north of the island of Las Desertas in the Madeiras. *Sea King* was sold to the Confederate States and renamed C.S.S. *Shenandoah*, after which guns, powder, supplies, and crewmembers from *Laurel* were loaded. Lieutenant Waddell, who had sailed from England in *Laurel*, assumed command of the cruiser and remarked: "Each of us asked himself instinctively, what great adventures shall we meet in her? What will be her ultimate fate?" *Shenandoah*, one of Bulloch's greatest successes, was destined to become one of the most effective commerce raiders of the war and the last warship to sail under the Confederate flag.

U.S.S. *Mobile*, Acting Lieutenant Giraud, captured schooner *Emily* off San Luis Pass, Texas, with cargo of 150 bales of cotton.

Even in the midst of blockade duty afloat, Union sailors were able to vote in the presidential election. Rear Admiral Dahlgren ordered Acting Master John K. Crosby, U.S.S. *Harvest Moon* to "proceed with the U.S.S. *Harvest Moon* under your command to Savannah River, Wassaw,

Ossabaw, Sapelo, and Doboy [Sounds], and communicate with the vessels there, in order to collect the 'sailors' votes already distributed for that purpose. A number of ballots will be given you, in order to enable the men to vote."

19–20 Boat expedition under Acting Master George E. Hill, U.S.S. *Stars and Stripes*, ascended the Ocklockonee River in Western Florida and destroyed an extensive Confederate fishery on Marsh's Island, capturing a detachment of soldiers assigned to guard the works. In small and large operations, assault from the sea destroyed the South's resources.

21 U.S.S. *Fort Jackson*, Captain Sands, captured steamer *Wando* at sea east of Cape Romain, South Carolina, with cargo of cotton.

U.S.S. *Sea Bird*, Ensign E. L. Robbins, captured blockade running British schooner *Lucy* off Anclote Keys, Florida, with assorted cargo.

22 Rear Admiral Porter, in a confidential letter to Commander Macomb, commanding naval forces in Albemarle sound, set down instructions for engaging C.S.S. *Albemarle*, should the ram again come out to challenge Union control of the Sounds: "There is but one chance for wooden vessels in attacking an ironclad. You will, in case she comes out, make a dash at her with every vessel you have, and 'lay her on board', using canister to fire into her ports, while the ram strikes her steering apparatus and disables her. You will see that every vessel is provided with proper grapnels, to hold on by while going alongside, and a boarding party will be appointed to lash the vessels together. Even if half your vessels are sunk you must pursue this course." Porter added: "I have directed Lieutenant Cushing to go down in a steam launch, and if possible destroy this ram with torpedoes. I have no great confidence in his success, but you will afford him all the assistance in your power, and keep boats ready to pick him up in case of failure."

In answer to the objections of Major General Whiting and Governor Vance of North Carolina (see September 1864), Secretary Mallory wrote to President Davis defending the use of C.S.S. *Tallahassee* and *Chickamauga* as commerce cruisers rather than holding them for the defense of Wilmington: "Though the *Tallahassee* captured thirty-one vessels her service is not limited to the value of these ships and cargoes and the number of prisoners; but it must be estimated in connection with other results—the consequent insecurity of the United States coastwise commerce, the detention and delay of vessels in port, and the augmentation of the rates of marine insurance, by which millions were added to the expenses of commerce and navigation, the compulsory withdrawal of a portion of the blockading force from Wilmington in pursuit of her. A cruise by the *Chickamauga* and *Tallahassee* against northern coasts and commerce would at once withdraw a fleet of fast steamers from the blockading force off Wilmington in pursuit of them, and this result alone would render such a cruise expedient."

Union shore batteries on the north bank of the James River at Signal Hill opened fire suddenly on Ships of the Confederate Squadron, anchored in the river at that point. Wooden gunboat C.S.S. *Drewry*, Lieutenant Wall, sustained moderate damage, and after engaging the batteries for about one hour, the Southern vessels retired under the protection of the guns of Fort Darling, on Chaffin's Bluff.

British blockade running steamer *Flora*, after being chased by U.S.S. *Wamsutta*, *Geranium*, and *Mingoe* off Charleston, was run ashore and destroyed next day by fire from monitors and the batteries on Morris Island.

U.S.S. *Eolus*, Acting Master William O. Lundt, captured Confederate blockade running steamer *Hope* near Wilmington with cargo of machinery.

22–24 Acting Ensign Sommers, U.S.S. *Tacony*, led a reconnaissance party up the Roanoke River, North Carolina. While returning, the party was fired on by Confederates and forced to seek

John K. Mitchell
Captain, CSN

Melancton C. Smith
Captain, USN

cover in a swamp. After constructing a make-shift raft to support his wounded, Sommers succeeded in reaching the mouth of the river, where he was picked up by Union forces. Four other members of his party, missing in the swamp for four days, were rescued by Union scouts on 29 October.

23 Blockade runner *Flamingo*, aground off Sullivan's Island, South Carolina, was destroyed by shell fire from Forts Strong and Putnam, Battery Chatfield, and ships of Rear Admiral Dahlgren's South Atlantic Blockading Squadron.

24 In light of the increased difficulty of manning his ships and mounting danger from Union torpedoes in the James River, Flag Officer Mitchell considered withdrawal of his squadron upriver closer to Richmond. In response to the Flag Officer's request for his views on the subject, General Robert E. Lee wrote: "If the enemy succeeds in throwing a force to the south bank [of the James River] in rear of General Pickett's lines, it will necessitate not only the withdrawal of General P.'s forces, but also the abandonment of Petersburg and its railroad connections, throwing the whole army back to the defenses of Richmond. . . . I fully appreciate the importance of preserving our fleet, and deprecate any unnecessary exposure of it. But you will perceive the magnitude of the service which it is thought you can render, and determine whether it is sufficient to justify the risk. . . . As I said before, I can forsee no state of circumstances in which the fleet can render more important aid in the defense of Richmond at present than by guarding the river below Chaffin's Bluff."

U.S.S. *Nita*, Acting Lieutenant Robert B. Smith, captured schooner *Unknown* off Clearwater Harbor, Florida, after her crew had escaped.

U.S.S. *Rosalie*, Acting Ensign Henry W. Wells, captured an unidentified blockade running sloop off Little Marco, Florida, with cargo of salt and shoes.

25   Expedition from U.S.S. *Don*, Commander F. A. Parker, landed at Fleet's Point, in the Great Wicomico River, Virginia, and burned houses, barns, and outbuildings formerly used as shelter by the home guards of Northumberland County while firing on vessels of the Potomac Flotilla. Four boats were also burned and five others captured.

    Rear Admiral George F. Pearson assumed command of the Pacific Squadron relieving Rear Admiral C. H. Bell.

26   U.S.S. *Adolph Hugel*, Acting Master Sylvanus Nickerson, captured schooner *Coquette* with cargo including tobacco and wheat at Wade's Bay on the Eastern shore of the Potomac River. Two days later sloop *James Landry* was also seized by Nickerson for violation of the blockade regulations. Nickerson took sloop *Zion* as a prize on 2 November, as the Potomac Flotilla alertly continued its ceaseless efforts to stifle even the smallest trickle of goods flowing from Southern sympathizers in Union dominated areas to the beleaguered Confederate forces in Virginia.

27   Boat expedition commanded by Lieutenant William Barker Cushing destroyed C.S.S. *Albemarle* at Plymouth, on the Roanoke River, North Carolina. Cushing reported to Rear Admiral Porter on 30 October: "I have the honor to report that the rebel ironclad *Albemarle* is at the bottom of the Roanoke River." In July the redoutable Cushing, only 21 years old, had been sent to Washington by Rear Admiral Lee to discuss with the Navy Department his plans for sinking the Confederate ram. He proposed at that time two plans, one involving a boarding party to travel overland and attack with india rubber boats, and the other calling for two steam launches to approach the ram's moorings on the river. Both plans envisaged the capture of the ram, since Cushing wanted to destroy her only if it became necessary. Secretary Welles assented to the plan, and gave the daring Lieutenant permission to proceed to New York to procure the necessary boats.

    Cushing finally decided upon two thirty-foot steam picket launches, each fitted with a fourteen-foot spar and a torpedo, and mounting a twelve-pounder howitzer in the bow. Moving south by the inland water route, one of the picket boats was lost to the Confederates (see 8 October 1864), but the other arrived in the sounds of North Carolina on 24 October. As Cushing later reported: "Here I, for the first time, disclosed to my officers and men our object and told them that they were at liberty to go or not as they pleased. These, seven in number, all volunteered."

    The imaginative attack seemed at first doomed to failure. Cushing departed the night of 26 October, but grounded at the mouth of Roanoke River, and spent most of the hours of darkness freeing his small craft. The attempt was postponed until 27 October.

    That night was dark and foul. Cushing was accompanied by fourteen men, an additional seven having been recruited from the blockading squadron. Among them were his old companion, Acting Master's Mate William L. Howorth, and that veteran of Roanoke reconnaissance patrols, Acting Master's Mate John Woodman. Towed behind the torpedo boat was a cutter from U.S.S. *Shamrock* whose duty, as Cushing described it, ". . . was to dash aboard the *Southfield* at the first hail and prevent any rocket from being ignited." *Southfield* had been captured by Confederates in an earlier action with *Albemarle* (see 19 April 1864) and was sunk in the Roanoke a mile below the ironclad's berth. With the steam engine's throb muffled by a heavy tarpaulin, the expedition moved out to cover the eight miles between Albemarle Sound and Plymouth, keeping close to the bank and anticipating discovery at any moment. Cushing's renowned good fortune held, however, and he succeeded in passing within twenty feet of *Southfield* without being challenged. The lieutenant still hoped to board *Albemarle* and "take her alive", but as he steamed up to the ram, an alert picket saw the dim form of the boat and challenged. Cushing instantly changed his plan: ". . . just as I was sheering in close to the wharf a hail came sharp and quick from the ironclad, in an instant repeated. I at once directed the cutter to cast off and go down to capture the guard left in our rear [on board *Southfield*], and ordering all steam, went at the dark mountain of iron in front of us. A heavy fire at once opened upon us, not only from the ship,

(Above) C.S.S. Albemarle *sunk at Plymouth, North Carolina.*
*(Right) Lieutenant William Barker Cushing, USN, commanded the
daring expedition that destroyed the awesome Confederate ram.*

Cushing drives home the spar torpedo that sinks C.S.S. Albemarle.

but from the men stationed on the shore, but this did not disable us and we neared them rapidly.'' A large fire now blazed up on shore, and Cushing discovered a large boom of protective logs surrounding the Confederate ship. Amid the mounting fire, he cooly turned the boat around in order to run at the obstructions at full speed. ''As I turned the whole back of my coat was torn out by buck shot and the sole of my shoe was carried away. The fire was very severe. In the lull of the firing the Captain hailed us, again demanding what boat it was. All my men gave comical answer and mine was a dose of canister which I sent amongst them from the howitzer, buzzing and singing against the iron ribs and into the mass of men standing fire-lit upon the shore.'' According to the recollections of Acting Ensign Thomas Gay, later captured, Cushing shouted: ''Leave the ram, or I'll blow you to pieces!'' No response was heard, and Cushing ran through the hail of fire at full speed, his boat lurching over the log barrier. ''The torpedo boom was lowered and by a vigorous pull I succeeded in diving the torpedo under the overhang and exploding it at the same time that the *Albemarle*'s gun was fired. A shot seemed to go chasing through my boat, and a dense mass of water rushed in from the torpedo, filling the launch and completely disabling her.''

Albemarle, a gaping hole in her port quarter, began to sink rapidly. Lieutenant Warley, commanding *Albemarle* reported: ''The water gained on us so fast that all exertions were fruitless, and the vessel went down in a few moments, merely leaving her shield and smokestack out.'' Cushing found his own boat sinking but, refusing to surrender in the midst of the enemy, ordered his men to save themselves and started to swim for shore. Although he had exploded the torpedo virtually staring down the muzzle of *Albemarle*'s gun, he was miraculously unharmed. Making for shore, he tried to save the gallant John Woodman, who was unable to swim any longer, but Woodman sank. Cushing finally pulled himself half onto the bank and lay exhausted until morning. Finding himself near a Confederate picket station, he managed to seize a skiff and rowed the eight miles downstream to Albemarle Sound. There he was picked up by U.S.S. *Valley City*.

When news of the dashing young lieutenant's feat reached the squadron, rockets were set off, and all hands called to ''cheer ship''. Elated, Porter said that Lieutenant Cushing had ''displayed a heroic enterprise seldom equalled and never excelled. . . . He has shown an absolute disregard of death or danger, and will no doubt be suitably rewarded by the Government, which reward he well deserves.'' The Admiral's enthusiasm was well founded, for the destruction of *Albemarle* paved the way for the capture of Plymouth and firm control of the entire Roanoke River area. It also released ships that had been guarding against the ram for other blockade duties.

Congress commended Cushing for his bravery and enterprise, and promoted him to Lieutenant Commander. Edward J. Houghton, the only other man to escape death or capture, was awarded the medal of honor.

28 U.S.S. *General Thomas*, Acting Master Gilbert Morton, engaged Confederate batteries near Decatur, Alabama, on the Tennessee River. Paddle-wheeler *General Thomas* sustained damage but passed the batteries, rounded to and, with Army gunboat *Stone River*, poured such a withering crossfire into the emplacements that the Southerners abandoned them. Brigadier General Robert Granger, commanding Union troops in the area, described the action: ''It was impossible for men to withstand this attack. They deserted their guns, a portion of them retreating to their main line, while many of them rushed down the bank and sought the protection of the trees at the waters edge. The guns of the boats, double-shotted with canister, were turned upon them at a distance of scarcely 300 yards, and poured in a terrible fire.'' As the Confederates under General Hood neared the Tennessee River in their campaign to divert Sherman by invading Tennessee, patroling Union gunboats, invaluable not only in guarding against river crossings, but also in collecting vital information about troop movements, were attacked by mobile field batteries with increasing frequency and intensity.

Captain Pennock, temporarily in command of the Mississippi Squadron, issued an order stressing: "The enemy must not be allowed to cross the [Mississippi] river. Officers in command will develop their utmost vigilance and activity, and take every precaution to prevent such a movement. Vessels must be kept in motion night and day." The inability of major Confederate forces to cross the Mississippi from the West in the face of patroling Union gunboats illustrated the vast importance of Union naval control of the river, and was a major factor in the developing Tennessee campaign.

C.S.S. *Chickamauga*, Lieutenant John Wilkinson, sortied from Wilmington harbor, eluded the blockading vessels off the bar, and put to sea as a commerce raider.

U.S.S. *Calypso*, Acting Master Stuart, and U.S.S. *Eolus*, Acting Master Lundt, captured blockade running British steamer *Lady Sterling* at sea off Wilmington with cargo of cotton and tobacco.

29 C.S.S. *Olustee*, formerly C.S.S. *Tallahassee*, Lieutenant William H. Ward, eluded the blockaders off Wilmington. Ward returned to Wilmington on 7 November after a brief but successful cruise, having destroyed bark *Empress Theresa*, schooners *A. J. Bird*, *E. F. Lewis*, and *Vapor*, ship *Arcole*, and brig *T. D. Wagner* during the first three days of November.

29–1 November Capitalizing on Lieutenant Cushing's success in destroying C.S.S. *Albemarle*, Commander Macomb moved upon Plymouth, North Carolina, capturing the town and its defenses after a heated engagement. Immediately after Cushing's return, on 29 October, Macomb steamed up the Roanoke with six ships. U.S.S. *Valley City*, Acting Master John A. J. Brooks, proceeded via Middle River and entered the Roanoke above Plymouth to cut off the garrison's escape by water. Macomb's gunboats engaged the lower batteries protecting the town, but, seeing that two schooners had been sunk abreast the wreck of U.S.S. *Southfield*, obstructing the river, withdrew to Albemarle Sound. On the 30th, Macomb took his fleet through the Middle River to attack the city and its defenses from above, spending the entire day in navigating the treacherous channels and shelling the Confederate works at long range. On 31 October, Macomb formed his line of battle, with converted ferryboat U.S.S. *Commodore Hull*, Acting Master Francis Josselyn, in the van, followed by side-wheel double-enders U.S.S. *Tacony*, Lieutenant Commander Truxtun, U.S.S. *Shamrock*, Commander Macomb, U.S.S. *Otsego*, Lieutenant Commander Henry N. T. Arnold, and U.S.S. *Wyalusing*, Lieutenant Commander English. Tinclad U.S.S. *Whitehead*, Acting Master Barrett, was lashed to the port side of *Tacony*, with tugs *Bazely* and *Belle* lashed to *Shamrock* and *Otsego*. The fleet steamed boldly up and engaged the Plymouth batteries and rifle pits at close range. A violent battle ensued in which *Commodore Hull* sustained heavy damage. The Union cannonade detonated a large magazine ashore with a tremendous explosion shortly thereafter. The Southerners began to evacuate their fortifications. Macomb reported: "I then made signal to cease firing, and then to land and take possession of the batteries, which was done without resistance." A landing party from U.S.S. *Wyalusing* entered Fort Williams, captured prisoners and raised the Stars and Stripes again over Plymouth.

At Plymouth Macomb captured 37 prisoners, 22 cannon, a large quantity of stores, 200 stand of arms, and the sunken but still important C.S.S. *Albemarle*. For his dashing and timely action, Macomb was praised by Secretary Welles and advanced ten numbers in grade by Congress. President Lincoln enthusiastically recommended the advancement, speaking of Commander Macomb's "distinguished conduct in the capture of the town of Plymouth, North Carolina. . . ." The Union again held this strategic town and thus commanded the Roanoke River, Albemarle Sound, and threatened the interior of North Carolina from the sea.

30 C.S.S. *Shenandoah*, Lieutenant Waddell, captured and scuttled bark *Alina* due south of the Azores and due west of Dakar. *Alina*, a new bark on her maiden voyage, was *Shenandoah*'s first prize. She carried a cargo of railroad iron. Waddell wrote: "It was fortunate my first capture could be scuttled, for the steamer's position was good and a bonfire would have given alarm to all Yankees

With C.S.S. Albemarle *destroyed, the Union's wooden gunboats recapture Plymouth, North Carolina.*

within 30 miles, and then, too, a cruiser might have been in the neighborhood, which would have [been] attracted by the red glare of the sky and interfered with our fun . . . we were forced to destroy our prizes because we were not allowed to take them into a neutral port [for] adjudication."

Confederate batteries on the Tennessee River near Johnsonville, Tennessee, fired on and captured U.S.S. *Undine*, Acting Master Bryant, and transports *Venus* and *Cheeseman*, after a sharp engagement. *Undine* had convoyed transport *Anna* to a point below Sandy Island, and was returning upstream when the sound of artillery was heard further down the Tennessee. Bryant came about to investigate, and near Paris Landing was attacked by a battery of several guns and volleys of musketry. While *Undine* was fiercely engaging the Confederates, transport *Venus* steamed down the river, and notwithstanding Bryant's warning passed by the batteries and joined him in the engagement. About twenty minutes later, another transport, *Cheeseman*, also came down river, and was immediately disabled and captured. *Undine* continued to fire on the batteries for nearly three hours, when her ammunition was nearly exhausted and her engine disabled. Unable to resist further, Bryant hauled down his flag but, when this was not observed by the Confederates and firing continued, he unsuccessfully attempted to destroy his vessel. *Undine* was taken intact, as well as the two transports, which could be put to good service in ferrying troops across the Tennessee River. The attacking Southern troops, operating in territory long under Union control, were part of General Nathan B. Forrest's cavalry, who were attempting to cross the Tennessee River and join forces with General Hood for the large-scale Confederate assault on Tennessee. By this drive into Tennessee, Hood and Forrest hoped to sever General Sherman's supply lines, forcing him to abandon the march across Georgia.

31 C.S.S. *Chickamauga*, Lieutenant Wilkinson, captured and burned off the northeast coast of the United States the ship *Emma L. Hall*, with cargo of sugar and molasses, and ship *Shooting Star*, with cargo of coal. Wilkinson transferred the passengers of *Shooting Star* to a passing vessel, *Albion Lincoln*, which headed directly for New York to spread the alarm. Wilkinson later wrote of the transfer of prisoners: "In truth, I was relieved from an awkward dilemma by the opportune capture of the *Albion Lincoln* for there was absolutely no place for a female aboard the *Chickamauga*. I do not doubt, however, that the redoubtable Mrs. Drinkwater [wife of *Shooting Star*'s Master]

would have accommodated herself to the circumstances by turning me out of my own cabin. Heavens! what a tongue she wielded! The young officers of the *Chickamauga* relieved each other in boat duty to and fro and she routed every one of them ignominiously."

U.S.S. *Katahdin*, Lieutenant Commander John Irwin, captured British blockade runner *Albert Edward* off Galveston with cargo of cotton.

U.S.S. *Wilderness*, Acting Master Henry Arey, and U.S.S. *Niphon*, Acting Master Kemble, seized blockade running British steamer *Annie* off New Inlet, North Carolina, with cargo of tobacco, cotton, and turpentine. Concerned by reports that the two captains had failed to signal other patroling ships in the vicinity during the chase of *Annie* in order to obtain a larger share of the prize money, Rear Admiral Porter wrote: "This war is not being conducted for the benefit of officers or to enrich them by the capture of prizes, and every commander is deficient in the high moral character which has always been inherent in the Navy who for a moment consults his private interests in preference to the public good, hesitates to destroy what is the property of the enemy, or attempts to benefit himself at the expense of others . . . Honor and glory should be the watchword of the Navy, and not profit."

NOVEMBER

1 C.S.S. *Chickamauga*, Lieutenant Wilkinson, captured and scuttled off the northeast coast of the United States schooners *Goodspeed* in ballast and *Otter Rock* with cargo of potatoes.

Dr. W. A. W. Spotswood, Surgeon in Charge, Office of Medicine and Surgery, C.S.N., reported the effect of the continuing blockade: "It affords me much satisfaction to report that, by the operations of the purveyor's department, an ample supply of medicines, instruments, and everything to meet the wants of the sick has been furnished up to the present time, but owing to the strict blockade of the seacoast and harbors of the Confederacy, rendering it impossible to procure medical supplies from abroad, I feel that there will necessarily be much difficulty in procuring many valuable articles soon required for the use for the sick. Every effort has been made to procure a large supply, but in vain, and it is to be regretted that the supply of cotton placed in the hands of the Navy agent at the port of Wilmington can not be sent to Bermuda to purchase more or to pay for the medicines that have been received."

Rear Admiral Lee assumed command of the Mississippi Squadron at Mound City, Illinois.

2 Paddle-wheelers U.S.S. *Key West*, Acting Lieutenant King, and U.S.S. *Tawah*, Acting Lieutenant Jason Goudy, patrolling the Tennessee River, encountered *Undine* and *Venus*, which the Confederates had captured three days earlier. After a heated running engagement, *Venus* was retaken, but *Undine*, though badly damaged, escaped. Carrying Southern troops, *Undine* outran her pursuers and gained the protection of Confederate batteries at Reynoldsburg Island, near Johnsonville, Tennessee. King wired his district commander, Lieutenant Commander Shirk, "Weather so misty and dark, did not follow her."

C.S.S. *Chickamauga*, Lieutenant Wilkinson, captured bark *Speedwell* off the New Jersey coast and bonded her for $18,000.

U.S.S. *Santiago de Cuba*, Captain Glisson, captured blockade running steamer *Lucy* at sea east of Charleston with cargo of cotton and tobacco.

4 Paddle-wheelers U.S.S. *Key West*, Acting Lieutenant King, U.S.S. *Tawah*, Acting Lieutenant Goudy, and small steamer U.S.S. *Elfin*, Acting Master Augustus F. Thompson, were destroyed after an engagement with Confederate batteries off Johnsonville, Tennessee, along with several transport steamers and a large quantity of supplies. Acting Lieutenant King, in command of the naval group, was patrolling the river and protecting the Union depot and headquarters at Johnsonville as the forces of Confederate General Forrest suddenly struck the city. On 3 November,

King discovered a strong Confederate field battery emplaced to command a narrow channel in the Tennessee River between Reynoldsburg Island and the west bank two miles below Johnsonville. Confederate gunboat *Undine*, lately captured from the Union (see 30 October), twice attempted on the 3rd to lure King and his gunboats downriver in range of the batteries without success. On the morning of 4 November, *Undine* again came upriver from the Confederate batteries, and this time King took his three ships down to engage her. At about the same time, Lieutenant Commander Fitch, commanding U.S.S. *Moose* and five other small steamers, *Brilliant*, *Victory*, *Curlew*, *Fairy*, and *Paw Paw*, approached the downstream side of Reynoldsburg Island, to support King. The Confederates burned *Undine* and opened on the Union gunboats with shore fire. Because of the narrowness of the channel and the commanding position occupied by the batteries, Fitch could not bring his ships closer to Johnsonville to aid *Key West*, *Tawah*, and *Elfin*, which had retired to a position off the town to protect the transports and supplies. The Confederates then moved their main batteries along the river to positions opposite Johnsonville, leaving sufficient guns to block Fitch's passage, and commenced a fierce bombardment of the gunboats, transports, and wharf area. After fighting for nearly an hour against great odds, King at last ordered his three riddled gunboats fired. Army Assistant Quartermaster Henry Howland, a witness to the action from ashore, described it: ". . . for nearly thirty minutes the cannonading was the most terrific I have ever witnessed. The gunboats fought magnificiently and continued firing for more than twenty minutes after they were all disabled, when Lieutenant Commander King was compelled to order them abandoned and burned." King and most of his men escaped to the waterfront, which by this time was itself a roaring inferno as Union officers put the torch to supplies on the wharves to prevent them from falling into Southern hands. The gunboats and transports were lost, but General Forrest was prevented from capturing them intact, and was thus unable to cross the river in force and capture Johnsonville. Instead, the Confederate commander,

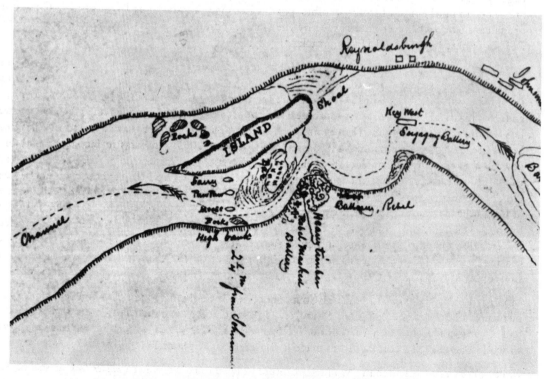

Manuscript map of the Reynoldsburg Island area, Tennessee River.

IV–130

anxious to press his advantage, moved his batteries downstream to cut off Fitch and the gunboats below Reynoldsburg Island. Fitch, nevertheless, succeeded in withdrawing his forces safely. Later reflecting on the action at Johnsonville, he commented: "The *Key West, Tawah,* and *Elfin* fought desperately and were handled in magnificent style, but it is impossible for boats of this class, with their batteries, to contend successfully against heavy-rifled field batteries in a narrow river full of bars and shoals, no matter with what skill and desperation they may be fought." By this time it was clear that the Confederates were moving in force, and that Forrest was threatening to close the Tennessee and Cumberland rivers completely. Decisive events both on the rivers and the hills of Tennessee were imminent.

5 In General Order No. 34 to the North Atlantic Blockading Squadron, Rear Admiral Porter wrote: "The gallant exploits of Lieutenant Cushing previous to this affair will form a bright page in the history of the war, but they have all been eclipsed by the destruction of the *Albemarle.* The spirit evinced by this officer is what I wish to see pervading this squadron. . . . Opportunity will be offered to all those who have the energy and skill to undertake like enterprises."

Secretary Mallory reported to President Davis on the continuing contribution of the Confederate Naval Academy which was training young midshipmen not only in the classroom but under fire: "In my last report I brought to your notice that the steamship *Patrick Henry* had been organized as a school and practice ship for the education of midshipmen in the several essential branches of their profession. The system of instruction conforms, as nearly as practicable, to that of the most approved naval schools, and this institution will serve as a nucleus for an establishment which the necessities of a naval service and the interests of the country will at an early day render necessary. Under the efficient command of Lieutenant Commander Parker, aided by zealous and competent officers, the beneficial results of the school are already visible in the progress, tone, and bearing of our midshipmen. Though but from 14 to 18 years of age, they eagerly seek every opportunity presented for engaging in hazardous enterprises, and those who are sent upon them uniformly exhibit good discipline, conduct, and courage." Classroom ordnance theory was often interrupted by the very real ordnance "drills" of helping to man ship and shore batteries to repel Union attack.

W. G. Fargo, Mayor of Buffalo, New York, telegraphed Secretary Welles that ship *Georgian* had been purchased in Toronto by a Southern sympathizer, Dr. James Bates: "My information is that she will be armed on the Canada shore for the purpose of encountering the U.S.S. *Michigan* and for piratical and predatory purposes on the Lakes. . . ." Though Commander Carter, U.S.S. *Michigan,* discounted the rumors, *Georgian* continued to arouse grave concern in the Great Lakes area. To be commanded by Master John Y. Beall, CSN, she was in fact to be part of a new plot on the part of Confederate agent Jacob Thompson to capture U.S.S. *Michigan* and attack the cities on Lake Erie, but the suspicions of Union authorities and the strict surveillance under which the ship was placed by Union agents prevented the plot from being carried out. Welles ordered Carter to seize *Georgian* if she ventured into American waters, but she was searched twice by local American and Canadian authorities without any hint of her true character being detected. Nevertheless, Union intelligence and close surveillance prevented this Confederate scheme from bearing fruit, and *Georgian* was laid up at Collingwood, on the Canadian side, eventually to be sold again to private parties.

Monitor U.S.S. *Patapsco,* Lieutenant Commander John Madigan, bombarded and set afire an unidentified sloop aground off Fort Moultrie, Charleston. Madigan noted: "She seems to have had a cargo of cotton and turpentine." Rear Admiral Dahlgren wrote: ". . . the work was so well done that the conflagration made a considerable appearance at night."

C.S.S. *Shenandoah,* Lieutenant Waddell, captured and burned schooner *Charter Oak* at sea off the Cape Verde Islands, after removing her passengers and a quantity of fruit, vegetables, and other provisions. Waddell remained near the burning prize to make sure she was consumed, and then, suspecting that Union cruisers might be attracted by the blaze, stood southward.

U.S.S. *Fort Morgan*, Lieutenant William B. Eaton, captured blockade runner *John A. Hazard* off the Texas coast (27° N, 96° W) with cargo including coffee, rice, oil, dry goods and medicines.

6 U.S.S. *Fort Morgan*, Lieutenant Eaton, captured blockade running schooner *Lone* off Brazos Pass, Texas, with cargo including iron and bagging.

Boats from U.S.S. *Adela*, Acting Lieutenant Louis N. Stodder, captured schooner *Badger* attempting to run the blockade out of St. George's Sound, Florida, with cargo of cotton.

7 Upon learning that Confederate officers were quartered in a house on the Arkansas side of the Mississippi River near Island 68, Acting Lieutenant Frederic S. Hill led an expedition from U.S.S. *Tyler* to capture them. However, they had departed. The mother of one of them boldly showed Hill her permit to transport cotton up the Mississippi and a request, officially endorsed by Major General Cadwallader C. Washburn, USA, for gunboat protection. Hill reluctantly complied with the request, remarking to Rear Admiral Lee: ". . . in the face of all these documents, as I was upon the spot and a steamer then at hand ready to take the cotton, I considered it proper to give her the required protection, although with a very bad grace. Permit me, admiral, respectfully to call your attention to the anomaly of using every exertion to capture rebel officers at 2 a.m., whose cotton I am called upon to protect in its shipment to a market at 10 a.m. of the same day, thus affording them the means of supplying themselves with every comfort money can procure ere they return to their brother rebels in arms with Hood."

8 Rear Admiral Farragut, writing Secretary Welles, expressed his deeply held conviction that effective seapower was not dependent so much on a particular kind of ship or a specific gun but rather on the officers and men who manned them: ". . . I think the world is sadly mistaken when it supposes that battles are won by this or that kind of gun or vessel. In my humble opinion the *Kearsarge* would have captured or sunk the *Alabama* as often as they might have met under the same organization and officers. The best gun and the best vessel should certainly be chosen, but the victory three times out of four depends upon those who fight them. I do not believe that the result would have been different if the *Kearsarge* had had nothing but a battery of 8-inch guns and 100-pound chase rifle. What signifies the size and caliber of the gun if you do not hit your adversary?"

Acting Master Francis Josselyn, U.S.S. *Commodore Hull*, landed with a party of sailors at Edenton, North Carolina, under orders from Commander Macomb to break up a court session being held there. Josselyn described the unique expedition: "I landed with a detachment of men this afternoon at Edenton and adjourned *sine die* a county court which was in session in the court house at that place under so-called Confederate authority. This court, the first that has been held at Edenton since the breaking out of the war, the authorities had the impertinence to hold under my very guns."

C.S.S. *Shenandoah*, Lieutenant Waddell, captured and burned bark *D. Godfrey* southwest of the Cape Verde Islands with cargo of beef and pork.

9 U.S.S. *Stepping Stones*, Acting Lieutenant Daniel A. Campbell, captured blockade running sloops *Reliance* and *Little Elmer* in Mobjack Bay, Virginia.

10 Rear Admiral Dahlgren wrote to Secretary Welles regarding plans for another joint attack on Charleston. Dahlgren well understood the great advantage in mobility and supply enjoyed by the Union through its strong control of the sea: "Part of the troops could be landed at Bull's Bay, whence there is a good road for some 15 miles; part would enter the inlet seaward of Sullivan's Island, seize Long Island, and with the aid of the Navy, land in the rear of Sullivan's Island,

join the force coming from Bull's Bay, and occupy Mount Pleasant. . . . This operation would require 30,000 to 50,000 good men, because it is reasonable to admit that the present small force of the rebels would receive large additions. Still, we have the unquestioned advantage of being able to bring here additional forces more promptly in the present position of the main armies. Hood must pass around Sherman in order to give any aid, and General Grant equally obstructs the road from Richmond.''

C.S.S. *Shenandoah*, Lieutenant Waddell, captured and scuttled brig *Susan* at sea southwest of the Cape Verde Islands with cargo of coal. Waddell recalled later: ''She leaked badly and was the dullest sailor I had ever seen; really she moved so slowly that barnacles grew to her bottom, and it was simply impossible for her crew to pump her out as fast as the water made.''

11 Commander Henry K. Davenport, U.S.S. *Lancaster*, captured Confederates on board steamer *Salvador*, bound from Panama to California, after having been informed that they intended to seize the ship at sea and convert her into a raider. *Salvador*'s captain had warned naval authorities at Panama Bay that the attempt was to be made, and Davenport and his men arranged to search the baggage of the passengers after the vessel passed the territorial limits of Panama. The search revealed guns and ammunition, along with a commission from Secretary Mallory for the capture; the Confederates were promptly taken into custody. This daring party, led by Acting Master Thomas E. Hogg, CSN, was one of many attempting to seize Union steamers and convert them into commerce raiders, especially with a view toward capturing the gold shipments from California. Union warships usually convoyed the California ships to prevent their capture.

U.S.S. *Wachusett*, Commander Collins, arrived at Hampton Roads with the captured commerce raider C.S.S. *Florida*.

12 A boat expedition from U.S.S. *Hendrick Hudson*, Acting Lieutenant Charles H. Rockwell, and U.S.S. *Nita*, Acting Lieutenant Robert B. Smith, attempted to destroy Confederate salt works on a reconnaissance near Tampa Bay, Florida, but the sailors were driven back to their boats by Southern cavalry.

C.S.S. *Shenandoah*, Lieutenant Waddell, seized and bonded clipper ship *Kate Prince* and brig *Adelaide* in mid-Atlantic near the equator.

13 C.S.S. *Shenandoah*, Lieutenant Waddell, captured and burned schooner *Lizzie M. Stacey* in mid-Atlantic near the equator with cargo of pinesalt and iron. *Lizzie*'s mate, an unabashed Irishman, told Waddell: ''. . . my hearty, if we'd had ten guns aboard her, you wouldn't have got us without a bit of a shindy, or if the breeze had been a bit stiffer, we'd given her the square sail, and all hell wouldn't have caught her.'' Two of the schooner's seamen joined *Shenandoah*'s crew voluntarily and another was impressed. She was the last prize the raider would take for some three weeks.

14-15 Acting Master Lothrop Wight and Acting Ensign Frederick W. Mintzer reconnoitered Confederate naval dispositions above Dutch Gap on the James River, Virginia. Work was going ahead rapidly on the Dutch Gap Canal, which would allow Union gunboats to bypass the obstructions at Trent's Reach, and the work of Wight and Mintzer provided valuable information regarding the positions of Confederate ships and troops.

15 Governor William A. Buckingham of Connecticut wrote Secretary Welles of the ''defenseless condition of Stonington.'' The citizens of the city, he reported, ''feel that the *Tallahassee* having been near them, that or some other vessel may make them a piratical visit at any hour, and urge that an ironclad be stationed in their harbor not only for their protection, but for the protection of other towns on the sound and of the sound steamers.'' The Governor's letter typified the grave concern caused by the infrequent but devastating Confederate raids near Northern seaports.

Contemporary wash drawing shows ships of the James River squadron operating below the obstructions at Farrar's Island. Not shown to the right of this scene, the Dutch Gap canal was being dug.

17 Side-wheelers U.S.S. *Otsego*, Lieutenant Commander Arnold, and U.S.S. *Ceres*, Acting Master Foster, ascended the Roanoke River to Jamesville, North Carolina, on a reconnaissance. The smaller *Ceres* continued upriver to Williamston. Although Confederates had been reported in the area, no batteries or troops were encountered.

19 C.S.S. *Chickamauga*, Lieutenant Wilkinson, ran the blockade into Wilmington under cover of heavy fog. He has miscalculated his position the day before and successfully run through the blockade to Masonboro Inlet instead of New Inlet. Wilkinson dropped down the coast and early in the morning of the 19th anchored under the guns of Fort Fisher to await high tide when *Chickamauga* could cross the bar and stand up Cape Fear River to Wilmington. As the fog lifted, blockaders U.S.S. *Kansas*, *Wilderness*, *Cherokee*, and *Clematis* opened on what they at first took to be a grounded blockade runner. *Chickamauga* broke the Confederate flag and returned the fire, joined by the heavy guns of Fort Fisher. Fog and the range of the Fort's guns thwarted efforts to destroy the cruiser; by mid-morning *Chickamauga* was safely in the river and nearing Wilmington.

20 Edward La Croix of Selma, Alabama, writing Secretary Welles from Detroit, reported that a torpedo boat had been constructed at Selma for use against the Union forces in Mobile Bay. He described her: "Length, about 30 feet; has water-tight compartments; can be sunk or raised as desired; is propelled by a very small engine, and will just stow in 5 men. It has some arrangement of machinery that times the explosions of torpedoes, to enable the operators to retire to a

The beginnings of the Dutch Gap canal. The canal was attempted by General Grant as a means of bypassing the heavy obstructions in the James River.

safe distance. The boat proves to be a good sailer on the river and has gone to Mobile to make last preparations for trying its efficacy on the Federal vessels." La Croix was referring to the submersible torpedo boat *Saint Patrick* built by John P. Halligan who was also her first commander. *Saint Patrick* was a source of concern to Federal naval officers in the vicinity of Mobile and early in the following year, under command of a Confederate naval officer, she did attempt to destroy a blockader.

Rear Admiral Porter directed Commander Macomb to send U.S.S. *Louisiana* to Beaufort, North Carolina. *Louisiana* was to become the powder ship with which Porter and General Butler hoped to level Fort Fisher and obviate the necessity of a direct attack. Early in December she was taken to Hampton Roads, where she was partially stripped and loaded with explosives.

21 Boats from U.S.S. *Avenger*, Acting Lieutenant Charles A. Wright, captured a large quantity of supplies on the Mississippi River near Bruinsburg, Mississippi, after a brief engagement. Union gunboats maintained a vigilant patrol to prevent Confederate supplies from crossing the Mississippi River for the armies in Alabama and Tennessee.

U.S.S. *Iosco*, Commander John Guest, captured blockage running schooner *Sybil* with cargo of cotton, at sea off the North Carolina coast.

23 Constantly alert to the need to strengthen his squadron for the difficult work of convoying and patrolling on the Western Rivers, Rear Admiral Lee this date detached Lieutenant Commander Greer, Acting Naval Constructor Charles F. Kendall, Acting Fleet Engineer Samuel Bickerstaff,

and Paymaster Calvin C. Jackson to proceed on a confidential mission to Cincinatti, Pittsburgh, "and to other places if necessary, for the purpose of purchasing ten sound, strong, and swift light-draft steamers, to be converted into gunboats." Ten were subsequently bought, converted, and added to the Mississippi Squadron in early 1865.

24 Lieutenant James McC. Baker's preparations for the capture of Fort Pickens at Pensacola were terminated by Secretary Mallory: "Major-General Maury having withdrawn his men from the enterprise to the command of which you were assigned, its prosecution became impracticable." It was a bitter blow to the daring young Confederate naval officer who had first undertaken the scheme in April and had fought persuasively for months to bring it off. By mid-August, still unable to obtain authorization from the local command to proceed with the plan, the bold lieutenant wrote Mallory outlining his scheme to seize Fort Pickens: "Not dreaming that we have any designs upon it, and deluding themselves with the idea that its isolated position renders it safe from attack, they have become exceedingly careless, having only two sentinels on duty. . . ." Baker proposed to take a landing force of sailors and soldiers in small boats and, ". . . pulling down the eastern shore of the bay into Bon Secours, and, hauling the boats across a narrow strip of land into Little Lagoon, I would enter the Gulf at a point 20 miles east of Fort Morgan and be within seven hours' pull of Fort Pickens, with nothing to interrupt our progress." A month later, after having conferred with President Davis and General Braxton Bragg, Mallory ordered Baker to proceed with the mission. On 25 October Baker departed Mobile with a number of sailors on steamer *Dick Keys* and rendezvoused with 100 soldiers from General Dabney Maury's command that night at Blakely, Alabama. As the daring group was preparing to get underway, Maury ordered a temporary delay because of information received which reported that Union forces had landed at the Pensacola Navy Yard near Fort Pickens. By the 30th this intelligence was demonstrated to be inaccurate, but Maury still was reluctant to go ahead with the operation. Concerned that the Northerners now had knowledge of the planned attempt, he suggested that the soldiers return to their companies to give the appearance of having had the expedition called off. At a future date they could be ordered back to Blakely suddenly, as Baker reported, "when the expedition might proceed, he thought, with more secrecy and certainty of success." This date, 24 November, Mallory reluctantly advised the intrepid Baker: "I regret that circumstances beyond the control of the Department or yourself should have thus terminated an enterprise which seemed to promise good results."

U.S.S. *Chocura*, Lieutenant Commander Meade, sighted schooner *Louisa* and chased her ashore on the bar off San Bernard River, Texas. A heavy gale totally destroyed the schooner before she could be boarded.

27 An explosion and fire destroyed General Butler's headquarters steamer *Greyhound*, on the James River, Virginia, and narrowly missed killing Butler, Major General Schenck, and Rear Admiral Porter, on board for a conference on the forthcoming Fort Fisher expedition. Because of the nature of the explosion, it is likely that one of the deadly Confederate coal torpedoes had been planted in *Greyhound*'s boiler. "The furnace door blew open," recalled Butler, "and scattered coals throughout the room." The so-called "coal torpedo" was a finely turned piece of cast iron containing ten pounds of powder and made to resemble closely a lump of coal, and was capable of being used with devastating effect. As Admiral Porter later described the incident: "We had left Bermuda Hundred five or six miles behind us when suddenly an explosion forward startled us, and in a moment large volumes of smoke poured out of the engine-room." The Admiral went on to marvel at the ingenuity which nearly cost him his life: "In devices for blowing up vessels the Confederates were far ahead of us, putting Yankee ingenuity to shame." This device was suspected of being the cause of several unexplained explosions during the war.

Blockade running British steamer *Beatrice* was captured by picket boats under Acting Master Gifford of the South Atlantic Blockading Squadron, off Charleston. The prize crew accidentally grounded *Beatrice* near Morris Island and she was soon a total wreck. In reporting the capture to Secretary Welles, Rear Admiral Dahlgren noted the fact that the blockade runner was captured by small boats and not by seagoing vessels, adding: "The duty is severe beyond what is imagined. In the launches the men may be said to live in the boats, and all of them are, in these long nights, exposed to every hardship of sea, wind, and weather; in the stormiest nights they are cruising around close in to the rebel batteries." The Federal Navy spared no efforts to tighten the blockade now that final victory was coming in sight.

Ram U.S.S. *Vindicator*, Acting Lieutenant Gorringe, and small stern-wheeler U.S.S. *Prairie Bird*, Acting Master Burns, transported and covered a successful Union cavalry attack on Confederate communications in western Mississippi. Thirty miles of track and the important railroad bridge over the Big Black River, east of Vicksburg, were destroyed. Major General Dana praised the part of the gunboats in the expedition: "The assistance of the vessels of the Sixth Division Mississippi Squadron rendered the expedition a complete success."

U.S.S. *Princess Royal*, Commander Woolsey, seized blockade running British schooner *Flash* in the Gulf of Mexico off Brazos Santiago with cargo of cotton. Later in the day, *Princess Royal* also captured blockade running schooner *Neptune*. Woolsey reported: "The vessel was empty, having just lost a cargo of salt, said salt having, according to the master's statement, 'dissolved in her hold.'"

U.S.S. *Metacomet*, Lieutenant Commander Jouett, captured blockade running steamer *Susanna* in the Gulf of Mexico off Campeche Banks. Half her cargo of cotton was thrown overboard in the chase. Rear Admiral Farragut had regarded *Susanna* as "their fastest steamer."

29 Double-turret monitor U.S.S. *Onondaga*, Commander William A. Parker, and single-turret monitor U.S.S. *Mahopac*, Lieutenant Commander Edward E. Potter, engaged Howlett's Battery, on the James River, Virginia, for three hours. This was part of the continuing action below Richmond.

Double-turretted monitor U.S.S. Onondaga *operates off Exchange Point on the James River.*

As Major Francis W. Smith, CSA, remarked, "I think the monitors (although they retired under our fire below Dutch Gap) will probably return. . . ."

A ship's boat under the command of Acting Ensign A. Rich from U.S.S. *Elk*, Acting Lieutenant Nicholas Kirby, captured an unidentified small craft with cargo of whiskey and opium near Mandeville, Louisiana.

30 Naval Brigade composed of 350 sailors and 150 Marines from ships of the South Atlantic Blockading Squadron and commanded by Commander George H. Preble joined in an Army action at Honey Hill, near Grahamville, South Carolina. In order to aid General Sherman in his march toward Savannah, Major General Foster had proposed to Rear Admiral Dahlgren a campaign up the Broad River to cut the Charleston-Savannah Railway and establish contact with Sherman. Preble organized an artillery and two naval infantry battalions to operate with the Army, and they were landed at Boyd's Landing on Broad River on 29 November. Sailors and Marines played a vital role in the ensuing battle of Honey Hill on 30 November, after which they entrenched on the Grahamville Road. General Foster then decided with Dahlgren, who accompanied his Brigade as far as Boyd's Landing, that the main thrust should come up the Tulifinny River toward Pocotaligo.

Boat expedition under the command of Acting Master Charles H. Cadieu, U.S.S. *Midnight*, landed at St. Andrew's Bay, Florida, destroyed a salt work and took prisoners.

U.S.S. *Itasca*, Lieutenant Commander George Brown, seized blockade running British schooner *Carrie Mair* off Pass Cavallo, Texas.

30–4 December Acting on intelligence that Union prisoners were attempting to reach the blockading vessels after having escaped from a prisoner train en route to Savannah, Acting Master Isaac Pennell, with 5 boats and nearly 100 men from U.S.S. *Ethan Allen* and *Dai Ching*, scoured the South Altamaha River, South Carolina, without finding any of the reported escapees. After encountering and engaging a considerable Confederate force, Pennell was compelled to withdraw to the ships.

DECEMBER

1 In order to cope with the powerful rifled batteries erected by Confederates along the Cumberland and Tennessee Rivers, Rear Admiral Lee, commanding the Mississippi Squadron, strengthened the

U.S.S. Carondelet *was one of the seven gunboats built for duty on the western waters by James B. Eads.*

forces of Lieutenant Commander Fitch with ironclads U.S.S. *Neosho* and U.S.S. *Carondelet*. Major General Thomas, responsible for halting General Hood's advance at Nashville, wired Major General Halleck this date: "I have two ironclads here, with several gunboats, and Commander Fitch assures me that Hood can neither cross the Cumberland or blockade it. I therefore think it best to wait here until Wilson can equip all his cavalry." In the coming battle, as in the whole Tennessee campaign, the Mississippi Squadron played a key role in covering Union armies, engaging shore batteries in support of troop movements, and insuring river lines of supply.

U.S.S. *Rhode Island*, Commander Stephen D. Trenchard, captured blockade running British steamer *Vixen* off Cape Fear, North Carolina, with cargo including arms.

2-3 U.S.S. *Pequot*, Lieutenant Commander Braine sighted blockade running steamer *Ella* off the coast of South Carolina and pursued her for nearly seven hours before darkness halted the chase. Early in the morning, 3 December, U.S.S. *Emma*, Acting Lieutenant Thomas Dunn, sighted *Ella* steering for the western bar of the Cape Fear River, and, attempting to intercept her, forced the runner aground near the light at Bald Head Point. Ships of the blockading squadron shelled the grounded *Ella* for two days before a boarding party commanded by Acting Ensign Isaac S. Sampson burned *Ella* on 5 December.

2-6 Joint Army-Navy expedition, including sailors from U.S.S. *Chicopee*, Commander Harrell, captured and burned a large quantity of Confederate supplies and equipment near Pitch Landing, on the Chowan River, North Carolina. In addition, a quantity of cotton and over $17,000 in Confederate money and bonds were brought off.

3 As Union pressure on Savannah increased, the Squadron under Captain W. W. Hunter, CSN, played an increasing role in the defense of the city and the important railway above it. This date Hunter wrote Lieutenant Joel S. Kennard, C.S.S. *Macon:* "The Charleston and Savannah Railway Bridge at the Savannah River is a very important point to defend, and, should it become necessary, endeavor to be in position there to defend it. In order to do so, and also to patrol the Savannah River, watch carefully the state of the river, and do not be caught aground or be cut off from the position at the bridge."

Boat expedition from U.S.S. *Nita, Stars and Stripes, Hendrick Hudson, Ariel,* and *Two Sisters*, commanded by Acting Lieutenant Robert B. Smith, destroyed a large salt work at Rocky Point, Tampa Bay, Florida.

U.S.S. *Mackinaw*, Commander Beaumont, captured schooner *Mary* at sea east off Charleston with cargo of cotton, tobacco, and turpentine.

3-4 U.S.S. *Moose*, Lieutenant Commander Fitch, U.S.S. *Carondelet*, Acting Master Charles W. Miller, U.S.S. *Fairplay*, Acting Master George J. Groves, U.S.S. *Reindeer*, Acting Lieutenant Henry A. Glassford, and U.S.S. *Silver Lake*, Acting Master Joseph C. Coyle, engaged field batteries on the Cumberland River near Bell's Mills, Tennessee, silenced them, and recaptured three transports taken by the Confederates the preceding day. Fitch and his gunboats, employed protecting Major General Thomas' right flank before Nashville, had started downriver on the night of 2 December after hearing that Confederate troops under Major General Forrest had erected a battery on the river at Bell's Mills. Fitch succeeded in surprising the batteries and a sharp engagement ensued. With visibility severely limited by darkness, smoke, and steam, small paddle-wheelers *Moose* and *Reindeer* and stern-wheeler *Silver Lake* nevertheless drove the Southern gunners from the bank. *Carondelet* and *Fairplay* passed below the batteries and after a short battle recaptured the three transports *Prairie State, Prima Donna,* and *Magnet* and many of the prisoners taken earlier from the transports. In addition, Fitch was able to return to Nashville with valuable intelligence on the composition and strength of Southern forces opposing Thomas' right flank, information which was to prove vital in the coming battle for Nashville.

4 Major General Maury, CSA, commanding troops at Mobile, wired Secretary of War Seddon: "Farragut has gone North. The *Hartford* and other heavy vessels have disappeared from down bay." Maury also commented on John P. Halligan, builder of torpedo boat *Saint Patrick:* "Halligan, recently appointed lieutenant, has not yet used his torpedo boat. I do not believe he ever will. His boat is reported a most valuable invention." Next day, Maury wrote Commodore Farrand, commanding naval forces at Mobile: "Every opportunity and facility having been afforded Mr. Halligan to enable him to use his boat against the enemy, and he evidently not being a proper man to conduct such an enterprise, please order a suitable officer of your command to take charge of the *Saint Patrick* at once and attack without unnecessary delay." In January 1865 *Saint Patrick* was transferred to Maury's authority and an energetic young naval officer, Lieutenant John T. Walker, put in command.

C.S.S. *Shenandoah*, Lieutenant Waddell, captured and burned whaling bark *Edward* off Tristan da Cunha in the South Atlantic. Waddell recorded in his journal: "Her outfit was of excellent quality, and I lay by her two days supplying the steamer with deficiencies. . . . Two of her boats were new, and took the place of my old and worthless ones."

U.S.S. *Chocura*, Lieutenant Commander Meade, captured schooner *Lowood* south of Velasco, Texas, with cargo of cotton. Calling *Lowood* "a notorious blockade runner", Meade said: "We had been watching this schooner for some time and finally laid a trap for her, which has proved successful."

U.S.S. *Pembina*, Lieutenant Commander James G. Maxwell, seized blockade running Dutch brig *Geziena Hilligonda* near Brazos Santiago, Texas, with cargo including medicines, iron, and cloth.

Boats from U.S.S. *Pursuit*, Acting Lieutenant George Taylor, captured *Peep O'Day* near Indian River, Florida, with cargo of cotton.

U.S.S. *R. R. Cuyler*, Commander Caldwell, U.S.S. *Mackinaw*, Commander Beaumont, and U.S.S. *Gettysburg*, Lieutenant R. H. Lamson, captured blockade running steamer *Armstrong* at sea (33° N., 78° W.). *Cuyler* and *Gettysburg*, joined by U.S.S. *Montgomery*, picked up a number of bales of cotton thrown over by *Armstrong* during the chase. *Mackinaw* had earlier in the day captured brig *Hattie E. Wheeler* with cargo of sugar.

5 In his fourth annual report to the President, Secretary Welles noted the great impact on the Confederacy made by Union seapower. Of the tireless blockaders he wrote: "The blockade of a coast line . . . greater in extent than the whole coast of Europe from Cape Trafalger to Cape North, is an undertaking without precedent in history." Welles observed that while successful runs through the blockade brought huge profits, "the blockade has not been violated with impunity. Heavy losses have befallen most of those who have been engaged in the illicit trade. Sixty-five steamers, the aggregate value of which, with their cargoes, will scarcely fall short of thirteen millions of dollars, have been captured or destroyed in endeavoring to enter or escape from Wilmington. Over fifty such results have occurred since Rear-Admiral Dahlgren anchored his monitor inside of Charleston bar and closed that port to commerce." By this date the United States Navy, consisting of only 42 ships on active duty in March 1861, had grown to 671 ships mounting more than 4,600 guns. A total of 203 ships had been built for the naval service since March 1861, including 62 ironclads. This growing force had ringed the South with an increasingly close blockade which by December 1864 had taken nearly 1,400 prizes. In addition, the Secretary noted four ships had been lost to the Southern naval cause in the course of the year: the commerce raiders *Alabama*, *Florida*, and *Georgia*, and the fearsome ram *Albemarle*. Moreover, the last major Gulf port had been closed with the Union victory at Mobile Bay. The fierce engagement, Welles wrote, was one which "in many respects [is] one of the most remarkable on record, and which added new lustre even to the renown of Rear-Admiral Farragut. . . ."

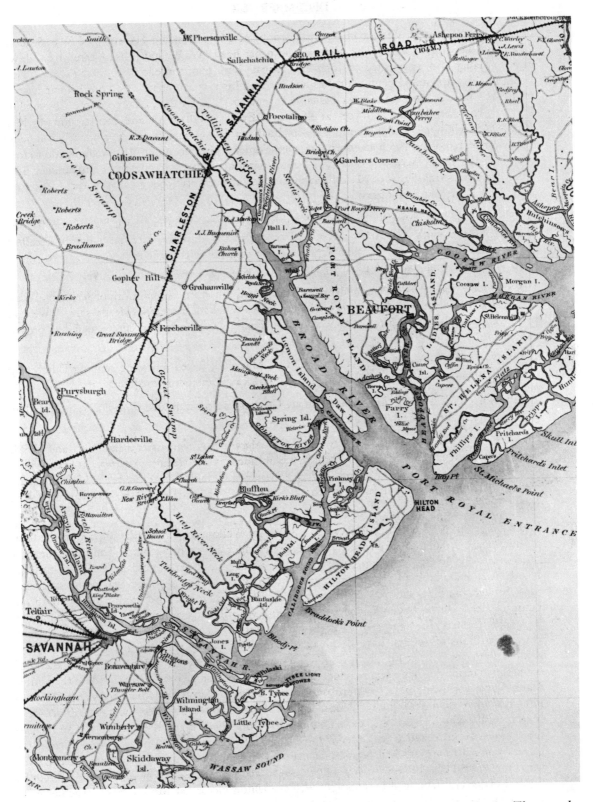

Map showing the South Carolina-Georgia coastal area from the Coosaw River to Wassaw Sound. The map also shows the Tullifinney River, where the Naval Brigade operated.

Confederate force under Acting Master William A. Hines, CSN, captured tug *Lizzie Freeman* by boarding near Smithfield, Virginia. The daring raid took place shortly before midnight while the Union tug, with two Army officers on board, lay at anchor.

U.S.S. *Chocura*, Lieutenant Commander Meade, seized blockade running British schooner *Julia* south of Velasco, Texas, with cargo including bar iron, medicines, cotton bagging, and rope.

5–9   The naval landing force under Commander Preble participated in heavy fighting around Tulifinny Crossroads, Georgia, while Federal troops attempted to cut the Savannah-Charleston Railway and join with the advancing forces of General Sherman. The Naval Brigade was withdrawn from Boyd's Landing, Broad River, on 5 December, and while Union gunboats, made a feint against the Coosawwatchie River fortifications, soldiers and sailors landed up the nearby Tulifinny River. During the next four days, the versatile naval brigade participated in a series of nearly continuous heavy actions, though plagued by rain and swampy terrain. Union forces advanced close enough to the strategic railway to shell it but failed to destroy it.

5–6   Monitors U.S.S. *Saugus*, *Onondaga*, *Mahopac*, and *Canonicus* participated in a lively engagement with strong shore batteries at Howlett's, James River, Virginia. *Saugus* received a solid 7-inch shot which disabled her turret.

6   U.S.S. *Neosho*, Acting Lieutenant Howard, with Lieutenant Commander Fitch embarked, with the three small steamers U.S.S. *Fairplay*, *Silver Lake*, and *Moose* and several army transports in company, moved down the Cumberland River from Nashville and engaged Confederate batteries near Bell's Mills, Tennessee. With ironclad *Neosho* in the lead and lightly protected ships to the rear, Fitch steamed slowly up and single-handedly engaged the Southern artillery. As the gallant officer reported later: "I had also great faith in the endurance of the *Neosho*, and therefore chose this position [directly in front of the main Confederate battery] as the most favorable one to test her strength and at the same time use canister and grape at 20 to 30 yards range. Our fire was slow and deliberate, but soon had the effect to scatter the enemy's sharpshooters and infantry, but owing to the elevated position of the batteries directly over us we could do but little injury. The enemy's fire was terrific, and in a very few minutes everything perishable on our decks was completely demolished." After holding his position for about two and a half hours, Fitch withdrew upstream, and aware that his lighter-armed vessels would not survive a passage of the batteries, returned with them to Nashville. During this fierce action, Quartermaster John Ditzenback, seeing *Neosho*'s ensign shot away by the concentrated Southern fire, coolly left the pilot house, and, despite the deadly shot raking *Neosho*'s decks, took the flag which was drooping over the wheelhouse and made it fast to the stump of the highest mast remaining. For this courageous act Ditzenback was awarded the Medal of Honor. Later in the day, Fitch in the *Neosho* joined by *Carondelet* again engaged the batteries, and, choosing a different firing position disabled some of the Confederate guns. Attesting to the endurance of *Neosho* under fire, Fitch was able to report to Rear Admiral Lee: "During the day the *Neosho* was struck over a hundred times, but received no injury whatever."

Major General Grant wrote Major General Butler regarding the objectives of the proposed joint expedition against Wilmington, one of the most ambitious of the war: "The first object of the expedition under General Weitzel is to close the port of Wilmington. If successful in this, the second will be to capture Wilmington itself. . . . The object of the expedition will be gained by effecting a landing on the mainland between Cape Fear River and the Atlantic north of the north entrance to the river, then the troops should intrench themselves, and by cooperating with the Navy effect a reduction and capture of those places. These in our hands, the Navy could enter the harbor and the port of Wilmington would be sealed."

U.S.S. *Chocura*, Lieutenant Commander Meade, seized blockade running British schooner *Lady Hurley* off Velasco, Texas, with cargo including bar iron, steel, salt, and medicines. *Lady Hurley*, according to Meade was the "consort to the *Carrie Mair*, captured by the *Itasca* few days since off Pass Cavallo [see 30 November]." She was the third prize taken by Meade in as many days as the Union naval forces pulled ever tighter the blockade of the Texas coast.

U.S.S. *Princess Royal*, Commander Woolsey, captured blockade running schooner *Alabama* after forcing her aground near San Luis Pass, Texas. Her crew abandoned ship, Woolsey's boarding party worked her free and took the prize to Galveston. Her cargo included iron bars, rope, flour, and soda.

U.S.S. *Sunflower*, Acting Master Charles Loring, III, seized blockade running sloop *Pickwick* off St. George's Sound, Florida.

7 U.S.S. *Narcissus*, Acting Ensign William G. Jones, struck a Confederate torpedo in a heavy storm while lying off the city of Mobile. Jones reported: ". . . the vessel struck a torpedo, which exploded, lifting her nearly out of water and breaking out a large hole in the starboard side, amidships . . . causing the vessel to sink in about fifteen minutes." The tug went down without loss of life and was raised later in the month. Mobile Bay was in Union hands, but Southern torpedoes took a heavy toll of Northern ships.

Blockade running steamer *Stormy Petrel* was run ashore and fired upon by gunboats of the North Atlantic Blockading Squadron while attempting to enter Wilmington. *Stormy Petrel* was totally destroyed a few days later by a gale. In his report of the incident, Rear Admiral Porter remarked: "Within the last fifty days we have captured and destroyed $5,500,000 worth of enemy's property in blockade runners. To submit to these losses and still run the blockade shows the immense gains the runners make and the straits the enemy are in."

8 Rear Admiral Porter wrote to Lieutenant Commander Watmough, senior officer off New Inlet, North Carolina, regarding the plan to explode a vessel laden with powder off Fort Fisher: "I propose running a vessel drawing 8½ feet (as near to Fort Fisher as possible) with 350 tons of powder, and exploding her by running her upon the outside and opposite Fort Fisher. My calculations are that the explosion will wind up Fort Fisher and the works along the beach, and that

U.S.S. Neosho *engages Confederate batteries on the Cumberland River below Nashville, Tennessee.*

we can open fire with the vessels without damage.'' Major General Butler had suggested the powder ship late in November, and Porter, anxious to get the long-delayed Wilmington attack underway, agreed to attempt this unlikely means of reducing the fort before the landing.

U.S.S. *J. P. Jackson*, Acting Lieutenant Pennington, with U.S.S. *Stockdale*, Acting Master Thomas Edwards, in company, captured blockade running schooner *Medora* in Mississippi Sound with cargo of cotton.

U.S.S. *Cherokee*, Lieutenant William E. Dennison, captured blockade running British steamer *Emma Henry* at sea east of North Carolina with cargo of cotton.

U.S.S. *Itasca*, Lieutenant Commander George Brown, chased blockade running sloop *Mary Ann* ashore at Pass Cavallo, Texas. Brown removed her cargo of cotton and destroyed her.

9 U.S.S. *Otsego*, Lieutenant Commander Arnold, sank in the Roanoke River near Jamesville, North Carolina, after striking two torpedoes in quick succession. Double-ender *Otsego*, along with U.S.S. *Wyalusing*, Lieutenant Commander English, *Valley City*, Acting Master John A. J. Brooks, and tugs *Belle* and *Bazely*, had formed an expedition to capture Rainbow Bluff, on the Roanoke River, and the Confederate ram rumored to be building at Halifax, North Carolina. Commander Macomb anchored his squadron at Jamesville to await the arrival of cooperating troops, and *Otsego* struck two torpedoes while anchoring. *Bazely*, coming alongside to lend assistance, also struck a torpedo and sank instantly. Lieutenant Commander Arnold and part of his crew remained on board the sunken *Otsego* to cover that portion of the river with her guns above water on the hurricane deck, and the rest of the group slowly moved upriver, dragging for torpedoes, to commence the attack on Rainbow Bluff (see 20 December).

U.S.S. Bazely *and* Otsego *strike torpedoes and sink while on an expedition up the Roanoke River in company with U.S.S.* Wyalusing *and other gunboats.*

10 U.S.S. *O. H. Lee*, Acting Master Oliver Thacher, captured blockade running British schooner *Sort* off Anclote Keys, Florida, with cargo of cotton.

10–12 C.S.S. *Macon*, Lieutenant Kennard, C.S.S. *Sampson*, Lieutenant William W. Carnes, and C.S.S. *Resolute*, Acting Master's Mate William D. Oliveira, under Flag Officer Hunter, took Union shore batteries under fire at Tweedside on the Savannah River. Hunter attempted to run his gunboats downriver to join in the defense of Savannah, but was unable to pass the strong Federal batteries. *Resolute* was disabled in this exchange of fire, 12 December, and was abandoned and captured. Recognizing that he could not get his remaining two vessels to Savannah, and having destroyed the railroad bridge over the Savannah River which he had been defending, Hunter took advantage of unusually high water to move upstream to Augusta.

11 Commander Preble, commanding the Naval Brigade fighting ashore with the forces of Major General Foster up the Broad River, South Carolina, reported to Rear Admiral Dahlgren concerning a unique "explosive ball" used by Confederate forces against his skirmishers: "It is a conical ball in shape, like an ordinary rifle bullet. The pointed end is charged with a fulminate. The base of the ball separates from the conical end, and has a leaden standard or plunger. The explosion of the charge drives the base up, so as to flatten a thin disk of metal between it and the ball, the leaden plunger is driven against the fulminate, and it explodes the ball. . . . It seems to me that use of such a missile is an unnecessary addition to the barbarities of war."

12 Rear Admiral Dahlgren wrote to President Lincoln, reporting news of the greatest importance to the Union: "I have the great satisfaction of conveying to you information of the arrival of General Sherman near Savannah, with his army in fine spirits. . . . This memorable event must be attended by still more memorable consequences, and I congratulate you most heartily on its occurrence." The value of seaborne supply to Sherman was inestimable. His army switched from rail logistics at Chattanooga to sea logistics on the Atlantic.

13 Rear Admiral Farragut arrived in New York on board his battle-scarred veteran flagship, U.S.S. *Hartford*. A New York newspaper hailed him in verse:

> To Farragut all glory!
> The Sea-King's worthy peer,
> Columbia's greatest seaman,
> Without reproach or fear.

Returning to the Confederacy from London, Captain Semmes had landed a month before at Bagdad, Mexico, near Matamoras. This date, en route to his home at Mobile for a brief respite before making his way to Richmond, Semmes crossed the Mississippi River with his son, Major O. J. Semmes. He later wrote: "We reached the bank of the Mississippi just before dark. There were two of the enemy's gunboats anchored in the river, at a distance of about three miles apart . . . the enemy had converted every sort of a water craft, into a ship of war, and now had them in such number, that he was enabled to police the river in its entire length, without the necessity of his boats being out of sight of each other's smoke. . . ." Semmes described the night crossing of the river in a crowded skiff: "Our boat was scarcely able to float the numbers that were packed into her. . . . As we shot within the shadows of the opposite bank, our conductor, before landing, gave a shrill whistle to ascertain whether all was right. The proper response came directly, from those who were to meet us, and in a moment more, we leaped on shore among friends." Federal naval forces on the river had been alerted in an effort to capture the elusive Captain Semmes of C.S.S. *Alabama*, but he succeeded in getting home, and later to Richmond, to receive the thanks of the Confederacy and promotion to the rank of Rear Admiral.

The Union fleet massed for the bombardment of Fort Fisher departed Hampton Roads for Wilmington. Wooden double-ender U.S.S. *Sassacus*, Lieutenant Commander John L. Davis, was assigned the duty of towing the powder ship *Louisiana* to Beaufort, North Carolina, where she was to take on more powder. Army transports carrying the invasion force commanded by Major General Butler left Hampton Roads at approximately the same time as the supporting naval group.

14 Foreseeing the fall of Savannah, Secretary Mallory wrote Flag Officer Hunter, commanding the naval squadron at that city: "Should the enemy get and hold Savannah, and you can do no further service there, you are expected to dispose of your squadron to the greatest injury to him and the greatest benefit to our country. If necessary to leave Savannah, your vessels, except the *Georgia*, may fight their way to Charleston. Under no circumstances should they be destroyed until every proper effort to save them shall have been exhausted." Three days later, Captain S. S. Lee, CSN, addressed a similar letter to Hunter: "Under any circumstances, it is better for the vessels, for the Navy, for our cause and country, that these vessels should fall in the conflict of battle, taking all the risks of defeat and triumph, than that they should be tamely surrendered to the enemy or destroyed by their own officers."

14–21 Union gunboats supporting General Sherman aided in the capture of Forts Beaulieu and Rose-dew in Ossabaw Sound, Georgia, the outer defenses of Savannah. Wooden steamer U.S.S. *Winona*, Lieutenant Commander Dana, U.S.S. *Sonoma*, Lieutenant Commander Scott, and mortar gunboats shelled the forts until they were abandoned by the defenders on 21 December. *Winona's* log recorded on that date: "At 10:05 saw the American Ensign flying on Fort Beaulieu. Ships cheered; captain left in the gig and proceeded up to the fort."

15 President Lincoln wrote in a message to Congress: "I most cordially recommend that Lieutenant William B. Cushing, U.S. Navy, receive a vote of thanks from Congress for his important, gallant, and perilous achievement in destroying the rebel ironclad steamer *Albemarle* on the night of the 27th October, 1864, at Plymouth, N.C. The destruction of so formidable a vessel, which had resisted the continued attacks of a number of our vessels on former occasions, is an important event touching our future naval and military operations, and would reflect honor on any officer, and redounds to the credit of this young officer and the few brave comrades who assisted in this successful and daring undertaking."

An expedition under Acting Master William G. Morris, including U.S.S. *Coeur De Lion* and U.S.S. *Mercury*, seized and burned more than thirty large boats which the Confederates had been massing on the Coan River, Virginia, and drove off defending soldiers in a brief engagement.

15–16 As Major General Thomas opened his offensive in the pivotal battle of Nashville, gunboats of the Mississippi Squadron, commanded by Lieutenant Commander Fitch, operated closely with the Union Army by engaging batteries on the Cumberland River and helping to secure a resounding victory for Thomas. On the night of 14 December, Fitch, together with the seven gunboats of his command, had moved down toward the main Confederate battery guarding the river and Major General Forrest's far left. Fitch described the joint effort: "Acting Volunteer Lieutenant Howard then returned to where I was, just above their works, and reported but four guns in position. These I could easily have silenced and driven off, but our army had not yet sufficiently advanced to insure their capture. I therefore maneuvered around above them till the afternoon, when our cavalry had reached the desired position in the rear; the *Neosho* and *Carondelet* then moved down again and the rebels, finding the position they were in, had tried to remove the guns, but were too late; our cavalry closed in and took them with but little resistance." The Union gunboats then engaged other batteries down the river, in some cases silencing them with gun-fire and in others absorbing the attention of the Confederate gunners while Union cavalry encircled them. By the afternoon of 15 December, Hood's batteries on the Cumberland had been captured and his left flank, further inland, was in full retreat. In reply to congratulations from President Lincoln on his important victory, Thomas remarked: "I must not forget to report the operations of Brigadier-General Johnson in successfully driving the enemy, with the cooperation of the gunboats, under Lieutenant Commander Fitch, from their established batteries on the Cumberland River below the City of Nashville. . . ."

16   U.S.S. *Mount Vernon*, Acting Lieutenant James Trathen, in company with U.S.S. *New Berne*, Acting Lieutenant T. A. Harris, captured and burned schooner *G. O. Bigelow* in ballast at Bear Inlet, North Carolina.

16–17   Acting Master Charles A. Pettit, U.S.S. *Monticello*, performed a dangerous reconnaissance off New Inlet, North Carolina, removing several Confederate torpedoes and their firing apparatus near the base of Fort Caswell. Pettit's expedition was part of the extensive Union preparations for the bombardment and assault on Fort Fisher and the defenses of Wilmington, planned for late December.

18   U.S.S. *Louisiana*, Commander Rhind, arrived off Fort Fisher, having that day been towed from Beaufort, North Carolina, by U.S.S. *Sassacus*, Lieutenant Commander J. L. Davis, in company with Rear Admiral Porter and his fleet. *Louisiana* had been loaded with powder and was to be blown up as near Fort Fisher as possible in the hope of reducing or substantially damaging that formidable Confederate work. The day before, Porter had sent detailed instructions to Commander Rhind, adding: "Great risks have to be run, and there are chances that you may lose your life in this adventure; but the risk is worth the running, when the importance of the object is to be considered and the fame to be gained by this novel undertaking, which is either to prove that forts on the water are useless or that rebels are proof against gunpowder. . . . I expect more good to our cause from a success in this instance than from an advance of all the armies in the field." Rhind and his brave crew of volunteers proceeded in toward Fort Fisher towed by U.S.S. *Wilderness*, Acting Master Henry Arey, but finding the swells too severe, turned back. Major General Butler, seeing the worsening weather at Beaufort, asked Porter to postpone the attempt until the sea was calm enough to land his troops with safety.

19   C.S.S. *Water Witch*, captured from the Union on 3 June, was burned by the Confederates in the Vernon River near Savannah, in order to prevent her capture by General Sherman's troops advancing on the city.

U.S.S. *Princess Royal*, Commander Melancthon B. Woolsey, captured schooner *Cora* off Galveston with cargo of cotton.

20   U.S.S. *Hartford* was turned over to Rear Admiral Paulding at the New York Navy Yard for repairs. Rear Admiral Farragut wrote Secretary Welles: ". . . my flag [was] hauled down at sunset. . . ." Thus did the two, man and ship, who had served so heroically for so many months together, close their active Civil War careers.

Boats from U.S.S. *Chicopee*, *Valley City*, and *Wyalusing* under the command of Commander Macomb on an expedition to engage Confederate troops at Rainbow Bluff, North Carolina, were fired upon while dragging for torpedoes, seven miles below the Bluff. Macomb then put out skirmishers to clear the banks, but made only slow progress against the Southern force along the river. After the destruction of U.S.S. *Otsego* and *Bazely* (see 9 December), the Union gunboats moved laboriously up the tortuous river, dragging for torpedoes in small boats and being harassed by Confederate riflemen. As many as 40 torpedoes were found in some bends of the river. Union troops intending to operate with the gunboats were delayed. By the time they were ready to advance on Rainbow Bluff, the Confederate garrison there had been strongly reinforced. Torpedoes in the river, batteries along the banks below that point, and the difficulty of navigating the river forced abandonment of the operation. The wrecks of *Otsego* and *Bazely* were destroyed to prevent their falling into Confederate hands on 25 December. The expedition got back to Plymouth three days later.

Confederate ironclad floating battery Georgia *defended the approaches to Savannah.*

20–21   Boat expedition under the command of Acting Master Pennell, U.S.S. *Ethan Allen*, carried out a reconnaisance of the Altamaha River, South Carolina, engaging Confederate pickets and bringing off prisoners and horses.

21   The Confederate Navy continued vigorous efforts to save the remnants of the Savannah squadron still at that city on the eve of its capture. On 10 December Commander Thomas W. Brent, C.S.S. *Savannah*, ordered the torpedoes in Savannah harbor removed in order that his vessels might fight their way to Charleston. As Brent later reported to Flag Officer Hunter: "... after every endeavor he [Lieutenant McAdam] found that with all the appliances at his command, grapnels, etc., he was unable with the motive power of the boats to remove any one of them, the anchors to which they are attached being too firmly embedded in the sand. ... Under these circumstances it did not seem to me possible to carry out the instructions of the Department in regard to taking the *Savannah* to sea and fighting her way into this [Charleston] or some other port." After attempting futilely to move the smaller of his vessels upriver, Hunter this date destroyed C.S.S. *Savannah*, *Isondiga*, *Firefly*, and floating battery *Georgia*. General Sherman occupied Savannah on 23 December having fought his way across Georgia to the sea where he knew the mobility of naval power would be ready to provide him with support, supplies, and means of carrying out the next operation.

Blockade runner *Owl*, Commander Maffitt, departed Wilmington through the Federal blockaders with large cargo of cotton. *Owl*, owned by the Confederate government, was one of several blockade runners commanded by Southern naval officers.

23   President Lincoln signed a bill passed the preceding day by Congress which created the rank of vice admiral. A fortnight before Secretary Welles had written in his report to the President: "In recommending, therefore, that the office of vice-admiral should be created, and the appointment conferred on Rear-Admiral David G. Farragut, I but respond, as I believe, to the voice and wishes of the naval service and of the whole country." Thus was Farragut made the first vice admiral in the Nation's history as he had been its first rear admiral. The *Army and Navy Journal* wrote of him: "In Farragut the ideal sailor, the seaman of Nelson's and Collingwood's days, is revived, and the feeling of the people toward him is of the same peculiar character as that which those great and simple-hearted heroes of Great Britain evoked in the hearts of their countrymen."

U.S.S. *Acacia*, Acting Master William Barrymore, captured blockade running British steamer *Julia* off Alligator Creek, South Carolina, with cargo of cotton.

Samuel P. Lee
Rear Admiral, USN

John Wilkinson
Lieutenant, CSN

23–24   After many days of delay because of heavy weather, powder ship U.S.S. *Louisiana*, Commander Rhind, towed by U.S.S. *Wilderness* late at night, anchored and was blown up 250 yards off Fort Fisher, North Carolina.   After Rhind and his gallant crew set the fuzes and a fire in the stern, they escaped by small boat to *Wilderness*.   Rear Admiral Porter and General Butler, who was waiting in Beaufort to land his troops the next morning and storm Fort Fisher, placed great hope in the exploding powder ship, hope that Dahlgren as an ordnance expert no doubt disdained. The clock mechanism failed to ignite the powder at the appointed time, 1:18 a.m., and after agonizing minutes of waiting, the fire set by Rhind in the stern of *Louisiana* reached the powder and a tremendous explosion occured.   Fort Fisher and its garrison, however, were not measurably affected, although the blast was heard many miles away; in fact, Colonel Lamb, the fort's resolute commander, wrote in his diary:"A blockader got aground near the fort, set fire to herself and blew up."   It remained for the massed gunfire from ships of Porter's huge fleet, the largest ever assembled up to that time under the American flag, to cover the landings and reduce the forts.

24   Rear Admiral Lee, commanding the Mississippi Squadron, arrived off Chickasaw, Alabama, in an attempt to cut off the retreat of Confederate General Hood's army from Tennessee.   At Chickasaw, U.S.S. *Fairy*, Acting Ensign Charles Swendson, with Lee embarked, destroyed a Confederate fort and magazine, but even this small, shallow-draft river boat was unable to go beyond Great Mussel Shoals on the Tennessee River because of low water.   On 27 December, gunboats engaged and destroyed two fieldpieces near Florence, Alabama, but by this time the water of the Tennessee River had fallen drastically, and Lee's vessels were compelled to withdraw toward Eastport.

24–25   Naval forces under the command of Rear Admiral Porter and Army units under Major General Butler launched an unsuccessful attack against Fort Fisher.   Transports carrying Butler's troops had retired to Beaufort in order to avoid the anticipated effects of the explosion of the powder boat *Louisiana*, and fleet units had assembled in a rendezvous area 12 miles from the fort.   At daylight on 24 December, the huge fleet got underway, formed in line of battle before the formidable Confederate works, and commenced a furious bombardment. The staunch Southern defenders, under the command of Colonel William Lamb, were driven from their guns and into the bombproofs of Fort Fisher, but managed to return the Federal fire from a few of their heavy cannon. Transports carrying the Union soldiers did not arrive from Beaufort until evening; too late for an assault that day. Accordingly, Porter withdrew his ships, intending to renew the attack the next day. Most of the casualties resulted from the bursting of five 100-pounder Parrott guns on board five different ships. By taking shelter the defenders, too, suffered few casualties, despite the heavy bombardment.

At 10:30 the following morning the ships again opened fire on the fort and maintained the bombardment while troops landed north of the works, near Flag Pond Battery. Naval gunfire kept the garrison largely pinned down and away from their guns as Butler landed about 2,000 men who advanced toward the land face of the fort.

Meanwhile, the Admiral attempted to find a channel through New Inlet in order to attack the forts from Cape Fear River. When Commander Guest, U.S.S. *Iosco* and a detachment of double-ender gunboats encountered a shallow bar over which they could not pass, Porter called on the indomitable Lieutenant Cushing, hero of the *Albemarle* destruction, to sound the channel in small boats, buoying it for the ships to pass through. Under withering fire from the forts, even the daring Cushing was forced to turn back, one of his boats being cut in half by a Confederate shell.

Late in the afternoon, Army skirmishers advanced to within yards of the fort, supported by heavy fire from Union vessels. Lieutenant Aeneas Armstrong, CSN, inside Fort Fisher, later described the bombardment: "The whole of the interior of the fort, which consists of sand, merlons, etc., was as one eleven-inch shell bursting. You can now inspect the works and walk on nothing but iron." Union Army commanders, however, considered the works too strongly defended to be carried by assault with the troops available, and the soldiers began to reembark. Some 700 troops were left on the beaches as the weather worsened. They were protected by gunboats under Captain Glisson, U.S.S. *Santiago de Cuba*, who had lent continuous close support to the landing. By 27 December the last troops were embarked; the first major attack on Fort Fisher had failed. Confederate reinforcements under General R. F. Hoke were in Wilmington and arrived at Confederate Point just after Union forces departed. The Army transports returned to Hampton Roads to prepare for a second move on the Confederate bastion, while Porter's fleet remained in the Wilmington-Beaufort area and continued sporadic bombardment in an effort to prevent repair of the fort.

26 Blockade runner *Chameleon*, formerly the dread raider C.S.S. *Tallahassee*, under the command of Lieutenant Wilkinson, slipped out of Wilmington amid the confusion in the aftermath of the first attack on Fort Fisher. In Bermuda, *Chameleon* loaded badly needed foodstuffs for the Confederate armies, but by the time Wilkinson could get her back to Wilmington in January, the port had already fallen.

27 Shortly after midnight a boat crew under the command of Acting Ensign N. A. Blume from U.S.S *Virginia*, cut out schooner *Belle* in Galveston harbor with cargo of cotton. *Belle* was at anchor only some 400 yards from Confederate guard boat *Lecompte* when Blume's party boldly boarded and sailed her out of the harbor.

28 The military situation having been stabilized in the Tulifinny River area of South Carolina (see 5–9 Dec.), Rear Admiral Dahlgren withdrew the naval brigade under Commander Preble and returned the sailors and marines comprising it to their respective ships. The 500-man brigade, hastily brought together and trained in infantry tactics, performed vital service in the arduous four-week campaign. Major General Foster, commanding the Military District of the South, complimented Dahlgren on the Brigade's courage and skill: ". . . its gallantry in action and good conduct during the irksome life in camp won from all the land forces with which it served the

highest praises." Although the Savannah-Charleston railroad was not cut by the expedition, it did succeed in diverting Confederate troops opposing Sherman's march across Georgia.

U.S.S. *Kanawha*, Lieutenant Commander Taylor, forced an unidentified blockade running sloop ashore near Caney Creek, Texas, and destroyed her.

29 Major General Thomas, summarizing the successful repulse of General Hood's Confederate Army in Tennessee, paid tribute to the assistance of the Navy in a letter to Rear Admiral Lee: "Your efficient cooperation on the Tennessee River has contributed largely to the demoralization of Hood's army." With the big guns and mobility of the river warships efficiently aiding his forces ashore, General Thomas had succeeded in virtually destroying the most effective Confederate force in the West, thus protecting General Sherman's line of communications on his march to Georgia.

C.S.S. *Shenandoah*, Lieutenant Waddell, captured and destroyed bark *Delphine* in the Indian Ocean with cargo of rice. *Delphine* was Waddell's last capture of the year and ninth prize in eight weeks.

30 Determined to take Wilmington and close the South's last important harbor but dissatisfied with General Butler's leadership, Rear Admiral Porter strongly urged the General's removal from command. General Grant wrote Porter: "Please hold on where you are for a few days and I will endeavor to be back again with an increased force and without the former commander." Ships of Porter's squadron kept up a steady bombardment of Fort Fisher to restrict the erection of new works and the repair of the damaged faces of the fort.

U.S.S. *Rattler*, Acting Master Willets, parted her cables in a heavy gale, ran ashore, struck a snag and sank in the Mississippi River near Grand Gulf. Willets, after salvaging most of *Rattler*'s supplies and armament, was forced to abandon his small paddle wheeler, which was subsequently burned by Confederates.

31 Vice Admiral Farragut received a gift of $50,000 in government bonds from the merchants of New York as a symbol of the esteem in which he was held by them. A letter from the merchants added: "The citizens of New York can offer no tribute equal to your claims on their gratitude and affection. Their earnest desire is, to receive you as one of their number, and to be permitted, as fellow citizens, to share in the renown you will bring to the Metropolitan City."

Two launches from U.S.S. *Wabash* and *Pawnee* under the command of Acting Master's Mates Albert F. Rich and William H. Fitzgerald ran aground and were captured in Charleston harbor by Confederate pickets. While on guard duty in the harbor, the two launches were driven aground close to Fort Sumter by a strong flood tide and freshening wind. Rich later reported: "I made every attempt that lay in my power to work the boat off shore; but all my efforts proved unsuccessful. A total of 27 sailors were captured."

U.S.S. *Metacomet*, Lieutenant Commander Jouett, captured schooner *Sea Witch* southeast of Galveston, Texas, with cargo of coffee and medicine.

As the year 1864 ended at sea, far from the Confederacy, Lieutenant Waddell, captain of the raider C.S.S. *Shenandoah*, wrote in his journal: "Thirty-first of December closed the year, the third since the war began. And how many of my boon companions are gone to that bourne from whence no traveler returns. They were full of hope, but not without fears, when we last parted." Even the tireless Waddell could by this time sense the impending defeat of the South, despite great gallantry, overwhelmed by Union advantages especially the ceaseless, crushing power of the sea.

IV–152

1865

I.—SOME SIGNIFICANT EVENTS OF 1865

13–15 January The joint amphibious assault under Rear Admiral David D. Porter and Major General Alfred H. Terry took Fort Fisher, the key in the defense of Wilmington, North Carolina, which was the last port by which supplies from Europe could reach General Lee's troops at Richmond.

23–24 January The Confederate fleet under Flag Officer John K. Mitchell attempted to dash down the James River to attack General Grant's headquarters at City Point, Virginia. The bold attack was thwarted when the heaviest of the ironclads ran aground.

17–18 February Charleston, confronted by General William T. Sherman's soldiers approaching from the rear and a Navy supported amphibious assault from Bull's Bay, was evacuated.

18 February C.S.S. *Shenandoah*, Lieutenant James I. Waddell, departed Melbourne to resume her commerce raiding career in the Pacific.

22 February Wilmington, North Carolina, was evacuated as Rear Admiral Porter's ships steamed up the Cape Fear River and General Terry's soldiers marched on the city.

24 March C.S.S. *Stonewall*, Captain Thomas J. Page, put to sea from Ferrol, Spain, en route to Havana. The ironclad was intended to raise the blockade of one or more southern ports.

28 March Rear Admiral Porter joined Generals Grant and Sherman for a conference with President Lincoln on board steamer *River Queen* at City Point, Virginia. They discussed the strategy to be followed in the closing days of the war and how the South would be treated at the close of the conflict.

2–4 April Secretary of the Navy Stephen R. Mallory ordered the destruction of the Confederate James River Squadron and directed its officers and men to join General Lee's troops then in the process of evacuating Richmond and retreating westward toward Danville.

3 April Midshipmen at the Confederate Naval Academy, under the command of Lieutenant William H. Parker, escorted the archives of the government and the specie and bullion of the treasury from Richmond to Danville and southward.

4 April Rear Admiral Porter accompanied President Lincoln up the James River to Richmond on board flagship *Malvern*. Vice Admiral David G. Farragut had already arrived in the Confederate capital.

9 April General Lee met General Grant at Appomattox Court House and formally surrendered the Army of Northern Virginia.

11–12 April Batteries Tracy and Huger, up the Blakely River from Spanish Fort, fell to Union forces and Confederate troops evacuated Mobile, which was surrendered by the mayor.

14 April President Lincoln was shot shortly after 10 p.m. while watching "Our American Cousin" at Ford's Theatre, Washington. He died at 7:22 a.m. the next morning.

14 April	Major General Anderson, Commander of the Union Army garrison at Fort Sumter on 14 April 1861, raised above Sumter's ruins "the same United States flag which floated over the battlements of that fort during the rebel assault. . . ."
23–24 April	C.S.S. *Webb*, Lieutenant Read, dashed from the Red River and entered the Mississippi in a heroic last-ditch effort to escape to sea. Trapped below New Orleans, *Webb* was grounded and fired to avoid capture.
27 April	The body of John Wilkes Booth, President Lincoln's assassin, was delivered on board U.S.S. *Montauk*, anchored in the Anacostia River off the Washington Navy Yard.
3 May	Secretary of the Navy Mallory submitted his resignation to President Davis at Washington, Georgia.
10 May	President Jefferson Davis was captured by Union troops near Irwinville, Georgia.
19 May	C.S.S. *Stonewall*, Captain T. J. Page, was turned over to Cuban officials at Havana.
2 June	Terms of surrender of Galveston were signed on board U.S.S. *Fort Jackson* by Major General E. Kirby Smith on behalf of the Confederacy.
22 June	Secretary Welles announced to the naval forces that France and Great Britain had "withdrawn from the insurgents the character of belligerents", and that the blockade of the coast of the United States would soon be lifted.
28 June	This date marked the most successful single day C.S.S. *Shenandoah*, Lieutenant Waddell, enjoyed as a commerce raider during her long cruise that spanned 13 months and covered 58,000 miles. On this field day Waddell captured 11 American whalers near the narrows of the Bering Strait.
18 July	Rear Admiral Louis M. Goldsborough arrived at Flushing, in the Netherlands, where he hoisted his flag on U.S.S. *Colorado* and assumed command of the reinstated European Squadron. The East India Squadron was reactivated on 31 July.
2 August	Lieutenant Waddell, C.S.S. *Shenandoah*, spoke the English bark *Barracouta* and for the first time learned positively that the war was over He determined to make a nonstop voyage to Liverpool, England, via Cape Horn.
12 August	Brazil Squadron reactivated under Rear Admiral Godon in flagship *Susquehanna*.
11 September	Emperor Maximilian approved the "Regulations and Instructions" prepared by Matthew Fontaine Maury to encourage emigration of Southerners to Mexico. The Emperor also appointed Maury director of the proposed National Observatory.
3 November	Secretary Welles ordered all naval vessels to resume rendering honors when entering British ports and to begin again exchanging official courtesies with English men of war.
6 November	C.S.S. *Shenandoah*, Lieutenant Waddell, arrived at Liverpool, England, 123 days and 23,000 miles from the Aleutians. Waddell lowered the last official Confederate flag, and his ship was ultimately turned over to American authorities.
4 December	Secretary Welles announced that the West India Squadron was to be reestablished under Commodore James S. Palmer, in that area "where we have so large a trade, owing to the proximity of the islands to our shores, it is essential that we cultivate friendly relations."
31 December	In his annual report to the President, Secretary Welles wrote: "It is still wise—the wisest—economy to cherish the navy, to husband its resources, to invite new supplies of youthful courage and skill to its service, to be amply supplied with all needful facilities and preparations for efficiency, and thus to hold within prompt and easy reach its vast and salutary power for the national defence and self-vindication "

II.—DETAILED CIVIL WAR NAVAL CHRONOLOGY

1865

JANUARY

1   As the new year opened, General Robert E. Lee clung doggedly to his position defending Richmond, conscious that world opinion had come to regard the fate of the Confederacy as inseparable from that of its capital city.   Equally determined that Richmond should fall, General Ulysses S. Grant, with great superiority in numbers, pressed against Petersburg, the key to the capital's southern defense line.   Grant also sought to break through to the westward, encircling Lee and Richmond, and cutting the Weldon, Southside (Lynchburg), and Danville railroads by which the city and the soldiers were supplied.

That Grant lay in front of Petersburg and less than 20 miles from Richmond was wholly due to Federal naval control of the James and Potomac Rivers.   His waterborne line of supply extended up the James to City Point, only seven miles from Petersburg.   From this principal base at City Point, Grant coordinated the joint movements of the Army of the Potomac and the Army of the James.

In Richmond, the prospect of a naval attack was so threatening that the government assembled for the city's defense the strongest naval force it ever placed under one command.   The James River Squadron, commanded by Flag Officer John K. Mitchell, consisted of three ironclads, seven gunboats, and two torpedo boats.   In addition to its defensive functions, Mitchell's squadron also constituted a potentially formidable threat to the security of the vital City Point base.   It operated behind a protective minefield at Chaffin's Bluff, some 35 miles upriver from City Point.

To counter Mitchell's warships and protect Grant's waterborne supply line, the Fifth Division of the North Atlantic Blockading Squadron lay on the James guarding the sunken hulk obstruction line at Trent's Reach and the pontoon crossings of the James and Appomattox Rivers and protecting supply vessels against sharpshooters and hidden batteries on shore.   Normally the Fifth Division consisted of five monitors and some 25 gunboats.   However, in January four of the monitors and a number of the gunboats were away from the James with the fleet being assembled by Rear Admiral David D. Porter for the second attack on Fort Fisher.   Hence the Confederate squadron above City Point enjoyed an unprecedented opportunity for offensive operations on which it sought to capitalize before the month ended.

Receiving General Grant's 30 December notification of a renewed Army assault by sea on Fort Fisher with an "increased force and without the former commander [General Benjamin F. Butler]", Rear Admiral Porter acted vigorously to set up a massive and overwhelming attack behind the fleet's heavy guns.   He directed that his 43 warships concentrated at Beaufort, North Carolina, and the 23 on station off the Cape Fear River send in their operations charts for corrections and onload "every shell that can be carried" for shore bombardment.   Porter replied immediately to the Army commander-in-chief: ". . . thank God we are not to leave here with so easy a victory at hand . . . ."   He assured his old Vicksburg colleague that he would "work day and night to be ready."   At Fort Fisher, mindful of General Lee's message that the work must be held at all costs or the Army of Northern Virginia could not be supplied, Colonel William Lamb and his garrison readied themselves for the further attacks forecast by the sizeable Federal naval force which had remained off the Cape Fear River entrances since the first attempt to take the fort had been broken off.

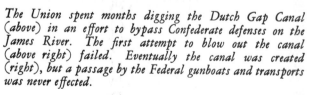

The Union spent months digging the Dutch Gap Canal
(above) in an effort to bypass Confederate defenses on the
James River. The first attempt to blow out the canal
(above right) failed. Eventually the canal was created
(right), but a passage by the Federal gunboats and transports
was never effected.

On the James River, Commander William A. Parker, commanding the double-turreted monitor *Onondaga*, reported that 12,000 pounds of gunpowder had been detonated in an effort to remove the end barriers of the canal excavation at Dutch Gap, Virginia. "The earth was thrown up into the air about 40 or 50 feet," he noted, "and immediately fell back into its original place. This earth will have to be removed to render the canal passable for vessels." Major General Butler had begun the canal in 1864 (see Part IV, pages 115 and 133–135) with a view to passing Confederate obstructions above Trent's Reach. If the passage had been effected, Butler's Army of the James could have bypassed key positions in Richmond's southern defense system and moved on the city in a diversionary threat aimed at reducing General Lee's resistance to the main Union thrust under General Grant.

U.S.S. *San Jacinto*, Captain Richard W. Meade, ran on a reef at Green Turtle Cay, Abaco, in the Bahamas. She was found to be seriously bilged and was abandoned without loss of life. Meade was able to salvage the armament, ammunition, rigging, cables, and much of the ship's copper. At an early period of the war, *San Jacinto* had gained fame when her commanding officer, Captain Charles Wilkes, stopped the British ship *Trent* and removed Confederate commissioners James M. Mason and John Slidell (see 8 November 1861).

2 In September 1864, Secretary of the Navy Gideon Welles had discussed with Vice Admiral Farragut the importance of seizing Wilmington to cut General Lee's vital link with Europe and to stop the Confederacy's credit-producing cotton shipments abroad. He now called Secretary of War Stanton's attention to the present "fit opportunity to undertake such an operation." Pointing to the availability of troops, "as the armies are mostly going into winter quarters," he urged on Stanton a proposal of Rear Admiral Porter to land an assault force at Fort Caswell, guarding the west entrance to the Cape Fear River, and stressed that the naval blockaders, which thus would be able

to lie inside the river, would close Wilmington, "the only port by which any supplies whatever reach the rebels."

Rear Admiral Dahlgren returned to Savannah after a brief visit to Charleston where he had gone because of the threat of a breakout by the Confederate ironclads. He had wanted to be on hand to help check them from a foray against Savannah and to insure "the perfect security of General Sherman's base." After stationing a force of seven monitors there, sufficient to meet such an emergency, "and not perceiving any sign of the expected raid, I returned to Savannah to keep in communication with General Sherman and be ready to render any assistance that might be desired.

"General Sherman has fully informed me of his plans, and so far as my means permit, they shall not lack assistance by water. . . .

"The general route of the army will be northward, but the exact direction must be decided more or less by circumstances which it may not be possible to foresee.

"My cooperation will be confined to assistance in attacking Charleston or in establishing communication at Georgetown in case the army pushes on without attacking Charleston, and time alone will show which of these will eventuate.

"The weather of the winter, first, and the condition of the ground in the spring, would permit little advantage to be derived from the presence of the army at Richmond until the middle of May. So that General Sherman has no reason to move in haste, but can choose such objects as he prefers, and take as much time as their attainment may demand."

3   U.S.S. *Harvest Moon*, Acting Master John K. Crosby, transported the first group of men from Major General William T. Sherman's army from Savannah, Georgia, to Beaufort, South Carolina, below Charleston. Sherman had marched across Georgia from Atlanta to the sea where he knew the Navy would be able to supply and support his troops.

General Grant ordered Major General Alfred H. Terry to command the troops intended for the second attack on Fort Fisher. "I have served with Admiral Porter," he wrote, "and know that you can rely on his judgment and his nerve to undertake what he proposes. I would, therefore, defer to him as much as is consistent with your own responsibilities." The same day Grant wrote Porter that he was sending Terry to work with him and wished the Admiral "all sorts of good weather and success. . . ."

4   Rear Admiral Porter, laying meticulous plans for the second Fort Fisher attack, ordered each of his commanding officers to "detail as many of his men as he can spare from the guns as a landing party." Armed with cutlasses and revolvers, the sailors and Marines were to hit the beach when the assault signal was made "and board the fort in a seaman-like way. The marines will form in the rear and cover the sailors. While the soldiers are going over the parapets in front, the sailors will take the sea face of Fort Fisher."

The impact of Union seapower throughout the war strongly influenced the views of Confederate naval commanders as to their own capabilities. This date, Flag Officer Mitchell, commanding the South's James River Squadron, expressed his estimate of the military situation on the river below Richmond: "The enemy, with his large naval establishment and unlimited transportation, has, in all his expeditions against us, appeared in such overwhelming force as to render a successful resistance on the part of ours utterly out of the question, as witness his operations on the Mississippi from New Orleans up, and more recently at Mobile. Would he be likely to do less on the James in any naval enterprise he undertakes against us? Surely not, and we can never hope to encounter him on anything like equal terms, except by accident. It behooves us, therefore, to bring to our aid all the means in our power to oppose his monitors in any advance they may attempt up the river." Mitchell recommended the placing of additional obstructions and torpedoes as the most reliable means of preventing a waterborne movement on Richmond. However, he added that his own squadron, which was the largest assembled at one point by the South, "will be expected to take a part, not only in opposing the advance of the enemy, but held in readiness to

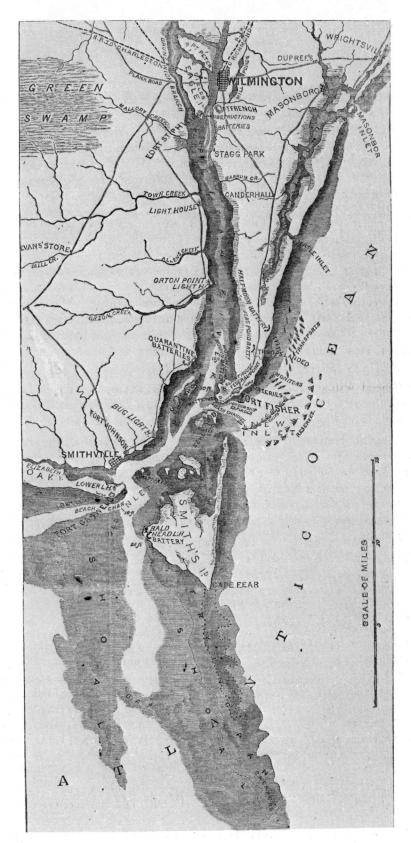

Wilmington and its defenses.

V–7

move and act in any direction whenever an opportunity offers to strike a blow.'' Mitchell would have this opportunity three weeks later.

A landing party under Acting Master James C. Tole from U.S.S. *Don* captured several torpedoes and powder on the right bank of the Rappahannock River about six miles from its mouth. The success of Confederate torpedo warfare—beginning with the destruction of U.S.S. *Cairo* (see 12 December 1862)—had led to increased efforts in this new area of war at sea, first under the genius of Commander Matthew Fontaine Maury, then under Commander Hunter Davidson. Throughout the remaining months of the war—and for some time thereafter—Southern torpedoes (or mines) would take a heavy toll of Union shipping.

5 A boat expedition under Acting Ensign Michael Murphy from U.S.S. *Winnebago* seized copper kettles used for distilling turpentine, 1300 pounds of copper pipes, and four sloop-rigged boats at Bon Secours Bay, Alabama.

Acting Lieutenant James Lansing succeeded in refloating U.S.S. *Indianola* in the Mississippi River. *Indianola* had been sunk by the Confederates almost two years before (see 24 February 1863) and the Union had been attempting to float her ever since. Rear Admiral Porter, who, as commander of the Mississippi Squadron, had been particularly interested in salvaging the ironclad, warmly congratulated Lansing on his success: "There are triumphs of skill such as you have displayed as glorious as if the result were from combat, and as such you have my highest commendations.'' *Indianola* was taken upriver to Mound City, Illinois.

7 Secretary Welles and Vice Admiral Farragut visited President Lincoln in the White House. The three discussed the capture of Mobile Bay which the Admiral had effected the previous August.

General Sherman wrote something of his plans to Rear Admiral Dahlgren, revealing his understanding of the importance of sea communications and the support of concentrated naval gunfire where possible:

"The letter you send me is from Admiral Porter, at Beaufort, N.C. I am not certain that there is a vessel in Port Royal from Admiral Porter, or I would write him. If there be one to return to him I beg you to send this, with a request that I be advised as early as possible as to the condition of the railroad from Beaufort, N.C., back to New Berne, and so on, toward Goldsboro; also all maps and information of the country above New Berne; how many cars and locomotives are available to us on that road; whether there is good navigation from Beaufort, N.C., via Pamlico Sound, up Neuse River, etc. I want Admiral Porter to know that I expect to be ready to move about the 15th; that I have one head of column across Savannah River at this point; will soon have another at Port Royal Ferry, and expect to make another crossing at Sister's Ferry. I still adhere to my plan submitted to General Grant, and only await provisions and forage.

"The more I think of the affair at Wilmington the more I feel ashamed of the army there; but Butler is at fault, and he alone. Admiral Porter fulfilled his share to admiration. I think the admiral will feel more confidence in my troops, as he saw us carry points on the Mississippi where he had silenced the fire. All will turn out for the best yet.''

8 Commander James D. Bulloch, Confederate naval agent in England, ordered Lieutenant John Low, who had previously served on board C.S.S. *Alabama* and as captain of C.S.S. *Tuscaloosa*, to assume command of the twin screw steamer *Ajax* upon her arrival in Nassau. Scheduled to sail from Glasgow on 12 January, *Ajax* had been built in Scotland under a contract of 14 September 1864 and had been designated a tug boat "to deceive Federal spies''. Minor alterations were planned to make her—and her sister ship *Hercules*—useful in the defense of Wilmington. However, *Ajax* never reached the Confederacy, and *Hercules* was never completed. On 1 March Secretary Mallory wrote Bulloch: "A notice of the arrival of the *Ajax* at a port in Ireland has reached me through the United States papers, but no further advices as to her or the *Hercules* or other vessels have come to hand.''

I have received a letter from Sherman — he wants me to time my operations by his, which I think a good plan — we will make a sure thing of it — but the troops and its navy must be ready to strike at a moment's notice, and when the enemy least expects us. We will have the report spread that the troops are to cooperate with Sherman in the attack on Charleston

I hope Sherman will be allowed to carry out his plans — he will have Wilmington in less than a month, and Charleston will fall like a ripe pear. I expect you understand all this better than I do. I have made arrangements to keep communication open with Sherman from the time he starts.

I am, General
very truly & sincerely
David D. Porter
Rear Admiral

Rear Admiral Porter writes General Grant of the proposed second attack on Fort Fisher and cooperation with General Sherman.

Rear Admiral Dahlgren advised Secretary Welles: "Among the articles found here [Savannah] after our troops entered was a torpedo boat, which I have received from General Sherman and sent to Port Royal. As yet it is only the unfinished wooden shell; no machinery was found about the place, but may be among some that was thrown overboard.

"There is also another torpedo boat in the yard of the builder, not finished, which I may be able to secure."

9   Secretary Welles notified Commander F. A. Parker, commanding the Potomac Flotilla, of intelligence received that Confederate agents enroute Richmond were crossing the Potomac River by India rubber boats at night in the vicinity of Port Tobacco, Maryland. "These messengers," the report warned, "wear metal buttons, upon the inside of which dispatches are most minutely photographed, not perceptible to the naked eye, but are easily read by the aid of a powerful lens."

Lieutenant Commander Earl English, U.S.S. *Wyalusing*, reported the capture of schooner *Triumph* at the mouth of the Perquimans River, North Carolina, with cargo including large quantity of salt.

10 Commander Bulloch wrote Secretary Mallory that he had obtained one of the French ironclads which Louis Napoleon, unwilling to provoke the United States government, had previously refused to release to the South. The ironclad had been sold to Denmark for the Schleswig-Holstein War, but when that conflict ended abruptly before the ship could be delivered, the Danes refused to accept her, and she was sold secretly to the Confederacy. Captain Thomas Jefferson Page took command of her in Copenhagen. "I have requested Captain Page," Bulloch wrote, "to name the ironclad *Stonewall*, an appellation not inconsistent with her character, and one which will appeal to the feelings and sympathies of our people at home." *Stonewall*, with a temporary crew and under another name (*Sphinx*) to divert suspicion as to her real ownership, had departed Copenhagen on 7 January.

Bulloch wrote Commander Hunter Davidson, one of the South's ablest naval officers who had directed the Torpedo Service and was now captain of the blockade runner *City of Richmond*, regarding an anticipated rendezvous between her and *Stonewall* at Belle Ile, Quiberon Bay, France. *City of Richmond* carried officers and men as well as supplies for the ironclad. It was hoped that *Stonewall* could break the blockade off Wilmington and then attack New England shipping.

U.S.S. *Valley City*, Acting Master John A. J. Brooks, seized steamer *Philadelphia* in the Chowan River, North Carolina, with cargo including tobacco and cotton.

12 "The great armada," as Colonel Lamb described Rear Admiral Porter's fleet, got underway from Beaufort, North Carolina, where a rendezvous had been made with 8,000 Union troops under the command of Major General Terry. The fleet, up to that time the largest American force to be assembled under one command, proceeded along the Carolina coast northeast of Wilmington and arrived off Fort Fisher the same night. Preparations were made for commencing a naval bombardment the following morning and for the amphibious landing of 10,000 soldiers, sailors, and Marines.

The new and formidable Confederate ram *Columbia*, ready for service, grounded while coming out of her dock at Charleston. Extensive efforts to refloat her failed and she was abandoned when Charleston was evacuated in mid-February. *Columbia* was saved by Union forces after much effort and was floated on 26 April. Rear Admiral Dahlgren described the ram: "She is 209 feet long (extreme), beam 49 feet, has a casemate 65 feet long, pierced for six guns, one on each side and one at each of the four corners, pivots to point ahead or astern and to the side. She has two engines, high pressure, and [is] plated on the casemates with 6 inches of iron in thickness, quite equal, it is believed, to the best of the kind built by the rebels."

James M. Mason, Confederate Commissioner in England, reported to Secretary of State Judah P. Benjamin, that France had proposed to Great Britain that each power permit Confederate prizes, having cargo in whole or in part claimed by English or French citizens, to be taken for adjudication into the ports of either nation.

13   Lieutenant Commander Stephen B. Luce, U.S.S. *Pontiac*, was ordered to report for duty with General W. T. Sherman. *Pontiac* steamed 40 miles up the Savannah River to protect the left wing of Sherman's army which was crossing the river at Sister's Ferry, Georgia, and cover its initial movements by water on the march north that would soon cause the fall of Charleston. Luce later credited his meeting with General Sherman as the beginning of his thinking which eventually resulted in the founding of the Naval War College. He said: "After hearing General Sherman's clear exposition of the military situation, the scales seemed to fall from my eyes . . . . It dawned on me that there were certain fundamental principles underlying military operations , . . . principles of general application whether the operations were on land or at sea."

13-15   Early on the morning of the 13th, the second amphibious assault on Fort Fisher was begun. Rear Admiral Porter took some 59 warships into action; Major General Terry commanded 8,000 soldiers. The naval landing party of 2,000 sailors and Marines would raise the assaulting force to 10,000. Colonel Lamb's valiant defenders in the fort numbered 1,500.

    U.S.S. *New Ironsides*, Commodore William Radford, led monitors *Saugus*, *Canonicus*, *Monadnock*, and *Mahopac* to within 1000 yards of Fort Fisher and opened on the batteries. A spirited engagement ensued. Porter wrote to Secretary Welles: "It was soon quite apparent that the iron vessels had the best of it; traverses began to disappear and the southern angle of Fort Fisher commenced to look very dilapidated." U.S.S. *Brooklyn*, Captain Alden, and U.S.S. *Colorado*, Commodore Thatcher, led the heavy wooden warships into battle and the Federal fleet maintained a devastating bombardment throughout the day until after dark. In the meantime, General Terry selected a beachhead out of the fort's gun range and made naturally defensible on the northern side by a line of swamps and woods extending across the peninsula where he landed his 8000 troops unopposed. By daybreak on the 14th he had thrown up a line of defensive breastworks facing Wilmington in order to protect his rear from possible attack by the 6000 troops stationed in that city under the command of General Bragg. Porter wrote to Secretary Welles: "We have a respectable force landed on a strip of land, which our naval guns completely command, and a place of defense which would enable us to hold on against a very large army."

    The monitors had maintained an harassing fire during the night of the 13th; then at daylight of the second day of the attack the fleet's big guns reopened the bombardment in full fury. General W. H. C. Whiting who had come to "counsel" with Colonel Lamb and share his fate inside the fort, remarked: "It was beyond description, no language can describe that terrific bombardment." The Confederates were hardly able to bury their dead, much less repair the works, as the fleet poured in, according to one estimate, 100 shells a minute. The defenders suffered some 300 casualties from the naval bombardment and had but one gun on the land face of the fort still serviceable. During the day C.S.S. *Chickamauga* fired on the recently landed Union troops from her position in the Cape Fear River, but on the 15th U.S.S. *Monticello*, Lieutenant Commander William B. Cushing, drove the former Confederate raider out of range.

    On the evening of the 14th General Terry visited Porter on the flagship *Malvern*, and the two planned the timing of the next day's operations. The fleet would maintain the bombardment until the moment of attack in mid-afternoon. Then half of the 8000 soldiers would assault the land face on the western front of the fort and the 2000 sailors and Marines from the ships would attack the "northeast bastion". The remaining troops would hold the defensive line against a possible attack from Wilmington.

    At 3 p.m. on the 15th the signal to cease firing was sent to the fleet, and the soldiers, sailors, and Marines ashore charged the Confederate fortifications. Because the Army advanced through a wooded area while the Naval Brigade dashed across an open beach, the defenders opened a concentrated fire at point blank range on the naval attack, "ploughing lanes in the ranks." Leading the assault, Lieutenant Samuel W. Preston, one of the war's ablest young naval officers, and Lieu-

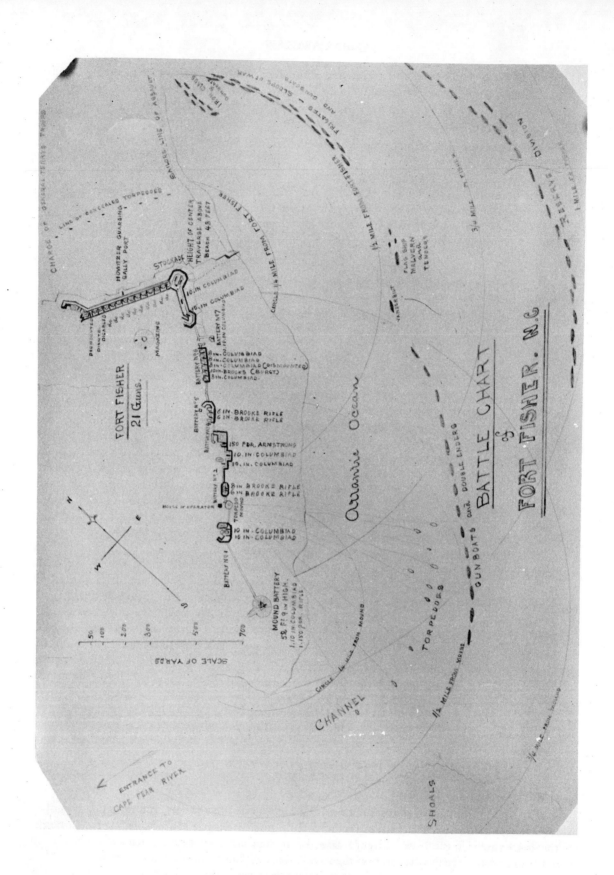

BATTLE CHART
of
FORT FISHER, N.C.

FORT FISHER
21 Guns.

tenant Benjamin H. Porter, commanding officer of the flagship U.S.S. *Malvern*, were among those killed. Unchecked, however, the assaulting force under the command of Lieutenant Commander K. Randolph Breese pressed forward. Ensign Robley D. Evans—later to become a Rear Admiral with the well-earned sobriquet "Fighting Bob"—suffered four wounds, two crippling his legs. He later vividly described the naval assault: "About five hundred yards, from the fort the head of the column suddenly stopped, and, as if by magic, the whole mass of men went down like a row of falling bricks. . . . The officers called on the men, and they responded instantly, starting forward as fast as they could go. At about three hundred yards they again went down, this time under the effect of canister added to the rifle fire. Again we rallied them, and once more started to the front under a perfect hail of lead, with men dropping rapidly in every direction." Some 60 men under Lieutenant Commander Thomas O. Selfridge reached and broke through the palisade, but it was the high water mark of the charge. They were hurled back and others recoiled under the withering fire after approaching the stockade and the base of the parapets. "All the officers," Evans wrote, "in their anxiety to be the first into the fort, had advanced to the heads of the columns, leaving no one to steady the men in behind; and it was in this way we were defeated, by the men breaking from the rear." The significance of the naval assault was perceived by Colonel Lamb when he wrote that "their gallant attempt enabled the army to enter and obtain a foothold, which they otherwise could not have done."

Cries of victory rose from the brave defenders, who thought they had beaten back the main attack, but their exultation was short lived. For General Terry's troops had meanwhile taken the western end of the parapet. The Confederates at once launched a counter-attack, and desperate hand-to-hand fighting followed.

Now the naval shore bombardment intervened decisively. The guns of Porter's assembled ships—firing at right angles to the direction of the Union charge—opened with "deadly precision" into the Confederate ranks. Other ships lifted their fire to neutralize the river bank behind the fort and prevent the dispatch of reinforcements. Lamb later recorded that "as the tide of the battle seemed to have turned in our favor, the remorseless fleet came to the rescue of the faltering Federals."

General Whiting was mortally wounded during the engagement and Colonel Lamb was felled with a bullet in his hip. Major James Reilly assumed command and fought "from traverse to traverse" before finally being forced to retreat from the fort. He and his men surrendered later that night. "Fort Fisher," Porter wired Welles, "is ours."

It had not been taken without considerable losses. The Union forces—Army and Navy—sustained some 1000 casualties, more than twice as many as the defenders suffered. Porter wrote: "Men, it seems, must die that this Union may live, and the Constitution under which we have gained our prosperity must be maintained."

More than 35 sailors and Marines were awarded the Medal of Honor for their heroism in this action that closed the Confederacy's last supply line from Europe.

The second Federal assault on Fort Fisher revealed again the inherent ability of a fleet-supported amphibious force to capitalize on the superior mobility conferred by command of the sea, forcing the defenders to spread their forces thinly in a vain effort to be strong at all threatened points simultaneously. This operation also provided dramatic demonstration of a fleet's ability to mass superior firepower at any point of a shore defense position. Fear of concentrated naval gunfire forced inaction on General Hoke's Confederate division stationed between the fort and Wilmington, forestalling any interference with the landing of the Federal expeditionary force and enabling General Terry to split the Confederate defense forces.

Colonel Lamb, the fort's gallant commandant, later recorded: "For the first time in the history of sieges the land defenses of the works were destroyed, not by any act of the besieging army, but by the concentrated fire, direct and enfilading, of an immense fleet poured into them without intermission, until torpedo wires were cut, palisades breached so that they actually afforded cover for assailants, and the slopes of the work were rendered practicable for assault." The second

The fleet opens the second attack on Fort Fisher...

Sailors, Marines and soldiers are landed..

And storm the mighty bastion.

attack became a classic example of complete Army-Navy coordination. In his telegram to Secretary Welles announcing the capture of the fort, Porter stated: "General Terry is entitled to the highest praise and the gratitude of his country for the manner in which he has conducted his part of the operations. . . . Our cooperation has been most cordial. The result is victory, which will always be ours when the Army and the Navy go hand in hand." Terry began his own report: "I should signally fail to do my duty were I to omit to speak in terms of the highest admiration of the part borne by the Navy in our operations. In all ranks, from Admiral Porter to his seamen, there was the utmost desire not only to do their proper work, but to facilitate in every manner the operations of the land forces."

14   Blockade runner *Lelia* foundered off the mouth of the Mersey River, England. Flag Officer Samuel Barron wrote Secretary Mallory from Paris: "The melancholy duty devolves on me of reporting the death on the 14th instant, by drowning of Commander Arthur Sinclair, C. S. Navy, and Gunner P. C. Cuddy, late of the *Alabama*." Commander Hunter Davidson, learning of the accident while in Funchal, Madeira, early in February, commented: "What an awful thing the loss of the *Lelia*. To death in battle we become reconciled, for it is not unexpected and leaves its reward; but such a death for poor Sinclair, after forty-two years' service . . .!"

U.S.S. *Seminole*, Commander Albert G. Clary, captured schooner *Josephine* bound from Galveston to Matamoras with cargo of cotton.

15   At the request of Major General William T. Sherman, Rear Admiral John A. Dahlgren, commanding the South Atlantic Blockading Squadron, issued orders to prepare for a combined naval and military demonstration before Charleston in order to draw attention from General Sherman's march to the north. Before making the demonstration, it was necessary to locate and mark the numerous obstructions in the channel of Charleston harbor. Accordingly, this date orders were issued charging the commanders of the monitors with this duty. That evening, while searching for the Confederate obstructions, U.S.S. *Patapsco*, Lieutenant Commander Stephen P. Quackenbush, struck a torpedo (mine) near the entrance of the lower harbor and sank instantly with the loss of 64 officers and men, more than half her crew. She was the fourth monitor lost in the war, the second due to enemy torpedoes. Thereafter, only small boats and tugs were used in the search for obstructions and the objective of the joint expedition was changed to Bull's Bay, a few miles northeast of Charleston.

16   With Fort Fisher lost and foreseeing that the Union fleet's entrance into the Cape Fear River would cut the waterborne communications system, General Bragg ordered the evacuation of the remaining Confederate positions at the mouth of the river. At 7 a.m. Forts Caswell and Campbell were abandoned and destroyed. Fort Holmes on Smith's Island and Fort Johnson at Smithville were likewise destroyed by the retreating garrisons, which fell back on Fort Anderson, on the west bank of the Cape Fear River between Fort Fisher and Wilmington. "The Yankees," wrote one Confederate, not perceiving the full import of the fateful results, "have made a barren capture. . . ." In fact, however, Wilmington, the last major port open to blockade runners, was now effectively sealed and General Lee was cut off from his only remaining supply line from Europe. Rear Admiral Porter recognized the implications of the Union victory more clearly. He wrote Captain Godon: ". . . the death knell of another fort is booming in the distance. Fort Caswell with its powerful batteries is in flames and being blown up, and thus is sealed the door through which this rebellion is fed."

Seeking to take advantage of the reduced Union naval strength in the James River, Secretary Mallory wrote Flag Officer Mitchell to encourage him to pass the obstructions at Trent's Reach and attack General Grant's base of operations at City Point. "From Lieutenant Read," Mallory noted, "I learn that the hulk which lay across the channel [at Trent's Reach] and the net also have been washed away, and I think it probable that there is a passage through the obstructions. I deem the opportunity a favorable one for striking a blow at the enemy, if we are able to do so.

Samuel W. Preston
Lieutenant, USN

Benjamin H. Porter
Lieutenant, USN

The Union fleet celebrates the surrender of Fort Fisher.

In a short time many of his vessels will have returned to the river from Wilmington and he will again perfect his obstructions. If we can block the river at or below City Point, Grant might be compelled to evacuate his position." City Point was essential to Grant's anticipated movement on Richmond. The supplies to the Union soldiers on the Petersburg front reached City Point by water, assured of free passage by the Navy, and then were sent to the front by rail. If the North were forced to abandon the base at City Point, it might also have to abandon a spring offensive against the Confederate capital. Mallory added: "I regard an attack upon the enemy and the obstructions of the river at City Point, to cut off Grant's supplies, as a movement of the first importance to the country and one which should be accomplished if possible." Mitchell replied that he was having the obstructions examined to ensure that Read's report was correct. "Should information be obtained that the passage of these obstructions is practicable," the flag officer wrote, "I shall gladly incur all the other hazards that may attend the proposed enterprise that promises, if successful, such bright results to our cause."

The Twenty-Third Army Corps, Major General John M. Schofield, commenced embarking on transports at Clifton, Tennessee. The corps was being ordered by General Grant to move by water and rail to Washington, D.C.–Annapolis area and thence by water south for further operations. These troops assaulted Wilmington and formed a juncture with General Sherman's northward moving army.

17 Delayed in departure from Savannah, General Sherman wrote Rear Admiral Dahlgren: "When we are known to be in rear of Charleston, about Branchville and Orangeburg, it will be well to watch if the enemy lets go of Charleston, in which case Foster will occupy it, otherwise the feint should be about Bull's Bay. We will need no cover about Port Royal; nothing but the usual guard ships. I think that you will concur with me that, in anticipation of the movement of my army to the rear of the coast, it will be unwise to subject your ships to the heavy artillery of the enemy or to his sunken torpedoes. I will instruct Foster, when he knows I have got near Branchville, to make a landing of a small force at Bull's Bay, to threaten, and it may be occupy, the road from Mount Pleasant to Georgetown. This will make the enemy believe I design to turn down against Charleston and give me a good offing for Wilmington. I will write you again fully on the eve of starting in person."

Rear Admiral Porter wrote Secretary Welles regarding Fort Fisher: "I have since visited Fort Fisher and the adjoining works, and find their strength greatly beyond what I had conceived; an engineer might be excusable in saying they could not be captured except by regular siege. I wonder even now how it was done. The work . . . is really stronger than the Malakoff Tower, which defied so long the combined power of France and England, and yet it is captured by a handful of men under the fire of the guns of the fleet, and in seven hours after the attack commenced in earnest." He concluded his report by proclaiming that Wilmington was hermetically sealed against blockade runners, "and no *Alabamas* or *Floridas*, *Chickamaugas* or *Tallahassees* will ever fit out again from this port, and our merchant vessels very soon, I hope, will be enabled to pursue in safety their avocation."

News of the capture of Fort Fisher reached Washington and talk of the Army-Navy success dominated President Lincoln's cabinet meeting. Secretary Welles noted in his diary, "The President was happy."

Knowing that many blockade runners, unaware of Fort Fisher's fall, would attempt to run in to Wilmington, Porter ordered the signal lights on the Mound "properly trimmed and lighted, as has been the custom with the rebels during the blockade." He added: "Have the lights lighted to-night and see that no vessel inside displays a light, and be ready to grab anyone that enters." Three days later the Admiral's resourcefulness paid dividends with the capture of two runners (see 20 January).

Office U. S. Military Telegraph,
WAR DEPARTMENT.

The following Telegram received at Washington 11.35 A.M. Jany 17 1865.

From Fort Fisher Jany 15 1865.

Hon Gideon Welles Secy Navy

Sir. Fort Fisher is ours. I send a bearer of despatches with a brief account of the affair. Genl Terry is entitled to the highest praise and the gratitude of his Country for the manner in which he has conducted his part of the operations. He is my beau ideal of a soldier and a General. Our cooperation has been most cordial. The result is victory which will always be ours when the Army and Navy go hand in hand. The Navy loss in the assault was heavy. The Army loss is also heavy

95,295 Paid

D. D. Porter
Rear Admiral

Rear Admiral Porter telegraphs Secretary Welles the news of the capture of Fort Fisher.

Admiral Porter kept Confederate signal lights on the Mound "properly trimmed and lighted" to lure in unsuspecting blockaders after Fort Fisher fell.

Naval forces, commanded by Lieutenant Moreau Forrest of the Mississippi Squadron, cooperated with Army cavalry in a successful attack on the town of Somerville, Alabama. The expedition resulted in the capture of 90 prisoners, 150 horses and one piece of artillery.

Two armed boats from U.S.S. *Honeysuckle*, Acting Master James J. Russell, captured the British schooner *Augusta* at the mouth of the Suwannee River as she attempted to run the blockade with cargo of pig lead, flour, gunny cloth and coffee.

17–19 Confederate steamers *Granite City* and *Wave* (ex-U.S. Navy ships, see 6 May 1864) eluded block-ading ship U.S.S. *Chocura*, Lieutenant Commander Richard W. Meade, Jr., on a "dark, foggy, and rainy" night and escaped from Calcasieu Pass, Louisiana. *Granite City* was reported to carry no cargo but *Wave* had a load of lumber for the Rio Grande. Meade gave chase for 60 miles, "but our boilers being in a disabled condition, and leaking badly, the speed of the ship was so much reduced that I reluctantly gave up the hope of overtaking the *Granite City* before she could make a port."

18 J. B. Jones, a clerk in the Confederate War Department, wrote in his diary: "No war news. But blockade-running at Wilmington has ceased; and common calico, now at $25 per yard, will soon be $50. . . . Flour is $1250 per barrel, to-day." Only five days before he had recorded: "Beef (what little there is in market) sells to-day at $6 per pound; meal, $80 per bushel; white beans, $5 per quart, or $160 per bushel." These figures bore eloquent witness to the decisive role played by Federal seapower in the collapse of the Confederacy. A giant amphibious assault had closed Wilmington, General Lee's last hope for sufficient supplies to sustain his soldiers. Control of the Mississippi River and the western tributaries by omnipresent Union warships, coupled with the destruction of the South's weak railway system, prevented the transfer of men and supplies to strengthen the crumbling military situation in the East. Thus, blockade of the coasts and continuing attack from afloat as well as on land surrounded and divided the South and hastened its economic, financial, and psychological deterioration. Just as civilians lived in

deep privation, so, too, were the armies of the Confederacy gravely weakened from a shortage of munitions, equipment, clothing, and food.

Lieutenant Commander William B. Cushing, commanding U.S.S. *Monticello*, landed at Fort Caswell, hoisted the Stars and Stripes, and took possession for the United States.

19   Blockade runner *Chameleon* (formerly C.S.S. *Tallahassee*), Lieutenant John Wilkinson, put to sea from Bermuda loaded to the rails with commissary stores and provisions for General Lee's hard-pressed, ill supplied army. Wilkinson had departed Cape Fear on this special blockade running mission on 24 December 1864 in the aftermath of the first Fort Fisher campaign. Upon his return, he successfully ran the blockade (as he had done on 21 separate occasions during 1863 with *Robert E. Lee*) and had entered the harbor before learning that Union forces had captured Fort Fisher during his absence. *Chameleon* reversed course and safely dashed to sea. Wilkinson later said that he had been able to escape only because of the ship's twin screws, which "enabled our steamer to turn as if on a pivot in the narrow channel between the bar and the rip." After an unsuccessful attempt to enter Charleston and in the absence of orders from Secretary Mallory, Wilkinson took *Chameleon* to Liverpool and turned the ship over to Commander Bulloch, the Confederate naval agent. Ironically, he arrived on 9 April, the same day that Lee surrendered to Grant at Appomattox.

In orders to U.S.S. *Canonicus*, *Mahopac*, and *Monadnock*, having arrived to join the Charleston blockaders, Rear Admiral Dahlgren showed his concern for the threat of Confederate torpedoes: "You will lose no time in securing the *Canonicus* against the possible action of the rebel torpedo boats; temporary fenders must be used until permanent fixtures can be provided. Boat patrol must be used with vigilance, and such other measures resorted to as are in common practice here."

20   Flag Officer Mitchell wrote Major James F. Milligan of the Confederate signal corps seeking information "as to the number and disposition of the enemy's ironclads, gunboats, armed transports, torpedo boats, and vessels generally on the James. . . ." The commander of the South's James River Squadron was readying his ships for a thrust downriver at the major Union supply base, City Point. It was hoped that a successful attack on General Grant's supply base would force him to withdraw and abandon his plans for a spring offensive against Richmond.

Blockade runner *City of Richmond*, Commander Davidson, anchored in Quiberon Bay, France, to await the arrival of C.S.S. *Stonewall*. Davidson permitted no communication with the shore in order to preclude the possibility of others learning that the ironclad would rendezvous with him and effect a transfer of men and supplies. Flag Officer Barron described *Stonewall* as "a vessel more formidable than any we have yet afloat. . . ."

Flag Officer Barron reported to Secretary Mallory that he had ordered Commanders James H North and G. T. Sinclair and Lieutenant Commander C. M. Morris, Confederate agents abroad, to return to the Confederacy, ". . . there being in my judgement no prospect of any duty for them."

Blockade runners *Stag* and *Charlotte*, unaware that Fort Fisher and the works at Cape Fear had fallen, anchored in the harbor at Smithville near U.S.S. *Malvern*, flagship of Rear Admiral Porter, and were captured. Porter wrote: "I intrusted this duty to Lieutenant [Commander] Cushing, who performed it with his usual good luck and intelligence. They are very fast vessels and valuable prizes." *Stag* was commanded by Lieutenant Richard H. Gayle, CSN, who had previously been captured while commanding blockade runner *Cornubia* (see 8 November 1863).

21   Secretary Mallory again wrote Flag Officer Mitchell urging an immediate movement by the James River Squadron past the obstructions at Trent's Reach and assault on General Grant's base of operations at City Point. "You have an opportunity, I am convinced, rarely presented to a naval officer, and one which may lead to the most glorious results to your country." The same day Mitchell sent a telegram to General Lee, whose troops depended heavily on a successful completion of the attack, informing him that the squadron would attempt to pass the obstructions on the 22nd.

"I have not time to visit you," he wrote, "and would therefore be glad to meet on board of the flagship or at Drewry's Bluff any officer whom you could appoint to meet me, to give me your views and wishes as to my cooperation with the army down the river in the event of our being successful."

U.S.S. *Penguin*, Acting Lieutenant James R. Beers, chased steamer *Granite City* ashore off Velasco, Texas. The blockade runner was under the protection of Confederate shore batteries. Beers reported that, since he was "of the opinion that the steamer could not be got off, and would eventually go to pieces, as there was a heavy sea rolling in and continually breaking over her, I did not think it was prudent to remain longer under the enemy's fire, as their guns were of longer range than ours."

Elements of the Twenty-Third Army Corps, Major General Schofield, disembarked from transports at Cincinnati, Ohio, which they had reached in five days via the Tennessee and Ohio Rivers from Clifton, Tennessee. The troops entrained for Washington, D.C., Alexandria, Virginia, and Annapolis, Maryland, where the first echelon arrived 31 January.

22   Flag Officer Mitchell reported that he was unable to get underway to pass the obstructions at Trent's Reach as he had planned because of heavy fog. Mitchell had also received no report from Boatswain Thomas Gauley, whom he had dispatched on the 21st to remove a number of Confederate torpedoes that had been placed in the channel near Howlett's Landing. He wrote Major General George Pickett: "To-morrow night, if the weather is sufficiently clear for the pilots to see their way, our movement will be made, and I will be glad to have your cooperation as agreed upon for to-night." A successful downriver thrust by Mitchell's squadron could spell disaster for the Union cause as General Grant would be deprived of his great water-supplied base at City Point and his armies would be divided by Confederate control of the James River.

Rear Admiral Porter ordered Commander John Guest, U.S.S. *Iosco*, to "regulate the movements of the vessels in the Cape Fear River above Fort Fisher. . . ." Porter sought to move the line of ships as near Fort Anderson, the position to which the Confederates had withdrawn following the fall of Fort Fisher and adjacent forts, "as is consistent with safety, and in doing so care must be taken of the torpedoes and other obstructions." The same day U.S.S. *Pequot*, Lieutenant Commander Daniel L. Braine, steamed upriver and opened on Fort Anderson to reconnoiter and test its defenses. The Confederates brought only two "small rifle pieces" in action, but, Braine reported: "I observed 6 guns, evidently smoothbore, pointing down the river, protected by the ordinary sand traverses." Having sealed off Wilmington, the last major port in the South, the Union was now moving to occupy it.

A boat expedition from U.S.S. *Chocura*, Lieutenant Commander R. W. Meade, Jr., captured blockade running schooner *Delphina* by boarding in Calcasieu River, Louisiana. *Delphina* was carrying a cargo of cotton.

The steamer *Ajax*, with Lieutenant John Low, CSN, on board as a "passenger", put out of Dublin, Ireland, for Nassau. *Ajax* had been built for the Confederacy in Dumbarton, Scotland, for use in harbor defense. She had been detained in Dublin for more than a week because the U.S. Consul there suspected that the light-draft vessel was bound for the South. However, two inspections failed to substantiate this belief and the 340 ton would-be gunboat was released. Nevertheless, Charles F. Adams, the American Ambassador in England, and Secretary of State Seward prevailed upon British Foreign Minister Earl Russell to prevent the armament of *Ajax* in Halifax, Bermuda, or Nassau (see 4 May).

23   U.S.S. *Fox*, Acting Master Francis Burgess, seized British schooner *Fannie McRae* near the mouth of the Warrior River, Florida, where she was preparing to run the blockade.

23-24   Flag Officer Mitchell's James River Squadron launched its downstream assault with high hopes in Richmond that victory afloat would turn the tide ashore. The Union squadron defending

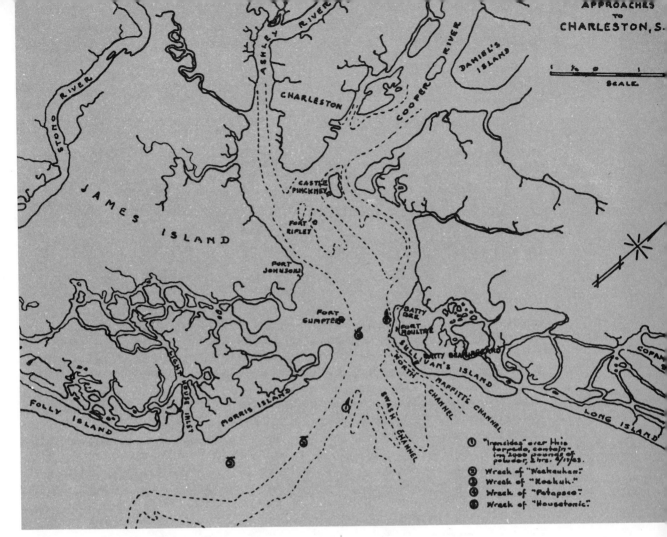

APPROACHES
TO
CHARLESTON, S.

SCALE

ASHLEY RIVER

COOPER RIVER

CHARLESTON

DANIEL'S ISLAND

JAMES ISLAND

CASTLE PINCKNEY

FORT RIPLEY

FORT JOHNSON

FORT SUMTER

BATTY GEE

FORT MOULTRIE

BATTY BEAUREGARD

SULLIVAN'S ISLAND

MAFFITT'S CHANNEL

NORTH CHANNEL

SWASH CHANNEL

LIGHTHOUSE INLET

MORRIS ISLAND

FOLLY ISLAND

LONG ISLAND

COPAH'S

① "Ironsides" over this torpedo, contain- in 3000 pounds of powder, 2 hrs. 4/17/63.

② Wreck of "Weehawken."

③ Wreck of "Keokuk."

④ Wreck of "Patapsco."

⑤ Wreck of "Housatonic."

Map of the approaches to . . .

. . . and view of the harbor of Charleston.

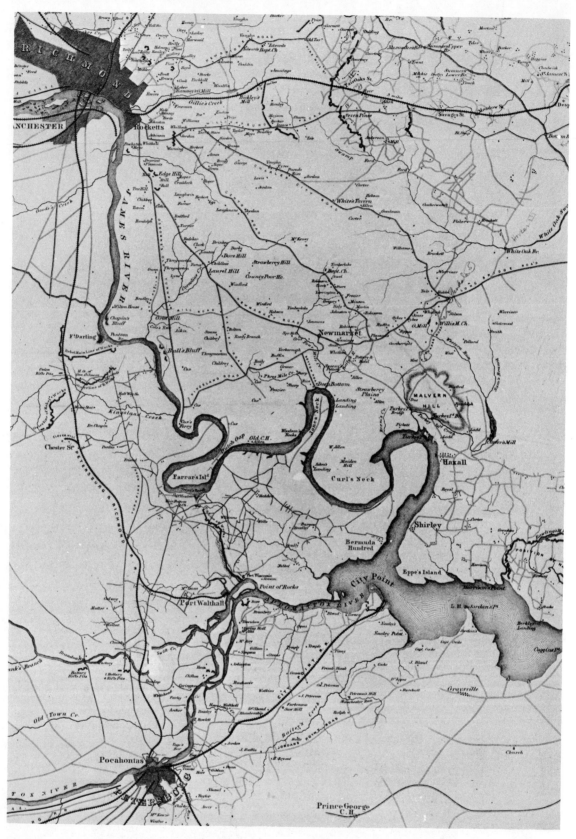

Map of the James River showing Petersburg, City Point, and Richmond.

Attempting to take Grant's City Point supply base, the Confederate James River Squadron steams past Fort Brady. . . .

. . . only to be halted when the heaviest of the ironclads ground while forcing the obstructions.

the lower James and City Point had been greatly reduced for the Fort Fisher-Wilmington opera-tions. It now included only one monitor, the double-turreted *Onondaga*. She and the ten gunboats withdrew upon the approach of Mitchell's formidable force. Commodore W. A. Parker explained that he moved downstream "because I thought there would be more room to maneuver the vessel and to avoid the batteries bearing on Dutch Gap." The eleven ship Con-federate squadron was built around the three heaviest ironclads now in the Southern Navy: C.S.S. *Richmond*, Commander John McIntosh Kell, *Virginia No. 2*, Lieutenant John W. Dunning-ton, and *Fredericksburg*, Lieutenant Francis E. Shepperd. The serious Confederate thrust, however, was turned back when both *Virginia No. 2* and *Richmond* ran aground while passing the obstructions at Trent's Reach and were brought under heavy fire from the Union shore batteries. Gunboat *Drewry*, Lieutenant William H. Wall, and torpedo boat *Scorpion*, Lieutenant Edward Lakin, also went aground. *Drewry* was shattered by an explosion resulting from a mortar shell penetrating her magazine, and *Scorpion*, thought to be damaged by that nearby explosion, was abandoned. *Onondaga*, flagship of Parker's squadron, returned to Trent's Reach the following morning and took the stranded Confederate ironclads under fire. Her 15-inch Dahlgren guns spoke with devastating effect, and the damaged *Virginia No. 2* and *Richmond* withdrew upriver as soon as they were refloated.

Although Parker was severely criticized for failing to engage the Confederates at once, the war's last battle of ironclads ended favorably for the North. Grant's supply lines remained unbroken and he could move inexorably toward Richmond. Control of the James and Potomac Rivers was of inestimable value to the North. Had they been in the hands of the South, the campaigns of McClellan and Grant could not have been undertaken. Indeed, with Confederates controlling these rivers Washington, and not Richmond, would have been on the defensive.

24 At mid-morning, C.S.S. *Stonewall*, Captain T. J. Page, put into Quiberon Bay to rendezvous with blockade runner *City of Richmond*. The two ships remained there until 28 January when *Stonewall*, still short of coal but unable to obtain more, "considered it prudent to sail." *City of Richmond* remained in company with the ironclad, but by the morning of the 30th had become separated by five miles because of heavy weather. Page signalled Commander Davidson on board *City of Richmond* that he was short of coal and would put into Ferrol, Spain. Davidson deemed it wiser not to follow *Stonewall* and signalled "Adieu". Page replied, "Many thanks. Adieu." The runner then continued toward Bermuda, while the ironclad sailed for Ferrol.

President Lincoln dispatched Vice Admiral Farragut to the James River to investigate the with-drawal of the Union squadron in the face of an offensive movement by the Confederate flotilla. The Admiral's son, Loyall, later wrote: "Late in December, 1864, the Richmond papers announced that a movement was on foot which would astonish the world. This turned out to be a scheme for the Confederate iron-clads and gunboats in the James to descend the river, break through the obstructions at Howlett's, destroy the pontoon bridges at Aiken's Landing, and cut off both the Army of the James and the Army of the Potomac (the former being on the left bank, and the latter on the right) from their base of supplies at City Point." However, upon Farragut's arrival on the James the next day, he found that the Confederate thrust had been turned back and the emer-gency had passed. The gap in the obstructions through which the Southerners had threatened to pass was filled with sunken coal barges, and, as young Farragut remarked, "the Confederate opportunity was lost forever." Finding the Union naval force in firm control of the lower river, the Admiral returned to Washington.

Secretary Welles ordered Commodore Henry K. Thatcher to relieve Commodore James S. Palmer as Commander, West Gulf Blockading Squadron. Welles cautioned that the "Rio Grande is a great avenue through which supplies of every description reach the insurgents. Being a neutral highway, unscrupulous parties avail themselves of it to enrich themselves and aid the rebel cause. . . . But by vigilance and the maintenance of an adequate blockading fleet in the vicinity of the mouth of the river and in the route to and from Havana this trade may be seriously interrupted."

James Waddell
Lieutenant, CSN

Hunter Davidson
Commander, CSN

Major General W. T. Sherman commenced his march to the north from Savannah while the ships of the South Atlantic Blockading Squadron operated in the rivers in the proximity of his army. These naval operations served to protect Sherman's army and simultaneously forced the Confederate commanders to spread thin their remaining forces. Rear Admiral Dahlgren reported to Secretary Welles the deployment of the naval vessels supporting the advance of Sherman's men: "I have the *Dai Ching* and a tug in the Combahee to assist the move at that ferry. The *Sonoma* is in the North Edisto, and the *Pawnee* leaves at early light with a tug for the Ashepoo, where a battery and obstructions are reported. The orders of all are to drive in the rebel pickets and knock down his batteries where they can be reached. The *Tuscarora, Mingoe, State of Georgia*, and *Nipsic* are at Georgetown, with orders to prevent the erection there of any batteries. The *Pontiac* is in the Savannah River at Purysburg, advancing with General Sherman's extreme left. The demonstrations desired by General Sherman at Charleston may be said to be begun by the collection there of so many ironclads."

25 C.S.S. *Shenandoah*, Lieutenant Waddell, put into Melbourne for repairs and provisions 108 days out of England. Although the cruiser had taken no prizes for four weeks and remained considerably undermanned—Waddell reported that the berthing spaces would accomodate 150 men comfortably but that he had only 51 crew men on board—the Lieutenant promptly wrote Flag Officer Barron in Paris: "I am getting along boldly and cheerfully." To Secretary Mallory he reported: ". . . when I have done all that which you have directed me to do I shall be better able to decide what ought to be done with the *Shenandoah*. I shall keep her afloat as long as she is, in my opinion, serviceable." Without the dry docking and machinery repairs accomplished at Melbourne, Waddell would not have been able to carry out his mission against American whalers in the Pacific.

Captain T. J. Page reported that C.S.S. *Stonewall* was now at sea off the coast of France and wrote Secretary Mallory: "You must not expect too much of me; I fear that the power and effect of this vessel have been too much exaggerated. We will do our best."

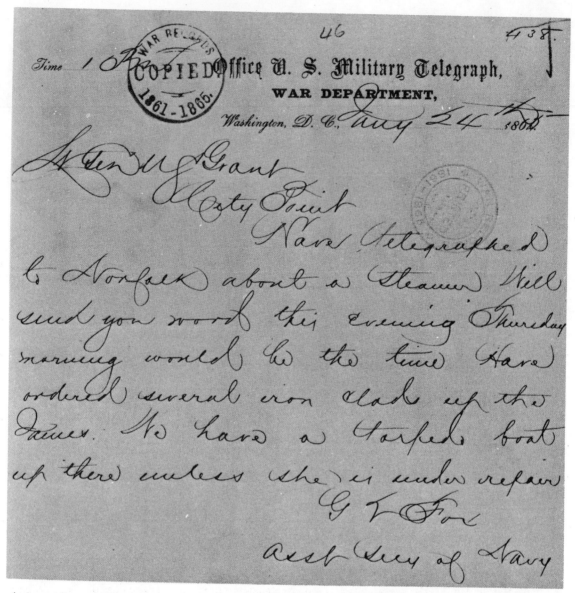

46

438

Time 1 0

WAR RECORDS 1861-1865.

COPIED Office U. S. Military Telegraph,

WAR DEPARTMENT,

Washington, D. C., Aug 24 1864.

Lt Gen U S Grant
City Point

Navy telegraphed to Norfolk about a Steamer Will send you word this evening Thursday morning would be the time Have ordered several iron clads up the James. We have a torpedo boat up there unless she is under repair

G V Fox

Asst Secy of Navy

Assistant Secretary Gustavus Fox responds to General Grant's request for naval support to protect his City Point headquarters on the James River.

Shortly after dawn, a boarding party from U.S.S. *Tristram Shandy*, Acting Lieutenant Francis M. Green, seized blockade running steamer *Blenheim* just inside the bar at New Inlet, North Carolina. *Blenheim* had run into the approach to Wilmington unaware that Federal forces now controlled the area and anchored off the Mound battery. "At the time of boarding," Green reported, "they were endeavoring to get the vessel underway." *Blenheim* was the third prize to be lured into Union hands by the Confederate range lights at the Mound which Rear Admiral Porter had kept burning.

26 Confederate picket boat *Hornet* was sunk and Lieutenant Aeneas Armstrong, CSN, was drowned as a result of the collision between *Hornet* and the steamer *Allison* on the James River.

U.S.S. *Dai Ching*, Lieutenant Commander James C. Chaplin, operating on the right flank of General W. T. Sherman's army in the Combahee River, ran aground while engaging Confederate batteries. After a 7 hour battle, and only after all her guns were out of operation, *Dai Ching* was abandoned and fired by her crew. The tug U.S.S. *Clover*, Acting Ensign Franklin S. Leach, which had been in company with *Dai Ching*, captured blockade running schooner *Coquette* with cargo of cotton.

27 After dark, a launch commanded by Acting Ensign Thomas Morgan from U.S.S. *Eutaw* proceeded up the James River past the obstructions at Trent's Reach and captured C.S.S. *Scorpion*. The torpedo boat had run aground during the Confederate attempt to steam downriver on the 23rd and 24th and had been abandoned after Union mortar fire destroyed C.S.S. *Drewry* which was similarly stranded nearby. Morgan reported: "Finding her hard aground, I immediately proceeded to get her afloat and succeeded in doing so, and repassed the obstruction on my return to the fleet about 10:30 p.m." *Scorpion* was found to be little damaged by the explosion of *Drewry*, contrary to Confederate estimates, and Chief Engineer Alexander Henderson, who examined her, reported approvingly: "She has fair speed for a boat of her kind, and is well adapted for the purpose for which she was built." *Scorpion* was reported to be 46 feet in length, 6 feet 3 inches beam, and 3 feet 9 inches in depth.

28 Confederate torpedo boat *St. Patrick*, Lieutenant John T. Walker, struck U.S.S. *Octorara*, Lieutenant Commander William W. Low, off Mobile Bay but her spar torpedo failed to explode. Although attacked by ship guns and small arms, Walker was able to bring *St. Patrick* safely back under the Mobile batteries.

U.S.S. *Mattabesett*, Commander John C. Febiger, dispatched U.S.S. *Valley City* to Colerain, North Carolina, on the Chowan River to protect an encampment of Union troops there.

30 Returning from an afternoon reconnaissance of King's Creek, Virginia, Acting Ensign James H. Kerens, U.S.S. *Henry Brinker*, and his two boat crews "discovered 5 men, who, upon seeing us, immediately fled." His suspicions aroused, Kerens determined to return under cover of darkness to search the vicinity. That night he and two boat crews returned to the mouth of King's Creek and, after more than an hour of careful searching, found "two very suspicious looking mounds. . . ." Removing the earth Kerens found two galvanic batteries and torpedoes, each containing some 150 pounds of powder. Acting Third Assistant Engineer Henry M. Hutchinson and Landsman John McKenna cut the connections from the batteries to the torpedoes and the weapons were safely removed and taken on board *Henry Brinker*. Risk of life in little heralded acts such as this happened throughout the war.

U.S.S. *Cherokee*, Acting Lieutenant William E. Dennison, exchanged gunfire with Confederate troops at Half Moon Battery, Cape Fear, North Carolina. Earlier in the month, 19 January, U.S.S. *Governor Buckingham*, Acting Lieutenant John MacDiarmid, opened on the battery in support of Army efforts ashore to clear the area of Confederates following the fall of Fort Fisher.

INCIDENT ON BOARD THE "OCTORARA," January 26, 1865.

INCIDENT ON BOARD THE "OCTORARA."

THE incident illustrated in the above cut is thus narrated by our correspondent: "On the night of the 26th a torpedo-boat came out from Mobile Bay, and made an unsuccessful attack upon the *Octorara*. At about 2 A.M., though the night was very dark, an object was discovered not many yards astern, and making direct for the vessel. The look-out hailed lustily, 'Boat ahoy!' The response came, 'Ay, ay!' as though from one of our own boats. The officer of the deck immediately sang out to them to 'lie on their oars;' to which they answered, 'Ay, ay!' A moment after they rasped along the vessel's side from aft forward to the guards. The knowledge that it was the torpedo-boat of the rebels now flashed upon all. The intrepidity of the captain of the after-guard is worthy of the highest praise. Though all expected momentarily to be blown up, this man, seeing how readily they could gain an advantage over the enemy by prompt action, grasped her smoke-pipe as it came by the guards of the ship, at the same time crying out lustily for a rope to make the devil fast with. The remaining sailors, acting under different impulses, recoiled to the opposite side of the deck. Several shots were fired at this brave man, and as his exertions were hardly sufficient to retain his hold upon the hot pipe, he preferred to let go rather than be dragged overboard."

FEBRUARY

1–4 A boat expedition from U.S.S. *Midnight*, Acting Master John C. Wells, landed and destroyed salt works "of 13,615 boiling capacity" at St. Andrews Bay, Florida. The making of salt from sea water became a major industry in Florida during the Civil War as salt was a critical commodity in the Confederate war effort. Large quantities were needed for preserving meat, fish, butter, and other perishable foods, as well as for curing hides. Federal warships continuously destroyed salt works along the coasts of Florida. The expedition led by Wells was the finale in the Union Navy's effective restriction of this vital Confederate industry.

2 Having failed to pass the obstructions at Trent's Reach in order to attack the Union supply base at City Point, Flag Officer Mitchell confronted another kind of difficulty in maintaining communications with his own capital, Richmond. In the bitter cold the James River began to freeze over and the ice threatened Wilton Bridge. This date, Mitchell ordered C.S.S. *Beaufort*, Lieutenant Joseph W. Alexander, to break up the ice near the bridge and remain near it "to insure its safety." Two days later, Mitchell noted that C.S.S. *Torpedo* was of special importance because "she is now the only boat in connection with the *Beaufort* (that is crippled) that we can use to protect the Wilton Bridge from ice and to keep open our communication with the city."

U.S.S. *Pinola*, Lieutenant Commander Henry Erben, captured blockade running British schooner *Ben Willis* at sea in the Gulf of Mexico with cargo of cotton.

3 Flag Officer William W. Hunter reported to the Confederate Navy Department that he was ordering C.S.S. *Macon*, Lieutenant Joel S. Kennard, and C.S.S. *Sampson*, Lieutenant William W. Carnes, to turn over their ammunition to the Confederate Army at Augusta, Georgia. The shallow upper Savannah River made it impossible to use the vessels effectively in the defense of the city against the threatened attack by General Sherman's army which was working northward from Savannah. Sherman had spent January in Savannah preparing for the march to North Carolina and ensuring that he would have the necessary support from the sea coast. After preparatory combined operations, in which Rear Admiral Dahlgren lost U.S.S. *Dai Ching* to gunfire and subjected other gunboats to the threat of the ever-present torpedoes in shallow river and coastal waters, Sherman crossed the Savannah River and on 1 February continued his march. When Savannah fell, Hunter had brought *Macon* and *Sampson* upriver with difficulty, determined to fight them as long as possible. Now, however, he had run out of navigable water.

To speed the collapse of the faltering South, another giant thrust gathered from the sea off Wilmington. During the lull before the planned spring assault on Richmond when the road conditions improved, General Grant came down to confer with Rear Admiral Porter, his old Vicksburg shipmate. The General had spent several hours on board the flagship *Malvern* on 28 January where plans took shape for the push into North Carolina up the Cape Fear River as Sherman marched inland parallel to the coast. When Grant returned to Virginia he quickly dispatched General Schofield by sea with an army which, with the big guns of the fleet, would be large enough to push on to Wilmington. This date, Porter, in U.S.S. *Shawmut* preparing for the campaign, engaged Fort Anderson to test the strength of the Confederate defenses on the west bank of the Cape Fear which guarded the approach to Wilmington.

From City Point, Virginia, General Grant requested the Navy to keep two or three vessels patrolling between Cape Henry and the Cape Fear River during the transit of General Schofield's Twenty-Third Army Corps. The Corps was embarking from Annapolis, Maryland, and Alexandria, Virginia, for North Carolina to participate in the attack on Wilmington. "It is barely possible," Grant wrote, "for one of the enemy's privateers to be met on that route and do us great injury." Two steamers were stationed as requested to protect the troop transports.

In anticipation of the movement on Wilmington, Porter wrote Dahlgren requesting that the monitors he had dispatched to Charleston after the fall of Fort Fisher be returned for duty on the Cape

General Sherman's Army marches through South Carolina within supporting distance from the fleet on the coast.

Fear River. Although each squadron commander wanted the sturdy warships to spearhead his own efforts, Dahlgren prevailed in his belief that his problem was the greater before the heavily fortified Charleston harbor. Thus Porter had to plan on the services of only U.S.S. *Montauk*, the lone monitor he had retained.

Monitors, with their big guns and massive armor, appealed more to naval and military commanders for fighting forts than they did to many of their crews. An officer on board U.S.S. *Canonicus* had written earlier: "I will never again go to sea in a monitor. I have suffered more in mind and body since this affair commenced than I will suffer again if I can help it. No glory, no promotion can ever pay for it."

Brigadier General John P. Hatch, one of General Sherman's subordinates, turned to Dahlgren for naval assistance: "If you can spare a tug or two launches, to cruise in upper Broad River during the stay of this command near here [Pocotaligo, South Carolina], it would be of service to us. Night before last three of our boats were stolen, and I fear some scamps in the vicinity of Boyd's Neck or Bee's Creek are preparing to attempt to capture some of our transports."

U.S.S. *Matthew Vassar*, Acting Master George E. Hill, captured blockade running schooner *John Hale* off St. Marks, Florida, with cargo including lead, blankets, and rope.

4 U.S.S. *Wamsutta*, Acting Master Charles W. Lee, and U.S.S. *Potomska*, Acting Master F. M. Montell, sighted an unidentified blockade runner aground near Breach Inlet, South Carolina; on being discovered, the runner's crew fired and abandoned her.

4-6 A boat expedition under Lieutenant Commander Cushing, U.S.S. *Monticello*, proceeded up Little River, South Carolina, placing the small town of All Saints Parish under guard and capturing a number of Confederate soldiers. On the 5th Cushing destroyed some $15,000 worth of cotton.

The next day he sent two boat crews under Acting Master Charles A. Pettit to Shallotte Inlet, North Carolina, where they surprised a small force of Confederates collecting provisions for the troops at Fort Anderson below Wilmington. Six of the soldiers were taken prisoner and the stores they had gathered were destroyed. The Southerners reported that troops previously stationed at Shallotte Inlet had been ordered to Fort Anderson; there the South hoped to stall the Army-Navy movement on Wilmington.

5   Blockade runner *Chameleon*, Lieutenant Wilkinson, attempted to run through the blockade of Charleston to deliver desperately needed supplies for General Lee's troops but was unsuccessful. Having run into the Cape Fear River the previous month only to find Fort Fisher in Union hands (see 19 January), the bold Wilkinson had returned to Nassau and learned on 30 January that Charleston was still held by the South. He departed on 1 February, evaded U.S.S. *Vanderbilt* after a lengthy chase, but found that the blockade of Charleston had been augmented by so many ships from the Wilmington station that he could not get into the harbor while the tide was high. "As this was the last night during that moon, when the bar could be crossed during the dark hours," Wilkinson later wrote, "the course of the *Chameleon* was again, and for the last time, shaped for Nassau. As we turned away from the land, our hearts sank within us, while the conviction forced itself upon us, that the cause for which so much blood had been shed, so many miseries bravely endured, and so many sacrifices cheerfully made, was about to perish at last!"

U.S.S. *Niagara*, Commodore Thomas T. Craven, learned that "the pirate ram" *Stonewall* was repairing at Ferrol, Spain. He departed Dover, England, for Spain next day but because of foul weather did not reach Coruña, Spain, some nine miles from Ferrol, until 11 February. He requested assistance in blockading the ironclad from U.S.S. *Sacramento* but found that she was at Lisbon repairing and would not be ready for sea for ten days. Craven himself put into Ferrol on the 15th and maintained a close watch on *Stonewall*.

U.S.S. *Hendrick Hudson*, Acting Lieutenant Charles H. Rockwell, reported locating the sunken wreck of U.S.S. *Anna*, Acting Ensign Henry W. Wells, south of Cape Roman, Florida. *Anna* had departed Key West on 30 December and had not been heard from since. Apparently, an accidental explosion had ripped the schooner apart. Rockwell found no survivors.

6   Secretary Mallory wrote General Braxton Bragg in Wilmington that Chief Naval Constructor John L. Porter had advised him that a new Confederate vessel could be completed within 90 days. Machinery for the ship was available in Columbus, Georgia, but Mallory sought assurance from the General that Wilmington would be held long enough for machinery to be transported and the ship built so that it could get into action. On the 8th Bragg replied: "This place will be held so long as our means enable us. There is no indication of any movement against it, and our means of defense are improving." However, Rear Admiral Porter and General Grant had other plans; Wilmington would be evacuated exactly two weeks later.

A joint Army-Navy expedition up Pagan and Jones Creeks, off James River, Virginia, captured a Confederate torpedo boat, a torpedo containing some 75 pounds of powder, and Master William A. Hines, CSN. Hines had led an expedition late in 1864 that destroyed the tug *Lizzie Freeman* off Pagan Creek (see 5 December 1864). The naval force, consisting of eight cutters and two launches conveying 150 troops, was commanded by Lieutenant George W. Wood of U.S.S. *Roanoke*.

Rear Admiral Porter, having received intelligence that a new Confederate ram was near completion at a shipyard on the Roanoke River and would soon enter Albemarle Sound, ordered Commander William H. Macomb, commanding the squadron in the Sound, to make every preparation to destroy her when she came down to Roanoke. Porter directed Macomb to fit a spar "to the bow of every gunboat and tug, with a torpedo on it, and run at the ram, all together. No matter how many of your vessels get sunk, one or the other of them will sink the ram if the torpedo is coolly exploded. Have your large rowboats fitted with torpedoes also, and . . . put your large vessels alongside of her, let the launches and small torpedo boats run in and sink her. . . . You can sling a good sized anchor to an outrigger spar, and let it go on her deck, and by letting go your own anchor keep her from getting away until other vessels pile in on her. Five or six steamers getting alongside of a ram could certainly take her by boarding. If you can get on board of her, knock a hole in her smokestack with axes, or fire a howitzer through it, and drop shrapnel down into the furnaces. . . . Set torpedoes in the river at night, so that no one will know where they are. Obstruct the river above Plymouth, and get what guns are there to command the approaches. Get a net or two across the river, with large meshes, so that when the ram comes down the net will clog her propeller. . . . It is strange if we, with all our resources, can not extinguish a rebel ram." With the South struggling to complete ironclads one by one, the North was able to bring massive strength to bear against each potential threat. However, if the Confederacy had been able to import machinery and iron freely, she would have completed a number of effective ironclad warships that could have changed the whole complexion of the war.

7   Well on his way toward Columbia, General Sherman advised Rear Admiral Dahlgren of the possibilities of having to turn back to the coast: "We are on the railroad at Midway [S.C.], and will break 50 miles from Edisto toward Augusta and then cross toward Columbia. Weather is bad and country full of water. This cause may force me to turn against Charleston. I have ordered Foster to move Hatch up to the Edisto about Jacksonboro and Willstown; also to make the lodgment about Bull's Bay. Watch Charleston closely. I think Jeff Davis will direct it to be abandoned, lest he lose its garrison as well as guns. We are all well, and the enemy retreats before us. Send word to New Berne that you have heard from me, and the probabilities are that high waters may force me to the coast before I reach North Carolina, but to keep Wilmington busy."

Sherman and his subordinates utilized water transport and naval support as much as possible during his move northward. This date, Lieutenant Colonel Alexander C. McClurg, Chief of Staff of the Fourteenth Army Corps, wrote Lieutenant Commander Luce of U.S.S. *Pontiac*: "All the transports will, by this afternoon or evening, be unloaded and ordered to return to Savannah. General Morgan, commanding the rear division, has been ordered to withdraw his pickets on the Georgia shore of the [Savannah] river as soon as the transports have passed the lower landing. The general commanding requests that you assist and cover the crossing of these troops. The general commanding takes this opportunity to express to you and your officers his thanks for your efficient cooperation during your stay and movements at this point." Two days later, Major General Cuvier Grover added in a letter to Luce: "Understanding that you have in view leaving this station, I would respectfully request that, if it be consistent with your instructions, you would remain here until some such time as you can be relieved by some other naval vessel, as I consider it quite necessary that there should be at least one gunboat here at all times."

Boat expedition under Acting Ensign George H. French from U.S.S. *Bienville*, assisted by a cutter from U.S.S. *Princess Royal*, entered Galveston harbor silently at night intending to board and destroy blockade runner *Wren*. Because of "the strong current and wind . . ., and the near approach of daylight", French and his daring men were unable to reach *Wren* but did board and take schooners *Pet* and *Annie Sophia*, both laden with cotton.

8   Flag Officer Barron received orders from Secretary Mallory to return to the Confederacy, These orders symbolized the abandonment of the long-cherished hopes of obtaining ironclad ships from Europe with which to break the ever-tightening blockade. Originally selected to be the flag officer in command of the turreted ironclads "294" and "295", Barron had arrived in England during October 1863. The Laird rams, however, had been seized by the British government on 9 October 1863 and Barron thereafter served the Confederacy in Paris. On 15 February, a week after receiving Mallory's dispatch, Barron replied to the Secretary in words that gave clear evidence of the degree to which the shores of the South were sealed by the Union squadrons: "I am endeavoring to get ready to leave in the Southampton steamer of March 2, which will take

PART OF THE
Military Department
OF
THE SOUTH
AND OF
SOUTH ATLANTIC COAST

me to Cuba, and from that point I shall see how the land lies and make such arrangements as will most probably insure my earliest arrival in the Confederacy, where I feel every man is needed who can pull a pound. The closing of the port of Wilmington does, I fear, render the route through Texas the only one of security, but I shall not determine positively until after my arrival in Havana.'' Barron, however, did not return to the South, for on 28 February he resigned as senior Confederate naval officer on the continent.

The first troops of General Schofield's Twenty-Third Army Corps were landed at Fort Fisher. By mid-month the entire Corps had moved by ocean-transport from Alexandria and Annapolis to North Carolina. The protection of the Federal Navy and the mobility of water movement had allowed the redeployment of thousands of troops from Tennessee to the eastern theater for the final great struggles of the war.

9 U.S.S. *Pawnee*, Commander George B. Balch, U.S.S. *Sonoma*, Lieutenant Commander Thomas S. Fillebrown, and U.S.S. *Daffodil*, Acting Master William H. Mallard, engaged Confederate batteries on Togodo Creek, near the North Edisto River, South Carolina. *Pawnee* took ten hits and the other ships two each, but the naval bombardment successfully silenced the Southern emplacements. The action was one of several attacks along the coast that helped to clear the way and keep the South's defenses disrupted while General Sherman's army advanced northward. With assurance of aid from the sea when needed, Sherman could travel light and fast. On this date he was marching toward Orangeburg, on the north side of the Edisto River, and would capture it on the 12th.

10 Captain Raphael Semmes was appointed Rear Admiral in the Provisional Navy of the Confederate States of America "for gallant and meritorious conduct, in command of the steam-sloop *Alabama*." Secretary Mallory had created the Provisional Navy as a means of instituting selection to higher rank on the basis of ability rather than strict seniority. Semmes later wrote: "After I had been in Richmond a few weeks, the President was pleased to nominate me to the Senate as a rear-admiral. My nomination was unanimously confirmed, and, in a few days afterward, I was appointed to the command of the James River Fleet. . . . An old and valued friend, Commodore J. K. Mitchell, had been in command of the James River Fleet, and I displaced him very reluctantly. He had organized and disciplined the fleet, and had accomplished with it all that was possible, viz., the protection of Richmond by water." Except for this powerful fleet backing up the forts and the extensive obstructions in the river, Richmond would have long since fallen.

The Confederate Navy began its last attempt to gain control of the James River and thus force the withdrawal of General Grant's army by cutting its communications at City Point. The expedition of 100 officers and men was led by the audacious naval lieutenant, Charles W. Read. He loaded four torpedo boats on wagons and started overland from Drewry's Bluff. The plan called for marching to a place below City Point on the James River where the party would launch the boats, capture any passing tugs or steamers, and outfit these prizes with spars and torpedoes. The expedition would then ascend the river and attack and sink the Union monitors, leaving the Union gunboats at the mercy of the Confederate ironclads. The James, without which Grant would be denied transport and supplies, would be under Confederate control from Richmond to Hampton Roads.

On the night of the 11th Read and his men endured bitter cold as the weather worsened. On the 12th sleet slowed and finally stopped the expedition only a few miles from the place they were to ford the Blackwater River and rendezvous with Lieutenant John Lewis, CSN, who had been reconnoitering the area ahead of the main body of sailors. Master W. Frank Shippey wrote that while the men sought refuge from the storm in a deserted farmhouse, "a young man in gray uniform came in and informed us that our plan had been betrayed, and that Lewis was at the ford to meet us, according to promise, but accompanied by a regiment of Federals lying in ambuscade and awaiting our arrival, when they were to give us a warm reception. Had it not been for the storm and our having to take shelter, we would have marched into the net spread for us . . . ."

Read directed the rest of the expedition to retrace their steps for about a mile; then he ventured forth alone to confirm the report of the young Confederate. Late in the afternoon of the 13th Read, "cool and collected as ever," returned to the campsite where his men were, informed them that the intelligence of the day before had been correct, and that they would have to fall back to Richmond. Thus, the bold Confederate thrust failed. Moreover, the constant exposure to the inclement weather took a heavy toll of the men. Shippey later wrote that "of the hundred and one men who composed this expedition, fully seventy-five were in the naval hospital in Richmond, suffering from the effects of their winter march, on the sad day on which we turned our backs upon that city."

U.S.S. *Shawmut*, Lieutenant Commander J. G. Walker, engaged Confederate batteries on the east bank of the Cape Fear River while U.S.S. *Huron*, Lieutenant Commander Thomas O. Selfridge, bombarded Fort Anderson. Fleet attacks were building up preliminary to full naval support of General Schofield's advance on Wilmington. Schofield planned to outflank General Hoke's defense force by marching from Fort Fisher up the outer bank and, with the aid of pontoons to be landed by the Navy on the coast side, cross Myrtle Sound to the mainland of the peninsula behind the Confederate lines. From the Cape Fear River and the sea coast the Navy was to contain the defenders in their trenches by shore bombardment.

Rear Admiral Porter issued an operations plan for the move up the Cape Fear River which revealed the high degree to which naval gunfire support doctrine had been developed during the Civil War: "The object will be to get the gunboats in the rear of their intrenchments and cover the advance of our troops. When our troops are coming up, the gunboats run close in and shell the enemy in front of them, so as to enable the troops to turn their flanks, if possible. . . . As the army come up, your fire will have to be very rapid, taking care not to fire into our own men. . . . Put yourself in full communication with the general commanding on shore, and conform in all things to his wishes. . . ."

To the 16 gunboats in the Cape Fear River Porter issued an operation plan for an attack on Fort Anderson that was to coincide with the naval bombardment of General Hoke's flanks and the launching of Schofield's turning movement. The gunboats were directed to make a bows-on approach, to minimize the target presented Southern gunners, while the monitor U.S.S. *Montauk* would lay down a covering fire from close in. When the fort's fire should slacken, the light-hulled gunboats were to close and drive the gunners from their positions with grapeshot and canister. With the enemy's battery thus silenced, the fleet would shift to carefully aimed point fire to dismount the guns. So swiftly had the build up of force been effected by sea that only two weeks after the meeting between Porter and General Grant on board U.S.S. *Malvern*, which shaped the Union strategy, an irresistible juggernaut was already being forged.

Boat expedition from U.S.S. *Princess Royal* and *Antona* led by Lieutenant Charles E. McKay boarded and destroyed blockade runner *Will-O'-The Wisp*, a large iron screw steamer hard aground off Galveston.

10–14 The monitor U.S.S. *Lehigh*, Lieutenant Commander Alexander A. Semmes, and smaller wooden vessels including U.S.S. *Commodore McDonough*, *Wissahickon*, *C. P. Williams*, *Dan Smith*, and *Geranium*, supported Brigadier General Alexander Schimmelfennig's troop movements in the Stono and Folly River, South Carolina, area. The Army had requested the assistance of naval gunfire in the operations preparatory to the final push on Charleston.

11 U.S.S. *Keystone State*, *Aries*, *Montgomery*, *Howquah*, *Emma*, and *Vicksburg* engaged Half Moon Battery, situated on the coastal flank of the Confederate defense line which crossed the Cape Fear Peninsula six miles above Fort Fisher. This bombardment contained General Hoke's division while General Schofield's troops moved up the beach and behind their rear (see 10 February). Deteriorating weather, however, prevented the landing of the pontoons, and Schofield withdrew his troops to the Fort Fisher lines. Porter's gunboats also engaged the west bank batteries.

Secretary Welles warned Acting Rear Admirals Cornelius K. Stribling, commanding the East Gulf Blockading Squadron, and Henry K. Thatcher, commanding the West Gulf Blockading Squadron, that information had been received that the ram *Stonewall*, built at Bordeaux, France, had been transferred to the Confederate government. "Her destination," he wrote, "is doubtless

U.S.S. Commodore McDonough *and mortar boat shell Confederate positions on James Island, South Carolina.*

some point on our coast, and it behooves you to be prepared against surprise , as she is represented to be formidable and capable of inflicting serious injury."

U.S.S. *Penobscot*, Lieutenant Commander A. E. K. Benham, captured blockade running British schooner *Matilda* in the Gulf of Mexico with cargo of rope, bagging, and liquors.

12 The blockade runners *Carolina, Dream, Chicora, Chameleon,* and *Owl,* heavily laden with supplies desperately needed by General Lee's army, lay at anchor in Nassau harbor. During the day the five captains, including Lieutenant John Wilkinson and Commander John Maffitt, held a conference and formulated plans for running the blockade into Charleston. After putting to sea that night, the five ships separated and stood on different courses for the South Carolina port. Only *Chicora*, Master John Rains, Shipmaster, got through and became the last blockade runner to enter and leave Charleston prior to its evacuation during the night of 17–18 February. Two and a half months later *Owl*, Commander Maffitt, slipped past 16 Federal cruisers and entered the harbor at Galveston. After off-loading his cargo, Maffitt again evaded the blockaders and safely reached Havana on 9 May, where after coaling his ship he continued to give Union warships the slip on his return voyage to Nassau and ultimately to Liverpool (see 14 July).

Captain T. J. Page, C.S.S. *Stonewall*, wrote Commander Bulloch from Ferrol of the arrival of U.S.S. *Niagara*, Commodore T. T. Craven, at Corunna the preceding day. "I wish with all my heart we were ready now to go out," Page said. "We must encounter her, and I would only wish that she may not be accompanied by two or more others." Craven was equally apprehensive about a possible engagement. "The *Stonewall*," he wrote at month's end, "is a very formidable vessel, about 175 feet long, brig-rigged, and completely clothed in iron plates of 5 inches in thickness. Under her topgallant forecastle is her casemated Armstrong 300-pounder rifled gun. In a turret abaft her mainmast are two 120-pounder rifled guns, and she has two smaller guns mounted in broadside. If as fast as reputed to be, in smooth water she ought to be more than a match for three such ships as the *Niagara*. . . ."

In small boats, Lieutenant Commander Cushing and a patrol party passed the piling obstructions and reconnoitered the Cape Fear River as far as Wilmington.

13 General Sherman's on-rushing army approached the Congaree River, South Carolina. The soldiers would cross it on the 14th, heading for Columbia. With the fall of Columbia assured and with the supply route to Augusta, Georgia, already cut, General Hardee speeded up his preparations to evacuate Charleston and to take the troops he brought from Savannah to North Carolina where he planned to join Generals Joseph E. Johnson and Beauregard. Since Charleston would have to be abandoned and the Confederate naval squadron there scuttled, Commodore John R. Tucker, detached 300 men and officers from C.S.S. *Chicora*, *Palmetto State*, and *Charleston*, as well as the Navy Yard, and dispatched them, under the command of Lieutenant James H. Rochelle, to assist in the final defense of Wilmington. This naval detachment was assigned to Major General Robert F. Hoke's division which held the defensive line across the peninsula between Fort Fisher and Wilmington.

14 The blockade runner *Celt* ran aground while attempting to run the blockade from Charleston harbor.

15 U.S.S. *Merrimac*, Acting Master William Earle, was abandoned in a sinking condition at sea off the coast of Florida in the Gulf Stream. The tiller had broken in a gale, the pumps could not keep the ship free of water, and two boilers had given out. Having fought for 24 hours to save his ship, Earle finally ordered her abandoned. The mail steamer *Morning Star*, which had been standing by the disabled gunboat for several hours, rescued the crew.

Steamer *Knickerbocker*, aground near Smith's Point, Virginia, was boarded by Confederates, set afire, and destroyed. U.S.S. *Mercury*, Acting Ensign Thomas Nelson, had thwarted a previous attempt to destroy the steamer.

16 U.S.S. *Penobscot*, Lieutenant Commander A. E. K. Benham, forced blockade running schooners *Mary Agnes* and *Louisa* ashore at Aransas Pass, Texas. Two days later the runners were destroyed by a boat crew from *Penobscot*.

16–17 As the combined operation to capture Willington vigorously got underway, ships of Rear Admiral Porter's fleet helped to ferry General Schofield's two divisions from Fort Fisher to Smithville, on the west bank of the Cape Fear River. Fort Anderson, the initial objective for the two commanders, lay on the west bank mid-way between the mouth of the river and Wilmington. On the morning of the 17th, Major General Jacob D. Cox led 8,000 troops north from Smithville. In support of the army advance on the Confederate defenses, the monitor *Montauk*, Lieutenant Commander Edward E. Stone, and four gunboats heavily bombarded Fort Anderson and successfully silenced its twelve guns. Unable to obtain other monitors for the attack (see 3 February), Porter resorted to subterfuge and, as he had on the Mississippi River (see 25 February 1863), improvised a bogus monitor from a scow, timber, and canvas. "Old Bogey", as she was quickly nicknamed by the sailors, had been towed to the head of the bombardment line, where she succeeded in drawing heavy fire from the defending Southerners.

Ships of the South Atlantic Blockading Squadron, including U.S.S. *Pawnee*, *Sonoma*, *Ottawa*, *Winona*, *Potomska*, *Wando*, *J. S. Chambers*, and boats and launches from these vessels supported the amphibious Army landing at Bull's Bay, South Carolina. This was a diversionary movement in the major thrust to take Charleston and was designed to contain Confederate strength away from General Sherman's route. Such diversions had been part of Sherman's plan from the outset as he took full advantage of Northern control of the sea. A naval landing party from the fleet joined the troops of Brigadier General Edward E. Potter in driving the Confederates from their positions and pushing on toward Andersonville and Mount Pleasant, South Carolina.

As Captain Daniel B. Ridgely later reported to Rear Admiral Dahlgren: "I am confident that the expedition to Bull's Bay embarrassed the rebels from the great number of men-of-war inside and outside of the bay and the great number of boats provided by the navy to disembark a large land force. . . . I am of the opinion that the evacuation of Charleston was hastened by the

Dispatch No. 69.
Flag Steamer Harvest Moon
Port Royal Harbor S.C.
February 13th 1865 —

Honorable Gideon Welles.
Secretary of the Navy.
Sir—

The Army of General Sherman
may now be considered as having
begun its movement Northward
from Savannah.

I had sent the "Pontiac"
to cover these troops and their
crossing at Sisters Ferry, 41 miles
from the City where this vessel
arrived on the 24th January,
about three days in advance of

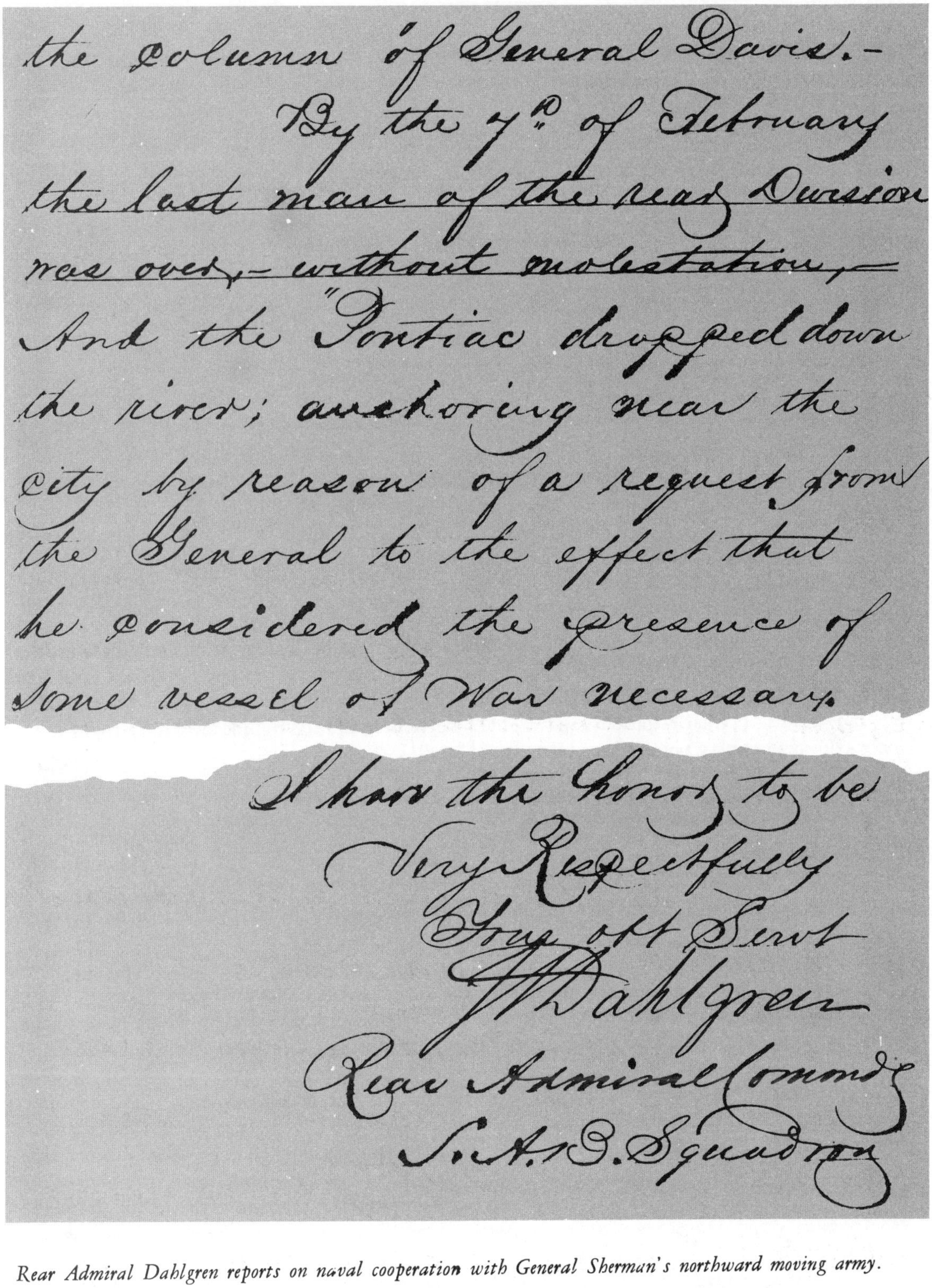

the column of General Davis.—

By the 7th of February the last man of the rear Division was over,— without molestation,— And the "Pontiac dropped down the river; anchoring near the City by reason of a request from the General to the effect that he considered the presence of some vessel of War necessary.

I have the honor to be
Very Respectfully
Your obt Servt
JA Dahlgren
Rear Admiral Commdg
S.A.B. Squadron

Rear Admiral Dahlgren reports on naval cooperation with General Sherman's northward moving army.

Bombardment of Fort Anderson on the Cape Fear River guarding the approach to Wilmington.

demonstration made by the army and the navy at that point in strong force.'' Ridgely also pointed out another example of one of the aspects of Northern control of the sea throughout the war, the fact that the very capability of the Union to move wherever water reached forced the South to spread itself thin in an attempt to meet the Federals on all possible fronts. ''The rebels signaled our movements to Charleston day and night,'' he wrote, adding significantly, ''and threw up intrenchments at every point where boats could land.''

17 U.S.S. *Mahaska*, Lieutenant Commander William Gibson, seized schooner *Delia* off Bayport, Florida, with cargo of pig lead and sabers.

17–18 Charleston, South Carolina, was evacuated by Confederate troops after having endured 567 days of continuous attack by land and sea. The long siege witnessed some of the most heroic fighting of the war, including the sinking of U.S.S. *Housatonic* by the valiant, hand-powered submarine *H. L. Hunley* (see 17 February 1864).

 During the night, Forts Moultrie, Sumter, Johnson, Beauregard, and Castle Pinckney were abandoned as the Confederates marched northward to join the beleaguered forces of General Lee. The Southern ironclads *Palmetto State, Chicora,* and *Charleston* were fired and blown up prior to the withdrawal, but C.S.S. *Columbia,* the largest of the ironclads at Charleston, was found aground and abandoned near Fort Moultrie and was eventually salvaged.

 Lieutenant Commander J. S. Barnes later wrote that the occupation forces also captured several ''David'' torpedo boats, one of which had damaged U.S.S. *New Ironsides* off Charleston on 5 October 1863. She was subsequently taken to the Naval Academy, Barnes wrote, ''where she is preserved as one of the relics of the war. These vessels were built of boiler iron, and were of the shape known as 'cigar shape.' They presented but a very small target above the surface, but were usually clumsy and dangerous craft in a seaway. Under full steam they could attain a speed of seven knots per hour.''

 The steamers *Lady Davis, Mab,* and *Transport* were taken after the evacuation. U.S.S. *Catskill,* Lieutenant Commander Edward Barrett, seized blockade runner *Celt,* which had run aground trying to get out of Charleston on the night of the 14th; *Catskill* also took the British blockade runner *Deer.* The steamer had been decoyed into Charleston that night by the same ruse—keeping the Confederate signals lighted—employed at Wilmington. *Deer* ran aground and on being boarded

The diversionary and effective amphibious attack at Bull's Bay, South Carolina.

her master told Barrett: "Well, we give it up; she is your prize. Strange we did not smell a rat, as we could not make out your signal on Fort Marshall." Also in the aftermath of the fall of Charleston, U.S.S. *Gladiolus*, Acting Ensign Napoleon Boughton, captured blockade runner *Syren* in the Ashley River where she had successfully run in through the blockade the night before.

The capture of these blockade runners underscored Dahlgren's letter to Rear Admiral Porter: "You see by the date of this [18 February] that the Navy's occupation has given this pride of rebeldom to the Union flag, and thus the rebellion is shut out from the ocean and foreign sympathy." To Secretary Welles, Dahlgren added: "To me the fall of Charleston seems scarcely less important than that of Richmond. It is the last seaport by which it can be made sure that a bale of cotton can go abroad. Hence the rebel loan and credit are at an end." Learning of the fall of Charleston a week later in Nassau, Lieutenant Wilkinson, the daring Confederate sea captain, agreed: "This sad intelligence put an end to all our hopes. . . ." At last the city that had symbolized the South's spirit was in Union hands.

18 Upon orders to evacuate Charleston, Commodore John R. Tucker scuttled the ironclads *Palmetto State*, *Charleston* and *Chicora*, took charge of the remaining sailors in the area, and set out by train for Wilmington to join the naval detachment that had previously proceeded there under Lieutenant Rochelle (see 13 February). Tucker's detachment got as far as Whiteville, about 50 miles west of Wilmington, where he learned that Union troops had cut the rail line between the two cities and that the evacuation of Wilmington was imminent. After unsuccessfully trying to obtain rail transportation for his detachment, which he pointed out was "unused to marching," Tucker set out across country on a 125 mile march to Fayetteville, North Carolina.

The big guns of Rear Admiral Porter's fleet in the Cape Fear River silenced the Confederate batteries at Fort Anderson. Under a relentless hail of fire from the ships and with Union troops investing the fort from two sides, the Southerners evacuated their defensive position and fell back to Town Creek. Simultaneously, the Confederates dug in at Sugar Loaf Hill on the east bank of the river, adjacent to Fort Anderson, withdrew to Fort Strong, a complex of fortifications comprising several batteries some three miles south of Wilmington. The combined Army-Navy movement was now pushing irresistibly toward the city.

Fort Sumter after the Confederate evacuation of Charleston.

Rear Admiral Semmes assumed command of the Confederate James River Squadron. "My fleet," he wrote, "consisted of three iron-clads and five wooden gunboats." The ironclads, each mounting four guns, were C.S.S. *Virginia No. 2*, *Richmond*, and *Fredericksburg*. The wooden ships included C.S.S. *Hampton*, *Nansemond*, *Roanoke*, *Beaufort*, and *Torpedo*; all mounted two guns except *Torpedo* which was armed with one. Semmes noted: "The fleet was assisted, in the defence of the river, by several shore batteries, in command of naval officers. . . ."

C.S.S. *Shenandoah*, Lieutenant Waddell, having completed repairs at Melbourne, Australia, got underway before daybreak and steamed out of Port Philip Bay to resume her career on the high seas. As soon as the cruiser discharged her pilot and entered international waters, more than 40 stowaways—who had come on board late the previous night—appeared on deck. *Shenandoah*'s log recorded: "Forty-two men found on board; thirty-six shipped as sailors and six enlisted as marines." This represented a net gain when balanced against the desertions induced by gold from the American consul. However, *Shenandoah* paid a considerable price for the three week stay in Melbourne. Waddell later wrote in his memoirs: "The delay of the *Shenandoah* had operated against us in the South Pacific. The whaling fleet of that ocean had received warning and had either suspended its fishing in that region or had taken shelter in the neighboring ports. The presence of the *Shenandoah* in the South Pacific," however, he added, "dispersed the whaling fleet of that sea, though no captures were made there."

A boat expedition under Acting Ensign James W. Brown from U.S.S. *Pinola* boarded and fired armed schooner *Anna Dale* in Pass Cavallo, Texas. The prize had been fitted out as a cruiser by the Confederates. The long reach of the sea closed its iron grip on the South in events great and small from the Potomac to the Rio Grande and throughout the western waters.

U.S.S. *Forest Rose*, Acting Lieutenant Abraham N. Gould, dispersed a number of Confederates who had fired on the ship *Mittie Stephens* attempting to load cotton at Cole's Creek, Mississippi.

Sweeping for torpedoes and buoying a channel in Cape Fear River.

19 The Confederate steamer *A. H. Schultz*, used as a flag-of-truce vessel to carry exchange prisoners between Richmond and the Varina vicinity on the James River and as a transport by the Southern forces below the Confederate capital, was destroyed by a torpedo near Chaffin's Bluff on the James River. Ironically, she met the fate intended for a Union ship. The torpedo was one laid by Lieutenant Beverly Kennon of the Torpedo Service that had drifted from its original position. When torpedoed, *Schultz* was returning to Richmond after delivering more than 400 Federal prisoners; because of an administrative error, there were no Confederate prisoners ready to be taken on board at Varina. Thus, the loss of life was considerably minimized. Had the steamer struck the torpedo going downriver or picked up the Southern soldiers to be exchanged as expected, the casualties might well have been frightful.

U.S.S. *Gertrude*, Acting Lieutenant Benjamin C. Dean, captured Mexican brig *Eco* off Galveston. *Eco*, suspected of attempting to run the blockade, carried a cargo of coffee, rice, sugar, and jute baling cord.

19–20 Following the evacuation of Fort Anderson, Rear Admiral Porter's gunboats steamed seven miles up the Cape Fear River to the Big Island shallows and the piling obstructions and engaged Fort Strong's five guns. Ship's boats swept the river for mines ahead of the fleet's advance. On the night of the 20th, the Confederates released 200 floating torpedoes, which were avoided with great difficulty and kept the boat crews engaged in sweeping throughout the hours of darkness. Although many of the gunboats safely swept up torpedoes with their nets, U.S.S. *Osceola*, Commander J. M. B. Clitz, received hull damage and lost a paddle wheel box by an explosion. Another torpedo destroyed a boat from U.S.S. *Shawmut*, inflicting four casualties. The next day, 21 February, one of Porter's officers wrote that ''Old Bogey'', the make-shift monitor fashioned by the Admiral to deceive the defenders (see 16–17 February), had taken part in the action: ''Johnny Reb let off his torpedoes without effect on it, and the old thing sailed across the river and grounded in the flank and rear of the enemy's lines on the eastern bank, whereupon they fell back in the night. She now occupies the most advanced position of the line, and Battery Lee has been banging away at her, and probably wondering why she does not answer. Last night after half a days fighting, the rebs sent down about 50 [sic] torpedoes; but although 'Old Bogey' took no notice of them, they kept the rest of us pretty lively as long as the ebb tide ran."

21-22 The gunboat fleet of Rear Admiral Porter closed Fort Strong and opened rapid fire "all along the enemy's line" to support the Army attack ashore as it had throughout the soldiers' steady march up both banks of the Cape Fear River. The next day, 22 February, the defenders evacuated the fort and Porter's ships steamed up to Wilmington, which earlier in the day had been occupied by General Terry's men after General Bragg had ordered the evacuation of the now defenseless city. The same day the Admiral wrote Secretary Welles: "I have the honor to inform you that Wilmington has been evacuated and is in possession of our troops. . . . I had the pleasure of placing the flag on Fort Strong, and at 12 o'clock noon today shall fire a salute of thirty-five guns this being the anniversary of Washington's birthday." As Raphael Semmes later wrote: ". . . we had lost our last blockade-running port. Our ports were now all hermetically sealed The anaconda had, at last, wound his fatal folds around us."

22 In Richmond, Confederate War Department clerk J. B. Jones wrote in his diary: "To-day is the anniversary of the birth of Washington, and of the inauguration of Davis; but I hear of no holiday. Not much is doing, however, in the departments; simply a waiting for calamities, which come with stunning rapidity. The next news, I suppose, will be the evacuation of Wilmington! Then Raleigh may tremble. Unless there is a speedy turn in the tide of affairs, confusion will reign supreme and universally." Material suffering and the unwavering pressure of Union armies ashore and Federal ships afloat destroyed Southern hopes. In the Union's strength at sea the Confederacy faced a doubled disadvantage. Not only did the fleet provide the North with massed artillery, great mobility, easy concentration, and surprise in attack, but it also provided a safe fortress to which the soldiers ashore could retreat—as had been most recently shown during General Butler's amphibious failure at Fort Fisher as 1864 ended.

23-25 Rear Admiral Dahlgren dispatched a squadron from Charleston, commanded by Captain Henry S. Stellwagen in the U.S.S. *Pawnee*, to capture and occupy Georgetown, South Carolina, in order to establish a line of communications with General Sherman's army advancing from Columbia, South Carolina, to Fayetteville, North Carolina. Fort White, guarding the entrance to Winyah Bay leading to Georgetown, was evacuated upon the approach of the naval squadron and was occupied by a detachment of Marines on the 23rd. The following day Stellwagen sent Ensign Allen K. Noyes with the U.S.S. *Catalpa* and *Mingoe* up the Peedee River to accept the surrender of the evacuated city of Georgetown. Noyes led a small party ashore and received the surrender of the city from civil authorities while a group of his seamen climbed to the city hall dome and ran up the Stars and Stripes. This action was presently challenged by a group of Confederate horsemen. More sailors were landed. A skirmish ensued in which the bluejackets drove off the mounted guerrillas. Subsequently, the city was garrisoned by five companies of Marines who were in turn relieved by the soldiers on 1 March.

In December the ships of the powerful Federal Navy, now in such numbers that they could attack anywhere along the coast when needed, had made it possible for Sherman "to march to the sea" with confidence, since they gave him any part of the coast he chose as a base. Now Dahlgren's warships provided the general with unlimited logistic support, rapid reinforcement, and the defensive line of their massed guns to fall back on if he was defeated. Easing and speeding his progress to the North, the fleet therefore helped to bring the cruel war more quickly to an end. From Savannah to Wilmington the whole Southern sea coast—with its irreplaceable defenses, heavy coastal cannon that could not be moved, and superior means of communication— swiftly fell. Although it was not clear to General Lee at the time, the accelerated speed with which the solders were able to move inevitably forecast the frustration of his plan to send part of his veterans to join the Confederate Army in North Carolina in an attempt to crush Sherman while still holding the Petersburg-Richmond lines with the remainder.

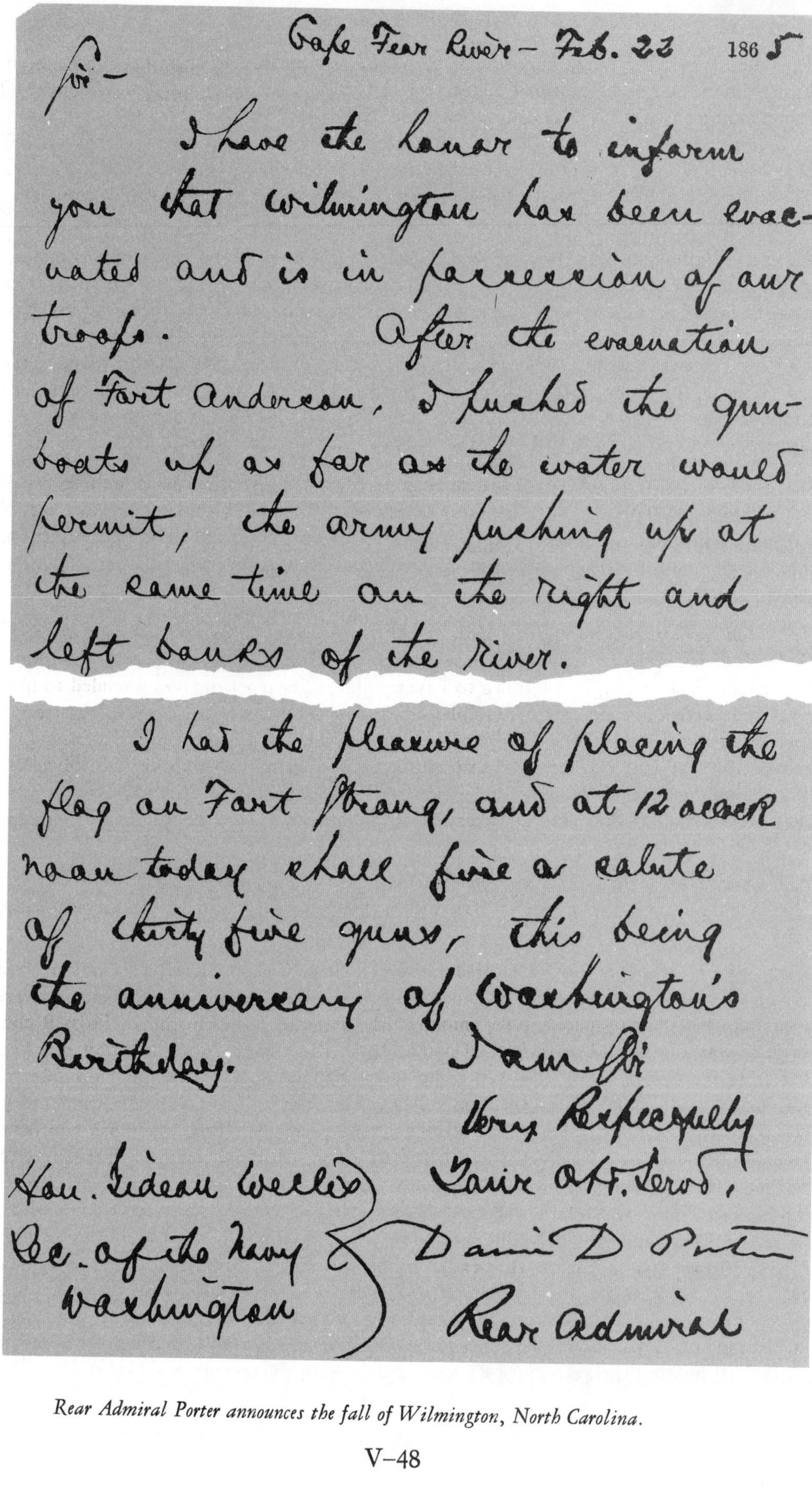

Cape Fear River – Feb. 23   186 5

Sir –

I have the honor to inform you that Wilmington has been evacuated and is in possession of our troops.   After the evacuation of Fort Anderson, I pushed the gunboats up as far as the water would permit, the army pushing up at the same time on the right and left banks of the river.

I had the pleasure of placing the flag on Fort Strong, and at 12 o'clock noon today shall fire a salute of thirty five guns, this being the anniversary of Washington's Birthday.   I am Sir

Very Respectfully
Your Obt. Servt,
David D Porter
Rear Admiral

Hon. Gideon Welles
Sec. of the Navy
Washington

Rear Admiral Porter announces the fall of Wilmington, North Carolina.

24 The intention of the Navy Department to reduce the size of the operating forces as the end of hostilities neared was indicated in Secretary Welles' instruction to Rear Admiral Thatcher, commanding the West Gulf Squadron, to "send North such purchased vessels as appear by surveys to require very extensive repairs . . . and all those no longer required. These will probably be sold or laid up. You will also send home any stores that are not required. Further requisition must be carefully examined before approval, and the commanders of squadrons are expected to use every possible exertion and care to reduce the expenses of their squadrons."

Secretary Welles similarly directed Rear Admiral Dahlgren to send north vessels under his command that were no longer required, especially the least efficient. "The Department is of opinion that the fall of Fort Fisher and Charleston will enable it to reduce the expenses of the maintenance of the Navy." Even as the Union could begin to cut back its huge fleet, the effect of Northern sea power was felt more and more acutely in General Lee's army. With its last access to the sea, Wilmington, now controlled by the North, the shortage of essential supplies—including shoes, artillery, blankets, lead, medicines, and even food for men and horses—became increasingly desperate. By now, much of Lee's famed cavalry, for want of horses, had become infantry.

25 U.S.S. *Marigold*, Acting Master Courtland P. Williams, captured blockade running British schooner *Salvadora* with an assorted cargo in the Straits of Florida between Havana and Key West.

In a letter to Secretary Welles, Commander F. A. Parker, Commander of the Potomac Flotilla, reported that "within the past week three boats, with three blockade runners, have been captured by the *Primrose*, commanded by Acting Ensign Owen."

C.S.S. *Chickamauga* was burned and sunk by her own crew in the Cape Fear River just below Indian Wells, North Carolina. The position selected by the Confederates was above Wilmington on the Northwest Fork of the river leading to Fayetteville. The scuttling was intended to obstruct the river and prevent the Union from establishing water communications between the troops occupying Wilmington and General Sherman's army operating in the interior of the state. The effort proved abortive as the current swept the hulk around parallel to the bank and by 12 March the water link between Wilmington and Fayetteville had been opened (see 12 March). Every river that would float a ship was an artery of strength from the sea for Sherman in his rapid march north.

A boat expedition from U.S.S. *Chenango*, Lieutenant Commander George U. Morris, captured blockade running sloop *Elvira* at Bullyard Sound, South Carolina, with cargo of cotton and tobacco.

27 Commodore Tucker and his 350 Confederate sailors from Charleston arrived safely in Fayetteville, North Carolina, where he received orders to have Lieutenant James H. Rochelle's naval detachment join his and to proceed to Richmond with the entire Naval Brigade. From Richmond the brigade was sent on to Drewry's Bluff on the James River to garrison the formidable Confederate batteries positioned there. Tucker commanded the naval forces ashore while Rear Admiral Raphael Semmes commanded the James River Squadron. These two commands, through the course of the long war, had successfully protected Richmond from attack via the James River. General Lee desperately needed staunch fighters more than ever before. With his supply line from Europe cut, hunger, privation, sickness, and desertion steadily shrank his army. Meanwhile, General Grant's army increased as ships poured in supplies to his City Point base in preparation for the spring offensive.

U.S.S. *Proteus*, Commander R. W. Shufeldt, seized the steamer *Ruby*—purportedly en route from Havana to Belize, Honduras, but, according to some of the officers and passengers, actually bound for St. Marks, Florida. It appeared that part of her cargo had been thrown overboard during the chase; the remainder consisted of lead and sundries.

Flag Steamer 'Harvest Moon'
Off the City of Charleston.
February 18th 1865.

My Dear Porter.
                Your very acceptable
letter of the 28th Jan'y reached me
duly — and was very gratifying. —
                In return you will
see by the date of this, that the
Navy's occupation has given this
pride of Rebeldom to the Union
Flag, and thus the Rebellion is shut
out from the Ocean, and foreign
Sympathy.
                They went from it —
unheralded by a Shot, and to-day,
I quietly Steamed up to the wharves,
and walked through the town. —

                I have just walked
over the City — every house Shut up
— the few persons in the Streets
were foreigners, and negroes. —

"As they have made their beds, so let them lie.

General Sherman desires me to let you know, that I had heard from him. He was at Midway on the 7th February, ten miles East of Branchville — and the evacuation of Charleston shows that he must have pressed them very hard since, in advance on some point that they deemed vital.

You have indeed struck a glorious blow at Wilmington, — and no one will rejoice more in your having done so, than myself.

With my best wishes I am most truly yours.

Dahlgren

Rear Admiral Comd'g S. A. B. Squadron.

Rear Admiral Dahlgren writes to Rear Admiral Porter announcing the fall of Charleston and congratulating him on the capture of Wilmington.

C.S.S. Chickamauga.

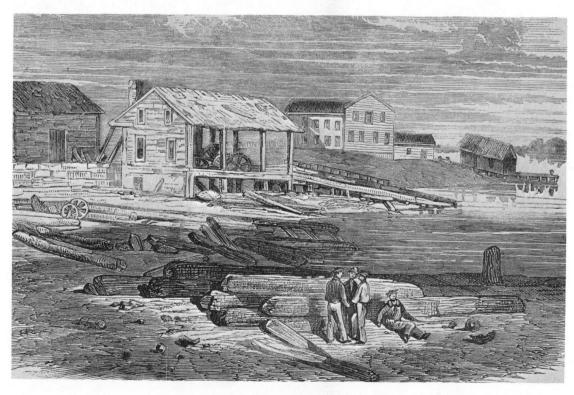

Ruins of the Confederate Navy Yard, Wilmington.

John Randolph Tucker
Captain, CSN

James H. Rochelle
Lieutenant, CSN

28 Rear Admiral Dahlgren issued instructions to Captain Stellwagen, U.S.S. *Pawnee*, on operations in the vicinity of Georgetown, South Carolina, coordinated with General Sherman's march north: "I leave here for Charleston, and you remain the senior officer. The only object in occupying the place, as I do, is to facilitate communication with General Sherman, if he desires it here, or by the Santee. When the *Chenango* and *Sonoma* arrive, station one in each river by the town to assist the force ashore; one vessel should be near the fort and one at the light-house to look for communication with me. Keep up information from the Santee by a courier over the Santee road or by water. I leave you three tugs, the *Sweet Brier*, *Catalpa* and *Clover*, with a dispatch boat. Let parties be pushed out by land and water, to feel the rebel positions, and drive back his scouts and pickets."

Armed boats under Acting Ensign Charles N. Hall from U.S.S. *Honeysuckle* forced the blockade running British schooner *Sort* aground on a reef near the mouth of Crystal River, Florida, where she was abandoned. *Sort* was the same schooner captured in December 1864 by U.S.S. *O. H. Lee*.

U.S.S. *Arizona*, Lieutenant Commander George Brown, was destroyed by fire in the Mississippi River below New Orleans. In his report, the unlucky Brown, who had also lost U.S.S. *Indianola* (see 24 February 1863), noted: "Not a soul attempted to leave the vessel until I gave the order for them to do so, and the marines were of much service in preventing the boats from being overloaded."

Lieutenant George W. Gift, CSN, on sick leave at his wife's home in Georgia, reflected on the fate of the South: "It is all too disheartening! The press brings accounts of new defeat for us. The *Water Witch* has been captured and destroyed. Mobile has fallen, so that all the ports in the Confederacy are lost! That goes for the Navy. . . ."

MARCH

1 As the month of March opened, General Grant was preparing for a massive spring attack against General Lee's lines defending Richmond. Throughout the North optimism ran high and the feeling prevailed that the offensive would be the final thrust and that Grant would take Richmond. It was widely believed that the Confederacy was on the threshold of defeat. Since

the beginning of the new year Charleston and Wilmington had fallen, sealing off the South from the sustaining flow of supplies from Europe. Moreover, General Sherman's army had devastated the heart of the Confederacy in its march through Georgia and South Carolina; by the end of February Sherman was preparing to enter North Carolina. The Union's confidence was further fed by the wide spread knowledge that General Lee and Confederate officials were openly grappling with the problem of desertions. During the winter these had become considerable as men became concerned about their families in areas invaded by the Union armies. Finally, Lee further revealed his hardpressed position by appealing to the civilian population to search their households for any spare guns, cutlasses, equestrian gear and tools.

The Southern spirit, on the other hand, remained unshaken by what was regarded in the North as portents of defeat. The Richmond *Daily Examiner* editorialized on March 1: "We cannot help thinking that 'our friends, the enemy,' are a little premature in assuming the South to be at their feet. There are Southern armies of magnitude in the field, and Richmond, the capitol, is more impregnable at this hour than it has been at any period of the war."

A week later the Richmond *Daily Dispatch* expressed its confidence in the Confederate cause by comparing the South's position in the spring of 1865 with that of the American patriots in 1781. "In the American Revolution," wrote the editor, "three-fourths of the battles were gained by the British [and they] held all the major seaports and cities. They marched through South Carolina, precisely as Sherman is doing now. . . . They had the most powerful empire in the world at their back; had the aid of armed tories in every county; they excited the blacks to insurrection; and let loose the scalping knife of the Indian. . . . What is there in our condition as gloomy, as terrible, as protracted, as the long and dreary wilderness through which they marched to freedom and independence?"

President Jefferson Davis sent a Resolution adopted by the Confederate Congress to Mr. John Lancaster of England thanking him for his gallant and humane conduct in the rescue of Captain Raphael Semmes and 41 of his officers and men after the sinking of C.S.S. *Alabama* by U.S.S. *Kearsarge* (see 19 June 1864). It was particularly gratifying to the Confederacy that Lancaster's yacht *Deerhound* had sailed for England with the rescued Confederates rather than turning them over to *Kearsarge* as would have been customary under international law. This incident became even more galling for the Union Navy after Semmes and his officers were socially lionized during their stay in England.

Rear Admiral Dahlgren, upon receiving the report that his naval forces had occupied Georgetown, South Carolina, decided to proceed there and have a personal "look at things." He inspected the formidable but evacuated Fort White and the four companies of marines which held Georgetown. This date, Dahlgren's flagship *Harvest Moon* was steaming down Georgetown Bay enroute Charleston; the Admiral was awaiting breakfast in his cabin. "Suddenly, without warning," Dahlgren wrote in his diary, "came a crashing sound, a heavy shock, the partition between the cabin and wardroom was shattered and driven in toward me, while all loose articles in the cabin flew in different directions. . . . A torpedo had been struck by the poor old *Harvest Moon*, and she was sinking." The flagship sank in five minutes, but fortunately only one man was lost. The Admiral got off with only the uniform he was wearing.

Because of the loss of Charleston and Wilmington, Secretary Mallory directed Commander Bulloch, the regular agent of the Confederate Navy in England, to dispose of the deep draft steamers *Enterprise* and *Adventure* and to substitute for them two light draft vessels for use in the small inlets along the East coast of Florida. He wrote: "We can not ship cotton at present, but with light-draft vessels we could at once place cotton abroad. Moreover, we need them to get in our supplies now at the islands, and the want of which is seriously felt." Mallory added: "We are upon the eve of events fraught with the fate of the Confederacy, and without power to foresee the result. . . . The coming campaign will be in active operation within fifty days and we can not close our eyes to the dangers which threaten us and from which only our united and willing hearts and arms and the providence of God can shield us. We look for no aid from any other source."

The capture of ports on the Confederate coast injured the South and aided the North in many ways throughout the war. One was the availability to the Union Navy of nearby "advance bases" for operations and repairs. This date, Commander William H. Macomb, writing Rear Admiral Porter from the North Carolina Sounds, reported the arrival of U.S.S. *Shokokon*, Acting Lieutenant Francis Josselyn, at Plymouth. "She arrived yesterday," he wrote, "and I sent her to New Berne to have her decks shored up and breeching bolts fitted for her IX-inch guns."

2   In an effort to avoid capture by an armed boat from U.S.S. *Fox*, the crew of the blockade runner *Rob Roy*, from Belize, Honduras, ran her ashore and fired her in Deadman's Bay, Florida. The cargo removed from the blazing wreck consisted of cavalry sabers and farming and mechanical implements.

The steamer *Amazon*, "quite recently used as a rebel transport," surrendered to U.S.S. *Pontiac*, Lieutenant Commander Luce, on the Savannah River. *Amazon* was carrying a cargo of cotton when she was given up by David R. Dillon, her owner.

On this date the Chattanooga *Gazette* carried an account of the capture on the Tennessee River of a Confederate torpedo boat, accessory equipment, and a nine man party. The expedition had been organized in Richmond in early January and had gone by rail to Bristol, Tennessee, where a boat was obtained and launched in the Holston River. Its mission was to destroy Union commerce and key bridges on the Tennessee River. The expedition was captured near Kingston, Tennessee, by a local group of armed civilians. With little means the South sought desperately to strike at the Union stranglehold.

Because of difficulties in communications, small fast warships (often captured blockade runners) were in great demand for courier service. This date Assistant Secretary Fox wrote President Lincoln from Norfolk: "General Grant would like to see you and I shall be in Washington to-morrow morning with this vessel, the *Bat*, in which you can leave in the afternoon. She is a regular armed man-of-war, and the fastest vessel on the river. I think it would be best for you to use her."

Bat was a long, low sidewheeler which Commander Bulloch, CSN, had built in England. She fell victim in October 1864 to the concentrated blockaders off Wilmington as she made her first run with supplies for the Confederate Government. Bought by the Navy from the Boston Prize Court for $150,000, she was commissioned in mid-December 1864 and was in great demand because of her high speed.

3   General Sherman's large army, marching parallel to the coast from Columbia in order to keep sea support near at hand, steadily approached Fayetteville, N.C. The Navy continued to clear Cape Fear River of torpedoes and obstructions so as to provide him with a base at Wilmington for sea supply comparable to Savannah. As the river was cleared light draft gunboats bumped up the river to be ready to open communications. This date Lieutenant Commander Ralph Chandler, U.S.S. *Lenapee*, reported to Lieutenant Commander George W. Young, Senior Naval Officer at Wilmington: "In obedience to your order of the 1st instant, I got underway with this vessel on the 2d instant and proceeded up the North West Branch to a point where the Cape Fear River forms a junction with the Black River. The bends in the river I found too short to attempt to get the vessel higher without carrying away the wheelhouses and otherwise damaging the ship. I remained there until 1 o'clock p.m. to-day. During the night some negroes came down, and, on questioning them, they informed me that they had been told that General Sherman's forces were at a town called Robeson, 20 miles from Fayetteville."

U.S.S. *Glide*, Acting Master L. S. Fickett, captured schooner *Malta* in Vermilion Bayou, Louisiana, with cargo of cotton on board.

U.S.S. *Honeysuckle*, Acting Master James J. Russell, sighted the sloop *Phantom* as she attempted to enter the Suwannee River on the west coast of Florida. An armed boat from the ship overhauled and captured the blockade runner and her cargo of bar iron and liquors.

3–4 A naval squadron consisting of twelve steamers and four schooners commanded by Commander R. W. Shufeldt joined with Army troops under Brigadier General John Newton in a joint expedition directed against St. Marks Fort below Tallahassee, Florida. Although the expedition was not successful, in part because shallow water prevented the naval guns from approaching the Fort, the ships did succeed in crossing the bar and blockading the mouth of the St. Marks River, thus effectively preventing access to the harbor.

4 Major General E. R. S. Canby requested mortar boats from Rear Admiral S. P. Lee's Mississippi Squadron to participate in impending joint operations against the city of Mobile. Admiral Lee made the mortar boats available from Mound City naval station.

U.S. transport *Thorn* struck a torpedo below Fort Anderson in the Cape Fear River. Brigadier General Gabriel J. Rains, Superintendent of the Confederate Torpedo Corps and a pioneer in the development of torpedoes, reported: "The vessel sunk, as usual in such cases, in two minutes, but in this the crew escaped, but barely with their lives." The loss of the 400 ton Army steamer within two weeks of the damage to U.S.S. *Osceola* and destruction of a launch from U.S.S. *Shawmut* by torpedoes (see 20–22 February 1865) underscored the fact that although the Union controlled the waters below Wilmington it did not have complete freedom of movement. The presence—or even the suspected presence—of Confederate torpedoes forced the Navy to move more slowly than would otherwise have been possible.

Lieutenant Moreau Forrest, in his flagship U.S.S. *General Burnside* and accompained by U.S.S. *General Thomas*, Master Gilbert Morton, led a Tennessee River expedition which followed the course of that river across the state of Alabama. At Mussel Shoals the naval force attacked and dispersed the encampment of Confederate General Philip D. Roddey and captured horses, military equipment and cotton. Forrest then proceeded to Lamb's Ferry where he destroyed Confederate communications and transportation facilities. He also destroyed numerous barges, boats and scows encountered along the course of the river. Finally, Forrest penetrated the Elk River, deep into the state of Tennessee, where he "found a rich and populous country" in which "a great deal of loyal sentiment was displayed".

U.S.S. Harvest Moon, *Admiral Dahlgren's flagship.*

A. M.							
1							
2							
3							
4							
5							
6							
7							
8							
9							
10							
11							
12							

Distance per Log

Latitude, D. R.

Longitude, D. R.

Latitude observed

Longitude

Current

Variation

P. M.							
1							
2							
3							
4							
5							
6							
7							
8							
9							
10							
11							
12							

Commences & till 4 A M
At 1. Am. Saw a light
in the direction of Battery
White. thick & foggy weather
D B Arey

From 4. to 8. A M
At 6. 31. Am. A Boat from
Pawnee came down the river
and landed At Battery
White At. 7. Am Pawnee fired
a gun At. 7. 15. Am got underway
& proceeded down the river through
Marsh Channel Tug Clover in Company
At. 7. 45. Am when about 3 miles
from Battery White we ran on
to a torpedo. It blowed a hole
through the Starboard Quarter
tearing away the Main deck
over it which caused this ship
to sink in 5 minutes. In (2½)
two & half fathoms water. Tug
Clover. Immediately came to
our assistance The Admiral
& Staff went on board Clover
the Ship's Officers remaining on
Board to save every thing possible
Sent Gig in charge of Act Ensign
D B. Arey. to USStr Pawnee.
for Assistance. Sent three (3) boats
up the river to drag for torpedoes.
John Hayzard Ward Room Steward.
Missing supposed to be drowned
he being in the Hold at the time
of the Explosion

A. N. Bates

From. 8. Am. to Midnight
Ship sunk. in Swash Channel Winyah
Bay. 3 Miles S E. by E. from Battery White in (2½) two & half fathoms
water At. 9. Am Tug Clover. Cast off & proceeded down the river
the Officer & crew remaining by the Ship to save the furniture &c.
Boats returned without finding torpedoes. Tug Sweet Brier came alongside
delivered to her furniture. rigging. sails &c. She cast off. & went alongside
USStr Pawnee At. 5. Pm Tug Sweet Brier came alongside All the
Ship Officers & men went on board. for Passage to U S Str Pawnee for
Quarters for the night Pawnee Sent Boat with armed crew to this
Ship. for the night   L A Cornthwait

Log of the Harvest Moon records that Confederate torpedo "blowed a hole through the Starboard Quarter."

4–5 Spring floods in the James River made it possible for the heavy draft Confederate ironclads to strike at City Point, as they had attempted to do in January, or for the Union monitors to drive upstream. On 3 March Secretary Welles had asked Captain Oliver S. Glisson, senior naval officer at Hampton Roads, if ironclads *Montauk* and *Monadnock* had reported to him. "When they arrive," he directed impatiently, "send them up James River immediately." On the evening of the 4th General Grant, hoping to take advantage of the rising water, wired Assistant Secretary Fox: "The James River is very high, and will continue so as long as the weather of the past week lasts. It would be well to have at once all the ironclads that it is intended should come here [City Point]." Within half an hour of the arrival of Grant's message at the Navy Department, Secretary Welles ordered Glisson: "Send off a steamer to Cape Fear River to bring the *Montauk*, ironclad, to James River immediately, and let the same steamer go with great dispatch to Charleston to bring up two ironclads from there; all for James River."

The next morning, 5 March, Glisson replied to the Secretary: "Your telegram was received this morning at fifteen minutes after midnight; blowing a gale of wind at the time. U.S.S. *Aries* sailed at daylight this morning. The monitors are expected every moment from Cape Fear, and I shall send them up the river immediately."

One of the monitors from the southern stations, U.S.S. *Sangamon*, arrived in Hampton Roads that afternoon and sped up the James—a quick response to Grant's request. Within several days three additional monitors joined the squadron in the James River.

5 Landing party from U.S.S. *Don* under Acting Ensign McConnell destroyed a large boat in Passpatansy Creek, Maryland, after a brief skirmish with a group of Colonel Mosby's raiders. Commander F. A. Parker, commanding the Potomac Flotilla, reported that the boat was "a remarkably fine one, painted lead color, and capable of holding fifty men. It had been recently brought from Fredericksburg, and its rowlocks carefully muffled for night service. Five boxes of tobacco were found near the boat, which I have distributed to the captors."

6 Commodore F. A. Parker ordered Lieutenant Commander Edward Hooker to take U.S.S. *Commodore Read*, *Yankee*, *Delaware*, and *Heliotrope* up the Rappahannock River to cooperate with an Army detachment in conducting a raid near Fredericksburg, Virginia. Parker cautioned: ". . . you will be particularly careful in looking out for torpedoes; having all narrow channels and shoal places carefully swept by the small boats kept in advance of the flotilla. At points where torpedoes may be exploded from the shore, you will land flanking parties, and you are to shell as usual all heights . . ."

U.S.S. *Jonquil*, Acting Ensign Charles H. Hanson, was damaged by a torpedo while clearing the Ashley River, near Charleston, of obstructions and frame torpedoes. *Jonquil* had secured three torpedoes while dragging the Ashley that day. Hanson reported: "I hooked on to the log which had the fourth one on, but the log came up with the end, not having the torpedo on. I hoisted it to the bows of the steamer and started for shore. On shoaling the water, the torpedo being down struck the bottom and exploded directly under and about amidships of the steamer. Its force was so great as to raise the boilers 5 inches from their bed and knocked nine men overboard and completely flooded the vessel." Hanson added that the explosion took place in ten feet of water and "had it been any shoaler the vessel would have been entirely destroyed." *Jonquil*'s hull, however, was "not materially damaged" and she resumed dragging operations again the next day.

7 Lieutenant Commander Hooker, commanding a naval squadron consisting of U.S.S. *Commodore Read*, *Yankee*, *Delaware*, and *Heliotrope*, joined with an Army unit in conducting a raid at Hamilton's Crossing on the Rappahannock River six miles below Fredericksburg. Hooker reported that the expedition succeeded in "burning and destroying the railroad bridge, the depot, and a portion of the track . . .; also the telegraph line was cut and the telegraphic apparatus brought away. A train of twenty-eight cars, eighteen of them being principally loaded with tobacco, and an army wagon train were also captured and burned. A considerable number of mules were captured

and some thirty or forty prisoners taken. A mail containing a quantity of valuable information was secured." Throughout the war, rivers were avenues of strength for the North, highways of destruction to the South, which enabled warships and joint expeditions to thrust deep into the Confederacy.

Rear Admiral Porter testified before Congress. He had arrived in Washington the day after the Inaugural, having left his flagship off North Carolina on the 3rd. He scorched the congressional walls with some seagoing comments on Generals Banks and Butler. He then left town for City Point to direct the operations of the James River Squadron in coordination with Grant's final assault on Lee's lines.

7-8 U.S.S. *Chenango*, Lieutenant Morris, conducted a reconnaissance mission up the Black River from Georgetown, South Carolina, for a distance of some 45 miles. Morris reported that: "Upon reaching the vicinity of Brown's Ferry [a company of Confederate cavalry] opened upon us from behind a levee or bluff with rifles. We immediately responded with broadside guns and riflemen stationed in the tops."

10 Lieutenant Commander Young reported to Porter progress in clearing Cape Fear River for support of Sherman's army now near Fayetteville. Only small ships or steam launches could provide upriver service. "The gate obstructions are all clear, so that three or four vessels can pass abreast. The obstructions on the line of the two sunken steamers, where the buoy flags were planted, it will be necessary to take great pains to raise carefully. We have succeeded in destroying some four torpedoes which were found lodged in the logs of the obstructions."

One of Young's gunboats had noted that upriver "the stream is very narrow and tortuous, with a strong current. Finding that I could not make the turns without using hawsers, and then fouling paddle boxes and smokestack in the branches of large trees, I concluded to return. The people, white and black, whom I questioned, state that the *Chickamauga* is sunk across the stream at Indian Wells, with a chain just below. Her two guns are on a bluff on the western bank of the river." Operating conditions on these low, shallow rivers, often backed by swamp and forest, had many similarities with those encountered 100 years later in South Vietnam by the U.S. Navy Advisory group.

The Federals had long held New Bern, 80 air miles northeast of Wilmington (but some three times that by water), near where the Neuse River abruptly narrows from a main arm of Pamlico Sound. The city was the gateway for another supply route from the sea on General Sherman's route North to unite with Grant. This date, at the request of the Army, a small naval force got underway up the river to cut a pontoon bridge the Confederates were reported building below Kinston.

11 The steamer *Ajax* put into Nassau. Lieutenant Low, who had been on board as a "passenger", assumed command, and on 25 March transferred her registry. Governor Rawson W. Rawson of Bermuda carefully examined the ship and concluded that "nothing [was] found on her. . . . She now appears to be intended for a tug. It is suspected that she was intended as a tender to the Confederate Iron-clad vessel [*Stonewall*], said to be now in a Spanish Port, watched by two Federal cruisers." By early April *Ajax* was ready to sail for Bermuda.

11-12 Lieutenant Commander George W. Young, senior officer present off Wilmington, led a naval force consisting of U.S.S. *Eolus* and boat crews from U.S.S. *Maratanza*, *Lenapee*, and *Nyack* up the Cape Fear River to Fayetteville, where the expedition rendezvoused with General Sherman's army. The naval movement had been undertaken at the request of Major General Terry, who, Young reported, had said on the morning of the 11th "that he was about starting an expedition up the North West Branch [of the Cape Fear River] for the purpose of clearing the way to Fayetteville, and wished to have one of the gunboats, as a support, to follow." The expedition was halted for the night at Devil's Bend because of "the circuitous nature of the river", but resumed the next morning and arrived at Fayetteville on the evening of the 12th. In addition to opening communications between Sherman and the Union forces on the coast, the naval units arrived in time to protect the General's flank while he crossed the river.

12   At the request of Brigadier General Schofield, Acting Master H. Walton Grinnell, leading a detachment of four sailors, succeeded in delivering important Army dispatches to General Sherman near Fayetteville.   Grinnell and his men began their trip on the 4th in a dugout from Wilmington. About 12 miles up the Cape Fear River, after passing through the Confederate pickets undetected, the men left the boat and commenced a tedious and difficult march towards Fayetteville.   Near Whiteville, Grinnell impressed horses and led a daring dash through the Confederate lines. Shortly thereafter, the group made contact with the rear scouts of Sherman's forces, successfully completing what Grinnell termed "this rather novel naval scout."   Naval support, no matter what form it took, was essential to General Sherman's movements.

U.S.S. *Althea*, Acting Ensign Frederic A. G. Bacon, was sunk by a torpedo in the Blakely River, Alabama.   The small 72-ton tug had performed duties as a coaling and supply vessel since joining the West Gulf Blockading Squadron in August 1864.   She was returning from an unsuccessful attempt to drag the river's channel when she "ran afoul of a torpedo".   *Althea* went down "immediately" in 10 to 12 feet of water.   Two crewmen were killed and three, including Bacon, were injured.   *Althea* had the dubious distinction of being the first of seven vessels to be sunk by torpedoes near Mobile in a five week period.   The Confederate weapons took an increasing toll of Union ships as they swept for mines and pressed home the attack in shallow waters.   *Althea* was later raised and recommissioned in November 1865.

U.S.S. *Quaker City*, Commander William F. Spicer, captured blockade running British schooner *R. H. Vermilyea* in the Gulf of Mexico with cargo of coffee, clothes, rum, tobacco, and shoes.

13   Commander Rhind, Senior Naval Officer at New Bern, reported to Commander Macomb, commanding in the North Carolina sounds, that the expedition up the Neuse River had returned the previous

U.S.S. Malvern, *Admiral Porter's flagship.*

evening. "A deserter from a North Carolina regiment came on board the [Army steamer] *Ella May* yesterday morning. He states that the whole rebel force under Bragg (estimated by him at 40,000) had evacuated Kinston, moving toward Goldsboro, but that Hoke's division returned when he left. The ironclad [*Neuse*] is afloat and ready for service; has two guns, draws 9 feet. No pontoon was found in the Neuse. If you can send me a torpedo launch at once he may have an opportunity of destroying the ironclad. The bridge (railroad) at Kinston has been destroyed by the enemy."

General Johnston, recalled to duty, had been sent to North Carolina to oppose General Sherman. Troops withdrawn from Kinston were part of his consolidation of divided armies seeking to gain a force of respectable size to fight effectively against Sherman's large army. The withdrawal, however, left a vacuum which the Federals promptly filled. They occupied Kinston on the 14th; meanwhile the Confederates had destroyed the ram *Neuse* to prevent her capture

Lieutenant Commander Hooker led a naval expedition, consisting of the U.S.S. *Commodore Read, Morse, Delaware,* and Army gunboat *Mosswood,* up the Rappahannock River to assist an Army detachment engaged in mopping-up operations on the peninsula formed by the Rappahannock and Potomac Rivers. At Tappahannock, a landing party from *Delaware,* Acting Master Joshua H. Eldridge, destroyed eight boats including a large flatboat used as a ferry. The bridge connecting Tappahannock with evacuated Fort Lowry was then destroyed by the well directed gunfire from *Delaware* and *Morse,* Acting Master George W. Hyde. During these operations the squadron exchanged fire for two hours with two rifled field pieces concealed in a wooded area. The vessels also opened on Confederate cavalry units in the vicinity and, Hooker reported, "emptied some of their saddles."

14 Having dispatched a large number of troops to White House, Virginia, General Grant requested the Navy to send additional gunboats into the York and Pamunkey Rivers "to keep open free navigation between White House and the mouth of York River." Commodore Radford replied at once: "Will send vessels required immediately." U.S.S. *Shawmut* and *Commodore Morris* were detailed for this duty which, like control of the waters of the James, assured the Army of rapid communications and logistic support.

U.S.S. *Wyandank,* Acting Lieutenant Sylvanus Nickerson, seized schooner *Champanero* off Inigoes Creek in Chesapeake Bay. The Federal Customs Office at Port of St. Mary's had cleared the schooner and endorsed the accuracy of its manifest. Nickerson alertly examined the cargo and found more than one half of it not manifested, including a large quantity of powder. He also discovered that the customs official who had signed the clearance had $4,000 worth of liquor and other readily salable merchandise on board.

15 Rear Admiral S. P. Lee, commanding the Mississippi Squadron, warned of the receipt from "the highest military sources" of the information "that the rebel Navy is reported to have been relieved from duty on the Atlantic coast and sent to operate on the Western rivers." He added: "The design of the enemy is believed to be to interfere with the naval vessels and the transports on these rivers, or to cover the transfer of rebel troops from the west side of the Mississippi."

Acting Lieutenant Robert P. Swann, U.S.S. *Lodona,* reported to Rear Admiral Dahlgren that he had destroyed an extensive salt work on Broro Neck, McIntosh County, Georgia. Destroyed were 12 boilers, 10 buildings, 100 bushels of salt, a large quantity of timber and a number of new barrels and staves.

16 Major General Canby requested Rear Admiral Thatcher to provide naval gunfire and transport support to the landing and movement of Federal troops against Mobile. The response again demonstrated the close coordination with ground operations which was so effective throughout the conflict; Thatcher replied: "I shall be most happy and ready to give you all the assistance in my power. Six tinclads are all the light-draft vessels at my disposal. They will be ready at any moment."

No. 93.

U.S. Mississippi Squadron
Flag Ship "Black Hawk"
Mound City Feby 21st 1864

Sir

The following is the present disposition of the vessels of this Squadron, viz:—

Name of Vessel	No. of Guns	Name of Comdg Officer
Flag Ship "Black Hawk"	14	A.V.Lt. W.G. Saltonstall, temporarily
Myrtle (tug)		Acty Ensign A. N. Goldsmith

1st District. New Orleans to Donaldsonville; Lieut. Comdr. Byron Wilson Commanding.

Ouichita	39	Lt. Comdr. Byron Wilson
Alexandria	2	Acty Master D.P. Rosenmiller
Argosy	9	" " J. C. Morong

2nd District; Donaldsonville to Morganzia; Lieut. Comdr. J. B. Cornwell, Commanding.

Choctaw	8	Lt. Comdr. J.J. Cornwell
Genl. Price	4	A.V.Lt. W.R. Wells

Extracts from Rear Admiral Lee's report of the disposition of the Mississippi Squadron.

9th District; Mound City to Muscle Shoals; Tenn: River, Lieut. Comdr. R. Boyd, Jr. Comdg

Name of Vessel	No. of Guns	Name of Comdg Officer
	"305	
Peosta	15	A. V. Lt. Jno. E. Smith
Brilliant	6	" " Chas. G. Perkins
Silver Lake	6	Actg Master J. C. Coyle
Reindeer	8	A. V. Lt. H. A. Glassford
Fair Play	8	Actg Master G. J. Groves
Carondelet	7	A. V. Lt. Jno. Rogers
Tensas	2	Actg Ensign E. C. Van Pelt
Naumkeag	7	" Master A. F. Thompson
St. Clair	6	A. V. Lt. J. S. French
Curlew	8	Actg Master, M. Hickey

10th District; Cumberland River & Upper Ohio; Lieut. Comdr. Le Roy Fitch, Commanding.

Name of Vessel	No. of Guns	Name of Comdg Officer
Springfield	12	Actg Ensign Ed. Morgan
Moose	11	Lieut. Comdr. Le Roy Fitch
Victory	6	Actg Master Fredk. Read

V–63

U.S.S. *Pursuit*, Acting Lieutenant William R. Browne, captured British schooner *Mary* attempting to run the blockade into Indian River on the East Coast of Florida. Her cargo consisted of shoes, percussion caps, and rum.

U.S.S. *Quaker City*, Commander Spicer, captured small blockade running sloop *Telemico* in the Gulf of Mexico with cargo of cotton and peanuts.

16–18   A naval expedition, led by Lieutenant Commander Thomas H. Eastman, consisting of the U.S.S. *Don*, *Stepping Stones*, *Heliotrope* and *Resolute*, proceeded up the Rappahannock River and its tributary, Mattox Creek, to the vicinity of Montrose, Virginia, where it destroyed a supply base that had been supporting Confederate guerrillas on the peninsula between the Rappahannock and Potomac Rivers. Eastman led a landing force of 70 Marines and sailors up the right fork of Mattox Creek where he found and destroyed four boats. The landing party, led by Acting Ensign William H. Summers, that cleared the left fork encountered heavy musket fire but successfully destroyed three schooners. Houses in the vicinity were also searched and contraband destroyed. Acting Ensign John J. Brice, who led the 40 man search party, "found himself opposed by about 50 cavalry. He formed his men to receive their attack. While doing this, 8 or 10 cavalry came down on his left flank, which he drove off. The main portion, on seeing this, retired to the woods."

17   Coast Survey steamer *Bibb*, commanded by Charles O. Boutelle, struck a submerged torpedo in Charleston harbor. "Fortunately for us," Boutelle reported, "the blow was upon the side. To this fact and the great strength of the vessel may be ascribed our escape from serious injury." Nevertheless, as Rear Admiral Dahlgren noted a few days later, *Bibb* "was much jarred" by the impact and required considerable repairs.

U.S.S. *Quaker City*, Commander Spicer, captured blockade running schooner *George Burkhart* in the Gulf of Mexico with cargo of cotton, bound from Lavaca, Texas for Matamoras, Mexico.

U.S.S. *Wyalusing*, Lieutenant Commander Earl English, while engaged in clearing and opening the tributaries of Albemarle Sound, removed 60 nets and captured a Confederate schooner in Scuppernong and Alligator Rivers.

19   U.S.S. *Massachusetts*, Acting Lieutenant William H. West, struck a torpedo in Charleston harbor; "fortunately," West reported, "it did not explode." The incident took place only two days after Coast Survey steamer *Bibb* had been damaged by a torpedo in the harbor and occurred within 50 yards of the wreck of U.S.S. *Patapsco*, which had been sunk by a torpedo two months before (see 15 January 1865). The danger to those attempting to clear torpedoes from the waters previously controlled by the South was constant, as was the risk to ships that were simply operating in these waters.

20   Commander Macomb, U.S.S. *Shamrock*, reported the successful raising of the Confederate ram *Albemarle*. The formidable ironclad had been sunk the previous autumn in a daring attack led by Lieutenant William B. Cushing in an improvised torpedo boat (see 27 October 1864).

21   C.S.S. *Stonewall*, Captain T. J. Page, having been detained in Ferrol, Spain, for several days because of foul weather, attempted to put to sea. However, the seas outside were still too heavy and the ironclad put back into port. Two days later another attempt to get to sea was made with similar results. Page off-loaded some 40 tons of coal to make her more seaworthy.

Lieutenant Commander Arthur R. Yates, commanding U.S.S. *J. P. Jackson*, in Mississippi Sound, reported to Rear Admiral Thatcher that he had issued food from his ship's stores to relieve the destitute and starving condition of people in Biloxi, cut off from Mobile from which provisions had been formerly received. Yates illustrated the humanitarian heritage of the Navy.

The heavy guns of Union gunboats supported the landing of troops of General Canby's command at Dannelly's Mills on the Fish River, Alabama. This was a diversionary operation intended to prevent the movement of additional Confederate troops to Mobile during the week prior to the opening of the Federal attack against that city.

22 Assistant Secretary Fox directed Commodore Montgomery, Commandant of the Washington Navy Yard, to have U.S.S. *Bat* ready to convoy steamer *River Queen* at noon the next day: "The President will be in the *River Queen*, bound to City Point." Lincoln was headed for a conference with his top commanders. In a hard fought battle (19–22 March), General Sherman had just defeated a slashing attack by General Johnston at Bentonville, mid-way between his two river contacts with the sea at Fayetteville and Goldsboro. At Goldsboro Sherman was joined by General Schofield's army, which had been brought to Wilmington by ships. Confident of the security of his position, Sherman could leave his soldiers for a few days and take steamer *Russia* to City Point and the meeting with Lincoln, Grant, and Porter.

23 From the James River Rear Admiral Porter directed Commander Macomb, commanding in the North Carolina Sounds: "It seems to be the policy now to break up all trade, especially that which may benefit the rebels, and you will dispose your vessels about the sounds to capture all contraband of war going into the enemy's lines. You will stop all supplies of clothing that can by any possibility benefit a soldier; sieze all vessels afloat that carry provisions to any place not held by our troops and send them into court for adjudication. Recognize no permits where there is a prospect of stores of any kind going into rebel hands. . . . For any capture, send in prize lists and make full reports. You will see by the law (examine it carefully) that an officer is authorized to send all property 'not abandoned' into court, especially property afloat."

U.S.S. *Constellation*, approaching the 68th birthday of her launching and already the United States' oldest warship afloat, as she still is today, continued to serve a useful purpose in the new era of steam and iron. This date Commodore Radford reported from Norfolk to Rear Admiral Porter: "I have ordered the men transferred from the *Wabash* to this ship [U.S.S. *Dumbarton*] for the James River Flotilla on board the *Constellation*."

24 The heavily armed Confederate ironclad *Stonewall*, Captain T. J. Page, put to sea from Ferrol, Spain, after two previous attempts had been frustrated by foul weather. Page cleared the harbor at mid-morning and attempted to bring on an engagement with wooden frigate, U.S.S. *Niagara* and sloop-of-war *Sacramento*, under Commodore T. T. Craven. *Sacramento* was commanded by Captain Henry Walke, who had gained fame as captain of the Eads gunboat U.S.S. *Carondelet* in the Mississippi River campaigns. Craven kept his ships at anchor in nearby Coruña, Spain, and refused to accept *Stonewall*'s challenge. Page wrote Commander Bulloch in Liverpool: "To suppose that these two heavily armed men-of-war were afraid of the *Stonewall* is to me incredible. . . ." However, as Craven explained to Secretary Welles: "At this time the odds in her favor were too great and too certain, in my humble judgment, to admit of the slightest hope of being able to inflict upon her even the most trifling injury, whereas, if we had gone out, the *Niagara* would most undoubtedly have been easily and promptly destroyed. So thoroughly a one-sided combat I did not consider myself called upon to engage in." Craven was subsequently courtmartialed and found remiss in his duties for failing to engage *Stonewall*. Serving as President of this court was Vice Admiral Farragut and sitting as a member was Commodore John A. Winslow who had sunk the Confederate raider *Alabama*. The court sentenced Craven to two years suspension on leave pay. Secretary Welles refused to approve what he regarded as a "paid vacation" for an officer who had been found guilty and instead he restored Craven to duty.

President Lincoln visited General Grant at City Point, Virginia, arriving at this all important water-supported supply base at 9 p.m. on board the steamer *River Queen*. Accompanied by Mrs. Lincoln and his son Tad, he was escorted up the James River by U.S.S. *Bat*, Lieutenant Commander John S. Barnes. Two days later Barnes accompanied Grant and the President on a review of part of the Army of the James. General Horace Porter, serving on Grant's staff, later recalled: "Captain Barnes, who commanded the vessel which had escorted the President's steamer, was to

C.S.S. Stonewall *departing Lisbon harbor.*

be one of the party, and I loaned him my horse. This was a favor which was usually accorded with some reluctance to naval officers when they came ashore; for these men of the ocean at times tried to board the animal on the starboard side, and often rolled in the saddle as if there was a heavy sea on; and if the horse, in his anxiety to rid himself of a sea-monster, tried to scrape his rider off by rubbing against a tree, the officer attributed the unseaman-like conduct of the animal entirely to the fact that his steering-gear had become unshipped. . . . Navy officers were about as reluctant to lend their boats to army people, for fear they would knock holes in the bottom when jumping in, break the oars in catching crabs, and stave in the bows through an excess of modesty which manifested itself in a reluctance to give the command 'Way enough!' in time when approaching a wharf.''

U.S.S. *Republic*, Acting Ensign John W. Bennett, was dispatched up the Cape Fear River from Wilmington to check reports that detachments of General Wheeler's cavalry were operating in the area. About six miles up the river a cavalry squad was driven away with gunfire. Bennett then landed a reconnoitering party. It was learned that the mounted Confederates had broken into small squads and were plundering the country. The reconnaissance party also made contact with a rear guard detachment of General Sherman's army en route to Fayetteville.

U.S.S. *Quaker City*, Commander Spicer, captured blockade runner *Cora* with cargo of lumber off Brazos Santiago, Texas.

25 General Grant wired Rear Admiral Porter that General Lee's soldiers had broken through the right of the Union's line and that he thought they would strike toward the essential James River supply base at City Point a few miles from the breakthrough. ''I would suggest putting one or two gunboats on the Appomattox up as high as the pontoon bridge,'' he told the Admiral. Porter

immediately ordered gunboats up the Appomattox River to guard the pontoon bridge "at all times." Simultaneously, U.S.S. *Wilderness*, Acting Master Henry Arey, was ordered up the Chickahominy River to communicate with General Sheridan, carry intelligence about any Confederate activity along the river, and bring back dispatches from Sheridan for Grant.

Lee's attack was his last bold gamble for great stakes. Never one to submit tamely to even the most formidable odds, he sought in the surprise assault to cripple Grant's army so that the overwhelming spring attack the Federals were building up could not be launched. Lee hoped that then he could speed to North Carolina with part of his veterans, join General Johnston and crush Sherman while still holding the Richmond-Petersburg front. Had the attack gone as well in its later stages as it did in the first onslaught, he would have been within range of City Point, only some ten miles away. The wholesale destruction of the host of supply ships, mountains of stores, and vast arsenal would have ended Grant's plant for seizing Richmond that spring.

26–27 A detachment of sailors led by Acting Ensign Peyton H. Randolph of U.S.S. *Benton* joined troops under the command of Brigadier General B. G. Farrar in a combined expedition to Trinity, Louisiana, where they captured a small number of Confederate soldiers as well as horses, arms and stores.

27 Captain Stellwagen, the senior naval officer at Georgetown, South Carolina, reported to Rear Admiral Dahlgren "the return of another expedition of four days' duration up the Waccamaw River some 50 miles, to Conwayboro." Detailing the nature of one of the ceaseless naval expeditions in coastal and inland waters that facilitated the land campaign, Stellwagen continued: "Having heard that threats of a visit in force had been made by the guerrillas against the plantations and settlements, in view of which great alarm was felt on the whole route by blacks and whites, I dispatched the *Mingoe*, having in tow some ten armed boats, to proceed as high as Buck's Mills, and leaving it discretionary with Lieutenant-Commanders G. U. Morris and William H. Dana to proceed the remaining distance by boats or land. The arrival of the steam launch and two large row launches from the Santee [River] enabled me to follow with them, and the steam tug *Catalpa* determined to ascend as far as the water would permit. I found the *Mingoe* ashore near her destination, towed her off, and caused her to drop to a point where she could anchor. The shore expedition had gone on, and I took the remainder of boats in tow as far as practicable, then causing them to row. After incredible labor and difficulty, succeeded in getting to Conwayboro at nightfall, just after the marching division. No enemies were encountered, but it was reported many small parties fled in various directions on our approach by river and land.

"The people of the town were glad to see us; even those having relatives in the army professed their joy at being saved from the raiding deserters. They assure us that the penetration of our parties into such distances, supposed to be inaccessible to our vessels, has spread a saluatory dread, and that our large force of *Catalpa*, 4 large launches, and 10 boats, with about 300 men in all, at the highest point, presented such a formidable display, with 7 howitzers, that they thought they would be completely prevented [from] returning to that neighborhood."

Secretary Welles ordered U.S.S. *Wyoming*, Commander John P. Bankhead, then at Baltimore, to sail in search of C.S.S. *Shenandoah*. So delayed were communications between the Pacific and Washington that although *Wyoming* was ordered to cruise from Melbourne, Australia, to China, *Shenandoah* had departed Australia more than five weeks before and was now nearing Ascension Island. *Wyoming* would join U.S.S. *Wachusett* and *Iroquois* on independent service in an effort to track down the elusive commerce raider.

Captain T. J. Page, C.S.S. *Stonewall*, wrote Commander Bulloch in England that he would sail from Lisbon, Portugal, to Teneriffe and then to Nassau where his subsequent movements "must depend upon the intelligence I may receive. . . ." That evening, U.S.S. *Niagara* and *Sacramento*, which had followed *Stonewall* from Coruna, Spain, entered Lisbon. The Confederate ram, however, was able to put to sea the next day without interference because international law required the two Union ships to remain in port for 24 hours after *Stonewall* had departed.

Brig. Gen. Davidson sent Lieut. Comdr McCauley a copy of Brevet Brig. Gen. Scaran's report of the expedition, in which the services of the Navy are acknowledged in complimentary terms, to which Gen. Davidson adds his thanks, concluding, "I take advantage of this occasion to testify to you my regard for the uniform co-operation you have afforded me during my command here, and for the cordial harmony which exists between the two branches of the service."

I have the honor to be, Sir,
Very Respectfully,
Your obt Servt
S. P. L.
Acty. R Admiral
Comdg Miss. Squadron.

Rear Admiral Lee informs Secretary Welles of the joint expedition to Trinity, Louisiana (see 26–27 March) and reports the Army's reaction to the Navy's contribution to the movement.

27-28 Combined Army-Navy operations, the latter commanded by Rear Admiral Thatcher, aimed at capturing the city of Mobile commenced. The objective was Spanish Fort, located near the mouth of the Blakely River and was the key to the city's defenses. Six tinclads and supporting gunboats steamed up the Blakely River to cut the fort's communications with Mobile while the army began to move against the fort's outworks. The river had been thickly sown with torpedoes which necessitated sweeping operations ahead of the advancing ironclads. These efforts, directed by Commander Peirce Crosby of U.S.S. *Metacomet*, netted 150 torpedoes. Nevertheless, a number of the Confederate weapons eluded the Union—with telling results. In the next five days three Northern warships would be sunk in the Blakely.

28 Rear Admiral Porter visited President Lincoln with Generals Grant and Sherman on board steamer *River Queen*, the President's headquarters during his stay at City Point. The four men informally discussed the war during the famous conference, and Lincoln stressed his desire to bring the war to a close as quickly as possible with as little bloodshed as possible. He added that he was inclined to follow a lenient policy with regard to the course to be pursued at the conclusion of the war. After the conference Sherman returned to New Bern, North Carolina, on board U.S.S. *Bat*, a swifter ship than the steamer on which he had arrived at City Point. Porter had ordered Lieutenant Commander Barnes: "You will wait the pleasure of Major-General W. T. Sherman . . . and when ready will convey him, with staff, either to New Berne, Beaufort, or such place as he may indicate. Return here as soon as possible." Sherman's troops at Goldsboro were little more than 125 miles in a direct line from the front south of Petersburg.

Following the Presidential conference on board *River Queen*, Rear Admiral Porter ordered Commander Macomb, commanding in the North Carolina Sounds, "to cooperate with General Sherman to the fullest extent" during operations soon to be opened in the area. "They will want all your tugs, particularly, to tow vessels or canal boats up to Kinston, [North Carolina]. . . . It will be absolutely necessary to supply General Sherman by the way of Kinston." Porter continued: "There will be a movement made from Winton after a while. It is necessary for us to get possession of everything up the Chowan River, so that Sherman can obtain his forage up there. . . . I trust to Captain Rhind to remove the obstructions at New Berne and to tow up rapidly all the provisions, and General Sherman can supply his army for daily use by the railroad, and you can get up the stuff required for the march."

Commander Macomb received the Admiral's orders via the swift steamer U.S.S. *Bat* on 30 March, and the following day replied from Roanoke Island: "I immediately had an interview with the general and arranged that Captain Rhind would attend to everything relating to the Navy in the Neuse. I am on my way to Plymouth to carry out your orders as regards sending vessels to Winton, on the Chowan, and holding the same. The *Shokokon* and *Commodore Hull* are on their way up from New Berne. As soon as possible after my arrival at Plymouth I shall proceed up the Chowan, dragging ahead for torpedoes." Control of the sea and rivers continued to be as invaluable to the North in operations at the end of the war as it had from the start.

U.S.S. *Milwaukee*, Lieutenant Commander James H. Gillis, struck a torpedo in the Blakely River, Alabama, while dropping downstream after shelling a Southern transport which was attempting to supply Spanish Fort. Just as Gillis returned to the area that had been swept for torpedoes and "supposed the danger from torpedoes was past," he "felt a shock and saw at once that a torpedo had exploded on the port side of the vessel . . . ." *Milwaukee*'s stern went under within three minutes but the forward compartments did not fill for almost an hour, enabling the sailors to save most of their belongings. Although the twin turreted monitor sank, no lives were lost.

U.S.S. *Niagara*, Commodore T. T. Craven, was fired upon by one of the forts in the harbor of Lisbon, Portugal. In a report to James E. Harvey, U.S. Minister Resident in Lisbon, Craven stated: "With view of shifting her berth farther up the river, so as to be nearer the usual landing stairs, at about 3:15 p.m. the *Niagara* was got underway and was about being turned head upstream

U.S. Grant
Lieutenant General, USA

David D. Porter
Rear Admiral, USN

William T. Sherman
Major General, USA

when three shots were fired in rapid succession directly at her from Castle Belem." Portugal later apologized for the incident.

Secretary Welles advised Commodore Sylvanus W. Godon that he had been appointed an acting Rear Admiral and was to command the Brazil Squadron. Welles' letter was a significant commentary on the progress of the war afloat: "It is proposed to reestablish the Brazil Squadron, as circumstances now admit of the withdrawal of many of the vessels that have been engaged in the blockade and in active naval operations and sending them on foreign service . . . ."

29 In a downpour, General Grant launched his wideswinging move to the southwest of Petersburg to roll up Lee's flank. Ever concerned about his lifeline on the James River, he wrote Rear Admiral Porter: "In view of the possibility of the enemy attempting to come to City Point, or by crossing the Appomattox at Broadway Landing, getting to Bermuda Hundred during the absence of the greater part of the army, I would respectfully request that you direct one or two gunboats to lay in the Appomattox, near the pontoon bridge, and two in the James River, near the mouth of Bailey's Creek, the first stream below City Point emptying into the James." Porter complied with double measure, sending not one or two but several ships to Grant's assistance.

U.S.S. *Osage*, Lieutenant Commander William M. Gamble, upped anchor and got underway inside the bar at the Blakely River, Alabama. Gamble was trying to avoid colliding with U.S.S. *Winnebago*, which was drifting alongside in a strong breeze. Suddenly a torpedo exploded under the monitor's bow, and, Gamble reported, "the vessel immediately commenced sinking." *Osage* lost four men and had eight wounded in the explosion. She was the third ship to be sunk in the

President Lincoln confers with the three commanders on board steamer River Queen *at City Point, Virginia.*

U.S.S. Niagara *and* Sacramento *are fired upon by shore batteries in Lisbon harbor.*

U.S.S. Osage *sinking in Blakely River, Alabama, after striking torpedo on 29 March 1865. Wreck of U.S.S.* Milwaukee, *torpedo casualty of the day before, is in background.*

Blakely during March and the second in two days as torpedo warfare cost the North dearly even though its ships controlled waters near Mobile.

30 Lieutenant Charles W. Read took command of the ram C.S.S. *William H. Webb* in the Red River, Louisiana. Read reported to Secretary Mallory that he found the ship "without a single gun on board, little or no crew, no fuel, and no small arms, save a few cutlasses." Characteristically, the enterprising officer obtained a 30 pound Parrott rifle from General Kirby Smith and readied *Webb* for her bold dash out of the Red River, intended to take her down the Mississippi some 300 miles, past New Orleans, and out to sea.

31 *St. Mary's*, a 115 ton schooner out of St. Mary's, Maryland, loaded with an assorted cargo valued at $20,000, was boarded and captured off the Patuxent River in Chesapeake Bay by a Confederate raiding party led by Master John C. Braine, CSN. The disguised Southerners were in a yawl and had come alongside the schooner on the pretext that their craft was sinking. Braine took *St. Mary's* to sea where they captured a New York bound schooner *J. B. Spafford*. The latter prize was released after the raiders had placed *St. Mary's* crew on board her and had taken the crew members' personal effects. The Confederates indicated to their captives that their intention was to take *St. Mary's* to St. Marks, Florida, but they put into Nassau in April.

U.S.S. *Iuka*. Lieutenant William C. Rogers, captured blockade running British schooner *Comus* off the coast of Florida with cargo of cotton.

APRIL

1   The positions of the opposing forces on this date demonstrated vividly what superiority afloat had meant to the North in this giant struggle that decided the future of the nation. From his overflowing advance bases on the James at City Point, only a few miles from General Lee's lines, General Grant was on the move for the final battle of the long saga in Virginia.

To the south in North Carolina backed by his seaport bases at New Bern and Wilmington, General Sherman's massive armies were joined to strike General Johnston at the capital city, Raleigh. In South Carolina and Georgia, Charleston and Savannah, key ports from colonial times, were Union bases fed from the sea.

Far down on the Gulf of Mexico General Canby, with 45,000 soldiers brought and supplied by transports, lay at the gates of the crumbling defenses of Mobile manned by 10,000 Confederates under General Dabney Maury.

Although constantly under attack by guerrillas along the Mississippi and its eastern tributaries, Federal gunboats kept the river lifeline open to the occupying armies. Trans-Mississippi, still largely held from invasion by the Confederates, was tightly blockaded by the Union Navy. Without control of the water, to paraphrase John Paul Jones, alas! united America. Fortunate indeed was the nation to have men ashore like Lincoln and Grant who made wide use of the irreplaceable advantages to the total national power that strength at sea imparted.

C.S.S. *Shenandoah*, Lieutenant Waddell, put into Lea Harbor, Ascension Island, (Ponape Island, Eastern Carolines). A number of sail had been sighted from the cruiser's decks as she approached the island, and, Waddell reported, ". . . we began to think if they were not whale ships it would be a very good April fool." The Confederates had sighted only one vessel between 20 February, shortly after departing Melbourne, and this date. They were not disappointed. Waddell found whalers *Pearl, Hector, Harvest* and *Edward Carey* in the harbor and seized them. The Confederates obtained vital charts from the four ships showing the location of the whaling grounds most frequented by American whalers. "With such charts in my possession," Waddell wrote, "I not only held a key to the navigation of all the Pacific Islands, the Okhotsk and Bering Seas, and the Arctic Ocean, but the most probable localities for finding the great Arctic whaling fleet of New England, without a tiresome search." In addition to obtaining this intelligence and the charts essential to future operations, Waddell stocked *Shenandoah*'s depleted storerooms with provisions and supplies from the four prizes. The ships were then drawn upon a reef where the natives were permitted to strip them from truck halyards to copper sheathing on the keels. Of the 130 prisoners, 8 were shipped on board *Shenandoah*; the remainder were set ashore to be picked up by a passing whaler. The four stripped vessels, totaling $116,000 in value, were then put to the torch.

Fighting gamely on all fronts, the South also inflicted maritime losses elsewhere. U.S.S. *Rodolph*, temporarily commanded by her executive officer, Acting Ensign James F. Thompson, struck a torpedo in the Blakely River, Alabama, and "rapidly sank in 12 feet of water." The tinclad was towing a barge containing apparatus for the raising of U.S.S. *Milwaukee*, a torpedo victim on 28 March. Acting Master N. Mayo Dyer, *Rodolph*'s commanding officer, reported that "from the

Confederate torpedo in the waters around Mobile claims tinclad U.S.S. Rodolph *as a victim.*

effects of the explosion that can be seen, I should judge there was a hole through the bow at least 10 feet in diameter. . . ." Four men were killed as a result of the sinking and eleven others were wounded. *Rodolph*, the third warship in five days to be lost in the same vicinity due to effective Confederate torpedo warfare, had played an important role in the continuing combined operations after the fall of Mobile Bay to Admiral Farragut on 5 August 1864. Arriving in the Bay, from New Orleans on 14 August, she had participated in forcing the surrender of Fort Morgan on 23 August. Acting Master's Mate Nathaniel B. Hinckley, serving on board *Rodolph*, told his son many years after the war that he had carried the Confederate flag from the captured fort and turned it over to a patrol boat. *Rodolph* had remained in the Bay and its tributaries as Union seapower projected General Canby's powerful army against the final defenses of the city of Mobile. Hinckley was stationed in the tinclad's forecastle when she struck the torpedo that sank her, but he escaped injury.

The development of torpedoes had been encouraged by Matthew Fontaine Maury, John Mercer Brooke and others early in the war. Had the Confederate government at this time perceived the all-embracing influence of the Union Navy in combined operations, it would have vigorously developed this strange new weapon. The early use of torpedoes could have greatly, perhaps decisively, delayed the devastating joint operations. Successive Confederate disasters at Hatteras Inlet and at Port Royal, in the sounds of North Carolina and in the Mississippi Valley, and at New Orleans, shocked Richmond into action. Losses eventually became severe for the Union Navy, but they were too late to affect the outcome.

A Federal naval officer writing soon after the war summarized this development: "With a vast extent of coast peculiarly open to attack from sea; with a great territory traversed in every part by navigable streams . . . the South had no navy to oppose to that of the Union—a condition which, from the very commencement of the struggle, stood in the way of their success, and neutralized their prodigious efforts on land. Their seaports were wrested from them, or blockaded, fleets of gunboats, mostly clad with iron, covered their bays and ascended their rivers, carrying dismay to their hearts, and success to the Union cause . . . Under such a pressure, the pressure of dire distress and great necessity, the rebels turned their attention to torpedoes as a means of defense against such terrible odds, hoping by their use to render such few harbors and streams as yet remained to them inaccessible, or in some degree dangerous to the victorious gunboats."

1–2　As spring blossomed in Virginia, General Grant's powerful army, outnumbering Lee's several times, unleashed its final attack.　On 1 April he outflanked Lee's thin lines southwest of Petersburg in the battle of Five Forks.　He ordered an all-out assault on Petersburg along the entire front for the 2nd.　Union batteries fired all night preparing for the attack—and Fort Sedgwick's heavy fire again earned it the nickname "Fort Hell."　Porter's fleet made a feint attack.　The Confederates fought fiercely in Petersburg throughout the 2nd, but one by one the strong points fell.　That night Lee withdrew.

Mrs. Lincoln had returned to Washington on *River Queen* on 1 April.　The President embarked in *Malvern* with Porter.　His "bunk was too short for his length, and he was compelled to fold his legs the first night," but Porter's carpenters remodeled the cabin on the sly, and the second morning Lincoln appeared at breakfast with the story that he had shrunk "six inches in length and about a foot sideways."　During the evening of the 2nd the two sat on the upper deck of the ship listening to the artillery and musket fire ashore as General Grant's troops, having rendered Richmond untenable with a crushing victory in the day long battle at Petersburg, closed in on the Confederate capital.　Lincoln asked the Admiral: "Can't the Navy do something at this particular moment to make history?"　Porter's reply was a tribute to the officers and men throughout the Navy who all during the war made history through vital if often unheralded deeds: "The Navy is doing its best just now, holding the enemy's four [three] heavy iron-clads in utter uselessness.　If those vessels could reach City Point they would commit great havoc. . . ."　Grant's position on the Petersburg—Richmond front had long depended on holding City Point where water borne supplies could be brought.　The Federal fleet maintained this vital base.

2　Supporting General Sherman in North Carolina, Commander Macomb reported to Porter: "In obedience to directions contained in your letter of the 28th ultimo, I started yesterday evening from Plymouth with the *Shamrock, Wyoming, Hunchback, Valley City,* and *Whitehead* and proceeded up this river as far as the Stumpy Reach (about 10 miles from the mouth), where we came to anchor

Rear Admiral Semmes destroys his James River ironclads as the Confederacy evacuates Richmond.

for the night. We had proceeded this far without dragging for torpedoes, in order to make quicker time (the river being broad and not suitable for torpedoes), but on starting this morning we dragged the channel ahead of us, in which manner we advanced all day, and reached this place about 5 p.m. without having encountered any resistance or finding any torpedoes . . . I have brought up with me three large flats, with which I can ferry the regiment over. I left orders at New Berne for the *Commodore Hull* and *Shokokon* to join me as soon as possible.

"On our way up the river this morning we were overtaken by three canal boats loaded with troops (which had come from Norfolk, I believe), which followed us up and are now lying along the western shore, the troops having debarked on that side." He concluded with a request for coal for the warships. Happily, two coal schooners from Philadelphia arrived at New Bern that same day and were soon enroute to him. Coal was a problem all during the war. Without bases for supply on the Confederate coast the Union Navy could not have carried out its ceaseless attacks and blockade.

2–4 Secretary of the Navy Mallory ordered the destruction of the Confederate James River Squadron and directed its officers and men to join General Lee's troops then in the process of evacuating Richmond and retreating westward toward Danville. As Mallory left Richmond with Davis and his cabinet late at night on the 2nd, the train passed over the James River. Later, as a prisoner of war at Fort Lafayette, the Secretary reflected on his thoughts at that time: "The James River squadron, with its ironclads, which had lain like chained bulldogs under the command of Rear Admiral Raphael Semmes to prevent the ascent of the enemy's ships, would, in the classic flash of the times, 'go up' before morning . . . ; and the naval operations of the Confederacy east of the Mississippi would cease."

Mallory's orders to destroy the squadron were carried out by Semmes. After outfitting his men with arms and field equipment, the admiral burned and scuttled the three formidable ironclads, C.S.S. *Virginia No. 2*, *Fredericksburg*, and *Richmond* near Drewry's Bluff. By 3 a.m. on 3 April the ironclads were well afire, and Semmes placed his 400 men on the wooden gunboats. Semmes later wrote: "My little squadron of wooden boats now moved off up the river [to Richmond], by the glare of the burning iron-clads. They had not proceeded far before an explosion, like the shock of an earthquake, took place, and the air was filled with missiles. It was the blowing up of the *Virginia* [No. 2], my late flag-ship. The spectacle was grand beyond description. Her shell-rooms had been full of loaded shells. The explosion of the magazine threw all these shells, with their fuses lighted, into the air. The fuses were of different lengths, and as the shells exploded by twos and threes, and by the dozen, the pyrotechnic effect was very fine. The explosion shook the houses in Richmond, and must have waked the echoes of the night for forty miles around."

Semmes disembarked his men at Richmond, then put the torch to the gunboats and set them adrift. The naval detachment, seeking transportation westward out of the evacuated Confederate capital, was forced to provide its own. The sailors found and fired up a locomotive, assembled and attached a number of railroad cars, and proceeded to Danville, arriving on the 4th. Semmes was commissioned a Brigadier General and placed in command of the defenses that had been thrown up around Danville. These defenses were manned by sailors who had been organized into an artillery brigade and by two battalions of infantry. This command was retained by Semmes until Lee's surrender at Appomattox.

3 Fifty of the sixty Midshipmen at the Confederate Naval Academy, under the command of Lieutenant William H. Parker, escorted the archives of the government and the specie and bullion of the treasury from Richmond to Danville. There, Midshipman Raphael Semmes, Junior, was detached from the escort corps and detailed to the staff of his father. The Midshipmen Corps continued to be entrusted with this select guard duty during subsequent moves of the archives and treasury to Charlotte, North Carolina; Washington, Georgia; Augusta, Georgia; and finally to Abbeville, South Carolina (see entries for 8–11, 17–19, and 24–29 April). The ten Midshipmen

Two of the outstanding Confederate naval officers—Matthew Fontaine Maury and Raphael Semmes.

who remained in Richmond under the command of Lieutenant James W. Billups, CSN, fired and scuttled C.S.S. *Patrick Henry*, schoolship of the Naval Academy.

3-4　As General Lee withdrew from the lines he had so long and brilliantly held, the Federal fleet sought to move on with the Army into Richmond; however, many hazards lay in the course. Rear Admiral Porter had ordered: "Remove all torpedoes carefully and such of the obstructions as may prevent the free navigation of the river, using our torpedoes for this purpose if necessary. Be careful and thorough in dragging the river for torpedoes and send men along the banks to cut the wires."

Sweeping for the torpedoes (mines) was conducted by some 20 boats from 10 ships in the flotilla. Lieutenant Commander Ralph Chandler, directing the sweeping operations, gave detailed orders: "Each boat's bow laps the port quarter of the boat just ahead and will lap within the 2 or 3 feet of her. Each vessel will send an officer to take charge of the two boats. Lieutenant Gillett of the *Sangamon*, and Lieutenant Reed, of the *Lehigh*, will have charge of shore parties to keep ahead of the boats and cut all torpedo wires. The wires should be cut in two places. Lieutenant Gillett will take the right bank going up and Lieutenant Reed the left. Twenty men from the *Monadnock* will be detailed for this service and will be armed as skirmishers with at least twenty rounds of ammunition. Two pairs of shears should be furnished the shore parties. The officer in charge will throw out the pickets, leaving two men to follow the beach to cut the wires." With the upper river cleared of torpedoes and obstructions, Union ships steamed up to Richmond.

3-6　General Lee, in his hardpressed and hurried evacuation of Richmond, neglected to apprise Commodore John R. Tucker, commanding the Confederate Naval Brigade at Drewry's Bluff on the James River, of the projected evacuation of the capital. Tucker maintained his station until the 3rd when he saw the smoke from the burning ironclads and learned that Confederate troops were streaming out of Richmond. Tucker then joined the Naval Brigade to Major General Custis Lee's division of Lieutenant General Richard S. Ewell's corps. The brigade participated in Ewell's rear guard stand at Sailor's Creek on 6 April which was intended to cover the westward retreat. The Naval Brigade was captured along with Ewell's entire corps but was the last unit in the corps to surrender. Tucker tendered his sword to Lieutenant General J. Warren Keifer. Some years after the war, when Keifer had become a prominent member of Congress, he returned the sword to the ex-Confederate naval officer.

4　Rear Admiral Porter accompanied President Lincoln up the James River to Richmond on board flagship *Malvern*. When obstructions blocked the flagship's way, the two embarked in Porter's barge, with three aides and boat crew of twelve. Thus, in a single small boat under oars, significantly by water, the President reached the Southern capital that for four years had been so near for conquest by the Union armies, yet had so long been held safe by the remarkable Lee and his hard fighting armies.

"It was a mild spring day. Birds were singing in the orchards on either side of the river, and the trees were in bloom. As the party pulled up the river they saw a wide curtain of smoke rise on the horizon ahead. Richmond was on fire. On evacuating the city the Confederates had fired their magazines and warehouses of cotton and tobacco; and bursting projectiles had dropped over the town, setting fire to a wide swath of dwellings and buildings in the business district.

"The party landed about one block above Libby Prison. Porter formed ten of the sailors into a guard. They were armed with carbines. Six marched in front and four in rear, and in the middle with the President and the Admiral walked Captain Penrose, Lincoln's military aide, Captain Adams of the Navy, and Lieutenant Clemens of the Signal Corps. Lincoln with his tall hat towered more than a foot above the thick-set Admiral, whose flat seaman's cap emphasized his five feet seven inches. The President "was received with the strongest demonstrations of joy." In his report to Secretary Welles, Porter wrote: "We found that the rebel rams and gunboats had all been blown up, with the exception of an unfinished ram, the *Texas*, and a small tug gunboat, the *Beaufort*, mounting one gun."

Boat crews from the Union fleet regularly patrolled the James River.

The ships destroyed included the 4-gun ironclads *Virginia No. 2*, *Richmond*, and *Fredericksburg;* wooden ships *Nansemond*, 2 guns; *Hampton*, 2 guns; *Roanoake*, 1 gun; *Torpedo*, *Shrapnel*, and school-ship *Patrick Henry*. "Some of them are in sight above water, and may be raised," Porter wrote. "They partly obstruct the channel where they are now, and will either have to be raised or blown up." He added: "Tredegar Works and the naval depot remain untouched." With its James River Squadron destroyed and its capital evacuated, the Confederacy was certain to fall soon. As Vice Admiral Farragut, who had preceded the President and Porter to Richmond, said: "Thank God, it is about over."

General Canby requested Rear Admiral Thatcher to provide assistance in the form of "eight or ten boats . . . and fifty or sixty sailors to row them" for the purpose of moving troops to assault Batteries Tracy and Huger, part of Mobile's defenses. The Admiral agreed to supply the boats but noted: "To send sixty men in these boats to row them will be nearly a load for them, at least they will be nearly filled with their own crews, so that an assaulting party would find but little room in them, particularly as our vessels are all small and their boats proportionally so. I would therefore respectfully suggest that your assaulting party be drilled at the oars."

A naval battery of three 30-pounder Parrott rifles, seamen manned and commanded by Lieutenant Commander Gillis, the former captain of the torpedoed monitor *Milwaukee*, was landed on the banks of the Blakely River to join in the bombardment of Spanish Fort, the Confederate strong-

President Lincoln visits the Richmond house recently occupied by President Jefferson Davis.

point in the defense of Mobile. General Canby reported that the "battery behaved admirably." (See 8 April.)

5 Steamer *Harriet DeFord* was boarded and seized in Chesapeake Bay, 30 miles below Annapolis, Maryland, by a party of 27 Confederate guerrillas led by Captain T. Fitzhugh. A naval detachment under Lieutenant Commander Edward Hooker was sent in pursuit and found *Harriet DeFord* trapped in Dimer's Creek, Virginia, burned to the water's edge. A captive reported that a pilot had taken the steamer into the creek and that she went aground several times. Some of the cargo was thrown overboard to lighten the ship and the remainder was unloaded with the help of local farmers before the torch was put to the steamer.

Commander Macomb steadily pushed up the narrowing Chowan River and its tributaries preparing for General Sherman's move north. This date he reported from "Meherrin River, near Murfreesboro, N.C." near the Virginia border and far inland: "The steamer *Shokokon* arrived at Winton yesterday, and I have stationed her a short distance below here near an ugly bluff some 60 or 80 feet high, on which I thought the rebels might give us some trouble on our return. There were some rifle pits on the brow of this bluff, but I sent a party down there and had them filled up. There is also an old earthwork, made to mount six guns, a short distance below here, which I have had partially destroyed. The river is rather narrower than the Roanoke, but not quite so crooked. I got 50 men (soldiers) from Winton to hold the bluff till we have passed, the river being very crooked and narrow at this point, so much so that we are unable to steam by, but will have to warp the ship round."

6   Acting Lieutenant John Rogers, commanding both U.S.S. *Carondelet* and Eastport, Mississippi, station, wrote Brigadier General Edward Hatcher about joint operations in the area and expressed a desire to cooperate to the extent of his ability: ". . . if you are in danger of being attacked by the Enemy . . . send timely notice to us, that everything connected with the Army and Navy may work harmoniously together." From the early moments of the war, such as the Battle of Belmont (see 7 November 1861), to the last days of conflict, the usual close coordination of the Army and Navy enabled the Union to strike quickly and effectively in the West—first against Confederate positions and later against Confederate threats.

    Lieutenant Commander Ramsay indicated the extent of the Confederate underwater defences of the James River as he reported to Rear Admiral Porter on an expedition aimed at clearing out the torpedoes: "All galvanic batteries were carried off or destroyed. At Chaffin's Bluff there was a torpedo containing 1,700 pounds of powder. At Battery Semmes there were two, containing 850 pounds each, and at Howlett's one containing 1,400 pounds. I cut the wires of them all close down, so that they are now perfectly harmless."

7   Commander Macomb reported to Rear Admiral Porter on developments in North Carolina near the Virginia border: "We arrived here [Winton] from Murfreesboro last night without accident. The army force has returned and we are going back to Suffolk. They found Weldon too strong for them, but succeeded in cutting the Seaboard Railroad near Seaboard for about a mile. I shall lie here some time longer in order to be ready for any more troops that may wish to cross."

8   Invested by General Canby's troops and bombarded heavily by the big guns of Rear Admiral Thatcher's ships, Spanish Fort and Fort Alexis, keys to Mobile, finally fell. In reporting the capture to Secretary Welles, Thatcher noted the efficiency of the naval battery on shore under Lieutenant Commander Gillis. He added: "Eighteen large submerged torpedoes were taken by our boats from Apalachee or Blakely River last night in the immediate vicinity of our gunboats. These are the only enemies that we regard." The loss of half a dozen vessels near Mobile since *Tecumseh* was sunk in August 1864 during Admiral Farragut's celebrated battle, which gave the Union control of Mobile Bay, had taught Northern naval officers an unforgettable lesson about torpedo warfare. The Confederate defenders, who suffered heavy casualties during the siege of the forts, were supported by a squadron under Flag Officer Ebenezer Farrand, including C.S.S. *Nashville, Morgan, Huntsville, Tuscaloosa,* and *Baltic* (see 11–12 April).

8–11   Lieutenant W. H. Parker, commander of the Midshipmen who were escorting the Confederate archives and treasury, arrived in Charlotte, North Carolina, from Danville (see 3 April) and deposited the important cargo in the Confederate Mint located in that city. While awaiting further orders, Parker learned that a Union cavalry detachment was nearby and since the city was without military protection, the naval officer, on his own initiative, prepared to move the archives and treasury southward. He added the uniformed personnel of the local Navy Yard to his escort, bringing its numbers up to 150 and drew quantities of provisions from the naval warehouse. Parker offered the protection of his command to Mrs. Jefferson Davis, who had only recently arrived in Charlotte, and strongly urged that she accompany him southward. Mrs. Davis accepted Parker's offer, and on the 11th the Navy-escorted entourage bearing the archives, treasury, and first lady of the Confederacy set out from Charlotte (see 17–19 April).

9   General Lee met General Grant at Appomattox Court House and formally surrendered the Army of Northern Virginia. Rear Admiral Semmes and his naval brigade charged with the defense of Danville were included in the surrender. Lee's struggle to break free from Grant's overwhelming armies, well fed and supplied from City Point, had failed. His effort to join Johnston, hopefully far enough from the sea to limit Grant's logistic advantage, had come fatefully to the end. One of the greatest armies and leaders of history without an adequate Navy had succumbed to the united power of land and sea.

Robert E. Lee
General of the Armies, CSA

President Jefferson Davis

The contrast between the two Generals at the confrontation in the living room of the McLean House was most striking. Grant's mud splattered uniform was that of a private with only the shoulder straps of a Lieutenant General to designate his rank. His uniform was unbuttoned at the neck and was unadorned by either sword or spurs. Lee on the other hand had taken special pains for this last act of the drama as if dressing for execution. His uniform was immaculate, his jewel studded sword of the finest workmanship. His well-polished boots were ornamented with red stitching and set off by a handsome pair of spurs.

After conversing about their Mexican War experiences, Lee asked the terms upon which his surrender would be accepted. Grant replied: "The terms I propose are those stated substantially in my letter of yesterday,—that is, the officers and men surrendered to be paroled and disqualified from taking up arms again until properly exchanged, and all arms, ammunition and supplies to be delivered up as captured property." Lee agreed to the terms and Grant then wrote them out. He specifically provided that Confederate officers would be permitted to retain their side arms, horses and luggage. This exemption was further broadened, at Lee's suggestion, to permit the men in the ranks to retain their horses and mules. Lee observed that these exemptions "were very gratifying and will do much toward conciliating our people." The long, bitter war was ending ashore, although fiery drama still awaited in far off Northern seas.

Blockade runner *Chameleon* (formerly C.S.S. *Tallahassee*), Lieutenant Wilkinson, put into Liverpool, England. With the fall of both Fort Fisher and Charleston in January and February respectively, Wilkinson had been unable to deliver his cargo of provisions destined for General Lee's destitute army defending Richmond (see 19 January and 5 February). Sealed off from the Confederacy, Wilkinson off-loaded his cargo at Nassau, took on board extra coal and set a course for Liverpool with the intention of turning the ship over to Commander Bulloch. However, the news of the fall of Richmond reached England on the 15th, followed a week later by the news of General Lee's surrender at Appomattox. Thus, the ship was seized by the British government and her officers and men, reported Wilkinson, "were turned adrift with the wide world before them where to choose." Wilkinson established his residence in Nova Scotia where he lived for a number of years before eventually returning to his native Virginia. The ex-Confederate ship was subsequently sold by the English government and was being prepared for service in the merchant marine under the name *Amelia* when the American government initiated court action to gain possession of the vessel. The court awarded the ship to the United States and she was turned over to the American consul at Liverpool on 26 April 1866.

10 Brigadier General Schimmelfennig, upon retiring from command of Charleston District, wrote Rear Admiral Dahlgren, commanding the South Atlantic Squadron, commending the Navy for its "hearty and most efficient assistance." He added: "When my troops advanced on to the enemy's ground, your gunboats and ironclads went up the rivers and creeks, covering my flanks, entirely regardless of the enemy's fire within most effective range. Under its cover I safely retreated, when necessary, over marshes and creeks without losing a man."

11 President Lincoln issued a proclamation warning nations that the continued denial of privileges and immunities to American naval vessels in foreign ports would result in the United States taking like action against foreign warships. "In the view of the United States," wrote the President, "no condition can be claimed to justify the denial to them [U.S. naval ships] by anyone of such nations of customary naval rights . . ." This document disputing the validity of any view attributing beligerent status to American warships was to be the President's last proclamation dealing with the Navy.

U.S.S. *Sea Bird*, Acting Master Ezra L. Robbins, seized sloops *Florida* and *Annie* with cargoes of cotton off Crystal River, Florida. Both were subsequently destroyed.

11–12 Batteries Tracy and Huger, up the Blakely River from Spanish Fort, fell to the Union forces on the 11th and the Confederate troops retreated through Mobile to Meridian, Mississippi. U.S.S. *Octorara*, with Commodore Palmer embarked, and the ironclads proceeded up the Blakely River to its intersection with the Tensas River and steamed down the latter to Mobile where they took bombarding position in front of the city. The gunboats, meanwhile, were conveying 8,000 troops across the head of the bay for the final attack on Mobile. The city, having been evacuated by the retreating Confederates, was surrendered to the Federal forces by the Mayor. Secretary Welles extended the Navy Department's congratulations to Rear Admiral Thatcher and Major General Granger "for this victory, which places in our possession, with but one exception, all the chief points on the Southern coast, and bids fair to be the closing naval contest of the rebellion." Before the evacuation of the city, ironclads C.S.S. *Huntsville* and *Tuscaloosa* were sunk in Spanish River. C.S.S. *Nashville*, *Baltic*, and *Morgan* sped up the Tombigbee River to avoid capture. With the Stars and Stripes raised over Mobile, the Union ironclads steamed upriver in pursuit of the Confederate ships (see 28–29 April).

12 Commander Bulloch, Confederate naval agent in England, wrote Secretary Mallory that wherever possible he had ordered all work on naval accounts stopped and that he intended to transfer the remainder of his outstanding balance to the account of the Confederate Treasury Department. Like the Confederate government itself, after a long and gallant effort the Southern Navy was going out of existence.

Having completed preparations for sailing from Lea Harbor, Lieutenant Waddell made his farewell call on the local "king" with whom he had become friendly. "His majesty," Waddell recorded, asked, "what was to be done with our prisoners. He supposed they would all be put to death, as he considered it right to make such disposition of one's enemies.

"I told him they would not be harmed, and that in civilized warfare men destroyed those in armed resistance and paroled the unarmed.

"'But,' said his Majesty, 'war cannot be considered civilized, and those who make war on an unoffending people are a bad people and do not deserve to live.'

"I told the king I would sail the following day, the 13th of April, and should tell our President of the kind hospitality he had shown to the officers of the *Shenandoah* and the respect he had paid our flag.

No. 61.

West Gulf Squadron,

U. S. Flag Ship Stockdale

Off Mobile

April 15th   1865.

Sir,

In my last despatch of the 12th instant
I had the honor to inform the Department that General
Granger and myself had demanded the immediate and
unconditional surrender of the City of Mobile and that
it would undoubtedly be accorded as the City was at
her mercy and we were in possession of the outside
Forts. The Officers detailed by General Granger and
myself were met by the mayor and other authorities near
the entrance of the City and the demand for its surrender
was there made. The parties then repaired to the City
Hall where the Mayor addressed us the following communication.

Mayor's Office, City of Mobile. April 12th 1865.

Gentlemen,

I have the honor to acknowledge the

Rear Admiral Thatcher announces the surrender of the city of Mobile.

"receipt of your communication at the hands of Lt.Col:
" R.G. Laughlin, Staff of Major General Granger Comdg:
" 13th Army Corps, and Lieut: Commander S.R. Franklin
" U.S. Navy, Staff of Admiral Thatcher, demanding the
" immediate and unconditional surrender of this City. The
" City has been evacuated by the Military Authorities, and
" its municipal authority is now within my control. Your
" demand has been granted, and I trust, Gentlemen, for
" the sake of humanity, all the safeguards which you can
" throw around our People will be secured to them."

Very Respectfully

Your Obdt: Servt.

(Signed)   R.H. Slough

Mayor of the City of Mobile

Maj.Genl. Gordon Granger

Commanding 13th Army Corps

Acting Rear Admiral H.K. Thatcher

Commanding West Gulf Squadron ".

The Flag of the United States was then hoisted
on the City Hall and a portion of the troops immediately
advanced to preserve order and to prevent pillage. The

"He said, 'Tell Jeff Davis he is my brother and a big warrior; that (we are) very poor, but that our tribes are friends. If he will send your steamer for me, I will visit him in his country. I send these two chickens to Jeff Davis (the chickens were dead) and some cocoanuts which he will find good.'"

13 After Appomattox, Confederate resistance elsewhere rapidiy gave way. From the North Carolina Sounds, Commander Macomb reported: "The rebels have evacuated Weldon, burning the bridge, destroying the ram at Edwards Ferry, and throwing the guns at Rainbow Bluff into the river. Except for torpedoes the [Roanoke] river is therefore clear for navigation. The floating battery, as I informed you in my No. 144, has got adrift from Halifax and been blown up by one of their own torpedoes."

U.S.S. *Ida*, Acting Ensign Franklin Ellms, struck a torpedo on her starboard side and sank in Mobile Bay. *Ida* was the fifth vessel in less than five weeks to be sunk by a Confederate torpedo in the vicinity of Mobile.

14 President Lincoln was shot shortly after 10 p.m. while watching "Our American Cousin" at Ford's Theatre. He died at 7:22 a.m. the next morning. Rear Admiral Porter, who had departed Hampton Roads on the 14th, learned, when his flagship, U.S.S. *Tristram Shandy* put into Baltimore on the morning of the 15th, that the President had been shot. The Admiral immediately went to Washington, where he learned that the President had died. The reaction of the tough, battle hardened sea dog to the news expressed the grief of a nation: Porter, who had bid the President a merry farewell exactly one week before at City Point, bowed his head and wept.

Union fleet standing off battered Fort Morgan, Mobile Bay.

In accordance with a previous directive of President Lincoln, Major General Anderson, commander of the Union Army forces at Fort Sumter on 14 April 1861, raised above Sumter's ruins "the same United States flag which floated over the battlements of that fort during the rebel assault, and which was lowered and saluted by him and the small force of his command when the works were evacuated on the 14th of April, 1861." As U.S.S. *Pawnee* had witnessed that event four years before, naval forces of Rear Admiral Dahlgren participated in this ceremony.

U.S.S. *Sciota*, Acting Lieutenant James W. Magune, struck a torpedo and sank off Mobile. Magune reported: "The explosion was terrible, breaking the beams of the spar deck, tearing open the waterways, ripping off starboard forechannels, and breaking fore-topmast." Dragging for and destroying torpedoes continued to be extremely hazardous duty. A launch from U.S.S. *Cincinnati*, Lieutenant Commander George Brown, was blown up and three men killed when a torpedo which was being removed accidentally swung against the boat's stern.

C.S.S. *Shenandoah*, Lieutenant James I. Waddell, departed Ascension Island, Eastern Carolines and set a northerly course for the Kurile Islands. Unaware that General Lee had surrendered at Appomattox on the 9th, *Shenandoah* would inflict crippling damage to the American whaling fleet in the North Pacific. The havoc wrought on Union commerce by Confederate raiders dealt the whaling industry a blow from which it never recovered.

15 Secretary Welles announced the assassination of President Lincoln to the officers and men of the Navy and Marine Corps. Welles wrote: "To him our gratitude was justly due, for to him, under God, more than to any other person, we are indebted for the successful vindication of the integrity of the Union and the maintenance of the power of the Republic." The President had continually demonstrated a keen interest in the Navy and far-seeing appreciation of seapower. Late in the afternoon of the 14th he had taken what was to be his last trip to the Washington Navy Yard to view three ironclads there that had been damaged during the Fort Fisher engagement. In the summer of 1863 he had written: "Nor must Uncle Sam's web feet be forgotten. At all the watery margins they have been present. Not only on the deep sea, the broad bay, the rapid river, but also up the narrow, muddy bayou, and wherever the ground was a little damp, they have been and made their tracks."

Welles sent a telegram to Commodore John B. Montgomery, Commandant of the Washington Navy Yard: "If the military authorities arrest the murderer of the President and take him to the Yard, put him on a monitor and anchor her in the stream, with strong guard on vessel, wharf, and in yard. Call upon commandant Marine Corps for guard. Have vessel immediately prepared to receive him at any hour, day or night, with necessary instructions. He will be heavily ironed and so guarded as to prevent escape or injury to himself."

16 Secretary Welles directed: "To prevent the escape of the assassin who killed the President and attempted the life of Secretary of State, search every vessel that arrives down the bay. Permit no vessel to go to sea without such search, and arrest and send to Washington any suspicious persons." Response was immediate; ships took stations "on the coast of Maryland and Virginia."

The Navy Department directed that on 17 April a gun be fired in honor of the late President Lincoln each half hour, from sunrise to sunset, that all flags be kept at half-mast until after the funeral, and that officers wear mourning crepe for six months.

17 The Confederate ironclad *Jackson* (previously *Muscogee*) was destroyed at Columbus, Georgia, after Union Army forces overran Southern defenses at the city in an attack that began the preceeding night. Major General George H. Thomas reported: "The rebel ram *Jackson*, nearly ready for sea, and carrying six 7-inch [rifled] guns, fell into our hands and was destroyed, as well as the navy yard, founderies, the arsenal and armory, sword and pistol factory . . . all of which were burned." Twelve miles below the city the Union troops found the burned hulk of C.S.S.

Chattahoochee which the Confederates themselves had destroyed. The navy yard at Columbus had been a key facility in the building of the machinery for Southern ironclads.

Sunken obstructions placed in the channel of Blakely River, Mobile Bay, Alabama, were removed by blasting directed by Master Adrian C. Starrett, U.S.S. *Maria A. Wood*, thus clearing navigational hazards from Mobile Bay.

Acting Master J. H. Eldridge, U.S.S. *Delaware*, reported that information had been received that the murderer of the President was in the vicinity of Point Lookout, Maryland. Secretary Welles promptly ordered the Commanding Officer of Naval Force, Hampton Roads, to send all available vessels to assist in the blockade of the eastern shore of Virginia and Maryland from Point Lookout to Baltimore.

17–19   Lieutenant W. H. Parker, commanding naval escort entrusted with the Confederate archives, treasury, and President Davis' wife, successfully evaded Federal patrols en route southward from Charlotte (see 8–11 April) and arrived at Washington, Georgia, on the 17th. Parker, still without orders as to the disposition of his precious trust and unable to learn of the whereabouts of

The Presidents' funeral cortege moves up Pennsylvania Avenue, Washington.

C.S.S. Jackson *(or Muscogee), ironclad steamer built at Columbus, Georgia, was destroyed in 1865 when Union overran Confederate positions on the Chattahoochee River, Georgia.*

President Davis and his party (including Secretary Mallory), decided to push on through to Augusta, Georgia, where he hoped to find ranking civilian and military officials. The escort commander recorded: "We left the ladies behind at the tavern in Washington for we expected now a fight at any time." The escort again, however, managed to elude Federal patrols and arrived without incident at Augusta where Parker placed his entrusted cargo in bank vaults and posted a guard around the building. Having learned upon arrival that armistice negotiations between Generals Sherman and Johnston were in progress, the escort commander decided to remain in the city and await the outcome of the conference.

17–25 Four of the five Lincoln assassination suspects arrested on the 17th were imprisoned on the monitors U.S.S. *Montauk* and *Saugus* which had been prepared for this purpose on the 15th and were anchored off the Washington Navy Yard in the Anacostia River. Mrs. Mary E. Surratt was taken into custody at the boarding house she operated after it was learned that her son was a close friend of John Wilkes Booth and that the actor was a frequent visitor at the boarding house. Mrs. Surratt was jailed in the Carroll Annex of Old Capitol Prison. Lewis Paine was also taken into custody when he came to Mrs. Surratt's house during her arrest. Edward Spangler, stagehand at the Ford Theater and Booth's aide, along with Michael O'Laughlin and Samuel B. Arnold, close associates of Booth during the months leading up to the assassination, were also caught up in the dragnet. O'Laughlin and Paine, after overnight imprisonment in the Old Capitol Prison, were transferred to the monitors at the Navy Yard. They were joined by Arnold on the 19th and Spangler on the 24th. George A. Atzerodt, the would-be assassin of Vice President Andrew Johnson, and Ernest Hartman Richter, at whose home Atzerodt was captured, were brought on board the ships on the 20th. João Celestino, Portuguese sea captain who had been heard to say on the 14th that Seward ought to be assassinated, was transferred from Old Capitol Prison to *Montauk* on the 25th. The last of the eight conspiracy suspects to be incarcerated on board the monitors was David E. Herold. The prisoners were kept below decks under heavy guard and were manacled with both wrist and leg irons. In addition, their heads were covered with canvas hoods the interior of which were fitted with cotton pads that tightly covered the prisoners' eyes and ears. The hoods contained two small openings to permit breathing and the consumption of food. An added security measure was taken with Paine by attaching a ball and chain to each ankle.

18 Vice Admiral Farragut, in whom President Lincoln had placed great confidence, wrote to his wife: "All the people in the city are going to see the President in state. I go tomorrow as one of the pall bearers." Meanwhile, the Navy was carrying out Secretary Welles instructions to search "all vessels going out of the [Potomac] river for the assassins. Detain all suspicious persons. Guard against all crossing of the river and touching of vessels or boats on the Virginia shore."

19 Secretary Welles recorded President Lincoln's funeral in his diary: "The funeral on Wednesday, the 19th, was imposing, sad, and sorrowful. All felt the solemnity, and sorrowed as if they had lost one of their own household. By voluntary action business was everywhere suspended, and the people crowded the streets . . . . The attendance was immense. The front of the procession reached the Capitol, it was said, before we started, and there as many, or more, who followed us. A brief prayer was made by Mr. [P.D.] Gurley in the rotunda, where we left the remains of the good and great man we loved so well."

U.S.S. *Lexington*, Acting Lieutenant William Flye, conveyed Colonel John T. Sprague, Chief of Staff to General John Pope, from Cairo and up the Red River to meet Confederate General Kirby Smith. At the ensuing conference, Smith was given the terms under which the surrender of his forces would be accepted.

Captain Benjamin F. Sands, commanding the ships of the West Gulf Blockading Squadron stationed off Galveston, reported that the blockade runner *Denbigh* had grounded on the Galveston bar attempting to put to sea under cover of night. "She succeeded in getting off by throwing over some 200 bales of cotton, about 140 of which were recovered by the *Cornubia* and *Gertrude* . . . ." Sands added that *Denbigh* was "next seen under Fort Point and returned to the city." However, the well known blockade runner, which Admiral Farragut had been especially anxious to capture prior to the fall of Mobile when *Denbigh* shifted to Galveston, shortly succeeded in running through the Union cordon and put into Havana on 1 May.

21 Major General Gillmore wrote Rear Admiral Dahlgren that he had received dispatches from Major General Sherman that a convention had been entered into with General Johnston, CSA, on the 18th whereby all Confederate armies were to be disbanded and a general suspension of hostilities would prevail until terms of surrender were agreed upon in Washington.

U.S.S. *Cornubia*, Acting Lieutenant John A. Johnstone, captured blockade running British schooner *Chaos* off Galveston with cargo of cotton.

22 Secretary Welles warned the Potomac Flotilla that "[John Wilkes] Booth was near Bryantown last Saturday [15 April], where Dr. Mudd set his ankle, which was broken by a fall from his horse [*sic*]. The utmost vigilance is necessary in the Potomac and Patuxent to prevent his escape. All boats should be searched . . . ." The condition of alert remained in effect until word of the assassin's death on 26 April was received.

Thomas Kirkpatrick, U.S. Consul at Nassau, New Providence, reported to Rear Admiral Stribling of the East Gulf Blockading Squadron that schooner *St. Mary's* had arrived in Nassau. The Baltimore schooner had been seized in Chesapeake Bay during a daring raid on 31 March by ten Confederates led by Master John C. Braine, CSN. Kirkpatrick pressed British authorities to seize the vessel and apprehend her crew for piracy. *St. Mary's* was permitted to put to sea, however, after being adjudged a legitimate prize.

23 In response to a telegram from Secretary Welles urging the utmost vigilance to prevent the escape of Jefferson Davis and his cabinet across the Mississippi, Rear Admiral S. P. Lee, commanding the Mississippi Squadron, directed: "The immediate engrossing and important duty is to capture

Jeff. Davis and his Cabinet and plunder. To accomplish this, all available means and every effort must be made to the exclusion of all interfering calls."

As the Navy vigorously sought to apprehend the assassin of President Lincoln, Secretary Welles directed Rear Admiral Porter: "Booth is endeavoring to escape by water. Send a gunboat or some tugs to examine the shore of Virginia and all vessels in that direction, and arrest and seize all suspicious parties. If you have any tugs to spare, send them into the Potomac."

23–24 C.S.S. *Webb*, Lieutenant Read, dashed from the Red River under forced draft and entered the Mississippi at 8:30 at night in a heroic last-ditch effort to escape to sea. Before departing Alexandria, Louisiana, for his bold attempt, Read wrote Secretary Mallory: "I will have to stake everything upon speed and time." The sudden appearance of the white-painted *Webb* in the Mississippi caught the Union blockaders (a monitor and two ironclads) at the mouth of the Red River by surprise. She was initially identified as a Federal ship; this mistake in identification gave Read a lead in the dash downstream. A running battle ensued in which *Webb* shook off the three Union pursuers. As Read proceeded down the Mississippi, other blockading ships took up the chase but were outdistanced by the fast moving *Webb*, which some observers claimed was making 25 knots. While churning with the current toward New Orleans, Read paused at one point to cut the telegraph wires along the bank. This proved futile as word of his escape and approach passed southward where it generated considerable excitement and a flurry of messages between the Army and Navy commanders who alerted shore batteries and ships to intercept him. About 10 miles above New Orleans Read hoisted the United States flag at half mast in mourning for Lincoln's death and brought *Webb*'s steam pressure up to maximum. He passed the city at about midnight, 24 April, going full speed. Federal gunboats opened on him, whereupon Read broke the Confederate flag. Three hits were scored, the spar torpedo rigged at the steamer's bow was damaged and had to be jettisoned, but the *Webb* continued on course toward the sea. Twenty-five miles below New Orleans Read's luck ran out, for here *Webb* encountered U.S.S. *Richmond*. Thus trapped between *Richmond* and pursuing gunboats, Read's audacious and well-executed plan came to an end. *Webb* was run aground and set on fire before her officers and men took to the swamps in an effort to escape. Read and his crew were apprehended within a few hours and taken under guard to New Orleans. They there suffered the indignity of being placed on public display but were subsequently paroled and ordered to their respective homes. Following the restoration of peace, Read became a pilot of the Southwest Pass, one of the mouths of the Mississippi River, and pursued that occupation until his death.

Engulfed in flames below New Orleans, C.S.S. Webb's *spectacular but futile dash for the open sea ends.*

The body of John Wilkes Booth examined on board U.S.S. Montauk *in Anacostia River off Washington Navy Yard.*

24-29   While in Augusta, Georgia, with the Confederate archives and treasury (see 17-19 April 1965), Lieutenant W. H. Parker learned that the Federal Government had rejected the convention of surrender drawn up by Generals Sherman and Johnston.   Parker withdrew his valuable cargo from the bank vaults, reformed his naval escort (consisting of Naval Academy midshipmen and sailors from the Charlotte Navy Yard) and on the 24th set out for Abbeville, South Carolina, which he had previously concluded to be the most likely city through which the Davis party would pass enroute to a crossing of the Savannah River.   Near Washington, Georgia, Parker met Mrs. Jefferson Davis, her daughter and Burton Harrison, the President's private secretary, proceeding independently to Florida with a small escort.   Gaining no information on the President's whereabouts, Parker continued to press toward Abbeville, while Mrs. Davis' party resumed its journey Southward.   On the 29th he arrived in Abbeville, where he stored his cargo in guarded rail cars and ordered a full head of steam be kept on the locomotive in case of emergency.   Parker's calculations as to the probable movements of President Davis' entourage proved correct; the chief executive entered Abbeville three days after Parker's arrival.

25   The search for President Lincoln's assassin followed rumors in all directions, and warships in the large Union Navy were available to speed the investigation.   The Navy Department ordered Commodore Radford at Hampton Roads: "Send a gunboat to the mouth of the Delaware for one week to examine and arrest all suspicious characters and vessels."

27   The body of John Wilkes Booth, Lincoln's assassin, and David E. Herold, who had accompanied Booth in the escape from Washington and was with the actor when he was shot, were delivered on board U.S.S. *Montauk*, anchored in the Anacostia River off the Washington Navy Yard.   Booth had been slain and Herold captured at John M. Garrett's farm three miles outside Port Royal,

Disastrous explosion destroys steamer Sultana *above Memphis with heavy loss of life.*

Virginia, in the early morning hours of the previous day. While the body was on board the monitor, an autopsy was performed and an inquiry conducted to establish identity. Booth's corpse was then taken by boat to the Washington Arsenal (now Fort McNair) where it was buried in a gun box the following day. Herold was incarcerated in the hold of *Montauk* which, along with U.S.S. *Saugus*, was being utilized for the maximum security imprisonment of eight of the suspected assassination conspirators.

Secretary Welles informed Commander F. A. Parker of the Potomac Flotilla that the "special restrictions relative to retaining vessels are removed." He advised the Flotilla commander that "Booth was killed and captured with Herold yesterday, 3 miles southwest of Port Royal, Va." With the search for President Lincoln's assassin ended, further south the Navy focused its attention to another end. This date, Rear Admiral Dahlgren ordered nine ships of his South Atlantic Blockading Squadron to patrol along the Southern coast to prevent the escape of Jefferson Davis and his cabinet.

River steamer *Sultana* blew up in the Mississippi River above Memphis, Tennessee, killing 1,450 out of 2,000 passengers—all but 50 of whom were former prisoners of war. She was en route to Cairo when a violent explosion ripped her apart and turned her into a sheet of flame. The cause of the explosion was never determined, but one of the theories advanced was that a coal torpedo—such as the one that was suspected of having destroyed Army steamer *Greyhound* (see 27 November 1864)—had been slipped into the steamer's coal bin.

Commodore William Radford, commanding the James River Flotilla, stationed U.S.S. *Tristram Shandy*, Acting Lieutenant Francis M. Green, at Cape Henry to watch for C.S.S. *Stonewall*. The next day Secretary Welles warned Radford that *Stonewall* had sailed from Teneriffe, Canary Islands, on 1 April and had steamed rapidly to the south. ". . . Every precaution should be taken to guard against surprise and to prevent her inflicting serious injury should she make her appearance anywhere within the limits of your command. . . ." Welles sent the same directive to Commander F. A. Parker of the Potomac Flotilla.

28 Secretary Welles directed Rear Admiral Thatcher of the West Gulf Blockading Squadron: "Lieutenant General Grant telegraphs to the War Department under date of the 26th instant, from Raleigh, N.C., that Jeff Davis, with his Cabinet, passed into South Carolina, with the intentions, no doubt, of getting out of the country, either via Cuba or across the Mississippi. All the vigilance and available means at your command should be brought to bear to prevent the escape of those leaders of the rebellion."

Rear Admiral Thatcher reported to Secretary Welles that U.S.S. *Octorara*, *Sebago*, and *Winnebago* were up the Tombigbee River, Alabama, blockading C.S.S. *Nashville* and *Morgan*. The Confederate ships had steamed upriver when Mobile fell. The Admiral concluded: "They must soon fall into our hands or destroy themselves."

29 Secretary Welles congratulated Rear Admiral Thatcher and his men on their part in bringing about the fall of Mobile: "Although no bloody strife preceded the capture . . ., the result was none the less creditable. Much has been expended to render it invulnerable, and nothing but the well-conducted preparations for its capture, which pointed to success, could have induced the rebel commander to abandon it with its formidable defenses, mounting nearly 400 guns, many of them of the newest pattern and heaviest caliber, its abundant supply of ammunition and ordnance stores, and its torpedo-planted roads and waters, without serious conflict."

U.S.S. *Donegal*, Acting Lieutenant George D. Upham, was ordered to cruise from Bull's Bay, South Carolina, to the Savannah River in search of C.S.S. *Stonewall*.

Acting Master W. C. Coulson, commanding U.S.S. *Moose* on the Cumberland River, led a surprise attack on a Confederate raiding party, numbering about 200 troops from Brigadier General Abraham Buford's command. The raiders under the command of a Major Hopkins, were crossing the Cumberland River to sack and burn Eddyville, Kentucky. Coulson sank two troop laden boats with battery gunfire and then put a landing party ashore which engaged the remaining Confederates. The landing force dispersed the detachment after killing or wounding 20 men, taking 6 captives, and capturing 22 horses.

30 The eight suspects in the Lincoln assassination plot who had been imprisoned on monitors U.S.S. *Montauk* and *Saugus* were transferred to the Arsenal Penitentiary, located in the compound of what is today Fort McNair. This was also the site of their trial by a military tribunal which returned its verdict on 30 June 1865. Three of the eight, along with Mrs. Mary E. Surratt, were hanged in the prison yard of the penitentiary on 7 July—Lewis Paine who made the unsuccessful assassination attempt on Secretary of State Seward; George A. Atzerodt who had been designated by Booth to murder Vice President Johnson; and David E. Herold who had accompanied Booth in his escape from the city. Michael O'Laughlin and Samuel B. Arnold, boyhood friends of Booth and conspirators in the actor's earlier plans to abduct President Lincoln and in his later plans to assassinate the government's top officials, were sentenced to life in prison. Another accomplice, Edward Spangler, stagehand at the Ford Theater was sentenced to six years in prison. The remaining two of the eight who had been incarcerated on the monitors—Ernest Hartman Richter, a cousin of Atzerodt, and Joao Celestino, a Portuguese sea captain—were released without being brought to trial.

MAY

1-15 During this period, *Shenandoah* "made northings" towards the Bering Sea whaling ground through pleasant seas that would soon change in the high parallels. After departing Lea Harbor, Ponape, in the Caroline Islands, on 13 April, the lone raider had experienced fine cruising—except for lack of prizes. Waddell wrote:

"Never in our various experience of sea life had any of us seen such or more charming weather than we now enjoyed. The sun shone with a peculiar brilliancy and the moon shed that clear, soft light which is found in this locality, in which the heavens seem so distant and so darkly blue, while the vast expanse of ocean was like a great reflecting mirror. The track for vessels bound from San Francisco and many of the ports on the west coast of America to Hong Kong lies between the parallels in north latitude of 17° and 20°. Here the winds are better than are found in a more northerly route, while the track to San Francisco and other ports along the west coast of America from China lies between the parallels of 35° and 45°, because here west winds prevail . . .

"After the vessel had reached the parallel of 43° north the weather became cold and foggy and the winds were variable and unsteady, and that ever reliable friend of the sailor, the barometer, indicated atomspheric changes.

"The ship was prepared for the change of weather which was rapidly approaching. Soon the ocean was boiling with agitation, and if the barometer had been silent, I would have called it only a furious tide but a dark, then a black cloud,was hurrying towards us from the N. E. and so close did it rest upon the surface of the water that is seemed determined to overwhelm the ship, and there came in it so terrible and violent a wind that the *Shenandoah* was thrown on her side. . . .

"Squall after squall struck her, flash after flash surrounded her, and the thunder rolled in her wake. It was the typhoon. The ocean was as white as the snow and foamed with rage. A new close-reefed main topsail was blown into shreds, and the voice of man was inaudible amid this awful convolution of nature. . . ."

2 Commander Matthew F. Maury sailed from England carrying $40,000 worth of electric torpedo equipment which he was confident could be used to keep Galveston harbor open for the Confederacy. He had developed what today is known as a controlled mine system during the two and a half years that he served in Europe with Commander Bulloch. It was a harbor defense system consisting of a planted mine field with each mine in a charted position and capable of being separately detonated by closing an electrical circuit from ashore when the target ship is within a mine's lethal range. Maury, a pioneer in mine warfare as well as oceanography, had devised the system working in close conjunction with British naval engineers. He prophetically appraised the system as being "as effective for the defense as ironclads and rifled guns are for the attack. . . . I feel justified in the opinion that hereafter in all plans for coast, harbor, and river defense . . . the electrical torpedo is to play an important part." Upon arriving at Havana, Maury learned of the collapse of the Confederacy and he stored the equipment in the city.

President Davis, accompanied by most of his cabinet and other ranking officials of the Confederacy, entered Abbeville, South Carolina, escorted by the remnants of four brigades of cavalry commanded by Brigadier General Basil Duke. The President's cavalry train was met there by Lieutenant W. H. Parker, commanding the 150 man naval escort which had safely transported and guarded the Confederate archives and treasury during the thirty day journey from Richmond (see 24-29 April). Parker transfered his cargo to Acting Secretary of the Treasury John Reagan and was instructed by him to deliver it to General Duke. Upon completing the transfer, Parker disbanded his command; but with a lingering optimism for the Confederacy's future, he ordered each of his Midshipmen: "You are hereby detached from the naval school, and leave is granted you to visit your home. You will report by letter to the Hon. Secretary of the Navy as soon as practicable." Later in the day, Parker conferred with the President and advised him that his chances for escape would be greatly enhanced if he would abandon his large cavalry escort and leave "now with a few followers and cross the Mississippi, as you express a desire to do eventually, and there again raise the standard." President Davis, after proceeding to Washington, Georgia, from Abbeville, did replace the cavalry train with a 10 man mounted escort. However, rather than immediately setting out for the trans-Mississippi west, the President detoured and overtook his wife fleeing toward the Florida coast. He travelled with his family until the 10th in an effort to see them safely through threatening marauders, and was captured by a unit of the Fourth Michigan Cavalry while encamped near Irwinville, Georgia, on the eve of his intended departure for the west.

2–3 Secretary Mallory penned a brief letter of resignation while at Abbeville and handed it to President Davis on the 3rd at Washington, Georgia, where Mallory took leave of his chief. "The misfortunes of our country," wrote the Navy Secretary, "have deprived me of the honor and opportunity longer to serve her, and the hour has approached when I can no longer be useful to you personally. Cheerfully would I follow you and share whatever fate may befall you, could I hope thereby in any degree to contribute to your safety or happiness. The dependent condition of a helpless family prevents my departure from the country, and under these circumstances it is proper that I should request you to accept my resignation as Secretary of the Navy." President Davis accepted the resignation with deep regret and added: "For the zeal, ability and integrity with which you have so long and so constantly labored, permit one who had the best opportunity to judge, to offer testimonial and in the name of our country and its sacred cause to return thanks." Mallory then set out for La Grange, Georgia, to join his family and "to await the action of the [United States] government."

3 Secretary Welles ordered the reduction of the Potomac Flotilla to one-half its strength; however, execution of the order was temporarily postponed while C.S.S. *Stonewall* was reported to be still at large.

As Commodore J. S. Palmer was detached from the West Gulf Blockading Squadron, Major General Canby wrote him: "The relations that have existed between the two services for the past year have been of the most intimate and cordial character and have resulted in successes of which the friends of both the Army and the Navy have reason to be proud."

4 C.S.S. *Ajax*, Lieutenant Low, entered St. George's, Bermuda, from Nassau. The Confederate captain had not yet learned that his government had collapsed, that Generals Lee and Johnston had surrendered the preceding month. He attempted to obtain guns for delivery to Havana but Governor W. G. Hamley refused to permit it. He advised Low: "The *Ajax* has been a suspected vessel ever since she was launched. She has the appearance of a gunboat; she has never carried merchant cargo; she changed owners at Nassau; she is now commanded by an officer in the service of the Confederate States; in short, she wants nothing but armament to be in a position to take the seas as a privateer."

Rear Admiral Thatcher accepted an offer from Commodore Ebenezer Farrand, CSN, to surrender "all Confederate naval forces, officers, men, and public property yet afloat under his command and now blockaded by a portion of our naval forces in the Tombigbee River [Alabama]." The formal capitulation took place on the 10th and included C.S.S. *Nashville*, *Morgan*, *Baltic*, and *Black Diamond*.

8 U.S.S. *Isonomia*, Lieutenant L. D. D. Voorhees, captured blockade running British bark *George Douthwaite* off the Warrior River, Florida, with cargo of sugar, rum, wool, ginger, and mahogany.

10 The blockade of the coast of the states east of the Mississippi was partially raised in accordance with President Johnson's Executive Order of 29 April, 1865. General Order No. 53, which implemented the President's instruction, directed: "The entrance of vessels into ports within the designated territory will not be interrupted or interfered with when the same are provided with a regular United States customhouse clearance, and there is no reasonable ground for suspicion that they have contraband of war on board."

Signs of battle are visible on turret of U.S. monitor Catskill *anchored in Charleston harbor.*

11–19 The escape of the ram C.S.S. *Stonewall* from Ferrol, Spain, and Lisbon, Portugal (see 24 and 27 March), which created a great deal of excitement at the time, did not lead to battle. The ironclad put into Havana on the 11th without having spoken a single Union ship enroute from the Canary Islands. Upon learning of *Stonewall*'s arrival, Rear Admiral Cornelius K. Stribling, commanding the East Gulf Blockading Squadron, dispatched a squadron, led by U.S.S. *Powhatan* and commanded by Commander Reed Werden, to cruise off Havana and engage the Confederate ram when she departed. However, Captain T. J. Page, *Stonewall*'s commander, learning of the collapse of the Confederacy, delivered the ship over to the Governor General of Cuba and in turn received $16,000—the amount of money Page required to pay off his officers and crew. Subsequently the ship was turned over to the United States and was ultimately sold to Japan.

13 C.S.S. *Shenandoah*, then south of the Kuriles, steadily headed North, her position unknown in the vast distances of the Pacific. The threat of this single raider, however, created consternation far across the world. The merchants of New London, Connecticut, requested Secretary Welles to protect their whaling vessels in the Arctic and Pacific Oceans from the destructive raids

of C.S.S. *Shenandoah*. Previously New England ship owners had sought protection by purchasing additional insurance. When the news arrived from England that *Shenandoah* was on her way to the Arctic, the leading maritime insurance carrier in New England did a booming business. In a three day period the Atlantic Mutual Insurance Company collected $350,000 in premiums from shipowners increasing coverage on their vessels. During the course of one day alone, the company received $118,978 in premiums—the largest sum written by the company during a 24 hour period until the start of World War I.

15 Secretary Welles wrote Rear Admiral Thatcher of the West Gulf Blockading Squadron that "it appears that blockade running at Galveston is still carried on with much success." Between 15 April and 1 May six runners, including the elusive *Denbigh*, were reported to have put into Havana with cargoes of cotton, all from Galveston.

16 President Davis, his family, and Confederate officials captured with him at Irwinville, Georgia, on the 10th were taken down the Savannah River to Port Royal. They were placed on board the steamer *William P. Clyde*, Master John L. Kelly, Shipmaster. The steamer was escorted on her passage to Hampton Roads by U.S.S. *Tuscarora*, Commander James M. Frailey.

17 After weathering an earlier typhoon (see 1–15 May), C.S.S. *Shenandoah* encountered a second less violent blow. "The weather continued so threatening that it looked impossible for the *Shenandoah* to get north of the parallel of 45, but the last gale, like its predecessor, had worked to the westward, and the ship began to make her northing again," Waddell wrote. "On the 17th of May we were north of the parallel of 45 and the weather, though cold, looked more settled, and we took a long breath."

20 A board appointed by Secretary Welles and headed by Vice Admiral Farragut began a comprehensive investigation and review of the Naval Academy. Its normal functioning, like almost everything in the nation, had been greatly disrupted by the war. The Academy had suffered especially through the enforced move to Newport of staff and students in *Constitution* early in the war and the telescoping of the academic course. The Board had been commissioned to report its findings and make recommendations for improving the school as a training institution for naval officers. The study and the resulting report covered the material condition and adequacy of the buildings, grounds and training ships; administration and finance; sanitation and medical care; system of appointments and entrance requirements; and the quality of classroom and shipboard instruction.

The Board's studies and the changes that followed achieved the goals. In the ensuing years the Academy would produce some of the nation's great leaders. These not only included those who led the Navy, adapted it to the changing times and directed it in the great task of world leadership that swiftly flowered for the United States in the next century. They also included some of the nation's famous leaders in industry, engineering, education, science. Within little more than a decade, Albert A. Michelson, Class of 1873, would conduct the first of his notable experiments on the speed of light at Annapolis. Returning as a young officer from sea duty to teach, he developed the apparatus and conducted the experiments with midshipmen associates.

Secretary Welles indicated the Navy Department's continuing concern about blockade running from Galveston in his order to Rear Admiral Thatcher: "Seven large steamers have arrived abroad from Galveston in nine days. As this is the only port in the United States where traffic can be carried on to any extent, it is desirable that the majority of vessels and the best officer you have should be on duty as senior officer off that port."

Former Secretary Mallory was arrested at the home of Benjamin H. Hill in La Grange, Georgia, and charged with "treason and with organizing and setting on foot piratical expeditions." He was taken to New York and imprisoned at Fort Lafayette, where he remained until paroled in March 1866. Mallory was the last Confederate cabinet officer to gain his freedom. Returning to Pensacola he entered into law practice with Augustus E. Maxwell and wrote newspaper articles attacking the reconstruction policies. Mallory died in November 1873.

Steadily breasting northward, C.S.S. *Shenandoah*, Lieutenant Waddell, sighted the Kuriles "covered with snow".

21 C.S.S. *Shenandoah* entered the Sea of Okhotsk "and ran along the coast of Kamchatka under sail. There is a strong current along the Pacific side of these islands setting to the N. E. which clings to the eastern shore on to the Arctic Ocean, and how much further northward man knoweth not."

22 Commander Macomb, commanding in Albemarle Sound, reported U.S. Picket Boat No. 5 had seized steamers *Skirwan*, *Cotton Plant*, *Fisher* and *Egypt Mills*, as well as a small, unfinished steamer, near Halifax, Roanoke River, North Carolina.

Commander Matthew Fontaine Maury arrived in Havana in S.S. *Atrato* and learned of General Johnston's surrender. Realizing the futility of his intended efforts, he abandoned plans to proceed with his electric torpedo equipment to Galveston for the defense of that harbor. He placed the material ashore in custody for Commander Bulloch. As he wrote later to his wife: "I left $30,000 or $40,000 worth of torpedoes, telegraphic wire, etc. which I bought for the defense of Richmond. Bulloch paid for them but they were left in Havana at the breakup, subject to my orders. I write by this mail directing that they be turned over to Bulloch. Now they don't belong to him, neither do they to me. But it is quite a relief to get rid of them by transferring them to a man who I am sure will make the most proper use of them. I did not want any of the $10,000 or $20,000 which they will bring, though some one will get it who has no more right to it than I have."

Maury's keen sense of honor was borne out by the audit of his accounts delivered to him shortly before he sailed for England. Bulloch's assistant wrote: "Although the custom here would have sanctioned your receiving a large per centum in the way of commission on contracts, purchases and disbursements made by me, yet you consistently set your face against it and never, to my certain knowledge, received a shilling."

23 U.S.S. *Azalea*, Acting Master F. W. Strong, seized British brig *Sarah M. Newhall*, attempting to put into Savannah with a cargo of West Indies produce. She had cleared from Inagua, Bahamas, ostensibly for New York.

24 The blockade runner *Denbigh*, once described by Admiral Farragut as "too quick for us", was found aground at daylight on Bird Key Spit, near Galveston. She had attempted to run into the Texas port once again under cover of darkness. She was destroyed during the day by gunfire from U.S.S. *Cornubia* and *Princess Royal*, and later boarding parties from *Kennebec* and *Seminole* set her aflame. Prior to the capture of Mobile Bay, *Denbigh* had plagued Farragut by running regularly from Mobile to Havana. He narrowly missed taking her on 7 June 1864, and Farragut expressed his feelings in a letter to Rear Admiral Theodorus Bailey: "We nearly had the *Denbigh;* she has not moved from the fort [Morgan] yet, so she must have been hit by some of the shots fired at her; but he is a bold rascal, and well he may be, for if I get him he will see the rest of his days of the war in the Tortugas." William Watson, a Confederate blockade runner who shipped on *Rob Roy* and other elusive runners, later wrote of *Denbigh*: "I may safely say that one of the most successful, and certainly one of the most profitable, steamers that sailed out of Havana to the Confederate States was a somewhat old, and by no means a fast, steamer, named the *Denbigh*. This vessel ran for a considerable time between Havana and Mobile; but when the latter port was captured by the Federals she ran to Galveston, to and from which port she made such regular trips that she was called the packet. She was small in size, and not high above water, and painted in such a way as not to be readily seen at a distance. She was light on coal, made but little smoke, and depended more upon strategy than speed. She carried large cargoes of cotton, and it was generally allowed that the little *Denbigh* was a more profitable boat than any of the larger and swifter cracks." Nevertheless, in the end she met the same fate as hundreds of her sister runners.

U.S.S. Genesee *swept the waters near Mobile for Confederate torpedoes long after the surrender at Appomattox. She is rigged with anti-torpedo nets.*

U.S.S. *Cornubia*, Lieutenant John A. Johnstone, captured and destroyed C.S.S. *Le Compt* off Galveston. The Confederate schooner, which had been used as a port guard ship, was abandoned by her crew as *Cornubia* approached her station. *Le Compt* drifted ashore, bilged, and next day was reported "a total wreck."

25 An ordnance explosion and the resulting fires caused extensive damage in Mobile. The explosion originated in Marshall's warehouse, which contained surrendered Confederate ammunition. Rear Admiral Thatcher noted that although the explosion occurred three quarters of a mile from the flagship, fragments of shell fell on board. Commander Edward Simpson was immediately dispatched with a number of sailors to render all possible aid. Simpson reported: "I visited the scene of the fire, and with a large force of sailors was enabled to do some service, the presence of the sailors in the neighborhood of the exploding shells tended much to restore a partial feeling of confidence to the firemen and others." He called particular attention to the bravery of Quartermaster John Cooper who "at the risk of being blown to pieces by exploding shells" entered the fire and carried a wounded man to safety on his back. For this heroic deed, Cooper was awarded the Medal of Honor for a second time—his first award was for courageous devotion to duty on board U.S.S. *Brooklyn* at Mobile Bay in 1864. The tug U.S.S. *Cowslip*, Acting Master W. T. Bacon, towed three vessels to safety.

Because of his activities as a Confederate agent abroad and his torpedo activities, that many then considered dastardly, Commander Maury decided he would not be granted amnesty. Before the war, when he headed the Naval Observatory and was world famous for his pathfinding in oceanography, he had corresponded with many leaders from Europe including Heads of State. One of these had been Maximilian of Austria. In England he had renewed this correspondence and had dabbled in political intrigue with Emperor Napoleon and Maximilian before the latter proceeded in 1864 on his ill-fated venture as Emperor of Mexico. Hence Maury had continued on board *Atrato* which had departed Havana on the 24th for Mexico. This date Maury drafted a note to the United States Consul at Vera Cruz, enclosing a letter addressed "To the officer in command of the U.S. Naval forces in the Gulf of Mexico". He wrote:

"In peace as in war I follow the fortunes of my native old state [Virginia]. I read in the public prints that she has practically confessed defeat and laid down her arms. In that act mine were grounded also. I am here without command, officially alone, and am bound on matters of private concern abroad. Nevertheless, and as I consider further resistance worse than useless, I deem it proper formally so to confess, and to pledge you in the words of honor that, should I find myself before the final inauguration of peace within the jurisdiction of the United States, to consider myself a prisoner of war, bound by the terms and conditions which have been or may be granted to General Lee and his officers. Be pleased to send your answer through my son (Colonel R. L. Maury), a prisoner of war on parole in Richmond. In the meantime, and until I hear to the contrary, I shall act as though my surrender had been formally accepted on the above named terms and conditions."

Rear Admiral Thatcher reported that this date the defensive works at Sabine Pass, Texas, were evacuated and that the United States flag was hoisted at Forts Mannahasset and Griffin. The flags were raised by men from the U.S.S. *Owasco*, Acting Lieutenant Commander Lewis W. Pennington.

U.S.S. *Vanderbilt*, Captain C. W. Pickering, arrived at Hampton Roads with the captured Confederate ram *Columbia* in tow. She was one of the largest ironclads built by the Confederacy but had never seen service as she grounded when being outfitted at Charleston (see 12 January). *Columbia* was captured when Charleston capitulated and was subsequently salvaged (see 17–18 February).

27 Reporting to Secretary Welles that he had visited C.S.S. *Stonewall* in Havana, Rear Admiral Stribling wrote: "I . . . . do not consider her so formidable a vessel as had been represented. In a seaway she would be powerless, and unless her speed was greater than that of her opponent her ram could do no harm."

U.S.S. *Pontiac*, Lieutenant Commander Luce, delivered several relics of Confederate warfare to the United States Naval Academy. These were sent from Charleston by Rear Admiral Dahlgren and included a torpedo boat similar to the one "that exploded a torpedo under the *Ironsides* on the night of October 10, 1863, and afterwards menaced our vessels constantly." He also sent two torpedoes similar to those which had sunk U.S.S. *Patapsco* and *Harvest Moon*. He credited Confederate torpedo warfare as "most troublesome" to the Union naval forces. Secretary Welles reported that "torpedoes have been more destructive of our naval vessels than all other means combined."

Rear Admiral Stribling, commanding the East Gulf Squadron, reported to Secretary Welles the surrender to his forces of C.S.S. *Spray*. The gunboat had been stationed in the St. Marks River guarding the water approaches to Tallahassee, Florida. *Spray*'s commanding officer, Lieutenant Henry H. Lewis, surrendered the vessel upon learning that the troops at Tallahassee had capitulated.

C.S.S. *Shenandoah*, Lieutenant Waddell, captured whaling bark *Abigail* near Shantarski Island in the northwestern reaches of the Sea of Okhotsk. *Abigail*'s master, Ebenezer Nye, had been captured earlier in the war by C.S.S. *Alabama*. One of Nye's mates turned to him and said, "You are more fortunate in picking up Confederate cruisers than whales. I will never again go with you, for if there is a cruiser out, you will find her." The following day, after taking on a stove from *Abigail* to warm Waddell's cabin, a large quantity of liquor found on board the prize to warm the men, and winter clothing essential to continued operations in these northern waters, the whaler was burned. Waddell proceeded southward along the Siberian Coast and Sakhalin.

29 Charles Francis Adams, American Minister to Great Britain, claimed that the cruiser policy England had encouraged during the war had destroyed the United States thriving merchant marine. In a letter to the British Foreign Minister, Adams held English policy directly responsible for the 110,000 tons of American shipping burned or sunk then went on to broaden the indictment by adding that "the action of these British built, manned and armed vessels has had the indirect effect of driving from the sea a large portion of the commercial marine of the United States." Although the American flag disappeared from the sea the merchant ships that had flown it (except for the destroyed prizes) did not. More than 800,000 tons of American owned shipping was either trans-

ferred to foreign registry or sold to foreign shipowners in order to gain the shelter of a neutral flag. Prior to the Civil War, the United States had become the world's leading maritime carrier measured by both tonnage of bottoms and value of cargo. The Civil War cost the nation this number one position.

31 Assistant Secretary Fox ordered a reduction in the East Gulf Blockading Squadron to ten steamers and four tug boats. The same order redesignated the Squadron as the East Gulf Squadron. The South Atlantic Blockading Squadron to 15 steamers and 6 tugboats and was redesignated the South Atlantic Squadron. The West Gulf Squadron was reduced to 15 steamers, one monitor and one river ironclad, and 6 tugs.

JUNE

1 In his report regarding the surrender of Confederate forces, Major General Edward R. Canby, commanding the Military Division of West Mississippi, noted—"during the whole period of my command in the Southwest, I was materially aided by the zealous and efficient cooperation of the naval forces of the West Gulf and Mississippi squadrons, and a more effective acknowledgement than mine is due to Admiral Farragut, Commodore Palmer, Admiral Thatcher, successive commanders of the West Gulf, and Admirals Porter and Lee, of the Mississippi Squadron, and to their subordinates in both squadrons."

1–4 Lieutenant Commander Nathaniel Green, in U.S.S. *Itasca*, commanded the naval units in a combined Army-Navy movement to occupy Apalachicola, Florida. Brigadier General Alexander Asboth, commanding the expedition, commended Green highly for his "nautical skill and efficiency, as well as his friendly willingness to aid" which, the General reported, "materially contributed to the successful" execution of the mission.

1–6 Lieutenant William E. Fitzhugh, in U.S.S. *Ouachita*, led a naval expedition of seven gunboats up the Red River escorting 4,000 troops under Major General Francis J. Herron. These troops were moving into the trans-Mississippi theater to garrison the forts and posts surrendered by Confederate General Kirby Smith and to establish law and order in the region. At Alexandria, Louisiana, Fitzhugh met with Lieutenant Jonathan H. Carter, the senior Confederate naval officer in the trans-Mississippi department and received the surrender of all naval vessels, equipment, and personnel in that region. The most formidable vessel surrendered was the sternwheel ironclad, C.S.S. *Missouri*, commanded by Carter. The ship had been built in Shreveport and late in March, when the river had risen sufficiently, had steamed down river to Alexandria. There Carter had written enthusiastically to General Simon B. Buckner: "I will . . . be pleased to welcome you on the deck of the *Missouri*, when we arrive at Grand Ecore . . . I hope to be a valuable [addition] to your forces defending the valley." *Missouri*, however, never had this opportunity for battle, although she had the distinction of being the last Confederate ironclad to be surrendered in home waters.

1–13 Before burning *Abigail*, Lieutenant Waddell obtained a stove from her for his cabin, one of the many items that had not been provided when C.S.S. *Shenandoah* hastily left Liverpool the previous autumn. He needed it in the ensuing days as he navigated along the frozen shores of Siberia. "I continued as far as the Chi-jinskiki Bay, but found it so full of ice the steamer could not be entered. I then stood along the land of eastern Siberia as far as Tausk Bay, when she was forced away by the ice, and I left for Shantaski [Shantarski] Island, but I found ice in such quantities before we reached the 150° meridian of east longitude that she was forced to the southward finding ice in almost every direction and apparently closing on her.

"The situation caused anxiety of mind, and I solved the seamanship problem before us. The scene was cold, the mercury several degrees below zero, the ice varied in thickness from fifteen to thirty feet and, although not very firm, was sufficiently so to injure the *Shenandoah* if we were not very careful. I wanted to reach Shantarski Island (called by whalers Greer Island) for there is fishing there and in the bays southwest of it."

In this chill sea, *Shenandoah* met severe gales. "The damage from these gales is much increased by the heavy ice which a vessel is likely to be driven on and wrecked. We encountered the first one of those gales to windward of twenty miles of floe ice, and if we had been lying to with the ice under our lea, the *Shenandoah* would probably have been lost with her entire crew.

"It became imperatively necessary to relieve the ship of her perilous situation. She was run a little distance from and along the floe until a passage was seen from aloft through it with open water beyond. Into this passage she was entered and in a short time she was lying to under close reefed sails with the floe to windward, and this was the solution of that seamanship problem alluded to a little time before, for our dreaded enemy was now become our best friend, the fury of the sea was expended on it and not against the *Shenandoah*. It was a breakwater for the ship.

"She laid perfectly easy, the water was as smooth as a pond, while the seas on the weather edge of the floe broke furiously, throwing sheets of water twenty feet high, to all appearances a fog bank.

"It was so far away we could only hear the hurrying of wind as it piped louder and carried in it a penetrating mist. The *Shenandoah* being relieved of the threatened danger, the next thought was to prevent her from going into the ice during the thick weather, which now came on in fine rain and sleet. The wind was bitter cold, turning the rain into ice and forming a crust everywhere. The braces, blocks, yards, sails, and all the running rigging was perfectly coated with ice from a half to two inches thick, so that it was impossible to use the braces and icicles of great length and size hung from every portion of the rigging.

"The gale had passed over, and it was calm, the clouds were exhausted, the rosy tints of morn opened upon a scene of enchantment, and when the sunlight burst on us, the flash and sparkle from truck to deck, from bowsprit to topsail awakened exclamations of enthusiastic delight over the fair ship.

"The disposition was evidently not to disturb, but leave to enjoyment the crystal mantle of the *Shenandoah*. Finally the crew was sent aloft with billets of wood to dislodge the ice and free the running rigging. The large icicles falling from aloft rendered the deck dangerous to move upon, and it soon became covered with clear, beautiful ice, which was removed to the tanks, casks, and every vessel capable of receiving it."

2 The terms of surrender of Galveston, Texas, were signed on board U.S.S. *Fort Jackson* by Major General E. Kirby Smith on behalf of the Confederacy. Brigadier General E. J. Davis represented the Union Army.

Assistant Secretary Fox ordered the Mississippi Squadron reduced to 15 ships "with all possible dispatch." In his letter to Rear Admiral S. P. Lee of the Mississippi Squadron, Fox concluded: "Economize in the use of coal and give directions to all vessels to keep steam down, except in an emergency. . . ." With the war completed, a number of similar steps were taken to cut expenditures to a minimum and reduce drastically what had become during the years of conflict the strongest Navy afloat.

5 Captain Benjamin F. Sands, with U.S.S. *Cornubia* and *Preston*, crossed the bar at Galveston, landed and raised the United States flag over the custom house. *New London* and *Port Royal* were ordered to follow immediately. Terms of the surrender had been agreed upon by Major General E. Kirby Smith, CSA, on 2 June on board U.S.S. *Fort Jackson*. The surrender of Galveston, combined with the capitulation of Sabine Pass and Brownsville, enabled Rear Admiral Thatcher to write Secretary Welles that "blockade running from Galveston and the coast of Texas is at an end."

6 After landing in Vera Cruz, Matthew Fontaine Maury proceeded to Mexico City. He was confident that Emperor Maximilian would give him a warm welcome. In December 1857 the then Archduke and head of the Austrian Navy had sent a present to Maury for his wife, and wrote:

"I have observed, with intense interest and admiration, your noble and unequaled efforts, in order to forward the improvement of the scientific part of our profession. I trust you will accept this little present as a token of my gratitude towards a man whom all seafaring nations are bound to look upon with respect and thankfulness."

Maury proposed to offer his services not only as a torpedo expert but also on a broader scale that would be of far reaching benefit to his own loved people and to the new Empire—the emigration of Confederates to Mexico. At the time, it appeared to him that he might never be able to return home because of the several categories that applied to exclude him from the amnesty, including his leadership in the development of torpedoes and his overseas intrigue. Throughout this summer he received communications from home advising against his return. For example, on 19 June his daughter Elizabeth Herndon Maury wrote: "Don't trust to any parole or any promise. General Curtis of the U.S. Army, who is staying here, said to me this morning that you ought not to come under any circumstances. General Lee said to me the other day, 'Mrs. Maury, tell your father from me not to think of coming home.'"

7   Lieutenant Commander William E. Fitzhugh, U.S.S. *Ouachita*, seized the Confederate ship *Cotton* (*No. 2*) and took her to the mouth of the Red River. She had been purchased by the Confederate Navy but the stipulated payment had not been made and for this reason she was returned to her former owners by Lieutenant Carter, CSN, prior to surrendering the naval forces (see 1–6 June). Fitzhugh justified his seizure of the vessel on the basis that she had been employed in military operations against the Union.

9   Secretary Welles ordered that the East Gulf and the West Gulf Squadrons be combined and redesignated the Gulf Squadron. He directed Rear Admiral H. K. Thatcher to relieve Rear Admiral C. K. Stribling and assume command of the newly formed Squadron with headquarters at Pensacola.

The Welles also directed that the North and South Atlantic squadrons be combined and redesignated the Atlantic Squadron. At the same time he ordered Rear Admiral Dahlgren to return to Washington and Rear Admiral William Radford to assume command of the squadron. Dahlgren recorded in his diary under the date of 17 June: "And so ends a command of two years of one of the largest fleets ever assembled under American colors—as many as 96 at one time."

C.S.S. *Ajax*, Lieutenant Low, arrived at Liverpool, England, from Bermuda. *Ajax* had been detained at Bermuda by the British Governor after Low had made an unsuccessful attempt to arm his ship under the guise of taking a shipment of guns to Havana (see 4 May). The vessel was released after the news reached Bermuda that the American war had ended in the capitulation of the Confederacy. Upon his arrival at Liverpool, Low turned the ship over to the local port authorities. The former lieutenant of C.S.S. *Alabama* chose to remain in England rather than return to his homeland. He established his residence in Liverpool where he subsequently became a prosperous shipping and cotton mill executive. Years later Low was presented *Alabama*'s pennant by a Frenchman who had witnessed the Confederate cruiser's sea battle with U.S.S. *Kearsarge* from a yacht, and had salvaged her pennant. Today this pennant, seventy-five feet in length and bearing twenty-seven white stars on a blue field, with a red and white tail, is in the possession of John Low's grandson.

12   The steamer *Sonora* arrived in Tampico, Mexico, after running the blockade from Matagorda Bay, Texas. Although originally loaded with 300 bales of cotton, disbanded Confederate troops had seized all but 38 bales.

14   Lieutenant Waddell had worked C.S.S. *Shenandoah* free of the dangerous ice field that had provided him a safe breakwater in the icy storm (see 1–13 June) by running out warps "on the floe and grapnels hooked to large blocks of ice. . . . One gathers experience under certain circumstances, and becomes accustomed to certain situations which create anxiety at first."

After meeting increasingly heavy drift ice that flowed to the westward, Waddell became convinced that to continue sailing in that direction would be useless. "She was therefore run to the

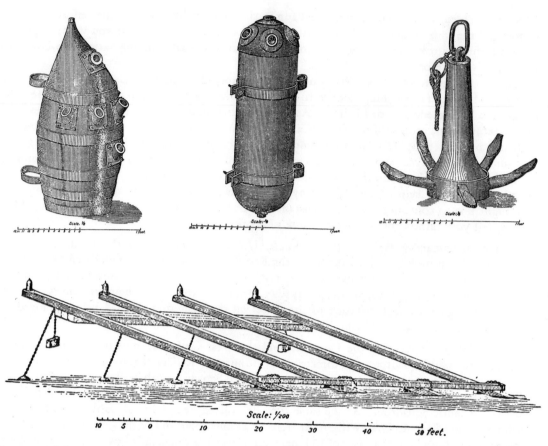

Weapons and obstructions found in Charleston harbor after the surrender of the city in February: (top left) torpedo attached to the bow of C.S.S. Charleston; (top center) copper torpedo attached to the bow of a torpedo boat; (top right) obstruction anchor; (bottom) frame torpedoes found in the Ashley River, Hog Island Channel, and elsewhere.

eastward and after knocking about till the 14th of June, I left the sea of Okhotsk and entered the North Pacific Ocean by the fiftieth parallel passage of Amphitrite Strait, and steering N.E. with a cracking southwester after us.

"When I gave the course N.E. it was to run the ship midway of the most western of the Aleutian and the most eastern of Komandorski Islands, because currents about islands are irregular in direction as well as in force. In a few hours after leaving Amphitrite Strait the wind hauled more to the south and then east of south, producing a condensation of the atmosphere which closed around the *Shenandoah* an impenetrable mist."

16 For two days C.S.S. *Shenandoah* had sailed northward in fog that fortunately lifted partly just in time to enable her to miss running aground as she passed west of the Aleutians. Three days later, half way across the world, Commander Bulloch wrote to Lieutenant Waddell, ordering him to desist from further destruction of United States property upon the high seas and all offensive operations against U.S. citizens. These were orders that could not be delivered for many weeks under the best conditions. Therefore, whalers were destined to suffer disastrous blows.

20 Lieutenant Commander John J. Cornwell of U.S.S. *Grossbeak* reported the capture of the steamer *Idaho* "a few days since" by Southern guerrillas near Greenville, Mississippi. She was a small trading steamer and was loaded with 400 bales of cotton which had belonged to the Confederacy.

C.S.S. Shenandoah *sailed through ice-clogged Arctic waters to deal Union whalers a devastating blow.*

22 Secretary Welles announced to the naval forces that France and Great Britain had "withdrawn from the insurgents the character of belligerents." He also announced that the blockade of the coast of the United States would soon be lifted and the belligerent right of search abrogated.

C.S.S. *Shenandoah*, Lieutenant Waddell, cruising off Cape Navarin, found "a current setting to the N.E. and soon after seeing blubber we concluded the whale vessels south of us were cutting out, and steam was ordered. This calculation was correct." Within an hour they sighted two American whalers which were the first spoken since entering the Bering Sea. Coming up on the two New Bedford whalers in close proximity, he captured and placed a prize crew on board *William Thompson* and then stood in pursuit of *Euphrates*. After a two hour chase, she was captured, stripped of supplies and set ablaze. Waddell then returned to *William Thompson* and subjected her to the same fate. The following day which, as her log recorded, remained the 22nd as *Shenandoah* had crossed the international date line, Waddell continued to light the Arctic skies with the flaming hulks of American whalers. He first captured the ship *Milo* of New Bedford. It was from this vessel that Waddell first heard rumors that the South had surrendered and the war had ended. The Confederate captain sought documentary evidence from the master to authenticate these rumors. "He had none, but 'believed the war was over.' I replied that was not satisfactory . . . ." Waddell bonded *Milo*, took most of her crew to insure against escape, and gave chase to two other whalers in the vicinity. They entered the ice flow seeking to escape, but he soon cut out the bark *Sophia Thornton*, placed a prize crew on board with orders to keep company with *Milo*, and continued in pursuit of *Jerah Swift*. Waddell recorded in his memoirs: "We chased her for three hours before getting in shelling distance of her, but Captain Williams, who made every effort to save his bark, saw the folly of exposing the crew to a destructive fire and yielded to his misfortune with a manly and becoming dignity." *Shenandoah* burned the two barks and transfered all prisoners to *Milo* for passage to San Francisco.

Upon learning of the final collapse of the Confederacy, Master John C. Braine, CSN, took passage for Liverpool, England, from Kingston, Jamaica. On several occasions during the war Braine had led naval parties in the successful seizures of Federal merchantmen and quite likely would have been prosecuted for piracy had he been apprehended by the Federals. The schooner *St. Mary's*, which he seized in Chesapeake Bay and had sailed to Nassau, was abandoned in Kingston just prior to his booking passage for Liverpool (see 31 March and 22 April 1865). Previous to the *St. Mary's* incident, he had seized the steamers *Chesapeake* off Cape Cod (7 December 1863) and the *Roanoke* off Havana (29 September 1864) while leading Confederate naval parties masquerading as passengers.

C.S.S. *Shenandoah*, Lieutenant Waddell, captured *Susan Abigail*, recently from San Francisco. A newspaper was found on board dated April 17, 1865. It told of the capture of Richmond but also contained President Davis' Danville Proclamation declaring that the war would be continued with renewed vigor. Moreover, the raider's captain observed: "Three of the *Susan Abigail*'s crew joined the *Shenandoah*, which was good evidence at least that they did not believe the war had ended." The master of the prize stated that in San Francisco, "Opinion is divided as to the ultimate result of the war. For the present the North has the advantage, but how it will all end no one can know, and as to the newspapers they are not reliable." After burning the trader, Waddell continued northward to the Bering Strait, the northern exit to the Arctic Sea.

Waddell burned most of the ships captured in the northern seas. Earlier in his journal he had discussed the destruction of prizes.

According to the freighting for some ships one could simply "knock a hole in her bottom from in board below the water line and the vessel sinks rapidly and finally disappears leaving only a few pieces of plank floating over the great abyss which has closed over her.

"It frequently occurs that to destroy a prize, fire must be resorted to, and there is no escape from that ruthless element. However much it may be condemned, it is better than to leave a prize so disabled and injured as to be formidable enough to endanger the navigation of the ocean. Fire serves as a beacon to inform the sailor of danger, but it leaves a small portion of the vessel, the floor and the keel to float upon the surface of the water.

"To prepare a vessel for destruction by fire, first remove all living animals, take out all useful equipment which may be wanted, discover what combustibles are in her hold, such as tar, pitch, turpentine, and see to the removal of gunpowder. All of these things should be thrown into sea. Combustibles are then scattered throughout the vessel, bulkheads torn down and piled up in her cabins and forecastle. All hatches are opened and all halyards let go that the sails may hang loosely and the yards counter braced. Fire is then taken from the galley or cooking stove and deposited in various parts of her hold and about her deck.

"If she is very old she burns like tinder. This painful duty which sometimes became necessary would have been avoided had we been allowed to take our prizes into port for adjudication."

23 Rear Admiral Samuel F. DuPont died unexpectedly at the age of 61 while on a visit to Philadelphia. He had commanded the South Atlantic Squadron during the first two years of the war

Samuel F. DuPont
Rear Admiral, USN

John C. Braine
Master, CSN

and had led the naval forces in the important capture of Port Royal by amphibious assault on 7 November 1861. The author J. T. Headley wrote of DuPont: "A gentleman of the old school . . . whose bearing was that of dignified courtesy to all. Chivalrous in his own feelings, he was incapable of wounding those of others.—Insensible to fear, he never shrank from encouraging any danger, while he was absolutely incapable of thrusting himself forward to obtain notoriety."

Lieutenant Commander Cushing received orders to U.S.S. *Lancaster*, flagship of Rear Admiral George F. Pearson, commanding the Pacific Squadron. Shortly after reporting on board the ship at San Francisco, the people of that city extended to Cushing the freedom of the city in recognition of his courageous and heroic war record. On five separate occasions he led daring raids and each time was successful in destroying a Confederate ship. The most famous of these was conducted 27 October 1864, when he sank the C.S.S. *Albemarle* with a spar torpedo. He also led one of the assaulting columns of sailors and Marines against the sea face of Fort Fisher on 15 January 1865.

C.S.S. *Shenandoah*, Lieutenant Waddell, captured and burned at sea ship *General Williams* near St. Lawrence Island in the Bering Sea. In this area "several Esquimaux canoes with natives from the island visited us and our crew struck up a brisk trade with them for furs and walrus tusks" using sign language.

25 Secretary Welles ordered the further reduction of the Mississippi Squadron to 5 ships, and directed the abandonment of all the naval stations of the Mississippi Squadron, except that at Mound City, Illinois.

26 Shortly after midnight C.S.S. *Shenandoah*, Lieutenant Waddell, commenced a highly successful day of operations. At one thirty a.m. she sailed alongside three becalmed whalers. In short order Waddell put *Nimrod*, *William C. Nye*, and *Catherine* to the torch, ordered their crews into small boats to be towed astern of the raider, and set out in pursuit of three other sails sighted to the northward. He captured barks *General Pike*, *Isabella*, and *Gipsey* before noon, and, after making a cartel ship out of *General Pike* and bonding her, the other two whalers were burned. "Within forty-eight hours," Waddell wrote, "the *Shenandoah* has destroyed and ransomed property to the value of $253,500."

Waddell described the usual whaler of that period: "The whaling vessels vary from 90 to 100 feet in length with great beam, consequently they can be turned around more easily than vessels of greater length; powerful in construction, dull sailers, and sheathed for forty feet from the stern, which is generally shod with iron, they are calculated to resist contact with ice which floats in detached floes or pilot ice some sixteen feet in thickness and in an abundance in Bering Sea and northwards. They are equipped with boats much elevated at either end and strongly built. On the stempost are fitted collars for lines to pass over when attached to a whale. These lines are made of white hemp from 1½ to 2½ inches in circumference, varying from 100 to 250 fathoms (600 to 1,500 feet) in length, and coiled in large tubs, (made to fit the boats expressly for this purpose) a precautionary measure to secure their easy flight and keep them from being entangled, which might cause the boat to capsize, so rapidly does the whale move when struck by a harpoon, the lance, and a two-inch muzzle blunderbuss, of short barrel, constructed of iron, and weighing about 40 pounds.

"The projectile used is an elongated explosive shell of 12 inches in length. The blunderbuss is handled by a powerful and expert whalesman and discharged into the animal when near enough. The fuse is short, burns quickly, and explodes the shell causing instant death.

"The whale floats to the surface of the water when the men attach a line to the head by sharp hooks, and tow the fish alongside the vessel when they proceed to cut it up.

"A part of the midship section of the vessel is converted into a blubber room and into which the fish, after being cut up, is thrown. The boiling process for oil is proceeded with as quickly as possible. The arrangements for boiling the blubber are found on deck between the fore and mainmast, built of masonry and barred against accident in heavy weather. In the center of the masonry are one or more large cauldrons into which the blubber is placed, and after the oil is extracted, the refuse is used for making fire and produces an intense heat. The whalers carry hogs and this refuse is used for fattening them and they eat ravenously. The hogsheads used for receiving the oil vary in size from two to three hundred gallons. The greater part of these are shaken up when delivered to the vessels in port and put together upon the ship when wanted, consequently their stowage is closer.

"Those hogsheads which have contained flour in bags, hams, cordage, clothing, shipbiscuits, when emptied, are filled with oil. The odor from a whaling ship is horribly offensive, but it is not worse than that of the green hide vessels from South America, which can be smelt [sic] fifty miles in a favorable wind.

"The bones of the whale are taken on board and placed in the bone room; from these the offensive exhalation is too horrible to relate."

27 Emperor Maximilian was absent from Mexico City when Matthew F. Maury arrived early in the month. In the last week he arrived and promptly saw the noted American. After other short meetings, he granted Maury a long audience to present his emigration plan in full. Then he had Maury leave a written draft for study.

Commander Macomb, commanding the Union naval forces in Albemarle Sound, reported to the commander of the Atlantic Squadron that he had captured all the Confederate naval vessels in the Roanoke River. He took possession of the sternwheel steamer *Cotton Plant*, the screw steamer *Egypt Mills*, the unfinished gunboat *Halifax*, and one lighter. He also seized 99 bales of cotton. The two steamers had been privately owned at one time but had been taken over by the Confederate Navy during the latter stages of the war.

28 This date marked the most successful single day C.S.S. *Shenandoah* enjoyed as a commerce raider during her long cruise that spanned 13 months and covered 58,000 miles, and during which Waddell often successfully followed his conviction that "nothing is to be gained if risk is not taken." Near the narrows of the Bering Strait, Lieutenant Waddell fell in with a rendezvous of eleven American whalers. The ship *Brunswick* of New Bedford had been stove in by an ice floe and the others had gathered either to render assistance or to bid on supplies and oil in the event the master

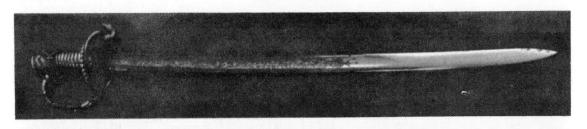

(Top) Sword belonging to Admiral David Dixon Porter. (Bottom) Jeweled sword presented to Lieutenant General U.S. Grant by friends in Kentucky. (Both from the collections of Mr. Jay Altmayer of Mobile, Alabama.)

decided to abandon ship and offer bargains. To insure that none escaped, Waddell entered the bay under the American flag and while five boats were being quickly armed and manned, he maneuvered the ship to a position in which the raider's guns commanded the whalers. As soon as the armed boats were away, the Confederate commander lowered the American flag and ran up the Stars and Bars. Ten of the whalers immediately struck their colors. The single exception was *Favorite* of New Haven whose flag remained at the gaff defended by her drunken master flourishing a harpoon gun. The resistance was shortlived as the whaler was carried by boarding without bloodshed. Waddell then bonded the ship *James Murray* and the bark *Nile* and placed his 336 prisoners on board for passage to San Francisco. The latter whaler was selected for this mission because her master had died, leaving a widow and two small children on board; "the poor widow had the remains of her husband on board preserved in whiskey". Waddell stripped the vessels of supplies, and recruited 9 men. He noted that their enlistment was "evidence that if they had heard any report of the military failure of the South, they considered it unreliable". Waddell put the torch to the ships *Hillman, Nassau, Brunswick, Isaac Howland* and barks *Waverly, Martha, Favorite, Covington* and *Congress*. Waddell records in his memoirs that "the horizon was illuminated with a fiery glare presenting a picture of indescribable grandeur, while the water was covered with black smoke mingled with flakes of fire". This field day against American commerce climaxed a highly successful cruise in which *Shenandoah* captured a total of 38 American vessels valued at $1,361,983.

Matthew F. Maury dined with the Emperor and Empress Charlotte at the Chapultepec Palace in Mexico City. The Emperor extended the unusual courtesy to Maury of requesting that from then on, unlike others, he "remain seated when the Emperor was in the room". Empress Charlotte, the daughter of Leopold I of Belgium and first cousin of Queen Victoria, asked for his photograph for her album.

29 Rear Admiral Thatcher sent the Navy Department the Confederate flag flown from C.S.S. *LeCompt* captured by U.S.S. *Cornubia* off Galveston, Texas, on 24 May. Thatcher wrote: "It is believed to be the last rebel flag on the coast afloat captured from the rebels during this war."

JULY

1–3 After destroying the large fleet of Arctic whalers (see 26 and 28 June), Waddell stood south "amid snow and icebergs" looking for more victims. There he wrote, in "the immensity of the ice and floes", threatened with "danger of being shut up in the Arctic Ocean for several

NORTH ATLANTIC SQUADRON,
January 1, 1865.

Name.	Guns.	Class.	Commanding officer.	Present duty or station.
Agawam	10	3	Comdr. A. C. Rhind	Norfolk, repairing.
Alabama	10	3	Actg. Vol. Lt. A. R. Langthorne	Off Beaufort.
Anemone	4	4	Actg. Ens. W. C. Borden	Do.
Alert	2	4	Actg. Ens. J. Bishop	James River.
Atlanta	3	3	Actg. Vol. Lt. T. J. Woodward	Hampton Roads.
Aries	7	3	Actg. Vol. Lt. F. S. Wells	Off Wilmington.
Augusta	10			Not reported.
Adger, James				Do.
Arletta (schooner)			Lt. Comdr. W. C. West	Beaufort, N. C.
Albemarle (hulk)				Sounds, North Carolina.
Alpha		4	Actg. Ens. N. R. Davis	James River.
Beta, destroyed (formerly called Picket Boat No. 2, or Bazely).				
Berberry	4		Actg. Ens. R. W. Rowntree	Beaufort, N. C.
Britannia	6	4	Actg. Vol. Lt. S. Huse	Off Wilmington.
Banshee	3	4	Actg. Vol. Lt. W. H. Garfield	Norfolk, repairing.
Bignonia	3	4	Actg. Vol. Lt. W. D. Roath	Off Wilmington.
Belle	2	4	Actg. Mast. J. G. Green	Sounds, North Carolina.
Brooklyn	26	2	Capt. James Alden	Off Beaufort.
Ben Morgan (hulk)			Actg. Mast. A. B. Mulford	Norfolk, Va.
Charles Phelps (coal bulk).		4	Actg. Ens. W. Ottiwell	Craney Island, Va.
Canonicus	2	3	Lt. Comdr. G. E. Belknap	Off Beaufort.
Chicopee	10	3	Comdr. A. D. Harrell	Do.
Clematis	3	4	Actg. Vol. Lt. E. D. Bruner	Norfolk, repairing.
Commodore Hull	6	4	Actg. Mast. F. Josselyn	Sounds, North Carolina.
Ceres	2	4	Actg. Mast. H. H. Foster	Do.
Colorado	50	1	Commo. H. K. Thatcher	Off Beaufort.
Cherokee	6	4	Actg. Vol. Lt. W. E. Dennison	Off Wilmington.
Calypso	6	4	Actg. Mast. F. D. Stuart	New York Navy Yard.
Cambridge	10	3	Actg. Vol. Lt. J. F. Nickels	Norfolk Navy Yard.
Commodore Barney	7	4	Actg. Vol. Lt. G. B. Livingston	James River.
Cactus	3	4	Actg. Mast. and Pilot Jno. Evans	Naval Station, Norfolk.
Commodore Morris	7	4	Actg. Mast. R. G. Lee	James River.
Crusader	7	4	Actg. Vol. Lt. Peter Hays	York River.
Commodore Perry	5	4	Actg. Vol. Lt. A. P. Foster	James River.
Cuyler, R. R	12	3	Comdr. C. H. B. Caldwell	Norfolk Navy Yard.
Chippewa	6	4	Lt. Comdr. A. W. Weaver	Off Wilmington.
Cohasset	1	4	Actg. Ens. and Pilot G. B. Griffin	Norfolk, Va.
Clinton		4	G. W. Hadden	Do.
Dumbarton	4	4	Actg. Vol. Lt. H. Brown	Do.
Delaware	4	4	Actg. Mast. J. H. Eldridge	James River, Va.
Dawn	3	4	Actg. Mast. J. A. Jackaway	Do.
Daylight	8	4	Actg. Mast. H. A. Phelon	James River, Va.
Dictator	2	1	Commo. Jno. Rodgers	Hampton Roads.
Dacotah				Not reported.
Delta		4	Actg. Mast. Mate W. F. Gragg	James River, Va.
Epsilon		4	Actg. Ens. E. M. Boggs	Do.
Emma	8	4	Actg. Vol. Lt. J. M. Williams	Off Wilmington.
Eolus	4	4	Actg. Mast. E. S. Keyser	Beaufort, N. C.
Eutaw	10	3	Lt. Comdr. H. C. Blake	James River.
Fort Jackson	11	2	Capt. B. F. Sands	Off Wilmington.
Florida				Not reported.
Fort Donelson	1	4	Actg. Vol. Lt. T. Pickering	Beaufort, N. C.
Fahkee	5	4	Actg. Mast. F. R. Webb	Off Wilmington.
Grand Gulf				Not reported.
Gettysburg	7	3	Lt. R. H. Lamson	Beaufort, N. C.
Governor Buckingham	6	3	Actg. Vol. Lt. J. MacDiarmid	Do.
General Putnam	4	4	Actg. Mast. H. H. Savage	James River.
Granite (sloop)			Actg. Mast. E. Boomer	Guard ship, Hatteras Inlet.
Glance			Actg. Ens. H. Wheeler	James River.
Gamma		4	Actg. Ens. H. F. Curtis	Do.
Howqnah		4	Actg. Vol. Lt. J. W. Balch	Off Wilmington.
Huron	5	4	Lt. Comdr. T. O. Selfridge	Beaufort, N. C.
Hunchback	5	4	Lt. Jos. Fyffe	James River.
H. Brinker	3	4	Actg. Ens. J. H. Kerens	Do.
Heliotrope	1	4	Actg. Ens. and Pilot Norman	Norfolk, Va.
Hoyt		4	Actg. Ens. H. B. Twambly	Sounds, North Carolina.
Hetzel	2	4	Actg. Mast. Thompson	Norfolk, Va.
Harcourt				Do.
Iosco	10	3	Comdr. Jno. Guest	Off Wilmington.
Juniata	14	2	Capt. W. R. Taylor	Off Beaufort.
I. N. Seymour	2	4	Actg. Ens. F. B. Allen	Hampton Roads.
Kansas	8	4	Lt. Comdr. P. G. Watmough	Off Wilmington.
Keystone State	6	3	Comdr. H. Rolando	Do.
Lilian		4	Actg. Vol. Lt. T. A. Harris	Do.
Launch 4				James River.
Launch 5				Sounds, North Carolina.
Launch 6				New Berne, N. C.

Name.	Guns.	Class.	Commanding officer.	Present duty or station.
Lockwood	3	4	Actg. Ens. J. Q. A. Davidson	Sounds, North Carolina.
Lilac				Norfolk, Va.
Little Ada	2	4	Actg. Mast. S. P. Crafts	Beaufort, N. C.
Monticello	6	4	Lt. W. B. Cushing	Do.
Maumee	8	4	Lt. Comdr. R. Chandler	Do.
Mohican	9	3	Comdr. D. Ammen	Do.
Minnesota	46	1	Commo. J. Lanman	Do.
Mackinaw	10	3	Comdr. J. C. Beaumont	
Massasoit	10	3	Comdr. R. T. Renshaw	James River.
Mount Vernon	5	4	Actg. Vol. Lt. J. Trathen	Off Wilmington.
Moccasin	3	4	Actg. Ens. J. Brown	Beaufort, N. C.
Mattabesett	10	3	Comdr. J. C. Febiger	Sounds, North Carolina.
Montgomery	6	3	Actg. Vol. Lt. T. C. Dunn	Off Wilmington.
Maratanza	6	3	Lt. Comdr. G. W. Young	Do.
Morse	6	4		Repairing at Baltimore.
Miami	8	3	Actg. Vol. Lt. G. W. Graves	James River.
Mendota	10	3	Comdr. E. T. Nichols	Do.
Mount Washington	1	4	Actg. Mast. and Pilot H. H. Haynie	Do.
Mystic	7	4	Actg. Mast. W. Wright	York River.
Monadnock	4	3	Comdr. E. G. Parrott	Beaufort, N. C.
Mahopac	2	3	Lt. Comdr. E. E. Potter	Do.
Martin				Norfolk Navy Yard.
Mercedita	9	3	Lt. Comdr. M. Haxtun	Baltimore, Md.
Malvern	12	4	Lt. B. H. Porter	Beaufort, N. C.
Nyack	8	4	Lt. Comdr. L. H. Newman	Do.
Nansemond	3	4	Actg. Mast. J. H. Porter	Do.
Niphon	9	4	Actg. Mast. E. Kemble	Repairing at Boston.
New Ironsides	20	1	Commo. W. Radford	Off Beaufort, N. C.
New Berne				Supply steamer.
Osceola	10	3	Comdr. J. M. B. Clitz	Off Beaufort, N. C.
Onondaga	4	3	Comdr. W. A. Parker	James River.
Phlox		4		Do.
Powhatan	24	1	Commo. J. F. Schenck	Off Beaufort, N. C.
Pequot	8	4	Lt. Comdr. D. L. Braine	Do.
Pawtuxet	10	3	Comdr. J. H. Spotts	Off Wilmington.
Poppy	2	4	Actg. Ens. W. Clarke	James River.
Pontoosuc	12	3	Lt. Comdr. W. G. Temple	Off Wilmington.
Quaker City	7	2	Comdr. W. F. Spicer	Do.
Rhode Island	12	2	Comdr. S. D. Trenchard	Beaufort, N. C.
Release	3	4	Actg. Mast. J. Baker	Do.
Renshaw		4	Gunner E. A. McDonald	Sounds, North Carolina.
Seneca	5	4	Lt. Comdr. M. Sicard	Beaufort, N. C.
State of Georgia				Not reported.
Saco	12	4	Lt. Comdr. J. G. Walker	Hampton Roads.
Shenandoah	6	2	Capt. D. B. Ridgely	Beaufort, N. C.
Susquehanna	18	1	Commo. S. W. Godon	Do.
Santiago de Cuba	11	2	Capt. O. S. Glisson	Do.
Samuel Rotan	5	4	Actg. Mast. W. G. Nutting	York River, Va.
Saugus	2	3	Comdr. E. R. Colhoun	Beaufort, N. C.
Shamrock	11	3	Comdr. W. H. Macomb	Sounds, North Carolina.
Saffron		4	Actg. Ens. H. M. Pishon	Hampton Roads.
Spuyten Duyvil (torpedo boat)			First Asst. Eng. [J. L.] Lay	James River.
Shokokon	6	4	Actg. Vol. Lt. W. B. Sheldon	Beaufort, N. C.
Sassacus	12	3	Lt. Comdr. J. L. Davis	Do.
St. Lawrence	13	1	Comdr. D. Lynch	Naval Magazine, Norfolk.
Tallapoosa	10	3	Lt. Comdr. DeHaven	Boston.
Tuscarora	10	3	Comdr. J. M. Frailey	Off Wilmington.
Tristram Shandy	4	4	Actg. Vol. Lt. E. F. Devens	Do.
Tacony	12	3	Lt. Comdr. W. T. Truxtun	Beaufort, N. C.
Ticonderoga	14	2	Capt. C. Steedman	Do.
Unadilla	6	4	Lt. Comdr. F. M. Ramsay	Do.
Unit		4	Actg. Ens. H. P. Hathaway	James River.
Vanderbilt	16	2	Capt. C. W. Pickering	Beaufort, N. C.
Victoria	3	4	Actg. Ens. W. Moody	Norfolk, Va.
Vicksburg	6	3	Lt. Comdr. [F. H.] Baker	Off Wilmington.
Valley City	6	4	Actg. Mast. J. A. J. Brooks	Sounds, North Carolina.
Vance, A. D	5	4	Lt. Comdr. J. H. Upshur	Savannah, Ga.
Wabash	44	1	Capt. M. Smith	Beaufort, N. C.
Western World	5	4	E. Herrick	James River.
William Badger (hulk)				Beaufort, N. C.
Wilderness	4	4	Actg. Mast. H. Arey	Off Wilmington.
Wyalusing	14	3	Lt. Comdr. E. English	Sounds, North Carolina.
Whitehead	4	4		Do.
Wyandotte	5	4	Actg. Mast. T. W. Sheer	Norfolk, Va.
Young America	2	4	Actg. Ens. O. Lasher	James River.
Yantic	5	4	Lt. Comdr. T. C. Harris	Off Wilmington.
Zouave	2	4		Norfolk, Va.
Zeta		4	Actg. Ens. F. W. Mintzer	James River.

The list of vessels appearing on these two pages constituted the North Atlantic Blockading Squadron on 1 January 1865. It contrasts sharply with the list of vessels attached to the Squadron on 1 July 1865, which is printed on the following page.

List of vessels composing the North Atlantic Squadron, July 1, 1865.

Name.	Guns.	Class.	Commanding officer.	Present duty or station.
Agawam	10	Paddle	Lieut. Com. C. L. Franklin	Hampton Roads.
Anemone	4	Screw	Acting Ensign A. O. Kruge	Beaufort, N. C.
Arletta	3	Schooner	Lieut. Com. W. C. West	Do.
Albemarle		Hulk	Acting Asstant Paymaster G. R. Watkins.	Sounds, North Carolina.
Alpha		Screw	Acting Ensign Jno. Brown	Hampton Roads.
Chicopee	10	Paddle	Commander H. N. T. Arnold	Repairing, navy yard, Norfolk.
Charles Phelps		Hulk	Acting Ensign W. Ottiwell	Craney Island coal station.
Delta		Screw	Acting Ensign W. F. Gragg	Sounds, North Carolina.
Glance	1	....do	Acting Ensign H. Wheeler	Hampton Roads.
Gamma		....do	Acting Ensign H. F. Curtis	Sounds, North Carolina.
Harcourt		....do	Acting Ensign I. Miller	Hampton Roads.
Iosco	10	Paddle	Lieut. Com. J.·[S.] Thornton	Sounds, North Carolina.
Lenapee	10	....do	Lieut. Com. T. S. Phelps	Cape Fear River.
Malvern	12	....do	Act. Vol. Lieut. G. W. Graves	Flagship.
Phlox		....do	Acting Master H. North	Hampton Roads.
Picket launch No. 5	1	Screw	Acting Ensign [J. H.] Chapman	Navy yard, Norfolk; ordered to Philadelphia.
Renshaw		Schooner	Gunner E. A. McDonald	Sounds, North Carolina.
Shamrock	11	Paddle	Commander W. H. Macomb	Do.
Sangamon	2	Screw	Lieut. Com. R. Chandler	Repairing, navy yard, Norfolk.
William Badger		Hulk	Acting Ensign S. G. Swain	Beaufort, N. C.
Yantic	5	Screw	Lieut. Com. T. C. Harris	Hampton Roads (Philadelphia at present).
Boxer	4	Paddle	Act. Vol. Lieut. F. M. Green	Hampton Roads.
Tahoma	4	Screw	Lieut. Com. W. P. McCann	Off Newport News.

Very respectfully,

J. C. HOWELL,
Commander and Senior Officer.

U.S.S. Iosco *was one of the war ships remaining in the North Atlantic Squadron on 1 July 1865. She was a double-ender of the* Sassacus *class, with a length of 240 feet; beam, 35 feet, displacement, 1173 tons.*

months, I was obliged to turn her prow southward and reached East Cape just in time to slip by the Diomedes when a vast field of floe ice was closing the strait. . . . The sun was in his highest northern declination, and it was perpetual daylight, when he sank below the northern horizon, a golden fringe marked his course until his pale and cheerless face came again, frosted from icebergs and snows.

"When the *Shenandoah* reached the Island of St. Lawrence there was a fine northwest wind. Sail was made, and the propeller triced up. While to the westward of that island, the ship making six knots per hour, a dense fog came on. . . ."

Trying to beat out of the ice the ship ran into a large floe and damaged her rudder when, with sails aback to avoid sudden collision with thick ice, "she gathered sternboard." The crew placed heavy rope mats around the prow. "Steam was gently applied and with a large block of ice resting against her cutwater she pushed it along to open a passage, and in this way we worked the *Shenandoah* for hours until she gained open water."

To avoid being trapped by Federal cruisers, if not the ice, Waddell decided to run for "more open seas". On 3 July "a black fog closed upon us and shut out from our view the heavens and all things terrestrial." It clung about them thick and ominous for the next two days as the raider steamed south depending on dead reckoning.

5   C.S.S. *Shenandoah*, Lieutenant Waddell, steamed out of the hostile Bering Sea via the Amukta Passage in the Aleutian chain and set a southeasterly course across the commerce lanes of the Eastern Pacific. A captain at sea day and night never rests from the all encompassing responsibility for safety of his ship and men. Escaping from the clutches of the ice Waddell felt deep relief: "Again in the North Pacific with fine weather and the Aleutian Islands astern, I looked back in thankfulness towards those seas in which we had seen hard and dangerous service, and I felt a sensation of freedom on that vast outstretched water before us, no longer dreading the cry from the masthead of "ice ahead". We had run from gloomy fogs into a bright, cheerful, sparkling ocean, and as soon as a hot sun thawed the frosty timbers and rigging of ship and man, we should feel ourselves more than a match for anything we might meet under canvas."

During Waddell's last week in the Bering Sea an idea had occurred to him and as the raider proceeded across the North Pacific he developed it into an audacious plan of action. The idea germinated from reading a San Francisco newspaper that he had obtained on 23 June from *Susan Abigail*. From the newspaper article he learned that U.S.S. *Saginaw*, Commander Charles McDougal, was the only Union warship in San Francisco harbor and constituted the city's sole means of defense. Waddell had been second officer in her prior to the war and was thoroughly familiar with her capabilities and limitations. Moreover, the vessel's captain was "an old and familiar shipmate" whom Waddell remembered as being "fond of his ease." The bold Confederate planned to bring *Shenandoah* into San Francisco harbor under cover of darkness, ram *Saginaw*, and carry her by boarding. Beginning at daylight, the raider would subject the city to a prolonged bombardment, after which Waddell would send a negotiating party ashore "to parlay for a sizable ransom."

Rear Admiral Stribling turned over command of the East Gulf Squadron to Rear Admiral Thatcher of the West Gulf Squadron. In accordance with Navy Department orders dated 9 June 1865, the two squadrons were joined to form the newly designated Gulf Squadron. Stribling proceeded to Boston on U.S.S. *Powhatan* and hauled down his flag on the 12th.

6   U.S.S. *Sacramento*, Captain Henry Walke, intercepted steamer *Beatrice*, formerly C.S.S. *Rappahannock*, off the coast of Wales. She was enroute to Liverpool, England, from Calais, France, and was disarmed and under English colors. When intercepted, the former Confederate cruiser was steaming well within the three mile limit which Walke respected by refraining from either attacking or attempting to seize the vessel. *Sacramento* trailed the steamer through territorial waters until her arrival off Liverpool where Walke broke off the chase. *Rappahannock* had been purchased for the Confederacy by Commander Matthew F. Maury in the fall of 1863. However, she never

Distribution of vessels of the South Atlantic Blockading Squadron,
January 1, 1865.

Vessel.	Station.	Remarks.
	Murrell's Inlet	No vessel.
Canandaigua	Georgetown	
Do	Cape Romain	
*Mungham	Bull's Bay	
Chambers	do	
Adger	Charleston	Outside the bar.
Wamsutta	do	Do.
Nipsic	do	Do.
Sanford	do	Do.
South Carolina	do	Do.
Flambeau	do	Do.
Memphis	do	Do.
Potomska	do	Do.
Laburnum	do	Do.
Azalea	do	Do.
Sweet Brier	do	Do.
Patapsco	do	Inside the bar.
Montauk	do	Do.
Nahant	do	Do.
Passaic	do	Do.
Nantucket	do	Do.
Lehigh	do	Do.
Home	do	Do.
*Bruen	do	Do.
*Adams	do	Do.
*Orvetta	do	Do.
*Sea Foam	do	Do.
Gladiolus	do	Do.
Catalpa	do	Do.
Hydrangea	do	Do.
Jonquil	do	Do.
Geranium	do	Do.
Oleander	do	Do.
Catskill	do	Repairing.
*Ward	Light-House Inlet	
Wissahickon	Stono	
McDonough	do	
*Smith	do	
*Williams	do	
*St. Louis	North Edisto	
Percy Drayton	do	Tender.
Stettin	St. Helena	
*Norfolk Packet	do	
*New Hampshire	Port Royal	
Philadelphia	do	
Pawnee	do	
Arethusa	do	
Carnation	do	
Larkspur	do	
Pettit	do	
*Houghton	do	
Chatham	Port Royal	
Sonoma	Savannah River	
*Racer	do	
*Thunder	do	Tender.
*Griffith	Wassaw Sound	
*Lightning	do	Tender.
Flag	Ossabaw	
*Para	do	
*Fernandina	St. Catherine's	
Lodona	Sapelo	
Saratoga	Doboy	
Altamaha		
*Allen	St. Simon's	
Dai Ching	St. Andrew's	
*Perry	Fernandina	
Norwich	St. John's	
Hale	do	
	Mosquito [Inlet]	No vessel.
Sangamon	Port Royal	Repairing.
Cimarron	do	Do.
Ottawa	do	Do.
Winona	do	Do.
Acacia	do	Do.
Amaranthus	do	Do.
Iris	do	Do.
Camelia	do	Do.
Clover	do	Do.
*George W. Rodgers	do	Do.
*Braziliera	do	Do.
*Wild Cat	do	Tender.
*Swift	do	Do.
*Valparaiso	do	Hulk.
Mingoe		Expedition, Broad River.
Pontiac		Do.
Daffodil		Do.
Dandelion		Do.
Harvest Moon		Special duty.
*Blunt		Do.
*Hope		Do.

*Sailing vessels.

Just as the North Atlantic Squadron was severely reduced in numbers in the final months of the war and early post-war period, the South Atlantic Blockading Squadron was similarly cut back. Above is Rear Admiral Dahlgren's list of vessels attached to his command on 1 January 1865. On the following page is list containing the ships of the Squadron as of 1 July.

Vessel.	Station.	Remarks.
Hydrangea	Georgetown	
Catskill	Charleston Harbor	
Calypso	do	
Philadelphia	do	
*Adams	do	
*Blunt	do	
*Hope	do	
Catalpa	do	
Mab	do	Preparing to go north.
Jonquil		Do.
Clover		Quarantine and light vessel.
Home	Port Royal	
*New Hampshire	do	
Conemaugh	do	
Wando	do	
Daffodil	do	
Arethusa	do	
Amaranthus	do	
Laburnum	do	
Three Newport boats	do	Quarantine vessel.
*Chambers	do	
*Racer	Tybee	Tender.
Thunder	do	
Griffith	Wassaw Sound	Tender.
Lightning	do	
Donegal	Savannah River	
Cimarron	Fernandina	
George W. Rodgers	do	
Gladiolus	St. John's	Repairing.
Nahant	Port Royal	Do.
Emma	do	Repairing, East Gulf Squadron.
Sophronia	do	Repairing.
Preston	do	Do.
Para	do	Do.
McDonough	do	Do.
Pettit	do	Do.
Ottawa	do	Do
Chatham	do	Hulk.
Valparaiso	do	Laid up.
Swift	do	Do.
Percy Drayton	do	Do.
Coquette	do	Do.
Mail		Supply stores.
Oleander		North, to tow monitor.
Fahkee		With Rear-Admiral Dahlgren.
Pawnee		Detached and sent north since last list.
Wissahickon		Do.
Carnation		Do.
Larkspur		Do.
Geranium		Do.
Iris		Do.
Canonicus		Do.
Azalea		Do.
Sweet Brier		Do.
Norfolk Packet		Do.
Ward		Do.
Dandelion		Do.
Camelia		Preparing to go north.
Nahant	Port Royal	Do.
Para	do	Preparing to go north to dredge.
Preston	do	Do.
Patapsco	do	
Juniata		Left for other squadrons.
Fort Donelson		Do.
Transport		Transferred to Army.

WILLIAM REYNOLDS,
Commander and Senior Officer Present.

went to sea as the French government detained the vessel in Calais where she had been taken to avoid seizure in England.

7 Secretary Welles ordered Rear Admiral Radford of the Atlantic Squadron to further reduce his command to a total of 10 vessels. Welles also ordered the further reduction of the Gulf Squadron to a total of 12 vessels.

Rear Admiral Thatcher reported to Secretary Welles that U.S.S. *Sciota* had been raised, repaired and sent to Pensacola for rearming. This vessel had been sunk by a torpedo in Mobile Bay while conducting sweeping operations, 14 April (see 13 April 1865).

11 Secretary Welles advised Rear Admiral S. P. Lee, commanding the Mississippi Squadron, that officers against whom no charges were pending could leave the service at once, with honorable discharges and receive a month's leave for each year of service.

14 Blockade runner *Owl*, Commander Maffitt, steamed up the Mersey River and came to anchor in Liverpool harbor. He had brought the ship from Nassau through a Union Navy that had been alerted by Secretary Welles to exert all efforts to capture him. The following day, Maffitt had his boatswain pipe all hands aft where he appeared in an immaculate uniform and addressed the crew. "This is the last time we meet as sailors of the Confederate States Navy. . . . The Confederacy is dead. Our country is in the hands of the enemy, and we must accept the verdict. . . . I am grateful to you for your loyalty to me and to the South." He then paid off the crew, spliced one last mainbrace for the Confederacy and then personally struck the colors to three resounding cheers from the crew. Maffitt turned the ship over to Fraser, Trenholm and Company and established residence in Liverpool. After qualifying for a Master's License, he was employed by a shipping company and commanded the merchant steamer *Widgeon* trading between Liverpool and South American ports.

Maffitt finally returned to the United States in 1868 and made an unsuccessful attempt to secure restitution of confiscated property valued at $75,000. With the money he earned while serving in the British merchant marine, he purchased a 212 acre farm outside Wilmington, North Carolina, where he lived his remaining years. During these sunset years, Maffitt engaged in some very perceptive reflecting. On one occasion he summarized the important role played by sea power in the war. "The Northern navy," he wrote, "contributed materially to the successful issue of the war. The grand mistake of the South was neglecting her navy. All our army movements out West were baffled by the armed Federal steamers which swarmed on western waters, and which our government provided nothing to meet. Before the capture of New Orleans, the South ought to have had a navy strong enough to prevent the capture of that city, and hold firmly the Mississippi and its tributaries. This would have prevented many disastrous battles; it would have made Sherman's march through the country impossible and Lee would have still been master of his lines . . . the errors of our government were numerous but her neglect of the navy proved irremediable and fatal."

Maffitt also astutely commented on the lasting contributions made by the navy he represented. "The Confederate Navy," he wrote, "minute though it was, won a place for itself in history. To the Confederates the credit belongs of testing in battle the invulnerability of ironclads and of revolutionizing the navies of the world. The *Merrimack* did that. And though we had but a hand full of light cruisers, while the ocean swarmed with armed Federal vessels, we defied the Federal navy and swept Northern commerce from the sea." For this latter achievement, Maffitt personally merited a large share of the credit. As captain of C.S.S. *Florida* during her 1863 cruise he captured 24 American merchant ships and he commissioned tender *Clarence*, Lieutenant Charles W. Read, whose subsequent exploits accounted for 23 additional merchantmen.

15-31 After crossing the hazardous Bering Sea, C.S.S. *Shenandoah* made slow headway at first on the daring venture to attack San Francisco. Lieutenant Waddell wrote: "Prudence indicated communicating with a vessel recently from San Francisco before attempting the enterprise. The *Shenandoah* moved gently along with light winds or dashed before occasional gales until we reached the meridian of 129 W. when with the north wind that sweeps down the California coast her course was parallel with the land and we kept a sharp lookout, for we were then in waters frequented by the enemy's vessels."

16 The more he saw of Mexico the more Matthew Fontaine Maury became convinced that emigration of Confederates would prove a blessing. In all his many large undertakings through life, Maury

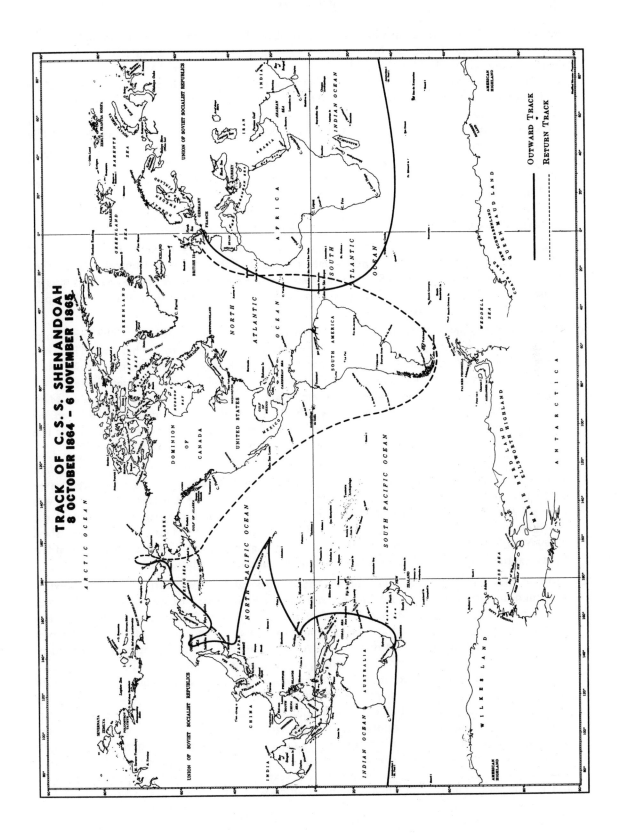

TRACK OF C.S.S. SHENANDOAH
8 OCTOBER 1864 – 6 NOVEMBER 1865

OUTWARD TRACK
RETURN TRACK

worked with the welfare of mankind in general in his heart. Emigration, he thought, would benefit his fellow Confederates who here could lead useful, productive lives, instead of languishing in mouldy dungeons, like Mallory and Davis. Emigration would benefit Mexico. The leadership able, educated men of energy and vision could provide might work wonders. As he wrote: "I saw corn in all its stages, from the time of its scattering by the hand of the sower, till it was gathered in the arms of the reaper. But agriculture is in a rude state. I saw them ploughing with a stick, and sawing with an axe, hoeing their corn with a shovel, and grinding it with a pebble. A few of our clever farmers, bringing with them their agricultural apprentices, would give new life and energy to the country. By sprinkling the Empire with settlers of this sort, they and their improved implements of husbandry and methods of culture would serve as so many new centres of agricultural life, energy, and improvement."

The emperor liked the plan, considering no nation could have enough men like Maury. On this date Maury wrote to a friend: " 'Max' enters heartily into my ideas."

18 Rear Admiral Louis M. Goldsborough arrived at Flushing, in the Netherlands, where he hoisted his flag on U.S.S. *Colorado* and assumed command of the reinstituted European Squadron. The Squadron consisted of U.S.S. *Niagara, Sacramento, Kearsarge, Frolic* and *Guard* and was to cruise from the North Sea to the Canary Islands, as the U.S. Navy resumed its historic role of protecting the nation's interests.

20 Lieutenant Commander William C. West, commanding the naval station at Beaufort, North Carolina, took charge of a large scale rescue operation off the entrance to the harbor. The Army transport *Quinnebaug*, loaded with troops, struck a reef and sank off Shackleford Banks while putting out of Beaufort. Participating in the rescue were U.S.S. *Anemone*, Acting Ensign A. O. Kruge, U.S.S. *Corwin*, Acting Master Robert Platt, and the boats from *Benjamin Adams* under the charge of the ship's second officer, Charles Freckrall. West singled out these officers for "rendering invaluable service in saving life" at the scene of the disaster. He reported the loss of 25 lives which he attributed to "the panic at the time of the steamer first striking."

Whaler *Milo* arrived in San Francisco Bay from the Bering Sea with 200 passengers who had formerly manned ten whalers captured and burned by C.S.S. *Shenandoah*. *Milo* had been seized on 22 June and bonded by Lieutenant Waddell for $30,000. Having departed promptly she was over a fortnight ahead of *Shenandoah*, which was beating down the North Pacific toward the Northwestern United States. Captain David McDougal, Commandant of the Mare Island Navy Yard, telegraphed this arrival to Secretary Welles and reported: "Great apprehension felt by mercantile community of San Francisco in consequence of depredations of *Shenandoah*."

22 Most of Maury's family and many of his friends opposed his colonization plan for Mexico. Although his family did not want him to return to Virginia to be "hanged or manacled," they also opposed his staying in Mexico because of the instability of Maximilian's rule. Overseas friends offered stronger and, perhaps seeing clearer from that distance, truer advice. One wrote: "The people of Virginia have shown themselves to be as brave as any people ever have been; but courage is coupled, in patriotism, with perseverance in suffering until better times come for Virginia. All who love her for what she has done ought to love her enough to suffer with her and for her sake. If the best people who have made Virginia what she is desert her at this critical moment, it would be like children leaving their mother in distress. There is no virtue without sacrifice, and if the Virginians possess the virtue of patriotism, they ought to bring her now the sacrifice of pride. Don't emigrate! Stand by your country with stern courage; learn the patience to bear without shame and with all the dignity of self-command . . . I don't think you can now return to Virginia; but in three or four years great changes will take place in opinions, and you nor your family won't find a country which would be able to give you anything like her sympathy, or to take Virginia out of your hearts and souls. You ought to go back to your dear state as soon as you can do so safely; and if you had followed my advice you would never have left England."

30 General Lee wrote Maury's son, Colonel Richard L. Maury: "I received by the last packet from Richmond your letter of the 22d enclosing an extract from a letter of your Father to you dated June 27 and a project of a decree of the Emperor of Mexico to encourage emigration of the planters of the South to that country.

"I was very glad to learn of the well being of your Father and of his safe arrival in Mexico and had felt assured wherever he might be that he deeply sympathized in the suffering of the people of the South and was ready to do all in his power to relieve them. I do not know how far their emigration to another land will conduce to their eventual prosperity although their prospects may not now be cheering. I have entertained the opinion that it would be better for them and the country to remain at their homes and share the fate of their respective States. I hope however the efforts of your father will facilitate the wishes and promote the welfare of all who find it necessary or convenient to expatriate themselves but should sincerely regret that either he or his should be embraced in that number."

31 Commodore Henry H. Bell was appointed by Secretary Welles to command the East India Squadron, consisting of Admiral Farragut's former flagship U.S.S. *Hartford*, and U.S.S. *Wachusett*, *Wyoming*, and storeship *Relief*. The command extended from the Strait of Sunda to the shores of Japan.

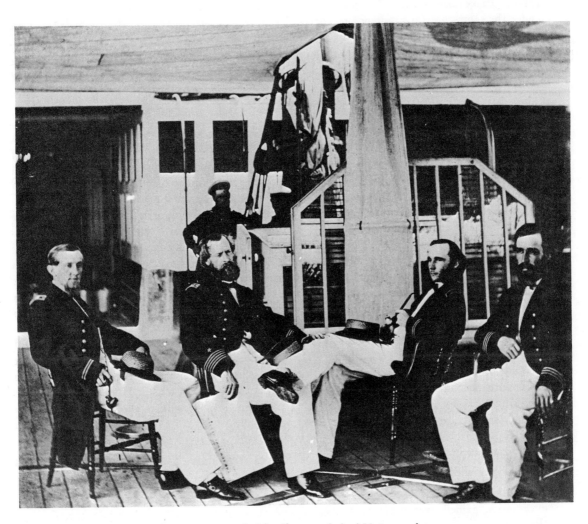

Canvas awning shields officers on deck of Union gunboat.

Wachusett and *Wyoming* were already in the Pacific at the time having been ordered there by Secretary Welles to search for C.S.S. *Shenandoah*. Thus the East India Squadron was reactivated after being discontinued upon the outbreak of the Civil War. The squadron had been initially established in 1835 when Commodore Edmond P. Kennedy commanded the sloop U.S.S. *Peacock* and the schooner *Boxer* on a cruise of Far Eastern waters. Secretary Welles directed the new squadron commander "to guard with jealous care the honor and interests of your flag and country, defend the citizens of the United States, and protect and facilitate the commerce thereof within the limits of your command." The squadron was an ancestor of today's Seventh Fleet, which alertly guards the long troubled shoreline of Asia from Siberia to Singapore.

In a General Order to the officers and men of the Potomac Flotilla, Commander F. A. Parker, announced the disbanding of the flotilla: "The war for the preservation of American liberty being at an end, the Potomac Flotilla, which took its rise with it and grew with its growth until it had become a fleet rather than a flotilla, this day happily ceases to exist." This squadron had made significant contributions to the Union victory by safeguarding the water approaches to Washington, by denying the use of the Potomac to the Confederacy, by maintaining control of the Rappahannock which rendered secure General Grant's supply base at Fredericksburg, and by conducting numerous amphibious operations which secured Virginia's Northern Neck for the Union. Parker concluded: "To those of you who are about to return to civil life I would say, render the same cheerful obedience to the civil that you have rendered to the naval law. Cast your votes as good citizens, regularly and quietly at the polls; so keeping in your hearts 'with malice toward none, with charity for all,' that after each Presidential election, whether it be with you or against you, you may be able to respond heartily to our old navy toast: 'The President of the United States: God Bless Him!' "

AUGUST

2 C.S.S. *Shenandoah*, Lieutenant Waddell, having quit her Arctic hunting grounds early the previous month, spoke English bark *Barracouta*, some 13 days out of San Francisco. For the first time Waddell learned positively that the war which he had been doing his part to prosecute had been over since April. He abandoned his daring and prospectively successful plan to lay San Francisco under ransom. The log of *Shenandoah* recorded: "Having received by the *Barracouta* the sad intelligence of the overthrow of the Confederate Government, all attempts to destroy the shipping or property of the United States will cease from this date, in accordance with which the first lieutenant, William C. Whittle, Jr., received the order from the commander to strike below the battery and disarm the ship and crew." Lieutenant Whittle, *Shenandoah*'s executive officer, wrote in his journal: "We were bereft of ground for hope or aspiration, bereft of a cause for which to struggle and suffer." Having terminated the raider's commerce destroying mission, Waddell was next confronted with the problem of what to do with the ship—a decision "which involved not only our personal honor, but the honor of the flag entrusted to us which had walked the waters fearlessly and in triumph." In addition to avoiding capture as a matter of honor and pride, Waddell was intent on insuring that the raider's crew should be accorded fair and unprejudiced treatment upon surrendering. After much consideration, he decided that these various purposes could best be served by attempting a nonstop voyage to Liverpool, England, via Cape Horn.

3 At the request of the United States agent in San Domingo, Rear Admiral Thatcher sent U.S.S. *Mercedita*, Lieutenant Commander Milton Haxtun, to the Dominican Republic with orders "to take all necessary steps to protect the lives and property of American citizens" in San Domingo. Now that the war was over, the Navy resumed its peacetime duty of protecting American citizens and property throughout the world.

4 Rear Admiral George F. Pearson of the Pacific Squadron reported to Secretary Welles that the information gained from whaler *Milo* on depredations of C.S.S. *Shenandoah* had brought him (Pearson) to San Francisco (see 20 July). He also reported that he immediately dissolved a general

court martial being conducted by squadron officers and sent every available ship to sea to search for the last of the raiders.

12 Rear Admiral Godon arrived in flagship *Susquehanna* in the harbor of Bahia, Brazil, pursuant to orders of the Navy Department appointing him to command the Brazil Squadron. This squadron dating back to the early 1820's was reactivated after being temporarily discontinued during the Civil War. Its station extended from the Amazon River to the Magellan Straits and its commander was directed to protect "our flag from insult and the property of our citizens from unlawful seizure." Godon's command consisted of U.S.S. *Monadnock, Chippewa, Monticello, Canonicus, Shawmut, Fahkee* and *Wasp.*

14 Rear Admiral S. P. Lee hauled down his flag on U.S.S. *Tempest* and the Mississippi Squadron ceased to exist. The squadron had played a major role in fashioning the Union's ultimate victory. In the Tennessee and Cumberland Rivers campaign, naval actions had been decisive in rolling back the Confederacy's northern frontier from Kentucky to Mississippi and Alabama. Its Mississippi River operations at Vicksburg and elsewhere, combined with Admiral Farragut's victory at New Orleans, had severed the Confederacy and denied to the eastern portion the vital supplies of the provision-rich western half. Finally, the squadron's operations on the tributaries of the Mississippi, including support of the Army, had projected Union striking power into the deepest reaches of the Confederacy. The five remaining vessels of the former eighty ship fleet were placed under the operational control of Commodore John W. Livingston, commanding the Mound City Naval Station, the only remaining station on the western rivers.

15–31 C.S.S. *Shenandoah* stood steadily for the empty South Atlantic. Up to the time of deciding to steer for England, Lieutenant Waddell wrote, the successful raider "had made more than forty thousand miles without an accident. I felt sure a search would be made for her in the North Pacific and that to run the ship south was important to all concerned. Some of the people expressed a desire that I should take the *Shenandoah* to Australia or New Zealand or any near port rather than attempt to reach Europe. There seemed however to me no other course to pursue but the one I had decided upon, and I considered it due the integrity of all to reject anything and everything like flinching under the severe trial imposed upon us. It was my duty as a man and a commanding officer to be careful of the honor as well as the welfare of the one hundred and thirty-two men placed in my hands."

19 Maury's sage friend, Captain Marin Jansen of the Netherlands Navy, writing from Delft, Holland, proved a prophet when he gave an added reason for Maury's not proceeding with his plan for the colonization of Mexico. He would probably lose his head with the Emperor if he remained. "As long as Maximilian tries to make what is called a civilized government his position is unstable and I should not like you to stay there, however sweet and pleasant it may be in the shade of an Emperor's crown. . . You may run the chance as his Prime Minister to be a Prince of Empire or to be hung or shot or something worse."

The members of Maury's family again urged him to abandon the plan and go to Russia, accepting the invitation of the Grand Duke Constantine, or to France where Napoleon III had invited him to live. Many nations sought the great mind of Maury, leading naval scientist of his time. Before the Civil War he was the most honored and possibly most noted living American among other nations of the world.

Maury's reply to his family was characteristic of the stout integrity and dedication of so many naval officers on both sides in the Civil War. He did not want to be a court drone, but to *earn* a living—and to help make a better world. "I have come here to provide a home for such of the conquered people as like to emigrate," he wrote. "Suppose they do not thank me—well, there is still useful and honourable occupation for me here. There are many things here with which I may identify myself and do good, such as organizing the census, a land survey for the Empire, a system of internal improvements; and though last, not least, the introduction of chinchona cultivation."

Introduction of chinchona was a long cherished idea. Before leaving England Maury had discussed it with a distinguished geographer who had developed plantations in India. In Mexico, he had early applied himself to study of the country's geography, one purpose being to determine the best location for chinchona cultivation. "Bark of this tree, variously called Calisava, Jesuit's or Peruvian Bark, was a source of quinine vitally needed in the treatment of malaria." Maury left a continuing heritage of good in his wake through life.

28 Rear Admiral Porter, who had commanded the Mississippi Squadron in the early part of the war and the South Atlantic Squadron in the latter part of the conflict, was appointed Superintendent of the Naval Academy. Under his supervision the school was returned to its pre-war location at Annapolis, Maryland. At the outbreak of the war the Academy had been moved to Newport, Rhode Island, where the resort hotel Atlantic House and the historic frigate U.S.S. *Constitution* were utilized for housing and classrooms. Porter was also confronted with the task of refurbishing the buildings and grounds which, during the war, had been used as an army post and field hospital. Porter served as Superintendent for four years and while at the Academy was promoted to the rank of Vice Admiral.

SEPTEMBER

5 Steadily proceeding with the colonization plan proposed by Maury, whom he deeply respected, Emperor Maximilian issued a decree that began "We, Maximilian, Emperor of Mexico, in consideration of the sparseness of the population in the Mexican territory, in proportion to its extent, desiring to give to immigrants all possible security for property and liberty . . . do decree as follows: Mexico is open to immigrants of all nations. Immigration agents shall be appointed, whose duty it will be to protect the arrival of immigrants, install them on the lands assigned them, and assist them in every possible way in establishing themselves. These agents will receive the orders of the Imperial Commissioner of Immigration, especially appointed by us, and to whom all the communications relative to immigration shall be addressed."

6 General Lee advised Maury against remaining in Mexico. He wrote: "We have certainly not found our form of government all that was anticipated by its original founders; but this may be partly our fault in expecting too much, and partly due to the absence of virtue in the people. As long as virtue was dominant in the Republic, so long was the happiness of the people secure. I cannot, however, despair of it yet; I look forward to better days, and trust that time and experience—the great teachers of men under the guidance of our ever-merciful God—may save us from destruction, and restore to us the bright hopes and prospects of the past. The thought of abandoning the country, and all that must be left in it, is abhorrent to my feelings, and I prefer to struggle for its restoration, and share its fate rather than to give up all as lost." He admired Mexico but still loved Virginia.

"I shall be very sorry if your presence will be lost to Virginia. She has now sore need of all her sons, and can ill afford to lose you. I am very much obliged to you for all you have done for us, and hope your labours in the future may be as efficacious as in the past, and that your separation from us may not be permanent."

11 Emperor Maximilian approved Maury's "Regulations and Instructions" prepared to accompany the Immigration decree. The pamphlet provided general information on Mexico's climate, topography, mineral wealth, agricultural possibilities. That evening after dinner with the royal family, in private conference with the Emperor, Maury told him: "I can't manage immigration through the Ministers. I must transact business with you directly, and not through them; nor must they have anything to do with it. 'That's what I intend,' said he. Said I, 'I have not seen my wife and children for three years; I want to be quick, organize immigration, and take the

Matthew Fontaine Maury, naval officer-scientist, Pathfinder of the Seas, headed Maximilian's efforts to encourage immigration of Southerners to Mexico after the conflict.

Maximilian, Emperor of Mexico.

steamer of 13th November for France.' 'Certainly,' said he. Then he said, 'I wish you to continue the conversation with the Empress; I have something pressing to do. She will make notes, give me verbal explanations, and have it all ready for me by four o'clock in the morning, when I will attend to it.' Carlotta was walking in the garden. He referred me to some books on the table, and went to look for her. She came, and we commenced discussing matters, she making notes nearly as fast as I could talk . . . we discussed, with approbation, my going to see you [Maury's wife]; the appointments of agents in the South and their salaries, and the organization of a land office. She is very clever, practical and businesslike. I told her I thought she could do more business in a day than all of the Ministers put together could do in a week. She said, 'I believe I could'.''

16 C.S.S. *Shenandoah*, Lieutenant Waddell, rounded Cape Horn and entered the Atlantic enroute to Liverpool, England. In the Pacific, the *Shenandoah* had struck the New England whaling industry a blow as devastating as that administered the English whaling industry in 1813 by U.S.S. *Essex* commanded by Captain David Porter. There was hard truth in the boast made by Waddell in later years when he said, "I made New England suffer."

17–30 After rounding Cape Horn *Shenandoah* took a northeast gale which forced her "to west longitude of 24°40' before she reached the parallel of 40°S . . ." Day after day icebergs and savage blocks of ice came near. "We were without a moon to shed her cheerful light over our desolate path, and the wind blew so fiercely that the ship's speed could not be reduced below five knots. It was more prudent to go ahead than to heave to, for I was without observations for several days and in an easterly current. Some of the icebergs were castellated . . . ." The struggles of the ship accorded with the struggles that "filled our minds." Alone on the friendless sea, "we were without a home or country, our little crew all that were left of the thousands who had sworn to defend that country or die with her, and there were moments when we would have deemed that a friendly gale which would have buried our sorrowful hearts and the beautiful *Shenandoah* in those dark waters. What a contrast to those gay hopes and proud aspirations with which we had entered upon the cruise. How eager we had been to court danger. Now gloomily and cautiously we avoided recognition. The very ship seemed to have partaken our feelings and no longer moved with her accustomed swiftness."

18 Emperor Maximilian's imperial decree appointed Commander Maury "Honorary Counselor of the State". He was becoming more and more the trusted confidant of both the Emperor and Empress, which did not help him with the rest of the Administration.

22 Planning to build a National Observatory and wanting to have the right man on hand to direct it, Emperor Maximillian appointed ex-Commander Maury, CSN, one time world famous head of the U.S. Naval Observatory while Lieutenant, USN, as "Director of the National Observatory.

26 Several of Maximilian's ministers objected to Maury's immigration plans and effectively stalled them. Maury, accustomed to getting things done, took shortcuts through the imperial household. Empress Carlotta handled many of the plans. This date she agreed to Maury's request to have former Major General John Bankhead Magruder appointed to head a land office at a salary of $3,000 a year, with a large number of surveyors under him who were needed to assist in the clarification of land titles. Magruder, a native of Virginia, had graduated from West Point, and served the United States Army with distinction until 1861, then serving ably in the Confederate Army. He had announced that he would bring his family to Mexico to live.

OCTOBER

10 Command of the Atlantic Squadron passed from Rear Admiral Radford to Commodore Joseph Lanman. Radford reported to Washington and assumed command of the Washington Navy Yard.

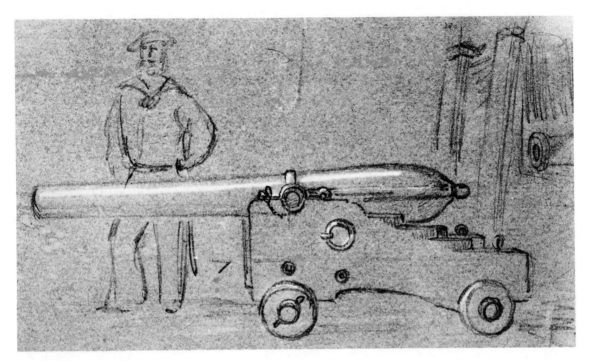

Pencil drawing by Alfred Waud of new rifled cannon at Washington Navy Yard.

11 C.S.S. *Shenandoah* crossed the equator about midway between South America and Africa as she steered for England. Application had been made to Waddell to take the ship to Capetown. He inflexibly held to his decision to sail back to England, believing this best served the welfare and honor of all.

12–24 C.S.S. *Shenandoah* fell in "with a great many sail but kept at a polite distance from them, working her way along under sail through calms and light airs. In latitude 10° N. we took the trades."

24 Commander Maury's oldest son, Richard, and the only member of the family who voiced any enthusiasm for his Mexican plan, arrived in Mexico with his wife. He, crippled like his father, would be understudy in directing immigration and would run the office when his father departed for England to see Mrs. Maury.

25 When C.S.S. *Shenandoah* had "nearly run out of the trades and her sails fanning her along, a mast-head lookout cried sail O! The cry sail O! brought many to their feet who were indulging repose, and their anxious glances evinced their state of mind, for if a Federal cruiser was to be found anywhere she would be in that region of ocean . . ." The stranger was a steamer, apparently a warship. If of the U.S. Navy, *Shenandoah* had to avoid her, but the courses converged. "The sun was thirty minutes high and the sky was cloudless. We could make no change in the course of the ship or the quantity of sail she carried, for to arouse the suspicions of the sail might expose the *Shenandoah* to investigation. Whatever she was she had seen our ship and might be waiting to speak her. The *Shenandoah* was perceptibly shortening the distance between herself and the sail, and there was danger that she would approach too near during daylight for she could already be seen from our deck. The propeller had been lowered to impede her progress, but the favoring night seemed to come on more slowly than I had ever before known it . . . There was but one hope, and that was in a drag, two ends of a hawser made fast and the bite thrown overboard would retard in some degree her progress through the water . . . When darkness closed between us we

could not have been more than three miles distant. The *Shenandoah*'s head was turned south and steam was ordered. At nine o'clock while our sails were being furled the moon rose and the surface presented a little before by the *Shenandoah* being greatly diminished by that maneuver it would be difficult to find where she lay.

"The Cardiff coal makes a white vapor which could not be seen two hundred yards off, and now that the engines were working and the steamer heading east, we had all the advantages to be expected. It was the first time our ship had been under steam since crossing the line in the Pacific Ocean, indeed the fires were not lighted during a distance of over thirteen thousand miles. The *Shenandoah* was five hundred miles southeast of the Azores, and if there was an American cruiser in that locality on the 25th day of October, 1865, we were probably in sight of each other. I have been told that the U.S. steamer *Saranac*, Captain Walke, was probably the vessel."

As he wrote elsewhere, Waddell again felt: "I believe the Divine will directed and protected that ship in all her adventures."

NOVEMBER

1 James Brooks, formerly of the U.S. Ram Fleet and Mississippi Marine Brigade, wrote a brief sketch of the ram fleet history to Brigadier General L. B. Parsons, Chief of Transportation Department in St. Louis: "The idea . . . of destroying the enemy's fleet by the use of rams originated with Colonel Charles Ellet, Jr. . . . About the last of March, 1862, the Secretary of War invited him to his office to consult on the subject, and ordered him . . . to procure the boats and make the necessary alterations . . . It (the ram fleet) . . . was at Memphis on the morning of the 6th of June (1862) and participated in the battle. . . . The result was a great triumph for the rams, and fully came up to the expectations of Colonel Ellet and the Government. . . . In November, 1863, the Secretary of War decided upon enlarging the fleet by . . . what was known as the Mississippi Marine Brigade. . . . The fleet was continued in the service until August 1864, when the War Department thought the necessity of such an organization no longer existed, and it was mustered out of the service and the boats turned over to the quartermasters . . . to be used as transports."

2 A special squadron of four vessels commanded by Commodore John Rodgers departed from Hampton Roads for the Pacific via Cape Horn. The ships consisted of the U.S.S. *Vanderbilt*, *Tuscarora*, *Powhatan* and *Monadnock* and were intended to increase the Pacific Squadron to a fourteen ship force. Even so, this was a small number for the vast responsibilities of the United States already rapidly increasing in this mighty ocean where so much history would be written.

3 Secretary Welles ordered all naval vessels to resume rendering honors when entering British ports and to begin again exchanging official courtesies with English men of war. Early in the war, the Navy had been ordered to cease rendering these traditional courtesies to the national flag of any nation that accorded recognition to Confederate belligerency. This order continued in effect against Great Britain until that nation lifted the last of the restrictions that had been placed on American naval vessels entering British ports or waters.

6 C.S.S. *Shenandoah*, Lieutenant Waddell, sailed up the Mersey River into Liverpool, 123 days and 23,000 miles from the Aleutians. This had been a non-stop cruise made primarily under sail. The raider resorted to steam only on the one occasion at night in the mid-South Atlantic to evade U.S.S. *Saranac*. The following morning the boiler fires were banked and Waddell proceeded under sail and arrived at his destination without sighting another vessel. *Shenandoah* entered Liverpool harbor with the Confederate flag flying and became the only ship to circumnavigate the globe under the Stars and Bars. Waddell reported his arrival to the British Foreign Ministry and was officially informed that the war had ended. He thereupon lowered the last official Confederate flag and turned over ship, himself and crew to Captain J. G. Paynter, RN, commanding H.M.S. *Donegal*. After a few days' confinement to the ship, Waddell and his crew were set at liberty by the English government.

ably distant from us. The ship was continued under sail during the daylight, because if we had gotten up steam it would have been observed, and as each sail was ignorant of the character of the other, it would have directed attention to the steamer, and one of them might have been a Federal cruiser. As soon as night received us in her friendly folds steam was applied and we were off for St. George's Channel. The weather continued calm and beautiful, and I entered the channel on the 5th of November, just 122 days from the Aleutian Islands. The chronometers had not been rated since we left Melbourne, and we had not seen land since we had left the Aleutian Islands, and yet we could not have made a more beautiful land fall; the beacon in St.George's Channel was seen where and at the time looked for. I received a pilot after midnight, and when he was informed it was the Shenandoah he exclaimed, "I was reading a few days ago of your being in the Arctic Ocean." I asked for the news from America. His statements corroborrated the Barracouta's intelligence. I desired the pilot to take the ship into the Mersey that I might communicate with her British Majesty's Government. On the morning of the 6th of November, 1865, the Shenandoah steamed up the River Mersey in a thick fog under the Confederate flag, and the pilot had orders to anchor her near H.M. ship-of-the-line Donegal, Captain Paynter, R.N. Shortly after we anchored a lieutenant from the Donegal visited us to ascertain the name of the vessel and gave me official intelligence of the termination of the American war. He was polite. The flag was then hauled down.

An extract from the typescript of the Waddell Journal. This typescript is in the holdings of the National Archives, Washington, D.C.

Before reaching port Waddell had divided prize money "captured prior to the surrender of the Southern armies and other money which had been captured after the surrender of the Southern armies. The former I directed to be divided among the officers and crew according to the law on the subject of prize money, of which I declined to receive the portion which I would be entitled to, and it was divided among the officers and crew with the rest of the money. That which was captured after the surrender of the Southern armies was surrendered to Paymaster Robert W. Warwick, H.M. ship *Donegal*."

Secretary Welles bitterly denounced the release of the Confederates in a letter to Secretary of State Seward and urged that demands be made for Waddell and his crew to be delivered over to the United States. "The close of the career of the *Shenandoah* on the high seas," wrote Welles, "was notoriously and indisputably that of a pirate, and the piracy was of the most odious and despicable character. It was not the plunder of richly laden barks belonging to 'merchant princes,' who could afford the loss, though they might feel it, but the wanton destruction of the property of individuals seeking a humble subsistence in one of the most laborious and perilous of callings, and who could make no show of resistance to the overwhelming force of the pirate. No other description of robbery upon the high seas could have inflicted so much individual distress upon persons so little able to bear it, and so little deserving of it."

Shenandoah was subsequently delivered over to the American Minister, Charles Francis Adams, who, after an abortive attempt to have her sent to the United States, ordered her sold at auction. She was purchased for $108,632.18 by the Sultan of Zanzibar who intended to convert her into a luxury yacht. After this proved economically unfeasible, the Sultan placed the ex-raider in the Indian Ocean ivory trade under the name *Majidi*.

For a number of years she sailed out of this far off Muslim island kingdom where in 1963 U.S.S. *Manley* sped from a Southeast African visit to rescue Americans threatened by a Communist infiltrated revolution that destroyed the Muscat monarchy long sustained by British law and order. *Shenandoah*'s career ended in 1879, eighty-four years ahead of the Sultan's rule, when she ripped her bottom out on an uncharted reef in the Indian Ocean.

Waddell chose to remain in England rather than return to his homeland where Secretaries Welles and Stanton were publicly calling him the "Anglo-Rebel Pirate Captain". He finally returned to the United States in 1875 and was employed as a master by the Pacific Mail Steamship Company.

23 The former Confederate ram *Stonewall* arrived at the Washington Navy Yard under her own power, escorted by U.S.S. *Rhode Island* and *Hornet*. Commander Alexander Murray, commanding the *Rhode Island*, had taken possession of the ship in Havana after reimbursing Spanish authorities for all expenses incurred during her detention. The reimbursement totaled $18,000 which included $16,000 which the Governor General of Cuba had given Captain T. J. Page, CSN, to pay off his officers and crew, and an additional $2,000 for tug services, dock fees and preservation expenses (see 11–19 May). *Stonewall* was subsequently sold to Japan and used in her naval service.

27 By this date Maury could report that "about 40 of our people" had already arrived at New Virginia, the name he gave his proposed colony. He described it as "a garden spot" between Mexico City and Vera Cruz. Maury didn't leave for England this month as he originally planned. It took longer than he had anticipated for him to establish the administrative organization for the emigration program and to get it going smoothly. He did go later and events conspired that he would never return.*

---

* A study summarizing his subsequent career overseas along with those of some other leading Confederate and U.S. Naval Officers after the war will appear in the final volume of the series. It will contain other special studies and a full index covering all volumes of the series.

This photograph of Confederate naval officers was taken late in 1865 at Leamington Spa, England, after the return of C.S.S. Shenandoah to Liverpool. Seated (center) is Dr. Edwin Gilliam Booth, who had served with Franklin Buchanan and was Assistant Surgeon on board C.S.S. Selma. Others are: (left to right) Acting Master Irvine S. Bulloch of C.S.S. Alabama and Shenandoah; Passed Assistant Surgeon Bennett W. Green of C.S.S. Stonewall; Lieutenant William H. Murdaugh, one of James Bulloch's aides in Great Britain; and Passed Assistant Surgeon Charles E. Lining of Shenandoah.

DECEMBER

4 Secretary Welles announced that the West India Squadron was to be reestablished in that area "where we have so large a trade, and where, owing to the proximity of the islands to our shores, it is essential that we cultivate friendly relations". Commodore James S. Palmer was designated to command this squadron with U.S.S. *Rhode Island* serving as his flagship. The eight additional vessels comprising the squadron were: U.S.S. *De Soto, Swatara, Monongahela, Florida, Augusta, Shamrock, Ashuelot*, and *Monocacy*.

27 Secretary Welles observed in his diary that his orders to arrest Raphael Semmes had been carried out and that the ex-Confederate raider captain was being brought to Washington to stand trial for breaking parole. "He did not belong in the Rebel region," wrote Welles, "and has not therefore the poor apology of those who shelter themselves under the action of their States; he was educated and supported by that government which he deserted in disregard of his obligations and his oath; he made it his business to rob and destroy the ships and property of his unarmed countrymen engaged in peaceful commerce; when he finally fought and was conquered he practiced a fraud, and in violation of his surrender broke faith, and without ever being exchanged fought against the Union at Richmond. . . ." Semmes was released from prison in April, 1866 without being brought to trial. The government considered its legal case against him inadequate as Semmes had never been in the actual custody of the Union forces when *Alabama* was sunk off Cherbourg on 19 June 1864.

In his fourth annual report to the President, Secretary Welles summarized naval activity during 1865 and reviewed the contributions of the Navy to the North's war effort. "The demands upon the naval service," he wrote, "which for four years had been exacting, were relaxed upon the fall of Fort Fisher. That event, and the possession of Cape Fear river, closed all access to Wilmington, the port of rebel supplies, put an end to illicit traffic with the States in insurrection, and extinguished the last remnants of that broken commerce which foreign adventurers had, notwithstanding constant and severe losses persisted in carrying on by breach of blockade."

Welles noted that the evacuation of Wilmington "was preliminary to the fall of Richmond and the surrender of the rebel armies, which were thenceforward deprived of supplies from abroad." But while General Lee's soldiers were thus cut off from their source of supplies, the Union troops were assured full logistic support and freedom of movement because the North dominated the waterways at General Grant's vital base at City Point.

Farther down the coast, Welles continued, ". . . Rear Admiral Dahlgren was engaged in assisting in the transfer of the right wing of the army to Beaufort, S.C., and in the course of General Sherman's march northward that officer and his army were aided by all needful naval operations. On the 12th and 13th of February a joint movement was made along the approaches from Bull's Bay to Mount Pleasant, with a view of embarrassing the military commandant at Charleston, and blinding him as to the actual military design . . . . Other less extensive movements than that at Bull's Bay were made about that period. . . . They were intended simply to attract the attention of the rebels and aiding General Sherman in accomplishing his great purpose of moving towards Richmond. . . . The morning of the 18th [of February] revealed the fact that Charleston was evacuated. Thus, without a final struggle, the original seat of the rebellion, the most invulnerable and best protected city on the coast, whose defenses had cost immense treasure and labor, was abandoned, and the emblem of unity and freedom was again reinstated upon the walls of Sumter."

The Secretary reported the joint operations leading to the evacuation of Mobile and the capitulation of the Confederacy through the Gulf coast. "On the 2d of June, Galveston was surrendered, and the supremacy of the government was once more established on the entire coast, from Maine to and including Texas."

"With only limited means at the command of the department to begin with," he wrote, "the navy became suddenly an immense power."

During the war, the Navy had increased from 42 active commissioned ships to a fleet of nearly 700. Welles noted that 208 ships had been built or begun during this period, and 418 others, primarily steamers, had been purchased. The number of men in the service grew from 7,600 at the outset of the war to 51,500 at its close.

"An unrelaxing blockade was maintained for four years from the capes of the Chesapeake to the Rio Grande, while a flotilla of gunboats, protecting and aiding the army in its movements, penetrated and patrolled our rivers, through an internal navigation almost continental, from the Potomac to the Mississippi. After the capture of Forts Hatteras and Clark, in August, 1861, port after port was wrested from the insurgents, until the flag of the Union was again restored in every harbor and along our entire coast, and the rebellion was eventually wholly suppressed."

Welles continued: "As soon as our domestic troubles were overcome, the duty of attending to out interests abroad prompted the re-establishing of the foreign squadrons which had been suspended. The European, the Brazil, and the East India squadrons have been organized anew upon as economical a scale as is consistent with their efficiency, the interests of commerce, and a proper regard for our position as a nation."

He wisely added: "In time of peace our naval force should be actively employed in visiting every commercial port where American capital is employed, and there are few available points on the globe which American enterprise has not penetrated and reached. But commerce needs protection, and our squadrons and public vessels in commission must not be inactive. One or more of our naval vessels ought annually to display the flag of the Union in every port where our ships may trade. The commerce and the navy of a people have a common identity and are inseparable companions. Wherever our merchant ships may be employed, there should be within convenient proximity a naval force to protect them and make known our national power."

The Secretary concluded his report: "As peace is being restored among us, the country now puts off the formidable naval armor which it had assumed to vindicate upon a mighty scale that supremacy of the national law which is the very life of our Union. In the details of the policy and the measures by which our naval power is now brought down to the dimensions and distributed to the important operations of a peace establishment, the country will see with relief and gratitude a large and signal reduction of national expenditure. I need hardly say that this great object is kept constantly and carefully in view by this department.

"Such alleviations of the public burdens is the plain dictate of a wise policy. Yet true wisdom directs that this policy of retrenchment in the naval branch of the public service must not be carried too far. It is still wise—the wisest—economy to cherish the navy, to husband its resources, to invite new supplies of youthful courage and skill to its service, to be amply supplied with all needful facilities and preparations for efficiency, and thus to hold within prompt and easy reach its vast and salutary power for the national defence and self-vindication."

SUMMARY OF SIGNIFICANT EVENTS
AND
CALENDAR FOR 1861–1865

Firing on Fort Sumter

Fleet bombards Fort Fisher

Monitor-Virginia *Engagement*

SOME SIGNIFICANT CIVIL WAR EVENTS AND CALENDAR 1861-1865

12 April 1861	Fort Sumter fired on by Confederate batteries—the conflict begins.
19 April 1861	President Lincoln issued proclamation declaring blockade of Southern ports from South Carolina to Texas.
20 April 1861	Norfolk Navy Yard, after being partially destroyed, was abandoned by Union forces. This gave the Confederacy a major installation and a quantity of guns and ordnance supplies.
22 April 1861	Union troops, coming by water, land at Annapolis and save Washington.
16 May 1861	Commander John Rodgers ordered to form a Union naval force on the western rivers. The three ships purchased and outfitted by Rodgers were the nucleus of the fleets which split the Confederacy along the Mississippi.
30 June 1861	C.S.S. *Sumter*, Commander Raphael Semmes, ran blockade out of Mississippi River to begin successful commerce raiding.
6 July 1861	C.S.S. *Sumter*, arrived at Cuban port with seven captured Union merchantmen.
29 August 1861	Union forces under Flag Officer S. H. Stringham and General B. F. Butler received the unconditional surrender of Confederate-held Forts Hatteras and Clark, closing Pamlico Sound to commerce raiding and blockade running.
7 November 1861	Naval Forces under Flag Officer S. F. DuPont captured Port Royal Sound, S.C., which gave the Union forces an important operating base on the Southern coast.
11 November 1861	Thaddeus Lowe made balloon observation of Confederate forces from Balloon-Boat *G. W. Parke Custis* anchored in Potomac River.
6 February 1862	Naval forces under Flag Officer A. H. Foote captured strategic Fort Henry on the Tennessee River. This breached the Confederate line and opened the flood gates for the flow of Union power deep into the South.
7–8 February 1862	Joint amphibious expedition under Flag Officer L. M. Goldsborough and Brigadier General A. E. Burnside captured Roanoke Island—the key to Albemarle Sound. The operation cut off Norfolk from its main supply lines and led to eventual evacuation of the city.
14 February 1862	Gunboats under Flag Officer A. H. Foote attacked Fort Donelson on the Cumberland River in conjunction with troops under Brigadier General U. S. Grant. The Fort capitulated on 16 February, opening the way to the fall of Nashville with its large stockpile of stores and munitions.
8 March 1862	Ironclad ram C.S.S. *Virginia*, Captain F. Buchanan, destroyed wooden blockading ships U.S.S. *Cumberland* and *Congress* in Hampton Roads.
9 March 1862	U.S.S. *Monitor*, Lieutenant J. L. Worden, engaged C.S.S. *Virginia*, Lieutenant C. ap R. Jones, in the historic first battle of ironclads—the age of the wooden warship ended.
22 March 1862	C.S.S. *Florida*, sailing as British steamer *Oreto*, cleared Liverpool for Nassau.

7 April 1862	Island No. 10, key to the Confederate defense of the upper Mississippi, surrendered to the naval forces of Flag Officer A. H. Foote. The capture opened the river to Union gunboats and transports south to Fort Pillow.
24 April 1862	Flag Officer D. G. Farragut's fleet ran past Fort Jackson and St. Philip, destroyed the defending Confederate flotilla below New Orleans, and, next day, compelled the surrender of the South's largest and wealthiest city. Farragut had achieved a brilliant victory.
10 May 1862	Confederates destroyed the Norfolk and Pensacola Navy Yards in actions caused by the forced Southern withdrawal from her coasts.
11 May 1862	C.S.S. *Virginia* was blown up by her crew off Craney Island to prevent her capture by advancing Union forces.
15 July 1862	C.S.S. *Arkansas*, Lieutenant I. N. Brown, engaged and ran through the Union fleet above Vicksburg, partially disabling U.S.S. *Carondelet* and *Tyler*. Brown's heroic dash was one of great heroism and high professional ability.
16 July 1862	David Glasgow Farragut promoted to Rear Admiral, the first officer to hold that rank in the history of the U.S. Navy.
24 August 1862	Captain Semmes placed the commerce raider C.S.S. *Alabama* in commission at sea off the Azores.
26 August 1862	Franklin Buchanan promoted to Admiral, ranking officer in the Confederate Navy.
12 December 1862	U.S.S. *Cairo*, Lieutenant Commander T. O. Selfridge, was sunk in Yazoo River, the first ship to be destroyed by a Confederate torpedo.
31 December 1862	U.S.S. *Monitor*, Commander J. P. Bankhead, foundered and was lost at sea off Cape Hatteras.
1 January 1863	C.S.S. *Bayou City* and *Neptune* engaged the Union fleet at Galveston, forcing the North's withdrawal from that foothold on the Texas coast. U.S.S. *Harriet Lane* was captured and U.S.S. *Westfield* was destroyed.
21 January 1863	C.S.S. *Josiah Bell* and *Uncle Ben* captured U.S.S. *Morning Light* and *Velocity*, temporarily lifting the blockade of Sabine Pass, Texas.
31 January 1863	C.S.S. *Palmetto State* and *Chicora* boldly attacked the blockading fleet off Charleston; U.S.S. *Mercedita* and *Keystone State* were heavily damaged and struck their flags.
12 February 1863	C.S.S. *Florida*, Lieutenant John N. Maffit, captured *Jacob Bell* with cargo from China valued at more than $2,000,000.
14 March 1863	Rear Admiral D. G. Farragut passed the heavy batteries at Port Hudson with U.S.S. *Hartford* and *Albatross* to establish an effective blockade of the vital Red River supply lines.
7 April 1863	Rear Admiral S. F. Du Pont's ironclad squadron engaged strong Confederate forts in Charleston harbor in an attempt to penetrate the defenses and capture the city. The ironclads were heavily damaged and the attack was broken off; U.S.S. *Keokuk* sank the next day.
3 May 1863	C.S.S. *Alabama*, Captain Semmes, captured and burned bark *Union Jack* and ship *Sea Lark* off Brazil. Semmes estimated the value of *Sea Lark* and cargo at $550,000.
4 July 1863	Vicksburg surrendered after a lengthy bombardment and siege by Union naval and land forces. President Lincoln wrote: "The Father of Waters again goes unvexed to the sea."

Memorandum.

Bureau Med Surgery
August 4, 1863

I am of opinion the issue of whiskey to men under the circumstances mentioned by Fleet Surgeon Holmes, is neither wise nor conducive to anything more than a merely temporary result of no beneficial character, though I dissent with diffidence from so judicious, and intelligent an Officer.

The issue of whiskey to men exhausted by labor, and heat proves a momentary comfort, and stimulus it is true; but the depression soon recurs to make its repetition necessary.

Whiskey is a simple stimulant, and nothing more.

It appears to me a judicious plan to follow in the Fleet operating before Charleston would be as follows:

When the men are turned out in the morning let them go into the water; immediately on coming out issue a draught of strong coffee.

Breakfast at the usual hour with coffee.

Dinner at the usual hour, when coffee, iced, and sweetened, or tea, prepared in like manner, may be served for drink.

Supper. If possible in these long days at a later hour.

As it is understood the Department proposes to supply Ice liberally, tea or coffee of good strength, and iced, might be allowed as at common drinks for the men.

This memorandum from the Chief of the Bureau of Medicine and Surgery was in response to a request from Rear Admiral John Dahlgren that men serving in monitors off Charleston Harbor be permitted a whiskey ration, despite the fact that Congress had outlawed the "spirit ration" in July 1862. It is not known how the hard bitten sailors took to the iced coffee and tea or oatmeal recommended by the Bureau Chief, but they did not get their whiskey.

A bath before turning in at night might prove refreshing, and aid the sailor to recover his energies by sound sleep.

Liquor should only be served out in special cases, when the judgement of the Medical Officer suggests its use.

Oatmeal, mixed with water, is familiar to sea-going men, and Engineers as a means of assuaging, or diminishing thirst.

The ship's decks should be kept as dry as possible that the sailor in profuse perspiration from hard work should have a place to rest himself where he will not be exposed to Rheumatism, or cold.

Frequent changes of clothing would conduce as much to the comfort of sailors in hot weather as they do to all other persons.

Very respectfully &c

W. Whelan.

9 July 1863	Port Hudson, Louisiana, surrendered after prolonged attack by Northern sea and land forces. The Union now had control of the entire Mississippi and had won the war in the West.
29 August 1863	Confederate submarine *H. L. Hunley*, Lieutenant J. A. Payne, CSN, sank for the first time in Charleston harbor after making practice dives preparatory to attacking the blockading fleet. Another crew volunteered to man her.
6 September 1863	Morris Island, Charleston harbor, was evacuated by Confederate forces after nearly 2 months of intensive bombardment from afloat and ashore. Union forces were now entrenched within full view of the city.
5 October 1863	C.S.S. *David*, Lieutenant W. T. Glassell, exploded a spar torpedo against U.S.S. *New Ironsides* in an attempt to destroy the heavy blockader off Charleston. *New Ironsides* was damaged but not destroyed.
15 October 1863	Submarine *H. L. Hunley* sank for the second time in Charleston harbor. The part owner, for whom she was named, and a crew of seven perished in the accident, but she was again recovered and a third crew volunteered to man her.
17 February 1864	Confederate submarine *H. L. Hunley* sank Union blockader *Housatonic* off Charleston—the first submarine to sink a ship in combat.
12 March 1864	Ships of Rear Admiral D. D. Porter's Mississippi Squadron moved up the Red River to commence the unsuccessful Army-Navy campaign to gain a foothold in the Texas interior and cut off the flow of supplies to the Confederate forces.
19 June 1864	U.S.S. *Kearsarge*, Commander J. A. Winslow, sank C.S.S. *Alabama*, Captain R. Semmes, off Cherbourg, France, ending the career of the South's most

famous commerce raider. *Alabama* had captured and burned 55 Union merchantmen valued at four and one-half million dollars, and had boarded 10 others to the value of 562 thousand dollars.

11 July 1864	Raid on Washington by General Jubal Early, CSA, thwarted by ships of the Potomac Flotilla and the rapid movement of Union reinforcements by water.
5 August 1864	Rear Admiral D. G. Farragut's fleet steamed by Forts Morgan and Gaines, through the deadly torpedo field blocking the channel, and into Mobile Bay. In the fierce engagement with the forts and Admiral F. Buchanan's small squadron, Farragut won a victory worthy of his great name and closed the South's last major Gulf port.
19 October 1864	C.S.S. *Shenandoah*, Lieutenant J. I. Waddell, commissioned off the Madeira Islands. *Shenandoah* was the last of the successful commerce raiders.
27 October 1864	Torpedo launch commanded by Lieutenant W. B. Cushing destroyed ram C.S.S. *Albemarle* in the Roanoke River, assuring the North of renewed control of the waters around Plymouth, North Carolina.
24–25 December 1864	A joint Army-Navy operation under Rear Admiral Porter and Major General B. F. Butler unsuccessfully attempted to take the Confederate stronghold of Fort Fisher, Wilmington, by amphibious assault.
13–15 January 1865	The joint amphibious assault under Rear Admiral David D. Porter and Major General Alfred H. Terry took Fort Fisher, the key in the defense of Wilmington, North Carolina, which was the last port by which supplies from Europe could reach General Lee's troops at Richmond.
23–24 January 1865	The Confederate fleet under Flag Officer John K. Mitchell attempted to dash down the James River to attack General Grant's headquarters at City Point, Virginia and disrupt the Union's waterborne supply line. The bold attack was thwarted when the heaviest of the ironclads ran aground.
17–18 February 1865	Charleston, confronted by General William T. Sherman's soldiers approaching from the rear and a Navy supported amphibious assault from Bull's Bay, was evacuated.
22 February 1865	Wilmington, North Carolina, was evacuated as Rear Admiral Porter's ships steamed up the Cape Fear River and General Terry's soldiers marched on the city.
2–4 April 1865	Secretary of the Navy Stephen R. Mallory ordered the destruction of the Confederate James River Squadron and directed its officers and men to join General Lee's troops then in the process of evacuating Richmond and retreating westward toward Danville. Thus ended Confederate naval operations east of the Mississippi.
9 April 1865	General Lee met General Grant at Appomattox Court House and formally surrendered the Army of Northern Virginia.
14 April 1865	President Lincoln was shot shortly after 10 p.m. while watching "Our American Cousin" at Ford's Theatre, Washington. He died at 7:22 a.m. the next morning.
10 May 1865	President Jefferson Davis was captured by Union troops near Irwinville, Georgia.
28 June 1865	C.S.S. *Shenandoah*, Lieutenant Waddell, captured 11 American whalers near the narrows of the Bering Strait. This was *Shenandoah*'s most successful day as a commerce raider during her long cruise that spanned 13 months and covered 58,000 miles.

2 August 1865	Lieutenant Waddell of C.S.S. *Shenandoah*, last ship to fly the Confederate flag on the sea, spoke the English bark *Barracouta* and for the first time learned positively that the war was over. He determined to make a nonstop voyage to Liverpool, England, via Cape Horn.
6 November 1865	C.S.S. *Shenandoah*, Lieutenant Waddell, arrived at Liverpool, England, 123 days and 23,000 miles from the Aleutians. Waddell lowered the last official Confederate flag, and his ship was ultimately turned over to American authorities.

One hundred pound gun on U.S.S. Teaser.

THE NAVY IN THE DEFENSE
OF WASHINGTON

The dome of the Capitol, unfinished when this photograph was taken in 1860, was completed in 1863 while the Navy patrolled the Potomac River and its tributaries.

THE NAVY IN THE DEFENSE OF WASHINGTON

During the winter preceding the outbreak of war, while the Army was taking steps to protect the capital from internal revolt by reorganizing the militia and bringing a few regulars into the city, the Navy was taking measures to defend and prepare the area against potential attack. On January 5, 1861, Secretary of the Navy Isaac Toucey ordered Marines to garrison Fort Washington on the Maryland side of the Potomac River—a vital link in the defense of the city by either land or water. Four days later, other Marines from the Washington Navy Yard garrisoned Fort McHenry in Baltimore until Army troops could relieve them. By the end of January, Commander John A. Dahlgren had gathered all ordnance at the Navy Yard—Washington's primary arsenal—in the attic of the main building, a sort of elevated fort, in the event of attack on either Washington or the yard itself.

As early as April 2, President Lincoln, in office only a month, began going personally to the Navy Yard to confer with Dahlgren, with whom he established a close working relationship. It was to the Yard Commander that the President entrusted the responsibility of holding the Anacostia Bridge against assault and guarding the river approaches to the Capital.

One of President Lincoln's first actions following the fall of Fort Sumter was to declare a naval blockade of the Southern ports. The Navy was at first limited in its ability to enforce the proclamation because of its small size—only 42 active ships at the outset and these were scattered on the seven seas serving the United States' world interests. Under the dynamic drive in Washington of Gideon Welles and Gustavus Fox, naval officers in shipyards, and civilian ship owners and builders, the fleet grew rapidly both in numbers and effectiveness. Eventually the squadrons would deny the Confederacy the use of its vast coastline, thereby cutting off the flow of supplies from Europe necessary for the prosecution of the war. Equally important, they would divide the Confederacy along the Mississippi River and steadily sap its strength by amphibious assault from the sea.

James H. Ward
Commander, USN

Stephen C. Rowan
Commander, USN

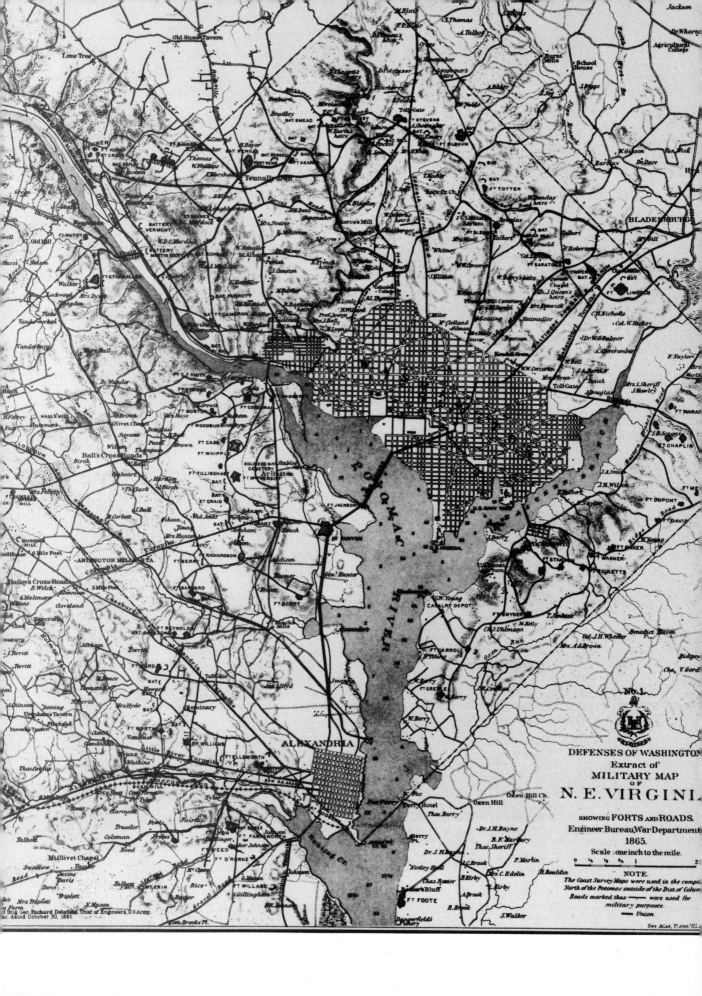

DEFENSES OF WASHINGTON
Extract of
MILITARY MAP
OF
N. E. VIRGINIA
SHOWING FORTS AND ROADS.
Engineer Bureau, War Department
1865.
Scale : one inch to the mile.

NOTE.
The Coast Survey Maps were used in the compila
North of the Potomac outside of the Dist. of Colum
Roads marked thus ———— were used for
military purposes
———— Union

Andrew A. Harwood
Commander, USN

Foxhall A. Parker
Commander, USN

The Anacostia Bridge was one of the first links in the defense of the city which the President sought to protect. Commander (later Rear Admiral) John Dahlgren was charged with responsibility of guarding it.

Samuel F. Du Pont
Rear Admiral, USN

John A. Dahlgren
Rear Admiral, USN

These events lay in the future, but the impact of mobility at sea made itself powerfully felt at once. In the tense mid-April days of the Baltimore riots, which prevented reinforcements from reaching Washington by rail, control of the waters of the Chesapeake swung the balance in the North's favor.

After the 6th Massachusetts Infantry had arrived in the Capital, the railroad bridges in Baltimore were destroyed and Washington was virtually isolated. Maryland opposed the passage of soldiers and Confederate sympathy ran strong. There was danger of her quitting the Union. In these dramatic moments when Washington was an island in a hostile sea, Captain Samuel F. DuPont, Commandant of the Philadelphia Navy Yard, and others transported troops by ship to relieve the Capital.

The steamer *Boston* departed Philadelphia with New York 7th Regiment on board to proceed via the Chesapeake Capes; and the railroad ferryboat *Maryland* embarked General Butler's Massachusetts 8th at Perryville, at the head of the Chesapeake, for Annapolis on the 19th. *Maryland* promptly arrived and towed U.S.S. *Constitution*, the Naval Academy station ship into Chesapeake Bay to prevent her capture by Confederate sympathizers. *Maryland*, however, ran aground. On the 22nd, *Boston*, coming up the Chesapeake, arrived at Annapolis, helped *Maryland* get free, and the Regiments from both ships disembarked at the Naval Academy, safe Federal territory in a pro-Confederate region. Soon other regiments arrived by ship. The soldiers repaired the torn up railroad from Annapolis, reopened Washington's ruptured communications with the North, and exercised a stabilizing influence on the explosive situation in Maryland. Thus, use of the sea probably saved Washington and, as Dahlgren wrote on the arrival of the troops in the Capital, "dispelled all fears of an assault."

The Navy promptly began to build up strength at Washington. With the fall of Norfolk Navy Yard, April 20, U.S.S. *Pawnee* returned to Washington to bolster its defenses. Her arrival on the 23rd with her powerful battery brought important strength at a critical hour. Nothing in the area ashore or afloat could stand up to her heavy guns.

Meanwhile, on 21 April four steamers were obtained and fitted out as gunboats under Commander Dahlgren's supervision at the Navy Yard for the defense of the Capital. On 22 April, Commander James H. Ward proposed the creation of a "flying flotilla" for service in the Washington and Chesapeake Bay area. Secretary of the Navy, Gideon Welles approved the recommendation, and in May

In early April, troops of the Massachusetts Sixth Regiment were fired on while passing through Baltimore.

Thereafter, troops were sent by sea and bay to Annapolis, where U.S.S. Constitution—"Old Ironsides"—lay off the Naval Academy.

The soldiers were put ashore . . .

. . . and fed and organized on the Academy grounds prior to pushing on to Washington.

The Long Bridge over the Potomac was a strategic point in the defense of the Capitol.   The planks could be taken up at night to guard against surprise attack.

Commander Ward arrived at the Washington Navy Yard on board U.S.S. *Thomas Freeborn* with two small craft in tow. The Potomac Flotilla was formed. Following in the wake of Dahlgren's gunboats and *Pawnee*, it would well serve the Union in keeping open this mighty river highway to the Capital.

On May 11, Dahlgren ordered *Pawnee*, Commander Stephen C. Rowan, to Alexandria to protect vessels in the vicinity from attack. On the night of the 23rd, Dahlgren launched the war's first amphibious operation, under Rowan, from the Navy Yard aimed at the seizure of Alexandria. The next morning soldiers and sailors landed as other troops marched over the "Long Bridge" and occupied the city. Admiral David Dixon Porter later noted that the operation was affected under cover of the gunboats U.S.S. *Thomas Freeborn*, *Anacostia*, and *Resolute*, that the Confederates had evacuated the city upon Rowan's demand, and that the American flag had been hoisted on the custom house and elsewhere in the city by the naval officers in charge of a landing party of sailors. "This," he wrote, ". . . gave indication of the feelings of the Navy, and how ready was the service to put down secession on the first opportunity offered."

Later in May the Potomac Flotilla under Commander Ward engaged Confederate batteries at Aquia Creek, less than 35 miles south of the Capital, and again on June 27, in action in which Ward became the first naval officer to lose his life in the war. As Admiral Porter observed in retrospect, ". . . the ordinary events taking place on the Potomac . . . formed the small links in the chain, which in the end, shackled the arms of the great rebellion." The Flotilla restricted to a great extent communication between opposite shores, thus closing the river for all practical purposes to the Confederacy.

Throughout the remainder of the war, under Commodore Andrew Harwood and, later, Commander Foxhall Parker, the Potomac Flotilla continued to render what Secretary Welles termed "active service." With the opening of the Peninsula Campaign in the spring of 1862, Southern attention

The Stars and Stripes were hoisted over Alexandria, Virginia, following the first amphibious landing of the war— an expedition launched from the Washington Navy Yard.

U.S.S. Mount Vernon *reconnoiters Mathias Point, Aquia Creek, where Commander James H. Ward became the first U.S. naval officer to be killed in the war.*

was drawn away from the Potomac—and Washington—and focused on the James and York Rivers—and Richmond. Never again was the South to possess strong batteries along the waterways that served as the vital communication and logistic artery for the nation's Capital. The Union Navy was too well established, and its mobility and fire power were too great, to give the Confederacy renewed entree to such a strategic position.

In 1863, however, when Washington was again threatened by a series of Southern successes in Maryland and Pennsylvania, ships of the Potomac Flotilla reassured the North by their presence at Annapolis and Washington, by their appearance in the Susquehanna at Havre de Grace, and by their positions up the Gunpowder and Backwater Rivers. In July Gettysburg brought this critical period to a close, but the Navy continued to sweep the Potomac and its tributaries—often in operations with the Army, as at Fredricksburg in 1864. It kept the river open for commercial as well as military purposes, not only by preventing its use by the Confederates but by removing torpedoes (mines) that were planted by the Southerners.

When General U. S. Grant made his wide flanking move to strike at Robert E. Lee from Petersburg to the South he shifted his base of supply (by ship) to the James. City Point became a great logistic center where ships poured a steady stream of munitions, equipment, food, and fresh reserves for his besieging armies. The Chesapeake and tributaries continued to be arteries of power and life.

Seeking to reduce the pressure exerted by Grant's growing Army, Lee sent General Jubal Early out of the Shenandoah Valley to attack Washington.

In July 1864, when Early crossed into Maryland at Harper's Ferry and General Bradley Johnson's forces split off to head south toward the Capital, the Federals thought the two pronged attack was designed to destroy Washington and capture the Point Lookout prison camp at the mouth of the Potomac.

To meet the greater threat, widespread troop movements got underway. Control of the Chesapeake, and the swiftness of the mass transport provided by ships, made the difference between disaster and arrival in the nick of time.

Ordered to pursue Early, General Philip Sheridan moved across the York Peninsula where naval

THE SEAT OF WAR.

Drawn from Nature and Lith. by John Bachmann.

BIRD'S EYE VIEW OF
Part of MARYLAND, DISTRICT OF COLUMBIA and Part of VIRGINIA,
A. Rumpf, Publisher 175 Broadway.
Agent for John Bachmann's Publications

Distance from
imore to Harpers Ferry 81 Miles
Washington 38
Point of Rocks 69

Distance from
Washington to Ft Monroe 170
Richmond 130
Petersburg 152

support provided necessary munitions and supplies at White House, a base that many times had served the North well. Even with this assistance, however, he had no chance to catch Early. Meanwhile, reinforcements arrived in Washington directly by ships. Wright's 6th Corps embarked and sped up to the Capital from Petersburg. Emory's 19th Corps, coming in transports by long sea voyage from Louisiana, reached Hampton Roads just in time to sail on to Washington. When Early saw the Capitol dome on 11 July, he was too late; the mobility of the sea had defeated him.

In addition, Secretary Welles had acted promptly to help counter both threats in other ways. U.S.S. *Currituck* was sent to protect Havre de Grace; U.S.S. *Fuchsia* and *Teaser* were dispatched to the Bush River and Gunpowder River bridges respectively, both being objects of General Johnson's attack. The bridge over the Gunpowder was burned nevertheless, but *Fuchsia* did succeed in saving

This drawing by the famous Civil War artist Alfred R. Waud shows the Potomac River and Washington Arsenal (now Fort McNair). Waud's pencil notations at the bottom read: "Washington arsenal. Insane Asylum in the distance. The arsenal stands on a point running out into the river at the junction of the eastern branch [Anacostia River]."

The Georgetown wharves as seen from Mason's Island in mid-November 1865.

VI–22

that over the Bush River.   U.S.S. *Commodore Read*, stationed in the southern Potomac, was ordered to steam to Washington and "shell all suspicious places" on July 11; and U.S.S. *Bibb*, then without ordnance at the Washington Navy Yard, was rapidly fitted with guns from another ship and sent to join the rest of the Flotilla in defense of the Capital.

As Lincoln wrote of "Uncle Sam's web feet" after the fall of Vicksburg, "At all the watery margins they have been present."

Besides the activities of the Potomac Flotilla the Navy made other important contributions in the Washington area.   From the Navy Yard, which Dahlgren characterized as a place "of great importance . . . as a position in the general defenses of the city," came many of the guns and much of the munitions which, by war's end, helped make the U.S. Fleet the most powerful force afloat in the world.   The genius of Commander (later Rear Admiral) Dahlgren guided these efforts at the Yard through the first half of the war and influenced the concepts of naval ordnance to the present day. Under his guidance, too, the *G. W. Parke Custis* was purchased before the war was six months old and fitted out at the Navy Yard for balloon reconnaissance observations of Confederate positions in Virginia.   She was in a very real sense the forerunner of the modern aircraft carrier.

The Civil War ran its course from Sumter to Appomattox; from its beginning—and before—until its close, the Navy played a decisive role in the defense of Washington.   It did so through the vigorous activity of the Potomac Flotilla, the vital contributions of the Navy Yard, and the vast dedication of individual officers and men such as James Ward and John Dahlgren.

Control of Washington's waterways provided the North with the flexibility and mobility that enabled it to thwart Confederate threats and mount overwhelming offensive movements.   It was so wherever water reached any theatre of operations.

These two photographs taken the year following the end of the war, show various parts of the Washington Navy Yard. The Yard was an essential facility in the defense of the Capital throughout the conflict.

The body of John Wilkes Booth is examined on board USS Montauk *in the Anacostia River, 27 April 1865.*

"THE POSITIVE IDENTIFICATION OF THE BODY OF JOHN WILKES BOOTH"

By

John F. May

                    The Positive Identification of
                     THE Body of John Wilkes Booth
                              BY
                    Doctor John Frederick May
                              Of
                     Washington Coty DC

Captain Dudley Knox
Navy Dept Washington DC

My Dear Captain Knox

            I read in the Star of last Sunday
May 17 an article by George Battey Jr relating to r
relicks belonging to John Wilkes Booth,and stating
also in his article that there had existed and still
exists in the minds of many people,doubt as to whether
or not the dead body brought to the Navy Yard at
Washington DC and placed on a Monitor there ,really
was the body of John Wilkes Booth .Mr. Battey says
in his article that the body of Booth was identified
by Dr John Frederick May of Washington DC .This
statement is absolutely correct and I have thought
that it might interest the public too hear from
me the facts appertaining to this identification.

            I am the son of Dr JF May and my Father
before and after the Civil War and in fact up to th e
time when his health began to fail ,had all the
surgical practice of this city and the surroundim
country as well .He was a great surgeon and had a
National reputation.During his surgical career
he performed two major operations on the hunan body
which up to his time had not been performed successfully
in this country by any other surgeon.One was an
amputation at the hip joint (which was done in thirty
seconds)the man surviving the operation and living
for some years afterwards;and the other was a ligation
(tyin or tying) of the popliteal artery which Sir
Astley Cooper the most celebrated surgeon of his day
spoke of as a feat of the dissecting room,meaning
thereby to say that it was impossible to perform it
on the living subject.

                            VI-26

I distindtly remember the operation he performed
on John Wilkes Booth in fact I assisted him (although
only a boy of fourteen years of age) by holding
the basin to receive the blood from the wound.We did
not have trained nurses in those days.The operation
was a minor one and was done for the removal of a f
fibroid tumor on the back of his neck,it was done w
without any anesthetic of any kind.Booth at the tim e
was playin g with Charlotte Cushman in Romeo & Juliet
and during the play she embraced him with so much
ardor that she tore out the stitches and tore open
the wound.It then healed by what we call second intention
and left a wide large scar that looked like the scar
made by a burn.It was by this scar that his remains
were identified.

    When the body of Booth was brought
to the Navy Yard there was doubt in the mind of Genl
Barns and other officers whether or not they really
had the right man .A soldier was sent to our house
312 C Street NW with a su mmons for my Father to
come to the Navy Yard and if possible identify the
body that they had on the Monitor .I drove him to
the yard in his Doctors Gig and was present at
the identification of the body and the autopsy
which followed afterward.

    When we were on the deck of the
Monitor before looking at the body Dr May said to
Genl Barns "If the body lying under that tarpauling
is the body of John Wilkes Booth you will find a
scar on the back of his neck ,and let me describe
the scar before it seen by me" Dr May then described
the scar and Genl Barns then said "you have described
the scar as well as if you were looking at it"
"it looks more like the scar made by a burn than
the cicatrix made by asurgical operation.Further
speaking Dr May "the body being turned off the back
of the neck was examined and my mark was unmistakeably
found by me upon it ;and it being ###########
afterwards at my request placed in a sitting posture
standing and looking down upon it I was finally
enabled to recognize the features of Booth.But never
in a human body had greater change taken placefrom
the man whom I had seen in the vigor of life and health
than in that of the haggard corpse which was before
 me with its yellow discolored skin, its unkempt
and matted hair, and its whole facial expression
 sunken and sharpened by the exposure and starvation

3

that it had undergone.The right lower limb was
greatly contused and per fectly blackfrom the fracture
of one of the long bones of the leg(the fibula)
The autopsy was then made by the assistants of
Genl Barnes which proved that the bullet which
killed him,passed through two of the vertebrae
of the neck causing their fracture and lesion of
the spinal cord.The body was secretely and at night
burried in the yard of the penetentiary which was
not known until some time afterward.

You must thus see from the statements
of my Father Dr John Frederick May that the body
of John Wilkes Booth was positively identified
and any doubts upon the subject should be put at
rest forever .1 was present at the identification
of the body and also at the autopsy which followed,
and 1 remember well what transpired upon both
occasions.

Very Truly Yours

Wm May.

Washington City DC
May 18 1925
1411 Hopkins Place

This interesting letter sent in 1925 to Captain Dudley Knox, USN, is reproduced here in its original typed form. Captain Knox, the distinguished naval historian, was at that time director of the Office of Navy Records and Library, forerunner of the present Naval History Division, Navy Department.
The writer was the physician son of Doctor John Frederick May, prominent Washington surgeon. Doctor May received his medical degree in 1834 from Columbian College (now George Washington University). He served Columbian and the University of Maryland as a professor of surgery.
During the Civil War, Doctor May's association with the Washington Infirmary and his reputation led to the remarkable experience recounted in his son's letter.

The White House—President Lincoln's home and office.
From here he ordered the blockade of the thousands of miles
of Confederate coastline.

PRESIDENT LINCOLN AND THE NAVY

by

Charles Oscar Paullin

PRESIDENT LINCOLN AND THE NAVY

by Charles Oscar Paullin

FROM March 4, 1861, to April 15, 1865, Abraham Lincoln was the commander-in-chief of the navy of the United States. During these years the duties of this office were more important, varied and difficult than at any other period of the history of our nation. Early in the Civil War the task of administering the navy was suddenly augmented and complicated by a large increase in the number of ships, officers, and seamen, by far-reaching changes in the art of naval construction, and by the employment of the fleet in actual warfare. From 1861 to 1865 the naval ships increased from 90 to 670, the officers from 1300 to 6700, and the seamen from 7500 to 51,500. Some two hundred vessels were built either at the navy-yards by the government or at private shipyards under contract, and more than three hundred vessels were purchased. The net annual expenditures of the navy rose from $12,000,000 to $123,000,000.[1]

During the Civil War naval architecture was in a state of transition. Iron was superseding wood as a material of construction, and steam engines were taking the place of sails as a means of propulsion. When the war began more than one-half of our naval vessels were sailing-ships; when it ended four-fifths of them were steamships. Many of the latter were ironclads, the modern type of war-vessel, now first introduced into our navy. Of the ironclads, not a few were monitors, the well-known invention of that distinguished engineer and naval architect, John Ericsson. The construction of naval machinery and of ordnance was rapidly improved. Nearly every variety and type of engine, valve-gear, screw-propeller and boiler were tried. A chief engineer was sent to Europe to collect information relating to steam engineering. The various kinds of coal in the seaboard states were experimented with in order to ascertain their comparative value for naval vessels. New cannon of different kinds were introduced, the largest of which were the 15-inch guns brought into use by Assistant Secretary of the Navy Gustavus V. Fox. These numerous changes in the art of naval construction greatly increased the difficulties of administration.[2]

The naval operations of the Civil War were the most extensive ever undertaken by our navy. A blockade of the Southern States was successfully enforced, many important naval expeditions were projected and executed, numerous rivers of the South and West were actively patrolled, and the commerce-destroyers of the enemy were tracked over distant seas. At the beginning of the war the blockading of the extensive coast of the Confederacy was deemed impossible by many men both at home and abroad. To their surprise this difficult undertaking was soon accomplished. The length of the coast blockaded, measured from Alexandria, Virginia, to the Rio Grande, was 3549 miles. One hundred and eighty-nine harbors, openings to rivers, or indentations of the coast were guarded. On the Mississippi and its tributaries the gunboats traversed and patrolled 3615 miles; and on the sounds, bayous, rivers and inlets of the Atlantic and Gulf coasts, about 2000 miles.[3] Next in importance to the blockade, were the naval operations against the batteries, forts and fortified towns and cities on the sea-coast and rivers of the Confederacy. As examples of this class of operations, it it sufficient to mention the memorable achievements of Farragut at New Orleans, Vicksburg and Mobile, of Porter at Fort Fisher, and of Dupont and of Dahlgren at Charleston. The most important event of the war

---

[1] *Senate Ex. Doc.*, 45 Cong., 1 sess., no. 3, pp. 156–157; *House Ex. Doc.*, 40 Cong., 2 sess., no. 280; *Annual Report of the Secretary of the Navy*, for 1864, pp. xii–xxiv; for 1865, pp. xii–xiii; *Navy Registers*, for 1860, pp. 18–81; for 1865, pp. 12–216.

[2] *Annual Report of the Secretary of the Navy*, for 1864, p. xxix.

[3] *Annual Report of the Secretary of the Navy*, for 1863, p. iii.

in connection with the Confederate commerce-destroyers was of course the capture of the *Alabama* by the *Kearsarge*, off Cherbourg, in June, 1864.

President Lincoln has briefly described the work of the navy in a letter written on August 26, 1863, in response to an invitation to attend a mass-meeting of "unconditional Union men", to be held at Springfield, Illinois, the President's home-town. Having referred to the achievements of the army at Antietam, Murfreesboro and Gettysburg, and on fields of lesser note, he paid his respects to its sister-service.

Nor must Uncle Sam's web-feet be forgotten. At all the watery margins they have been present. Not only on the deep sea, the broad bay, and the rapid river, but also up the narrow, muddy bayou, and wherever the ground was a little damp, they have been and made their tracks. Thanks to all.[4]

The immediate representatives of the President in naval affairs were the two leading officials of the Navy Department, Secretary of the Navy Gideon Welles and Assistant Secretary of the Navy Gustavus V. Fox. These two men, with the assistance of their bureau chiefs, largely conducted the naval business of the war. Their relations with the President were exceedingly cordial and intimate. They saw him almost daily, visited him at all hours at the White House, and discussed with him the various phases of naval policy and administration. Upon them largely depended the success or failure of the navy. Differing widely in temperament, training and experience, the two men were complementary. Each would have been weak without the other. Together they were a remarkably strong force in conducting the war. So closely were they associated with the President, and so large and predominant a part in naval affairs did they play, that no account of Lincoln and the navy would be be complete without some reference to their work and character.

Gideon Welles was descended from the best stock of Connecticut. The original emigrant of his family to that state, Thomas Welles, held many important public offices between 1639 and 1659, being twice elected governor of the infant colony. Gideon was educated at the Episcopal Academy in Cheshire, Connecticut, and at the Norwich University in Vermont. He read law, and at the age of twenty-three became editor and one of the proprietors of the *Hartford Times*, which he edited until 1837. From 1827 to 1835 he was a member of the Connecticut legislature. For several years Welles served his state as comptroller of public accounts, and for some five years he was postmaster of Hartford. From 1846 to 1849 he was chief of the Bureau of Provisions and Clothing in the Navy Department at Washington.

In politics Welles was for many years a Jacksonian Democrat. His anti-slavery views carried him into the Republican party when it was organized, and in 1856 he was its candidate for governor of Connecticut. He was at that time the leading contributor to the *Hartford Evening Press*, the Republican organ of his state. For several years Welles was a member of the Republican National Committee. He was a delegate to the Republican National Conventions of 1856 and 1860, and during the presidential campaign of 1860 he labored earnestly for the election of Lincoln.[5]

In November, 1860, when Lincoln began to consider various men for places in his Cabinet, Welles's name was one of the first presented to him, and was the subject of a special consultation. Vice-President Hannibal Hamlin urged his appointment. Senator John P. Hale, a New Hampshire politician, was rather earnestly pressed upon the President for Secretary of the Navy, and he was somewhat mortified that his pretensions for the place were not more seriously regarded. Other names may have been considered for the naval portfolio. Lincoln from the first was convinced of Welles's fitness, availability and representative character.[6]

The assignment of Welles to the Navy Department instead of to some other Cabinet position may be ascribed to his three years' experience as chief of the Bureau of Provisions and Clothing, and to his residence in New England, whose maritime interests have given her a claim upon the naval secretaryship. In making up his Cabinet, Lincoln apportioned its members according to their sectional residence and their party antecedents. Welles was chosen as the New England member, and as a

---

[4] Nicolay and Hay, *Complete Works of Abraham Lincoln* (Gettysburg ed.), IX, 101.

[5] Boynton, *History of the Navy during the Great Rebellion*, I. 22–24.

[6] Papers of Gideon Welles, in the possession of his son Edgar T. Welles, of New York City; Nicolay and Hay, *Abraham Lincoln*, II. 367.

Executive Mansion.

Washington, Nov. 8. 1864.

The Managing Committee of the
Sailor's Fair:
Boston, Mass.

Allow me to wish you a great success. With the old fame of the Navy, made brighter in the present war, you can not fail. I name none, lest I wrong others by omission. To all, from Rear Admiral, to honest Jack, I tender the Nation's admiration and gratitude

A. Lincoln

This is the original of the telegram sent by the President to managers of the National Sailors' Fair at its opening in Boston. It reflects his warm regard for the Navy.

representative of the Democratic element of the Republican party. The Whig faction of the party was not generally friendly to him. No love was lost between Lincoln's Secretary of the Navy and his Secretary of State, William H. Seward. Thurlow Weed, one of the leaders of the Whigs in New York, was not kindly disposed towards Welles and opposed his selection for the naval secretaryship. In December, 1860, Weed said to the President that if he would on his way to his inauguration in Washington stop long enough in New York, Philadelphia, or Baltimore to select an attractive figure-head from the prow of a ship, would adorn it with an elaborate wig and luxuriant whiskers, and would transfer it to the entrance of the Navy Department, this figure-head would be quite as serviceable to the navy as Welles, and much less expensive. "Oh", Mr. Lincoln replied, "wooden midshipmen answer very well in novels, but we must have a live secretary of the navy." [7]

Welles's "elaborate wig and luxuriant whiskers" gave him a patriarchal appearance, which his age and vigor of intellect belied. When he entered the Cabinet, he was in his fifty-ninth year. Secretary of State Seward and Secretary of War Cameron were older than the Secretary of the Navy, and Attorney-General Bates was ten years his senior. Among the naval officers and seamen Welles's paternal and benevolent aspect won for him the familiar appellation of "Father Welles," or the "Old Man of the Sea." Mr. Charles A. Dana, for a time an assistant of Secretary of War Stanton, has left us one of the best characterizations of Lincoln's naval secretary.

---

[7] Weed, *Autobiography*, I. 606–607, 611.

Welles was a curious-looking man: he wore a wig which was parted in the middle, the hair falling down on each side; and it was from his peculiar appearance, I have always thought, that the idea that he was an old fogy originated. I remember Governor Andrew, of Massachusetts, coming into my office at the War Department one day and asking where he could find "that old Mormon deacon, the Secretary of the Navy." In spite of his peculiarities, I think Mr. Welles was a very wise, strong man. There was nothing decorative about him; there was no noise in the street when he went along; but he understood his duty, and did it efficiently, continually, and unvaryingly. There was a good deal of opposition to him, for we had no navy when the war began, and he had to create one without much deliberation, but he was patient, laborious, and intelligent at his task.[8]

Welles has sometimes been unjustly regarded as a time-serving and routine-loving executive. It is true that he was not one of those dashing administrators, who reach conclusions by intuition, put their decisions into effect with great strenuosity, and are at once the inspiration and the terror of their subordinates. Rather, he was the quiet, unswerving, fearless executive, who reasons carefully from the evidence presented and draws temperately his conclusions therefrom, who enforces his judgments with firmness and uniformity, and who gains the esteem of his fellows by reason of his patience, integrity and justice. While Welles had his antipathies, he nevertheless administered the navy as a rule with great impartiality. He applied the laws of the navy fearlessly and without favor, no matter what the rank of the offender. He stood, as few secretaries have, for naval discipline and an impartial administration of the naval code. More than once he rebuked a naval court for bringing in a verdict contrary to the evidence presented to it. A court-martial, of which Farragut was president, found the captain of a certain ship guilty of failing to do his utmost in overtaking and capturing a certain Confederate vessel, an offense punishable with death. The court sentenced the offending officer to be suspended from the navy for two years on leave-of-absence pay—a merely nominal penalty. Welles in reviewing these absurd findings pointed out that the sentence of the court would be too mild for a trivial offense, and declared that such punishment as the court had prescribed "no officer could obtain from the Department as a favor".[9]

No man could be more generous than the Secretary of the Navy in praise of gallant and meritorious conduct. His congratulatory messages to the victorious naval officers were warm and hearty, and felicitously phrased. As a newspaper writer he had acquired considerable facility in composition. All of his writings reveal a faculty for lucid expression, clear thinking, and the discernment of the gist of any subject. His official reports are more interesting reading than are most documents of that sort. Unlike some of the naval secretaries, Welles did not depute to his subordinates the composition of his annual reports, although he availed himself of their criticisms and suggestions. From the diary which he kept during and after the war, an unpublished document of great historical value, one infers that its author was a methodical man, painstaking and honest, and fearless and coldly precise in estimating the character and ability of his colleagues.[10]

In determining the policy of the government, Welles's advice was valued by the President, and his judgment was sober and well-balanced. His counsel, however, may not always have been politic. It is recollected that at the time of the Mason and Slidell episode he wrote a warmly-congratulatory letter to Captain Wilkes. That the Secretary of the Navy should have a profound knowledge of international law, was, however, hardly to be expected. Regarding the government's powers under the Constitution, Welles took a middle ground, being neither a strict nor a broad constructionist. He and the Secretary of State were instinctively opposed to each other, and were usually on opposite sides of the questions that came before the Cabinet. Welles regarded Seward as an intriguing and designing politician. He held, on plausible grounds, that Seward's conduct during the first weeks of Lincoln's administration was, if not traitorous, certainly highly unpatriotic. The Secretary of the Navy possessed none of those superb delusions that sometimes afflicted Lincoln's brilliant Secretary of State On matters lying within the field of his information his judgment was certainly as reliable as that of his more famous colleague.

---

[8] Dana, *Recollections of the Civil War*, p. 170.
[9] *Official Records of the Union and Confederate Navies*, first series, vol. III., pp. 467–470.
[10] Diary of Gideon Welles, in possession of Edgar T. Welles.

Abraham Lincoln, the sixteenth President of the United States, "kept in close touch with the navy."

To a technical and intimate knowledge of the navy, Welles made no pretensions. He, however, was better equipped than most naval secretaries have been. His three years' service in one of the naval bureaus had given him a considerable acquaintance with the business of the navy and the department. Fortunately, the limitations of Welles's naval knowledge were adequately compensated by the extensive professional information of his Assistant Secretary of the Navy, Gustavus V. Fox, whose selection by President Lincoln as Welles's assistant was a most happy one.

At the beginning of the war Fox was in his fortieth year. He was born in Saugus, Essex County, Massachusetts. His father was a country physician, in moderate circumstances. At the age of sixteen young Fox was appointed a midshipman in the navy, where he remained for eighteen years. During a varied career he saw service in the squadrons of the Mediterranean, the East Indies, the Pacific, the coast of Brazil and the west coast of Africa; and he participated in the naval operations of the Mexican War. For a time he was attached to the Coast Survey. In 1853 and 1854 he commanded a mail steamer plying between New York and the Isthmus of Panama and belonging to one of the three lines subsidized at that time by the United States government. In July, 1856, having reached the rank of lieutenant, he resigned from the navy and accepted the position of "agent" of the Bay State Woolen Mills, of Lawrence, Massachusetts. Early in 1861, he came to Washington with a plan for the relief of Fort Sumter, and in April President Lincoln permitted him to put it into operation. In planning, promoting and conducting this daring adventure, he displayed such energy and initiative that the President formed a high estimate of his character. The Fort Sumter expedition paved the way to his political preferment. On May 9, 1861, he was appointed chief clerk of the Navy Department, and on July 31 he was promoted to be Assistant Secretary of the Navy, a newly-created position.[11]

Fox's career both in and out of the navy admirably fitted him for the assistant secretaryship. His long service in the navy gave him a wide acquaintance among the naval officers. He had acquired the habit of the navy and of the sea, and knew well the practice of the naval profession. On the other hand, his experience as a New England manufacturer had familiarized him with the currents of thought and action outside of the navy; with the methods of business, its economies and administration, and the qualities of commercial men. In the science of the naval profession, in contradistinction to its art, Fox was not specially well-grounded. His knowledge of naval architecture was naturally limited, and his strategy proved to be at times faulty. To Rear-Admiral C. H. Davis he appeared more ready to plan, than laboriously to execute. Fox was decisive, quick of mind, and self-confident. No matter how dark and gloomy were the prospects of the North, the buoyancy of his spirits never failed him. Urbane and suave, the amenities of social life came easy to him. His brother-in-law was Lincoln's Postmaster-General, Montgomery Blair. Few men, who in the eventful spring of 1861 came to the surface of that tempestuous political sea at Washington, were so likely as Gustavus V. Fox to survive in its rough waters and ride its waves to preferment and eminence.[12]

Both the Secretary and the Assistant Secretary of the Navy had a great capacity for work, and each wrote with his own hands a vast number of letters. To their subordinates they often appeared fatigued and overworked. Night after night they toiled over their desks at the department. In the course of his duties Fox now and then visited the navy-yards or some of the principal seaports of the North. Infrequently, Welles or his assistant went to the "front", the latter more often than the former. The Assistant Secretary of the Navy witnessed the fight at Hampton Roads, in March, 1862, between the *Monitor* and the *Merrimac*. In May of that year the Secretary of the Navy invited two or three members of the Cabinet, the chief clerk of the department, and several naval officers with the ladies of their families to make a special cruise on the steamer *City of Baltimore* and visit the Union fleets between Washington and Richmond. Such excursions must have brought to the Secretary and his assistant a welcome relief from the anxieties, vexations and arduous toil of their offices.

Throughout the war Lincoln's gaunt form was a familiar figure in the Old Navy Department Building, situated a stone's throw to the westward of the White House. The rooms of Welles and Fox were on the second floor, in easy reach of each other. Here the President often called and chatted

---

[11] Biographical details in Boynton, *History of the Navy during the Great Rebellion*, pp. 58–59.
[12] Nicolay and Hay, *Abraham Lincoln*, V. 4–5; Davis, *Life of Charles Henry Davis*, pp. 132–133.

Secretary of the Navy Gideon Welles (left) and Assistant Secretary Gustavus V. Fox: "Upon them largely depended the success or failure of the navy."

VI–36

in the most informal way. A clerk, who is still living, remembers seeing him appear in the department with "carpet slippers" on his feet. Sometimes he wore a shawl around his shoulders. Of a visit of Lincoln to the department made in April, 1863, Rear-Admiral Dahlgren writes: "The President came into Fox's room while I was there, and sat some time, talking generally of matters. . . . Abe was in good humor, and at leaving said, 'Well I will go home; I had no business here; but as the lawyer said, I had none anywhere else'." [13]

The following entry occurs in the diary of Dahlgren for March 29, 1863:

> I went to the Department. Found the President in the Chief Clerk's room with the Secretary and Fox. He looks thin and badly, and is very nervous. Complained of everything. They were doing nothing at Vicksburg or Charleston. Dupont was asking for one iron-clad after another, as fast as they were built. He said the canal at Vicksburg was of no account, and wondered that a sensible man would do it. I tried my hand at consolation, without much avail. He thought the favorable state of public expectation would pass away before anything was done. Then levelled a couple of jokes at the doings at Vicksburg and Charleston. Poor gentleman! [14]

Lincoln kept in close touch with the navy. Almost every day, and often several times a day, he consulted with the Secretary, the Assistant Secretary, the officials of the naval bureaus, and the officers holding important commands. Of these, the most frequent visitor at the White House was the Assistant Secretary, to whom fell, among many other duties, that of obtaining from Congress proper naval legislation. Whenever the leading naval officers were in Washington they always called upon the President and found him an eager listener to all that they had to relate about their plans and operations. Chief among the President's naval advisers were Farragut, Porter, Dahlgren, Dupont, Davis, Foote and Wise. In the conferences on naval affairs Lincoln took an active part, and as a result of them he often reached a decision or issued an order. As no minutes of them were kept, it is impossible in most cases to determine precisely what was said or done. The voluminous papers of Welles and Fox, only a small part of which was accessible to me, will doubtless throw some additional light upon the President's achievements in naval administration.

The planning of the naval operations was largely a composite work. Lincoln's share in it was confined for the most part to criticisms and suggestions respecting the plans formulated by others. As to naval movements upon the Mississippi, however, he seems to have had original opinions of his own, derived doubtless from his early experiences as a flatboatman on that river. In the summer of 1861 the Commission of Conference, composed chiefly of naval officers, served as a board of strategy. The commanding officers often originated their own plans, and the Assistant Secretary was always fertile in suggestions respecting naval operations. In all co-operative movements with the army, much consultation took place between the officers of the army and the navy, the officials of the two departments, and the President.

As a rule, the orders to the officers were drafted in the Navy Department and were issued and signed by either Welles or Fox. Sometimes, however, when the need of action was very great, the President himself wrote or dictated orders. For instance, in April, 1863, when Admiral Dupont was operating against Charleston, South Carolina, Lincoln, fearing that the admiral was about to abandon the movement against the city, telegraphed him to hold his position "inside the bar near Charleston." [15] Before the telegram reached him Dupont had withdrawn his ships from the bar. He regarded it as a reflection upon his management of the fleet, and he soon retired from the command of the South Atlantic Blockading Squadron. It was unusual for the President to interfere in this manner with the work of his officers.

Early in 1862 Commodore Foote, who was then in command of the Mississippi flotilla and had his headquarters at Cairo, Illinois, encountered many difficulties in procuring mortars at Pittsburgh. Much exasperated by the slowness with which the work proceeded, the President ordered Foote to

---

[13] Dahlgren, *Memoir of John A. Dahlgren*, p. 390.
[14] *Ibid.*, p. 389.
[15] *Official Records*, first series, vol. XIV., p. 132.

telegraph daily to Captain H. A. Wise, the assistant inspector of naval ordnance at Washington, his progress in obtaining the mortars. For several weeks Wise went to the White House every day, read the telegrams to the President, and received orders for Foote. In this way Lincoln conducted a small part of the business of the navy independent of both Welles and Fox. "With reference to the mortar rafts", Wise wrote to Foote on January 27, 1862, "Uncle Abe, as you already know, has gone into that business with a will, making his first demonstration, *entre nous*, by pitching General Ripley out of his Ordnance Bureau." On January 31 Wise wrote of the President thus, "He is an evidently practical man, understands precisely what he wants, and is not turned aside by anyone when he has his work before him."[16]

In selecting officers for the higher commands Lincoln generally followed the advice of the department. Admiral Porter, however, was of the opinion that the President selected him to command the Mississippi squadron, in opposition to the wishes of Welles. Porter said that Lincoln seemed to be familiar with the name, character and reputation of every officer of rank in the army and navy, and "appeared to understand them better than some whose business it was to do so; he had many a good story to tell of nearly all, and if he could have lived to write the anecdotes of the war, I am sure he would have furnished the most readable book of the century."[17]

The Navy Department was conspicuously successful in selecting officers for the higher commands. Its good fortune in this respect as compared with the bad fortune of the War Department was commented upon by President Lincoln. He once said to Welles that the qualities of the officers of the navy must run more even, and the task of selecting officers for the higher commands must be less difficult, than in the army. The Secretary of the Navy assured the President that this was not true, and that the good fortune of the navy in choosing commanders had resulted from the wise judgment exercised by his department.[18] It is a fact that the Navy Department did no experimenting corresponding with that of the War Department with McClellan, Halleck, Hooker and Pope. Before the end of 1862 the navy officers who achieved fame had already received the highest position within the gift of the President. Even at this early date the roll of great naval names could have been made out— Farragut, Porter, Foote, Davis, Dahlgren, Rodgers and Lee.

When Lincoln and Welles entered upon their duties in March, 1861, they found the Navy Department and the navy in a deplorable condition. Many of the clerks of the department were hostile to the new Secretary of the Navy. The disaffected naval officers on duty at the department maintained a rallying-point in the Bureau of Ordnance, whose chief, Captain George A. Magruder, and whose clerks, almost to a man, later allied themselves with the Confederacy. The Naval Observatory in Washington, under the command of Commander Matthew F. Maury, the famous meteorologist, and a warm friend of the South, was another centre for the propagation of Secessionist doctrines. The officers of the navy were more or less demoralized. Already a number of them had resigned, and many of those that remained in the service were suspected of disaffection to the Union. Captain Samuel Barron, one of the leaders of a clique of Southern officers, who were favorable to the interests of the Confederacy, was exercising a considerable influence on naval affairs. It was impossible for Welles to tell his friends from his foes. The Pensacola navy-yard was in the hands of the Confederates. The situation at the Norfolk yard was by no means reassuring, and among the officers of the Washington yard sentiments of disloyalty were common. All the navy-yards were in bad repair, since no appropriations for their improvement had been made in 1859 or 1860. The national treasury was bankrupt. In pursuance of President Buchanan's policy of non-resistance and temporizing, Secretary of the Navy Toucey had failed to place the navy in a posture of defense. As was customary in peace, most of the vessels in commission were on foreign stations. The home-squadron consisted of twelve ships, carrying one hundred and eighty-seven guns and about two thousand man.

A sharp turn in naval policy might have been expected to signalize the advent of the new administration. The public records, however, disclose no sudden change of any sort. For the first three weeks Welles did almost nothing to increase or improve the naval defense of the country, and for the

[16] *Official Records*, first series, vol. XXII., pp. 516, 518, 522, 523, 527, 549.
[17] Porter, *Incidents and Anecdotes of the Civil War*, p. 283.
[18] Papers of Gideon Welles, in possession of Edgar T. Welles.

second three weeks he did little. In the first days of April he prepared an expedition for the relief of Fort Sumter, and opened several rendezvous for the enlistment of seamen. Until the firing on Fort Sumter the policy of Lincoln differed but little from that of Buchanan. It was one of conciliation and waiting; it was passive, hesitant, expectant, uncertain, cautious and tentative. Lincoln and the members of his Cabinet were not familiar with federal administration, nor with each other; and at first they did not pull well together. They were strangely awkward at their new work, how awkward it is painful to tell. The attempts of the Secretary of State to manage the government and the President are well known.

Seward's influence on naval affairs greatly added to the confusion of the first weeks of the new administration. On April 1, without consulting the Secretary of the Navy, he obtained Lincoln's signature to a most remarkable naval document. It was addressed to Welles. The body of the document was in the handwriting of Captain Montgomery C. Meigs, of the army; and the postscript in that of Lieutenant David D. Porter, of the navy. The body of the document was an order of Lincoln to Welles to make certain details of naval officers. Of special significance was the direction to Welles to detach Captain Silas H. Stringham from the Secretary's office, to order him to Pensacola, and to supersede him as detailing officer of the department by Captain Samuel Barron. The postscript, which related to the organization of the department, read as follows:

> As it is very necessary at this time to have a perfect knowledge of the personal of the navy, and to be able to detail such officers for special purposes as the exigencies of the service may require, I request that you will instruct Captain Barron to proceed and organize the Bureau of Detail in the manner best adapted to meet the wants of the navy, taking cognizance of the discipline of the navy generally, detailing all officers for duty, taking charge of the recruiting of seamen, supervising charges made against officers, and all matters relating to duties which must be best understood by a sea officer. You will please afford Captain Barron any facility for accomplishing this duty, transferring to his department the clerical force heretofore used for the purposes specified. It is to be understood that this officer will act by authority of the Secretary of the Navy, who will exercise such supervision as he may deem necessary.[19]

These orders went far towards supplanting Welles as Secretary of the Navy by Barron. In the management of the department they made the naval officer the more important official. Upon receiving them, Welles was greatly astonished; and he immediately, on the night of April 1, carried them to the White House for an explanation. Lincoln was much surprised to find that he had signed a document of such import. He said that Seward, with two or three young men, had been at the White House during the day on a matter which the Secretary of State had much at heart; and that he had signed the document without reading it or knowing what it was, supposing that it related to an enterprise of Seward. Welles told the President that he had no confidence in the fidelity of Barron, who was by the order forced into an official and personal intimacy with him and who was virtually given charge of the department; that the establishment of a bureau by executive order was unlawful; and that the proposition to make a naval officer secretary of the navy *de facto* was illegal and in his view "monstrous". Lincoln replied that he knew nothing of Barron, that the document was not his although he had signed it, and that Welles should treat it as cancelled. He expressed regret that he had blundered, and was wont afterwards to say that during the first weeks of his administration he and the members of his Cabinet were all new to their work and naturally made mistakes. Welles believed that the attempt of Seward and Porter to place the principal business of the department in the hands of Barron was a movement in behalf of the Confederacy and the Southern naval officers. Barron was shortly dismissed from the naval service. He entered the Confederate navy, taking rank as captain from March 26, 1861, five days before the date of the executive order giving him charge of the federal Navy Department.[20]

---

[19] *The Galaxy*, vol. X. (1870), p. 624.
[20] *The Galaxy*, vol. X. (1870), pp. 624–626.

Seward's interference with the department was not confined to measures for its reorganization and to the detailing of naval officers. He planned a naval expedition for the relief of Fort Pickens, Florida, which was officered and fitted out and had sailed before Welles got wind of it. This was the enterprise to which Lincoln supposed the above-mentioned document related when he signed it. On April 1 Seward had obtained Lincoln's signature to a second document, ordering Lieutenant Porter to proceed to the New York navy-yard and prepare an expedition for the relief of Fort Pickens. At this time Welles was fitting out at the New York navy-yard an expedition for the relief of Fort Sumter, which was to be under the command of Gustavus V. Fox. Both Welles and Seward intended that the ship *Powhatan* should sail as one of the vessels of their respective fleets. It therefore happened that the orders respecting her conflicted. The commandant of the New York yard was naturally confused. Since the President's orders were superior to those of the Secretary of the Navy, he gave Porter possession of the vessel. Welles was completely in the dark as to Porter's movements until about the time that Porter's fleet sailed from New York for Fort Pickens on April 6. On receiving intelligence of them, he in company with Seward, went to the White House and asked for an explanation of the diverting of the *Powhatan* from the Fort Sumter expedition, which venture, he said, would fail if this ship was taken from Fox's fleet. Lincoln, after explaining that he had confused the name of the *Powhatan* with that of another ship, decided that Porter should turn the vessel over to Fox. An order to this effect was signed by Seward and sent to Porter at New York, but he had already sailed. A tug was procured, and the orders reached him berore he got to sea. He however declined to detach the *Powhatan* from his fleet on the ground that he was acting under orders signed by the President, while the countermanding orders were signed by the President's subordinate, the Secretary of State. The *Powhatan* therefore proceeded to Fort Pickens. Welles and Fox always maintained that the sending of Porter's expedition was one of the main causes of the failure of Fox's.[21]

Porter cannot be freed from all blame for the part that he played in these strange proceedings. He was a man of mature years and long experience in the navy. The postscript of one of the documents was in his handwriting. Knowing well the routine of the department, he must have been aware of the irregularity of Seward's acts, and he must have foreseen that they would likely cause confusion. One might suppose that he had some knowledge of the character of Barron and of that officer's unfitness for the management of the navy during the crisis of the spring of 1861. On the other hand, it may be said in Porter's favor that he was acting under his superiors, the President and the Secretary of State, and that under the extraordinary circumstances that then existed irregularities were to be expected.[22] When he accepted the command of the Fort Pickens expedition, he was under orders to proceed to the Pacific Coast and report for duty on the Coast Survey, a detail which he had sought. Welles did not forget the part that Porter played in Seward's machinations. That he did not permit it to prevent the advancement of that gallant and ambitious officer is a tribute to his fairness.

In retrospect, one can now see that during the first months of Lincoln's administration no matter deserved more consideration than the holding and defending of the Norfolk navy-yard, one of the three principal navy-yards of the United States. It contained numerous dwellings, sheds, storehouses and machine shops. Here were large quantities of tools, machines, naval stores and provisions, and some two thousand pieces of artillery. Connected with the yard was a commodious dry dock constructed of granite, and near it were twelve ships. One of these, the *Merrimac*, when equipped for sea, was worth $1,200,000. The total value of the yard and its property was estimated by the department at $9,780,000. The Norfolk yard was strategically situated for the use of either the Unionists or the Confederates. To the latter, at the beginning of the war, its ordnance stores were worth far more than their value in money. These facts did not receive the consideration that they deserved. It is not here urged that the President should have provided for the defense of this yard without regard to his general policy, but certainly he should not have formulated his general policy without regard to its effect upon the holding of the yard.

During the first weeks of his administration Lincoln's policy was to do nothing that might offend those Southern states that still remained in the Union. He was especially considerate of the

_____

[21] *The Galaxy*, vol. X. (1870), pp. 627, 637; vol. XI. (1871), pp. 105–107; *Official Records*, first series, vol. IV., pp. 228–241.
[22] Soley, *Admiral Porter*, pp. 101–102.

The Norfolk Navy Yard, photographed above in 1862, was abandoned by the Union in April 1861 and retaken in May 1862. ". . . during the first months of Lincoln's administration no matter deserved more consideration than the holding and defending of the Norfolk navy-yard, one of the three principal navy-yards of the United States."

feelings of the Virginians. While some slight measures of defense were taken late in March and early in April, 1861, not until about the time that the Old Dominion seceded from the Union was any vigor and decision respecting the Norfolk yard shown by the administration. On April 16 Welles ordered Commodore Hiram Paulding to proceed from Washington to Norfolk and consult with the commandant of the yard, Captain C. S. McCauley, about its defense and the protection of its ships. Paulding carried an order to McCauley that rang with true mettle, the first issued by the department for several months of which this may be said. "The vessels and stores under your charge", the order read, "you will defend at any hazard, repelling by force, if necessary, any and all attempts to seize them, whether by mob violence, authorized effort, or any assumed authority." During the next four days the department showed considerable activity, but unfortunately its efforts were too late. McCauley and Paulding, who were in positions of authority, did not rise to the occasion. They were too old, too long schooled in routine, to accomplish great things in a sudden emergency. McCauley lacked energy and initiative, and he was largely under the influence of his disaffected officers, who were Southerners and who did their utmost to deceive him as to the real situation of the yard. On April 20, fearing an attack on the ships, he ordered them to be scuttled. They were sinking when Paulding arrived from Washington with fresh orders. The two officers now decided not to attempt a defense, but to destroy all the public property and to abandon the navy-yard. Their work of destruction, however, was hasty and ill-executed, and much property fell into the hands of the Confederates.

Possession of the Norfolk navy-yard with its valuable supplies was of great service to the South. Its cannon were used in fortifying the forts and batteries of the Confederacy on the Atlantic and Gulf coasts and on the Potomac, York, James, Rappahannock, and Mississippi rivers. The *Merrimac* was raised and converted into a terrible engine of war. Its dramatic contest with the *Monitor* made its name famous. The dry dock was but little injured. Many of the workshops with their valuable machinery escaped harm. Admiral Porter said that "but for the misfortune of losing, or we may say throwing away, the Norfolk Navy Yard, all the unarmed ports of the South would have easily fallen into our hands." [23]

With no other naval officer was Lincoln so intimate as with Rear-Admiral John A. Dahlgren, who early in the war was commandant of the Washington navy-yard, and later was chief of the Bureau of Ordnance. For many years before the outbreak of the war Dahlgren had been in charge of the Ordnance Department of the Washington yard. He was the chief ordnance expert of the Old Navy, and had invented the Dahlgren gun. The friendship between him and the President was established during the first months of the war when the Washington navy-yard was the chief defense of the capital. In the latter part of April, 1861, almost all of the officers of this yard, including its commandant, Captain Franklin Buchanan, resigned from the navy, and most of them cast in their lot with the Confederacy. Dahlgren almost alone remained faithful to the flag, and he was given command of the yard. Later, when some of the higher officers of the navy wished to displace him and obtain his position, Lincoln refused them, saying that it should not be taken from Dahlgren, that he had held it when no one else would, and that he should keep it as long as he wished. During the first two years of the war the President visited the yard almost every week. He would take Dahlgren to ride with him, invite him to the White House to dine, and seek his advice upon naval matters. Often the two men were together during short voyages which Lincoln now and then made down the Potomac on one of the naval vessels. When the news reached Washington on Sunday morning, March 9, 1862, that the *Merrimac* had destroyed the *Cumberland* and the *Congress*, and that she might next move upon Washington or one of the Northern ports, the President was excited; he could not be satisfied with the opinions of Welles and other civilian advisers, but ordered his carriage and drove to the navy-yard to consult its commandant. [24]

The diary of Dahlgren, for the years 1861–1863, is exceedingly interesting and valuable because of his close association with Lincoln during that period. From its pages one may glean much information regarding Lincoln's propensity for joking, the tragedy of his life during the war, his love of good reading, and his careless informality of manners. How the conflict between the States exhausted him and wore his heart away is painfully clear from such sentences as these: "Poor gentleman, how thin and wasted he is"; "I observe the President never jokes now"; "He looks thin and badly, and is very nervous"; "Mr. Lincoln frequently passed sleepless nights." Often, however, the President was in good spirits and would "let off a joke." On the trips down the Potomac he was usually jolly and full of anecdotes. Regarding one of these voyages Dahlgren writes: "Meanwhile we had a gay evening in the little cabin, and then went to bed. Five of us stowed away in a place like a box! The President in his usual way, and telling many a joke." Sometimes on these trips the President would read aloud to the assembled officers and officials some favorite piece of literature. He is said to have read with much dramatic power, and with much pathos or humor according to the character of the selection. His choice on one occasion was Halleck's spirited lyric, *Marco Bozzaris*, the closing lines of which have been thought prophetic of Lincoln's own career and fate:

> "For thou are Freedom's now, and Fame's;
> One of the few, the immortal names,
> That were not born to die." [25]

When the war began, Lincoln was entirely ignorant of military and naval affairs, but before its close he had acquired a considerable knowledge of them. He was especially interested in ordnance and ammunition. A resident of Washington tells me that he has seen the President in the White

[23] *The Galaxy*, vol. X. (1870), pp. 112–119; *Senate Reports*, 37 Cong., 2 sess., no. 37, pp. 1–123; *Official Records*, first series, vol. IV., pp. 272–313; Sands, *From Reefer to Rear Admiral*, pp. 225–229; Porter, *The Naval History of the Civil War*, p. 62; Parker, *Recollections of a Naval Officer*, pp. 206–207.

[24] Dahlgren, *Memoir of John A. Dahlgren*, p. 358.

[25] Dahlgren, *Memoir of John A Dahlgren*, pp. 364, 368.

*Advisors to the President: (left) Rear Admiral
John A. Dahlgren; (top right) Rear Admiral
Charles H. Davis; (bottom right) Captain Henry
A. Wise.*

Lot firing at a target with a Spencer gun. The diary of Dahlgren contains many references to Lincoln in connection with naval ordnance. On one day he drives to the navy-yard with Assistant Secretary of the Navy Fox to see a 150-pounder fired off; shortly he comes down with the Secretary of State and the Secretary of the Treasury and examines ''guns, iron plates, etc.''; next, he goes to the Bureau of Ordnance ''to see about some new powder''. On January 29, 1863, Dahlgren records that the President sent for him. ''Some man in trouble about arms. President holding a breech-loader in his hand.'' On February 16 Dahlgren is again sent for: ''Some inflammable humbug had been poked at him; from it he went off easily to Charleston matters. Dupont and Fox differ as to plan of attack, and he insists on Fox going down to Charleston to talk it over.'' On April 28 Dahlgren writes thus: ''The President came down in the afternoon, to learn about Ames, one of the hunters for a heavy ordnance contract. It is unfortunate that the President will meddle in such matters. No adventure on the Treasury now stands on its merits. Projects for new cannon, new powder, and devices of all kinds are backed by the highest influences.'' [26]

Dahlgren's account of a visit to the White House on December 22, 1862, affords an excellent view of the variety and vexation of Lincoln's tasks:

> The President sent for me about ten. Entering his cabinet room, Forney, Secretary of Senate, was in conversation with him, and saying that it would be well to publish report of committee on fight at Frederick, as the people were excited.
>
> The President answered warmly, ''that he did not want to swear, but why will people be such damned fools?'' Forney remarked, going, ''that he hoped the President would not let Mr. Chase resign'', and added, ''nor Mr. Seward''. The President paused and reddened, then said suddenly, ''If one goes, the other must; they must hunt in couples.'' So Forney made his bow.
>
> The President, much glad to drop such troublesome business, and relaxing into his usual humor, sat down and said, ''Well, Captain, here's a letter about a new powder'', which he read, and showed the sample. Said he had burned some, and there was too much residuum. ''Now, I'll show you.'' He got a small sheet of paper, placed on it some of the powder, ran to the fire, and with the tongs picked up a coal, which he blew, specs still on nose. It occurred to me how peaceful was his mind, so easily diverted from the great convulsion going on, and a nation menaced with disruption.
>
> The President clapped the coal to the powder and away it went, he remarking, ''There is too much left there.'' He handed me a small parcel of the powder to try, and, in noticing the late imbroglio, said, ''it was very well to talk of remodelling the Cabinet, but the caucus had thought more of *their* plans than of *his* benefit'', and he had told them so. [27]

The President's interest in naval details was by no means confined to arms and ammunition. On September 15, 1861, Dahlgren writes: ''Last night Professor Way took his electro-mercury light down the river, and I had the President out in a steamboat to see it.'' Several months later the same authority records that the President came down to the navy-yard to look at ''some invention.'' Lincoln often inspected the vessels of the navy that visited Washington or Alexandria. Rear-Admiral Daniel Ammen relates that on one occasion when the President, in company with Dahlgren and Thurlow Weed, was passing Alexandria on board the *Philadelphia*, he happened to see our war-ship *Pawnee* abreast the wharf. On hearing her name he asked if she were not the vessel with the ''curious bottom having bilges coming down below the line of the keel, and then drew roughly on the marble

---

[26] Dahlgren, *Memoir of John A. Dahlgren*, pp. 386, 388, 390–391.
[27] *Ibid.*, pp. 383–384.

top of a table, with a lead-pencil, a cross-section of the vessel, and asked Dahlgren whether the bottom was not something like that, and on receiving an affirmative answer he made one of the humorous comparisons for which he was famous".[28]

Several naval officers who saw much of the President during the war have left us their impressions of him and their estimates of his character. Shortly after Lincoln's death, Dahlgren wrote: "I can say, from an intimate acquaintance with the President, that he was a man of rare sagacity, good genial temper, and desirable firmness; that he possessed qualities of the highest order as a ruler; indeed, we know of no man who was so well fitted to carry the country through her trial." [29]

On several occasions Admiral Porter had good opportunities for observing the President. Early in 1865, a few weeks before the war ended, Lincoln spent several days with him on board of his flagship *Malvern*, on the James River. Porter was impressed with the kindness of heart, the habit of story-telling, and the unassuming simplicity of his distinguished visitor. Long after the war he wrote of Lincoln as follows:

> To me, he was one of the most interesting men I ever met. He had an originality about him which was peculiarly his own, and one felt when with him as if he could confide his dearest secret to him with absolute security against its betrayal. There, it might be said, was "God's noblest work—an honest man", and such he was all through. I have not a particle of the bump of veneration on my head, but I saw more to admire in this man, more to reverence, than I had believed possible. He had a load to bear that few men could carry, yet he traveled on with it, footsore and weary, but without complaint; rather, on the contrary, cheering those who would faint on the roadside. He was not a demonstrative man, so no one will ever know amid all the trials he underwent how much he had to contend with and how often he was called upon to sacrifice his own opinions to those of others who he felt did not know as much about matters at issue as he did himself. When he did surrender, it was always with a pleasant manner, winding up with a characteristic story.[30]

Rear-Admiral C. H. Davis was for the larger part of the war attached to the Navy Department, in Washington. He was an officer of cultivated mind and acute observation. His descriptions of the President are especially valuable since they were penned without view to their publication and before the Lincoln tradition had more or less obscured the real man. The following words, written on March 9, 1861, give Davis's first impressions:

> Yesterday morning, Friday, I set off early for the department, in and about which I passed the day. I found that the officers of the navy were to be formally received by the Secretary and President, and being in uniform (though the others were in full dress), I fell in and had the pleasure of seeing the President and Mrs. Lincoln. In the former I was agreeably disappointed. His likenesses, such as are seen in prints, etc., give no idea of his appearance,—I might almost say, none whatever. His countenance is far from ugly, and its expression is decidedly attractive. The play of features and the easy smile are more engaging than the pictures make him. He is awkward in his figure and manners, but his awkwardness is not *gaucherie*. It is by no means vulgar. The impression he makes is altogether favorable.[31]

---

[28] Dahlgren, *Memoir of John A. Dahlgren*, pp. 343, 378; Ammen, *The Old Navy and the New*, p. 341.
[29] *Ibid.*, p. 509.
[30] Soley, *Admiral Porter*, pp. 445–446.
[31] Davis, *Life of Charles Henry Davis*, pp. 114–115.

In a letter of December 13, 1863, apparently to his wife, Davis wrote the following prophetic words.

> You may be assured that in future times Lincoln will be regarded as the very greatest of all the blessings bestowed on this country in these sad times,—as God-sent, appointed by God, like the prophets of old, to do his work, to save the nation and regenerate the people, to remove the curse of slavery, and to set another example of the profound wisdom that lies hidden and unrevealed in simplicity, truthfulness, uprightness before God, humility, conscientiousness, even when unaccompanied with great talents or great learning. In his and similar examples consists the political life of the nation and its safety,—the safety of our republican institutions.[32]

---

[32] *Ibid.*, p. 301.

Farragut's fleet engages C.S.S. Tennessee *in Mobile Bay.*

THE JOURNAL

OF

PRIVATE CHARLES BROTHER, USMC

THE JOURNAL OF PRIVATE CHARLES BROTHER

Introduction

The dramatic Battle of Mobile Bay on 5 August 1864 is one of the most famous engagements in American naval history. The various aspects of that action—the dash of the Union squadron past Forts Morgan and Gaines, the sudden destruction of the monitor *Tecumseh* and David Glasgow Farragut's bold decision to "Damn the torpedoes!", the spirited defense by the small Confederate squadron led by indomitable Franklin Buchanan in the ram *Tennessee,* and the eventual surrender of the forts—have all been well recorded in the documents of the time and in subsequent historical treatments.

But these descriptions of the battle have been told primarily from the point of view of the officers in the squadron, for it is their action reports and official and personal letters that dominate the historical record. That is one reason that the journal published below is a particularly welcome addition to the documents of the Civil War. It was kept on board U.S.S. *Hartford* by Charles Brother, a young Marine Private, who penciled in its pages his impressions of what he saw as Farragut's squadron prepared to take the last major Confederate port on the Gulf coast and battered its way to victory on 5 August. Thus, it not only presents an enlisted man's views of the battle and the careful preparations Farragut made that helped to ensure his success, but it also gives an illuminating glimpse of daily shipboard life and routine—which is essential for those who would understand and appreciate fully the Civil War Navy.

Charles Brother was born in Bath, New York, on 10 August 1844. He was just over 18 years of age when he enlisted in the Marine Corps for four years in New York City on 13 October 1862. He was described in his enlistment papers as being five feet eight and one-quarter inches tall, of fair complexion, with light hair and hazel eyes.[1]

Brother was first assigned to the Marine Barracks at the Brooklyn Navy Yard where he was trained for a fortnight and treated briefly for a sore throat. On 4 November he was transferred to U.S.S. *Vanderbilt.* Two days later, under Acting Lieutenant Charles H. Baldwin, *Vanderbilt* steamed out of New York in search of Raphael Semmes and his celebrated Confederate commerce raider *Alabama.* Brother's first taste of sea duty was uneventful, however, for *Vanderbilt* cruised off Nova Scotia, then sailed for Bermuda where she stayed overnight on 21 November, and returned to New York on the 30th. During the cruise of more than 3,500 miles, perhaps the only incident he would have found worthy of recording had he maintained a journal at this time would have been a minor collision with the British bark *Symmetry* on the 15th. The accident occurred while Baldwin was attempting to board the merchantman, and the damage to the warship was only "trifling".[2]

On 6 December Secretary of the Navy Gideon Welles ordered *Vanderbilt* to "resume the search for the pirate *Alabama*" and to take Captain John Winslow and two other officers to Fayal, Spain.[3] Brother saw the only European port he was to visit during his Marine Corps career when his ship put into Fayal in December. After taking on 350 tons of coal and spending several days in the Spanish harbor, *Vanderbilt* put out to sea again in pursuit of the elusive *Alabama.* The cruiser recrossed the

---

[1] Unless otherwise cited, the biographical information regarding Brother is derived from his service and pension records, both of which are held in the Army and Marine Corps Branch, National Archives.

[2] Lieutenant Baldwin's report of the November cruise is in the *Official Records of the Union and Confederate Navies in the War of the Rebellion,* Series I, Volume 1, pages 563–564; hereinafter cited as ORN.

[3] ORN I, 1, 575–576.

Charles Brother as he appeared later in life.

Atlantic, refueled briefly at Hampton Roads, Virginia, and was underway for the Caribbean Sea by the end of January 1863.[4]

Vanderbilt touched at Havana on 4 February and St. Thomas on the 13th as she criss-crossed the Caribbean searching for commerce raiders and blockade runners. Her tireless efforts did not go unrewarded, for on 25 February she took the British steamer *Peterhoff* near St. Thomas—a capture that was to prove controversial indeed.[5]

On the 26th, *Peterhoff* was ordered to the United States for adjudication in a prize court, and Charles Brother was one of five Marines who were ordered from *Vanderbilt* as part of her prize crew. *Peterhoff* was taken first to Key West and then to New York, where she arrived on 28 March. All five of the Marines were detached and assigned to the Barracks at the Brooklyn Navy Yard on 31 March.[6]

There young Brother remained until 6 June when he was transferred to the receiving ship *North Carolina* in New York harbor. He returned to the Barracks on 25 July for a short time, again going on board *North Carolina* on 3 August.[7]

While Charles Brother was spending an uneventful summer and fall in New York far from any action, U.S.S. *Hartford* was engaged constantly in the struggle on the Mississippi River, where Vicks-

---

[4] For details of *Vanderbilt*'s cruise, see *ORN* I, 2.

[5] See *ORN* I, 2, 97 *ff.*

[6] See *Marine Muster Rolls*, January–June 1863, pages 186 and 195; Army and Marine Corps Branch, National Archives; hereinafter cited as *MMR*.

[7] *MMR*, July–December 1863, 33 and 163.

I, *Charles Brother*

do acknowledge that I have voluntarily enlisted myself to serve four years in the Marine Corps of the **UNITED STATES**, unless sooner discharged, upon the terms mentioned in the act passed the 11th day of July, 1798, entitled "An act for establishing and organizing a Marine Corps;" also the act passed the 2d day of March, 1833, entitled "An act to improve the condition of the non-commissioned Officers and Privates of the Army and Marine Corps of the United States, and to prevent desertion;" also the act passed 30th June, 1834, entitled "An act for the better organization of the United States Marine Corps;" and also the acts passed the 2d day of March, 1837, entitled "An act to provide for the enlistment of boys for the Naval service, and to extend the term of the enlistment of seamen;" and February 20, 1845, entitled "An act to amend an act entitled 'An act to provide for the enlistment of boys for the Naval service, and to extend the term of the enlistment of seamen;'" and also the 9th section of an act passed March 3, 1845, "making appropriations for the Naval service for the year ending the 30th of June, 1846;" and that I have had read to me the Rules and Articles of the Army and Navy against Mutiny and Desertion.

Witness my hand, this *Thirteenth* day of *October* 186*2*

IN THE PRESENCE OF—

Wm Walsh
Sergt U.S.M. Corps

Cha Brother

I, *Charles Brother*

do solemnly swear or affirm, (as the case may be,) that I will bear true allegiance to the United States of America, and that I will serve them honestly and faithfully against all their enemies or opposers whosoever, and observe and obey the order of the President of the United States, and the orders of the officers appointed over me, according to the Rules and Articles for the government of the Army and Navy of the United States. ~~And further, that I am of the full age of twenty-one years.~~

Cha Brother

Sworn before me, at *New York*
this *Thirteenth* day of *October* 186*2*

Capt Com as Rendezvous

SIZE ROLL.

Charles Brother a private, born in the *U.S.*
State of *New York* County of *Steuben* Town of
Bath enlisted *October Thirteenth 1862* at
New York for four years, by *Capt A N Brevoort*
aged *Eighteen* years, *Five* feet *Eight½* inches high, *Hazle* eyes,
Light hair, *Fair* complexion, by trade or occupation a *Clerk*

REMARKS.

I CERTIFY, That the above recruit is free from bodily defects, and is qualified to perform the duty of a soldier.

George Peck
Surgeon

Charles Brother's enlistment paper.

U.S.S. Vanderbilt *was the first warship on which Marine private Charles Brother served.*

burg was the object of a massive Army-Navy siege and bombardment. When the Southern stronghold finally fell on 4 July 1863, other Confederate positions in the area (primarily at Port Hudson) quickly collapsed as well; and Farragut seized the opportunity to take his battered flagship to New York for much needed repairs before undertaking the task of capturing Mobile Bay. The Admiral departed New Orleans on 1 August and reported his arrival in New York on the 10th.[8] In this way was the opportunity presented for Brother to serve with Farragut on board *Hartford*.

On 15 December, Charles Brother was transferred from the Marine Barracks at the Brooklyn Navy Yard and ordered to *Hartford*.[9] That same afternoon Farragut's flagship was recommissioned, but only a shortage of sailors prevented her from sailing for the Gulf until early January. Finally, on 5 January 1864, *Hartford* departed New York, arriving at Pensacola on the 17th. Two days later, Farragut commenced a tour of his squadron, visiting New Orleans and the blockading ships off Mobile before returning to Pensacola on 9 February.[10] Here Brother was treated for a remittent fever from 12 to 18 February before he was returned to duty. And it was while the ship was at Pensacola that the Marine Private began his journal, a daily record of events from 14 March through 5 August.

Although the journal ends with a narrative of the Battle of Mobile Bay, Brother continued to serve in *Hartford* until she returned to New York in December. On 20 December, with the gallant warship once more undergoing repairs and destined to see no more action during the conflict, Brother was reassigned to the Marine Barracks in Brooklyn.[11] He was on duty there when Lee surrendered to Grant at Appomattox on 9 April 1865 and the war drew to a close.

With the war over, Brother sought to obtain his release from the Marine Corps prior to the end of his four year enlistment. On 28 May 1865, however, his father wrote him:

---

[8] *ORN* I, 20, 442–443.
[9] *MMR*, July–December 1863, 539.
[10] *ORN* I, 21, 796.
[11] *MMR*, July–December 1864.

I obtained through R. B. Van Valkenburgh [12] an introduction to Assistant Secretary Fox [13] and stated your case to him accompanied with a request for your discharge on the grounds first that you had not been paid your bounty & secondly that the war being over I supposed the Govt could dispense with your services.

His reply was that insted [sic] of having too many Marines they had too few and were enlisting more all the time, that they had not discharged any Marines except for other causes & he could do nothing for me in the matter. [14]

Thus, Brother was transferred to the Marine Barracks at the Boston Navy Yard on 20 June. While stationed in Boston he apparently persuaded (or paid) an acquaintance to serve out the rest of his tour of duty—a not uncommon practice in those days—for he was "honorably discharged, a private, October 21, 1865 at Boston, Mass., by order of the Secretary of the Navy, on settlement of accounts upon furnishing a substitute."

Brother returned to his home in Bath, New York, where he lived for perhaps ten years. [15] He then moved to the Middle West, living in several Iowa towns: New Hanford, Cedar Falls, Sioux City, Des Moines. He was employed as a railroad postal clerk, commonly travelling 250 miles a day for a week and then having a week off. He married and had four children.

In the 1890's he was injured in a train wreck, and, also suffering from rheumatism and "general dibility", in October 1896 he applied for a pension from the Marine Corps because he was "to a material extent unable to earn support. . . ." He was granted a monthly pension of six dollars, an amount that was increased only slightly during the next 20 years. Brother never regained his health and was residing with his son-in-law, John W. Toyne, in South Bend, Indiana, at the time of his death on 21 November 1917.

Charles Brother left little information about himself, but he did leave an interesting journal. A number of editorial insertions have been made to clarify and in some cases to correct it. The only editorial alterations of the text that are not immediately apparent have to do with the beginning and ending of sentences. The young Marine seldom began a sentence with a capital letter or ended one with a period, and these have been added in the interest of readability. Where his spelling is corrected for the sake of accuracy—as in the names of people and ships—brackets ([ ]) and footnotes have been used to indicate it. The journal tells its own story, however, and tells it well.

U.S. SLOOP *HARTFORD* WESTERN GULF BLOCKADING SQUADRON

ADMIRAL FARRAGUT'S FLAGSHIP

Monday March 14th 1864

Had the Morning and 2d dog watches. [1] Pork & beans for dinner. General quarters in the forenoon at three bells. Took my station at the Cabin door as usual. Retreat at half past ten. Knapsack inspection on the berth deck after quarters, were inspected by Lieut. [Charles L.] Sherman. Capt. [Charles] Heywood is sick. [George] Bickfort [2] was sent on shore in charge of Sargt. [John] Cavendish, is to remain there till his punishment is over. At six bells all hands triced up the Propeller. I hear they are going to put a knife in it but for what purpose I dont know. The auxly. steamer *Union* arrived about one o'clock. Brought a Mail. Rec'd a letter & paper from Mary. Got up wash clothes in the evening.

---

[1] Watches were stood from midnight to 4 a.m. (the mid watch); 4 to 8 (morning watch); 8 to 12 noon (forenoon watch); 12 to 4 p.m. (afternoon watch); 4 to 6 (first dog watch); 6 to 8 (second dog watch); and 8 to 12 midnight (night watch). The bell was rung to mark the passage of each half hour of the watch: one bell was rung half an hour after the watch commenced, two bells after an hour, and so on, until eight bells marked the end of the watch. Thus, in this journal entry for example,

[12] Robert Bruce Van Valkenburgh was a Republican member of the U.S. House of Representatives from New York State, 4 March 1861–3 March 1865.

[13] Assistant Secretary of the Navy Gustavus Vasa Fox.

[14] This is one of a few letters to and from Brother which, along with the journal, are held by the Historic Mobile Preservation Society, Mobile, Alabama.

[15] Brother's pension records indicate that he was a resident of Bath for 30 years "until came to Iowa."

"in the forenoon at three bells" meant 9:30 a.m.; "half past ten" was five bells in the forenoon; and "six bells [in the forenoon]" was 11 a.m.

[2] Marine Private George W. Bickford had been found guilty on 8 March of disobedience of orders. "Had to forfeit one months' pay. One month solitary confinement on bread and water, except Sundays when he got full ration for Navy." (*MMR*, January–June, 1864, 266.)

Tuesday March 15th

Washed clothes in the morning. [Charles] Bol[l]ing washed three pieces for me while I stood his post for him. The *Union* went out about seven o'clock. Had the forenoon and 1st night watch. Piped down wash clothes at four bells in the afternoon, found several dead inhabitants on my shirt. Cheated us out of our duff [1] & gave us bullion beef for dinner.

[1] Duff is a flour pudding boiled in a bag.

Wednesday March 16th

Weather quite cool. Mark & Eugene were tried by a summary court martial today.[1] Quarters & drill in the forenoon at three bells. Had the afternoon watch. Pork & beans for dinner.

[1] Orderly Sergeant Alfred Mark was found guilty on 16 March of striking Corporal Edward Eagan and was to forfeit one month's pay and do three months of "police" duty. Eagan was found guilty on the same date of striking Sergeant Mark and was to forfeit two months' pay and do three months of "police" duty. (*MMR*, January–June 1864, p. 266) See journal entry for 19 March.

Thursday Mar 17th, St Patricks day.

Weather cold, like to froze in the mid watch. Had the mid & 1st dog watches. Duff for dinner. The steamers *Onida* [*Oneida*] & *Tennesee* [1] came in to day. A Sargt Smith belonging to the barracks was buried & the drummer & fifer went on shore to attend his funeral.[2] Came back just after sundown slightly intoxicated, especialy the fifer. The cooper and armorer also half seas over.

[1] *Tennesee* was a 1,275 ton side wheel steamer seized on 25 April 1862 after the capture of New Orleans. Farragut frequently used her as his flagship when he was not on board *Hartford*.

[2] Sergeant George Smith died 16 March 1864. The drummer from *Hartford* was George Ryall and the fifer was James McKivitt. (*MMR*, January–June 1864, 234, 266.)

Friday March 18th

Had the morning and 2d dog watches. Duff again for dinner. The gun boat *Ossippee* [*Ossipee*] came in about six bells in the morning. [About two lines have been erased] word was passed that a mail would leave the ship at two P.M. Wrote a letter to Father & took it aft at half past one but the mail had gone so did not sent it. The *Ossipee* went out about half past two. [More erasures] fire quarters at six P.M.

Saturday March 19,

Had the forenoon & first night Watches, pork and beans for dinner. [Sergeant Alfred] Mark & [Corporal Edward] Eagan have received their sentences & gone to duty again. Mark is to lose one months pay & receive three months extra duty. Eagan forfits two months pay & get three mn's extra duty.[1] What the extra duty will be is more than I can tell. The *Glasscow* [*Glasgow*] came in at a bout two o'clock. *Pembina* at noon. Cleaned belts &c in afternoon. Wrote a letter to Father.

[1] See footnote 1 to journal entry of 16 March.

Sunday March 20th.

Weather warm & pleasant. Marines in full uniform at quarters. Ships company in clean blue & white cap covers. Sarg't Bhernsen [Orderly Sergeant August Behrensen] gave the order to clean & mark our uniform hats & turn them in to him as they are going to be done away with for the present.

Bully for that. Had the afternoon watch. Bullion and coffee for dinner. The *Bermuda* came in at three P.M. Will probably take our mail for the North.

Monday March 21st,

Weather very unpleasant. Cold & raining all day. Had the mid & first dog watches. Pork & beans for dinner. All hands scrub & wash clothes. Did not wash any. [Private Joseph] Williams came back from the hospital this afternoon. Hoisted colors at 8 A.M. Two or three gun boats arrived during the day. The *Jessimine* [*Jasmine*] came in about five o'clock P.M. Brought no mail. Says the weather is very rough outside.

Tuesday March 22d 1864,

Had the Morning and second dog watches. Duff for dinner. Ship *Corina* went out in the Morning. Gunboat *Sebago* arrived in the afternoon. General quarters at 5.50 P.M. This morning found my belts turned black. They say it is the bilge water in the hold. Several other belts are the same way though not so bad as mine. The paint work about the last lockers is blackened. Weather cold.

Wednesday March 23d, 1864,

[Dennis] Morrison & [Epenitus] Devoe [1] went to Hospital. Had the forenoon & first night watches. Pork and beans for dinner. Bought a bucket of[f] the bum boat [2] for sixty cents. Loosed sail in forenoon at three bells. Cleaned belts.

[1] Marine privates.
[2] Slang for a private boat with supplies for sale.

Thursday March 24th

Weather cold. Had the Afternoon watch. Bullion & coffee for dinner. The last of the spuds for breakfast. Rain & wind in the afternoon. Winch[e]ll went on shore yesterday. Was to come abbaft sun down. Has not come yet.

Friday March 25th.

Weather pleasant, washed shirt, drawers & pr socks in the morning. Had the mid and 1st dog watches. Duff for dinner. General quarters in the forenoon at four bells. All the port guns fired at a target five times, some splendid shots were made, distance eleven hundred yards. The *Glasscow* [*Glasgow*] arrived in the evening with a mail from New Orleans. Rec'd a letter from Mary dated Mar 6th.

Saturday March 26th

Weather warm and pleasant. Last night [Charles] Bol[l]ing was taken sick while on post at the door—had to be relieved. [Private Isaac B.] Lawrence 2d [1] takes his place. Turned out at two o'clock this morning to go to the head. Was gone about three minutes, when I came back my blanket was gone and I could not find it any-where. This is the third one I have lost in the service besides the comforter sent me from home. Fire quarters in the forenoon at four bells. General quarters at six bells and target practice. Each of the starboard guns had two shots at it. The firing was very good but not so good as yesterday. Cleaned belts & epauletts in the Afternoon. Had the Morning & 2d dog watches. Pork and beans for dinner, in the afternoon wrote a letter to Mary.

[1] There were two Marine Privates named Lawrence on board *Hartford*. Brother refers to "Lawrence 2d" on 26 March and on 12 July. It is possible to determine that this was Isaac B. Lawrence because the *Marine Muster Rolls* (July–December 1864, 59) corroborate Brother's 12 July entry by noting that Isaac B. Lawrence was "transferred to Navy Hospital" on that date. On 20 May Brother refers to "Lawrence on the sick list." Because the "2d" designation does not appear, it is likely that he is identifying George Lawrence, who was also reported "sick in June" in the *Marine Muster Rolls* (January–June 1864, 640).

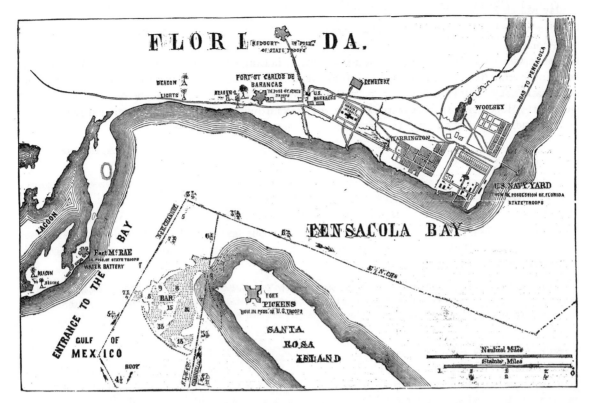

(top) *This contemporary chart of Pensacola Bay was drawn early in the war while Southern troops occupied key facilities in the area.* (bottom) *The Pensacola Navy Yard as seen from Fort Pickens on Santa Rosa Island.*

Sunday March 27th

Weather warm & pleasant. At Muster Marines in full uniform & fatigue caps with white covers. Ships company in clean blue with white cap covers. The Chaplain came on board from the *Potomac* & held service after quarters. Had the forenoon and first night watches. Bullion beef & coffee for dinner. Several Mortar schooners arrived during the day.[1] Rec'd a paper from Mary. The New York papers say that Farragut is to be relieved from here to take command of the South Atlantic squadron. Hope it is not so or if it is that he may take us with him. In the evening a ship was seen outside sending up rockets, she afterward went further out and anchored.

[1] The mortar schooners came from Grant's Pass in Mississippi Sound. They were: *Sea Foam, O. H. Lee, Henry James,* and *Orvetta.*

Monday March 28th

One Year ago today I sailed into New York Harbor on board the *Peterhoff*. Heard yesterday that she had been sunk off Galveston.[1] Commenced raining at about seven A.M. Rained all day. Had the Afternoon watch. Pork & beans for dinner. Gun boat *Itasca* arrived in the afternoon. Scrubed shirt, drawers & socks.

[1] U.S.S. *Peterhoff* had been purchased from the prize court in New York in February 1863. On 7 March 1864, commanded by Acting Lieutenant Thomas Pickering, *Peterhoff* was in collision with U.S.S. *Monticello* south of New Inlet Bar, North Carolina, and sank in five fathoms. She was a total loss, although all officers and men were saved. (See *ORN* I, 9, 535-538.)

Tuesday March 29th 1864.

Had the Mid & 1st dog watches. Duff for dinner. At 1.15 A.M. let go the starboard anchor on account of the winds blowing strong from the N.W. At 6.30 got up the starboard anchor again. Quarters at three bells, & a long drill for us after retreat. Wind blowing hard all day, no boats ashore but the *Loyal,* an army transport arrived in the afternoon. Put down to day for 1 blk slk hdkf, 1 pr shoes & 2 prs socks from the purser.

Wednesday March 30th

All hands called at three bells. Breakfast at 6 o'clock. Weather pleasant. Had the Morning & 2d dog watches. Pork & beans for dinner. The Sloop of war *Richmond* came in in the afternoon. She has encountered a heavy storm and lost two of her boats. Capt [Thornton A.] Jenkins came on board as soon as she had anchored. We Orderlies now have charge of the keys of the Magazine.

Thursday March 31st. 64

Weather pleasant. All hands called at three bells, breakfast at four bells. Had the forenoon and first night watches. Bullion beef for dinner. The *Jassimine* [*Jasmine*] came in about eleven o'clock in the evening. Marines fired at target in the afternoon. I fired five times & hit it once, the last time.

Friday April 1st, 1864

Weather pleasant but rather windy. All hands called at three bells, breakfast at four. Scrubed & washed clothes, [I] did not wash any. The mail came on board from the *Jasimine* [*Jasmine*]. Rec'd a letter from Mary, one from Ellie & one from Ella Wixom. Had the Afternoon watch. Duff for dinner, ate my own ration & Willcox's [Private Rufus E. Wilcox] too. Corporal [Edward] Eagan went on shore to barracks to-day [1] and a private [John McCrystall] came on board in his place.

[1] See footnote 1 to journal entry of 16 March.

Saturday April 2d.

Weather pleasant. All hands called at three bells, breakfast at four. [Lemeal M.] Mason was made Act'g Corporal today in [Edward] Eagans [1] place. Cleaned belts in the afternoon. Had the mid & 1st dog watches. Pork and beans for dinner. The Admiral, Capt, flag Lieut, Mr McKinley, Mr Dennis, Mr Brownell & Willis, Wilson & Brooks went on board the steamer *Tennessee* & left for New Orleans.[2] We now fly a lonely pennant at the main instead of a blue one at the mizzen. Mr Kimberley [Lieutenant Commander Lewis A. Kimberly] is now Commanding officer. It is expected the Admiral will be gone a month or more. Strike the bell now by the *Richmond*. Wrote a letter to Mother.

[1] See footnote 1 to journal entry of 16 March.

[2] Those going on board *Tennessee* included: Rear Admiral David G. Farragut, Captain Percival Drayton, Flag Lieutenant John Crittenden Watson, Flag Secretary Alexander McKinley, Flag Ensign Theodore W. Davis, Flag Master's Mate Henry H. Brownell and Pilot Martin Freeman. (*Hartford* Log; ORN I, 21, 796–797.)

Sunday April 3d 1864.

Weather warm & pleasant. At quarters at four bells in the forenoon. Marines in full uniform & white cap covers, ship company in clean blue and white cap covers. Gen'l muster after quarters. First Leuff [Lieutenant] read articles of war. Ships company mustered around the Capstern. Had the Morning and 2d dog watches. Bullion & coffee for dinner. In the afternoon some of the Marines and ships company went on board of the *Richmond* & some of the *Richmond*'s men came on board on us. Her Marines have ten & twelve hours off, have no drill, wear no uniform & wear nothing but a wrist belt on post. Dirty Dick must be a pretty good man after all. Wrote a letter to E. W. [Ella Wixom?] & commenced one to Miss Hess.

Monday April 4th 1864.

Had the forenoon and first night watches. Pork & beans for dinner. General quarters at three bells, retreat at four. Order given for Marines to wear no box belt on post in the future. No knapsack inspection. Signed for $37.01.

Tuesday April 5th 1864.

Called all hands at 2 bells. Breakfast at 8, then scrub & wash clothes. Washed shirt, drawers & socks. Ship *New England* went out in forenoon. Quarters at three bells. Quite a long drill after retreat. Had the afternoon watch. Duff for dinner.

Wednesday April 6th 1864.

Weather warm & pleasant, all hands called at two bells, scrubed hammocks after breakfast. Had the Mid & 1st dog watches. Pork & beans for dinner. Quarters in the morning at three bells, a short drill afterwards, double quick to "Pop goes the weazel". Scrubed hammocks [were] piped down at one o'clock.

Thursday April 7th 1864

Had the morning & 2 dog watches. Bullion, coffee & soft tack for dinner. Supply steamer *Admiral* arrived at 7 a.m. Mail came on board in forenoon. Rec'd a letter & several New York *Heralds* from Cameron. Commenced raining about seven A.M. Rained at intervals all day, no quarters. Got a lot of fresh beef, ice & vegitables from the *Admiral*. Our mess got two barrels of spuds.

Friday April 8th 1864,

Weather stormy & rainy all day. Fresh grub for dinner & potatoe sause for breakfast. Had the forenoon & first night watches. Dispatch boat *Glasscow* [*Glasgow*] arrived in the afternoon from

This 1864 photograph, taken looking aft, shows the main deck of U.S.S. Hartford.

New Orleans, brought us a small mail. I did not get any-thing. A ship said to be the *Pensacola* has anchored outside with her Jack up for a pilot.

Saturday April 9th
The *Pensacola* arrived this morning[.] She is homeward bound, has been out here about two years, is said to have three hundred sick men on board & two hundred men whose times are out. Wrote a letter to Val.

[Sunday, 10 April 1864]
Marines at quarters in full uniform, fatigue caps with white covers, ships company in clean blue & white cap covers. Had the Mid & 1st dog watches. Fresh grub for dinner. A number of the men went on board the *Richmond* in the afternoon.

Monday April 11th,
Weather warm & pleasant. Quite a long drill after quarters, & then knapsack inspection on the berth deck. Had the Morning & 2d dog watches. The *Pensacola* went out in the afternoon. Tug *Jassimine* [*Jasmine*] arrived in afternoon, brought us a small mail, nothing for me. An atack upon the yard being anticipated we were ordered to have our belts & muskets in order, ready to go on shore in a moments warning. At evening quarters the gun were loaded with ten second shell, word was

passed when hammocks were piped down for the men to stand by for a call to general quarters during the night. Pork & beans for dinner. Bickfort came on board.[1]

[1] Private George Bickford. See footnote 2 to 14 March journal entry.

Tuesday April 12th 1864.

Wash morning, scrubed a shirt[,] pr of drawers & pr of stockings. The Rebels did not disturb us last night. Quarters in forenoon a little before three bells. Marines drilled as usual after quarters. Wash clothes piped down in the afternoon at 7 bells. In the morning we were ordered to put our fatigue coats away and put on jumpers. Weather quite warm, about the warmest day we have had yet. Had the forenoon and first watches. Duff for dinner.

Wednesday April 13.

Weather warm and pleasant. Had the afternoon watch. Pork and beans for dinner. Drill on the quarter deck in the morning, an atack is expected on the [Navy] yard tonight. The bark *Carn* & ship *Sportsman* have moved up out of the way.

Thursday April 14th 1864.

Had the Mid & 1st dog watches. Firing was heard on shore in the direction of Fort Barrankas [Barrancus] between two & three o'clock A.M. At three the *Potomac* and *Richmond* beat to quarters & then we did. The guns were cast loose. All the boats sent on shore with the Marines. Some of the sick & myself were left on board. The Men stayed at the guns untill about five o'clock when they were piped down. Shortly after the boats returned in with the Marines. Breakfast at half past six, quarters at two bells but no drill. The report is that we are going on shore tonight with knapsacks. Comenced raining at about noon. In the afternoon scrubed a pr of pants for myself & one for Sergt, [John] Cavendish. At about half past five Marines fell in with cross belts, mess kits & watch coats & went on shore in the first cutter. We marched up to Barracks and stacked arms, broke ranks & went to the canteen which was opened for us. A Marine who I used to know in Brooklyn lent me a matrass & watch coat, and spreading them on the floor I turned in about eight o'clock. Turned out again at nine to answer roll call, turned in again but could not get to sleep for some time on account of the fleas. Pork & beans for dinner.

Friday April 15th 1864,

Turned out at revelie. [Private Denis] Foley was put in the brig during the night for being drunk and disorderly. In the morning took a walk around the yard with [Private John] Knox. Fell in about half past six and marched down to the basin, where we found the first cutter wating for us. [Private Dennis] Sullivan and McCuistle [John McCrystall] could not be found so we went off without them. Got on board about seven o'clock and after a little delay got breakfast, no coffee. The *Glasscow* [*Glasgow*] arrived last evening. Brought us a mail. Was distributed this morning. Rec'd a letter from Mary dated March 29th. [Private Thomas] Hunt is cooking in Sullivans place. In the forenoon cleaned belts, brasses &c &c. Had the 2d dog watch Duff for dinner.

Saturday April 16th '64

Had the forenoon & first watches. [Dennis] Sullivan & McCeistle [John McCrystall] were brought on board in the afternoon, were put on double duty immediately. Pork and beans for dinner. Hunt makes a tip top cook. Hope he will stay there.

Sunday April 17th 1864.

Had the afternoon watch. Quarters at 4 bells. Marines in full uniform, fatigue caps & white cap covers, ships company in clean blue & white cap covers. The Commodore's Sec'y belong[ing] to

This photograph, taken in August 1864, shows part of the "after guard" on board Hartford. *Charles Brother was assigned to this guard.*

the yard came on board with his wife a mighty good looking lady. Wrote a letter to Mary. In the afternoon some of the Marines & sailors went on board the *Richmond* and *Potomac*. Some of their men came on board of us, [Private Patrick] Malloy among them. He belongs on board the *Potomac*, says he likes her first rate. The *Arkansas* arrived in the evening. Had bullion beef & boiled spuds for dinner and dandyfunk[1] for supper. [Dennis] Sullivan is off double duty and takes the cooking again.

[1] Dandyfunk is sailors' slang for hardtack soaked in water and baked with molasses and salt pork.

Monday April 18th 1864.

Weather pleasant, no knapsack inspection. General quarters in the forenoon at two bells. Relieved Bolyn [Charles Bolling] & took my station at the Cabin door. Retreat in about fifteen minutes, went below & did not fall in to drill. Rest of the guard drilled about an hour. Had the mid & 1st dog watches. Pork and beans for dinner, The *Seminole* came in about six P.M. She is, I believe, from off Galveston.[1] Word passed to wear white pants next Sunday.

[1] Earlier in the year, *Seminole* had served on the Texas coast, but she was ordered to Mobile by Rear Admiral Farragut on April 5 from New Orleans, where she had been undergoing repairs. (*ORN* I, 21, 168.)

Tuesday April 19th.

Had the Morning & 2d dog watches. Duff for dinner. In the morning about seven bells the schooner *Kittatiny* [*Kittatinny*] & bark [*William G.*] *Anderson* at the Bayou fired several times towards shore. Dont know what the firing was for.

Wednesday April 20th,

Had the forenoon and first watches. Pork & beans for dinner. The supply steamer *Admiral* arrived in the forenoon, brought a mail from New Orleans, Rec'd a letter from Mary and 14 N.Y. *Ledgers* from New York. [John] Kelly & [Joseph] Williams went on board the *Admiral*. Are going north by the doctors order, Williams with a blind eye & Kelly with varicose veins in his legs & his foot.

Thursday April 21st,

Weather warm and pleasant. Had the afternoon watch. Bullion beef & coffee for dinner. Drill on the quarter deck in the forenoon. Those of the guard who were not there drew white pants & jumpers in the forenoon. Langdon came off the sick list this morning.

Friday April 22d 1864,

Wash morning. Washed a mattress cover, shirt, drawers & pr of socks. Had the mid and 1st dog watches. Duff for dinner. Fire quarters at two bells in the forenoon. A short drill after[wards]. The Capt [Heywood] taught us how to stack arms without bayonetts. Wrote a letter to Mary in the afternoon.

Saturday April 23d,

Cleaned belts &c in the afternoon. Had the Morning and 2d dog watches. Pork & beans for dinner.

Sunday April 24th,

Had the forenoon & first watches. Marines in full uniform & cap covers at muster. Ships company in clean blue & winter cap covers. A army transport landed[.] Part of soldiers arrived in the morning. An army transport came in in the forenoon. Boiled rice for dinner. Rec'd a paper from Mary.

Monday April 25th 1864,

Weather warm & pleasant. General quarters at two bells in the forenoon. Drill after quarters. Had the afternoon watch. Pork & beans for dinner. Deveaux [1] came on board from the hospital.

[1] Probably Private Epenitus Devoe; see journal entry of 23 March.

Tuesday April 26th 1864

Wash morning, washed a jumper. The *Tennes[s]ee* came in and anchored at six P.M. Suppose the Admiral will be on board of us tomorrow. Rec'd a N.Y. *Times* from Mary. Had the mid & first dog watches. Pork & beans [for dinner].

Wednesday April 27th.

The Admiral, Captain & all hands came on board this morning & once more we fly the blue penant from our Mizzen mast head. [1] Quarters at two bells in the forenoon and drill after. Got up the awning posts & built on the awning. 'Tis a very nice one, because new. The *Sebago* came in. Had the morning and 2d dog watches. Pork & beans for dinner.

[1] See footnote 3 to journal entry of 2 April.

Thursday April 28th,

Had the forenoon & 1st watch. Bullion and coffee for dinner. The *Rachel Seaman*[,] schooner[,] came in about one bell in the first watch. She is said to have a lot of spuds on board, hope we will get some. The *Tennes[s]ee* went out at four P.M. bound on a cruise.

Friday April 29th '64.

Weather pleasant. Quarters at two bells in forenoon. After retreat all hands aired bedding. Wash morning, washed a blue shirt & pr of socks. Wrote a letter to Mother. Had the Afternoon watch. Duff for dinner.

Saturday April 30th,

Weather pleasant, cleaned belts &c for tomorrows inspection. Got up anchor at ten o'clock & steamed from Pensacola, arrived off Mobile & came to anchor about seven o'clock P.M. The Capt of the Os[s]ipee [Captain William M. Walker] came on board as soon as we dropped anchor. Had the mid & 1st dog watches. Pork & beans for dinner.

Sunday May 1st,

Got up anchor last night & got under weigh at 12.30. A Pensacola pilot came on board about seven o'clock, said that the steamer Union had gone into Pensacola about an hour before. We came to anchor off the Navy Yard about eight o'clock. Got some fresh beef, vegitables & ice from the Union. She left in the evening for New Orleans. Quarters for inspection at six bells in the forenoon. Marines in full uniform & white cap covers. Ships company in clean blue & white cap covers. Had the Morning & 2d dog watches. Bullion beef & rice for dinner. Clean hammocks served out at evening quarters & word passed to scrub the dirty ones in the morning.

Monday May 2d 1864,

Scrubed hammocks in the morning. Had the forenoon & first watches. Fresh grub for dinner. Scrubed hammocks piped down at 7 bells in the forenoon. Small stores served out. Drew three plugs tobacco, 1 bar soap, 1 cake beeswax & 1 hot pepper. Turned in our clean hammocks at evening quarters. Glasgow went out at 12.

Tuesday May 3d 1864,

Had the Afternoon watch. Duff for dinner. Quarters at the usual hours. About a dozen men whose time is out were to-day sent on board one of the mortar schooners [Orvetta] which is going north and several men were sent on board here in their places from the mortar schooner. Wrote a letter to Mary in the afternoon. The Ossipee came in.

Wednesday May 4th,

Weather pleasant. Had the mid & 1st dog watches. Pork & beans for dinner. [Private Lewis] Langdon on the [sick] List. [Private Abraham] Thompson relieved me at six o'clock. The Anchor chains were got up & cleaned to-day & sent below again. The boom boats were got out. Guess we will lay here some months yet. The Mettacomet [Metacomet] came in about six P.M.

Thursday May 5th

Weather pleasant. Had the Morning & 2d dog watches. Pork & beans for dinner. Quarters at the usual hours but fortunately for us, no drill. Drew a pair of shoes from the orderly sargent.

Friday May 6th 1864,

Weather warm & pleasant. The Union came in at about half past five, brought us a mail from New Orleans. Rec'd a letter from Mary & one from Vep Deubing. Cleaned belts in the afternoon. Had the forenoon & first watch. Duff for dinner. The Richmond went out about eight o'clock in the morning. Suppose she is bound for the blockade off Mobile. The Glasgow came in about five P.M.[,] brought us another mail. Rec'd a letter from Mary written about a Month before those I got this morning.

Saturday May 7th 1864,

Weather warm & pleasant. Had the afternoon Watch. Pork & beans for dinner. Loosed sail in the morning[.] Money served out, drew five dollars.

Captain Percival Drayton and Rear Admiral David Farragut photographed on board U.S.S. Hartford *in August 1864. Drayton commanded the Admiral's flagship at the battle of Mobile Bay.*

Sunday May 8th

Weather very pleasant. Marines in full uniform & white cap covers at muster, ships company in clean blue & white cap covers. Were inspected by the Captain and then by the Admiral. In the afternoon about twenty men & boys went ashore on liberty untill sundown. Came off in the sundown boat nearly all slightly intoxicated. We are all to have liberty here, a few every day. Had the mid & 1st dog watches. Bullion & rice for dinner. Wrote a letter to Mary.

Monday May 9th

General quarters & fire quarters in the morning. Some more of the ships company went on shore in the afternoon. Had the morning & 2d dog watches. Pork & beans for dinner.

Tuesday May 10th

Weather very pleasant. Gunboat *Penguin* came in in the morning. Wash morning, washed a shirt pr of socks & pr of pants. In the forenoon the bark *Harry Booth* of New York came along side loaded with coal & all hands commenced coaling ship.[1] There is a report that Grant has gained a great victory in Virginia.[2] Hope it is true. Had the forenoon & first watches. Sea pie [3] for dinner. About thirty more men ashore on liberty. *Seminole* came in.

[1] Farragut reported on 2 June that the monthly coal consumption by the squadron off Mobile was 2,000 tons. *ORN* I, 21, 314.
[2] This may refer to Grant's victory at the Battle of the Wilderness, 5–6 May 1864.
[3] Sea pie is a meal of crust and meat baked in alternate layers.

Wednesday May 11th,

Weather rather cool. Still coaling ship. Knocked off about half past twelve. John Howell [1] was on board this morning[,] saw him on the quarter deck, did not speak to him. Had the afternoon watch. Pork & beans for dinner. More men ashore on liberty. [Private Lewis] Langdon off the sick list.

[1] Probably Lieutenant John C. Howell who was executive officer on board U.S.S. *Ossipee*.

Thursday May 12th,

Weather pleasant. Had the mid & 1st dog watches. More men ashore on liberty. The coal bark hauled away from us this morning. [Lieutenant] John Howell came on board while we were at quarters, after we were dismissed he sent for me. Went up on the quarter deck & had a short talk with him. He is a fine looking man in uniform, has a rousing mustache. Said his ship [*Ossipee*] was to sail soon or he would ask me to come & see him. The *Albatros[s]* came in & *Glasgow*. Bullion beef for dinner.

Friday May 13th 1864.

Had the Morning watch. Sea pie for dinner. On liberty to-day, went ashore in the 3d cutter about one o'clock with Corpl O'Connor[,] Knox & Tailor. We first had a bath on the beach at the Navy Yard, then went out at the Woolsey Gate, went in to a house & had some ale, then went up to Ft Barrankas. The roads were filled with Black & white troops & refugees. The ground was covered all over with sand which made it hard work walking. The town dont amount to much. There are only a few shanties in it. Came back to the town about half past five, bought some ink, paper & envelopes, thread[,] needles & sewing silk. Went on board the *Bermuda* to see Corpl McCandles [Robert McCandlass] but he had gone on shore. Got on board about seven o'clock. The *Bermuda* came in in the morning. Got some fresh beef, ice & vegitables from her. The *Buckthorn* came in in the afternoon, brought a large mail for the squadron, nothing for me.

As a Captain, Charles Heywood—shown here three decades later as a Major General and Commandant of the Marine Corps—commanded the Marine guard on board Hartford *while Brother served in her.*

Lieutenant John A. Howell, USN, executive officer of U.S.S. Ossipee, *was a friend of the Brother family.*

Saturday May 14th,

More men ashore on liberty. Weather pleas[a]nt. General quarters in the morning & target practice. Joe Pinto made the best shot, he struck the target. Had the forenoon & first watches. Pork & beans for dinner. Cleaned belts &c in the afternoon.

Sunday May 15th 1864,

Weather pleasant. Marines in full uniform & white cap covers, ships company in white shirts, white cap covers & blue pants. After quarters all hands mustered aft & listened to some remarks from the chaplain of the *Potomac*. More men ashore on liberty. Had the afternoon watch. Fresh grub for dinner, dandyfunk for supper.

Monday May 16th 1864.

Weather pleasant. General quarters in the morning at two bells. Had the Mid & 1st dog watches. Fresh grub for dinner. Wrote a letter to Val. Bollyn [Charles Bolling] went ashore to barracks to-day, & another man came on board in his place. Drill about an hour in the afternoon. *Ten[n]es[s]ee* came in

Tuesday May 17th,

Fresh grub for dinner. Wash morning, did not wash any. Had the Morning & 2 dog watches. Fresh grub for dinner. Quarters at the usual hours. Wrote a letter to Ellie, one to Cameron & one to Darling. Sergt [John] Mackie of the *Seminole* on board in the afternoon, The *Port Royal* came in in the forenoon.

Wednesday May 18th,

Weather pleasant. Had the forenoon & first watches. Pork & beans for dinner. The *Glassgow* [*Glasgow*] went out in the evening. The *Itasca* & another double ender arrived in the forenoon from Mobile. The *Itasca* had broken down [1] & had to be towed in by another one [U.S.S. *Conemaugh*].

  [1] *Itasca* had fouled her propeller while pursuing a blockade runner off Mobile early on 18 May. (*ORN* I, 21, 285–286.)

Thursday May 19th,

Weather pleasant. The *Galena* came in in the afternoon. Had the afternoon watch, bullion & coffee for dinner. Clean hammocks served out at evening quarters with orders to scrub dirty ones in the morning. Fire quarters.

Friday May 20th,

All hands scrubbed hammocks & washed clothes, scrubbed mine & washed a shirt, jumper & pr of socks. Had the Mid & 1st dog watches, duff for dinner. General quarters in night at eleven o'clock, did not wake up. After all the rest were on deck the Orderly Sargent came down & woke me up. Went on deck. Whil[e] at quarters the tug boat *Narcis[s]us* came in. Her capt [Acting Ensign William G. Jones] came on board & reported that the rams were out at Mobile. Caused considerable excitement on board.[1] Retreat beat at about half past eleven, went below & turned in. [Private George] Lawrence on the sick list, [Private Robert A.] Taylor goes on the door in his place.

  [1] The Confederate ram *Tennessee*, Admiral Franklin Buchanan, succeeded in getting over the Dog River Bar and into Mobile Bay on 18 May. On 21 May Farragut wrote: "I shall leave the port [Pensacola] this morning and repair off Mobile, where I understand the ram *Tennessee* has made her appearance." (*ORN* I, 21, 291.)

Saturday May 21st.

Had the morning & 2d dog watches. Steam was up when I went on watch, got under weigh & left Pensacola about half past six A.M. About ten o clock met the *Glassgow* [*Glasgow*]. She brought us mail, rec'd a letter & N.Y. *Times* from Mary, cleaned belts in forenoon, arrived off Mobile & anchored in the afternoon. Weather very warm. Pork & beans for dinner.

Sunday May 22d,

Weather warm. Had the forenoon & first [dog] watches. Wrote a letter to Mary. Muster in the morning at ten, Marines in uniform, white pants & white cap covers, ships company in blue pants, white frocks & cap covers. In the afternoon the two hundred pound rifles were got up on the forecastle & the 30 pdr was put on the poop. Report is that we are going in to feel the forts [Morgan and Gaines]. Bullion & dandyfunk for dinner.

Monday May 23d,

Weather very warm. Jumpers & white pants. Aired bedding in the morning, put up splinter nettings, looks as if we expected to see hot work soon. The *Glassgow* [*Glasgow*] came along side in the morning from Pensacola. Bro't us a small mail, did not get anything. In the afternoon about six o'clock we with nearly all the other vessels of the fleet got under weigh & stood away in a southerly direction & then back again to nearly the same place we were before. Suppose it was done for a drill. Had the afternoon watch. Pork & beans for dinner.

Tuesday May 24th,

Weather very warm, washed a shirt, pr of socks & pr of white pants. The *Admiral* arrived last night. Got some ice, vegitables & fresh beef from her. Had the mid & 1st dog watches. Duff for dinner.

Ossipee & several other ships fired at target. From what I heard the Admiral say to day I think we are going to run past the forts soon.[1]

[1] Brother does not record that on this date Farragut "ran inshore . . . and took a good look at the ironclad *Tennessee*." The next day, 25 May, Farragut advised Secretary Welles of his reluctance to attack the Confederate squadron at this moment. ". . . I would not hesitate to run in and attack him; but if I were to run in, and in so doing get my vessels crippled, it would be in his power to retire to the shoal water with his ironclads (in fact, all their vessels draw much less water than ours), and thus destroy us without our being able to get at him; but if he takes the offensive and comes out of port, I hope to be able to contend with him." (*ORN* I, 21, 298.)

Wednesday May 25,

The *Bermuda* arrived last night, brought us a mail. Recd a letter from Father & Mary containing sad news about Henry, also rec'd a N.Y. *Times* for April 16th. There is a report that Grant has taken Richmond, hope it is true.[1] Had the Morning & 2d dog watches. Fresh grub for dinner. Wrote a letter to Father.

[1] This inaccurate report may have been based on early news from the Spottsylvania, Virginia, battlefield in mid-May. Union troops briefly held the outer works at the vital Confederate batteries on Drewry's Bluff, which dominated the James River approach to Richmond, and cut the railroad and telegraph on the Danville road south of the Confederate capital. By 17–18 May, however, the Northern soldiers had been forced to withdraw and, as one observer in Richmond recorded, ". . . we drove them back to Bermuda Hundred, behind their fortifications, and near their ships." (See J. B. Jones, *A Rebel War Clerk's Diary*, II, 213.)

Thursday May 26th '64

Weather warm, clean blue clothes. Had the forenoon & first watches, fresh grub for dinner. [Dennis] Sullivan has a sore finger & Smitty [Private Charles C. Smith] is cook in his place "pro tem."

Friday May 27th 1864

Weather warm. Had the afternoon watch. Cleaned musket & bayonet in the forenoon. Clean blue & white cap covers. In the evening. about half past five the fleet got under weigh & drilled & maneuvered about two hours, came to anchor again a little closer in. Fire quarters in forenoon, loosed sail in evening. Fresh grub for dinner.

Saturday May 28th,

Weather warm. Had the Mid & 1st dog watches. About one bell in the mid watch a light was seen bearing W.S.W. Capt [Drayton] and Admiral came on deck. It blazed up once very bright & disappeared shortly afterward. The *Seminole* went to quarters about two bells, made no signal. Cleaned belts, brasses &c in forenoon. In the 1st dog watch about three bells fleet got under weigh, drilled a short time, anchored at the old spot again about seven o'clock. Pork & beans for dinner.

Sunday May 29th,

Weather warm. Quarters at 4 bells. Marines in uniform. White pants & cap covers. Ships company all whites. Wrote a letter to Mother. Had the morning and 2d dog watches. Bullion & dandyfunk for dinner.

Monday May 30th,

Had the forenoon & first watches. Pork & beans for dinner. Some Rebel prisoners were brought down from up the sound by the tug *Narcis[s]us* in the afternoon. At evening quarters the guns were cast loose & the men were ordered to sleep by their guns during their watch on deck.[1] About one bell in the first watch a bright light was seen in the vicinity of Ft. Gaines. About an hour after, two green lights were seen near Ft Morgan. They disappeared about four bells. A picket boat went out about one bell. Lieut. Munday [Acting Lieutenant George H. Munday] & Masters Mate [William H.] Childs in chg.

Acting Lieutenant George H. Mundy and Acting Ensign LaRue P. Adams on Hartford's *quarterdeck in 1864. Both officers were mentioned by Brother a number of times.*

[1] The fleet was concerned about a possible attack by the Confederates under Admiral Franklin Buchanan. This date Captain Percival Drayton, commanding *Hartford*, wrote Captain Thornton Jenkins: "I think 'Buck' will come out the next dark night." (*ORN* I, 21, 310.)

Tuesday May 31st 1864,

Wash morning, turned out at four o'clock & scrubed 2 prs wht pants, 1 pr drawers, 1 pr socks & a blue shirt. Guard in white pants & cap covers, ships company in white frocks & cap covers. The *Glassgow* [*Glasgow*] arrived in the morning from Pensacola, brought Deveaux & Perry the Quartermasters. Pentonys [1] sentence is three years penitentary at hard labor. Had the afternoon wa[t]ch. Duff & salt horse [2] for dinner. The *Brooklyn* came in about four o'clock P.M. & anchored near us. She fired a salute of sixteen guns.[3] Wrote a note to [Private Theodore R.] Harris & sent it off by the coxswain of her gig.

[1] Perhaps Private John Pentoney, who at this time was assigned to the Marine Barracks at the Pensacola Navy Yard.

[2] Salt horse is sailors' slang for salted beef.

[3] *Hartford*'s log recorded that *Brooklyn* fired fifteen guns at 3:25 P.M.

Wednesday June 1st,

Fleet got under weigh in the forenoon & drilled about three hours. Rec'd a note from [Joshua C.] Gregg in the afternoon. He & [Private Theodore R.] Harris, [Private George H.] Bandfield, Aulpes[?], [Private William M.] Smith & Oviate [Corporal Miles M. Oviatt] are on board the *Brooklyn*. Oviate [Oviatt] is a corporal. The *Port Royal* came in the afternoon. Had the Mid & 1st dog watches. Pork & beans for dinner. All the Captains of the fleet were on board in the afternoon.

Thursday June 2d,

Sent a note on board the *Brooklyn* to [Josiah C.] Gregg. Had the morning & 2d dog watches. Bullion & coffee for dinner. The *Kanawha* arrived & brought quite a large mail for the Fleet. Rec'd a letter from Ella W[ixo]m.

Friday June 3d 1864,

Had the forenoon & first watches, washed a mattress cover & pr of white pants in the morning. Duff for dinner. The Capt & Admiral went on board the *Brooklyn* in the afternoon; Serg't [John] Cavendish went on board the *Ossipee* yesterday, is to be her Orderly Sergent. Her old serg't comes on board of us in Cavendish's place. His name is Beard.[1] They can not get along with him there, Fire quarters.

[1] According to the *Marine Muster Rolls* (January–June 1864, 640), this exchange took place on 1 June. The Sergeant coming on board *Hartford* from *Ossipee* was Robert G. Baird.

Saturday June 4th,

Had the afternoon watch. Cleaned belts &c in forenoon. The *Admiral* arrived in the morning from New Orleans. Brought us a small mail, nothing for me. While on her way from Galveston to New O's she captured a prize, was taking her up to New Orleans when she sunk in the river.[1] Tis thought that her Capt scuttled her to prevent the captors getting anything for her. Pork & beans for dinner. [Private Rufus E.] Wilcox in brig.

[1] On the night of 28 May *Admiral* seized blockade running steamer *Isabel* near San Luis Bay, Texas. For reports of the capture and subsequent sinking of *Isabel*, see *ORN* I, 21, 305–310.

Sunday June 5th,

Had the Mid & 1st dog watches, fresh grub for dinner. At quarters Marines in full uniform, white pants & cap covers, ships company [in] all white. Rec'd a letter from [Josiah C.] Gregg, wrote one to Mary.

Monday June 6th '64

Had the morning & 2d dog watches. Last night during the Mid watch a great comotion was seen among the vessels in shore, lights were burnt & rockets fired off. In the morning the *Metacomet* and one or two other vessels were not to be seen. About half past eight the *Metacomet* came up with a good sized side wheel steamer in company. She proved to be a prize which tried to run in last night but was turned back by our gun boats & the *Metacomet* chased her & captured her after a run of five hours. She is no doubt a valuable prize, is said to be from Havana.[1] The supply steamer *Circassian* arrived this forenoon, brought us a small mail, recd a N.Y. *Times* from Mary. Pork & beans for dinner.

[1] The prize, Farragut reported, was the "famous blockade runner, the *Donegal*, or *Austin*. The first is her English name and the last her American." According to Lieutenant Commander James E. Jouett, captain of U.S.S. *Metacomet*, the chase took four hours, not five. (See *ORN* I, 21, 321–323.)

Tuesday June 7th 1864.

Wash morning. Washed a pr of white pants, pr of drawers[,] pr of socks, blue shirt & two cap covers. Had the forenoon & first watches, Duff & fresh grub for dinner. The *Glasgow* arrived from New Orleans in the afternoon. Prize [*Donegal*] left for Phila. [for adjudication].

Wednesday June 8th,

Had the afternoon watch. Fresh grub for dinner. Capts [James] Alden, [Thornton] Jenkins, [John] Marchan[d] & [William] Leroy [LeRoy] came on board in the afternoon and dined with the Admiral & Capt. Aired bedding in the forenoon, piped down in the afternoon at two bells. *Tennessee* arrived. Rec'd a letter from Mary.

Thursday June 9th,

Had the Mid & 1st dog watches. Fresh grub for dinner. The *Circas[s]ian* arrived in Morning.

Friday June 10th 1864.

Had the morning & 2d dog watches. Salt horse for dinner, no duff.

Saturday June 11th.

Had the forenoon & first watches. Pork & beans for dinner. The *Glasgow* arrived in forenoon, brought a mail, recd a "comm" [communication] from Mary, wrote her a letter. Cleaned belts, brasses, Mess kits &c in the afternoon. Clean hammocks served out at evening quarters,

Sunday June 12th,

Had the afternoon watch, about two o'clock some of the *Brooklyns* men came on board, [Theodore R.] Harris & [Josiah C.] Gregg among them; was of course very glad to se[e] them & we had a long talk. Talked about old times. Bullion & dandyfunk for dinner. Marines at muster in full uniform, white pants & cap covers, ships company in all white.

Monday June 13th,

Twenty months in the service to-day. Scrubed hammocks in the morning. General quarters in forenoon. Had the Mid & 1st dog watches. Pork & Beans for dinner.

Tuesday June 14th.

Port watch[.] Scrubed hammocks. Had the morning & 2d dog watches. Duff for dinner.

Wednesday June 15th

Had the forenoon & first watches. The *Glassgow* [*Glasgow*] arrived from Pensacola & left in the afternoon for New Orleans. Drill in the afternoon. Pork & beans for dinner. Wash morning, washed pr drawers, 1 shirt & pr socks.

Thursday June 16th

Had the afternoon watch. Bullion & coffee for dinner. Saw Lieut John A. Howell [of *Ossipee*] on board in the forenoon. The *Tennessee* arrived & left again.

Friday June 17th 1862 [4],

The *Glassgow* [*Glasgow*] arrived in the afternoon, brought a mail, recd a letter from Val with some postage stamps I sent for some time ago. Genl Canby came on here & took dinner with the Admiral.[1] Left at four o'clock. Marines gave him a present[2] as he went over the side. He is enroute for Pensacola. Had the Mid & 1st dog watches. Sea pie for dinner. Aired bedding.

[1] Major General Edward R. S. Canby commanded the U.S. Army Military Division West Mississippi. The next day, 18 June, Canby reported to Major General Henry W. Halleck, Army Chief of Staff in Washington: "The preparations for a demonstration against Mobile are progressing favorably. . . . I have just returned from the fleet off Mobile. Admiral Farragut will render any assistance that may be in his power, and is now quietly conducting some preliminary examinations that are necessary." (*ORN* I, 21, 339.)

[2] Brother is apparently referring to "present arms," a traditional military salute.

Saturday June 18th

Had the morning & 2d dog watches. Pork & beans for dinner. Cleaned belts in forenoon, fire quarters in the forenoon.

Sunday June 19th 1864,

Rained in the morning. Quarters for inspection at the usual hours, ships company in blue pants, white frocks & cap covers. Guard in clean blue. Had the forenoon & first [dog] watches. Bullion & coffee for dinner. Wrote a letter to Val & one to Ella Wixom (Sherman [on] Richmond).[1]

[1] Second Lieutenant Charles L. Sherman was transferred to U.S.S. *Richmond* on 17 June. (*MMR*, January–June 1864, 640.)

Monday June 20th.

Had the afternoon watch. Pork & beans for dinner. Wrote a letter to Ed Church & one to Ed May. The *Glasgow* arrived here in the forenoon and left for New Orleans. Drill in the afternoon by Capt [Charles] Heywood. S.C. Tobacco.

Tuesday June 21,

Had the Mid & 1st dog watches. Sea-pie for dinner. Drill in the afternoon by Capt [Charles] Heywood. Wrote a letter to Will Hess.

Wednesday June 22d,

Had the Morning & 2d dog watches. Pork & beans for dinner. Drill in the afternoon by the orderly Sergent. Wrote to Bonner of the N.Y. *Ledeger* for some papers. In the evening the *Lackawana* came in from Pensacola.

Thursday June 23d

Had the forenoon & first watches. Bullion for dinner. The *Circassian* came in in the morning, left in the afternoon. Mr Dennis left.

Friday June 24th 1864,

Had the afternoon watch. Duff for dinner. The *Glasgow* & the *Genesee* arrived. Each brought a mail. Rec'd a letter from Mary and one from Tom Seymour. *Genesee* and *Glassgow* [*Glasgow*] both left in the afternoon for Pensacola. Cleaned musket in forenoon, aired bedding. *Conemaugh* arrived in P.M. from Pensacola.

Saturday June 25th,

Had the mid & 1st dog watches. Pork & beans for dinner. Cleaned belts &c in the forenoon for Sundays inspection.

Sunday June 26th,

Weather very warm. Had the Morning & 2d dog watches. Bullion for dinner & boiled rice. Marines at muster in uniform and white pants, ships company in white. Wrote a letter to Mary & one to Tom Seymour. The *Richmond* & *Metacomet* came in from Pensacola in the morning.

Monday June 27th

Glasgow & *Philip*[*p*]*i* came in in the forenoon. *Glasgow* left for ship island & *Philip*[*p*]*i* for New Orleans. Had the forenoon & first watches. Pork & beans for dinner. Genl Q's in eve.

Tuesday June 28th,

Had the Afternoon watch. Duff for dinner. Drill in the Afternoon by O.S. *Cowslip* arrived in evening, also *Glasgow*. Washed in morning two prs white pants, 1 pr drawers & 1 pr socks, & cap cover. *Clyde* [U.S. Army transport] went to Pensacola.

Wednesday June 29th,

Had the mid & 1st dog watches. Pork & beans for dinner. Steamer *Clyde* passed us this morning on her way to New Orleans. Drill in the afternoon by Capt [Charles] Heywood.

Thursday June 30th,

Had the morning and 1st dog watches. Bullion & coffee for dinner. Drill in the afternoon by Capt [Charles] Heywood.

Friday July 1st 1864

Had the forenoon and night watches. Last night a steamer tried to run in but was run ashore by the *Glasgow*. This morning she can be seen plainly about a mile from Ft Morgan. Several of the gun boats are firing at her and at a four gun battery on the beach but they do not seem to hit her. The fort has fir'd at them several times but done no damage. Then in the afternoon the Admiral & Capt went on board the *Glassgow* [*Glasgow*] & went in to where the gun boats were firing. In the evening an armed boat crew left the ship in chg of Lieut [LaRue P.] Adams & Ensign [William S.] Dana. I suppose they are going to try and board the steamer & distroy her.[1] The supply steamer *Bermuda* arrived here [in the] evening.

> [1] The blockade runner was the steamer *Ivanhoe*. She was finally destroyed on 6 July. (See *ORN* I, 21, 353–357.)

Saturday July 2d 1864.

Lieut Adam's boat returned this morning early. They went so near the prize that they could hear the men talking who were at work unloading her, did not try to board her. The gun boats fired at intervals all day but we could not see that they did any damage. In the evening another boat left the ship in chg of Lieut Munday [George Mundy]. I believe they are giong to board her tonight

"IVANHOE" RUNNING THE BLOCKADE, JUNE 30, '64. COPYRIGHT, 1902 BY GEO. S. WATERMAN

On 30 June, U.S.S. Glasgow *forced* Ivanhoe *aground near Fort Morgan. As Brother's journal entries indicate, Farragut at first tried to destroy her from long range with gun fire but was unable to end her career as a blockade runner until a boarding party put* Ivanhoe *to the torch on 6 July. The above illustration is one of several used in these pages drawn by George Waterman, a Confederate sailor who was present at Mobile Bay.*

sure. Had the afternoon watch. Fresh grub for dinner. The *Philip[p]i* arrived last night from New Orleans. Cleaned mess kit in forenoon, belts in morning before hammocks were up. The *Ossipee* arrived in afternoon from Pensacola.

Sunday July 3d 1864.
Had the Mid & 1st dog watches. Fresh grub for dinner. The steamer [*Ivanhoe*] is there yet. During the mid watch shots were fired from our gun boats & from Ft Morgan but the blockade runner does not seem to be damaged any. Mr Mundays [Mundy's] boat does not seem to have done any more than Mr Adam's did. Marines [at] quarters in full uniform, white pants, white cap covers & packed knapsacks. Ships company in all whites. Wrote a note to Mother in the afternoon.

Tuesday July 5th,

Had the forenoon and 2d dog watches. Duff for dinner. The *Glasgow* arrived in the afternoon, brought a mail. Rec'd a letter from Mary & one from Mrs Metcalfe. The Admiral is sixty three years old to-day, had all the officers in the cabin drinking his health.

Wednesday July 6th.

Had the afternoon watch. Pork & beans for dinner. Two boats went from this ship last night in chg of Lieuts [James C.] Watson & [Herbert B.] Tyson & Ensign [William S.] Dana & [William H.] Whiting.[1] They boarded the blockade runner [about 1:00 A.M.] & set her on fire. She burned about two hours. Did no[t] burn much I guess for we can still see her.[2] The *Pinola* and *Ten[n]es[s]ee* arrived from Pensacola. *Glasgow* left for same place. It is reported that two Monitors are expected down here soon. Hope so.

[1] In his report of the incident, Farragut also called attention to Ensign George D. B. Glidden and Acting Master's Mate Richard P. Herrick of *Hartford* and "a boat from the *Brooklyn* in charge of Ensign C. H. Pendleton and [from *Hartford*] Assistant Surgeon William Commons." Of the destruction of *Ivanhoe* Farragut said: "The whole was performed with great judgement and discretion." (*ORN* I, 21, 355.)

[2] Captain J. B. Marchand's journal revealed why *Ivanhoe* "did not burn much": "She burned for a few hours; but as she is an iron vessel, the conflagration was not very magnificent." (*ORN* I, 21, 817.)

Thursday July 7th '64,

Had the morning and 1st dog watches. Bullion & coffee for dinner. Wrote a letter to Mary and one to J. C. Gregg. An expedition is going in tonight to blow up the steamer [*Ivanhoe*]. Drill at evening quarters.

Friday July 8th 1864,

The boats which went in to blow up the steamer last night were fired upon by some men on board of her. One of our men [William] Hawkins of the Main top was dangerously wounded, none of the others were hurt.[1] Had the forenoon & 1st dog watches. Duff for dinner. In the forenoon at nine o'clock the *Jessimine* [*Jasmine*] arrived from Pensacola, brought news of the arrival of the *Bienville* & the Monitor iron clad *Manhatten* [*Manhattan*]. The Admiral is in high glee about it.[2] The *Glassgow* [*Glasgow*] left at seven bells for New Orleans without mail. About half past two P.M., the man Hawkins died in the sick bay, he did not have his senses from the time he was hit untill he died. Rec'd a letter from [Josiah C.] Gregg with his photo'h for me to forward to Mary. It is one of the best pictures I ever saw. In the afternoon about five o'clock a steamer arrived from New Orleans bringing Major General's [Edward] Canby & [Gordon] Granger and several other officers. They came aboard to see the Admiral & of course the Marines had to turn out to receive them. Comodore [James S.] Palmer was also with them. General [Daniel E.] Sickles was on board the steamer but did not come aboard of us. They left about seven o'clock.

[1] According to Captain Percival Drayton's 8 July report to Farragut, "only one man, William Hawkins, was struck. . . ." (*ORN* I, 21, 356.)

[2] Farragut immediately wrote Secretary Welles: "I am most happy to announce the arrival of the U.S. ironclad *Manhattan*, in tow of the *Bienville*, at Pensacola, but needing some repairs, coal, etc." (*ORN* I, 21, 366.)

Saturday July 9th 1864.

Had the Afternoon watch. Rained in forenoon. Cleaned belts, musket &c after supper. The *Philip[p]i* left for Pensacola in the morning taking the corpse of [William] Hawkins for burial, four sailors & Mr Herrick [Master's Mate Richard P. Herrick] went with it. Pork & beans for dinner.

Sunday July 10th.

Had the Morning & 1st dog watches. [Lewis] Langdon takes his regular turn again. Bullion & coffee for dinner. Marines at inspection in uniform & white pants, ships company all [in] white.

A little after day light in the morning another blockade runner [1] was discovered on shore about a quarter of a mile from Ft Morgan. The *Monongahela*, the *Galena* & *Genesee* were ordered in to shell her. They made some splendid shots and hit her several times although they had to fire at long range. The Rebels could be seen busy unloading her. In the afternoon a steamer came out from behind the fort and went along side of the Blockade runner apparantly to tow her off. The *Seminole* & *Metacomet* were sent in to shell her and they soon drove her inside again. In the afternoon wrote a letter to Father, one to Mrs Metcalfe & one to [Josiah C.] Gregg. The *Glassgow* [*Glasgow*] arrived from New Orleans about four o'clock, brought a mail. Rec'd a N.Y. *Times* from Mary but no letters. In the evening a picket boat was put out in charge of Mr Herrick. Bickfort [George Bickford] & [Rufus E.] Wilcox were black listed for not having their muskets clean in the morning.

[1] According to the log of U.S.S. *Tennessee*, this was blockade runner *Virginia* (*ORN* I, 21, 936). The Union called her *Virgin* (See *ORN* I, 21, 642; 22, 60, 263).

Monday July 11th,
Had the Morning and 2d dog watches. The *Glassgow* [*Glasgow*] left for New Orleans. A steamer came out from behind the fort & towed the blockade runner [*Virginia*] in. The Admiral[,] flag Lieut [J. C. Watson] & Steward, Cook &c went on board the *Ten[n]es[s]ee* in the afternoon, expect we will leave for Pensacola to-night. Pork & beans for dinner.

Tuesday July 12th 1864.
Got up anchor & got under weigh in the morning about three o'clock.[1] Had the forenoon & first watches. A Pensacola pilot came on board about eight o'clock, came to anchor in the bay off the Navy Yard at eleven o'clock. The *Manhatten* [*Manhattan*] is here & several of our gun boats. We are not allowed to hold any communication with those on shore. Bolyn [Charles Bolling] & [Private William] Leodan came along side at noon but would not be let on board. About half past two P.M. a coal bark came along side and the Port watch comenced coaling ship. [Private Isaac B.] Lawrence 2d[2] was sent on shore to the hospital this P.M. About seven o'clock in the evening an officer came from the *Manhatten* [*Manhattan*] and said that she was on fire below and that they could not get at the fire to put it out. We could see the men all crowded on her deck and smoke coming out of her smoke stack. Capt Drayton went away in the third cutter to her. Came on board again about half past ten, said the fire was all put out & that nothing was injured, that it was only some oil & stuff that was burning.[3]

[1] Farragut remained on station off Mobile on board small steamer *Tennessee* while *Hartford* was at Pensacola.
[2] See footnote 1 to journal entry of 26 March.
[3] According to Farragut's report of 15 July to Secretary Welles, the fire took place "in the engineer's storeroom on the night of the 10th [12th], but it was extinguished in a few hours, and the damage amounts to very little. She will be ready for service by the 19th or 20th." (*ORN* I, 21, 375.) The court of inquiry that probed the fire's origin concluded that "it was the result of spontaneous combustion." (*ORN* I, 21, 381.)

Wednesday July 13th.
Twenty one months since I enlisted. All hands called & hamocks piped up at four o clock. Commenced coaling ship. Breakfast at seven. Had the afternoon watch. Pork & beans for dinner. Hoisted up propeller in the forenoon. Wrote a letter to Val in Afternoon. Had the afternoon watch. Pork and beans for dinner.

Thursday July 14th.
Still coaling ship. Watch & watch. Had the mid & 1st dog watches. Bullion for dinner. In the mid watch about one bell a rocket was sent up by a vessel outside. She burned her lights, proved to be the supply steamer *Admiral*. She came in after day light, brought news of the destruction of the

Pirate "290" [C.S.S. *Alabama*] by the U.S.S. *Keysarge* [*Kearsarge*]. Dont know whether it is true or not.[1] The gunboat *Estrella* arrived here in the afternoon.

[1] *Kearsarge* sank *Alabama* in a historic engagement off Cherbourg, France on 19 June 1864, ending the Confederate raider's career on the high seas. Farragut recorded his reaction to the report in a letter to Rear Admiral Theodorus Bailey on 16 July: "The capture of the *Alabama* is glorious news." Referring to the fact that *Alabama*'s commanding officer, Captain Raphael Semmes, and many of the Confederate officers and men had been taken on board the English yacht *Deerhound*, thus evading capture, Farragut added: "I only wish [Captain John A.] Winslow had bagged that looker on, Mr. *Deerhound*." (*ORN* I, 21, 377.)

Friday July 15th 1864.

Had the morning & 2d dog watches. Fresh grub for dinner, got a barrel of spuds from Str *Admiral*.[1] Got through coaling ship about two o'clock in the Afternoon, washed down decks.[2] Seven months to day since we went into commission.

[1] Farragut also received another welcome replenishment: sailors. In his letter of this date to Secretary Welles (*op. cit.*), he noted: "I have the honor to acknowledge receipt of the draft of men, 230 in number, by the *Admiral*. This will make us comfortable for a short time, but the expiration of service and the medical surveys take men North very rapidly." (*ORN* I, 21, 374–375.)

[2] In his Journal entries for 12, 13, 14, and 15 July, Brother recorded the coaling of *Hartford*. In his letter to Welles, Farragut wrote: "My great apprehension now is want of coal. I have been writing Commodore [Henry A.] Adams for some time, urging a supply, and today received a letter informing me that there are only two or three hundred tons at Pensacola. Will the Department please urge it forward?" (*ORN* I, 21, 375.)

Saturday July 16th.

Had the forenoon & first watches. Fresh grub for dinner, potatoe sause for breakfast. Loosed sail at eight A.M. The *Narcissus* came in during the forenoon, got in a lot of provisions & stores, a quantity of Marine clothing also came on board. The *Bermuda* came in in the afternoon.

Sunday July 17th,

Had the afternoon watch. Ten of our sailors and one fireman went on board the *Bermuda* in the forenoon, are going north. Quarters in the forenoon at ten, Marines in Jumpers, blue pants, white caps. In the afternoon sixteen new recruits came on board from the *Potomac*. Dandyfunk for dinner.

Monday July 18.

Had the Mid & 1st dog watches. Pork & beans for dinner. Got in provisions[,] ammunition &c. Doctor Gibson is detached from this ship, he goes I believe on board the *Seminole*. Another man comes here in his place.

Tuesday July 19th

Had the morning & 2d dog watches. The washer woman was off from shore yesterday with the wash clothes. I was asleep, did not know she was here so she took mine ashore with her again.

Wednesday July 20th 1864

The *Bienville* & *Manhatten* [*Manhattan*] left about seven o clock, A.M. We got under weigh & left Pensacola about nine a.m. About half past ten we met the *Brooklyn* bound for Pensacola, passed the *Manhatten* [*Manhattan*] in tow of the Bienville at noon. The Monitor's was all under water. Arrived off Mobile & anchored in about the old spot about four P.M. Had the forenoon & first watches. Pork & beans for dinner. The *Bienville* & *Manhatten* [*Manhattan*] arrived about an hour after. The Admiral & staff came on board before dark, several Army officers were on board in the evening.

Thursday July 21st 1864.

Had the afternoon watch. Bullion & coffee & ham for dinner. Willcox [Rufus E. Wilcox] & [John]

McCrystal[1] were let out of the brig.   The Monitor [*Manhattan*] went in near sand island & anchored. Wrote a letter to Mary.

Friday July 22d, 1864,

Weather very warm.   The *Glassgow* [*Glasgow*] left for New Orleans.   Had the Mid & 1st dog watches. Sea pie for dinner.

Saturday July 23d 1864,

Had the Morning & 2d dog watches.   Pork & beans for dinner.   Cleaned belts[,] epauletts &c in the forenoon.   The *Philip*[*p*]*i* arrived from Pensacola.   A severe rain squall visitisited [visited?] us about seven P.M.   The Admiral was out in it & got wet through.

Sunday July 24th,

Weather somewhat cooler than of late.   Wind blew hard all last night & to-day.   Ship rolls heavily. Had the forenoon & first watches.   Bullion & coffee for dinner.   Wrote a letter to Ed Church.   Marines at inspection in uniform, blue pants & white caps.   Ships company in clean blue & white caps. The *Glassgow* [*Glasgow*] arrived in afternoon from New Orleans, brought no mail for us.   Clean hammocks served out at evening quarters.

Monday July 25th

Had the Afternoon watch.   Pork & beans for dinner.   *Glassgow* [*Glasgow*] left in forenoon for New Orleans.   Genl quarters in A.M.

Tuesday July 26th

Had the mid & 1st dog watches.   Duff for dinner.   The *Ossipee* left for Pensacola at 2.30 A.M.   Port watch scrubed hammocks, scrubed mine, rec'd a paper from Mary but no letters.   The *Admiral* left again for the North at noon.   Wrote a letter to Father.   Sargt Bhernson [Orderly Sergeant August Behrensen] went home on her, has been sick for some weeks.   Beard [Robert G. Baird] is now our Orderly Sergent.   McSweny [James McSweeney] is act'g corporal.   The *Octorara* arrived in the afternoon, left again in a few hours.

Wednesday July 27th

Had the morning & 2d dog watches.   Pork & beans for dinner.   The *Oneida* came in from Pensacola, *Glasgow* arrived in afternoon from New Orleans.   Aired bedding in P.M.

Thursday July 28th

Had the forenoon & first watches.   Bullion & coffee for dinner.   Guard at quarters & eight o'clock relief in fatigue coats.   The Capt wanted to see who had them and who had not.   The *Glassgow* [*Glasgow*] left for New Orleans about eleven A.M.   About ten A.M. tug boat *America* of Phil'a arrived with dispatches for the Admiral.   The *Brooklyn* arrived about four P.M.   *Buckthorn* arrived in eve.

Friday July 29th.

White pants.   Had the Afternoon watch.   Duff for dinner.   Got our sheet chain up & comenced putting it over the starboard side for protection of the boilers when we go into action.   Shifted No's 1 & 2 broadside guns from the port side to the starboard side.

Saturday July 30th.

Had the mid & 1st dog watches.   Pork & beans for dinner.   The *Glasgow* arrived from New Orleans in forenoon.   Cleaned musket in forenoon, belts &c in afternoon.   Marines are stationed at the two afterguns.[1] Took the Monitor [*Manhattan*] around to the other side of Sand island in the forenoon. There is another Monitor the *Tecumpsa* [*Tecumseh*] at Pensacola,[2] came down in tow of the steamer *Eutaw*.

[1] In his 6 August report of the Battle of Mobile Bay, Captain Percival Drayton of *Hartford* noted: "The two after guns were entirely manned by Marines, who, under the direction of Captain Charles Heywood, performed most efficient service." (*ORN* I, 21, 427.)

[2] *Tecumseh* had been detained for six days at Port Royal, South Carolina, by "injuries to the engines." (*ORN* I, 21, 390.)

Sunday July 31st,

Weather warm. Uniform & white cap covers at quarters. Ship's company in clean blue & white cap covers. The *Mettacomet* [*Metacomet*] arrived about half past nine A.M. In the afternoon one of the iron clads from New Orleans arrived & went around inside of sand island. The *Tennes[s]ee* arrived in the afternoon from New Orleans, brought us a mail, rec'd a bundle of [New York] *Ledgers* which I sent for some time ago but no letters. I guess the people at home have forgotten me alltogether. Had the morning and 2d dog watches. Bullion & coffee for dinner.

Monday Aug 1st,

Had the forenoon & first watches. Pork & beans for dinner. The other Monitor [*Chickasaw*] from New Orleans arrived to day & went around inside sand island. In the Afternoon about three bells we were all hustled into uniform coats, blue pants, fatigue caps, waist belts & muskets & lined up on deck to receive Genl [Gordon] Granger. He came after we had been up about half an hour, gave him a present as he came over the side. A Colonel & Capt were with him. We were allowed to break ranks but must stay on the quarter deck untill he left. He went over the side about half past five. We then got out of uniform & got our suppers.

Tuesday Aug 2d,

Had the Afternoon watch. Duff for dinner. The *Glasgow* arrived from New Orleans about two o'clock. Brought us a mail. Recd a letter & paper from Mary, a letter from Ella W[ixom], one from Tom Seymour & one from Ed May. Mary writes that Mother's health is improving, very welcome news indeed. Guess we are going to fight soon. Everything is being got ready for fighting & I guess a few days more will tell whether we are to take Mobile or not. Transports loaded with troops are at Ship island. Wrote a letter to Mary in afternoon. Small stores served out, drew a scrub brush, 4 P H'dkfs & bar soap.

Wednesday Aug 3d,

Wash morning. Washed 1 pr drawers, pr socks & 1 shirt. Had the Mid & 1st dog watches. Pork & beans for dinner. In the morning some officers & men belonging to the Army signal corps came on board, they are to be distributed among the different ships in the fleet.[1] Mr [J. C.] Watson was out in picket [boat] last night [2] & returned this morning with four deserters from Ft Gaines, all

[1] In joint operations Army signal officers were frequently used to coordinate Army-Navy movements and keep the ship commanders in constant communication. *Hartford*'s log for this date recorded: "Lieutenant [John C.] Kinney, of the Signal Corps, U.S. Army, and 8 privates reported for duty on board this ship." With regard to the services which the Signal Officers rendered during the Battle of Mobile Bay, Farragut wrote on 10 October 1864: "During the action of the 5th August I had not myself the opportunity of observing these gentlemen [Captain Frank W. Marston and Lieutenant J. C. Kinney] as I might otherwise have done, owing to the difficulties that surrounded me, but I am informed by my flag-lieutenant, Mr. Watson, that he is indebted to them for a number of signals which they made to individual ships during the action. Sometimes they were in the foretop, sometimes on the forecastle, wherever their signals could best be seen. At all times they were prompt in the discharge of their duties, and never backward in exposing themselves when in the least necessary." (*ORN* I, 21, 518.)

[2] Farragut's Flag Lieutenant, John Crittenden Watson, had led daylight reconaissances of the channel into Mobile Bay during 27–30 July. This night Watson and his men sought to deactivate as many torpedoes [mines] as they could under the guns of Fort Morgan.

Rear Admiral Farragut and Major General Gordon Granger, photographed here on board U.S.S. Hartford, *coordinated the sea-land offensive to seal off Mobile.*

stout healthy looking men.[3] In the afternoon the Admiral & Capt sent all their valuables on board the *Ten[n]essee*. Guess we will get some hard knocks & that pretty soon. Towards evening one of the New Orleans iron clads [4] came out quite near us & went back again.

[3] This date Farragut wrote: "Four deserters came off from Gaines last night, and they say they do not expect any landing there; but they are working like beavers on Morgan." (*ORN* I, 21, 403.)

[4] Either *Winnebago*, which had been stationed inside of Sand Island since her arrival on 31 July, or *Chickasaw*, which had arrived on 1 August after being delayed near New Orleans due to rudder weaknesses and heavy weather.

Thursday Aug 4th 1864,

Had the morning & 2d dog watches. Bullion & coffee for dinner. In the afternoon got out boats. The report is that we are going to fight tomorrow morning. Guess we are. God grant that we may have good luck.

Battle of Bay

Friday Aug 5th 1864.

All hands called at 3 o'clock, at 5.30 the *Mettacomet* [*Metacomet*] came alongside & made fast to us.[1] Other vesels of the fleet paired off in the same manner, got under way about 6.30 & steamed in toward Ft Morgan[,] the *Brooklyn* taking the lead, we following her & the *Richmond* next after us. The fort opened fire at us at about ten minutes past seven. Just after we comenced firing one of the monitors the *Tecumpseh* [*Tecumseh*] sunk[.] She had her bottom blown out by a torpedo & went down like a shot. We passed the *Brooklyn* in front of the fort & so had the honor of being the first ship in.[2] As soon as we passed the fort the gun boats [U.S.S. *Morgan*, *Gaines*, and *Selma*] pitched into us and the

[1] *Hartford*'s log recorded that all hands were called at 3:00; *Metacomet* lashed alongside at 4:30; *Hartford* underway at 5:40; Fort Morgan opened fire at 7:06; *Hartford* commenced firing at 7:11; *Tecumseh* was sunk at 7:40. (See *ORN* I, 21, 799–800.)

[2] It was at this point that *Brooklyn* had stopped and backed because of the sinking of *Tecumseh*. Thus, the entire fleet was in danger of being stalled directly under Fort Morgan's guns. Farragut made his instant decision: "Damn the torpedoes!" For an account of the battle, see *Civil War Naval Chronology*, Part IV, 1864, 95–97.

FORT MORGAN

GAINES BEACHED

TORPEDOES

OBSTRUCTION

TENNESSEE

CHANNEL

GAINES

FORT GAIN

MORGAN

SELMA

PEN DRAWING 1864 BY
GEO.S.WATERMAN C.S.N.

MIDDLE GROUND

Battle of Mobile Bay, August 5, 1864

Mettacomet [*Metacomet*] cast off from us [at 8:02] and went after one of them. About twenty minutes past eight we had passed out out of range of the gun boats & batteries and ceased firing. Anchored about 8.35. The rest of the fleet soon came up. In a little while we discovered the Rebel ram *Tennes*[*s*]*ee* coming up after us. We signaled for the monitors to go after her and also to the other vessels & then got up anchor. The Admiral gave the order for us to run at her and run her down if we could. We made for her but did not strike her fairly. She swung round against us & fired a shell into us which killed & wounded eight men. Luckily her other guns did not go off or she must have swept our berth deck clean. As she passed us we gave her our port broadside but I could not tell whether it did her any harm or not. Some of the other ships then engaged her & shot away her smoke stack. She seemed to be disabled otherwise and appeared to be making for the fort again. We loaded up the starboard guns with solid shot and got under weigh to go after her again when the *Lackawan*[*n*]*a* ran into us. She struck us just abaft the main rigging, crushing in our bullwarks, dismounting 2 guns and raising the d—l generaly. I thought sure she would sink us but she did no damage below the water line. As soon as we got clear of her[,] disabled as we were[,] we started for the ram again. But before we got to her she showed the white flag. I was very glad to see it for I did not at all like the idea of risking another broadside from her. At the time the *Ossipee* was nearly onto her and one of the monitors [was] close at hand. We then came to anchor about five miles above Ft Morgan.

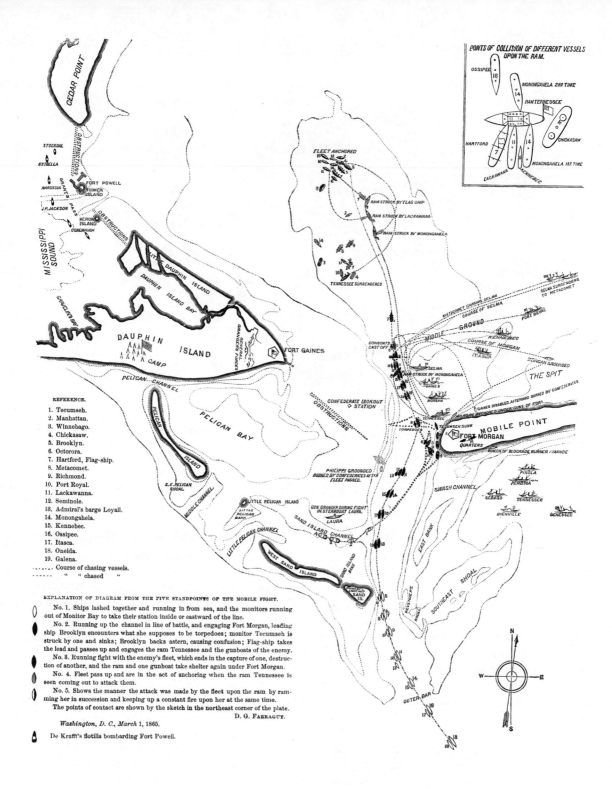

POINTS OF COLLISION OF DIFFERENT VESSELS UPON THE RAM.

REFERENCE.

1. Tecumseh.
2. Manhattan.
3. Winnebago.
4. Chickasaw.
5. Brooklyn.
6. Octorora.
7. Hartford, Flag-ship.
8. Metacomet.
9. Richmond.
10. Port Royal.
11. Lackawanna.
12. Seminole.
13. Admiral's barge Loyall.
14. Monongahela.
15. Kennebec.
16. Ossipee.
17. Itasca.
18. Oneida.
19. Galena.
.... Course of chasing vessels.
— " " chased

EXPLANATION OF DIAGRAM FROM THE FIVE STANDPOINTS OF THE MOBILE FIGHT.

No. 1. Ships lashed together and running in from sea, and the monitors running out of Monitor Bay to take their station inside or eastward of the line.

No. 2. Running up the channel in line of battle, and engaging Fort Morgan, leading ship Brooklyn encounters what she supposes to be torpedoes; monitor Tecumseh is struck by one and sinks; Brooklyn backs astern, causing confusion; Flag-ship takes the lead and passes up and engages the ram Tennessee and the gunboats of the enemy.

No. 3. Running fight with the enemy's fleet, which ends in the capture of one, destruction of another, and the ram and one gunboat take shelter again under Fort Morgan.

No. 4. Fleet pass up and are in the act of anchoring when the ram Tennessee is seen coming out to attack them.

No. 5. Shows the manner the attack was made by the fleet upon the ram by ramming her in succession and keeping up a constant fire upon her at the same time.

The points of contact are shown by the sketch in the northeast corner of the plate.

D. G. FARRAGUT.

Washington, D. C., March 1, 1865.

De Krafft's flotilla bombarding Fort Powell.

Diagram showing the entrance of Farragut's fleet into Mobile Bay, 5 August 1864.

Surrender of Ram Tennessee

After gallantly carrying the fight to the Union fleet in Mobile Bay, C.S.S. Tennessee *finally surrenders, assuring Farragut control of the last important Confederate Gulf port.*

Capt Johnson the commanding officer of the ram [3] came on board with the Capt of the *Ossipee* & delivered up his sword to the Admiral. He reported that Admiral Buchanan was on board the ram & had lost a leg during the action. [4] He sent his sword on board by one of the *Ossipee's* officers. [5] Our ship presented a fearful sight after the action. A shell burst in the steerage tearing everything to pieces. The powder division suffered worse than any other. A great many shots came in on the berth deck. The shell from the ram burst as it came through killing the Docts Stew'd instantly[,] wounding one of the engineers & Mr Higginbothem [Acting Ensign William H. Heginbotham] & killing & wounding several others. Mr [Lieutenant LaRue P.] Adams, Mr Herrick [Master's Mate Richard P. Herrick] & Mr Dickson [Boatswain Robert Dixon] were all slightly wounded, not one of the Marines were hurt, boy [Henry] Clark had both legs taken off, lived but a short time. [James] Alexander had both legs & both arms taken off & died shortly after. Very few were slightly wounded, all were either killed instantly or horribly mangled. Our cockpit [sick bay] looked more like a slaughter house than any thing else. At night twenty one dead bodies were sewed up in hamocks, sent on board the *Selma*[,] the *Mettacomet's* [*Metacomet*] prize[,] and taken away for burial. About twenty more were sent to Pensacola badly wounded. [6] At night the Rebs abandoned Ft Powell ruining every thing they could. The Monitor *Tecumseh* was blown up by a Torpedo during the first part of the engagement and immediately sunk, only about ten of her crew were saved. The *Philip[p]i* attempted to run by the fort after we had all got in but finding the fire too hot for her she turned back and got aground. Her Capt and crew left her, leaving their signal books & everything else to fall into the hands of the enemy. The Rebels boarded her and after taking everything they wanted set her on fire.

[3] Commander James D. Johnston had assumed command of C.S.S. *Tennessee* when Admiral Buchanan was severely injured.

[4] Buchanan's leg suffered a compound fracture. Even Farragut "supposed" it would have to be amputated, but Buchanan insisted that it not be and medical treatment at the U.S. Naval Hospital, Pensacola, saved the leg.

[5] On 17 September, Buchanan, writing from the hospital at Pensacola, observed: "After the surrender of the *Tennessee*, Captain Giraud [Acting Lieutenant Pierre Giraud of *Ossipee*], the officer who was sent on board to take charge of her, said to me he was directed by Admiral Farragut to ask for my sword, which was brought from the cabin and delivered to him by one of my aids." (*ORN* I, 21, 578.)

[6] Farragut reported (8 August) 25 killed on *Hartford* and 28 wounded. He enclosed Surgeon Philip Lansdale's report which named 23 killed, 20 seriously wounded and eight slightly wounded. (*ORN* I, 21, 406–407.)

AN AUGUST MORNING WITH FARRAGUT AT MOBILE BAY

By

Harrie Webster

AN AUGUST MORNING WITH FARRAGUT AT MOBILE BAY

by Harrie Webster, Third Assistant Engineer, U.S.S. Manhattan

The Battle of Mobile Bay was fought on the fifth of August 1864 under the leadership of our greatest Admiral, the victorious Farragut. My point of view, and field of action will of necessity be somewhat limited, for I propose to describe that part of the great "Bay Fight," as the poet Brownell[1] calls it, which was taken by the Monitor *Manhattan*, on which I was serving as a third assistant engineer.

That portion of the Gulf of Mexico extending into the southern part of Alabama a distance of about thirty-five miles, offers to the student of American history a most interesting field.

The celebrated Spanish voyager and discoverer, Hernan[do] de Soto, first came in contact here with the aborigines of Alabama; and it is related that the gigantic chief, Tuscaloosa, received the Spanish Commander seated, his pride, as stern as that of De Soto, giving a dignity to the savage equal to that of his civilized adversary.

The Battle of the fifth of August, 1864, was not the first which Mobile Bay had witnessed, for almost fifty years before, on September 15, 1814, the roar of English guns woke the echoes of the bay in an attack by Perry, the British Admiral,[2] on a small work called Fort Bowyer, in which one vessel and upward of two hundred men were lost.[3] Fort Morgan occupies the site of old Fort Bowyer, and is situated on the main land at the western extremity of Mobile Point, and mounted, in August 1864 eighty-six guns of all calibers. In addition to this a "water battery," or supplementary work at the water's edge, mounted seven heavy guns which infiladed the channel.[4]

Fort Gaines stands on the opposite side of the channel from Fort Morgan, distant about three miles, at the eastern end of Dauphine Island. It mounted thirty guns,[5] and had a garrison of forty-six officers and eight hundred and eighteen men. The channel past Fort Gaines had been obstructed by the rebels with numberless piles, leaving but a single narrow channel open for the passage of vessels, and that channel lay so near to Fort Morgan that all ships were forced to run close to that fort on their way into the bay. About six miles northwest of Fort Gaines a narrow cut, called Grant's Pass, afforded passage between Mississippi Sound and Mobile Bay. A small work called Fort Powell was partly completed and located here.

In addition to the regular and visible means of offense and defense, the rebel authorities had planted the narrow channel thickly with torpedoes, and, as was found during the battle, not in vain.

The preparations for an attack on the defenses of Mobile Bay had been for a long time in view by the Navy Department, and as usual in those days, Admiral Farragut was looked upon as the man for the duty.

---

[1] Henry Brownell was a Rhode Island poet whose verse published in the Hartford *Evening Press* caught Farragut's eye. The Admiral secured Brownell a commission as master's mate, and he advanced to ensign with special duties as Farragut's secretary. Brownell was one of the most popular war poets.

[2] The writer meant Captain William H. Percy, commander of H.M.S. *Hermes*.

[3] In his *Historical Memoir of the War in West Florida and Louisiana, 1814-1815* (Philadelphia: 1816), Major A. L. Latour lists British killed and wounded as 232 (p. 40).

[4] Alfred Thayer Mahan has written that Fort Morgan's "armament at this time cannot be given with absolute certainty. He estimated its strength as follows: "Main fort seven X-inch, three VIII-inch and twenty-two 32-pounder smooth-bore guns, and two VIII-inch, two 6.5-inch and four 5.82-inch rifles. In the water battery there were four X-inch and one VIII-inch columbiads and two 6.5-inch rifles. Of the above, ten X-inch, three VIII-inch, sixteen 32-pounders and all the rifles, except one of 5.82 calibre, bore upon the channel. There were also twenty flanking 24-pounder howitzers and two or three light rifles, which were useless against the fleet from their position. A. T. Mahan, *The Gulf and Inland Waters* (New York: 1883), pp. 219-220.

[5] Mahan lists 27 guns of all kinds. *Ibid.*, p. 219.

Harrie Webster, photographed above as a First Assistant Engineer and at right as a Rear Admiral, served on board the monitor Manhattan *at Mobile Bay.*

Consequently as soon as the campaign on the Mississippi river had been brought to its brilliant conclusion by the surrender of Vicksburg and Port Hudson, the former on July 4th, and the latter four days later, it was generally understood that the next point of attack was to be the forts at the entrance to Mobile Bay.

Following the splendid achievements at Forts Jackson and St. Phillip, and Port Hudson, and the developement of the novel tactics for passing well manned fortifications under fire, it was felt that if the problem was left to Farragut the task was already half done.

During the spring and summer of 1864, a large fleet of vessels had been gradually collected for the blockading of Mobile, in anticipation of the time when the blow was to be struck for the capture of this important rebel stronghold.

Among the vessels doing duty in the blockading fleet was the double-ender gunboat *Genesee*, Commander Edward C. Grafton, on board of which I had been serving since the preceding year. The *Genesee* had taken part in the campaign against Port Hudson, and following the capture of that important point, she had gone to Vicksburg, thence to Ship Island, and from there, late in 1863, to blockade duty off Mobile. Admiral Farragut had joined the fleet in the spring of 1864, in the *Hartford*, and renewed activity followed his arrival. Frequent rumors from shore, through deserters, and occasional newspapers, had convinced the Admiral that the enemy was improving [during] our delays, and it was known in April that the rebels were preparing to give us a warm reception should the union fleet attempt a repetition of the tactics of the previous year on the Mississippi.

Taking the experience of the blockading fleet off Charleston as a guide, it was held that without ironclads it was worse than useless to attack such fortifications as those at the entrance of Mobile Bay.

General Order

For passing "Port Hudson"

The Ships will each take a Gunboat on the Port Side and secure her as well aft as possible, so as to leave the Port Battery clear for the enemy's Battery on the Port side of the River going up, after we round the point opposite Port Hudson —

Each Ship will keep a very little on the Starboard Quarter of her next ahead, so as to give free range to her chase guns, without risk of damage from premature explosion of Shrapnel or Shells —

The Captains will bear in mind that the object is to run the batteries at the least possible damage to our ships, and thereby secure an efficient force above for the purpose of rendering such assistance as may be required of us by the Army at Vicksburg or if not required there, to our Army at Baton Rouge —

If they succeed in getting past the Batteries, The Gunboats will proceed up to the mouth of the Red River and keep up the police of the River between that River and Port Hudson, capturing anything they can. Should any vessel be disabled so that she is unable to pass Port Hudson, she will use the Gunboat to the best advantage, if the Captain thinks he can get by, try it — if he thinks not, let the Gunboat drop her down below the range of the Batteries —

If both are disabled, then club down with a light anchor or use the sails, as

Harrie Webster served under Farragut at the passage of Port Hudson as well as at Mobile Bay. Farragut employed much the same strategy for passing Forts Morgan and Gaines that he did at Port Hudson, as indicated by his above orders and sketch.

VI–88

as in his judgment may seem best — but
I expect all to go by, who are able, and I think
the best protection against the enemy's fire,
is a well directed fire from our own Guns,
Shell and Shrapnel at a distance, and
Grape when within 4 or 500 Yards —

D. G. Farragut
Rear Admiral

Port Hudson

Diagram of Port Hudson

For various reasons it was a difficult matter to get ironclads for use on that part of the blockade, so that the days rolled up into weeks, and the weeks into months, before reports began to reach the West Gulf Squadron that the Navy Department had determined to reinforce that portion of the blockading fleet with Monitors.

During the months of waiting, the routine of blockade life went on, and May became June and June gave place to July before definite information reached us that two Monitors, the *Tecumseh* and *Manhattan*, had been detailed for duty in the Gulf of Mexico.

About the same time news from shore was received of the completion and successful trial of a formidable iron-clad ram by the rebels at Mobile, followed shortly afterward by the information that, although drawing considerable more water than was found on Dog River Bar, below Mobile, the ram had been safely taken into deep water, and the work of fitting her to attack the blockading fleet was in progress. [*Tennessee* crossed Dog River Bar on 18 May 1864.]

Of course, all such rumors and reports strengthened the feeling that without ironclads success was problematical, and the news from the north was watched with no little anxiety while waiting for the arrival of the needed reinforcement.

One day early in July the rebel ram made her first appearance to the Union fleet just inside the entrance to the bay, and, through the numerous glasses which were at once levelled at the formidable looking craft, it could be seen that the *Tennessee* was no mean adversary even for a Monitor.   Later events proved the correctness of these surmises.

The continued delay in the arrival of our Monitors seemed to invite attack from the enemy, and it was not until long afterward that the reason for their non-activity was developed.

Among the blockading fleet was the *Galena*, at one time a partially protected corvette.   Her want of success at Drury's Bluff on the James River had caused the Navy Department to remove her armor plating, leaving the ship an ordinary wooden sloop of war.   But it appeared that the rebels were not aware of this change and still believed her to be [the] armored craft which had so stubbornly withstood the battering below Richmond.   Acting on this belief Admiral Buchanan counseled against the policy of attempting to raise the blockade by an attack on the Union fleet, deeming it unwise to "risk too much upon a single throw, and win or lose it all."

Following this advice the rebel fleet remained inside of Forts Morgan and Gaines waiting for the opportunity which never came.

By the first of July the blockading fleet had reached such proportions that the celebration of the National Holiday of 1864 off [Mobile Bay] presented to the eyes of the rebels guarding the bay the

Tennessee, *photographed here after her capture by the Union, was the key in Confederate naval defenses of Mobile Bay*.

The monitor Manhattan *was the ship on which Webster served at Mobile Bay. Commander J. W. A. Nicholson, shown at right as a Commodore in the 1870's, was Webster's commanding officer.*

sight of more stars and stripes than had been assembled under one commander since the beginning of the blockade. By order of Admiral Farragut every ship in the squadron steamed as near to Fort Morgan as practicable, and fired the National Salute with shotted guns. From this time active preparations were made for the attack on the rebel works, and the movements of the four Monitors which were reported to have been assigned to the West Gulf Squadron were watched with the greatest interest. These ironclads were the *Manhattan, Tecumseh, Chickasaw* and *Winnebago*, the first two being regular Ericsson Monitors, built in New York, each carrying two fifteen inch guns in a single turret. The two last named were modifications of the monitor principle, were of much less draft, were armed with eleven inch guns mounted in the Eads turret on the disappearing plan, and their armor was much thinner than that of the *Manhattan* and *Tecumseh*. Their decks, instead of being flat, were heavily crowned. They were familiarly called "Turtle Back" Monitors. Each vessel was propelled by four screws and could steam five or six knots an hour.

These novel craft contained many of the ideas of their eminent designer, Captain James B. Eads, who long afterward became famous as constructor of the jetties at the southwest pass of the Mississippi River. The *Chickasaw* and *Winnebago* were armed with four guns each, mounted in [two] revolving [turrets], but the turrets were of but ten inches in thickness. Their eleven inch smooth bore guns, instead of being mounted in the usual way, were arranged with their muzzles projecting through a circular port in the turret, their elevation and depression being affected by hydraulic gear at the breech. This same gear took up the recoil of the gun, and also lowered the piece into the turret chamber for sponging and loading. The gun was hoisted into position and trained with the turret by the same force.

The *Manhattan* arrived at Pensacola about the tenth of July, and after making some needed repairs, rendered necessary by her long journey from New York, proceeded at once to her station off Mobile.

The *Tecumseh* did not arrive with the *Manhattan*, and the other two ironclads were detained at New Orleans by repairs and adjustments to their machinery.

On the twelfth of July I made official application to be transferred to the *Manhattan*, and on the twenty-second I was detached from the *Genesee* and ordered to report to Commander J. W. A. Nicholson on board the *Manhattan*. I joined the ironclad two days later, on the twenty-fourth, inside of Sand Island, at the entrance to Mobile Bay.

My first experience on the Monitor was somewhat dampening. I had taken passage from Pensacola where the *Genesee* was at that time, in the *Monongahela*, and in one of her boats I was taken in to the *Manhattan*. A light swell was running, not enough to incommode a small boat, but on going alongside the ironclad, what with her naturally small freeboard and being prepared for action with full coal bunkers and shot lockers, her decks were completely awash, and as I stepped aboard I was wet to my knees, and my humble packing box, containing all my worldly goods, was swept by a gentle wave against the turret, where it was sized by a couple of sailors and speedily taken to a place of safety.

The fourth of August was busy. The *Tecumseh* had joined the fleet, the *Chickasaw* and *Winnebago* had arrived, and the wooden ships had completed their preparations for the fight which was to come off on the morrow. The following general orders were sent to each ship in the fleet, and show, as had already been shown at Forts Jackson and St. Philip, and at Port Hudson, what tactics were to be relied upon for victory, as on those memorable battlefields.

> Strip your vessels and prepare for the conflict. Send down all your superfluous spars and rigging. Trice up or remove the whiskers. Put up the splinter nets on the starboard side, and barricade the wheel and steersman with sails and hammocks. Lay chains and sand bags on the deck over the machinery to resist a plunging fire. Hang the sheet chains over the side, [. . .] Land your starboard boats or lower and tow them on the port side, and lower the port boats down to the water's edge. [. . .] The vessels will run past the forts in couples, lashed side by side, as hereinafter designated. [. . .] each vessel will keep a very little on the starboard quarter of his next ahead, and when abreast of the fort, will keep directly astern [. . .] It will be the object of the admiral to get as close to the fort as possible before opening fire. The ships, however, will open fire the moment the enemy opens upon us [. . .] Use short fuzes for the shell and shrapnel, and as soon as within three or four hundred yards give them grape. [. . .] If one or more of the vessels be disabled, their partners must carry them through, if possible; but if they can not then the next astern must render the required assistance; but as the admiral contemplates moving with the flood tide, it will only require sufficient power to keep the crippled vessels in the channel. [. . .] [6]
>
> Should any vessel be disabled to such a degree that her consort is unable to keep her in her station, she will drop out of line to the westward and not embarrass the vessels next astern by attempting to regain her station. Should she repair damages, so as to be able to reenter the line of battle, she will take her station in the rear as close to the last vessel as possible. [. . .]

Following these instructions, every ship carrying spars left nothing standing above the top masts, and the *Richmond* struck and landed even her top masts and topsail yards.

The wooden ships which took part in the battle were arranged as follows: *Brooklyn* with the *Octorara; Hartford* with the *Metacomet* alongside; *Richmond* and *Port Royal; Lackawana* and *Seminole; Monongahela* with the *Kennebec; Ossippe* and *Itasca;* and bringing up the rear was the *Oneida* and *Galena.*

The fifth of August broke clear and calm, and from where we lay, inside of Sand Island, with our consorts, the *Tecumseh, Chickasaw,* and *Winnebago,* the sounds of preparations in the fleet came floating over the water long before daybreak.[7] About five o'clock the first of the wooden fleet made their appearance, the *Brooklyn,* with the *Octorara* secured to her port side abaft the beam, steaming slowly in with the flood tide.

---

[6] This was Farragut's General Order No. 10, dated 12 July 1864. As indicated by the bracketed ellipses [. . .], Webster omitted sections of Farragut's orders. The author also unaccountably fails to indicate that the last paragraph comes from Farragut's General Order No. 11, dated 29 July 1864. The full text of both orders is published in the *Official Records of the Union and Confederate Navies in the War of the Rebellion*, Volume 21 (Washington, D.C.: Government Printing Office, 1906), pp. 397–98. Hereafter cited *ORN.*

[7] The log of *Manhattan* recorded ". . . called all hands up at 3." *ORN* I, 21, 824.

As one ship followed another it was a glorious and inspiriting sight, and one never to be forgotten.

At each masthead floated an American flag, and in the soft morning stillness each drum beat, calling to quarters the crews of the advancing ships, could be heard with perfect distinctness.

In stately line and in compact order the fleet came steadily on, the hoarse shouts of command mingling with the sounds of rattling gun tackles as they lessened the distance between us.

At half past five the drum of the *Manhattan* beat to General Quarters,[8] and, as all preparations for the coming fight had been carefully made in advance, in a few minutes everybody was at his station, the battle hatches were secured in place, and we were ready for the fray. Early that morning it had been discovered that one of our fifteen inch guns had been disabled during the night, some traitor having spiked the gun by forcing a small rat-tail file far into the fuse vent putting that gun out of commission most effectually.[9]

Already the *Tecumseh* had weighed anchor, and had steamed slowly away for the channel, keeping well off toward Fort Morgan.

Commander T. A. M. Craven, in command of the *Tecumseh*, was senior to Commander Nicholson of the *Manhattan*, consequently took the head of the ironclads and kept well in advance of the oncoming fleet. At forty-seven minutes past six o'clock the boom of the first shot from the *Tecumseh*'s fifteen inch guns reached our ears, and we knew that the momentous battle had begun. A few minutes later the *Brooklyn* became engaged, and the fight was on. The first shot from the *Manhattan* was fired at five minutes past seven, and as it was the beginning of my fighting experience on a monitor I may be pardoned for a few words descriptive of the sensations and effects of a shot from a fifteen inch gun.

With the recoil of the gun a sudden tremor ran through the ship as though in collision followed an instant later by the roar of the explosion mingled with deep voiced rushing note of the shot as it leaves the muzzle of the gun. The turret chamber, or space directly below the gun was instantly filled with blinding smoke mingled with particles of burning powder, and in a few minutes the smell was forced into every part of the ship by the blowers which take their air for ventilation through the turret. The effect in the engine room was perhaps more marked than in other parts of the ship, being near the extreme after part of the vessel.

Shot followed shot in rapid succession, and the steady roar which filled the air told that every ship was under fire, and that the rebels behind the ramparts of Fort Morgan were doing their best to undo the tactics, which, under the gallant Admiral leading us today, had been so disastrous to their cause at New Orleans and Port Hudson. Our magazines were open, the officers and men were cool and collected, and but for the tremendous noises of the battle and the ever increasing clouds of powder smoke enveloping the ship, the situation below resembled ordinary drill.

On account of the terrible heat in the engine room, which was 150 F. except directly beneath the blower-pipe, the engineers were assigned short periods of duty at their stations, and following a turn in the engine room, we were given a breathing spell in the turret chamber, then a spell in the turret at the handling levers, and then into the engine room again.

I had completed my first service in the engine room and in the turret chamber, and about fifteen or twenty minutes after seven I was at the levers in the turret. The turret was being slowly moved, first "right," then "left," as the guns were being brought to bear on the fort, near which we lay, and the gallant *Tecumseh* was a short distance ahead and on the starboard bow.

The frequent blows on our turret told that the enemy was not idle, and the steady roar from the guns of our wooden fleet was accented at frequent intervals with the savage explosion of a bursting shell, and once in a while could be dimly heard the peculiar crackling, singing noise made by shot smashing through the wooden walls of some unfortunate ship on our port side. The combination of sounds is impossible to describe, and each instant brought a new one. Shot, shell, grape and canister from the guns of our fleet flew over and past our turret, and as our huge piece sent its compliments ashore, the effect was almost deafening.

---

[8] *Manhattan*'s log recorded: "At 6 called all hands up anchor. At 6:20 beat to quarters, cleared ship for action." *Ibid.*

[9] Neither the log nor any of Commander Nicholson's reports mention this episode.

The fleet of Rear Admiral Farragut passes Fort Morgan.   Tecumseh, *leading the line of monitors, is shown sinking after striking a torpedo.   Webster's ship,* Manhattan, *is directly astern of her.*

About half past seven, while the action was at its height, our gun had just been revolved for a shot at Fort Morgan, a momentary view was had of the *Tecumseh,* and in that instant occurred the catastrophe whereby a good ship filled with men, with a brave captain, in the twinkling of an eye vanished from the field of battle.

A tiny white comber of froth curled around her bow, a tremendous shock ran through our ship as though we had struck a rock, and as rapidly as these words flow from my pen the *Tecumseh* reeled a little to starboard, her bows settled beneath the surface, and while we looked her stern lifted high in the air with the propeller still revolving, and the ship pitched out of sight like an arrow twanged from the bow.   We were steaming slowly ahead when this tragedy occurred and, being close aboard of the ill-fated craft, we were in imminent danger of running foul of her as she sank.   "Back hard" was the order shouted below to the engine room, and, as the *Manhattan* felt the effects of the reversed propeller, the bubbling water round our bows, and the huge swirls on either hand, told us that we were passing directly over the struggling wretches fighting with death in the *Tecumseh.*

The effect on our men was in some cases terrible.   One of the firemen was crazed by the incident. But the battle was not yet over.   After coming to a standstill for a few minutes, during which the commotion of the water set up by the foundered ship passed away, the *Manhattan* steamed ahead into line and took the duty but now being performed by her lost consort.   As the *Tecumseh* sank to the bottom, the crew of the *Hartford* sprang to her starboard rail and gave three ringing cheers in defiance of the enemy and in honor of the dying.

Perhaps some drowning wretch on the *Tecumseh* took that cheer in his ears as he sank to a hero's grave, and we may imagine the sound as it pierced the roar of battle, giving courage to some fainting heart as his face turned for the last time to the light of that sun whose rising and setting was at an end for him.

But Mobile Bay was yet before us.   Immediately following the events just related, my tour of duty in the turret ended for the time being, and I once more returned to the engine room.   The first effect of going from the cool air of the turret to the terrible heat of the engine room was that of a curious chilliness.   This, in a minute or two, was succeeded by a most copious perspiration, so violent that one's clothing became soaking wet, and the perspiration coursing down the scantily clothed body and limbs, filled the shoes so that they "chuckled" as one walked.

At 150 F. the glass in a lantern will crackle and break, the lamps burn dimly, and it is impossible to handle any metal with the bare hands.   Pieces of canvas, like flat-iron holders alone enable one to grasp a hand-rail or valve handle. Of course frequent bulletins of the fight were brought to the poor devils sweating their lives out in the engine room, and we got some idea of what was going on, through the signal which at frequent intervals [came] from the pilot house.

"Ahead slow," "stop," "back," these told the phases of our part in the battle, and we knew that we were employed in quelling the fire of Fort Morgan at pistol shot range while the wooden fleet passed in by the ship channel on our starboard side.

During one of my turns at the training gear our gun was served with grape and canister, and it was marvelous to note the effect of the cart-load of iron sent hissing into the enemy's works from a fifteen inch gun. In the first place the noise of this mass of missiles tearing through the air was in striking contrast with the roar of a smooth projectile, and its effects even more marked: A cloud of dust marked by flying debris, the sound of smashing and tearing coming back from the point of impact, and, as the smoke lifted, destruction and ruin.

Of course it will be understood by this that we lay pretty close in shore, for our orders were to "silence everything at the water level during the passage of the wooden ships." [10]

So the formidable water battery commanding the channel received especial attention from our big gun, and gave no trouble after the first infliction of fifteen inch grape and canister.

And thus the battle raged, minute after minute, and we continued in serviceable condition, no one hurt thus far, and the turret intact, though heavily struck at frequent intervals.

The sounds produced by a shot striking our turret were far different from what I had anticipated. The scream of the shot would arrive at about the same time with the projectile, with far from a severe thud, and then the air would be filled with that peculiar shrill singing sound of violently broken glass, or perhaps more like the noise made by flinging a nail violently through the air. The shock of discharge of our own guns was especially hard on the ears of those in the turret, and it seemed at times as though the tympanumus must give way. The sensations of the manipulator of the turning gear were not particularly pleasant. In addition to the frequent shocks to his ears, his position was such that the huge gun, as it was discharged, recoiled to the limit of the turret, and the space was so contracted that at first it appeared certain that a shocking death would follow every round. But it was really a place of perfect safety, and no one was injured at this station throughout the battle.

At about eight o'clock the fire on our port hand began to slacken, and the word was passed below that the wooden fleet had entered the bay and that the fight was over.

"Ahead slow" was the signal to the engine room, and as we gathered headway, steering for the wooden fleet inside, the guns of Fort Morgan again opened fire, and quite a number of shot and shell fell around us as we drew out of the line of fire.

Of course, after more than two hours of confinement below in the smoky torrid atmosphere of the monitor, we were all glad to take advantage of the lull in affairs and catch a breath of fresh air on deck. The sight there was inspiriting. Astern lay the comparatively narrow entrance through which the fleet had but just passed, on the starboard quarter lay Fort Morgan, and sheltered by its protecting guns could be seen the huge ram *Tennessee* with her two consorts, the *Morgan* and *Gaines*, while some distance up the bay, in the direction of Mobile, lay the *Selma*, hotly engaged with the double ender gunboat *Metacomet* under Lieutenant Commander James E. Jouett.

The sky had become overcast in the bay, but outside the sun could be seen shining in fitful patches, and the fleet, under orders from the Flagship, had come to anchor in a sort of irregular circle, ready for further combat in case the enemy decided to stake the result upon a single-handed fight between the *Tennessee* and the Union fleet.

Every flag was flying, as when we saw the line slowly advancing in battle array at sunrise, and the number was undiminished save by the ship of the gallant Craven, the *Tecumseh*, which lay at the bottom but a few hundred yards away.

The gentle westerly breeze which had prevailed all the morning had gradually drifted the smoke of battle across the fort and so out to sea, and the rebel flag lazily flapped against the single staff within

---

[10] Farragut's instructions of 4 August to Commander T. H. Stevens of *Winnebago* indicated what he expected from the monitors: "The service that I look for from the ironclads is, first, to neutralize as much as possible the fire of the guns which rake our approach; next to look out for the [Southern] ironclads when we are abreast of the forts, and lastly, to occupy the attention of those batteries which would rake us while running up the bay." *ORN* I, 21, 404.

the works, and from the halyards of the ram. We had barely come to anchor, and were congratulating ourselves that the hard work of the day was over when, about a quarter of nine, a signal from the *Hartford* of "prepare to engage the enemy" told us that the fight was not yet over. As we hastened below, previous to securing our battle hatches, a glance toward Fort Morgan gave the reason for the signal.

The rebel ram *Tennessee* was slowly steaming from under the fort into the open bay, and as her direction became plain, it was evident that the final struggle was about to begin.

The ram was headed directly for the flagship, and by the time our gun was ready for action, the sharp firing told us that the fleet was engaged. Our anchor was weighed and we were well underway by nine o'clock, and as we entered the melee [at 9:20] the steady roar of big guns, the shrill whistle of shot and shell, and the occasionally heard hoarse voice of command, were evidences that all the fighting was being done at close quarters.

Shortly after going into action, word was sent below to secure everything for ramming, and we waited for breathless minutes for the shock which never came. The speed of the *Manhattan* was so low that the attempt to ram was a failure. Our engines were kept in motion, however, and the peculiar smashing sound which succeeded every discharge of our fifteen inch gun told us below that the ram was not far away. Several times the sound of cheering came below to us, but the most prominent sounds were those of shrieking shell and booming cannon. The battle had raged for nearly an hour, and the only news we had from deck was that the wooden ships were pouring an ineffectual fire from their eleven inch guns into the ram, and that several of the vessels had rammed her, with what effect, however, was not known. The fact, however, that the combat still raged was proof that no serious injury had been done to either side, and for aught we knew the fight might last for hours yet.

My tour of duties had once more brought me into the turret, and from occasional glimpses caught through our gun ports, I could see that the ram, battered and dented in a hundred places, her smoke pipe shot away flush with the top of her casemate, was keeping up the fight with the greatest vigor, but was stationary. Several shots at very close range had been delivered, and Captain Nicholson had said that the rebel flag was shot away when, almost on the stroke of ten, the command came "cease firing," and I saw that we were almost in contact; peering past the muzzle of one of our guns the flutter of a tiny white flag told that the ram had stopped fighting.

"For God's sake, don't fire; I surrender, I surrender," came faintly from the *Tennessee*, and as Captain Nicholson stepped to the side of the monitor with the question, "Who [*sic*] do you surrender to?" the answer came on the instant, "I surrender to you, sir; for God's sake, don't fire again; we are disabled."

By direction of our Captain, the First Lieutenant [11] stepped aboard the ram, now alongside, and, seizing the rebel flag lying in the starboard scuppers, brought it aboard the *Manhattan* and tossed it into the turret through a gun port.

The Battle of Mobile Bay was over. The surrender of the *Tennessee* took place on the stroke of ten o'clock, and as soon as the fact became known throughout the fleet every throat gave out its cheers in honor of the glorious victory.

A motly throng poured on deck from our engine room and turret chamber, but in whatever condition a man appeared, he broke into a cheer as soon as his eyes caught sight of the helpless shape of the ram lying near us, and showing so plainly the terrible ordeal through [which] she had passed in the fierce fight just ended. Cheer upon cheer broke from every ship as the ram was taken in tow by the *Chickasaw*, and slowly carried to the *Hartford*, a trophy of victory.

The condition of the *Tennessee* was in sorry contrast with her appearance a few hours before. Her smoke pipe had been shot away, giving her a particularly shorn, stubby look. Many indentations in her sloping armor showed where our shots had struck, and in a general way this formidable craft looked anything but warlike; and, as her steering gear was disabled, her movements were controlled by the *Chickasaw*. Her humiliation was complete.

---

[11] According to *Manhattan's* log: "Acting Master Robert B. Ely boarded her [*Tennessee*] by order of Commander Nicholson and received her colors which he brought on board this vessel." *ORN* I, 21, 824.

The water batteries at Fort Morgan, photographed after the battle of 5 August 1864.

The subsequent stages and results of this famous battle are now familiar history, and have been dealt with by abler pens than mine.

The total loss of life was one hundred and sixty three, of whom one hundred and eleven were drowned in the *Tecumseh*.[12]

The wounded numbered one hundred and seventy. But for living and dead alike "it was a glorious victory."

---

[12] Exclusive of the more than 100 who went down in *Tecumseh*, A. T. Mahan lists (from official reports) 52 dead and 170 wounded. Mahan, *op. cit.*, p. 244.

SHIPBOARD LIFE IN THE CIVIL WAR

APPENDIX VI

VI–99

The life of a sailor on board a warship has never been easy. In the Civil War it was particularly difficult. Officers and men alike in both navies faced new challenges and had additional burdens placed upon them as the mode of war at sea changed with the shift from sail to steam, from wood to iron, and from smoothbore guns to increasing use of the new rifled weapons.

Progress brought with it new hazards. Although steam engines provided warships with the maneuverability in action which they had lacked with sail, a shot in the boilers could leave the vessel virtually helpless or scald many of the men in the engine spaces. C.S.S. *Chattahoochee* was not even engaged in combat in May 1863 when her boiler exploded, killing 18 men. Ironclads gave the crew greater protection from enemy shot than ships had ever before possessed, but their construction imposed grave hardships on the men as well. The early monitors did not ride well even in moderate seas and the interior spaces were usually damp. If dampness was not a problem, heat from the engines was. Temperatures below deck frequently rose above 100 degrees; indeed, as Harrie Webster, then a Third Assistant Engineer, reported in another chapter of this work, at Mobile Bay the thermometer in U.S.S. *Manhattan*'s engine spaces read 150 degrees and the men had to be rotated in and out during the battle of 5 August to prevent collapse. Even in the better ventilated and comparatively spacious gunboats, yellow fever was a constant problem for men serving extended tours on the blockade lines.

Moreover, the physical demands on the crews were compounded by a chronic shortage of men and material. Too few were often asked to do too much with too little, which usually happens at sea in war. More often than not the men (and boys like the powder monkey at right), under the indomitable leadership of such officers as John Rodgers, David Glasgow Farragut, Andrew Hull Foote and David Dixon Porter, rose gallantly to the tasks assigned them, but the effort took its toll.

Confronted with the necessity of having to create a navy where none had existed before, the Confederacy was placed on the defensive at sea from the outset of the conflict. The lack of resources, facilities and time never let Southern sailors get a sustained naval offensive underway. Thus it was the North that felt the operational hardships more often.

Frequently operating in cooperation with the Army in amphibious assaults along the Southern coast, Federal sailors had to engage strong fortifications ashore and stand up to their heavy guns.

A daily threat to the wooden gunboats operating in coastal waters and rivers were the rams which the South constructed. These warships were few in number but their capacity to wreak havoc on the small Union vessels was great. Above, C.S.S. *Albemarle*, having sunk U.S.S. *Southfield* near Plymouth, North Carolina, early on 19 April 1864, turns to engage U.S.S. *Miami*.

Landing parties constantly probed Confederate shores to gain vital intelligence of Southern strengths, positions, and possible operational intentions, to overrun mine control positions, to destroy resources, munitions and defenses.

The peril presented to Union ships by torpedoes made it mandatory for the North to clear channels of the lethal weapons. Boat crews were called upon for this hazardous duty by day . . .

. . . while by night, especially off the major ports, they acted as pickets to guard against blockade runners and low slung "David" torpedo boats that might attempt to strike units of the inshore blockading fleet. Often the same men had to perform both duties, working virtually around the clock.

Even when the crew was not engaged in action, the day to day aspects of shipboard life required attention. Watches had to be stood . . .

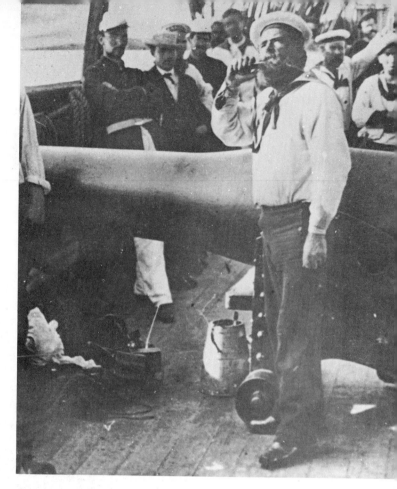

. . . the boatswain piped the men to drill.

. . . on monitors ironworks forged repairs for old casualties or provided spare parts for those that were anticipated . . .

. . . not only did ships have to be
repaired but canvas and clothes had
to be mended . . .

. . . and all hands did their laundry.

B-2011

. . . but throughout the fleet (photo above taken on board U.S.S. *Hunchback*) almost every ship had at least one banjo or guitar player who helped to while away leisure hours.

And not all of one's shipmates were regulation members of the crew.

Nevertheless, there were times when the men could relax. On such occasions checkers was a favorite pastime, both on gunboats . . .

. . . and on battered monitors.

U.S.S. *Wabash* (and probably some other ships as well) had a large minstrel group . . .

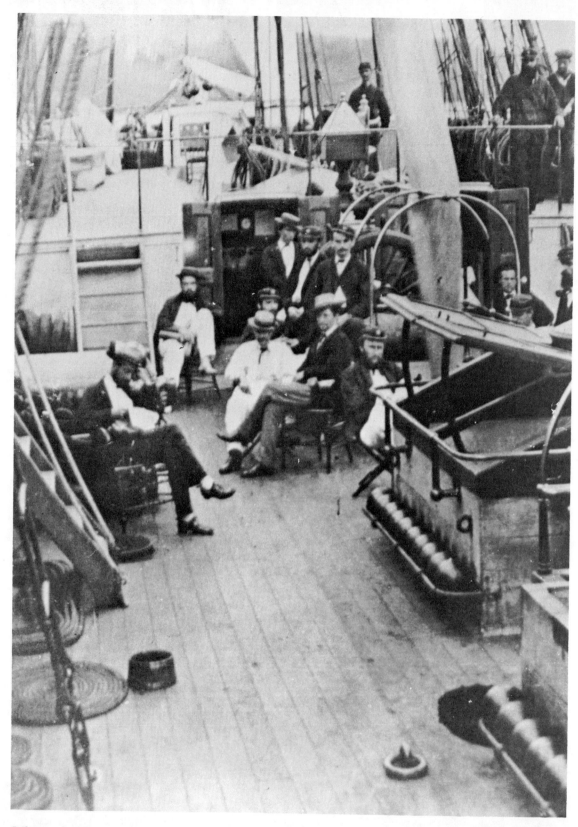

Officers often spent their spare time on deck, catching up on the news in the papers forwarded to the fleet, reading letters from home, or simply getting some sun.

At other times they relaxed in their quarters.

The visits of dignitaries and high ranking members of the government—such as that of Vice President Andrew Johnson to U.S.S. *Susquehanna*—provided a major change in daily routine.

And religious services were held regularly to give each member of the crew an opportunity to exercise his faith.

Alternately hazardous and tedious, cruelly hard and pleasantly enjoyable, always exacting and of utmost importance to the nation—this was shipboard life during the Civil War.

NAVAL
SHEET MUSIC
OF THE
CIVIL WAR

NAVAL SHEET MUSIC OF THE CIVIL WAR

Sheet music is an overlooked phase in the study of history. Important events and obscure happenings were all recorded in patriotic music. Hence the sheet music of a particular period interests the historian as well as the musician for he finds portrayed in it the wars, the military and political campaigns, the presidents, ships and the sea, the opening of railroads and canals, the California gold rush, advent of the telegraph and ocean cable and much else important or minor.

This music is classified by publisher, composer and lyricist. However, the historian finds especially interesting the illustrated title page. Drawings by James A. McNeill Whistler, Winslow Homer, D. C. Johnston, Robert W. Weir and many other artists appeared on them.

Many buyers of sheet music carefully and handsomely colored the engravings, thereby adding to the dramatic quality of the art work. A number of the title sheets which are published below were so colored, and it is regrettable indeed that we have had to confine ourselves to black and white reproduction. Nevertheless, the title sheets are of sufficient interest themselves to warrant publishing them even though space considerations have necessitated the omission of some of the music. The songs that are published in full, however, are representative of Civil War naval song and music.

Among the most popular subjects have been the wars this country has fought, and ships and the sea. During the Civil War composers frequently combined these themes and described naval actions and naval heroes. Some of this sheet music is reproduced here, and it will be noted that the saga of the sea is told not only in the lyrics but also specifically in the music itself.

Mr. Lester S. Levy of Pikesville, Maryland, has the most comprehensive private collection of American sheet music. Through his kindness, a selected group of Civil War naval sheets, Federal and Confederate, are reproduced for this centennial publication. We are grateful to Mr. Richard E. Townsend of Annapolis for entrée to this remarkable collection and the foregoing brief summary. Mr. Townsend himself has a wide reputation as a discriminating and knowledgeable collector of Americana, including sheet music.

THE
BANNER OF THE SEA.
a
NATIONAL SONG AND CHORUS.

Philadelphia LEE & WALKER 722 Chesnut St

TO THE GALLANT OFFICERS AND TARS

OF THE

UNITED STATES NAVY,

THE BANNER OF THE SEA

Is heartily dedicated by the Author

D. BRAINERD WILLIAMSON.

The Music composed   By Geo. W. Hewitt.

NATIONAL & PATRIOTIC SONGS, No. 22.

With animation but not too fast.

1. Of all the flags that float aloft O'er Neptune's gallant tars, That
2. Beneath its folds we fear no foe, Our hearts shall never quail; With
3. On ev'ry wave to ev'ry shore, Columbia's Flag shall go, And
4. Its enemies our own shall be Upon the land or main; Its

wave on high in victory, A-bove the sons of Mars, Give
bosoms bare, the storm we'll dare, And brave the battle gale: And
through all time, its fame sublime, With brighter hues shall glow: For
star-ry light shall gild the fight And guide our iron rain. Nor

us the flag—Columbia's Flag! The emblem of the free, Whose
though the cannon plough our decks, The planks with gore run red, Still
Freedom's Standard is our flag— Its guardians, Freedom's Sons, And
for-eign pow'r, nor treason's arts Shall shake our patriot love; While

flashing Stars blazed through our wars For TRUTH and LIB_ER _ TY! Then
through the fray, our Flag al_way, Shall gleam far o_ver_head. Then
wo be_tide th'in_sulter's pride, When we un_loose our guns. Then
with our life, in peace or strife, We'll keep that flag a_bove. Then

dip it, lads, in o_cean's brine, And give it, give it three times three, And
dip it, lads, in o_cean's brine, And &c.
dip it, lads, in o_cean's brine, And &c.
dip it, lads, in o_cean's brine, And &c.

fling it out 'mid song and shout, The Ban_ner of the

sea! Then dip it lads in O_cean's brine, And give it, give it

Then dip it lads in O_cean's brine, And give it, give it

three times three, And fling it out, 'mid song and shout, The Banner of the Sea!

three times three, And fling it out, 'mid song and shout, The Banner of the Sea!

VI–117

BATTLE OF PORT ROYAL.

CH. GROBE. Op. 1385.

First page of sheet music only.

THE BATTLE OF ROANOKE ISLAND.
Story of an Eye Witness.

MUSICALLY PORTRAYED

BY

CHARLES GROBE.

BOSTON
Published by OLIVER DITSON & Co. 277 Washington St.

THE BATTLE OF ROANOKE.

CH. GROBE. Op. 1395.

Seven O'Clock, Tuesday evening, Feb. 4th 1862.— The steamer "PATUXENT" delivers the orders to the fleet to get rea-

-dy for sailing from Hatteras Inlet the morning following.

Great is the joy manifested from the Colonel down to the cook.

Allegro.

"We know the way."

First page of sheet music only.

GENERAL BURNSIDE'S GRAND TRIUMPHAL MARCH.

BOSTON
Published by HENRY TOLMAN & C° 291 Washington St.

CHICAGO
ROOT & CADY

NEW YORK
S.T. GORDON

ALBANY
J. H. H. PARKHURST

MARCHE MILITAIRE.

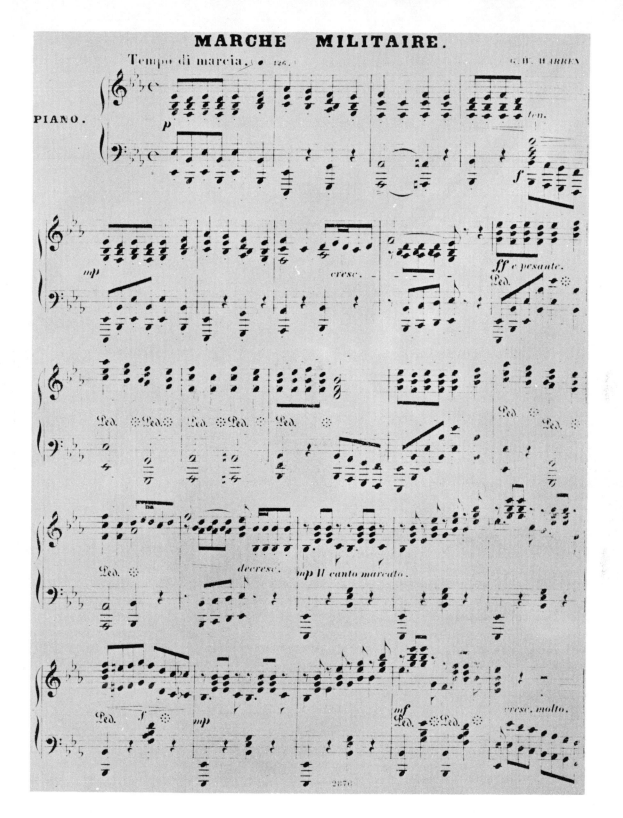

First page of sheet music only.

The Last Broadside

The following lines were written upon hearing of the heroism of the noble crew of the "FRIGATE CUMBERLAND", in the engagement at "Hampton Roads," who bravely fired a last "Broadside" while their ship was sinking, in compliance with the order of their Commanding Officer, the gallant hero. LIEUTENANT MORRIS.

"SHALL WE GIVE THEM A BROADSIDE AS SHE GOES?"

WORDS BY

Elizabeth T. Porter Beach.

MUSIC BY

FREDERICK BUCKLEY.

2½

NEW YORK
Published by Firth, Pond & Co 547 Broadway.

Boston.	Syracuse.	Pittsburgh.
O. DITSON & CO.	T. HOUGH.	H. KLEBER & BRO.

Entered according to Act of Congress A.D. 1862 by Firth. Pond & Co in the Clerks Office of the Dt Ct of the Sn Dt of N.Y.

THE
LAST BROADSIDE.

Words by ELIZABETH T. PORTER BEACH.

Music by FREDERICK BUCKLEY.

Marziale.

Con Spirito.

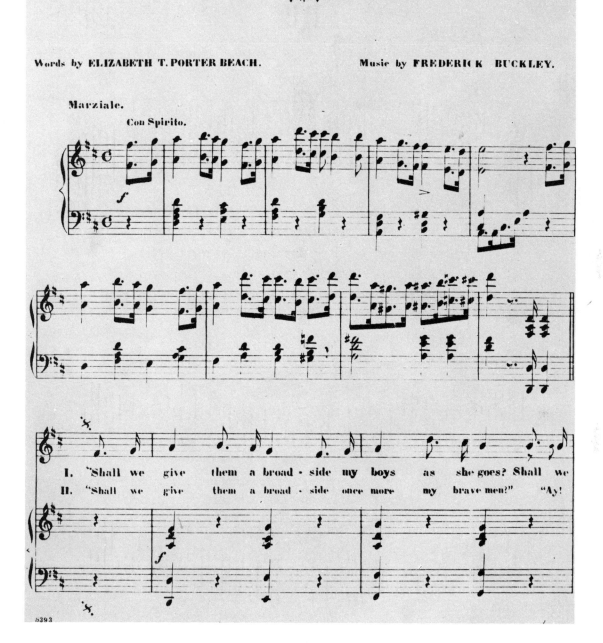

I. "Shall we give them a broad-side my boys as she goes? Shall we

II. "Shall we give them a broad-side once more my brave men?" "Ay!

5393

hearts! mighty spi- rits! "tried gold" of our land! A ha - lo of glo- ry your

meed; All hon- or'd the no- ble - soul'd

Cum- ber - land band; So true in Co - lum - bia's need,

To Capt. Ericsson.

Monitor Polka

BY

G. WEINGARTEN.

NEW YORK

Published by H.B. DODWORTH, 6 Astor Place.

POLKA.

MONITOR POLKA.

By G. Weingarten.

First page of sheet music only.

The ERICSSON GALOP

Dedicated to the **INVENTOR** of the celebrated STEAM BATTERY

MONITOR,

{"N.B. In preparing for action, the awning over the turret is removed and the square smoke stacks as well as the short pipes, through which air is drawn into the vessel, are taken down."}

BY V. TINAN.

Engd by H F Greene.

BOSTON.
Published by Oliver Ditson & Co. 277 Washington St.

Firth Pond & Co.   J. Church Jr.   J.C. Haynes & Co.   J.E. Gould.   C.C. Clapp & Co.
N. York.   Cin.   Boston.   Philad⁰   Boston.

ERICSSON GALOP.

V. TINANS.

First page of sheet music only.

THE ADIEU

MARCH OF THE U.S.SHIP "NORTH CAROLINA"

ARRANGED FOR THE PIANO AND

LITH. OF SARONY, MAJOR & KNAPP, 449 BROADWAY, N.Y.

DEDICATED TO

CAPT. R.W. MEADE

COMMANDING U.S. SHIP "NORTH CAROLINA."

BY

LUIGI DE PERINI.

NEW YORK

Published by Wm. A. POND & Co. 547 Broadway.

BOSTON,
O. DITSON & Co.

PITTSBURGH,
H. KLEBER & BRO.

MONTREAL
BOUCHER & MANSEAU

CHICAGO
ROOT & CADY

MILWAUKEE

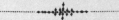

"THE ADIEU"
MARCH.

Tempo di marcia.

LUIGI de PERINI.

5919

First page of sheet music only.

GUN-BOAT QUICK STEP.

"Fort Henry,"   "Fort Donelson,"   "Island Nº 10."

inscribed to

COMMODORE FOOTE

BY

LELIA.

NEW YORK.

GUN-BOAT QUICK STEP.

Tempo di Marcia.

Entered acc:to Act of Congress AD.1862 by Firth, Pond & Cº in the Clerk's Office of the Dᵗ. Court of the Soutᵗⁿ Dᵗ of N.Y.

First page of sheet music only.

MONITOR

GRAND MARCH,
COMPOSED BY
E. MACK,
LEE & WALKER

RESPECTFULLY DEDICATED TO
CAPTAIN JOHN L. WORDEN.

THE

MONITOR

GRAND MARCH

CAPTAIN WORDEN WAS PARTIALLY STUNNED BY THE CONCUSSION, AND WAS CARRIED AWAY. ON RECOVERING, HE ASKED, "HAVE I SAVED THE MINNESOTA" THE REPLY WAS "YES, AND WHIPPED THE MERIMAC" HE RESPONDED "THEN I DON'T CARE WHAT BECOMES OF ME"

COMPOSED BY

E. MACK.

5   3

Philadelphia LEE & WALKER 722 Chesnut St.

VI–139

MONITOR GRAND MARCH.

COMPOSED

BY E. MACK.

Fine.

Entered according to Act of Congress A.D. 1862 by Lee & Walker at the Clerk's Office of the Dt. Ct. of the Ea. Dt. of Pa.

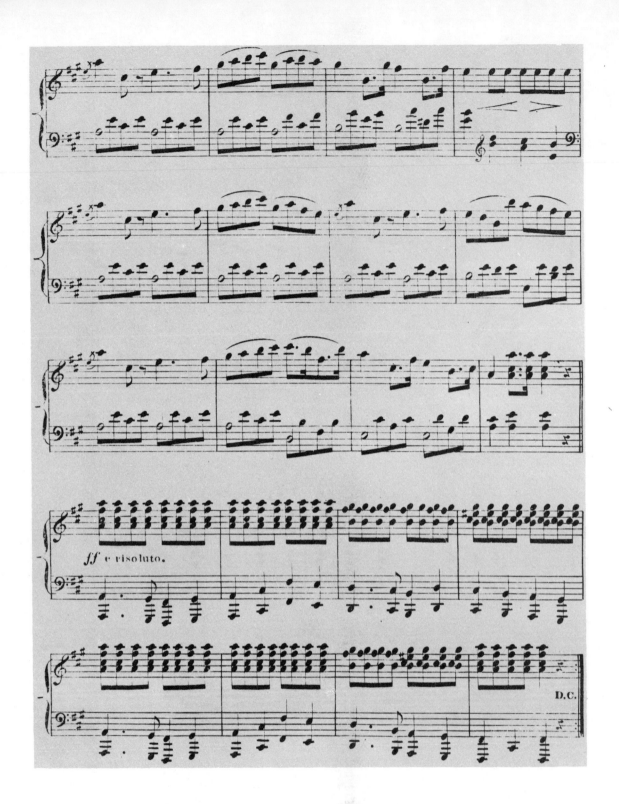

TO CAPT. JOHN ERICSSON
Inventor of the Monitor.

OH! GIVE US A NAVY OF IRON

THE POPULAR NAVAL BALLAD

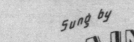

Sung by

J. H. RAINER

AT SANFORD'S NEW OPERA-HOUSE

Words by

D. Brainerd Williamson

Music by

JAS. W. PORTER.

Geo. Swaim

PHILADELPHIA
Publd by J. W. LAWTON & Co. 19 So. 8th St

O GIVE US A NAVY OF IRON.

Poetry by
D. BRAINERD WILLIAMSON.

Music by
JAMES W. PORTER.

O give us a Na-vy of I-ron, And to man it our Yankee

x

Ent. according to Act of Congress AD. 1862 by D.B.Williamson, in the Clerks Office of the Dis.^t Court of the Eastern Dis.^t of Penn.^a

VI–144

CHORUS.

2.v. Old England the foe of our fathers, The foe of their children to day, Is gloat-ing in hopes that our Un-ion In darkness is passing a-way. But Trea-son shall die in its ash-es, And stronger than ev-er be-fore; We'll turn on the jealous old ty-rant, And punish John Bull at his door. (Chorus.)

3.v. And where in the wide world a nation, That could cope with our I-ron Jacks! We would sweep all their seas and harbors, Of their Warriors and Mer-ri-macs. Then give us a Na-vy of I-ron, And we'll fling our Flag to the breeze, And prove to the des-pots of Eu-rope, That free-dom must reign on the seas. (Cho:)

THE
BATTLE OF NEW ORLEANS

Philadelphia LEE & WALKER 722 Chestnut St

THE BATTLE OF NEW ORLEANS

Musically illustrated.

CH. GROBE.

Op. 1412.

"DONA NOBIS PACEM." — Conclusion of **High Mass** at the

Cathedral in New Orleans.

GEN. LOVELL'S COMMAND, "Strike up the

drum and let the tongue of war plead for our interest."

ST. CHARLES HOTEL. " Lord Lovell the town had vowed to defend,

Vivace.

and waving his sword on high, He swore that his last ounce of powder he'd spend,

and in the last ditch he'd die. He swore by black and he swore by blue. He

swore by the stars and bars, that he'd never fly from a Yankee crew while he

was a son of Mars. He had Forts that no Yankee alive could take,

Attack on the VARUNA by the rebel fleet.   She successfully

fights and sinks six rebel steamers, and goes down firing her guns, which are nearly

under water. The Missisippi runs the rebel ram Manassas ashore and destroys her.

Cheer after cheer rends the air as the Fleet behold the gallantry of

the Varuna and the Mississippi.

New Orleans in sight.

"Fire rafts" coming down the river, which however do our fleet no injury.

cres — — — cen — — — do.

ANIMATO.

Large crowds gather on the levees and cheer the ships,

as they approach. The fleet take possession of the city. Great rejoicing

among the loyal citizens.

— cen — do.

The Star Spangled Banner again floats over the City and Forts.

"Oh tarry, Lord Lovell!" Sir Farragut

VIVACE.

Retreat of Gen: Lovell.

cried, "Oh tarry, Lord Lovell!" said he; "I rather think not," Lord Lovell

replied, "For I'm in a great hurry!"

The Victory.   The story of the capture of New Orleans will make a

ALLº MODERATO.

chapter in our naval annals that will be read with wonder and pride by all future generations of

our glorious country. No navy has ever done deeds of greater valor and skill, than were done by our

fleet, under the command of the gallant Farragut and Porter, supported by such heroes as Boggs,

Bailey, Morris, Wainwright, Lee, Harrison, Perkins, Martin, Nichols, Russell, Thornton, Harris,

Kortz, Brown, Pennington, Samson, etc. "They have demeaned themselves like men born to renown, by life or death."

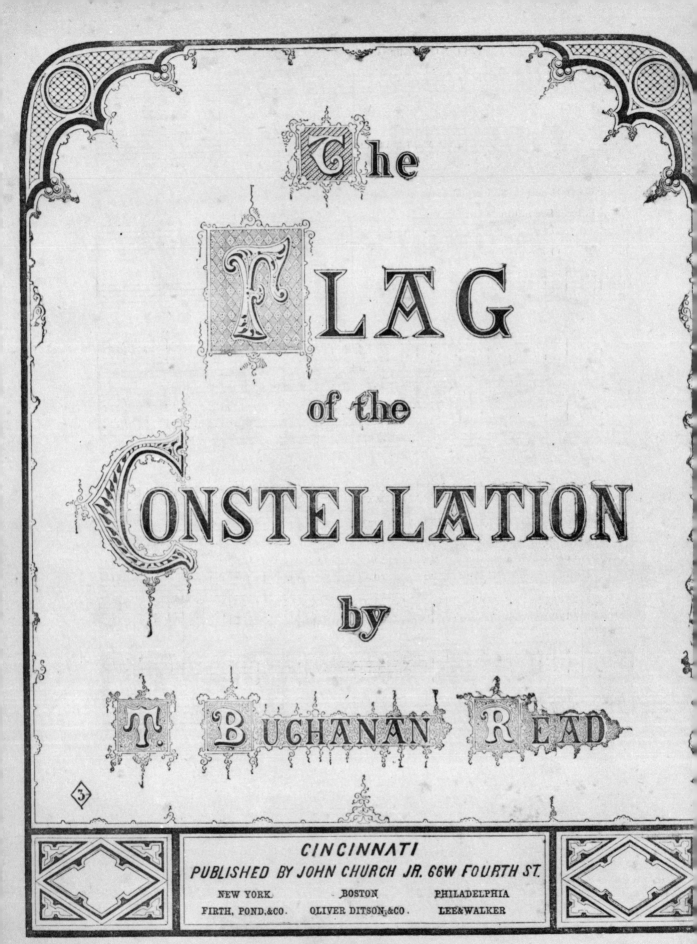

The Flag of the Constellation

of the

Constellation

by

T. Buchanan Read

CINCINNATI
PUBLISHED BY JOHN CHURCH JR. 66 W FOURTH ST.

| NEW YORK. | BOSTON | PHILADELPHIA |
| FIRTH, POND, & CO. | OLIVER DITSON & CO. | LEE & WALKER |

FLAG OF THE CONSTELLATION.

A

NATIONAL SONG

Poetry by T. Buchanan Read. ———————— Music by Chs. R. Crosby.

Allegretto marcia.

1. The stars of morn, On our banner borne, With the iris of Heaven are blended, The
2. What hand so bold, As strike from its fold, One star or one stripe of its brightning? For
3. Its meteor form, Shall ride the storm, Till the fiercest of foes sur-ren-der, The
4. Peace to the world, Is our motto unfurled, Tho'we shun not the field that is go-ry, At

Ent. acc. to act of Congress A.D. 1861 by John Church jr. in the Cl'ks. office of the Southern Dis. Ct. of O.

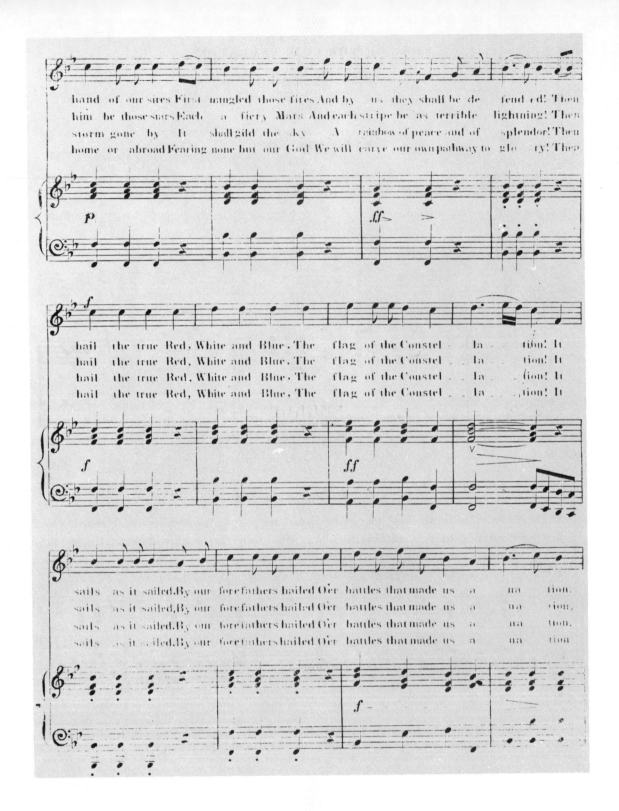

hand of our sires First mangled those fires And by us they shall be defended! Then
him be those stars Each a fiery Mars And each stripe be as terrible lightning! Then
storm gone by It shall gild the sky A rainbow of peace and of splendor! Then
home or abroad Fearing none but our God We will carve our own pathway to glory! Then

hail the true Red, White and Blue, The flag of the Constel la tion! It
hail the true Red, White and Blue, The flag of the Constel la tion! It
hail the true Red, White and Blue, The flag of the Constel la tion! It
hail the true Red, White and Blue, The flag of the Constel la tion! It

sails as it sailed, By our forefathers hailed O'er battles that made us a na tion.
sails as it sailed, By our forefathers hailed O'er battles that made us a na tion.
sails as it sailed, By our forefathers hailed O'er battles that made us a na tion.
sails as it sailed, By our forefathers hailed O'er battles that made us a na tion.

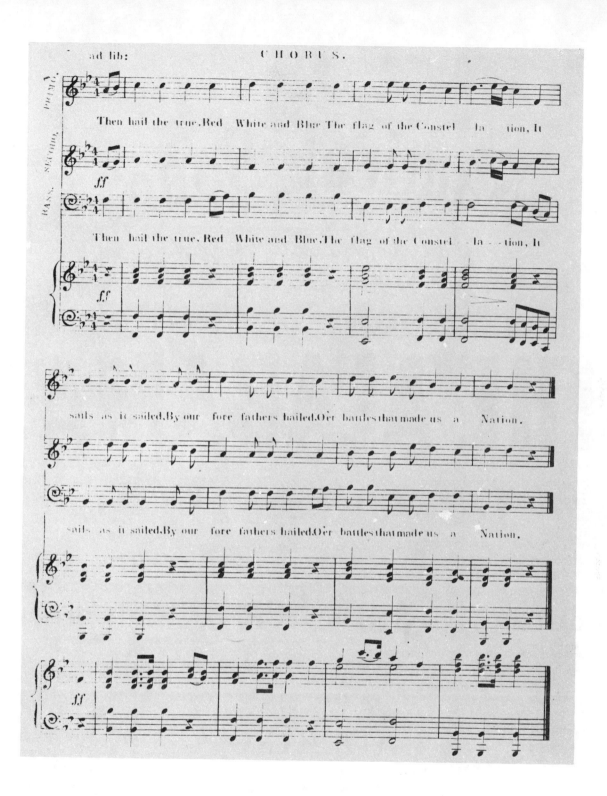

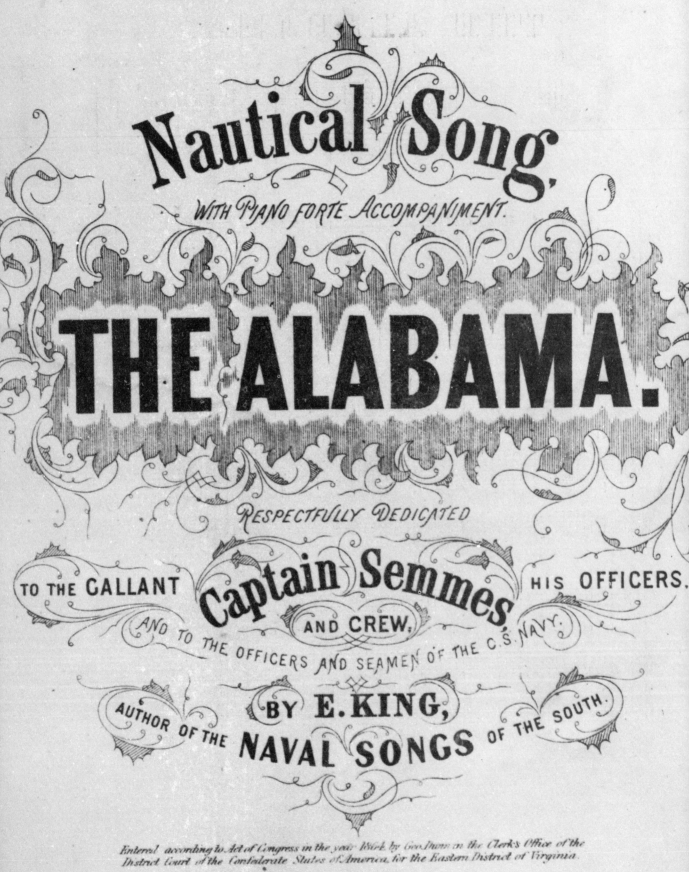

Nautical Song,
WITH PIANO FORTE ACCOMPANIMENT.

THE ALABAMA.

RESPECTFULLY DEDICATED

TO THE GALLANT Captain Semmes HIS OFFICERS,
AND CREW,
AND TO THE OFFICERS AND SEAMEN OF THE C.S. NAVY.

BY E. KING,
AUTHOR OF THE NAVAL SONGS OF THE SOUTH.

Entered according to Act of Congress in the year 1864 by Geo.Dunn in the Clerk's Office of the
District Court of the Confederate States of America, for the Eastern District of Virginia.

RICHMOND, VA. LITHOGRAPHED AND PUBLISHED BY GEO. DUNN & COMPY

THE ALABAMA.

POETRY BY E. KING

MUSIC BY F. W. ROSIER.

The wind blows off yon rock....y shore, Boys! set your sails all free; And

soon our boom ing can...non's roar Shall ring out mer...ri....ly.

Run up your bunt....ing taught a...peak, And swear, lads, to de fend her; 'Gainst

ev....ry foe, where....'er we go, Our mot....to "No Sur....ren....der!"

TENOR I. *ff*
Then sling the bowl, drink ev....'ry soul, A toast to the A....la

TENOR II. *ff*
Then sling the bowl, drink ev....'ry soul, A toast to the A....la

BASS. *ff*
Then sling the bowl, drink ev....'ry soul, A toast to the A....la

CHORUS. *ff*

....ha....ma; What....e'er our lot, through storm or shot, Here's suc....

....ba.....ma; What....e'er our lot, through storm or shot, Here's suc....

....ba....ma; What....e'er our lot, through storm or shot, Here's suc....

cess to the A la ba ma!

cess to the A la ba ma!

cess to the A la ba ma!

Our country calls all hands to arms,
    We hear but to obey ;
Nor shall home's most endearing charms
    Steal one weak thought away.
Our saucy craft all roam the deep,
    We've sworn, lads, to defend her ;
Trim, taught and tight, we'll brave the fight,
    Our motto "No Surrender!"
        Then sling the bowl, &c.

Our home is on the mountain wave,
    Our flag floats proudly free ;
No boasting despot, tyrant, knave,
    Shall crush fair Liberty.
Firmly we'll aid her glorious cause,
    We'll die, boys, to defend her ;
We'll brave the foe, where'er we go,
    Our motto "No Surrender!"
        Then sling the bowl, &c.

Boys! if perchance it may befall,
    When storm of battle raves,
By shot or shell our noble hull
    Shall sink beneath the waves,
Yet while a plank to us is left
    To death we will defend her;
Facing the foe, down, down we'll go,
    But still cry "No Surrender!"
        Then sling the bowl, &c.

SECOND EDITION.

THE

ALABAMA

3

NEW ORLEANS:

BLACKMAR & CO., 74 Camp Street.

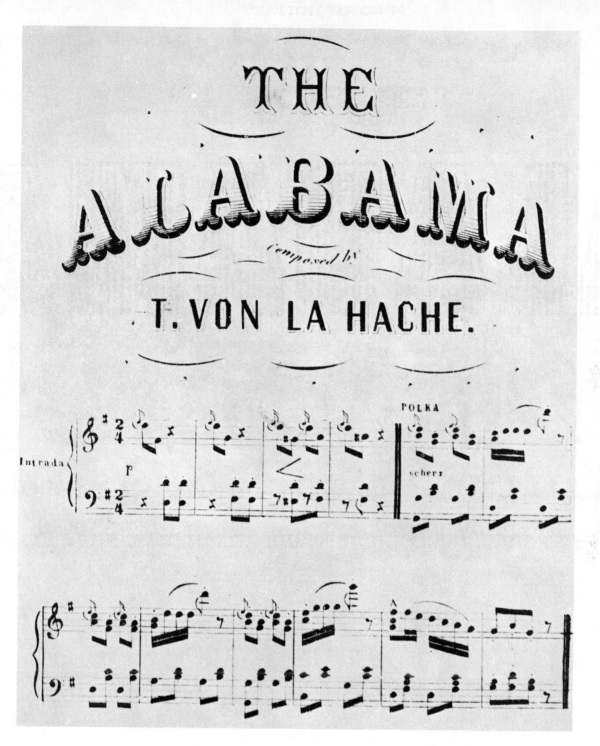

First page of sheet music only.

Last of the Alabama

RESPECTFULLY INSCRIBED TO THE CREW OF THE KEARSARGE

COMMODORE WINSLOWS GRAND VICTORY MARCH

Published by J. Marsh No. 1102 Chestnut St. Philada.

L.N. Rosenthal lith.

1. Off Cherbourg Port one summer day, Our noble ship the Kearsarge lay, Quite
2. Brave(?) Captain Semmes had saild the sea, O'er many a Merchant Vessel, he, Had

anx_ious her res_pects to pay, Un_to the Al_a_bam_a; She
won a bril_liant vic_to_ry With his great Al_a_bam_a; He

ad lib:

had as bold and brave a crew, As ev_er saild o'er o_cean blue, Whose
had a thiev_ing Brit_ish crew, Who un_to na_ture's in_stinct true, Could

ad lib:

Chorus

hearts were bent on "put_ting through," The Pi_rate Al_a_bam_a.
pil_lage, rob, and mur_der too, Up_on his Al_a_bam_a.

✱ Pronounced Keer-sarge.

Alabama

CHORUS.

Then mes-mates let your voi-ces swell, And let us now in mu-sic tell, Of

Then mes-mates let your voi-ces swell, And let us now in mu-sic tell, Of

"Winslow" whom we love so well, Who sunk the Al - a - bam - a.

"Winslow" whom we love so well, Who sunk the Al - a - bam - a.

3.

Her guns were cast in British sand,
By British sailors they were manned,
And British shipwrights built and planned,
　　This Pirate Alabama;
And let the truth be plainly told,
How she was bought with British gold,
By British merchants armed and coaled,
　　This Pirate Alabama.
　　　　　Chorus.

4.

So Captain Semmes quite confident,
That British crews was excellent,
Sent out a challenge insolent,
　　From his great Alabama;
And boastingly did he aver,
He'd meet the Kearsarge — punish her,
And "thrashing sound" administer,
　　With his dear Alabama.
　　　　　Chorus.

5.

Poor devil! little had he thought,
The combat which he had besought,
Could end in victory for aught,
　　Save his great Alabama;
So steaming outward in the bay,
To where the gallant Kearsarge lay,
Went — dashing from her bow the spray,
　　The Pirate Alabama.
　　　　　Chorus.

6.

Brave "Winslow" and his noble crew,
Their feelings scarcely could subdue,
As they saw coming to their view,
　　The Pirate Alabama;
For Yankee tars had heretofore,
Met crews such as the Pirate bore,
And in their hearts the sailors swore,
　　They'd sink the Alabama.
　　　　　Chorus.

7.

The Ship for action was prepared,
The "Stars and Stripes" raised overhead,
From cannons mouth a ball was sped
　　Unto the Alabama;
Then flew a storm of Iron hail,
Which caused the Pirate crew to quail,
As "Winslow" boldly did assail,
　　The Pirate Alabama.
　　　　　Chorus.

8.

The battle raged an hour or so,
When Captain Semmes began to show,
That he had met his overthrow,
　　And lost his Alabama;
Then "Winslow" in her hull, did pour,
A broadside — as she steered for shore,
She sunk, and Semmes shall never more,
　　Behold his Alabama.
　　　　　Chorus.

9

The coward "Deerhound" now bereft
Of hope, commenced her sneaking theft,
And stole what pris'ners we had left,
　　From the Great Alabama;
A day of reck'ning yet will come,
When Yankee fife, and Yankee drum,
Will cause the British to succumb,
　　And give up Alabama.
　　　　　Chorus.

MORAL.

Now Britishers do you beware,
And don't to combat Yankee's dare,
Or you perhaps the fate may share,
　　Of Semmes' Alabama;
For "Uncle Sam" will never stand,
An insult on the sea or land;
The men and ships at his command,
　　Can sink all Alabama's
　　　　　Chorus.

FARRAGUT'S GRAND MARCH.

J. STRAUSS.

Marsch.

Trio.

p

pp *cres.*

f

1.

2.

Marsch D.C.

U.S. NAVY QUADRILLE.

As played with great Success at Wallack's Theatre NEW YORK.

By the same Author

Composed by ROBERT STŒPEL.

"U.S. ARMY Quadrille"

U.S. NAVY QUADRILLE.

ROBERT STOEPEL.

The Departure. *Outward Bound!*

First two pages of sheet music only.

HOMEWARD BOUND.

COMPOSED

and respectfully dedicated to

CURTIS GUILD Esqr.

(AUTHOR OF THE WORDS)

BY

HIS FRIEND.

L.H. Bradford & C's Lith.

Price 38 Cents neft.

BOSTON,
Published at the Musical Exchange by Nathan Richardson, No. 282 Washington Street.

HOMEWARD BOUND.

Hur -
Swift
Far,

con brio.

- rah my lads the live - ly breeze now bloweth fresh and   free,   And through the rattling
out up - on the heav - ing waves our stout ship now shall ride,   Tri - um - pha nt o'er
far be hind the dis - tant shore has fa ded from the view,   As   forth up - on our

cor - dage all it pipes right mer - ri - ly   It pipes   right
each billows crest up - on the o - cean wide   Up - on   the
home ward course we plough the bil lows blue   We plough   the

mer - - - ri - ly right mer - ri - ly   right mer - ri -
o - - - - cean wide o - cean wide   o - - - cean
bil - - - lows blue bil - lows blue   bil - - lows

- ly .
wide .   Up with the hea - vy   an - chor then and
blue .   A - bout her prow the blue waves curl and
    So spread the can vass to the breeze and

let the air re - sound   And let the air re - sound   with a
lift their heads of foam   And lift their heads of foam   the live-
let the air re - sound   And let the air re - sound   with a

mer - ry song and cho - rus lads for we are homeward bound   with a
- ly breeze still fol lows on hur rah we're homeward bound   the live-
mer - ry song and cho - rus lads hur rah we're homeward bound   with a

mer - ry song and cho - rus lads for we are homeward bound   we're
- ly breeze still fol lows - - on hur - rah we're homeward bound   we're
mer - ry song and cho - rus lads hur - rah we're homeward bound   we're

C.S.S. Stonewall

CONFEDERATE FORCES AFLOAT

APPENDIX VIII

CONFEDERATE FORCES AFLOAT

From Dictionary of American Naval Fighting Ships, Vol. II

The Government of the Confederate States of America got underway in the spring of 1861, totally unprepared from a naval standpoint to uphold the independence it had declared. The Confederacy lacked adequate means to conduct an offensive or defensive war, wanting in ships to defend its long coastline and inland waters, to carry the war to Northern shores, or to conduct the foreign trade vital to existence. To this bleak outlook was added but limited hope and possibility for constructing or acquiring a navy. Nevertheless, inspired determination and ingenuity, evinced particularly by the more than 300 able officers who resigned from the United States Navy to support the Southern cause, culminated in the rapid appearance of many varied types of forces afloat under the Confederate flag.

The State navies provided the foundation for events to follow. The seceding States confiscated small United States ships, such as revenue cutters, coast survey ships, and lighthouse tenders, that were still within their grasp; they purchased others from Northern as well as Southern owners; and they quickly began to build additional vessels better suited to warfare. These actions were repeated in Virginia, North Carolina, Georgia, Alabama, Louisiana, Texas and elsewhere. Between 20 February 1861 when the Confederate Navy was authorized and the following summer, the State navies were gradually turned over to the central Government. More ships were purchased or captured and added to this nucleus, while construction of ironclads and other war vessels began.

Some ships served under direct army control. The Mississippi River Defense Fleet, composed of 14 ships manned by the army and under the overall command of Capt. J. E. Montgomery, CSN, was one such organization which operated during 1862. A second army group, the Texas Marine Department, established in 1861, was charged with the defense of coastal waters and rivers, especially in the vicinity of Galveston. The Department employed more than 25 ships, including gunboats, transports, repair ships, and coal barges. Elsewhere, the army carried men and material over the river highways in transports that they controlled, manned, and sometimes captained.

To compensate for the relatively small number of ships and inadequate construction facilities and supplies, the South improvised with marked daring. Their resourcefulness produced the first submarine to sink an opposing warship, and numerous types of torpedoes which wrought heavy damage against United States ships. Confederate cruisers proved venturesome and successful in weakening the North's war effort by damaging her trade, and luring Union ships from the blockade to facilitate the passage of runners.

The Confederacy, like the Union, pioneered in constructing the seagoing as well as river ironclads which significantly influenced the war's outcome: In the West, the Union's partially ironclad ships figured decisively in the crucial campaigns that divided and pierced to the heart of the Confederacy. In the East and along the Gulf, ironclads were the spearhead of victory for the North, and those of the South a constant threat. The first battle between ironclads, *Monitor* and *Virginia*, had world repercussions that revolutionized naval warfare.

A realistic appraisal of Southern naval strength has necessitated a broader scope for this undertaking than inclusion of only naval ships operated by the central Government. Thus "Confederate Forces Afloat" considers a wide range of militarily employed craft and ships, whether under Navy, Army, Confederate States Government, or State government control.

In categorizing these forces the editors do not try to impose a system of nomenclature which the Confederates themselves did not employ; classification was arbitrary with them and had not yet crystallized into hard and fast rule. The important thing is that the ships here included were all part of the struggle of the South—all "Public Vessels" and justly called "Confederate Forces Afloat." In this struggle the efforts of each element demonstrated a keen realization by certain southern leaders of the vital import of effective offensive and defensive measures on the high seas, in coastal waters and inland rivers—but leaders as a group never fully realized the tremendous importance that control of the sea and inland waters played in the ultimate destiny of the South.

Along with the histories of over 500 ships of the Confederate forces, this section contains four annexes which provide the reader with additional information. In the case of the River Defense Fleet (Annex II), the Texas Marine Department (Annex III), and some Confederate privateers (Annex I), histories of the ships listed in these annexes are included in the body of the section. In the case of some Confederate privateers (Annex I) and "Stone Fleet" ships (Annex IV), histories are not included in the body of the section. The reader, therefore, not finding a ship listed in the alphabetical section, should also consult Annex I and Annex IV for its listing there. Ships' histories appearing in the body of the work are cross-referenced to an appropriate annex.

No listing of Confederate ships prepared in the mid-twentieth century can be considered definitive; and necessarily, the histories of many remain incomplete statistically and operationally. Frequently, exhaustive research produced the most meager returns, or at best conflicting data. It has been difficult to find data that can be totally relied upon, especially when it comes to type, size, number of guns, extent and thickness of armor, speed, tonnage, and complement. Conscientious effort was made to consult primary sources, an endeavor which was persistently complicated by the destruction of many Confederate records, the dispersal of others among museums, private individuals, and historical societies of the land, and the conflict among those still extant and accessible. It is hoped that readers who hold authentic pertinent documents will send us copies to insure historical accuracy and completeness in a future revision.

In considering the statistics included with these Confederate ships' histories, the reader should remember that they often changed, sometimes radically, during a ship's lifetime. When ships were taken over, and frequently renamed, they were often altered and fitted for war with generous additions of metal, wood, or cotton. The addition of a ram, for example, increased a ship's offensive capability. These same materials were also used to increase a ship's defenses by protection of vital parts and spaces. Armament was often added or changed.

Lengths are not uniform and cannot be assumed to be "overall" rather than "between perpendiculars" or "water-line length." Neither can anyone give assurance in all cases that "extreme beam" (including paddle-box of a sidewheeler) is shown. Depths and drafts vary beyond recognition.

"Tonnage" is the most vexatious set of concepts the reader will ever encounter in dealing with ships of any period—but never more baffling than during the Civil War. It should be understood at the outset that the "t." is to be interpreted as an index figure rather than a known quantity, solely for identification, not in order to visualize size. Wherever known to be displacement, tonnage is shown by "dp" rather than "t."

Generally speaking today: Tonnage of the ship alone, without contents, is "light weight" or "light displacement"; her light plus "deadweight" (her cargo, stores, fuel, water, personnel, etc.) is "load displacement." No arbitrary yardstick such as "standard" or "normal displacement" can be readily applied to ships of mercantile origin except as an educated estimate by a specialist, even today.

If the picture now is legal science fiction, it was legal fiction merely in 1861–65. Conceive of the chaos implicit in five different systems of measuring "registered" tonnages (gross and net) obtaining at that time. A reader who wishes to understand the unbelievably confused principles of measuring such tonnages can do no better than to consult Dr. John Lyman's clear expositions of *Register Tonnage & its measurement* in *The American Neptune*, Vol. V (1945), pp. 223–34, 311–25. Suffice it to say that the figures given under "t" herein could be "carpenter's measurement," "builder's old measurement," "Thames measurement," tons according to New York, Philadelphia or New Orleans custom house rules; Moorsom system, which was made mandatory in the United States on 6 May 1864 and brought with it "net tonnage" alongside gross, after deduction or exemption of non-earning spaces. Army records sometimes specify "capacity," which is usually taken to mean the more modern deadweight, largely introduced by World War I, yet the colloquial term "tons burden" is by no means always an equivalent but may refer to the vexing gross register tons. But no one can be sure in what category a "tonnage" figure belongs at the time of the Civil War whether the ship be sail or steam, British or American, river, lake or oceanside-built. Even the expert must take it in faith believing for whatever it may be worth—an identification label usually, not a size tag.

In addition to the staff of the Naval History Division which labored long and diligently in preparing this compilation, several persons merit special recognition and thanks for their contributions. First among many, Mrs. Alma Lawrence worked before and subsequent to her retirement in 1959 from the Naval History Division to launch the project. She prepared the basic study of Confederate warships from which our expanded version, based on changed "rules of the road" has grown; the Navy Department and scholars who use this work will continue to be indebted to her for this latest of her many enduring contributions to the country in naval research. Valuable research assistance, recommendations, and review were rendered at various periods by Capt. Neville T. Kirk, USNR, of the Naval Academy faculty, Comdr. Alexander C. Brown, USNR, literary editor of the Newport News *Daily Press*, and Mr. William E. Geoghegan, Exhibit Specialist of the Division of Transportation, Smithsonian Institution; Mr. Geoghegan's many years of Confederate naval research, particularly into the design and construction methods of John L. Porter and the placement of contracts in foreign yards by Commander Bulloch, have been indispensable to this study. Mr. and Mrs. Edwin C. Bearss of Vicksburg, Miss., and Mr. Henry A. Meyer of Evansville, Ind., have helped with particulars of steamboats on the western rivers, while Prof. William N. Still of Mississippi State College for Women, Columbus, has kindly reviewed various points in the manuscript, and Mr. William H. Davis' painstaking Confederate compilations have been consulted frequently. Finally, Captain John Lyman, USNR, formerly of the National Science Foundation, and now of the Department of the Interior's Bureau of Commercial Fisheries; Mr. Thomas E. R. Stribling of NASA, and Lt. Comdr. Richard S. Pattee, USN, have been ever willing to keep our sights straight when asked technical questions beyond the scope of research possible in a study covering so many ships.

SOME MAJOR CLASSES AND TYPES OF THE CONFEDERATE STATES NAVY

Single-screw unless otherwise indicated; lengths between perpendiculars unless noted "O.A." (overall).

IRONCLAD GUNBOATS

150'; 4 guns; *Richmond* Type

Richmond (Gosport Navy Yard, Va.), *Raleigh* (J. L. Cassidy, Wilmington, N.C.), *North Carolina* (Berry & Sons, Wilmington), *Chicora* (James M. Eason, Charleston), *Palmetto State* (Cameron & Co., Charleston), *Savannah* (Henry F. Willink, Savannah): First and most numerous type. Designed by (Chief) Naval Constructor John L. Porter, CSN.

180'; 6 guns

Charleston: built by James M. Eason, Charleston, 1863 [Model extant in Naval Academy Collection at U.S. National Museum.]

180'; 4 guns

Virginia (No. 2): Built at Navy Yard, Richmond, from plan as altered in 1863. Plans (and perhaps construction) by Acting Naval Constructor William A. Graves, CSN.

180'; O.A.; 6 guns; Small *Charleston* Type

(No name yet confirmed). Similar to *Charleston* but length reduced. Drawing by Graves exists in the Willink Papers, Atlanta. [Whether keel ever laid is unknown.]

139'; 2 guns; twin-screw; *Albemarle* Type

Albemarle (Gilbert Elliott, Edwards Ferry [-on-Roanoke], N.C.), *Neuse* (Elliott, Smith & Co., Kinston [-on-Neuse], N.C.); several sisters destroyed before completion: J. L. Porter design, diamond-shaped hull. [Model in U.S. National Museum.]

139'; 4 guns; twin-screw; Heavy *Albemarle* Type

Huntsville, Tuscaloosa: Built at Navy Yard, Selma, Ala., by Henry D. Bassett. Type of *Albemarle* with 2 more guns in broadside: *Muscogee*, built by Lt. Augustus McLaughlin (Columbus, Ga.) Similar diamond-shaped construction; never completed.

170'; 4 guns; twin-screw; Enlarged *Albemarle* Type

Fredericksburg: Built at Navy Yard, Richmond. J. L. Porter design. [Model in U.S. National Museum.]

260'; 20 guns triple-screw

Mississippi: Simplified hull form conceived and produced by Nelson and Asa F. Tift, Jefferson City, La. Drawings by J. L. Porter, assisted by Joseph Pierce and E. M. Ivens.

204'; 4 guns

Atlanta: Hull of SS *Fingal* (James & George Thomson, Clyde Bank Iron Shipyard, Glasgow, 1861, for Hutcheson's W. Highland service). Converted into ironclad by Tift brothers; construction from bottom of knuckle up: similar to *Mississippi.*

264'; 20 guns; twin-screw and double center-wheels

Louisiana: Built by E. C. Murray, New Orleans. (Destroyed at New Orleans 28 April 1862, almost complete).

189'; 6 guns; single/twin-screw; *Columbia* Type

Columbia (single-screw; F. M. Jones J. M. Eason, Charleston); *Texas* (twin-screw), Navy Yard, Richmond (Casemates shortened from original plans because of scarcity of iron); *Tennessee* (No. 2) (single-screw with adapted sidewheel engines but casemate and arrangement of battery different), built by Henry Bassett, Selma, Ala., J. L. Porter design. [Model of *Tennessee* in U.S. National Museum.]

224'; 2 guns; double-casemate; twin-screw

Wilmington: Built at Wilmington, N.C.; designed by J. L. Porter, 1863. Machinery built at Columbus, Ga., naval works.

220'; 1 gun; short-casemate; quadruple-screw

(Names probably unassigned): Double-ended,

armored ram-gunboat; one building at Navy Yard, Richmond. Engines and boilers ordered in England for two of this type, Sept. 1864. (Designed for 27' beam, 11'6'' draft).

175'; 4 guns

Milledgeville: Built by Henry F. Willink, Savannah; unnamed sister begun by Krenson & Hawkes, Savannah; two more unfinished at Charleston (one or both launched but names unknown). J. L. Porter design; plan in Willink Collection, Emory University.

271'; O.A.; 7 guns (designed); sidewheel; *Nashville* Class

Nashville: Built at Montgomery; unnamed sister contracted 28 March 1863 by John T. Shirley & D. D. DeHaven at Selma, irreparably damaged in launching and sold for scrap April 1864. (*Nashville* was only new sidewheel ironclad, so designed from keel up, which saw actual service.)

310'; twin-screw and 4 sidewheels

(Name unknown): Built at Navy Yard, Yazoo City, Miss., to use sidewheel engines available; destroyed before completion, 21 May 1863. Construction supervised by Comdr. Isaac Newton Brown, CSN, to J. L. Porter's (?) design. 70' beam, designed speed: 16 k.

165'; 8 guns; twin-screw; *Arkansas* Type

Seagoing ironclad ram-gunboat: Built by John T. Shirley, Memphis; available information indicates *Arkansas* and *Tennessee* (No. 1) were intended to be of this type; completed for 10 guns. J. L. Porter design, 1862.

234'; 8 guns

Seagoing ironclad ram-gunboat; designed by J. L. Porter as combination war vessel-blockade runner ("to be built in England of iron"): George N. Sanders to finance 6 of these rams; contract approved 19 April 1862 by Confederate Congress but never consummated.

270'; 20 guns

Santa Maria or *Glasgow*, while building at James & George Thomsons, Clydebank (intended Confederate name unknown): Ironclad Frigate (No. 61), sold to Denmark, rechristened HDMS *Danmark.* [Selected and supervised by Commander James H. North, CSN, through undercover agents.]

224'; 4 guns; twin-turret; *North Carolina* Class

North Carolina (Laird Hull 294; later Khedivial *El Tousson;* ultimately HMS *Scorpion*), *Mississippi* (295; *El Mounassir*, HMS *Wivern*): Built at John Laird & Sons, Birkenhead, but seized by British Admiralty before delivery to Confederacy.

171'; 3 guns; twin-screw; *Stonewall* Class

Stonewall (ex-*Sphinx*, ex-*Staerkodder*, ex-*Olinde;* ultimately HIJMS *Azuma*), *Cheops* (Confederate name unassigned; ultimately Prussian Navy's *Prinz Adalbert*): Built by L. Arman, Bordeaux, "for the China trade" (secretly for Confederacy); contract voided by personal intervention of Emperor Napoleon III.

143'; 1 gun; twin-screw

Manassas (ex-*Enoch Train*): Converted at Algiers, La., to Capt. John A. Stevenson's design, 1861.

183'; 3 guns; centerwheel

Missouri: Built by Thomas Moore and John Smoker, Shreveport, La., 1863. Protection for wheel never completed.

WOODEN GUNBOATS

106' O.A.; 2 guns; twin-screw; *Hampton* Class

Hampton, Nansemond, Norfolk, Portsmouth: Built or building at Navy Yard, Gosport (Norfolk); several destroyed before naming or completion (*e.g.,* at Ollinger & Bruce and F. G. Howard in Pensacola Bay; Gilbert Elliott, Edwards Ferry and Elizabeth City, N.C.); 100 of these "Maury Gunboats" were planned at various yards. (*Norfolk* and *Portsmouth* had to be burned on stocks.) Government to provide engines.

150' O.A.; 5-6 guns; twin-screw; *Chattahoochee* Class

Chattahoochee (Navy Yard, Saffold, Early County, S.W. Ga.), *Peedee* (E. J. Means at Peedee Navy Yard, Mars Bluff, S.C.), *Macon* (ex-*Ogeechee;* H. F. Willink, Savannah). J. L. Porter design. (Another contracted at $50 per ton (carpenter's meas.), 22 October 1861) to use steamer *Empire's* engines: Gilbert Elliott as agent for J. G. Martin and Flag Officer W. F. Lynch, signatories, on board *Sea Bird;* ship apparently burned when Elizabeth City was evacuated.

196'; 8 guns; sidewheel; *Morgan* Class

Morgan, Gaines: Built by Bassett & Oates, Mobile. Alabama area Flag Officer, V. M. Randolph, CSN, stopped further wooden construction of this type in favor of an ironclad-only policy.

5 guns; sidewheel; *Bienville* Class

Bienville, Carondelet: Built by John Hughes & Co., Bayou St. John, La., under Acting Constructor Sidney D. Porter's supervision, 1862.

TORPEDO LAUNCHES

46'; spar torpedo; *Squib Class;* b. 6'3''; dph. 6'9''

Squib, Hornet, Scorpion, Wasp: Wooden hulls built and fitted out at Richmond, late 1864. Engines also fabricated in Confederacy, apparently: condensing engine comprising twin oscillating cylinders (7''-dia., 6''-stroke) and driving a 4-bladed propeller; 1 tubular boiler. *Note:* Improvement over Cushing's *Launch No. 1* in that both spar torpedo operator and boiler were not exposed, although Secretary Mallory thought the Federal spar more maneuverable and versatile (questionable that it was, actually).

40' 50'; 1 or 2 light howitzers, spar torpedo; b. 5' to 6'; dr. 3'

(Names unassigned): 12 wooden hulls reported building by end 1864: 4 at Richmond (2 completed), 1 each at Peedee River Bridge, S.C., and Columbus, Ga., 6 at unidentified yards in Confederacy. *Engines:* 12 ordered 16 April 1864 from Clyde Bank Iron Foundry (Thomsons) and all forwarded by Bulloch in 3 blockade runners from Glasgow circa September 1864 to save transshipment at British Islands—whether delivered is not known. Of direct-acting, condensing type, 2-cylinder (10''-dia., 10''-stroke), connecting at right angles to 20', 3''-dia. shaft, driving 3'-dia., 3-bladed wheel, with 6'-pitch, at 200 rpm. *Boiler:* Locomotive, tubular type, not over 10' long by 3'6'' high by 3'6'' wide; fire-door on starboard side (sic!); 4 pair also ordered by Lt. William Fitzhugh Carter, CSN, 27 June 1864, delivery in two months. [To SecNav Welles, 22 Feb. '65: "Paroled prisoners report that 6 large launches, each armed with a 12-pounder and manned by a crew of 15 men, have been sent from Mobile to the Yazoo River * * *"]

dp. 9.18 on less than 3' draft; [loaded for action]; spar torpedo; [40# to 100# powder]; cpl. 5; s. 10 k.

(No names): 6 iron boats, light as possible, ordered in U.K., 18 June 1864, by Bulloch to Graves' design, with stem strengthened and rake of stern changed to fit iron construction; completed January or February 1865—very light steel hull, sectionalized for shipment to Confederacy.

Engines: Too heavy due to Engr.-in-Chief William P. Williamson's careless drawings without descriptive back-up (8'' instead of 7''-dia. cylinders shown). *Boiler:* Too small and space for firing it much too cramped. Wilmington was closed in mid-January 1865, so there is little probability these ever arrived. (Second trio were to have longer floors to accommodate larger boilers, but draft of boats unaltered.)

60'; twin-screw; b. 12'; dph. 7'; spar torpedo

"Semi-submersibles" with bizarre bow form criticized by Bulloch—drawings by Lt. Joseph Fry, CSN. (6 discussed with J. & W. Dudgeon, Millwall, in late 1864, but order never confirmed)—"The plan admits of immersing the vessel to nearly her decks and of elevating her by the rapid admission and exclusion of water." (Mallory also empowered Bulloch, 21 Nov. 1864, to use his own judgment and "order the construction of six torpedo boats of the best plan you can devise, in addition to other orders, and send them to us at once").

1 gun; spar torpedo

"In designing the six steam launches for picket and general service, alluded to in your dispatch of November 17, 1864, I will consult with Mr. [Michael] Quinn, and will endeavor to arrange them so as not only to carry a gun when necessary, but to be capable of use as torpedo boats."—Bulloch to Mallory, 26 Jan. 1865.

CRUISERS AND COMMERCE RAIDERS
Built or Bought Abroad

191'; 8 guns

Florida (ex-*Manassas*, ex-*Oreto*): Built by William C. Miller & Sons, Liverpool, 1861; engined by Fawcett, Preston & Co., Liverpool. [Model in U.S. National Museum.]

214'; 8 guns

Alabama (ex-*Enrica*): Laird Hull 290, Birkenhead (Liverpool).

230'

Texas (known as *Pampero* or *Canton* in yard): Built by James & George Thomson, Clydebank (Glasgow); seized by British Government. (*Texas* [inf.], perhaps from same plans, modified.)

200'; 5 guns

Rappahannock (ex-HMS *Victor*): Thames-built. [*Georgia*'s battery was to have been transferred to her.]

200′; 5 guns

Georgia (ex-*Japan*): Built by William Denny & Bros., Dumbarton.

t. 280

Alexandra: Built by William C. Miller & Sons, Liverpool. "Tonnage: 280"; no other dimensions available. Became blockade runner *Mary*.

223′; 8 guns

Shenandoah (ex-*Sea King*): Built by Alexander Stephen & Sons, Kelvinhaugh, Glasgow, Hull No. 42, completed 1863 for Robertson & Co., Glasgow. Composite (iron/teak) hull; lifting screw propeller and collapsible funnel.

205′; pierced for 14 guns

Georgiana: Completed in Glasgow, December 1862 by Lawrie (subcontract from Laird?); iron hull, coppered bottom. Wrecked off Charleston, S.C., 19 March 1863.

200′; 5 guns; twin-screw

Tallahassee (ex-*Atalanta*): Built by J. & W. Dudgeon, Cubitt Town, Millwall, for London, Chatham & Dover Rly. Co. (Calais ferry). Became cruiser *Olustee*, then blockade runner *Chameleon*.

?; 3 guns

Chickamauga (ex-*Edith*): "Tonnage: 585"; no other dimensions available.

170′; 2 guns; twin-screw; *Ajax* Class

Ajax (intended ultimately to be *Olustee*), *Hercules* (to become *Vicksburg*): Built by Denny, Dumbarton; to be converted into gunboats by minor alterations at Wilmington, N.C.; temporary names picked by Cdr. Bulloch for security reasons—common names for British registry and running blockade; ultimate names assigned by Secretary Mallory. (Ships completed too late for Confederate use.) [Cost £117,500 each, complete except for coal and stores; contract dated 16 September 1864.]

250′; ? guns; twin-screw; *Enterprise* Class

Enterprise (ultimately *Black Warrior*), *Adventure* (to become *Waccamaw*): Designed for conversion to cruisers after running blockade. Built somewhere in the United Kingdom (ordered disposed of, 1 March 1865, in favor of "light-draft, handy vessels").

220′; 12 guns; *Louisiana* Class

Louisiana (ex-*Osacca;* later: Prussian *Victoria*), *Mississippi* (ex-*Yeddo;* Prussian *Augusta*), *Texas*

(ex-*San Francisco;* ultimately: Peruvian Navy's *Union*); *Georgia* (ex-*Shanghai;* became Peruvian *America*).

SIDEWHEEL BLOCKADE RUNNERS

Steel or Iron-Hulled, Built Abroad

(For CSN account; operation with CSN commanders and pilots; carrying C.S. Treasury Dept. cargo under CSA Ordnance management and cloak of British, commercial registry.*)

230′; *Owl* Class; 2 stacks; steel hull

Owl, Bat, Stag, Deer: Jones, Quiggin & Co., Liverpool, Hulls 167–170, "bought on the stocks too far advanced to be modified in any material way but are good ships"—Bulloch to Mallory, 15 Sept. 1864; 800 to 850-bale capacity on 7′6″ draft.

225′; *Curlew* Class

Curlew, Plover, Widgeon, Snipe: Jones, Quiggin Hulls 177–180, all launched same day, 1865; 700 to 800-bale capacity on 6′ draft; 180 nominal h.p.

* There was always the dilemma of presenting different faces on opposite sides of the water—toward the blockading squadron on this side and the British and colonials on the other. Policy governing ships of this category had to be directed toward achieving two essential but opposite objectives: 1) to camouflage transports of war as peaceful merchantmen in British ports and yet 2) to insure captured Confederate seamen the immunities of prisoners-of-war as CS Navy officers or ratings—instead of hanging as "pirates."

Prior to the impact of the *Cornubia* (q.v.) papers in 1863, foreign nationals, seamen or passengers, taken prisoner in blockade runners were released after interrogation, upon taking oath as bona fide aliens. Endorsing 11 January 1864 letter of transmittal of correspondence captured in *Cornubia*, Secretary Welles set in motion new policy: "British blockade violaters will be henceforth detained, and not released, etc. Any orders inconsistent herewith countermanded."

As for the other jaw of the pincers, Colonel Josiah Gorgas, Chief of Ordnance, CSA, promulgated a standing order, copy to *Cornubia's* captain thus: "You are requested when in foreign ports to carefully guard against all acts tending in any manner to cause issuance of orders by the authorities curtailing the facilities and privileges our vessels now enjoy. Your conduct should be such as to leave the impression that your steamer does not belong to the Government, but is simply used by it as a carrier.

Shifting of cargo procurement and control to the Treasury is explained in part by Secretary Mallory to Bulloch, 16 December 1864: "The trade regulations adopted by the Government provide, as you have been advised, that all shipments of cotton on public account shall be made by the Treasury. No more, therefore, will be shipped by this Department [Navy], but funds will be provided for your operations and to fill orders of the Department in sterling exchange."

240'; *Albatross* Class; Steel, iron-bottomed

Albatross, Penguin: Lairds, Birkenhead, Hulls 319–320; 1,000-bale capacity on 9' draft; 150 tons additional cargo on 10'. ("Framed and plated from light loadline up with steel, bottoms plated with iron"—Bulloch-Mallory, 15 Sept. 1864.)

260'; *Rosina* Class

Rosina, Ruby: Jones, Quiggin Hulls 174–175; 1,500-bale capacity on 9' draft.

210'; *Lark* Class; 2 stacks

Lark, Wren: Lairds, Birkenhead, Hulls 317–318; 650 to 750-bale capacity on 6' draft for Texas and Florida shoal waters.

270'; *Condor* Class; 3 raked stacks; iron hull

Condor, Flamingo, Falcon, Ptarmigan: Built in Scotland (perhaps in Greenock?): 1,000-bale capacity on 7' draft.

LIST OF SHIPS

A. B. Seger

SwStr: t. 30; l. 55'; a. 2 guns

A. B. Seger, also referred to as *Seger, Segar,* and *Segur,* was acquired by the Confederate States Navy in 1861 for service as a gunboat in Berwick Bay, La. The steamer operated with the naval force of Flag Officer G. N. Hollins, CSN, who was charged with the defense of the Mississippi River and Louisiana coast.

The little gunboat was powered by two locomotive engines with "cylinders bolted to the top of and axis parallel to" her boiler—also from a railroad locomotive.

During 1862 *A. B. Seger* served as a dispatch boat, commanded by Acting Master I. C. Coons. As the Federal flotilla under Lt. Comdr. Buchanan proceeded up Atchafalaya Bay on 1 November 1862, *A. B. Seger* was run aground and abandoned near Berwick Bay. She was then seized and placed in service by the Union.

A. C. Gunnison, see Gunnison

A. D. Vance

SwStr:

A. D. Vance, often written *Advance,* was the former Clyde packet *Lord Clyde,* built by Caird & Co., Greenock. She was owned in large part by the State of North Carolina and named in honor of a leading North Carolinian; some portion of her ownership rested in Power, Lord & Co.—a Fayetteville newspaper once stated two-thirds—but she was locally considered a public vessel.

A. D. Vance was one of the most successful blockade runners and her loss, after more than 20 voyages and 40-odd hairbreadth escapes, was a blow keenly felt by the State. Gov. Zebulon B. Vance attributed her capture, 10 September 1864, to the use of low grade North Carolina bituminous coal and denounced Secretary Mallory for giving the stockpile of smokeless anthracite to *Tallahassee* so that none was left for *Advance* to run out of Wilmington safely: Writing 3 January 1865, Vance complained, "Why a State struggling for the common good, to clothe and provide for its troops in the public service, should meet with no more favor than a blockade gambler passes my comprehension."

She was commanded by Capt. Tom Crossan when taken by USS *Santiago de Cuba,* becoming USS *Advance* and eventually *Frolic.* Lt. John J. Guthrie, CSN, commander of *Chattahoochee* at the time of her disaster, was her earlier captain.

A. H. Schultz, see Schultz

A. S. Ruthven

(SwStr: t. 144; l. 127'; b. 30'; dph. 4'8")

A. S. Ruthven was privately built at Cincinnati, Ohio, in 1860. By October 1863 she had been chartered for operation with the Texas Marine Department [See Annex III] under the Superintendent of Transports, J. H. Sterrett, and was operating effectively, one of six such shallow draft steamers in Galveston Bay. On 23 August 1864 she was under the control of the Quartermaster Department, running on Galveston Bay and tributaries, carrying guns, stores and personnel.

Records of the Commerce Department show that she was lost in 1869.

A. W. Baker

(SwStr: t. 112; l. 95'; b. 25'; dph. 4'6")

A. W. Baker was built in 1856 at Louisville, Ky., and served the Confederates as a cargo ship carrying salt and bacon from the Red River to Port Hudson, La., to supply the Confederate Army in that area. With a number of Confederate officers on board, *A. W. Baker* was approached 15 miles below the mouth of the Red River on 2 February 1863 by the Federal ram *Queen of the West* under Col. C. R. Ellet, USA. *A. W. Baker* ran ashore allowing some of the officers to escape but was herself captured by the Union ram and burned by her captors.

Acacia

(Str)

Acacia was a Confederate transport captured by Union Army forces under Col. G. N. Fitch near Memphis, Tenn., in early June 1862. Union records report her sunk in August 1862.

Adkin, see *Yadkin*

Admiral

(SwStr)

Admiral, a small steamer, was employed as a picket boat in the Mississippi River in the vicinity of New Madrid, Mo. She was captured by Flag Officer Foote's naval forces on 7 April 1862. Valued at $10,000 she was taken into the Union Army.

Admiral, see *Morgan*

Advance, see *A. D. Vance*

Adventure

(ScStr: t. 972; l. 250′; b. 28′; dph. 15′6″; cl. *Enterprise*)

Adventure and *Enterprise* were the larger pair of vessels which Confederate oversea agent James D. Bulloch, CSN, writing from Liverpool, 15 November 1864, reported to Secretary Mallory as "* * * the four steamers I am now building for the Navy Department specially, which are progressing very favorably." Having run the blockade into a Confederate port, they were quickly to become cruisers "fully able to repeat the operations of the *Tallahassee*." Mallory told Bulloch to choose any common name for her to run the blockade; her permanent name was to be *Waccamaw*.

But, "upon the eve of events fraught with the fate of the Confederacy," Mallory was forced to advise Bulloch, 1 March 1865: "You will have to dispose of the other two steamers as best you can for the public interests, and send us two light-draft, handy vessels instead of them * * * With light-draft vessels we could at once place cotton abroad."

They were to be iron hulls, twin-screw, and each to be driven by two pairs of 130-hp. disconnected engines. [cf. *Ajax* and *Hercules, infra.*]

Agrippina

(Bark: t. 285; l. 97′; b. 24′4″; dph. 16′5″)

Agrippina was a British bark built at Scarborough by the Tindall yard in 1834 and engaged in the Mediterranean trade when bought or chartered secretly by the Confederacy in 1862; she acted as the first and principal tender to the raider *Alabama* throughout her meteoric career. One distinguishing mark recorded of her is hull painted "black with a yellow bead along the sides."

Orders of 28 July 1862 written by Commander Bulloch and signed by the ostensible "owner," Mr. A. Hamilton, St. Helen's Place, London, told British Capt. Alexander McQueen—whom the U.S. Consul dubbed "a most active rebel agent"—to proceed to Praya, Island of Terceira in the Azores and await the *Enrica (Alabama)*, which he should recognize when she should "stop a white English ensign to the after shroud of the main rigging * * * you will answer with your number, after which you can communicate freely." Captain McQueen was told that Capt. Matthew S. Butcher (master until relieved by Semmes at Praya) would give him written orders thereafter but, "You are to consider all orders from the commander of the steamer [*Alabama*] as authorized by us, with or without any other letter of advice."

Later *Agrippina* coaled and rearmed *Alabama* at uninhabited Blanquilla Island in the Caribbean, at Praya again in mid-January 1864, and elsewhere, while Federal cruisers searched in her wake all over the Caribbean and South Atlantic. Once in May-June 1863 USS *Mohican* and *Onward* cornered both *Agrippina* and *Castor (Georgia's* tender) in Bahia and stayed there in Brazilian waters until their presence forced the two barks to sell their coal and gunpowder in consideration of a clearance from the port; *Agrippina* loaded "pecava" and rosewood for London, thus being unable to meet Semmes at the Cape of Good Hope as ordered.

Aid

(Sch)

Aid, a schooner of Mobile, Ala., was captured by a boat expedition from USS *Niagara* off Mobile on 5 June 1861. She was sunk by Union forces to obstruct the pass at the east end of Santa Rosa Island in August 1861.

(Str: a. 1 42-pdr.)

Aid, bought by private individuals in 1861 for the express purpose of driving off the Union blockading ships in defense of Charleston, often carried the British Consul out of Charleston Harbor to visit British ships over the bar. In addition to her crew of six or eight, she was reported to carry out Charleston pilots who would gather information vital to ships interested in running the blockade of that port. In November 1862 it was reported that her engines like those of *Lady Davis* had been removed to power the ironclad rams *Palmetto State* and *Chicora*.

Aiken, William, see Petrel

Ajax

(ScStr: t. 515; l. 170′; b. 25′; dph. 12′6″; dr. 7′6″; s. 12 k.; a. des. for 1 9″ r., 1 8″ r.)

Ajax and her sister, *Hercules*, were twin-screw, iron gunboats built under contract of 14 September 1864 with an old-line Scottish yard, William Denny & Brothers, Dumbarton, for £17,500. "Designed as towboats to deceive Federal spies," they were the smaller pair ordered with *Adventure* (q.v.) and *Enterprise*, powered by "two pair of 120-horsepower collective" engines. Secretary of the Navy Mallory said they would "require insignificant alterations to convert them into serviceable gunboats for local work."—merely "fill up the space between the beams and add a few permanent stanchions under the permanent position of the guns."

Mallory wrote Commander Bulloch at Liverpool, 30 July 1864: "We require for the port of Wilmington two small steamers with low-pressure engines for service in and about the harbor. Their draft should not exceed . . . 7 feet 6 inches, and it would be well if they could have at least 18 inches or 2 feet drag, so that they might be tipped by the head when they get ashore. With this light draft and pressure, two screws would be necessary to give them high speed.

"It is proposed to place upon them a single-pivot gun, weighing about 5 tons, on a circle, and the arrangements for quarters, etc., should be designed accordingly . . . [or] a pivot gun forward and aft . . . at least one large-shell gun, say a IX-inch pivot. . . . They should be small, snug, strong, fast, and handy vessels for quick working with light crews . . . dimensions and details are left to your judgement. Four com-

mission and six warrant officers would probably be required for each."

Bulloch reporting the contract signing to Mallory, 16 September, revealed: "They will be very strongly built, with heavy decks and beams, so as to carry a gun at each end, of from 5 to 6 tons weight, and the internal and deck arrangements will be such as to suit them for gun vessels, and yet not to excite suspicion. They will be designed for a speed of 12 knots on a draft of 7 feet 6 inches aft, but can be loaded to 8 feet 6 inches with safety as seagoing boats . . . one [*Ajax*] to be delivered on January 1, 1865, and the other [*Hercules*] 6 weeks later." Mallory wished her to be *Olustee* ultimately.

A Briton, Captain Adams, was in command, representing "Mr. Denny, the ostensible owner," in order to hold *Ajax'* mercantile register, but Lt. John Low, CSN, went along as "supercargo" and actual commander, under orders to take over officially at Nassau. *Ajax* slipped out of the Clyde 12 January 1865 for the Bahamas via Madeira, but apparently the shadows of impending Confederate defeat deterred her; finis is written in Mallory to Bulloch, 1 March 1865: "A notice of the arrival of the *Ajax* at a port in Ireland has reached me through the United States papers, but no further advices as to her or the *Hercules* or other vessels have come to hand."

Alabama

(ScBark: t. 1,050; l. 220′; b. 31′8″; dph. 17′8″; dr. 14′; s. 13 k.; cpl. 145; a. 6 32-pdrs., 1 110-pdr., 1 68-pdr.)

CSS *Alabama* was a screw sloop-of-war built at Lairds dockyard, Liverpool, England, in 1862 for the Confederacy. The famous Hull "290" was launched under the name *Enrica*, put to sea from Liverpool on 29 July 1862 and proceeded to Porto Praya in the Azores where Captain R. Semmes, CSN, and her other officers boarded and fitted her out as a cruiser. She was commissioned at sea off Terceira, Azores on 24 August as the Confederate cruiser *Alabama*.

Semmes spent the next 2 months in the North Atlantic where he captured and burned some 20 ships, including a dozen whalers. From there he departed for the Newfoundland Banks to intercept American grain ships bound for Europe, and thence to the West Indies and the coast of Texas where he sank *Hatteras* and captured her crew. Cruising along the coast of Brazil, he used the desolate island of Fernando de Noronha as a base. Shrewdly calculating the length of time necessary for word of his deeds to reach the United States Government, Semmes next put in at Cape Town and sailed for the East Indies where he spent 6 months and destroyed 7 ships before redoubling the Cape en route to Europe. Arriving at Cherbourg, France, on 11 June 1864, he hoped to be allowed to dock and overhaul his ship.

As Semmes awaited permission from French authorities, *Kearsarge*, Capt. J. A. Winslow commanding, arrived at Cherbourg, brought there by word of *Alabama's* presence. *Kearsarge* took up a patrol at the harbor's entrance awaiting Semmes' next move. *Alabama's* log for 15 June 1864 tells succinctly of her skipper's decision:

"The admiral sent off his aid-de-camp to say to me that he considered my application for repairs withdrawn upon making application for coal, to which I assented. We commenced coaling this afternoon. The *Kearsarge* is still in the offing. She has not been permitted to receive on board the prisoners landed by me, to which I had objected in a letter to the admiral. Mailed a note yesterday afternoon for Flag-Officer Barron, informing him of my intention to go out to engage the enemy as soon as I could make my preparations, and sent a written notice to the U.S. consul, through Mr. Bonfils, to the same effect. My crew seem to be in the right spirit, a quiet spirit of determination pervading both officers and men. The combat will no doubt be contested and obstinate, but the two ships are so equally matched that I do not feel at liberty to decline it. God defend the right, and have mercy upon the souls of those who fall, as many of us must. Barometer low, and weather unusually cold and blustering for the middle of June."

On 19 June 1864, *Alabama* stood out of Cherbourg Harbor for her last action. Careful of French neutrality, Winslow took *Kearsarge* well clear of territorial waters, then turned to meet the Confederate cruiser. *Alabama* opened fire first while *Kearsarge* held her reply until the range had closed to less than 1,000 yards. Steaming on opposite courses the ships moved around a circle as each commander tried to cross the bows of his opponent to deliver deadly raking fire. The battle quickly turned against *Alabama*, for the quality of her long stored powder and shells had deteriorated while *Kearsarge* had been given added protection by chain cable triced in tiers along her sides abreast vital spaces. One hour after she

The war's most famous raider, Captain Raphael Semmes, on board C.S.S. Alabama *at Capetown.*

loosed her first salvo *Alabama* had been reduced to a sinking wreck. Semmes struck his colors and sent a boat to *Kearsarge* with a message of surrender and an appeal for help. *Kearsarge* rescued the majority of *Alabama's* survivors, but Semmes and 41 others were picked up by the British yacht *Deerhound* and escaped in her to England.

In her 21-month cruise to the four corners of the globe, *Alabama* wrought havoc among United States merchant shipping, taking more than 60 prizes valued at nearly $6,000,000. The most famous of the Confederate cruisers, her very existence caused the Federal Navy Department to divert warships from the blockade to intercepting positions at focal points on the world's trade routes. Northern shipowners were compelled to delay sailings, to pay increased maritime insurance premiums and, in many cases, to transfer ships to foreign registry. *Alabama's* exploits buoyed the morale of the South during some of its darkest days, and wrote a chapter of daring in the brief history of the Confederate States Navy. [cf. also *Texas* (#4), inf.]

———

Alabama, see under *James Battle*

Alabama, see *Florida*

Alamo

(Str)

Alamo was employed during the course of the war primarily as a government transport to move troops and supplies on the Arkansas River between Little Rock and Van Buren, Ark. During the summer of 1863 she operated briefly in the area of Matagorda Bay in connection with the Texas Marine Department [See Annex III].

Alar

(SwStr: t. 150 [86]; l. 134'; b. 17'; dph. 9'3")

Alar was an iron steamer believed to have been acquired by the Confederacy by purchase or charter through the Fraser, Trenholm secret channel as a tender to CSS *Georgia*. Welsh built about 1847 at Neath in Glamorganshire, her bottom appears to have been coppered a decade later. She is listed under a Capt. J. Black in 1863, sailing out of London, nominal owner an "H. Maples."

Albatross

(SwStr: t. 1,063; l. 240'; b. 30'; dph. 13'; dr. 10'; cl. *Albatross*)

Albatross was the first of a pair of fast (260 nominal h.p.) ships designed for the Confederate Navy to the order of Fraser, Trenholm & Co., Liverpool, and negotiated by Comdr. James D. Bulloch, CSN. Ordered in the well known Birkenhead yard, she was built as Lairds Hull No. 319 early in 1865, but it is unlikely that she was delivered in time to serve the Confederacy. Later she was sold to an Admiral Grenfell, RN, and was renamed *Isabel*.

Albemarle

(StwStr: t. 183)

Albemarle was built in 1855 at Wheeling, Va. She served the Confederates as a cargo ship and transport off Hatteras Inlet and New Bern, N.C. *Albemarle* was captured on 15 March 1862 off New Berne by USS *Delaware*. Federals employed her in the same area but on 5 April, while transporting wounded servicemen, she accidentally ran on the piles in New Berne harbor and sank immediately. Being hopelessly damaged, *Albemarle's* destruction was ordered by Lt. A. Murray, USN, commanding USS *Louisiana*.

———

(IrcRam: l. 152', 139 b.p.; b. 34'; dr. 9'; a. 2 6.4" r.; type *Albemarle*)

CSS *Albemarle* was built in the Roanoke River at Edwards Ferry, N.C., in 1863–64 under supervision of Comdr. J. W. Cooke, CSN, who became her first commanding officer. She was commissioned on 17 April 1864 and 2 days later played the leading role in an attack on the Union forces at Plymouth, N.C., during which *Southfield* was rammed and sunk, and *Miami*, *Ceres*, and *Whitehead* were forced to withdraw. The following day Plymouth surrendered to the Confederate forces.

On 5 May *Albemarle*, accompanied by CSS *Bombshell*, former United States Army transport, attacked a Federal squadron below Plymouth during which *Bombshell* was captured, but *Albemarle* received only damage to one gun and several hits on her smokestack which seriously reduced her speed. She was taken up the Roanoke River

C.S.S. Albemarle.

for repairs; before their completion, however, she was torpedoed and sunk by Lt. W. B. Cushing, USN, whose daring crew of 14 officers and men sailed an improvised torpedo boat in the night exploit of 27–28 October 1864.

Albemarle was raised after the Union forces captured Plymouth. Following the end of hostilities, she was towed to Norfolk Navy Yard by USS *Ceres*, arrived there on 27 April 1865, was condemned as a prize, and purchased by the Navy who sold her in October 1867.

Alena

(Slp)

Alena, a small sloop used to transport Confederate troops from Maryland across to Virginia, was seized in June 1861 in the Pamunkey River by Union forces in the steamer *Mount Vernon* under Lt. J. M. Prichett, USN. She was then towed to the Navy Yard for Federal service.

Alert

(Sch: cpl. 31; a. 1 32-pdr.)

Alert was a lighthouse tender seized by State authorities at Mobile, Ala., in 1861. During 1861–62 she served under Acting Master A. Pacetty, CSN, on the Mobile Station then commanded by Flag Officer V. Randolph, CSN.

Alexandra

(ScStr: t. 280)

Alexandra, a prospective cruiser, was a bark-rigged, very strong, wooden steamer with "rakish masts, round stern, very straight stem." Built in the United Kingdom by William C. Miller & Sons, Liverpool, to the order of Charles K. Prioleau of Fraser, Trenholm & Co., the Liverpool firm with Charleston roots whose partner, George A. Trenholm, was the able Confederate Secretary of the Treasury, *Alexandra* was built through the agency of Fawcett, Preston & Co. She quickly became a *cause célèbre* in testing British policy toward Confederate building in British shipyards to fight the United States at sea.

Alexandra was intended to be a gift from the Trenholm firm to the Confederacy. Commander Bulloch to Secretary Mallory, 30 June 1863, explains: "The gunboat presented to the Confederate Government by Messrs. Fraser, Trenholm & Co. happend to be launched on the day [7 March 1863] the present Princess of Wales entered London, and in compliment or in commemoration

of that event, was named *Alexandra* . . . while the *Alexandra* was fitting in the Toxtetle dock, the customs officer of this port seized her in obedience to orders from London" on 5 April under the "Foreign Enlistment Act." Bulloch continues bitterly," * * * such was the apparent haste of the British authorities to carry out the wishes of the American minister that the seizure was effected on Sunday. The *Alexandra* . . . was still the actual property of the contractors, Messrs. Fawcett, Preston & Co. * * * but the British authorities showed a further disposition to favor the United States through its officials here by causing the ship to be 'exchequered,' a proceeding by which there would be indefinite delay in obtaining the release of the ship, even if she should not be condemned, and by which the Government, even though it failed to prove its case, would debar the defendants from any right or claim for damages or costs. The trial resulted in favor of the defendants . . . but this ship is still held pending the issue of the attorney-general's 'bill of exceptions,' which cannot be argued until November." Meanwhile the Russians had made overtures to buy her at a bargain from Comdr. James H. North, CSN, in Britain. That the Confederacy still had friends in high places is shown by North to Mallory, 3 July: "Judging from the speech of Sir Hugh Cairns and the charge of the Lord Chief Baron to the jury, anyone has a right to buy arms and build ships." Litigation dragged on while all Confederate shipbuilding in Britain marked time awaiting the decision. Agents such as Bulloch, North et al. shifted their sights increasingly to France not only as a source of ships but of new "owners" and "fences" for the hulls building in Britain "as a probable and very plausible means of security." *Alexandra* was not released for a full year; by May 1864 seizure of the Laird rams the previous October was ancient history and a scapegoat had been discovered in Clarence R. Yonge, a deserter from CSS *Alabama* who had turned informer. The new political climate must have ended hope of using *Alexandra* as a commerce destroyer. In the meantime, she had become *Mary* of Liverpool, ostensibly a peaceful merchant vessel owned by Henry Lafone, another secret agent of the Confederacy. U.S. Consul Thomas H. Dudley, not deceived, reported to London, 10 July: "*Alexandra* has had her insides taken out and houses put up on her decks and has sailed." He thought she would be armed in Bermuda or Nassau, but there is no evidence she ever was. Consul M. M. Jackson at Halifax telegraphed Secretary Seward, 9 September: "Steamer *Mary*, formerly *Alexandra* . . . is now at Liverpool, Nova Scotia, and carries, as is reported, 4 guns." She had arrived that night in ballast from Bermuda with a crew of 24. The U.S. Consul in Nassau on 16 November remarked she was a "very slow boat," 8 days Hailfax-Nassau. But her slow passage did not deter the United States from arranging to have her libeled at Nassau, 13 December 1864, and *Mary* was not released again until after war's end, 30 May 1865.

Alfred Robb

(StwStr: t. 79; l. 114'9"; b. 20'; dph. 4'; s. 9 k.)

Alfred Robb, built at Pittsburgh, Pa., in 1860, was used by the Confederates as a transport on the upper Tennessee River. She was captured 19 April 1862, at Florence, Ala., by USS *Tyler*, a unit of Lt. W. Gwin's division of gunboats. Her fine condition prompted the Union leaders to arm her with a howitzer from USS *Lexington* and, after conversion and commissioning as USS *Alfred Robb* to use her in transporting goods and patrolling on the Tennessee River. She briefly carried the name *Lady Foote*, but instruction from Flag Officer A. H. Foote restored the original name. She was also referred to frequently as *Robb* in later Union correspondence.

Alice, see Matagorda

Alice Vivian, see under James Battle

Alliance

(Sch)

Alliance, D. Ireland, master, was boarded at Eastville, Va., on the night of 19 September 1863 by a party of 25 Confederate guerrillas under Acting Master J. Y. Beall, C.S. Navy. Loaded with valuable military stores and provisions, she was used to capture schooner *J. J. Houseman* on 21 September, as well as the schooners *Samuel Pearsall* and *Alexandria* on the 22d. The helms of the three prizes were lashed by the Confederate raiders who started them over the bar at Wachapreague Inlet, Va.

On 23 September 1863, *Alliance* was discovered in Old Haven Creek by the Union ships of the Potomac Flotilla. Taken under fire, she was run ashore where some 30 or more small boats became busily employed in removing her cargo.

USS *Freeborn* fired three shells in an effort to scatter the boats but could not land an armed party to stop the proceedings because of a heavy sea. The Richmond *Globe* reported cargo valued at approximately $10,000 was saved by the small boats before *Alliance* was burned at Milford Haven in the Chesapeake Bay to prevent capture by Union forces.

(Str)

Alliance was listed by the Commander of the Federal North Atlantic Blockade Squadron in January 1863 as being fitted out and purchased by the Confederate States to run the blockade at Wilmington. She was still on the wanted list of the Union Fleet in December of the same year, said to be very active on sea lanes running from Nassau and Bermuda to Wilmington and other Atlantic ports of the Confederacy. She was captured some time prior to 3 May 1864 when Acting Rear Adm. S. P. Lee was ordered by the Secretary of the Navy to send the prize steamer *Alliance* to Boston if not already sent out.

Allison

(Str)

CSS *Allison* was employed as a transport in the James River area. While operating with the James River Squadron under Flag Officer J. Mitchell, CSN, she took an active part in the attempted passage through the obstructions at Trent's Reach on 23–24 January 1865. On 26 January 1865 she collided with the steam torpedo boat *Hornet*, causing that ship to sink.

Alonzo Child

(SwStr: t. 493; l. 222'; b. 36'; dph. 6'; a. 8", 10", and 6" rifles)

Alonzo Child, which is also frequently cited as *A. Childs* or *Childs*, was built in 1857 at Jeffersonville, Ind., and fell under Confederate control in the Mississippi River area. Near Yazoo City, Miss., in May 1863 her engines and machinery were taken out and sent to Mobile, Ala., for *Tennessee* (No. 2). The Confederates used *Alonzo Child*'s hulk to obstruct the channel at Haynes' Bluff on the Yazoo River. She was found there in the same month by units of a Federal naval force under Acting Rear Adm. D. D. Porter, USN, and taken into Union service.

Amazon

(SwStr: t. 372; dr. 2')

Amazon, a high pressure, iron-hulled steamer was built at Wilmington, Del., in 1856, for the cotton trade. Taken into Confederate service, she was used in transporting material and laying torpedoes in the Savannah River. On 2 March 1865 she surrendered to USS *Pontiac* and was sent into Savannah as a prize.

Amelia, see *Tallahassee*

America, see *Memphis*

America, see under *Texas* (corvette)

Anglo-Norman

(SwStr: t. 558; l. 176'2''; b. 29'5''; dr. 9'; cpl. 35; a. 1 32-pdr.)

Anglo-Norman, built at Algiers, La., in 1850 and employed as a towboat by the Southern Steamship Company, New Orleans, La., was impressed for public service by order of the Confederate Secretary of War. The order was implemented by Maj. Gen. M. Lovell on 15 January 1862 when 14 ships were seized for the Mississippi River Defense Fleet for possible conversion to gunboats and rams.

At the time of the action at Forts Jackson and St. Philip, April 1862, *Anglo-Norman* was not mentioned as one of the River Defense Fleet, however, the gunboat *Anglo-Norman* is one of the 22 listed in the prize cases before arbitrators on 1 May 1862.

Anglo-Saxon

(SwStr: t. 508; l. 120'3''; b. 28'; dph. 11')

Anglo-Saxon, built in New York City in 1848 and owned by the Southern Steamship Company, was one of 14 steamers seized in January 1862 by Maj. Gen. M. Lovell, CSA, under orders of the War Department. While participating in the defense of Forts Jackson and St. Philip on 24 April 1862, she was taken under vigorous attack by the Union Mortar Flotilla. *Anglo-Saxon* caught fire and drifted downstream in a sinking condition. The Federals seized and repaired her for use as an army transport during the rest of the war.

Anna Dale

(Sch: t. 70; a. 1 12-pdr.)

The schooner, *Anna Dale* was operated by the Confederates off the Texas coast and may have engaged in privateering. She was commanded by Master J. E. Stevenson when surprised and captured in February 1865 off Pass Cavallo, Tex., by a boarding party from USS *Pinola* in charge of Acting Ensign J. Brown, USN. The captors set sail in her but running aground they set her afire on 18 February to prevent recapture.

Anna Perrette

(StwStr: t. 173; l. 130'; b. 32'; dr. 4'6'')

Anna Perrette, built in 1857 at Jeffersonville, Ind., operated in the Mississippi and Red Rivers under Confederate control from 1863 to 1865. During March 1865 she was permitted by Union officials to transport cotton from the Red River to New Orleans under a flag-of-truce. The Confederates seized her cargo and imprisoned her captain in late March 1865 while ordered to treat all persons trading cotton under Yankee permits as spies.

Appleton Belle

(Str)

Appleton Belle is known to have served Confederate forces under Lt. Col. J. H. Miller, CSA, at Paris, Tenn., where she was burned with two other steamers on 7 February 1862 to prevent her falling into Union hands. All on board escaped safely. She may have been the 103-ton stern-wheel steamer built in 1856 at West Newton, Pa., which operated out of Pittsburgh, Pa., prior to the outbreak of Civil War.

Appomattox

(Tug: a. 2 guns)

Appomattox, as *Empire*, was bought at Norfolk in 1861, converted to a gunboat, and assigned to the waters along the North Carolina coast, under the command of Lt. C. C. Simms, CSN. *Appomattox* helped to obstruct channels in the Hatteras area by towing block-ships to strategic points for sinking. Immediately afterward, she fought valiantly during the battles of Roanoke Island on 7–8 February 1862 and Elizabeth City, N.C., 2 days later. Following the rout of the Confederate fleet in the Pasquotank River on 10 February 1862, *Appomattox* tried to escape but her beam was 2 inches too great to let her into the lock and so prevented passage through the Dismal Swamp Canal. Accordingly Lieutenant Simms set her on fire and she blew up. [See *Empire*, infra.]

Arcadia

(Str)

Arcadia may have served the Confederates as a transport in the Yazoo River, Miss., under the control of Comdr. I. N. Brown, CSN, in charge of Confederate vessels in the Yazoo. Commander Brown burned and scuttled *Arcadia* in the Yazoo River in July 1863 to keep her from falling into the hands of a Union naval force under Acting Rear Adm. D. D. Porter, USN.

Archer

(Sch: t. ca. 90; a. 1 12-pdr. how.)

Archer, a fishing schooner, was captured on 24 June 1863 off Portland, Maine, by the bark *Tacony* under Lt. C. W. Read, CSN. Realizing that the U.S. Navy was carrying on an intensive search for his raiding ship, Lieutenant Read, in order to elude his pursuers, transferred his force to *Archer* and burned *Tacony*.

Archer was piloted into Portland, Maine, by two unsuspecting fishermen from whom Lieutenant Read learned of the presence in port of the U.S. Revenue Cutter *Caleb Cushing*. In the early morning hours of 27 June, Read and his men quietly boarded and seized *Caleb Cushing*, and locked her crew below in irons. It was Read's plan to get the cutter away from Union shore batteries and then return before daylight and set fire to merchant shipping in the harbor. *Archer* with three of Read's men on board, and *Caleb Cushing* with the rest of Read's crew were unable to clear the Union forts before daybreak and found it impossible to return to carry out their plan.

About 20 miles at sea in late morning of 27 June *Caleb Cushing*, surrounded by Federal ships, was fired by Lieutenant Read to prevent capture. He and his prisoners in small boats surrendered to the steamer *Forest City*. *Archer*, in which Lieutenant Read had intended to send his prisoners back after transferring his supplies to *Caleb Cushing*, was also captured later on in the day by *Forest City*.

Arctic

(IrcFltBtry: a. 3 guns)

CSS *Arctic*, built at Wilmington, N.C., in 1863, was an ironclad floating battery which performed additional duty as receiving ship for Flag Officer Robert F. Pinkney's North Carolina defense force. She was stationed in the Cape Fear River from 1862 to 1864, with Lt. C. B. Poindexter, CSN, in command. Her machinery had been removed in the latter part of 1862 for the ironclad CSS *Richmond* then completing at Richmond, Va.

With the threat to Wilmington, created by the arrival off Fort Fisher of the joint army-navy expedition under Rear Admiral Porter and Major General Butler, *Arctic* was sunk on 24 December 1864 to obstruct the river channel.

Argo

(StwStr: t. 99)

Argo was built in 1856 at Freedom, Pa. She operated on the Yazoo River, Miss., during the Civil War and may have been under the control of Comdr. I. N. Brown CSN, commanding Confederate ships on the river. *Argo* was burned near the middle of 1863, 75 miles up the Sunflower River, Miss., by the Federal ship *Linden* of the force of Acting Rear Adm. D. D. Porter, USN.

Argosy

(Str)

Argosy was burned and destroyed in the Sunflower River, Miss., in the middle of 1863 by the Confederates to keep her from falling into the hands of a Union naval force under Acting Rear Adm. D. D. Porter, USN. *Argosy* may have been employed by the Confederates as a cargo ship or army transport.

Argosy No. 2, see *Wave*

Argus

(StwStr)

Argus, a small steamer, was used as a Confederate Army transport in the Mississippi River area. On 7 October 1863 she was surprised and captured along with *Robert Fulton* at the mouth of the Red River, La., by a boat dispatched from USS *Osage*. Unable to get her beyond a river shoal which existed at that time, her captors burned *Argus* immediately.

Arizona

(SwStr: t. 578 [582, 670, 959]; l. 200'; b. 34'; dph. 17'6''; dr. 8')

Arizona was one of the well known 14 Southern S. S. Co. ships and tugs "impressed for public service" at New Orleans, 15 January 1862, by Maj. Gen. Mansfield Lovell, CSA, acting under Secretary of War Benjamin's orders.

An iron paddle-steamer, barkentine rigged, she was built on the Delaware for Charles Morgan by Harlan and Hollingsworth as Hull No. 57 in 1858, with a beam engine and single boiler. As a "sea steamer" she was not the best choice for a river gunboat; from the spring of 1862, she became very valuable as a Government-operated blockade-runner to the Caribbean, carrying over a thousand bales of cotton per voyage under command of a Captain Forbes of New Orleans.

On 28 October 1862, USS *Montgomery* caught the former *Arizona* trying to run into Mobile from Havana with saltpeter and other munitions. She had become *Caroline* under "provisional British register"—the usual routine cloak for blockade running—but like many others made it an open secret by carrying the Confederate ensign forward, British colors aft, as she was reported at Havana in October 1862.

She brought $84,500 in Philadelphia prize court 23 June 1863 and followed the familiar pattern: Commodore C. K. Stribling sent her back to her old locale as USS *Arizona*, an armed member of the West Gulf Blockading Squadron that captured her. She took part in the fight at Sabine Pass, Tex., in September 1863. On 27 February 1865 she burned 38 miles below New Orleans.

Arkansas

(IrcRam: l. 165'; b. 35'; dr. 11'6"; s. 8 k.; cpl. 200; a. 2 9" sb., 2 9" 64-pdr., 2 9" shell guns, 2 6" r., 2 32-pdr sb.; type *Arkansas*)

CSS *Arkansas*, a twin-screw ram, was laid down at Memphis, Tenn., in 1861 by J. T. Shirley. When the Union fleet imperiled that city in May 1862 she was taken up the Yazoo River for completion.

On 26 May 1862 Lt. Isaac Newton Brown, CSN, took command; displaying great energy he finished plating the "long and rakish" ram with utmost speed; for example: "Without waiting for the apparatus to bend the railway iron to the curve of our quarter and stern, and to the angles of the pilot house . . . we tacked boilerplate iron over it (the stern) and very imperfectly covered the pilot-house shield with a double thickness of bar iron . . ."

Brown further noted *Arkansas* "now appeared as if a small seagoing vessel had been cut down to the water's edge at both ends, leaving a box for guns amidships. The straight sides of the box, a foot in thickness, were covered with one layer of railway iron; the ends closed by timber one foot square, planked across by 6" strips of oak, were then covered by one course of railway iron laid up and down at an angle of 35 degrees . . . shield flat on top, covered with plank half-inch iron . . . large smoke-stack came through top of shield . . . pilot-house raised about one foot above shield level. Through the latter led a small tin tube by which to convey orders to the pilot."

One of *Arkansas*' junior officers, George W. Gift, wrote candidly of her "very incomplete condition. The iron of her armor extended only a foot or a little more above the water line, and there was not a sufficiency of iron on hand to finish the entire ship . . . gotten up under . . . haste and incompetency . . . I imagine that she was designed for a powerful iron-clad gunboat, with an iron beak . . . and several heavy guns . . . before she had arrived at anything like a state of completion, the plan was altered and she was made into an hermaphrodite iron-clad . . . instead of finishing the ship with an ordinary rail and bulwark all round, her sides were 'built on' amidships for 50 or 60 feet in length, so as to give an apology for protection for 3 guns in each broad side . . . The sides, it must be understood, were perpendicular. . . . The ends of this 'castle' or 'gun-box' were sloping or inclined from which were thrust 4 more guns, 2 at each end . . . battery of 10 guns . . . 4 of the carriages on railroad iron chassis."

Opportunely a number of Confederate Army artillerists volunteered to act as gunners on board *Arkansas*. On 15 July, *Carondelet*, *Tyler*, and *Queen of the West*, carrying Army sharpshooters on a reconnaissance of the Yazoo River, encountered the ram and a spirited engagement took place. *Queen of the West* got away but *Carondelet*, Comdr. Henry Walke, USN, exposed his unprotected stern to *Arkansas*' efficient fire long enough to be put out of command and went aground; *Arkansas*, of deeper draft, could not ram her there but was already too close aboard to use her guns to finish off *Carondelet* ("could train our guns laterally very little"). Furthermore, Brown maintained afterward that Walke had struck his colors, which the latter hotly denied. *Arkansas*, under the circumstances, properly pursued *Tyler* instead, inflicting heavy casualties.

Entering the Mississippi, *Arkansas* ran through the Union fleet to take refuge under the Vicksburg batteries, but she was heavily damaged and sustained many casualties.

Gift noted that since her boilers were "not lined on the fire-front with non-conducting material . . . the whole mass of iron about the boilers became red hot." Brown further explained, "The connections between the furnace and smoke-stack (technically called the breechings) were shot away, destroying the draught and letting the flames come out into the shield, raising the temperature to 120 degrees, while it had already risen to 130 degrees in the fire-room . . . We went into action with 120 pounds of steam . . . came out with 20 pounds."

Admiral Farragut reported: "it was so dark by the time we reached the town that nothing could be seen except the flashes of the guns." In the heavy cannonade as Farragut's ships continued down the river below Vicksburg, *Winona* and *Sumter* were substantially damaged—probably as much by *Arkansas'* guns as by the shore batteries.

Confederate Secretary of the Navy Mallory said of the event: "Naval history records few deeds of greater heroism or higher professional ability than this achievement of the *Arkansas*."

Arkansas evoked amazement and praise, however grudging, from her adversaries also: Walke wrote, "Strange to say, the *Arkansas*, in spite of her strength and weight, is quite fast—nearly as much so as the *Tyler*. . . . Her bow is made sharp . . . and her stern tapers so as to permit the water to close readily behind her. In the center of her hull she is broad and of great capacity, and for nearly 80 feet along the middle she is almost flat-bottomed, like an ordinary freight or passenger boat on the Western waters.

"The engines of the *Arkansas* are low pressure and of 900 H.P., all placed below the water-line, and well protected from injury by hostile missiles. Her cylinders are said to be 24" diameter and 7-foot stroke. She is provided with two propellors, working in the stern and acting independently. . . . 7 feet in diameter and are each provided with 4 wings or flanges, and are capable of making 90 revolutions to the minute. In consequence of the independent action of the engines, one propellor can be revolved forward while the other is reversed, thus permitting the boat to be turned in little more than her own length.

"Forward she carries an enormous beak of cast iron, which is so made that the entire bow of the boat fits into it like a wedge into a piece of timber. . . . A sharp cast-iron beak, about 3 feet deep on her stem, projecting 4 feet therefrom,

and clasping the bow 6 feet on either side, and bolted through solid timber about 10 feet. Her cut-water was heavily iron-shod. . . . The supporting sides of this beak are perforated in numerous places, to admit huge bolts that pass completely through the bow and are riveted at either end. The entire beak weighs 18,000 pounds, and is of sufficient strength to penetrate the hull of any war vessel on the river. The sides of the boat are of 18 inches solid timber, and, with their mail covering of railroad and plate iron, are proof against any but the heaviest projectiles. . . . Thoroughly covered with T-rail iron upon heavy timber bulwarks, and cotton pressed casementing, almost impervious to shot. Her port-holes were small, with heavy iron shutters."

Another of her officers, Actg. Master's Mate John A. Wilson, CSN, preserved for posterity that *Arkansas*, "being painted a dull brown color could not be seen at a distance." Her protective coloration attracted Admiral Farragut's attention also: "The ram is chocolate color, very low." Gift said, "Our sides were the color of rust."

On 22 July *Essex* and *Queen of the West* ran down past Vicksburg and unsuccessfully attacked *Arkansas*. Again on 6 August 1862 she was engaged by *Essex* about 5 miles above Baton Rouge, La. Plagued by engine trouble, she was unable to fight or flee and drifted ashore. There she was abandoned and fired to prevent capture.

Arrow

(Str: a. 1 32-pdr.)

Arrow was seized by the Governor of Louisiana in 1861 and turned over to the Confederate Army. Fitted out as a gunboat, *Arrow* operated in Mississippi Sound protecting the water route between New Orleans and Mobile. On 13 July 1861 she steamed in company with *Oregon* to the vicinity of Ship Island Light where they sought unsuccessfully to lure USS *Massachusetts* under the shore batteries. She aided in removing Confederate troops from Ship Island, Miss., during September 1861. When the Confederacy evacuated New Orleans in April 1862 she sailed up the West Pearl River. There on 4 June 1862 she was burned to prevent capture.

———

(Str)

Arrow, a tug, was operated by the Virginia State Navy at Norfolk, Va. early in 1861. She was ordered on picket duty in the vicinity of

Confederate ironclad Atlanta *in the James River after her capture by the Union.*

Craney Island under command of Lt. Peter U. Murphey. Deemed "inefficient" as a picket she may have rendered towing service in that area. There is no evidence that she was actually taken into the Confederate States Navy.

Atalanta, see *Tallahassee*

Atlanta

(IrcRam: t. 1,006; l. 204'; b. 41'; dr. 15'9''; s. 7 to 10 k.; cpl. 145; a. 2 7'' r., 2 6.4'' r.)

CSS *Atlanta* was originally the English blockade runner *Fingal*, built at Glasgow, Scotland, in 1861. She was procured by the Confederate Government in 1862 and converted into an ironclad ram at Savannah by Messrs. N. and A. F. Tift. This vessel, with Commander W. McBlair, CSN, in command, was active on the Savannah station, usually flying the flag of Commodore Tattnall, who lived ashore in Savannah. On 17 June 1863 she was captured at dawn in Wassaw Sound, Ga., by monitors *Weehawken* and *Nahant*.

Atlantic

(SwStr: t. 623 or 660)

Atlantic was a wooden steamer, one of 14 belonging to Charles Morgan's Southern S. S. Co. seized for "public service" by order of Maj. Gen. Mansfield Lovell at New Orleans, 14 January 1862. Surprisingly, she became a Government-owned blockade runner instead of a gunboat: Her engines being low-pressure—easier to protect against shot and offering relative fuel economy— would have made her a logical choice for a cottonclad, but General Lovell the following day found her "small and poor" and asked for *Galveston* (q.v.) in her place. Apparently Secretary of War Benjamin honored his request, for *Atlantic*, under Captain Smith, turned up in Havana, 19 April, and again in May and September, with over 1,000 bales of cotton. The U.S. Consul in

Havana mentions her again in June 1863 as leaving for Nassau. It is not altogether clear when her name was changed to *Elizabeth* under British registry, Capt. Thomas J. Lockwood; owned by the Confederacy's secret office abroad, Fraser, Trenholm & Co., Liverpool. Her operations changed to Wilmington, N.C.; running in there 24 September 1863 she grounded and was burned to escape capture at Lockwood's Folly in the Cape Fear River, 12 miles from Fort Caswell.

Augusta (see under *Texas* (corvette))

Austin

(SwStr: t. 1,150 gr, 604 dw.; l. 200' bp.; b. 34'; dph. 10'; dr. 8'; s. 7–10 k.)

Austin was an iron sidewheeler, Harlan & Hollingsworth's Hull 65, built on the Delaware at Wilmington in 1859, sailing on the New Orleans-Galveston line of Southern S. S. Co. and similar to *Arizona*, with vertical beam engine. Seized at New Orleans by order of Secretary of War Benjamin, 14 January 1862, as one of 14 steamers belonging to the Charles Morgan interests, she apparently was intended for a gunboat by Maj. Gen. Mansfield Lovell, CSA, but ended as a Government-owned blockade-runner under Master's Mate Charles Fowler, CSN, formerly commanding CSS *Neptune*. She was unarmed when captured by USS *Metacomet* off Mobile Bay, 6 June 1864, operating under British registry as *Donegal*, her name also in the U.S. Navy, where she finished out the war. She served the Morgans again from 1865 to 1876.

Azuma, see *Stonewall*

B. M. Moore

(SwStr: t. 38; l. 81'5''; b. 17'1''; dr. 3'8''; a. 2 12-pdr. how.)

B. M. Moore was a small steamer which may have served the Confederates in the Mississippi

River area. She was captured on 30 September 1862 at Cairo, Ill., and transferred to the U.S. War Department as *General Pillow*. She was sold for $2,000 on 25 November 1865 at an auction at Mound City, Ill.

Bahama

(ScBark: t. 888 [1,530; 716]; 226'; b. 29'2''; dph. 20'8''; dr. 16–19')

Bahama of London was a "very fast," iron bark-rigged propeller built in the Pearse yard at Stockton-on-Tees in 1862—in one month—most modern in design and near-sister to *Bermuda*. Acquired by the Confederacy as a new ship, late the following year she became tender to CSS *Alabama* (q.v.). The U.S. Consul at London wrote, 24 February 1863, that she had sailed the 21st in ballast with a crew of 34, "double the number required for working the vessel. Her clearance was for Hong Kong, but I understand she goes to meet the *Alabama*. Cunard, Wilson & Co., the same house that cleared her before, cleared her this time. Her captain is W. Rowe. She is bound on mischief and should be captured wherever found."

Bahama had already been transporting munitions for the Confederate Government for nearly a year. Her first load, under Capt. Eugene L. Tessier, formerly of *Bermuda*, was "a large and valuable cargo of cannons and small arms" from Hamburg, 27 March 1862, to Nassau via Funchal, for the U.S. Minister in Brussels was so interested in *Bahama* and her million-dollar load, "the most valuable cargo yet shipped by the rebels," that he drew a priceless sketch of the ship, thus preserved to this day in official records with a description, in unaccustomed detail, of "a new screw steamer of about a thousand tons measurement, painted black, with a narrow red stripe around her waist; yellowish-grey below the waterline; yellow houses and boats; much gilt and filigree work about her bows and stern; upper half of her chimney red, lower half black; name gilded on light blue ground on each bow and upon her stern; roofs of her houses rounded and painted white; three masts, two of them square-rigged, carrying topgallant sails; heads and yards painted black; five boats in sight." The consul in Hamburg, J. H. Anderson, also reported her to Secretary Seward.

Baker, see *A. W. Baker*

Baltic

(IrcRam: t. 624; l. 186'; b. 38'; dr. 6'5''; s. 5 k.; cpl. 86; a. 2 Dahlgrens, 2 32-pdr., 2 smaller pieces)

CSS *Baltic*, an iron-and-cottonclad sidewheeler, was built in 1860 as a river tow boat, and belonged to the Southern Steamship Co. She was purchased by the State of Alabama, converted to an armored ram, and turned over to the Confederate States Navy in the middle of 1862. Her first commanding officer was Lt. J. D. Johnston, CSN.

Throughout the war *Baltic* operated in Mobile Bay and the Mobile, Alabama and Tombigbee Rivers. Reported unfit for service in February 1863, her sinking condition prevented her joining the defense of Mobile Bay in June 1864. She was dismantled by July 1864 and her armor transferred to CSS *Nashville*.

Baltic was captured at Nanna Hubba Bluff, Tombigbee River, Ala., on 10 May 1865, and sold to the U.S. Government on 31 December 1865.

Barataria

(StwIrcGbt: t. 400; l. 125'; dr. 3'6''; a. unknown)

An unaccountable blackout of information prevails as to the origin and role of little gunboat *Barataria* (as the name is consistently spelled by Army; *Barrataria* in Navy records), before she was captured by the U.S. Army at New Orleans in April 1862. It is generally accepted that she must have been ironclad under the Confederates [cf. Vol. I]: In April 1863 she was cited once as "completely covered with iron one inch thick," yet the recorded repair bill of $409.90 would scarcely cover a partial one-inch shield of mail for a vessel of any appreciable size. Confederate published documents shed no light on her during this period. The little sternwheel ironclad was transferred by Lt. Col. A. N. Shipley, USA, to Farragut's command as of New Year's 1863 and is invariably spelled *Barrataria* thereafter. On 7 April next, she met disaster at 6 a.m. on a snag in Lake Maurepas at the mouth of the Amité River, La. Alternately lightening ship and fighting off guerrillas all day with her two guns and rifle fire by Col. Thomas S. Clark and a company of the 6th Michigan Volunteers, Acting Ensign James F. Perkins, USN, and his command were unable to free *Barrataria*, even after jettisoning the bow gun and emptying her boiler. The ship was fired at sunset and her magazine blew up soon after all hands had escaped in small boats. Capt. Gadi Herren, CSA, of the Mississippi Cavalry, inspected her the next day and reported her "a complete wreck" but still exhibiting the numerals "291" and the remaining brass rifled gun; reporting to Colonel J. M. Simonton, CSA, at Ponchatoula, he called *Barataria* (291) "one of the enemy's most formidable boats on the lake" but seemed unaware that she had been Confederate only a year ago.

Bartow, see *F. S. Bartow* (Annex I)

Bat

(SwStr: t. 771 or 330; l. 230'; b. 26'; dph. 9'6" or 10'9"; dr. 7'6"; s. 16 k.; cl. *Owl*)

Bat and her sisters—*Owl, Stag, Deer*—were side-wheelers, long, low, molded steel hulls, schooner-rigged, fore and aft, with two funnels. They had twin, 180-nominal h.p., vertical, double-oscillating, Watt engines and capacity for 800 to 850 bales of cotton, plus enough anthracite to return from Nassau, Havana or Bermuda.

The quarto was built by Jones, Quiggin & Co., Liverpool, for Capt. James D. Bulloch, CSN, principal Confederate Navy purchasing agent in Britain. They were Government-owned ships, reporting to the Army Chief of Ordnance, were commanded by CSN captains, carried pilots and as many other CSN regulars as available—but keeping a British master to bring the ship out of the United Kingdom and "front" for them so as not to lose her mercantile register before she reached Confederate waters and until any outstanding liens were paid in full. The *Owl* class was the first new building program after this pattern and, despite the Army's presence in their management, Navy kept a good share of control: Secretary Mallory speaks of the *Owls* as "under this Department" and of "this Department having to defray the expenses of the vessels sailing under its direction." [cf. *Cornubia*]

Bat, the second ship, reached Halifax on her maiden voyage and ran down to the Cape Fear River, attempting entrance the night of 8 October 1864 with a cargo of shoe machinery and 200 tons of coal; she was turned back by the blockaders *Eolus* and *Emma* and chased by *Vicksburg*. The morning of the 10th, Captain A. Hora, an "old blockade runner," tried again and was hit by USS *Montogomery* in the forecastle before her speed,

double that of *Montgomery*, could save *Bat*. The 30-pounder amputated the leg of seaman Match Madick, an Austrian, who had been captain of the forecastle in *Alabama* during her battle with *Kearsarge;* Captain Hora surrendered and called *Montgomery*'s surgeon but Madick died.

Less than a month old, *Bat* was taken into Beaufort and bought by the Navy from the Boston Prize Court in November for $150,000. Valuable to the Union the remainder of the war in the North Atlantic Blockading Squadron, USS *Bat* was sold at public auction in New York, 25 October 1865. One time in March 1865 she had been Admiral Porter's flagship. Renamed *Teazer*, 1865–72, she next became *Miramichi*, for the New Brunswick river, and a Canadian institution in the St. Lawrence and Gulf of Newfoundland trade, avoiding the breakers until after 1902.

Bayou City

(Str: dr. 3'; a. 1 32-pdr.)

Bayou City, originally a mail boat that ran between Galveston and Houston, Tex., was chartered on 26 September 1861 by Comdr. W. Hunter, CSN, commanding the Texas Marine Department, from the Houston Navigation Co. Fitted with cotton cladding, she was operated by the State of Texas [See Annex III] in the area of Galveston harbor and the Trinity River until October 1862 when she was taken over by the War Department. *Bayou City* played an important part in the battle of Galveston during which she attacked USS *Harriet Lane*, ramming and boarding her to effect capture on 1 January 1863. Thereafter, the Marine Department employed her as gunboat and guardboat along the coast of Texas until the end of the war.

Beaufort

ScTug: t. 85 (80); l. 85'; b. 17'5"; dph. 6'11"; a. 1 gun)

CSS *Beaufort*, built at Wilmington, Del., in 1854, as *Caledonia*, was put in commission at Norfolk, Va., on 9 July 1861, by Lt. R. C. Duvall, North Carolina Navy, and sailed immediately for New Bern, N.C. While en route she engaged the large steamer *Albatross*, in an inconclusive battle off Oregon Inlet.

After North Carolina seceded, *Beaufort* was turned over to the Confederate States Navy and on 9 September Lt. W. H. Parker, CSN, was placed in command. Thereafter she participated in the battles of Roanoke Island on 7-8 February 1862, and Elizabeth City, N.C., 2 days later. Escaping via the Dismal Swamp Canal to Norfolk, she was tender to CSS *Virginia* (ex-*Merrimack*) off Hampton Roads, Va., on 8–9 March 1862. The Confederate Congress tendered thanks to the officers and crew for their gallantry during the action.

From May 1862, *Beaufort* operated on the James River, her commander in November 1863 being Lt. W. Sharp, CSN. She served until the evacuation of Richmond 3 April 1865 when she was taken into the United States Navy. She was sold 15 September 1865.

Beauregard

(Sch: t. 101; s. 7 k.; cpl. 40; a. 1 24-pdr. rifle)

C. S. privateer brig *Beauregard*, formerly the schooner *Priscilla C. Ferguson*, owned by a group headed by A. F. W. Abrams of Charleston, S.C., was commissioned there 14 October 1861. She sailed short in complement on 5 November, commanded by Capt. Gilbert Hay as master, with two lieutenants, a purser and 23 seamen. *Beauregard* ran the blockade unobserved, although reported 24 October by a Northern shipmaster to Secretary of the Navy Welles in Washington as fitting out at Charleston along with *Dixie*, destined for longer life as a privateer than *Beauregard*.

One week out of home port, Captain Hay was surprised in the Bahama Channel by U.S. bark *W. G. Anderson*, Lt. William C. Rogers, whose attention was attracted to the schooner when only 4 miles off by "many men on her decks." Rogers overhauled *Beauregard* after a 2-hour chase and recorded that Hay "brought a letter of marque from J. Davis which he surrendered with his vessel. We put a prize master and crew on board and transferred the prisoners to our ship. * * * On boarding her the crew * * * committed all the destruction they could, throwing overboard the arms and ammunition, spiking the gun, and cutting the sails and rigging to pieces. She was otherwise in bad order and poorly found. * * * Took prisoners and vessel to Key West." Arrived there the 19th, the $15,000 *Beauregard* was in due course condemned by the prize court, sold to the U.S. Navy for $1,810 on 24 February 1862 and, name unchanged, ably served Flag Officer McKean thereafter in the Eastern Gulf Blockading Squadron.

———

(SwStr)

Certain references to CSN transport *Beauregard* in official documents where area of operation is not specified, are difficult to separate from those pertaining to the larger C.S. Army steamer of the same name plying the western rivers. Apparently an old vessel whose former name has not been preserved, she was operated by the C.S. Navy carrying troops, guns and munitions along the Georgia and South Carolina coasts. From November 1861 or earlier until Savannah fell, 21 December 1864, it is frequently noted that her services were much in demand, although neither their nature nor her particulars are precisely described. Her last known assignment, along with *General Lee* and *Jeff Davis*, was to tow the floating battery *Georgia* to a better position. Less than 2 weeks later she and *General Lee* were both captured by General Sherman's forces entering Savannah.

———

(Sch)

C.S. Schooner *Beauregard* is several times referred to in Confederate records as "one of our transports," moving cargo for both Navy and Army along the Virginia-North Carolina coast early in 1862. On 4 May Capt. J. Milligan, CSA, Signal Officer at Norfolk, reported to Richmond, "Schooner *Beauregard*, bound from City Point to Norfolk with a cargo of coal for the *Virginia*, was burned by the enemy off Ragged Island this morning at 2 a.m. * * *"

———

(Str)

Official references as early as March 1864 indicate C.S. Army steamer *Beauregard* had been for some time an outstanding unit of the western river fleet serving the Confederate Army's Quartermaster Department. On 22 March she is mentioned as "the most valuable boat" transporting cannon and ammunition from Grand Ecore to Shreveport, La. She and steamers *General Quitman* and *Countess* moved two divisions of infantry, cavalry and artillery across the Red River in mid-April 1865. Maj. Gen. F. J. Herron, USA, found her with the pump boat *Champion* at Mound City, 6 June, and took possession of both.

Beauregard, see also *General Beauregard*

Bee, see *General Bee*

Beebe, [*Junius*], see *General Sumter*

Bell, see *Josiah A. Bell*

Belle Algerine

(Str)

Belle Algerine operated in conjunction with the River Defense Fleet under Capt. J. A. Stevenson at Forts Jackson and St. Philip. Following action early in April 1862 she was represented as unfit for service having sustained bow damage while landing guns at Fort St. Philip, and handling the fire rafts with which the Confederates illuminated the channel below the forts against the passage of Farragut's fleet assembled there.

Comdr. Beverly Kennon in the *Governor Moore* reported that, during the engagement at Forts Jackson and St. Philip, *Belle Algerine* had twice run afoul of his ship and he eliminated the danger by ramming and sinking her on 24 April 1862.

Ben McCulloch

(StwStr: t. 80)

Ben McCulloch, a small river steamer built in 1860 at Cincinnati, Ohio, was impressed into Confederate Army transport service. Early in 1863 she conveyed supplies on the Tallahatchie and Sunflower Rivers and on Tchula Lake.

Following the capture of Yazoo City by the Federals, she was one of the four remaining Confederate vessels that escaped up the Tallahatchie and Yalobusha Rivers. In July 1863 she was burned on Tchula Lake by Confederate cavalry to avoid capture.

Bermuda

(ScBrig: t. [888]; l. 226'; b. 29'; dph. 20'; dr. 16'–19'—see note)

Bermuda was at one time in her career as a Confederate blockade runner indicated as tender to CSS *Florida*, then known as *Oreto*, and was expected to deliver her battery to her in Palermo, since she was officially bound there, in March and April 1862. She seems to have been the ship that made the delivery to *Florida* in the Bahamas, under command of Capt. Eugene L. Tessier and Capt. C. W. Westendorff.

Bermuda, with 5 watertight bulkheads and first "owned" by cotton man Edward Haigh, was built, 1861, in 7 months as near-sister to *Bahama* in the same yard (the particulars given in parentheses above are based on that assumption) but is also mentioned as sister to *Czar*, which has not been verified. That *Bermuda* and *Bahama* were true public vessels operated by the Confederate Government all of part of the war is not certain

though plausible. Fraser, Trenholm & Co., Confederate agency in Great Britain, officially bought them.

Note: If she was tender to *Florida*, this ship was clearly a different *Bermuda* from the one captured by USS *Mercedita*, 27 April 1862, and sent to Philadelphia for adjudication. One *Bermuda* became *General Meade* later.

Berosa

(Str)

Berosa was an antiquated and worn out craft used by the Confederates to transport cargo. While sailing from St. Mary's River on 8 April 1863 she sprang a leak and defied attempts to save her. *Berosa* was abandoned in the Gulf Stream at latitude 29°50', longitude 79°50'.

Berwick Bay

(Str: t. 64)

Berwick Bay was a steamer engaged in transporting supplies for the Confederates in the Mississippi River area. She was captured and destroyed on 3 February 1863 by Ellet's Ram Fleet as she came out of the Red River heavily laden with supplies for Port Hudson.

Bienville

(SwStr: a. 5 guns; cl. *Bienville*)

Bienville was a light draft steamer "substantially built" of yellow pine and white oak under contract by John Hughes and Co., at Bayou St. John, La., in 1861–62. Collaborating and inspecting for the Government in the Hughes yard was S. D. Porter, Acting Constructor, CSN. She was launched in February 1862 and delivered on 5 April. Her commanding officer was Lt. C. B. Poindexter, CSN. On 21 April 1862, as the battle of New Orleans impended, *Bienville* was still without a crew, consequently her officers were obliged to destroy her in Lake Pontchartrain to prevent capture.

Black Diamond

(SwStr: l. 156'; b. 48'; dph. 5'6")

Black Diamond was constructed in 1865 for river navigation. She was one of four ships that were surrendered formally on 10 May 1865 by Commodore E. Farrand, commanding Confederate Naval Forces in the State of Alabama, at Nanna Hubba Bluff in the Tombigbee River. As she was not suitable for Navy use, *Black Diamond* was sold by December 1865.

Black Warrior

(Sch: a. 2 32-pdr.)

Black Warrior was a large schooner pressed into service by the Confederates to assist in the defense of Roanoke Island on 7–8 February 1862 and Elizabeth City, N.C., 2 days later. She was commanded by Acting Master F. M. Harris, CSN. At the end of the fighting on 10 February she was set on fire to prevent capture by Union forces. Her crew escaped through the marshes of the Pasquotank River.

———

Black Warrior, see [*Enterprise*] under *Adventure*

Blanche, see *General Rusk*

Blue Wing

(SwStr: t. 170)

Blue Wing, employed by Confederates near Helena, Ark. in November 1862, was found to be carrying contraband for planters. In December 1862 she was seized for violating the river blockade and then employed as a Union army transport. In late December 1862 while towing army coal she was fired upon by the Confederates near Napoleon. Her captain being sympathetic to the southern cause ran her into the bank and there delivered her over to them.

Bombshell

(Str: l. 90'; dr. 3'6''; cpl. 37; a. 3 how., 1 20-pdr.)

Bombshell—believed to have been an Erie Canal steamer—as a U.S. Army transport was sunk by the Confederate batteries in Albemarle Sound, N.C., on 18 April 1864. She was raised by the Confederate forces and taken into their navy under the command of Lt. A. G. Hudgins, CSN. *Bombshell* was recaptured in Albemarle Sound by *Mattabesett* and *Sassacus* on 5 May 1864 and sent to New York.

Boston

(ScTug: dr. 6'–9' est.)

Boston was a U.S. naval towboat captured by Acting Master James Duke, CSN, in a famous exploit, 8 June 1863, in Pass à l'Outre, La. Duke and his men left Mobile in a launch, 28 May, and returned there in triumph in *Boston,* 11 June, with 19 prisoners—crewmen from three captured ships; the other two, barks *Lenox* and *Texana,* were burned and sunk. From the latter part of August 1863 until the next February the Federal blockading squadron was keeping close watch outside Mobile to intercept *Boston,* believed to be armed as a privateer [see Annex I] with 2 to 5 boat howitzers, hull "painted lead color" and ready to escape with "a double crew of 56 men" through Grant's Pass. She had been lengthened about 25 feet, but delayed by fire damage on the ways a mile above Mobile; when this was done is not altogether clear, nor is there agreement on *Boston's* speed and draft among Union sources, on which we now depend largely for data on her. Capt. Thornton A. Jenkins, USN, commanding off Mobile in mid-January 1864, thought she "appeared to be fast (when seen in the bay)". It is not fully established whether this was the *Boston* that fell prize 8 July 1864, between Bermuda and Wilmington, to USS *Fort Jackson.* [cf. Cutter *Teaser, infra*]

Bracelet

(SwStr: t. 169)

Bracelet, a steamer built in 1857 at Louisville, Ky., was outfitted with cotton-cladding by the Confederates who used her as a transport in the White and Arkansas Rivers during the early part of 1863.

Bradford

(Gbt)

Bradford was used by the Confederates as a storeship at Pensacola, Fla., in early 1862, and as part of the defense of Deer Point before its evacuation in February of that year.

Breaker

(Sch: cpl. 3)

Breaker was employed by the Confederates as a pilot boat at Pass Cavallo off the Texas coast. On 12 August 1862 USS *Corypheus,* under Lt. J. Kittredge, USN, gave chase to *Breaker* which was returning from a reconnoitering expedition with a detachment of men under Capt. R. Jones. *Breaker* was run ashore and fired by her crew, but Union forces succeeded in saving her for later use as a tender along the Texas coast.

Breckinridge, see *General Breckinridge*

Burton, see *W. Burton*

Caleb Cushing

(Sch: dp. 153; l. 100'4''; b. 23'; dph. 8'8''; dr. 9'7''; a. 1 32-pdr., 1 12-pdr. Dahlgren)

Caleb Cushing, a U.S. revenue cutter built by J. M. Hood in Somerset, Mass., in 1853, was quietly boarded and seized in the early morning hours of 27 June 1863 while in the harbor at Portland, Maine, by Lt. Charles W. Read, CSN, and his men who had entered the harbor undetected on board their prize schooner *Archer*. It was Read's plan to get the cutter away from Union shore batteries before daylight, and then set fire to Union shipping in the harbor. As it was dawn before Read's force cleared the Union guns, he found it impossible to carry out his plan, and instead he set out for sea.

Lt. "Savez" Read intended to send his prisoners back on *Archer* after transferring his supplies to *Caleb Cushing*. However, when about 20 miles at sea, *Caleb Cushing* was overtaken by 2 steamers. Read ran out of ammunition and was unable to put up a resistance. Ordering his men and prisoners into small boats he fired the cutter after setting a powder train to her magazine. He, his men and his prisoners were captured by the steamer *Forest City*. *Archer* was captured later, and *Caleb Cushing* soon exploded and was destroyed.

Caledonia, see *Beaufort*

Calhoun (*J. C. Calhoun*)

(SwStr: t. 509; cpl. 85; a. 1 18-pdr., 2 12-pdr., 2 6-pdr.)

CSS *Calhoun*, built at New York in 1851 as *Cuba*, was commissioned by the Confederate Government as a privateer on 15 May 1861; Capt. John Wilson and his 150 men, during the next 5 months, captured and sent in six prizes. She was then chartered by the Confederate States Navy and placed under the command of Lt. J. H. Carter, CSN. *Calhoun* served as flagship for Commodore G. N. Hollins, CSN, during a successful engagement between his fleet and five Union ships at the Head of the Passes into the Mississippi River, 12 October 1861.

Calhoun was captured off South West Pass, La., on 23 January 1862 by schooner *Samuel Rotan*, a tender to frigate *Colorado*. Subsequently, she served as USS *Calhoun*.

Camilla, see *Memphis*

Canton, see *Texas* (#4)

Capitol

(SwStr: t. 499; l. 224'; b. 32'; dph. 6'6'')

Capitol was built in Jeffersonville, Ind., in 1855. Seized by the Confederates, she burned on 28 June 1862, at Liverpool, Miss., and in July 1862 was sunk as an obstruction in the Yazoo River. The engines and machinery removed from *Capitol* were kept at Yazoo City until early 1863 when they were sent to Selma, Ala., for use in the further defense of Mobile Bay and the Alabama River.

Carolina, see *Theodora*

Caroline, see *Arizona*

Carondelet

(SwStr: a. 5 42-pdr., 1 32-pdr. r.; cl. *Bienville*)

CSS *Carondelet* was a light draft steamer built by John Hughes and Acting Constructor S. D. Porter, CSN, at Bayou St. John, La., in 1861–62. She was put into service in March 1862 with Lt. W. Gwathmey, CSN, in command. On 4 April this ship, accompanied by CSS *Oregon* and *Pamlico*, engaged the Federal gunboats *New London, John P. Jackson* and *Hatteras* at Pass Christian, Miss. The Confederates were unable to prevent the landing of 1,200 Union men at the Pass and the destruction of the camp there.

Carondelet was destroyed by her own officers on Lake Pontchartrain just before the fall of New Orleans to escape capture by the Federals.

Carr, see *John F. Carr*

Castor

(Bark: t. 252)

Castor was a Maltese sailing vessel of fir with coppered bottom, built on the island in 1851 and bought in Liverpool by Confederate agents about 1863. Commanded by a Captain G. Attard, she acted as tender and storeship to CSS *Georgia*. The best known incident during that duty, which of necessity she performed with as little ostentation as possible, was at remote Fernando de Noronha Island, belonging to Brazil: On 16 May 1863 as she commenced coaling *Georgia*, she was forced by the Brazilian authorities, under diplomatic pressure from the United States, to cease operations. *Georgia* got away and USS *Mohican* stood guard thereafter over *Castor* and her companion, *Agrippina* (q.v.), until they were induced to sell their coal and ammunition locally in return for permission to depart in peace. *Castor* began discharging 22 June, following *Agrippina's* example.

Caswell

(SwStr: cpl. 32)

CSS *Caswell* was a wooden steamer which operated as a tender on the Wilmington station, 1861–62, Acting Master W. B. Whitehead, CSN, in command. She was burned to avoid capture when Wilmington, N.C., fell in February 1865.

Catawba

(Str)

The steamer *Catawba* was used by the Confederates as a flag-of-truce boat in Charleston Harbor during April 1861. She transported personnel who arranged the transfer of Major Anderson's command from Fort Sumter to USS *Baltic*. In February 1862 she arrived at Nassau bearing a cargo of cotton and rice, and took on arms and powder from the British steamer *Gladiator*. It is possible that she passed to Union control, for a ship of the name was reported in February 1865 as getting underway from Annapolis with Union troops on board.

Cerro Gordo, see *Muscle*

Chameleon, see *Tallahassee*

Charles Morgan, see *Governor Moore*

Charleston

(IrcStSlp: l. 180'; b. 34'; dph. 14'; s. 6 k.; cpl. 150; a. 4 r., 2 9" sb.)

CSS *Charleston* was built at Charleston, S.C., where she was laid down in December 1862, and commissioned 9 months later. She was not ready for service until early in 1864 when she became the flagship of the squadron on the South Carolina coast with Comdr. I. N. Brown, CSN, in command. This ram was set on fire and abandoned in Charleston Harbor when the city was evacuated by the Confederates on 18 February 1865.

Charleston was widely known as the "Ladies' Gunboat" because of the zeal with which the distaff side of the Charleston populace made sacrifices to contribute to her building.

Charm

(SwStr: t. 223)

Charm was built in 1860 at Cincinnati, Ohio and served the Confederates as an ammunition and gun carrier and troop transport in the Mississippi River area. Under Capt. W. L. Trask, *Charm* participated with high distinction in the Battle of Belmont, Mo., on 7 November 1861, as part of the Confederate force under Maj. Gen. L. Polk, CSA. Under heavy Union fire, *Charm* stood firmly at her post, carrying troops and ammunition back and forth across the Mississippi River in the course of the battle. Although grounded in the furor of battle she was pulled free and saved by the Confederate transport *Prince*.

She was scuttled, secured to *Paul Jones* (q.v.), 17 May 1863. Substantial traces of the two hulks, burned to the waterline, are visible now a century later in a bank of the Big Black River.

Chattahoochee

(ScGbt: l. 150'; b. 25'; dph. 10'; dr. 8'; s. 12 k.; cpl. 120; a. 4 32-pdr., 1 32-pdr. r., 1 9")

Twin-screw *Chattahoochee* was built in 1862–63 at Saffold, Ga., by D. S. Johnson and W. O. Saffold under supervision of Lt. C. R. Jones, CSN. Lt. J. J. Guthrie succeeded to command 4 February 1863. She was variously reported rigged as a two-masted schooner and as a barkentine.

Chattahoochee was plagued by machinery failures, one of which, a boiler explosion which killed 18, occurred on 27 May 1863 as she prepared to sail from her anchorage at Blountstown, Fla., to attempt retaking the Confederate sloop *Fashion*, captured by the Union. On 10 June 1864 she was moved to Columbus, Ga., for repairs and installation of engines and a new boiler.

While she was undergoing repairs at Columbus, 11 of her officers and 50 crewmen tried unsuccessfully to capture *Adela* blockading Apalachicola, Fla. USS *Somerset* drove off the raiders, capturing much of their equipment. When the Confederates evacuated the Chattahoochee River in December 1864, *Chattahoochee* was destroyed to prevent capture. This thwarted plans to use boilers from the wreck of CSS *Raleigh* in the Cape Fear River to power *Chattahoochee*.

Cheney

(Str)

Cheney operated with Confederate forces in and about the Mississippi River from 1861 to 1863. In August 1861 she carried army dispatches to General Pillow at New Madrid, Mo. In April 1863 she was reported as one of four cotton-clad steamers preparing to attack Union naval forces in the Arkansas River.

(IrcRam: t 900; l. 171'10"; b. 32' 8"; dr. 14'4";
s. 10 k.; cl. *Stonewall*)

Cheops was sister to *Sphinx* (see *Stonewall*), built
by L. Arman de Rivière in Bordeaux "for the
China trade," under an involved secret contract
with Comdr. James D. Bulloch, CSN, and his
agent, French Capt. Eugene L. Tessier.

Bulloch to Secretary of the Navy Mallory, 10
June 1864, reveals: "As Denmark was then at
war it had been arranged that the nominal ownership of the rams should vest in Sweden . . .
[which had] consented to do this piece of good
service for Denmark . . . a Swedish naval officer
was then at Bordeaux superintending the completion of the rams as if for his own Government."
Delivery was to be at Gothenburg; M. Arman
explained: "When the first ram is ready to sail,
the American minister will no doubt ask the
Swedish minister if the vessel belongs to his
Government; the reply will be 'yes'; she will
. . . arrive at her destination according to contract. This will distract all suspicion from the
second ram and when she sails under like circumstances with the first, my people . . . will
deliver her to you or your agent at sea." Also
settled were "the best mode of shipping the guns,
the engagement of reliable captains, and the
possibility of getting seamen from the ports of
Brittany." But the whole structure of intrigue
was dashed when, "Mr. Arman obtained his
promised or anticipated interview with the Emperor [Napoleon III], who rated him severely,
threatened imprisonment, ordered him to sell the
ships at once, 'bona fide,' and said if this was not
done he would have him seized and carried to
Rochefort . . . the two corvettes at Nantes
[*Texas* and *Georgia*] were also ordered to be sold
. . . The order is of the most peremptory kind,
not only directing the sale but requiring the
builders to furnish proof to the minister of foreign
affairs that the sale is a real one . . . in a style
of virtuous indignation; specifies the large scant-
ling, the power of the engines, the space allotted
to fuel and the general arrangements of the ships,
as proving their war-like character . . . *une
véritable corvette de guerre* . . . When you call to
mind the fact that this same minister of marine
on the 6th day of June, 1863, wrote over his own
official signature a formal authorization to arm
those very ships with 14 heavy guns each ('canons
rayé de trentes'), the affectation of having just

discovered them to be suitable for purposes of
war is really astonishing."

Cheops became *Prinz Adalbert* of the Prussian
Navy, but *Sphinx* finally did get to sea as CSS
Stonewall (q.v.).

Chesapeake

(ScStr: t. 460)

Chesapeake was the wooden steamer *Totten*, built
in Philadelphia in 1853 and first registered there.
She was rebuilt in 1857, being renamed *Chesapeake*
27 August and described at that time as schooner-
rigged with single funnel, owned by H. B. Crom-
well & Co., New York. She was involved in the
Caleb Cushing (q.v.) affair in June 1863, being one
of the ships that set out from Portland, Me., to
recapture the revenue cutter.

She was sailing as a regular New York-Portland
liner on 7 December 1863 when she became a *cause
célèbre* upon being taken over as a Confederate
vessel by a group acting in the name of the Confederacy under alleged authority of a second-hand
letter of marque issued 27 October to the former
captain of a privateer sold as unseaworthy in
Nassau some months earlier—whereas her relief
captain, mastermind of this later expedition, was
found to be a British subject, having acted under
an assumed name and without authorization by
the Confederacy. The Halifax, N.S., Court of
Vice-Admiralty found, 15 February 1864, that the
capture "was undoubtedly a piratical taking.
But in its origin, . . . in the mode of the recapture, in short, all the concomitant circumstances, the case is very peculiar." *Chesapeake*
was restored to her owners and served in commerce until 1881. The captors were dismissed:
"This court has no prize jurisdiction, no authority
to adjudicate between the United States and the
Confederate States, or the citizens of either of
those States." The prisoners were not surrendered to the United States under the Ashburton
treaty for trial "on charges of murder and piracy."

"Colonel" John Clibbon Braine, Henry A. Parr
and a dozen fellow-conspirators took over *Chesapeake* 20 miles NNE of Cape Cod, 7 December,
having boarded her two nights before in New
York as passengers. In the takeover, her second
engineer was killed and her chief officer and chief
engineer wounded; Captain Isaac Willett, his bona
fide passengers and all but five of his crew were
landed at St. John, N.B., 8 December; Capt John
Parker (actually Vernon G. Locke) joined in the
Bay of Fundy and took command. They coaled

In December 1863 a daring Confederate expedition captured the steamer Chesapeake, *she was recaptured by the North on 17 December.*

at Shelburne, N.S., the 12th, shipped four men and were seeking enough fuel to make Wilmington, N.C., when USS *Ella & Annie* (v. *William G. Hewes*) captured *Chesapeake*, the morning of the 17th, in Sambro, a small harbor near the entrance to Halifax, N.S., with three crewmen—only one being of the boarding party.

Comdr. A. G. Clary, USS *Dacotah*, prevented *Ella & Annie* from taking the recaptured prize into Boston and accompanied her that day to Halifax, where she was turned over to local authorities the 19th—conceding that her recovery in neutral waters of Canada had been extra-legal—and the prisoners with her.

Eight Federal ships hastily summoned to search out *Chesapeake* returned home the 19th; the same day Secretary of State J. P. Benjamin appointed James B. Holcombe special commissioner to represent the alleged Confederate raiders in Halifax and try to gain possession of the prize steamer. Holcombe found ultimately, "That the expedition was devised, planned, and organized in a British

colony by Vernon G. Locke, a British subject, who, under the feigned name of Parker, had been placed in command of the privateer *Retribution* by the officer who was named as her commander at the time of the issue of the letter of marque. . . . Locke assumed to issue commissions in the Confederate service to British subjects on British soil, without . . . authority for so doing, and without being himself in the public service of this Government. . . . there is great reason to doubt whether either Braine, who was in command of the expedition, or Parr, his subordinate, is a Confederate citizen . . . Braine . . . after getting possession of the vessel and proceeding to the British colonies, instead of confining himself to his professed object of obtaining fuel for navigating her to a Confederate port, sold portions of the cargo at different points on the coast, thus divesting himself of the character of an officer engaged in the legitimate warfare. . . . The capture of the *Chesapeake*, therefore, . . . is disclaimed. . . . men who, sympathizing with us in a righteous cause, erroneously believed themselves authorized to act as belligerents against the United States by virtue of Parker's possession of the letter of marque issued to the privateer *Retribution*'' could not be accepted after the fact as Confederate volunteers.

Chesterfield

(SwStr: t. 204)

Chesterfield, a light draft side-wheel cargo steamer built at Charleston, S.C., in 1853, was privately owned by Mr. John Ferguson, and chartered monthly by the Confederate Army as early as 1 June 1861 for South Carolina coast defense. Army-operated, she moved ammunition, ordnance, general supplies and troops from Charleston to Edisto, from Port Royal to Cole's Island and among the various military posts in the harbor.

Chesterfield participated in the defense of Charleston from 1–20 August 1863, and was often under heavy fire while bringing in troops and supplies and removing sick and wounded. She continued to operate along the South Carolina coast throughout 1864.

Chickahominy, see *Fredericksburg*

Chickamauga

(ScStr: t. 585; cpl. 120; a. 3 r.)

CSS *Chickamauga*, originally the blockade runner *Edith*, was purchased by the Confederate Navy at Wilmington, N.C., in 1864. In September when she was nearly ready for sea the Confederate Army sought unsuccessfully to retain her at that place for use as a troop and supply transport. On 28 October 1864, she put to sea under Lt. J. Wilkinson, CSN, for a cruise north to the entrance of Long Island Sound, thence to St. Georges, Bermuda, for repairs and coal. She took several prizes before returning to Wilmington on 19 November.

During the bombardment of Fort Fisher, 24–25 December 1864, a portion of *Chickamauga's* crew served the guns at the fort. Although not immediately engaged in defense of Fort Fisher, the ship rendered further aid in transporting ammunition. She lent support to the fort when it was bombarded again on 15 January 1865.

After the evacuation of Wilmington, *Chickamauga* went up the Cape Fear River where she was sunk by the Confederates on 25 February at Indian Wells, perhaps 50 miles above the city.

Chicora

(IrcRam: l. 150'; b. 35'; dph. 14'; s. 5 k.; cpl. 150; a. 2 9'', 4 32-pdr. r.; cl. *Richmond*)

CSS *Chicora* was built under contract at Charleston, S.C., in 1862, by James M. Eason to J. L. Porter's plans, using up most of a $300,000 State appropriation for construction of marine batteries; Eason received a bonus for "skill and promptitude." Her iron shield was 4'' thick, backed by 22'' of oak and pine, with 2-inch armor at her ends. Keeled in March, she was commissioned

C.S.S. Chickamauga.

in November, Comdr. John R. Tucker, CSN, assuming command.

In thick, predawn haze on 31 January 1863, *Chicora* and CSS *Palmetto State* raided the Federal blockading force of unarmored ships lying just outside the entrance to Charleston Harbor. With ram and gun, *Palmetto State* forced *Mercedita* to surrender, then disabled *Keystone State*, which had to be towed to safety. *Chicora* meanwhile engaged other Union ships in a long-range gun duel, from which she emerged unscathed to withdraw victoriously to shelter inside the harbor.

She took part in the defense of the forts at Charleston on 7 April when they were attacked by a squadron of ironclad monitors under Rear Adm. S. F. DuPont, USN. The Federal ships were forced to retire for repairs and did not resume the action.

Chicora was actively employed in fighting around Charleston during 1863 and 1864. Her valuable services included the transporting of troops during the evacuation of Morris Island, and the bombardment of Forts Sumter, Gregg, and Wagner. In August 1863 she had the distinction of furnishing the first volunteer officer and crew for the Confederate Submarine Torpedo Boat *H. L. Hunley*.

She was destroyed by the Confederates when Charleston was evacuated on 18 February 1865.

Child, see *Alonzo Child*

City of Richmond

(Str)

City of Richmond was a blockade runner which the Confederacy chartered, probably in London, during the last year of war. Sailing under Comdr. Hunter Davidson, CSN, she conveyed officers, crew, and military stores to the ironclad *Stonewall* off Quiberon, France, in early January 1865.

_____

City of Richmond, see *George Page*

City of Vicksburg, see *Vicksburg*

Clara Dolsen

(SwStr: t. 939; l. 268'; b. 42'; dph. 8'9'')

Clara Dolsen was "a magnificent river steamer" in which half interest was owned by Bart Able and Albert Pearce of St. Louis. She was built in 1861 at Cincinnati, Ohio. Used in the service of

the Confederate States out of Memphis, Tenn., she was captured by Federal ships of the St. Charles Expedition on the White River, 14 June 1862. Later she operated with the Union army and eventually as USS *Clara Dolsen* (frequently written *Dolson*).

Clarence

(Brigantine: t. 253; l. 114'; b. 24'; dr. 11'; a. 1 12-pdr. how.)

Clarence, also known as *Coquette*, was built at Baltimore, Md., in 1857 for J. Crosby, a Baltimore fruit dealer. While transporting a cargo of coffee from Rio de Janeiro, Brazil, to Baltimore, Md., she was captured by CSS *Florida* on 6 May 1863. Comdr. J. N. Maffitt, CSN, commanding *Florida*, placed *Clarence* under Lt. C. W. Read, with 20 men as a prize crew. Lieutenant Read had requested that, rather than burn *Clarence*, he might try, with the ship's papers, to sail into Hampton Roads, Va., and if possible destroy or capture a Federal gunboat and burn Union merchant vessels congregated at Fortress Monroe. Commander Maffitt armed *Clarence* with one gun so that Read might capture prizes on his way to Hampton Roads.

En route to Virginia, *Clarence* captured the bark *Windward*, also known as *Whistling Wind*, on 6 June 1863, and on the next day the schooner *Alfred H. Partridge*. On 9 June she captured the brig *Mary Alvina*. From his prisoners Read learned that all vessels were restricted from Hampton Roads which was unusually well guarded, and he decided that his original plan would be impossible.

On 12 June *Clarence* captured the bark *Tacony*, and then immediately captured the schooner *M. A. Shindler*. Lieutenant Read transferred his force to *Tacony*, a better sailer than *Clarence*, and while this was being done, *Clarence* intercepted her last prize, the schooner *Kate Stewart*. *Clarence* was then burned after her short but unusually successful career, and Lieutenant Read and his men continued on *Tacony* to harass Union commerce along the Atlantic coast.

Clarendon

(Str: t. 143)

Clarendon, a ferryboat, was built in 1860 at Portsmouth, Va. She served the Confederacy as a dispatch vessel and transport during operations off Fort Fisher, N.C., in late December 1864. On 14 March 1865 she was seized by Union forces and burned.

Clifton

(SwStr: t. 892; l. 210′; b. 40′; dph. 13′6″; dr. 7′6″; cpl. 120; a. 4 32-pdr., 2 9″ sb., 1 30-pdr. r.)

Clifton, a ferryboat, was built in Brooklyn, N.Y., in 1861, and purchased 2 December 1861 by the U.S. Navy. Placed in commission late in 1861 or early 1862, she served with the Mortar Flotilla of the West Gulf Blockading Squadron, joined in the bombardment and capture of Forts Jackson and St. Philip, and attacked the Confederate batteries at Vicksburg, Miss., during which action on 28 June 1862 she took a shot through her boiler which killed seven men. She also assisted in the capture of Galveston in October 1862.

Clifton was seized by the Confederates at Sabine Pass, Tex., on 8 September 1863. She was then employed as a gunboat by the Texas Marine Department [See Annex III]. On 21 March 1864, while attempting to run the blockade off Sabine with a cargo of cotton she grounded on a bar, and to prevent capture by the blockading vessels was set on fire and burned by her crew after ineffectually disposing of her deckload to refloat her.

Clinch, see *General Clinch*

Colonel Hill

(Str)

Colonel Hill transported Army troops and supplies in the Cape Hatteras area in August 1861. On 20 July 1863 she was boarded and burned by Union army forces near Tarboro on the Tar River, N.C.

Colonel Lamb

Col. William Lamb, CSA, commanding Fort Fisher, N.C., was the blockade runner's best friend: he saved many such daring ships not only by the guns of the fort but by a mobile battery of Whitworth rifles with which he often drove off Federal blockade ships attempting to capture a stranded runner within view of safety in the haven.

(SwStr: t. 1,788; l. 281′; b. 36′; dph. 15′6″)

Colonel Lamb, one of the most famous and successful of the Confederate Navy's own blockade runners—a fine model of which can be seen in the Science Museum at Liverpool—was built in 1864 at that city as Jones, Quiggin & Company's Hull No. 165—a near sister to *Hope* which preceded her that year, but with much longer deckhouse and lacking the customary turtleback foredeck which *Hope* had.

She is identified with the dashing Captain Tom Lockwood and was christened by his wife. The shipbuilder, William Quiggin, registered *Colonel Lamb* in his name, then quietly transferred her to Confederate agent J. B. Lafitte in Nassau, where she fitted out. She survived the war intact and was sold as *Ariel* through Fraser, Trenholm & Co. to the Greek Government for a "ship of war." Now *Bouboulina*, after loading a cargo of explosives at Liverpool, she blew up, 29 November 1867, at anchor in the Mersey.

Colonel Lovell

(SwRam: t. 521; l. 162′; b. 30′10″; dr. 11′)

Colonel Lovell, previously named *Hercules*, was built in Cincinnati, Ohio, in 1843 and was owned by the Ocean Towing Co. of New Orleans. She was taken over in 1861 by Maj. Gen. M. Lovell, commanding the New Orleans military district, and converted to a cottonclad ram by installation of double pine bulwarks filled with compressed cotton and one-inch iron plates on each bow. She operated under the direction of the Confederate War Department and was attached to the Mississippi River Defense Fleet [See Annex II], commanded by Commodore J. E. Montgomery, a former river steamboat captain.

On 10 May 1862, while operating off Fort Pillow, Tenn., in defense of the river approaches to Memphis, *Colonel Lovell*, in company with seven of Montgomery's vessels, attacked the ironclad gunboats of the Federal Mississippi Flotilla. The action of Plum Point Bend which followed witnessed successful ramming tactics by the Confederates, though each of their vessels mounted at least four 8-inch guns. The Federal gunboats *Cincinnati* and *Mound City* were run on the banks in sinking condition. Later, Montgomery's force held off the Federal rams and gunboats until Fort Pillow was successfully evacuated on 1 June, and the Confederate rams fell back on Memphis to take on coal.

Following the Federal capture of Fort Pillow, Flag Officer Charles H. Davis, USN, commanding the Mississippi Flotilla, pressed on without delay and appeared off Memphis with superior force on 6 June. Included in his force were two of the Federal Army's rams, commanded by Col. C. R. Ellet. Montgomery, unable to retreat to Vicksburg because of his shortage of fuel and unwilling to destroy his boats, determined to fight against heavy odds. In the engagement that followed, one of *Colonel Lovell*'s engines malfunctioned and she became unmanageable. She was then rammed amidships by USS *Queen of the West*, and immediately struck again by USS *Monarch*, both of the Ellet fleet. *Colonel Lovell* sank in deep water in the middle of the river. Capt. J. C. Delancy and a number of his crew were able to swim ashore.

Colonel Stell

(SwStr: t. 199; l. 138′; b. 24′; dph. 4′8″)

Colonel Stell, also known as *Colonel Stelle* and *J. D. Stelle*, was built in 1860 at Pittsburgh, Pa., and owned by C. and F. A. Gearing of Galveston, Tex. Chartered by the Confederate Government on 30 September 1861 she was employed first on the Trinity River, Tex. On 3 April 1862 the Texas Marine Department chartered her. [See Appendix III]. Cooperating with the Army, she transported military stores and soldiers, and served on picket stations in the Galveston area during 1862–63.

Colonel Stell was accidentally sunk off Pelican Island in Galveston Bay on 10 February 1864. Quickly raised and repaired, she resumed her duties as a cargo ship and transport. In May 1864 she received orders to raise the hollow forged shafts of the wreck USS *Westfield*, which were converted to gun barrels by the hard-pressed Confederate Ordnance Department.

After the Civil War, *Colonel Stell* was in the possession of the U.S. Treasury Department who sold her on 12 July 1866. She was lost on 21 December 1867.

Colonel Stelle, see Colonel Stell

Columbia

(IrcRam: l. 216′; b. 51′4″; dph. 13′; dr. 13′6″; a. 6 guns; type *Columbia*)

CSS *Columbia*, an uncommonly strong ironclad ram, was constructed under contract at Charleston, S.C., in 1864, of yellow pine and white oak with iron fastenings and 6-inch iron plating.

Hull work was done by F. M. Jones to J. L. Porter's plans, plating and machinery by James M. Eason; her casemate was shortened to conserve precious metal and clad with 6″ iron.

When the Union forces took possession of Charleston on 18 February 1865 they found the greatly prized *Columbia* in jeopardy near Fort Moultrie; in coming out she had run on a sunken wreck and been damaged on 12 January 1865. Once she had been nearly ready for commissioning but when seized was found to have had her guns and some armor plating removed and shipworms already at work.

She was raised on 26 April and towed by USS *Vanderbilt* to Hampton Roads, Va., where she arrived 25 May 1865.

Condor

(SwStr: t. 300; l. 270′; b. 24′; dr. 7′; cpl. 50; cl. *Condor*)

Condor was the ill-fated precursor of a class of fast iron ships, the largest design of seven contracted out by the Confederate Navy Department to British shipbuilders. From Scotland she sailed on her maiden voyage—from the port of Greenock, which has led to the belief that she may also have been built there.

She was long and low, with three raked stacks fore and aft, turtleback forward, midship house, poop deck, one mast, straight stem and painted elusive white—all in all, presenting a striking appearance. Chased on her maiden voyage by blockaders, she arrived safely 1 October 1864 under the guns of Fort Fisher, on Swash Channel Bar at the entrance to Wilmington, N.C., only to run aground—it has been said to avoid the wreck of blockade-runner *Night Hawk*, which all accounts agree was stranded nearby. Lookouts appear to have been stationed on board *Condor* at low tide as late as December, but by this time any hope of getting her off must have been abandoned, for Colonel Lamb noted in his diary for 3 December that his battery had practiced with 150-pounder Armstrong rifles, their first shot hitting her forward stack, the second her after stack.

More famous than the ship herself was one of her passengers, the patriot and courier Rose Greenhow, who died in the surf—weighed down, tradition maintains, with vital dispatches for President Davis and $2,000 in gold received as royalties from her bestselling book on Confederate womanhood. The ship is forever linked also to the colorful personality of her captain, August Charles Hobart-Hampden, RN, VC, alias "Captain Roberts" or "Samuel S. Ridge", a younger son of the Duke of Buckingham and a favorite of Queen Victoria. He apparently cleared *Condor* under the alias of "Captain Hewitt"; ever a chameleon, another trip he answered to "Gulick." Captain Hobart-Hampden survived until 1886, when he was buried in Scutari as "Hobart Pasha", retired Admiral-in-Chief or Marshal of the Ottoman Empire's Navy, and Vice-Admiral, RN (Ret.)

Confederate States, see Laurel

Confederate States, see *United States*

Conrad, see *Tuscaloosa*

Coquette

(ScStr: t. 300; l. 228′; b. 25′; dph. 12′2″; dr. 10′; s. 13.5 k.)

Coquette was a 200-horsepower, twin-screw, iron steamer, with three masts, schooner rigged, built in Scotland at Renfrew—perhaps by Hoby & Son. Her purchase by the Confederate Navy was arranged through Comdr. James D. Bulloch, CSN agent in Britain, in September 1863. She carried large cargoes of cotton—up to 1,259 bales—out of the Confederacy, running back in with indispensable loads of munitions. In 1864 she was under the command of Lt. Robert R. Carter, CSN, and in the spring of that year she imported two marine engines past the Federal blockade into Wilmington.

Although successful for some months, her boiler tubes became clogged with scale from inadequate maintenance in this most exacting service. Secretary Mallory, fearing she would be captured, wrote Commander Bulloch 10 August 1864 that she must be "sold in consequence of her decreasing speed." Bulloch confirmed in his reply that, "this vessel was bought for a special purpose and, notwithstanding some defects has been a very profitable piece of property to the [Navy] Department." But she "broke down and had to return to Bermuda and . . . waited three months for machinery from England." At this juncture, Messrs. W. W. Finney, B. F. Ficklin and J. R. Anderson & Co. (Tredegar Iron Works, Richmond), consented to take her for £16,000.

Coquette was laid up in Nassau at war's end, when a Southern agent of the owners went there to try to get possession of her before she was seized by the United States. A certain Capt. Richard Squires accordingly took her into Baltimore, where he arrived six days later, 17 December 1865, and turned her over to the Government, for which he had been an undercover agent all along.

———

Coquette, see *Clarence*

Cornubia

Cornubia is the Latinized name for Cornwall, an ancient Celtic kingdom, today the southwesternmost county of England and noted for its rugged coastline and survival of picturesque folkways from pre-Roman times.

(SwStr: t. 411 [589, 359, 259]; l. 190′; b. 24′6″; dph. 12′6″; dr. 9′; sp. 18 k.)

Cornubia was a fast, powerful, iron steamer of 230 h.p., long and low, painted white, with two funnels close together. She was built in Hayle, Cornwall, in 1858 for ferry service from there to nearby St. Ives under the house flag of the Hayle Steam Packet Co. The Confederacy bought her in the United Kingdom and she proved a very good investment, bringing 22 vital cargoes through the blockade in 1863.

Her 23d voyage was disastrous, having repercussions far beyond those stemming from the loss of a precious cargo: Blockader USS *Niphon* gave chase as she sought to run in to Wilmington, N.C., Lt. Comdg. Richard H. Gayle, CSN, beached his ship at 0230, 8 November, 11 miles north of New Inlet; the captain, carpenter and one seaman remained on board while the officers, crew and passengers escaped to shore. By 0300, USS *James Adger* had towed *Cornubia* free on the flood tide still intact and she was duly sent to Boston as a prize, along with a bag of watersoaked mail, which one of her officers had tried to dispose of in the surf, and the three captives.

Cornubia was more correctly *Lady Davis* (confused by Secretary Welles in one letter with *Jeff Davis*) when captured, having been renamed when a new *Cornubia* came out in June or July, but she was known to her captors by her old, familiar label while the *Cornubia* papers quickly became a rosetta stone to unlock the management secrets of the Confederate Army-Navy-Treasury blockade-running fleet on the eve of the Mallory-Trenholm-Bulloch newbuilding program in Britain. The most immediate result was a new, tough policy toward British seamen caught challenging the blockade. U.S. District Attorney Richard Henry Dana, Jr., at Boston, was designated to receive a sealed packet of all papers taken in the prize. Transmitting them to Secretary Welles, 26 December, after study, Dana wrote: "We have found in the prize steamer *Cornubia* letters which prove that that steamer, the *R. E. Lee,* and *Ella & Annie* and others of their class are the property of the Confederate Government and that their commanders are in the service of the Confederate Navy Department. This raises the question whether, in like cases, the Government will detain foreign seamen found on board as prisoners of war. The letters also show that they are under orders to conceal these facts while in neutral ports, in order to escape the rules applicable to public vessels of belligerents." Welles endorsed the letter: "The persons captured on the boats mentioned and others in like cases to be detained as prisoners."

Comdr. Thomas H. Patterson, USN, of *James Adger* noted, "Her captain remarked to my executive officer that 'though the *Cornubia* is a small vessel the Confederate Government could better have afforded to lose almost any other vessel.' " He was not referring merely to essential cargo. The operational pattern of the Confederate Army transport service developed as follows: The ship's Confederate register showed the Secretary of War, "James A. Seddon, of Richmond, Va., is her sole owner." Commanders of these transports were C. S. Navy officers—either regulars or officers such as Gayle, commissioned "Lt. for the War, CSN," reporting to Col. Josiah Gorgas, Chief of Ordnance, CSA, through special War Department Agent J. M. Seixas in Wilmington, N.C. "The entire ship's accounts will be forwarded through this agency" (War Dept., Ordnance Bureau, CSA), including monthly reports of stores and quarterly inventories.

Cornubia had been commanded by a Briton, Capt. J. M. Burroughs, to keep her British register, as Commander Bulloch explained to Secretary Mallory the following year: "I would suggest that as fast as the ships are paid for, Navy officers be put in command as a general rule," adding that such vessels "ought to be kept registered in the names of private individuals, otherwise serious embarrassment may arise, as Lord Russell has stated in the House of Lords that if it could be shown that the steamers trading between the Confederate States and the British Islands were owned by the Confederate States Government, they would be considered as transports and would be forbidden to enter English ports, except under the restrictions imposed upon all men-of-war of the belligerent powers."

In accordance with this pattern we read—Gorgas to Gayle care of Seixas, Wilmington, June 1863: "You will assume command of the Steamer *Cornubia* relieving Capt. J. M. Burroughs . . . (whose contract) terminates on reaching Bermuda . . . you should assume command at Wilmington before starting, making the voyage terminate there hereafter. Captain Burroughs has been requested to accompany you, giving you the benefit of his experience and advice. He will also be able to assist you very much in acquiring good

officers and crew. Take immediate steps to change your flag and register under Confederate colors. . . . Those who decline to reship will be discharged and furnished with free passage to Bermuda." Appended for "the steamers of the War Department" was a scale of wages and bounties (60 to 100% of base wages, earned on completion of voyage) effective 1 July 1863; articles to be signed for six months. The intent of the whole system was revealed in, "Being in the Confederate service, they are entitled to be exchanged as prisoners-of-war."

Corpus Christi

(Gbt)

Corpus Christi was listed by Confederate army sources among the gunboats which operated with the Texas Marine Department late in 1864. [See Annex III].

Corypheus

(Sch: t. 81; l. 72'; b. 20'; dph 6')

Corypheus, a yacht built at Brook Haven, N.Y., in 1859, was seized under orders of Gen. M. Lovell, CSA, outfitted as a gunboat, and operated in Lakes Borgne and Pontchartrain. On 13 May 1862, a cutter from USS *Calhoun* proceeded to Bayou Bonfouca and cut out the gunboat. Following appraisal, the prize was purchased that month from the Key West prize court for $14,724, and promptly taken into the Union Navy.

Cotton, see *J. A. Cotton*

Cotton, Jr., see *J. A. Cotton*

Cotton Plant

(SwStr: t. 59)

Cotton Plant, built at Rochester, Pa., in 1859, was used by the Confederate Army as a transport and supply boat in the Tallahatchie and Yazoo Rivers during 1862–63. During the expedition of the Union Mississippi Squadron into the Yazoo, and consequent destruction of the fleet and Navy Yard at Yazoo City there in May 1863, *Cotton Plant* was one of four that escaped into the Tallahatchie. Two months later she was ordered burned by the Confederate Army command to prevent capture.

————

(StwStr: t. 85; l. 107'; b. 18.9'; dr. 4.5')

Cotton Plant, sometimes referred to as *Cotton Planter*, was built at Philadelphia, Pa., in 1860 and reportedly carried troops in the Pamlico River as early as September 1861. She sailed with CSS *Albemarle* when that ironclad ram attacked Union forces at Plymouth, N.C., sank *Southfield* and drove off *Miami, Ceres* and *Whitehead* 18–19 April 1864. On 5 May 1864 she steamed as convoy to *Albemarle* from the Roanoke River en route to Alligator River. The convoy was engaged by ships of the North Atlantic Blockading Squadron but both the ram and *Cotton Plant* with several launches in tow escaped into the Roanoke River.

In May 1865 *Cotton Plant* was surrendered to Union officials near Halifax, N.C., by parties claiming that she had been appropriated by Confederate authorities. Ownership was adjudicated at Plymouth and she was turned over to the U.S. Treasury purchasing agent to transport cotton and provisions. She was later delivered to the U.S. Navy at Norfolk.

Cotton Planter, see Cotton Plant

Countess

(SwStr: t. 198; l. 150'; b. 30'; dph. 4'9'')

Countess was built in 1860 in Cincinnati, Ohio, and served the Confederates in the Mississippi River area. Maj. Gen. J. G. Walker, CSA, retained *Countess* to help evacuate Alexandria, La., before the arrival of Union forces, and set fire to her after she grounded in the rapids at Alexandria.

Crawford, see W. W. Crawford

Crescent

(SwStr: t. 171)

Crescent was built in 1858 at Mobile, Ala., and served the Confederate army there as a workboat, tow boat, and flag-of-truce boat. Often she unloaded cargo from arriving blockade runners so that they could get over the bar into port.

Cuba, see Calhoun

Curlew

(SwStr: t. 260; l. 150'; dr. 4'6''; s. 12 k.; a. 2 guns)

CSS *Curlew*, built at Wilmington, Del., in 1856, was a tug purchased at Norfolk, Va., in 1861 by the Confederate Government. She was ordered to duty under command of Comdr. T. T. Hunter, CSN, in North Carolina waters and participated in the battle of Roanoke Island on 7 February 1862. She was sunk in shoal water by the Con-

federates the following day to prevent capture by United States forces.

———

(SwStr: t. 645; l. 225'; b. 24'; dph. 11'; dr. 6'; cl. *Curlew*)

Curlew was ordered by the Confederate Navy in England. As Jones, Quiggin & Co.'s Hull No. 177, she was laid down at Liverpool in 1864, and launched with her three sisters the same day in 1865, but is believed to have been delivered too late to serve the Confederacy.

Currituck

(Str)

The tug *Currituck* was active as a dispatch, flag-of-truce and towboat along the coast of North Carolina during the early years of the war.

Curtis Peck

(SwStr: t. 446)

The fast steamer *Curtis Peck* built in 1842 at New York was employed in reconnaissance duty by the Confederates on the James River during August 1861. She operated as a flag-of-truce boat in May 1862, delivering exchanged Union prisoners to Fortress Monroe. The Confederates sank her in September 1862 along with the steamers *Jamestown* and *Northampton* to obstruct the James River below Drewry's Bluff against passage of advancing Union forces.

D. Bentley

(Gbt)

D. Bentley, an aged craft, was reputedly outfitted as a gunboat at Port Hudson in February 1863 to assist *Frank Webb* in a proposed attack on USS *Conestoga* and other Union ships near the mouth of the Red River.

Dalman

Dalman, also known as *Dalma*, served as receiving ship in Mobile Harbor in 1862. She continued her duty on the Mobile Station with Adm. Franklin Buchanan's force. *Dalman* was surrendered to Union authorities 4 May 1865.

Damascus

Damascus was one of several ships reported to have been sunk by the Confederates late in 1862 to obstruct the James River near Drewry's Bluff.

Dan

(Str: t. 112)

Dan, a small river steamer built in 1858 at Calcasieu, La., was in Confederate service on the Calcasieu River and Lake in early October 1862 when she was captured by a launch from USS *Kensington* and sent in as a prize. She was sunk in the Mississippi during February 1863 while in Union service.

Danmark, see *Santa Maria*

Danube

(FltBtry: t. 980; l. 170'4"; b. 30'11"; dr. 16'11"; a. 4 42-pdr.)

Danube was built at Bath, Maine, in 1854. She was confiscated in Mobile Bay by the Confederate authorities in May 1861.

In 1863 *Danube* was anchored at the Apalachee Battery as part of the defense of Mobile. The Confederates ordered her sunk in Mobile Bay in November 1864 in the upper line of obstructions in the Spanish River gap.

Darby

(Str)

Darby served as a transport for stores, ordnance, and troops on Bayou Teche and in Berwick Bay, La., in support of Confederate army forces at Camp Bisland, Bayou Teche, which fell to combined Army-Navy forces of the Union on 14 April 1863.

Darlington

(SwStr: t. 298)

Darlington, built at Charleston, S.C., in 1849, was probably employed by the Confederate Army along the Florida coast. She was captured by launches of USS *Pawnee* under Comdr. C. R. P. Rodgers on 3 March 1862 while trying to escape with military wagons, mules, and stores from Fernandina, Fla., when that town fell to the Union. She was transferred to the U.S. Army for use as a transport.

David

(ScTB: l. 50'; b. 6'; dr. 5'; cpl. 4; a. 1 spar torpedo)

David [1] was built as a private venture by T. Stoney at Charleston, S.C., in 1863, and put under the control of the Confederate States Navy. The cigar-shaped boat carried a 60- or 70-pound explosive charge on the end of a spar projecting forward from her bow. Designed to operate very low in the water, *David* resembled in general a submarine; she was, however, strictly a surface vessel.

On the night of 5 October 1863 *David*, com-

[1] The term "David" came to be the generic term for any torpedo boat resembling *David*, the prototype of others built in Charleston. The names, if any, that were given to these other boats are not known. Their existence caused some concern among Union naval officers but they were never a serious threat to the blockade. The exact number of "Davids" built is not known. One was taken to the U.S. Naval Academy and was there for some years after the war.

A David torpedo boat is shown aground in Charleston Harbor.

manded by Lt. W. T. Glassell, CSN, slipped down Charleston Harbor to attack the casemated ironclad steamer *New Ironsides*. The torpedo boat approached undetected until she was within 50 yards of the blockader. Hailed by the watch on board *New Ironsides*, Glassell replied with a blast from a shotgun and *David* plunged ahead to strike. Her torpedo detonated under the starboard quarter of the ironclad, throwing high a column of water which rained back upon the Confederate vessel and put out her boiler fires. Her engine dead, *David* hung under the quarter of *New Ironsides* while small arms fire from the Federal ship spattered the water around the torpedo boat.

Believing that their vessel was sinking, Glassell and two others abandoned her; the pilot, W. Cannon, who could not swim, remained on board. A short time later, Assistant Engineer J. H. Tomb swam back to the craft and climbed on board. Rebuilding the fires Tomb succeeded in getting *David's* engine working again, and with Cannon at the wheel, the torpedo boat steamed up the channel to safety. Glassell and Seaman J. Sullivan, *David's* fireman, were captured. *New Ironsides*, though not sunk, was seriously damaged by the explosion. Lt. Glassell was "promoted for gallant and meritorious conduct", to rank as Commander from 5 October.

The next 4 months of *David's* existence are obscure. She or other torpedo boats tried more attacks on Union blockaders; reports from different ships claim three such attempts, all unsuccessful, during the remainder of October 1863. On 6 March 1864, *David* attacked *Memphis* in the North Edisto River, S.C. The torpedo boat struck the blockader first on the port quarter but the torpedo did not explode. *Memphis* slipped her chain, at the same time firing ineffectively at *David* with small arms. Putting about, the torpedo boat struck *Memphis* again, this time a glancing blow on the starboard quarter; once more the torpedo missed fire. Since *Memphis* had now opened up with her heavy guns, *David*, having lost part of her stack when rammed, retreated up the river out of range. *Memphis*, uninjured, resumed her blockading station.

David's last confirmed action came on 18 April 1864 when she tried to sink the screw frigate *Wabash*. Alert lookouts on board the blockader sighted *David* in time to permit the frigate to slip her chain, avoid the attack, and open fire on

the torpedo boat. Neither side suffered any damage.

The ultimate fate of *David* is uncertain. Several torpedo boats of this type fell into Union hands when Charleston was captured in February 1865. *David* may well have been among them.

Day, see *James L. Day*

De Soto

(SwStr)

De Soto was a sidewheel steamer, one of the many taken over by the Confederate forces for use on the Mississippi and other rivers. In April of 1862 she was busy ferrying troops to evacuate the area near Island No. 10 and was used, under a flag of truce, to communicate with the Union gunboats. On 7 April 1862 she carried Confederate officers who surrendered possession of Island No. 10 to Flag Officer Foote. It was at night, and *De Soto* approached cautiously, giving four blasts of her whistle, repeatedly, until answered, whereupon Federal officers came on board to accept surrender.

She then became USS *De Soto*, with a later name change to *General Lyon*.

Deer

(SwStr: t. 857 [771]; l. 238'; b. 26'2''; dph. 17'10''; dr. 7'6''; cl. *Owl*)

Deer was the last ship of the first class of steel blockade runners procured for Secretary of the Navy Mallory by Comdr. James D. Bulloch, CSN, in United Kingdom shipyards; four hulls were bought in Liverpool, well along on the ways at Jones, Quiggin & Co., and finished up on schedule without alterations; *Deer* was Hull No. 170. The financial *raison d'être* of these vessels is explained in Commander Bulloch's letter to Secretary Mallory 15 September 1864: that they "are not . . . to be paid for out of the funds of the Navy Department, but the cost of construction and outfit is provided for by the Treasury Department, through its financial agent, General C. J. McRae . . . the management and navigation of the ships to and from the Confederate ports will be under the control of the Navy Department." [Gen. McRae was special agent to regulate disbursement of the "Erlanger loan" and sell Confederate Treasury bonds.]

Deer carried a particularly sensitive Navy cargo on her maiden voyage out of Liverpool, early in

November 1864: "goods . . . almost exclusively for submarine defense," consigned to Comdr. Hunter Davidson, CSN, the torpedo (mine) specialist, and an "Ebonite machine" for Comdr. Matthew F. Maury.

Her second trip, *Deer* was not so lucky: Running into Charleston with a valuable load of copper and arms, 18 February 1865, her lookout failed to spot a trio of monitors, USS *Canonicus*, *Catskill* and *Monadnock*, lying across the channel entrance; the fleet *Deer* submitted to the ultimate humiliation of surrendering to slow "cheese boxes on rafts." The prize court in Boston sold *Deer* to Nickerson's line of steamers whom she served locally as *Palmyra;* resold to the Argentine in June 1869, she disappears from the registers before 1875.

Defiance

(SwRam: t. 544; l. 178'; b. 29'5"; dph. 10'11"; a. 1 32-pdr.)

Defiance, a high pressure steamer, was built at Cincinnati, Ohio in 1849. She was purchased for the Confederate Army, probably from the Southern Steamship Co., New Orleans, La., in the latter part of 1861. Capt. J. E. Montgomery, a former river steamboat captain, selected her to be part of his River Defense Fleet [See Annex II]. On 25 January 1862 he began to convert her into a cottonclad ram by placing a 4-inch oak sheath with a one-inch iron covering on her bow, and by installing double pine bulkheads filled with compressed cotton bales.

On 10 March 1862, *Defiance's* conversion was completed and she steamed from New Orleans to Fort Jackson on the lower Mississippi to operate in the Confederate defense of New Orleans. *Defiance*, with five other ships of Montgomery's fleet in that area was under the overall command of Capt. J. A. Stevenson, who operated under Capt. J. K. Mitchell, commanding Confederate naval forces on the lower Mississippi.

When Flag Officer D. G. Farragut, USN, ran his fleet past Forts Jackson and St. Phillip on 24 April 1862 on his way to New Orleans, *Defiance*, under Capt. J. D. McCoy, was the only river defense vessel to escape destruction or capture. On 26 April Captain Stevenson turned her over directly to Captain Mitchell after her captain, officers, and crew left her. On 28 April, Captain Mitchell, not having enough men for a crew, and realizing that capture was inevitable after the forts' surrender, burned her to keep her from falling into Union hands.

Delight

(Sch)

Delight, a fishing smack which sailed under Confederate papers was captured by USS *New London* on 9 December 1861 near Cat Island Passage in Mississippi Sound.

Dew Drop

(SwStr: t. 184)

Dew Drop, built at Cincinnati, Ohio, in 1858, was used by Confederate army forces in western waters. Early in May 1863 she was ordered to transport commissary stores up the Sunflower River. While so engaged knowledge came of approaching Federal gunboats and on 30 May 1863 she was burned to the water's edge to prevent capture. Union forces led by Acting Lt. G. W. Brown later effected her complete destruction.

Diana

(StRam: dr. 3'2"; cpl. 61; a. 2 12-pdr. how.)

Diana was a steamer offered for charter or sale at Galveston, Tex. on 23 September 1861 by the Houston Navigation Co., along with steamers *Bayou City* and *Neptune No. 2*. She was mentioned as a steamer of the Houston Line on 19 December 1861 when she took the seized Federal metal life boat *Francis* in tow for San Jacinto, Tex., to be put in condition for CSS *General Rusk* fitting out in that port. Mentioned as a steamer under Captain Blakmen, she was ordered to carry the crew of CSS *General Rusk* from Galveston to Houston on 20 January 1862.

Diana and *Bayou City* where eventually fitted out as rams and used as gunboats of the Texas Marine Department [See Annex III] for the defense of Galveston Bay. One-inch iron protected their bows and their decks were barricaded with cotton. The two warships, listed by the Texas Marine Department as gunboats, were still on duty in Galveston Bay as of 27 October 1863.

———

(SwIrcGbt: t. 239)

Diana was a steamer reported to have escaped from Farragut's passage of Fort St. Philip and Fort Jackson, 24 April 1862, into the city of New Orleans. She was taken possession of by USS *Cayuga* on the 27th.

Diana was appraised for Union service at New Orleans on 5 May 1862 and became a transport on interior waters. Finally assigned to assist Federal ships in Berwick Bay, La., she was sent into Grand Lake, 28 March 1863, to make reconnaissance down the Atchafalaya to the mouth of Bayou Teche. When she had passed the mouth of Bayou Teche, near Pattersonville, La., Confederate shore batteries cut away her tiller ropes, disabled her engine, and caused her to drift ashore where she surrendered. Her Union commander, Acting Master T. L. Peterson, along with five other men were killed and three were wounded in this brave 2-hour action.

Diana was taken into the Confederate army service on Bayou Teche in support of troops at Camp Bisland, La. On 11 April 1863 under Lieutenant Nettles of Valverde Battery, CSA, she showed great skill as a gunboat in driving Union troops back on Bayou Teche from Camp Bisland. Nettles, taken severely ill, was relieved on 13 April 1863 by gallant Captain O. J. Semmes of the Artillery as thousands of Union troops moved in with the support of Federal gunboats for a fierce action on Bayou Teche and Camp Bisland that lasted until sundown. She concentrated on the center of the advancing Union line with a battery of Parrott guns until a 30-pounder shell penetrated her forward plating and exploded in the engine room to kill the first and assistant engineer and damage her engine. Pulling beyond range of the Union guns, she completed repairs near midnight and was ordered the following morning to move up to Franklin, La., to support the right flank of Confederate troops by sweeping the fields and woods formerly held by Union forces. When badly outnumbered Confederate forces began their withdrawal from Franklin, she maintained her position near an already burning bridge until General Mouton and his staff followed their troops across to safety. Semmes and his brave crew then abandoned and burned *Diana* to prevent her capture by Union forces.

Dick Keys

(Str)

Dick Keys, sometimes reported as *Dick Keyes*, was captured by the Confederate fleet off Mobile on 8 May 1861, sold into private ownership and chartered to assist blockade runners out of that port. She joined steamer *Crescent* in saving 30,000 pounds of powder and a million musket caps from the British steamer *Ann*, 29–30 June 1862, when that ship grounded under the guns of Fort Morgan. *Ann* floated out on the ebb tide to be taken by Union ships before all of her cargo could be removed. In the following years *Dick Keys* gave valuable service in Mobile Bay as a transport between the forts and the city of Mobile. She assisted in towing CSS *Tennessee* down the Mobile River on 29 February 1864 and came under Federal gunfire off Fort Gaines on 5–6 August 1864.

On the night of 24 October 1864 *Dick Keys* was to leave Mobile carrying Lt. J. M. Baker, CSN, bound for Blakely, Ala., whence a boat expedition of 100 men would be launched overland in wagons to sail the Perdido River for a landing near Fort Pickens, Fla. No further record of her service has been found.

Dime

(Str)

Dime, used to transport Confederate army troops and materiel was assigned in October 1863 to the Texas Marine Department for service as a tender and transport [See Annex III].

Dixie

(Sch: t. 110; cpl. 35; a. 3 guns)

Dixie was originally the Baltimore-built schooner *H. & J. Neild*, completed in 1865. Capt. Thomas J. Moore of Virginia bought her in 1860 and operated in the West Indian trade until war broke. Then he rechristened her *Dixie*, ran the blockade into Charleston, formed a syndicate and petitioned for a letter of marque. *Dixie* was commissioned a privateer 26 June 1861, Captain Moore still commanding.

Her month's cruise netted two valuable prizes out of three taken: Bark *Glenn*, the 23rd, was run into Morehead City, N.C., and condemned; schooner *Mary Alice* fully laden with sugar surrendered the 25th, but was recaptured by USF *Wabash* before making a Confederate port; *Rowena* of Philadelphia had a complement that would endanger his small prize crew, so Captain Moore took command of her himself and brought with him all but a skeleton crew of 5 to man *Dixie*. After some narrow escapes, *Dixie* and prize together slipped back into Charleston through Bull's Bay and up under the guns of Fort Pinckney, 27 August. *Dixie* was sold as well as *Rowena*, very satisfactorily; on 15 October the little privateer schooner ended her successful chapter as a privateer, went to A. J. White & Son, locally, later becoming *Kate Hale* and *Success*.

Doctor Beatty

(SwStr: t. 281; l. 171'; b. 28'9''; dph 6'; a. 1 20-pdr.)

Dr. Beatty, spelled variously as *Doctor Beaty*, *Doctor Batey*, and *Dr. Battie*, was built at Louisville, Ky., in 1850. She was described as a frail steamer by the Confederates who had outfitted her with 900 bales of cotton for use as a transport and boarding ship.

Dr. Beatty was a unit of the expeditionary force that included the rams *Queen of the West* and *Webb*, and the steamer *Grand Era* which attacked USS *Indianola* near New Carthage, Miss., on 24 February 1863. During the engagement this steamer, commanded by Lt. Col. F. Brand, CSA, and carrying a volunteer boarding party of 250 men closed *Indianola* only to receive word of her sinking condition and surrender.

During July 1863 *Dr. Beatty* escaped capture by USS *Manitou* and *Petrel* by running under the guns of the fort at Harrisonburg in the Ouachita River.

Dodge

(Sch: t. 153 [71.5]; l. 100'4''; b. 23'; dph. 8'8''; cpl. 26; a. 1 9-pdr.)

Dodge was originally USRC *Henry Dodge* serving under the command of Capt. W. F. Rogers of the U.S. Revenue Marine.

She was seized by the State of Texas on 2 March 1861 and subsequently turned over to the Confederate Navy. Remaining in Rogers' command, she assisted the Confederate Army in defending the Texas coast until December 1862 when she was officially transferred to the control of the Confederate Army's Quartermaster at Houston.

In 1864 *Dodge* passed into private hands and under the name *Mary Sorley* operated as a blockade runner. She was captured by USS *Sciota* off Galveston, Tex., on 4 April 1864 en route to Havana with a cargo of cotton.

Dollie Webb

(StwGbt: t. 139; a. 5 guns)

Webb—only twice referred to in published official records by any but her last name, once as *Dollie* and once as *Dolly*—is believed to have been a Wheeling, Va., steamer built there in 1859. [It does not seem likely she was *Frank Webb*, as

one compiler has suggested, unless there were two different ships involved]. In the one available description of her, she was a large sternwheeler, "ship built", "a regular gunboat" with "five pieces of artillery and a complement of 200 men, and is commanded by Major [George T.] Howard. I judge her . . . to be a towboat altered," wrote Lt. George H. Preble, USN, on 22 July 1862. *Webb* appears to be inseparable from *Music* for about two weeks and then both fade into obscurity again. [See *Music, inf.*]

Dolly

(Str)

Dolly was a steamer which served Confederate authorities in the Roanoke River. She was seized by the U.S. Navy near Edwards Ferry, N.C., in May 1865; on the 27th it was reported that she had been sunk in a canal along with a lighter of iron plates. Her dimensions and importance are not recorded.

Don

(ScStr: t. 390; l. 162'; b. 23'; dph. 12'3''; dr. 6'; cpl. 43; s. 10–14 k.)

Don was the iron, twin-screw, two-stacked running-mate of *Hansa*—both of which were blockade-runners operated and partly owned by the State of North Carolina and are generally considered to have been public vessels for all practical purposes. A Captain Cory commanded *Don* when, as a still new, $115,000 ship carrying a $200,000 cargo of Army uniforms, blankets and shoes in from Nassau, she fell prey to USS *Pequot*, 4 March 1864, on her third attempt that voyage to run into Wilmington, N.C.

She was purchased from the Boston prize court next month and commissioned USS *Don*, assigned to the North Atlantic Blockading Squadron which had captured her. She was sold to commercial interests 28 August 1868 after being stricken from the Navy register.

Doubloon

(SwStr: t. 293; l. 165'; b. 33'; dph. 5')

Doubloon, built in 1859 at Cincinnati and taken over at New Orleans in 1861, served as a Confederate Army transport in the western rivers throughout the war. She is last mentioned in the records by U.S. gunboat *Lafayette* in the Red River on 30 May 1863 as being hemmed in somewhere "in the rivers above."

Drewry

(Gbt: t. 166; l. 106'; b. 21'; dph. 8'; dr. 5'; a. 1 6.4" r., 1 7" r.)

Drewry was a wooden gunboat with foredeck protected by an iron V-shaped shield. Classed as a tender, she was attached to Flag Officer F. Forrest's squadron in the James River sometime in 1863 with Master L. Parrish, CSN, in command.

In addition to transporting troops and other routine service, she took part in several engagements along the river prior to 24 January 1865, when, in Trent's Reach, she was destroyed by two shots from a 100-pounder rifle in a battery of the 1st Connecticut Artillery. The second hit exploded her magazine as she assisted CSS Richmond to get afloat; all but two of her crew had reached safety before the explosion.

Duane

(Sch: dp. 153; l. 102'; b. 23'; dph. 8'8"; dr. 9'7")

Duane was the schooner-rigged United States Revenue Cutter William J. Duane, seized by the Confederates at Norfolk, Va., on 18 April 1861. She was built at Philadelphia by Jacob Tees.

Dunbar

(Str)

Dunbar, a steamer under Captain Fowler, was dispatched from Fort Henry, Tenn., on 4 February 1862 in company with steamer Lynn Boyd to embark two regiments stationed at Paris Landing, Tenn. General Tilghman, CSA, and Major Gilmer, CSA, debarked in a small boat the morning of 6 February 1862 to direct the defense of Fort Henry which surrendered to Union forces that same day. Dunbar was sunk off the Tennessee River, in Cypress Creek, to prevent her capture by the Federal Gunboat Fleet. She may have been the 213-ton side-wheel steamer that was built in 1859 at Brownsville, Pa., and first home ported in Pittsburgh, Pa.

E. J. Gay, see Edward J. Gay

Earl Van Dorn, see General Earl Van Dorn

Eastport

(SwStr: t. 700 [570]; l. 280' dr. 6'3")

Eastport, a well modeled, fast Louisville, Ky., steamer built at New Albany, Ind., in 1852, was acquired by Navy in January 1862 and underwent conversion to an ironclad gunboat at Cerro Gordo on the Tennessee River prior to duty with Lt. I. N. Brown's flotilla. Her alterations were about half completed when on 7 February 1862 she was captured by the Union gunboats, Conestoga, Tyler, and Lexington, together with the materials to finish the job.

Eastport was sent in to Cairo, Ill., and her conversion finished. She then served with the Union Army until 9 January 1863, when she was turned over to the Navy to be part of the Mississippi Squadron. Eastport steamed on western waters until sunk on 15 April 1864 in the Red River by a Confederate torpedo. Efforts to salvage her failed and she was blown up and destroyed to prevent capture on 26 April 1864.

It has been suggested that Eastport may formerly have been C. E. Hillman. This seems highly unlikely. Hillman was probably the 420-ton Wheeling sidewheeler built in 1860 at Shousetown, Pa., and abandoned in 1867.

Eclipse, see Petrel

Ed Howard, see General Polk

Edith, see Chickamauga

Edward J. Gay

(SwStr: t. 823)

Edward J. Gay, known also as E. J. Gay, was built at St. Louis, Mo., in 1859 and impressed into Confederate States service on 1 February 1863 for duty with Commodore Brown's fleet. The Union expedition up the Yazoo River caused her to be scuttled and burned in July 1863 to obstruct the Yalobusha River and avoid capture.

Edwards (steam tug), see Forrest

Edwards (steamer), see Weldon N. Edwards

Egypt Mills

(ScStr: t. 70)

Egypt Mills, probably built at Poplar Neck, Md., in 1856 and first enrolled at Philadelphia, was seized by Confederate authorities and operated as a river transport. After Confederate withdrawal from the Roanoke River, she was captured there with Cotton Plant (q.v.), 22 May 1865, by Shamrock, Comdr. W. H. Macomb, USN, who maintained that the two steamers, whether "purchased or seized from their owners . . . were certainly rebel Government property." Egypt Mills had on board a quantity of Confederate Government cotton salvaged from the Halifax, N.C., Navy

Yard during evacuation. Both were "claimed as private property by citizens of Halifax and elsewhere"—without success; Macomb sent both to Norfolk in June 1865. *Egypt Mills'* documentation shows she was forfeited "for breach of laws" but redocumented as *Alida* (consistently though unaccountably shown as a sidewheeler) 14 December next and returned to commercial operation. She ended her active service in 1869.

El Paraguay, see *Ivy*

Eliza G.

(Str)

Eliza G. was used as a Confederate transport. On 16 June 1862 she was sunk together with *Maurepas* and *Mary Patterson* to obstruct the White River near St. Charles, Ark., against the advance of Union gunboats.

Eliza Simmons, see *Pontchartrain*

Ellis

(SwStTug: a. 1 32-pdr. r., 1 how.)

CSS *Ellis* was purchased at Norfolk, Va., in 1861 by the State of North Carolina and turned over to the Confederacy when that State became a member. With Comdr. W. T. Muse, CSN, in command she played an important part in the defense of Forts Hatteras and Clark in Hatteras Inlet, N.C., 28–29 August 1861, of Roanoke Island, 7–8 February 1862 and of Elizabeth City, N.C., on 10 February 1862; that day she was captured by the Union Army after a desperate struggle in which her commander, Lt. J. W. Cooke, CSN, was badly wounded.

Ellis was taken into the Navy and assigned to the North Atlantic Blockading Squadron. She served well until 25 November 1862 when she grounded above the mouth of New River, N.C. She was set afire to prevent recapture and demolished by the explosion of her own magazine. Lt. William B. Cushing, USN, was her last commander.

Elma

(Sch)

Elma, also referred to as *Major Minter*, was taken into Confederate army service in July 1862 under plans for arming and manning her to prevent Union forces from entering Corpus Christi Bay. On 11 August 1862 *Elma* was run into the channel of Nueces Bay where she grounded and on the following day she was fired and destroyed to prevent capture.

Elmira

(StwStr: t. 139; l. 125'; b. 27'; dr. 4'6")

Elmira, built at Pittsburgh, Pa., in 1858, was acquired by the Confederates in 1861 for use as a transport. On 13 July 1863 she was seized by *Forest Rose* and *Petrel* in the Tensas River and sent into Cairo as a prize.

Emma Bett, see *Emma Betts*

Emma Betts

(Str: t. 79)

Emma Betts, also known as *Emma Bett*, was built in 1858 at Pittsburgh, Pa., and used to transport supplies and ammunition for the Confederate army during 1862 and 1863 on the Mississippi and Sunflower Rivers. On 30 May 1863 she was captured and burned in Quiver Bayou by three boats from USS *Linden* and USS *Forest Rose*.

Empire

(Str)

Empire was chartered by the Virginia State Navy under Captain Milligan. She towed ballasted ships into position to assist in obstructing the channels of the river between the forts at Norfolk in May 1861. In that same month she twice sailed under a flag-of-truce with Capt. T. T. Hunter of the Virginia Navy to arrange with the Union commander off Fortress Monroe exchange of wounded Union prisoners and passage north from Norfolk of certain families wishing to return to their Northern friends. In the latter part of June 1861 she again served as the bearer of a flag-of-truce off Fortress Monroe, this time for Brigadier General Huger, CSA. In September 1861 *Empire* was to be provided with four guns transported by *Superior* and two rifled guns transported by *Harmony* to assist in a plan to drive Union forces from Roanoke Island. [See *Appomattox, supra*]

On 22 October 1861 Commodore W. F. Lynch, in his flagship *Sea Bird* off Roanoke Island, signed a contract with Gilbert Elliott, as agent for J. G. Martin, to build at Elizabeth City, N.C., a gunboat hull "to be fitted to machinery" out of steamer *Empire*. The engines were never transferred because the hull was not ready to receive them before Federal armies took the area. *Empire*, becoming *Appomattox* (q.v.), had further need of her power plant.

Empire Parish

(SwStr: t. 279; l. 56'; b. 31'; dph. 6'2'')

Empire Parish was built at New Albany, Ind., in 1859, to operate out of New Orleans, La. She continued duty there as a tow, flag-of-truce and dispatch boat for the Confederacy on the outbreak of the Civil War. On 23 June 1863 she carried dispatches from Semmes' famed Confederate raider *Sumter* into the city. *Empire Parish* came into Union possession with the fall of New Orleans in April 1862 and was taken into the United States Navy for duty as a towboat of the West Gulf Blockading Squadron in that same locale.

Enoch Train, see Manassas

Enterprise

(ScStr: t. 972; l. 250'; b. 28'; dph. 15'6'')
[Described under *Adventure*, q.v. *supra*].

Equator

(SwTug: a. 1 gun)

CSS *Equator* was a wooden steamer fitted for gunboat service in Cape Fear River in March 1864. When Wilmington, N.C., fell to the Union in January 1865, she was burned to prevent capture.

Era No. 3

(Str: t. 144; l. 129'; b. 28'4''; dph. 4'4'')

Era No. 3, built at Freedom, Pa., in 1858, for service out of New Orleans, became a unit of Comdr. W. Hunter's Texas Marine Department. [See Annex III]. She was one of 25 light draft ships that patrolled rivers and coastal waters and carried troops and supplies for the State of Texas. Her operations were largely on the Brazos River, between Columbia and Velasco.

Era No. 5

(StwStr: t. 115)

Era No. 5, a shallow-draft steamer built in 1860 at Pittsburgh, Pa., was chartered by the Confederates early in 1863 to transport corn from the Red River to Camden, Ark. As the steamer, laden with 4,500 bushels of corn, proceeded to her destination on 14 February 1863, she rounded a sharp bend 15 miles above the mouth of the Black River, came upon and was captured by USS *Indianola*. *Era No. 5* was then assigned to Col. C. R. Ellet's river fleet, fitted out with protective cotton baling and used by the Union as a dispatch boat and transport in the Mississippi.

Etiwan

(SwStr: t. 132)

Etiwan, *Etwan*, *Etowah*, *Etowan* or *Hetiwan*, was built at Charleston, S.C., in 1834. She operated in Charleston Harbor throughout the Civil War as a transport and cargo ship between the forts and city. She was damaged by striking a torpedo in the harbor in the spring of 1863 and was run ashore to prevent her sinking. She resumed her transport duties in the fall of 1863. *Etiwan* was said to be the steamer moored at the wharf at Fort Johnson on 29 August 1863 when Confederate Submarine Torpedo Boat *H. L. Hunley* came alongside and attached mooring lines to her. *Etiwan* unexpectedly moved away from the wharf, drawing the submarine over on her side, and the *H. L. Hunley* filled and went down, drowning five seamen of CSS *Chicora* who formed a part of her volunteer crew. At the close of the Civil War *Etiwan* was found wrecked in Charleston Harbor. She was fitted for service to the Army Quartermaster Department engaged in clearing the harbor after the Civil War and was documented in April 1867 as the merchant steamer *St. Helena*.

Etta, see Uncle Ben

Everglade, see Savannah (old)

Express

(Slp)

Express, a fishing smack which sailed under Confederate papers, was captured by USS *New London* on 9 December 1861 near Cat Island Passage in Mississippi Sound. She may or may not have been a public vessel.

F. S. Bartow, see Annex I

Fairplay

(SwStr: dp. 156; dr. 5'; s. 5 mph.)

Fairplay was built in 1859 at New Albany, Ind., for service out of Vicksburg, Miss. She served as a Confederate transport on the Yazoo and other tributaries of the Mississippi. In August 1862 she was ordered out of the Yazoo to convey arms, munitions, and stores from Vicksburg to Milliken's Bend, thence up the Mississippi River for a load of corn which she safely delivered to the same landing. She transported arms from Vicksburg to Milliken's Bend a second time, and had arrived with a third shipment on 18 August 1862 when she was surprised and captured with her cargo intact by a Federal gunboat fleet which had sailed from Helena, Ark. At that time, *Fairplay* was under command of Captain White, a citizen of Milliken's Bend. Her prize cargo was said to include 5,000 Enfield rifles and muskets, much ammunition and quartermaster stores.

Fairplay was armed with four 12-pounder howitzers and taken into the Federal Western Gunboat Flotilla which was transferred to the jurisdiction of the United States Navy on 1 October 1862 and redesignated the Mississippi Squadron. She spent the remainder of the Civil War on patrol as a Federal gunboat in the Cumberland, Tennessee, and Ohio Rivers. *Fairplay* was decommissioned at Mound City, Ill., on 9 August 1865 and sold on 17 August 1865.

Falcon

(SwStr: t. 285; l. 270'; b. 24'; dr. 7'; s. 14–18 k.; cpl. 45; cl. *Condor*)

Falcon belonged to the largest type of Confederate Government blockade runner placed in United Kingdom shipyards by Commander James D. Bulloch, CSN. *Falcon* was striking in appearance—long, low, with straight stem, hull painted white, three red funnels fore and aft, a single mast sloop rigged and straight stern; she was extremely fast, being said to have done 20 knots on her trials with her pair of oscillating sidewheel engines. She attracted considerable attention from August to October 1864 and then faded from the limelight, although she is said to have continued running into Wilmington, N.C., from Halifax, N.S.

Fanny

(ScStr: cpl. 49; a. 1 32-pdr., 1 8-pdr. r.)

CSS *Fanny* was originally a United States Army steamer. She was captured by the Confederates in Loggerhead Inlet, N.C., on 1 October 1861 with a large quantity of commissary and quartermaster's stores on board. Taken into the Confederate Navy, she was placed in command of Acting Master J. L. Tayloe, CSN, and participated in the battles of Roanoke Island, 7–8 February 1862, and Elizabeth City, N.C., on the 10th when she was run aground and blown up by her captain, who escaped with his crew to shore.

Fanny Morgan

(Yacht: t. ca. 8; l. 26'; b. 11')

Fanny Morgan was a very fast sailboat loaned to the Confederate government by her owner W. H. Beazley, who remained on board as her captain. She was accepted for the Confederate service on 22 October 1861 by Acting Master P. F. Appel, CSN, commanding the Confederate steamer *Bayou City*, and was ordered fitted out for service by Comdr. W. W. Hunter, CSN, commanding naval defenses on the coast of Texas. *Fanny Morgan* served as a guard and dispatch boat off Galveston, Tex., and was part of the Texas Marine Department [See Annex III].

Ferd Kennet

(SwStr: t. 591)

Ferd (or "*Ferd.*") *Kennet*, built in 1861 at St. Louis, and seized by the Confederate Army in May 1861, served in the western waters as a transport. In July 1863 she was burned and scuttled in the mouth of the Yalobusha River by order of Comdr. I. N. Bown, CSN.

Fingal, see *Atlanta*

Firefly

(SwStr: cpl. 15; a. 1 gun)

Firefly, a wooden sidewheeler, was purchased by the State of South Carolina in 1861 and transferred to the Confederate Navy in May of that year. On 13 August 1863 authority was granted to mount a small gun and construct the magazine necessary for it.

Firefly was used as a small tender on the Savannah station from March 1863 to 21 December 1864, commanded by Acting Master's Mate R. M. C. Kennedy, pilot W. Thomas, and Acting Master's Mate S. F. Hebbard. She was burned by her officers at the fall of Savannah.

Fisher

(StGbt: t. 66)

The small wooden gunboat captured while building at Edwards Ferry, N.C., has been presumed to have been CSS *Fisher*. "New and with good machinery," she reached Hampton Roads 27 June 1865. She may have been the sidewheeler *Alexander Oldham*, documented for commerce 27 September 1865 in Philadelphia and lost in 1873.

Flamingo

(SwStr: t. 284; l. 270'; b. 24'; dr. 7'; cpl. 45; s. 16 k.; cl. *Condor*)

Flamingo was one of the striking, three-stacked, sloop-rigged steamers, usually painted white to obscure their movements at night through the blockade, which were delivered to the Confederacy's order in the United Kingdom—very likely on the Clyde—sometime in 1864; they were negotiated by Comdr. James D. Bulloch, in close correspondence with Navy Secretary Mallory. *Flamingo* was one of the largest type of blockade runners placed by the Confederate Navy in foreign yards.

Sailing from Glasgow under Captain T. Atkinson in July, she put in at Queenstown in nearby Northern Ireland and at Ponta Delgada in the Azores before beginning her runs into Wilmington, N.C., with high priority cargoes. *Flamingo* suffered a serious setback probably for several weeks or longer in the autumn: she was at Bermuda in September, along with her sister, *Ptarmigan*, while their crews battled yellow fever.

While two of her last runs in 1865 were into the Gulf, *Flamingo* must have attempted one more into Charleston, for a contemporary Coast Survey chart shows the wreck of a *Flamingo* off Battery Rutledge on the north side of Charleston harbor.

Florida

(Sch: a. 1 6-pdr. rifle)

The pilot schooner *Florida* was not issued a letter of marque but gave better account of herself as a "junior privateer" than did many a larger vessel better armed after formal commissioning. Maj. W. Bevershaw Thompson, CSA, chief engineer of the Coast Defense Department fortifying Hatteras Inlet approaches, in a report from Fort Hatteras, N.C. to the Military Secretary, Col. Warren Winslow, 25 July 1861 described her: "We have also a saucy-looking little pilot schooner, the *Florida*, mounting one 6-pounder rifled cannon. She captured a prize 2 days since, took her crew out, and sent her in with her own men. A U.S. Government steamer gave chase to the prize, and they were obliged to beach her near Nag's Head. She, of course, is a total loss." After this brief moment on stage during the early days of the war, history says no more of the enterprising pilot boat-privateer; it is impossible at this distance even to be sure that she was privately owned and not a North Carolina public vessel.

———

(ScStr: t. 429 or 460; l. 171'; b. 29'11''; dph. 9'6'')

CSS *Florida*, built at Greenpoint N.Y. in 1859, was thrice considered for a gunboat before she became one. Contrary to previous interpretation of the official records, closer comparison of entries reveals that she did not serve the Mississippi River Defense Fleet as originally intended ,but became a Government-owned blockade runner; most authors have confused her with the Mobilian CSS *Florida* who did not receive her name *Selma* (q.v.) until July 1862. CSS *Florida* of New Orleans was one of 14 steamers of Charles Morgan's Southern Steamship Co. which Maj. Gen. Mansfield Lovell "impressed for public service" at New Orleans, 15 January 1862, acting on Secretary of War Benjamin's orders.

The colorful Lt. Beverly Kennon, CSN, had sought her command but had to be content with *Governor Moore*. He nostalgically described *Florida* to a court of inquiry as "a very fast and a very handsome vessel indeed. . . . A direct-acting screw of about 100 horsepower . . . about the same size in all respects as the U.S. steam sloop *Pocahontas*."

Of the several ships of the same name, she apparently is the *Florida* who arrived at Havana 23 March 1862 with 1,000 bales of cotton. Attempting to repeat her success, she had loaded 211 bales in St. Joseph's Bay near Pensacola when captured by Acting Master Elnathan Lewis with armed boats from US Bark *Pursuit*, 6 April. The boarders had just captured a sloop, *Lafayette*, at St. Andrew's, 20 miles below, and the latter's Captain Harrison volunteered to pilot Lewis' party on up to capture *Florida*. Surprised at 4 o'clock Sunday morning, *Florida*'s crew were unable to fire their ship.

It later appeared that the pilot, chief mate, first and second engineers were Union sympathizers. Mr. Lewis, after running *Florida* aground twice and jettisoning 30 bales of cargo, found "it was impossible to bring her out without the assistance of the engineers, pilot, and mate; so rather than burn her he considered it prudent to bargain with them, and gave his word that they would receive $500.00 each. They were faithful."

In the 30-mile passage to the bar, *Florida* and *Lafayette* were almost recaptured by the Confed-

The famed commerce raider C.S.S. Florida *is shown at anchor at St. George's, Bermuda in 1863.*

erates on 8 April after Capt. R. L. Smith, CSA, and his company of dragoons had galloped 24 hours from Marianna, Fla. to intercept them off St. Andrew's. A ship's boat was ambushed with four casualties, one dead, but the prizes continued on to Key West. There, 19 April 1862, Commodore McKean reporting to Secretary Welles confirms that *Florida* had never been converted: "I have examined her, and find that her upper deck is too light to carry guns of any weight. I have not the means to strengthen her sufficiently, or I should retain and convert her into a gunboat." Despite this rejection, the U.S. Navy brought *Florida* from the Philadelphia prize court, 20 September, changed her name to *Hendrick Hudson* (q.v.) and placed 4, later 5, guns on board.

(ScSlp: l. 191'; b. 27'2''; dph. 14'; dr. 13'; s. 9.5 k. (12 under canvas); cpl. 146; a. 6 6'' r., 2 7'' r., 1 12-pdr.)

CS Cruiser *Florida* was built by the British firm of William C. Miller & Sons and purchased by the Confederacy from Fawcett, Preston & Co., also of Liverpool, who engined her. Known in the shipyard as *Oreto* and initially called by the Confederates *Manassas*, the first of the foreign-built commerce raiders was commissioned *Florida*; Union records long continued to refer to her as *Oreto* or to confuse her with *Alabama* although, fitted with two funnels, she was readily distinguishable from single-stacked *Alabama*.

Florida departed England 22 March 1862 for Nassau to coal and contrived to fill her bunkers, although entitled only to enough to make the nearest Confederate port. The Governor drew the line, however, at an attempted rendezvous with her tender in Nassau harbor; so she transferred stores and arms at isolated Green Cay. There she commissioned as *Florida* 17 August, with veteran Lt. John Newland Maffitt, CSN, in command. During her outfit, yellow fever raged among her crew, in 5 days reducing her effective force to one fireman and four deckhands. In desperate plight, she ran across to Cuba. There in Cardenas Maffitt too was stricken with the dread disease.

In this condition, against all probability, the intrepid Maffitt sailed her from Cardenas to Mobile. In an audacious dash the "Prince of Privateers" braved a hail of projectiles from the Union blockaders and raced through them to anchor beneath the guns of Ft. Morgan for a hero's welcome by Mobile. *Florida* had been unable to fight back not only because of sickness but because rammers, sights, beds, locks and quoins had, inadvertently, not been loaded at the Bahamas. Having taken stores and gun accessories she lacked, along with added crew members, *Florida* escaped to sea 16 January 1863.

After coaling at Nassau, she spent 6 months off North and South America and in the West Indies, with calls at neutral ports, all the while making captures and eluding the large Federal squadron pursuing her. (See also the exploits of Lieutenant Read under *Clarence, Tacony, Archer* and *Caleb Cushing*.)

Florida sailed 27 July from Bermuda for Brest, where she lay in the French Government dock from 23 August 1863 to 12 February 1864. There broken in health, Maffitt relinquished command to Lt. C. M. Morris. Departing for the West Indies, *Florida* bunkered at Barbados, although the 3 months specified by British law had not elapsed since last coaling at an Empire port. She then skirted the U.S. coast, sailed east to Teneriffe in the Canaries and thence to Bahia, 4 October 1864.

Anchored in the Brazilian haven, on 7 October *Florida* was caught defenseless in a night attack by Comdr. Napoleon Collins of USS *Wachusett*, while her captain was ashore with half his crew. Towed to sea, she was sent to the United States as a prize despite Brazil's protests at this violation of neutral rights.

At Newport News, 28 November 1864, *Florida* reached the end of her strange career when she sank in a collision with the USAT *Alliance*, a troop ferry, and thus could not be delivered to Brazil in satisfaction of the final court order. Commander Collins was courtmartialed but won fame and eventual promotion for his daring.

Florida captured 37 prizes during her impressive career; her prizes *Tacony* and *Clarence* in turn took 23 more.

———

Florida, see *Selma*

Florida No. 2, see *Tacony*

Florilda

(Str)

Florilda was employed by the Texas Marine Department [See Annex III] in 1863 as a troop transport. Capt. J. Price and his officers were commended by Col. Leon Smith, CSA, for their role in the Battle of Sabine Pass, 8 September, in which USS *Clifton* and *Sachem* were captured. The citation said *Florilda* "assisted in placing the reinforcements at disposal in time to effectually intimidate the enemy from further attack."

Fly Catcher, see *Flycatcher*

Flycatcher

(ScStr: t. 37)

Flycatcher, sometimes written *Fly Catcher*, was sunk by Confederate forces in November 1862 as an obstruction on the Atchafalaya River, La.

Forrest

(StTug: a. 2 guns, 1 32-pdr.)

Forrest, known originally as *Edwards*, was bought at Norfolk in 1861. *Edwards/Forrest* operated off the North Carolina coast in 1861–62. She participated in the battle of Roanoke Island on February 7, 1862 during which her commanding officer, Lt. J. L. Hoole, CSN, was seriously wounded. *Forrest* was disabled during the action and towed to Elizabeth City, N.C., for repairs. There, 3 days later, while out of water on the marine railway, she was burned to prevent capture by Union forces.

Fredericksburg

(IrcRam: l. 188' [170']; b. 40'3''; [34']; dr. 9'6''; cpl. 150; a. 11'' sb., 1 8'' r., 2 6.4'' r.; type Enlarged *Albemarle*)

CSS *Fredericksburg* was built at Richmond, Va., 1862–63. At the time of her launching in mid-June 1863, intelligence reports erroneously associated the name *Chickahominy* with her. On 30 November 1863 she was reported completed and awaiting armament. In March 1864 she was taken down to Drewry's Bluff to be fitted out, and placed in command of Comdr. T. R. Rootes, CSN.

Fredericksburg, one of the ships of the squadron commanded by Commodore J. K. Mitchell, CSN, was actively engaged in the James River from mid-1864 until the end of the war. She participated in an action with Union ships in Trent's Reach on 21 June 1864 but little damage was inflicted on either side due to the distance between them. Similar inconclusive encounters took place in August, October, December, and the following January. With the evacuation of Richmond on 3 April 1865 the Confederates blew up *Fredericksburg* and other ships in the vicinity the following day.

Frigate No. 61, see *Santa Maria*

Frolic

(SwStr: t. 296)

Frolic was built in 1860 at Wheeling, Va. She served the Confederacy in the Red River above Fort de Russy in May 1863. She was still in the Red River, below Alexandria, La., in June 1864, having come out of the mouth into the Mississippi under a flag-of-truce to deliver Union casualties suffered during engagements with Confederate batteries on the banks of the Red River.

Fulton

(SwStr: t. 698; l. 180'; b. 34'8''; dr. 10'6''; s. 10 k.; cpl. 130; a. 4 32-pdr.)

Fulton was a sidewheeler built at Brooklyn Navy Yard in 1837 and rigged as a fore-topsail schooner.

Fulton, formerly of the United States Navy, was captured by the Confederates when they seized the Pensacola Navy Yard on 12 January 1861. She was selected for Confederate Navy service but never finished refitting. The Confederates destroyed her while evacuating the yard before Union reoccupation on 10 May 1862.

Fulton, see *Robert Fulton*

G. H. Smoot

(Sch: t. 36)

G. H. *Smoot,* a schooner, was captured May 18, 1862 in Potecasi Creek, N.C., by USS *Hunchback* and *Shawsheen,* of the naval force under Comdr. S. C. Rowan, USN. She was reported by her captors "as being the property of the rebel citizens of North Carolina . . . engaged in the transportation of troops and supplies. . . ."

G. W. Bird, see *Governor Milton*

Gaines

(SwStr: t. 863; l. 202'; b. 38'; dph. 13'; dr. 6; s. 10 k.; cpl. 130; a. 1 8'' r., 5 32-pdr.; cl. *Morgan*)

CSS *Gaines* was hastily constructed by the Confederates at Mobile, Ala., during 1861–62, from unseasoned wood which was partially covered with 2-inch iron plating. *Gaines* resembled CSS *Morgan* except that she had high pressure boilers. Operating in the waters of Mobile Bay, under the command of Lt. J. W. Bennett, CSN, she fought gallantly during the battle of 5 August 1864 until finally run aground by her own officers to avoid surrender to the Union forces.

Gallatin

(Sch: t. 112 [150]; l. 73'4'' bp; b. 20'6''; dph. 7'4''; cpl. 40; a. 2 12-pdr.; cl. *Morris*)

Gallatin was a foretopsail schooner, sister to *Caleb Cushing* (q.v.) and built at New York Navy Yard in 1831 as a revenue cutter. Originally on the Mobile station, she had been rushed to Charleston at the time of the South Carolina nullification incident, November 1832. In 1840, she went to the Coast Survey, back to the Revenue Marine in 1848 and to the Survey once more in 1849.

She was seized upon Georgia's secession, she and *Hallie Jackson* becoming, 18 April 1861, the first privateers commissioned under the law of 17 April. A letter of marque was issued to William Hone, acting for fellow-owners F. W. Simms, D. H. Baldwin, J. A. Courvoisie and William Stamch, all of Savannah. *Gallatin's* further activity is not recorded in official documents.

Gallego

(Sch: t. 596; l. 144'; b. 30'; dph. 15')

Gallego was built in 1855 at Newburyport, Mass., and was operating out of New Orleans when acquired by the Confederates. She was employed primarily as a cargo and store ship on the James River, Va.

In a sinking condition and badly in need of repairs *Gallego* was run aground by the Confederates below the obstructions at Drewry's Bluff on the James River late in 1864. With the use of steam pumps the waterlogged schooner was successfully floated on 18 January 1865 and the next day was returned to an officer of the Confederate Engineering Corps stationed at Drewry's Bluff.

Galveston, see *General Quitman*

General Beauregard

(SwRam)

General Beauregard, often called *Beauregard,* was selected in January 1862 by Capt. J. E. Montgomery, former river steamboat master, for his

River Defense Fleet. [See Annex II]. At New Orleans, 25 January, Captain Montgomery began her conversion to a cottonclad ram, installing 4-inch oak and 1-inch iron sheathing over her bow, with cotton bales sandwiched between double pine bulkheads to protect her boilers.

Conversion completed 5 April, *General Beauregard* steamed to Fort Pillow, Tenn., to defend the approaches to Memphis. On 10 May 1862, *General Beauregard*, Capt. J. H. Hart, and seven more of Montgomery's fleet, attacked the Federal Mississippi ironclad flotilla. This Plum Point Bend action witnessed effective ramming tactics by the Confederates, although *General Beauregard* succeeded only in keeping her four 8-inch guns bravely firing in the face of a withering hail of Union shells. Montgomery's force held off the Federal rams until Fort Pillow was safely evacuated, 4 June, then fell back on Memphis to coal, the fifth.

After Fort Pillow fell, Flag Officer C. H. Davis, USN, commanding the Mississippi Flotilla, lost no time in appearing off Memphis, 6 June 1862. Montgomery, with a smaller squadron short of fuel, was unable to retreat to Vicksburg; unwilling to destroy his boats, he fought against heavy odds. In the ensuing Battle of Memphis, "witnessed by thousands on the bluff," *Beauregard* unluckily missed ramming USS *Monarch* and "cut away entirely the port wheel and wheelhouse" of her partner, *General Sterling Price*, also engaging *Monarch*. *General Beauregard*, backing out, gave Union flagship *Benton* a close broadside with a 42-pounder, and *Benton* replied with a shot into the Confederate's boiler, killing or scalding many of her crew, 14 of whom, in agony, were rescued by *Benton*. *General Beauregard* exploded and was sinking fast as *Monarch* captured the rest of her complement and took her in tow towards the Arkansas shore, where the wreck remained for a short time partially visible in shoal water.

(Gbt)

On 16 December 1863, Admiral Porter noted, "From a refugee who escaped from Mobile, Ala., I learned the following particulars in relation to the rebel gunboats . . . in that vicinity. . . . A wooden gunboat called *General Beauregard* carries four guns, and is commanded by Lieutenant Milligan. . . ." No further evidence to corroborate the existence of this warship has yet been discovered, but even this modicum of information does not suggest identification with any of the other *Beauregards* better known to history.

General Bee

(Gbt)

General Bee, under Capt. T. Harrison, recruited a crew at Corpus Christi, Tex., in July 1862 and was assigned to guard the ship channel to prevent Federal gunboats from entering Corpus Christi Bay.

General Bragg

(SwRam: t. 1,043; l. 208'; b. 32'8''; dph. 15'; dr. 12'; s. 10 k.; a. 1 30-pdr. r., 1 32-pdr., 1 12-pdr. r.)

General Bragg, originally *Mexico*, was built at New York, N.Y., in 1851. She was owned by the Southern Steamship Co. before Maj. Gen. M. Lovell, CSA, under orders from Secretary of War J. Benjamin, impressed her for Confederate service at New Orleans, La., on 15 January 1862. Capt. J. E. Montgomery, a former river steamboat captain, selected her to be part of his River Defense Fleet [See Annex II] and on 25 January ordered her conversion to a cottonclad ram with 4-inch oak sheath, 1-inch iron covering on her bow and double pine bulkheads filled with compressed cotton bales.

On 25 March 1862 *General Bragg*'s conversion was completed and she was sent from New Orleans to Fort Pillow, Tenn., where she operated in defense of the river approaches to Memphis, Tenn. On 10 May 1862, off Fort Pillow, *General Bragg*, in company with seven other vessels under Captain Montgomery, attacked the ironclad gunboats of the Federal Mississippi Flotilla. In the engagement of Plum Point Bend *General Bragg*, Capt. W. H. H. Leonard, went into the lead and closed USS *Cincinnati*. The Union ship retreated to shallow water, but *General Bragg* pursued despite vicious fire from nearly the whole Union fleet and rammed *Cincinnati*, preventing her further retreat. *General Bragg* received *Cincinnati*'s broadside, and, as her tiller rope was cut, drifted down river out of action leaving *General Sterling Price* and *General Sumter* to finish off the Union ship.

Later, Montgomery's force held off the Federals until Fort Pillow was evacuated on 1 June. The Confederate rams then fell back on Memphis to take on coal. Following the Union capture of Fort Pillow, Flag Officer C. H. Davis, USN, commanding the Mississippi Flotilla, pressed on without delay and appeared off Memphis with a

C.S.S. General Bragg *after her capture by the Union.*

superior force on 6 June. Montgomery, unable to retreat to Vicksburg, Miss., because of his shortage of fuel, and unwilling to destroy his boats, determined to fight against heavy odds. In the ensuing Battle of Memphis on 6 June 1862, *General Bragg,* called by Brig. Gen. M. Jeff Thompson, MSG, "the best and fastest" of Montgomery's vessels, was fired by a Union rifle shot bursting in her cotton protection. In the ensuing Union victory against the small Confederate force, *General Bragg* grounded on a sand bar was captured by Union forces, who, with great difficulty, managed to save her. She was taken into Federal service and sold after the war, 2 September 1865.

General Breckinridge

(StwRam: cpl. 35; a. 1 24-pdr.)

General Breckinridge, also called *R. J. Breckinridge* or *Breckinridge,* was selected at New Orleans, La., by Capt. J. E. Montgomery to be part of his River Defense Fleet [See Annex II]. On 25 January 1862 Captain Montgomery began to convert her into a cottonclad ram by placing a 4-inch oak sheath with a 1-inch iron covering on her bow, and by installing double pine bulkheads fiilled with compressed cotton bales.

On 22 April 1862, as soon as her conversion was completed, *General Breckinridge,* under Capt. J. B. Smith, left New Orleans for Fort Jackson on the lower Mississippi to cooperate in the Confederate defense of New Orleans. *General Breckinridge,* with five other ships of Montgomery's River

Defense Fleet in that area, was under the overall command of Capt. J. A. Stevenson. On 24 April 1862, when Flag Officer D. G. Farragut, USN, ran his fleet past Forts Jackson and St. Philip on his way to capture New Orleans, *General Breckinridge* was abandoned by her crew and burned to keep her from falling into Union hands.

General Clinch

(SwStr: t. 256; a. 2 brass guns)

General Clinch, also called *Clinch,* was built at Charleston, S.C., in 1839, and acquired in January 1861 by the State of South Carolina. She operated throughout the war in the Charleston harbor area and off the South Carolina coast, as a tender, harbor transport, and patrol boat. One of her earlier commanders was Lt. Thomas P. Pelot, CSN.

In April 1861 before the hostilities of the Civil War, *General Clinch,* in conjunction with *Lady Davis* and *Gordon,* all under the command of Comdr. H. J. Hartstene, CSN, guarded the approaches to Charleston harbor to prevent the Federal Government from reinforcing Fort Sumter. In the spring of the following year *General Clinch* worked with *Marion* in moving the obstructions off Battery Island to near Elliott's Cut running into Wappoo Creek and into Charleston harbor.

On 31 January 1863 *General Clinch* participated with two other tenders *Chesterfield* and *Etiwan,* and the ironclad rams *Palmetto State* and *Chicora* in a daring expedition under Flag Officer D. Ingraham, CSN. The tenders, under Commander Hartstene, assisted the rams in leaving and re-entering the narrow channels of Charleston harbor in their bold and damaging attack on Federal blockaders.

There is evidence that *General Clinch* sank in Charleston harbor and was raised before October 1864 by her owner, Mr. McCormick, for use as a blockade runner.

General Earl Van Dorn

(SwRam: a. 1 32-pdr.)

General Earl Van Dorn, Van Dorn, Earl Van Dorn or *General Van Dorn,* was fitted out at New Orleans in 1862 for Confederate service. She operated under the direction of the Confederate army and was attached to the Mississippi River Defense Fleet commanded by Capt. J. E. Montgomery, a former river steamboat captain [See Annex II].

General Earl Van Dorn left New Orleans on 25 March 1862 and was detained at Memphis, Tenn., until 10 April, when her ironwork was completed. She then steamed north and operated off Fort Pillow, Tenn., in defense of the river approaches to Memphis. On 10 May 1862, *General Earl Van Dorn* under Capt. I. D. Fulkerson, with seven other vessels of Montgomery's fleet, attacked the ironclad gunboats of the Federal Mississippi Flotilla off Fort Pillow. In the action of Plum Point Bend which followed, *General Earl Van Dorn,* with skillful fire from her 32-pounder, succeeded in silencing Federal *Mortar Boat No. 16.* She then rammed USS *Mound City* forcing her to run aground to keep from sinking. *General Earl Van Dorn* herself ran ashore and sustained a terrific cannonade for a few minutes until she was able to back off.

On 1 June 1862 a large number of Federal rams and gunboats appeared at Fort Pillow. *General Earl Van Dorn* and the other ships of Montgomery's fleet held them off until Fort Pillow was successfully evacuated. The Confederate force then fell back on Memphis to take on coal.

Following the Federal capture of Fort Pillow, Flag Officer Charles H. Davis, CSN, commanding the Mississippi Flotilla appeared off Memphis on 6 June with a superior force. Montgomery, unable to retreat because of his fuel shortage and unwilling to destroy his boats, engaged the Federal force against heavy odds. All of the vessels of the Confederate River Defense Fleet at this engagement were either captured or destroyed except for *General Earl Van Dorn* which managed to escape because of her superior speed. She was chased down the Mississippi and up the Yazoo River by the rams *Monarch* and *Lancaster* under Col. C. Ellet, Jr., USA. They arrived below Yazoo City on 26 June 1862 in time to see *General Earl Van Dorn* being burned along with *Polk* and *Livingston* to prevent capture. According to *Lancaster's* log, they were "all oiled and tarred ready to be fired on our arrival," and, when first seen by the Federals rounding the bend, "all on fire and turned adrift . . . within a few hundred yards of the battery at Liverpool. . . . We backed down under the point, when the *Van Dorn* blew up, which shook the hills."

General Lee

(SwStr)

General Lee, a small steamer, was used as a Confederate Army transport until captured at Savannah, Ga., in December 1864.

General Lovell

(SwRam: cpl. 40-50; a. 1 32-pdr.)

General Lovell, a gunboat ram, had been a tugboat on the Mississippi River before she was purchased and fitted out at New Orleans for Confederate service. She was part of the River Defense Fleet [See Annex II] under the overall command of Capt. J. E. Montgomery, a former river steamboat captain.

On 22 April 1862, as soon as her conversion was completed, *General Lovell,* commanded by Capt. B. Paris, left New Orleans for Fort Jackson on the lower Mississippi. *General Lovell* and the other ships of Montgomery's River Defense Fleet in that area were under the command of Capt. J. A. Stevenson, CSA. On 24 April 1862 they were all destroyed when the Union fleet under Flag Officer D. G. Farragut, USN, ran past Forts Jackson and St. Philip on its way to New Orleans. *General Lovell* was abandoned by her crew after being set on fire to keep her from falling into Union hands.

General M. Jeff Thompson

(SwRam)

General M. Jeff Thompson, often referred to as *Jeff Thompson,* was selected in January 1862 by Capt. J. E. Montgomery to be part of his River Defense Fleet [See Annex II]. At New Orleans, La., on 25 January, Captain Montgomery began to convert her into a cottonclad ram by placing a 4-inch oak sheath with a 1-inch iron covering on her bow, and by installing double pine bulkheads filled with compressed cotton bales.

When *General M. Jeff Thompson*'s conversion was completed on 11 April, she steamed to Fort Pillow, Tenn., where she operated in defense of the river approaches to Memphis, Tenn. On 10 May 1862, *General M. Jeff Thompson*, in company with seven other vessels of Montgomery's fleet, attacked the ironclad gunboats of the Federal Mississippi Flotilla. The action of Plum Point Bend which followed witnessed successful ramming tactics by the Confederates, but *General M. Jeff Thompson*, under Capt. J. H. Burke, was not able to get into the battle except with her guns. These she manned coolly and effectively despite the discouraging effect of heavy Union fire.

Later Montgomery's force held off the Federal rams and gunboats until Fort Pillow was successfully evacuated on 1 June. Then the Confederate vessels fell back on Memphis to take on coal. Following the Federal capture of Fort Pillow, Flag Officer C. H. Davis, USN, commanding the Mississippi Flotilla pressed on without delay and appeared off Memphis with a superior force on 6 June 1862. Montgomery, unable to retreat to Vicksburg, Miss., because of his fuel shortage, and unwilling to destroy his boats, determined to fight against heavy odds. In the ensuing Battle of Memphis *General M. Jeff Thompson* was heavily damaged and set afire by Union shells. She ran aground and was abandoned by her crew. She burned to the water's edge and her magazine blew up violently, strewing the shore with iron braces and fastenings, with charred remains of broken timbers, and leaving her wrecked remains half buried and half sunk.

General Miramon, see under McRea

General Pillow, see B. M. Moore

General Polk

(Gbt: t. 390; a. 3 to 7 guns, progressively)

CSS *General Polk* was originally a side-wheel river steamer which some authorities cite as the *Ed Howard* or *Howard*, built in New Albany, Ind., in 1852. Purchased for $8,000 by the Confederates at New Orleans, La., in 1861, she was converted into a ship of war, which involved stripping her to a "mere shell."

Her first service was under Flag Officer G. N. Hollins who took his Louisiana defense fleet up the Mississippi in December to cooperate with the Army in the vicinity of New Madrid, Mo. At that time Lt. J. H. Carter, CSN, commanded *Polk*, as she was usually known.

In April, 1862 Commodore Hollins returned to New Orleans and command of the river fleet devolved on Comdr. R. F. Pinkney, CSN. After the fall of Island No. 10, *Polk*, *Livingston* and Army ram *General Earl Van Dorn* escaped 75 miles up the Yazoo River where they were burned at Liverpool, 25 miles below Yazoo City, on 26 June 1862 to prevent capture.

General Price, see General Sterling Price

General Quitman

(SwStr: t. 946; l. 233'3''; b. 34'3''; dph. 12'3''; dr. 9'; cpl. 90; a. 2 32-pdr.)

General Quitman was probably built at Brooklyn, N. Y. in 1857 and sailed as *Galveston* for the Texas Line of Charles H. Morgan's Southern S. S. Company before the war. Commodore Hunter, surveying her for a Confederate Navy gunboat in June 1861 at New Orleans, found her space too cramped for mounting guns. *Galveston* may have been substituted for the "small and poor" *Atlantic*, among 14 ships "impressed for public service" at New Orleans by Secretary of War Benjamin's order of 14 January 1862. On the 16th, Maj. Gen. Mansfield Lovell reported to the Secretary thus: "Captain Huger, of the Navy, who accompanied the party that took possession of the [14] ships, thinks the *Atlantic* will hardly answer as a war vessel, and I telegraphed yesterday to know whether I should substitute the *Galveston* for her." But it seems fairly certain *Galveston* soon became *General Quitman* of Capt. John K. Mitchell's lower Mississippi squadron. *General Quitman* continued under Louisiana State ownership, however, like *Governor Moore*, still her running mate, with whom her identity has been confused for a century.

Early in April 1862, cotton-clad and fitted with an iron prow to act as a ram, *General Quitman* steamed to support Forts Jackson and St. Philip, keys to the river position of New Orleans. Under Capt. Alexander Grant, an experienced riverboat master, she reconnoitered the Union fleet downriver and stood by the forts. She was burned to prevent capture in the confusion of 24 June 1862, when New Orleans fell to the Union.

(SwStr: t. 615 [1,076]; l. 246 [261'6"]; b. 36' [40'2"]; dph. 7'3" ['4"])

General Quitman was a river transport whose history from mid-January to 24 June 1862 is difficult to disentangle in official records from that of the former "sea steamer" *Galveston*, burned under the name *General Quitman* to escape capture when New Orleans fell to Farragut's forces. *General Quitman* is believed to have been built at New Albany, Ind. in 1859 for a New Orleans shipowner. She was "one of the best and most powerful boats on the river" in 1862 and one of the last to escape from the city the 24th, evacuating upriver "a good many ladies, some officers, and some ordnance stores." *General Quitman* continued to serve the Confederate Army as a troop and supply ship on the western rivers until war's end. Passed to private ownership, she sank at New Texas Landing, near Morganza, La., 23 October 1868.

General Rusk

(SwStr: t. 750; l. 200'; b. 31'; dph. 12'; dr. 5'7")

General Rusk, built as a merchantman at Wilmington, Del., in 1857, was seized from the Southern Steamship Co., by the State of Texas at Galveston in 1861. She served as reconnaissance and signal boat with the Texas Marine Department [See Annex III] in and about the waters of Galveston Harbor during the latter half of 1861, trying unsuccessfully on several occasions to slip past the Federal blockade. In early November 1861 she rendered aid to *Royal Yacht* following that vessel's capture and firing by Union forces from USS *Santee*, and managed to save her from complete destruction and tow her to safety. In December 1861 she was ordered to take part in the defense of Buffalo Bayou, San Jacinto River.

Her most memorable exploit was the capture on 17 April 1861 off Indianola, Tex., of USS *Star of the West*, the first Union transport to make news in the Civil War. [See *St. Philip*.]

During the early part of 1862 *General Rusk* was placed by General Hebert, commanding Texas Marine Department, under the control of Maj. T. S. Moïse, Assistant Quartermaster, who colluded to transfer the steamer to his associates, authorizing them to place her under the British flag and employ her in blockade running. After a single successful round-trip there under the name *Blanche*, she was bound for Havana in October 1862 when pursued by USS *Montgomery*, Comdr. C. Hunter, USN. While attempting to escape, the steamer

was run aground near Marianao, Cuba, and seized by a *Montgomery* boat crew. Efforts to get her towed off the bar and underway again ended when fire broke out and consumed both ship and cargo. The incident occasioned strong protest from England under whose flag she sailed, and Spain in whose territorial waters she was captured.

General Scott

(Str)

General Scott, a guard boat and transport in Confederate army service, was fired and abandoned by her crew in the York River, Va., in May 1862 to prevent capture.

General Sterling Price

(SwRam: t. 633 [483]; l. 182'; b. 30'; dph. 9'3")

General Sterling Price, often referred to as *General Price*, or *Price*, was built as *Laurent Millaudon*, *L. Millandon*, or *Milledon*, at Cincinnati, Ohio, in 1856. She was acquired for Confederate service and fitted out at New Orleans, La., for the River Defense Fleet under Capt. J. E. Montgomery. [See Annex II] On 25 January 1862 Captain Montgomery began to convert her into a cottonclad ram by placing a 4-inch oak sheath with a 1-inch iron covering on her bow, and by installing double pine bulkheads filled with compressed cotton bales. On March 25 *General Price*, Capt. J. H. Townsend, sailed from New Orleans to Memphis, Tenn., where she stayed until 10 April having her ironwork completed. She was then sent to Fort Pillow, Tenn., where she operated in defense of the river approaches to Memphis.

On 10 May 1862, off Fort Pillow, *General Price*, under First Officer J. E. Henthorne (or Harthorne), in company with seven other vessels under Captain Montgomery, attacked the ironclad gunboats of the Federal Mississippi Flotilla. In the action of Plum Point Bend, which followed, the Confederate ram *General Bragg* struck USS *Cincinnati* halting her retreat. This allowed *General Price* to violently ram the Federal gunboat, taking away her rudder, stern post, and a large piece of her stern, thus disabling her. At the same time *General Price's* well directed fire silenced Federal *Mortar Boat No. 16*, which was being guarded by *Cincinnati*. *General Price* was heavily hit in this action. Her upper works were severely damaged, and she was struck by a 128-pound shell which cut off her supply pipes and caused a dangerous leak.

C.S.S. General Sterling Price *was sunk on a sand bar at the battle of Memphis, 6 June 1862. She was later raised and, as this photograph shows, taken into Union service.*

The Confederates quickly repaired *General Price* and later she participated with Montgomery's force in holding off Federal vessels until Fort Pillow was successfully evacuated on 1 June. The Confederate vessels then fell back on Memphis to take coal.

Following the Federal capture of Fort Pillow, Flag Officer C. H. Davis, USN, commanding the Mississippi Flotilla, pressed on without delay and appeared off Memphis with a superior force on 6 June. Montgomery, unable to retreat to Vicksburg, Miss., because of his shortage of fuel, and unwilling to destroy his boats, determined to fight against heavy odds. In the ensuing Battle of Memphis, *General Sterling Price* charged the Federal ram *Monarch*, but instead collided with the Confederate ram *General Beauregard*, also attacking *Monarch*. *General Price* lost one wheel and was disabled. While the two Confederate vessels were entangled, Federal rams attacked them mercilessly. *General Price* collided with the Federal ram *Queen of the West*, under Col. C. Ellet, Jr., USA, commander of the two rams of the Davis Flotilla. As *Queen of the West* captured her

crew, *General Sterling Price* sank slowly onto a sand bar. She was later raised by Union forces and taken into Federal service.

General Sumter

(SwRam: t. 525; l. 182'; b. 28'4''; dph. 10'8''; a. 1 32-pdr.)

General Sumter—as often *Sumter* in common parlance—is known to have been the river towboat *Junius Beebe*, with low-pressure machinery—quite likely a vessel built at Algiers, La., in 1853. Acquired by the State of Louisiana from Charles H. Morgan's Southern Steamship Co. early in 1861, *Junius Beebe* was useful to the Confederate cause in such details as diverting foreign shipping preparatory to closing Southwest Pass, operating under Stanton & Co., New Orleans, managing for the Governor, until selected by Capt. James E. Montgomery for his River Defense Fleet [see Annex II]. On 25 January 1862, in the James Martin yard at Algiers, across the Mississippi from New Orleans, Montgomery began her conversion to a cottonclad ram featuring 4-inch oak sheathing, an inch of iron over her bows and cotton bales between double pine bulkheads.

Alterations completed, *General Sumter* went up to Ft. Pillow, Tenn., 17 April, to be armed. On 10 May, defending the main avenue to Memphis, Montgomery's fleet of eight attacked the Federal ironclads. In this action at Plum Point Bend, 4 miles above Ft. Pillow, it was probably *General Sumter* under Capt. W. W. Lamb that bravely steamed up within 20 yards of *Mortar Boat No. 16*, whose projectiles were threatening the fort, and fired everything she had, including a rifle volley; two 32-pound shot actually pierced the iron blinds of the Union floating battery. Then *General Sterling Price* and *General Sumter* cooperated in a well executed coordinated attack, one after the other ramming USS *Cincinnati* at full speed so that she lost her rudder and much of her stern; *Cincinnati* (whom Montgomery reported as *Carondelet*) had to be run ashore to save her from sinking. Thus the Montgomery rams held off the Federal flotilla until the fort was successfully evacuated, 1 June, before falling back on Memphis to refuel.

Quickly following up capture of Ft. Pillow, Flag Officer Charles H. Davis, USN, appeared off Memphis in force on 6 June. Montgomery, cornered, without coal enough to retreat to Vicksburg yet unwilling to scuttle his fleet, fought it out desperately in the Battle of Memphis: *General Sumter* rammed and seriously damaged USS *Queen of the West* but eventually most of the Confederate vessels were destroyed or bowed to the inevitable. *General Sumter* did not sink; badly shot up, she ran up on the Arkansas shore, was captured and became, briefly, USS *Sumter*. In August she grounded again, downriver off Bayou Sara, La., and was abandoned except for sparepart raids on her machinery by the rest of the squadron at periods of low water; before the local populace completed stripping her, Confederate authorities succeeded in setting fire to the hulk.

(SwStr)

The passenger steamer *General Sumter*, also commonly abbreviated to *Sumter*, is reputed to have been under more or less direct Confederate Army control as a transport in the upper Florida Lakes-Ocklawaha River area but specific details of her service are lacking today. To avoid confusion in the roster of *Sumter*s, already too frequently misidentified over the past century, this *Sumter* cannot

well be omitted here, especially since she became a notable ship from the time of her capture by USS *Columbine* in Big (Great) Lake George, Fla., 23 March 1864. *Sumter's* Capt. W. W. Tumblin, after his surrender, piloted *Columbine* and, together with the *Sumter* as a prize and armed with a howitzer, searched out and captured the Confederate steamer *Hattie Brock* in the difficult inland waters of Florida.

General Van Dorn, see General Earl Van Dorn

George Buckhart
(Sch: a. 1 6-pdr.)

George Buckhart was armed by the Confederates for duty in conjunction with the Texas Marine Department [See Annex III] along the Texas Coast, particularly in the Matagorda Bay area. She was described as a good vessel, but riding extremely low in the water so that she could be boarded easily. On 17 March 1865, a schooner, *George Burkhart*, probably the same ship, was captured by USS *Quaker City* off Brazos Santiago while running the blockade.

George Page
(SwStr: t. 410; a. 2 guns)

George Page, built as a transport at Washington, D.C., in 1853, was attached to the Quartermaster's Department of the United States Army, until captured by the Confederates at nearby Aquia Creek, Va., in May 1861. Acquired by the Confederate States Navy, *George Page*, Lt. C. C. Simms, CSN, was fitted out for river defense service, and sometime later renamed *City of Richmond*. Her upper works may have been removed at this time.

She operated in the Potomac in the vicinity of Quantico Creek until 9 March 1862 when she was destroyed by her crew upon abandonment of the Evansport batteries at that place.

Georgia
(ScStr: t. 600 [700]; l. 212'; b. 27'; dph. 13'9''; a. 2 100-pdr., 2 24-pdr., 1 32-pdr.)

Georgia was built in 1862 as the fast merchantman, *Japan*. The Confederate Government purchased her at Dumbarton, Scotland, in March 1863. On 1 April she departed Greenock, reputedly bound for the East Indies and carrying a crew of fifty who had shipped for a voyage to Singapore. She rendezvoused with the steamer *Alar* off Ushant, France, and took on guns, ordnance and other stores. [cf. also *Castor* and *Agrippina*].

On 9 April 1863 the Confederate flag was hoisted and she was placed in commission as CSS *Georgia*, Comdr. W. L. Maury, CSN, in command. Her orders read to prey against United States shipping wherever found.

Calling at Bahia, Brazil, and at Trinidad, *Georgia* recrossed the Atlantic to Simon's Bay, Cape Colony, Africa, where she arrived 16 August. She sailed next to Santa Cruz, Teneriffe, thence up to Cherbourg, arriving 28 October. During this short cruise she captured nine prizes.

Georgia had a round stern, iron frame, fiddle-bow figurehead, short, thick funnel and full poop. Being an iron hull, she was clearly unsuited to long cruises without drydocking during a period when antifouling underbody coatings were yet unknown. Commander James D. Bulloch, key Confederate procurement agent overseas, would have nothing to do with iron bottoms, but Commander Maury settled for *Japan* because wood (which could be coppered) was being superseded in Great Britain by the new metal; consequently wooden newbuilding contracts were not easy to buy up in British shipyards.

While she was undergoing repair at Cherbourg in late January 1864, it was decided to shift her armament to CSS *Rappahannock*. The transfer was never effected and *Georgia* was moved to an anchorage 3 miles below Bordeaux. On 2 May 1864 she was taken to Liverpool and sold on 1 June to a merchant of that city over the protest of Charles F. Adams, United States Minister to Great Britain. The steamer again put to sea on 11 August and 4 days later was captured by the frigate *Niagara* off Portugal. She was sent into Boston, Mass., where she was condemned and sold as a lawful prize of the United States.

She was documented as a U.S. merchant vessel in New Bedford, Mass., 5 August 1865.

[N.B.: *Georgia* was often called *Virginia*, erroneously, by Union writers early in her career.]

———

(IrcFltBtry: l. 250'; b. 60'; cpl. 200; a. 4 to 9 guns)

Georgia, also known as *State of Georgia* and *Ladies' Ram*, was an ironclad floating battery built at Savannah, Ga., in 1862–63. Placed under command of Lt. W. Gwathmey, CSN, she was employed in defending the river channels below Savannah, Ga., training her batteries against the Union advance. Since she lacked effective locomotive power the Confederates found it necessary to fire and destroy her during the evacuation of Savannah on 21 December 1864.

Georgia, see under *Texas* (corvette)

Georgian

(ScStr: t. 350)

Georgian might easily have headed the entire roster of Confederate cloak-and-dagger ships—had it not been for treachery and bungling. Intended for quick conversion to a cruiser by being "strengthened in the bow for a ram somewhere on Lake Huron", she was purchased in Toronto, Ont., by the Confederate agent Col. Jacob Thompson through a Dr. James Bates of Louisville, "at one time a captain of the steamer *Magnolia* on the Mississippi River." Delivery to the Confederate fifth column was effected at Pt. Colborne, Upper Canada (Ont.), 1 November 1864. The price paid was $16,000 or $16,500 to A. M. Smith & Co., who had labeled themselves Southern sympathizers two years earlier by selling a ship for blockade running.

Georgian was described by U.S. Vice Consul Gen. Thurston, Montreal, as "a new vessel, built some year and a half since on the Georgian Bay, by [George] H. Wyatt and others, and has, I believe, made one trip across the Atlantic. She is a splendid vessel, built with great care, a fast sailer, and would . . . be capable of doing immense injury to the shipping on the Lakes." He noted, the Confederate agents "claim that she is particularly adapted to the lumber trade, as she carries heavy loads with light draft and . . . intend to strengthen her beams for towing."

Word traveled quickly; by 5 November, Mayor W. G. Fargo of Buffalo, N.Y., where *Georgian* arrived the 3d., telegraphed *Michigan's* Comdr. John C. Carter at Sandusky, O., that the steamer would "be armed on the Canada shore for the purpose of encountering the USS *Michigan* and for piratical and predatory purposes." Carter, known to some of the conspirators as "Jack," a former shipmate, had just foiled the *Philo Parsons* (q.v.) plot and was unimpressed by a second lightning bolt impending; he wrote routinely to Secretary Welles two days later, "These reports are gotten up for the purpose of alarming the citizens on these Lakes." Welles retorted the 16th, "This may be so, but past experience teaches us to be on our guard," and ordered him to seize *Georgian* on the smallest pretext.

C.S.S. Georgia *off Cherbourg, France.*

C.S. gunboat Governor Moore.

Carter's relief, Lt. Comdr. F. A. Roe, followed the scent and wrote Welles, 6 December: "Her captain, Bates, is a notorious secessionist and rebel sympathizer. When the *Georgian* put to sea from Buffalo her propeller became loose. She went into Port Stanley, when it again became loose . . . to Sarnia, and Bates went to Toronto and ordered a new wheel . . . sent to Collingwood . . . On her passage by Detroit [Lt.] Colonel [Bennett H.] Hill [Detroit post commander], who was on the lookout with two armed tugs, caught her, overhauled and examined her, and reports to me that he found nothing about her to justify her seizure. At Collingwood she was a second time examined—by the Canadian authorities—and they could not condemn her. Here it was given out that she was going into the Saginaw lumber trade, but this was a blind. She has not carried a pound of freight or earned a dollar in legitimate trade since she fell into her present owner's hands." She went to Bruce Mines and back to lay up for the winter in Collingwood, highly suspect but untouchable.

On 6 April Canadian authorities seized *Georgian*, transferred to a new owner, "G. T. Denison", and "being altered for the purpose, as it was said, of carrying more freight"; a new mast was being stepped "and she was intended to sail among the fishing vessels of the United States to attack and destroy them." So prophesied Consul Thurston on 7 April, but he had been nearer right the first time about her intentions. This time a letter of October to Bates was captured on board containing patent references to procuring "Greek Fire" and "finest waterproof caps for the troops." By the time this furor had subsided, the war was over.

Colonel Thompson's own confidential report of the plot is more amazing: "Desiring to have a boat on whose captain and crew reliance could be placed, and on board of which arms could be sent to convenient points for arming such vessels as could be seized for operations on the Lakes, I aided Dr. James T. Bates, of Kentucky, an old steamboat captain, in the purchase of the steamer *Georgian*. She had scarcely been transferred when the story went abroad that she had been purchased and armed for the purpose of sinking the *Michigan* [only warship on the Lakes], releasing the prisoners on Johnson's Island [off Sandusky], and destroying the shipping on the Lakes and the cities on their margin. The wildest consternation prevailed in all the border cities. At Buffalo two

tugs had cannon placed on board; four regiments of soldiers were sent there—two of them represented to have been drawn from the Army of Virginia; bells were rung at Detroit, and churches broken up on Sunday. The whole lake shore was a scene of wild excitement. Boats were sent out, which boarded the *Georgian* and found nothing contraband on board; but still the people were incredulous."

The outline of the plot was essentially the same as the February '63 plan of Lt. William H. Murdaugh, CSN, partly carried through that November—as far as Halifax, N.S.—by Lt. John Wilkinson, CSN, 21 other naval officers and 32 escaped prisoners from Johnson's Island. The Wilkinson expedition (cf. *Robert E. Lee*, infra) had substituted an Ogdensburg-Chicago liner, to be boarded in the Welland Canal, for the Detroit-Sandusky steamer they had planned to join at Windsor; they too might have succeeded but for the treachery of a Canadian—one McCuaig—who informed the Governor General, which led him, Lord Monck, to alert Secretary of War Stanton. Colonel Thompson never gave up although he lamented bitterly to Secretary of War Benjamin in the 3 December report quoted above: "The bane and curse of carrying out anything in this country is the surveillance under which we act. Detectives, or those ready to give information, stand at every street corner. Two or three can not interchange ideas without a reporter."

Thompson was abysmally disappointed that the "Order of the Sons of Liberty" had been unable "to throw off the galling dynasty at Washington", seize and hold "the three great Northwestern States of Illinois, Indiana and Ohio" besides freeing Bates' Kentucky—since such a coup "in 60 days would end the war." Undaunted by the *Philo Parsons* and *Georgian* debacles, Thompson in January 1865 was busy promoting "The Order of the Star", a new, "purely military" organization based on his belief that, "There is no ground to doubt that the masses, to a large extent, of the North are brave and true and believe Lincoln a tyrant and usurper."

Georgiana

(ScStr: t. 519 [407]; l. 205.6′; b. 25.2′; dph. 14.9′; dr. over 14′)

Georgiana was a brig-rigged, iron propeller of 120 horsepower and had clipper bow, jib, and two masts, hull and stack painted black. She was built by the Lawrie shipyard at Glasgow—perhaps under subcontract from Lairds of Birkenhead (Liverpool)—and registered at that port in December 1862 as belonging to N. Matheson's Clyde service. The London *American* took special note of her in its 28 January 1863 edition as a "powerful" steamer and remarked that her officers wore gold lace on their caps, considered a sure indication she was being groomed for a man-o'-war. The U.S. Consul at Teneriffe was rightly apprehensive of her as being "evidently a very swift vessel."

Attempting to run into Charleston, S.C., through Maffitt's Channel on 19 March 1865, she was spotted by the yacht *America* which quickly brought gunfire from USS *Wissahickon*, crippling *Georgiana*. Capt. A. B. Davidson flashed a white light in token of surrender, thus gaining time to beach his ship in 14 feet of water, three-quarters of a mile offshore and escape on the land side with all hands; this was construed as "the most consummate treachery" by the disappointed blockading crew.

Capt. Thomas Turner, station commodore, reported to Admiral S. F. du Pont that *Georgiana* was evidently "sent into Charleston to receive her officers, to be fitted out as a cruiser there. She had 140 men on board, with an armament of guns and gun carriages in her hold, commanded by a British naval retired officer." There seems to be no reason to dispute his facts or figures.

Lt. Comdr. J. L. Davis, USN, commanding *Wissahickon*, decided to set the wreck afire lest guerrilla bands from shore try to salvage her or her cargo: she burned for several days accompanied by large explosions when lots of powder succumbed to the flames.

Germantown

(Ship: t. 939; l. 150′; b. 36′9″; dr. 17′; s. 12 k; a. unarmed)

CSS *Germantown*, formerly the United States 22-gun sloop-of-war of that name, was built at Philadelphia Navy Yard in 1846. In 1861 she lay at Gosport (Norfolk) Navy Yard ready for sea but had to be scuttled and burned by the Federal Navy, evacuating Gosport, 20–21 April.

The Confederates raised her in June of that year but she lay at anchor off Craney Island until May 1862 when she was filled with sand and sunk in the Elizabeth River for the protection of Norfolk.

She was raised again by Federal forces in April 1863.

Gibraltar, see *Sumter*

Giraffe, see *Robert E. Lee*

Golden Age

(Str)

Golden Age was probably in use as an Army transport in the Mississippi River area. She was sunk in May 1863 as an obstruction in the Yazoo River about 15 miles below Fort Pemberton to impede advancing Union forces.

She is mentioned as being "prepared with cotton bales" to carry 500 soldiers, in April 1863.

Gordon, see *Theodora*

Gordon Grant

(Tug)

Gordon Grant was used by Confederate army forces in emplacing batteries at Columbus, Ky., late in 1861. She also served as a scout boat on the Mississippi River during the early months of 1862.

Gossamer

(StwStr)

The small steamer *Gossamer* was used as a Confederate transport in Bayou Teche during the early months of 1863.

Governor Aiken

Governor Aiken, a sailing ship which had served as United States lighthouse tender at Charleston, was seized by South Carolinian forces following that state's secession from the Union on 20 December 1860. She was found to be of little value.

Governor Milton

(SwStr: t. 68; l. 85′; b. 20′; dph. 4′8″)

Governor Milton was a wooden river steamer seized by the State of Florida as *G. W. Bird*, renamed and used for a transport by the Confederacy. She was unarmed when captured by a boat from USA Transport *Darlington*, 7 October 1862, in a creek above Hawkinsville, Fla.

Governor Moore

(SwGbt: t. 1,215; cpl. 93; a. 2 32-pdr. r.)

CSS *Governor Moore* had been Southern S. S. Company's *Charles Morgan*, named for the firm's founder and built at New York in 1854 as a schooner-rigged, low pressure, walking beam-engined, seagoing steamer. She was seized at New Orleans by Major General Mansfield Lovell, CSA, in mid-January 1862 "for the public service." As a gunboat, renamed for the State's Governor, her stem was reinforced for ramming by two strips of flat railroad iron at the waterline, strapped and bolted in place, with pine lumber and cotton-bale barricades to protect her boilers.

The larger of two similar cotton-clads owned and operated by the State of Louisiana, *Governor Moore* was commanded for some time by Lt. Beverly Kennon, CSN, then serving as Commander in the Louisiana Provisional Navy without pay. She distinguished herself in the battle of 24 April 1862, when Admiral Farragut passed Forts Jackson and St. Philip before dawn en route to capture New Orleans. After a furious exchange of raking fire, *Governor Moore* twice rammed USS *Varuna* and a third thrust from another cotton-clad forced *Varuna* aground. Next attacking *Cayuga*, *Governor Moore* exposed herself to fire from most of the Union flotilla. With practically her whole upper hamper shot away and 64 men dead or dying, she went out of command, drifting helplessly to shore, where her captain, pilot, and a seaman set her afire. *Governor Moore* blew up while they and three other survivors were being captured by *Oneida's* boats to be imprisoned on board *Colorado;* two-thirds of the two dozen or more crew members escaped into the marshes, the rest being captured by other ships' launches; no one drowned.

"The pennant and remains of the ensign were never hauled down," wrote Kennon from *Colorado.* "The flames that lit our decks stood faithful sentinels over their halyards until they, like the ship, were entirely consumed. I burned the bodies of the slain. Our colors were shot away three times. I hoisted them myself twice; finally every stripe was taken out of the flag, leaving a small constellation of four little stars only, which showed to our enemy how bravely we had defended them." (The flag referred to was the Louisiana State banner.)

Governor Morehead

(StwStr)

Governor Morehead, a fast river steamer, was used by the Confederates as a tow boat and transport in the area of the Pamlico and Neuse Rivers, N.C. She was destroyed by Union army forces under Gen. E. E. Potter, USA, in July 1863.

Grampus

(StwGbt: t. 352; a. 2 brass 12-pdr.)

Grampus, a stern-wheeler, served with Confederate army forces as a scout boat and transport on the Mississippi. Late in March 1862 she took an active part in the defense of Island No. 10 where the Confederates finally sank her to prevent capture, 7 April. Captain Marsh Miller was in command. The Union Gunboat Flotilla set out to raise her during May 1862 and did so but she is believed to be the *Grampus No.* 2 which burned the following 11 January.

Grand Bay

(StwStr: t. 135; l. 121'; b. 26'; dr. 4')

Grand Bay was built in 1857 at Mobile, Ala. Taken into the Texas Marine Department [See Annex III] to assist in defending the coastal waters of that State, she was employed as a transport in the Sabine River and Sabine Lake until the end of the war.

Grand Duke

(SwStr: t. 508; l. 205'; b. 35'; dr. 7'6'')

Grand Duke, a steamer built at Jeffersonville, Ind., in 1859, was outfitted as a cotton-clad gunboat for service with the Confederate army in February 1863. She transported troops to Fort Taylor, La., late in February. On 14 April 1863 she was in company with the steamer *Mary T.*, and ram *Queen of the West* when they were taken under attack on the Atchafalaya River, La., by Union vessels *Estrella*, *Calhoun*, and *Arizona*. Her speed, turning power, and superior piloting allowed *Grand Duke* to escape up river.

On 4 May 1863 *Grand Duke* and *Mary T.* were taking on guns, ordnance stores, and other public property prior to the evacuation of Fort De Russy, La., when a Union reconnaissance force that included *Albatross*, *Estrella* and *Arizona* hove into view. In the ensuing hour-long engagement, each of the principal contestants sustained damage, but the Union ships withdrew, allowing the Confederates to remove their materiel further up the Red River and to delay the Federal advance by obstructing the river. *Grand Duke* was ordered to Shreveport, La., where she burned late in 1863.

Grand Era

(Str)

Grand Era was armed and outfitted with cotton-cladding for use as a tender in the Red River area. She was a unit of the Confederate squadron under Maj. J. L. Brent, CSA, that included the rams *Queen of the West*, and *Webb*, and the boarding ship *Dr. Beatty*, ordered to attack USS *Indianola*. In the evening of 24 February 1863 the battle was joined near New Carthage, Miss. Tender *Grand Era* came down carrying troops for boarding but they proved unnecessary to the success of the mission. When the Union crew wisely allowed the heavily damaged *Indianola* to fill with water and sink, *Grand Era* received prisoners on board.

Confederate interest in raising and restoring the valuable *Indianola* was demonstrated in feverish efforts, joined by *Grand Era*, but a clever Union ruse foiled the project. The Federals floated a barge, disguised as a gunboat, down near the site where work was proceeding. The working party at once abandoned the effort and departed in the ships present. They later returned only to eventually destroy their valuable prize.

Granite City

(SwStr: t. 450(463); l. 160'; b. 23'; dph. 9'2''; dr. 5'6''; a. 6 24-pdr. how., 1 24-pdr. r., 1 20-pdr. r.)

Granite City was an iron sidewheeler which the Confederates recaptured 6 May 1864 at Calcasieu Pass, La. USS *Tioga* had caught her off Eleuthera I. in the Bahamas, 22 March 1863, under Capt. John McEwan and in British disguise. The U.S. Navy bought *Granite City* from the New York prize court for $55,000.

Working for the Confederacy again in April 1864, she was disarmed and loaded at Galveston. She ran out of the Calcasieu River, 20 January 1865, only to be chased ashore next day by *Penguin* off Velasco, Tex.; this time she is believed to have broken up. It is alleged that by this time she had actually been renamed *Three Marys*.

Great Republic

(Str)

Great Republic, a Confederate cotton-clad steamer rigged for boarding purposes and sharpshooters, was captured by units of the Mississippi Squadron in late summer of 1864. Later she was placed in service by Union army forces in the Gulf of Mexico.

Grey Cloud

(Str)

Grey Cloud, a Confederate transport on the Mississippi River operated in the vicinity of Ship Island in July 1861 and eluded capture by running into Biloxi on 11 December 1861. By the following July she had been captured and placed in service by Union forces.

Greyhound

(ScStr: t. 290 [400])

Greyhound was "a three-masted propeiler", known also as "a fast sailer" and noticeable on account of the red streak along her light lead colored hull; she was built in Liverpool in 1863. Whether J. B. Lafitte, Confederate agent in Nassau, managed her for the Government or owned part or all of her has not been established, but she did carry Government cargo and is here assumed to have acted as a public vessel.

She left Liverpool for the Confederacy 5 January 1864 on her maiden voyage, and ran between there and the British islands nearby. Commanded by "Captain Henry", more accurately known as Lt. George Henry Bier, CSN, on 9 May 1864 she ran out of Wilmington, N.C. with 820 bales of cotton, 35 tons of tobacco and 25 casks of turpentine—presumably to pay for Confederate ships of her type being built in Britain. Captured next day by USS *Connecticut*, she became celebrated as the ship that carried a mysterious "Mrs. Lewis", soon recognized as "the famous rebel lady, Miss Belle Boyd, and her servant", Belle was a Southern heroine and Government agent who had been captured by the Union before.

"Captain Henry," commanding *Greyhound*, was recognized also—as late Lieutenant, U.S. Navy. The prize master, Acting Ensign Samuel Harding, Jr., USN, who took *Greyhound* to Boston, was persuaded by his charming prisoner to let Captain Bier escape from Boston to Canada; for this Harding was dismissed from the Navy in disgrace but eventually married Belle Boyd in England.

Greyhound and cargo were assessed at $484,000 in prize money. Some sources indicate this was the *Greyhound* that became General Ben Butler's floating headquarters on the James in the late fall of 1864 and that on her Butler visited Admiral Porter at Dutch Gap. *Greyhound* being faster than Porter's *Malvern* at this period, Butler gave the admiral a ride to Fortress Monroe to confer with

Asst. Secretary Gustavus V. Fox. Admiral Porter mentioned in his memoirs that *Greyhound* "deserved her name, for she was a long, lean-looking craft and the fastest steamer on the river." But not much longer; Porter relives her dramatic last trip: a few miles below Bermuda Hundred, Va., a "torpedo" blew out the engine room and set the ship afire, the admiral, general, their staffs and the crew barely escaping as *Greyhound* was "wrapped in flames from one end to another" in a final "grand spectacle." Some Southern saboteurs had planted one or more torpedos in the bunkers camouflaged as chunks of coal, which the stokers dutifully shoveled into the fires.

Grosse Tete, see *Maurepas*

Gunnison

(ScTug: t. 54; l. 70'; b. 15'; dph. 7'; cpl. 10; a. 2 6-pdr., 1 spar torpedo)

Probably built in Philadelphia and first owned in Troy, N.Y., *Gunnison* became the Confederate privateer *A. C. Gunnison* [See Annex I], commissioned at Mobile, Ala., on 25 May 1861 and commanded by Capt. P. G. Cook, a part owner. Sometime in 1862 she was acquired by the Confederate Navy and fitted out as a dispatch and torpedo boat, carrying 150 pounds of powder on a spar over her bow. Her upperworks were protected by boiler iron sheathing.

Gunnison was commanded first by Acting Master's Mate F. M. Tucker, CSN, and after 9 November 1863 by Midshipman E. A. Swain, CSN.

Plans for her to attack *Colorado*, one of the Mobile Bay blockade ships, fell through. She was turned over to the United States Navy in April, 1865 and kept in naval rather than army service as a good example, in Rear Adm. H. K. Thatcher's phrase, "of the heavier class of vessels."

H. D. Mears

(StwStr: t. 338)

H. D. Mears, also known as *Mears* and *Meares,* and not infrequently confused in Union dispatches with the *Mars,* was built in 1860 at Wheeling, Va. She was among the Confederate steamers active in western waters through August 1863 when the Confederates scuttled her in the Sunflower River to escape capture by Porter's forces.

H. J. King, see *Henry J. King*

H. L. Hunley

(SS: l. 40'; b. 3½'; dph. 4'; s. 2½ mph.; cpl. 9)[1]
(SS: l. 30'; b. 4'; dph. 5'; s. 4 mph.; cpl. 9)[2]

The submarine *H. L. Hunley* was privately built in the spring of 1863 in the machine shop of Park and Lyons, Mobile, Ala., under the direction of Confederate Army Engineers, Lts. W. A. Alexander and G. E. Dixon, 21st Alabama Volunteer Regiment, from plans furnished by Horace L. Hunley, James R. McClintoch and Baxter Watson.

[1] McClintock, James R., in a letter to Matthew F. Maury, 1868, in a collection of Matthew F. Maury's papers, Vol. 46, Folios 9087 through 9094, Library of Congress.
[2] Alexander, William A. "The Hunley", in the *Mobile Daily Herald*, July 6, 1902; contains author's recollection of ship's dimensions.

H. L. Hunley *was the first submarine to sink an enemy ship in combat.*

H. L. Hunley was fashioned from a cylindrical iron steam boiler as the main center section, with tapered ends added, and expressly built for hand-power. She was designed for a crew of 9 persons, eight to turn the hand-cranked propeller and one to steer and direct the boat. A true submarine, she was equipped with ballast tanks at each tapered end which could be flooded by valves or pumped dry by hand pumps. Iron weights were bolted as extra ballast to the underside of her hull; these could be dropped off by unscrewing the heads of the bolts from inside the submarine if she needed additional buoyancy to rise in an emergency. *H. L. Hunley* was equipped with a mercury depth gage, was steered by a compass when submerged, and light was provided by a candle whose dying flame would also warn of dwindling air supply. When near the surface, two hollow pipes equipped with stop cocks could be raised above the surface to admit air. Glass portholes in the coamings of her two manholes were used to sight from when operating near the surface with only the manholes protruding above the water. Her original armament was a floating copper cylinder torpedo with flaring triggers which was towed some 200 feet astern, the submarine to dive beneath the target ship, surface on the other side, and continue on course until the torpedo struck the ship and exploded.

After successful trials under Lieutenant Dixon in Mobile Bay, General Beauregard ordered railway agents on 7 August 1863 to expedite *H. L. Hunley* to Charleston for defense of that city. She arrived in Charleston on two flat-cars and under the management of part owners, B. A. Whitney, J. R. McClintock, B. Watson and others unknown. B. A. Whitney was a member of the Secret Service Corps of the Confederate States Army, his compensation to be half the value of any Union property destroyed by torpedoes or submarine devices.

Finding the intended target, Union blockader *New Ironsides*, in too shallow water for the submarine to pass beneath her keel, the torpedo-on-a-towline was abandoned in favor of a spar torpedo which was a copper cylinder holding 90 pounds of powder and equipped with a barbed spike. The submarine would drive the torpedo into the target by ramming, back away, and by a line attached to the trigger, explode the charge from a safe distance. The submarine was based at Battery Marshall, Beach Inlet, Sullivan's Island, in Charleston Harbor where smooth waters

of interior channels were particularly favorable to the operations of the under-powered submarine which could, at best, make only about four knots in smooth water.

H. L. Hunley was soon given to a volunteer crew of Confederate sailors commanded by Lt. J. A. Payne, CSN, of CSS *Chicora*.

After several dives about the harbor on 29 August 1863, the submarine moored by lines secured to steamer *Etiwan* at the dock at Fort Johnson. The steamer unexpectedly moved away from the dock, drawing *H. L. Hunley* on her side and she filled and went down. Five seamen of the CSS *Chicora* were officially reported to have drowned but Lieutenant Payne and two others escaped. The submarine was raised, and on 21 September 1863, turned over to Horace L. Hunley for fitting out and manning. He brought a crew from Mobile which had previous experience in handling the submarine and was to be headed by Lt. G. E. Dixon, 21st Alabama Volunteers, CSA.

In the absence of Lieutenant Dixon, 15 October 1863, Hunley took charge of the submarine for practice dives under the Receiving Ship *Indian Chief*. After several successful dives, *Hunley* again went under *Indian Chief* but air bubbles traced the downward course of the submarine which failed to surface. Hunley and his entire crew of seven lost their lives as the water was nine fathoms deep and nothing could immediatly be done to aid them.

H. L. Hunley was raised and reconditioned by Lt. G. E. Dixon and Lt. W. A. Alexander but General Beauregard refused to permit her to dive again. She was fitted with a "Lee spar-torpedo" and adjusted to float on the surface, being ballasted down so that only her manholes showed above the water. For more than 3 months the submarine went out an average of 4 nights a week from Battery Marshall, Beach Inlet, Sullivan's Island. Steering compass bearings taken from the beach on Federal ships anchoring for the night, she failed time and time again because of circumstances: the distance of the closest blockader often 6 to 7 miles away, the conditions of tide, wind and sea, or physical exhaustion of her crew, who sometimes found themselves in danger of being swept out to sea in the under-powered craft.

Then on the night of 17 February 1864 she found her destiny in the Federal steam sloop-of-war *Housatonic* anchored in about 27 feet of water some 2 miles from Battery Marshall in the north channel entrance to Charleston Harbor. Approaching silently through calm waters, *H. L. Hunley* made a daring attack in bright moonlight and approached within a hundred yards of the blockader before *Housatonic's* lookouts spied the Confederate craft. By the time observers determined she was not a log or other harmless object, she was so close that the heavy guns of *Housatonic* could not be depressed sufficiently to come to bear. She approached the keel of her victim at right angles and came under small arms fire from the watch officers and men of *Housatonic*.

Housatonic slipped her cable in great haste to try to back away. Her maneuver proved vain as *H. L. Hunley's* torpedo struck home under water just abaft the mizzenmast. There was a stunning crash of timbers and a muffled explosion like the report of a 12-pound howitzer and a severe shock. Some of *Housatonic's* crew reported pieces of timber hurtling to the top of the mizzenmast itself while a dark column of smoke rose high in the sky. *Housatonic*, in shallow water, settled rapidly to the bottom as all her crew, save five who were killed by drowning or explosion, scrambled to the safety of the rigging which remained above the water's surface.

H. L. Hunley failed to return from her mission. The exact cause of her loss is not known; she may have gone down beneath *Housatonic;* or in backing away, been swamped by waves caused by her sinking victim; or she may have been swept out to sea. In giving their lives the heroic crew wrote a new page in history—the first submarine to sink a warship in combat—and cast a shadow far ahead to the enormous new factor of seapower in undersea war.

H. R. W. Hill

(SwStr: t. 602)

H. R. W. Hill, also known as *Hill*, was built in 1852 at New Albany, Ind., and employed by the Confederates as a transport in the Mississippi River area. Under Captain Newell she participated in the Battle of Belmont, Mo., on 7 November 1861. As part of the force under Maj. Gen. L. Polk, CSA, she stood fearlessly at her post while under heavy Union fire ready to transport troops back and forth across the river in the course of the battle. *H. R. W. Hill* fell into Union hands at the Battle of Memphis on 6 June 1862.

Habana, see *Sumter*

Halifax

(StGbt: l. 91')

Halifax, a steam towboat completing as a gunboat at the Confederate Navy Yard, Halifax, N.C., was taken captive on the ways, 12 May 1865, when forces under Comdr. W. H. Macomb, USN, in *Shamrock* advanced up the Roanoke River. Commodore Macomb commended Carpenter Mark W. Paul, USN, "who managed, with the small means at his command, to launch this craft without any injury, though on account of the low state of the river the vessel was full 30 feet above the level of the water and only a few yards distant from the bank. The ways he constructed are 200 feet long and very steep."

She was towed to Norfolk by *Ceres* about 25 June and was in Philadelphia 18 July. *Halifax* does not appear further in published naval records.

Hallie Jackson

(PvtrBrig)

Privateer brig *Hallie Jackson* is alleged to have been built in 1860 of the strongest available materials—white and live oak, copper fastened—to the specifications of a B. S. Sanchez of Savannah. Sanchez applied for a letter of marque 18 April 1861, one of the first two citizens to do so under President Jefferson Davis' 17 April proclamation, although he expressed his preference for selling *Hallie Jackson* for $9,000 "as a coast guard." [cf. Annex I]

More important, there seems to be no particular reason to challenge Mr. Sanchez' claim that, "This vessel has the exalted honor of having hoisted the first Confederate flag within the limits of a foreign country . . . for one week while in the port of Matanzas [Cuba] . . . although not yet recognized, it was respected."

But *Hallie Jackson* never got back to Georgia to arm: en route she was captured by USS *Union* and sent to New York for condemnation by the prize court.

Hampton

(ScGbt: dp. 166; l. 106'; b. 21'; dph. 8'; dr. 5'; cl. *Hampton*)

CSS *Hampton* was a wooden gunboat built at Norfolk Navy Yard in 1862 and based there until May when the yard was abandoned and the fleet moved up the James River. With Lt. J. S. Maury, CSN, in command, *Hampton* participated in significant river actions including the battle at Dutch

Gap on 13 August 1864; operations against Fort Harrison, 29 September–1 October; and the engagement at Chaffin's Bluff, 22 October.

Hampton was burned by the Confederates as they evacuated Richmond on 3 April 1865.

Hampton Class: Known as "Maury Gunboats," 100 of which were planned—brain children of Comdr. Matthew Fontaine Maury, CSN, the father of hydrography. These "Jeffersonian-type" gunboats were a "contemporary manifestation of a recurrent theory that wars may be fought economically with mosquito fleets." Flag Officer L. M. Goldsborough, USN, wrote Secretary Welles, 14 February 1862, "I forward herewith a very remarkable letter [19 January] from Mr. M. F. Maury, late of our Navy, to Flag Officer Lynch, which was found among the papers of the latter gentleman when his vessel, the *Sea Bird*, was captured by our forces . . . [Enclosure: Comdr. George] 'Minor has the guns in hand; most of the engines and boilers are provided for, and by the end of this week I hope to be able to say that in 90 days or less all the hulls will be ready for the machinery . . . for 100 steam launches. . . . A call has been made upon the Army for a transfer to us of all the sailors in the State [N.C.], and a law has been passed offering a bounty of $50 . . . also a law for the appointment of 50 lieutenants and masters . . . considering . . . that all the vessels are steamers of the same model, and that they are intended for bay and river navigation only, I think that we can manufacture a pretty good set of officers and capital guns' crews . . . I expect my son John [v. penult. para. supra], your pet, here in a day or two. I shall propose to him to try for a master's place in one of these boats . . . . At any rate, if you can take him as a supernumerary and work him up as a middy, requiring him to do any and everything, it will be the "very dandy" . . . . The boat that is at present proposed as the model for all, is 21 feet beam, 112 feet long, and 6 feet draft, with 171 tons and an armament of a 9-inch gun forward and a 32-pounder aft. I am protesting with all my might against such a large boat and such a feeble stern gun.' "

Surprisingly, no drawings have come to light to support the very detailed specifications extant, despite the notation thereon that "the inboard plans will be furnished by the Department," for many sets must have been issued. Individual yards may have made minor modifications, but nothing approaching what Maury himself sought. Only *Hampton* and *Nansemond* saw service, *Norfolk*, *Portsmouth* and others being burned on the stocks. Such mass production of "standard ships" as Maury desired was not achieved until 1918.

N.B.: Contracts preserved to us for 106-ft. gunboats are revealing—

Contractor	No. boats/cost	1861
Myers & Co., Washington, N.C.	2 @ $16,000...	5 Oct.
Ollinger & Bruce, (Fla.) (110')	1 @ $15,850...	4 Nov.
W. A. Graves, Norfolk, Va..	1 @ $9,986....	28 Nov.
		1862
G. Elliott, Edwards Ferry, N.C.	3 @ $10,000...	13 Jan.
N. Nash, Norfolk, Va.......	4 @ $12,000...	7 & 9 Feb.
Krenson & Hawkes, Savannah	3 @ $16,000...	4 Mar.
F. M. Jones, Charleston......	3 @ $14,000...	5 Mar.
W. O. Saffold, Early Co., Ga.	2 @ $50,000*..	25 Mar.

* Complete with engines.

Secretary Mallory to Pres. Davis, 29 Mar. '62, recommends that the "$2,000,000 appropriated for the [Maury] gunboats . . . be expended upon building iron-clad vessels; and I suggest . . . the expediency of completing those vessels already commenced according to the original design but of making iron-clad gunboats of the others as far as the appropriation will allow. Fifteen of these boats have been commenced—these vessels cannot advantageously be plated—but will be serviceable as originally designed."

Hannah

(Sch)

Hannah was an armed schooner under Captain Jack Sands, CSA. She attempted to get over the reef into Nueces Bay on 12 October 1862 when the Federal fleet advanced on Corpus Christi, Tex. Finding the channel made dangerously narrow by a grounded steamer which was reportedly loaded with powder, Sands was unable to enter the bay and ran *Hannah* ashore about 7 miles above Corpus Christi. A party of unarmed men were driven away from salvage efforts by shots from a Federal ship which anchored 400 yards out and commenced manning a boat to land an armed party. Fearing this party would cut out *Hannah*, Captain Sands immediately fired her and she was consumed.

C.S.S. Harriet Lane *prior to her capture by Confederate forces at Galveston.*

Hansa

(SwStr: t. 257; s. 12 k.)

Hansa was operated by the State of North Carolina (cf. *Don supra*), running to Havana and Nassau for munitions, out of Wilmington. She was commanded by Captains James E. Randle, T. Atkinson and Murray during the course of the war, which it may be assumed that she survived, in the absence of evidence to the contrary. She had two stacks and must have been a fast steamer when acquired by the Confederates, but she appears to have fouled her boilers—by February 1864, if not earlier—and may have been retired to less hazardous service; many steamers ruined their tubes by burning turpentine-soaked cotton from their cargo to get steam for flank speed in a dire extremity such as might be encountered any or every run through the blockade.

Harmony

(SwTug: t. 78; a. 2 32-pdr. r.)

CSS *Harmony*, a small steam tug built at Philadelphia, Pa., in 1859, was placed under exclusive control of A. B. Fairfax, Confederate Inspector General of Naval Ordinance at Norfolk Navy Yard on 24 April 1861 and was used primarily for ordinance transport throughout the war; Flag Officer Forrest, CSN, wrote in September 1861, "Her services are indispensable as an ordnance transportation boat."

On 30 August 1861 Commander Fairfax took command, armed her with a rifled gun and attacked sloop-of-war *Savannah*, riding at anchor off Newport News. *Harmony* inflicted considerable damage on *Savannah* who was unable to train her guns effectively upon her attacker.

Harriet Lane

Miss Lane was Pres. James Buchanan's niece and acted as First Lady in the White House during the administration of America's only bachelor First Executive.

(SwStr: t. 674; l. 180'; b. 30'; dr. 12'6''; s. 11 k.; a. 3 9'', 2 24-pdr., 1 30-pdr. r.)

CSS *Harriet Lane* was built for the United States Revenue Cutter Service in 1857-58 by the celebrated William H. Webb, New York, and was the only steam vessel in that service at the time. Taken over by the Navy on 17 September 1861, she performed valiant service on the Atlantic coast, the Mississippi River, and coast of Texas. Following the battle at Galveston on 1 January 1863 in which her commanding officer, Comdr. Jonathan M. Wainwright, USN, was killed, she surrendered to the Confederates.

The Confederate Secretary of War turned *Harriet Lane* over to the Confederate Navy Department, and Lt. J. N. Barney, CSN, was given command. She served with the Confederate Army's Marine Department of Texas [See Annex III] until 31 March 1863 when all naval officers were detached and she was turned back to the Confederate War Department.

Early in 1864 she was converted into a blockade runner to carry cotton to Havana to pay for war supplies. She lay in wait at Galveston until 30 April to escape, arriving safely, only to remain idle at Havana the duration of the war under the name *Lavinia*.

In 1867, recovered from Cuba and taken to New York, she was converted from brigantine to bark rig and named *Elliott Richie*. In 1884, being waterlogged, she was abandoned off Pernambuco, Brazil.

Harriet Pinckney

(ScBrig: t. 715[682]; l. 190'; b. 28'5''; dph. 17'5'')

Harriet Pinckney (more often spelled *Pinkney* in official naval records) was a fast, new, British brig, of iron with coppered bottom and a 90-horsepower auxiliary steam engine; she was completed in Richardsons yard at Middlesbrough in Yorkshire, 23 July 1862, registered at London next day and was alleged to have done 18 knots on her builders' trials. Because of her speed and other characteristics she was immediately bought up by Confederate agents working through Fraser, Trenholm & Co., Liverpool, and Comdr. James D. Bulloch, CSN, as secretly as possible. Her "owner," therefore, was a "Mr. Thomas Sterling Begbie of 4 Mansion House Place, London," to whom Lloyd's Register adds a "Mr. R. Hamilton" [cf. *Agrippina*]. But "Begbie" was a red light to Consul F. H. Morse, who lost no time in relaying the new Confederate steamer's particulars to Washington: he described her as having "one deck, two masts, brig rig, elliptic stern, clench build, no gallery, no head; iron frame." He also seemed to be aware that she promptly loaded 24,000 rifles, 18 cannon and a cargo of other vital munitions in the Thames, transhipped from the *Sylph*, just in from Hamburg, and was off about 9 August for Bermuda.

On 8th and 9th August 1862, assiduous Consul Morse sent Secretary of State Seward sketches and descriptions of a new mine which he thought "H.P.," as she was frequently called, would certainly be carrying: these "infernal machines or torpedoes" were "an invention for destroying ships in harbor" and he warned that "if the explosion takes place at the right distance, the consequences will be most horrible." The horrendous contraptions employed an unknown "poisonous fluid and explosive balls filled with poisonous matter." While it is doubtful that this intelligence was released in Bermuda, "H.P." caused a considerable stir there on 5 October when the whole populace turned out to watch her and fellow blockade-runner *Minho* try to escape, only to be chased back into port by USS *Sonoma*, there for that purpose.

Harriet Pinckney was diverted from her transport functions through the blockade when a tender was chosen for CSS *Rappahannock* (q.v.) but when the raider was held indefinitely in port at Brest, "H.P." was no longer seen in the area and presumably disappeared back into the demimonde of the blockade runner to deliver essential cargoes to the Confederacy.

Hart

(Str)

Hart, an iron-clad steamer under Lt. E. Montague, CSA, transported stores, ordnance and troops in support of Camp Bisland on Bayou Teche and in Berwick Bay, La. On 1 November 1862 she gallantly went to the assistance of Confederate gunboat *J. A. Cotton* in her unequal contest with Federal gunboats until ordered to resume towing a government sugar barge up Bayou Teche. Later in the month she transported from Camp Bisland to Petite Anse Island, four guns of a Confederate army battery for operations against Federal gunboats. She was sunk on 14 April 1863 to avoid capture when Camp Bisland, Bayou Teche, La., fell to the combined efforts of Federal gunboats and troops under Maj. Gen. N. P. Banks, USA. On 28 July 1863, an intelligence report from USS *Clifton* stated that *Hart* had been nearly raised but sunk again on reappearance of the Federal gunboats.

Hartford City

(Str: t. 150)

Hartford City was a small river steamer built at McKeesport, Pa., in 1856 and first homeported at Cincinnati, Ohio. In May 1862 she was impressed into Confederate service out of Vicksburg, Miss., to tow rafts and other craft for obstruction of Union gunboat navigation in the Yazoo River. She later transported supplies out of that same Confederate base, but sought refuge in the Yalobusha in July 1863 as the Federal fleet took over control of the Yazoo. On 18 July 1863 Capt. A. H. Forrest, CSA, at Carrollton, Miss., was ordered to send a detachment to burn the steamboats, including *Hartford City*, said to be located in the Tallahatchie and Yazoo Rivers.

Hawley

(Sch)

Hawley was used as a Confederate transport in coastal waters of North Carolina during the latter part of 1861.

Helen

(Str)

Helen, a small steamer employed as guard boat and transport, was burned by Confederate army troops at Pensacola in May 1862 to prevent capture.

(Slp)

Helen used in transporting Confederate provisions along the Florida coast was captured with a cargo of corn by a boat from USS *Sagamore* near Bayport on 2 April 1863. She was then destroyed by fire.

Henry Dodge, see *Dodge*

Henry J. King

(Str)

Henry J. King, also known as *H. J. King* and *King*, served as a Confederate transport between Selma and Mobile, Ala., during 1864. On 14 April 1865 she was captured with a valuable cargo of provisions by Union Army forces on the Coosa River, Ala., and sent in to Montgomery as a prize.

Hercules

Ajax (ScStr: t. 515; l. 170′; b. 25′; dph. 12′6′′; dr. 7′6′′; s. 12 k.; a. 1 9′′ r. 1 8′′r.; cl.)

Hercules was building on the Clyde at Denny's and presumably nearly finished at war's end in 1865 [v. *Ajax supra*]. She was intended to become *Vicksburg*.

(N.B.: Not to be in any way confused with the tug *Hercules* which delivered arms to *Alabama* in Beaumaris Bay, Wales, in July 1862.)

Hercules, see *Colonel Lovell*

Hibben

(Str)

Hibben was operated by Confederate army forces in transporting men and materials in the vicinity of Charleston harbor during 1863–64. During the Federal attack on that city in August 1863 *Hibben* sustained damage while lying at the wharf of Fort Sumter. However, a year later army officials reported her in good condition and she apparently continued to operate.

Hill, see *H. R. W. Hill*

Hine, see *T. D. Hine*

Hope

(StwStr: t. 193; l. 128′; b. 34′; dr. 5′)

Hope, built in Louisville, Ky., in 1855, was operated in the Mississippi and Yazoo Rivers during 1862–63, successfully eluding capture by Admiral Porter's squadron until August 1863.

(SwStr: t. 1,800 [1,200; 1,000; 1,697bom]; l. 281.5 bp; b. 35′; dr. 11′; cpl. 66)

Hope was a "very large" and "very strong" Wilmington, N.C., iron and steel paddlewheeler, called the "finest and fastest steamer in the trade" by one observer in Britain. She was procured there for the Confederate Government shortly before or after she left the Liverpool yard of Jones, Quiggin & Co. She was Hull No. 159, sister to the noted *Colonel Lamb* (q.v.), which she resembled except for the presence of the usual turtleback forward.

The name *Hope* was already well known from a recent blockade-runner. She could carry over 1,800 cotton bales on a draft of only 11 feet and possessed the safety factor of five watertight compartments—highly unusual in her day. She first appeared in U.S. consular dispatches 10 July as consigned to Fraser, Trenholm & Co., the Confederate Government "front" in Liverpool. USS *Sacramento* hurried over from Cork to Falmouth to try to capture *Hope* at sea but she reached Nassau unscathed early in August, having avoided Bermuda because of yellow fever raging there that summer.

Two fore-and-aft engines of 350 nominal horsepower, supplied by 4 boilers, gave *Hope* power to outrun most of her contemporaries. Yet she was cornered on 22 October 1864 by USS *Eolus*, trying to enter Cape Fear River; the loss of her cargo and particularly her mail bags was a blow to the Confederacy. A week later she was sighted near New York bound to Boston for adjudication, under a prize master.

An excellent model of *Hope* is on permanent display at Mariners Museum, Newport News, Va.

Hornet

(ScTB: l. 46′; b. 6′3″; dph. 3′9″; a. 1 18′ spar torpedo, percussion type, 5″ dia.; cl. *Squib*)

CSS *Hornet* was a steam launch fitted out as a torpedo boat on the James River late in 1864. Under Master Samuel P. Blanc, CSN, she took an active part in the attempted passage through the obstructions at Trent's Reach on 23 and 24 January 1865. She sank 2 days after colliding with the flag-of-truce steamer *Allison*.

Howard, see *General Polk*

Hunley, see *H. L. Hunley*

Huntress

(SwStr: t. 500; l. 230′; b. 24′6″; dr. 6′6″; s. 16–20 k. (flat calm); a. 1 to 3 guns)

CSS *Huntress* was purchased in New York City in March 1861 for the State of Georgia, which later relinquished her to the Confederate States Navy. Her first commanding officer was Lt. Wilburn B. Hall, CSN, in that he went North to buy and bring her South; Hall was then detached and reported to *Savannah*, being succeeded by Lt. C. Manigault Morris, CSN.

Huntress had been a crack Boston-Portland mail packet, "very narrow beam, low in the water, immense sidewheels, painted black"; she had been built at New York City in 1838.

Huntress—first ship to raise the Confederate flag on the high seas, it is claimed—served on the Charleston station during 1861–62, taking part in the battle of Port Royal, S.C., 7 November 1861. During the summer of 1862 she served as a transport in Charleston harbor, taking the duty of *Planter* (q.v.) which fell into Federal hands. *Huntress* had been advertised for sale in May but was not sold until 29 October, when she finally went for $133,650 to A. J. White & Son, Charleston merchants. Converting to a blockade runner, she was renamed *Tropic*.

Attempting to escape to sea with turpentine and cotton on 18 January 1863, she was accidentally burned off Charleston; USS *Quaker City* rescued passengers and crew.

Huntsville

(IrcStFlBtry: l. 150′; dr. 7′; s. 4 k.; cpl. 40; a. 4 32-pdr.; type Heavy *Albemarle*)

Huntsville, launched 7 February at Selma, was completed at Mobile Ala., and commissioned in 1863, Lt. J. Myers, CSN, in command. Although designed an iron-clad she was only partially armored. Owing to defective engines and the lack of a full complement of guns *Huntsville* rendered no active service although she guarded the waters around Mobile. After the battle of Mobile Bay on 5 August 1864 she escaped up the Spanish River only to be sunk 12 miles from Mobile on 12 April 1865, upon the evacuation of that city.

Huntsville was a propeller ordered by the Confederate Navy from Henry D. Bassett, 1 May 1862, for $100,000 and delivered about 1 August 1863. Her high-pressure engines are believed to have been transferred from a river steamer, although it had been intended to supply them from Columbus, Ga., Naval Iron Works, commanded by Lts. Julian Myers and James McC. Baker, CSN. Her armor plate was delivered at Mobile by Shelby Iron Co. and Schofield & Markham of Atlanta.

I. C. Landis, see *Landis*

Ida

(SwStr)

Ida, a small steamer, operated in conjunction with Commodore Tattnall's squadron in the Savannah River. She served as a transport, dispatch, and tow boat from 1862 until 10 December 1864, when, during the Union attack on Savannah, she was captured by a party of foragers and cavalrymen under Captain Gildersleeve, USA, and burned near Argyle Island.

Indian Chief

CSS *Indian Chief* was used as receiving ship at Charleston, S.C., from 1862 to 1865. One of her additional details in 1863 was support of the local torpedo (mine) operations. Flag Officer J. R. Tucker, CSN, wrote her commander, Lt. W. G. Dozier, CSN, 24 August 1863, "You will be pleased to have as many boats fitted with torpedoes as you can hoist up to the davits of the *Indian Chief* . . ." Her first commanding officer was Lt. J. H. Ingraham, CSN. She was burned by the Confederates prior to the evacuation of Charleston on 18 February 1865.

Infanta, see *Squib*

Iron King

(Str)

Iron King, a Confederate States naval coal transport operating on the Alabama River between Selma and Mobile in late 1864 was commanded by Master's Mate J. E. Mayhew.

Isaac Smith, see *Stono*

Isabella

(Slp)

Isabella was captured in Waccasassa Bay, Florida, by USS *Fort Henry* on 22 May 1863, while en route from Tampa, Fla., to Island No. 4 in the Keys. She was sent in to Key West as a prize.

Isabella, see Annex I

Isabella Ellis

(Sch: t. 340)

Isabella Ellis was reported early in the war to be transporting armament for the Confederacy along the North Carolina coast. She is listed as a Union ship in October 1864.

Island City

(SwStr: t. 245)

Island City, owned by the Texas Marine Department, was used as a supply boat in Galveston Bay and tributaries from 1863 through the end of the war. [See Annex III].

Isondiga

(StwGbt: dr. 6'6''; s. 5 k.; cpl. 60; a. 1 9'' shell gun, 1 6.4'' r.)

CSS *Isondiga* was a small wooden gunboat without masts which operated in waters around Savannah, Ga., and in St. Augustine Creek, Fla., from April 1863 to December 1864, Lt. J. S. Kennard commanding.

She escaped from Savannah on 21 December 1864 before the city fell to the forces of Gen. W. T. Sherman. She was later burned by her commanding officer and crew to prevent seizure by the Union.

Ivy

(SwStr: t. 454; l. 191'; b. 28'; dph. 9'; cpl. 60 (as pvtr.); 1 8''. 1 32-pdr. r., 2 24-pdr. brass how.)

CSS *Ivy,* formerly *El Paraguay,* was commissioned 16 May 1861 at New Orleans as the Confederate privateer *V. H. Ivy,* Capt. N. B. Baker. She was purchased later in the year by the Navy, renamed *Ivy* and placed under the command of Lt. J. Fry, CSN.

On 12 October 1861 she joined in attacking the Federal blockading squadron lying at the Head of the Passes in the Mississippi River and achieved notable success with her long range gun and maneuverability. *Ivy* remained active in the lower Mississippi until May 1863 when she was destroyed by her officers near Liverpool Landing in the Yazoo River in order to foil plans for her capture.

J. A. Bell, see *Josiah A. Bell*

J. A. Cotton

(IrcSwStr: t. 549; a. 1 32-pdr. sb., 1 9-pdr. r.)

J. A. Cotton, also known as *Cotton,* was built at Jeffersonville, Ind., in 1861 for use on the bayous of Louisiana. She was purchased by the Confederate Navy in 1862, clad at least partially with iron, and placed under the command of Lt. E. W. Fuller, CSN.

She operated in Berwick Bay and Bayou Teche where from 1 to 6 November 1862, she fought a series of actions against Union gunboats *Calhoun,* *Colonel Kinsman,* *Diana,* and *Estrella.* Casualties and damage were light on both sides. On 15 January 1863, off Brashear City, La., *J. A. Cotton,* after a 2-day engagement with her adversaries of the previous November, was burned to prevent capture.

(SwStr: t. 372; l. 185'; b. 34'6''; dph. 8'9''; dr. 4'10''; a. 2 24-pdr., 2 12-pdr., 1 how.)

J. A. Cotton, also known as *Mary T.,* *Cotton,* and *Cotton Jr.,* was built at Jeffersonville, Ind., in 1860, as *Mary T.* for the New Orleans, Coast, and La Fourche Transportation Co. She was seized by the Confederate Army in the Red River early in 1863.

Renamed *J. A. Cotton* she was fitted out as a gunboat and protected with cotton bales. On 4 May 1863 at Fort De Russy, in company with CSA Steamer *Grand Duke,* she fought a sharp but inconclusive action with the Federal gunboat *Albatross,* during which *J. A. Cotton* suffered minor damage. She served in various capacities until the end of the war when she was surrendered to Union forces at Alexandria, La.

J. D. Clarke

(SwStr)

J. D. Clarke, a sidewheel steamer, operated as a Confederate army transport in the Red River. On 9 April 1863 Admiral Farragut on board USS *Hartford* gave chase to two steamers outside the mouth of the Red River and captured *J. D. Clarke*. On 10 April the captors removed the steamer's machinery and scuttled her.

J. D. Stelle, see *Colonel Stell*

J. D. Swaim

(SwStr: t. 350; l. 150'6''; b. 30'; dph. 6')

J. D. Swaim, also known as *J. D. Swain* and *Swaim*, a steamboat of New Orleans, was built at Jeffersonville, Ind., in 1859. She was taken into Confederate service and sunk sometime in 1862 in the mouth of McCall's River where Union forces raised her early in April 1864. Considered a fine prize, she was used thereafter as a Union transport.

J. D. Swain, see *J. D. Swaim*

J. E. Coffee, see *Winslow*

J. F. Carr, see *John F. Carr*

J. F. Pargoud, see *Pargoud*

J. H. Jarvis

(Str)

The main particulars and fate of *J. H. Jarvis* or *Jarvis* are an enigma: She may have been the embryo of "the new steamer built at" Columbus, Ga., early in 1864. It seems certain that she did exist and was commanded by Lt. John W. Bennett, CSN, in June 1863 in the Mobile-West Florida area. If she was the same ship as the newbuilding, she was later commanded by daredevil mastermind Lt. George W. Gift, CSN; it is matter of record that he was detached from *Chattahoochee* just before or after the famous boiler explosion that sank her, 27 May 1863, for he was principal informant to the press following the disaster. It is known that Gift reported to Bennett, Commanding Officer "on board the *Jarvis*", 8 June, for duty, because Bennett so endorsed Gift's orders from Capt. John K. Mitchell, CSN. On 15 February 1864 Lt. Gift was detached from Naval Station, Charleston, S.C., to command "the new steamer at Columbus, Ga.", relieving Lt. Augustus McLaughlin, CSN, who appears to

have been commanding *Chattahoochee* concurrently; then on 5 March Captain Mitchell in Richmond directed Gift to relieve McLaughlin in *Chattahoochee*. Apparently this change in command enabled Gift to take the luckless gunboat to Eufaula, Ala., for on 10 June he was ordered to bring her back to Columbus "and turn her over to Lt. Comdr. A. McLaughlin for repairs," while Chief Constructor J. L. Porter was to come from Wilmington as soon as possible to inspect her.

These bits of fact establish little directly about *Jarvis* herself but define an intriguing area of probability which could eternally link *Jarvis* and the interesting personality of George Gift. Two letters from Gift published in official records point to him as a colorful, unrecognized idea man of the Confederate Navy: On 9 May he proposed to Lt. John J. Guthrie, CSN, *Chattahoochee's* captain, a daring raid by the latter's men using the yawl *Swan* to capture USS *Port Royal* in Apalachicola, Fla. Two days later he suggested to Secretary Mallory a plot to purchase secretly and operate a Confederate cruiser on Lake Erie and to terrorize Union commerce throughout the Great Lakes, "although," he added, "the scheme may be as Quixotic as it is audacious." Whatever his confréres may have thought of Gift's daydreams—probably not much—his Lake Erie stratagem just might have succeeded at that time: witness the *Georgian* (q.v.) affair which so nearly did 18 months later, although the sands of time were running out for the Confederacy. Gift did participate in the abortive Wilkinson raid of November 1863, which might well have taken USS *Michigan* had it not been for treachery (see: *Georgian*).

J. J. Crittenden

(Sch)

J. J. Crittenden was serving the Confederacy in 1862 when captured off Newbegun Creek, N.C., by USS *Whitehead*. She was subsequently "sunk as an obstruction."

Jackson

(SwStr: t. 297; cpl. 75; a. 2 32-pdr.)

Jackson, a fast river tug built at Cincinnati in 1849, called *Yankee*, was purchased at New Orleans, La., on 9 May 1861 by Capt. L. Rousseau, CSN, strengthened and fitted for service in the Confederate Navy. On 6 June Lt. W. Gwathmey, CSN, was ordered to her command, and after shipping a crew, took her up the Mississippi to

Columbus, Ky., to join the squadron under Capt. G. N. Hollins charged with the defense of the river.

On 4 September 1861 *Jackson* supported by shore batteries briefly and inconclusively engaged gunboats *Lexington* and *Tyler* off Hickman, Ky. The Federal ships finding the current fast setting them down upon the Confederate batteries returned to their former position. Six days later the little gunboat took part in a spirited engagement at Lucas Bend, Mo., between Confederate artillery and cavalry and Union gunboats *Lexington* and *Conestoga* during which she received an 8-inch shell in her wheel house and side which forced her to retire on one engine.

Jackson sailed with Hollins' squadron to attack five of the Federal blockaders at the Head of the Passes, Mississippi River, on 12 October 1861. They successfully routed the Union forces and proceeded to the defense of Forts Jackson and St. Philip which the United States Mortar Flotilla under Comdr. David D. Porter bombarded from 18 to 24 April 1862. On 23 April *Jackson* was despatched to make the canals above the fort inaccessible to Union ships.

When the commanding officer, Lt. F. B. Renshaw, CSN, found it impossible to stem the Federal advance he retired to New Orleans. After the surrender of that city, *Jackson* was destroyed by the Confederates.

Jacob Musselman

(StwStr: t. 144)

Jacob Musselman, built in 1860 at Paducah, Ky., was a Union steam transport serving near Memphis, where a Confederate guerrilla band captured her on 6 January 1863. Capt. J. H. McGehee's Arkansas cavalry band was acting under orders to reconnoiter the area, "burning cotton in that country and annoying the enemy on the Mississippi River" wherever possible. The Confederates ran the steamer in to Bradley's Landing and there destroyed her.

James Battle

(SwStr: t. 407)

James Battle or *Battle* was a fast, shallow-draft river steamer of Mobile, built in New Albany, Ind., in 1860 with high pressure machinery. Considered for arming as a gunboat to defend Mobile, *Battle* was not armed like the *Morgan* class only because of the farsighted policy of Flag Officer Victor M. Randolph, CSN, who rejected palliatives and would have nothing to do with anything but ironclads for his fleet.

Turned down finally as a gunboat, *Battle* undoubtedly served the Confederate Army in varied transport services, under Capt. Jesse J. Coxe, until captured running the blockade; she was laden with naval stores and over 600 bales of cotton on 18 July 1863 70 miles southeast of Mobile bar when overhauled by USS *De Soto* and *Ossipee*. Armed with four 12-pounders and kept for "temporary use . . . to scour the coast" from Tampa to St. Marks, Fla., prize steamer *Battle* under Lt. Comdr. A. A. Semmes, USN, was instrumental in bringing about the destruction of another blockade runner, a cotton warehouse at Bayport and assisting other naval operations in Florida.

Battle, in the words of Adm. Theodorus Bailey, USN, was "the finest packet on the Alabama River and was altered to suit her for a blockade runner at a large expense." As such, whether within the scope of this listing as fully Confederate Government-owned or not, *Battle* deserves special mention as representative of a class of the newer river steamers with high-pressure plants whose light hulls the Confederates converted at great expense but with relative success for quick dashes across the Gulf to Havana or Nassau with cotton. Admiral Bailey complained: "The *Warren, Fannie, William Bagley* [captured same day as *Battle* by same blockaders], *W. H. Smith, Alabama, Alice Vivian* and *St. Mary's* are other vessels of the same class. The *De Soto* is the only vessel I have with sufficient speed to overtake any of these traders." Farragut's *Ossipee* apparently was another. Histories of these ships are omitted since it is not certain they all were public vessels, but *Alice Vivian* at least did some troop carrying, as evidenced at the time of her capture by *De Soto*, 16 August 1863, with the whole staff and baggage of Brig. Gen. James E. Slaughter, CSA—only by merest accident missing the general too.

James Funk

(Str: t. 120)

James Funk, Pilot Boat No. 22 of New York, was captured by the audacious CSS *Tallahassee* off Montauk Point on 11 August 1864. She may have been used briefly as a tender before being burned by her captor.

James Gray, see *Lady Davis*

James Johnson

(SwStr: t. 526)

James Johnson, built in 1856 at Jeffersonville, Ind., was one of several steamers purchased at Nashville, Tenn., late in 1861 by Lt. I. N. Brown, CSN, for conversion to a gunboat. She was not yet completed in February 1862 when the advance of Union gunboats caused Brown to order her destruction.

James L. Day

(SwStr: t. 414; l. 187'; b. 25'6''; dr. ca. 6'; dph. 9')

James L. Day, also known as *Day*, was a Mississippi river towboat which was built in 1843 at New York, N.Y. She was seized at New Orleans, La., by the Confederates and used under the control of Flag Officer G. N. Hollins, CSN, as a gunboat in that area. On 12 October 1861, in conjunction with *Ivy* and other vessels of Hollins' "Mosquito Fleet," she engaged in a harassing action with Federal blockading ships near Head of the Passes, La.

James Wood, see James Woods

James Woods

(SwStr: t. 585)

James Woods, also known as *James Wood*, was built at Jeffersonville, Ind., in 1860 and operated out of Nashville, Tenn. Offered by her owner for sale to the Confederacy, she was purchased by Lt. I. N. Brown, CSN, for use as a gunboat. The approach of Union forces interrupted her conversion and caused the Confederates to destroy her at Nashville in February 1862.

Jamestown

(SwStr: t. 1,300; l. 240'3''; b. 33'6''; dph. 23'5''; a. 2 guns)

Jamestown, originally a passenger steamer, was built at New York, N.Y., in 1852, and seized at Richmond, Va., in 1861 for the Commonwealth of Virginia Navy. She was commissioned by the Confederate Navy the following July, renamed *Thomas Jefferson* but was generally referred to as *Jamestown*.

Brigantine-rigged *Jamestown* was designed and constructed by Jacob Westervelt, with machinery by Morgan Iron Works, for the New York & Virginia S. S. Co. as a near-sister to *Yorktown* (v. *Patrick Henry*).

With Lt. J. N. Barney, CSN, in command, she was actively employed until the end of her career in May 1862. Her service was highlighted by the battle of Hampton Roads on 8–9 March 1862 during which she assisted CSS *Virginia* in attacking *Congress* and *Cumberland* and stood by during the battle between *Monitor* and *Virginia*. The Confederate Congress tendered special thanks to the officers and crew of *Jamestown* for their "gallant conduct and bearing" in combat.

Some four weeks later, on 11 April 1862, *Jamestown*, CSS *Virginia*, and five other Confederate ships sailed from Norfolk into Hampton Roads in full view of the Union squadron there. When it became clear that the Federal ships were not going to attack, *Jamestown*, covered by *Virginia* and the others, moved in, captured three merchant ships, and helped by CSS *Raleigh*, towed them to Norfolk. Later that month *Jamestown* was dispatched from Norfolk to cooperate with Major General Magruder, CSA, in the James River and early in May she was used to transport army sick and wounded to Richmond.

On the night of 5 May, *Jamestown* and CSS *Patrick Henry* proceeded to Norfolk and returned the following night with CSS *Richmond*, CSS *Hampton* and ordnance store boats, passing the Federal battery at Newport News unobserved on both occasions. A second attempt to return to Norfolk met with failure.

On 8 May *Jamestown* was ordered to notify the Secretary of the Confederate States Navy of the continuing engagement of two Federal gunboats and ironclad *Galena* with the Confederate batteries at Day's Point. Unable to carry out her assignment *Jamestown* retired up the James River as far as Drewry's Bluff where on 15 May 1862 she was sunk to obstruct the channel.

Japan, see Georgia

Jeff Davis

(StGbt)

Jeff Davis, a steam gunboat, was employed by the Confederates on the Ohio and Mississippi Rivers during the early years of the war. She was captured at Memphis by gunboats of the Mississippi Squadron in early June 1862, and later taken into Union service.

(Str)

The chartered steamer *Jeff Davis* used as a transport by the Texas Marine Department [See

Annex III] was reported in poor condition in October 1863.

(Sch)

Jeff Davis, a small Confederate schooner, was captured off New Bern, N.C., in early June 1864 and taken into Union service.

(Str)

The steamer *Jeff Davis* was used by Confederate Navy and Army forces near Savannah, Ga. Late in 1864 she assisted operation of the ironclad *Georgia*, and remained in that area through the end of the war.

Jeff Thompson, see *General M. Jeff Thompson*

Jefferson Davis

(Brig: t. 187; dr. 10'6"; cpl. 75; a. 2 32-pdr., 2 24-pdr., 1 18-pdr.)

Jefferson Davis or *Jeff Davis* was a New Orleans full-rigged brig, built in Baltimore about 1845 as *Putnam* and captured off Cuba 21 August 1858 by Lt. John Newland Maffitt, USN, in USS *Dolphin* as the slaver *Echo*; her cargo of 271 Negroes was returned to Africa in *Niagara* and *Echo* forfeited to the United States. Auctioned in January 1859, *Echo* reverted to her original name, *Putnam*, and was owned by Capt. Robert Hunter of Charleston, S.C.

Hunter signed up 27 shareholders, including the elite of Charleston, and 10 of them applied for a letter of marque for *Putnam* to be known as *Rattlesnake*, but a name change to *Jefferson Davis* was approved by the State Department, 23 May, and the brig commissioned a privateer 18 June 1861 at Charleston. [See Annex]. I She was armed with five 60-year old, British, iron cannon.

Jeff Davis was described by a prisoner as having "black mastheads and yards and a black hull" and being "very rusty." Another victim was misled by her "French-cut hempen sails." Master and shareholder was the "impudent sea robber," Louis M. Coxetter, a name soon to be placed high on the list of "pirates" most wanted by the U.S. Navy, although he treated his prisoners well, by their own account. His mate, Lt. William Ross Postell, once pride of the Republic of Texas Navy, also ex-Lieutenant, USN, was equally sought.

On 28 June, celebrated by Charleston as the anniversary of driving off Admiral Sir Peter Parker in the Revolution, *Jeff Davis* received a gala send-off as she escaped to sea through Maffitt's Channel, "notwithstanding," as the *Mercury* quipped, "the very efficient blockade of Abraham I." Coxetter took 9 sail in 7 weeks in "the last truly classic cruise in the history of private-armed sea power." These included 3 brigs, 3 schooners, 2 ships and a bark, causing consternation on the coast from Maine to Delaware. Seeking to make Florida, *Enchantress* was recaptured by USS *Albatross* and her prize-master, William W. Smith, a Savannah pilot, was nearly hanged as a pirate, along with his prize-crew, by a Philadelphia court—perhaps the most celebrated case of its type during this war. Bark *Alvarado* was chased ashore by *Jamestown* at Fernandina, Fla., and burned to prevent recapture. Coxetter released schooner *Windward*, brig *Mary E. Thompson*, schooner *Mary Goodell* with prisoners, but had to burn *John Carver*, an Army ship with anthracite for the blockade. Schooner *S. J. Waring* was taken into New York by her cook, who killed the three leaders of her prize crew with an ax 100 miles off Charleston. Brigs *John Welsh* and *Santa Clara* got into Savannah safely as prizes and were auctioned at handsome figures. *Jeff Davis'* crew was augmented by deserters from several of her prizes.

Jeff Davis arrived off St. Augustine, Fla., 16 August but had to wait nearly two days for a half-gale to blow over; going in, finally, she grounded and even jettisoning the starboard guns did not save the brig; only stores and small arms were saved. Church bells rang and the town gave the shipwrecked privateersmen an ovation as heroes with a celebration lasting for days; on returning to Charleston, two weeks later, Captain Coxetter was honored with heavy gold watch and fob by hero-worshippers. Crowed Charleston *Mercury*, 26 August 1861, "The name of the privateer *Jefferson Davis* has become a word of terror to the Yankees. The number of her prizes and the amount of merchandise which she captured have no parallel since the days of the *Saucy Jack*," a Charlestonian privateer schooner in the War of 1812.

Coxetter attempted to organize a new privateering expedition without success, but putting to sea in steamer *Herald* he only added steadily to his fame by blockade running the remainder of the war.

Jenny Lind

(Str)

Jenny Lind, a steamer operated by the Union army, was used in lightering stores in the Rappahannock River area in April 1862. In February 1863 reference is made to a steamer of this name being used as a troop transport at New Orleans. The steamer was captured by the Confederates at the Passes in the Mississippi in June 1863.

(Sch)

The Confederate schooner, *Jenny Lind* is listed among five captured by USS *Lockwood*, Acting Volunteer Lt. G. W. Graves commanding, on 16 June 1864 at Mount Pleasant, Hyde County, N.C. She was sent in as a prize to New Bern, N.C.

Jewess, see *William G. Hewes*

John B. White

(Tug)

John B. White, a Confederate steam tug, surrendered to Union army forces near Hampton Roads, Va., on 8 May 1862, and was used thereafter by the War Department in the Virginia area.

John F. Carr

(Str)

John F. Carr, also referred to as *J. F. Carr,* or *Carr,* served the Confederates as a transport and cotton-clad gunboat off the coast of Texas. She was part of the Texas Marine Department [See Annex III].

John Roach

John Roach was one of several ships reported to have been sunk by the Confederates late in 1862 to obstruct the James River near Drewry's Bluff.

John Simonds

(Str: t. 1,024)

John Simonds, built in 1852 at Freedom, Pa., was used as a Confederate army support ship in the Mississippi River. She was sunk following the battle at Island No. 10 in September 1862.

John Walsh

(SwStr: t. 809; l. 275'; b. 38'; dph. 8')

John Walsh was built at Cincinnati, Ohio in 1858. She served the Confederates as a transport in the Mississippi River area, and was part of the force under Comdr. Isaac N. Brown, CSN, commanding the Confederate vessels in the Yazoo River. In July 1863, *John Walsh* was burned to the water's edge by Commander Brown, and sunk in the Yazoo River, 15 miles below Greenwood, Miss., to block the channel and delay the advance of Union forces under Gen. W. T. Sherman, USA, towards Vicksburg, Miss., and to escape the hands of the Union naval force under Acting Rear Adm. D. D. Porter, USN.

Joseph E. Coffee, see *Winslow*

Joseph Landis, see *Landis*

Josiah A. Bell

(SwStr: t. 412; dr. 4'6''; cpl. 35; a. 1 to 2 guns)

Josiah A. Bell, also known as *J. A. Bell*, was built in Jeffersonville, Ind., in 1853 and cotton-clad at Sabine Pass the summer of 1862 for service with the Texas Marine Department [See Annex III.] On 20 January 1863, acting as flagship for the Second Squadron, she steamed under command of Capt. C. Fowler and in company with *Uncle Ben* to engage the blockading sloop-of-war *Morning Light* and armed schooner *Fairy*, formerly *Velocity*. A lively 2-hour fight ensued in which army sharpshooters on board *Josiah A. Bell* repeatedly swept the decks of USS *Morning Light* and soon caused her to strike her colors, while *Uncle Ben* effected the schooner's unconditional surrender.

Josiah A. Bell remained a worry and threat to the blockading vessels off Sabine Pass. At the end of the war she was operating in Sabine Lake.

Julia A. Hodges

(Sch: t. 8)

Julia A. Hodges, a small, fast vessel, was used by the Confederacy as a dispatch, mail, and flag-of-truce ship along the Texas coast. On 6 April 1864 she was captured by the Union gunboat *Estrella* near Indianola, Tex.

Julius

(Str)

Julius was reported by the Richmond *Dispatch* on 12 February 1862, to have been a Confederate boat burned at Florence, Ala., on 7 February 1862, to escape capture by Federal gunboats.

Junaluska

(ScTug: t. 79; a. 2 guns)

CSS *Junaluska*, also known as *Younalaska*, was built at Philadelphia, Pa., in 1860, purchased at Norfolk, Va., in 1861 and assigned to duty in the coastal waters of Virginia and North Carolina. She assisted CSS *Curlew* and CSS *Raleigh* in capturing the United States tug *Fanny* in Loggerhead Inlet, N.C., on 1 October 1861. She continued to operate along the coast of North Carolina until August 1862, when she was dismantled and sold.

Junius Beebe, see *General Sumter*

Juno

(Str: dr. 4'; cpl. c. 50; a. 1 how.)

Juno, a fast, iron-framed paddle-wheeler, operated as a mail steamer between London and Glasgow, sailed as a British blockade runner but was purchased by Confederate agents, probably in May 1863. Successfully evading blockaders, she ran into Charleston where she served as a dispatch, picket, and flag-of-truce boat. In July 1863 she was outfitted with a spar torpedo to permit attacks against Union monitors then threatening the defense works on Morris Island, Charleston Harbor. In August 1863 she rammed and sank a launch from USS *Wabash*, taking its crew captive. *Juno* returned to running the blockade in the fall of 1863, reportedly suffering capture by USS *Connecticut* on 22 September off Wilmington, N.C.

K. L. Bruce, see *Kate L. Bruce*

Kahuha, see *Kahukee*

Kahukee

(ScTug: t. 150; l. 95', 85'bp; b. 17'; dph. 7'; s. 9 k.)

Kahukee, also called *Kakakee*, and *Kahuha*, was a Confederate Army screw tug in service at Norfolk, where she was purchased by the Confederate Navy in July 1861. She had been built as Harlan & Hollingsworth's hull 34 in 1855 for a Scotland Neck, N.C., owner.

Kahukee was sent on 5 September to join the forces under Commander Sinclair, CSN, at New Bern, N.C., and assist in the attempt to drive Union forces from Hatteras Inlet.

She became a cause célèbre in inter-service rivalry between Capt. W. F. Lynch, CSN, and Brig. Gen. H. A. Wise, CSA, when the former

charged that he had been treated badly by the Army in the acquisition of *Kahukee*. *Kahukee* probably was built at Wilmington, Del., in 1855, and homeported at Plymouth, N.C.

Kakakee, see *Kahukee*

Kanawha Valley

(Str)

Kanawha Valley served in the Mississippi River as a Confederate watch or hospital boat. She was present at Madrid Bend, Mo., in March 1862, when Union gunboats entered the area.

Kaskaskia

(SwStr: t. 49)

Kaskaskia, built in 1859 at Cincinnati, Ohio, was used by the Confederates as a tow boat and troop transport in the White River and Little Red River area. On 14 August 1863 USS *Cricket* captured *Kaskaskia* and the steamer *Tom Sugg*, the only means of river transportation remaining to the Confederates in that vicinity. She was then placed in Federal service.

Kate Bruce, see *Kate L. Bruce*

Kate Gregg, see *Stag*

Kate L. Bruce

(Sch: t. 310; dr. 10')

Kate L. Bruce, also known as *Kate Bruce* and *K. L. Bruce*, sailed under the English flag as a blockade runner from Havana to Apalachicola, Fla., during 1861 and early 1862. During the latter half of 1862 she was converted to an armed steamer at Columbus, Ga. She was later sunk to obstruct the Chattahoochee River.

Keene, see *Mary E. Keene*

Kentucky

(SwStr: t. 500)

The name *Kentucky* being commonly used on the Mississippi, we have not been able to determine the origin, main particulars, length of service or fate of the specific *Kentucky* that rendered distinguished service to the Confederacy as a troop transport in November 1861 and March 1862. On the former occasion, her Captain Lodwick "exhibited fearlessness and energy deserving of the highest praise" for ten hazardous days and nights ferrying Major General Leonidas Polk's troops and some Union prisoners between Columbus, Ky. and Belmont, Mo., frequently under fire, and may have been a decisive factor in winning a battle. Again at Madrid Bend early the following March, when Brigadier General J. P. McCown sought to hold Island Number 10 at all costs, *Kentucky* dodged shells to get the battalions through. The rest of her career is not recorded in official records.

It seems clear that *Kentucky* fell into the hands of the Western Gunboat Flotilla at Memphis, 6 June 1862—not at Island Number 10, as some records state. Although a U.S. Navy survey at Memphis, 10 June, had found her "very much out of repair," she was being considered for refit as a receiving ship at St. Louis the end of October: "She is now advertized for sale," having been "turned over a few days ago to the U.S. Marshall," the document continues.

A U.S. Army report of 30 June 1862 notes *Kentucky* as "returned to owners." The same source erroneously states that the transport was captured at Island Number 10. Whether she saw commercial service in the interim or not, another entry three years later briefly alludes to the tragic end, perhaps from a boiler explosion, of a transport *Kentucky* between the mouth of the Red River and Alexandria, La., sometime during June 1865, in which at least 30 "paroled rebel soldiers" met death. This may have been the same *Kentucky*.

King (schooner), see *William B. King*

King (steamer), see *Henry J. King*

L. Millandon, see *General Sterling Price*

Ladies' Gunboat, see *Charleston*

Ladies' Ram, see *Georgia*

Lady Davis

(ScTug: t. 250; a. 1 24-pdr., 1 12-pdr. r.)

Lady Davis, formerly the Richmond iron, steam tug *James Gray,* built at Philadelphia in 1858, was purchased in March 1861 by Governor Pickens of South Carolina, who armed her and placed in command Lt. W. G. Dozier, South Carolina Navy, with orders to thwart reinforcement of Fort Sumter by Union troops.

On 7 May 1861 *Lady Davis* was purchased by the Confederacy for $32,000 and commissioned in the Confederate Navy, operating thereafter along the Georgia as well as the South Carolina coasts. Lt. T. P. Pelot, CSN, took command about 5 days later, relieving Lt. E. C. Stockton, South Carolina Navy. At that time, the little gunboat served as flagship of Commodore Tattnall's Savannah Defense Squadron, consisting of CSS (Old) *Savannah, Samson* and *Resolute.*

On 19 May *Lady Davis* began her career with distinction by capturing and taking into Beaufort the *A. B. Thompson,* a full-rigged ship of 980 tons and a crew of 23 out of Brunswick, Maine, whom she encountered off Savannah while on an expedition seeking the U.S. armed brig *Perry.* The exploit culminated in acrimonious litigation to decide whether an Army captain and a dozen of his soldiers should share in the prize money. Capt. Stephen Elliott, Jr., CSA, happened to be on board and acted as pilot during the capture and afterward, while his men claimed to have helped bring in the prize.

On the following day, the crew were reenlisted into the Confederate States Navy, the State officers being replaced by regulars between then and 1 June. *Lady Davis's* rifled gun remained the property of South Carolina, on loan, while the other, a 24-pounder howitzer, was a gift outright to the Confederacy. By November, Lt. John Rutledge commanded her.

She joined in the battle of Port Royal, S.C., 7 November 1861. Although her engines were transferred to CSS *Palmetto State* late in 1862, well built iron hulls were in great demand and she was able to continue her successful career as a privately owned blockade runner out of Charleston. With the occupation of Charleston in 1865 by Federal forces, *Lady Davis* was captured and turned over to the Light House Board by Adm. J. A. Dahlgren, who praised her hull, while noting that she was, again, minus her machinery, disposition of which is not recorded.

Lady Foote, see *Alfred Robb*

Lady Walton

(StwStr: t. 150)

Lady Walton, built in 1858 at Cincinnati, Ohio, operated as a Confederate steamer until 6 June 1863 when she came down the Little Rock River and surrendered to USS *Tyler* at the mouth of the White River. The prize was sent to Cairo, Ill., for appraisal.

Landis

(SwStr: t. 377; l. 190′; b. 30′; dph. 9′; cpl. 75)

Landis, also known as *Joseph Landis*, *I. C. Landis*, and *Landes*, was a high pressure steamer built in 1853 at Cincinnati, Ohio. She was partly owned by her master, M. Davis, until acquired at New Orleans by the Confederate States in 1862 to be used primarily as a tender to CSS *Louisiana*. On 22 April 1861, Captain Davis had applied for a letter of marque, with Peter Marcy and others, at New Orleans, alleging *Joseph Landis* was "very fast." [See Annex I.]

Under Captain Davis, *Landis* was attached to the force of Capt. J. K. Mitchell, CSN, commanding Confederate naval forces in the lower Mississippi in the area of the Confederate forts St. Philip and Jackson. On 20 April 1862 she helped tow the unfinished and still unmanageable Confederate warship *Louisiana* into place near the guns of Fort St. Philip, in anticipation of a defensive engagement with Union forces. *Landis* also served as living quarters for many of the officers and crew of *Louisiana* while the latter, with mechanics on board day and night, was being prepared for battle.

Flag Officer D. G. Farragut, USN, ran his fleet up the lower Mississippi past the Confederate forts on 24 April 1862, and inflicted great damage on the Confederate ships. *Landis*, although remaining seaworthy, was seriously hurt. Captain Davis and his crew left her and turned her over to Captain Mitchell to be operated directly by the Confederate Navy.

The Confederate forts, Jackson and St. Philip, surrendered on 28 April 1862 to Comdr. D. D. Porter, USN. Captain Mitchell set fire to *Louisiana* on the east bank of the Mississippi near Fort St. Philip to keep her from falling into Union hands. He and his men, realizing that capture was inevitable, retired to the opposite shore with the unarmed tenders *Landis* and *W. Burton*. After three Federal gunboats fired over them, *Landis* and *W. Burton*, under Captain Mitchell, surrendered to Commander Porter.

Landis was used by the U.S. Army as a tugboat and transport in the Mississippi River and Gulf areas for the rest of the war.

Lapwing

(Bark)

Lapwing sailed from Boston, Mass., en route to Batavia, Java, with a cargo of coal, tobacco, and provisions when she was captured by CSS *Florida* on 28 March 1863. Lt. J. N. Maffitt, CSN, commanding *Florida*, transferred two howitzers, two officers, and 18 men to the prize and placed Lt. S. W. Averett, CSN, in command with orders to meet him in longitude 30° W. on the Equator or at the island of Fernando de Noronha. At that time Averett was addressed as commanding officer of the C.S. tender *Oreto* but thereafter this ship was referred to as *Lapwing*.

Florida fell in with *Lapwing* off the coast of Brazil on 14 April and again on 3 May. Lieutenant Averett reported the capture on 20 April of the American ship *Kate Dyer* bonded by him because she bore a neutral cargo. His ship was leaking so badly at the time that she was unfit for cruising; consequently her armament was returned to *Florida*. Averett was replaced by Acting Master R. S. Floyd, CSN, who was directed to anchor under the Rocas, 80 miles west of Fernando de Noronha where *Florida* would coal. Floyd waited the stipulated 30 days, but faced with a shortage of provisions, burned his ship on 20 June 1863. He and his men went ashore in the ship's boats and reported to the Confederate agent on Barbados.

Launch No. 1

Launch No. 1, Acting Master J. M. Rogers in command, was present with CSS *Cotton*, *Hart*, and *Segar* in Berwick Bay when Union gunboats came up to engage in early November 1862. *Launch No. 1* was ordered up Lake Teche to Indian Bend where she continued her service.

Launch No. 3

(StLch: cpl. 20; a. 1 how.)

Launch No. 3, Acting Master Tilford in command, was one of the units of J. K. Mitchell's Confederate States River Defense Force in the lower Mississippi. She served as a picket and scout below New Orleans and was lost in the defense of Forts St. Philip and Jackson on 24 April 1862.

Launch No. 6

(StLch: cpl. 20; a. 1 how.)

Launch No. 6, Acting Master Fairbanks in command, was a ship of the Confederate States River Defense Force assigned to the lower Mississippi. She was charged by General Duncan, CSA, with keeping fires lighted on the bank of the river below Fort St. Philip on 22–23 April 1862, and with maintaining a vigilant lookout for the Federal fleet under Farragut. *Launch No. 6* was lost in the defense of Forts St. Philip and Jackson on 24 April 1862.

Laura

(Sch)

Laura, a Confederate schooner, sailed to Key West from the mainland on 23 October 1861. There her crew deserted and she was taken into custody by the United States schooner *Wanderer*. It is not at all certain that she was a public vessel.

Laurel

(ScStr: t. 386 dw.; dr. 11′; s. 13 k.)

Laurel was a new reputedly fast, 140-horse-power, Liverpool packet, Clyde-built by A. and J. Inglis to ply the Irish Sea to Sligo. The Confederacy's Comdr. James D. Bulloch bought her on 4 October 1864 at Liverpool. She cleared the 9th, ostensibly "for Matamoras, Mexico, via Havana and Nassau," the same day as *Sea King* from London and carrying a larger than ordinary crew.

Commanded in fact by Lt. John F. Ramsay, CSN, whoever her titular "master," *Laurel* rendezvoused at Funchal, Madeira, with *Sea King*, about to be commissioned CSS *Shenandoah*. The steamer brought the cruiser her new commander, Lt. James I. Waddell, CSN, all but one of her officers, her prospective crew members (British), guns, ammunition and stores. In the group was a nucleus of veterans from *Alabama*, including her Chief Bos'n George Harwood to persuade his fellow-countrymen to enlist—including as many as possible of *Laurel's* surplus hands.

Laurel arrived first, coaled and went outside to meet *Sea King* upon her arrival; she transferred men and gear to *Sea King*, then departed for Teneriffe to land 33 crewmen unwilling to ship under Confederate articles. Continuing on to Nassau to keep up appearance of completing a commercial voyage, *Laurel* then ran into Wilmington, N.C., prepared to load cotton.

Secretary Mallory, deciding 16 December that *Laurel's* 11.6-knot actual top speed was not enough and 11 feet with only 500 bales was too deep draught for the Cape Fear entrances, wrote Comdr. Bulloch, "I have directed the sale of the *Laurel*." Next day he wrote, "Lt. Ramsay arrived in Richmond and upon his representations the Secretary of the Treasury [George Trenholm] decided to take the *Laurel* at cost to us, and load her with cotton for Liverpool on account of the

Treasury. Her register will be changed and she will be consigned to Messrs. Fraser, Trenholm & Co. [Liverpool]. Lieutenant Ramsay will remain in command." *Laurel* was duly renamed *Confederate States* and survived the war, becoming *Walter Stanhope*, still under British register, and finally Peter Hutcheson's *Niobe* of Glasgow, also losing a mast at this time.

Lavinia, see *Harriet Lane*

Le Grand

(SwStr: t. 235)

Le Grand or *La Grand*, built at New Albany, Ind., in 1856 and first enrolled at Mobile, served the Confederacy, probably as an Army transport or store ship in the Western rivers; little is known of her but the fact that in September 1864 she was carrying some heavy chain for the Army Engineer Department somewhere in the Mobile-Tensas River area.

Lecompt

(Sch)

Lecompt, also known as *Lecompte* or *Le Compt*, was chartered at Matagorda, Tex., by the Confederate army on 12 February 1862, to guard and patrol the different channels of the area and along the Matagorda peninsula.

Lecompt was captured by USS *Westfield* and *Clifton* in Matagorda Bay, a few days before they bombarded Lavaca, Tex., in a futile effort to take that town. *Lecompt* returned to Confederate ownership when Galveston was recaptured from Union forces in January 1863.

Lecompt ran aground on Bird Key Spit in Galveston Bay on 24 May 1865 while being chased by USS *Cornubia*. She wound up a wreck on Bolivar Point Beach.

Leesburg

(Str)

Leesburg, alternatively spelled *Leesburgh*, was employed in the Savannah River as a transport from 1862 through the end of the war. While under temporary command of Lieut. Joel S. Kennard, CSN, she figured in laying and removing torpedoes from the river during the last months of the war.

Leviathan

(ScTug: dr. 9′–11′)

Leviathan was a new, fast steamer belonging to the U.S. Army Quartermaster Department; she became the shortest-lived Confederate privateer on record, not excepting *Caleb Cushing*. *Leviathan* was captured 22 September 1863 by Acting Master David Nichols, CSN, an engineer and 18 men in *Teaser* (q.v.) during a daring raid off the mouths of the Mississippi but recaptured a few hours later by USS *De Soto*.

Lewis Cass

(Sch: cpl. 45; a. 1 68-pdr.)

CSS *Lewis Cass*, originally the United States Revenue Cutter *Lewis Cass*, was seized by the Alabama authorities on 31 January 1861 and later turned over to the Confederate States Navy.

Capt. J. J. Morrison, commanding the cutter *Lewis Cass* at Mobile, decided, like General Lee, to cast his lot with the Confederacy, and accordingly turned over his ship to Alabama, 30 January 1861. The crew remained loyal to the United States and made its way through the hostile South to reach Northern territory.

Little Rebel

(ScRam: t. 159; dr. 12'; s. 10 k.; a. 3 12-pdr. r.)

Little Rebel was built as *R. E. & A. N. Watson* at Belle Vernon, Pa., in 1859. She was acquired at New Orleans, La., by the Confederate Army, and selected by Capt. J. E. Montgomery, CSN, to be part of his River Defense Fleet. On 25 January 1862 Montgomery began her conversion to a cottonclad ram by placing a 4-inch oak sheath with a 1-inch iron covering on her bow, and by installing double pine bulkheads filled with compressed cotton bales. [See Annex II.]

On 11 April *Little Rebel's* conversion was completed and she steamed from New Orleans to Fort Pillow, Tenn., where she operated in defense of the river approaches to Memphis, Tenn. On 10 May 1862, off Fort Pillow, *Little Rebel*, in company with seven other vessels under Captain Montgomery, attacked the ironclad gunboats of the Federal Mississippi Flotilla. The action of Plum Point Bend witnessed successful ramming tactics by the Confederates, but *Little Rebel*, under Capt. J. White Fowler, serving as Montgomery's flagship, was unable to get into the battle except with her guns. Brig. Gen. M. J. Thompson, MSG, who witnessed the battle said that *Little Rebel*, under a shower of enemy missiles, "ran amid the storm as heedlessly as if charmed." Meanwhile her guns supported Montgomery's other vessels ramming their opponents.

Later Montgomery's force held off the Federal rams and gunboats until Fort Pillow was evacuated on 1 June. Then the Confederate vessels fell back on Memphis to take on coal. Following the Federal capture of Fort Pillow, Flag Officer C. H. Davis, USN, commanding the Mississippi Flotilla, pressed on without delay and appeared off Memphis with a superior force on 6 June 1862. Montgomery, unable to retreat to Vicksburg, Miss., because of his shortage of fuel, and unwilling to destroy his boats, determined to fight against heavy odds. In the ensuing Battle of Memphis, *Little Rebel* attacked the ram *Monarch*, one of two vessels in the Union force under Col. C. Ellet Jr., USA. *Monarch* met the attack and ran *Little Rebel* towards the Arkansas shore. The Confederate vessel was hit by fire from USS *Carondelet* and then was struck by *Monarch* and beached by the blow. *Little Rebel* was captured and taken into Federal service.

Livingston

(SwStr: l. 180'; b. 40'; dph. 9'6''; a. 2 30-pdr. r., 4 shell guns)

CSS *Livingston* was constructed at New Orleans, La., during 1861, a ferryboat converted to a warship on the ways by John Hughes and Co. In January 1862 she was taken up the Mississippi River to Columbus, Ky., to be fitted for service and during much of that year operated in the vicinity of Island No. 10, with Comdr. R. F. Pinkney, CSN, in command. She formed part of the flotilla, at one time numbering 17 vessels, under command of Major Gen. M. Lovell, CSA. Secretary of the Navy S. R. Mallory wrote General Lovell on 23 January 1862: "The *Livingston* you will find to be, I think, a superior steamer, capable of doing capital service . . ." Later she ascended the Yazoo River in Mississippi where she was burned by the Confederates on 26 June 1862 to prevent capture.

An opinion of her somewhat divergent from Sec. Mallory's was expressed by Midshipman James M. Morgan, CSN, who served in her: "There had also been built (from designs by a locomotive roundhouse architect, I suppose) the most wonderful contraption that was ever seen afloat, called the *Livingston;* she carried 6 guns, 3 for'd and 3 abaft the paddle boxes, and she was almost circular in shape. She was so slow that her crew facetiously complained that when she was going downstream at full speed they could not sleep on account of the drift logs catching up with her and bumping against the stern."

Lizzie Simmons, see *Pontchartrain*

Logan

(SwStr: t. 514; l. 160' bp.; b. 26'; dph. 7')

Logan, an iron steamer, was built in 1855 at Wilmington, Del., as Harlan & Hollingsworth's hull 35. In 1861 she was chartered by the State of Virginia and served the Confederate army as a transport in the Virginia rivers.

Logan was burned at Barrett's Landing, 25 miles above White House, Va., on the Pamunkey River by Confederate forces evacuating the area at the approach of *Currituck* and *Seth Low* under Lt. A. Murray, USN.

Lone Star

(SwStr: t. 126)

Lone Star, a light draft steamer built in 1854 at Louisville, Ky., was operated out of Galveston, Tex., where she was chartered by the Texas Marine Department [See Annex III] in July 1863. She served as a transport in Texas coastal waters for the remainder of the war.

Lord Clyde, see *A. D. Vance*

Louis d'Or

(SwStr: t. 343; l. 180'; b. 32'; dph. 7')

Louis d'Or was built in 1860 at Cincinnati, Ohio, and operated as a New Orleans steamboat.

She was taken over by the Confederate Government and operated by the Navy as a cargo ship on the Mississippi and Red Rivers.

Louisiana

(IrcSc & CenterwheelStr: t. 1,400; l. 264'; b. 62'; cpl. ca. 300; a. 2 7-inch rifles, 3 9-inch shell guns, 4 8-inch shell guns and 7 32-pdr. r.)

Louisiana was designed for four engines, two paddlewheels in a center-well and two propellers, with twin rudders. Her casemate—all four sides sloping sharply at nearly a 45° angle—extended her full length, less 25 feet at each end, and was covered by "T" railroad iron in two courses, while its top was encompassed by sheet iron bulwarks nearly four feet high.

CSS *Louisiana* was begun by E. C. Murray at New Orleans in mid-October 1861, but lack of materials impeded her completion. On 20 April 1862 after Union mortar boats under Comdr. D. D. Porter, USN, had been shelling Fort St. Philip and Fort Jackson incessantly for two days, *Louisiana*, although unfinished and unready for action, was towed to Fort St. Philip. There, in anticipation of a Federal drive past the forts, up the lower Mississippi and into New Orleans, she was to participate with the Confederate naval force, in conjunction with the River Defense Fleet and the forts, in defending the passage to the city.

Louisiana, still incomplete, had insufficient power to maneuver as a warship in any naval action. Capt. J. K. Mitchell, CSN, commanding the naval forces in the lower Mississippi, decided

DIMENSIONS:
4000 Tons,
4 Engines,
2 Wheels,
2 Propellers.

ARMAMENT
16 Guns.

Confederate ram Louisiana.

that she should be operated as a floating battery. Accordingly he had her tied to the eastern bank of the Mississippi a half mile above Fort St. Philip. With mechanics on board working furiously night and day to prepare her batteries for action, *Louisiana* lay just clear of the line of fire of Commander Porter's mortar boats which continued bombarding the forts.

On 24 April 1862, Flag Officer D. G. Farragut, USN, ran his fleet past the forts on his way to capture New Orleans. Almost all of the Confederate ships were destroyed in the action. *Louisiana*, under Comdr. C. F. McIntosh, CSN, might have posed a serious threat to the Union fleet, but her lack of maneuverability and the inadequacy of some of her gun mountings which limited the direction of her fire made it impossible for the Confederates to make use of her full potential. Yet, for the most part the ironclad remained impregnable, and posed a constant danger to any Federal ship coming within her range and line of fire. USS *Iroquois* which came against her delivered a full broadside at a distance of a few feet, but did her little serious damage, while she herself was riddled by *Louisiana's* fire.

After Farragut's fleet passed the forts on 24 April, Commander Porter remained in the lower Mississippi with his mortar boats, completely isolating the Confederate force. Meanwhile Captain Mitchell worked frantically to get *Louisiana's* propellers ready for service so that she might sail effectively against the Federals. On 28 April 1862 just before this work was completed, the forts, with their communications cut off, surrendered to Commander Porter. Captain Mitchell, realizing that the defeat of his force was now inevitable, and not considering himself bound by the surrender of the military garrison, set fire to *Louisiana* and retired on her two tenders to the opposite bank, where he was later captured. Meanwhile, as the articles of capitulation of the forts were being drawn up under flags-of-truce on board Commander Porter's flagship, the burning *Louisiana* broke loose and drifted downstream. Her guns fired as the flames reached their charges, and then the whole ship exploded violently in front of Fort St. Philip, and was seen and heard for many miles.

Louisiana (corvette), see under *Texas*

Louisville
(SwStr: t. 743; l. 231.5′; b. 38.6′; dph. 7.5′)

Louisville, later known as *Ouachita* and *Vicksburg*, was built at New Albany, Ind., in 1861 and served privately in the Mississippi River area. Adm. D. D. Porter, USN, described her as "one of the largest and best steamers in western waters," and "the pride of the Mississippi." The Confederate army fitted her out at Port Hudson, La., in February 1863, and used her in the Mississippi River area as a cargo ship.

Louisville was captured on 13 July 1863 on the Little River, La., by *Manitou* and *Rattler*. These had sailed from the junction of the Black, Ouachita and Tensas Rivers, and were part of a gunboat force under Lt. Comdr. T. Selfridge, USN, sent by Acting Rear Admiral Porter.

Louisville was renamed *Ouachita* on 29 September 1863 at Admiral Porter's request, and was commissioned in the U.S. Navy on 18 January 1864. She was operated privately after the war as *Vicksburg*, and sold abroad in 1869.

Lucy Gwin
(StwStr: t. 152)

Lucy Gwin, also called *Lucy Gwynn*, *Lucy Gwinn*, and *Gwinn*, was built in Freedom, Pa., in 1859. Her home port was Galveston, Tex., and in 1861 she passed into the Texas Marine Department under Confederate army control. [See Annex III.]

Lucy Gwin served as a transport and cargo ship along the Texas coast. She was surrendered at Matagorda to Union forces in late spring of 1865 but was carried off and anchored at Bagdad, on the Mexican side of the Rio Grande, where demands for her return were made of the controlling French authorities.

Lynn Boyd
(Str)

Lynn Boyd, under Captain Smedley, proceeded in company with *Dunbar* on 4 February 1862 from Fort Henry to Paris Landing, Tenn., for two Confederate Army regiments stationed there. Fort Henry was surrendered on 6 February and *Lynn Boyd* was burned on the Tennessee River, at the mouth of Duck River, 7 February to prevent her capture by Federal gunboats.

Lynx
(SwStr)

Lynx was a long, very fast paddle-steamer with two stacks and two masts, all painted white. Managed by John Fraser & Co., Charleston, she carried Confederate Government cargo and is believed to have been a public vessel for all practical purposes.

She met her end bound for Bermuda running out of Wilmington, N.C., under Captain Reid, 25 September 1864, with 600 bales of cotton, passengers and special cargo, including $50,000 in Government gold. She was hit eight times, six below the waterline, by the 100-pounder and 30-pounder rifles of much slower USS *Howquah*, assisted by *Niphon* and *Governor Buckingham;* sinking, with one of her wheels damaged, *Lynx* had to be beached about six miles below Fort Fisher. The Confederates all escaped, along with the gold, although Federal sharpshooters got near enough to wound one crew member. The ship's remains were set afire.

Ironically, an intelligence report to Secretary Welles, about 1 September 1864, had warned that, "the swift steamers *Lynx* and *Badger* were being fitted out at Wilmington to make a dash at our blockaders . . . their machinery protected by compressed cotton . . . each vessel having about 200 men, will sally forth early in September, and, by boarding, attempt the capture of one or more of our vessels. If precautions are not taken this plan will certainly succeed." It was a false alarm, although Lt. J. W. Balch, *Howquah's* captain, in this instance made one of the rare charges that a blockade runner had fired back at him— but only two shots and they could have been cross-fire from the fort.

M. C. Etheridge

(Sch: t. 144; l. 92′; b. 24′; dr. 7′; a. 2 guns)

M. C. Etheridge was built in 1859 at Plymouth, N.C. She was used by the Confederates, probably as a storeship for their fleet, in North Carolina waters. Carrying a valuable cargo of naval stores, she was attacked by USS *Whitehead* in the Pasquotank River, N.C., on 10 February 1862, and fired by the Confederates to prevent her from falling into Union hands. Despite attempts to extinguish the fire, nothing was saved and she was scuttled by her Union captors.

M. E. Dowing

(Str)

M. E. Dowing, or *M. E. Downing* served as a Confederate dispatch boat off the coast of North Carolina in 1861.

Mab, see *Queen Mab*

Macon

(StGbt: l. 150′; b. 25′; dph. 10′; dr. 8′; a. 6 guns)

CSS *Macon,* a wooden steamer formerly named *Ogeechee,* was fitted out at Savannah, Ga., early in 1864, with Lt. J. S. Kennard, CSN, in command. In June her name was changed to *Macon* and on 3 August she was reported ready for duty, although still lacking a full complement. Savannah capitulated on 21 December and 3 days later *Macon* departed for Augusta, Ga., where she remained until the end of the war.

Magenta

(SwStr: t. 782; l. 269′; b. 39′; dph. 7′ 9″)

Magenta was built in 1861 at New Albany, Ind. She may have served the Confederates as a transport in the Mississippi River area while under the control of Comdr. I. N. Brown, CSN, commanding Confederate vessels in the Yazoo River. Called one of the best Confederate transports by Maj. Gen. William T. Sherman, USA, *Magenta* was burned on the Yazoo River in July 1863 by Commander Brown, to keep her from falling into the hands of a Union naval force under Acting Rear Adm. D. D. Porter, USN.

Magnolia

(SwStr: t. 843; s. 12 k.)

Magnolia was a seagoing, wooden sidewheeler with typical walking-beam engine, built at Greenpoint, N.Y., in 1857. One of the 14 ships belonging to Charles Morgan's Southern S. S. Co., she was impressed as a public vessel at New Orleans, 15 January 1862, by Maj. Gen. Mansfield Lovell, CSA, acting for Secretary of War Benjamin. The original intention was to arm them all as cottonclad rams to defend the Delta, but further consideration argued in favor of smaller, low-pressure steam towboats, with lower fuel consumption and easier to shield for battle, and few of the high-pressure sea-going steamers were used for this essentially inappropriate role.

Rejected as a ram but probably still Government-owned, *Magnolia* made at least two successful runs to nearby British islands in 1861 with extremely large cargoes. Escaping through Pas à l'Outre, she was overhauled, 19 February 1862, by USS *Brooklyn* and *South Carolina* as a rich prize carrying 1,210 bales of cotton. USS *Magnolia* entered the U.S. Navy 22 July 1862 at New York, following Key West prize court proceedings in April. After expensive repairs, she was a valuable gunboat carrying 2 to 5 guns the rest of the war. Sold at auction 12 July 1865, she was enrolled for commercial transportation 23 August, going out of service in 1866.

(SwStr: t. 824)

New Orleans sidewheeler *Magnolia*, built at New Albany, Ind., in 1859, was "one of the finest steamboats in the West" and served the Confederacy well as a river transport until destroyed in the Yazoo City area to escape Porter's flotilla, the spring of 1863. Admiral Porter wrote that the chief gain from his Yazoo Pass expedition was its "harm to the enemy" in causing them "to sink the *Star of the West*, *Magnolia*, and *Natchez*, three of their best vessels."

Major Minter, see *Elma*

Manassas

(Sch)

Manassas, formerly the U.S. Revenue Cutter *Minot*,[1] was seized by the Confederates at New Bern, N.C., on 27 August 1861. With the launches *Mosquito* and *Sand Fly*, she was placed under Lt. W. H. Murdaugh, CSN, who was seriously wounded in the Federal attack on Fort Hatteras the next day, and was unable to assume his command. *Manassas* was active on the coast of North Carolina during 1861–62 and then dismantled by the Confederates.

(IrcRam: t. 387; l. 143'; b. 33'; dph. 17'; cpl. 36; a. 1 64-pdr. Dahlgren, later replaced by 1 32-pdr.)

CSS *Manassas*, formerly the steam propeller *Enoch Train*, was built at Medford, Mass., by J. O. Curtis in 1855. A New Orleans commission merchant, Capt. J. A. Stevenson, acquired her for use as a privateer and fitted her out at Algiers, La., as an ironclad ram of radically modern design. Covered with 1½-inch iron plating, her hull projected only 2½ feet above the water, and her plated top was convex causing cannon shot to glance off harmlessly. She was provided with sharp irons on her bow to stave holes through

[1] This is stated in the *Official Records of the Union and Confederate Navies*. No other record, official or unofficial, of U.S. Revenue Cutter *Minot* has been found.

enemy vessels. Fast moving, lying low in the water and a difficult target, virtually bomb-proof, she looked like a floating cigar or egg shell and was described by Union intelligence as a "hellish machine."

Commissioned as a Confederate privateer on 12 September 1861 *Manassas* was seized soon afterwards by Flag Officer G. N. Hollins, CSN, for use in the lower Mississippi River. With Lieutenant A. F. Warley, CSN, in command she participated in Flag Officer Hollins' surprise attack on the Federal blockading squadron at Head of Passes, Mississippi River, on 12 October 1861. In the action *Manassas* violently rammed USS *Richmond* damaging her severely below the water line. *Manassas*, however, suffered the loss of her prow and smokestack and had her engines temporarily thrown out of gear by the impact. She managed to retire under heavy fire from USS *Preble* and *Richmond* whose shells glanced off her armor. Two months after this engagement *Manassas* was purchased for direct ownership by the Confederate Government.

Under Lieutenant Warley, *Manassas* joined the force of Capt. J. K. Mitchell, CSN, commanding Confederate naval forces in the lower Mississippi. She participated in the engagement of 24 April 1862 during which Flag Officer Farragut, USN, on his way to New Orleans, ran his fleet past the Confederate Forts Jackson and St. Philip. In the action *Manassas* attempted to ram USS *Pensacola* which turned in time to avoid the blow and deliver a broadside at close range. *Manassas* then ran into murderous fire from the whole line of the Union fleet. She next charged USS *Mississippi* and delivered a long glancing blow on her hull, firing her only gun as she rammed. Firing again, she rammed USS *Brooklyn*, injuring her rather deeply, but not quite enough to be fatal.

After this action *Manassas* followed the Union fleet quietly for a while but as she drew closer *Mississippi* furiously turned on her. *Manassas* managed to dodge the blow but was run aground. Her crew escaped as *Mississippi* poured her heavy broadsides on the stranded Confederate vessel. Later *Manassas* slipped off the bank and drifted down the river in flames past the Union mortar flotilla. Comdr. D. D. Porter, USN, in command of the mortar boats, tried to save her as an engineering curiosity but *Manassas* exploded and immediately plunged under water.

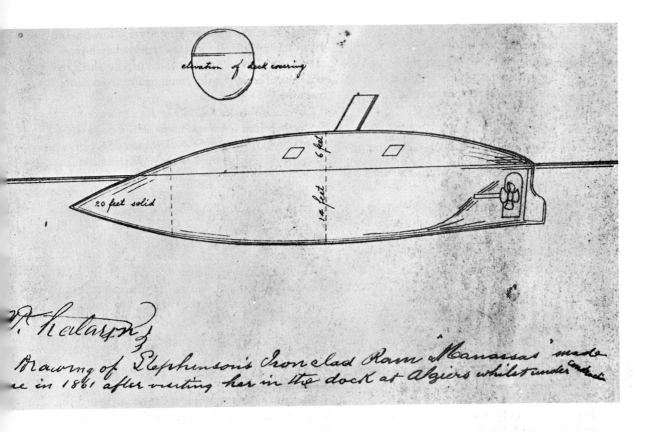

elevation of deck covering

6 feet

12 feet

20 feet solid

Drawing of Stephenson's Ironclad Ram "Manassas" made e in 1861 after visiting her in the dock at Algiers whilst under c...

C.S.S. Manassas.

VI–267

Manassas, see *Florida*

Marianna

(SwStr: dr. 3′3″)

Marianna was an unarmed river steamer which served the Confederates as early as February 1862 in towing schooners to the gaps or passes of the Mississippi River to assist them in running the Union blockade. She was reported under repair at Columbus, Ga., in November 1864.

Marion

(SwStr: t. 258)

Marion was built at Charleston, S.C., in 1850, and passed to Confederate control in 1861. She helped lay the obstructions around Charleston, S.C., and was used by the Confederate army as a transport and cargo ship in that area.

Marion sank accidentally on the night of 6 April 1863 in the Ashley River after drifting from her moorings off Charleston.

Marqués de la Habana, see *McRae*

Mars

(SwStr: t. 329)

Mars, .built in 1856 at Cincinnati, Ohio, was among Confederate transports captured at Island No. 10 on 7 April 1862. She then was taken into Federal service as a tender to the Mississippi Squadron. [Similarity of names occasioned by pronunciation in local dialects has caused confusion with the *H. D. Mears.*]

Mary, see *Alexandra*

Mary E. Keene

(SwStr: t. 659; l. 238′; b. 38; dph. 7′8″)

Mary E. Keene, known also as *Keene, Mary Keene,* and *Mary Keane,* was built at New Albany, Ind., in 1860 and enrolled as a New Orleans steamboat. She served as a transport on the western rivers and was a unit of Comdr. I. N. Brown's fleet that was scuttled in July 1863 at Yazoo City to prevent capture.

Mary Hill

(Gbt: t. 234; dr. 2′; a. 1 24-pdr., 1 12-pdr.)

Mary Hill was a side-wheel steamer built in 1859 at Smithfield, Tex., and operated out of Galveston. She was chartered by Comdr. W. W. Hunter, CSN, for service with the Texas Marine Department [See Annex III] and outfitted as a cotton-clad gunboat. She served during the entire war as a transport, look-out, and guard ship in Texas coastal regions, principally from Matagorda Bay to Galveston.

Mary Keane (or Keene), see *Mary E. Keene*

Mary Patterson

(Str)

Mary Patterson, built in 1859 at Grand Glaise, Ark., was used as a Confederate transport on western waters early in the war. On 16 June 1862 she was sunk along with *Maurepas* and *Eliza G.* to obstruct the White River near St. Charles, Ark., against the advance of Union gunboats.

Mary T., see *J. A. Cotton*

Matagorda

(SwStr: t. 616 dw., 1,250 gr.; l. 220′; b. 30′; dph. 10′6″)

Matagorda, also known as *Alice,* was an iron sidewheeler built in 1858 as their Hull No. 53 by Harlan & Hollingsworth, Wilmington, old Delaware River shipbuilders. One of 14 owned by Charles Morgan's Southern S.S. Co., she was "impressed for public service" 15 January 1862 by Maj. Gen. Mansfield Lovell, CSA, acting on orders from Secretary of War Benjamin. Too valuable as a Government-owned blockade runner, *Matagorda* was not one of the trio chosen for conversion to cottonclad rams—small towing steamers with low-pressure power plant serving more satisfactorily as gunboats. Under a Captain Cole, she made successful runs with 1,000 bales of cotton to Havana from Gulf ports such as Sabine Pass, Tex. Under Capt. William Stumminger, she was chased for 6½ hours, while she jettisoned her whole deck cargo of 200 bales in an attempt to increase speed and tempt her pursuer, but was finally run down and captured, 10 September 1864, by USS *Magnolia* (q.v. supra as Confederate), 75 miles off Cape San Antonio, Cuba.

Maurepas

(SwStr: t. 399; l. 180′; b. 34′; dr. 7′; a. 5 guns)

Maurepas, built as *Grosse Tete* at New Albany, Ind., in 1858, was purchased at New Orleans, La., in 1861. Early in 1862 she was assigned to duty with the fleet in the lower Mississippi River under Flag Officer G. N. Hollins, CSN. Her commanding officer was Lt. J. Fry, CSN.

Maurepas operated with the fleet at Island No. 10 and New Madrid, Mo., from 12 March to 7 April 1862. She was then sent up the White River where she was sunk as an obstruction near St. Charles, Ark., 16 June 1862.

"Maury Gunboats", see *Hampton*-class

"Maury's Ship", see *Georgia*

May
(Str)

May, "presumed to be cotton-clad," which Lt. Gen. J. C. Pemberton, CSA, mentions prominently in a telegram of 12 March 1863, cooperated with Confederate Army forces and Comdr. I. N. Brown's fleet in the Mississippi in 1863. It may be inferred from the General's order that she and *Magenta* were transports of great value in ferrying large troop concentrations at short notice.

McRae

(ScSlp: t. 830; a. 1 9″, 6 32-pdr., 1 6-pdr.)

McRae, often erroneously identified by Union leaders as *Miramon* or *General Miramon*, was former Mexican rebel screw bark *Marqués de la Habana* which had been captured by USS *Saratoga* in March 1860. She was purchased by the Confederate States at New Orleans on 17 March 1861 and fitted out as CSS *McRae*. She was placed under command of Lt. T. B. Huger, CSN, and assigned to the fleet under Flag Officer G. N. Hollins, CSN, entrusted with the defense of the lower Mississippi River. Part of this time, as in her last battle, she was Hollins' flagship.

McRae gave protection to blockade runners slipping in and out of the Mississippi and Mobile Bay. She gave a good account of herself in a spirited engagement with ships of the Federal blockading fleet at the Head of the Mississippi River Passes on 12 October 1861. Her last fight was a gallant defense of Forts Jackson and St. Philip on 24 April 1862. In this engagement the conduct of her officers and crew was reported "rarely surpassed in the annals of naval warfare." With their ship cut to ribbons they fought on and would not surrender in an unequal contest which was conducted simultaneously against several Union warships and which left most of her crew dead or injured on her deck.

Though severely damaged, *McRae* came up river

to New Orleans under a flag-of-truce on the evening of 27 April 1862, landing Confederate wounded from the forts below. There she was left to her fate and was found the following morning by Union forces sunk alongside the city wharf.

Meares (or *Mears*), see *H. D. Mears*

Memphis

(Sch: t. 100, 208 (Thames meas.); l. 111′; b. 25′; dr. 12′; a. 1 12-pdr. r., 2 24-pdr. sb.)

Memphis was constructed as the racing schooner *America* and launched 3 May 1851 by W. H. Brown, of New York for a local yacht club syndicate. She was the namesake of the "America's Cup." In 1857 she appears in the Royal Yacht Squadron as *Camilla*, owned by a Viscount Templetown and registered in Portsmouth, Hants. Henry Sotheby Pitcher bought and rebuilt her the following year. On 30 July 1860 she was reported sold to another Briton, Henry E. Decie. Lord Decie, as he was known in the Confederacy, arrived at Savannah in *Camilla* in the spring of 1861 and allied himself with the Southern cause. Running the blockade out of Savannah piloted by A. F. Marmelstein, *Camilla* carried a Confederate purchasing commission to Britain, took part in the Queenstown (Ulster) Yacht Club regatta 28 June 1861 and raced the schooner *Alarm* around the Isle of Wight, 5 August.

Local rumor maintained Lord Decie sold his yacht to the Confederacy later in 1861 and she was renamed *Memphis*—all quite consistent with the next documentation now available although details of her Confederate Government service are lacking.

It is a fact that in March 1862, gunboat USS *Ottawa* and other vessels discovered her scuttled in St. John's River, Fla. She was raised, towed to Port Royal, S.C., and outfitted for service in the United States Navy under her original name, with acting Master J. Baker in command.

Until May 1863 *America* served with the South Atlantic Blockading Squadron, capturing one prize. She then reported to the Naval Academy as a school ship. She continued on that service until sold 20 June 1873. On 1 October 1921 *America* was presented to the Navy Department by the Eastern Yacht Club, Marblehead, Mass., for preservation as a relic. She was stationed at the Naval Academy until scrapped in 1945.

C.S.S. McRae.

(FltBtry: a. 18 guns)

Memphis was converted from a floating drydock in 1861 at New Orleans. In November 1861, she was "under construction or alteration" and in December was noted as having been at New Orleans "without any armament." By February 1862, *Memphis* was evidently fitted out, as she was noted as being one of the units of Flag Officer George N. Hollins, who commanded the naval defenses of the Mississippi and the coast of Louisiana.

The records are naturally laconic on a unit of such small size. The battery, however, can be surmised to have been one of those that took part in the defense of New Orleans, and was probably destroyed or captured when Farragut's fleet captured the city.

Merite

(Str)

Merite, a common steamboat encased with thick timbers, was employed as a gunboat on the Mississippi River above New Orleans in April 1865.

Merrimac

(SwStr: t. 635; l. 230'; b. 30'; dr. 8'6''; s. 16–18 k.)

Merrimac, less often reported as *Merrimack*, was one of the original group of Confederate Government-owned blockade-runners operated by the Ordnance Department, CSA (cf. *Cornubia*). She was an iron paddle-steamer with two stacks "hinged for lowering," a short foremast only, which could be square-rigged, and was said to have done 18 knots on her trials. Her pair of 9-ft. stroke, oscillating sidewheel engines and 4 boilers were considered "very superior and valuable" until her flues became clogged by burning naval stores in emergencies—as so often happened in this dangerous service. It is said *Merrimac* was built for opium running on the China coast.

Apparently she was bought for the Confederacy by Commissioner James M. Mason and N. S. Reneau in or before September 1862. By the time of her capture by USS *Iroquois* 24 July 1863 off Cape Fear she had lost her speed and been sold with her cargo to new owners—one of whom, a Mr. Roberts, was taken in her—for $2,200,000 Confederate. She was loaded deeper than prudence directed for running the blockade, with 642 bales of cotton plus turpentine and tobacco.

Merrimack, see *Virginia*

Merrimack No. 2, see *Richmond*

Mexico, see *General Bragg*

Milledgeville

(IrcStr: l. 175′; b. 35′3′′; dph. 12′; dr. 9′; a. des. for 4 guns; type *Milledgeville*)

CSS *Milledgeville* was in process of construction at Savannah, Ga., by H. F. Willink. Launched just before the evacuation of that city on 21 December 1864, she was burned and sunk to prevent her capture by Union forces.

Milledon, see *General Sterling Price*

Minot, see *Manassas*

Miramichi, see *Bat*

Miramon, see under *McRae*

Mississippi

(IrcStr: t. 1,400; l. 260′; b. 58′; dph. 15′; dr. 12′6′′ (incomplete); s. 14 k.; a. des. for 20 guns incl. 4 7′′ pivots)

CSS *Mississippi* was built by N. and A. F. Tift in a shipyard erected for the purpose in Jefferson City, La., just beyond the city limits of New Orleans. Construction was started on 14 October 1861 and she was launched on 19 April 1862. A fast, triple-screw steamer, she was far from complete at that time, having neither her 20 guns nor ammunition on board.

"The celebrated ram," as Admiral Porter called *Mississippi* in his battle dispatch, was later described by Commander Sinclair as "a formidable ship—the finest of the sort I ever saw in my life; she would, in my opinion, not only have cleared the river of the enemy's vessels but have raised the blockade of every port in the South."

There took place in September following her loss a lengthy and intense investigation of *Mississippi's* builders, brothers Nelson and Asa Tift, and all officers and civilians responsible for her construction, premature launching and destruction; transcript of the hearings, readily accessible in libraries, is excellent background reading on the early Confederate Navy.

Only at the last minute Comdr. Arthur Sinclair, Sr., CSN, designated as her commanding officer, attempted to take her up the river when the Federal fleet under Flag Officer Farragut appeared from below Forts Jackson and St. Philip on 25 April, but his objective thwarted, he fired her to prevent capture.

Machinery was fabricated by Jackson & Co. and by Patterson Foundry, locally. The last two guns, bow and stern 7′′-rifles, pivoted, were a late addition. Schofield & Markham, Atlanta, rolled 1,000 tons of armor plate and the bolts alone weighed another 80 short tons; plating ranged from 1¼′′ to 3¾′′. Hull thickness was 2 feet at the sides, 3 at bow and stern.

———

Mississippi (corvette), see under *Texas*

Missouri

(IrcRam: l. 183′; b. 53′8′′; dph. 10′3′′; dr. 8′6′′; a. 1 32-pdr., 1 11′′ Dahlgren, 1 9′′ Dahlgren)

CSS *Missouri,* a centerwheel steam sloop, was launched at Shreveport, La., on 14 April 1863. Her commanding officer was Lt. J. H. Carter, CSN. *Missouri* never saw action but engaged in transport and mining details between Alexandria and Shreveport, La., above the Red River obstructions. At the end of hostilities *Missouri* came down to Shreveport and surrendered to U.S. naval forces on 3 June 1865—last Confederate ironclad to do so in home waters. She was taken into the U.S. Navy and sold at Mound City, Ill., on 29 November 1865.

Missouri's casemate or citadel was 130′6′′ by 53′8′′ at base, but only 105′ by 29′ at the top, creating a slope of 30°. Railroad T-iron, 4½′′ thick, was laid diagonally (to avoid cutting) over this structure, with rail crowns facing alternately inward and outward in order to interlock when spiked to the 23′′ yellow pine backing. The pilot-house in the forepart of the casemate projected 19′′ above its deck, which was not armored at all, although the exposed 50-odd feet of the ship's main deck was plated like the citadel's sides. No time having been available to build a wheel-box, the big centerwheel, 22′6′′ in diameter, projected for 8′4′′ above any protection out of a recess at the after end of the casemate. Three balanced rudders were located under the fantail; her steering wheel on the gun deck beneath the pilothouse.

Mobile

(ScGbt: t. 283; a. 3 32-pdr. sb., 1 32-pdr. r., 1 8′′ sb., probably 1 addl. r.)

Mobile was a wooden steamer built at Philadelphia in 1860; home port: Mobile. Alleged to be worth $40,000, she apparently was picked up for a $5,000 lien by Comdr. W. W. Hunter, CSN, in July 1861, already having been under seizure in Berwick Bay, La., since 4 May.

Her chronology thereafter has piqued many a researcher: She made five successful dashes—no doubt only to Cuba or the Bahamas—as a blockade runner, yet on 8 October she had "been fitting out there [Berwick City] for some time" under Lts. Francis E. Shepperd and George S. Shryock, CSN, reporting to Flag Officer G. N. Hollins; engines and boilers were already protected by 12-inch timbers clad with railroad iron. On 19 December, Union intelligence learned she was a ship of "about 400 tons, thoroughly strengthened and armed with 4 or 6 heavy guns, two of them rifled."

By 1 February 1862, when she engaged USS *Hatteras* in Atchafalaya Bay, La., *Mobile* was described as a "long, low, three-masted steamer," ostensibly able to give a good account of herself. From June 1862 to the following May, all sources place her up the Yazoo River under command of Lieutenant Shepperd but variously alleged to be laid up at Yazoo City or ordered to sink any vessel attempting to pass the barrier at Liverpool. Whatever his information or motives, a deserter as late as 13 May 1863 thought it news that she was a "small boat" still "being converted into an ironclad gunboat" in the Yazoo. Scarcely more than a week later, the 21st, it is certain she was burned to escape capture by Admiral D. D. Porter's approaching squadron, taking the evidence to the bottom.

Mohawk

(StwStr)

Mohawk served as a watch boat, possibly a gunboat, in the Mississippi River and tributaries during 1862. She was sunk 7 April 1862 by Union forces under Flag Officer Foote following the battle at Island No. 10, Tenn.

Morgan

(Sch: a. 3 guns)

CSS *Morgan*, originally United States Revenue Cutter *Morgan*, was seized by the Confederates in 1861. She was listed as one of the ships of Flag Officer G. M. Hollins' squadron in the lower Mississippi River in November 1861.

———

(SwGbt: t. 863; l. 202'; b. 38'; dph. 13'; dr. 7'2''; s. 10 k.; a. 10 guns when outfitted, 6 guns when surrendered; cl. *Morgan*)

CSS *Morgan* was a partially armored gunboat built at Mobile, Ala., in 1861–62. She operated in the waters around Mobile from the time of her completion early in 1862 to the close of hostilities. One reference of October 1862 gave her name as *Admiral*.

Morgan, Comdr. G. W. Harrison, CSN, took an active part in the battle of Mobile Bay on 5 August 1864. Situated well to the right of the Confederate line of battle as the enemy proceeded up the channel she was able to deliver a telling broadside raking fire against USS *Hartford* and others. Toward the end of the engagement she was pursued by USS *Metacomet* but succeeded in driving her off. *Morgan*, attempting to avoid capture, then turned toward shallow water, grounded briefly, but continued on her perilous route and reached the guns at Fort Morgan. She dispatched a boat which effected the destruction of Union gunboat *Philippi* below the fort. Captain Harrison then saved *Morgan* by boldly running the gauntlet up to Mobile. Although hotly pursued and shelled by cruisers for a large part of the 25-mile starlight voyage, she reached the outer obstructions near Mobile at daybreak and that afternoon was permitted to pass through.

Morgan continued to serve in the Mobile area. In April 1865 she participated in the battle near Blakely, Ala., sustaining considerable damage. On 4 May 1865 Commodore E. Farrand, commanding Confederate Naval Forces in the State of Alabama, ordered the surrender of *Morgan* to the United States Navy. She was sold the following December.

Morning Light

(Ship: t. 937; l. 172'; b. 34'3''; dr. 19'; dph. 24'; a. 8 32-pdr., 1 rifled Butler gun)

Morning Light, a wooden sailing ship, was built at Kensington, near Philadelphia, Pa., in 1853 and launched on 15 August 1853. She was purchased by the U.S. Navy on 2 September 1861 and commissioned on 21 November of that year. Assigned to the West Gulf Blockading Squadron she was captured off Sabine Pass, Tex. on 21 January 1863 by two cottonclad Confederate steamers, *Uncle Ben* and *Josiah A. Bell*. *Morning Light* was under Confederate control for 2 days before she was burned on 23 January off Sabine Pass.

Moro

(SwStr: t. 132; l. 122'; b. 24'10''; dph. 4'9'')

Moro, built at Louisville, Ky., in 1858, transported cargo for the Confederate armies along the Mississippi River and tributaries. She was seized by Union army forces near Vicksburg in November 1862, but apparently escaped to resume operations in the lower Mississippi. On 4 February 1863 she was intercepted near the mouth of the Red River by Col. C. R. Ellet, commanding USS *Queen of the West*, and was captured with a large cargo of food supplies intended for delivery at Port Hudson.

Morris, see *Caleb Cushing*

Mosher

(ScTug: t. 49; cpl. 40)

Mosher, Confederate States Army-chartered but Navy-controlled, had been built at Philadelphia in 1857.

Mosher, a small unarmed screw tug owned by the Southern Steamship Co., operated with the Confederate Navy under Comdr. J. K. Mitchell during the bombardment of Forts Jackson and St. Philip. On 24 April 1862 the tug, commanded by Capt. H. Sherman, was towing a fire boat against a heavy sloop-of-war, probably USS *Hartford*, when she received a broadside shot and sank instantly.

Mosquito

(Launch)

Mosquito, together with the launch *Sand Fly* and the schooner *Manassas*, was assigned to the command of Lt. W. H. Murdaugh on 27 August 1861 by Flag Officer S. Barron, commanding the naval defenses of Virginia and North Carolina. On 29 August 1861 Lieutenant Murdaugh was seriously wounded in the attack on Fort Hatteras and unable to assume his command.

Moultrie

(Str)

Moultrie served the Confederate Navy on the Charleston Station. A report on her condition by Lieutenant Dozier, CSN, resulted in her release from the Confederate Navy and consignment to her owners on 24 August 1863.

Muscle

(Str: t. 125)

Muscle, a cargo steamer also referred to as *Cerro Gordo*, was built at Allegheny, Pa., in 1856. She was captured early in February 1862 at Chickasaw, north of Eastport, Miss., by USS *Conestoga*, *Lexington*, and *Tyler*. While being towed to Cerro Gordo, Tenn., with a load of kindling she sprang a leak and sank in the Tennessee River.

Muscogee

(ScStr: cl. heavy *Albemarle*)

Muscogee, until recently presumed to have been a centerwheel ironclad steamer, was begun at Columbus, Ga. during 1863–64. Her unusual casemating and dimensions prevented a successful launching and she remained incomplete through the end of the war when she was burned. In 1960 her wreck was rediscovered some 25 miles down the Chattahoochee River. *Muscogee* has been raised and returned to Columbus where she is on exhibit.

Music

(SwStr: t. 330; l. 172'; b. 29'; dph. 6'; cpl. 25–40, 50 max., as pvtr.; a. 2 6-pdr.)

The New Orleans sidewheel towboat *Music*, driven by high-pressure machinery, was delivered from the builders at Jeffersonville, Ind., in 1857, and was serving Charles Morgan's Southern S. S. Co. when war broke. Within a month her owner and master, Capt. Thomas McLellan, had applied for a letter of marque and reprisal and was commissioned a privateer, 15 May 1861 [See Annex I]. By next reports, *Music* was in rundown condition but busy as an unarmed tender to Forts Jackson and St. Philip—also custodian, with tugs *Mosher* and *Belle Algerine*, of the fire rafts. But *Music* reappears late in July—apparently the same big towboat, for two New Orleans predecessors of that name, built in Jeffersonville also, are recorded as having finally turned in their documents, prewar.

In her new role in the Atchafalaya-Red River area under Lt. E. W. Fuller, *Music* attracted constant attention and comment for a week or two—along with gunboat *Dolly Webb* or *Webb*, although accounts differ as to whether she carried three pieces of artillery, only two or merely a large company of riflemen. The greatest fear expressed by Farragut's forces was that the armed pair would join the menacing ram, *Arkansas*. Again, observers differ as to whether these armed tugs were *Arkansas*' only support during her death throes or failed to arrive in time to turn her about when she went out of command. Said to be,

C.S. sidewheel steamer
Nashville.

Ram C.S.S. Nashville.

with *Mobile* and *Webb*, one of the last three Confederate gunboats on the river, *Music* is heard of no more in published official records.

Nansemond

(ScGbt: t. 166; l. 106'; b. 21'; dph. 8'; dr. 5'; a. 2 8''; cl. *Hampton*)

CSS *Nansemond* was a small wooden steamer built at Norfolk, Va., in 1862, and assigned to duty with the James River Squadron under Flag Officer S. Barron, CSN. With Lt. J. Rutledge, CSN, in command, she sailed from Norfolk with the other vessels of the squadron on 4 May 1862, just prior to the evacuation of the navy yard.

Nansemond continued on active duty in the James River until the end of the war. Her commander in November 1863, Lt. J. H. Rochelle, CSN, was relieved by Lt. C. W. Hays, CSN, sometime after March 1864. She took part in engagements at Howlett's, Va., 21 June 1864, Dutch Gap, 14 August 1864, and Fort Harrison, 29 September–1 October 1864.

Upon evacuation of Richmond on 3 April 1865 she was destroyed to preclude capture by the Union.

Nashville

(SwStr: t. 1,221; l. 215'6''; b. 34'6''; dph. 21'9''; cpl. 40; a. 2 12-pdr.; cl. *Nashville*)

CSS *Nashville* was a brig-rigged, passenger steamer, running between New York and Charleston, S.C. After the fall of Fort Sumter the Confederates seized her at Charleston and fitted her out as a cruiser. Under the command of Lt. R. B. Pegram, CSN, she braved the blockade on 21 October 1861 and headed across the Atlantic to Southampton, England, the first ship of war to fly the Confederate flag in English waters. *Nashville* returned to Beaufort, N.C., on 28 February 1862, having captured two prizes worth $66,000 during the cruise. In this interval she was sold for use as a blockade runner and renamed *Thomas L. Wragg*.

On 5 November 1862 she was commissioned as the privateer *Rattlesnake* [See Annex I]. Union forces destroyed her in the Ogeechee River, Ga., 28 February 1863, under the guns of Fort McAllister.

———

(Irc Ram: l. 271'; b. 62'6''; dph. 13'; dr. 10'9''; a. 3 7'' r., 1 24-pdr.)

CSS *Nashville* was a large side-wheel steam sloop built by J. G. Montgomery and A. Anderson at Montgomery, Ala., in 1864 and taken to Mobile for completion. Her first commander was Lt. C. C. Simms, CSN.

Still fitting out, she took no part in the battle of Mobile Bay on 5 August 1864, but was one of the vessels formally surrendered by Commodore E. Farrand, CSN, at Nanna Hubba, Ala., on 10 May 1865.

Although never finished, she had been heavily armored with triple 2-inch plating forward and around her pilot house, only a single thickness aft and there had been some doubts expressed that her builders might have overestimated her structural strength. Rear Adm. H. K. Thatcher, USN, wrote on 30 June 1865, after survey, ''She was hogged when surrendered and is not strong enough to bear the weight of her full armor.'' He was certain ''she could not live in a seaway.''

Nashville was purchased by the Navy Department and sold at New Orleans, La., on 22 November 1867, her iron sheathing having been removed for naval use.

Natchez

(SwStr: t. 800; l. 273'; b. 38'; dph. 8')

Natchez, built at Cincinnati, Ohio, in 1860, was impressed by order of Comdr. I. N. Brown, CSN, for Confederate States service as a cotton-clad armed boat in the Yazoo River. *Natchez* was burned by the Confederates in April 1863 in the Yazoo River near Burtonia, Miss., in order to avoid capture by the advancing gunboats of Admiral Porter's command.

Neafie

(SwStr: dr. 8'; cpl. 60; s. 6 k.)

Neafie, also spelled *Neaffie*, was an iron steamer which operated as a transport and tug in coastal waters of the Gulf of Mexico during 1861. For part of the year she was under the command of Major Lovell, CSA. She sustained some damage during the action off Fort Pickens, Fla. on 22 November 1861, but managed to escape. By February 1863 she had been seized by the Union and was serving as a tug.

Nelms

(Gbt)

Nelms, a steamboat present at the Navy Yard at Fort McRee, Fla., on 22 November 1861 when that site was taken under attack by Union forces, proceeded safely to Pensacola, remaining there until the evacuation of that port in March 1862.

It was then suggested that she be run into Mobile Bay where she may have been lost.

Nelson

(Str)

Nelson was anchored with *Dr. Beatty* in the Red River, La., when early in July 1863, news of the arrival of USS *Manitou* and *Petrel* forced their hasty withdrawal to the fort at Harrisonburg, in the Ouachita River.

Neptune

(Str: a. 2 guns)

Neptune, a wooden steamer, was seized by Col. E. B. Nichols for duty with Comdr. W. W. Hunter's Texas Marine Department. [See Annex III]. She operated as a tug, lookout, and transport in coastal waters, especially in the Galveston area.

On New Year's Day 1863, the Confederates, having determined to recapture Galveston which had fallen to the Union during the previous October, launched their attack. *Bayou City* and *Neptune*, with their decks well protected by cotton bales and loaded with troops, moved down to engage the Federal fleet in the harbor.

Bayou City first closed with USS *Harriet Lane*, one of two principal Union ships in the harbor, and tried to board her, but the strong tide swung the ships into a collision which damaged both. *Neptune*, Capt. W. Sangster, then rammed the Federal gunboat but was herself injured by the impact and began to take water rapidly. Making for the edge of the channel she sank there in 8 feet of water. The ensuing capture of *Harriet Lane* triggered a series of events which forced Union withdrawal and proved a mighty morale factor for the Confederates.

Neuse

(IrcRam: l. 152'; b. 34'; dr. 9'; a. 2 6.4'' or 8'' r.; type *Albermarle*)

CSS *Neuse* was a steam sloop built in 1862–64 for the Confederate Navy by Howard & Ellis at Whitehall and Kinston, N.C., on the Neuse River. Launched in November 1863, *Neuse* sailed in April 1864 for duty on the inland waters of North Carolina as part of the force under Comdr. R. F Pinkney, CSN. Shortly thereafter she grounded off Kinston and remained fast for almost a month. She never left the river, and in March 1865 she was burned by the Confederates to escape capture

by the Union army under Maj. Gen. W. T. Sherman, USA.

New Falls City

(SwStr: t. 880; l. 301'4''; b. 39'9''; dph. 7'7'')

New Falls City was built in 1858 at Paducah, Ky. She lay near Coushatta Chute, La., on 18 March 1864, when ordered by Lieutenant General E. Kirby Smith, CSA, Department of Trans-Mississippi, to be towed to Scopern's Cut-off in Red River and held in readiness to be sunk as an obstruction upon approach of the Federals. It was suggested that her machinery be removed and her hull be filled with rock to make her more stable [cf. *Osceola*]. Rear Admiral Porter, leading the naval force on the Red River Expedition, found the way blocked 10 April by the huge steamer. He later described it to General W. T. Sherman: "When I arrived at Springfield Landing I found a sight that made me laugh. It was the smartest thing I ever knew the rebels to do. They had gotten that huge steamer, *New Falls City*, across the Red River, 1 mile above Loggy Bayou, 15 feet of her on shore on each side, the boat broken down the middle, and a sand bar making below her. An invitation in large letters to attend a ball in Shreveport was kindly left stuck up by the rebels, which invitation we were never able to accept." Before he could clear the wreck, Porter was forced to turn back by the defeat of the Federals at Sabine Cross Roads.

New Merrimack, see *Richmond*

New National

(Str)

New National, a transport, was seized by Union gunboats at Memphis on 6 June 1862 after the withdrawal of the Confederate flotilla.

New Orleans

(FltBtry: a. 17 8'', 1 9'', 2 32-pdr. r.)

CSS *New Orleans* was a floating battery fitted out at New Orleans, La., in 1861. She featured "two small boilers with pump connections," designed to repel boarders by drenching them with scalding water from her hoses. She deployed under Lt. S. W. Averett, CSN, in the Mississippi in time to assist joint army-navy operations at Island No. 10 and New Madrid, Mo., 12 March to 7 April 1862. The final day of this engagement, the Confederates avoiding capture, sank

New Orleans during the evacuation of Island No. 10.

Nina Simms

(SwStr: t. 327; l. 177′; b. 33′; dph. 6′)

Nina Simms, spelled variously *Nina Simmes* and *Nina Sims*, was built at New Albany, Ind., in 1860 and operated out of New Orleans in 1861. She was placed under Army control and transported provisions on the Mississippi, principally in the Port Hudson, La., region.

Norfolk

(ScGbt: dp. 166; l. 106′; b. 21′; dph. 8′; dr. 5′; a. 1 9″, 1 32-pdr.; cl. *Hampton*)

Norfolk was a sister to *Portsmouth*, paralleling her progress in Gosport (Norfolk) Navy Yard. Both of these early "Maury Gunboats" were burned on the ways to escape capture by entering Federal forces, 10 May 1862.

North Carolina

(IrcStSlp: l. 150′; b. 32′; dph. 14′; dr. 12′; cpl. 150; a. 4 guns; type *Richmond*)

CSS *North Carolina* was built by Berry & Bros. at Wilmington, N.C., in 1863. She was placed in commission during the latter part of the year with Comdr. W. T. Muse, CSN, in command. Structurally weak and unable to cross the bar, she remained in Cape Fear River until about 27 Sept. 1864 when she developed a leak and sank, her hull riddled by teredos, off Smithville, where she had been serving as a guard ship. [cf. *Uncle Ben*.]

————

North Carolina, see under *Texas* (corvette)

Northampton

(SwStr: t. 405)

Northampton was built in 1860 at Baltimore, Md. Under Captain Gibbs she was used by the Confederates as a cargo ship for military stores on the James River, Va., and purchased by the State of Virginia in June 1861 for its own use. The Confederates sank *Northampton* in the latter part of 1862 as an obstruction below Drewry's Bluff on the James.

Oconee, see *Savannah*

Ogeechee, see *Macon*

Ohio Belle

(SwStr: t. 406)

Ohio Belle, a small second class steamer built in 1855 at Cincinnati, and used as an Army watch boat on the Mississippi, was captured by the Federals at Island No. 10 on 7 April 1862.

Old Savannah, see *Savannah*

Olinde, see *Stonewall*

Olustee, see *Tallahassee*

Oregon

(SwGbt: l. 216′10″; b. 26′6″; dph. 9′6″; t. 532; a. 1 8″, 1 32-pdr., 2 how.)

Oregon, a wooden steamer similar to *California*, was built at New York City in 1846 for the Mobile Mail Line, 60 percent owned at the end of April 1861 by the Geddes family of New Orleans and Cincinnati, the remainder by R. A. Heirn and Samuel Wolff of Mobile. Described as having "one deck, one mast, no galleries and a billethead," she was permanently enrolled (coastwise) at New Orleans, 20 June 1858. Seized by Louisiana's Governor Moore sometime in 1861, she was an early and successful blockade runner, apparently only in the Gulf. Under Capt. A. P. Boardman she had somehow contrived to make 92 "entrances and clearances" at blockaded ports before being picked for arming as a man-of-war; how much of this coastal service was under Confederate Army auspices is not altogether clear. Capt. A. L. Myers succeeded to her command.

After being converted into a gunboat, *Oregon* operated in Mississippi Sound on various assignments. On 13 July 1861 she steamed in company with *Arrow* to the vicinity of Ship Island Light where they vainly attempted to lure USS *Massachusetts* within range of shore batteries. During September 1861 she evacuated Confederate property and troops from Ship Island, Miss. When Confederate forces evacuated New Orleans in April 1862, *Oregon* was destroyed to prevent capture.

Oreto, see *Florida* (#3)

Oreto, see *Lapwing*

Orizaba

(SwStr: t. 595)

The Confederate Government Steamer *Orizaba*, formerly belonging to the Texas Line of Charles

Morgan's Southern Steamship Co., seems to have been the low-pressure, seagoing packet built in Brooklyn, N.Y., in 1858. Some writers have tried to identify her with the big, 1,200-passenger, predecessor Morgan liner *Orizaba* delivered in New York in 1854 to Morgan & Harris, sent to California two years later and scrapped there in 1887, never having returned to the Atlantic; her only war service having been short, transporting Union troops to the Isthmus of Panama.

Orizaba was seized by the Confederacy at Galveston prior to mid-September 1861, according to Confederate Army records. Released under gentleman's agreement with her owner to sail Galveston-New Orleans coastwise, her captain—once underway—made known Morgan's sub rosa countermand and tried to head for New York, but his Mate and passengers kept the pact for him by putting in to New Orleans anyway.

Whether *Orizaba* continued to ply to Galveston the next three months or was interned in the Mississippi is not authenticated by available documents. On 15 January 1862, she was commandeered a second time, appearing on the list of 14 ships Secretary of War Benjamin ordered Maj. Gen. Mansfield Lovell to "impress for public service" at New Orleans. Her status confused even her contemporaries for, the end of May 1862, when her owners pressed Richmond for the last payment on *Orizaba* and erstwhile running mate *Mexico*, Secretary of War G. W. Randolph had to ask General Lovell, "Are they a part of the River Defense Fleet?" Judging by official Navy records' silence about *Orizaba* thereafter, the answer must have been negative. Earlier in May, a Union spy had reported her in Texas; that is all.

Although clearly Government-owned the rest of her career, she apparently was never armed as a gunboat. As a blockade-runner, *Orizaba* is believed to have carried at least 16 essential Confederate cargoes out of Havana into the Gulf and to have been lost in 1865.

Osceola

(SwStr: t. 157)

Osceola was built in 1858 at Louisville, Ky., and passed to Confederate control in 1861. She was reported by USS *Lafayette* to be in the river above Alexandria, La., on 30 May 1863. On 18 March 1864, Lt. W. E. Marshall, Engineer Troops, was ordered to proceed in *Osceola* from Shreveport to the vicinity of Coushatta Chute where the steamer *New Falls City* lay. He was to fill *New Falls City* with dirt and rock for stable ballast, and hold her in readiness to be sunk on approach of the Federals at the foot of Scopern's Cut-off to block their passage up Red River.

(Slp)

Osceola, a fishing smack which sailed under Confederate papers, was captured by USS *New London* on 9 December 1861 near Cat Island Passage in Mississippi Sound. She may not have been a public vessel.

Ouachita, see *Louisville*

Owl

(SwStr: t. 771; l. 230'; b. 26'; dph. 9'6" or 10'9"; dr. 7'6"; s. 14–16 k.; cl. *Owl*)

Maffitt's last command, "long, low and painted light-red color," *Owl*, sister to *Bat* (q.v. supra for background) was more fortunate than her twin which followed her closely: *Owl* succeeded in running into Wilmington, N.C., some time in September, 1864, although U.S. Consul M. M. Jackson in Halifax wired Washington that *Owl* had "a large, valuable cargo" cleared 31 August—officially for Nassau. She escaped to sea from Wilmington, 3 October; her masts were visible all the while she lay in port loading. The blockaders wounded her captain and several crewmen but 9 shots failed to stop *Owl*.

She was now commanded by Comdr. John Newland Maffitt, CSN—the "Prince of Privateers"—detached from CS Ram *Albemarle* at Plymouth, N.C., on or about 9 September. Secretary Mallory, telegraphing 19 September, warned Maffitt: "It is of the first importance that our steamers should not fall into the enemy's hands . . . these vessels, lightly armed, now constitute the fleetest and most efficient part of his blockading force off Wilmington." [cf. *Bat*] Maffitt was to take no passengers, as a rule, and Asst. Paymaster Adam Tredwell, CSN, would deliver "5,000 pounds in sterling bills before sailing," Mallory concluded.

Owl was at Bermuda with cotton, 24–29 October, as the U.S. Consul faithfully reported. Mallory on 5 December instructed Maffitt to pick up *Florida's* men in Bermuda. A letter to Mallory captured, along with Asst. Paymaster Talley, CSN, by USS *Forest Rose*, 7 May 1865, bears an endorsement by her commander, Lt. A. N. Gould,

Rams C.S.S. Chicora *and*
Palmetto State *in Charleston
Harbor.*

USN, "It shows that Maffitt has been landing on the Florida coast with the *Owl*." U.S. Consul W. T. Minor at Havana reported 20 May 1865 that Maffitt was to leave there in a day or two for Galveston. This last trip *Owl* was almost captured at Wilmington by a Federal cruiser and had to jettison valuable mail as well as sustain 12 casualties; Maffitt then tried Galveston, grounded on Bird Island Shoals at the entrance within range of 16 enemy cruisers. Capt. James H. MacGarvey, CSN, in little *Diana*, got *Owl* off barely in time; she not only ran into port but ran out safely too. There is some evidence *Owl's* last two runs through the blockade were made under the name of *Foam*.

Owl was delivered to Fraser, Trenholm & Co. in Liverpool after war's end and Maffitt took the Board of Trade examinations to command British merchant ships to South America.

Palmetto State

(IrcRam: l. 150'; b. 34'; dph. 14'; dr. 12'; s. 6 k.; a. 2 7" r., 2 9" sb.; type *Richmond*)

CSS *Palmetto State*, an ironclad ram, was built by Cameron and Co., Charleston, January 1862, under the supervision of Flag Officer D. N. Ingraham, CSN. She was readied for service by September 1862 when Lt. Comdr. J. Rutledge, CSN, was placed in command. Her armor was 4" thick on the shield, backed by 22" of wood, 2" of iron elsewhere. Her pilothouse was located abaft the stack.

Before dawn on 31 January 1863, *Palmetto State* and her sister ram CSS *Chicora* crept through thick haze to surprise the Union blockading force off Charleston. Taking full advantage of her low silhouette, the ironclad stole in under the guns of *Mercedita*, ramming as well as firing into her. Completely disabled, with no guns that would depress enough to fire at *Palmetto State*, the Union ship surrendered. The ram then turned her attention to *Keystone State* and put several shells into that blockader. Her steam chests punctured, *Keystone State* lost all power and had to be towed to safety. A long-range gun action between the Confederate rams and other Federal blockaders then took place, but little damage was inflicted by either side before *Palmetto State* and *Chicora* withdrew to safety within Charleston Harbor. The attack of the Confederate rams caused the temporary withdrawal of the blockaders from their inshore positions and led to the claim by the Confederate Government, unsuccessfully advanced, that the blockade of Charleston had been raised.

Palmetto State also joined in the defense of Charleston during Adm. S. F. Du Pont's unsuccessful attack on the harbor forts, 1–7 April 1863. Her officers and men were cited for valuable services rendered during the removal of troops from Fort Wagner and Battery Gregg on the night of 6–7 September 1863.

Palmetto State was burned by the Confederates upon the evacuation of Charleston on 18 February 1865.

Pamlico

(SwStr: t. 218; a. 3 8" sb., 1 6.4" r.)

CSS *Pamlico*, a side-wheel steamer purchased in New Orleans, La., on 10 July 1861, was placed in commission on 2 September with Lt. W. G.

Dozier, CSN, commanding. She operated in the vicinity of New Orleans, clashing ineffectually with vessels of the Federal blockading squadron on 4 and 7 December 1861, and 25 March and 4 April 1862. *Pamlico* was burned by her officers on Lake Pontchartrain, La., when New Orleans fell to the Union [cf. *Selma* and *Carondelet*].

Pampero, see *Texas*   (#4)

Parallel, see *Thirty-fifth Parallel*

Pargoud

(SwStr: t. 523; l. 319'; b. 36'; dph. 7')

Pargoud, also known as *J. F. Pargoud*, was built in 1860 at Jeffersonville, Ind. She may have served the Confederates in the Mississippi River area, probably as a cargo ship or transport, and may have been under Comdr. I. N. Brown, CSN, commanding Confederate vessels in the Yazoo River, Miss. *Pargoud* was burned and scuttled by Commander Brown in the Yazoo River in July 1863, in order to prevent her from falling into the hands of a Union naval force under Acting Rear Adm. D. D. Porter, USN.

Patrick, see *Patrick Henry*

Patrick Henry

(SwStr: t. 1,300; l. 250'; b. 34'; dph. 17'; dr. 13'; cpl. 150; a. 1 10'' sb.; 1 64-pdr., 6 8'', 2 32-pdr. r.)

CSS *Patrick Henry*, sometimes referred to as *Patrick*, was the former side-wheel passenger and freight steamer *Yorktown* which ran between Richmond, Va., and New York. When Virginia seceded from the Union on 17 April 1861 *Yorktown*, then in the James River, was seized by that State and subsequently turned over to the Confederate Navy.

Brigantine-rigged *Yorktown* was built at New York City by the renowned William H. Webb in 1859 for the New York & Old Dominion S.S. Line; the Webb plans of her are still extant.

Commander J. R. Tucker, CSN, who commanded the newly organized James River Squadron, directed that *Yorktown* be converted into a lightly protected ship-of-war and renamed *Patrick Henry*. She was assigned to a position near Mulberry Island in the James to protect the right flank of the Confederate Peninsular Army, and during the following months remained vigilant against possible attack by Federal vessels from Newport News.

On 13 September 1861 and again on 2 December, Commander Tucker took *Patrick Henry* down the river to a point about a mile and a half above Newport News and opened fire on the Federal squadron at long range, hoping to draw out some of the gunboats. The lure was refused, but Tucker inflicted some minor damage.

During the battle of Hampton Roads, Va., on 8 March 1862 when ironclad *Virginia* inflicted such damage on the Union fleet, *Patrick Henry* approached *Congress*, run aground and flying a white flag, but she herself came under fire from other Federal ships and shore batteries, a shot through her steam chest killing four of her crew. Towed out of action long enough to make repairs, she resumed her former position.

In the engagement between CSS *Virginia* and *Monitor* the following day, *Patrick Henry* fired long range at *Monitor* maneuvering against *Virginia*. The Confederate Congress later accorded special thanks to all officers and men for their gallant conduct during the 2-day battle.

After the surrender of Norfolk on 10 May 1862, the James River Squadron retired up the river to Drewry's Bluff where pursuing Federal ships were repulsed on 15 May. In October 1863 *Patrick Henry* housed the floating Confederate States Naval Academy at Drewry's Bluff, where instruction for 52 midshipmen began under the superintendency of Lt. W. H. Parker, CSN. She had been designated as academy ship in May 1862 and had undergone alterations to this end. She was burned by the Confederates when Richmond was evacuated 3 April 1865.

Paul Jones

(SwStr: t. 353; l. 172'; b. 34'; dph. 6'6'')

Paul Jones, built in 1855 at McKeesport, Pa., served as a Confederate transport in the Mississippi, Yazoo, and Red Rivers until she was burned and scuttled by the Confederates, 17 May 1863.

One of her last details was helping *Grand Era* to raise *Indianola* in early March 1863. She last appears "at Allan's Mills in a disabled condition" with *Anna Perrette* on the 19th.

Paul Jones ferried Confederate troops across the Big Black River in company with *Charm* and the two transports were believed to have been lashed together when sunk. The wreck of *Charm* was exposed 99 years later, in 1962, and in 1965 a further portion of the river bank caved away

C.S.S. Patrick Henry *served as the school ship for midshipmen at the Confederate States Naval Academy.*

revealing long anticipated relics of her running mate: firebricks, part of a pitman strap, paddle-wheel spiders and charred white oak timbers.

Pauline

(Str)

Pauline operated as an Army transport in Louisiana waters during 1863 and 1864.

Peedee

(ScSlp: l. 170′; b. 26′; dph. 10′; s. 9 k.; cpl. 91; a. 1 7″ r., 1 6.4″ r., 1 9″ sb.)

CSS *Peedee* was a wooden gunboat built at Mars Bluff near Marion Court House, S.C., on the Great Peedee River, to the design of Acting Naval Constructor John L. Porter, CSN, late in 1862. Lt. Edward J. Means, CSN, commanding the naval station there, superintended construction of the twin-screw gunboat; one engine was ordered from the Naval Iron Works, Richmond, and the other is believed to have run the blockade from Great Britain. Her battery was intended to be four 32-pdrs. broadside and two 9-inch pivots.

Although little information concerning her has been preserved, reports indicate that she was completed and in commission as early as 20 April 1864 with Lt. O. F. Johnston, CSN, in command. She remained in the Peedee River where the Confederates destroyed her 110 miles above Georgetown upon the evacuation of Charleston, 18 February 1865.

Penguin

(SwStr: t. 1,063; l. 240′; b. 30′; dph. 13′; dr. 10′; cl. *Albatross*)

Penguin was built in Liverpool for Fraser, Trenholm & Co., as secret agents for the Confederacy, and was negotiated by Comdr. J. D. Bulloch, CSN. She was Lairds No. 320, from the Birkenhead yard early in 1865, but probably never reached the Southern States before war's end.

Petrel

(Sch: t. 82; cpl. 38; a. 2 guns)

Petrel was the U.S. Revenue Cutter *William Aiken*, taken over by South Carolina in December 1860, on secession. She had been Charleston pilot boat *Eclipse* when purchased for the Revenue Service.

Sold by the State to Henry Buist, Maier Triest and eight other Charlestonians, who were issued a letter of marque, 10 July 1861 at Charleston, *Petrel*'s life as a privateer was short: off her home port on her first cruise, 28 July, she was overhauled and sunk by USS *St. Lawrence*, after a four-hour chase. Capt. William Perry ran up the Confederate flag and fired three shots; one passed through the pursuer's "mainsail and took a splinter out of the main yard," whereupon *St. Lawrence* unlimbered her fo'c'sle battery, made two hits, "one of which struck her bows." *Petrel* sank in 30 minutes. Capt. Hugh Y. Purviance, USN, noted laconically in his log, "Got out the boats and picked up the crew," thus learning *Petrel's* name and the fact that two of her men had drowned; he took no time then to file a report. The 36 prisoners were transferred to *Flag* at Savannah, then taken to Philadelphia to be tried for their lives as "pirates"—one of the early test cases by which this doctrine of "piracy" proved impracticable to enforce.

Peytona

(SwStr: t. 685; l. 256'; b. 37'; dph. 7'6'')

Peytona was built in 1859 at New Albany, Ind. She was chartered by the Confederates on 17 April 1862 as a towboat and tender to the newly launched CSS *Mississippi*. When the Union fleet under Flag Officer D. G. Farragut, USN, approached New Orleans and after *Mississippi* was fired to prevent capture, *Peytona*, on 25 April 1862, escaped up the Mississippi River.

Peytona may have served the Confederates further under Comdr. I. N. Brown, CSN, commanding Confederate vessels in the Yazoo River. She was burned and scuttled in the Yazoo River in July 1863 by Commander Brown, to keep her from falling into the hands of a Union naval force under Acting Rear Adm. D. D. Porter, USN.

Phantom

(ScStr: t. 266 [500]; l. 190' bp.; b. 22'; dph. 13'4''; dr. 8'6''; cpl. 33; s. 18 k.)

Phantom is said to have been one of the original line of Confederate Government steamers operated between Wilmington, N.C., and Bermuda by the Ordnance Bureau, CSA (cf. *Cornubia*).

She was a "very handsome," steel-plated, screw steamer of 170 horsepower, constructed at Liverpool late in 1862 as "Hull No. 167" by a "G. Hillman"; drawings of her lines, captioned in German, do not specify the builder's yard. She seems to have left Liverpool early in April 1863.

Chased ashore by USS *Connecticut*, she was lost on her third run into the Cape Fear, 23 September 1863, near Rich or New Topsail Inlet, above Fort Fisher, and fired by her crew, who made good their escape in the lifeboats. Boats from *Connecticut* could not get near her, "hard and fast . . . and done for," to put out the fires or get her off, although one landsman in a boat making the attempt was killed by Confederate sharpshooters behind the dunes.

Philo Parsons

(Str)

Philo Parsons was a Detroit-Sandusky steamer seized on Lake Erie by Confederate raiders in an attempt to capture USS *Michigan*, only United States war vessel on the Great Lakes, and liberate Confederate prisoners she was guarding on Johnson's Island, off Sandusky, O.

The commandos boarded at Malden, Upper Canada (Ont.), in the guise of passengers, 19 September 1864. Their leader was Acting Master's Mate John Y. Beall, CSN, who had helped Capt. Charles H. Cole, CSA, of Gen. Nathan B. Forrest's command—an escapee from Johnson's I. in July—organize the plot under chief Confederate agent in Canada, Col. Jacob Thompson (v. *Georgian* supra). Cole also claimed to have a commission as Lieutenant, CSN.

Cole was drinking with officers of *Michigan* when Beall took over *Parsons;* the scheme went awry, Cole was arrested and failed to send a messenger, as agreed, to Beall, but the latter proceeded according to plan regardless. Beall, in *Parsons*, had to stop at Middle Bass Island for wood; *Island Queen* "with a large number of passengers and 32 soldiers" tied up alongside them with the same intent. The *Parsons* raiders took them all prisoner, paroled the soldiers and left the civilians on the isle sworn not to leave for 24 hours. *Island Queen* was towed out to deep water and sunk; *Parsons* finally headed for Sandusky, but for some reason now unknown the crew all backed out, refusing to attack *Michigan*.

Nothing was left for it but to retreat: at Sandwich, Ont., the 20th, "after plundering and cutting her pipes to scuttle" her, *Philo Parsons* was left to founder while, according to Colonel Thompson, "most of" the Confederate conspirators escaped below the Mason-Dixon Line; Acting Master's Mate Bennett G. Burley, CSN, did not: Comdr. John C. Carter, USN, of *Michigan* telegraphed of Burley, "I have got the principal agent prisoner on board and many accomplices." Canada sought at the Burley trial to force Colonel Thompson's expulsion from the country as the espionage mastermind behind the *Parsons*, *Georgian* and other incidents.

Phoenix

(IrcFltBtry: a. 6 guns)

Phoenix, an ironclad floating battery, was built by the Confederates probably in 1863 and outfitted as a ram. She was sunk at Mobile, Ala., in August 1864 as an obstruction, and later burned.

(SwTug: cpl. 75)

Phoenix, an unarmed high-pressure tender to CSS *Manassas*, was under the command of Capt. James Brown. She took part in the engagement at Forts Jackson and St. Philip and was destroyed there on 24 April 1862 as a part of Comdr J. K. Mitchell's flotilla.

Pickens

(Sch: a. 1 to 5 guns variously)

Pickens, originally the United States Revenue Cutter *Robert McClelland*, was seized by the State of Louisiana on 31 January 1861 and subsequently turned over to the Confederate States Navy and renamed *Pickens*. Capt. J. G. Breshwood, CSN, formerly an officer in the United States Revenue Service, was retained in command.

Pickens operated in the lower Mississippi during 1861 and early 1862, in Commodore Hollins' squadron, fighting Federal gunboats in the engagement of 12 October 1861 off the Head of the Passes, Mississippi River.

Pine

(Slp: t. ca. 40)

Pine may have remained under private ownership in serving the Confederates as a cargo ship along the North Carolina coast. On 30 August 1861 she was ordered to report to Captain Leech, CSA, at Fort Ocracoke, N.C. On 3 February 1863 she was under orders of Major General Foster, CSA, carrying nonmilitary provisions for the use of the officers and soldiers in Washington, N.C.

Pioneer

(SS: 1. 20' [34']; b. 3'2'' [4']; dph. 6' [4']; a. clockwork torpedo)

Pioneer, a privateer two-man submarine, was begun in New Orleans in 1861 to meet the menace of the United States steamers *New London* and *Calhoun* on Lake Pontchartrain. She was completed in early 1862, having been constructed from quarter-inch rivited iron plates that had been cut from old boilers.

Some reports indicate that *Pioneer* was built in the Leeds Foundry but her principal inventor, J. R. McClintock, stated that she was built in his Machine Shop at 21 Front Levee Street, where, in partnership with B. Watson, he manufactured steam gages and turned out "minnie balls" on a high speed machine of his own invention.

According to a post Civil War interview with McClintock, *Pioneer* was 30 feet long, of which a 10-foot midship section was cylindrical. From either end of the cylinder was a tapered section that gave her conical ends and resulted in a kind of "cigar shape." There was a conning tower with manholes in the top and small windows of circular glass in her sides. One man propelled the submarine by turning the manual crank of the screw and her iron ballast keel, detachable from the inside, was so heavy that it barely enabled the submarine to float on the surface with the conning tower awash. She was equiped with diving planes and was armed by a clock-work torpedo, carried on top of the submarine, and intended to be screwed into the bottom of the enemy's ship by gimlet-pointed screws of tempered steel. Actual inside measurements of *Pioneer* made on the spot by W. M. Robinson in 1926, were reported by him to be: length of 20 feet; maximum inside width of 3 feet, 2 inches; and a maximum depth of 6 feet.

There is little clear evidence on the operations of *Pioneer*. She was granted a commission as a privateer by F. H. Hatch on 12 March 1862 and the application for a letter of marque was forwarded to Richmond on 1 April 1862. Her register of commission listed J. K. Scott as *Pioneer's* commander, and she was described by him as 34 feet in length, 4 feet breadth, 4 feet deep; measuring about 4 tons, with round conical ends and painted black. Her part-owners were identified as J. K. Scott, R. F. Barrow (brother-in-law of H. L. Hunley), B. Watson and J. R. McClintock. A surety bond of $5,000 was put up by H. L. Hunley and his lifelong friend and college classmate, Henry J. Leovy, who was then a New Orleans attorney of the law firm of Ogden and Leovy.

The application for letter of marque for *Pioneer* called "for authority to cruise the high seas, bay, rivers, estuaries, etc., in the name of the government, and aid said Government by the destruction or capture of any and all vessels opposed to or at war with the said Confederate States, and to aid in repelling its enemies." In an interview after the Civil War, McClintock stated *Pioneer* made several descents in Lake Pontchartrain and succeeded in destroying a small schooner and several rafts during experiments. Before she could attack a Union ship, Farragut captured New Orleans

President of the Confederate States of America

TO ALL WHO SHALL SEE THESE PRESENTS,

GREETING

Know Ye that reposing special Trust and Confidence in the Patriotism, Valour, Fidelity, and Abilities of   I do appoint him

in the Navy of the **CONFEDERATE STATES**

to rank as such from the   day of   18   He is therefore carefully and diligently to discharge the Duties of   by doing and performing all Manner of Things thereto belonging

And I do strictly charge and require all Officers Seamen and Marines under his Command to be obedient to his Orders as   And he is to observe and follow such Orders and Directions from time to time as he shall receive from me or the future **PRESIDENT** *of the Confederate States of America or his Superior Officer set over him according to the Rules and Discipline of* **THE NAVY.**

BY THE PRESIDENT   *Given under my Hand at   this*

day of   in the Year of our Lord One Thousand Eight Hundred and

Secretary of the Navy

Registered N°

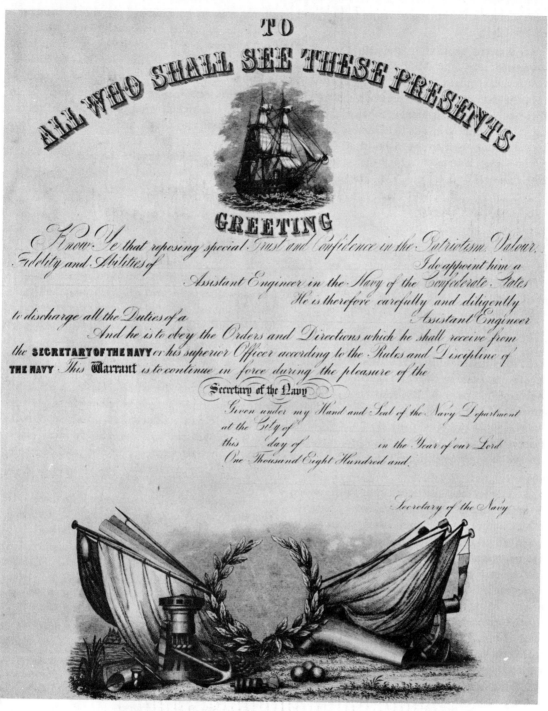

TO
ALL WHO SHALL SEE THESE PRESENTS
GREETING

Know Ye that reposing special Trust and Confidence in the Patriotism, Valour, Fidelity and Abilities of   I do appoint him a Assistant Engineer in the Navy of the Confederate States   He is therefore carefully and diligently to discharge all the Duties of a   Assistant Engineer And he is to obey the Orders and Directions which he shall receive from the **SECRETARY OF THE NAVY** *or his superior Officer according to the Rules and Discipline of* **THE NAVY** *This* **Warrant** *is to continue in force during the pleasure of the*

Secretary of the Navy

Given under my Hand and Seal of the Navy Department at the City of this   day of   in the Year of our Lord One Thousand Eight Hundred and.

Secretary of the Navy

During 1965 the U.S.S. Alabama *Battleship Commission in Mobile came into possession of two rare engraving plates, made in England during the Civil War, for producing commission certificates in the Confederate States Navy. The plates were obviously handsomely designed but were badly pitted and corroded. While helping to trace the history of the plates, the Naval History Division located at the Library of Congress copies of commissions struck from plates similar to those now held in Mobile. Apparently, these artistically designed commissions were never used by the South, perhaps arriving from England too late in the war (November 1864); nevertheless their existence is of historical interest and the commissions held by the Library of Congress are reproduced on these two pages.*

and she was sunk to prevent her from falling into Federal hands.

Pioneer was recovered long after the Civil War and removed to Camp Nicholls, the Louisiana Home for Confederate Soldiers. On 24 April 1957 she was transferred to her present site in the Presbytere Arcade, Louisiana State Museum, New Orleans, La. She was the forerunner of two other submarines which were built at Mobile, Ala., one the unnamed submarine sometimes called "*Pioneer II*" (q.v.) and *H. L. Hunley* (q.v.).

"Pioneer II"

(SS: 1. 36'; b. 3'; dph. 4'; cpl. 5; s. 2.5 k.; a. clockwork torpedo)

An unnamed submarine sometimes called "*Pioneer II*" was built during 1863 in the machine shop of Park and Lyons, Mobile, Ala., on plans said to have been furnished by H. L. Hunley, B. Watson and J. R. McClintock. Her principal builder was probably W. A. Alexander who claimed this distinction after close of the Civil War, stating that he was a Confederate Army Engineer of Company B, 21st Alabama Volunteer Regiment, CSA. He also stated he was assisted by Lt. G. E. Dixon, Company A, 21st Alabama Volunteer Regiment, who had also been detailed to do work in the machine shop of Park and Lyons.

H. L. Hunley has left record that he provided the "entire means" for this five-man submarine and McClintock stated that much money was spent in an unsuccessful attempt to power with an electro-magnetic engine. He afterwards fitted cranks to turn the propeller by hand, working four men at a time, but was unable to get a speed sufficient to make the submarine of service against Union ships blockading Mobile. In a letter to M. F. Maury in 1868, McClintock gave her dimensions as 36 feet long, 3 feet wide, 4 feet deep, with 12 feet of each end being tapered to facilitate underwater movement. She was towed off Fort Morgan to be manned for an attack on the Federal Fleet but foul weather and rough seas swamped her, without any loss of life.

"*Pioneer II*" was probably the submarine described by a Confederate deserter on 26 February 1863 to the Senior Officer of the Federal Blockade off Mobile: "On or about the 14th, an infernal machine, consisting of a submarine boat, propelled by a screw which turned by hand, capable of holding 5 persons, and having a torpedo

which was to be attached to the bottom of a vessel and exploded by means of clockwork, left Fort Morgan at 8 p.m. in charge of a Frenchman who invented it. The intention was to come up at Sand Island, get the bearing and distance of the nearest vessel, dive under again and operate upon her; but on emerging they found themselves so far outside the island and in so strong a current (setting out) that they were forced to cut the torpedo adrift and make the best of their way back." She was second in line of three submarines that included *Pioneer* (q.v.) and *H. L. Hunley* (q.v.).

Planter

(SwStr: t. 313; dr. ca. 3½–4'; a. 1 32-pdr., 1 24-pdr. how.)

Planter was built in 1860 at Charleston, S.C., and served as an armed dispatch boat and transport attached to the engineer department at Charleston, under Brig. Gen. Ripley, CSA. On 12 May 1862 at 0400, while her captain, C. J. Relyea, was absent on shore, Robert Smalls, a Negro slave who was *Planter*'s pilot, quietly took *Planter* from the wharf, and with a Confederate flag flying, steamed past the successive Confederate forts, saluting as usual by blowing her steam whistle. As soon as she was out of range of the last Confederate gun, Smalls hauled down the Confederate flag and hoisted a white one. Then he turned *Planter* over to the U.S. ship *Onward* of the Union blockading force. On the next day *Planter* was sent to Flag Officer S. F. DuPont, USN, at Port Royal Harbor, S.C., who kept Robert Smalls as *Planter*'s pilot. At the time she was taken over by the Federals, *Planter* had on board a valuable cargo, four guns, one of them a 7-inch rifle, besides her usual armament.

The Senate and House of Representatives of the United States passed a Private Law on 30 May 1862, granting Robert Smalls and *Planter*'s Negro crew one half of the value of *Planter* and her cargo.

Plover

(SwStr: t. [645]; 1. 225'; b. 24'; dph. 11'; dr. 6'; cl. *Curlew*)

Plover was one of four sisters ordered for the Confederate Navy in Great Britain by Comdr. J. D. Bulloch, CSN, in 1864. The quarto was launched the same day in 1865 at Jones, Quiggin & Co., Liverpool. *Plover* was Hull No. 178, second in the series. It is doubtful that any of

C.S.S. Planter.

them were finished in time to serve the Confederacy.

Plymouth

(Ship: t. 974; l. 147'6"; b. 38'1"; dph. 16'4"; a. 22 guns)

CSS *Plymouth*, originally the sailing sloop-of-war *Plymouth*, was built at the Boston Navy Yard in 1843 and sailed for the Mediterranean on 3 April 1844, returning to the United States in October 1846. Between that date and December 1858, she made several cruises in foreign waters. In 1859 and 1860 she was in use as practice ship for midshipmen at Annapolis and in April 1861 was at the Gosport (Norfolk) Navy Yard where she was scuttled and partially burned at the evacuation of the yard.

Plymouth was raised by the Confederates who planned to sail her up the James River to Richmond; however, when the Navy Yard was recaptured by the Union on 10 May 1862 she had not been moved and the Confederates scuttled her to avoid capture.

Polk, see *General Polk*

Pontchartrain

(SwStr: t. 454; l. 204'; b. 36'6"; dr. 10'; a. 7 guns)

CSS *Pontchartrain*, formerly named *Lizzie Simmons* or *Eliza Simmons*, was purchased by the Confederates at New Orleans, La., on 12 October 1861 and converted to a ship-of-war. When ready for service in March 1862, she was placed under the command of Lt. J. W. Dunnington, CSN, and assigned to the fleet under Flag Officer G. N. Hollins, CSN, for the defense of the Mississippi River and Louisiana coast.

Pontchartrain fought at Island No. 10 and New Madrid, Mo., during March and April 1862. After the evacuation of New Madrid on 7 April she and CSS *Maurepas* were sent up the White River into Arkansas.

On 17 June 1862 *Pontchartrain* cooperated with the army in a hard fought battle at St. Charles, Ark. During the engagement two of her 32-pounder rifled guns were transferred to the fort; Lieutenant Dunnington and his men joined the army in its defense and were among the prisoners taken.

Pontchartrain moved farther up the river and remained inactive until the following summer when she was burned to prevent capture, 9 October 1863, at or near Little Rock.

Portsmouth

(ScGbt: dp. 166; l. 106'; b. 21'; dph. 8'; dr. 5'; a. 1 9", 1 32-pdr.; cl. *Hampton*)

Portsmouth was one of the first of the 100 "Maury Gunboats" begun to defend the Virginia-North Carolina coastline. At Gosport (Norfolk) in 1862, almost completed, *Portsmouth* had to be burned on the stocks when the Navy Yard was evacuated by the Confederates, 10 May.

Post Boy

(Str)

Post Boy served the Confederacy as a dispatch and tow boat in coastal waters of North Carolina during late 1861 and early 1862.

Powhatan

(ScTug)

"The large and comfortable tug *Powhatan*," as she is described by Brig. Gen. H. A. Wise, CSA, was acquired by the Confederate States Navy in January 1862, apparently from a proprietor of the Currituck Canal. She was propeller driven, we learn from Flag Officer W. F. Lynch, CSN, who intended to arm her as "an auxilliary means of defense" of Roanoke Island, N.C., against a fleet Gen. Ambrose Burnside, USA, was assembling. This plan is outlined in Lynch's report to Secretary of the Navy Mallory. Of seven such tugs we have only the names of *Powhatan* and *Kakakee* and those thanks entirely to a picturesque verbal skirmish between Commodore Lynch and General Wise. The brigadier charged, "It would have been well for the service to have employed his (Lynch's) boats as tugs for transports instead of vainly trying to turn tugs into gunboats to encounter a Burnside fleet of 60 vessels, any one large steamer of which could easily have taken his seven boats." Commodore Lynch bought *Powhatan* for $12,000 from a Mr. Parks who, according to General Wise, had just sold her to the Army Quartermaster for $10,000. The Army had taken possession of *Powhatan* but she was overtaken in Currituck Canal by Commodore Lynch and taken over. (CSS *Ellis'* log mentions *Powhatan* operationally—when she delivered cable for ballast on 10 January.) Outraged, General Wise protested at length to Major General Huger, his superior at Norfolk, and on up through Secretary of War to President Davis. Commodore Lynch, however, had written Secretary Mallory from CSS *Sea Bird*, 22 January, "The crisis will soon be over, and desirable as it is to keep the *Powhatan* until some of the new gunboats are ready, I have no wish to detain her unjustly." Whether he relinquished *Powhatan* can only be conjectured without further documentation.

Price, see *General Sterling Price*

Prince

(SwStr: t. 223)

Prince was built in 1859 at Cincinnati, Ohio, and served the Confederates as a troop transport in the Mississippi River area. She participated valiantly in the Battle of Belmont, Mo., on 7 November 1861, as part of the Confederate force under Maj. Gen. L. Polk, CSA. *Prince*, under Captain Butler, stood firmly and fearlessly at her post amidst heavy Union fire, ready to ferry troops and ammunition back and forth across the Mississippi River in the course of the battle. She saved the Confederate transport *Charm* by pulling her free after she had been grounded, and took Brig. Gen. B. F. Cheatham, CSA, across the river from Columbus, Ky., to Belmont, Mo., to rally the Confederate forces for a flanking attack.

Prince was sunk by the Confederates before the battle for Island Number 10 in April 1862 to prevent her from falling into Union hands.

Prince of Wales

(SwStr: t. 572)

Prince of Wales, built in 1860 at Cincinnati, Ohio, and pronounced one of the finest river steamers in the West, served as a transport with Comdr. I. N. Brown's flotilla. She was burned at Yazoo City in mid-July 1863 to escape capture by the advancing Union forces under Admiral Porter.

Ptarmigan

(SwStr: t. 284; l. 270′; b. 24′; dr. 7′; sp. 15–18 k.; cpl. 50; cl. *Condor*)

Ptarmigan, later *Evelyn*, was probably the last of the *Condor* class of fast, triple-funneled, sloop-rigged paddle steamers delivered to the Confederate Navy through Comdr. James D. Bulloch, CSN, in the United Kingdom. She was ready about October 1864 and is conjectured to have reached the Confederacy via Halifax and Bermuda before December, with invaluable munitions and "a large quantity of medicines." She is known to have made at least four runs into the Gulf in 1865, apparently from Havana or Nassau to Galveston.

Her name change some time during this period has made her record the more elusive and was undoubtedly a part of a blockade runner's repertoire of disguises. In Halifax 27 October she was still *Ptarmigan;* in Bermuda, 16 November, she was *Evelyn* and acquired a coat of white paint the better to conceal her movements. Her crew had a siege with yellow fever at Bermuda, along with the men of *Flamingo*, her sister, during that autumn, but the ship seems to have gotten underway again and is believed to have survived the war.

Queen Mab

(SwStr)

Queen Mab, also known as *Mab*, was a very small side-wheeler whose shallow draft made her useful in shoal waters. She served the Confederacy as a transport in the Charleston area until the evacuation of that city in February 1865, when she was seized by Union forces. She was surveyed and condemned in July 1865.

Queen of the West

(SwRam: t. 212 or 406; l. 180′; b. 37′6″; dph. 8′; cpl. 120; a. 1 30-pdr., 1 20-pdr., 3 12-pdr. how.)

Queen of the West, Cincinnati-built in 1854, was purchased and converted into a ram by the United States Army in 1862. She was one of the vessels of Ellet's Ram Fleet operating in conjunction with the U.S. Navy. The Confederates sank her off Fort de Russy, La., on the Red River, on 14 February 1863, and later raised her.

Queen of the West, cottonclad with iron protection around her machinery, operated thereafter under the Confederate Army. In conjunction with another Confederate ram, *Webb*, she forced the surrender of USS *Indianola* off the Red River on 24 February 1863. On 14 April 1863 she was attacked on the Atchafalaya River, La., by the Union vessels *Estrella*, *Calhoun*, and *Arizona*. A shell from *Calhoun* set fire to *Queen of the West's* cotton and her burning wreck drifted down the river for several hours before she grounded and exploded.

R. E. & A. N. Watson, see *Little Rebel*

R. J. Breckinridge, see *General Breckinridge*

R. J. Lockland

(SwStr: t. 710; l. 265'; b. 40'; dph. 7')

R. J. Lockland was built at Cincinnati, Ohio, in 1857. She served the Confederates as a transport in the Mississippi River area, and was part of the force under Comdr. I. N. Brown, CSN, commanding Confederate vessels in the Yazoo River. In July 1863, R. J. Lockland was burned to the water's edge by Commander Brown, and sunk in the Yazoo River, 15 miles below Greenwood, Miss., to block the channel and delay the advance of Union forces under Gen. W. T. Sherman, USA, towards Vicksburg, Miss., and to escape the hands of the Union naval force under Acting Rear Adm. D. D. Porter, USN.

R. T. Renshaw, see Renshaw

Raleigh

(ScGbt: t. 65; a. 1 to 4 guns, variously)

CSS Raleigh was originally a small, iron-hulled, propeller-driven towing steamer operating on the Albemarle and Chesapeake Canal. She was taken over by the State of North Carolina in May 1861, and transferred to the Confederate States the following July. Her commanding officer during 1861–62 was Lt. J. W. Alexander, CSN. Her entire service was in coastal waters of North Carolina and Virginia and in the James River.

Raleigh supported Forts Hatteras and Clark on 28–29 August 1861; took part in an expedition on 1 October to capture United States Army steamer Fanny with valuable stores on board; and accompanied CSS Sea Bird when she reconnoitered Pamlico Sound 20 January 1862. She was also active in defense of Roanoke Island, N.C., against an amphibious assault by overwhelming Federal forces on 7–8 February 1862 at Elizabeth City, N.C., 2 days later. Thence Raleigh escaped through Dismal Swamp Canal to Norfolk, Va.

On 8–9 March 1862 Raleigh was tender to CSS Virginia during the historic battle of ironclads at Hampton Roads, for which she received the thanks of the Confederate Congress.

With the Federal recapture of Norfolk Navy Yard in May 1862, Raleigh steamed up the James River but thereafter a shortage of crew members restricted her to flag-of-truce or patrol service.

Raleigh, renamed Roanoke near the end of the war, was destroyed by the Confederates on 4 April 1865 upon the evacuation of Richmond.

(IrcRam: l. 150'; b. 32'; dph. 14'; dr. 12'; cpl. 188; a. 4 6" r.; type Richmond)

CSS Raleigh, a steam sloop, was constructed by the Confederate States Navy at Wilmington, N.C., in 1863–64, with Lt. John Wilkinson, CSN, commanding. She was reported in commission on 30 April 1864 under the command of Lt. J. P. Jones, CSN.

Built to Constructor John L. Porter's plans, similar to those of North Carolina, she had been laid down and launched at the foot of Church Street, completed at the shipyard of J. L. Cassidy & Sons.

On 6 May, she emerged from Cape Fear River accompanied by CSS Yadkin and Equator and inconclusively engaged six Federal blockaders off New Inlet, N.C. When the six reappeared the following day, Raleigh hastily withdrew up river, struck Wilmington Bar and "broke her back." Her iron plating was salvaged.

Randolph

(Str)

The steamer Randolph was operated in the Charleston, S.C., area by private parties but under the control of Maj. Gen. S. Jones, CSA, during 1863–64.

Rappahannock

(SwStr: t. 1,200; a. 1 gun)

Rappahannock, originally the passenger steamer St. Nicholas, was captured in the Potomac River on 28 June 1861. On a regularly scheduled run between Baltimore and Georgetown, D.C., she was boarded at various points along the Potomac by Confederates posing as passengers. Leaders of this group were Col. R. Thomas, CSA, who came on board disguised as a woman, and Capt. G. N. Hollins, CSN. They seized the steamer near Point Lookout and Captain Hollins took command, sailing the ship down to Chesapeake Bay, where she took three prizes on 29 June. Condemned as a prize, purchased by the Confederate Navy and commanded by Lt. H. H. Lewis, CSN, she operated in the Potomac and Rappahannock until April 1862 only to be burned by the Confederates at Fredericksburg.

———

(ScBark: t. 857; l. 200 bp.; b. 30'2''; dph. 14'6'')

Rappahannock, a steam sloop-of-war, was built in the Thames River in 1857 for the British Government and named Victor. Although a

C.S.S. Rappahannock *photographed in the harbor at Calais, France.*

handsomely modeled vessel, numerous defects occasioned her sale in 1863. An agent of the Confederate States Government purchased her ostensibly for the China trade, but British authorities suspected she was destined to be a Confederate commerce raider and ordered her detention. Nevertheless, she succeeded in escaping from Sheerness, England, on 24 November, with workmen still on board and only a token crew. Her Confederate Naval officers joined in the Channel.

When he bought her from the Admiralty through his secret agent on 14 November, Comdr. M. F. Maury had intended *Rappahannock* to replace unwanted, iron *Georgia* and was about to transfer *Georgia's* battery to her. She was ideal for a cruiser—wooden hull, bark-rigged, two engines and a lifting screw propeller—but she was doomed to serve the Confederacy no more glamorously than a floating depot.

She was commissioned a Confederate man-of-war underway, but while passing out of the Thames Estuary her bearings burned out and she had to be taken across to Calais for repairs. There Lt. C. M. Fauntleroy, CSN, was placed in command.

Detained on various pretexts by the French Government, *Rappahannock* never got to sea and was turned over to the United States at the close of the war.

Rattlesnake, see *Nashville*

Raven

(Yawl)

Raven, under Acting Master Edward McGuire, CSN, belonged to the "Confederate Volunteer Coast Guard," as it was locally known in Mathews County, Va. He served under the derring-do specialist, Master John Yates Beall, CSN. Particulars of *Raven* are nowhere given in official records; she may have been another yawl or even a skiff made to serve the purpose of the guerrillas, but she was at all times inseparable from *Swan,* commanded by Beall.

Rebel

(SwStr)

Rebel served the Confederates as a troop transport in the rivers and coastal waters of Virginia and North Carolina.

Red Rover

(SwStr: t. 786; dr. 8'; s. 8 k.)

Red Rover was built as a sidewheeler steamer at Cape Girardeau, Mo., in 1859 and purchased at New Orleans by the Confederacy on 7 November 1861 to serve as a barracks and accommodation ship for the crew of the floating battery *New Orleans.* Lt. J. J. Guthrie, CSN, had joint command of both ships, having placed *New Orleans* in commission at New Orleans on 14 October 1861.

Red Rover assisted in the defense of Columbus, Ky., then joined the formidable Confederate blockade of the Federal Western Gunboat Flotilla at Island Number 10 in the Mississippi River. She was put out of service early in the Federal naval bombardment which began on 15 March 1862, being pierced through all her decks and bottom by a shell fragment which caused considerable leakage. She was moored on the opposite side of Island Number 10 after this action and remained there until captured on 7 April by Acting Master C. Dominy of the Federal Gunboat *Mound City.* Fitted out by the United States Army in St. Louis as a temporary summer floating hospital for the Western Gunboat Flotilla, she was later converted to winter use and commissioned the first hospital ship of the United States Navy on

26 December 1862. Her nursing staff was headed by Sisters of the Order of the Holy Cross, forerunner of the Navy Nurse Corps. The first of her kind to carry women nurses, *Red Rover* gave comfort to only three less than 2,500 patients during an illustrious career with Acting Rear Adm. D. D. Porter's Mississippi Squadron that terminated on 17 November 1865.

Reliance

(ScStr: t. 90; l. 88'2''; b. 17'; dph. 7'5''; cpl. 40; a. 1 30-pdr. r., 1 24-pdr. how.)

Reliance was built at Keyport, N.J., in 1860 and first enrolled at New York City.

Originally a Federal gunboat stationed in lower Chesapeake Bay, *Reliance* was surprised, boarded, and captured early on 23 August 1863 at the mouth of the Rappahannock River by a Confederate naval assault party led by Lt. John Taylor Wood. With *Satellite*, captured at the same time, *Reliance* was taken to Port Royal, Va., where she was destroyed on 28 August to prevent recapture by Kilpatrick's advancing Federal cavalry.

Renshaw

(Sch: t. 75; l. 68'; b. 20'; dph. 5'4'')

Renshaw, also known as *R. T. Renshaw*, was in Confederate service near Washington, N.C., in the Tar River on 20 May 1863, when she was seized by a launch from USS *Louisiana*. Sent in as a prize, she was acquired by the Union for carrying ordnance.

Republic

(SwStr: t. 699; l. 249'; b. 40'; dr. 7.3')

The steamboat *Republic*, owned in New Orleans in 1861, had been built at Jeffersonville, Ind., in 1855. Confederate Navy records do not reveal the length or nature of her mission but Union intelligence unmistakably credited *Republic* with being one of the largest troop transports on the upper Yazoo River until she was selected, prior to May 1863, for conversion to a ram. Thus *Republic* was being armored at Yazoo City when Federal forces threatened; her charred remains were found at the navy yard there when Admiral Porter's forces took possession, 21 May. Porter's 24 May report to Secretary Welles notes, "Three powerful rams were burned . . . (including) the *Republic*, being fitted for a ram with railroad iron plating."

Resolute

(SwRam: cpl. 40; a. 2 32-pdr. r., 1 32-pdr sb.)

Resolute, a side-wheel gunboat ram, had been a tugboat on the Mississippi River before she was acquired by the Confederate Government. Capt. J. E. Montgomery selected her to be part of his River Defense Fleet [See Annex II]. On 25 January 1862 Montgomery began to convert her into a cottonclad ram by placing a 4-inch oak sheath with a 1-inch iron covering on her bow, and by installing double pine bulkheads filled with compressed cotton bales.

Resolute's conversion was completed on 31 March 1862. Under Capt. I. Hooper, she was detached from Montgomery's main force and sent to Forts Jackson and St. Philip on the lower Mississippi to cooperate in the Confederate defense of New Orleans. There, with five other vessels of Montgomery's fleet, all under Capt. J. A. Stevenson, she joined the force under Capt. J. K. Mitchell, CSN, commanding Confederate naval forces in the lower Mississippi.

On 24 April 1862 a Union fleet under Flag Officer D. G. Farragut, USN, ran past Forts Jackson and St. Philip on its way to capture New Orleans. *Resolute* was run ashore a mile above Fort Jackson by her crew who raised a white flag and then abandoned her. A party of 10 men under Lieutenant T. Arnold, CSN, sent from CSS *McRae*, boarded her, hauled down her white flag, and manned her guns. Later, while attempting to get her afloat, *Resolute* was attacked by long range Union fire and was pierced by several rifle shot, some below her water line. *Resolute's* damage could not be repaired quickly, and since another Union attack was expected, and since she lay dangerously exposed to land and sea, the Confederates burned her on 26 April 1862 to keep her from falling into Union hands.

(SwStr: t. 322; cpl. 35)

CSS *Resolute* was a tugboat built in 1858 at Savannah, Ga. She entered Confederate service in 1861 and operated as a tow boat, transport, receiving ship, and tender to the sidewheeler CSS *Savannah* on the coastal and inland waters of Georgia and South Carolina.

On 5–6 November 1861, *Resolute*, under Lt. J. P. Jones, CSN, in company with *Lady Davis*, *Sampson* and *Savannah*, under the overall command of Flag Officer J. Tattnall, CSN, offered harassing resistance to a much larger Union fleet preparing to attack Confederate strongholds at Port Royal Sound, S.C.

On 7 November 1861, while *Resolute* had been sent to Savannah with dispatches, the Union fleet under Flag Officer S. F. Du Pont, USN, pounded the Confederate Forts Walker and Beauregard until they were abandoned. Upon her return, *Resolute* helped evacuate the garrison of Fort Walker and then returned to spike the Confederate guns at Pope's Landing on Hilton Head Island.

On 26 November 1861, *Resolute*, in company with *Sampson* and *Savannah*, under Flag Officer Tattnall, weighed anchor from under the guns of Fort Pulaski, Ga.; and made a brief attack on Union vessels at the mouth of the Savannah River. On 28 January 1862, accompanied by *Sampson* and *Savannah*, she delivered supplies to the fort despite the spirited opposition of Federal ships.

On 12 December 1864 while on an expedition with the gunboats *Macon* and *Sampson*, under Flag Officer W. W. Hunter, CSN, to destroy the Charleston and Savannah Railway bridge spanning the Savannah River, *Resolute* received heavy fire from a Union field battery. Although hit twice she was not seriously damaged until she was disabled by colliding with the two gunboats during their retreat. Although the gunboats escaped, *Resolute* ran aground on Argyle Island in the Savannah River. She was captured the same day by the 3d Wisconsin Regiment under Col. W. Hawley, USA, of General Sherman's forces, and taken into Federal service. Colonel Hawley described her as an "armed tender" when captured.

Retribution, see Uncle Ben

Richmond

(IrcRam: l. 150' (bp.), 172'6''; b. 34' (molded); dph. 14'; dr. 12'; cpl. 150; s. 5 to 6 k.; a. 4 rifled guns, 2 on each side, and 2 shell guns, one on each side; 1 spar torpedo; type *Richmond*)

CSS *Richmond* was built at Gosport (Norfolk) Navy Yard to the design of John L. Porter with money and scrap iron collected by the citizens of Virginia, whose imagination had been captured by the ironclad *Virginia*. Consequently she was sometimes referred to as *Virginia II*, *Virginia No. 2* or *Young Virginia* in the South and as *Merrimack No. 2*, *New Merrimack* or *Young Merrimack* by Union

writers, months before the actual *Virginia II* was ever laid down.

Begun in March 1862, *Richmond* was launched 6 May and towed up to the Confederate capital that very night to escape Federal forces again in possession of Norfolk Navy Yard and the lower James River. *Richmond* was thus finished at Richmond in July 1862 and placed in commission by Comdr. R. B. Pegram, CSN. Twenty-two inches of yellow pine and oak plus 4 inches of iron protected her roof and "she is ironed 3½ feet below her load lines," wrote Shipyard Superintendent John H. Burroughs.

During 1863 and early 1864 the James front was quiet but from May 1864 momentous events followed in quick succession. The Confederates had three new ironclads in Capt. French Forrest's squadron there and minor actions were frequent.

During 1864 *Richmond*, under Lt. William H. Parker, CSN, took part in engagements at Dutch Gap, 13 August; Fort Harrison, 29 September–1 October; Chapin's Bluff, 22 October. On 23–24 January 1865, she was under heavy fire while aground with *Virginia* above the obstructions at Trent's Reach—fortunately at an angle that encouraged Federal projectiles to ricochet harmlessly off their casemates. But *Richmond's* tender, *Scorpion*, not thus armored, was severely damaged by the explosion of CSS *Drewry's* magazine as *Drewry* ended her life, lashed alongside *Richmond*. The ironclads withdrew under their Chapin's Bluff batteries for a few weeks but *Richmond* had to be destroyed by Rear Admiral Raphael Semmes, CSN, squadron commander, prior to evacuation of the capital, 3 April.

Roanoke

(Str)

The small steamer *Roanoke* was chartered in June 1861 from the Albemarle and Chesapeake Canal Co. by Comdr. F. Forrest to keep open Confederate communications on the Nansemond River in Virginia. She carried on similar duties off the North Carolina coast in 1862.

Roanoke, see Raleigh

Robb, see Alfred Robb

Robert E. Lee

(SwStr: t. 900; l. 283′; b. 20′; dph. 13′; dr. 10′; s. 9–13.5 k.)

Robert E. Lee was a schooner-rigged, iron-hulled, oscillating-engined paddle-steamer with two stacks, built on the Clyde during the autumn of 1862 as a fast Glasgow-Belfast packet. Alexander Collie & Co., Manchester, acquired her for their blockade-running fleet but were persuaded by renowned blockade-runner Lt. John Wilkinson, CSN, to sell her, as *Giraffe*, to the Navy Department for the same £32,000 just paid.

Her first voyage, for the Confederate Navy, was into Old Inlet, Wilmington, N.C., in January 1863 with valuable munitions and 26 Scot lithographers, eagerly awaited by the Government bureau of engraving and printing. On 26 January, Union intelligence maintained she "could be captured easily" at anchor in Ossabaw Sound, but this was not to be for another 10 months. Running out again, *R. E. Lee* started to establish a nearly legendary reputation by leaving astern blockader USS *Iroquois*. Lt. Richard H. Gayle, CSN, assumed command in May, relieving Lt. John Wilkinson but the latter was conning the ship again out of Cape Fear River from Smithville, N.C., on 7 October 1863, as recounted by Lt. Robert D. Minor, CSN, in a letter to Admiral Franklin Buchanan, 2 February 1864, detailing the first venture to capture USS *Michigan* and liberate 2,000 Confederate prisoners at Johnson's Island, Sandusky, Ohio (cf. *Georgia*, *Philo Parsons* and *J. H. Jarvis*): *R. E. Lee* transported Wilkinson, Minor, Lt. Benjamin P. Loyall and 19 other naval officers to Halifax, N.S., with $35,000 in gold and cotton cargo "subsequently sold at Halifax for $76,000 (gold) by the War Department—in all some $111,000 in gold, as the sinews of the expedition."

Thus Wilkinson was in Canada and Gayle commanding when *Robert E. Lee's* luck ran out, 9 November 1863, after 21 voyages in 10 months carrying out over 7,000 bales of cotton, returning with munitions invaluable to the Confederacy. She left Bermuda five hours after her consort, *Cornubia* (q.v.), only to be run down a few hours after her by the same blockader, USS *James Adger*. The two runners were conceded to be easily "the most noted that ply between Bermuda and Wilmington."

Robert E. Lee was bought by the U.S. Navy from the Boston prize court for $73,000 in January 1864. On 27 February she was renamed *Fort Donelson* and served out the war as a blockader.

Robert Fulton

(SwStr: t. 158)

Robert Fulton, also known as *Fulton*, was built in 1860 at California, Pa. She served as a Confederate army transport in the Mississippi River.

Robert Fulton, Capt. J. F. Saunders commanding, was surprised and captured along with *Argus* at the mouth of the Red River, La., on 7 October 1863 by a boat crew dispatched from USS *Osage*. She was burned with all her stores when her captors were unable to pass a shoal in taking her out of the Red River.

Robert Habersham

(SwStr: t. 173)

Robert Habersham was built in 1860 at Savannah, Ga. She served the Confederates as a transport in the Savannah area.

Robert E. Lee *was one of the most successful Confederate blockade runners of the war.*

Ram C.S.S. Selma.

Robert McClelland, see *Pickens*

Roebuck

(SwStr: t. 164; l. 147'; b. 23'; dph. 5')

Roebuck was built in 1857 at Brownsville, Pa., and chartered during the Civil War by the Texas Marine Department [See Annex III]. She served the Confederate Army as an unarmed cottonclad transport off the coast of Texas.

Rosina

(SwStr: t. 1,391; l. 260'; b. 33'; dph. 15'; dr. 9'; s. 14 k.; cl. *Rosina*)

Rosina was on order for the Confederate Navy in Great Britain when war ended. She was Jones, Quiggin & Co.'s Hull No. 174, begun at Liverpool in 1864 or 1865; little else is known of her except that she was one of a pair, the largest of the Navy's blockade-runner designs, and would have carried 1,500 bales of cotton.

Roundout

(SwStr)

Roundout, a Confederate transport, was captured in the Rappahannock River by the Potomac Flotilla in April 1862.

Royal Yacht

(Sch: t. 40; dr. 6'6''; cpl. 15; a. 1 12-pdr.)

On 10 October 1861 *Royal Yacht*, reputed to be the fastest schooner on the Texas coast, was chartered by Comdr. W. W. Hunter, CSN, for naval patrol duty off Galveston. Five days later she was damaged by a violent squall which caused the loss of her bowsprit. She was armed by the 23d and went on station between Bolivar and East Points. About 0230, 8 November, *Royal Yacht* was surprised at anchor outside Bolivar Point Lighthouse and, "after a desperate encounter," set afire by Lts. J. E. Jouett and J. G. Mitchell, commanding the first and second launches from USS *Santee*, blockading the port. Capt. T. Chubb and others were captured, but eventually paroled. At 0330, the watch on CSS *Bayou City* lowered their boats to investigate and extinguished the fire with a few buckets of water, minutes before the magazine would certainly have exploded. At 0900, *Royal Yacht* was towed alongside *General Rusk* to remove arms and ammunition; her upper hamper was ruined but hull intact. On 11 November she was returned to Captain Charles Chubb, father of her captain, also part owner.

On 10 May 1862, Col. J. J. Cook, Confederate States Artillery, asked Commander Hunter to "deliver to Capt. Thomas Chubb as many arms and equipment as will suffice him to fit out his schooner, the *Royal Yacht*, for harbor service." She is known to have served again with *Bayou City* off Galveston as late as the end of October. Some time during the next 5 months, she was fitted out as a blockade runner for, on 15 April 1863, the schooner was overhauled by a boat from U.S. Bark *William G. Anderson* and sent to be condemned by the Key West prize court, along with her 97 bales of best cotton. The bark had not been able to outsail *Royal Yacht* but her second cutter, after a hard 6½-hour chase, placed the quarry within range of a one-pounder Butler rifle and induced Captain Chubb to surrender once more.

Ruby

(SwStr: t. 1,391; l. 260'; b. 33'; dph. 15'; dr. 9'; s. 14 k.; cl. *Rosina*)

Ruby would certainly have attracted attention as the Confederate Navy's largest blockade-runner design, had she been completed in time to serve. All that is now certain of her history is the fact that she was laid down at the Jones, Quiggin yard, largest builder for the Confederacy in the United Kingdom. She was ordered by Comdr. J. D. Bulloch, CSN, in Liverpool during 1864.

Ruthven, see *A. S. Ruthven*

Sachem

(ScStr: t. 197; l. 121'; b. 23'6''; dph. 7'6''; dr. 5'4''; cpl. 50; a. 2 32-pdr., 2 24-pdr.)

Sachem was built in 1844 at New York, N.Y., and was sold to the U.S. Navy in 1861 for use as a gunboat. On 8 September 1863 she participated with other Federal gunboats besieging Fort Manahassett at Sabine Pass, Tex. A shot from the fort blew up her boilers, and she was run down and captured by the Confederate steam gunboat *Uncle Ben*. At the time of her capture *Sachem* was armed with four 32-pounders and one 30-pounder Parrott rifle, which were immediately removed by the Confederates.

Sachem became part of the Texas Marine Department [See Annex III] and served the Confederate army at Sabine Pass. In the spring of 1864 she was fitted out to run the blockade and placed under the command of noted blockade runner John Davisson.

St. Francis No. 3

(SwStr: t. 219)

St. Francis No. 3, built at Jeffersonville, Ind., in 1858, served as an Army transport in western waters. In April 1862, while commanded by Captain Clendening she participated in a cotton burning expedition to prevent the capture and use of the valuable product by the Federals. Records of early 1863 indicate that she had been outfitted with cotton-cladding. *St. Francis No. 3* was lost in 1863.

St. Mary

(SwStr: t. 60; l. 89'9''; b. 15'; dph. 5'; dr. 4'; s. 3–4 k.; a. 1 24-pdr., 1 12-pdr.)

St. Mary, a small cotton-clad river steamer, was built at Plaquemine, La., early in 1862, and presented to the Confederate Government. Under the command of Lt. F. E. Shepperd, CSN, she operated in the Yazoo and Tallahatchie Rivers in 1863. She was captured at Yazoo City, Miss., on 13 July by a joint Army-Navy expedition consisting of four Federal ships and 5,000 troops. She was taken into the United States Navy under the name of *Alexandria* and commissioned in December at Cairo, Ill.

St. Mary's see under *James Battle*

St. Nicholas, see *Rappahannock*

St. Patrick

(ScTB: l. 30'; cpl. 6; a. 1 torpedo)

St. Patrick, a submersible torpedo boat which could "be sunk and raised as desired," was built privately at Mobile, Ala., by John P. Halligan in 1864. She was transferred to the Confederate States Army on 24 January 1865, but placed under the command of Lt. J. T. Walker, CSN. An hour after midnight on 28 January this little vessel struck the Federal ship *Octorara* abaft her wheelhouse with a torpedo which misfired and did no damage. When the Federals returned artillery and musket fire *St. Patrick* escaped to the protection of the Confederate batteries at Mobile.

St. Philip

(SwStr: t. 1,172; l. 228'4''; b. 32'8''; dph. 24'6''; s. 11.5 k.; a. 2 68-pdr., 4 32-pdr.)

St. Philip was originally *San Juan*, built for

$250,000 by Jeremiah Simonson at Greenpoint, N.Y., in 1852, brigantine-rigged, with two vertical beam engines, and sailed as the noted passenger steamer *Star of the West* which operated between New York and the California coast. In January 1861 she was chartered by the Federal Government to carry reinforcements to Fort Sumter in the harbor of Charleston, S.C. Within sight of the fort, she was greeted by fire from harbor defense guns manned by cadets from the Citadel Military Academy, and was compelled to return to New York without accomplishing her mission. The Federal Government again chartered her 3 months afterwards to carry troops from the coast of Texas to New York, but on 17 April she was captured by the Confederate Army steamer *General Rusk* and sent to New Orleans. There the Confederate Navy employed her as a receiving ship and renamed her *St. Philip*.

With the impending surrender of New Orleans in April 1862, *St. Philip* was sent up the Yazoo River with Confederate specie on board. In March 1863, when Rear Adm. D. D. Porter attempted to outflank Vicksburg by a naval expedition through the Yazoo Pass, the Confederates sank her to obstruct the channel of the Tallahatchie River, above the Yalobusha's mouth at Fort Pemberton.

Sallie Wood(s)

(SwStr: t. 256)

Sallie Wood, also referred to as *Sallie Ward*, was built in 1860 at Paducah, Ky. She operated as a Confederate transport but was laid up above Eastport, Miss., when captured on 8 February 1862 by USS *Conestoga* at Chickasaw, Alabama.

Sam Kirkman

(StwStr: t. 271)

Sam Kirkman was built in 1857 at Paducah, Ky. She operated on the Tennessee River, and may have served the Confederate Army, probably as a cargo ship. At the approach of Federal gunboats, Confederate troops burned *Sam Kirkman* at Florence, Ala., on 8 February 1862, to keep her from falling into Union hands.

Sampson

(SwStr: dr. 8'; cpl. 49; a. 1 32-pdr. sb., 1 12-pdr.)

CSS *Sampson*, sometimes spelled *Samson*, was employed as a tugboat, prior to her purchase by the Confederate Government in 1861.

On 7 November 1861 this ship, *Sampson*, Lt. J. S. Kennard, CSN stood out with other gunboats of Commodore Josiah Tattnall's squadron to engage the heavy ships of Rear Admiral DuPont at the battle of Port Royal, S.C. The Confederates finally were forced to withdraw to Skull Creek. After the naval bombardment and evacuation of Port Royal's defensive works, *Sampson* helped transport a number of the retreating garrison to Savannah. Later in the month she exchanged shots with Federal forces off Fort Pulaski, Ga., and in January 1862, with two others of Tattnall's squadron, ran past the Federal ships in the Savannah River to provision Fort Pulaski. *Sampson* received considerable damage in this encounter.

Thereafter she served as receiving ship at Savannah and on 16 November 1863 returned to combat duty, patrolling the Savannah River with the defense force of Flag Officer W. W. Hunter, CSN. In early December 1864 she joined with *Macon* and *Resolute* in an expedition to destroy the Charleston and Savannah Railway bridge spanning the Savannah River, and sustained considerable damage. Prior to the capture of Savannah by General Sherman on 21 December 1864 *Sampson* was taken up the river to Augusta, remaining there until the end of the war.

Samuel Hill

(Str)

Samuel Hill, a transport, served Confederate forces in the Mississippi and Yazoo Rivers.

Samuel Orr

(Str)

Samuel Orr was a steamer in use as a hospital boat on the Tennessee River at the time Fort Henry was surrendered to Union Forces on 6 February 1862. She was burned the following day at the mouth of the Duck River to prevent her capture by the Federal gunboats.

Sand Fly

(Launch)

Sand Fly, together with the launch *Mosquito* and the schooner *Manassas*, was assigned to the command of Lt. W. H. Murdaugh on 27 August 1861, by Flag Officer S. Barron, CSN, commanding the naval defense of Virginia and North Carolina. On 29 August 1861 Lieutenant Murdaugh was seriously wounded in the attack on Fort Hatteras and unable to assume his command.

Santa Maria

(IrcScFr: t. 3,200 gr.; l. 270'; b. 50'; dph. 22')

Santa Maria, also known as *Glasgow* or *Frigate No. 61* while on the ways at Clydebank, never received her Confederate name: To Secretary Mallory, Commander Bulloch and their circle, she was simply "North's ship," after Comdr. James H. North, CSN, who ordered and was largely responsible for her. The British Government, under diplomatic pressure from the United States, canceled the £182,000 contract of 21 May 1862, arranged through intermediaries by Commander North, and sold her to the Danish Navy, where she was long known as HDMS *Danmark*.

Satellite

(SwGbt: t. 217; l. 120'7''; b. 22'9''; dph. 8'6''; cpl. 40; a. 1 8'', 1 30-pdr. r.)

Satellite, a wooden sidewheeler bought by the U.S. Navy in July 1861, was commissioned 27 September 1861 and assigned to the Potomac Flotilla. She enjoyed a successful career, capturing five ships and aiding in the capture of four others. The night of 23–4 August 1863 she was surprised, boarded, and captured at the mouth of the Rappahannock River by a Confederate boat expedition led by Lt. J. T. Wood. *Satellite* aided in capturing three Union schooners in Chesapeake Bay before being sent into Port Royal, Va. There, 9 days after her capture, she was stripped and scuttled amidst bombardment from Union forces.

Savannah

(SwStr: t. 406; a. 1 32-pdr.)

Savannah, later called *Old Savannah*, was formerly the steamer *Everglade* built in 1856 at New York, N.Y. She was purchased early in 1861 by the State of Georgia and converted into a gunboat for coast defense. With Georgia's admission to the Confederacy, *Savannah*, under Lt. J. N. Maffitt, CSN, was commissioned by the Confederate States Navy. She was attached to the squadron of Flag Officer J. Tattnall, CSN, charged with the naval defense of South Carolina and Georgia.

On 5–6 November, *Savannah*, flying Tattnall's flag, in company with *Resolute*, *Sampson*, and *Lady Davis*, offered harrassing resistance to a much larger Union fleet, under Flag Officer S. F. Du Pont, USN, preparing to attack Confederate strongholds at Port Royal Sound, S.C. On 7 November *Savannah* fired on the heavy Union ships as they bombarded Forts Walker and Beauregard. Driven finally by the Federal gunboats into Skull Creek, S.C., Tattnall disembarked with a landing party in an abortive attempt to support the fort's garrison, and *Savannah* returned to Savannah to repair damages.

On 26 November 1861, *Savannah*, in company with *Resolute* and *Sampson*, all under Flag Officer Tattnall, weighed anchor from under the guns of Fort Pulaski, S.C., and made a brave but brief attack on Union vessels at the mouth of the Savannah River. On 28 January 1862 the same three vessels delivered supplies to the fort despite the spirited opposition of Federal ships. *Savannah* later assisted in the unsuccessful defense of Fort Pulaski on 10–11 April 1862, and for the remainder of the year served as a receiving ship at Savannah.

Her name was changed to *Oconee* on 28 April 1863 and in June she was loaded with cotton and dispatched to England to pay for much-needed supplies. After some delay she escaped to sea only to founder on 18 August during bad weather. A boat with four officers and 11 men was captured 2 days later; the remainder of her crew escaped.

(IrcRam: l. 150' bp.; b. 34'; dph. 14'; s. 7 k.; dr. 12'6''; s. 6 k.; cpl. 180; a. 2 7'' r., 2 6.4'' r.; type *Richmond*)

CSS *Savannah* was an ironclad steam sloop built by H. F. Willink for the Confederacy at Savannah, Ga., in 1863. On 30 June 1863 she was transferred to naval forces in the Savannah River under the command of Flag Officer W. W. Hunter, CSN. Under Comdr. R. F. Pinkney, CSN, she maintained her reputation as the most efficient vessel of the squadron and was kept ready for service. She remained on the river and was burned by the Confederates on 21 December 1864 when Savannah, Ga., was threatened by the approach of Gen. W. T. Sherman, USA.

(PvtrSch: t. 53; l. 56'; b. 17'; dph. 6'; cpl. 20; a. 1 pivot gun)

T. Harrison Baker and seven Charleston businessmen, owners of *Charleston Pilot Boat #7*, applied for letter of marque, 13 May 1861, received a privateer's commission the 18th, and cleared Charleston, S.C., 2 June. The following day, *Savannah* captured Rockland, Me., brig *Joseph*, Capt. Meyer, Cardenas to Philadelphia with muscovado sugar. Captain Baker put Pilot James Evans on board as prizemaster to sail *Joseph* and 6 prisoners into Charleston. There brig and cargo, valued at $30,000, were condemned by the South Carolina District Court sitting in Admiralty—as "a good and legal prize."

In the meantime, 3 June, U.S. Brig *Perry* caught *Savannah* and sent her under Midshipman R. S. McCook to New York, where she in turn was condemned and sold by the prize court. Captain Baker and crew were transferred from *Perry* to Blockading Squadron flagship *Minnesota* the 5th; after a 10-day patrol, the prisoners were transshipped in Hampton Roads to USRC *Harriet Lane* and eventually incarcerated in the Tombs, New York City, to await trial for "piracy."

On 6 July President Davis protested to President Lincoln, threatening retaliation if the 13 were executed. The "piracy" case was to set precedent: It attracted notoriety North and South— no less because the trial of privateer brig *Jefferson Davis'* William W. Smith and his prize-crew from recaptured schooner *Enchantress* was taking place concurrently at Philadelphia.

The "Baker's dozen" were arraigned, 17 July, in U.S. Circuit Court, New York, and all pleaded "not guilty." Trial began 23 October; by then one of the seamen, Albert G. Ferris, had turned state's evidence. The jury went out the seventh day but remained deadlocked after 20 hours. A new trial was called for. But the Confederate Congress, 30 August, authorized their President to employ the ultimate in retaliation. On 9 November, Brigadier General J. H. Winder, CSA, Provost Marshal of Richmond, responsible for all prisoner-of-war camps, was ordered to select 14 hostages, of the very highest rank available, to be hanged if Prizemaster Smith, already condemned to die in Philadelphia, and each of the unlucky 13 in New York were executed. In February 1862 the United States backed down, accorded *privateersman* status to all the arraigned. They were exchanged the following summer. Although "pirate" continued to be a popular, even overworked word in the North, there were no more "piracy" trials per se. *Savannah* was purchased from the New York Prize Court 2 July 1861 and became USS *Choptank* in the Potomac Flotilla.

Schultz

(SwStr: t. 164)

Schultz, also known as *A. H. Schultz*, was built

at New York, N.Y. She served the Confederates in the James River, Va., as a flag-of-truce boat, and was probably armed. *Schultz* was accidentally blown up in the James River by a Confederate torpedo which may have drifted from its original position.

Scorpion

(ScTB: l. 46'; b. 6'3"; dph. 3'9"; a. 1 5"-dia., 18' spar with percussion torp.; cl. *Squib*)

CSS *Scorpion* was procured late in 1864 by the Confederate States Navy and armed with a spar torpedo fitted to her stem. She performed picket duty in the James River under command of Lt. E. Lakin, CSN.

On 23–25 January 1865 torpedo boats *Scorpion*, *Hornet* and *Wasp*, under overall command of Lt. C. W. Read, CSN, joined Flag Officer J. K. Mitchell's James River Squadron in the abortive attack on General Grant's main supply base at City Point, Va. Attempting to rejoin her consort, ironclad *Richmond*, aground above Trent's Reach, *Scorpion* ended up fast ashore also and was severely damaged by the magazine explosion which destroyed nearby gunboat CSS *Drewry*, 24 January. Abandoned, she fell into Federal hands.

Scotland

(SwStr: t. 567; l. 230'; b. 27'; dph. 7')

Scotland was built in 1855 at Jeffersonville, Ind. She served the Confederates as a transport in the Mississippi River area, and became part of the force under Comdr. I. N. Brown, CSN, commanding Confederate vessels in the Yazoo River. In July 1863 *Scotland* was burned by Commander Brown, and her hulk sunk in the Yazoo River, 15 miles below Greenwood, Miss., to block the channel and delay the advance of Union forces under Maj. General W. T. Sherman, USA, towards Vicksburg.

Sea Bird

(SwStr: t. 202; cpl. 42; a. 1 32-pdr. sb., 1 30-pdr. r.)

CSS *Sea Bird*, built at Keyport, N.J., in 1854, was purchased by North Carolina at Norfolk, Va., in 1861 and fitted for service with the Confederate States Navy. She was assigned to duty along the Virginia and North Carolina coasts with Lt. P. McCarrick, CSN, in command. *Sea Bird* served as the flagship of Confederate Flag Officer W. F. Lynch's "mosquito fleet" during the hard-fought battles in defense of Roanoke

Island on 7–8 February 1862, and Elizabeth City, N.C., on the 10th when she was rammed and sunk by USS *Commodore Perry*.

Seaboard

(SwTug: t. 59)

Seaboard was a wooden towboat built at Philadelphia in 1859 and first owned in Norfolk, Va. Confederate military authorities acquired her in 1861 and turned her over to the Engineer Corps, CSA, for operation during most of the war. She was captured by the Federal army and USS *Lilac* at the upper or Tree Hill bridge over the James below Richmond, 4 April 1865.

As a prize of war, passing the obstructions at Drewry's Bluff, *Seaboard* hit a snag and had to be run aground to prevent her sinking in deep water. By July the little tug came to be remembered as a storm center of interservice acrimony when Col. J. B. Howard, local Army Quartermaster, raised and sent her to Norfolk for repairs; Admiral William Radford, USN, claimed her as "original captor."

Segar, Seger or Segur, see *A. B. Seger*

Selma

(SwGbt: l. 252′; b. 30′; dr. 6′; dph. 6′; s. 9 k.; cpl. 65 to 94; a. 2 9″ sb., 1 8″ sb., 1 6.4″ r.)

CSS *Selma* was a coastwise packet built at Mobile for the Mobile Mail Line in 1856. Little doubt now remains that she was originally named *Florida*. As the latter, she was inspected and accepted by Capt. Lawrence Rousseau, CSN, 22 April 1861, acquired by the Confederacy in June, cut down, strengthened by hog frames and armed as a gunboat—all, apparently, in the Lake Pontchartrain area. Her upper deck was plated at this time with ⅜″-iron, partially protecting her boilers, of the low-pressure type preferred for fuel economy and greater safety in battle. CSS *Florida* is cited on 12 November 1861 as already in commission and serving Commodore Hollins' New Orleans defense flotilla under command of Lt. Charles W. Hays, CSN.

The *Mobile Evening News* editorialized early in December on the startling change "from her former gay, first-class hotel appearance, having been relieved of her upper works and painted as black as the inside of her smokestack. She carries a jib forward and, we suppose, some steering sail aft, when requisite."

Although much of *Florida's* time was spent blockaded in Mobile, she made some forays into Mississippi Sound, two of which alarmed the U.S. Navy's entire Gulf command: On 19 October *Florida* convoyed a merchantman outside. Fortunately for her the coast was clear of Union ships and batteries, for *Florida* fouled the area's main military telegraph line with her anchor and had no sooner repaired the damage than she went aground for 36 hours. Luck returning, she tried out her guns on USS *Massachusetts*, "a large three-masted propeller" she mistook for the faster *R. R. Cuyler*. Being of shallower draft and greater speed, she successfully dodged *Massachusetts* in shoal water off Ship Island. The havoc caused by one well-placed shot with her rifled pivot gun is described by Commander Melancton Smith, USN, commanding *Massachusetts*: "It entered the starboard side abaft the engine five feet above the water line, cutting entirely through 18 planks of the main deck, carried away the table, sofas, eight sections of iron steam pipe, and exploded in the stateroom on the port side, stripping the bulkheads of four rooms, and setting fire to the vessel . . . 12 pieces of the fragments have been collected and weigh 58 pounds."

The first sortie by *Florida* caused consternation. Capt. L. M. Powell, USN, in command at Ship Island—soon to be main advance base for the New Orleans campaign—wrote to Flag Officer McKean, 22 October, "The first of the reported gun steamers made her experimental trial trip on the *Massachusetts*, and, if she be a sample of the rest, you may perhaps consider that Ship Island and the adjacent waters will require a force of a special kind in order to hold them to our use. . . . The caliber and long range of the rifled cannon from which the shell that exploded in the *Massachusetts* was fired established the ability of these fast steam gunboats to keep out of the range of all broadside guns, and enables them to disregard the armament or magnitude of all ships thus armed, or indeed any number of them, when sheltered by shoal water."

Protecting CSS *Pamlico*, in contrasting white dress and laden with some 400 troops, "the black rebel steamer" *Florida* on 4 December had a brush with USS *Montgomery* in Horn Island Pass that caused jubilation in the Southern press. Comdr. T. Darrah Shaw of *Montgomery*, finding his 10-inch shell gun no match for *Florida's* long-range rifles, signaled Comdr. Melancton Smith for assistance, and when it was not forthcoming, ran back to safety under the guns of Ship Island. Shaw saved *Montgomery* and lost his command for fleeing from the enemy: Commodore McKean promptly sent Lieutenant Jouett to relieve him and forwarded Shaw's action report to Secretary Welles, noting, "It needs no comment." Crowed *Richmond Dispatch* on 14 December, quoting *Mobile Evening News*, "The *Florida* fought at great disadvantage in one respect, owing to her steering apparatus being out of order, but showed a decided superiority in the effectiveness of her armament. That gun which scared the *Massachusetts* so badly, and had nearly proved fatal to her, is evidently a better piece or must be better handled than any which the enemy have." With the advent of cruiser *Florida*, she was renamed *Selma*, in July 1862, Lt. Peter U. Murphey, CSN, assuming command.

On 5 February 1863, while steaming down Mobile Bay with 100 extra men in search of a blockader to carry by boarding, *Selma* was bilged by a snag in crossing Dog River Bar, entrance to Mobile, and sank in 8 feet of water. Pumped out hastily, she was back in service the 13th— probably already a receiving ship.

By the following year, *Selma*, *Morgan* and *Gaines*, the only ships capable of defending lower Mobile Bay, were having a serious problem with deserting seamen, and intelligence reported *Selma's* crew as having fallen as low as 15 men about mid-February. At the crucial battle of 5 August 1864, *Selma* particularly annoyed Farragut by a steady raking fire as she stood off *Hartford's* bow. After passing the forts, Farragut ordered gunboat *Metacomet* cast loose from *Hartford* to pursue *Selma*. After an hour-long running fight, Murphey, unable to escape to shallows out of reach, had to surrender to faster, more heavily armed *Metacomet*. *Selma* lost 7 killed and 8 wounded, including her captain.

She was sold at New Orleans, 12 July 1865, being redocumented as a merchant ship the following month.

Sharp

(Str)

The Confederate steamer *Sharp* was employed by the army as a despatch boat and transport in the Tallahatchie River. She was used to transport troops and ammunition in the Yazoo River in March 1863. *Sharp* reportedly was burned and scuttled by order of Commander Brown, CSN, in the Sunflower River in August 1863.

Shenandoah

(ScStr: t. 1,152; l. 222'7''; b. 32'8''; dph. 20'6''; s. 9 k. under steam; cpl. 109; a. 4 8'' sb., 2 32-pdr. r., 2 12-pdr.)

CSS *Shenandoah*, formerly *Sea King*, was an iron-framed, teak-planked, full-rigged vessel with auxiliary steam power. She was designed as a British transport for troops to the East, built on the River Clyde, Scotland, and purchased by the Confederate Government in 1864 for use as an armed cruiser. On 8 October she sailed from London ostensibly for Bombay. India, on a trading voyage. She rendezvoused at Funchal, Madeira, with the steamer *Laurel*, bearing officers and the nucleus of a crew for *Sea King*, together with naval guns, ammunition, and stores. Commanding Officer Lt. J. I. Waddell, CSN, supervised her conversion to a ship-of-war in nearby waters. Waddell was barely able, however, to bring his crew to half strength even with additional volunteers from *Sea King* and *Laurel*. The new cruiser was commissioned on 19 October and her name changed to *Shenandoah*.

In accord with operational concepts originated in the Confederate Navy Department and developed by its agents in Europe, *Shenandoah* was assigned to destroy commerce in areas as yet undisturbed; thereafter her course lay in pursuit of merchantmen on the Cape of Good Hope-Australia route and of the Pacific whaling fleet. En route to the Cape she picked up six prizes. Five of these were put to the torch or scuttled; the other was bonded and employed for transport of prisoners to Bahia, Brazil. Still short-handed, though her crew had been increased by forced enlistments from prizes, *Shenandoah* arrived at Melbourne, Australia, on 25 January 1865, where she filled her complement and her storerooms.

Shenandoah had taken but a single prize in the Indian Ocean, but hunting became more profitable as she approached the whaling grounds. Waddell burned four whalers in the Carolines and another off the Kuriles. After a 3-week cruise in the ice and fog of the Sea of Okhotsk failed to yield a single prize, due to a warning which had preceded him, Waddell headed north past the Aleutian Islands into the Bering Sea and the Arctic Ocean. On 23 June he learned from a prize of Lee's surrender and the flight from Richmond of the Confederate Government 10 weeks previously. Nevertheless, he elected to continue hostilities, and captured 21 more prizes,

C.S.S. Shenandoah *destroys whalers off Cape Thaddeus in the Arctic Ocean, 23 June 1865.*

the last 11 being taken in the space of 7 hours in the waters just below the Arctic Circle.

Waddell then ran south to intercept commerce bound from the West Coast to the Far East and Latin America, and on 2 August received intelligence from a British bark of the war's termination some 4 months before. Immediately *Shenandoah* underwent physical alteration. She was dismantled as a man-of-war; her battery was dismounted and struck below, and her hull painted to resemble an ordinary merchant vessel. Waddell brought her into Liverpool on 6 November and surrendered her to British authorities who turned her over to the United States.

Shenandoah had remained at sea for 12 months and 17 days, had traversed 58,000 miles and captured 38 prizes, mostly whalers——two-thirds of them after the close of hostilities.

After the war, *Shenandoah* was sold and served various owners along the trade routes. She was lost in the Indian Ocean in 1879 while under the flag of the Sultan of Zanzibar.

Shrapnel

CSS *Shrapnel*, a small craft, apparently unarmed, was very actively employed in the James River, Va., with Acting Master J. Trower, CSN, in command. She served to tow fire craft, deliver mail and torpedoes, and as a picket boat in 1864–1865. She was among the ships destroyed by

the Confederates during evacuation of Richmond, Va., on 3 April 1865.

"Sinclair's Ship," see *Texas* (corvette)

Skirwan

(Str)

Skirwan appears to have been one of the smaller river steamers valuable to the Confederates on the Roanoke as a transport and storeship for most of the war. She was seized with *Fisher, Cotton Plant,* and *Egypt Mills* in May 1865 at Halifax, N.C., and became useful to Comdr. W. H. Macomb, USN, as a mail and despatch boat.

Slidell

(Gbt: a. 8 guns)

Slidell was built at New Orleans in early 1862. She was destroyed on the Tennessee River prior to 6 February 1863.

Snipe

(SwStr: t. [645]; l. 225'; b. 24'; dph. 11'; dr. 6''; cl. *Curlew*)

Snipe was the last ship christened in what may have been the only quadruple launching for the Confederate Navy. She was Hull No. 180 in the Jones, Quiggin yard at Liverpool on order for Comdr. J. D. Bulloch, CSN, and launched with her sisters the same day in 1865. Her completion could hardly have taken place before the war's close.

Sovereign

(SwStr: t. 336)

Sovereign, built in 1855 at Shousetown, Pa., performed transport duties in western waters for the Confederacy until 5 June 1862 when she was captured near Island No. 37 in the Mississippi River by a tug under Lt. J. Bishop. A member of her crew loyal to the Union remained on board after she had been run aground, her machinery set to explode, and abandoned near Memphis. He prevented her destruction and enabled the Federals to seize her for future employment as a storeship for the Mississippi Squadron.

Sphinx, see Stonewall

Spray

(StGbt: a. 2 guns)

CSS *Spray*, a small, high-pressure steamer, operated in the vicinity of the naval station at St. Marks, Fla., during 1863–65, and was the object of much attention by the Federal forces in that vicinity. She was commanded by Lts. C. W. Hays and Henry H. Lewis, CSN. *Spray* surrendered to the Federal forces late in May 1865.

Squib

(ScTB: l. 46'; b. 6'3"; dph. 3'9"; cpl. 6; a. 5" dia., 18'-spar with percussion torpedo; cl. *Squib*)

CSS *Squib*, also referred to as *Infanta*, was a small torpedo boat in the service of the Confederate States Navy in 1864. She operated in the James River. Her armament consisted of one spar torpedo.

On the night of 9 April 1864 Lt. H. Davidson, CSN, the Confederate torpedo expert, sailed *Squib* through the Federal fleet off Newport News, Va., and exploded 53 pounds of powder against the side of flagship *Minnesota* before returning up the James River to safety. The torpedo was exploded too near the surface to achieve maximum effect, and *Minnesota* escaped without serious damage. For his gallant and meritorious conduct in the performance of this exploit Hunter Davidson was promoted to the rank of commander in the Confederate States Navy. Final disposition of *Squib* has not been established.

Staerkodder, see Stonewall

Stag

(SwStr: t. 600 [771]; l. 230'; b. 26'; dph. 9'6" [10'9"]; dr. 7'6"; sp. 16 k.; cl. *Owl*)

Stag was a fast, modern, steel paddle-steamer built for the Confederate Navy at Liverpool as Jones, Quiggin & Co.'s Hull No. 169 in 1864 to the order of Comdr. James D. Bulloch, CSN. A superior ship, "one of a number of steamers to be run under the direction of the Navy Department," she sailed from the Mersey on her maiden voyage in August, getting away from Nassau about 1 September. She was busily running out of the Carolinas—Charleston and Wilmington—the rest of the year, to Nassau or Bermuda.

Secretary Mallory wrote Lt. Richard H. Gayle, Provisional Navy, C.S., 6 December 1864, "It is understood that the new steamer *Stag*, now at Wilmington, will be at once turned over to this Department." Gayle relieved British Captain J. M. Burroughs (cf. *Cornubia*,) formal transfer taking place about the 12th, as arranged by William H. Peters, special (fiscal) agent, C.S. Navy Department, Wilmington. Their correspondence, however, suggests this was not the *Stag* renamed *Kate Gregg* in October, as reported by the U.S. Consul in Nassau, but an older and larger *Stag* with capacity for 1,200 cotton bales whereas the new *Owl*-class *Stag* was unmistakably rated at only 850 bales on a draft of 7'6".

Capt. J. F. Green, USN, Senior Officer Offshore Blockade, can be thanked for preserving in Official records, "Rumor says that the *Stag* is to be converted into" a gunboat, along with *Badger* (destroyed about this time)—ironic in view of the sequel: five months later Admiral D. D. Porter, USN, victor over Fort Caswell that protected Wilmington, wrote from Smithville, N.C., 20 January 1865, "I had the blockade runners' lights lit last night, and was obliging enough to answer their signals, whether right or wrong we don't know . . . *Stag* and *Charlotte*, from Bermuda, loaded with arms, blankets, shoes, etc., came in and quietly anchored near the [flagship] *Malvern* [v. *William G. Hewes*] and were taken possession of . . . I intrusted this duty to Lt. [William B.] Cushing [in *Monticello*], who performed it with his usual good luck and intelligence. These two are very fast vessels and valuable prizes. They threw a portion of their papers overboard immediately on finding they were trapped . . . The *Stag* received three shots in her as she ran by our blockaders outside." Thus the curtain fell at 0200, the 20th, in New Inlet, N.C.; on the 24th, "hatches battened down" and hold "not entered", *Stag* was ordered to New York under a prize master, Actg. Master E. S. Goodwin, USN.

She was sold that year to F. Nickerson of Boston and became an asset to his coastwise service to New York and New Orleans as *Zenobia*. In 1867 George Savary & Co. bought her; resold 17 November in Buenos Aires for $82,000, she disappeared from the North American scene, although she is believed to have lived on until 1885 or later.

Star

(Tug: t. 250; cpl. 40)

Star, an unarmed high-pressure steam tug, was chartered by the Confederate Army from the Southern Steamship Co., New Orleans, La., in May 1861.

Early in April 1862 she was placed with several other steamers under Captain Stevenson, CSA, to handle the fire rafts with which the Confederates illuminated the channel below Forts Jackson and St. Philip against passage of Farragut's fleet assembled there. During the ensuing battle at the forts on 24 April *Star* was employed as a telegraph station attached to the command of Comdr. J. K. Mitchell, CSN. The steamer was destroyed by a Federal gunboat during the action.

Farragut's testimony in 1872 credited *Star* with one gun and 40 men; the gun is questionable but all sources agree she was commanded by a Captain LaPlace.

Star of the West, see St. Philip

Starlight

(Str)

Starlight, a Confederate steamer, was active in the Mississippi River. She reportedly transported released Confederate prisoners of war in the region of Port Hudson during early May 1863. On 26 May she was seized in Thompson's Creek, north of Port Hudson, by Union Army forces commanded by Colonel Prince. During the remainder of 1863 and 1864 *Starlight* was employed by the Union as a transport in the Red and Mississippi Rivers.

State of Georgia, see Georgia

Stonewall

(IrcRam: t. 900; l. 171'10"; b. 32'8"; dr. 14'4"; s. 10 k.; a. 1 300-pdr. r., 2 70-pdr. r.)

Stonewall, a powerful armored seagoing ram, was built by L. Arman at Bordeaux, France, in 1863–64 for the Confederate States Government; however, the French authorities refused to permit her delivery, following strong protests by American Ministers Dayton and Bigelow. The vessel was eventually sold to Denmark, via a Swedish intermediary, for use in the Schleswig-Holstein War. Because she failed to reach Copenhagen before the sudden termination of the war, the Danes refused acceptance, and title to the ram, now known as *Sphinxs*, was returned to her builder who then sold her to the Confederates.

In December 1864 Capt. T. J. Page, CSN, took command, renamed the vessel *Stonewall*, and in January sailed from Copenhagen for Quiberon Bay, France, to receive supplies. In this period she was called *Staerkodder* or *Olinde* to allay suspicion of her actual ownership and mission. *Stonewall* was assigned the considerable tasks of dispersing the Federal blockading fleet off Wilmington, N.C., intercepting Northern commerce between California and Northern ports, attacking New England coastal cities, and destroying the Yankee fishing fleet on the Newfoundland Banks.

Unable to replenish fully in French waters, *Stonewall* sailed for Madeira, but ran into a severe storm and had to put in to Ferrol, Spain, for coal and repairs. While she was there *Niagara* and *Sacramento* arrived at Coruña, only 9 miles distant. On 24 March *Stonewall* steamed out of Ferrol and prepared for battle; however when the Federals, believing her gun power to be too great, declined to close she bore away for Lisbon to coal before crossing the Atlantic.

She reached Nassau, New Providence, on 6 May and went from there to Havana where Page learned of the war's end. *Stonewall* was turned over to the Captain General of Cuba in return for money needed to pay off her crew. In July 1865 the Cuban authorities voluntarily delivered her to the United States Government which later sold her to Japan, where she was known as HIJMS *Azuma*. (See also *Cheops, supra.*)

Stonewall Jackson

(SwRam: cpl. 30; a. 1 32-pdr. or 1 24-pdr.sb.)

Stonewall Jackson was selected in January 1862, by Capt. J. E. Montgomery to be part of the

Ram C.S.S. Stonewall.

Stonewall Jackson *was part of the River Defense Fleet destroyed when*
the North seized New Orleans.

River Defense Fleet [See Annex II]. On 25 January Montgomery began to convert her into a cottonclad ram by placing a 4-inch oak sheath with 1-inch iron covering on her bow, and by installing double pine bulkheads fitted with compressed cotton bales.

Stonewall Jackson's conversion was completed on 16 March 1862. Under Capt. G. M. Phillips she was detached from Montgomery's main force and sent to Forts Jackson and St. Philip on the lower Mississippi to cooperate in the Confederate defense of New Orleans. There, with five other vessels of Montgomery's fleet, all under Capt. J. A. Stevenson, she joined the force under Capt. J. K. Mitchell, CSN, commanding Confederate naval forces in the lower Mississippi.

On 24 April 1862 a Union fleet under Flag Officer D. G. Farragut, USN, ran past Forts Jackson and St. Philip on its way to capture New Orleans. In the engagement *Stonewall Jackson* rammed USS *Varuna*, which had already been struck by *Governor Moore*. With *Varuna*'s shot glancing off her bow, *Stonewall Jackson* backed off for another blow and struck again in the same place, crushing *Varuna*'s side. The shock of the blow turned the Confederate vessel, and she received five 8-inch shells from *Varuna*, abaft her armor. *Varuna* ran aground in a sinking condition, and *Stonewall Jackson*, chased by USS *Oneida* coming to *Varuna*'s rescue, was driven ashore and burned.

Stono

(Patent ScStr: t. 453; l. 171'6"; b. 31'4"; dph. 9'; a. 1 30-pdr., 8 8")

Stono, formerly USS *Isaac Smith*, was captured by masked batteries while reconnoitering in Stono River on 30 January 1863. She was taken into the Confederate Navy and put in service in the waters around Charleston, S.C., with Lt. W. G. Dozier, CSN, in command. Because of her great speed she was loaded with cotton, and attempted to run the blockade on 5 June 1863. She was wrecked on the breakwater near Fort Moultrie, S.C., at that time.

Sugg, see Tom Sugg

Sumter

(ScStr: t. 374 (499?); l. 184'; b. 30'; dph. 12'; s. 10 k.; a. 1 8" shell gun, 4 32-pdr.)

CSS *Sumter* was originally the bark-rigged steamer *Habana* of New Orleans, built at Philadelphia in 1859 for McConnell's New Orleans & Havana Line. Purchased at New Orleans in April 1861 and converted to a cruiser by Capt. Raphael Semmes, CSN, *Sumter* was commissioned there 3 June and put to sea on the 30th to strike at Union shipping. Eluding sloop-of-war *Brooklyn* in hot pursuit, *Sumter* cruised the West Indies and south to Maranhao, Brazil, capturing several prizes. Returned to Martinique, she was discovered in the act of coaling by USS *Iroquois;* Capt. J. S. Palmer, USN, promptly protested to local authorities and took position to intercept *Sumter* leaving St. Pierre. But 9 days later the raider escaped by night and steered for Spain, anchoring at Cadiz, 4 January 1862. Allowed only to make necessary repairs there, without refueling, she was forced to run for Gibraltar and lay up. Disarmed and sold at auction 19 December 1862 to the Fraser-Trenholm interests, *Sumter* quietly continued her service to the Confederacy under British colors as the blockade runner *Gibraltar* of Liverpool.

Though her career as a fighting ship had lasted scarcely six months, *Sumter* had taken 18 prizes, of which she burned 8, released or bonded 9; only one was recaptured. The diversion of Federal blockade ships to hunt her down had been in itself no insignificant service to the Confederate cause.

As *Gibraltar*, she ran at least once into Wilmington, N.C., under Capt. E. C. Reid, a Southerner. He sailed from Liverpool 3 July 1863 with a pair of 22-ton Blakely guns and other particularly valuable munitions, returning with a full load of cotton. The beginning of this voyage is recorded only because the U.S. Consul at the British port passionately protested *Gibraltar*'s being allowed to sail—ostensibly for Nassau—days before formal customs clearance: "She is one of the privileged class and not held down like other vessels to strict rules and made to conform to regulations." The arrival at Wilmington is also accidental matter of record today because of the troop transport *Sumter* tragedy at Charleston the same summer—which, until November, Admiral Dahlgren's intelligence understandably confused with the former cruiser *Sumter*, now *Gibraltar*.

Mr. Trenholm's son-in-law long maintained *Sumter* finally "went down in a gale near the spot where the *Alabama* was sunk," but supplied no date; one source suggests 1867. The last official

C.S.S. Sumter, *first of the Confederate commerce raiders to take to the high seas, leaves New Orleans, 18 June 1861.*

report of her seems to have been by the U.S. Consul at Liverpool, 10 July 1864: "The pirate *Sumter* (called *Gibraltar*) is laid up at Birkenhead."

———

(? ScTug: l. 80′; b. 18′; dph. 7′; t. 90; a. 1 or 2 20-pdrs. ?)

The existence of this James River tug, "about the size of the *Teaser*," mounting either a smooth bore or rifled 20-pounder or both, on pivots, is not confirmed by a Confederate source. The alleged *Sumter* and three similar small tugs, in part identified as *Raleigh* and *Patrick Henry*, were operating in defense of Richmond according to Commodore Charles Wilkes, reporting to Secretary of the Navy Welles from USS *Wachusett*, 12 September 1862, the only mention of her in published official records.

———

(SwStr)

This transport with high-pressure steam plant was approaching completion near Charleston the end of March 1863—whether newbuilt or refitted remains uncertain. *Sumter* is mentioned relatively frequently in official records as being particularly useful in the tidal rivers of South Carolina because of her light draft. Apparently under Army control, she rendered the Confederacy yeoman service as a troop and munitions carrier, principally in the Stono River and the general area about Charleston, and was not infrequently a desirable target for Federal monitors and sharpshooters besieging the city throughout August. On the 30th, *Sumter* offloaded the 27th and 28th Georgia Regiments, an artillery company and stores at Morris Island, embarking the 20th South Carolina and 23d Georgia Regiments with another artillery company—740 in all—for Ft. Gregg on Sullivan's Island. The Military District Commander, Brig. Gen. Roswell S. Ripley, CSA, reporting to Chief of Staff, 22 September, recounts the tragedy which ensued that August day: "So much time had been taken up, however, [loading troops] that the tide had fallen so low as to necessitate going by the main channel, and unfortunately the necessity had not been provided against by giving information to and establishing a signal with the batteries on Sullivan's Island. The steamer had run safely to the enemy's fleet and was coming up the channel when, being observed from Ft. Moultrie, fire was opened upon her. Before the officers in charge had learned this error several shots took effect, sinking the boat and causing the loss of arms and equipments. The troops on board were rescued by the garrison of Ft. Sumter, under Col. Alfred Rhett, and boats sent down by the Navy. Eight men were reported missing the next morning . . . " The death toll came to 40. *Sumter's* wreck became a landmark used in target practice for some days afterward.

Sunflower

(Str: 105 t.; l. 121'6''; b. 25'; dr. 3'9'')

Sunflower, an unarmed, cotton-clad, Confederate steamer probably built at Louisville, Ky., in 1857, and described in official records as a "good boat," was employed in and around the Sabine River in the latter part of 1862. As a unit of the army controlled Texas Marine Department [See Annex III] she assisted in removing obstructions to navigation in the Sabine River in January 1863. Her efforts in this operation contributed to the ensuing victory of CSS *Uncle Ben* and *Josiah A. Bell* over the Union sloop *Morning Light*, and schooner *Fairy*, formerly *Velocity*. During Octo-

ber 1863 she underwent repairs at Beaumont and returned to duty with Commander Hunter's Marine Brigade, carrying supplies. In April 1865 *Sunflower* reportedly was engaged in the cotton trade on Sabine Lake.

Superior

(Barge: a. 4 guns)

Superior served the Confederates in the rivers and waters off the Virginia and Carolina coasts.

Swaim, see J. D. Swaim

Swan

(Str: t. 487)

Swan, a river cargo steamer of Mobile, Ala., served the Confederates as a flag-of-truce boat at Mobile on 28 May 1861. She was captured off Key West, Fla., on 24 May 1862, with a cargo of cotton and resin, by the U.S. bark *Amanda* and the U.S. brig *Bainbridge*, and later was used by the U.S. Army.

(Yawl)

No particulars of the small, white-hulled sailing craft *Swan* or her consort, the black *Raven*, nor of their armament have come to light, but neither could a history of the Confederate States Navy omit to mention the so-called "Volunteer Coast Guard", which they formed. *Swan's* captain and leader of the expedition was restless, daring, tubercular University of Virginia graduate John Yates Beall, Master, CSN, by special commission issued 5 March 1863. Acting Master Edward McGuire commanded *Raven*, apparently a yawl.

Private enterprise and legal expediency were thoroughly mixed in the expedition: at least two of their 16 volunteers, Scotsmen Bennett G. Burley and John Maxwell, were also appointed Acting Masters, CSN. Although they were more or less regularly commissioned, their cutters were not; while Beall was empowered to accept enlistments and draw gear from the Navy, yet he and his guerrilla band wore no uniforms, were required to procure their own sea vehicles and pay their own wages out of prizes and cargoes they might capture.

Mathews County, the Virginian peninsula between Mobjack Bay and the Piankatank River, was home soil for the Beall raiders. Setting out from there 17 September 1863, that very day they captured sloop *Mary Anne* and some fishing scows off Raccoon Island; the next day schooner *Alliance*, carrying $200,000 worth of ships' stores for Port Royal, fell into their hands. Schooner *J. J. Houseman* was carried by boarding the following day and two more schooners, *Samuel Pearsall* and *Alexandria*, were taken the 20th.

Beall in the end had to strip all his prizes but *Alliance* and send them to sea as derelicts, all sail set; 14 prisoners were safely delivered to Richmond. *Houseman* and *Pearsall* were, however, recovered at sea by blockaders. He himself almost succeeded in sailing *Alliance* up the Piankatank but grounded the last minute at the river's mouth, on the bar at Milford Haven, Va., and had to burn her when a Federal blockader approached—yet Beall's men still managed to salvage over $10,000 worth of goods.

The "Marine Coast Guard", as they called it, became such a thorn in the Union side that in October a joint U.S. Navy/Army expedition under General Isaac J. Winstar, USA, with the entire 4th U.S. Colored Infantry, Pennsylvania and New York cavalry and light artillery detachments, USS *Commodore Jones*, *Putnam* and *Stepping Stones*, and 4 Army gunboats sealing avenues of escape, finally got McGuire by a dragnet across Mathews County.

Undaunted, Beall and party in *Swan* and *Raven* entered Tangier Sound and divided up for scouting. A boatload of Beall's raiders was trapped and captured on 14 November and one man hanged; they were terrified into revealing Beall's hideout so that he and the remaining Coast Guardsmen were discovered next day. Secretary of War Stanton wrote that the captured personnel "will be held for the present, not as prisoners of war but as pirates or marauding robbers." Beall escaped the noose but not for long; he figured prominently in the *Philo Parsons* (q.v.) affray only to stand into danger again in the mid-December Buffalo-Dunkirk affair, for which he was secretly executed, 18 February 1865. The Union was not deterred this time by threat of reprisals but made sure Beall was dead before the news of his capture reached the Confederacy.

T. D. Hine

(SwStr: t. 205; l. 147'; b. 30'; dph. 6')

T. D. Hine, also called *Hine*, was built at Jeffersonville, Ind., in 1860 and taken into Confederate service as a transport. She operated principally in the Mississippi and Red Rivers until capture by the Federals during 1865.

Tacony

(Bark: t. 296; dr. 12'; a. 1 12-pdr. how.)

Tacony, also called *Florida No. 2*, was built in 1856 at Newcastle, Del. While traveling in ballast from Port Royal, S.C., to Philadelphia, Pa., she was captured on 12 June 1863 by the brig *Clarence*, under Lt. C. W. Read, CSN, which in turn had been captured and then detached by CSS *Florida*. Lieutenant Read, finding *Tacony* a far better vessel than his own, transferred his force to her and burned *Clarence*. Now called *Florida No. 2* by her captors, *Tacony* sailed northward along the New England coast to harass Union shipping.

Between 12 June and 24 June *Tacony* captured 15 vessels. Her last prize captured on 24 June was the small fishing schooner *Archer*. By now subject to a frantic and intensive search by the U.S. Navy, Lieutenant Read transferred his force to *Archer*, hoping to avoid his pursuers. He burned *Tacony* on the same day 25 June 1863.

Tallahassee

(ScStr: t. 500dw.; l. 220'; b. 24'; dph. 14'; s. 17 k.; cpl. 120; a. 3 guns)

CSS *Tallahassee*, formerly the blockade runner *Atalanta* built on the Thames River in England, had passed through the blockade at Wilmington, N.C., several times before being purchased in 1864 by the Confederate States Navy.

Twin-screw ferry *Atalanta* had the name of an "admirable sea boat," very stable yet fast, having made the Dover-Calais crossing in 77 minutes on an even keel. She had been turned out by J. & W. Dudgeon of Millwall for London, Chatham & Dover Rly. Co. to the design of Capt. T. E. Symonds, RN, with twin 100-h.p. engines.

After she was commissioned and prepared for sea *Tallahassee* was placed under Comdr. J. T. Wood, CSN, who took her through the blockade on 6 August 1864 and made a brilliant 19-day raid off the Atlantic coast as far north as Halifax, N.S. Being unable to procure enough coal to continue, Cdr. John Taylor Wood was forced to return to Wilmington where he arrived safely on the 26th. During this short cruise *Tallahassee* destroyed 26 vessels and captured 7 others which were bonded or released.

C.S.S. Tacony, *commanded by Lieutenant Charles Read, raised havoc with New England shipping during June 1863.*

C.S.S. Tallahassee.

Renamed *Olustee* and placed under the command of Lt. W. H. Ward, CSN, she ran through the blockade off Wilmington again on 29 October, but suffered some damage from Federal guns. She captured and destroyed six ships off the Capes of Delaware before having to return for coal. She thwarted attempts by *Sassacus* to capture her on 6 November and by four other United States ships on 7 November, finally passing into the safety of Wilmington harbor.

Following these cruises *Olustee's* battery was removed and she was renamed *Chameleon.* With Lt. J. Wilkinson, CSN, in command she ran through the blockade on 24 December 1864 while the United States fleet was preoccupied with bombarding Fort Fisher, and she proceeded to

Bermuda to obtain provisions for the Confederate army. Upon his return to the Confederate States, Wilkinson made two attempts to enter one of the Southern ports, but finding it impossible, he took *Chameleon* to Liverpool, England, and turned her over to Comdr. J. D. Bulloch, CSN, financial agent of the Confederate Navy Department.

On her arrival in England on 9 April 1865 *Chameleon* was seized and sold by the British authorities and was about to enter the merchant service when the United States instituted suit for possession. She was awarded to the United States Government and handed over to the consul at Liverpool on 26 April 1866.

Talomico

(SwStr: cpl. 20; a. 2 guns)

CSS *Talomico* was stationed at Savannah, Ga., 1861–63. Her commanding officer was First Assistant Engineer J. L. Fabian, CSN She was reported to have sunk accidentally at Savannah in 1863.

Teaser

(ScTug: t. 64; l. 80'; b. 18'; dph. 7'; a. 1 32-pdr. r., 1 12-pdr. r.)

CSS *Teaser* had been the aging Georgetown, D.C., tug *York River* built at Philadelphia. Purchased at Richmond by the State of Virginia in 1861, she was assigned to the naval forces in the James River with Lt. J. H. Rochelle, Virginia State Navy, in command. Upon the secession of that State *Teaser* became a part of the Confederate Navy and continued to operate in Virginian waters. With Lt. W. A. Webb, CSN, in command, she took an active part in the battle of Hampton Roads, Va., on 8–9 March 1862, acting as tender to CSS *Virginia*. She received the thanks of the Congress of the Confederate States for this action.

Teaser was a pioneer "aircraft carrier" (balloon ship); she also became a pioneer minelayer when ordered 17 June to assist Lee's Army of Northern Virginia. Under Lt. H. Davidson, CSN, she was used by the Confederate Naval Submarine Battery Service to plant and service "torpedoes" (mines) in the James River. While engaging *Maratanza* at Haxall's on the James 4 July 1862, a Union shell blew up *Teaser's* boiler and forced her crew to abandon ship. When seized by *Maratanza*, *Teaser* was carrying on board a balloon for aerial reconnaissance of Union positions at City Point and Harrison's Landing. *Teaser* was taken into the Federal Navy, and sold at Washington, D.C., on 24 June 1865.

(Cutter)

Surviving records of CS Cutter *Teaser* are limited to an order of 19 August 1863 from Adm. F. Buchanan, CSN, to Acting Master D. Nichols, CSN, Mobile: "You will proceed to sea in the cutter *Teaser* and cruise between this port and the Mississippi River for the purpose of destroying or capturing any of the enemy's vessels or boats you may fall in with. Should you succeed in making any captures you will convey them to a safe port, and on your arrival you will make a full report to me of your cruise." Scarcely more than a month later, Nichols captured "a new and very fast screw steamer," the *Leviathan* (q.v.), and nearly escaped to sea in her through Southwest Pass, 22 September. His daring exploit was reported by his captor, Capt. W. M. Walker, commanding USS *De Soto*, who enclosed a copy of Nichols' brand new commission, dated 5 August, as "acting master [without pay] in the Navy of the Confederate States" and the articles of enlistment of his crew. Captain Walker, who won the 35-mile, life-and-death race, noted in his report to Secretary Welles, "I feel great satisfaction in announcing this success, for when the *Boston*, a very much inferior vessel, was carried off some months ago by a similar enterprise we soon fell upon her track, and thus had the opportunity of witnessing the desolation she had spread in her path, blackening the seas in her wake with the charred memorials of many fine ships. I shall send the *Leviathan* with her desperate band to New Orleans."

Tennessee

(IrcRam: l. 165'; b. 35'; dr. 11'6''; s. 8 k.; cpl. 200; a. des. for 6 guns; type *Arkansas*)

Tennessee was begun by John T. Shirley and Co., at Memphis, Tenn., under fixed price contract for $76,920. Chief constructor of the twin-screw ironclad was a Mr. Prime Emerson.

In correspondence with Maj. Gen. Leonidas Polk, CSA, throughout January 1862, seeking Army workmen from Columbus, Ky., Secretary Mallory promised for *Tennessee* and her sister, *Arkansas*, building at Shirley's yard, that "with such aid as mechanics under your command can afford, they may be completed, I am assured, in

60 days." The desired "shipwrights, carpenters and joiners in the Army" were refused—"on furlough or otherwise"—although the general was reminded that, "One of them at Columbus would have enabled you to complete the annihilation of the enemy . . . Mr. Shirley," Mallory prophesied correctly, "will fail in completing them within the stipulated time entirely from the difficulty of obtaining workmen", although they "would be worth many regiments in defending the river."

Little more is known of the first *Tennessee;* she was never completed but was burned on the stocks by order of the provost marshal, 5 June 1862, to escape capture.

––––––

(IrcRam: t. 1,273; l. 209'; b. 48'; dr. 14'; cpl. 133; a. 2 7" r., 4 6.4"r.; type *Columbia,* modified)

Tennessee, a slow-moving ironclad ram, was built at Selma, Ala., where she was commissioned on 16 February 1864, Lt. J. D. Johnston, CSN, in command. *Baltic* towed her to Mobile where she fitted out for action.

Tennessee was laid down in October 1862, hull and other woodwork turned out by Henry D. Bassett, who launched her the following February, ready for towing to Mobile to be engined and armed. Her steam plant came from *Alonzo Child* (q.v.); only casemate design differed materially from *Columbia* and *Texas* (#5 inf.). Her iron mail was the same 2" by 10" plate used on *Huntsville* and *Tuscaloosa* but triple instead of double thickness. A fearsome detail of her armament was a "hot water attachment to her boilers for repelling boarders, throwing one stream from forward of the casemate and one abaft."

The vicissitudes implicit in creating such an ironclad are graphically conveyed by Admiral Franklin Buchanan, writing 20 September 1863 to Secretary Mallory: "The work on the *Tennessee* has progressed for some weeks past, under Mr. Pierce, as fast as the means in his power would permit. There is much delay for want of plate and bolt iron. It was impossible to iron both sponsons at the same time, as the vessel had to be careened several feet to enable them to put the iron on. Even then several of the workmen were waist deep in the water to accomplish it— to careen her, large beams 12 feet square had to be run out of her ports and secured, on which

several tons of iron had to be placed, and during the progress of putting on the sponson iron the shield iron could not be put on. The work has been carried on night and day when it could be done advantageously. I visited the *Nashville* and *Tennessee* frequently and, to secure and control the services of the mechanics, I have had them all conscripted and detailed to work under my orders. Previously, they were very independent and stopped working when they pleased . . ." Joseph Pierce referred to was Acting Naval Constructor in the Mobile area.

Tennessee became flagship of Adm. F. Buchanan, and served gallantly in action in the Battle of Mobile Bay on 5 August 1864. On that morning *Tennessee* and wooden gunboats CSS *Gaines,* CSS *Morgan,* and CSS *Selma,* steamed into combat against Adm. D. G. Farragut's powerful fleet of four ironclad monitors and 14 wooden steamers. Unable to ram the Union ships because of their superior speed, *Tennessee* delivered a vigorous fire on the Federals at close range. The Confederate gunboats were sunk or dispersed. Farragut's fleet steamed up into the bay and anchored. Buchanan might have held *Tennessee* under the fort's protection but bravely steamed after the Federal fleet and engaged despite overwhelming odds. The ram became the target for the entire Union fleet. *Tennessee* was rammed by several ships, and her steering chains were carried away by the heavy gunfire. Unable to maneuver, *Tennessee* was battered repeatly by heavy solid shot from her adversaries. With two of her men killed, Admiral Buchanan and eight others wounded, and increasingly severe damage being inflicted on her, *Tennessee* was forced to surrender.

Tennessee was taken into the Navy and was later commissioned on 19 August 1865. She was sold at public auction in New Orleans on 27 November 1867.

––––––

(SwStr: t. 1,275[1,149]; dr. 16'6")

Tennessee was a "very strong," oceangoing steamer built in Baltimore in 1854 for Charles Morgan's Texas Line and one of the 14 Morgan ships and tugs seized by Maj. Gen. Mansfield Lovell, CSA, 15 January 1862, at New Orleans. Inspected by Captain Lawrence Rousseau, CSN, she was ruled too deep for upriver service as a gunboat, but it was noted that she could carry enough fuel to reach Europe; appropriately, *Ten-*

The awesome ram Tennessee *after her capture by Farragut's fleet in Mobile Bay.*

nessee was reserved for a Government-operated blockade runner.

She probably made one trip to Havana in February, although four days after her alleged arrival there General Lovell was writing a memorandum that she could not get out of the Mississippi. But she was in New Orleans two months later, when Farragut's forces entered, 25 April. Sold in prize court for $96,000, she was commissioned 2 May 1862, still at New Orleans and name unchanged until 1 September 1864; her renaming was a natural result of the capture of Confederate ironclad ram *Tennessee* at Mobile Bay in August. As USS *Mobile*, she was sold at public auction in New York City, 30 March 1865.

Texas

(Str)

The Confederate Army operated a vessel by this name; several references in 1862–63 indicate she was a valued troop transport or supply steamer or both as local military needs directed. General Pemberton ordered her from the Red to the Big Black River in March 1863; Admiral Porter was alerted to capture her in that area

before 1 June but, whether burned or seized by the Federals, she does not appear again in records now available

_____

(SwStr: t. 800; a. 8 guns; cpl. 125 to 150)

CS Privateer *Texas'* prospective owner and captain, Charles de Montel of Castroville, Medina County, Tex., applied 8 January 1863 at San Antonio for a letter of marque to commission a vessel alleged to be already his property—although it appears from the documents that he was then a soldier "in a frontier company as captain and soon to be mustered out." Captain de Montel being "an old sailor who has seen service and is besides a very brave and energetic man," his application in absentia was apparently accepted by President Davis. *Texas*, therefore, may have served the Confederacy out of Corpus Christi or elsewhere, but subsequent activity has not been preserved in records now available.

_____

(Ship: t. 1,500; l. 220'; b. 30'; dr. 16'; s. 14 k.;
a. 14 30-pdr. r.)

The steam corvette *Texas* was intended for but

did not join the CSN. Secretary of the Navy S. R. Mallory, writing Comdr. James D. Bulloch, CSN, in Paris, 22 February 1864, directs that "... your four corvettes ... may be called *Louisiana, Mississippi, Texas* and *Georgia*." Two, camouflaged under the names of *Osacca* and *Yeddo*, were then building at Bordeaux by the firm of L. Arman, while the other pair, masquerading as *San Francisco* (presumably intended to be *Texas*) and *Shanghai*, took shape in the yards of Jollet, Babier, and of Th. Dubigeon & Sons at Nantes; their 400-h.p. engines were fabricated by Mazeline of Havre. The four are described as being full-rigged large ships with beautiful poop cabins, large topgallant foc'sles, iron spars and a large spread of canvas. Prussia bought the Bordeaux-built pair and Peru the Nantes corvettes when the French Government stopped their sale to the Confederacy.

Texas, rechristened *America* in the Peruvian Navy, was lost in the tidal wave and earthquake at Arica, Chile, in 1868.

(Composite [wood & iron] ScStr: t. 1,000; l. 230'; b. 32'; dph. 20')

The cruiser secretly assigned the name *Texas* was unable to serve the Confederacy at sea, but rumors of her potential as a commerce raider roused such hopes and fears that she is of considerable historical importance.

About 3 November 1863 she was Clyde-launched as *Pampero* at James & George Thomson's Clyde Bank Iron Shipyard, Glasgow. It was by then clear that the corvette *Texsa* (q.v.) would not be released by France. At Clydebank she was alternatively known as *Canton*, but more often referred to in Confederate correspondence as "Sinclair's ship" (Comdr. George T. Sinclair, CSN, supervised her construction). Flag Officer Samuel Barron, heading the CSN procurement commission in Paris, wrote just after her launch, "She is advertised for cargo, and there are hopes of getting her out of the waters of Great Britian without serious embarrassment. She is an uncommonly fine vessel in all respects, and if we get possession of her she will do good service against the commerce of our enemies ..." Notable features included a lifting screw to eliminate drag when under sail only and a handy telescopic funnel.

Texas' dimensions and appearance were very similar to *Alabama*'s except that the former had a poop and topgallant forecastle. Both were bark-rigged with iron fore and mainmasts, capable of a wide spread of canvas, and patent reefing topsails.

Too early fame proved *Texas*'undoing: a sketch of her, captioned with accurate dimensions from Clydebank, even appeared in *The Illustrated London News*, 2 January 1864. The U.S. Minister in London was only too well aware of the specter of a new and improved *Alabama;* both Union and British observers kept "*Pampero*" and the Confederate agents under closest surveillance. By November 1864, Commodore Barron had bowed to the inevitable and wrote from Paris on the 9th to Secretary of the Navy Mallory, "... I have discountenanced all idea of selling the *Texas*. True, we certainly can never get her out during the continuance of hostilities; but she is a fine vessel, and in the event of an armistice she could be got out in a week. I shall, therefore, retain Commander Sinclair out here until further orders from the department."

(IrcRam: l. 217'; b. 50'4''; loaded draft 13'6''; dph. 13'; cpl. 50; a. 4 pivots, 2 broadside guns; type *Columbia*)

CSS *Texas* was a twin-screw ironclad in an outfitting berth at Richmond which her builders failed to blow up before evacuating the Navy Yard in the Confederate capital on 3 April 1865. Launched about mid-January, *Texas* was seized by Union forces who moved her to Norfolk Navy Yard, where she was sold 15 October 1867. A sister to *Columbia* with shortened casemate, she is generally regarded as one of the most valuable hulls ever constructed for the Confederacy.

(SwStr: t. 1,223 [1,151])

Texas was one of the 14 Morgan liners seized at New Orleans by Maj. Gen. Mansfield Lovell, 15 January 1862, acting under Secretary of War Benjamin's oft quoted order. She was built at New York City in November 1852 as a wooden, full-rigged ship and altered in April 1856 to a paddlewheel steamer. One source indicates she was under foreign flag in 1860, however unlikely this may appear to be. Although equipped with low-pressure steam plant, *Texas* was considered too large for a cottonclad ram; she proved far more valuable as a Government-operated blockade runner, completing 13 runs to Havana with large cotton cargoes, returning with saltpetre, arms and ammunition.

Theodora

(SwStr: t. 518; l. 175'; dr. 7'; s. 16 k.; cpl. 50; a. 3 guns)

Theodora, originally named *Carolina*, then *Gordon*, *Theodora*, and finally *Nassau*, intermixed privateering with a blockade running and charter service to the Confederate States as a transport and picket ship. She was built as *Carolina* at Greenpoint, N.Y., in 1852 for service as a coastal packet out of Charleston, S.C., occasionally crossing to Havana, Cuba. Upon outbreak of Civil War she was strengthened and refitted as the *Gordon*, under Capt. T. J. Lockwood, and placed in commission as a privateer at Charleston on 15 July 1861.

Gordon captured the American brig *William McGilvery* off Charleston on 25 July 1861 and the American schooner *Protector* fell into her hands off Hatteras Inlet on the 28th. She was reported to have run the blockade out of Charleston 27 times by October 1861. At that time she was under charter to the Confederate States for daily reconnaissance of Union warships off that port. Of so light draft that she could slip over the bar without being confined to the channels, she kept barely out of reach of the guns of the Federal warships, which finally ignored her, being aware of her speed and the futility of chase. On 4 and 5 October 1861, with officers of *Nashville*, Mr. John Slidell and two young ladies of his family on board, she boldly approached to within 3 miles of the Federal fleet in broad daylight and found herself ignored. This set the stage for her charter by authority of Secretary of State Hunter, to run the Federal Blockade with Confederate diplomats, John Slidell and James M. Mason, to the West Indies.

Gordon, with her name changed to *Theodora*, slipped over the bar at Charleston at 1 a.m., 12 October 1861, having embarked Mason and Slidell and their parties to run the blockade to the West Indies. Too fast to be overtaken at sea, her light draft enabled her to hug the coast to escape the Federal blockading fleet. On 14 October she chased the American armed schooner *H. W. Johnson* into the mouth of the harbor at Nassau, New Providence, Bahamas. Two days later she came off Cardenas, Cuba, dipped the Confederate flag in salute to an approaching Spanish steamer, and was escorted into port where she landed her dis-

tinguished passengers on the 18th. This mission proved to be one in a chain of events that led to the famous "*Trent*" Affair" and brought on bitter relations between the United States and England.

Theodora continued to run the blockade out of Charleston and Wilmington, primarily to Nassau, where she caused consternation to observant commanders of Federal warships. By making herself a target of chase, she unsuccessfully attempted to lure USS *Flambeau* away from Nassau during 17–18 December 1861, hoping to allow opportunity for British steamer *Gladiator* to escape from that port with her cargo of munitions said to be sufficient to arm 25,000 Confederates. She got safely into Mobile, changed her name to *Nassau* under British colors, and continued to slip in and out of Wilmington until 28 May 1862. On that day she was discovered running for Fort Caswell, N.C., and was cut off by Federal warships *State of Georgia* and *Victoria*. She continued running close to land until stopped by direct shots by *Victoria*, then hauled down her British colors as her crew put off in boats for shore. A well directed shot from *Victoria* landed in the midst of the crew as they reached shore, killing one and injuring another. The remainder of the crew escaped into the woods.

Theodora was under command of the famous blockade runner, Captain Walker, when captured. On 28 May 1862, a prize crew of 24 officers and men from *Victoria* found her loaded with Enfield rifles, ammunition, clothing and medicines intended for the Confederate Army. She was sent to New York for adjudication as a prize of war.

Thirty-fifth Parallel

(SwStr: t. 419)

Thirty-fifth Parallel, also known as *Parallel*, was constructed at Cincinnati, Ohio, in 1859, and operated out of New Orleans. She was outfitted with protective cotton-baling, and taken into Confederate Army service in the Tallahatchie and Mississippi Rivers.

In March 1863 Comdr. I. N. Brown, CSN, took her 70 miles up the Tallahatchie where he transferred to the steamer *St. Mary* to make observations. *Thirty-fifth Parallel* proceeded ahead into Federal territory and, encountering an extremely narrow stream, was disabled, run ashore, and burned to prevent capture by advancing Union forces in *Chillicothe* and *Baron DeKalb*.

Thomas Jefferson, see *Jamestown*

Thomas L. Wragg, see *Nashville*

Time

(Str)

Time was a steamer used as a Confederate transport for conveying supplies into the Pensacola Navy Yard. When that yard was abandoned in March 1862, its stores were ordered loaded on *Time* for removal to the interior.

Tom Sugg

(SwStr: t. 62; l. 90'; b. 22'; dph. 3'6''; a. 2 guns)

Tom Sugg, also known as *Sugg,* a wooden river steamer built in Cincinnati, Ohio, was outfitted with protective cotton-cladding and armament for use as a Confederate gunboat in the White River, Ark. On 14 August 1863 while steaming in company with *Kaskaskia* she was captured by USS *Cricket* in the Little Red River. Purchased from the Illinois Prize Court by the Union Navy on 29 September 1863, and described as an "excellent vessel" by Adm. D. D. Porter, she served as USS *Tensas* during the remainder of the war.

Torch

(ScStr: cpl. 11; a. triple-torpedo spar)

Lt. Lewis R. Hill, CSN, commanded CSS *Torch* on the Charleston station 1863–64. As reported by a Confederate deserter in January 1864, *Torch,* a steamer, was "built like the other ironclads [*Charleston, Palmetto State, Chicora*], but is very small. Has no guns mounted, but has a pole projecting from her bow, with three branches at the end, with a torpedo on each. The pole is about 12 feet long. Each torpedo is about the size of the one on the *Charleston,* and contains about 70 pounds of powder."

The craft was launched at Charleston the summer of 1863, apparently unchristened, and "taken to Marsh's shipyard where a second-hand steam engine was placed in it and a spar designed to carry three 100-pound torpedoes was attached." Carrying six 75-pound torpedoes (mines), she left her moorings 20 August with a volunteer crew of Charlestonians under a naturalized Briton, experienced blockade runner Capt. James Carlin. At Fort Sumter they picked up Lt. E. S. Fickling, CSA, and 11 soldiers of the 1st South Carolina Artillery in case of attack by Federal launches. Passing the harbor obstructions after midnight, they sighted USS *New Ironsides,* Capt. Stephen C. Rowan, anchored "across the channel and heading for Morris Island," with five monitors moored nearby. The watch officer on the big ironclad was startled by "a strange vessel, sitting very low in the water and having the appearance of being a large boat, coming up astern very fast." Captain Carlin, 40 yards off, found *Torch* too slow in answering the helm and "discovered as we ranged up alongside that in consequence of the *Ironsides* being in the act of swinging to the ebb we must miss with our torpedoes, but feared that her chain cable would either ignite them or detain us alongside. In either case we must have been captured."

To repeated hails Carlin responded, "The steamer *Live Yankee*" from Port Royal. At this tense moment, *Torch's* engine caught on dead center; *Ironsides* beat to quarters, fired a rocket and threatened to board while Carlin's sharpshooters nearly let go a volley that would have betrayed the smaller craft; Carlin gave orders "in time to prevent the firing upon some sailors that were looking at us from the ports. I saw they were not boarding and I immediately ordered the men to hold and not fire. They dropped immediately, showing specimen of the effect of good discipline." In two minutes the little band drifted "just clear of his bow and out of danger of being boarded except by launches"; out of reach of the enemy's broadside, *Torch* was momentarily safe until *Ironsides'* "chain had been slipped, and backing astern, the bow guns were fired" at the retreating Confederates; for, in the nick of time, the recalcitrant engine started and *Torch* was off toward Fort Moultrie.

After this hairbreadth escape, Captain Carlin felt it his "duty most unhesitatingly to express my condemnation of the vessel and engine for the purposes it was intended, and as soon as she can be docked and the leak stopped, would advise making a transport out of her."

The following year, 1864, she continued to be commanded by Lt. Hill, but her role remains obscure. A contemporary reported long afterward that she had been a "tub-like model" with an inefficient, "second-hand and much worn engine" and "could only be kept afloat by bailing." A Lt. Clarence L. Stanton, CSN, had said of her that she had never been iron-plated, despite reports to the contrary, was structurally unsound and little used in consequence. Capt. F. D. Lee, CSA, from his report to General Beauregard seems to have obtained from Secretary Mallory the transfer of her unfinished hull on the ways and to have engined her, although originally she had been intended for a permanently anchored floating battery. The presumption is that *Torch* was relegated to such immobile status after her escapade of 21 August 1863.

Torpedo

(ScStr: t. 150; l. 70'; b. 16'; dph. 6'6''; a. 1 gun or 2 20-pdr.)

Torpedo, a screw steamer, was placed under the command of Lt. H. Davidson, CSN, and attached to the squadron of Flag Officer S. Barron, CSN. She served only in the James River as a torpedo boat tender.

Early in July 1863 she was stripped of her guns and made a flag-of-truce boat by Alexander H. Stephens, Vice President of the Confederate States, who hoped to bear a written communication from Jefferson Davis to Abraham Lincoln. Stephens' request to carry the message to Washington in *Torpedo* was refused.

She was cited as being in charge of James River submarine batteries in November 1863.

Torpedo's guns were remounted and she participated in the James River operations, including the attempted passage of the obstructions in Trent's Reach, 23–24 January 1865.

Torpedo was partially burned and sunk on 3 April 1865 to prevent her capture by the Union forces who entered Richmond. She was raised and sent to Norfolk Navy Yard in May 1865.

Towns

(Str)

Towns, a light draft steamer, was used in towing ships into the Warwick River, Va., where they were sunk as obstructions in September 1861.

Transport

(SwStr: c. t. 40)

Transport, a light draft tug, was in Confederate service in Charleston, S.C. She was captured by the Federals when Charleston fell in February 1865 and later served with the U.S. Navy before being transferred to the Army in July 1865.

Treaty

(Str)

Treaty, a Confederate tug, was captured by a boat from USS *Albatross* in the Santee River on 20 June 1862. She then was taken into Union service and used in coastal waters and rivers of South Carolina.

Trent

(Str)

Trent was used to transport Confederate provisions on the Mississippi and Red Rivers during 1862–63.

Tropic, see Huntress

Turel

(Str)

Turel was used as a transport by the Army between the forts, Navy Yard, and armed positions in the vicinity of Pensacola, Fla. When the yard at Pensacola was abandoned by the Confederates in March 1862, she carried stores, machinery and other military cargo up the Escambia River, having been ordered to cut down trees and place every obstruction possible in the river behind her. A steamer of very light draft, she arrived safely at a point deemed beyond Federal reach and unloaded her freight.

Tuscaloosa

(Bark: t. 500)

The American bark *Conrad*, en route from Buenos Aires to New York with a cargo of wool and goat skins, was captured by CSS *Alabama* on 20 June 1863. Being fast and well adapted for a cruiser, Capt. R. Semmes, CSN, commissioned her the next day as a cruiser and tender to the *Alabama*, renaming her *Tuscaloosa*. Three 12-pounders and a plentiful supply of rifles, pistols and ammunition were transferred to her with enough provisions for a 3-month cruise. Lt. J. Low, CSN, with 15 men, was ordered on board with instructions for an African cruise in the direction of the Cape of Good Hope.

On 31 July *Tuscaloosa* captured the American ship *Santee* with a cargo of rice and bonded her for $150,000. On 8 August, Low brought his ship into Simon's Bay in South Africa, departing thence for a 90-day cruise during which he stopped at Angra Pequena, Southwest Africa, to discharge *Tuscaloosa's* cargo of wool and goat skins. On 19 November he put into Santa Catarina, Brazil, for supplies but was not allowed to purchase them and was informed he must depart before nightfall.

From there *Tuscaloosa* returned to Simon's Bay on 26 December only to be seized by British authorities as an uncondemned prize which had violated the neutrality of Her Majesty's Government. They ordered her to be held until properly reclaimed by her original owners. Lieutenant Low and his men left the ship and an officer and men from HMS *Narcissus* were placed on board.

Her owners did not reclaim her and in March 1864 she was released by the British authorities, after Low and his crew had reached Britain; consequently she was never recovered by the Confederacy.

———

(IrcRam: l. 152′; b. 34; dph. 10′6″; dr. 8′; s. 3 k.; cpl. 120; a. 1 6.4″ r., 3 32-pdr. [planned]; type Heavy *Albemarle*)

CSS *Tuscaloosa*, an ironclad floating battery, was launched at Selma, Ala., 7 February 1863. She was designed as a ram to mount four guns and to have the protection of 4-inch iron plating supplied by Schofield & Markham and Shelby Iron Co.

Engined before launching, *Tuscaloosa* proceeded under her own power to Mobile for completion. Under Commander C. H. McBlair, CSN, she served in the Mobile area until Mobile's capitulation on 12 April 1865 when the Confederates sank her in the Spanish River 12 miles north of the city.

Tuscarora

(SwStr: a. 1 32-pdr., 1 8″ col.)

Tuscarora was purchased from the Southern Steamship Co. of New Orleans, La., in 1861 and converted into a ship-of-war. On 12 October, while under Commander Beverly Kennon, Louisiana State Navy, she participated in a spirited engagement between the Confederate fleet commanded by Flag Officer G. N. Hollins, CSN, and vessels of the Union blockading squadron at Head of the Passes, Mississippi River. She accidentally burned near Helena, Ark., on 23 November 1861.

Twilight

(Str: t. 392)

Twilight, a large Confederate steam transport, operated in the Ouachita River, La., during 1864–65.

Uncle Ben

(Gbt: t. 155; a. 1 gun)

CSS *Uncle Ben* was a Lake Erie tug which was chartered by the United States Government in April 1861 to accompany an expedition for the reenforcement of Fort Sumter in Charleston Harbor. She sailed from New York on 7 April but violent storms forced her to put in to Wilmington, N.C., where she was seized by the citizens and converted to a gunboat mounting one gun. When North Carolina seceded, *Uncle Ben* was turned over to the Confederacy and operated around Wilmington. In late summer of 1862, her engine was transferred to the ironclad *North Carolina* and her hull sold.

Under her new owners she was fitted out as a privateer schooner, renamed *Retribution*, and later *Etta*.

———

(Str: dr. 3′; a. 3 12-pdr.)

Uncle Ben, a cotton-clad steamer, operated with the Texas Marine gunboat fleet in and about Sabine City. [See Annex III]. On 20 January 1863 *Uncle Ben* came down Sabine Pass in company with *Josiah A. Bell* and stood out to engage the Union blockaders *Morning Light* and *Fairy*, formerly *Velocity*. In the heated battle which witnessed the capture of both blockaders, *Uncle Ben* concentrated her fire on *Fairy* and received her unconditional surrender.

The cotton-clad was used to remove obstructions from the Sabine River in June 1863. On 8 September, following another successful encounter with Federal blockaders off Sabine Pass, she went down to receive the surrender of USS *Sachem* and brought her into port. In October of that year *Uncle Ben* transported men and provisions in coastal waters.

Union, see Texas (corvette)

United States

(Fr: t. 1,576; l. 175′10″; b. 44′8″; dph. 21′2″; a. 44 guns)

United States was built at Philadelphia, Pa., under Act of Congress dated 27 March 1794. She was launched 10 May 1798 and commissioned 11 July 1798, one of the first 3 ships built for the U.S. Navy. The other two are still in existence: *Constellation* in Baltimore, *Constitution* in Boston.

At the beginning of the Civil War she lay in ordinary at Gosport Navy Yard. The Union, thinking it unnecessary to destroy a decayed relic, let her fall into Confederate hands when Norfolk surrendered. She was used as a receiving ship, Lt. V. R. Morgan, CSN, in command, and was oftentimes called *Confederate States*.

In April 1862 the Confederates sank her in the Elizabeth River, N.C., to obstruct approaching Union vessels. Later she was raised and broken up by the Navy.

V. H. Ivy, see Ivy

Velocity

(Sch: t. 87; a. 2 12-pdr. how.)

Velocity was a British blockade runner captured by USS *Kensington* at Sabine Pass, Tex., 30 September 1862, taken to Pensacola and Key West as a prize and finally returned armed as a blockader with two Dahlgrens. Recaptured by CSS *Bell* and *Uncle Ben* in the same locality, 21 June 1863, *Velocity* is believed to have continued to serve as a gunboat; one of her guns was recognized by Union naval officers when captured two years later in the fast Confederate privateer schooner *Anna Dale* (q.v.) by USS *Pinola*, 19 February 1865, in Pass Cavallo, Tex., but when it was transferred from *Velocity* or for what reason has not been explained in available records.

Vicksburg, see Louisville

Vicksburg

(SwStr: t. 635)

Vicksburg, sometimes noted as *City of Vicksburg*, was built in 1857 at New Albany, Ind., and owned and home ported in New Orleans. With the coming of the war she was evidently seized or bought for use on the river. A report of 19 February 1862 tells of her carrying guns up river to the forts above Memphis.

At Natchez, Miss., in May 1862, five Union ships were before the city. They had sent in a flag of truce. At this time, *Vicksburg* came down river with troops for the defense of Natchez. Brig. General C. G. Dahlgren, MSG, was on shore at the time and fired a musket to warn her off. She put about and went up river, being chased by two shots from gunboat USS *Oneida*.

Vicksburg made good her escape. In July 1862 she was spotted on the Black River in company with a Confederate gunboat, probably carrying troops and supplies. Early next year, February 1863, she was "lying at the landing" of the city of Vicksburg. Admiral Porter ordered his ram *Queen of the West* to run the defenses of Vicksburg, and attack the steamer *Vicksburg* in passing down.

Under the daring and gallant Col. Charles R. Ellet, *Queen of the West* got underway, after delays, and early in the morning of 2 February 1863, came in sight of *Vicksburg*.

The Confederates opened a heavy fire on *Queen of the West*, as she partially turned to make a better angle to deflect projectiles. In so doing, way was lost and the current took charge. But, with guns shotted with incendiary projectiles, Ellet directed a fire on *Vicksburg* and rammed her.

"The *Vicksburg*," reported Ellet, "was the largest and strongest steamer on this river, and I think they were preparing to use her against our transports, being very fleet." Deserters reported a large hole knocked in the side of *Vicksburg*. She was discovered to be on fire, and only held afloat by being buoyed up with coal barges.

Machinery removed, *Vicksburg* remained at Vicksburg as a wharf boat. On 29 March 1863, Federal units were sent to quarters, just after midnight. A steamer had been reported coming down river. The weather was squally, and *Vicksburg* had gone adrift. She passed by, "a harmless hulk," but was totally burned by three men who were seen chasing after her along the shore.

Vicksburg didn't die easily. The Federals sent a party to inspect the "totally consumed" hulk and found no machinery aboard. But, in December 1863, a report to Secretary of War E. M. Stanton gave intelligence of a "very formidable vessel" being finished near Mobile. Said the report: "This vessel is said to contain the machinery of the steamer *Vicksburg*, which was taken overland from Vicksburg to Mobile. These engines were constructed partially under my superintendence at New Albany, when the steamer *Vicksburg* was constructed, and I know the engine to be as powerful as any now on the Mississippi River."

Victor, see Rappahannock

Victoria

(SwStr: t. 405; l. 222'; b. 32'6''; dr. 5'10'')

Victoria, built in 1858 at Elizabeth, Pa., served the Confederate forces faithfully as a transport in the Mississippi until 6 June 1862 when captured by Union forces under Commodore C. H. Davis after the battle of Memphis. Following capture she was used as a storeship, wharf and inspection boat, with name changed to USS *Abraham*.

———

(SwStr: t. 487; dph. 9'6''; dr. 8')

Victoria, a seagoing steamer built at Mystic, Conn., in 1859, is cited in official records as owned or managed by Southern S. S. Co. at the outbreak of war and was one of 14 of their New Orleans ships inspected by Comdr. W. W. Hunter for possible conversion to a gunboat. Although he judged *Victoria*, "one of the best for that purpose we have inspected," there is no evidence of her being so altered or armed for river defense.

Instead, *Victoria* put to sea as a Government-operated blockade runner under Captain Lambert and appears to have been successful in getting Texan cotton into Havana; she disappeared after the fall of 1862 but survived the war and was lost in 1866.

———

Victoria (ex-*Louisiana*, ex-*Osacca*), see under *Texas* (corvette)

Virginia

(IrcRam: l. 275'; b. 38'6"; dr. 22'; s. 9 k.; cpl. 320; a. 2 7" r., 2 6" r., 6 9", 2 12-pdr. how.)

CSS *Virginia* was built at Boston Navy Yard as the frigate *Merrimack*, commissioned 20 February 1856, Capt. G. J. Pendergrast, USN, in command.

Departing Boston she cruised in West Indian and European waters in 1856–57. Following brief repairs she sailed in October 1857 as flagship of the Pacific Squadron, cruising the Pacific coasts of South and Central America until November 1859. Returning east she decommissioned at Norfolk 16 February 1860. On 20 April 1861 retiring Union forces burned *Merrimack* to the water line and sank her to preclude capture.

The Confederates, in desperate need of ships, raised *Merrimack* and rebuilt her as an ironclad ram, according to a design prepared by naval constructor Lt. J. M. Brooke, CSN. Commissioned on 17 February 1862, as CSS *Virginia*, the ironclad was the hope of the Confederacy to wreak havoc among the wooden ships in Hampton Roads and end the blockade's strangulation.

Despite all-out effort to complete her, *Virginia* still had workmen on board when she sailed out into Hampton Roads, 8 March 1862, tended by CSS *Raleigh* and *Beaufort*, accompanied by *Patrick*, *Jamestown*, and *Teaser*. Flag Officer F. Buchanan, CSN, commanding *Virginia*, chose as first victim sail sloop-of-war USS *Cumberland*, anchored west of Newport News, to test *Virginia*'s armor against a 70-pounder rifle. In taking position *Virginia* passed *Congress* and exchanged broadsides, suffering no injury while causing considerable. She crossed *Cumberland*'s bows, raking her with a lethal fire, finishing off the wooden warship with a thrust of her iron ram to conserve scarce gunpowder. *Cumberland* sank with colors flying, taking 121 men, one third of her crew, and part of *Virginia*'s ram down with her.

Virginia then turned her attention to *Congress*, which grounded while attempting to evade. Opening fire from a distance, assisted by the lighter ships of the James River Squadron, *Virginia*

C.S.S. Virginia (ex-Merrimack) *steams downriver on 8 March 1862 to engage the wooden blockading fleet in Hampton Roads.*

forced *Congress* to haul down her colors. As CSS *Beaufort* and *Raleigh* approached *Congress* to receive the surrender of her crew, Federal troops ashore, nct understanding the situation, opened a withering fire and wounded Buchanan, who retaliated by ordering hot shot and incendiary shell to be poured into *Congress*. The latter, ablaze and unable to bring a single gun to bear, hauled down her flag for the last time. She continued to burn far into the night and exploded about midnight.

Virginia did not emerge unscathed. Her stack was riddled causing loss of power—and she was initially underpowered. Two large guns were out of order, her armor loosened and her ram lost. Nevertheless, she went on to attack *Minnesota*, but because of depth of water could not close the range to do that steam frigate serious damage. *Virginia* anchored that night at Sewell's Point for repairs. Flag Officer Buchanan was taken ashore to the hospital and Lt. C. ap R. Jones, CSN, who had conned the ironclad after Buchanan had been wounded, assumed command.

On the following morning *Virginia* returned to battle. In the night the Union ironclad *Monitor*, after a hazardous trip from New York, had arrived in the nick of time to save the fleet in Hampton Roads. The ensuing inconclusive battle, the first ever fought between powered ironclads, revolutionized warfare at sea.

Flag Officer J. Tattnall, CSN, was ordered on 25 March 1862 to command in Virginia waters with the ironclad as his flagship. She and USS *Monitor* continued to stalemate each other for the next several weeks. However, *Merrimack* continued a major threat to Union military operations, acting as an important deterrent to the Union Army's advance. When forced to evacuate Norfolk, the Confederates tried to take *Virginia* up the James River but her draft prevented it. The crew ran her ashore near Craney Island, fired and destroyed her on 11 May 1862.

[Before *Virginia II* was built, CSS *Richmond* was constantly referred to by Union officers in their dispatches as *Virginia II*, *Virginia No. 2* or *Merrimack No. 2* and sometimes *Young Merrimack*, *New Merrimack* or *Young Virginia*. The preceding *Virginia* (ex-*Merrimack*) henceforth became *Virginia I*.]

"Virginia", see *Georgia* (cruiser)

Virginia II

(IrcStSlp: l. 197'; b. 47'6"; dr. 14'; s. 10 k.; cpl. 150; a. 1 11", 1 8" r., 2 6.4" r.)

CSS *Virginia II* was laid down at the Confederate Navy Yard at Richmond in 1863. Acting Constructor William A. Graves, CSN, superintended her building, but in order to conserve scarce metal, shortened the casemate called for in the original Porter plans; armor was 6" thick on the forward face and 5" on the sides and after face.

Virginia II, Comdr. Robert B. Pegram, CSN, went into action on 21 June 1864 as flagship of Commodore J. K. Mitchell, CSN, during the engagement between the Confederate James River Squadron and Federal ships in Trent's Reach. On 13 August and 22 October she exchanged fire with the enemy at Dutch Gap and on 17 August participated in the capture of Signal Hill.

Her final action took place on 23–24 January 1865 when the Confederate squadron in the James River, including ironclads *Virginia II*, CSS *Richmond*, and CSS *Fredericksburg*, with five smaller vessels, made a second unsuccessful attempt to circumvent obstructions in Trent's Reach. *Virginia II* suffered damage which required extensive repairs.

Virginia II was one of the ships destroyed in the James River before the evacuation of Richmond, Va., on 3 April 1865. She was raised by the United States after the war.

Virginia II (or *No. 2*), see *Richmond*

Volunteer

(SwStr: t. 209; d. 5')

Volunteer, acting under orders of the Depot Quartermaster's Office, CSA, Natchez, Miss., to procure and transport forage, was captured 25 November 1863 off Natchez Island, Miss., by Acting Volunteer Lieutenant Pearce, commanding USS *Fort Hindman*.

Volunteer was purchased by the Navy from the Springfield, Ill., prize court and served as USS *Volunteer* until sold at Mound City, Ill., 29 November 1865.

W. Burton

(SwStr: t. 253; l. 151'; b. 25'; dr. 5'6"; cpl. 75)

W. Burton, also known as *William Burton* and *Burton*, was built at New Albany, Ind., in 1857.

She was operating privately as a New Orleans steamboat prior to being acquired by the Confederate States. In April 1862 *W. Burton* is reported serving as an unarmed tender to CSS *Louisiana*.

Under Captain Hammond, *W. Burton* was attached to the force of Capt. J. K. Mitchell, CSN, commanding Confederate naval forces in the lower Mississippi near Confederate Forts St. Philip and Jackson. *W. Burton* was also used to berth many of the officers and crew of *Louisiana* while the latter, with mechanics on board working day and night, was being prepared as well as possible for battle.

Flag Officer D. G. Farragut, USN, ran his fleet up the lower Mississippi past the Confederate forts on 24 April 1862, and inflicted great damage on the Confederate ships. In the engagement *W. Burton* was badly damaged but remained seaworthy. Captain Hammond and his crew left her and turned her over to Captain Mitchell to be operated directly by the Confederate Navy.

Confederate forts Jackson and St. Philip surrendered on 28 April 1862 to Comdr. D. D. Porter, USN. Captain Mitchell, believing that he was not bound by the surrender of the army command at the forts, set fire to *Louisiana* on the east bank of the Mississippi near Fort St. Philip to keep her from falling into Union hands. He and his men, realizing that capture was inevitable, retired to the opposite shore with the unarmed tenders *W. Burton* and *Landis*. After three Federal gunboats fired at them, *W. Burton* and *Landis* surrendered to Commander Porter.

W. Burton was turned over to the U.S. Army and used as a transport in the Mississippi River.

W. H. Smith, see James Battle

W. W. Crawford

(SwStr: t. 123)

W. W. Crawford, also known as *Crawford*, was built in 1861 at Cincinnati, Ohio, and operated out of Louisville Ky. She transported supplies for the Confederacy between Memphis and Helena. By August 1863 she had passed to Union control and was used as a transport in western waters.

Waccamaw, see Adventure

Wade Water Belle

(Str)

Wade Water Belle was listed among the ships captured by USS *Conestoga* of the Mississippi gunboat flotilla prior to 25 September 1862.

Warren Winslow, see Winslow

Warrior

(SwRam: cpl. 40; a. 1 32-pdr.)

Warrior, a sidewheel gunboat-ram had been a tugboat on the Mississippi River before she was acquired by the Confederate Government. Capt. James E. Montgomery selected her to be part of his River Defense Fleet [See Annex II]. On 25 January 1862 Montgomery began to convert her into a cottonclad ram by placing a 4-inch oak sheath with a 1-inch iron covering on her bow, and by installing double pine bulkheads filled with compressed cotton bales to protect machinery and boilers.

Warrior's conversion was completed on 16 March 1862. In early April, under the command of Capt. J. A. Stevenson, she was detached from Montgomery's main force and sent to Forts Jackson and St. Philip on the lower Mississippi to cooperate in the Confederate defense of New Orleans. Captain Stevenson, who was also in charge of five other River Defense Fleet vessels in this area, placed his force under the overall command of Captain J. K. Mitchell, CSN, commanding Confederate naval forces in the lower Mississippi.

On 24 April 1862 Flag Officer D. G. Farragut, USN, ran his fleet past Forts Jackson and St. Philip on his way to capture New Orleans. In this action, *Warrior*, while under the guns of USS *Brooklyn*, received a broadside of eleven 5-second shells which exploded in her. *Warrior* was driven on the bank a little above Fort St. Philip, instantly began to burn, and was soon destroyed.

Washington

(Sch: a. 1 42-pdr.)

CSS *Washington* was formerly USRC *Washington* seized by the authorities at New Orleans, when Louisiana seceded on 31 January 1861. In June 1861, Lt. D. D. Porter, USN, commanding USS *Powhatan*, in a letter to Secretary of the Navy, reports her fitting out there and nearly ready for sea.

Wasp

(ScTB: l. 46′; b. 6′3″; dph. 3′9″; a. 1 18′ spar torpedo; cl. *Squib*)

Wasp, a torpedo boat commanded by Master's Mate J. W. Matherson, CSN, was attached to the James River Squadron in 1865. She was employed in the vain attempt to remove the obstructions in Trent's Reach on 23–24 January. Accompanying *Richmond* down the river, she neared Battery Semmes where she assisted in refloating *Hornet*. She also made an unsuccessful attempt to tow *Scorpion* off the shore and grounded herself. Later she retired to Battery Dantzler where she was used as a picket boat assigned to *Virginia II*, until the evacuation of Richmond, 3 April 1865.

Water Witch

(SwStr: t. 378; l. 150'; b. 23'; dr. 8'2''; s. 7 k.; a. 1 32-pdr. r., 1 12-pdr. r., 2 12-pdr. how.)

Water Witch was built at the Washington Navy Yard in 1852 and served in the United States Navy in home and foreign waters until 1860 when she was forced home by yellow fever and laid up at the Philadelphia Navy Yard. Recommissioned there on 10 April 1860, she sailed for southern waters. On 3 June 1864 she was captured in Ossabaw Sound, Ga., in a daring boarding attack from a small boat led by Lt. Thomas P. Pelot, who gave his life in the action.

She was taken into the Confederate States Navy, retained her original name, and was placed under the command of Lt. W. W. Carnes, CSN. It was planned to take her to Savannah, Ga., for a special assignment but she remained at White Bluff, Ga., until 19 December 1864, when she was burned to prevent capture.

Wave

(SwStr: t. 229)

Wave, originally *Argosy No. 2*, was built in 1863 at Monongahela, Pa., acquired by the Navy on 14 November 1863, and converted to a gunboat for service in western waters. The Confederates captured *Wave* and USS *Granite City* on 6 May 1864 at Calcasieu Pass, La. Thereafter she was in Confederate employ as a transport.

Webb

(SwTug: t. 655; l. 206'; b. 32'; dph. 13'; dr. 9'6''; a. 130-pdr. r., 2 12-pdr. how.)

Webb, also known as *William H. Webb*, was built in New York in 1856. She became the property of the Southern Steamship Co. In May 1861, arrived at New Orleans from Havana, she was issued a privateer's commission. She was never used in that capacity, but was employed in transport work until mid-January 1862 when

Major General Lovell, CSA, pressed her into Confederate service and converted her into a formidable ram which would operate henceforth in the Mississippi and Red Rivers.

Webb figured prominently in the sinking of *Indianola* near New Carthage, Miss., on 24 February 1863. Commanded at this time by Maj. J. L. Brent, CSA, she was fought by a detachment of soldiers and was part of the gunboat force of Maj. Gen. R. Taylor, CSA, consisting of two small cottonclad vessels and the other ram *Queen of the West*.

Early in 1865 she was transferred to the Confederate Navy, and in April was ordered to sea to cruise against Union commerce. On 23 April she ran the blockade at the mouth of the Red River, and by-passed the forts at New Orleans on the 24th, but Federal ships followed in close pursuit.

After a desperate race downriver which almost succeeded, her captain, the indomitable "Savez" Read of *Tacony* fame, ran *Webb* ashore and fired her.

Weldon N. Edwards

(Str)

Weldon N. Edwards, also known as *Edwards*, was probably named in honor of the President of the North Carolina Secession Convention. Assigned to the command of Capt. S. Barron who was charged with the naval defenses of Virginia and North Carolina, she operated in coastal waters of North Carolina during 1861 under Lt. James W. Cooke. In August 1861 she was pronounced generally worthless.

White Cloud

(Str)

White Cloud conveyed Confederate provisions in the Mississippi. She was captured on 13 February 1863 near Island No. 10 by USS *New Era* who sent her prize to Cairo, Ill., for adjudication. Acquired by the Union Navy, she served the North under the same name and in a similar capacity for the remainder of the war.

Widgeon

(SwStr: t. [645]; l. 225'; b. 24'; dph. 11'; dr. 6'; cl. *Curlew*)

Widgeon was the third of four sisters launched the same day in 1865 for the Confederate Navy at Liverpool in the Jones, Quiggin yard. It is doubtful whether this Hull No. 179 or any of the other three ever reached the Confederacy before hostilities ceased.

William B. King

(Sch)

William B. King, also referred to as *William R. King* and *King*, was authorized to be fitted out for service in St. James Parish, La., in July 1861. In October 1861 she was reported to be in Berwick Bay, possibly armed for coast guard duty.

William Bagley (or Bagaley)

(SwStr: t. 396; dr. 5'6''; cpl. 29)
See note under *James Battle*

William Burton, see W. Burton

William G. Hewes

(SwStr: t. 767[747, 795, 905]; l. 258'; b. 34')

William G. Hewes, *W. G. Hewes* or *Hewes* bore with her original name being misspelled *William G. Heness*, *William G. Hawes*, *William Heines* and was once even referred to in official records as *Jewess*—due, no doubt, to some local quirk of speech that elongated *Hewes* to two syllables. Despite any inducements to schizophrenia, Harlan & Hollingsworth's stout iron Hull No. 70 became a very distinct entity, leading a well integrated, even a charmed life lasting 35 years, the most harrowing and notable of which were her four serving the Confederacy. Known under many names and guises, she was built at Wilmington, Del., in 1860 for the Texas Line of Charles Morgan's Southern S. S. Co. in time to be interned at New Orleans upon Louisiana's secession. Governor Moore seized her 28 April 1861.

"*William Heines*" was one of the noted 14 Morgan ships and tugs "impressed for public service" by Secretary of War Judah P. Benjamin's order to Maj. Gen. Mansfield Lovell, CSA, 15 January 1862, with a view toward turning her into a cottonclad gunboat. Her economical, low-pressure steam plant with less exposed machinery was better adapted to such conversion than most of the seagoing steamers then in the area. Rejected as a gunboat prospect, with her speed and light draft coupled to large capacity, *Hewes* became much more valuable to the Confederacy as a successful blockade-runner to Havana and Nassau. She was presumably still Government-operated as a public vessel. A Captain Smith was commanding her in 1862. Few ships carrying cotton could match the 1,441-bale payload she transported to Havana in April 1862—probably a typical cargo.

April 1863, apparently, *Hewes* was renamed *Ella & Annie* and operated by W. C. Bee and C. T. Mitchell out of Charleston—perhaps partly owned by them, but still carrying Government cargo.

Master F. N. Bonneau, CSN, of Charleston, commanded *Ella & Annie* to Caribbean ports, reporting to Major N. S. Walker, CSA, for fiscal purposes. On 9 November 1863 *Ella & Annie* was cornered by USS *Niphon*, tried to ram the blockader and did succeed in slicing off her bowsprit and most of her stem along with a kedge anchor and other incidentals, but in so doing exposed herself to a boarding party which foiled Bonneau's attempt to blow up his ship—which he had been adjured to do at any cost to prevent capture. Thus *Ella & Annie* was taken with a valuable cargo of Austrian rifles, salt, beef, paper and saltpeter plus dispatches invaluable to the Federal blockaders.

It is largely due to the *Cornubia* (q.v.) and *Ella & Annie* papers that any clear picture is available today of the operation of the Confederate Army transport service. Crew members taken in the prize were put in irons on board USS *Niphon* and Captain Bonneau locked up in *Shenandoah*. A Boston prize court later was to convict him of "piracy"—probably the first time the extreme penalty was actually imposed—but the presiding judge, a retired flag officer, suspended sentence on the ground that he himself would have done the same under similar circumstances; fear of reprisal against high ranking Union officers held prisoner in the South would have prevented the execution in any case.

Ella & Annie was provisionally commissioned USS *Malvern* on 10 December 1863 at Boston Navy Yard and sent forth hastily to catch the *Chesapeake* (q.v.) After formal prize court proceedings and payment of $139,000 in claims, *Malvern* was commissioned with proper ceremony 9 February 1864 and became widely known as the flagship of the North Atlantic Blockading Squadron; she was also Admiral D. D. Porter's flagship at the capture of Fort Fisher, 15 January 1865, the death knell of the blockade runner. *Malvern* was placed out of commission 24 October 1865 and sold at public auction the 25th.

William H. Webb, see Webb

William H. Young

(SwStr: t. 179)

William H. Young or *Young* or *William G. Young* was built at Brownsville, Pa., in 1860 and served the Confederate Army as river transport and storeship in the West Florida-Georgia-Mobile area most of the war. In 1862 she was one of eight steamers that used to tow blockade-running schooners down to the passes to the sea.

Young came into prominence momentarily as the mercy ship from Ocheesee, Fla., that evacuated casualties after *Chattahoochee*'s boiler explosion, 27 May 1863; she stopped en route at Chattahoochee to inter the dead, carrying the survivors on to Columbus, Ga. In November 1864 she was floating headquarters for Capt. Joseph L. Dunham, CSA, his company of 140 men and four-gun battery, constantly patrolling the 50 miles between Chattahoochee and Iola, Fla. The U.S. Army, occupying the area early in June 1865, promptly seized *Young* to transport stores to Maj. Gen. J. H. Wilson, USA.

William J. Duane, see *Duane*

William R. King, see *William B. King*

Wilmington

(IrcGbt: l. 224' bp.; b. 42'6'' ext.; dph. 12'; dr. 9'6''; a. 2 guns)

Wilmington was building at Wilmington, N.C., to the design of Naval Constructor John L. Porter, CSN, in 1863–64. Four boilers and two engines "of sufficient power to insure good speed", driving 8-ft.-diameter propellers, were being finished by Chief Engineer J. H. Warner at the Naval Iron Works, Columbus, Ga.

Secretary Mallory's report, 30 April 1864, revealed: "A fast, light-draft, double-casemated steam ram is making good progress, with armor and machinery in readiness for the hull." In each casemate was to be mounted a gun in pivot. When Wilmington was evacuated, the city's namesake had to be destroyed on the ways to prevent capture by Federal forces.

Wilson

(SwStr: t. 58)

Wilson was built at Beaufort, N.C., in 1856. She served the Confederates in the transportation of troops and supplies until captured 9 July 1862, at Hamilton, N.C., on the Roanoke River by USS *Commodore Perry, Shawsheen* and *Ceres* under the command of Comdr. S. C. Rowan, USN.

Wilson was transferred July 22, 1862 to the Army for use by the U.S. Government.

Winchester

(SwStr: t. 180)

A Wheeling steamboat, probably built at Freedom, Pa., in 1851, *Winchester* is often reported as *Ohio Belle*'s running mate, serving as a transport in the Mississippi. In March 1862, Maj. Gen. J. P. McCown, CSA, had occasion to cite her master for disobeying an order to join Maj. Gen. J. G. Walker's forces. Not many days later, shortly before the battle for Island No. 10, the Confederates scuttled her to prevent capture. On 7 April 1862, Acting Masters E. W. Wheelock and H. A. Glassford, USN, accompanied by the pilots of *Mortar Boats Nos. 7* and *8,* boarded partly submerged *Winchester* and burned her to the water's edge. Over a century later, New Madrid County Historical Society members discovered what they now believe to be *Winchester*'s remains in a chute near Island No. 10.

Winslow

(SwStr: t. 207; a. 1 32-pdr., 1 6-pdr. brass rifle)

Winslow, also known as *Warren Winslow,* formerly the river steamer *Joseph E. Coffee,* also referred to as *J. E. Coffee* of Norfolk, was purchased and fitted out by the Governor of North Carolina after the State seceded on 20 May 1861—former Lt. T. M. Crossan, USN, in command. *Winslow* cruised off Hatteras Inlet, N.C., in search of Federal merchant shipping, taking several prizes including the Union steamer *Itasca.*

When North Carolina joined the Confederacy in July, her navy, consisting of *Winslow, Ellis, Raleigh* and *Beaufort,* was turned over to the Confederate States Navy, and *Winslow* continued taking prizes in the area of Hatteras and New Bern harbor.

Winslow carried Capt. S. Barron, commander of Forts Hatteras and Clark, and was under direct fire during the battle for the forts, 28–29 August 1861, escaping to Goldsboro with many wounded and refugees just prior to the fall of Hatteras.

On 7 November 1861 near Ocracoke Inlet *Winslow* was lost when she struck a sunken hulk, then was set afire by her crew.

Yadkin

(ScGbt: 1 or 2 guns variously)

Yadkin, "a wooden propeller steamer of about 300 tons", was built at Wilmington, N.C., in 1863–64. Under the command of Lt. William A. Kerr, CSN, and as flagship for Commodore W. F. Lynch, she operated in that locale as late as 20 December 1864, when she was ordered to carry reinforcements to Battery Buchanan. *Yadkin* was burned by the Confederates at the fall of Wilmington in February 1865.

Yankee, see *Jackson*

Yazoo

(SwStr: t. 371)

The first-class steamboat *Yazoo* transported Confederate troops and provisions on western waters until 7 April 1862 when she was left behind during the evacuation of Island No. 10. Seized by Union forces, she was later sunk by order of Commodore Foote.

York River, see *Teaser*

Yorktown, see *Patrick Henry*

Younalaska, see *Junaluska*

Young, see *William H. Young*

Young America

(StTug: t. 173)

Young America of Norfolk, Va., went out to aid the distressed schooner *George M. Smith* off Fortress Monroe on 24 April 1861 but was captured by USS *Cumberland* and placed in Union service.

Young Merrimack, see *Richmond*

Young Virginia, see *Richmond*

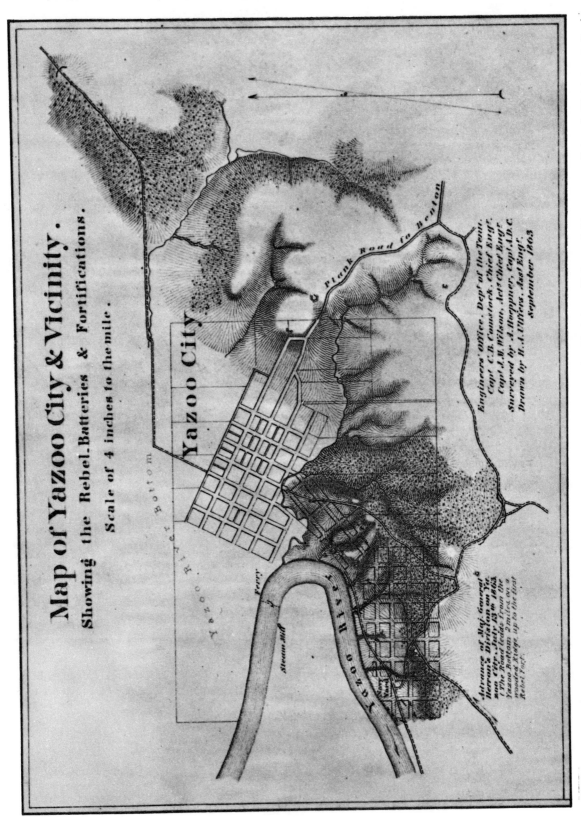

Map of Yazoo City & Vicinity.
Showing the Rebel Batteries & Fortifications.
Scale of 4 inches to the mile.

Yazoo City

Yazoo River Bottom

Yazoo River

Steam Mill

Ferry

G Plank Road to Benton

Engineers' Office. Dept. of the Tenn.
Capt. C.B. Comstock. Chief Engr.
Capt. J.M. Wilson. Act'g Chief Engr.
Surveyed by A. Hoeppner, Capt. A.D.C.
Drawn by H.A. Ulffers. Asst Engr.
September 1863

Advance of Maj. General
Herron's Division on Yazoo City, July 13th 1863.
(The Road leads from the
Yazoo Bottom 2 miles on a
wooded Ridge, up to the Boat
Rebel Fort.

Map of Yazoo City, Mississippi, showing (on the river at left) the location of the important Confederate Navy Yard there. (Existence of this map was called to the Division's attention by Commander Robert W. Collins, USN, Ret.).

VI–327

PRIVATEERS COMMISSIONED BY THE CONFEDERATE STATES GOVERNMENT

In answer to President Lincoln's de facto declaration of war and call-up of militia, Jefferson Davis issued a proclamation on 17 April 1861 inviting, "all those who may desire, by service in private-armed vessels on the high seas, to aid this Government in resisting so wanton and wicked an aggression, to make application for commissions or letters of marque and reprisal to be issued under the seal of these Confederate States." Confederate Congressional authorization was provided in an Act signed on 6 May 1861 which enabled the granting of letters of marque. Subsequent regulations extended inviting terms with but few restrictions to persons interested in the lucrative if hazardous pursuit. These actions, calculated in part to arouse fears among northern mercantile interests, achieved the desired objective. Further, they immediately prompted numerous requests for commissions from aspirants who, like buccaneers of the past, served the cause with a mixture of patriotic zeal and pecuniary interest.

Listed below are those ships which extant records indicate to have received letters of marque and reprisal between 1861 and 1864, none having been issued in the last few months of the war. Many of these ships had varied service during the war years, and some achieved greater fame as blockade runners, or Confederate States Navy ships. Only those in the latter group marked with a dagger (†) have histories in the body of the Appendix because of an established direct military association.

Ships marked with an asterisk (*) were found to have received commissions but no recorded service as privateers, having failed in fitting out, been taken into other employ, or fallen captive. Statistics, port of fitting out, and year of commission are indicated when available.

†*A. C. Gunnison* (StTug: t. 54; l. 70'; b. 15'; dph. 7'; Mobile; 1861)

†*Beauregard*, ex-*Priscilla C. Ferguson*, (Sch: t. 101; s. 7 k.; a. 1 24-pdr.; Charleston; 1861)

Bonita (Str: t. 1,110; a. 8 guns; 1862)

†*Boston* (Str: dr. 9'; a. 5 guns; Mobile, 1863)

Charlotte Clark (Str: t. 1,100; dr. 12'; a. 3 guns; 1863)

Chesapeake (Sch: t. 60; 4 guns; 1863)

†*Dixie* (Sch: t. 110; a. 3 guns; Charleston; 1861)

Dove (Str: t. 1,170; a. 8 guns; 1862)

F.S. Bartow (Sch: t. 74; a. 1 24-pdr., 1 6-pdr.)

†*Gallatin* (Sch: t. 150; a. 2 12-pdr.; 861)

General N. S. Reneau (Str: 1861)

Gibraltar Sch: t. 60, a. 2 guns; Mobile; 1864)

Gordon (SwStr: t. 518; l. 175'; dr. 7'; s. 16 k.; a. 3 guns; 1861)

Governor A. Mouton (Str: t. 125; a. 1 9-pdr., 1 6-pdr.; New Orleans; 1861)

†*Hallie Jackson* (Brig: 1861)

Isabella (ScStr: t. 801; a. 8 guns; New Orleans; 1861)

†*J. C. Calhoun* (*Calhoun*) (SwStr: t. 508; New Orleans; 1861)

J. M. Chapman (Sch: t. 90)

J. O. Nixon (Sch: t. 95; a. 1 18-pdr., 2 6-pdr.; New Orleans; 1861)

†*Jefferson Davis*, ex-*Echo*, ex-*Putnam*, (Brig; t. 187; dr. 10'6''; a. 2 32-pdr., 2 24-pdr., 1 18-pdr.; Charleston; 1861)

†*Joseph Landis* (Str: t. 400; 1861)

Josephine (Sch: 1861)

Judah (Sch: t. 250; a. 5 guns; Pensacola; 1861)

Lamar (Sch: 1861)

Lorton (Sch: t. 95; a. 1 pivot gun; Baltimore; 1861)

†*Manassas* (StRam: t. 387; l. 143'; b. 33'; dph. 17'; Algiers, La.; 1861)

Mariner (ScStr: t. 135; a. 2 12-pdr.; Wilmington, N.C.; 1861)

*Matilda (Bark: t. 400; a. 6 guns; New Orleans; 1861)

*MockingBird (Str: t. 1,290; a. 8 guns; New Orleans; 1862)

*Monticello (IrcStr; t. 460; 1861)

†*Music* (SwStr: t. 273; l. 172'; b. 29'; dph. 6'; a. 2 6-pdr.; New Orleans 1861)

*Onward (Sch: t. 70; a. 1 32-pdr.; 1861)

†*Paul Jones (Sch: t. 160; a. 2 guns; 1864)

*Pelican (Str: t. 1,479; a. 10 guns; 1862)

†*Petrel, ex-*William Aiken*, ex-*Eclipse*, (Sch: t. 82; a. 2 guns; Charleston; 1861)

*Phenix (Str: t. 1,644; l. 245'; b. 34'; dph. 19'; a. 7 guns; Wilmington, Del.; 1861)

†*Pioneer (SS: l. 30'; 1861)

†*Pioneer II (SS: l. 36'; b. 3'; dph. 4'; s. 2.5 k.; 1863)

†*Rattlesnake*, ex-*Thomas L. Wragg*, blockade runner; ex-CSS *Nashville* (SwStr: t. 1,221; l. 215'6''; b. 34'6''; dph. 21'9''; a. 2 12-pdr., 1862)

*Rescue (Sch: t. 120; l. 150')

St. Mary's (Sch: t. 115; St. Mary's, Md., 1865)

Sallie (Sch: t. 170; a. 1 gun; Charleston; 1861)

*Santiago (Sch: Brownsville[?]; 1863)

†*Savannah* (Sch: t. 53; l. 56'; a. 1 pivot gun; Charleston; 1861)

Sealine (Brig: t. 179; a. 1 gun; Baltimore; 1861)

*Stephen R. Mallory, ex-*Don Jose*, (Sch: t. 74; 1864)

*Stonewall Jackson (Sch: 1864)

†*Texas (SwStr: t. 800; a. 8 guns; 1863)

*Triton (Sch: t. 30; a. 1 6-pdr.; 1861)

†*V. H. Ivy* (SwStr: t. 454; l. 191'; b. 28'; a. 1 15-pdr.; New Orleans; 1861)

†*William H. Webb*, (*Webb*), (SwStr: t. 656; l. 195'; b. 31'6''; dr. 9'6''; 1861)

York (Sch: t. 68; a. 18-pdr.; Norfolk; 1861)

Annex B

RIVER DEFENSE FLEET

In 1862 the Confederate War Department purchased 14 vessels and converted them into lightly armed ships to defend the Mississippi River in cooperation with the Confederate Navy. Manned by Army personnel, they were under the overall command of Capt. J. E. Montgomery, CSN, a former river steamboat captain. (For details of their actions, see individual histories *supra*.)

Eight of the 14 ships, 6 of them equipped with rams, operated in the water around Memphis, Tenn., and participated in the battle at that place on 6 June 1862, with the following results:

Colonel Lovell—Sunk

General Beauregard—Sunk

General Bragg—Captured and taken into the U. S. Navy as *General Bragg*.

General Earl Van Dorn—The only vessel of the River Defense Fleet that avoided capture or destruction, escaping by means of her superior speed. Destroyed 26 June 1862 to prevent capture.

General M. Jeff Thompson—Set on fire during battle; blew up; abandoned.

General Sterling Price—Run ashore; abandoned; later taken into the U.S. Navy as *General Price*.

General Sumter—Run ashore; abandoned; later taken into the U.S. Navy as *Sumter*.

Little Rebel—Run ashore and captured; later taken into the U.S. Navy under the same name.

The remaining six ships, all of which were converted tug-boats, operated in the lower Mississippi and participated in the defense of Forts Jackson and St. Philip, 24-28 April 1862. These were:

Defiance—Emerged with little damage from the fighting on the 24th but was destroyed by her crew on the 28th.

General Breckinridge—Abandoned and burned on 24 April 1862.

General Lovell—Abandoned and burned on 24 April 1862.

Resolute—Abandoned and burned on 24 April 1862.

Stonewall Jackson—Destroyed by Union forces on 24 April 1862.

Warrior—Destroyed by Union forces on 24 April 1862.

Units of the River Defense Fleet are shown withdrawing from the Battle of Memphis, 6 June 1862.

Annex C

TEXAS MARINE DEPARTMENT, CONFEDERATE STATES ARMY

The Texas Marine Department, also called the Texas Marine Brigade, was organized by the Confederates early in the war to defend the coastal waters of that key State. In August 1861 Comdr. W. W. Hunter, CSN, was ordered to report to the Secretary of War for duty and assigned to superintend efforts to protect the Texas coast. An order of 21 September authorized his use of all available light draft vessels in that area to patrol the coastal waters and transport troops and supplies. Commander Hunter's first official act was to charter *Bayou City* on 26 September 1861. From that time until the end of hostilities more than 25 vessels became involved in these activities. A few were armed but most were used solely as transports. Some ships served only briefly with the Marine

Department; others for the war's duration. See details of their histories *supra*.

A. S. Ruthven
Alamo
Bayou City
Clifton
Colonel Stell
Corpus Christi
Diana
Dime
*Dodge
Era No. 3

*Dodge, originally USRC *Henry Dodge*, operated with the Texas Marine Department but maintained her identity as a ship of the Confederate States Navy.

Fanny Morgan	*Lone Star*
Florilda	*Lucy Gwin*
General Rusk	*Mary Hill*
George Buckhart	*Neptune*
Grand Bay	*Roebuck*
Harriet Lane	*Royal Yacht*
Island City	*Sachem*
Jeff Davis	*Sunflower*
John F. Carr	*Uncle Ben*
Josiah A. Bell	

Ships of the Texas Marine Department in action at Sabine Pass.

Annex D

THE CONFEDERATE STONE FLEET

The Confederate Army and Navy found it expedient at times to construct barricades at strategic points in inland waterways to permit the escape of their forces, prevent captures, and impede the Federal advance. During the first half of 1862, two areas of Virginia, Croatan Sound and the Pamunkey River, were obstructed with numerous ships which were seized from private owners specifically for this purpose, or which had served briefly as transports. Varied sizes and types of ships, having little if any previous service were loaded with stone and sand, or filled with dirt, then towed to a designated spot and sunk as a hazard to all craft that passed.

PART A

The following ships were seized by forces under Gen. J. E. Johnston, CSA, and employed to carry provisions and supplies while the army was at Yorktown. When the army withdrew toward Richmond, the transports were loaded with Government stores that were discharged at White House, Va., on the Pamunkey River. Most of the ships were then sunk in that vicinity during May 1862 to delay Union gunboats.

Vessels sunk at White House, Va., between 5 & 10 May 1862

Claudio, owned by M. J. Williams

Little Addie, sloop owned by John Montgomery

Vessels destroyed at Cooke's Island 5 & 10 May 1862

American Coaster, schooner owned by Robert W. Crockett, was loaded with dirt and prepared for sinking but was captured by USS *Currituck.* She was later used as a Union transport.

David Vaname, schooner owned by Cornelius V. Johnson

Diana Hopkins, schooner owned by Edward F. Phillips

Experiment, schooner owned by William C. Messick

Friendship, schooner owned by Allman and Watts

Hannah Ann, schooner

J. & G. Fair, schooner owned by William Lee

J. T. Connor, owned by John Bagby

Josephine, schooner owned by William Dansey

King William, schooner owned by William Sayre & James W. Fleming

Mary Elizabeth

Mary Luyster, owned by T. J. Bland

Ornament, sloop owned by G. H. Crittenden and Christopher Post

Palestine, schooner owned by Thomas

*Planter (cf: *American Coaster, supra*)

Princess, schooner owned by William Lee

R. P. Waller, schooner owned by T. W. Gilliam

Sarah Ann, schooner owned by William S. Ward

**Starlight

---

* *Planter,* a schooner, was prepared for sinking but was captured by USS *Currituck* on 7 May 1862. She was turned over by the Union to her former owner in recognition of assistance rendered in the York and Pamunkey Rivers.

** *Starlight,* also scheduled for destruction, was approached while underway for White House, Va., by USS *Corwin. Starlight* escaped up the Potopotank Creek where she was abandoned. She was seized by *Corwin* on 15 June and sent into Norfolk as a prize.

William Edward, schooner owned by Joel and William Thomas

William Shanberg, schooner owned by William C. Messick and Edward F. Phillips

Vessels destroyed at Garlick's Landing Between 5 & 10 May 1862

Jenny Lind, schooner owned by J. F. New & Co.

Star, owned by S. Moon

Vessels burned near Indian Town between 5 & 10 May 1862

Reliance

Way, schooner owned by Gresham and Bagby

Vessels burned at Newcastle on 17 May 1862

Jefferson, schooner owned by Garefoster & Braumly

Margaret Schultz, owned by Harrenn and Ballown

O. Whitmond, owned by John Wright

Walton, owned by John Warring

Watchman, owned by Jonh E. Brown

Wave, owned by R. Howard

William S. Ryland, owned by William Berkeley

Vessels burned at Cumberland between 5 & 10 May 1862

California, schooner owned by Blassingham

Caroline Baker, schooner owned by F. and Christopher Post

Vessels sunk near Bassett's Landing on 17 May 1862

Alert, owned by A. West

Ann Bell, owned by William Thomas

Betsey Richards, owned by Washington Smith

Francis and Theodore, owned by James Arrington

J. R. Baylis

James Braden, owned by S. Kimble

John Allen, schooner owned by S. Guy

Little Wave, owned by Thomas Hibble

Mary Alice, owned by Captain Gage

Mary Baxter, owned by C. W. Parks

Mirage, owned by estate of Wm. Johnson

Oxford, schooner of 85 tons and 7' draft built in 1855 at Dorchester County, Md., and owned by Claybrook and Dobyns

Paragon, sloop, owned by estate of William Johnson

Sarah Washington, schooner owned by Moore and Elliston

Sea Witch, owned by James Robins

Union, owned by Benjamin F. Gresham

Virginia, owned by E. Lawson

Wild Pigeon, schooner owned by William Messick

William and Wesley, schooner owned by J. D. Cronmonger

William Francis, schooner owned by C. Coleman

PART B

In January 1862 Flag Officer Lynch assessed the Confederate position about Hatteras Inlet where a large fleet of Union transports and steamers had assembled under Flag Officer L. M. Goldsborough, USN, to penetrate the Sound and take Roanoke Island. Lynch wrote to Secretary of the Navy Mallory: "Here is the great thoroughfare from Albemarle Sound and its tributaries, and if the enemy obtains lodgments or succeeds in passing here he will cut off a very rich country from Norfolk Market." Before the Union force departed its anchorage at Hatteras Inlet on 5 February in its successful amphibious expedition against Roanoke Island, the Confederates anxiously labored to sink piles and ships across the sound below Weir's Point. Included among those sunk as obstructions were the following schooners listed with the date of their scuttling:

A. C. Williams, schooner, 19 January

Carter, schooner, 21 January

Josephine, schooner, 20 January

Lydia and Martha, schooner, 1 February

Rio, schooner, 28 January

Southern Star, schooner, 31 January

Spuell and Moss, schooner, 26 January

Tripleet, schooner, 29 January

Zenith, schooner, 27 January

CIVIL WAR BLOCKADE RUNNERS

Blockade runners at anchor, St. Georges, Bermuda.

CIVIL WAR BLOCKADE RUNNERS

For the Confederacy, running the blockade of its coast, which President Lincoln had called upon his then small Navy to initiate, was one of the most vital aspects of the war. It was upon the availability of foreign supplies that the industrially deficient South depended to continue the conflict.

In this enterprise—which became both increasingly critical and, as more ships joined the blockading fleets, increasingly dangerous—Bermuda was a crucial point of transshipment. Goods and supplies were brought into Bermuda in neutral bottoms and reloaded on swift and shallow draft runners for the Confederacy. The usual trip to Wilmington or Charleston took only three or four days. Despite the alertness of Federal blockaders, during the course of the war millions of dollars worth of arms, supplies, cotton and tobacco shuttled back and forth between the Southern ports and Bermuda, where Confederate sympathy was strong.

It is fitting, therefore, that the excellent watercolor paintings of blockade runners collected by Sir Samuel Spurling are housed in the St. Georges Museum, St. Georges Histroical Society, Bermuda. Many of the more than thirty paintings in the collection are presented here through the courtesy of the Confederate Museum and the assistance of Captain Roy Belcher, USN, formerly commanding officer of the U.S. Naval Station, Bermuda, who arranged to have them photographed for this publication.

Overlooking the harbor at St. Georges, Bermuda.

The "Ad. Vance"

500 tons. Ran the blockade of Wilmington N.C. ten times and returned to Liverpool to repair machinery. Sailed again for Bermuda and put into Cork June 30th 1864. Coaled and proceeded July 2nd.

A notorious Runner, captured September 10th 1864 on her way to Halifax from Wilmington, by the U.S.S. "Santiago de Cuba." The Captain of the warship got $3,700.00 as his share of the prize money.

Advance

The *Advance* (also known as *A. D. Vance* or *ad Vance* and previously christened *Lord Clyde*) was a Clyde-built 500 ton iron paddlewheeler measuring some 230 feet in length and 26 feet at the beam. Her boilers drove her at the remarkable speed of 17 knots. Capable of carrying as many as 500 bales of cotton, she was purchased for the State of North Carolina and in the course of her 20 trips through the blockade to and from Bermuda she paid a handsome return on her purchase price of $171,000. Once, on her third voyage, inbound for Wilmington, she ran through the entire blockading squadron in broad daylight. But *Advance* was not always so successful. In the month following 8 August 1864 she made nine futile attempts to slip past the blockaders and over the bar at Cape Fear. On her ninth try, 10 September, she skirted the Federals only to encounter U.S.S. *Santiago de Cuba* sailing north to recoal. A nine and a half hour chase ensued, but finally *Advance* was taken and her career as a blockade runner ended.

The "Alliance"

Sailed from Cork for Nassau, N.P. September 1863. Grounded and was captured in the Savannah River April 12th 1864.

Alliance

With her three athwart ships funnels and whale-backed main deck, *Alliance* presented perhaps the most unusual silhouette of any of the Civil War runners. The Fraser-Trenholm blockade runner ran aground on Danfushie Island at Savannah, Georgia, on 12 April 1864.

The "Badger."
100 tons. From Liverpool to Nassau, N.P. Put into Cork April 6th and sailed April 7th 1864. Reached Nassau May 12th.

Badger

Badger was a conventional twin-stacked fast steamer whose funnels were probably built on the telescoping principle that would allow them to be lowered almost to deck level to make her less easily detected by the blockaders. She ran into various ports—including Wilmington and Galveston—and was never captured. She was sighted in Fayal harbor in the Azores in July 1865.

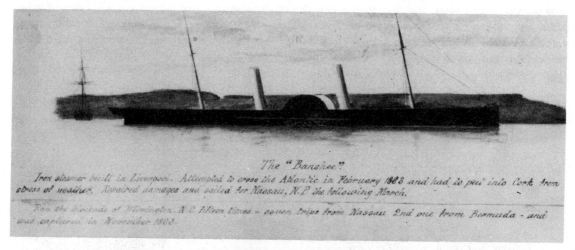

The "Banshee."
Iron steamer built in Liverpool. Attempted to cross the Atlantic in February 1863 and had to put into Cork from stress of weather. Repaired damages and sailed for Nassau, N.P. the following March.
Ran the blockade of Wilmington, N.C. fifteen times - seven trips from Nassau 2nd one from Bermuda - and was captured in November 1863.

Banshee No. 1

Banshee No. 1 was built in Liverpool, England, and painted a hard to sight dull grey, expressly for the purpose of running the blockade. She became the first steel vessel to cross the Atlantic. She was a small turtle back ship of 217 tons with a length of 214 feet and a beam of 20 feet. Her top speed was 11 knots and she burned 31 tons of coal a day while cruising at 10 knots. But she drew only 8 feet of water and her eight trips through the Union blockade into Wilmington earned her shareholders a 700 per cent profit on their investment. The desperate straits in which runners frequently found themselves is illustrated by U.S.S. *James Adger*'s pursuit of *Banshee No. 1* on one of her return trips to Bermuda. *Adger* chased *Banshee No. 1* for 15 hours, forcing her to burn coal at a rapid rate. When the Federal warship finally broke off the chase and the blockade runner headed south for the Bahamas, her coal supply was so low that the mainmast, bulwarks, and finally cotton soaked in turpentine were fed to her fires to bring her to an island 60 miles north of Nassau.

VI–338

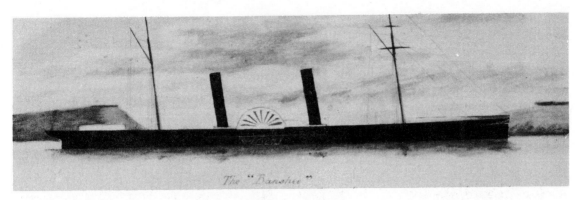

The "Banshee"

Banshee No. 2

Outwardly *Banshee No. 2* was similar to her namesake predecessor in the Anglo-Confederate Trading Company's fleet. But *No. 2* was larger, longer, faster and better built. She was double the tonnage at 439 tons. She was 252 feet in length with a beam of 31 feet. She drew 11 feet of water and was 4½ knots faster than *Banshee No. 1*'s 11 knot speed. T. E. Taylor of the Anglo-Confederate Trading Company, made 28 trips through the blockade. *Banshee No. 2* apparently was his favorite ship. On one occasion Taylor was taking *No. 2* quietly into the Cape Fear River below Wilmington, North Carolina. On board was a gift horse from Egypt, intended as a present for Jefferson Davis. As the ship drew near shore, the horse whinnied, alerting the blockader's gun crews. *Banshee No. 2* just managed to win a close race to the protection of Fort Fisher's guns. After Fort Fisher fell in January 1865, Taylor and *Banshee No. 2* began to operate out of Havana for Galveston, Texas, where she had another narrow escape. Forced into the middle of the blockaders in daylight, she ran aground on the Galveston Bar and it was feared that she had broken her back and would fall to the closing blockaders. However, the next crashing wave slammed her over the bar and into the harbor, safe for the time being. At the end of the war *Banshee No. 2* was sold into more prosaic work for less than one tenth of her original cost.

The "Bat"

Bat

Bat was one of the runners laid down by Jones, Quiggin and Company of Liverpool at the behest of Commander James D. Bulloch, CSN. She was 771 tons, 230 feet in length, 26 feet in the beam and drew only 7.6 feet of water. Her 180 horsepower Watt double oscillating engines drove *Bat* at 16 knots. She was constructed of steel, fore and aft schooner rigged with twin funnels. *Bat* could carry 800 to 850 bales of cotton and coal for a round trip to Nassau. Captured on 10 October 1864, she was purchased by the Navy from the prize court for $150,000 and was highly regarded because of her swift speed.

The "Charlotte"
Steamer of 400 tons. Put into Cork September 4th 1864 bound to Halifax, N. S.

Charlotte

Charlotte shared the forlorn distinction with *Stag* and *Blenheim* of being the last of the blockade runners to put into the Cape Fear River. The runners were already making for Wilmington when Fort Fisher fell to the Union. Rear Admiral D. D. Porter instructed a Lieutenant Commander William Cushing to rig the usual lights on the Confederate signal stations in the river and on the headlands so that any blockade runners would be unaware that control of the Cape Fear had changed hands. The run was successful, for on 19 January 1865 the 400 ton *Charlotte* anchored in the river, intending to continue to Wilmington at daybreak, and was captured.

The "Colonel Lamb"

Colonel Lamb

The sleek, graceful *Colonel Lamb*—named for the daring commander of Fort Fisher—was one of the most succussful runners in the war. She was laid down as hull #165 in 1864 by Jones, Quiggin and Company, builders of many other swift steamers. She was constructed with four water-tight bulkheads, was of 1788 tons, 281 feet in length and 36 feet at the beam. She was capable of making almost 17 knots. Dashing Captain Thomas J. Lockwood commanded *Colonel Lamb*. She was originally registered to William Quiggin, builder, but was secretly transferred to J. B. Lafitte, Confederate Agent at Nassau who kept title to her for the Confederate government. *Colonel Lamb* survived the war only to meet an abrupt end. She was sold by the firm of John Fraser and Company to the Government of Brazil. While loading explosives destined for South America *Colonel Lamb* blew up at her anchorage in the Mersey River.

The "Coquette"
Screw steamer 550 tons. From Glasgow to Bermuda. Sailed from Cork November 7th 1863.

Coquette

The single stacked, three masted, schooner rigged *Coquette* weighed 550 tons, was 220 feet long, 25 feet at the beam and drew 10 feet of water. The rakish *Coquette* was purchased for the Confederate States Navy by Commander J. D. Bulloch because she carried more than 1,200 bales of cotton and had a speed in excess of 13 knots. She made many successful runs for the Richmond government before word reached Secretary of the Navy Mallory that her boiler tubes were closing with scale and reducing her speed. Eventually she broke down in Bermuda and was sold for $16,000 to Messrs. W. W. Finney, B. F. Fichlen and J. R. Anderson (Tredegar Iron Works, Richmond). A union undercover agent, Captain Richard Squires, was engaged by her owners to rescue her for them at the end of the war, but Squires promptly seized her and took her into Baltimore, a prize for the United States.

The "Druid"
From Liverpool to Nassau. Put into Cork January 23rd and sailed January 28th 1864.

Druid

Druid, with her distinctive clipper bow and single tall stack was property of the Palmetto Company, Henry W. Felton, Master. She was able to run into Charleston as late as September 1864.

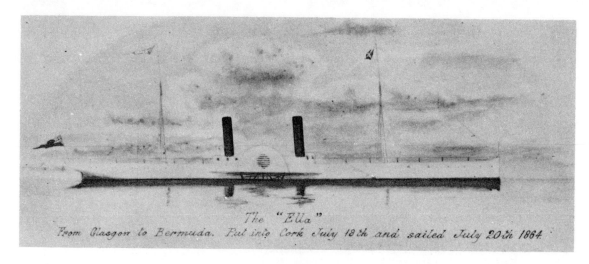

The "Ella"
From Glasgow to Bermuda. Put into Cork July 18th and sailed July 20th 1864

Ella

Although there were at least three *Ellas* involved in running the Union blockade, the *Ella* pictured above was the largest. She was the first runner to fly the Confederate Ensign in an English port. The 404 ton paddle-wheel steamer, owned by Fraser, Trenholm and Company, made just one successful run past the cruisers of the blockading squadron. On her second voyage *Ella* was sighted and chased aground near Fort Fisher.

The "Flamingo.
280 tons. From Glasgow to Bermuda. Put into Cork July 8th and sailed July 9th 1864.

Flamingo

The three funnels of *Flamingo*— and her sister *Ptarmigan*—are her most unusual and identifiable characteristics. Built on Commander Bulloch's orders, *Flamingo* was relatively light (280 tons) and was 270 feet long and 24 feet at the beam. She drew 7 feet of water and was able to cruise at 14 or 15 knots. *Flamingo* usually wore white paint rather than the dark hull pictured above. She carried the usual turtleback forecastle and a 45 man crew. In September of 1864 she was laid up in Bermuda because her crew was battling yellow fever. Nevertheless, *Flamingo* apparently ended her career attempting to run into Charleston, South Carolina, as a contemporary chart shows a *Flamingo* wrecked there off Battery Rutledge.

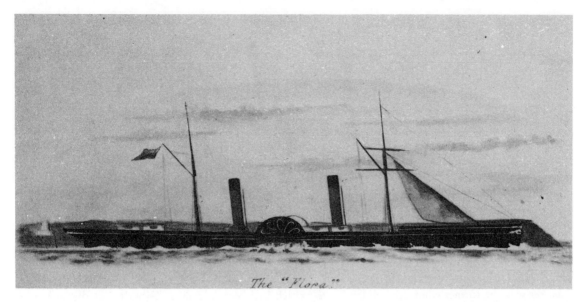

Flora

A *Flora*, with paddle-wheel and twin stacks, very long with a light draft, and reported as displacing 700 tons, was chased aground during the evening of 22 October 1864 by blockaders off Charleston's Fort Moultrie. She was completely wrecked by the combined shelling of the blockaders and the Union held forts on Morris Island.

Fox

Fox was a J. Fraser and Company runner, called by Captain J. F. Green, Senior Union Officer off Charleston, "an old and successful sinner". She presented the typical two funneled silhouette of the blockade runner but carried an extended poop that may have been "weather rounded" as was her forecastle turtleback. *Fox* broke down in July 1864 while attempting to run out of Charleston. She ran into Galveston from Havana as late as 22 April 1865. With her sister ship, *Badger*, *Fox* put into Fayal, Azores in July of 1865, her days as a runner ending with the fall of the Confederacy.

The "Gibraltar"

Formerly the Confederate States Cruiser "Sumter" 340 tons. Put into Cork short of coal December 5th 1863 ten days out from Wilmington, N.C. with a cargo of cotton. Coaled and proceeded to Liverpool December 6th.

Gibraltar

Gibraltar was the former commerce raider *Sumter* which had been laid up in Gibraltar in the spring of 1862 [see *Sumter* history in "Confederate Forces Afloat"]. The Fraser-Trenholm interest bought her in December 1862, and she was repaired and refitted as a blockade runner. *Gibraltar* made at least one trip into Wilmington under Captain E. C. Reid, apparently breaking down close to the Cape Fear and limping through the Union blockade to deliver two large Whitworth rifled guns. *Gibraltar* was never captured but sank at sea off Cherbourg, France.

The "Julia"

Clyde-built steamer of 117 tons. Put into Cork to repair machinery January 8th and sailed for Nassau, N.P. January 15th 1864.

Julia

Built in Renfrew, Scotland, in 1863, *Julia* displaced 117 tons and drew 7 feet of water forward and 8 feet aft while making a 12 knot speed. *Julia* was captured by U.S.S. *Acacia* off Charleston on 23 December 1864 as a result of her being sighted close inshore, blowing off steam. She was run aground and abandoned by her crew when taken under fire by *Acacia*. The boarding party and prize crew managed to pull the small steamer off the shoals and repair her damaged machinery. She was floated and towed to sea, her career as a runner ended.

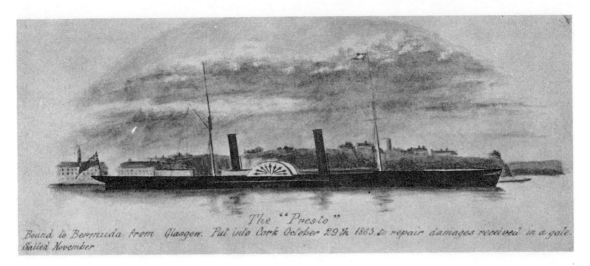

The "Presto"

Bound to Bermuda from Glasgow. Put into Cork October 29th 1863 to repair damages received in a gale. Sailed November

Presto

Presto was one of the smallest runners, displacing only 164 tons. On 2 February she was run aground off Fort Moultrie at Charleston where for the next two days she served as a practice target for Union monitors *Lehigh, Passaic, Catskill* and *Nahant*.

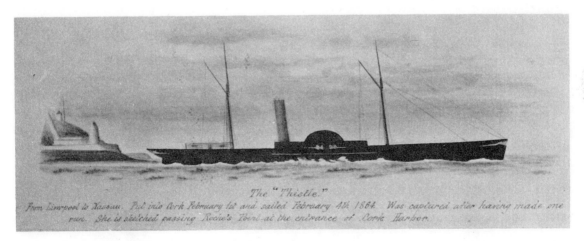

The "Thistle."

From Liverpool to Nassau. Put into Cork February 1st and sailed February 4th 1864. Was captured after having made one run. She is sketched passing Roche's Point at the entrance of Cork Harbor.

Thistle

Thistle's career as a blockade runner was disappointing. She made one run and was captured. She was commanded by Alexander Hora who managed to include 150 cases of champagne in her hold on her successful run. *Thistle* was a single-stacked sidewheeler of 700 tons. She was 204 feet in length and 29 feet in beam with a draft of 10 feet and a 12 knot speed. Her career as a blockade runner was cut short after one successful trip, when, on 4 June 1864, the Glasgow built steamer was captured by U.S.S. *Fort Jackson* at sea east of Charleston. *Thistle* was subsequently taken into the Navy and served in the North Atlantic Blockading Squadron.

VI–345

The *"Tristram Shandy."*
From Glasgow to Bermuda. Put into Cork March 10th and sailed March 19th 1864. Was captured
July 2nd 1864.

Tristram Shandy

Tristram Shandy was one of several vessels belonging to the Anglo-Confederate Trading Company, a joint stock enterprise backed by private citizens in England. *Tristram Shandy* was built in England of ⅜″ iron plating. She displaced 444 tons, was 222 feet in length with a beam of 23 feet and drew less than 6½ feet of water fully loaded. She was a sidewheeler with two boilers and eight furnaces of a peculiar design. On her second trip out of Wilmington she was loaded with cotton and $50,000 in gold. She began to throw off flames and sparks which attracted the attention of U.S.S. *Kansas*. After a long stern chase, *Kansas* captured her far east of Fort Fisher on 15 May 1864 (rather than the 2 July 1864 date which the artist indicated). *Tristram Shandy* was taken into the Navy and served vigorously on blockade duty for the remainder of the war.

The *"Iona"* and *"Flora"* and

CIVIL WAR SHIPS
SALVAGED or MEMORIALIZED

Salvage operations bring a section of U.S.S. Cairo *to the surface of the Yazoo River.*

CIVIL WAR SHIPS SALVAGED OR MEMORIALIZED

An object gives a dimension to history which the picture or the word can never impart. One can read of the vivid exploits of *Constellation* or *Constitution*, and a good picture presents the eye with an artist's conception of these grand frigates. But nothing compares to the thrilling and meaningful experience of actually walking the decks of the magnificent ships, of scanning the towering masts, of examining the great black guns. Here is no author's description or painter's rendition. This is living history which cannot be refuted.

Recent years have been marked by an increasing awareness of the historic ship or relic as a focal point in the nation's naval heritage. Whether it be a mighty World War II battleship memorialized by a state like *Alabama, Massachusetts, North Carolina, Texas;* a small lake gunboat of the American Revolution; a Civil War ironclad; or an enemy shot embedded in the sternpost of the *Kearsarge,* each relic is a priceless inheritance for generations of Americans to come.

Given the impetus of the Centennial observance, there has been feverish activity along the coast and on the inland waters to locate, salvage, and restore Civil War ships of both North and South. This is often a discouraging, and always costly, venture. Nevertheless the results have been splendid, and rich treasures have been added to the substance of the country's stirring history. It is strongly hoped that with encouragement and proper support, dedicated men will push this effort forward in the years ahead.

U.S.S. Cairo, *an ironclad river gunboat, was the first ship to be sunk in action by a torpedo (mine).*

U.S.S. *Cairo*

Cairo, an ironclad river gunboat, was built in 1861 by James Eads and Co., Mound City, Illinois, under an Army contract; and commissioned as an Army ship on 25 January 1862, Lieutenant James M. Prichett, USN, in command.

Cairo served with the Army's Western Gunboat Fleet, commanded by Flag Officer A. H. Foote, on the Mississippi and Ohio Rivers and their tributaries until transferred to the Navy on 1 October 1862 with the other river gunboats. Active in the occupation of Clarksville, Tennessee on 17 February 1862, and of Nashville, Tennessee on 25 February, *Cairo* stood down the river on 12 April escorting mortar boats to begin the lengthy operations against Fort Pillow, Tennessee. An engagement with Confederate gunboats at Plum Point Bend on 11 May marked a series of blockading and bombardment activities which culminated in the abandonment of the Fort by its defenders on 4 June.

Two days later, 6 June 1862, *Cairo* joined in the triumph of seven Union ships and a tug over eight Confederate gunboats off Memphis, Tennessee, an action in which five of the opposing gunboats were sunk or run ashore, two seriously damaged, and only one managed to escape. That night Union forces occupied the city. *Cairo* returned to patrol on the Mississippi until 21 November when she joined the Yazoo Expedition. On 12 December 1862, while clearing mines from the river preparatory to the attack on Haines Bluff, Mississippi, *Cairo* struck a torpedo and sank, the first warship to be so destroyed in combat.

For decades *Cairo* lay where she went down. Then, in the summer of 1956, she was rediscovered by National Park historian Edwin C. Bearss and geologist Warren Grabau. It was not until three years later, however, that attempts to actually salvage the ironclad from the mud of the Yazoo River were begun.

The attempts to raise *Cairo* proved tedious and expensive. With considerable effort the salvage crew brought bits and pieces, including the pilothouse, to the surface. The finds showed some of the wreck to be in a remarkable state of preservation.

An eight-inch naval gun was still charged with canister. The gun sight was set at 850 yards and the brass slide was deeply grooved at this point indicating that most of the ironclad's firing was done at short range.

The oaken gun carriage was in almost as good condition as it had been nearly a century before and impressions in the mud on the casabel and carriage indicated the hemp tackles used to absorb the recoil were intact until the gun was pulled from the casemate.

Powder canisters were found in the wreckage and a Navy explosives demolition team came from Indian Head, Maryland to investigate danger from other explosives which might have been on board. Surprisingly enough, *Cairo*'s powder was still dry—mute testimony to the care taken to keep it so a century before.

Cairo's wreckage was full of silt and the flotsam of decades was lodged against it. Freeing her from all the debris that held her to the bottom was impossible. Nevertheless, attempts were made to lift the hulk onto a barge, but the river's water level was low and the lifting wires cut the ship into three major sections.

Although *Cairo* sustained considerable damage during her resurrection, she can be restored to the condition she was in when she sank. Now at Pascagoula, Mississippi, for restoration, she will return to Vicksburg as the stellar attraction of what is expected to be an admirable local museum. Restoring the *Cairo* will be costly.

This contemporary sketch of ''Cairo submerged'' was drawn by the well known combat artist Frank Vizetelli who covered the war at first hand for the Illustrated London News.

The midship section of Cairo was lifted from the river separately after it was severed accidentally from the bow and stern sections during salvage operations in the latter part of 1964. This section contained the gunboat's boilers.

(Photo courtesy of Vicksburg *Evening Post*.)

One of the first items raised from Cairo was this 32 pounder gun.

A number of valuable artifacts and relics were saved when Cairo was salvaged. Balance scales and a two-handed meat cleaver are pictured above.

Above is a stove from Cairo bearing the label "Southern Belle." At the left are three of the gunboat's five boilers.

(Photo courtesy of Vicksburg Evening Post.)

(*Above*) Cairo's *casemate is raised from the Yazoo River.* (*Right*) *Workers examine a gunport cover.*

The bow of U.S.S. Cairo *is shown on a lifting barge after having been raised in 1964*

(Photo courtesy of Vicksburg *Evening Post.*)

C.S.S. *Chattahoochee*

The wooden sidewheel gunboat *Chattahoochee* was built in 1862-1863, but she was plagued with machinery failures [see "Confederate Forces Afloat," page 208], and was unable to get into action before being destroyed to prevent capture when the Confederates abandoned their defenses in the Apalachicola River area. In mid-April 1865 Union troops found her burned hulk some 12 miles below Columbus, Georgia.

A small section of the ship has been salvaged, as well as a number of artifacts. Of particular importance to Civil War historians are her engines, which were found intact and even show they had been struck with sledgehammers to destroy them prior to setting *Chattahoochee* afire.

C.S.S. Chattahoochee, *a wooden gunboat, was destroyed by Confederates to prevent her capture. Some of her machinery, shown here, reveals that sledge hammers were used to ruin the engines.*

(Photo courtesy of Confederate Salvage Association, Inc., Columbus, Georgia)

U.S.S. *Constellation*

The first *Constellation*, a frigate authorized by congressional enactment of 27 March 1794, was the design of naval constructors, J. Humphreys and J. Fox whose plans were altered in the execution by builder, D. Stodder, and supervisor of construction, Captain T. Truxtun. She was built at the Sterrett Shipyard, Baltimore, Md., and was launched on 7 September 1797, the second of the United States frigates to go down the ways.

Constellation's first cruise, from June through August 1798, in which she convoyed merchant ships to sea showed admirable qualities, including a sailing speed which could win her the nickname "Yankee Race Horse," and ensure an outstanding career of service.

Constellation figured actively in five wars. Her actions which closely parallel the course of American national involvement began with glorious achievement in the undeclared naval war against France. Here, as a unit of the newly reborn U.S. Navy, *Constellation* helped establish traditions of discipline and organization—the firm basis upon which United States naval power has grown to preeminence. Under the command of Captain T. Truxton, she departed for the Caribbean in December 1798 to join the West India Squadron in protection of American commerce. On 9 February 1799 she received her baptism of blood capturing the 40-gun frigate, *L'Insurgente* in battle off Nevis, West Indies, in a hard fought victory, and bringing her prize into port. In succeeding months, she also encountered and seized two French privateers, *Diligent* and *Union*.

After a brief voyage without incident under Captain S. Barron, *Constellation*, commanded again by Truxtun, sailed in December 1799 for the West India patrol. On the evening of 1 February 1800 she sighted the 52-gun frigate *Vengeance* and engaged her in a lengthy, furious battle. Although *Vengeance* twice struck her colors and was close to sinking, she was able to utilize the cover of darkness to escape from *Constellation* who, disabled by the loss of her mainmast, was unable to pursue. More success came to her in May 1800 with the recapture of three American merchantmen from French possession.

U.S.S. Constellation *as she appeared in the Civil War period.*

At the end of the Franco-American dispute, *Constellation* sailed back to home waters. Anchoring in Delaware Bay on 10 April 1801, the ship was caught in winds and an ebb tide which laid her over on her beam ends to ground, thereby occasioning need for extensive repair and refitting.

National interest next called her to serve in the Mediterranean Squadron which sought to eliminate depredations being inflicted by the Barbary pirates. Sailing with the squadron of Commodore R. Morris, and later, with that of Commodores S. Barron and J. Rodgers, *Constellation* acted in the blockade of Tripoli in May 1802; cruised widely throughout the Mediterranean in 1804 in demonstration of United States seapower; evacuated in June 1805 a contingent of Marines, as well as diplomatic personages, from Derne at the conclusion of a remarkable fleet-shore operation against Tripoli; and took part in a squadron movement against Tunis which culminated in peace terms in August 1805. *Constellation* returned to the States in November 1805, mooring at Washington where she later was placed in ordinary until 1812.

Constellation underwent an extensive repair in the Washington Navy Yard in 1812–13 which added 14″ to her beam.

With the advent of our second war with England, *Constellation*, now commanded by Captain C. Stewart, was dispatched to the Hampton Roads area. In January 1813 shortly after her arrival she was effectively blockaded by an imposing British fleet. Turning frustration into success, she took station between the enemy and the fortification at Craney Island and acted as a buffer, thwarting every British attempt to destroy the fort or to capture the ship.

The Treaty of Ghent ending the War of 1812 was followed closely by the renewal of naval action against the Barbary powers who had enriched themselves considerably during our struggle with England. *Constellation*, attached to the Mediterranean Squadron under Commodore S. Decatur, sailed from New York on 20 May 1815 and joined in the capture of the Algerian frigate, *Mashuda*, on 17 June 1815. With this demonstration of United States naval prowess, Decatur was enabled to exact treaties of peace from Algiers, Tunis, and Tripoli. *Constellation* was called upon to remain with the squadron under Commodores W. Bainbridge, I. Chauncey, and J. Shaw to enforce the agreements, returning to Hampton Roads only in December 1817.

With but brief periods of repair in 1828–29, 1832, 1834–35, and 1838–39, *Constellation's* career in the interval between this action against the pirates and the outbreak of the Civil War proved varied and colorful. From 12 November 1819 to 24 April 1820 she served as flagship of Commodore C. Morris on the Brazil Station patrolling to protect American commerce against privateers and to negotiate favorable trade agreements with the South American nations.

On 25 July 1820, she sailed for the first time to Pacific waters where she was attached to the Squadron of Commodore C. Stewart and remained for 2 years patrolling in defense of our trading ships off the coast of Peru, an area whose disquiet erupted into revolt against Spain.

In 1827 *Constellation* acted briefly as flagship for the West India Squadron on a twofold mission involving the eradication of the last of the pirates and the interception of slavers operating in the area. In August 1829 she cruised to the Mediterranean to exercise vigilant watch over American trade and to collect indemnities owing from previous losses suffered by United States merchantmen. While en route to her station, she carried the American ministers to France and England to their posts of duty. Returning to the United States in November 1831, she underwent minor repair and departed again for her Mediterranean station in April 1832 where she remained until outbreak of cholera forced her home in November 1834.

In October 1835 the frigate sailed for the Gulf of Mexico to assist in crushing the Seminole uprising. She landed shore parties to relieve the Army garrisons and sent her boats on amphibious expeditions. Mission accomplished, she then cruised with the West India Squadron until 1838 serving part of this period in the capacity of flagship for Commodore A. Dallas.

The decade of the 1840's saw *Constellation* circumnavigate the globe. As flagship of Captain Kearny and the East India Squadron, her mission, as assigned in March 1841, was to safeguard American lives and property against loss in the Opium War, and further, to enable negotiation of commercial treaties. En route home in May 1843 she entered the Hawaiian Islands in time to express American disapproval of the impending British annexation of the islands, and thereafter she sailed homeward making calls at South American ports.

Laid up in ordinary at Norfolk from 1845 through 1853, she was found to be greatly in need of extensive repair. Thus, in 1854 she was brought into the yard and, in keeping with the needs of the time, modified into a 22-gun sloop-of-war.

Constellation was recommissioned on 28 July 1855 and departed under the flag of Captain C. Bell for a 3-year cruise with the Mediterranean Squadron to protect American interests. This was followed in June 1858 by a brief tour in Cuban waters where she safeguarded United States ships against unlawful search on the high seas.

Decommissioned for a short time, she was placed back into service in June 1859 and named flagship of the African Squadron. Her mission was to obliterate the slave trade; and here she performed well, capturing the brig *Delicia* in 1859; the bark *Cora* in 1860; and the brig *Triton* in 1861.

The Civil War brought *Constellation* home in September 1861 whereupon she was ordered to serve in the Mediterranean guarding Union merchant ships against attack by Confederate cruisers and privateers. She was thus occupied from April 1862 through May 1864 when she returned to Hampton Roads via the Gulf Coast.

It was fitting indeed that this fine ship, resplendent in her own accomplishments and imbued with the spirit of the United States Navy, should be selected to serve as receiving and training ship. She carried out one or the other of these duties at Norfolk, Philadelphia, Annapolis, and Newport in various periods of commission between January 1865 and June 1933 with the exception of time devoted to six special missions.

The first of these special assignments was a cruise to France in March 1878, wherein she transported displays for the Paris Exposition and was an ambassador of good will. On 10 November 1879 she was placed in commission for a special voyage to Gibraltar, carring crew and stores for the flagship of the Mediterranean Squadron and thereafter returning to New York.

In March 1880 she sailed on a mission of charity occasioned by the famine in Ireland. Under Commander E. Potter, *Constellation* brought most welcome relief to the suffering with stores donated by generous Americans.

Again active in September 1892 she continued to arouse interest and win praise for her country when she sailed for Gibraltar in order to assemble works of art for the Columbian Exposition, stopping en route at Naples and Le Havre, and arriving home in New York in February 1893.

Following repairs at Norfolk in 1893, *Constellation* was towed to Newport, there resuming her duties as a receiving and training ship which she continued until 1914 when she was again overhauled at Norfolk. In September 1914 she sailed to Baltimore via Annapolis and participated in the centennial celebration of the "Star Spangled Banner."

It is an interesting fact that this venerable lady of the seas on 1 December 1917 was renamed "*Old Constellation*" in order to permit use of the original name for a projected new battle cruiser (CC–2), which, however, was scrapped before completion in accordance with the naval limitations agreement of 1922. Her original name was restored on 24 July 1925.

In the grave days of World War II President F. D. Roosevelt looked for a symbol of American glory to inspire American citizens to the task which lay ahead. One symbol was *Constellation*, recommissioned in August 1940, and classified IX–20 on 8 January 1941. From 1941–43 she was assigned as the shore-based relief flagship of Commander-in-Chief, U.S. Atlantic Fleet, and later of Commander, Battleship Division Five, Atlantic Fleet. Thus she rendered her final service to the Fleet.

Plans to memorialize *Constellation* brought her to Boston in October 1946 but lack of funds delayed the project. Decommissioned for the last time on 4 February 1955, this, the then-oldest ship in the United States Navy, arrived at Baltimore on 9 August 1955, was stricken from the Navy List on 15 August 1955, and transferred to a patriotic group of citizens who are restoring her as a visible evidence of the United States' enduring need of the sea.

U.S.S. *Constitution*

Constitution, one of six frigates authorized by act of Congress, approved 27 March 1794, was designed by Joshua Humphreys, and built at Hartt's Shipyard, Boston, Mass., under the supervision of George Claghorn with Captain Samuel Nicholson as inspector. She was launched on 21 October 1797 and christened by Captain James Sever.

Into the trim frigate's construction went timbers from States ranging from Maine to Georgia, as well as copper bolts and spikes supplied by Paul Revere. A ship of beauty, power, and speed thus was fashioned as a national expression of growing naval interest, and a symbol auguring the dedication, courage, and achievement of American fighting men and ships.

Constitution put to sea on 22 July 1798, commanded by Captain Samuel Nicholson, the first of many illustrious commanding officers. Following her trial runs in August, she was readied for action in the Quasi-War with France and ordered to patrol for French armed ships between Cape Henry and Florida. One year later she became flagship on the Santo Domingo station, making several captures including the 24-gun privateer *Niger*, the *Spender*, and the letter-of-marque *Sandwich*. At war's end, *Constitution* returned to the Charleston Navy Yard where she was placed in ordinary.

In 1803 amid growing demand for tribute and increasing seizures by the Barbary pirates, *Constitution* was recommissioned under Captain Edward Preble and sailed as flagship of the Mediterranean Squadron on 14 August. Preble took command of the squadron and vigorously brought the war to Tripoli, executing well-laid plans with brilliant success. On *Constitution's* decks tactics for destroying the captured frigate, *Philadelphia*, were laid as well as those for blockading and assaulting the fortifications of Tripoli. The small United States fleet on 3 and 7 August 1804 bombarded the enemy's ships and shore batteries with telling results.

Commodore Samuel Barron and later Captain John Rodgers were next to command the squadron and *Constitution*, continuing to blockade and take prizes. Naval action thus generated a favorable climate for the negotiation of peace terms with Algiers, ending for a time our tribute payments. After the Tunisians agreed to similar terms in August, *Constitution* spent 2 years patrolling in maintenance of the peace. She sailed for home under Captain Hugh Campbell and arrived at Boston in November 1807. Placed out of commission, the frigate was repaired in the succeeding 2 years.

U.S.S. Constitution, *shown in this post Civil War photograph with U.S.S.* Santee, *at the Naval Academy in Annapolis, Maryland.*

In August 1809 she was recommissioned and became flagship of the North Atlantic Squadron, Commodore J. Rodgers, and in 1810 Isaac Hull was appointed her captain. The following year she carried U.S. Minister, Joel Barlow, to France and returned to Washington in March 1812 for overhaul. War with Britain impended and *Constitution* was readied for action. On 20 June 1812 the declaration of war was read to her assembled crew and on 12 July she took the sea under Captain Hull to rejoin the squadron of Commodore J. Rodgers.

On 17 July *Constitution* sighted five ships in company; supposing them to be Rodger's squadron, Hull attempted to join up. By the following morning, however, the group was identified as a powerful British squadron which included the frigates *Guerriere* and *Shannon*. The wind failed, becalming within range of the enemy who opened fire. Disaster threatened until Captain Hull astutely towed, wetted sails, and kedged to draw the ship slowly ahead of her pursuers. For 2 days all hands were on deck in this desperate and successful attempt at escape, a splendid example of resolute command, superior seamanship, and indefatigable effort.

During the war, *Constitution* ran the blockade at Boston on seven occasions and made five cruises ranging from Halifax, Nova Scotia, south to Guiana and east to Portugal. She captured, burned, or sent in as prizes nine merchantmen and five ships of war. Departing Boston on 2 August she sailed to the coast of Nova Scotia, where she captured and destroyed two British trading ships. Cruising off the Gulf of St. Lawrence on 19 August, she caught sight of *Guerriere*, a fast British frigate mounting 49 guns. *Gurriere* opened the action, pouring out shot which fell harmlessly into the sea or glanced ineffectively from the hull of *Constitution* whose cheering crew bestowed on her the famous nickname "Old Ironsides," which has stirred generations of Americans. As the ships drew abreast, Hull gave the command to fire and successive broadsides razed *Guerriere's* mizzen mast, damaging her foremast, and cut away most of her rigging. *Guerriere's* bowsprit fouled the lee rigging of *Constitution*, and both sides attempted to board, but the heavy seas prevented it. As the ships separated *Guerriere* fired point blank into the cabin of *Constitution* and set it on fire, but the flames were quickly extinguished. *Guerriere's* foremast and mainmast went by the board and she was left a helpless hulk.

The flag of *Guerriere* was struck in surrender and when the Americans boarded her they found her in such a crippled condition that they had to transfer the prisoners and burn her. It was a dramatic victory for America and for *Constitution*. In this battle of only half an hour the United States "rose to the rank of a first-class power"; the country was fired with fresh confidence and courage; and union among the States was greatly strengthened.

Constitution, Commodore William Bainbridge, again stood out from Boston on 29 December 1812 to add to her conquest the British 38-gun frigate, *Java*, whom she engaged off the coast of Brazil. Despite loss of her wheel early in the fighting, *Constitution* fought well. Her superior gunnery shattered the enemy's rigging, eventually dismasting *Java*, and mortally wounding her captain. *Java* was so badly damaged that she, too, had to be burned. The seemingly invincible "Old Ironsides" returned to Boston late in February for refitting and her wounded commander was relieved by Captain Charles Stewart.

Constitution departed on 31 December for a cruise in the Windward Islands. On 15 February she seized and destroyed the schooner, *Pictou*, and 9 days later chased the schooner, *Pique*, who escaped. She also captured three small merchantmen on this cruise, characteristically successful despite a close pursuit by two British frigates along the coast of Massachusetts. *Constitution* moored safely at Boston only to be bottled up for nearly 9 months by the vigorous British blockade.

In December 1814 *Constitution* braved the forces of the enemy, and headed southeast. She seized the merchant brig *Lord Nelson* and later captured *Susannah* with a rich cargo on 16 February 1815. Four days later she gave close chase to the frigate *Cyane* and the sloop *Levant* bound for the West Indies. *Constitution* opened the action firing broadsides; as the contestants drew apart she maneuvered adroitly between the two, fighting each separately and avoiding raking by either. In less than an hour *Cyane* struck her colors and soon thereafter *Levant* surrendered. Sailing in company with her prizes, *Consti-*

tution encountered a British squadron which gave chase but was able to retake only *Levant*. En route to New York, she received confirmation of the ratification of peace terms and on 15 May arrived, confident in her success as protector of freedom of the seas.

Ordered to Boston, she was placed in ordinary for 6 years, undergoing extensive repair. In May 1821 she returned to commission, serving as flagship of the Mediterranean Squadron, under Commodore Jacob Jones, and guarding United States shipping until 1823. A second cruise on that station lasted from 1823 through July 1828, with a succession of commanding officers including Captain Thomas Macdonough and Daniel Patterson.

A survey in 1830 disclosed *Constitution* to be unseaworthy. Congress, considering the projected cost of repairs, relegated her for sale or scrapping. Public sentiment, engendered partly by the dramatization of her history in Oliver Wendell Holmes' memorable poem, elicited instead an appropriation of money for reconstruction which was begun in 1833 at Boston, where once again she was captained by the redoubtable Isaac Hull.

Returned to commissioned status in 1835, she served well in the ensuing 20 years in a variety of missions. In March 1835 she sailed to France where she embarked the U.S. Minister to France, Edward Livingston, for return to the States. In August she entered upon a 3-year tour as flagship of Commodore Jesse Elliott in the Mediterranean protecting trade and maintaining good relations. She served as flagship for the South Pacific Squadron from 1839 to 1841; and for the home station from November 1842 to February 1843. In March 1844 she began a memorable 30-month circumnavigation of the globe while under the command of Captain John Percival.

The fall of 1848 brought a resumption of duty as flagship of the Mediterranean Squadron, Commodore W. C. Bolton. Decommissioned briefly in 1851 she sailed under Captain John Rudd in 1852 to patrol the west coast of Africa in quest of slavers until June 1855.

Five years of decommissioned status followed. In August 1860 she was assigned to train midshipmen at Annapolis, and during the Civil War at Newport, R.I. Among her commanding officers in this period are listed Lieutenant Commanders David D. Porter, and George Dewey.

In, 1871 *Constitution* underwent rebuilding at Philadelphia; she was commissioned again in July 1877 to transport goods to the Paris Exposition.

Once more she returned to duty as a training ship, cruising from the West Indies to Nova Scotia with her youthful crews. In January 1882 she was placed out of commission and in 1884 was towed to Portsmouth, N.H., to become a receiving ship. Celebration of her centennial year brought her to Boston in 1897 where she was retained in decommissioned status.

A public grateful for her protective service once again rescued her from imminent destruction in 1905 and she was thereafter partially restored for use as a national museum. Twenty years later, complete renovation was initiated with the financial support of numerous patriotic organizations and school children.

On 1 December 1917, *Constitution* was renamed *Old Constitution* to permit her original name to be assigned to a projected battle cruiser. Given first to CC-1 (renamed *Lexington*) then to CC-5 (originally named *Ranger*), the name *Constitution* was restored to "Old Ironsides" on 24 July 1925, after the battle cruiser program had been canceled under the Washington naval treaty. *Constitution* (CC-5) was some 13.4 percent complete at the time of her cancellation.

On 1 July 1931, amid a 21-gun salute, *Constitution* was recommissioned. The following day she sailed on a triumphant tour of 90 United States' ports along the Atlantic, Pacific, and Gulf coasts, where thousands of Americans saw at first hand one of history's greatest fighting ships. On 7 May 1934 she returned to Boston Harbor, the site of her building. Classified IX-21 on 8 January 1941, *Constitution* remains in commission today, the oldest ship on the Navy List, proud and worthy representative of the Navy's great days of fighting sail, and symbol of the courage and patriotic service of generations of Americans at sea where much of the Nation's destiny will always lie.

Constellation *as she appears today in Baltimore harbor.*

U.S.S. Constitution *as she appears today in Boston harbor.*

U.S.S. *Hartford*

The *Hartford* was a steam sloop-of-war launched at the Boston Navy Yard on 22 November 1858. She was named in honor of Hartford, Connecticut. Her length was 225 feet; beam, 44 feet; depth, 18 feet 6 inches; draft (aft), 17 feet 2 inches; speed (max.), 13½ knots; tonnage, 1990; battery, 18 guns; complement, 302 officers and men.

She was commissioned on 27 May 1859 and on 25 June, with Captain Charles Lowndes in command and Flag Officer C. K. Stribling on board, proceeded to sea from Boston for a tour of duty in the East Indies where the United States kept a small squadron for the protection of American citizens and their property. She returned to the United States on 2 December 1861 and was immediately prepared for service in home waters and sailed from Philadelphia on 21 January 1862 as the flagship of Rear Admiral David G. Farragut who was in command of the West Gulf Blockading Squadron. She arrived at the mouth of the Mississippi River on 20 February and on 11 March anchored off South West Pass. From 7 to 16 April she was preparing for the passage of Forts Jackson and St. Philip, below New Orleans. Bombardment of the forts commenced on 16 April and continued until the 24th when the *Hartford* with the rest of Farragut's fleet passed them and on the 25th engaged Chalmette batteries. At 1 P.M. of the same day *Hartford* anchored before New Orleans and on the 28th accepted the surrender of the city.

The next objective of the West Gulf Blockading Squadron, of which *Hartford* was flagship, was to reduce the Confederate defenses at Vicksburg, Miss., and Port Hudson and join the Western Flotilla under Flag Officer Charles H. Davis moving down from above. Late in June, Farragut assembled his fleet below Vicksburg determined to run past its defenses and on the 28th, supported by the Mortar Flotilla under Commander David D. Porter, he succeeded, and on the first of July, Davis

This photograph, taken in Mobile Bay in August 1864, shows U.S.S. Hartford *stripped for battle.*

joined him with his gunboat squadron. This gain was only temporary however, and much hard fighting on land and water was in store before their control of the Mississippi became permanent by the capture of Vicksburg on 4 July 1863 and Port Hudson on the 9th.

After the opening of the Mississippi was accomplished and the Union flag was raised over Vicksburg and Port Hudson *Hartford* returned to New Orleans and on the first of August sailed for New York, arriving there on the 10th. After repairs were completed she returned south again on 3 January 1864 with Admiral Farragut on board and arrived at South West Pass on the 21st where she resumed her duties as the flagship of the squadron in that area.

Farragut now turned his attention to Mobile, Ala., one of the industrial centers of the Confederacy still in operation building ships and turning out other war supplies. On 5 August 1864 the battle of Mobile took place. Farragut led his fleet which consisted of four ironclad monitors and fourteen wooden vessels in his flagship *Hartford*. The Confederate naval force was composed of the newly built ram *Tennessee*, flagship of Admiral Buchanan, and the steamers *Selma*, *Morgan* and *Gaines* backed by the powerful guns of Forts Morgan and Gaines in the Bay, and protected by a field of more than 180 torpedoes. From the firing of the first gun by Fort Morgan to the raising of the white flag of surrender by the *Tennessee*, a little more than three hours elapsed, three hours of terrific fighting on both sides. The Confederate naval forces had twelve men killed and twenty wounded, including Admiral Buchanan. The Union forces suffered 335 casualties which included 113 men drowned in the monitor *Tecumseh* which struck a torpedo and sank at the beginning of the action.

Hartford returned to New York in December after the battle, where she was repaired and fitted out for a cruise as flagship of a newly organized squadron on the Asiatic Station. She departed from New York on 17 July 1865 and returned to the United States in August 1868 and was put out of commission preparatory to extensive repairs. She was recommissioned on 9 October 1872 and within the month was en route to the Asiatic Station where she was actively employed until her return home on 19 October 1875.

From November 1875 to June 1877 *Hartford* was the flagship of Captain Stephen B. Luce on the North Atlantic Station and from August 1877 to December 1879 was cruising on the South Atlantic Station. She was under repairs at the Boston Navy Yard from December 1879 to 26 June 1882 when she was commissioned as flagship of the Pacific Squadron. She put to sea on 5 August and arrived at her destination in January 1883, having passed through the Straits of Magellan en route. In March 1883, before she assumed her duties as flagship she visited the Caroline Islands with the Solar Eclipse party, then went on to Hawaii and Valparaiso, Chile, and arrived at San Francisco on 17 March 1884. She continued to cruise in the Pacific until 14 January 1887 when she was put out of commission at Mare Island where she was repaired and fitted for use as a training ship for landsmen in the Pacific.

During 1890–1894, she was laid up at Mare Island Navy Yard. On 17 December 1894 work of

Fife rail from U.S.S. Hartford.

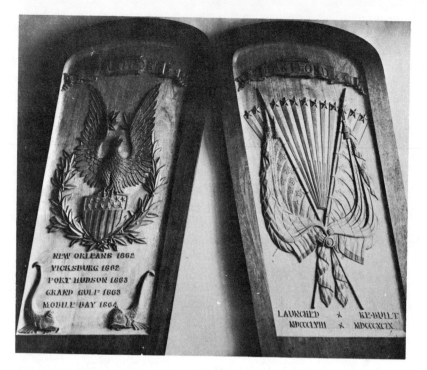

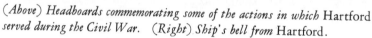
(*Above*) *Headboards commemorating some of the actions in which* Hartford *served during the Civil War.* (*Right*) *Ship's bell from* Hartford.

rebuilding her was commenced and it was not until 2 October 1899 that she was finally placed in commission as a training ship for landsmen and transferred to the Atlantic coast.

From 1900 to 1912 she was used for a variety of purposes including training ship for landsmen and apprentices, instruction ship for midshipmen at Annapolis and midshipmen cruises.

On 24 October 1912 Hartford was detached from the Naval Academy and taken to Charleston, S.C. for use as a station ship. In August, 1926 she was placed out of commission at that place but remained there until her removal to Washington, D.C., on 18 October 1938. She remained moored at the Washington Navy Yard until 19 October 1945 when she was taken down to the Norfolk Navy Yard and classified as a relic.

On 20 November 1956, she sank at her berth at Norfolk and has since been dismantled by salvage workers. A number of historic artifacts, however, have been preserved. One of Hartford's anchors is on display at the University of Hartford campus, while her ship's bell is in the Connecticut capital's Constitution Plaza. Another anchor may be seen by every visitor to the Naval Historical Display Center at the Navy Yard in Washington, D.C. A third anchor is exhibited at the entrance to Mystic Seaport's new yacht basin. Hartford's gilded billethead, fife-rail, and stanchion are housed in the famous Mariners Museum, Newport News, Virginia.

U.S.S. Harvest Moon *was Rear Admiral Dahlgren's flagship when she was sunk.*

U.S.S. *Harvest Moon*

Harvest Moon, a side-wheel steamer, was built in 1863 at Portland, Maine, and was purchased by Commodore Montgomery at Boston on 16 November 1863. She was fitted out for blockade duty at the Boston Navy Yard and was commissioned on 12 February 1864, Acting Lieutenant J. D. Warren, commanding.

Assigned to the South Atlantic Blockading Squadron, *Harvest Moon* departed Boston on 18 February and arrived off Charleston one week later. On 26 February Rear Admiral John A. Dahlgren, squadron commander, made her his flagship. After putting into Washington Navy Yard for repairs, *Harvest Moon* began her regular blockading duties off Charleston on 7 June 1864. For the next nine months the steamer served off Tybee Island, the North Edisto River, and Charleston harbor. During this period she also acted as a picket and dispatch vessel, as well as Admiral Dahlgren's flagship.

While proceeding in company with tug *Clover*, 1 March 1865, *Harvest Moon* struck a torpedo in Winyah Bay, South Carolina. Admiral Dahlgren, who had just started breakfast, saw a bulkhead in his quarters collapse before his eyes. The explosion blew a large hole in the ship's hull and she quickly sank in 2½ fathoms of water. One man was killed, but the Admiral and rest of the crew were taken on board U.S.S. *Nipsic*. *Harvest Moon* was stripped of her valuable machinery and abandoned on 20 April 1865.

Since 1963, the state of South Carolina and patriotic groups in the vicinity have been formulating plans to raise her and preserve her remains as a Civil War monument.

Divers probe the hulk of Harvest Moon *to determine the possibility of raising her.*

Intelligent Whale

Although *Intelligent Whale* was not completed and operational during the Civil War, she was the result of Union interest in submarines during that period—an interest that had been spurred by Southern experiments in undersea warfare. With the conclusion of the conflict, Northern desire to complete the vessel waned and she remained the last official Navy attempt to develop a submarine until John Holland began his pioneer work in the construction of submersibles.

Intelligent Whale was designed by Scovel S. Merriam, who agreed with Augustus Price and Cornelius Bushnell in 1863 to build a boat. Merriam would furnish the plans, while the other two were to provide some $15,000 in capital. In April 1864 the American Submarine Company was formed and assumed the interests of Price and Bushnell.

The submarine was eventually sold to the Navy Department on the following terms:

$12,500 to be paid on the conclusion of the agreement;

$12,500 to be paid on the successful completion of the experimental trials;

$25,000 to be paid for secrets and inventions, after this a fund was to be established from which any further compensation that might be determined could be paid.

The first payment was made by the Navy in October 1869, but when the first trial was made about three years later and proved unsuccessful, the Secretary of the Navy refused further payments. *Intelligent Whale*, as the submarine came to be known, was completed in Newark, New Jersey, by private interests.

Later the boat performed a successful experiment in which she submerged in 16 feet of water, one of her crew members clad in a diver's suit passed out through a manhole in her bottom, placed a torpedo under a scow, and after reentering the boat exploded the weapon by a lanyard and friction primer. The scow was totally destroyed. It is presumed that the lanyard was pulled by moving the submarine away from the target ship.

The water compartments were filled by opening a valve, which would cause the boat to submerge. Pumps and compressed air were used to eject the water to enable *Intelligent Whale* to surface. It was estimated that she could stay submerged for some ten hours. Thirteen men could be on board, but she was operational with a crew of only six. She was propelled by a hand crank at a speed of about four knots. *Intelligent Whale* is 30 feet long and approximately 9 feet in depth.

The submarine is presently on display at the Naval Historical Display Center, Washington Navy Yard, Washington, D.C.

Submarine Intelligent Whale *photographed at the New York Navy Yard. It is now on display at the Naval Historical Display Center, Washington, D.C.*

U.S.S. *Kearsarge*

The steam sloop-of-war *Kearsarge* was the first of three ships in the Navy thus far to bear the name. She was built by the Portsmouth Navy Yard, New Hampshire, and launched 11 September 1861 under the sponsorship of Mrs. McFarland of Concord, New Hampshire, wife of the editor of the Concord *Statement*.

Kearsarge had a length of 201 feet, 4 inches; beam, 33 feet, 10 inches; displacement of 1,550 tons; draft of 14 feet, 3 inches; depth in hold of 16 feet; and a complement of 163 officers and men. She was armed with two 11-inch Dahlgren guns, four 32-pounder guns of 42 centerweight, and one 30-pounder rifle.

Kearsarge commissioned at the Portsmouth Navy Yard on 24 January 1862 under the command of Captain Charles W. Pickering, USN. She sailed from Portsmouth, 5 February 1862, under orders to search in European waters for CSS *Sumter* and to capture all ships laden with munitions of war or contraband. Arriving off Algeciras, Spain, 7 March, via Funchal and Cadiz, *Kearsarge* joined USS *Tuscarora* and *Ino* in blockading CSS *Sumter* at Gibraltar. Because of being blockaded and unable to obtain coal, the Confederate cruiser was abandoned and sold at Gibraltar in December 1862.

Kearsarge received repairs at Cadiz, November 1862–March 1863, and on 8 April 1863, Captain John A. Winslow relieved Captain Pickering of command. She continued her search, calling at ports of Spain, France, Holland, Ireland, the Canaries, Madeira and Western Islands. Arriving at Cherbourg, France 14 June 1864, *Kearsarge* found the Confederate cruiser *Alabama*, under command of Captain Raphael Semmes, CSN, and immediately took up a blockading position off the harbor.

U.S.S. Kearsarge

On the morning of 19 June 1864, at 10:20 a.m., *Alabama* steamed out of the western entrance of Cherbourg Harbor to accept the challenge of the U.S. Sloop-of-War. She was escorted beyond the three mile limit of neutral waters by the French ironclad *Couronne* and followed at a distance by the English yacht *Deerhound*.

In an attempt to lure *Alabama* from shore, so that if disabled she could not return to port, Captain Winslow headed *Kearsarge* seaward until reaching a point seven miles off the coast, then turned to close the Confederate cruiser. This maneuver had barely taken place when *Alabama* sheered to present her starboard battery, and as *Kearsarge* closed within a mile, the Confederate cruiser opened with a full broadside. By the time *Kearsarge* had closed to within 900 yards, a third broadside had been fired by *Alabama* but the only effect was slight damage to rigging on the U.S. Sloop-of-War. *Kearsarge* sheered and opened fire as she came broadside to broadside with the Confederate cruiser. Keeping full speed, *Kearsarge* attempted to run under the stern of *Alabama* and rake, a maneuver which caused the Confederate cruiser to sheer and keep her broadside to the *Kearsarge*. Thus *Alabama* was forced with a full head of steam into a circular track throughout the engagament as she made the same response to this repeated maneuver of *Kearsarge*.

Alabama's fire was rapid and furious but the 370 or more shot and shell caused no serious damage aboard the *Kearsarge* who received only thirteen or fourteen in and about her hull and sixteen or seventeen about the masts and rigging. Two shots fired by the Confederate cruiser passed through *Kearsarge*'s ports in which 32-pounder guns were placed, with men stationed about them. One of these shots took effect in the hammock netting and the other passed through the port on the opposite side, its wind in the process knocking down the captain of one of the guns. No one was hit by these shots and *Kearsarge* had only three men wounded as the result of the engagement. Her fire was not as rapid as that of *Alabama* but almost every shot fired had a fearful effect on the Confederate cruiser. The U.S. Sloop-of-War fired only 175 shot but one shot alone wounded eighteen men and disabled a gun aboard the *Alabama*. Another shot entered *Alabama*'s coal bunkers where it exploded and completely blocked the engine room of the Confederate cruiser. Other shot and shell tore large holes by explosion in the sides of *Alabama* and she was completely at the mercy of *Kearsarge* by noon. With some forty men killed and wounded, *Alabama* was in a sinking condition. She went down within twenty minutes after sending her boat to *Kearsarge* to inform the sloop-of-war of surrender and to request aid in saving the Confederate crew. Seventy men were received on board *Kearsarge* while forty-two, including Captain Semmes and fourteen other officers, were rescued by the English yacht *Deerhound* and taken to England. Others were picked up by French boats.

Kearsarge remained at Cherbourg until 6 July 1864 when she departed for a cruise on the French coast in an unsuccessful search for C.S.S. *Florida*. In August she steamed southward and westward in search of the enemy, visiting various islands in the Atlantic and Caribbean, and arrived at Boston on 7 November. The ship was placed out of commission at the Boston Navy Yard 26 November 1864.

After undergoing repairs and refitting, *Kearsarge* was recommissioned 1 April 1865 under command of Commander A. D. Harrell, and on the 14th sailed from Boston for Coruna, Spain, to intercept and capture CS ram *Stonewall* and to cruise with the European Squadron for the protection of American interests and commerce. She arrived at Lisbon, Portugal, 1 May and learned that *Stonewall* was at Teneriffe when last heard from. The Confederate ram eluded Federal ships and surrendered to Spanish authorities at Havana on 19 May. *Kearsarge* continued to operate with the European Squadron until June 1866, cruising in the Mediterranean and from the English Channel down the coast of Africa as far as Monrovia, Liberia. She departed Fayal, Azores, 22 June and on 26 July arrived at the Boston Navy Yard where she was placed out of commission on 14 August 1866.

Recommissioned 16 January 1868, *Kearsarge* departed Boston on 12 February for the Pacific. She visited Rio de Janeiro and Montevideo en route, and arrived at Valparaiso, Chile, on 4 July. She was attached to the South Pacific Station until 1870, cruising principally on the west coast of South America. On 13 August 1868 a most devastating and extensive earthquake occurred in South America, destroying eight cities of Peru. *Kearsarge* at the time was at Caldera, Chile, where the earthquake

During their famed engagement off Cherbourg, a shot from C.S.S. Alabama *struck the sternpost of* Kearsarge; *it failed to explode, however, and remained embedded in the Union ship. The sternpost, with the shot from* Alabama, *is on display at the Naval Historical Display Center, Washington, D.C.*

was not so severe. On the 19th she got underway with provisions received from Chilean authorities for stricken areas in Peru, and arrived at Africa, Peru, on the 22nd. At Africa two U.S. ships, *Wateree* and *Fredonia*, had been wrecked by tidal waves caused by the earthquake. *Kearsarge* landed the provisions for the destitute citizens, assisted in transporting stores and provisions between the flagship *Powhatan* and shore, and on the 29th departed with part of the officers and crew of *Wateree* aboard for transportation to Callao. During the period 17 April–31 October 1869 *Kearsarge* made a cruise to the Marquesas, Society, Navigators and Feejee Islands, New South Wales and New Zealand to look after American interests in those distant regions. Departing Callao 21 July 1870, *Kearsarge* steamed to Mare Island, via the Sandwich (Hawaiian) Islands, and was placed out of commission 11 October 1870.

After repairs at the Mare Island Yard, *Kearsarge* was recommissioned 8 December 1873 and assigned to the Asiatic Squadron. She departed San Francisco 4 March 1874 and arrived at Yokohama, Japan, on 11 May. She cruised on the station three years, protecting American citizens and commerce on the coast of China, in Japan and the Philippine Islands. During the period 4 September–16 December 1874 she transported Professor Hall's scientific party from Nagasaki to Vladivostok to observe the transit of Venus. Departing Nagasaki 3 September 1877 *Kearsarge* returned to the United States via the Suez Canal, visiting many ports enroute, and arrived at Boston 30 December. On 2 January 1878 she proceeded to Portsmouth, New Hampshire, where she was placed out of commission on the 15th.

Recommissioned 15 May 1879, *Kearsarge* reported at New York 24 June for duty on the North Atlantic Station. She cruised on the east coast of the United States and Newfoundland, in the Caribbean and Gulf of Mexico, engaging in drills and exercises, protecting American interests, and participating in various celebrations and ceremonies. She established a coaling station at Bocas del Toro, Panama, 19 February–20 May 1880, and performed recruiting duty at New Orleans, Louisiana, 18 December 1881–15 March 1882. Necessary repairs were received at the Norfolk and New York Navy Yards.

On 31 May 1883 *Kearsarge* was detached from the North Atlantic Station and assigned to the European Station. After repairing at New York, she sailed for Europe on 21 August and arrived at

Gibraltar 8 October, after calling at Mogador and Casa Blanca, Morocco. During the following three years *Kearsarge* cruised extensively in the Mediterranean and northern European waters, protecting American commerce and exchanging courtesies and salutes with representatives and ships of other countries. She carried the flag to various ports in Spain, Portugal, Italy, Algeria, Minorca, Egypt, Syria, Greece, Austria, France, England, Sweden and Denmark. This duty was intervened by one cruise along the west coast of Africa. On this cruise she departed Lisbon, Portugal, 30 October 1844 visiting Cape Verde Islands, Liberia, Guinea, and Libreville, French Equatorial Africa. She arrived off Shark's Point, Congo River, on 16 December, and remained in the Congo, taking on coal and beef at Banana Creek until 22 December when she sailed for Cape Verde Islands. She was in that area from 7 January to 8 February 1885, when she returned to the Congo, via Monrovia Liberia.

Arriving off Shark's Point on 9 March 1885, *Kearsarge* stood up the Congo to Banana Creek where she took on coal and provisions. On the 15th Mr. Tisdale, United States Commissioner to the Congo, arrived from Stanley Pool and paid an official visit to the commanding officer. The following day, 16 March 1885, "Sir Francis De Winton, Chief of the Congo International Association, and Mr. Tisdel, U.S. Commissioner to the Congo, came on board and were received with the usual honors." On 17 March the commanding officer called upon Colonel Sir Francis De Winton and the following day Sir Francis returned his call. That afternoon (5:40 on 18 March) *Kearsarge* stood down the river and anchored off French Point where she remained until 18 April 1885. Departing the Congo on the 18th, she steamed to St. Paul de Loando, took on stores, and returned to anchorage off French Point, 27 April. United States Flagship *Lancaster*, Rear Admiral Earl English, arrived off French Point the next day.

On 30 April 1885 Admiral English receives Sir Francis Winton on board the *Lancaster*. At 11:40 a.m., the flagship fired a salute of 21 guns with the ensign of the Congo International Association at the fore. Upon departure of the Administrator General, at 12:40 p.m., the flagship fired a salute of 17 guns.

On 1 May *Kearsarge* stood up to Banana Creek, coaled then returned to anchor off French Point. The next day she received on board for passage north, Colonel Sir Francis de Winton and servant, and departed the Congo. She steamed by the way of Monrovia and Cape Verde Islands to Funchal, Madeira, where Sir Francis left the ship upon arrival, 29 May 1885. *Kearsarge* sailed from Funchal on 8 June and arrived at Gibralter the 14th. During the remainder of her stay on the Station she cruised in northern European waters and in the Mediterranean. *Kearsarge* departed Gibraltar on 7 October 1886 for return to the United States, arriving at Portsmouth, New Hampshire, 12 November. She was placed out of commission in the Portsmouth Navy Yard on 1 December 1886.

Kearsarge was recommissioned 2 November 1888 and made a cruise to the coast of South America with relief officers and crew for U.S.S. *Tallapoosa*, departing Portsmouth 11 November 1888 and returning to New York on 20 April 1889. She was assigned to the North Atlantic Station and sailed from New York 16 June for the Caribbean area. From 1889 to 1894 she cruised principally in the West Indies and on the coast of Venezuela and Central America, for the protection of American interests. She participated in squadron tactical drills and exercises, visited ports on the east coast and attended various celebrations, gave transportation to government officials, accompanied ships on trial trips, and was repaired at the Portsmouth Navy Yard. Early in 1894 *Kearsarge* was cruising in the West Indies. She departed Port au Prince, Haiti, 30 January for Bluefields, Nicaragua, and on 2 February 1894 was wrecked on Roncador Reef off Central America. Her officers and crew succeeded in getting safely ashore and were later rescued. Congress appropriated $45,000 to raise and tow *Kearsarge* to her home port and a contract was made with the Boston Towboat Company. However, a careful examination made it evident that the ship could not be raised and the wrecking company returned to the Norfolk Navy Yard, bringing back such articles as they were able to recover from the wreck and the surrounding reef. *Kearsarge* was stricken from the list of Navy ships in 1894.

Her sternpost, in which a shot from C.S.S. *Alabama* lodged but failed to explode, is on exhibit at the Naval Historical Display Center, Washington, D.C.

C.S.S. Virginia *destroys wooden blockaders* Congress *and* Cumberland, *8 March 1862.*

Monitor-Virginia Memorial

In September 1965 a 4′ x 8′ oil painting by muralist Sidney E. King was unveiled in Christopher Newport Park depicting the action in Hampton Roads on 8 March 1862 in which C.S.S. *Virginia* destroyed the wooden blockading ships U.S.S. *Congress* and *Cumberland*. This epic engagement signalled the end of the wooden warship and set the stage for the dramatic battle with U.S.S. *Monitor* the next day. The first engagement of ironclads will be similarly commemorated (probably in 1966) in an oil painting at *Monitor-Merrimack* Overlook near the mouth of Salters Creek.

The Monitor-Virginia *engagement, 9 March 1862.*

C.S.S. *Muscogee* (or *Jackson*)

Launched in December 1864 at Columbus, Georgia, this twin screw Confederate ironclad was captured and destroyed by Union troops on 17 April 1865 before she was commissioned.

Muscogee's hulk—then believed to be that of C.S.S. *Chattahoochee*—was located in 1960 in the Fort Benning Reservation. She was partially visible at low water, but almost half of the ironclad was under a ten foot bank on the Alabama side of the Chattahoochee River. State funds and contributions from private citizens and organizations enabled volunteer efforts to salvage *Muscogee* in two sections and return her to Columbus where she is mounted on concrete piers at the Confederate Naval Museum.

Although *Muscogee* was fired by the Federals, many of the construction details were preserved, as were tools, fuzes, tons of armor, cannon balls, and propellors. From this valuable material historians have been able to add considerably to their knowledge of Confederate ship construction and design.

C.S.S. Muscogee

C.S.S. Muscogee *was salvaged in two sections. First the stern section (shown above and below) was moved to Columbus, Georgia, and mounted on concrete piers. Later, a cofferdam (at right) was built some two-thirds of the way across the river and the bow section was salvaged and joined the rest of the ship in Columbus. Although the ironclad was effectively set afire many construction details and artifacts have been preserved.*

C.S.S. *Neuse*

On the afternoon of 23 April 1864 the Confederate ram *Neuse* got underway to steam down the muddy North Carolina river for which she had been named. Minutes later the ill-fated ship ran hard aground on a sand bar. The rapidly falling water level in the river frustrated the urgent Southern efforts to float *Neuse* and prevented her from contesting the Union's control of the Carolina Sounds.

It was a bitter blow to the Confederates who had been struggling to build and complete the ram since funds had been authorized for her construction in the fall of 1862. She had survived a Union assault on her construction site—far up the Neuse River at White Hall Landing—in mid-December 1862 and numerous difficulties that hampered her outfitting.

Late in 1862 the keel for C.S.S. *Neuse* was laid at White Hall Landing. She was to be 150 feet long, 40 feet wide, and have a draft of approximately 8 feet. After the December 13 attack on White Hall Landing by General John G. Foster, in which *Neuse* suffered minor damage, work on the warship was increased. A six foot long ram was fitted to the bow and the hull was made water-tight. She was then moved from her stocks into the river itself.

Although *Neuse* was only partially completed in November 1863, she was transferred downriver some 18 miles to Kinston to be fitted out. There she was pulled from the water again and placed on stocks where she received her boilers, motors, and rifled 6.24 inch cannon. *Neuse* never did receive all her iron plating—a fact which caused Flag Officer William F. Lynch to complain on 8 March 1864 that "the rights of the Navy are not respected, its wants are utterly disregarded, and it is in the power of an acting assistant quarter master to cause our transportation to be set aside at will." Finally in April 1864 she was refloated in the river.

It took a month to refloat the ram after her grounding on April 23, but late in May she was back at her Kinston mooring. Repairs and further outfitting were slowly made and early in 1865 *Neuse* was once more ready for action. Commander Joseph H. Price was ordered to take command and join in the defense of New Bern. By March 10, however, Price knew that Northern soldiers had advanced to within five miles of the river and that it would be virtually impossible to navigate the 60 miles to New Bern with any prospect of arriving safely. He futilely fired grape and cannister from *Neuse*'s cannon at the troops of General Jacob Cox and then ordered a charge in the ram's bow detonated and the ship set afire to prevent her falling into Union hands. The explosion blew a hole in the port side some eight feet in diameter and flames gutted the interior of the ship. She finally sank into the waters of the Neuse off Kinston.

For nearly a century little attention was paid to her. But late in 1961 a small group of men living in the area began serious efforts to raise the hulk of *Neuse*.

This aerial view shows the starboard after section of the ram that was exposed when salvage operations were begun in November 1961. In the background is the cofferdam which is being constructed to facilitate the work of freeing Neuse.

By mid-December 1961 much of the ram's bow was exposed. Almost all of the top decking was intact at the outset of the salvage work, but it and all compartments were removed to make the process of relocating Neuse easier. Here the base of the conning tower hatch and central passageway are shown.

(*Above*) Neuse *was successfully floated late in December 1961 by the use of steel barrels lashed to her hull. Heavy rains flooded the area, however, forcing the salvage crew to evacuate the area, and the hulk remained in the condition shown above during 1961 as further operations were halted by lack of funds.* (*Right*) *By May 1963 workmen were again engaged in the effort to salvage C.S.S.* Neuse. *Although water seeping through the cofferdam constantly hindered the work, above a workman drills a hole into which a cable was subsequently inserted to help free the Confederate warship.*

This stern view of Neuse *provides a clear view of the* rudder mounting. *The cables are attached preparatory to her removal from the river bed.*

In mid-May 1961 Neuse *had been hauled partially onto the river bank . . .*

. . . a task which was completed on 19 May. Above is an excellent stern view of the Confederate ram.

During the winter of 1963, rains flooded the lowlands near the river, but the hulk of Neuse *was secured to nearby trees until spring when salvage work would continue.*

In May 1964 the ram's hulk was weighed and found to be 207 tons. In order to comply with North Carolina State highway weight regulations, Neuse *was carefully cut into three sections and transported to Richard Caswell Memorial Park, two miles west of Kinston. Above, the stern section is being taken through Kinston—along with some errant tree limbs.*

At the park the ram was reassembled. In this photograph the flat bottom is clearly shown. Here C.S.S. Neuse is on public display, while plans are progressing for the construction of museum to house the valuable relics recovered from the ill-fated ram. Consideration is also being given to reconstructing the warship. Handsome bronze and silver commemorative coins bearing a representation of Neuse on one side and the Confederate Navy Department seal on the other have been struck; information regarding the sale of these medals may be obtained from the Lenoir County Confederate Centennial Commission, Box 210, Kinston, North Carolina.

C.S.S. *Pioneer*

The two-man privateer submarine *Pioneer* was begun in New Orleans in 1861 to offset the threat of U.S.S. *New London* and *Calhoun* on Lake Pontchartrain. When Farragut took the city in April 1862, however, *Pioneer* was scuttled to prevent her capture and lay forgotten for years on the bottom of Lake Pontchartrain. [For a brief history of *Pioneer*, see "Confederate Forces Afloat," page 181.]

Long after the war the submarine was raised and taken to the Louisiana Home for Confederate Soldiers at Camp Nicholls. In April 1957 she was again moved to her present site in the Presbytere Arcade, Louisiana State Museum in New Orleans.

C.S. Submarine Pioneer

CIVIL WAR ANTI-TORPEDO RAFT [1]

Lying in Dolly's Bay, St. David's Island, Bermuda there can be found a curious relic of the American Civil War, the remains of a Federal Navy torpedo-raft. According to local legend, in 1868 a group of men spotted the strange derelict off St. David's Island. Investigation showed the raft to contain much new timber, and it was towed in for salvage. After a few days, the salvage operations were forced to cease, owing to the sturdy construction of the raft. It was left to rot where it lay.

The Islanders had little idea of the origin and purpose of their find. Four years later, on January 11, 1872, Captain E. H. Faucon, a sea captain representing Boston underwriters, arrived in Bermuda on board the mail steamer *Alpha*. Captain Faucon readily identified the raft by its heretofore un-noticed U.S. government number, having been the officer-in-charge of the transportation of some rafts from New York to Port Royal, South Carolina. The traditional story tells of a man being lost overboard in trying to recover the raft, but the official report makes no mention of this.

During the Civil War, in order to deter and destroy the Union naval forces, the Confederates turned to underwater devices known as torpedos or mines. Heavy torpedo-searching rafts were built by the Federals for use in clearing paths through the mine fields in Charleston Harbor. On 27 December 1862, the Secretary of the Navy directed Rear Admiral F. H. Gregory to provide transportation by steamer for four rafts from New York to Port Royal, S.C. The steamer *Ericsson* was chartered under the command of Acting Volunteer Lieutenant E. H. Faucon, U.S. Navy, to tow them. Chief Engineer E. D. Robie was given special charge of the rafts until they reached Port Royal where Chief Engineer A. C. Stimers would relieve him.

On 30 January 1863, *Ericsson* left New York with the four rafts in tow. The next day, at dawn, one of them was discovered to be missing. Upon examination of the other rafts, it was evident that they need to be refastened. On 4 February, *Ericsson* anchored off Fortress Monroe, Virginia. The rafts were refitted with chains and a red and blue flag mounted on each bow.

On 10 February they proceeded towards Port Royal. At 10:45 p.m. on the 12th, the second and third rafts broke loose and were lost in heavy seas. *Ericsson*'s position was S.S.W. of Cape Hatteras, N.C., by 40 miles. (Through the use of drifting bottles, a surface current has been established between Cape Hatteras and Bermuda. The Civil War raft in Dolly's Bay gives further evidence of these currents.)

It was therefore a most discouraged Lieutenant who reported to Rear Admiral S. F. Du Pont of the South Atlantic Blockading Squadron on February 17th at Port Royal with only one of his four charges. Lieutenant Faucon was not held responsible for the loss of the rafts as his performance in the line of duty was beyond reproach.

The first employment of an anti-torpedo raft was on 7 April 1863 at Charleston. The ironclad *Weehawken*, with a raft attached to her bow, led eight other ships in the attack. After difficulties crossing the Charleston Bar, *Weehawken* approached the obstructions through which she was to clear a path. They proved too formidable and Captain John Rodgers turned *Weehawken* seaward. The raft was pitching and colliding against the bow in the seas; when it began to damage the bow, Captain Rodgers cut it adrift. This raft was later found by the Confederates on Morris Island. From their report we get this description of the 'devil', as they called it:

"The 'devil' floated ashore on Morris Island; the cables by which it was attached to the turret s bow were cut away. It is probable that the 'devil' becoming unmanageable, was the cause of the turret retiring early from the action, it being a massive structure, consisting of two layers of white-pine timbers, 18 inches square, strongly bolted together; a reentering angle 20 feet deep, to receive

---

[1] This account was prepared by First Lieutenant Donald R. Gardner, USMC, in March 1965. Lieutenant Gardner's excellent research was supplemented by first hand observation of the raft; he was on the staff of the Commander, U.S. Naval Station, Bermuda.

Two views of the Union's antitorpedo raft which drifted ashore at Dolly's Bay, Bermuda.

the bow of the vessel, 50 feet long, 27 feet wide; a layer of beveled timbers on the front, forming a bow, seven heavy iron plates, through which passed chains directly down and over the sides, through hawse pipes; to these were attached grappling irons with double prongs, suspended underneath, at the sides and bow; in the countersinks of the plates were loose iron rollers, apparently to facilitate the drawing of the chains through the holes over them, when the grapplings took hold, to drag up to the 'devil' whatever he may catch with his hooks.''

Using standard civil engineering data, the approximate weight of this wooden raft, reenforced with iron spikes, would have been 23 tons when new. Captain Rodgers reported that he thought the raft at Charleston displaced about 90 tons of water. Torpedo arms were originally intended to extend beyond the bow to destroy obstructions but they were not used for fear they might collide with a friendly vessel. Captain Rodgers later attempted to destroy *Keokuk* with the last of the *Ericsson's* rafts. Adverse sea conditions, straining and breaking the raft's lashings, thwarted the attempt.

The raft in Dolly's Bay now rests in a bed of sand, battered constantly by endless tides. For a while it was used as a slip for small boats and as a romping place for children; now it is only a deserted curiosity. There is little left of the massive structure but saturated decaying timbers held together by barnacle-encrusted spikes. In 1942 it was reported to measure 20 feet by 25 feet, with one of its ring bolts in excellent condition. Today the ring bolt is gone and the skeleton measures 18 feet by 23 feet. Two of the 16 inch ring plates are imbedded in the raft's timbers. These plates are five feet from the land edge of the raft. The bottom timbers seem to be in the best condition, with some fifteen of them remaining. A good number of the iron spikes have rusted off at deck level, although many of the original three foot ones remain. It is remarkable that this one hundred and three years old relic is in as good condition as it is.

A very small section of this raft can be seen in the Confederate Museum at St. George's, Bermuda. Another section has been recovered and brought to the Washington Navy Yard where it is on exhibit at the Naval Historical Display Center.

Close up of the anti-torpedo raft. A section from the anti-torpedo raft is on exhibit at the Naval Historical Display Center, Washington Navy Yard, Washington, D.C.

torpedo to the "Weehawken," during the attack upon Fort Sumpter unless I should receive positive orders to do so. I stated however that I thought the raft might be useful with Grapnels hanging from it, to catch obstructions. This accordingly I carried into action - and this I brought out.

The raft was cut so as to fit the bow of the vessel and secured by chains from ring bolts on the raft - a & c - to ring bolts on the bow of the "Weehawken", and further secured by rope lashings, to the same bolts. and also from the ring bolts - b & d. I presume as designed by the inventor.

In crossing Charleston bar the chains from - a & c - parted; all the lashings broke. this happened twice in the short period in crossing from the outside of the bar, to the anchorage inside.

When inside it was found that the sea converted the raft into a huge

Above is an extract from Captain John Rodgers' report of 20 April 1863 to Rear Admiral Samuel F. Du Pont. Rodgers described the difficulty he had encountered with the "anti-torpedo raft" attached to the bow of his monitor Weehawken *at Charleston. Rodgers' sketch, not drawn to scale, shows how the raft was supposed to be attached to the warship.*

SELECTED QUOTATIONS

Mallory
N. Maffitt
F. Maury

J. Alden

R. Semmes
D. G. Farragut
G. Welles

D. D. Porter

The high object of our country in this was is "that peace and happiness truth and justice, religion and piety may be established among us for all generations." In this sacred cause has fallen the Christian gentleman whose death we now lament; in this cause have fallen all the brave men whose blood has stained these decks—We cannot do our duty better, but let us at least try to do it as well.

> —Commander James Alden on the death of Lieutenant Commander Andrew B. Cummings during the passage of Port Hudson, 14 March 1863

The outward pressure of our Navy, in barring the enemy's ports, crippling the power and exhausting the resources of the States in rebellion; in depriving them of a market for their peculiar productions, and of the facilities for importing many vital requisites for the use of their Army and peoples, is slowly, surely, and unostentatiously reducing the rebellion to such straits as must result in their unconditional submission, even though our gallant Army does not achieve another victory.

> —Rear Admiral Theodorus Bailey, 9 December 1862

It is true that we have lost our ship; the ubiquitous gallant *Alabama* is no more, but we have lost no honor.

> —Flag Officer Samuel Barron on the sinking of C.S.S. *Alabama* by U.S.S. *Kearsarge*, 19 June 1864

We are at war with a brave, energetic adversary, fruitful in resources, ready to strike at any exposed point, and which, with one or two piratical cruisers, besides destroying a great amount of tonnage, has driven a large share of our commerce under the protection of the flags of other nations.

> —Governor Samuel Corry of Maine, 18 July 1864, on the effect of Southern commerce raiding

After you, pilot.

> —Commander T. A. M. Craven as his ship *Tecumseh* was sinking at Mobile Bay, 5 August 1864. The pilot was saved; Craven was not.

. . . we will beat the enemy or sink at our post.

> —Lieutenant William B. Cushing engaging Confederate batteries near Suffolk, Virginia, 14 April 1863

Now comes the reign of iron—and cased sloops are to take the place of wooden ships.

> —Captain John A. Dahlgren after *Monitor-Virginia* engagement, 9 March 1862

How busy is death—oh, how busy indeed!

> —Rear Admiral John Dahlgren after learning of the death of his son, Colonel Ulric Dahlgren, in battle on 6 March 1864

Success is the only thing listened to in this war, and I know I must sink or swim by that rule.

> —Flag Officer David G. Farragut, 10 March 1862

God alone decides the contest; but we must put our shoulders to the wheel.

> —Flag Officer Farragut, 19 March 1862

If I die in the attempt [to take New Orleans], it will only be what every officer has to expect. He who dies in doing his duty to his country, and at peace with his God, has played out the drama of life to the best advantage.

> —Flag Officer Farragut, 25 March 1862

Any man who is prepared for defeat would be half defeated before he commenced. I hope for success, shall do all in my power to secure it, and trust to God for the rest.

> —Flag Officer Farragut, 11 April 1862

The great man in our country must not only plan but execute.
—Flag Officer Farragut

I mean to be whipped or to whip my enemy, and not be scared to death.
—Rear Admiral Farragut, 29 July 1862

That we did our duty to the best of our ability, I believe; that a kind Providence smiled upon us and enabled us to overcome obstacles before which the stoutest of our hearts would have otherwise quailed, I am certain.
—Rear Admiral Farragut, 16 December 1863, commenting on his victory at New Orleans

Damn the torpedoes, full speed ahead!
—Rear Admiral Farragut at Mobile Bay, 5 August 1864

Discipline to be permanent must be based on moral grounds, and officers must in themselves, show a good example in morals, order, and patriotism to secure these qualities in the men.
—Flag Officer Andrew Hull Foote, 17 December 1861

We had nothing to fear from a land attack, but the gunboats are the devil.
—Flag Officer Andrew Hull Foote quoting the Nashville *Union and American* of 11 February 1862
(Source: *ORN* I, 22, 635–636)

The seamanship is of the utmost importance, in my opinion, notwithstanding steam, and ironclads. I share the old Jack Tar feeling that a sailor can do anything, and that a man is not good for much who is not a thorough seaman.
—Assistant Secretary Gustavus V. Fox regarding training at the Naval Academy, 30 September 1862

The Navy under Porter was all it could be during the entire [Vicksburg] campaign. Without its assistance the campaign could not have been successfully made with twice the number of men engaged.
—Lieutenant General U.S. Grant on the Navy's role in the fall of Vicksburg, 4 July 1863

We have no guns that can resist their [ships'] batteries, and have no resources but to prepare to meet them in the field.
—Major General Robert E. Lee, 9 November 1861

Wherever his fleet can be brought no opposition to his landing can be made except within range of our fixed batteries. We have nothing to oppose to its heavy guns, which sweep over the low banks of this country with irresistable force.
—Major General Robert E. Lee, 8 January 1862

The Father of Waters again goes unvexed to the sea. . . . Nor must Uncle Sam's web feet be forgotten. At all the watery margins they have been present. Not only on the deep sea, the broad bay, the rapid river, but also up the narrow muddy bayou, and wherever the ground was a little damp, they have been and made their tracks.
—President Lincoln, 26 August 1863, on the resumption of Union control of the Mississippi River

The grand mistake of the South was neglecting her navy.
—Commander John Maffitt, CSN

It will be remembered that the *Virginia* was a novelty in naval architecture, wholly unlike any ship that ever floated; that her heaviest guns were equal novelties in ordnance; that her motive power and obedience to her helm were untried, and her officers and crew strangers, comparatively, to the ship and to each other; and yet, under all these disadvantages, the dashing courage and consummate professional ability of Flag Officer Buchanan and his associates achieved the most remarkable victory which naval annals record.

—Secretary Mallory on the destruction of U.S.S. *Congress* and *Cumberland*, 8 March 1862

The destruction of the Navy at New Orleans was a sad, sad blow . . . .

—Confederate Secretary Mallory after the fall of New Orleans on 24 April 1862

Our necessities cry out for a Navy in war; and when peace comes, it will profit us but little to be affluent and free, if we are continually liable to be pillaged by all . . . the breadth of our plantations and the value of our staples will be of small advantage if the others may have the mastery in our own waters.

—Commander Matthew F. Maury, CSN

We cannot, either with cotton or with all the agricultural staples of the Confederacy put together, adopt any course which will make cotton and trade stand us as a nation in the stead of a Navy.

—Commander M. F. Maury, CSN

Enterprise, even with scant means, can accomplish much.

—Charleston *Mercury*, 7 May 1863

I am prepared to sacrifice life, and will only surrender when I have no means of defense.

—Brigadier General Richard L. Page refusing to surrender Fort Morgan despite overwhelming odds, 9 August 1864

To those of you who are about to return to civil life I would say, render the same cheerful obedience to the civil that you have rendered to the naval law. Cast your votes as good citizens, regularly and quietly at the polls; so keeping in your hearts "with malice toward none, with charity for all," that after each Presidential election, whether it be with you or against you, you may be able to respond heartily to our old navy toast: "The President of the United States: God Bless him!"

—Commander Foxhall A. Parker to his officers and men on the disbanding of the Potomac Flotilla, 31 July 1865

This was our first naval victory, indeed our first victory of any kind, and should not be forgotten. The Union cause was then in depressed condition, owing to the reverses it had experienced. The moral of this affair was very great, as it gave us a foothold on Southern soil and possession of the Sounds of North Carolina if we chose to occupy them. It was a death-blow to blockade running in that vicinity, and ultimately proved one of the most important events of the war.

—Admiral David D. Porter on the victory at Hatteras Inlet, North Carolina, 28–29 August 1861

You can't expect men to stand up against the fire of those gunboats.

—Rear Admiral Porter quoting a Confederate after the battle at Arkansas Post, 9–11 January 1863

We have met losses which we can not but deplore; still, we should not regret the death of those who died so nobly at their guns. Officers, and men, let us always be ready to make the sacrifice when duty requires it.

—Rear Admiral Porter, after the capture of Grand Gulf, 3 May 1863

Honor and glory should be the watchword of the Navy, and not profit.

—Rear Admiral Porter, 31 October 1864

. . . the death knell of another fort is booming in the distance. Fort Caswell with its powerful batteries is in flames and being blown up, and thus is sealed the door through which this rebellion is fed.

> —Rear Admiral Porter, 16 January 1865, after the fall of Fort Fisher and the closing of the Cape Fear River

. . . we had lost our last blockade-running port. Our ports were now all hermetically sealed. The anaconda had, at last, wound his fatal folds around us.

> —Rear Admiral Raphael Semmes on the fall of Wilmington, 22 February 1865

Of course we will get along together elegantly. All I have he can command, and I know the same feeling pervades every sailor's and soldier's heart. We are as one.

> —Major General William T. Sherman on the arrival of Lieutenant Commander S. L. Phelps for combined operations on the Tennessee River, 24 October 1863

We have no time, place, or means to build an effective navy. Our ports are, or soon will be, all blockaded. On land we do not fear Lincoln, but what shall we do to cripple him at sea?

> —John A. Stevenson to Secretary Mallory, 21 May 1861

Thus perished the *Virginia*, and with her many highflown hopes of naval supremacy and success.

> —Flag Officer Josiah Tattnall on the destruction of C.S.S. *Virginia*, 11 May 1862

The importance of a rigorous blockade at every point under your command cannot be too strongly impressed or felt. By cutting off all communication we not only distress and cripple the States in insurrection, but by an effective blockade we destroy any excuse or pretext on the part of foreign governments to aid and relieve those who are waging war upon the Government.

> —Secretary of the Navy Gideon Welles to Flag Officer Samuel F. Du Pont, 25 January 1862

If successful [at New Orleans], you open the way to the sea for the great West, never again to be closed. The rebellion will be riven in the center, and the flag to which you have been so faithful will recover its supremacy in every State.

> —Secretary Welles' instructions to Flag Officer David G. Farragut on the proposed attack on New Orleans, 10 February 1862

In the success which has attended your operations you have illustrated the efficiency and irresistible power of a naval force led by a bold and vigorous mind, and insufficiency of any batteries to prevent the passage of a fleet thus led and commanded.

> —Secretary Welles to Rear Admiral Farragut after the battle of Mobile Bay, 5 August 1864

To him our gratitude was justly due, for to him, under God, more than to any other person, we are indebted for the successful vindication of the integrity of the Union and the maintenance of the power of the Republic.

> —Secretary Welles, 15 April 1865, announcing to the Navy the assassination of President Lincoln

It is still wise—the wisest—economy to cherish the navy, to husband its resources, to invite new supplies of youthful courage and skill to its service, to be amply supplied with all needful facilities and preparations for efficiency, and thus to hold within prompt and easy reach its vast and salutary power for the national defense and self-vindication.

> —Secretary Welles, annual report to the President, 4 December 1865

We were bereft of ground for hope or aspiration, bereft of a cause for which to struggle and suffer.

—Lieutenant William C. Whittle, Jr., C.S.S. *Shenandoah*'s executive officer, on learning, 2 August 1865, that the war was over

As we turned away from the land, our hearts sank within us, while the conviction forced itself upon us, that the cause for which so much blood had been shed, so many miseries bravely endured, and so many sacrifices cheerfully made, was about to perish at last!

—Lieutenant John Wilkinson on the failure of his blockade runner *Chameleon* to get into Charleston, 5 February 1865

APPENDIX XII

TABLE OF
ILLUSTRATIONS

On the Tennessee River.

TABLE OF ILLUSTRATIONS

During the years in which this *Chronology* has been published, one of the most consistently praised aspects of the work has been the illustrations. The Naval History Division has received many requests for information regarding the illustrative material and copies of specific items. In some instances the inquirer has had to be directed to other agencies or individuals, for, as has been pointed out in the preface to each part, the illustrations have been drawn from a wide range of sources. By no means have all come from the Division's own extensive collection.

Thus, in the interest of enabling the reader to direct his inquiries to the appropriate office or person, the following table of illustrations has been compiled. It indicates the Part of the *Chronology* in which the illustration appears, the page within that Part on which it appears, the subject of the illustration, the source of the illustration, and, in the case of material found in the Naval History Division and the National Archives, the order number.

In order to be concise, the source has been abbreviated. The symbol and the organization each one designates are as follows:

CSA   Confederate Salvage Association, Inc., Columbus, Georgia
GHC   Georgia Historical Commission, Atlanta, Georgia
LC   Library of Congress, Washington, D.C.
MM   Mariners Museum, Newport News, Virginia
NA   National Archives, Washington, D.C. (RG indicates the Record Group in which the document or map is located.)
NHD   Naval History Division, Navy Department, Washington, D.C.
NHF   Naval Historical Foundation, Navy Department, Washington, D.C.
NN*DP*   Newport News, Virginia, Daily Press
NPC   Naval Photographic Center, U.S. Naval Station, Washington, D.C.
ORN   *Official Records of the Union and Confederate Navies in the War of the Rebellion* (followed by series, volume, and page number)
SUN   Baltimore *Sun*
V*EP*   Vicksburg, Mississippi, *Evening Post*

To order an 8″ x 10″ black and white glossy print of any item held by NHD or NPC, enclose check or money order in the amount of 90 cents per print ordered, indicate the order number, and mail the order to: Commanding Officer, U.S. Naval Photographic Center, U.S. Naval Station, Washington, D.C., 20390.

TABLE OF ILLUSTRATIONS

INTRODUCTION

Part III

Part V

Two "City" class gunboats under construction at the Carondelet
Marine Railway and Drydock Company, Carondelet, Mo.

VI–409

INDEX

The abbreviations used in this index are largely obvious: Lieut. for Lieutenant; Brig. General for Brigadier General; stmr. for steamer; schnr. for schooner; b.r. for blockade runner; Am. for American (Union); Conf. for Confederate; and so on.

All officers and enlisted men included in the index may be assumed to be in the U.S. Navy (USN) unless otherwise indicated. In this connection, the abbreviations used to identify a person's service are also familiar to most readers of the *Chronolgy*: USA for United States Army; CSA and CSN for Confederate States Army and Navy respectively; USMC and CSMC for the respective Marine Corps; RN for Royal Navy; RNN for Royal Netherlands Navy. Designations which some readers may not recognize at once are USRM, United States Revenue Marine (the predecessor of the present day Coast Guard), USRC, United States Revenue Cutter, and USCS, United States Coast Survey.

The upper case Roman numerals indicate to which of the six parts of the *Chronology* the subsequent page numbers refer. Page numbers that appear in italics indicate a pertinent illustration to which the reader's attention would not otherwise be directed.

Amaranth, b.r. schnr., **III:** 143
Amaranthus, USS (also *Christiana*), **V:** 116, 117
Amazon, Conf. stmr., **V:** 55, 123; **VI:** 197
Amazonian, Am. bark, **III:** 89
Amelia, Conf. b.r. ship, **I:** 17
Amelia, Conf. b.r. schnr., **III:** 78
Amelia, British stmr. (ex-CSS *Tallahassee*), **V:** 83
Amelia Ann, b.r. schnr., **III:** 157
Amelia, Emma, British b.r. schnr.; see: *Emma Amelia*
Amelia I., Fla., **II:** 28
America, C.S. yacht (also *Memphis*), **II:** 42; as USS; **II:** 103; **VI:** 77, 269
America, b.r. sloop, **II:** 47
America, b.r. schnr., **III:** 134
America, North, Am. schnr.; see: *North America*
America, Young, CSS; see: *Young America*
American Coaster, b.r. schnr., **II:** 61; **VI:** 332
Ames, Betsey, Am. brig; see: *Betsey Ames*
Amite River, La., **V:** 202
Ammen, Daniel, Rear Admiral, **II:** 20; **III:** 58–59; **V:** 113
Ammunition captured (see also: Arms cargoes, Gunpowder), **I:** 29, 37, 38; **II:** 11, 28, 33, 74; **III:** 45, 49
Ammunition, saving and shortages of, **II:** 7, 15–16, 26, 27, 52; **III:** 27, 84, 90, 92, 106, 115
Amphitrite Strait, So. China Sea, **V:** 106
Amukta Passage, Aleutians, **V:** 111, 115
Amy Warwick, Conf. brig, **I:** 19
"Anaconda Plan", x–xiii, xxix; **I:** 12; **VI:** 2
Anacostia, USS (ex-*M.W. Chapin*), **I:** 10, 15; **II:** 3, 31, 68, 112; **III:** 85, 89; **IV:** 5, 19
Anacostia River, D.C., **V:** 90, 93; **IV:** 12, *14*, 22
Anclote Keys, Fla., **III:** 81, 96; **IV:** 86, 122, 145
Anderson, Charles D., Colonel, CSA, **IV:** 98
Anderson, Fort, N.C.; see: Fort Anderson
Anderson, J.R. & Co. (Tredegar Iron Works), **VI:** 215
Anderson, James P., Major General, CSA, **IV:** 37
Anderson, Robert, Major General, USA, **I:** 6–7; **V:** 87; **VI:** 208
Anderson, Robert H., Major, CSA, **III:** 20
Anderson, William G., USS; see: *William G. Anderson*, USS
Andersonville, S.C., **V:** 39
Andrew, Henry, USS; see: *Henry Andrew*, USS
Andrews, George C., Acting Master, CSN, **III:** 66
Andrews, Thomas I., Acting Master, **III:** 32, 45, 74
Andromeda, b.r. schnr., **II:** 67
Anemone, USS (ex-*Wicaco*), **V:** 112, 114, 120
Angelina, b.r. sloop, **III:** 81
Anglia, b.r. stmr., **II:** 104
Anglo-Norman, CSS, **VI:** 197
Anglo-Saxon, USA stmr., **III:** 70; as Conf. stmr., **VI:** 197
Anglo Saxon, Am. ship, **III:** 131
Angra Pequena Bay, S.W. Africa, **III:** 134, 151; **VI:** 317
Anita, b.r. schnr., **III:** 150
Ann, British b.r. stmr., **II:** 74
Ann, b.r. schnr., **III:** 112
Ann, b.r. schnr., **III:** 126
Ann, Almira, b.r. schnr.; see: *Almira Ann*
Ann, Amelia, b.r. schnr.; see: *Amelia Ann*
Ann Bell, Conf. ship, **VI:** 332
Ann, Clara, b.r. sloop; see: *Clara Ann*
Ann, Corris, Am. brig; see: *Corris Ann*
Ann, E., Am. fishing schnr.; see: *E. Ann*

Ann, Emily, Conf. b.r. schnr., see: *Emily Ann*
Ann Hamilton, Conf. schnr., **IV:** 15
Ann Louisa, British b.r. schnr., **IV:** 110
Ann, Margaret, schnr.; see: *Margaret Ann*
Ann Maria, British b.r. schnr., **II:** 110
Ann, Martha, b.r. schnr.; see: *Martha Ann*
Ann Ryan, b.r. schnr., **I:** 18
Ann S. Davenport, b.r. schnr., **IV:** 60
Anna, Conf. stmr., **I:** 37
Anna, USA transport, **IV:** 128
Anna, USS; see: *Annie*, USS
Anna Belle, Conf. schnr., **II:** 29
Anna Dale, C.S. armed schnr., **V:** 45; **VI:** 197
Anna F. Schmidt, Am. ship, **III:** 105
Anna Maria, b.r. schnr., **III:** 104
Anna Perrette, Conf. stmr., **VI:** 197
Annapolis, Md. (cf. Naval Academy, U.S.), **I:** *9*, 10–11, 19; **III:** 104; **IV:** 89; **V:** 18, 22, 31, 35, 80, 99, 124; **VI:** 2, 208
Anne Sophia, Conf. schnr., **II:** 95
Annie, British b.r. sloop, **II:** 57
Annie, British b.r. schnr., **III:** 34
Annie, USS (or *Anna*; ex-b.r. *La Criolla*), **III:** 66, 149, 151, **V:** 33
Annie, b.r. stmr., **IV:** 118
Annie, British b.r. stmr. (later *Preston*, USS, q.v.), **IV:** 129
Annie, b.r. sloop, **V:** 83
Annie B., b.r. schnr., **III:** 67
Annie Dees, b.r. sloop (later USS *Thunder*), **II:** 110
Annie Sophia, b.r. schnr., **V:** 34
Annie Thompson, b.r. sloop, **IV:** 10
Annie Virdon, British b.r. schnr., **IV:** 118
Antelope, British b.r. schnr., **III:** 55
Antelope, USS, **IV:** 114
Antigua I., B.W.I., **I:** 19
Antoinette, British b.r. schnr., **III:** 163
Antona, British b.r. stmr., **III:** 6; as USS, **III:** 124, 159, 167; **V:** 37
Antonica, Conf. b.r. stmr. (ex-*Herald*, q.v.), **III:** 165–66
Antwerp, Belgium, **III:** 69
Apalachee River, Ga., **V:** 81
Apalachicola (and Bay), Fla., **I:** 24; **II:** 29, 42; **III:** 69, 85, 117, 129; **IV:** 59; **V:** 103; **VI:** 208, 253
Apalachicola River, Fla., **II:** 103; **VI:** 208
Appel, P. F., Acting Master, CSN, **VI:** 226
Appleton Belle, Conf. stmr., **II:** 18; **VI:** 197
Appomattox, CSS (ex-*Empire*, q.v.), **VI:** 197
Appomattox Court House, Va., **I:** 17; **V:** 21, 76, 81, 86, 87; **VI:** 6
Appomattox River, Va., **V:** 3, 66–67, 71
Aquia Creek, Va., **I:** 10–11, 15, 17, 18, 20; **VI:** 19, 20, 237
Aquilla, Conf. schnr., **II:** 89
Arabella, Am. brig, **III:** 93
Arago, Coast Survey schnr., **III:** 32
Arago, transport stmr., **III:** 117, 121
Aransas Pass, Tex., **I:** 10; **II:** 51, 80, 90, 93, 112; **III:** 156, 157; **IV:** 121; **V:** 39
Arcade, Am. schnr., **I:** 38
Arcadia, Conf. transport stmr., **III:** 115; **VI:** 198
Archer, Am. fishing schnr., **III:** 99, 113; as CSS, **III:** 101; **VI:** 198, 207
Archives, Conf., **V:** 76, 81, 89, 90, 93

Borden, William C., Acting Ensign, **V**: 112

Bormann fuze, **II**: 9

Boston, USA transport, **I**: 9, 11, 14; **IV**: 63; **VI**: 15

Boston, U.S. tug, **III**: 91; **VI**: 311; as Conf. privateer stmr., **VI**: 206, 328

Boston, British b.r. stmr., **IV**: 86

Boston, Mass., **II**: 3, 14; **III**: 8, 12, 39, 53, 54, 92, 93, 98, 113, 117, 166; **IV**: 23, 104, 105; **V**: 115; Navy Yard **VI**: 52

Boston prize court, **V**: 55; **VI**: 196, 203, 215

Boughton, Napoleon, Acting Ensign, **V**: 43

Bounty to privateers, CSN, **I**: 14

Bourne, John T., Conf. commercial agent, Bermuda, **IV**: 59

Boutelle, Charles O., Coast Survey shipmaster, **IV**: 59; **V**: 64

Bowers, Mary, British b.r. stmr.; see: *Mary Bowers*

Bowling Green, Ky., **II**: 28

Boxer, USS (ex-*Tristram Shandy*, q.v.), **V**: 114

Boyce, Sarah A., Am. schnr.; see: *Sarah A. Boyce*

Boyd, Miss Belle, **VI**: 243

Boyd, Lynn, Conf. stmr.; see: *Lynn Boyd*

Boyd's Landing, Broad River, S.C., **IV**: 138, 142

Boyd's Neck, S.C., **V**: 32

Boyer, Samuel P., Assistant Surgeon, **IV**: 54

Boyle, John, Acting Master's Mate, **III**: 81

Bracelet, Conf. river transport, **VI**: 206

Bradford, CSS **VI**: 206

Bradford, Abby, Am. schnr.; see: *Abby Bradford*

Bradley's Landing, Ark., **III**: 9

Brady, Lieu⁻., CSA, **II**: 23

Bragg, Braxton, General, CSA, **I**: 6; **II**: 24; **IV**: 136; **V**: 11, 16, 33, 47, 61

Bragg, General, USS; see: *General Bragg*, USS

Braine, Daniel L., Lt. Commander, **I**: 28, 37; **II**: 102, 110, 111; **III**: 32, 54, 67, 79; **IV**: 51, 89, 139; **V**: 22, 113

Braine, John C., Master, CSN, **III**: 162–63; **IV**: 116; **V**: 73, 91, *109*

Branchville, S.C., **V**: 18

Brand, Frederick B., Lt. Colonel, CSA, **III**: 3; **VI**: 222

Brandenburg, Ky., **III**: 111

Brandywine Hill, Va., **II**: 113

Brannon, John M., Brig. General, USA, **I**: 6; **II**: 100

Brashear City, La., **VI**: 252

Brasher, Thomas M., Commander, **I**: 14; **II**: 63, 66, 69

Braumly (Garefoster &), Conf. shipowners, **VI**: 332

Brave, British b.r. sloop, **III**: 10

Brayman, Mason, Brig. General, USA, **IV**: 34

Brazil, **III**: 134, 164; **IV**: 27, 78, 117; captures off, **III**: 47, 52, 53, 58, 67, 71, 72, 77, 81, 86, 111; **IV**: 49, **VI**: 207

Brazil Squadron, reestablished, **V**: 71, 123

Braziliera, USS, **III**: 147, 163; **IV**: 12, 108, 121; **V**: 116

Brazos, Tex., **IV**: 116

Brazos Pass, Tex., **IV**: 132

Brazos Santiago, Tex., **III**: 2, 88, 96, 127, 150, 151; **IV**: 110, 137, 140; **V**: 66

Bread cargo captured or destroyed, **IV**: 61

Breaker, CSS (later U.S. tender), **II**: 90; **VI**: 206

Breck, Joseph B., Acting Lieut., **III**: 122, 131, 153, 154; **IV**: 46, 109

Breckenridge, William K. M., Colonel, USA, **III**: 79

Breckinridge, CSS; see: *General Breckinridge*, CSS

Breach Inlet, S.C., **V**: 32

Bree, John de, Paymaster, CSN; see: de Bree, John

Breese, K. Randolph, Lt. Commander, **V**: 13

Breese, Oliver S., b.r. schnr.; see: *Oliver S. Breese*

Breese, S. Livingston, Lt. Commander, **III**: 72, 106; **IV**: 37, 48, 62

Bremen, Germany, **I**: 13, 14

Brennand, Edward E., Acting Lieut., **III**: 93

Brent, Joseph L., Major, CSA, **III**: 32–33; **VI**: 243, 323

Brent, Thomas W., Commander, CSN, **IV**: 148

Breshwood, John G., Captain, USRM (later CSN), **I**: 4; **VI**: 283

Brest, France, **III**: 121, 131, 149; **IV**: 4, 16, 26

Breton's Bay, Va., **I**: 16

Brewster, USA stmr., **IV**: 3

Bribery, attempted by blockade runners, **IV**: 12

Brice, James, b.r. schnr.; see: *James Brice*

Brice, John J., Acting Ensign, **V**: 64

Brick cargo captured, **II**: 61

Brick House Farm, Va., **IV**: 29

Bridgeport, Ala., **IV**: 121

Brigades; see: Marine Brigade; Naval Brigade

Bright, b.r. sloop, **III**: 71

Briggs, Smith, USA gunboat; see: *Smith Briggs*

Brilliant, Mexican schnr., **I**: 17

Brilliant, Am. ship, **II**: 100

Brilliant, British b.r. schnr., **II**: 112

Brilliant, USS, **III**: 23, 57; **IV**: 130

Brinker, Henry, USS; see: *Henry Brinker*, USS

Bristol, Tenn., **V**: 55

Britannia, British b.r. stmr., **III**: 100; as USS, **IV**: 34, 56; **V**: 112

British blockade runners; see individual ships

British Columbia, **III**: 148; **IV**: 4

British Empire, British b.r. schnr., **II**: 45

British Queen, British schnr., **II**: 27

Brittany, W. France, **VI**: 209

Broad River, S.C., **I**: 31, 34; **IV**: 138, 145; **V**: 32

Broadway Landing, Va., **V**: 71

Brock, Hattie, Conf. lake stmr.; see: *Hattie Brock*

Brockenborough, G. L., Conf. sloop; see: *G. L. Brockenborough*

Brodhead, Edgar, Acting Lieut., **III**: 88, 156

Brook Haven, N.Y., **VI**: 216

Brooke guns, **III**: 69, 89, 153, 165; **IV**: *17*, 64

Brooke, John Mercer, Commander, CSN, **I**: 16; **III**: 151, 159, 166; **IV**: *17*, 56; **V**: 74

Brooklyn, USS, **I**: 4–5, 7, 15, 17, 18; **II**: 24, 32, 53, 55, 67, 72, 90; **III**: 8, 17, 18, 36, 87, 157; **IV**: 95; **V**: 11, 101; **VI**: 69, 70, 77, 80, 92, 93, 322

Brooklyn, N.Y., **I**: 3, 11; Navy Yard **VI**: 49, 51

Brooks, Edwin F., Acting Ensign, **III**: 163

Brooks, Henry C., Conf. brig; see: *Henry C. Brooks*

Brooks, James, **V**: 128

Brooks, John A. J., Acting Master, **I**: 12; **IV**: 127, 144; **V**: 10, 113

Brookville, Fla., **IV**: 86

Broro Neck, McIntosh County, Ga., **V**: 61

Brother, Charles, Pvt., USMC; Journal of, **VI**: 48–83

Brothers, British b.r. schnr., **III**: 52

Brown, Alexander C., **VI**: 184

Brown, Charles H., Acting Lieut., **II**: 108; **III**: 26, 145, 150, 152; **IV**: 19, 25, 30, 31, 41, 44, 46, 51

Brown, Eugene H., Engineer, CSN, **III**: 104

Brown, George, Lt. Commander, **III**: 27, 32; **IV**: 138, 144; **V**: 53, 87

Brown, George W., Lieut., **III:** 22, 25, 29, 88, 115, 147; **VI:** 220

Brown, Henry, Acting Lieut., **V:** 112

Brown, Isaac N., Commander, CSN, **II:** 66, 81, 83, 84, 85–86, 89; **III:** 41, 84, 115; **VI:** 186, 198, 199–200, 208

Brown, James, Conf. shipmaster, **VI:** 283

Brown, James W., Acting Ensign, **V:** 45, 113; **VI:** 197

Brown, John, Acting Ensign, **V:** 114

Brown, John E., Conf. shipowner, **VI:** 332

Brown, Joseph E., Governor of Ga., **I:** 3

Brown, Louis A., Acting Master, **III:** 72

Brown, W. F., Captain, CSMC, **IV:** 116

Brown, W. H., N.Y. shipbuilder, **VI:** 269

Browne, George W., Acting Lieut., **I:** 40

Browne, William R., Acting Lieut., **III:** 131, 160, 163, 165; **V:** 64

Brown's Ferry, S.C., **V:** 59

Brown's Landing, Fla., **IV:** 62

Brownsville, Ky., **III:** 127

Brownsville, Pa., **VI:** 223, 295, 325

Brownsville, Tex., **III:** 2, 151; **IV:** 23, 110; **V:** 104

Bruce (Ollinger &), Conf. shipbuilder, **VI:** 186

Bruce, Robert, British b.r. brig; see: *Robert Bruce*

Bruce Mines, Ont., **VI:** 240

Bruinsburg, Miss., **III:** 74, 137; **IV:** 135

Bruner, Elias D., Acting Lieut., **II:** 116; **V:** 112

Brunswick, Am. whaling ship, **V:** 110–11

Brunswick, Ga., **II:** 31; **IV:** 12

Brunswick, Me., **VI:** 259

Brunswick, N.C., **III:** 158

Bryan, R. O., British b.r. schnr.; see: *R. O. Bryan*

Bryant, John L., Acting Master, **IV:** 90, 120, 128

Bryant, Nathaniel, Lieut., **II:** 26, 40

Bryantown, Md., **V:** 91

Bryson, Andrew, Commander, **III:** 156; **IV:** 14

Buchanan, Lighthouse tender, **I:** 9

Buchanan, Franklin, Admiral, CSN, resigns from USN, **I:** 11; Virginia service, **II:** 20, 23, 26, 29, 40, 71, *85*; promoted to Admiral, CSN, **II:** 94 **VI:** 3; at Mobile, Alabama, **III:** 135, 154, 160, 165, 166; **IV:** 1, 15, 58, 59, 61, 63, 82, 84, 95, 96, 97, 99; **VI:** 2, 6, 217

Buchanan, Thomas McK., Lt. Commander, **II:** 109; **III:** 9; **VI:** 189

Buckingham, Duke of, **VI:** 214

Buckingham, William A., Governor of Conn., **IV:** 133

Buckner, Simon Bolivar, Lt. General, CSA, **V:** 103

Buckthorn, USS; **VI:** 64, 77

Buck's Mills, Waccamaw River, S.C., **V:** 67

Budd, Thomas A., Acting Lieut., **I:** 38; **II:** 38

Budd, William, Acting Lieut., **I:** 15, 16, 17, 19, 20, 22, 38; **II:** 88, 108; **III:** 32; **IV:** 59, 60, 84

Buell, Samuel T., Colonel, USA, **II:** 26

Buenos Aires, Argentina, **I:** 19; **III:** 97

Buffalo, b.r. sloop, **IV:** 12

Buffalo, N.Y., **III:** 121; **IV:** 63, 131

Buffington I., Ohio River, **III:** 118

Buford, Abraham, Brig. General, CSA, **V:** 95

Buist, Henry, Conf. privateer owner, **VI:** 281

Bull Run, Va., **I:** 20, 24; **II:** 37

Bulloch, Irvine S., Acting Master, CSN; **V:** *131*

Bulloch, James D., Commander, CSN; ordered to England, **I:** 13; duty in England, **I:** 22; **II:** 38, 88, 89; **III:** 6–7, 69, 81, 91, 96, 112, 114, 116, 134, 149; **IV:** 21–22, 34, 44, 52, 67, 89, 102, 112, *113*, 119, 121; **V:** 8, 10, 21, 38, 55, 65, 67, 82, 83, 96, 100, 106; **VI:** 187, 188, 190–91, 193, 195, 203, 209, 215, 216, 219

Bull's Bay, S.C., **I:** 29, 40; **II:** 22, 57, 80, 104; **III:** 31, 54, 68; **IV:** 132–33; **V:** 16, 18, 34, 39, 42, 95; **VI:** 6

Bull's I., S.C., **II:** 67

Bullyard Sound, S.C., **V:** 49

Bunce, Francis M., Lt. Commander, **III:** 113

Bunner, John C., Acting Master, **III:** 94

Bunting, James H., Acting Ensign, **IV:** 47

Burgess, Francis, Acting Master, **III:** 134, 144, 153; **IV:** 7, 11, 31; **V:** 22

Burke, James H., Conf. shipmaster, **VI:** 234

Burke, Miles, **IV:** 99

Burkhart, George, b.r. schnr.; see: *George Burkhart*

Burley, Bennett G., Acting Master's Mate, CSN, **VI:** 282, 308

Burns, Thomas, Acting Master, **IV:** 90, 103, 137

Burnside, Ambrose E., Major General, USA, **II:** 6, 19, 33; **III:** 118; **VI:** 2, 288

Burnside, General, USS; see: *General Burnside*, USS

Burroughs, J. M., Conf. shipmaster, **VI:** 216, 303

Burroughs, John H., Richmond shipyard supt., **VI:** 293

Burton, CSS; see: *W. Burton*, C.S. tender

Burton, Mary P., British b.r. schnr.; see: *Mary P. Burton*

Burtonia, Miss., **VI:** 275

Butcher, Matthew S., British shipmaster, **VI:** 190

Butler, Benjamin F., Major General, USA, **I:** 9, 10, 11, 23–24, 27; **II:** 60, 66, 109, 110, 113; **III:** 119, 158; **IV:** 1, 3, 30, 51, 66, 72, 75, 134–35, 136, 142, 144, 146, 147, 149–50, 151; **V:** 3, 5, 8, 47, 59; **VI:** 2, 6, 198

Butler, William, Landsman, **IV:** 99

Butte à la Rose, La., **III:** 68

Butter shortage, **III:** 26

By George, British b.r. schnr., **II:** 112

Byzantium, Am. ship, **III:** 97

C. P. Knapp, Conf. schnr., **I:** 22

C. P. Williams, USS, **III:** 17, 20, 128, 167; **V:** 37, 116

C. Routereau, b.r. sloop, **III:** 81

Cabbage I., Ga., **IV:** 16

Cactus, USS (ex-*Polar Star*), **IV:** 78; **V:** 112

Cadieu, Charles H., Acting Master, **IV:** 138

Cadiz, Spain, **II:** 8; **VI:** 306

Cain, Tubal, British b.r. stmr.; see: *Tubal Cain*

Caird & Co., Greenock, Scotland, **VI:** 189

Cairns, Sir Hugh, **VI:** 195

Cairo, USS; sinking of, **II:** 113–14; **VI:** 3; mentioned, **I:** 22; **II:** 40, 68; **IV:** 30; **V:** 8; **VI:** *347, 349–53*

Cairo, Ill., **I:** 12, 22, 26; **II:** 14, 15, 16, 17, 18, 24, 32, 40, 46; **III:** 6, 7, 12, 17, 25, 36, 66, 101, 105, 107; **IV:** 34, 47, 63; **VI:** 202

Calais, France, **II:** 108; **IV:** 24, 25, 52, 93; **V:** 115, 117; **VI:** 118

Calcasieu, La., **VI:** 218

Calcasieu Pass, La., **III:** 144; **IV:** 57; **V:** 20, 22; **VI:** 323

Calcasieu River, La., **III:** 145; **IV:** 57; **VI:** 218

Calcium light, **III:** 122

Calcutta, India, **III:** 39, 47, 145

Caldwell, Charles H. B., Commander, **II:** 5, 8, 55, 68; **III:** 78, 105; **IV:** 140

Caleb Cushing, USRC, **III:** *101*, 104; **VI:** 207

Castle Belem, Lisbon, Portugal, **V:** 69, 71
Castle Pinckney, Charleston harbor, **III:** 127; **V:** 42
Castor, Conf. owned bark, **VI:** 190, 207–08
Castroville, Texas, **VI:** 313
Caswell, Coast Survey schnr., **III:** 32
Caswell, Conf. steam tender, **VI:** 208
Cat Island & Passage, Miss., **I:** 39; **II:** 25; **VI:** 220, 278
Catahoula Shoals, Ouachita River, La., **IV:** 26
Catalpa, USS (ex-*Conqueror*), **V:** 47, 53, 67
Catawba, C.S. stmr., & flag-of-truce boat, **VI:** 208
Cate, David, Lieut., **II:** 29, 45, 46, 67; **III:** 21, 54, 67, 115
Catherine, whaler, **V:** 109
Catherine Holt, b.r. sloop, **IV:** 25
Catskill, USS, **III:** 58, 59, 112, 113, 117, 129, 151; **IV:** 102; **V:** 42–43; **VI:** 220
Cattle, capture of, **II:** 103
Cavalry, CSA, **I:** 30, **II:** 57; **III:** 55, 96, 117, 126, 140, 148, 168; **IV:** 5, 24, 41, 50, 61, 78, 83, 86, 90, 92, 120, 121, 128, 133; **V:** 49, 59, 61, 66, 96, 97
Cavalry, USA, **II:** 104; **IV:** 29, 109, 146; **V:** 20
Cavendy, Edward, Acting Master, **I:** 27, 29; **II:** 37
Cayuga, USS, **II:** 40, 42, 55, 89; **III:** 57, 67, 97, 106, 119, 127, 132, 145; **VI:** 242
Cecelia, Conf. schnr., **I:** 27, 28
Cedar I., Neuse River, N.C., **III:** 119
Cedar Keys, Fla., **II:** 7, 9, 28, 70; **III:** 53; **IV:** 36
Celeste, USA transport, **IV:** 109
Celestino, João, **V:** 90, 95
Celt, British b.r. stmr., **V:** 39, 42
Ceres, USS, **II:** 69, 80; **III:** 44, 86; **IV:** 45, 54, 60, 75, 87, 134; **VI:** 193, 217
Ceres, British b.r. stmr., **III:** 161
Cerro Gordo, Tenn., **III:** 96; **VI:** 273
Chaffin's Bluff, Va., **II:** 71; **III:** 115; **IV:** 58, 116, 122, 123; **V:** 3, 46, 81; **VI:** 247, 293
Chain obstructions, river, **II:** 28, 50–51; **V:** 59
Chalmette, La., **II:** 54
Chambers, James S., USS; see: *James S. Chambers*, USS
Chambers, John W., Acting Ensign, **IV:** 46
Chambers, T. J., Conf. ship; see: *T. J. Chambers*
Chameleon, C.S. Govt. b.r. (ex-*Tallahassee*), **IV:** 150; **V:** 21, 33, 38, 82; **VI:** 311
Champanero, b.r. schnr., **V:** 61
Champion, b.r. sloop, **II:** 57
Champion, USS, **III:** 75, 141
Champion, b.r. schnr., **III:** 106
Champion, John C., Acting Master, **IV:** 32, 48
Champion, Little, U.S. pump steamer; see: *Little Champion*
Champion No. 3, U.S. pump steamer, **IV:** 48; as C.S. pump steamer, **VI:** 204
Champion No. 5, U.S. pump steamer, **IV:** 48
Chance, b.r. schnr., **II:** 74
Chandeleur Islands, La., **III:** 140
Chandler, Ralph, Lt. Commander, **III:** 140; **IV:** 4; **V:** 55, 78
Chaos, British b.r. schnr., **V:** 91
Chaplin, James C., Lt. Commander, **I:** 17; **II:** 20; **III:** 156; **IV:** 12
Chapman, J. P., privateer schnr.; see: *J. P. Chapman*
Chapman, John H., Acting Ensign, **V:** 114
Chapman, Robert T., Lieut., CSN, **I:** 6
Chapultepec Palace, Mexico City, **V:** 111
Charity, b.r. schnr., **I:** 39

Charity, b.r. schnr., **III:** 87
Charles City, Md., **II:** 77
Charles Henry, b.r. sloop, **I:** 22
Charles Henry, b.r. sloop, **II:** 57
Charles Hill, Am. ship, **III:** 53
Charles Morgan; see: *Governor Moore*, La. State gunboat
Charles Phelps, USS, **V:** 112, 114
Charleston, CSS, **II:** 91; **III:** 127, 137, 151; **IV:** 24; **V:** 39, 42, 43, *106;* **VI:** 208
Charleston-type, small, **VI:** 185
Charleston, b.r. stmr., **III:** 71
Charleston, S.C.; attack on, **III:** 55ff.; bombardment renewed, **III:** 117ff.; evacuation, **V:** 42ff.; mentioned, **I:** 2, 3, 6, 13, 14, 18, 20, 21, 23, 28, 29, 30, 31, 34, 39; **II:** 12, 15, 22, 38, 44, 51, 56, 57, 61, 62, 63, 66, 67, 71, 88, 89, 96, 98, 102, 103, 104, 110, 111, 112, 113; **III:** 2, 5–6, 12, 16, 17, 18–20, 27, 28, 29, 31, 38, 41, 44, 47, 49, 52, 55, 57–58, 59–60–61, 63, 64–65, 68, 69, 71, 74, 75, 77, 78, 79, 81, 83, 84, 90, 92, 93, 95, 96, 110, 111, 112, 114, 115, 117, 118, 119, 121, 122, 123, 124, 127, 128, 129, 131, 133, 134, 135, 137, 140, 141, 143–44, 145, 147, 148, 153, 154, 155, 156, 158, 159, 160, 164, 166, 168; **IV:** 2, 3, 5, 11, 13, 14, 15, 20, 21, 22, 24, 29, 31, 46, 47, 51, 66, 70, 85, 86, 102, 109, 118, 122, 129, 131, 132, 136, 139, 140, 146, 148, 151; **V:** 6, 10, 11, 16, 18, 21, 27, 31–32, 33, 34, 38, 39, 42, 43, 49, 53, 58, 64; **VI:** 3, 5, 6
Charleston (S.C.) *Daily Courier*, **IV:** 21
Charleston (S.C.) *Mercury*, **I:** 22; **III:** 78; **VI:** 256
Charleston & Savannah R.R., **IV:** 62–63, 85, 138, 139, 142, 151; **VI:** 293, 297
Charleston Pilot Boat #2, Conf. schnr.; see: *W. Y. Leitch*, British b.r.
Charlotte, b.r. schnr., **II:** 47; as USS, **II:** 116
Charlotte, British b.r. stmr., **V:** 21; **VI:** *340*
Charlotte, N.C., **III:** 159; **IV:** 56; **V:** 76, 81, 89, 93
Charlotte Clark, Conf. privateer stmr., **VI:** 328
Charlotte Harbor, Fla., **I:** 30; **III:** 44, 58, 77, 85, 136; **IV:** 48
Charm, CSS, **III:** 69; **VI:** 208, 280, 289
Charter Oak, Am. schnr., **IV:** 131
Chase, b.r. schnr., **II:** 56
Chase, Charles T., Acting Master, **IV:** 44, 51
Chase, Salmon P., Secretary of the Treasury, **II:** 61, 110; **III:** 154
Chassahowitzka Bay, Fla., **IV:** 63
Chassahowitzka River, Fla., **III:** 57
Chastelaine, Am. brig, **III:** 17
Chatfield, Battery, S.C.; see: Battery Chatfield
Chatfield, Thomas, Acting Master, **IV:** 5
Chatham, b.r. stmr. (later USS), **III:** 165
Chattahoochee, CSS, **III:** 86, 134; **V:** 89; **VI:** 100, 189, 208, 253, 354, *354*
Chattahoochee, Fla., **VI:** 325
Chattahoochee River, Ga./Fla., **III:** 86, 159
Chattanooga, Tenn., **III:** 156, 160; **IV:** 145
Chattanooga (Tenn.) *Gazette*, **V:** 55
Chauncey, John S., Captain, **I:** 26, 28
Cheatham, Benjamin Franklin, Brig. General, CSA, **VI:** 289
Cheeseman, USA transport, **IV:** 128
Cheesman, William S., Acting Lieut., **IV:** 85, 111
Chenango, USS, **V:** 49, 53, 59
Cheney, CSA stmr., **VI:** 208
Cheops, CSS, **VI:** 186, 209, 304

Cherbourg, France, **III**: 150; **IV**: 4, 27, 72, 74, 75, 78, 89, **VI**: 5, 192

Cherokee, b.r. stmr., **III**: 78; as USS, **IV**: 134, 144; **V**: 30

Cherry Grove, Va., **IV**: 36

Cherrystone Point, Va., **IV**: 29

Chesapeake, Am. stmr. (ex-*Totten*), capture of, **III**: *162*–63; **V**: 108; **VI**: 209–11, *210*, 324; mentioned, **III**: 101

Chesapeake, Conf. privateer schnr., **VI**: 328

Chesapeake Bay, Md./Va., **I**: 9–11, 15, 16, 17, 18, 27; **II**: 37, 104, 108; **III**: 99, 140; **IV**: 19, 29, 90, 119; **V**: 61, 73, 80, 108; **VI**: 196

Chesapeake Canal; see: Albemarle and Chesapeake Canal

Cheshire, British b.r. schnr., **I**: 39

Chester, Louis R., Acting Ensign, **IV**: 70

Chester, William E., b.r. sloop; see: *William E. Chester*

Chesterfield, CSA transport, **II**: 122; **VI**: 211, 232

Chicago, Ill., **II**: 15; **III**: 25

Chickahominy River, Va., **II**: 74, 79, 80, 91; **III**: 82; **V**: 67

Chickamauga, CSS, **IV**: 114–15, 122, 126, 128–29, 134; **V**: 11, 18, 49, *52*, 59; **VI**: 211, *211*

Chickasaw, USS, **IV**: 83, 95, 97, 98, 112; **VI**: 78, 91, 92, 96

Chickasaw, Ala., **II**: 20, 32, 50; **IV**: 149; **VI**: 273, 297

Chickasaw Bayou, Miss., **III**: 74

Chickasaw Bluffs, Miss., **II**: 116

Chicopee, USS, **IV**: 97-98, 139, 147

Chicora, CSS, **II**: 91; **III**: 18-*19*-20, 123, 127, 129, 133, 137, 140, 151; **IV**: 15; **V**: 39, 42, 43; **VI**: 3, 191, 211–12, 225

Chicora, C.S. Govt. b.r. stmr., **V**: 38

Chi-jinskiki Bay, Siberia, **V**: 103

Chillicothe, USS, **III**: 24, 32, 41, 47; **IV**: 30–31, 37–38, 59, 60, 70

China, **III**: 31; **IV**: 78; **V**: 67; **VI**: 3

Chincoteague Island & Inlet, Va., **I**: 28, 29, 30

Chippewa, USS, **II**: 56; **III**: 117, 159; **V**: 123

Chippewa Valley, Conf. river stmr., **III**: 29

Chippoak Creek, Va., **II**: 88

Chisholm, George, b.r. schnr.; see: *George Chisholm*

Choate, R., Am. fishing schnr.; see: *R. Choate*

Choctaw, USS, **III**: 72, 74, 82, 84, 91, 157; **IV**: 30–31

Choctawhatchee River, Fla., **II**: 8, 116

Chocura, USS, **II**: 61, 74; **III**: 15, 29, 77; **IV**: 51, 136, 140, 142; **V**: 20, 22

Chowan River, N.C., **II**: 24; **III**: 18; **IV**: 26, 92, 139; **V**: 10, 30, 69

Christian, Danish brig, **III**: 54

Christiana Keen, Am. schnr., **I**: 16

Chubb, Charles & Thomas, Conf. shipmasters, **VI**: 295–96

Chuckatuck Creek, Va., **III**: 15; **IV**: 36

Churchill, Thomas J., Brig. General, CSA, **III**: 8

Cienfuegos, Cuba, **I**: 18; **III**: 8, 17

Cilley, Greenleaf, Lt. Commander, **III**: 151

Cimarron, USS (ex-*Cimerone*), **II**: 84, 88, 97; **III**: 92, 129, 140; **IV**: 47

Cinchona, **V**: 124

Cincinnati, USS, **I**: 22; **II**: 17, 28, 37, 62, 116; **III**: 5, 7, 9, 10, 45, 86, 88, 100; **V**: 87; **VI**: 213, 231, 235

Cincinnati, Ohio, **I**: 14; **II**: 41; **III**: 111; **IV**: 136; **V**: 22; **VI**: 189, 205, 208, 212, 213, 217, 220, 222, 249, 253

Circassian, b.r. stmr., **II**: 57; as USS, **III**: 95, 163; **VI**: 70, 71

Circus Point, Rappahannock River, Va., **IV**: 44

Citadel, The, Charleston, S.C. **I**: 2

City of Bath, Am. ship, **III**: 104

City of Pekin, USA transport, **IV**: 120

City of Richmond, C.S. Govt. b.r. stmr., **V**: 10, 21, 26; **VI**: 212

City of Richmond; see: *George Page*, CSS

City of Vicksburg, CSS, **III**: 21, 22; **VI**: 319

City Point, Va., **II**: 77, 78; **IV**: 7, 102; **V**: 3, 16, 18, 21, 26, 31, 36, 49, 58, 59, 65, 66, 67, 69, 71, 73, 75, 81, 86; **VI**: 6, 20, 204

Civil War Ships Salvaged or Memorialized, **VI**: 347–84

Clara, b.r. schnr., **III**: 53

Clara Ann, b.r. sloop, **III**: 122

Clara Dolsen, b.r. stmr., **II**: 69; **VI**: 212; as USS, **II**: 85

Clara Eames, USA transport, **IV**: 62

Clara Louisa, British b.r. sloop, **III**: 126

Clarence, Am. brig. **III**: 77–78; as CSS, **III**: 91, 92, 93, 113; **V**: 118; **VI**: 212, 229

Clarendon, Conf. stmr., **VI**: 212

Clarendon, Ark., **II**: 74, 83; **III**: 127

Clarita, British b.r. schnr., **III**: 72

Clark, Henry E., Colonel, CSA, **IV**: 10

Clark, John, Am. ship; see: *John Clark*

Clark, Thomas S., Colonel, USA, **VI**: 202

Clark, W. C., Am. brig; see: *W. C. Clark*

Clark, William, Acting Ensign, **V**: 113

Clarke, J. D., Conf. transport; see: *J. D. Clarke*

Clarksville, Tenn., **II**: 21, 23; **III**: 17

Clary, Albert G., Commander, **II**: 112; **III**: 29, 52, 71, 104, 143; **V**: 16; **VI**: 210

Claudio, Conf. ship, **VI**: 332

Clay, Henry; see: *Henry Clay*

Clay Island, Md., **I**: 24

Clay Landing, Suwannee River, Fla., **IV**: 47, 70

Claybrook and Dobyns, Conf. shipowners, **VI**: 333

Clearwater, Fla., **II**: 23; **III**: 96, 111, 123

Clematis, USS (ex-*Maria Love*), **IV**: 134

Clemens, William W., Lieut. USA, **V**: 78

Clendening, Conf. shipmaster, **VI**: 296

Clifton, USS, **III**: 2, 68, 118, 121, 136, 137, 138; as CSS, **III**: 150; **IV**: 33; **VI**: 213, 229, 249, 330

Clifton, Tenn., **II**: 26; **IV**: 48, 90, 120; **V**: 18, 22

Clinch; see: *General Clinch*

Clinton, Mary, Conf. schnr.; see: *Mary Clinton*

Clipper ships, **I**: 37; **III**: 27, 155; **IV**: 133

Clitz, John M. B., Commander, **II**: 68, 89, 104, 107; **III**: 74, 93, 106; **IV**: 93, 95; **V**: 46

Clockwork torpedoes, **IV**: *100*, 102

Cloth and clothing cargoes, captured or destroyed, **II**: 81, 105; **III**: 6, 23, 105, 129, 131, 167; **IV**: 10, 27, 31, 49, 72, 140; **V**: 60

Cloth and clothing shortages, **II**: 107; **III**: 26, 155; **IV**: 17

Clover, USS (ex-*Daisy*), **V**: 30, 53

Clyde, b.r. schnr., **III**: 66

Clyde, USA transport, **VI**: 72

Clyde, USS (ex-*Neptune*), **III**: 143; **IV**: 70

Clyde River, Scotland, **IV**: 118; **VI**: 191, 227

Clydebank Shipyards, Glasgow, **VI**: 186, 187, 298, 314

Clyde, William P., U.S. transport, see: *William P. Clyde*

Coal, anthracite, **II**: 50, 111; **III**: 121, 131; **V**: 100; **VI**: 189, 203, 257

    bituminous, **VI**: 189

    blacksmith's, captured, **IV**: 72

    Coordinator of Supply, USN, Philadelphia, **II**: 111

Coal barges, **III**: 27, 32, 35, 49, 53, 67, 93; **VI**: 206

Dahlgren, John A., Rear Admiral; appointed Commandant, Washington N.Y., **I:** 11; with President Lincoln, **II:** 89, 110, 115; **III:** 10, 27; **IV:** 11 (letter), 145 (letter); on Du Pont's failure to take Charleston, **III:** 69, 77; appointed Commander, SABS, **III:** 98, 110; engages Charleston defenses, **III:** 112–13, 117, 119, 129, 131–32, 133, 135, 136, 137, 138, 140, 145, 148, 150, 152, 153, 156; **IV:** 85, 132–33, 138, 150; **V:** 16, 39; on the surrender of Charleston, **V:** 43; relieved of command SABS, **V:** 105; mentioned, **I:** 3, 5, 12, 13, 14, 15, 20, 23; **II:** 26, 30, 31, 77, 81; **III:** 44, 99, 104, 110, 113, 117, 120, 122, 124, 127, 134, 144, 160, 163, 166; **IV:** 2, 3, 5, 11, 12, 14, 20, 23, 29, 35, 47, 62, 66, 67, 70, 92–93, 98, 121, 123, 140, 149; **V:** 6, 8, 10, 18, 21, 27, 31–32, 34, 47, 49, 53, 54, 61, 64, 67, 83, 87, 91, 94, 102; **VI:** 4, 12, 14, 15, 19, 23, 37, 42–44, *43*

Dahlgren, Ulric, Colonel, USA, **IV:** 29

Dahlgren guns, **II:** *109*; **III:** 34, 44; **IV:** 7, 75; **V:** 26; **VI:** 202, 207

Dai Ching, USS, **III:** 119, 129, 156; **IV:** 12, 14, 62–63, 138; **V:** 30–31, 116

Dakar, Senegal, W. Africa, **IV:** 127

Dale, USS, **I:** 29, 37

Dale, Anna, C.S. armed schnr.; see: *Anna Dale*

Dale, Kate, b.r. stmr. & sloop; see: *Kate Dale*

Dalman, C.S. receiving ship, **VI:** 217

Damascus, Conf. blockship, **VI:** 217

Dan, USS, **II:** 105

Dan, Conf. river stmr., **VI:** 218; as USS, **II:** 105

Dan Smith, USS, **III:** 13; **IV:** 27; **V:** 37

Dana, USS, **I:** 18

Dana, Napoleon J. T., Major General, USA, **III:** 143, 151; **IV:** 137

Dana, Richard Henry, Jr., **VI:** 215

Dana, William Henry, Lt. Commander, **III:** 97, 106, 127, 132, 145; **IV:** 146; **V:** 67

Danmark, HDMS, **VI:** 298

Dannelly's Mills, Fish River, Ala., **V:** 64

Dansey, William, Conf. shipowner, **VI:** 332

Danube, C.S. floating battery, **VI:** 218

Danville, Va., **V:** 3, 76, 81; **VI:** 6

Danville Bridge, Tenn., **II:** 36

Danville R.R., Va., **V:** 3

Darby, Conf. transport, **VI:** 218

Dardanelle, Ark., **III:** 24

Dare, b.r. stmr., **IV:** 4

Darien, Ga., **I:** 31; **III:** 141, 148

Darien, S.C., **II:** 71

Darlington, Conf. stmr., **II:** 28; **VI:** 218; as USA transport, **II:** 42, 102, 108; **VI:** 241

Dart, b.r. schnr., **I:** 18; as USS, **I:** 27, 28

Dart, British b.r. schnr., **II:** 101

Dart, b.r. schnr., **III:** 74

Dashing Wave, British b.r. brig, **III:** 152

Daufuskie I., S.C., **IV:** 42

Dauphin I.. and Bay, Ala., **IV:** 64

Davenport, Henry K., Commander, **II:** 100, 105, 107; **III:** 44, 55, 86; **IV:** 46, 133

David, CSS, **III:** 114, 141, 143, 144, 146; **IV:** 5, 23; **VI:** 5, 218–19

David torpedo-boats, **IV:** 29, 46; **V:** 42; **VI:** 218–19

David Crockett, b.r. schnr., **II:** 103

David, Jules, Conf. sympathizer, Vancouver, **III:** 148

David Vaname, Conf. schnr., **VI:** 332

Davidson, A. B., Captain, RN (Ret.), Conf. shipmaster, **VI:** 241

Davidson, Hunter, Commander, CSN, **II:** 71, 76, 77, 105; **III:** 123; **IV:** 39; **V:** 8, 10, 16, 21, 26, 27; **VI:** 212, 220

Davidson, John Q. A., Acting Ensign, **V:** 113

Davis, Charles H., Rear Admiral; member, Blockade Strategy Board, **I:** 17; member, Ironclad Board, **I:** 21; assumes command Western Flotilla, **II:** 61, 70; operations of Western Flotilla, **II:** 68, 75, 88; relieved of command, Mississippi Squadron, **II:** 100; mentioned, **I:** 39; **II:** 12, 74, 81, 86; **III:** 5; **VI:** *43*, 45, 213, 231

Davis, Edmund J., Brig. General, USA, **V:** 104

Davis, George, Conf. Senator (N.C.), **III:** 58

Davis, Ike, Am. stmr.; see: *Ike Davis*

Davis, J. C., U.S. barge; see: *J. C. Davis*

Davis, J. L., USS; see: *James L. Davis*, USS

Davis, J. T., b.r. schnr.; see: *J. T. Davis*

Davis, Jefferson, C.S. privateer; see: *Jefferson Davis*

Davis, Jefferson, President; inaugural address, **I:** 5; instructions and remarks regarding war at sea, **I:** 7, 12, 14; **II:** 86; **III:** 25, 62, 105, 157; **IV:** 48, 50, 86–87, 98; **V:** 54; evacuation of Richmond, **V:** 76; effort to avoid capture, **V:** 90, 91–92, 93, 95, 96–97; capture of, **V:** 97, 99; **VI:** 6; mentioned, **I:** 23; **II:** 27, 28, 29, 80, 102; **III:** 16, 27, 78, 121, 151, **IV:** 12, 84, 116, 122, 131, 136; **V:** 34, 36, 47, *82*, 86, 94, 108

Davis, Mrs. Jefferson, **V:** 81, 89–90, 93

Davis, John, **II:** 20

Davis, John L., Lt. Commander, **II:** 110; **III:** 47, 90; **IV:** 145, 147; **V:** 113; **VI:** 241

Davis, Lady, CSS; see: *Lady Davis*

Davis, Lizzie, b.r. stmr.; see: *Lizzie Davis*

Davis, M., Conf. shipmaster and owner, **VI:** 260

Davis, Margaret Y., Am. schnr.; see: *Margaret Y. Davis*

Davis, William H., **VI:** 184

Davisson, John, b.r. shipmaster, **VI:** 296

Dawho River, S.C., **II:** 57

Dawn, USS, **II:** 110; **III:** 1, 20, 35, 38; **IV:** 57, 61, 62

Day, Benjamin F., Lieut., **III:** 62

Day, James L., CSS; see: *James L. Day*

Day's Point, Va., **VI:** 255

Daylight, USS, **I:** 19, 23, 28, 56, 113; **II:** 105, 108, 112; **III:** 15, 167; **IV:** 2, 5

Dayton, William L., U.S. Minister to France, **IV:** 11, 72; **VI:** 304

De Bree, John, Paymaster, CSN, **III:** 155

De Camp, John, Captain, **II:** 55, 68; **IV:** 46

De Ford, Harriet, Am. stmr.; see: *Harriet de Ford*

De Haven, D.D., Selma shipbuilder, **VI:** 186

De Haven, Joseph E., Lt. Commander, **II:** 57, 61, 63, 64; **III:** 114

De Kalb, Baron, USS; see: *Baron de Kalb*

De Krafft, James C.P., Lt. Commander, **IV:** 51

De Lion, Coeur, USS; see: *Coeur de Lion*

De Montel, Charles, Captain, CSA, & Conf. privateer master, **VI:** 313

De Soto, USS, **II:** 14, 75; **III:** 71, 72, 81, 82, 111, 118, 129, 140, 141; **IV:** 15, 61; **V:** 132

De Soto, USS (ex-Conf. transport); **VI:** 219

De Villeroy, Brutus, French inventor, **III:** 54

Deadman's Bay, Fla., **II:** 68, 71; **V:** 55

Enterprise, b.r. sloop, **III**: 39

Enterprise, CSN b.r. stmr., **VI**: 225

Eolus, USS, **IV**: 122, 127; **V**: 59; **VI**: 203, 250

Equator, CSS, **VI**: 225, 290

Equipment & Recruiting, Bureau of, **II**: 80

Era, U.S. stmr., **III**: 75

Era No. 3, Conf. stmr., **VI**: 225, 330

Era No. 5, Conf. supply stmr., **III**: 29; **VI**: 225

Erben, Henry, Lt. Commander, **II**: 81; **V**: 31

Ericsson, John, **I**: 30; **II**: 7, 14, 24; **III**: 44, 153; **VI**: 1, 30

"Ericsson Galop, The", sheet music, **VI**: 132-33

Erie, Pa., **III**: 25; **IV**: 36

Ernti, b.r. schnr., **III**: 131

Escambia River, Fla., **II**: 62; **VI**: 317

Essex, USS (ex-*New Era*, Am. stmr.), **I**: 6; **II**: 17, 40, 85-86, 89, 93, 95, 96; **III**: 26, 41, 86, 100, 105, 134; **IV**: 7, 30, 31, 32; **VI**: 200

Estelle, Am. brig, **III**: 12

Estrella, USS, **II**: 107; **III**: 9, 66, 68, 75, 121, 134, 168; **IV**: 38, 42

Ethan Allen, USS, **II**: 9, 23; **III**: 7, 49, 113, 166-67; **IV**: 47, 138, 148

Etiwan, b.r. schnr. (later USS *Percy Drayton*), **III**: 15

Etiwan (also: *Etowah, Etowan, Etwan, Hetiwan*), Conf. transport, **III**: 134; **IV**: 70; **VI**: 225, 232

Etta, b.r. schnr., **IV**: 36

Etta, C.S. privateer (ex-*Retribution*, ex-*Uncle Ben*), **VI**: 318

Etta Caroline, Am. schnr., **IV**: 105

Eufaula, Ala., **VI**: 253

Eufaula Sound, Ala., **III**: 163

Eugenia, Conf. schnr., **II**: 37

Eugenia, b.r. schnr., **II**: 66

Eugenie, b.r. stmr., **III**: 78; as USS *Eugenie*, **III**: 140, 147; as USS *Glasgow*, **IV**: 83; **VI**: 53, 54, 57, 59, 62, 64, 66, 70-75, 77, 78

Eugenie Smith, British b.r. schnr. (later USS *Eugene*), **II**: 18

Eunice, Ark., **II**: 95; **III**: 93

Eunice's Bluff, La., **IV**: 60

Euphrates, Am. whaler, **V**: 107

Eureka, b.r. stmr., **II**: 51; as USS, **IV**: 47

Eureka, b.r. river stmr., **III**: 106

Eureka, b.r. schnr., **III**: 157

Eutaw, USS, **IV**: 58; **V**: 30; **VI**: 78

Evans, Robley D., Ensign, **V**: 13

Evans, William E., Lieut., CSN, **IV**: 24

Evansport, Va., **II**: 31

Evansport batteries, Quantico Creek, Va., **VI**: 237

Evansville, Conf. river stmr., **II**: 107; as USA transport, suspected of smuggling, **III**: 27

Evansville, Ind., **II**: 85; **III**: 6

Evelyn, Conf. b.r. stmr., **VI**: 289

Evening Star, b.r. sloop, **III**: 88

Everson, Alfred, Acting Master, **IV**: 67

Ewell, Richard S., Lt. General, CSA, **V**: 78

Ewer, George W., Acting Master, **III**: 141

Excelsior, British b.r. schnr., **III**: 115

Exchange, b.r. schnr., **II**: 116

Exchange, b.r. schnr., **III**: 167

Exchange, USS, **IV**: 13, 15, 66

Experiment, Conf. schnr., **VI**: 332

Experiment, b.r. schnr., **IV**: 51

Express, Conf. fishing sloop, **I**: 39; **VI**: 225

Express, b.r. sloop, **III**: 77

Express, Am. ship, **III**: 111

Eytinge, Henry S., Lieut., **II**: 95; **III**: 83

Ezilda, Conf. schnr., **I**: 28; as USS, **II**: 68

F. S. Bartow, Conf. privateer schnr., **VI**: 328

F. W. Johnson, Conf. schnr., **I**: 15

Fabian, James L., First Assistant Engineer, CSN, **VI**: 311

Fahkee, USS, **III**: 147; **IV**: 2; **V**: 123

Fair Play, British b.r. schnr., **II**: 32

Fairbanks, Charles B., Acting Master, CSN, **VI**: 260

Fairfax, Archibald B., Commander, CSN, **VI**: 248

Fairfax, Donald McD., Commander, **III**: 58, 112

Fairfield, USS, **III**: 111

Fairhope, Ga., **II**: 108

Fairplay, Conf. stmr., **II**: 91; as USS, **III**: 23, 25, 112; **IV**: 43, 139, 142; **VI**: 225-26

Fairy, USS (ex-*Velocity*), **IV**: 43, 130, 149; **VI**: 257, 308, 318

Falcon, b.r. schnr., **I**: 18

Falcon, b.r. schnr., **II**: 51

Falcon, CSN b.r. stmr., **VI**: 199, 226

Fales, William, Acting Master, **IV**: 52

Falmouth, England, **III**: 122; **VI**: 250

Fannie, b.r. stmr., **III**: 128; **VI**: 254

Fannie Laurie, b.r. bark, **II**: 95

Fannie McRae, British b.r. schnr., **V**: 22

Fanny, Conf. schnr., **I**: 17

Fanny, USA tug, **I**: 21, 23, 36; as CSS, **I**: 28; **II**: 20; **VI**: 226, 258

Fanny, British b.r. schnr., **II**: 93

Fanny and Jenny, b.r. stmr., **IV**: 16-17

Fanny Lee, British b.r. schnr., **I**: 31

Fanny Morgan, C.S. yacht, **VI**: 226, 331

Farenholt, Oscar W., Seaman, **II**: 104

Fargo, W. G., Mayor, Buffalo, N.Y., **IV**: 131; **VI**: 238

Faries, Thomas A., Captain, CSA, **III**: 157

Farm tools, cargo of, destroyed, **V**: 55

Farquhar, Norman H., Lieut., **II**: 110

Farragut, David Glasgow, Vice Admiral, appointed Commander, WGBS, **II**: 5; captures New Orleans, *xvii;* **II**: 47-60; operations in Mississippi River, **II**: 63 ff; captures Mobile Bay, **IV**: 93-108; **VI**: 6; promoted to Rear Admiral, **II**: 83; **VI**: 3; to Vice Admiral, **IV**: 1, 148; mentioned, **I**: 9; **II**: 5, 8, 15, 21, 24, 29, 32, 38, 42, 45, 47-50, 51, 52-53, 54, 55, 56, 57, 60, 62, 63, 66, 72-73, 74, 75, 81, 83, *85*, 86, 88, 89, 90, 93, 105, 109, 110, 114, 115; **III**: 10, 17, 26, 36, 41, 44-45, 47, 48, 49, 52, 53, 54, 55, 57, 62, 68, 70-71, 72, 75, 77, 79, 83, 85, 86, 91, 92, 96, 100, 105, 108, 111, 112, 114, 116, 117, 121, 122, 126, 129, 136, 157, 160, 165, 166; **IV**: 5, 10, 17, 19, 20, 27, 47, 57, 58, 59, 61, 63, 66, 82, 83, 84, 88, 89, 90, 93, 95, 97, 98, 99, 102, 104, *107*, 108, 109, 110, 112, 113, 121, 132, 137, 140, 147, 151; **V**: 8, 26; **VI**: 3, 51, 57, 61, *63*, 67, 76, 77, 79, 87

Farragut, Loyall, **III**: 11, 62; **IV**: 27, 61, 121; **V**: 5, 26

"Farragut's Grand March", sheet music, **VI**: 170-73

Farrand, Ebenezer, Flag Officer, CSN, **I**: 6; **II**: 63, 97; **III**: 25; **IV**: 140; **V**: 81, 97; **VI**: 205

Farrar, B. G., Brig. General, USA, **V**: 67

Farrell, Thomas M., Acting Master, **IV**: 23

Fashion, b.r. sloop, **III**: 85; **VI**: 208

Fashion, b.r. schnr., **III**: 93

Fashion, Fla., **III**: 85

Faucon, Edward H., Acting Lieut., **IV**: 4, 20, 120

Faunce, John, Captain, USRM, **I**: 6-7, 15

Fauntleroy, Charles M., Lieut., CSN, **IV**: 93; **VI**: 291

Favorite, Conf. schnr., **I**: 19

Forbes, New Orleans shipmaster, **VI**: 199

Forbes, R. B., USS; see: *R. B. Forbes*, USS

Ford, Harriet de, U.S. stmr.; see: *Harriet de Ford*

Fordoche, Bayou, La.; see: Bayou Fordoche, La.

Ford's Landing, Ark., **IV**: 62

Ford's Theatre, Washington, D.C., **V**: 86, 90, 95; **VI**: 6

Foreign Enlistment Act, British, **VI**: 195

Foreign seamen sailing Conf. b.r.'s, **VI**: 215

Forest City, USS, **III**: 101, 104; **VI**: 198, 207

Forest King, Conf. schnr., **I**: 16

Forest Queen, U.S. transport, **III**: 67, 88

Forest Rose, USS, **III**: 11, 22, 25, 29, 32, 82, 84, 85, 87, 115; **IV**: 18; **V**: 45; **VI**: 224

Forrest, CSS (ex-*Edwards*), **II**: 20; **VI**: 229

Forrest, Andrew H., Captain, CSA, **VI**: 249

Forrest, French, Flag Officer, CSN, **II**: 11-12, 27; **IV**: 50; **VI**: 223, 293

Forrest, Moreau, Lieut., **V**: 20, 56

Forrest, Nathan B., Lt. General, CSA, **II**: 41-42; **III**: 6; **IV**: 120, 121, 128, 129-30, 130-31, 139, 146

Fort Alexis, Ala., **V**: 81

Fort Anderson, Cape Fear River, N.C., **III**: 44; **V**: 16, 22, 31, 33, 37, 39, 42, 43, 46, 56

Fort Barrancas, Pensacola, Fla., **I**: 2, 4; **II**: 62; **VI**: 59, 64

Fort Bartow, Pork Point, N.C., **II**: 19

Fort Beaulieu, Ossabaw Sound, Ga., **IV**: 146

Fort Beauregard, Port Royal Sound, S.C., **I**: 31, 32, 37; **III**: 65; **V**: 42

Fort Brady, James River, Va., **V**: 25

Fort Brooke, Tampa Bay, Fla., **II**: 50

Fort Burton, La., **III**: 68

Fort Campbell, N.C., **V**: 16

Fort Caswell, Cape Fear River, N.C., **II**: 22, 67, 74; **III**: 28, 32, 158; **IV**: 2, 3, 147; **V**: 5, 16, 21; **VI**: 201

Fort Clark, N.C., **I**: 23; **VI**: 2, 224

Fort Clifton, James River, Va., **IV**: 75

Fort Clinch, Amelia Island, Fla., **II**: 28

Fort Darling, James River, Va., **IV**: 63, 66, 122

Fort de Russy, Red River, La., **III**: 75, 77; **IV**: 7, 31, 32, 36; **VI**: 230, 242, 252, 289

Fort Defiance, Tenn., **II**: 24

Fort Delaware, Pea Patch Island, Del., **III**: 92

Fort Dixie, N.C., **II**: 33

Fort Donelson, Cumberland River, Tenn., **I**: 30; **II**: 8, 9, 18, 20, 22, 23, 28, 30, 36, 46, 61; **III**: 23, 98, 100; **VI**: 2

Fort Ellis, N.C., **II**: 33

Fort Ellsworth, Alexandria, Va., **I**: 23

Fort Fisher, N.C., first amphibious assault on, **IV**: 143-44. 145-46, 147, 149-50; **VI**: 6; second amphibious assault and capture of, **IV**: 151; **V**: 6, 10, 11-17, 19; mentioned, **II**: 113; **III**: 28, 29, 78, 119, 131, 158; **IV**: iv, 1, 3, 27, 60, 116, 118, 134, 135, 136; **V**: 3, 18, 21, 22, 30, 31, 35, 37, 39, 47, 49, 82, 109; **VI**: 198, 211, 212, 214

Fort Foote, Tenn., **II**: 18, 36

Fort Gaines, Mobile Bay, Ala., **II**: 109; **IV**: 1, 89, 97, 98, 100, 109; **VI**: 6, 86, 221

Fort Gates, Fla., **IV**: 48

Fort Gibson, Ark., **IV**: 74

Fort Greenwood, Miss., **III**: 47

Fort Gregg, Charleston harbor, S.C., **III**: 131, 136, 137; **VI**: 212

Fort Griffin, Sabine Pass, Tex., **V**: 102

Fort Harrison, James River, Va., **IV**: 116; **VI**: 275

Fort Hatteras, N.C., **I**: 23; **VI**: 2, 224, 227

Fort Henry, USS, **II**: 103; **III**: 53, 57, 85, 104, 106, 124, 127; **VI**: 252

Fort Henry, USS (ex-*Alick Scott*); see: USS *Lafayette*

Fort Henry, Tenn. (renamed Fort Foote, q.v.), **II**: 5, 8, 9, 14, 16, 17, 18, 20, 22, 28, 36, 46; **III**: 6, 7, 100, 112; **IV**: 44; **VI**: 2, 223

Fort Hindman, USS (ex-USS *Manitou*, q.v.), **III**: 159; **IV**: 25, 26, 30-31, 37, 38, 44, 48, 51, 70

Fort Hindman (or Arkansas Post), White River, Ark., **III**: 5, 7-8, 9; **IV**: 26

Fort Holmes, Smith's Island, N.C., **V**: 16

Fort Jackson, USS, **III**: 133; **IV**: 46, 70, 86, 122; **V**: 104; **VI**: 206, 232

Fort Jackson, La., **I**: 2; **II**: 21, 32, 38, 42, 45, 50, 51, 52-53, 54, 56, 57, 61, 70; **III**: 154; **IV**: 2; **VI**: 3, 197, 205, 213, 220, 233

Fort Jefferson, Key West, Fla., **I**: 2

Fort Johnson, Smithville, N.C., **V**: 16

Fort Johnson, Charleston harbor, S.C., **III**: 127, 134, 137, 151; **IV**: 70; **V**: 42; **VI**: 225

Fort Lafayette, N.Y., **V**: 76, 99

Fort Lane, Neuse River, N.C., **II**: 33

Fort Lee, Wilmington, N.C., **IV**: 3

Fort Livingston, Bastian Bay, La., **II**: 56

Fort Lowry, Northern Neck, Va., **III**: 32; **V**: 61

Fort Macon, N.C., **II**: 56

Fort Mannahassett, Tex., **V**: 102

Fort Marshall, Charleston harbor, S.C., **V**: 43

Fort McAllister, Ogeechee River, Ga., **II**: 110; **III**: 1, 17, 20, 35, 38, 44

Fort McHenry, Baltimore, Md., **I**: 2, 11; **VI**: 12

Fort McNair, D.C.; see: Washington Arsenal

Fort McRee, Pensacola, Fla., **I**: 4, 37; **II**: 62

Fort(ress) Monroe, Hampton Roads, Va., **I**: 12, 20, 30, 37; **II**: 32, 37, 42, 48, 61, 62, 93; **III**: 92; **IV**: 120; **VI**: 212

Fort Morgan, USS (ex-USS *Admiral*, q.v.), **IV**: 132

Fort Morgan, Mobile Bay, Ala., seizure of, **I**: 2; firing on, and passage of, by Union fleet, **IV**: 95; defense of, **IV**: 100, 102, 105; surrender of, **IV**: 108, 109; **VI**: 6; mentioned, **II**: 95; **III**: 34, 39, 58, 83, 147, 154; **IV**: 83, 87, 89, 90, 93, 97, 136; **V**: 74; **VI**: 73, 78, 80, 81, *85*, 86, 93-96, 221, 227

Fort Moultrie, Charleston, S.C., **I**: 2; **III**: 59, 64-65, 127, 132, 133, 135, 137, 140, 151, 160; **IV**: 14, 102, 131; **V**: 42; **VI**: 214

Fort Myers, Caloosahatchee River, Fla., **III**: 121

Fort No. 1, Tenn., **II**: 42

Fort Ocracoke, N.C., **VI**: 283

Fort Pemberton, Tallahatchie River, Miss., **III**: 1, 22, 23, 41, 47; **VI**: 241

Fort Pickens, Santa Rosa Island, Fla., **I**: 2, 4-7, 37; **IV**: 136; **VI**: 221

Fort Pike, La., **II**: 57, 60

Fort Pillow, Tenn., **II**: 46, 47, 50, 62, 68; **IV**: 41-42, 43; **VI**: 3, 213, 231, 233

Fort Pinckney, Charleston harbor, S.C.; see: Castle Pinckney

Fort Pitt Iron Works, Pittsburgh, Pa., **II**: *41*

Fort Point, Galveston, Tex., **V**: 91

Fort Powell, Tower Island, Mobile Harbor, Ala., **IV**: 20, 97, 99, 100, 109; **VI**: 86

Fort Powhatan, James River, Va., **II**: 38; **III**: 115; **IV**: 61

Fort Pulaski, Savannah, Ga., **I**: 38; **II**: 22, 25, 44, 45, 47, 90; **VI**: 298

Fort Putnam, Charleston harbor, S.C., **IV**: 123

Galveston, USS, **III**: 10

Galveston (and Bay), Tex., **I**: 5, 15, 18, 19, 21, 26, 28, 30, 34, 40; **II**: 92, 100-01; **III**: 3, 4, 8, *9*, 16, 17, 18, 26, 36, 41, 79, 83, 85, 116, 120, 157; **IV**: 25, 32, 36, 37, 50-51, 63, 86, 88, 129, 143, 147, 150, 151; **V**: 16, 34, 37, 38, 46, 91, 96, 99, 100, 104, 111; **VI**: 3, 189, 201, 203, 213, 220

Gamble, William M., Lt. Commander, **III**: 6, 39; **V**: 71

Gansevoort, Guert, Captain, **II**: 93; **III**: 123, 157-58

Gardner, Arthur S., Lieut., **II**: 93

Gardner, Franklin, Major General, CSA, **III**: 45

Gardner, Joseph, Lieut., CSN, **IV**: 82

Garefoster & Braumly, Conf. shipowners, **VI**: 332

Garfield, Walter H., Acting Lieut., **IV**: 15

Garlick's Landing, Va., **VI**: 332

Garonne, Conf. schnr., **I**: 40

Garrett, John M., farmer, **V**: 93

Garrison, S. T., Conf. schnr.; see: *S. T. Garrison*

Garrity, Joseph L., Am. schnr.; see: *Joseph L. Garrity*

Gaspar Strait, NEI, **III**: 155

Gatesville, Chowan River, N.C., **IV**: 92

Gaulden, William B., Colonel, CSA, **IV**: 93

Gauley, Thomas, Boatswain, CSN, **V**: 22

Gay, E. J., Conf. river stmr.; see: *Edward J. Gay*

Gay, Thomas, Acting Ensign, **IV**: 126

Gayle, Richard H., Lieut., CSN, **V**: 21

Gazelle, Conf. stmr., **I**: 26

Gazelle, b.r. schnr., **III**: 87

Gazelle, USS (ex-*Emma Brown*), **IV**: 30, 32

Gearing, C. and F. A., Galveston shipowners, **VI**: 214

Gem of the Sea, USS, **I**: 39; **II**: 32, 68; **III**: 41, 62, 67, 135, 136

Gemsbok, USS, **I**: 27, 29; **II**: 37, 56

General Beauregard, CSS, **II**: 62, 68; **VI**: 230-31, 329

General Beauregard, CSS, **VI**: 231

General Bee, CSS, **VI**: 231

General Berry, Am. bark, **IV**: 87

General Bragg, CSS (ex-*Mexico*), **II**: 62, 68, 91; **III**: 8-9, 36, 75; **IV**: 61, 74; **VI**: 231-32, *232*, 329

General Breckinridge, CSS (also, *R. J. Breckinridge* or *Breckinridge*), **II**: 54; **VI**: 232, 330

General Burnside, USS, **V**: 56

"General Burnside's Grand Triumphal March", **VI**: 122-23

General C. C. Pinckney, b.r. schnr., **II**: 61

General Clinch, CSS, **VI**: 232-33

General Earl Van Dorn, CSS, **II**: 62, 68; **VI**: 233, 329

General Finegan, b.r. sloop, **IV**: 63

General Green, Conf. bark, **I**: 16

General Hunter, USA transport, **IV**: 37

General Lee, CSA transport stmr., **VI**: 204, 233

General Lovell, CSS, **II**: 54, 62; **VI**: 233, 330

General M. Jeff Thompson, CSS, **II**: 62, 68; **VI**: 233-34, 329

General Meigs, USA transport, **III**: 99

General Pinckney, b.r. schnr.; see: *General C. C. Pinckney*

General N. S. Reneau, Conf. privateer stmr., **VI**: 328

General Parkhill, b.r. ship, **I**: 13

General Pike, Am. whaling bark, **V**: 109

General Polk, CSS (ex-*Ed Howard*), **II**: 32; **VI**: 234

General Price, CSS; see: *General Sterling Price*, CSS

General Prim, b.r. schnr., **III**: 71

General Putnam, USS (also, *Putnam* and *William G. Putnam*), **II**: 112; **IV**: 30, 51, 58

General Quitman (ex-*Galveston*), La. State gunboat, **II**: 54; **VI**: 234

General Quitman, Conf. river transport, **VI**: 204, 235

General Rusk, CSS (later *Blanche*, British b.r.), **VI**: 220, 235, 295, 331

General Scott, C.S. guard boat, **II**: 57; **VI**: 235

General Sterling Price, CSS (also, *Sterling Price* and *General Price*; ex-*Milledon*), **II**: 62, 68; **VI**: 231, 235; as USS, **III**: 67, 68, 75, 96, 105; **IV**: 30, 61; **VI**: 235-36, *236*, 329

General Sumter (or *Sumter*; ex-river tug *Junius Beebe*), Conf. river stmr., **II**: 62, 68; **IV**: 32; **VI**: 200, 231, 236-37, 329

General Sumter (or *Sumter*), CSA river stmr., **VI**: 237

General T. J. Chambers, Conf. schnr., **I**: 19

General Taylor, b.r. schnr., **III**: 32

General Thomas, USS, **IV**: 126; **V**: 56

General Van Dorn, CSS; see: *General Earl Van Dorn*, CSS

General Williams, Am. ship, **V**: 109

General Worth, b.r. schnr., **III**: 134

Genesee, USS, **III**: 41, 45, 86, 100, 140; **V**: 101; **VI**: 72, 75, 87, 92

Geoghegan, William E., **VI**: 184

George Buckhart, b.r. schnr., **V**: 64; **VI**: 237, 331

George Chisholm, b.r. schnr., **III**: 155; **IV**: 12

George Douthwaite, British b.r. bark, **V**: 97

George G. Baker, b.r. schnr., **I**: 18, 22

George Griswold, Am. ship, **III**: 91

George Latimer, Am. schnr., **IV**: 61

George M. Smith, Conf. schnr., **I**: 11

George M. Mangham, U.S. schnr., **III**: 166, 167

George Page, CSS (later *City of Richmond*), **I**: 18; **VI**: 237

George Peabody, USS, **I**: 24; **III**: 118

George Washington, b.r. schnr., **II**: 41

George Washington Parke Custis, U.S. Balloon Barge, **I**: 34, *35-36*, 37; **II**: 77; **VI**: 2, 23

Georgetown, D.C., **I**: 18; **VI**: 22-23, 290

Georgetown, S.C., **I**: 31, 39; **II**: 26, 32, 50, 71, 91; **V**: 6, 18, 27, 47, 53, 54, 59, 67

Georgia, CSS, **II**: 90-91; **III**: 66, 154; **IV**: 93, 146, *148*; **VI**: 238

Georgia, CSS (ex-*Japan*), **II**: 102; **III**: 71, 91, 93, 94, 99, 104, 117, 119, 135, 145, *150*; **IV**: 4, 5, 24, 37, 38, 52, 140; **VI**: 188, 193, 207, 237-38, *239*

Georgia, State of, USS; see: *State of Georgia*, USS

Georgian, C.S. stmr., **IV**: 131; **VI**: 238, 240, 253

Georgian Bay, Ont., **III**: 25; **VI**: 238

Georgiana, Conf. stmr., **III**: 47; **VI**: 240-41

Georgiana McCaw, b.r. stmr., **IV**: 67

Georgie, British b.r. schnr., **III**: 121

Geranium, USS (ex-*John A. Dix*), **III**: 166, 167; **IV**: 13, 122; **V**: 37

Gerdes, Ferdinand H., U.S. Coast Survey, **II**: 50

Gerhard, Benjamin, **III**: 17

Germantown, USS, **I**: 9, 16; **VI**: 241

Gertrude, British b.r. stmr., **III**: 67; as USS, **III**: 129; **IV**: 10; **V**: 46, 91

Getty, George W., Brig. General, USA, **III**: 68

Getty, Robert, Acting Lieut., **III**: 29, 93, 127

Gettysburg, USS (ex-*Margaret and Jessie*, q.v.), **IV**: 108, 140

Gettysburg, Pa., **III**: 104, 110, 134; **IV**: 29, 85

Geziena Hilligonda, Dutch b.r. brig, **IV**: 140

Gherardi, Bancroft, Lt. Commander, **IV**: 51

Gibbs, Conf. shipmaster, **VI**: 277

Gibraltar, b.r. stmr. (ex-CSS *Sumter*), **III**: 133; **VI**: 306, *344*

Gibraltar, Conf. privateer schnr., **VI**: 328

Gibraltar, **II**: 47, 50; **IV**: 11; **VI**: 306, 344

Gibraltar, Straits of, **II**: 8

Gibson, Thomas, Acting Master, **IV**: 29

Gibson, William, Lt. Commander, **II:** 88, 110; **III:** 148; **V:** 42

Gifford, John L., Acting Master, **IV:** 136

Gift, George W., Lieut., CSN, **II:** 66; **III:** 134; **IV:** 5, 13, 60; **V:** 53; **VI:** 199, 253

Gilbert's Bar, Fla., **III:** 126

Gildersleeve, Am. ship; see: *S. Gildersleeve*

Gildersleeve, Captain, USA, **VI:** 251

Gile, Frank S., Landsman, **III:** 156

Gilfillan, Robert, Am. schnr.; see: *Robert Gilfillan*

Gillespie, William T., Acting Master, **III:** 147, 163; **IV:** 12, 108, 121

Gillett, Simeon P., Lieut., **V:** 78

Gilliam, T. W., Conf. shipmaster, **VI:** 332

Gillis, James H., Lt. Commander, **III:** 15, 55, 77, 90; **IV:** 12; **V:** 69, 79, 81

Gillis, John P., Captain, **I:** 14, 27, 38; **III:** 105, 118

Gillmore, Quincy A., Major General, USA, **III:** 112–13, 117, 119, 123, 129, 131, 136, 145, 156; **IV:** 14, 34, 35; **V:** 91

Gilmer, Jeremy F., Major General, CSA, **III:** 136; **VI:** 223

Gilmore Meredith, Am. ship, **III:** 5

Gilpin, John, b.r. schnr.; see: *John Gilpin*

Gilpin, Thomas S., Conf. shipmaster, **IV:** 59

Ginger cargo, captured, **V:** 97

Gipsey, Conf. schnr., **I:** 40

Gipsey, Am. whaling bark, **V:** 109

Gipson, James C., Acting Master, **III:** 164; **IV:** 66

Giraffe, Conf. b.r. stmr. (later *Robert E. Lee*, q.v.), **III:** 29

Girardeau, Cape, Mo.; see: Cape Girardeau

Giraud, Pierre, Acting Lieut., **IV:** 99, 118, 121

Gladiator, Am. mail stmr., **II:** 104

Gladiator, British b.r. stmr., **VI:** 208, 315

Gladiolus, USS (ex-*Sallie Bishop*), **V:** 43

Gladstone, William, British Chancellor of the Exchequer, **II:** 102

Glamorganshire, Wales, **VI:** 193

Glasgow, HMS, **VI:** 186, 298

Glasgow, USS; see: *Eugenie*, b.r. stmr.

Glasgow, Scotland, **III:** 29, 134; **V:** 8; **VI:** 185, 201

Glass cargo captured, **IV:** 42

Glassell, William T., Lieut., CSN, **III:** 141, 143–44; **VI:** 5, 219

Glassford, Henry A., Acting Lieut., **III:** 167; **IV:** 121, 139

Gleason, John H., Acting Master, **IV:** 74

Glenn, Am. bark, **I:** 20; **VI:** 221

Glenavon, Am. bark, **IV:** 104

Glide, b.r. schnr., **II:** 51

Glide, USS, **III:** 5, 8, 25

Glide, b.r. schnr., **III:** 32

Glide, USS, **V:** 55

Glisson, Oliver S., Captain, **I:** 20, 27; **II:** 42, 66, 74, 88; **IV:** 111, 129, 150; **V:** 58

Gloin, William M., Acting Master, **IV:** 87

Gloucester, Mass., **IV:** 70

Gloucester, Va., **II:** 56, 57

Gloucester Point, Va., **I:** 13; **II:** 61

Glymont, Md., **II:** 108

Godfrey, D., Am. bark; see: *D. Godfrey*

Godon, Sylvanus W., Rear Admiral, **II:** 26, 31, 44, 100; **V:** 16, 71, 123

Goff's Point, Va., **IV:** 17

Golconda, Am. whaling bark, **IV:** 86

Gold shipments, **I:** 14; **IV:** 32, 59, 133

Golden Age, Conf. river stmr., **III:** 115; **VI:** 241

Golden Eagle, Am. ship, **III:** 32

Golden Liner, British b.r. schnr., **III:** 72

Golden Rocket, Am. ship, **I:** 18; **III:** 32

Golden Rod, Am. transport schnr., **III:** 133; **IV:** 19

Golden Rule, Am. bark, **III:** 16, 32

Goldsboro, N.C., **II:** 113; **V:** 8, 61, 65, 69

Goldsborough, John R., Captain, **I:** 15, 16, 17, 20, 22; **III:** 85

Goldsborough, Louis M., Rear Admiral, appointed Commander, NABS, **I:** 27; promoted to Rear Admiral, **II:** 83; relieved as Commander, NABS, **II:** 95; mentioned, **I:** 27; **II:** 5, 6, 8, 11, 14, 18, 20, 24, 37, 42, 61, 62, 71, 75, 80, 83, 93, 95; **V:** 120; **VI:** 2

Gondar, British b.r. ship, **II:** 56

Good Hope, Am. bark, **III:** 93

Good Hope, b.r. schnr., **IV:** 44

Goodman, William, Landsman, **IV:** 99

Goodrich's Landing, La., **III:** 155

Goodspeed, Am. bark, **III:** 97

Goodspeed, Am. schnr., **IV:** 129

Goodwin, Ezra S., Acting Master, **II:** 112; **VI:** 304

Goodwin, Nathaniel, Acting Lieut., **II:** 66

Goose Creek, Fla., **IV:** 24

Gordon, Conf. privateer, **I:** 20, 39; **VI:** 315, 328

Gordon Grant, CSA tugboat, **VI:** 241

Gordon's Landing, La., **III:** 29

Gorgas, Josiah, Colonel, CSA, **VI:** 188, 216

Gorman, Willis A., Brig. General, USA, **II:** 116; **III:** 9, 11, 29

Gorringe, Henry H., Acting Lieut., **IV:** 48, 137

Gosport (Norfolk) Navy Yard (see also: Norfolk Navy Yard), *xiii*; **VI:** 241

Gossamer, C.S. transport, **VI:** 241

Gothenburg, Sweden, **VI:** 209

Goudy, Jason, Acting Lieut., **IV:** 129

Gould, Abraham N., Acting Lieut., **III:** 147; **V:** 45; **VI:** 278–79

Governor, U.S. transport, **I:** 31

Governor A. Mouton, Conf. b.r. stmr., **II:** 63; **VI:** 328

Governor Aiken, C.S. tender, **VI:** 241

Governor Buckingham, USS, **III:** 165; **IV:** 5, 114; **V:** 30; **VI:** 265

Governor Milton, Conf. stmr. (ex-*G. W. Bird*), **II:** 102; **VI:** 241

Governor Moore (ex-*Charles Morgan*), La. State gunboat, **II:** 54; **VI:** 205, 227, 239, 241–42

Governor Morehead, C.S. river transport, **VI:** 242

Governor Peabody, U.S. stmr., **I:** 22

Grace, John R., Acting Master, **IV:** 83, 109

Grace E. Baker, b.r. schnr., **II:** 42

Grafton, Edward C., Commander, **VI:** 187

Graham, Charles K., Brig. General, USA, **IV:** 3–4

Graham, Newell, Acting Master, **IV:** 78

Graham, Robert F., Colonel, CSA, **III:** 113, 118

Grahamville, S.C., **IV:** 138

Grain destroyed or captured, **III:** 55; **IV:** 88

Grampus, CSS, **II:** 46; **VI:** 242

Grampus No. 2, USS, **III:** 8; **VI:** 242

Granada, Am. brig, **I:** 29

Grand Bay, C.S. transport, **VI:** 242, 331

Grand Duke, CSA stmr., **III:** 77; **VI:** 242, 252

Grand Ecore, Red River, La., **IV:** 32, 37, 38, 40, 43; **V:** 103; **VI:** 204

Grand Era, Conf. stmr., **VI:** 222, 243, 280

Grand Glaizer, Ark., **VI:** 268

Grand Gulf, USS (ex-*Onward*), **III:** 157; **IV:** 29, 57, 104; **V:** 112

Grand Gulf, Miss., abandoned by Conf., III: 75; mentioned, II: 64, 67, 68; III: 32, 48, 54, 55, 57, 63, 67, 68, 69, 72, 73, 74, 75, 77, 78, 82, 86; IV: 30, 151

Grand Lake, La., III: 66; VI: 221

Granger, Gordon, Major General, USA, IV: 100; V: 83; VI: 78, 79

Granger, Robert, Brig. General, USA, IV: 126

Granite, USS, V: 112

Granite City, British b.r. stmr., III: 52; as USS, III: 136, 137, 144, 150, 157, 168, 169; IV: 11, 57; as Conf. stmr., V: 20, 22; VI: 243

Grant, Alexander, Captain, La. State Navy (later Lieut., CSN), VI: 234

Grant, Gordon, Conf. tug; see: *Gordon Grant*

Grant, Ulysses S., Lt. General, USA, in the West, I: 22, 26, 34; II: 5, 14, 16, 17, 18–19, 22, 24, 36, 45; III: 6, 7, 18, 38, 45, 47, 48, 49, 54, 61, 66, 68, 72, 74, 75, 82, 83, 84, 87, 88, 90, 93, 105, 106, 108, 114, 145, 167; IV: 7, 27; in the East, IV: 66, 102, 133, 134, 142, 151; V: 3, 6, 8, 9, 16, 18, 21, 22, 26, 31, 36, 37, 53, 55, 59, 61, 65, 66–67, 69, 70, 71, 73, 75, 81–82, 95, 122; VI: 2, 6

Grant's Pass, Mobile Bay, Ala., II: 70; VI: 206

Granville, Lord, I: 15

Grapeshot, b.r. sloop, II: 108

Grapnels, III: 55, 58, 59; IV: 122, 148

Graves, George W., Acting Lieut., IV: 75, 93; VI: 257

Graves, William A., Acting Constructor, CSN, VI: 185, 187, 321

Gray, Samuel C., Acting Master, IV: 74

Great Lake George, Fla., VI: 237

Great Lakes, III: 25; IV: 131; VI: 238, 282

Great Mussel Shoals, Ala. (see also: Mussel Shoals), IV: 149

Great Peedee River, S.C., VI: 281

Great Republic, Conf. cottonclad stmr., VI: 243

Great Wicomico River, Md./Va., II: 97; III: 129; IV: 124

"Greek Fire," VI: 240

Green, Bennett W., Passed Assistant Surgeon, CSN, V: *131*

Green, Charles, Commander, I: 21, 24, 26, 39; II: 57

Green, Francis M., Acting Lieut., V: 30, 94

Green, G. W., b.r. sloop; see: *G. W. Green*

Green, General, Conf. bark; see: *General Green*

Green, James G., Acting Master, V: 112

Green, Joseph F., Captain, III: 58, 78, 81, 118, 166; VI: 503

Green, Nathaniel, Lt. Commander, V: 103

Green, Thomas, Brig. General, CSA, III: 143; IV: 41

Green Cay, Bahamas, VI: 228

Green I., Ga., II: 61

Green Turtle Cay, Abaco I., Bahamas, V: 5

Greene, Samuel Dana, Lieut., II: *34–35*

Greene, Theodore P., Captain, IV: 121

Greenhow, Mrs. Rose O'Neal, IV: 116; VI: 214

Greenland, Am. bark, IV: 87

Greenock, Scotland, VI: 189, 214, 237

Greenpoint, L.I., N.Y., I: 30; II: 14, 95; VI: 227, 265, 297, 315

Greenville, Miss., III: 75; V: 106

Greenville, N.C., II: 108

Greenwood, Miss., III: 22, 41; IV: 15; VI: 257, 290

Greer, James A., Lt. Commander, III: 83, 88, 90, 96; IV: 30, 32, 36, 80–81, 121, 135

Gregory, Samuel B., Acting Master, II: 76; III: 71, 74

Gregory, Thomas B., Acting Lieut., IV: 60

Gregory, William D., Acting Master, II: 18, 30, 63, 71, 74

Grenades, hand, Conf. use of, III: 140

Grenfell, Admiral, RN, VI: 193

Gresham, Benjamin F., Conf. shipowner, VI: 333

Gresham and Bagby, Conf. shipowners, VI: 332

Grey Cloud, Conf. river transport, VI: 243; as USS, II: 84

Grey Jacket, b.r. stmr., III: 168

Grey, Mary, Conf. sloop; see: *Mary Grey*

Greyhound, HMS, II: 89

Greyhound, Conf. b.r. stmr., IV: 59; as USS, IV: 136; V: 94; VI: 243–44

Grimball's, Dawho River, S.C., II: 57

Grimball's Landing, Stono River, S.C., III: 116

Grimes, James W., Senator (Iowa), II: 26, 28, 63, 67, 80, 97, 98, 111–12; IV: 35

Grinnell, H. Walton, Acting Master, V: 60

Griswold, George, Am. ship; see: *George Griswold*

Griswold, William N., Acting Master, II: 74; IV: 87

Grosbeak, USS (ex-*Fanny*), V: 106

Grove, Francis H., Acting Master, III: 147

Grover, Cuvier, Major General, USA, V: 34

Groves, George J., Acting Master, IV: 43, 139

Guano cargoes captured, II: 104; III: 32, 111; IV: 36, 47

Guard, USS (or *National Guard*), V: 120

Guerrilla forces, Conf., II: 85, 89, 93, 104; III: 9, 17, 39, 57, 62, 66, 75, 93, 105, 134, 136, 149, 153, 165; IV: 31, 37, 90, 92, 112, 120; V: 47, 64, 67, 73, 80, 106; VI: 196

Guest, John, Commander, II: 37; III: 55; IV: 33, 135, 150; V: 22

Gulf of Mexico, I: 17, 22; II: 24, 25, 26, 31, 37, 42, 52, 69, 75, 95, 97, 110, 116; III: 11, 66, 67, 71, 72, 77, 82, 83, 85, 88, 94, 116, 129, 140, 141, 157, 166, 168; IV: 1, 11, 15, 22, 31, 33, 47, 48, 84, 97, 108, 110, 136, 137, 140; V: 31, 38, 60, 64

Gulf of Newfoundland, VI: 203

Gulf of St. Lawrence; see: St. Lawrence

Gulf Squadron, V: 115, 117

Gulf Stream, III: 11; V: 39; VI: 205

Gun Foundry & Ordnance Works, CSN; see: Selma, Ala.

"Gunboat Quick Step"; march, sheet music, VI: 136–37

Gunboats, Conf., criticism of, III: 155

Gunnery, observations on, II: 7, 15, 19, 29, 51; III: 20, 25, 38, 98, 105–06; IV: 19, 44

Gunpowder, cargoes captured, II: 54, 67, 68, 74, 95; III: 97, 104, 145, 163; IV: 15, 17, 23, 24, 33, 63; V: 61; VI: 190

Gurley, P. D., Rev., V: 91

Guthrie, John J., Lieut., CSN, III: 86; VI: 189, 208, 253, 291

Guy, James, Am. stmr.; see: *James Guy*

Guy, S., Conf. shipowner, VI: 332

Gwathmey, Washington, Lieut., CSN, II: 45; III: 154; VI: 207, 238, 253

Gwin, William, Lt. Commander, I: 31, 34; II: 26, 27, 32, 36, 39, 45, 50, 51, 81, 116; VI: 196

Gwynn's I., Va., II: 108

Gypsy, British b.r. schnr., III: 49

H. & J. Neild, Am. schnr., VI: 221

H. D. Mears, Conf. river stmr., VI: 244

H. L. Hunley, C.S. submarine, at Mobile, III: 34; described, III: 124, 126; at Charleston, III: 128, 133; first sinking, III: 134; VI: 5; second sinking, III: 147; VI: 5; attack on USS *Housatonic* and third sinking, IV: 21; VI: 5; mentioned, I: 30; III: 114, 141, 149, 164; IV: 3, 20, 23, 39, 96; V: 42, VI: *144*, 212, 225, 244–46

H. R. W. Hill (or *Hill*), Conf. river transport, **VI:** 246
H. W. Johnson, U.S. armed schnr., **VI:** 315
H. McGuin, Conf. barge, **III:** 118
Habana; see: *Sumter*, CSS
Habersham, Robert, C.S. transport stmr.; see: *Robert Habersham*
Hagood, Johnson, Brig. General, CSA, **III:** 132
Haigh, Edward, British businessman, **VI:** 205
Haines, Edward L., Acting Master, **I:** 27; **III:** 124
Haiti, **II:** 27, 112; **III:** 16
Hale, E. B., USS; see: *E. B. Hale*, USS
Hale, John, b.r. schnr.; see: *John Hale*
Hale, Kate, b.r. schnr.; see: *Kate Hale*
Hale, John P., Senator (N.H.), **II:** 68; **VI:** 31
Half Moon Battery, Cape Fear Peninsula, N.C., **V:** 37
Halifax, CSS, **V:** 110; **VI:** 246
Halifax, N.C., **IV:** 7, 144; **V:** 86, 100; **VI:** 217, 223–24
Halifax, N.S., **II:** 104, 108; **III:** 18, 163; **IV:** 49, 105, 106, 109; **V:** 22
Hall, Charles N., Acting Ensign, **V:** 53
Hall, Emma L., Am. bark; see: *Emma L. Hall*
Hall, John L., Acting Ensign, **IV:** 90
Hall, Samuel, Acting Master, **IV:** 118
Hall, Wilburn B., Lieut., CSN, **VI:** 251
Hall, William, Colonel, CSA, **III:** 86
Halleck, Henry W., Major General, USA, **II:** 14, 16, 17, 21, 22, 24, 26, 28, 32, 38, 40, 41, 70, 93, 107; **IV:** 2, 102, 139
Hallie Jackson, Conf. privateer brig, **I:** 16; **VI:** 230, 246, 328
Halligan, John P., Lieut., CSN, **IV:** 42, 74, 135, 140; **VI:** 296
Hallock, Isaac, Acting Ensign, **IV:** 47
Hamblin's Landing, Ark., **II:** 103
Hamilton, A., Conf. agent in London, **VI:** 190
Hamilton, Ann, Conf. schnr.; see: *Ann Hamilton*
Hamilton, Bermuda, **II:** 102
Hamilton, John R., Acting Master, **III:** 147
Hamilton, N. C., **II:** 69, 80, 105, 107; **IV:** 32, 44
Hamilton, R., Conf. agent in London, **VI:** 249
Hamilton's Crossing, Va., **V:** 58
Hamley, W. G., Governor of Bermuda, **V:** 97
Hamlin, Hannibal, Vice President, USA; **VI:** 31
Hammond, Nathan W., Acting Master, **III:** 13
Hammond, Conf. shipmaster, **VI:** 322
Hampton, Conf. schnr., **III:** 9
Hampton, CSS, **IV:** 63, 82, 104; **V:** 45, 79; **VI:** 246–47
Hampton-class gunboats, **VI:** 247
Hampton, Wade, Lt. General, CSA, **IV:** 78
Hampton Roads, Va., **I:** 6, 11, 13, 15, 17, 18, 19, 21, 23; **II:** 5, 7, 14, 15, 24, 29, 30–31, 42, 47, 48–49, 61–62, 82, 94, 112, 116; **III:** 15, 78, 92, 99; **IV:** 30, 104, 116, 118, 133, 135, 150; **V:** 58, 86, 89, 93, 99, 102, 128; **VI:** 204, 212, 214, 216
Hancock, b.r. sloop, **III:** 167
Handy, British b.r. schnr., **III:** 70
Hanford, William C., Acting Ensign, **III:** 23, 29, 36, 96; **IV:** 35
Hannah, CSA armed sloop, **II:** 90; **VI:** 247
Hannah, British b.r. sloop, **IV:** 31
Hannah Ann, Conf. schnr., **VI:** 332
Hannah M. Johnson, b.r. schnr., **I:** 15
Hanover, Am. schnr., **III:** 20
Hanover, b.r. schnr., **III:** 79
Hansa, N. C., b.r. stmr., **VI:** 248
Hanson, Charles H., Acting Ensign, **V:** 58
Hard Times, Conf. river stmr., **IV:** 21

Hardee, William J., Lt. General, CSA, **II:** 20; **V:** 39
Harding, Abner C., Colonel, USA, **III:** 23
Harding, Samuel, Jr., Acting Ensign, **VI:** 243
Hardin's Point, Ark., **III:** 124
Hardware cargoes captured, **III:** 163; **IV:** 23
Harford, Conf. schnr., **I:** 27
Harlan & Hollingsworth, shipbuilders, Wilmington, Del., **VI:** 199, 201, 268, 324
Harmony, Conf. armed tug, **I:** 24; **VI:** 248
Harmony, b.r. schnr., **I:** 27
Harrell, Abram D., Commander, **I:** 28; **IV:** 97, 139
Harrenn & Ballown, Conf. shipowners, **VI:** 332
Harriet, Conf. river schnr., **III:** 15
Harriet, British b.r. schnr., **III:** 96
Harriet A. Weed, USA transport, **IV:** 48, 59
Harriet De Ford, Am. stmr., **V:** 80
Harriet Lane, USS (ex-USRC), **I:** 6–7, 11, 15, 23, 39; **II:** 26, 57, 100; **III:** 1, 3, 8; as CSS, **III:** 16, 150; **IV:** 50–51; **VI:** 3, 203, 248–49, *248*, 331
Harriet Pinckney (or *Pinkney*), CSS, **VI:** 249
Harriet Stevens, Am. bark, **IV:** 84
Harris, Arnold, Jr., Ensign, **IV:** 3
Harris, Francis L., Acting Ensign, **III:** 13
Harris, Frank M., Acting Master, CSN, **VI:** 206
Harris, Isham G., **II:** 18
Harris, John, Colonel, USMC Commandant, **I:** 2
Harris, Sarah B., Am. schnr.; see: *Sarah B. Harris*
Harris, Thomas A., Acting Lieut., **IV:** 72, 147
Harris, Thomas C., Lt. Commander, **III:** 159
Harris, W. F., b.r. schnr.; see: *W. F. Harris*
Harrison, Conf. shipmaster & pilot, **VI:** 227
Harrison, Burton, **V:** 93
Harrison, George W., Commander, CSN, **IV:** 95; **VI:** 272
Harrison, Napoleon B., Commander, **II:** 40, 42, 55; **IV:** 102
Harrison, T., Conf. shipmaster, **VI:** 231
Harrison, William H., Acting Master, **III:** 165
Harrison's Bar, James River, Va., **II:** 74, 78, 80
Harrisonburg, La., **III:** 75; **IV:** 26; **VI:** 222, 276
Harrison's Landing, James River, Va., **II:** 74, 75, 77, 80, 84, 88, 89, 91; **IV:** 95
Harry Booth, Am. bark **VI:** 64
Hart, CSS, **III:** 66; **VI:** 249
Hart, John E., Lt. Commander, **III:** 77
Hart, B.W., Co., London, **IV:** 59
Hart, J. H., Conf. shipmaster, **VI:** 231
Hartford, Conn., **I:** 6
Hartford, USS, *xvii*; **II:** 5, 15, *25*, 50, 52, 54, 55, 56, *58–60*, 109; **III:** 26, 36, 41, 44–45, 47, 48, 52, 53, 54, 55, 70, 77, 79, 83, 86, 112, 122, 157, 166; **IV:** 10, 90, 95, 96–97, 99, 140, 145, 147; **V:** 121; **VI:** 3, 48, 49, 50, 51, 52, 58, *80*, 87, 92, 94, 96, 253, 362–64, *362*
Hartford City, Conf. river stmr., **III:** 115; **VI:** 249–50
Hartstene, Henry J., Commander, CSN, **VI:** 232–33
Harvest, b.r. schnr., **III:** 74
Harvest, Am. whaler, **V:** 73
Harvest Moon, USS, sinking of, by torpedo, **V:** 54, *57*; mentioned, **IV:** 121–22; **V:** *56*, 102; **VI:** *365*
Harvey, James E., U.S. Minister Resident, Lisbon, **V:** 69
Harvey Birch, Am. clipper ship, **I:** 37
Harwood, Andrew A., Commodore, **II:** 100; **III:** 13, 16; **VI:** 14, 19
Hasker, Charles H., Lieut., CSN, **III:** 137

Hudson Place Salt Works, Darien, Ga., **III:** 141

Hugel, Adolph, USS; see: *Adolph Hugel,* USS

Huger, Battery, Ala.; see: Battery Huger, Ala.

Huger, Benjamin, Major General, CSA, **II:** 11; **VI:** 224, 288

Huger, Thomas B., Lieut., CSN, **II:** 7; **VI:** 269

Hughes, Aaron K., Lieut., **I:** 37; **II:** 29; **III:** 140

Hughes, John, & Co., Conf. shipbuilders, **VI:** 187, 205, 207, 262

Hulks to sweep torpedoes, proposed, **III:** 55 (cf: Torpedoes)

Hull, Commodore, USS; see: *Commodore Hull,* USS

Hull, Joseph B., Captain, **I:** 24, 26

Hunchback, USS, **II:** 6, 66, 100, 105; **III:** 44; **IV:** 83; **V:** 75, 112; **VI:** 106, 230

Hunley, H. L., Conf. submarine; see: *H. L. Hunley*

Hunley, Horace L., Conf. inventor, **III:** 2, 34, 124, 141, 147; **VI:** 244, 283

Hunter, b.r. schnr.; **III:** 82

Hunter, Charles, Commander, **II:** 45, 68, 102, 104, 110; **VI:** 235

Hunter, David, Major General, USA, **II:** 47; **III:** 23, 39, 61

Hunter, General, USA transport; see: *General Hunter*

Hunter, Robert, Conf. shipmaster, **VI:** 256

Hunter, Robert M. T., C.S. Secretary of State, **VI:** 315

Hunter, Thomas T., Commander, **VI:** 217, 224

Hunter, William W., Flag Officer, CSN, **I:** 11; **II:** 42; **III:** 105; **VI:** 1, 72, 139, 145, 146, 148; **V:** 31; **VI:** 203, 225, 226, 234

Huntress, CSS (later b.r. stmr. *Tropic,* q.v.), **VI:** 251

Huntsville, USS, **I:** 27, 28; **II:** 8, 80, 84, 85, 115; **III:** 44, 58, 66, 81, 83

Huntsville, CSS, **III:** 25, 160; **IV:** 112, *114;* **IV:** 83; **VI:** 251

Hurlbut, Stephen A., Major General, USA, **IV:** 2, 42

Hurley, Lady, British b.r. schnr.; see: *Lady Hurley*

Huron, USS, **II:** 51, 57, 67, 89; **III:** 58, 66, 165; **IV:** 2; **V:** 37

Huse, Samuel, Acting Lieut., **III:** 123

Hutchens, William D., Captain, USA, **IV:** 52

Hutcheson, Peter, Glasgow shipowner, **VI:** 185, 261

Hutchin's Bridge, Miss., **III:** 72

Hutchinson, Henry M., Acting Third Assistant Engineer, **V:** 30

Hyde, George W., Acting Master, **V:** 61

Hyde County, N.C., **VI:** 257

Hyde rocket, **II:** 110

I. C. Landis, Conf. stmr.; see: *Landis,* CSS

I. N. Seymour, USS, **II:** 3, 107, 113; **III:** 115

Iatan, U.S. transport, **II:** 95

Ictineo, proposed submarine, **III:** 62

Ida, CSS, **I:** 40; **II:** 22; **VI:** 251

Ida, b.r. schnr., **II:** 81

Ida, b.r. schnr., **III:** 38

Ida, b.r. stmr., **IV:** 86

Ida, USS, **V:** 86

Idaho, Am. river stmr., **V:** 106

Ike Davis, Am. passenger stmr., **IV:** 116

Illinois & Michigan Canal, **III:** 25

Illustrated London News, The, **VI:** 314

Imperial, Am. stmr., **III:** 117

Impressment of seamen, **IV:** 133

Inagua I., Bahamas, **V:** 100

Independence, Southern, b.r. schnr.; see: *Southern Independence*

Indian, British b.r. schnr., **IV:** 51

Indian Bend, La., **VI:** 260

Indian Chief, C.S. receiving ship, **III:** 147; **VI:** 245, 251

Indian Key, Fla., **I:** 38

Indian Ocean, **III:** 164; **V:** 130

Indian River & Inlet, Fla., **II:** 104, 111, 112, 113; **III:** 41 62, 67, 71, 97, 126; **IV:** 24, 60, 83, 140; **V:** 64

Indian Town, Va., **VI:** 332

Indian Wells, N.C., **V:** 49, 59; **VI:** 211

Indianola, U.S. ram, sunk, **III:** 32–35; refloated, **V:** 8; mentioned, **III:** 27, *28,* 38, 48, 68, *164;* **V:** 8, 53; **VI:** 222, 225

Indianola, Tex., **I:** 9

Industry, b.r. schnr., **III:** 22

Inez, British b.r. schnr., **III:** 67

"Infernal machines," **I:** 17; **II:** 14, 113; **III:** 34

Inflation (due to blockade), **I:** 38; **III:** 12, 110, 156; **IV:** 2

Inglis, A. & J., Clyde River shipbuilders, **VI:** 261

Ingraham, Duncan N., Flag Officer, CSN, **II:** 91; **III:** 18–20, 92, 119, 121; **VI:** 232–33, 279

Ingraham, John N., Lieut., CSN, **VI:** 251

Inigoes Creek, Md., **V:** 61

Ino, USS, **IV:** 87

Inspector General of Ordnance, CSN; see: Fairfax, A.B., Commander

Insurance rates, marine; **III:** iv; **IV:** 23, 89, 122; **V:** 99; **VI:** 193

Intelligent Whale, US submarine, **VI:** *366*

Intended, British b.r., **II:** 57

Investigator, Am. bark, **II:** 8

Iola, Fla., **VI:** 325

Iosco, USS, **IV:** 135, 150; **V:** 22

Iowa, b.r. schnr., **IV:** 75

Ireland, **III:** 149; **V:** 8

Ireland, D., Am. shipmaster, **VI:** 196

Irish Sea, **VI:** 261

Iron Age, USS, **IV:** 2, 4, 5

Iron, cargoes of, captured, **I:** 15; **III:** 93; **IV:** 70, 142, 143; **V:** 56; mentioned, **II:** 40, 66, 71, 92, 109; **III:** 15, 127, 131

Iron King, C.S. river stmr., **VI:** 252

Iron, shortage of, in South, **II:** 91–2; **III:** 15, 154, 159, 160; **IV:** 24, 33, 115; **VI:** 214

Iron works, Conf., **II:** 56; **III:** 89; **V:** 87; see also: Richmond Naval Iron Foundry

Iron works, Union, **II:** 113–14

Ironclad Board, USN, **I:** 21, 26

Ironclads, Conf., development, **I:** 13, 16, 19, 37; **II:** 18, 51; **III:** 6, 7, 25; early operations of, **II:** 12, 26, 27, 29, 30, 31, 34, 38, 47, 48, 49, 62, 63, 71, 85; Western River operations, **II:** 18, 50, 66, 81, 84, 85–86, 89, 90–91; **III:** 32–35, 160; **IV:** 7, 58–59, 61, 74–75, 84, 94–97, 99, 112; Rams, **II:** 54, 90–91, 96; **III:** 39, 94–95, 160; **IV:** 44–46, 47, 94–97; **V:** 10, 37–38; Eastern coastal operations, **III:** 18, 20, 52, 58, 63, 78, 105, 112, 114, 119, 121, 131, 133, 137, 140, 143, 153, 159, 166; **IV:** 20–21, 24, 32, 33, 38, 44–46, 54–56, 63, 66, 82, 85, 92, 115, 148; **V:** 6, 10, 25, 27, 34, 36, 43, 45, 64–65, 67. 76, 87, 89, 90; Union, development of, **I:** 5, 21, 26, 30; **II:** 22, 23, 62, 113–14; **III:** 153; early operations of, **II:** 5, 14, 23, 26, 27, 29, 30–31, 34, 42, 47, 48–49, 62, 82, 83; Western River operations, **II:** 16, 17, 18, 22, 29, 40, 41, 50, 90, 91, 96; **III:** 32–34, 44, 45, 47–48, 134, 157; **IV:** 7, 10, 30–32, 58–59, 64–65, 83, 89, 94–97, 100, 114, 139, 142, 146; **V:** 71; Eastern coastal operations, **II:** 64, 75, 97, 98, 104, 112, 116–17; **III:** 16, 17, 18, 19, 20, 23, 35, 38, 39, 44, 55, 57–61, 63–65, 69, 77, 81, 90, 91, 92, 110, 113, 117, 119, 122, 127, 129, 132, 133, 134, 137, 158, 160–61, 163; **IV:** 11, 23, 61, 62, 66, 68, 85, 86, 91, 102, 103, 104–05, 122, 124–26, 137–38, 140, 146; **V:** 3, 5, 11, 16, 31–32, 37, 39, 42, 46, 58, 64, 75, 78–79, 87, 93–94, 98, 102, 103

Iroquois, USS, **I:** 37; **II:** 45, 53, 55, 61, 63, 68; **III:** 28, 78, 121; **V:** 67; **VI:** 294

VI–442

King, Henry J., Conf. stmr.; see: *Henry J. King*
King, William B., Conf. schnr.; see: *William B. King*
King William, Conf. schr, **VI**: 332
Kingfisher, USS, **II**: 14, 26, 62, 68, 97; **III**: 79; **IV**: 36
Kingfisher, Am. whaling schnr., **III**: 52
King's Creek, Va., **V**: 30
Kingston, Am. stmr., **IV**: 90
Kingston, Jamaica, B.W.I., **V**: 108
Kingston, Tenn., **V**: 55
Kinsman, USS (ex-Conf. *Colonel Kinsman*), **II**: 107, 108; **III**: 9, 32; **VI**: 252
Kinston, Neuse River, N.C., **IV**: 12, 20, 47; **V**: 59, 61, 69
Kirby, Nicholas, Acting Lieut., **IV**: 72, 138
Kirkpatrick, Thomas, U.S. Consul, Nassau, **V**: 91
Kirkman, Sam, Conf. river stmr.; see: *Sam Kirkman*
Kitching, William H., Jr., Acting Master's Mate, **IV**: 24
Kittatinny, USS (ex-schnr. *Stars and Stripes*), **II**: 56, 63, 99, 111; **III**: 41, 149; **VI**: 60
Kittredge, John W., Acting Lieut., **II**: 12, 51, 80, 81, 90, 91, 92, 93; **VI**: 206
Klinck, Leonard G., Master, **II**: 95
Knapp, C. P., Conf. schnr.; see: *C. P. Knapp*
Knapp, Shepherd, USS; see: *Shepherd Knapp*, USS
Knapp, W. A., Conf. river stmr.; see: *W. A. Knapp*
Knickerbocker, Am. stmr., **V**: 39
Koehler, J. G., Acting Ensign, **IV**: 21
Komandorski Islands, North Pacific, **V**: 106
Kosciusko, U.S. ram; see: *Lancaster*, U.S. ram
Krenson & Hawkes, Savannah shipbuilders, **VI**: 186
Kruge, A. O., Acting Ensign, **V**: 120
Kurile Islands, Japan, **V**: 87, 98, 100

L. Rebecca, b.r. sloop, **II**: 71
La Coruña, Spain; see: Coruña, Spain
La Criolla, b.r. schnr. (later USS *Annie*, q.v.), **II**: 67
La Croix, Edward, **IV**: 134–35
La Fayette, b.r. sloop, **II**: 45
La Fourche, La., **VI**: 252
La Grange, Ga., **V**: 97, 99
La Mountain, John, aeronaut, **I**: 1, 20, 21, *36*
La Place, Conf. shipmaster, **VI**: 304
Labuan, b.r. stmr., **II**: 15
Lackawanna, USS, **III**: 94; **IV**: 87, 96–97; **VI**: 71, 81, 92
Ladies' Delight, b.r. schnr., **III**: 81
Lady Davis, CSS, **I**: 14; **V**: 42; **VI**: 259
Lady Davis, C.S. b.r. stmr.; see: *Cornubia*
Lady Hurley, British b.r. schnr., **IV**: 142
Lady Maria, b.r. schnr., **III**: 111
Lady Sterling, British b.r. stmr. (later USS *Hornet*, q.v.), **IV**: 127
Lady Walton, Conf. river stmr., **III**: 91; **VI**: 259
Lafayette, Am. bark, **II**: 104
Lafayette, USS (ex-*Fort Henry*, ex-*Alick Scott*), **III**: 67, 69, 72, 75, 90, 141, 143; **IV**: 30–31, 61; **VI**: 222
Lafayette, Am. whaler, **III**: 67
Lafayette, b.r. sloop, **VI**: 227
Lafitte, John B., Conf. agent, Nassau, **VI**: 213
Lafone, Henry, Conf. agent, Liverpool, **VI**: 195
Laird hull 290; see: *Alabama* (ex-*Enrica*), CSS

Laird hulls *294* & *295* (Conf. turreted ironclads), **III**: 149; **V**: 34; **VI**: 186
Laird, John, & Sons, dockyard, Liverpool, **VI**: 186–87, 189, 191, 241, 281
Lake Borgne, La., **VI**: 216
Lake Calcasieu, La., **VI**: 218
Lake Erie, **III**: 121; **IV**: 49, 63, 112, 131; **VI**: 253, 318
Lake Huron, **III**: 25; **VI**: 238
Lake Maurepas, La., **III**: 62; **VI**: 202
Lake Michigan, **III**: 25
Lake Monroe, Fla., **IV**: 32
Lake Ocala, Fla., **III**: 160
Lake Ontario, **III**: 25
Lake Pontchartrain, La., **II**: 61, 64; **IV**: 61; **VI**: 205, 207, 216, 280, 283, 300
Lake Providence, La., **III**: 18, 126
Lakin, Edward, Lieut., CSN, **V**: 26; **VI**: 299
Lamar, Conf. privateer schnr., **VI**: 328
Lamar, Tex., **II**: 81
Lamb, William, Colonel, CSA, **IV**: 149–50; **V**: 3, 10, 11, 13; **VI**: 214
Lamb, William W., Conf. shipmaster, **VI**: 237
Lambert, Conf. shipmaster, **VI**: 320
Lamb's Ferry, Ala., **V**: 56
Lammot du Pont, Am. schnr. (collier), **IV**: 104
Lamplighter, Am. bark, **II**: 103
Lamson, Charles W., Acting Master, **II**: 63, 99, 111; **III**: 41, 68, 136, 144, 150, 157, 168, 169; **IV**: 11, 57
Lamson, Roswell H., Lieut., **III**: 145, 149, 153; **IV**: 59, 108, 140
Lancaster, Conf. stmr., **I**: 11
Lancaster, U.S. ram (later U.S. ram *Kosciusko*), **III**: 52–53; **VI**: 233
Lancaster, USS, **IV**: 24, 133; **V**: 109
Lancaster, John, **IV**: 78; **V**: 54
Landis, CSS (also: *Joseph C. Landis, I. C. Landis*, or *Landes*; later, US tug), **II**: 54; **VI**: 260, 328
Landry, James, b.r. sloop; see: *James Landry*
Landry, Philippe, guerrilla leader, **II**: 90
Lane, British ship, **IV**: 87
Langthorne, Amos R., Acting Lieut., **III**: 75, 127; **IV**: 52, 59
Lanier, Edward, Commander, **I**: 39
Lanman, Joseph, Commodore, **V**: 126
Lansing, James, Acting Lieut., **V**: 8
Lapwing, Am. bark (later CSS *Oreto*, q.v.), **III**: 54; **VI**: 260
Lard cargoes captured or destroyed, **II**: 110; **IV**: 61
Lardner, James L., Rear Admiral, **I**: 38, 39; **II**: 44, 81; **IV**: 33
Lark, CSN b.r. stmr., **VI**: 189
Las Desertas I., Madeira Islands, **IV**: 121
"Last Broadside, The", song, sheet music, **VI**: 124–29
"Last of the *Alabama*, The", song, sheet music, **VI**: 166–69
Last Push, b.r. sloop, **IV**: 63
Last Resort, b.r. sloop, **IV**: 83
Last Trial, b.r. sloop, **III**: 144
Launches #1–6, Conf., **VI**: 260–61
Laura, b.r. stmr., **IV**: 10
Laura, British b.r. schnr., **IV**: 47
Laura, Conf. schnr., **VI**: 261
Lauraetta, Am. bark, **II**: 104

Laurel, Conf. stmr. (tender to CSS *Shenandoah*), **IV**: 119, 121; **VI**: 261
Lauretta, British b.r. stmr., **IV**: 26
Laurie, Fannie, b.r. bark; see: *Fannie Laurie*
Lavaca, Tex., **V**: 64
Lavender, USS (ex-*Mayflower*), **IV**: 74
Lavender, Captain, inventor, **IV**: 4
Laverty, John, Fireman, **IV**: 62
Lavinia, b.r. schnr., **II**: 94
Lavinia, b.r. stmr., **VI**: 249
Lavinia, Sarah, b.r. schnr.; see: *Sarah Lavinia*
Lawrence, Mrs. Alma, **VI**: 184
Lawrie, shipbuilders, Glasgow, **VI**: 188, 241
Lawson, E., Conf. shipowner, **VI**: 333
Lawson's Bay, Rappahannock River, Va., **III**: 89
Lay, John L., First Assistant Engineer, **II**: 108
Le Grande, Conf. stmr., **VI**: 261
Le Maire Straits, Argentina, **IV**: 37
Le Roy, William E., Commander, **II**: 17, 47, 50, 67, 71, 93; **III**: 18-19
Lea Harbor, Ascension I., Ponape, **V**: 83
Leach, Franklin S., Acting Ensign, **V**: 30
Lead cargoes captured, **II**: 14, 57; **III**: 97, 140, 153, 167; **IV**: 15; **V**: 20, 32, 42, 49
Lead, shortage of, Conf., **V**: 49
Leadership, **IV**: 121, 132
Lealtad, b.r. schnr., **IV**: 31
Leather cargo captured or destroyed, **IV**: 66
Leavenworth, Ind., **III**: 111
Leavitt, Charles P., CSA, **I**: 30
Lebanon, Am. river stmr., **IV**: 62
Lebby, Henry S., Conf. privateer master, **I**: 29
Lecompt, C.S. guard boat (also *Le Compt* or *Lecompte*), **IV**: 150; **V**: 101, 111; **VI**: 261
Lee, Battery, N.C.; see: Battery Lee
Lee, Charles W., Acting Master, **IV**: 67, 118; **V**: 32
Lee, Francis D., Captain, CSA, **VI**: 316
Lee, G. W. Custis, Major General, CSA, **V**: 78
Lee, David, Acting Ensign, **IV**: 13
Lee, Fanny, British b.r. schnr.; see: *Fanny Lee*
Lee, General, CSA transport; see: *General Lee*
Lee, Fitzhugh, Major General, CSA, **IV**: 78
Lee, O. H., USS; see: *O. H. Lee*, USS
Lee, Robert E., b.r. stmr.; see: *Robert E. Lee*
Lee, Robert E., General, CSA, surrender, **V**: 81; mentioned, **I**: 12, 16, 17; **II**: 5, 8, 12, 21, 24, 28, 47, 75, 77, 80; **III**: 78, 104; **IV**: 3, 5, 16, 21, 33, 38, 42, 47, 49, 53, 54, 105, 114, 115, 123; **V**: 59, 66-67, 71, 73, 78, 81, *82*, 87, 97, 102, 105, 124; **VI**: 6
Lee, Robert G., Acting Master, **IV**: 89
Lee, Samuel P., Rear Admiral, appointed to command NABS, **II**: 95; relieved, **IV**: 110, 120-21; appointed to command Mississippi Squadron, **IV**: 129; mentioned, **I**: 23; **II**: 55, 63, 64, 66, 95, 97, 100, 104, 107, 113; **III**: 7, 38, 39, 55, 63, 66, 68, 77, 90, 104, 110, 115, 131, 132, 135, 147, 154, 156, 158, 163, 165; **IV**: 2, 3, 4, 23, 25, 30, 32, 35, 36, 38, 45, 46, 51, 57, 58, 59, 62, 66, 68, 78, 82, 83, 86, 87, 102, 108, 110, 116, 120, 124, 129, 132, 135, 138, 142, *149*, 151; **V**: 56, 61, 91-92, 103, 104, 118, 123; **VI**: 196
Lee, Sidney Smith, Captain, CSN, **IV**: 146
Lee spar-torpedo, **VI**: 245
Lee, William, Conf. shipowner, **VI**: 332
Lee, William P., Acting Ensign, **III**: 163

Leech, Captain, CSA, **VI**: 283
Leeds Foundry, New Orleans, **VI**: 283
Leesburg, Conf. stmr., **VI**: 261
Leeward Islands, B.W.I., **I**: 38; **II**: 111
Legareville, S.C., **II**: 66; **III**: 18, 158, 167
Lehigh, USS, **III**: 115, 137, 156; **IV**: 14, 85; **V**: 37, 78
Leitch, W. Y., British b.r.; see: *W. Y. Leitch*
Leland, George W., Gunner's Mate, **III**: 156
Lelia, b.r. stmr., **V**: 16
Lenapee, USS, **V**: 55, 59
Lenox, Am. bark, **III**: 91; **VI**: 206
Lenty, Joseph, **IV**: 16
Leonard, William H. H., Conf. shipmaster, **VI**: 231
Leopard, Am. schnr., **IV**: 105
Leovy, Henry J., New Orleans attorney, **VI**: 283
Let Her Rip; see: *Wando*, British b.r. schnr.
Letters of marque & reprisal, **I**: 7, 12, 14, 28; **III**: 148; **VI**: 209-11, 221
Levi Rowe, b.r. schnr., **II**: 111
Levi Starbuck, Am. whaling ship, **II**: 107
Leviathan, USA stmr. (tug), **III**: 141; **VI**: 261-62, 311
Lewis, Conf. stmr., **I**: 13
Lewis, b.r. stmr., **I**: 38
Lewis, transport stmr., **II**: 45
Lewis, E. F., Am. schnr.; see: *E. F. Lewis*
Lewis, Elnathan, Acting Master, **VI**: 227
Lewis, Henry H., Lieut., CSN, **V**: 102; **VI**: 290, 303
Lewis, John, Lieut., CSN, **V**: 36
Lewis, Robert F. R., Lt. Commander, **III**: 97; **IV**: 37
Lewis Cass, USRC, **I**: 4; as CSS, **VI**: 262
Lewis Kilham, Am. ship, **I**: 18
Lexington, USS, **I**: 14, 22, 23, 26, 27, 28, 34; **II**: 9, 14, 17, 32, 39, 40, 45, 50, 70, 74, 116; **III**: 5, 7, 12, 17, 20, 23, 39, 57, 71, 91, 127, 151; **IV**: 25, 30, 32, 37, 38, 41, 51, 74, 82; **V**: 91; **VI**: 196, 223, 254
Libby Prison, Richmond, Va., **V**: 78
Liberty, U.S. barge, **III**: 13
Lida, Conf. sloop, **I**: 38
Lt. Commander, rank established, **II**: 83
Light House Board, U.S., **VI**: 259
Light House Inlet, S.C., **III**: 113, 129
Lightning, b.r. schnr. (later USS), **III**: 39
Lightships, **I**: 40; **II**: 11
Lilac, USS, **VI**: 300
Lilian, b.r. stmr. (later USS), **IV**: 108
Lilla, British b.r. brig, **II**: 76
Lillie Martin, b.r. stmr., **III**: 149
Lilly, British b.r. schnr., **IV**: 24
Lilly, British b.r. schnr., **IV**: 44
Lily, b.r. schnr., **II**: 95
Lily, U.S. tug (ex-*Jessie*, USA tug), **III**: 72
Lime cargo captured, **I**: 27
Limpet mines, prototype, **IV**: 42, 75
Lincoln, Abraham, President, assassinated, **V**: 86-87; **VI**: 6; mentioned, **I**: 6, 7, 12, 20, 21, 22, 24, 38, **II**: 13, 15, 26, 50, 61, 62, 77, 80, 81, 107, 110, 111, 112, 115; **III**: 10, 12, 27, 29, 35, 57, 58, 78, 93, 110, 113, 163; **IV**: 4, 11, 23, 35, 62, 109, 140, 145, 146, 148; **V**: 8, 18, 26, 55, 65, 69, 71, 75, 78, 80, 83, 86, 87, *88*, 89, 90, 91, 92, 94, 95; **VI**: 2, 3; and the Navy, **VI**: 30-46, *34*
Lincoln, Albion, Am. ship; see: *Albion Lincoln*
Lincoln, Mary Todd, **V**: 65, 75

Louisville, USS, **I**: 22; **II**: 22, 28, 36, 68, 103, 107, 116; **III**: 5, 7, 45, 67, 72, 86, 111, 155; **IV**: 30, 32, 37, 59, 60, 66, 70

Louisville, Conf. river stmr. (later USS *Ouachita* and Am. stmr *Vicksburg*), **III**: 115; **VI**: 264

Louisville, Ky., **III**: 112; **VI**: 189, 206, 222

Love, John, Major General, USA, **II**: 85

Lovell, Colonel, CSS; see: *Colonel Lovell*, CSS

Lovell, General, CSS; see: *General Lovell*, CSS

Lovell, Mansfield, Major General, CSA, **II**: 7, 38, 51; **VI**: 197-98, 201, 213, 231, 234, 242, 278, 313-14, 324

Low, John, Lieut., CSN, **II**: 38; **III**: 122, 134; **IV**: 27; **V**: 8, 22, 59, 97, 105; **VI**: 191, 317

Low, Seth, USS; see: *Seth Low*, USS

Low, William W., Lt. Commander, **IV**: 20; **V**: 30

Lowe, Thaddeus S. C., Prof., **I**: 1, 34, *36*, 37

Lowe, William W., Colonel, USA, **III**: 6

Lowood, b.r. schnr., **IV**: 140

Lowry, Reigart B., Lt. Commander, **I**: 15, 22, 24; **III**: 83

Loyal, transport stmr., **VI**: 56

Loyall, Benjamin P., Lieut., CSN, **IV**: 47; **VI**: 294

Lucas Bend, Mo., **I**: 26; **II**: 6; **VI**: 254

Luce, Stephen B., Lt. Commander, **V**: 11, 34, 55, 102

Lucy, British b.r. schnr., **II**: 71

Lucy, British b.r. schnr., **IV**: 122

Lucy, b.r. stmr., **IV**: 129

Lucy C. Holmes, b.r. schnr., **II**: 67

Lucy Gwin (or *Gwynn*), Conf. stmr., **III**: 3; **VI**: 264, 331

Lumber captured or destroyed, **I**: 19, 37; **III**: 26, 36, 82; **IV**: 75, 84, 102, 104, 111, 115; **V**: 65

Luminary, U.S. transport, **III**: 57

Lundt, William O., Acting Master, **IV**: 122, 127

Lutherville, Md., **IV**: iv

Lydia, b.r. sloop, **IV**: 15

Lydia and Martha, Conf. schnr., **VI**: 333

Lydia and Mary, b.r. schnr., **II**: 42

Lye cargoes captured, **IV**: 15

Lyford, Stephen C., Major, USA, **III**: 87

Lynch, William F., Flag Officer, CSN, **I**: 1, 28, 40; **II**: 9, 19, 20, 66; **III**: 58; **IV**: 50, 56-57, 82; **VI**: 186, 224, 333

Lynchburg, Conf. schnr., **I**: 15

Lynchburg, Va., **V**: 3

Lynn Boyd, Conf. river transport, **II**: 18; **VI**: 223, 264

Lynnhaven Bay, Va., **I**: 28

Lynx, C.S. Govt. b.r. stmr., **IV**: 114-15; **VI**: 264-65

Lyon, General, USS; see: *De Soto*, USS

M. A. Shindler, Am. schnr., **III**: 93

M. C. Etheridge, Conf. supply schnr.; **VI**: 265

M. E. Downing, Conf. dispatch stmr., **VI**: 265

M. J. Colcord, Am. bark, **III**: 54

M. Walt, b.r. river stmr., **IV**: 74

Mab, C.S. stmr. (later USS), **V**: 42

Mabel, British b.r. schnr., **I**: 37

MacDiarmid, John, Acting Lieut., **II**: 80; **III**: 147, 153, 155, 167; **IV**: 114; **V**: 30

MacDonnell, Richard G., Lt. Governor of Nova Scotia, **IV**: 106

Macedonia, USS, **I**: 5

MacGarvey, James H., Captain, CSN, **VI**: 279

Machias, Am. vessel, **I**: 18

Machias, Me., **IV**: 75

Machinery cargoes captured, **I**: 29; **III**: 94; **IV**: 120, 122

Machinery shops, floating, **II**: 99; **III**: 31, 81

Machodoc Creek, Va., **I**: 14; **III**: 26

Mack, Eugene, Ordnance Gunner, **III**: 91

Mack Canfield, b.r. schnr., **III**: 133

Mackall, William W., Brig. General, CSA, **II**: 46

Mackay's Point, S.C., **I**: 34

Mackie, John B., Corporal, USMC, **II**: 64

Mackinaw, USS, **IV**: 56, 105, 139, 140

Macomb, William H., Commander, **III**: 140; **IV**: 91, 102, 104, 118, 122, 127, 132, 135, 144, 147; **V**: 33, 55, 60, 64, 65, 69, 75, 79, 81, 86, 100; **VI**: 223-24

Macon, CSS (ex-*Ogeechee*), **IV**: 139, 145; **V**: 31; **VI**: 186, 265

Madagascar I., Indian Ocean, **IV**: 16

Madeira Islands, **IV**: 1, 119, 121; **VI**: 304

Madgie, USS, **II**: 71; **III**: 131, 147

Madick, Match, b.r. seaman, **VI**: 203

Madigan, John, Jr., Lt. Commander, **III**: 79, 97, 119; **IV**: 131

Madrid Bend, Mo., **VI**: 258

Maffitt, John N., Commander, CSN, commands CSS *Florida*, **II**: 89ff; relieved, **III**: 126; appointed Commander, CSN, **III**: 126; commands CSS *Albemarle*, **IV**: 85, 110; appointed to command b.r. *Owl*, **IV**: 110-11; mentioned, **II**: 38, 89, 95, 111; **III**: 10, 12, *13*, 15, 27, 39, 44, 54, 67, 71, 77-78, 81, 91, 92, 94, 95, 104, 111, 112, 113, 121, 124, 126, 131; **IV**: 85, 110-11, 113, 148; **V**: 38, 118; **VI**: 3, 212, 228-29, 256, 298

Maffitt's Channel, Charleston harbor, S.C., **II**: 12; **VI**: 256

Magaw, Samuel, Lt. Commander, **II**: 97, 100, 101, 107; **III**: 32

Magee, Sally, Conf. bark; see: *Sally Magee*

Magellan Straits, Argentina, **V**: 123

Magenta, Conf. river transport, **III**: 115; **VI**: 265

Maggie Fulton, British b.r. schnr., **III**: 62

Magnet, USA transport, **IV**: 139

Magnolia, Conf. stmr., **II**: 24; **VI**: 265-66; as USS, **II**: 88, 116; **IV**: 85, 111

Magnolia, b.r. schnr., **II**: 57

Magnolia, Conf. river stmr., **III**: 47, 115; **VI**: 238, 266

Magnolia, b.r. sloop, **III**: 165

Magnolia, Am. schnr., **IV**: 105

Magruder, J. Bankhead, Major General, CSA, **III**: 4; **V**: 126; **VI**: 255

Magune, James W., Acting Lieut., **V**: 87

Mahan, Alfred T., Rear Admiral, **I**: 14; **II**: 45, 61; **III**: 105, 110

Mahaska, USS, **II**: 105, 110, 112; **III**: 7, 34, 115, 129; **IV**: 14, 37; **V**: 42

Mahogany cargoes captured, **V**: 97

Mahopac, USS, **IV**: 137, 142; **V**: 11, 21

Mail, b.r. schnr. (later USS), **II**: 88

Mail, British b.r. stmr., **III**: 147

Mail, captured Conf., **II**: 110; **IV**: 38, 50, 82; **V**: 59; **VI**: 215, 250

Mail steamers, **II**: 104; **III**: 29; **IV**: 87, 111, 133; **V**: 39

Maillefert, Benjamin, **IV**: 20

Majidi (ex-*Shenandoah*), CSS), **V**: 130

Major Barbour, British b.r. schnr., **II**: 14

Major E. Willis, b.r. schnr., **III**: 68

Major Minter; see: *Elma*, CSA schnr.

Malabar Coast, India, **IV**: 5

Malacca Strait, **III**: 167

Malaria, **IV**: 103; **V**: 124

Malden, Ont., Canada, **VI**: 282

Malinda, b.r. schnr., **IV**: 70

Mallard, William H., Acting Master, **V**: 36

Mallory, Stephen R., CSN Secretary, appointed Secretary of the Navy, **I**: 5; resigns, **V**: 97; captured, **V**: 99; mentioned, **I**: 4–5, 11, 13, 14, 19, 22, 26, 28, 29, 37, 40; **II**: 9, 47, 54, 66, 71, 83, 89, 91–92, 95; **III**: 6–7, 16, 25, 29, 31, 69, 74, 77, 81, 91, 96, 112, 114, 115, 117, 121, 126, 131, 134, 136, 144, 149, 150, 151, 155, 156, 159, 165; **IV**: 4–5, 7, 13, 19, 21, 23, 24, 31, 34, 37, 38, 39, 44, 46, 50, 52, 56, 59, 67, 78, 84, 89, 92, 102, 112, 113, 115, 116, 120, 122, 131, 133, 146; **V**: 8, 10, 16, 21, 27, 33, 34, 54–55, 76, 83, 90, 92, 96, 97, 99, 100; **VI**: 6, 188–91, 200, 203, 215, 219, 227

Mallory, William, Conf. schnr.; see: *William Mallory*

Malta, b.r. schnr., **V**: 55

Malta, Mediterranean, **IV**: 39; **VI**: 207

Malvern, USS (ex-*Ella and Annie*; ex-*William G. Hewes*), **V**: 11, 13, 21, 31, 37, 60, 75, 78; **VI**: 45, 324

Malvern Hill, Va., **II**: 74, 75, 76, 89; **IV**: 89

Man-of-War Cay, Abaco, Bahama Islands, **II**: 93; **III**: 129; **IV**: 12, 83

Manassas, CSS (ex-*Enoch Train*), **I**: 29, **II**: 54; **VI**: 266, 267, 329

Manassas, C.S. cruiser; see: *Florida*, CSS

Manassas, C.S. schnr., **VI**: 266

Manassas, Va., **I**: 20

Manatee River, Fla., **III**: 112

Manchester, Am. ship, **II**: 102

Mandarin Point, Fla., **IV**: 37

Mandeville, La., **IV**: 138

Mandoline, b.r. schnr., **IV**: 42

Mangham, George M., U.S. schnr.; see: *George M. Mangham*

Manhasset, Am. schnr., **III**: 141

Manhattan, USS, **IV**: 74–78, 86–97, 91, 100, 105

Manhattan, NYC, N.Y., **III**: 114

Manila tobacco, **III**: 155

Manitou, USS (ex-*James Thompson*, later *Fort Hindman*, q.v.), **III**: 88, 115; **VI**: 222

Mann, A. Dudley, Conf. Special Commissioner, London, **IV**: 15

Manokin River, Md., **I**: 23

Maple Leaf, USA transport, **III**: 92; **IV**: 37

Maratanza, USS, **II**: 56, 76, 78, 102; **III**: 77; **V**: 59; **VI**: 311

Marblehead, USS, **II**: 57; **III**: 21, 32, 116, 158, 167

Marblehead, Mass., **VI**: 269

Marchand, John B., Captain, **II**: 66; **III**: 94; **IV**: 36, 87

Marco Pass, Fla., **IV**: 72

Marcy, Peter, New Orleans privateer owner, **VI**: 260

Marcy, Samuel, Lieut., **I**: 38

Mare I. Navy Yard, Cal., **IV**: 4; **V**: 120

Marengo, Am. fishing schnr., **III**: 97

Margaret, Am. schnr., **I**: 18

Margaret, Conf. sloop, **II**: 18

Margaret, British b.r. schnr., **III**: 21

Margaret and Jessie, b.r. stmr. (later USS *Gettysburg*, q.v.), **III**: 71, 87, 153

Margaret Ann, schnr. **IV**: 17

Margaret, Sarah, b.r. schnr.; see: *Sarah Margaret*

Margaret Schultz, Conf. ship, **VI**: 332

Margaret Y. Davis, Am. schnr., **IV**: 87

Maria, b.r. schnr., **II**: 57

Maria, British b.r. schnr., **II**: 108

Maria A. Wood, USS, **V**: 89

Maria Alberta, b.r. schnr., **III**: 159

Maria Alfred, British b.r. schnr., **IV**: 42

Maria, Ann, British b.r. schnr.; see: *Ann Maria*

Maria, Anna, b.r. schnr.; see: *Anna Maria*

Maria Bishop, b.r. schnr., **III**: 82

Maria J. Carlton, U.S. mortar schnr., **II**: 51

Maria, Lady, b.r. schnr.; see: *Lady Maria*

Maria Louise, b.r. sloop, **IV**: 4

Marianao, Cuba, **VI**: 235

Marianna, Conf. river stmr., **VI**: 268

Marianna, Fla., **VI**: 228

Marigold, USS, **V**: 49

Marine Brigade, **III**: 66, 85, 87, 97, 98, 135; **V**: 128

Marine Coast Guard, C.S., **VI**: 308

Marine Corps, C.S., **II**: 64; **III**: 66, 95, 159; **IV**: 13, 116

Marine Corps, U.S., **I**: 2, 3, 4, 7, 10, 20, 23, 26, 31, 37, 39, 40; **II**: 7, 20, 33, 64, 84, 93, 101, 112, 115; **III**: 57, 86, 117, 124, 138, 166, 168; **IV**: 56, 62–63, 72, 138, 150; **V**: 6, 11, 47, 53, 54

Mariner, Conf. privateer stmr., **I**: 20; **VI**: 329

Marion, b.r. schnr., **IV**: 32

Marion, CSA transport, **VI**: 232, 268

Marion, Ark., **III**: 9

Marion C.H., Great Peedee River, S.C., **VI**: 281

Markham (Schofield and), Atlanta ironworkers; see: Schofield and Markham

Marlborough Point, Va., **I**: 20

Marmaduke, John S., Brig. General, CSA, **III**: 24, 127; **IV**: 70

Marmelstein, Adolphus F., Conf. Pilot (later Master's Mate, CSN), **VI**: 269

Marmora, USS, **II**: 116; **III**: 5, 24, 29, 32, 93, 127; **IV**: 13, 15, 29

Marquesas Keys, Fla., **II**: 116; **III**: 89

Mars, British b.r. schnr., **II**: 17

Mars, Conf. river transport, **VI**: 268

Mars Bluff, Great Peedee River, S.C., **VI**: 186, 281

Marshall, James, Acting Master, **IV**: 41

Marshall Smith, b.r. schnr., **III**: 163

Marshall's warehouse, Mobile, Ala., **V**: 101

Marsh's I., Fla., **III**: 116, 122

Marsh's shipyard, Charleston, S.C., **VI**: 316

Marshall, William E., Lieut., CSA, **VI**: 278

Marston, Gilman, Brig. General, USA, **IV**: 5

Marston, John, Captain, **II**: 14

Martello tower, **I**: 38

Martha, Am. whaling bark, **V**: 111

Martha Ann, b.r. schnr., **III**: 71

Martha Jane, British b.r. schnr., **III**: 149

Martin, U.S. tug (ex-*James McMartin*), **IV**: 91

Martin, James, Algiers, La., shipbuilder, **VI**: 236

Martin, James, Elizabeth City, N.C., shipbuilder, **VI**: 186, 224

Martin, Lillie, b.r. stmr.; see: *Lillie Martin*

Martine, William L., Acting Master, **II**: 14; **IV**: 87

Martinique, French West Indies, **I**: 37; **II**: 110; **VI**: 306

Mary, USRC, **I**: 37

Mary, b.r. schnr., **III**: 147

Mary, b.r. sloop, **IV**: 10

Mary, British b.r. schnr., **V**: 64

Mary, b.r. schnr., **IV**: 139

Mary, Conf. Govt. b.r. stmr. (ex-*Alexandra*, q.v.)

Mary A. Howes, Am. schnr., **IV**: 105

Mary Agnes, b.r. schnr., **V**: 39

Mary Alice, Am. schnr., **I**: 20, 21; **VI**: 221

Mary Alice, Conf. ship, **VI**: 332

McClellan, George B., Major General, USA, **I**: 12; **II**: 23, 24, 26, 37, 42, 47, 56, 57, 64, 66, 71, 74, 75, 77, 80, 86, 89, 91, 95, 116; **V**: 26

McClellan, John, Landsman, **IV**: 99

McClelland, Robert, USRC; see: *Robert McClelland*

McClellanville, S.C., **IV**: 35, 47

McClernand, John A., Major General, USA, **II**: 18, 110; **III**: 7, 70

McClintock, James R., Conf. submarine designer & builder, **III**: 34, 124, 126; **VI**: 244–45, 283

McClurg, Alexander C., Lt. Colonel, USA, **V**: 34

McCombs, John T., Am. river stmr.; see: *John T. McCombs*

McConnell, George E., Acting Ensign, **II**: 108; **V**: 58

McConnell, Am. shipowner, **VI**: 306

McCook, Roderick S., Lieut., **II**: 33, 91

McCorkle, David P., Lieut., CSN, **IV**: 24, 56

McCormick, Charleston shipowner, **VI**: 233

McCown, John P., Major General, CSA, **II**: 32; **VI**: 259

McCoy, Joseph D., Conf. shipmaster, **VI**: 220

McCrea, Edward P., Lieut., **I**: 27

McCuaig, Mr., **VI**: 240

McCulloch, Ben, Conf. river stmr.; see: *Ben McCulloch*

McCullough, James, Colonel, CSA, **III**: 24

McDermut, David A., Lt. Commander, **III**: 57, 67

McDonough, USS; see: *Commodore McDonough*, USS

McDougal, Charles J., Lt. Commander, **IV**: 34

McDougal, David, Captain, **V**: 115

McElroy, Thomas, Acting Master, **IV**: 29, 44, 46

McEwan, John, British shipmaster, **VI**: 243

McGehee, James H., Captain, CSA, **III**: 6, 31; **VI**: 254

McGilvery, William, Am. brig; see: *William McGilvery*

McGirt's Creek, Fla., **IV**: 15

McGowan, John, Captain, USRM, **I**: 2

McGowan, John, Jr., Acting Master, **II**: 98

McGrath, James, Landsman, **IV**: 99

McGuin, H., Conf. barge; see: *H. McGuin*

McGuire, Edward, Acting Master, CSN, **III**: 140; **VI**: 291,308

McIntosh, Charles F., Commander, CSN, **VI**: 264

McIntosh County, Ga., **IV**: 105; **V**: 61

McIntosh C.H., Ga., **IV**: 92

McKay, Charles E., Lieut., **V**: 37

McKean, William W., Captain, **I**: 13, 15, 27, 37; **II**: 8, 25; **VI**: 204, 228

McKeesport, Pa., **VI**: 249, 280

McKenna, John, Landsman, **V**: 30

McKenzie, John M., Boy, CSN, **IV**: 75

McKinstry, James P., Captain, **II**: 78; **III**: 45

McLaughlin, Augustus, Lieut., CSN, **IV**: 24; **VI**: 185, 253

McLean House, Appomattox C.H., Va., **V**: 82

McLellan, Thomas, Conf. shipmaster, **VI**: 273

McLeod, Norman, Acting Ensign, **III**: 168

McNeil, J. J., Conf. schnr.; see: *J. J. McNeil*

McPhail, James L., Md. Provost-Marshal, **IV**: 15

McPherson, James B., Major General, USA, **III**: 155; **IV**: 48

McQueen, Alexander, British shipmaster, **II**: 88; **VI**: 190

McRae, CSS (ex-*Marqués de la Habana*), **I**: 11; **II**: 57; **VI**: 269, 270

McRae, Colin J., General Agent, Conf. Treasury Dept., **VI**: 219

McRae, Fannie, British b.r. schnr.; see: *Fannie McRae*

Meade, Richard W., Jr., Lt. Commander, **II**: 103–04, 107; **III**: 158, 167; **IV**: 121, 136, 140, 142, 143; **V**: 5, 20, 22

Means, Edward J., Lieut., CSN, **VI**: 281

Medal of Honor (Congressional), **I**: 39; **II**: 20, 64, 115; **IV**: 62, 83, 126; **V**: 13, 101

Medford, Mass., **VI**: 266

Medicine and Surgery, Bureau of, USN, **II**: 80

Medicine and Surgery, Office of, CSN, **IV**: 129

Medicine, CSN, supply of, **IV**: 129; see also: Drug cargoes captured

Medina County, Tex., **VI**: 313

Mediterranean Sea, **II**: 107; **III**: 102–03, 143; **IV**: 11, 66, 78

Medora, b.r. schnr., **IV**: 144

Meherrin River, N.C., **V**: 80

Meigs, Montgomery C., Major General, USA, **II**: 13, 32

Melbourne, Australia, **V**: 27, 45, 67, 73

Memphis, British b.r. stmr. (later USS), **II**: 88

Memphis, CSS; see: *America*, C.S. yacht

Memphis, USS, **III**: 18–19, 55, 93; **IV**: 29, 46; **VI**: 219, 269

Memphis, C.S. floating battery, **VI**: 270

Memphis, Tenn., **II**: 40, 41, 43, 56, 60, 68, 93, 112; **III**: 7, 8, 31, 32, 38; **IV**: 2, 67, 92, 115; **V**: 94, 128; **VI**: 190, 199, 213, 231, 233

Memphis & Charleston R.R., **II**: 50

Memphis & Clarksville R.R., **II**: 18

Memphis Salt Works, Salt House Point, Ala., **IV**: 110

Mendota, USS, **IV**: 89, 92

Mercedita, USS, **II**: 11, 42, 57, 81; **III**: 18–20; **V**: 122; **VI**: 3, 205, 212, 279

Mercer, Samuel, Captain, **I**: 6, 21

Mercury, USS, **I**: 31; **IV**: 114, 146; **V**: 39

Mercury, Conf. sloop, **III**: 6

Mercury depth gauge, **VI**: 245

Meriam, Frank B., Acting Master, **II**: 71; **III**: 131; **IV**: 15, 37

Meridian, Miss., **IV**: 13, 15; **V**: 83

Merite, C.S. river stmr., **VI**: 270

Mermaid, Am. schnr., **I**: 15

Mermentau River, La., **III**: 106; **IV**: 42

Merrett, John, Gunner's Mate, **II**: 88

Merrimac (ex-British), b.r. stmr., **III**: 71, 121; as USS, **IV**: 84; **V**: 39; **VI**: 270

Merrimack, US frigate; see also: *Virginia*, CSS; burned, **I**: 9; raised by Conf., **I**: 15, 16; mentioned, **I**: 7, 16, 17, 19; **II**: 5, 12, 14, 20, 21, 40, 41; **IV**: 2, 7, 46; **V**: 118

Merrimack II, CSS; see: *Virginia II*, CSS

Merryman, James H., Lieut., USRM, **III**: 104

Mersey, b.r. schnr., **II**: 56

Mersey River, England, **V**: 16, 118, 128; **VI**: 213

Mervine, William, Flag Officer, **I**: 14, 16

Messick, William G., Conf. shipowner, **VI**: 332, 333

Metacomet, USS, **IV**: 70, 83–84, 95, 137, 151; **V**: 69; **VI**: 62, 70, 72, 75, 78, 80, 81, 83, 92, 95, 201

Meteor, U.S. transport, **II**: 103

Meteor, British b.r. schnr., **III**: 151

Meto, Bayou; see: Bayou Meto, Ark.

Mexican "National Observatory", **V**: 126

Mexico, Conf. stmr., **VI**: 231, 278

Mexico, **I**: 17; **II**: 80; **III**: 12, 21, 62, 91, 120, 136, 150; **IV**: 2, 19, 24, 46, 145; **V**: 104–05, 110, 111, 118, 120, 124, 126, 127, 130

Moise, T. S., Major, CSA, **VI:** 235

Molasses cargoes captured, **I:** 16, 20, 38, 76; **II:** 112; **III:** 12, 22, 94, 106, 112, 128

Molloy, John, Conf. transport shipmaster, **IV:** 103

Monadnock, USS, **V:** 11, 21, 58, 78, 123, 128

Monarch, U.S. ram, **II:** 68, 91; **III:** 5, 7, 20, 117; **VI:** 214, 231, 233

Monck, Charles S., Viscount, Gov. General, Canada, **VI:** 240

Mondamin, Am. bark, **IV:** 115

Monitor, USS, construction recommended, **I:** 26; begun, **I:** 30; Worden ordered to command, **II:** 7; construction of, **II:** 9; launched, **II:** 14; trial, **II:** 24; ordered to Hampton Roads, **II:** 24; commissioned, **II:** 26; departs New York, **II:** 27, 29; arrives Hampton Roads, **II:** 30; engages CSS *Virginia*, **II:** 30–31; **VI:** 1, 2, *371*; operations in Virginia waters, **II:** 47, 61, 62, 64; lost at sea, **II:** 116–*17*; **VI:** 3

Monitor, b.r. sloop, **II:** 68

Monitor Bay, Mobile, Ala., **IV:** 94

"Monitor, The", song, sheet music, **VI:** 138–42

"Monitor Polka", sheet music, **VI:** 130–31

Monitors, *xi*, **III:** 14, 17, 44, 48, 59–61, 63, 65, 74, 83, 85, 94, 95, 104, 110, 113, 114, 118, 128, 133, 135, 136, 143, 160; **IV:** 10, 11, 14, 15–16, 25, 30, 66, 82, 85, 93, 96–97, 131; **IV:** 137–38, 140; **V:** 3, 5, 6, 11, 16, 26, 32, 58, 90

Monitors, imitation, **III:** 34–35, 68; **V:** 39, 46

Monocacy, USS, **IV:** 137; **V:** 5, 69, 132

Monohassett, USA transport, **III:** 159

Monongahela, USS, **III:** 36, 45, 86, 95, 111, 150, 151, 156, 159, 168; **IV:** 83, 87, 90, 96, 97, 132; **VI:** 75, 92

Monongahela, Pa., **VI:** 323

Monroe, La., **IV:** 26

Montague, Eli, Lieut., CSA, **VI:** 249

Montauk, USS, **III:** 17, 20, 35–36, 44, 48, 55, 58, 59, 112, 113, 117, 119, 133, 137; **IV:** 85; **V:** 32, 37, 39, 58, 90, 93–94, 95, 116

Montauk Point, N.Y., **VI:** 254

Montebello, b.r. schnr., **II:** 69

Monte Christo, Conf. schnr., **II:** 81

Montel, Capt. Charles de; see: De Montel, Capt. Charles

Montell, F. M., Acting Master, **V:** 39

Monterey, b.r. schnr., **II:** 51

Monterrey, Mexico, **III:** 62

Montevideo, Uruguay, **III:** 88–89

Montgomery, USS, **I:** 38; **II:** 15, 45, 68, 102, 104, 110; **IV:** 2, 4, 20, 120; **V:** 37; **VI:** 203,235

Montgomery (ex-*Habanero*), b.r. stmr., **III:** 128, 140

Montgomery, John, Conf. shipowner, **VI:** 332

Montgomery, James E., Captain, CSN, **II:** 62, 68; **VI:** 182, 213, 230–33

Montgomery, John B., Commodore, **III:** 113; **V:** 65, 87

Montgomery, Ala., **I:** 5, 7

Monticello, USS, **I:** 14, 23, 28, 29, 37; **II:** 102, 111; **III:** 29, 32. 54, 67, 72, 79; **IV:** 25, 29, 82–83, 87, 109, 147; **V:** 11, 21, 32, 123

Monticello, Am. brig, **I:** 18, 23

Monticello, Conf. privateer stmr., **VI:** 329

Montmorenci, Am. brig, **I:** 38

Montrose, Va., **V:** 64

Montario, Narciso, Barcelona inventor, **III:** 62

Moody's Wharf, Va., **IV:** 17

Moon Lake, Miss., **III:** 23, 25

Moon, S. P., Conf. shipowner, **VI:** 332

Moore, Henry T., Acting Lieut., **II:** 70

Moore, Thomas J., Conf. privateer master, **VI:** 221

Moore, Thomas O., Governor of Louisiana, **VI:** 200, 324

Moore & Elliston, Conf. shipowners, **VI:** 333

Moorhead, James K., **II:** 41

Moose, USS (ex-*Florence Miller* Am. river stmr.), **III:** 111–12 118, 165; **IV:** 43, 130, 139, 142; **V:** 95

Morehead City, N.C., **VI:** 221

Morgan, CSS (ex-USRC), **VI:** 186, 272

Morgan, CSS, **III:** 160; **IV:** 95; **V:** 81, 83, 95, 97; **VI:** 95, 230, 272

Morgan, Ben, USS; see: *Ben Morgan*, USS

Morgan, Charles H., shipowner, **VI:** 199, 201, 268, 273, 277–78, 324

Morgan, Edward, Acting Lieut., **IV:** 56

Morgan, Edwin, Governor of N.Y., **I:** 3

Morgan, Fanny, C.S. guard boat; see: *Fanny Morgan*

Morgan, Fort, Mobile, Ala.; see: Fort Morgan

Morgan, Fort, USS; see: *Fort Morgan*, USS

Morgan, James D., Brig. General, USA, **V:** 34

Morgan, James M., Midshipman, CSN, **II:** 102; **VI:** 262

Morgan, John H., Brig. General, CSA, **III:** 111–12, 118

Morgan, Thomas, Acting Ensign, **V:** 30

Morgan, Van R., Lieut., CSN, **VI:** 318

Morgan & Harris, N.Y. shipowners, **VI:** 278

Morganza, La., **III:** 134, 143, 145, 163; **VI:** 235

Morning Light, USS, **II:** 70; **III:** 1, 13, 62; **VI:** 3, 257, 272

Morning Star, b.r. schnr., **II:** 74

Morning Star, Am. ship, **III:** 52

Morning Star, Am. mail stmr., **V:** 39

Moro, CSA supply stmr., **III:** 21–22; **VI:** 273

Morocco, **IV:** 25, 52

Morong, John C., Acting Ensign, **III:** 137

Morris, Charles M., Lieut., CSN, **IV:** 4, 16, 26, 36, 61, 75, 84, 86, 87, 115, 118; **V:** 21; **VI:** 229, 251

Morris, Commodore, USS; see: *Commodore Morris*, USS

Morris, George U., Lt. Commander, **III:** 69, 85, 117; **V:** 49, 59, 67

Morris, Henry W., Captain, **II:** 7, 47, 55

Morris I., Charleston, S.C., **I:** 2, 3, 6, 39; **III:** 5, 58, 63, 71, 112, 113, 118, 119, 120, 121, 122, 123, 124, 131, 133, 136, 137, 145, 148, 152, 156, 166, 167; **IV:** 11, 70, 102, 122; **VI:** 5

Morris, William G., Acting Master, **III:** 87, 93, 140; **IV:** 70, 146

Morrison, John J., Captain, USRM, **I:** 4; **VI:** 262

Morse, USS (ex-*Marion*, Am. ferry), **II:** 6, 79; **III:** 77, 98, 115; **IV:** 17, 29, 30, 35, 51, 78; **V:** 61

Morse, Freeman H., U.S. Consul, London, **VI:** 249

Mortar Boat No. 16, USS, **II:** 62; **VI:** 233, 235

Mortar boats, **I:** 40; **II:** 6, 9, 13, 24, *36*, 46, 50, 51, 74, 86; **III:** 38, 41, 45, 72, *82*, 86, 91, 100, 105; **IV:** 28, 146; **V:** 56

Mortar Flotilla, U.S., **II:** 21, 32, 62; **III:** 78, 105; **VI:** 197, 213

Morton, Oliver P., Governor of Indiana, **II:** 85

Morton, Gilbert, Acting Master, **III:** 149; **V:** 56

Morton, Thomas, **III:** 145

Mosby, John S., Colonel, CSA, **V:** 58

Moses, Edward, Acting Master, **IV:** 10

Mosher, Conf. steam tug, **VI:** 273

Mosman, D. Frank, Acting Master, **II:** 93

Mosquito, C.S. launch, **VI:** 273

Mosquito Inlet, Fla., **II:** 8, 38, 75, 94; **III:** 39, 52, 96; **IV:** 31, 83

Mosquito Point, Va., **IV:** 30

Night Hawk, British b.r. stmr., **IV**: 116; **VI**: 214
Nightingale, slave ship, **I**: 11; as USS, **I**: 29
Nile, Am. whaling bark, **V**: 111
Nimrod, Am. whaler, **V**: 109
Nina, Conf. stmr., **II**: 91
Nina, British b.r. sloop, **IV**: 24
Nina Simms, CSA transport (also: *Sims* or *Simmes*), **VI**: 277
Niphon, USS, **III**: 122, 131, 153, 154; **IV**: 46, 109, 113, 114, 116, 118, 129; **VI**: 215
Nipsic, USS, **III**: 166, 167–68; **IV**: 24, 83, 118; **V**: 27
Nita, b.r. stmr., **III**: 127, 129; as USS, **IV**: 24, 40, 123, 133, 139
Niter Bureau, C.S., **IV**: 7
Noe-Daquy, Spanish stmr.; see: *Virginia*, Conf. b.r. stmr.
Nolan, Matthew, Captain, CSA, **III**: 13
Nolte, Fred, b.r. stmr.; see: *Fred Nolte*
Nomini Creek, off Potomac River, Va., **II**: 108
Nonsuch, b.r. schnr., **II**: 112
Nora, Am. ship, **III**: 53
Norfolk, CSS, **VI**: 186, 277
Norfolk, Va., **I**: 7, 17; **II**: 7, 9, 20, 47, 61–62, 81; **III**: 18; **V**: 55; **VI**: 2, 197, 217, 224, 229
Norfolk Naval Hospital, **IV**: 56
Norfolk Navy Yard, abandoned by USN, **I**: 9–11; by Conf., **II**: 61–62, 85; mentioned, **I**: 6, 9, 10, 11, 15, 17; **II**: 11, 14, 20, 27, 38, 61–62, 85; **VI**: 2, 40, 41, 41
Norfolk Packet, USS, **III**: 149; **IV**: 31, 83
Norman, Am. vessel, **III**: 155
North, James H., Commander, CSN, **III**: 29, 77, 134; **V**: 21; **VI**: 186, 195, 298
North America, Am. schnr., **IV**: 105
North Atlantic Blockading Squadron, **I**: 27; **II**: 49, 80, 93, 95, 107; **III**: 39, 63, 110, 135, 156; **IV**: 5, 58, 105, 109–10, 116, 120, 131, 143; **V**: 3, 112–13, 114; **VI**: 222, 224
North Bay, Fla., **II**: 46
North Cape, Norway, **IV**: 140
North Carolina, USS, **I**: 11; **VI**: 49
North Carolina, CSS, **III**: 58; **IV**: 82–83, 115; **VI**: 277, 290, 318
North East Providence Channel, Bahamas, **III**: 44; **IV**: 12
North Edisto & River, S.C. **I**: 38, 55; **III**: 58; **IV**: 29; **V**: 27, 36; **VI**: 219
North Inlet, S.C. **II**: 47; **IV**: 4
North Santee River, S.C., **III**: 34
North Sea, **V**: 120
Northampton, C.S. stmr., **VI**: 217, 277
Northern Neck, Va., **V**: 61, 64, 122
Northrup, William H., conf. schnr.; see: *William H. Northrup*
Northumberland County, Va., **IV**: 124
N.W. Providence Channel, Bahamas, **III**: 10
Norton, Charles S., Lieut., **I**: 27
Norval, William, Conf. pilot, **IV**: 4
Norwich, USS **III**: 39, 54, 131; **IV**: 14, 15, 37; **V**: 116
Nova Scotia Prov., Canada, **I**: 26, 27; **II**: 102, 103, 105; **III**: 2; **IV**: 106; **V**: 82; **VI**: 196
Noyes, Allen K., Ensign, **V**: 47
Nueces Bay, Tex., **VI**: 224, 247
Nueces River, Tex., **II**: 91
Nutfield, b.r. stmr., **IV**: 15
Nyack, USS, **V**: 59
Nyanza, USS, **IV**: 32, 42
Nye, Am. whaler, **III**: 71

Nye, Ebenezer, Am. shipmaster, **V**: 102
Nymph, b.r. schnr., **III**: 70

O. H. Lee, U.S. mortar schnr., **IV**: 145; **V**: 53; **VI**: 56
O.K., Conf. sloop, **II**: 28
O.K., b.r. schnr., **IV**: 48
O. Whitmond, Conf. ship, **VI**: 332
Oak Hill, Ala., **III**: 72
Oates (Bassett &), Mobile shipbuilders, **VI**: 186
Oats, cargoes of, captured or destroyed, **IV**: 35, 61
Ocala, Lake, Fla.; see: Lake Ocala
Occoquan, Va., **II**: 101
Ocean Bird, b.r. schnr., **III**: 149
Ocean Rover, Am. whaler, **II**: 97
Ocean Towing Co., New Orleans, **VI**: 213
Ocean View, Norfolk, Va., **II**: 62
Ocheesee, Fla., **VI**: 325
Ochlawaha River, Fla., **VI**: 237
Ocklockonee River, Fla., **III**: 168; **IV**: 10, 122
Ocmulgee, Am. ship, **II**: 96
Oconee, CSS, **III**: 131; **VI**: 277, 298
O'Connor, Timothy W., Second Assistant Engineer, **II**: 103
Ocracoke Inlet, N.C., **I**: 20, 26, 27; **VI**: 325
Octavia, b.r. sloop, **II**: 42
Octorara, USS, **II**: 88, 97; **III**: 8, 10, 44, 47, 48, 68, 70, 83; **IV**: 20, 42; **V**: 29, 30, 83, 95; **VI**: 77, 92
Odd Fellow, b.r. schnr., **III**: 67
Odd Fellow, b.r. schnr., **III**: 93
Odiorne, Walter C., Acting Ensign, **IV**: 16
Ogden and Leovy, New Orleans, attorneys, **VI**: 283
Ogdensburg, N.Y., **VI**: 240
Ogeechee, CSS; see: *Macon*, CSS
Ogeechee River, Ga., **II**: 110; **III**: 35
"Oh! Give Us a Navy of Iron", song, sheet music, **VI**: 143–47
Ohio Belle, Conf. stmr., **VI**: 277
Ohio River, **I**: 22, 27, **II**: 85; **III**: 111–12, 118; **IV**: 43, 63; **V**: 22; **VI**: 226
Oil cargoes captured, **II**: 45; **IV**: 51
Oil shortages, **II**: 12; **III**: 26
Okhotsk, Sea of, **V**: 73, 100, 106
Oklahoma, **IV**: 74
O'Laughlin, Michael, **V**: 90, 95
Old Bahama Channel, Bahamas, **I**: 34
Old Capitol Prison, D.C., **V**: 90
Old Haven Creek, Va., **VI**: 196
Old Inlet, Wilmington, N.C., **VI**: 294
Old Pass, Miss., **III**: 25
Old Point Comfort, Va., **II**: 26, 80
Old River, La., **III**: 74
Oleander, USS, **III**: 121
Olive, Conf. schnr., **I**: 37
Olive Branch, Conf. schnr., **I**: 17; **II**: 9
Olive Jane, Am. bark, **III**: 32
Oliveira, William D., Acting Master's Mate, CSN, **IV**: 145
Oliver H. Lee, U.S. mortar schnr.; see: *O. H. Lee*
Oliver S. Breese, b.r. schnr., **III**: 81
Ollinger & Bruce, Conf. shipbuilders, **VI**: 186
Olustee, CSS (ex-*Tallahassee*, q.v.), **IV**: 127
Oneida, USS, **II**: 53, 55, 63, 64, 95; **IV**: 90; **VI**: 53, 77, 92, 242, 319
Oneida, Am. ship, **III**: 71
O'Neil, A. Frank, Acting Lieut., **IV**: 34

Parks, Conf. shipbroker/owner, **VI**: 288

Parks, John A., Am. ship; see: *John A. Parks*

Parr, Henry A., Conf. privateersman, **VI**: 209–10

Parrish, Lewis, Master, CSN, **VI**: 223

Parrott, Enoch G., Commander, **I**: 15, 39; **III**: 19

Parrott rifled guns, **III**: 17, 41; **IV**: 51, 58, *69*, 150; **V**: 72, 79; **VI**: 221

Parsons, Lewis B., Colonel, USA, **IV**: 91; **V**: 128

Partridge, Alfred H., Am. schnr.; see: *Alfred H. Partridge*

Pascagoula (and River), Miss., **II**: 84; **III**: 140

Pasquotank River, N.C., **II**: 19, 20; **IV**: 111; **VI**: 197, 206

Pass à l'Outre, Mississippi River, **I**: 17, 18; **III**: 66, 91; **VI**: 206, 265

Pass Cavallo, Tex., **II**: 12; **III**: 70, 87, 149, 150, 159, 168; **IV**: 42, 138, 143; **V**: 45; **VI**: 197, 206, 319

Pass Christian, Miss., **II**: 45; **VI**: 207

Passaic, USS, **II**: 95, 104, 112; **III**: 21, 38, 55, 58, 59, 77, 129, 131, 133; **IV**: *14*, 66

Passapatansy Creek, Md., **V**: 58

Passenger, Conf. sloop, **I**: 18

Patapsco, USS, **III**: 38, 48, 55, 58, 59, 117, 119, 129, 133, 137, 150, 153; **IV**: 11, 16, 131; **V**: 16, 64, 102

Patapsco River, Md., **I**: 12

Pathfinder, British b.r. ship, **II**: 107

Patras, British b.r. stmr., **II**: 67

Patrick Henry, CSS (or *Patrick*, ex-*Yorktown*), **I**: 26, 38; **II**: 20, 26, 61; **III**: 151, *152*; **IV**: 50, 102, 131; **V**: 78, 79; **VI**: 255, 280

Patriot, Conf. schnr., **II**: 94

Patroon, USS, **II**: 97

Pattee, Richard S., Lt. Commander, **VI**: 184

Patterson Foundry, New Orleans area, La., **VI**: 271

Patterson, Mary, Conf. stmr.; see: *Mary Patterson*

Patterson, Robert O., Acting Master, **IV**: 29

Patterson, Thomas H., Commander, **II**: 74; **III**: 153, 159; **VI**: 216

Pattersonville, La., **VI**: 221

Patuxent River, Md., **V**: 73, 91

Paul, British b.r. schnr., **III**: 153

Paul, Mark W., Carpenter, **VI**: 246

Paul Jones, USS, **III**: 117, 119; **IV**: 89

Paul Jones, Conf. river transport, **VI**: 208, 280–81

Paul Jones, Conf. privateer schnr., **VI**: 329

Paulding, Hiram, Rear Admiral, **I**: 7, 10, 11, 21; **III**: 114; **IV**: 104, 147

Paulding, Leonard, Lieut., **II**: 6, 7

Pauline, CSA river transport, **VI**: 281

Paullin, Charles O.; "President Lincoln and the Navy", **VI**: 29–46

Paw Paw, USS (ex-*Fanny*, ex-*St. Charles*), **III**: 124, 151; **IV**: 34, 130

Pawley's I., S.C., **IV**: 67

Pawnee, USS, **I**: 1, 6–7, 10, 11, 13, 15, 17, 18, 23, 26, 31; **III**: 54, 58, 88, 116, *128*, 130, 158, 167; **IV**: 32, 48, 151; **V**: 27, 36, 39, 47, 53, 87; **VI**: 15, 19

Payne, John A., Lieut., CSN, **III**: 2, 123, 132, 134; **VI**: 5, 245

Paynter, J.G., Captain, RN, **V**: 128

Peace Creek, Fla., **III**: 135–36

Peach Orchard Bluffs, Ark., **IV**: 109

Peacock, USS, **V**: 122

Peanut cargo captured, **V**: 64

Pearce, Albert, St. Louis shipowner, **VI**: 212

Pearce, John, Acting Lieut., **III**: 159; **IV**: 70; **VI**: 321

Pearl, Am. schnr., **IV**: 105

Pearl, Am. whaler, **V**: 73

Pearl River, Miss., **III**: 118; **IV**: 72

Pearsall, Samuel, Am. schnr.; see: *Samuel Pearsall*

Pearse shipyard, Stockton-on-Tees, England, **VI**: 202

Pearson, George F., Rear Admiral, **IV**: 124; **V**: 109, 122–23

Pease, Captain, USRM, **I**: 37

Peck, Curtis, Conf. stmr.; see: *Curtis Peck*

Peck, John J., Major General, USA, **IV**: 45, 46

Peedee, CSS, **VI**: 186, 281

Peedee Navy Yard, Mars Bluff, S.C., **VI**: 186, 281

Peedee River, S.C., **III**: 159; **V**: 47; **VI**: 281

Peel, William, British b.r. stmr.; see: *William Peel*

Peep O'Day, b.r. ship, **IV**: 140

Pegram, Robert B., Commander, CSN, **I**: 30, 37; **II**: 17, 27, 37, 104; **VI**: 275, 321

Pelican, Conf. privateer stmr., **VI**: 329

Pelican Pass Channel, Mobile Bay, Ala., **IV**: 89

Pelot, Thomas P., Lieut., **I**: 14; **IV**: 67; **VI**: 232, 259, 323

Pemberton, John C., Lt. General, CSA, **II**: 5; **III**: 47, 106; **VI**: 313

Pembina, USS, **I**: 31, 39; **II**: 22, 47, 66, 68, 90; **III**: 71; **IV**: 140; **VI**: 53

Pendergrast, Austin, Lt. Commander, **IV**: 67

Pendergrast, Garrett J., Flag Officer, **I**: 7, 11, 12, 16; **VI**: 320

Penguin, USS, **I**: 22, 31, 38; **II**: 38; **IV**: 86; **V**: 22, **VI**: 64, 243

Penguin, CSN b.r. stmr., **VI**: 189, 281

Peninsular Campaign, **II**: 37, 42, 47, 56, 61, 62, 75, 93, 116

Pennell, Isaac A., Acting Master, **II**: 7, 49, 113; **IV**: 47, 138, 147

Pennington, Lewis W., Acting Lt. Commander, **II**: 98, 110; **III**: 149; **IV**: 11, 144; **V**: 102

Pennock, Alexander M., Captain, **II**: 40, 46, 85; **III**: 6, 7, 12, 20, 26, 39, 105; **IV**: 34, 47, 127

Pennsylvania, USS, **I**: 9

Penobscot, USS, **II**: 68, 89, 104, 107; **III**: 114, 168; **IV**: 24, 25, 88; **V**: 39

Penrose, Charles B., Captain, USA, **V**: 78

Pensacola, USS, **II**: 7, 39, 47, 55, *99*; **III**: 26, 121; **VI**: 58

Pensacola (and Bay), Fla., **I**: 2, 4, 6–7, 16, 26, 37; **II**: 32, 40, 53, 93, 104, 109, 110; **III**: 26, 72, 81, 140, 155; **IV**: 93, 136; **V**: 118; **VI**: *55*, 206, 227; Navy Yard, *55*

Peosta, USS, **III**: 151; **IV**: 34, 43

Pepper Creek, Va., **III**: 99

Pequot, USS, **IV**: 27, 58, 89, 139; **V**: 22; **VI**: 222

Percussion caps, cargoes of, captured, **II**: 68; **III**: 160; **IV**: 31, 44; **V**: 64; **VI**: 221

Perdido River, W. Fla./Ala., **III**: 155; **VI**: 221

Periscope, pioneer use of, **IV**: 41

Perkins, George H., Lt. Commander, **III**: 111, 114, 168; **IV**: 11, 37, 97, 98

Perkins, James F., Acting Ensign, **III**: 62; **VI**: 202

Perkins Landing, Miss., **III**: 88

Pernambuco (Recife), Brazil, **VI**: 249

Perquimans River, N.C., **III**: 18; **V**: 10

Perry, USS, **I**: 15; **III**: 75, 160; **VI**: 259

Perry, William, Conf. privateermaster, **VI**: 281

Perryville, Md., **I**: 9

Persis, b.r. sloop, **IV**: 32

Rappahannock, CSS, **IV:** 4, 5, 24, 25, 38, 52, 89, 93; **VI:** 238, 290-91

Rappahannock River, Va., **I:** 17, 20, 23; **II:** 50, 51, 104, 116; **III:** 5, 13, 32, 85, 89, 114, 115, 132, 133, 149; **IV:** 5, 30, 44, 50, 64, 114; **V:** 8, 61, 64, 122

Raritan, USS, **I:** 9

Ratliff's Landing, Miss., **IV:** 61, 74

Rattler, USS (ex-*Florence Miller*), **III:** 5, 7, 8, 24, 41, 75, 115, 140, 151

Rattlesnake, Conf. privateer (ex-CSS *Nashville*, q.v., ex-*Thomas L. Wragg*), **III:** 35-36; **VI:** 329

Rattlesnake Shoals, S.C., **IV:** 109

Raven, Conf. Volunteer C.G. yawl, **VI:** 291

Rawlins, John A., Assistant Adjutant General, USA, **III:** 6

Rawson, Rawson W., Governor of Bermuda, **V:** 59

Read, Abner, Commander, **I:** 37, 38, 39, 40; **II:** 25, 40, 68; **III:** 57, 67, 111

Read, Charles W., Lieut., CSN, **III:** 77, 91, *92*, 93, 94, 97, 98, 99, 101, 113, 118; **IV:** 23, 104; **V:** 16, 18, 36, 72, 92, 118; **VI:** 207, 212, 229, 309

Read, Frederick, Acting Master, **IV:** 43

Reagan, John, Conf. Acting Secretary of the Treasury, **V:** 96

Rebecca, b.r. schnr., **II:** 67

Rebecca, L., b.r. sloop; see *L. Rebecca*

Rebekah, b.r. schnr., **III:** 96

Rebel, C.S. transport, **VI:** 291

Red River, La., Union blockade of, **II:** 89, 110; **III:** 21, 26-27, 29, 31, 34, 36, 48, 49, 52, 55, 77, 82; **IV:** 7; Union expedition up, **IV:** 12, 23, 25, 26, 27, 29, 30, 31, 32, 33, 34, 36, 37, 39, 40, 41, 43, 48, 49, 50, 51, 52-53, 56, 59, 60, 61, 63; **VI:** 5; mentioned, **III:** 18, 66, 70, 75, 90, 120, 141, 145; **IV:** 106; **V:** 72, 91, 103, 105; **VI:** 189, 197-98, 204, 217, 222-23, 225, 230

Red Rover, CSS, **II:** 46; **VI:** 291-92; as USS, first hospital ship, **II:** *46*-47; **III:** 38; **VI:** 291-92

Reed, J. Frank, Acting Master, **III:** 106

Reed, John H., Lieut., **V:** 78

Reed, Louisa, Am. schnr.; see: *Louisa Reed*

Reed's Ferry, Va., **III:** 68

Reid, Conf. shipmaster, **VI:** 265

Reid, E. C., Conf. shipmaster, **VI:** 306

Reilly, James, Major, CSA, **V:** 13

Reilly, Thomas, b.r. sloop; see: *Thomas Reilly*

Reindeer, b.r. schnr., **I:** 28

Reindeer, b.r. sloop, **II:** 51

Reindeer, b.r. schnr., **II:** 80; as U.S. schnr., **II:** 92

Reindeer, b.r. schnr., **II:** 98

Reindeer, USS (ex-*Rachel Miller*), **III:** 112, 167; **IV:** 139

Relampago, Spanish b.r. sloop, **III:** 38, 115

Release, USS, **I:** 23, **V:** 113

Reliance, USS, **I:** 17, 18, 20; **II:** 105, 111; **III:** 132, 133; as Conf. stmr., **VI:** 292

Reliance, b.r. stmr., **II:** 85

Reliance, b.r. sloop, **IV:** 132

Reliance, Conf. ship, **VI:** 332

Relief, U.S. storeship, **V:** 121

Relyea, C. J., Conf. shipmaster, **VI:** 286

Remittance, Conf. schnr., **I:** 23

Reneau, N. S., Conf. ship buying agent, **VI:** 270

Renfrew, Scotland, **VI:** 215

Renshaw, Francis B., Lieut., **VI:** 254

Renshaw, Richard T., Acting Lieut., **II:** 96, 108

Renshaw, William B., Commander, **II:** 100-01; **III:** 3

Republic, C.S. transport stmr., **III:** 84; **VI:** 292

Republic, USS (later USS *Peony*, q.v.), **V:** 66

Rescue, Conf. privateer schnr., **VI:** 329

Rescue, USS, **I:** 27, 31, 34

Reserve, b.r. schnr., **III:** 149

Resolute, USS, **I:** 15, 16, 17, 19, 20, 22; **II:** 90, 108; **III:** 118; **V:** 64; **VI:** 19

Resolute, CSS, **I:** 40; **III:** 95, 153; **IV:** 145; **VI:** 259, 292-93, 298

Resolute, CSS, **II:** 54; **VI:** 292, 330

Resolute, b.r. sloop, **IV:** 60

Restless, USS, **II:** 22, 41, 42, 57, 80, 85, 95, 103; **III:** 112, 131, 160, 163, 165; **IV:** 11, 118

Restless, Am. schnr., **IV:** 105

Retribution, Conf. privateer, **III:** 5, 8, 20, 32, 162-63; **VI:** 210, 318

Revenge, b.r. schnr., **III:** 119

Revenue Marine, U.S., **I:** 2, 4, 5, 6, 15, 23, 37; **III:** 93, 101, 104; **IV:** 15, 37; **VI:** 207, 222

Revere, British b.r. schnr., **I:** 26

Reynolds, Alfred H., Acting Ensign, **II:** 112

Reynolds, John G., Major, USMC, **I:** 20, 31

Reynoldsburg Island, Tenn., **IV:** 129-31

Rhett, Alfred, Colonel, CSA, **III:** 59; **VI:** 308

Rhind, Alexander C., Commander, **II:** 57, 71; **III:** 58; **IV:** 147, 149; **V:** 60, 69

Rhoda H. Shannon, Am. schnr., **I:** 6

Rhode Island, USS (ex-*Eagle*, ex-*John P. King*), **I:** 30, 39; **II:** 80; **III:** 88, 129; **IV:** 139; **V:** 130, 132

Rice cargoes captured or destroyed, **I:** 29, 31; **II:** 22, 41, 42, 51, 63, 70, 71, 111; **III:** 70, 122, 167; **IV:** 47, 151; **V:** 46; **VI:** 208

Riceboro River, Ga., **II:** 57

Rich, Abraham, Jr., Acting Ensign, **IV:** 138

Rich, Albert F., Acting Master's Mate, **IV:** 151

Rich Inlet, N. C., **VI:** 282

Richard, b.r. sloop, **III:** 135

Richard Vaux, b.r. sloop, **III:** 97

Richards, b.r. sloop, **III:** 21

Richards, Am. brig, **IV:** 103

Richardson, J. E., Acting Lieut., **IV:** 29, 61

Richardson's shipyard, Middlesbrough, Yorkshire, England, **VI:** 249

Richmond, USS, **I:** 29, 37; **II:** 53, 55, 72, 114; **III:** 26, 36, 41, 44-45, 50, 62, 78, 86, 100, 105, 112; **IV:** 63, 95; **V:** 92; **VI:** 56-60, 62, 72, 80, 92

Richmond, CSS, **IV:** 82, 104, 105; **V:** 26, 45, 76, 79; **VI:** 198, 223, 293

Richmond, Va., Union plans and attempts to capture, **II:** 37, 42, 63, 64, 75; **III:** 115; **IV:** 115, 137; **V:** 13, 31, 53, 71, 73, 75 (see also, James River Squadron, C.S.); Conf. defenses, **II:** 38, 71; **III:** 105, 131, 159; **IV:** 63, *66*, 82, 105, 123; **V:** 3, 6, 16-18, 22, 25-26, 36-37, 49, 54, 67; Conf. evacuation of, **V:** 76, 78-79; **VI:** 6; mentioned, **I:** 9, 11, 17; **II:** 95, 101, 105; **III:** 9, 18, 115, 132, 136, 141, 156, 159; **IV:** 23, 43, 56, 86, 102, 109, 133, 145; **V:** 46, 55, 102, 108; **VI:** 204, 229-30

Richmond (Va.), *Daily Dispatch*, **V:** 54; **VI:** 257, 301

Richmond (Va.), *Daily Examiner*, **V:** 54

Richmond (Va.), *Enquirer*, **II:** 89; **IV:** 7

Richmond (Va.), *Globe*, **VI:** 196

Richmond (Va.), *Sentinel*, **III:** 137

Richmond (Va.), *Whig*, **III:** 59

Rowan, Stephen C., Commo. **I:** 1, 13, 15, 17, 26; **II:** 8, 20, 24, 33, 67, 81; **III:** 58, 131, 133, 137, 143; **IV:** 34, 35; **VI:** *12*, 19, 230

Rowe, W., British shipmaster, **VI:** 202

Rowena, Am. vessel, **VI:** 221

Rowena, b.r. schnr., **II:** 68

Rowena, Conf. transport stmr., **III:** 29

Rowe's Landing, La., **IV:** 109

Royal I., Bahamas, **IV:** 12

Royal Yacht, Conf. armed schnr., **I:** 34; **III:** 67, **VI:** 235, 295–96, 331

Rubber boats, **IV:** 86, 124; **V:** 10

Ruby, b.r. stmr., **V:** 49

Ruby, b.r. stmr., **VI:** 296

Rude, William R., Acting Ensign, **III:** 83

Russell, James J., Acting Ensign, **III:** 112; **IV:** 11, 63, 86, 112; **V:** 20, 56

Russell, Lord John, British Foreign Minister, **III:** 114, 119; **IV:** 5; **V:** 22; **VI:** 216

Russell, John H., Lt. Commander, **II:** 55; **III:** 77, 118

Russia, Am. stmr., **V:** 65

Russia, **III:** 5, 83, 84, 94; **V:** 123; **VI:** 195

Ruthven, A. S., Conf. stmr.; see: *A. S. Ruthven*

Rutledge, John, Lieut., CSN **III:** 18–19; **VI:** 259, 275

Ryan, Ann, b.r. schnr.; see: *Ann Ryan*

S. Gildersleeve, Am. ship, **III:** 86

S. H. Poole, Am. schnr., **II:** 108

S. J. Waring, Am. schnr., **I:** 18, 19

S. S. Jones, b.r. schnr., **II:** 90

S. T. Garrison, b.r. schnr., **I:** 28

Saber cargoes captured or destroyed, **V:** 42, 55

Sabine, USS, **I:** 7, 31

Sabine City, Tex., **II:** 92, 98, 101; **III:** 67; **VI:** 318

Sabine Crossroads, La., **IV:** 40

Sabine Lake, Tex., **VI:** 242, 257, 308

Sabine Pass, Tex., capture of b.r.'s at or near, **I:** 40; **II:** 75, 76, 91, 101, 105; **III:** 57, 97, 119; Conf. evacuation of, **II:** 98–99; capture of Union blockaders at and Conf. reoccupation of, **III:** 13; Union attempt to recapture, **III:** 136, 137, 138; Conf. ships at, **III:** 150; Union reoccupies, **V:** 102; mentioned, **II:** 103, 105; **III:** 141; **IV:** 33, 57; **V:** 104; **VI:** 3, 199, 213, 229

Sachem, USS, **II:** 29, 92, 112; **III:** 2, 121, 136, 137, 138; as CSS, **III:** 150; **VI:** 229, 296, 331

Sacramento, USS, **III:** 75; **IV:** 10, 89; **V:** 33, 65, 67, 115, 120; **VI:** 250

Saffold, Ga., **VI:** 186, 208

Sagamore, USS, **II:** 42, 97, 112; **III:** 6, 7, 17, 39, 72, 100, 121, 126, 153; **IV:** 36, 47, 70; **VI:** 250

Saginaw, USS, **IV:** 19; **V:** 115

Saginaw, Mich., **VI:** 240

Sailor's Creek, Va., **V:** 78

St. Andrew's, Fla., **III:** 163; **VI:** 227

St. Andrew's Bay, Fla., **II:** 29, 97; **III:** 163, 165; **IV:** 11, 118, 138; **V:** 31

St. Andrew's Sound, Ga., **II:** 99; **III:** 147

St. Augustine, Fla., **I:** 22; **II:** 32; **IV:** 48; **VI:** 256

St. Augustine Creek, Fla., **VI:** 252

St. Augustine Inlet, Fla., **III:** 149

St. Catherine's Sound, Ga., **III:** 131; **IV:** 10

St. Charles, USS (later USS *Paw Paw*, q.v.), **II:** 90

St. Charles, White River, Ark., **II:** 70, 74; **III:** 9–10; **IV:** 85; **VI:** 224

St. Charles River, Ark., **III:** 8

St. Clair, USS, **III:** 20, 23, 57; **IV:** 60

St. Francis No. 3, C.S. stmr., **VI:** 296

St. George, b.r. schnr., **III:** 70

St. Georges, Bermuda, **IV:** 59; **V:** 97; **VI:** 211, 335

St. George's Channel, British Isles, **V:** 129

St. George's I., Md, **III:** 157

St. George's Sound, Fla., **IV:** 132, 143

St. Helena, Conf. stmr., **VI:** 225

St. Helena Sound, S.C., **I:** 29; **III:** 79; **IV:** 36

St. Ives, Cornwall, England, **VI:** 215

St. James Parish, La., **VI:** 324

St. Jerome's Creek, Md., **II:** 110

St. John, N.B., Canada, **III:** 162; **VI:** 209

St. Johns, b.r. stmr., **III:** 67

St. John's Bluff, Fla., **II:** 97, 100, 102

St. John's River, Fla., **I:** 39; **II:** 27, 42, 100, 102; **III:** 39; **IV:** 14, 32, 37, 48, 59

St. Joseph, La., **II:** 57

St. Joseph's (and Bay), Fla., **II:** 45, 97; **III:** 7, 49, 75, 168; **VI:** 227

St. Joseph's I., Tex., **III:** 77

St. Lawrence, USS, **I:** 19, 20, *21*, 31

St. Lawrence, Gulf of, Canada, **IV:** 70, 106; **VI:** 203

St. Lawrence Island, Bering Sea, **V:** 109, 115

St. Louis, USS (later USS *Baron de Kalb*, q.v.), **I:** 22; **II:** 6, 7, 17, 22, 37, 42, 68, 70, 93

St. Louis, USS, **III:** 143; **IV:** 11, 26

St. Louis, Mo., **I:** 22; **II:** 16, 17, 40, 41; **III:** 117, 122, 157; **V:** 128; **VI:** 212, 223, 226

St. Mark's (and River), Fla., **II:** 28, 69, 116; **III:** 54, 90, 95, 128; **IV:** 21, 24, 51; **V:** 32, 49, 56, 73, 102; **VI:** 303

St. Mark's Fort, Fla., **V:** 56

St. Martin's Reef, Fla., **III:** 124

St. Mary, Conf. armed river stmr. (later USS *Alexandria*), **III:** 115; **VI:** 296

St. Mary's, Conf. b.r. stmr., **IV:** 15; **VI:** 254

St. Mary's, Conf. privateer schnr., **V:** 73, 91, 108; **VI:** 329

St. Mary's (and River), Fla., **II:** 28; **IV:** 21; **VI:** 205

St. Mary's, Chesapeake Bay, Md., **V:** 61, 73

St. Nicholas, Am. passenger stmr., **I:** 18; **VI:** 290

St. Patrick, C.S. torpedo boat, **IV:** 42, 74–75, 134, 140; **V:** 30; **VI:** 296

St. Petersburg, Fla., **III:** 21, 83, 147

St. Philip, CSS (ex-*Star of the West*, ex-*San Juan*), **III:** 41; **VI:** 235, 296–97

St. Pierre, Emily, British b.r. ship; see: *Emily St. Pierre*

St. Pierre, Martinique, **VI:** 306

St. Simon's I., Ga., **II:** 21, 31; **III:** 147

St. Simon's Sound, Ga., **I:** 38; **II:** 93

St. Thomas I., V.I., **III:** 35, 53

Sakhalin Peninsula, Siberia, **V:** 102

Sallie, Conf. privateer schnr., **I:** 29, 30; **VI:** 329

Sallie, British b.r. schnr., **III:** 166

Sallie Robinson, USS, **II:** 90

Sallie Wood, Conf. river transport, **II:** 20; **VI:** 297; as USS, **II:** 85

Sally, b.r. schnr., **III:** 119

Sally Magee, b.r. bark, **I:** 17

Sally Mears, b.r. schnr., **I:** 18

Smith, Charles F., Brig. General, **II:** 9, 16, 36

Smith, Edmund Kirby, General, CSA, **III:** 90, 127; **IV:** 2, 33, 80–81, 106; **V:** 72, 91, 103, 104; **VI:** 276

Smith & Co. (Elliot,), Kinston, N.C., **VI:** 185

Smith, Eugenie, British b.r. schnr.; see: *Eugenie Smith*

Smith, Francis W., Major, CSA, **IV:** 138

Smith, George, Conf. schnr.; see: *George Smith*

Smith, Isaac, USS; see: *Isaac Smith*, USS

Smith, J. Adams, Paymaster, **IV:** 73

Smith, J. B., Conf. shipmaster, **VI:** 232

Smith, J. P., b.r. stmr.; see: *J. P. Smith*

Smith, J. W., Acting Lieut., **III:** 128, 143, 155

Smith, Joseph, Commodore, **I:** 21

Smith, Leon, Colonel, CSA, **III:** 3, 150; **VI:** 229

Smith, Marshall, b.r. schnr.; see: *Marshall Smith*

Smith, Martin L., Brig. General, CSA, **III:** 104

Smith, Melancton, Captain, **I:** 16, 17, 19, 22; **II:** 47, 55; **III:** 45; **IV:** 54, 62, 86, 105, *123*; **VI:** 300

Smith, R. L., Captain, CSA, **VI:** 288

Smith, Robert B., Acting Lieut., **IV:** 40, 123, 133, 139

Smith, Thomas E., Acting Lieut., **III:** 18, 83, 88; **IV:** 34

Smith, Thomas K., Brig. General, USA, **IV:** 37, 40, 41, 63

Smith, W. H., b.r. stmr.; see: *W. H. Smith*

Smith, Washington, Conf. shipowner, **VI:** 332

Smith, Watson, Lt. Commander, **III:** 7, 8, 24, 27, 29, 32, 34, 38, 41

Smith, William, Commander, **II:** 5, 57, 61

Smith, William W., Conf. prizemaster & Savannah pilot, **VI:** 256

Smith Briggs, USA gunboat, **III:** 90, 98; **IV:** 12

Smithfield, Ky., **III:** 23, 25

Smithfield, Tex., **VI:** 268

Smithfield, Va., **IV:** 12, 43, 142

Smithland, Ky., **I:** 26; **II:** 14, 16; **III:** 6, 20

Smith's I., N.C., **III:** 114; **V:** 16

Smith's Landing, Tex., **IV:** 11

Smith's Mill, Fish River, Ala., **IV:** 111

Smith's Point, Chesapeake Bay, Va., **IV:** 90; **V:** 39

Smithville, N.C., **III:** 158; **IV:** 25, 115; **V:** 16, 21, 39; **VI:** 277

Smoot, G. H., b.r. schnr.; see: *G. H. Smoot*

Snead, Claiborne, Colonel, CSA, **I:** 28

Snell, Alfred T., Captain, **II:** 108

Snipe, CSN b.r. stmr., **VI:** 188, 302–03

Snow, Jabez, Am. collier; see: *Jabez Snow*

Snyder's Bluff, Miss., **III:** 82

Soap cargoes captured, **III:** 53, 147; **IV:** 42, 86

Soda cargoes captured, **III:** 93, 114, 115, 149; **IV:** 10, 143

Soledad Cos, b.r. schnr., **I:** 26

Somerset, Conf. schnr., **I:** 16

Somerset, USS, **II:** 31, 57, 68, 69, 70, 101; **III:** 116; **IV:** 59; **VI:** 208

Somerset, Ky., **III:** 12

Somerville, Ala., **V:** 20

Sommers, Rudolph S., Acting Ensign, **IV:** 122–23

Sonoma, USS, **II:** 97; **III:** 12, 23, 29, 66, 86, 146; **V:** 27, 36, 39, 53; **VI:** 249

Sonora, Am. ship, **III:** 167

Sonora, b.r. stmr., **V:** 105

Sophia, British b.r. bark, **II:** 108

Sophia, British b.r. schnr., **IV:** 27

Sophia, Anne, Conf. schnr., see: *Anne Sophia*

Sophia, Annie, b.r. schnr.; see: *Annie Sophia*

Sophia Thornton, Am. whaling bark, **V:** 108

Sophronia, U.S. mortar schnr., **III:** 83

Sort, British b.r. schnr., **IV:** 145; **V:** 53

South America, **I:** 27

South Atlantic Blockading Squadron, **I:** 27, 31; **II:** 12, 100, 111; **III:** 60, 98, 99, 110, 111, 145, 152; **IV:** 2, 85, 98, 123, 136, 138; **V:** 27, 39, 94, 103, 108

South Atlantic Squadron, **V:** 83, 103, 124

South Carolina, USS, **I:** 18, 19, 21, 26, 28, 29, 39; **II:** 24, 75, 94; **III:** 54; **IV:** 42

South Edisto River, S.C., **II:** 95; **IV:** 62

South Newport River, Ga., **IV:** 105

South River, Md., **IV:** 89

South Santee River, S.C., **II:** 68; **IV:** 35

Southampton, England, **II:** 14, 17; **IV:** 78; **V:** 34

Southeast Pass, Mississippi River entrance, **II:** 25

Southern Belle, b.r. schnr., **II:** 71

Southern Cross, Am. ship, **III:** 91

Southern Independence, b.r. schnr., **II:** 47

Southern Methodist, b.r. stmr., **II:** 112

Southern Rights, British b.r. schnr., **III:** 126

Southern Star, Conf. schnr., **VI:** 333

Southern Star, b.r. sloop, **III:** 124

Southern S.S. Co. (Morgan Line), New Orleans, **VI:** 197, 198, 201, 202, 220, 227, 231, 268, 273, 278, 318, 320, 323, 324

Southerner, b.r. schnr., **II:** 98

Southfield, USS, **II:** 6, 78, 113; **IV:** 26, 44, 45, 121; **VI:** 101, 193, 217; as CSS, **IV:** 124, 127

Southside R.R., Va., **V:** 3

Southwest Pass, Mississippi River entrance, **I:** 15, 28 29; **II:** 30, 63, 141; **V:** 92; **VI:** 207

Sovereign, b.r. river stmr., **II:** 68; **VI:** 303

Spain, **I:** 18; **II:** 8, 15; **III:** 38, 83, 157; **V:** 59

Spangler, Edward, **V:** 90, 95

Spanish Fort, Ala., **V:** 69, 79, 81, 83

Spanish River, Ala., **V:** 83; **VI:** 218, 251, 318

Spar-torpedoes, described, **V:** 91; mentioned, **I:** 17; **II:** 91, *106*; **III:** 2, 63, 124, 131, 133, 143–44, 151, 153; **IV:** 39, 63, 86, 89, 91, 124–26; **V:** 30, 33, 92, 109; **VI:** 187, 218, 244

Spaulding, b.r. stmr., **III:** 147

Spaulding's, Sapelo River, Ga., **II:** 108

Specie, Conf. schnr., **I:** 29

Speedwell, Am. bark, **V:** 129

Spicer, William F., Commander, **IV:** 15; **V:** 60, 64, 66

Spirit ration; see: Liquor

Spitfire, Conf. schnr., **II:** 23

Spitfire, U.S. tug (later USS *Hyacinth*), **II:** 69

Spokane, Am. ship, **IV:** 104

Sponges, cargo of, captured, **III:** 10

Spotswood, Charles F. M., Commander, CSN, **III:** 66

Spotswood, Dr. W. A. W., Surgeon-in-Chief, CSN, **IV:** 129

Spotts, James H., Commander, **I:** 38; **III:** 168

Sprague, John T., Colonel, USA, **V:** 91

Spray, CSS, **V:** 102; **VI:** 303

Spring Creek, N.C., **III:** 97

Springbok, British b.r. bark, **III:** 23

Springfield, USS (ex-*W. A. Healy*), **III:** 57, 111–12

Springfield Landing, La., **III:** 92; **IV:** 39

Taylor, George, Acting Lieut., **IV:** 140

Taylor, Richard, Lt. General, CSA, **IV:** 2, 7, 48, 50, 61, 106; **VI:** 323

Taylor, William R., Captain, **III:** 19, 68

Taylor's Bayou, Tex., **II:** 98, 103

Tchefuncta River, La., **IV:** 61

Tchula Lake, Miss., **VI:** 205

Tea cargoes captured, **III:** 27, 71, 165

Teaser, Conf. sloop, **I:** 18

Teaser, CSS, **I:** 17, 24; **II:** 26, 71, 76, 77; **VI:** 311; as USS, **II:** 108; **VI:** 9, 21

Teaser, CSS, **III:** 141; **VI:** 311

Technicians, Conf. shortage of, **III:** 115

Tecumseh, USS, **IV:** 82, 93, 95, *96*, 109, 112; **V:** 81; **VI:** 78, 80, 90–97

Tees, Jacob, Philadelphia shipbuilder, **VI:** 223

Telegraph, British b.r. schnr., **I:** 38

Telegraph, b.r. schnr., **III:** 122

Telemico, b.r. sloop, **V:** 64

Tempest, USS, **V:** 123

Teneriffe, Canary Islands, **V:** 67, 95, 98; **VI:** 229, 241

Tennessee, CSS, **II:** 56; **VI:** 311–12

Tennessee, CSS, *xxi*; **III:** 134, 160, 165, 166, **IV:** 2, 7, 10, 27, *58*, 59, 61, 83, 84, 89, 95–97, *98*; **VI:** 312; as USS, **IV:** 99, 100, 104, 112; **VI:** 66, 81, 83, 90, *90*, 95, 96, 196, 221

Tennessee, C.S. Govt. b.r. stmr., **VI:** 312–13; as USS (later USS *Mobile*), **II:** 93; **III:** 148; **VI:** 53, 57, 61, 65, 70, 71, 74, 78, 80

Tennessee Iron Works, **II:** 23

Tennessee River, **I:** 23, 26; **II:** 5, 7, 9, 14, 16, 17, 18, *19*, 26, 27, 32, 36, 42, 51, 75, 95; **III:** 6, 7, 17, 20, 39, 66, 79, *80*, 105, 145, 149, 151, 152, 160; **IV:** 34, 42, 44, 48, 90, 120, 121, 126, 127, 129, 131, 138, 149, 151; **V:** 22, 55, 56; **VI:** 2, 196, 223, 226

Tensas Bayou, Ala., **III:** 18

Tensas River, La., **III:** 115; **V:** 83; **VI:** 224

Terceira I., Azores, **II:** 93; **III:** 114; **VI:** 190–91

Teresa, British b.r. schnr., **III:** 67

Teresita, b.r. bark, **II:** 14

Teresita, Spanish b.r. bark, **III:** 157

Terrapin, British b.r. schnr., **IV:** 87

Terrapin Point, Va., **IV:** 17

Terry, Alfred H., Major General, USA, **III:** 116; **V:** 6, 10, 11, 13, 16, 47, 59; **VI:** 6

Terry, Edward, Lt. Commander, **III:** 86, 100

Terry, W. B., Conf. stmr.; see: *W. B. Terry*

Tessier, Eugene L., Conf. shipmaster, **VI:** 202, 205, 209

Texan Star, Am. bark (also *Martaban*), **III:** 167

Texana, Am. bark, **III:** 91; **VI:** 206

Texas, CSS, **V:** 78; **VI:** 312, 313, 314–15

Texas, Conf. transport, **VI:** 313

Texas, Conf. privateer stmr., **VI:** 313, 329

Texas, CSS, **VI:** 313–14

Texas, CSS (also known as *Canton*, launched as *Pampero*), **VI:** 314

Texas, CSS, **VI:** 314–15

Texas Marine Department, **III:** 150; **VI:** 330–31

Thacher, Oliver, Acting Master, **IV:** 145

Thames River, England, **IV:** 93; **VI:** 187, 290, 309

Thatcher, Henry K., Rear Admiral, **II:** 107; **IV:** 4; **V:** 11, 26, 37, 49, 61, 64, 79, 81, 83, 84–85, 95, 97, 99, 101, 102, 103, 104, 111, 112, 115, 118, 122; **VI:** 244

Theodora, CSS (ex-*Gordon*, ex-*Carolina*), **I:** 29; **VI:** 315

Theodore Stoney, Conf. schnr., **II:** 22

Theresa, b.r. schnr., **II:** 95

Theresa C., b.r. schnr., **I:** 12

Theresa, Empress, Am. bark; see: *Empress Theresa*

Thirty-fifth Parallel, CSS, **III:** 41, 47, 115; **VI:** 315

Thistle, b.r. stmr. (later USS *Dumbarton*, q.v.), **IV:** 70; **VI:** 345

Thomas, Conf. shipowner, **VI:** 332

Thomas, General, USS; see: *General Thomas*, USS

Thomas, George H., Major General, USA, **IV:** 121, 139, 146, 151; **V:** 87

Thomas, Joel and William, Conf. shipowners, **VI:** 332

Thomas, Nathaniel W., Lieut., **III:** 45

Thomas, Richard, Colonel, CSA, **I:** 18; **VI:** 290

Thomas, William, Pilot, CSN, **VI:** 226

Thomas B. Wales, Am. ship; see: *T. B. Wales*

Thomas Colyer, Conf. stmr., **I:** 15; as USA stmr., **IV:** 92

Thomas Freeborn (or *Freeborn*), USS, **I:** 11, 14, 15, 17, 21; **II:** 88, 97, 100, 101, 107; **III:** 32, 141; **IV:** 50, 114; **VI:** 19, 196

Thomas Jefferson; see: *Jamestown*, CSS

Thomas L. Wragg, b.r. stmr.; see: *Nashville*, CSS

Thomas Reilly, b.r. sloop; **II:** 100

Thomas Watson, b.r. bark, **I:** 29

Thompson, A. B., Am. ship; see: *A. B. Thompson*

Thompson, A. W., b.r. schnr.; see: *A. W. Thompson*

Thompson, Annie, b.r. sloop; see: *Annie Thompson*

Thompson, Augustus F., Acting Master, **III:** 124; **IV:** 129

Thompson, Egbert, Lieut., **II:** 46, 95

Thompson, General M. Jeff, CSS; see: *General M. Jeff Thompson*

Thompson, Jacob, Colonel, CSA, **IV:** 48–49, 112, 131; **VI:** 238, 240

Thompson, James F., Acting Ensign, **V:** 73

Thompson, John, Conf. sloop; see: *John Thompson*

Thompson, M. Jeff, Brig. General, Mo. State Guard (Conf.), **VI:** 232, 262

Thompson, Mary E., Am. brig; see: *Mary E. Thompson*

Thompson, W. Bevershaw, Major, CSA, **VI:** 227

Thompson, William, Am. whaler; see: *William Thompson*

Thomson, James & George, Glasgow shipbuilders, **VI:** 186–87, 314

Thorn, USA transport stmr., **V:** 56

Thornton, Sophia, Am. whaler; see: *Sophia Thornton*

Three Brothers, b.r. schnr., **III:** 129

Three Brothers, b.r. stmr., **III:** 149

Three Brothers, b.r. schnr., **IV:** 40

Three Marys (ex-Conf. stmr. *Granite City*), **VI:** 243

Thunderbolt, Ga., **III:** 21

Thurston, David, U.S. Vice-Consul General, Montreal, **VI:** 238

Tibbits, Howard, Acting Master, **III:** 136

Ticonderoga, USS, **IV:** 70

Tierra del Fuego, Argentina/Chile, **IV:** 37

Tift, Nelson & Asa F., Savannah shipbuilders, **VI:** 185, 201, 271

Tigress, USA stmr., **III:** 70

Tilford, Robert H., Acting Master, CSN, **VI:** 260

Tilghman, Lloyd, Brig. General, CSA, **II:** 17; **VI:** 223

Tilghman, William, Seaman, **I:** 19

Tillson, Myron W., Acting Ensign, **III:** 148

Tilton, McClain, Lieut., USMC, **II:** 93

Timbalier Lighthouse, La., **I:** 39

Time, b.r. schnr., **III:** 16

Time, Conf. transport stmr., **VI:** 316

Timmonds, R. H., Acting Master, **III:** 72

Tindall, British shipbuilders, Scarborough, **VI:** 190

Tindel, James M., Conf. agent, **III:** 105

Vigilant, Am. ship, **I**: 38

Villeroy, Brutus de; see: De Villeroy, Brutus

Vincennes, USS, **I**: 29, 38; **III**: 118

Vincent's Creek, Morris I., S.C., **III**: 123, 136

Vindicator, USS, **IV**: 30, 137

Violet, USS (ex-Am. stmr. *Martha*), **III**: 161; **IV**: 98

Virdon, Annie, British b.r. schnr.; see: *Annie Virdon*

Virgin, b.r. stmr., **IV**: 87; **VI**: 75

Virginia, CSS (ex-*Merrimack*, q.v.), design ordered, **I**: 16; reconstruction begun, **I**: 17; commissioned, **II**: 23; first attack on Union ships, **II**: 29; engages *Monitor*, **II**: 30–31; in James River, **II**: 40, 42, 47, 61; destroyed, **II**: 62–63, 71, 85; **VI**: 3; mentioned, **II**: 5, 20, 24, 26, 27, 57, 81, 90–91, 112, 116; **III**: 7; **IV**: 15, 30, 46; **VI**: 2, 204, 238, 320–21, *371*

Virginia (II), CSS, **II**: 97; **IV**: 56, 63, 82, 104, 105; **V**: 26, 45; **VI**: 238, 321

Virginia, Am. whaler, **II**: 98

Virginia, Conf. b.r. stmr. (ex-*Noe-Daquy*, Spanish stmr.), **III**: 12; as USS, **III**: 145, 150, 151, 152; **IV**: 19, 23, 25, 30, 31, 41, 44, 51

Virginia, Conf. ship, **VI**: 333

Virginia, CSS; see: CSS *Georgia* (cruiser)

Virginia, Governor of; see: Fletcher, John

Virginia Navy, **I**: 12; **VI**: 200, 224

Vista, b.r. schnr., **III**: 36

Vixen, U.S. Coast Survey ship (later USS), **I**: 31

Vixen, British b.r. stmr., **IV**: 139

Vogdes, Israel, Captain, USA, **I**: 7

Volante, British b.r. schnr., **II**: 76

Volante, British b.r. brig, **III**: 152

Volante, British b.r. schnr., **III**: 153

Volunteer, CSA river transport (later U.S.), **III**: 159; **VI**: 321

Voorhees, L.D.D., Lieut., **V**: 97

W. A. Knapp, b.r. river stmr., **III**: 23

W. B. Nash, Am. brig, **III**: 112

W. B. Terry, Conf. stmr., **I**: 23; as U.S. transport, **II**: 95

W. Burton, C.S. steam tender (also *Burton*, or *William Burton*; later, USA transport), **II**: 54; **VI**: 321–22

W. C. Clarke, Am. brig, **IV**: 75

W. F. Harris, b.r. schnr., **II**: 67

W. H. Smith, b.r. stmr., **VI**: 254

W. W. Crawford, Conf. river stmr., **VI**: 322

W. Y. Leitch, British b.r. schnr. (ex-*Charleston Pilot Boat #2*), **III**: 68

Wabash, USS, **I**: 21, 23, 30–31; **II**: 32, 104; **III**: 124, 128; **IV**: 46, 151; **V**: 65; **VI**: 107, 219, 221, 258

Waccamaw River, S.C., **V**: 67

Waccasassa Bay, Fla., **III**: 85; **VI**: 252

Waccasassa River, Fla., **III**: 57, 128

Wachapreague Inlet, Va., **III**: 140; **VI**: 196

Wachusett, USS, **II**: 57, 61, 79, 97; **III**: 12, 53; **IV**: *117*–18, 133; **V**: 67, 121–22; **VI**: 229

Waddell, James I., Lieut., CSN, takes command of *Shenandoah*, **IV**: 121; **VI**: 6; mentioned as her commander, **IV**: 119, 127, 131–32, 133, 140, 151; **V**: 27, 45, 73, 83, 87, 95, 98–99, 100, 102, 103–04, 106, 107–08, 109, 110–11, 115, 118, 120, 122, 123, 126, 127–28, 130; **VI**: 7

Wade, Henry C., Acting Master, **IV**: 10

Wade, Thomas, Acting Lieut., **IV**: 56

Wade, William, Colonel, CSA, **III**: 72

Wade Water Belle, Conf. river stmr., **VI**: 322

Wade's Bay, E. Shore, Potomac River, Md., **IV**: 124

Wadmalaw River, S.C., **II**: 71

Wagner, T. D., Am. brig; see: *T. D. Wagner*

Wainwright, Jonathan M., Commander, **II**: 26; **III**: 3; **VI**: 248

Wainwright, Richard, Commander, **II**: 55

Wales, T. B., Am. ship; see: *T. B. Wales*

Walke, Henry, Captain, **I**:1, 28; **II**: 42, 44, 45, 46, 113; **III**: 49, 52, 67; **IV**: 10; **V**: 65, 115, 128; **VI**: 199

Walker, Conf. b.r. master, **VI**: 315

Walker, Edward A., Midshipman, **I**: 27

Walker, John G., Major General, CSA, **III**: 91; **IV**: 116

Walker, John G., Lt. Commander, **II**: 112; **III**: 9, 11, 27, 41, 82, 84, 85, 114; **V**: 37

Walker, John T., Lieut., CSN, **IV**: 140; **V**: 30; **VI**: 296

Walker, Norman S., Major, CSA, **VI**: 324

Walker, William M., Captain, **II**: 75; **III**: 71, 72, 81, 82, 83, 111, 118, 129, 140, 141; **IV**: 61; **VI**: 62, 311

Walker, William S., Captain, **I**: 4, 7

Walkerton, Va., **III**: 90

Wall, Edward, Boy, **IV**: 99

Wall, William H., Lieut., CSN, **IV**: 82, 104, 122; **V**: 26

Wallace, Lewis, Major General, USA, **II**: 22

Wallis, P. C., b.r. stmr.; see: *P. C. Wallis*

Wallops I., Va., **I**: 28

Wall's Cut, Savannah River, Ga., **II**: 12, 25

Walsh, John, Conf. river stmr.; see: *John Walsh*

Walt, M., b.r. river stmr.; see: *M. Walt*

Walter, Henry, Acting Ensign, **III**: 132

Walton, Conf. ship, **VI**: 332

Walton, Lady, Conf. stmr.; see: *Lady Walton*

Wamsutta, USS, **II**: 57; **IV**: 67, 118, 122

Wanderer, USS, **I**: 38; **III**: 67

Wanderer, British b.r. schnr., **III**: 75

Wanderer, Am. fishing schnr., **III**: 97

Wando, British b.r. schnr. (ex-*Let Her Rip*), **IV**: 122; as USS, **V**: 39

Wandoo, b.r. schnr., **II**: 22

Wappoo Creek, S.C., **VI**: 232

War Department, Conf., **II**: 7; **III**: 105, 116; **VI**: 216

War Department, U.S., **I**: 22; **II**: 100

Ward, USS; see: *T. A. Ward*, USS

Ward, James H., Commander, **I**: 11, 14, 15, 17; **VI**: *12*, 15, 19, 20

Ward, Joanna, Conf. schnr., see: *Joanna Ward*

Ward, William H., Lieut., CSN, **IV**: 127; **VI**: 310

Ward, William S., Conf. shipmaster and owner, **VI**: 332

Wardrop, David W., Colonel, USA, **IV**: 104

Ware River, Va., **III**: 55

Waring, S. J., Am. schnr.; see: *S. J. Waring*

Warley, Alexander F., Lieut., CSN, **III**: 123; **IV**: 126; **VI**: 266

Warley, Ella, b.r. stmr.; see: *Ella Warley*

Warner, USA transport, **IV**: 56

Warner, James H., Chief Engineer, CSN, **VI**: 325

Warren, b.r. stmr., **VI**: 254

Warren, David, Coxswain, **IV**: 82

Warren, Fitz Henry, Brig. General, USA, **IV**: 42

Warren, Joshua D., Acting Master, **II**: 67, 105, 108, 112; **III**: 15

Yazoo City, Miss., II: 66; III: 2, 23, 24, 48, 84, 85, 87, 88, 114, 115; IV: 29, 44, 46; VI: 198, 207, 216, 233, 289, 292

Yazoo Pass (Miss.) Expedition, III: 22, 23, 24, 25, 27, 32, 36, 38, 40, 41, 45, 47, 54, 57

Yazoo River, Miss., II: 81, 91, 113-14, 116; III: 4, 8, 11, 16, 22, 23, 26, 48, 57, 61, 72, 74, 82, 84, 85, 87, 90, 114, 115, 159; IV: 13, 15, 30, 46; VI: 5, 196, 198, 199, 207, 216, 223, 225, 233

Yellow Bluff, Fla., IV: 121

Yeocomico River, Va., I: 19; III: 87

Yeopim River, N.C., III: 18

Yokohama, Japan, IV: 85

Yonge, Clarence R., VI: 195

York, Conf. privateer schnr., I: 20, 22; VI: 329

York, British b.r., II: 7

York River, Va., II: 42, 47, 56, 57, 61; III: 63, 77; IV: 17, 29, 30, 35, 51; V: 61

Yorktown, Conf. stmr., II: 94

Yorktown, Conf. stmr., VI: 280, 326

Yorktown, Va., II: 42, 47, 49, 56, 57; III: 63, 156; IV: 17, 30

Young, George W., Lt. Commander, V: 55, 59

Young, Horatio N., Seaman, III: 156

Young, Jonathan, Lt. Commander, III: 71

Young America, CSS, I: 11; VI: 326

Young Racer, British b.r. sloop; IV: 5

Young Republic, British b.r. stmr., IV: 57

Young's Point, La., III: 101

Yucatan Bank, Mexico, II: 80

Yucatan Peninsula, Mexico, III: 11

Zavalla, Conf. schnr., I: 28

Zeilin, Jacob, Colonel, USMC, III: 124; IV: 72

Zelinda, Am. bark, IV: 87

Zenith, Conf. schnr., VI: 333

Zenobia, Am. stmr., VI: 304

Zephyr, USA transport stmr., III: 151; IV: 42

Zerega, Alfred L. B., Acting Master, III: 115, 159, 167

Zion, b.r. sloop, IV: 124

Zollicoffer, Fort, Tenn.; see: Fort Zollicoffer

Zouave, USS, II: 5; III: 12

☆U.S. GOVERNMENT PRINTING OFFICE: 1970   O—397-495